WILEY

CW01669674

2020 Interpretation and Application of IFRS® Standards

Subscriber Update Service

BECOME A SUBSCRIBER!

Did you purchase this product from a bookstore?

If you did, it's important for you to become a subscriber. John Wiley & Sons, Inc. may publish, on a periodic basis, supplements and new editions to reflect the latest changes in the subject matter that you ***need to know*** in order to stay competitive in this ever-changing industry. By contacting the Wiley office nearest you, you'll receive any current update at no additional charge. In addition, you'll receive future updates and revised or related volumes on a 30-day examination review.

If you purchased this product directly from John Wiley & Sons, Inc., we have already recorded your subscription for this update service.

To become a subscriber, please call **1-877-762-2974** or send your name, company name (if applicable), address, and the title of the product to:

mailing address: **Supplement Department**
John Wiley & Sons, Inc.
One Wiley Drive
Somerset, NJ 08875

e-mail: **subscriber@wiley.com**
fax: **1-732-302-2300**
online: **www.wiley.com**

For customers outside the United States, please contact the Wiley office nearest you:

Professional & Reference Division
John Wiley & Sons Canada, Ltd.
22 Worcester Road
Etobicoke, Ontario M9W 1L1
CANADA
Phone: 416-236-4433
Phone: 1-800-567-4797
Fax: 416-236-4447
E-mail: canada@wiley.com

John Wiley & Sons, Ltd.
The Atrium
Southern Gate, Chichester
West Sussex, PO19 8SQ
ENGLAND
Phone: 44-1243-779777
Fax: 44-1243-775878
E-mail: customer@wiley.co.uk

John Wiley & Sons Australia, Ltd.
33 Park Road
P.O. Box 1226
Milton, Queensland 4064
AUSTRALIA
Phone: 61-7-3859-9755
Fax: 61-7-3859-9715
E-mail: brisbane@johnwiley.com.au

John Wiley & Sons (Asia) Pte. Ltd.
2 Clementi Loop #02-01
SINGAPORE 129809
Phone: 65-64632400
Fax: 65-64634604/5/6
Customer Service: 65-64604280
E-mail: enquiry@wiley.com.sg

WILEY

2020 Interpretation and Application of IFRS® Standards

Salim Alibhai
Erwin Bakker
T V Balasubramanian
Kunal Bharadva
Asif Chaudhry
Danie Coetsee
James Dougherty
Chris Johnstone
Patrick Kuria
Christopher Naidoo
J Ramanarayanan
Darshan Shah
Minette van der Merwe

WILEY

This edition contains interpretations and application of the IFRS Standards, as approved by the International Accounting Standards Board (Board) for issue up to 31 December 2019, that are required to be applied for accounting periods beginning on 1 January 2020.

This book is printed on acid-free paper.

For general information on our other products and services, please contact our Customer Care Department within the United States at 800-762-2974, outside the United States at 317-572-3993 or fax 317-572-4002.

Wiley also publishes its books in a variety of electronic formats. Some content that appears in print may not be available in electronic books. For more information about Wiley products, visit our website at www.wiley.com.

ISBN: 978-1-119-69936-1 (pbk) ISBN: 978-1-119-69939-2 (epdf)
ISBN: 978-1-119-69940-8 (epub) ISBN: 978-1-119-69941-5 (obook)

Printed in Great Britain by TJ International Ltd, Padstow, Cornwall, UK.

CONTENTS

AUTHOR BIOS

Salim Alibhai, FCCA, CPA (K), is an audit partner at PKF Kenya and heads the IT assurance including methodology function across the Eastern Africa PKF member firms.

Erwin Bakker, RA, is international audit partner of PKF Wallast in the Netherlands, mainly involved in international (group) audits. He serves as chairman of the IFRS working group of PKF Wallast and is a member of the Technical Bureau of PKF Wallast in the Netherlands.

T V Balasubramanian, FCA, CFE, Registered Valuer and Insolvency Professional, is a senior partner in PKF Sridhar & Santhanam LLP, and part of the technical team engaged in Ind AS / IFRS activities of the firm. He previously served on the Auditing and Assurance Standards Board of the ICAI, India and Committee on Accounting Standards for Local Bodies of the ICAI, India.

Kunal Bharadva, FCCA, CPA (K), ACA, is a Director at PKF Kenya and is responsible for technical training across the Eastern Africa PKF member firms.

Asif Chaudhry, FCCA, CPA (K), MBA, is an audit partner at PKF Kenya and heads the technical and quality control functions across the Eastern Africa PKF member firms. He is also a member of the Kenyan Institute's Professional Standards Committee and the PKF International Africa Professional Standards Committee.

Danie Coetsee, PhD (Accounting Sciences), CA (SA), is Professor of Accounting at the University of Johannesburg, specializing in financial accounting. He is former the chairs of the Accounting Practice Committee of the South African Institute of Chartered Accountants and the Financial Reporting Technical Committee of the Financial Reporting Standards Council of South Africa.

Chris Johnstone, a member of the ICAEW and also holds ICAEW's Diploma in IFRS. She is the Audit Technical Director at Johnston Carmichael. She joined Johnston Carmichael in 2014 having previously worked at Baker Tilly and MacIntyre Hudson in London. She is also a member of the Accounting and Auditing Technical Committee of the PKF firms in the United Kingdom and Republic of Ireland and ICAS's Corporate and Financial Reporting Panel.

Patrick Kuria, B/Ed (Hons), CPA (K), is a partner at PKF Kenya and specialises in the audits of financial services and the not-for-profit sector. He is a member of the Institute of Certified Public Accountants of Kenya (ICPAK), PKF Eastern Africa technical and CSR Committees. He is a Life Member of Award Holders Alumni Kenya (AHA - K) and a member of the finance committee for President's Awards Kenya.

Christopher Naidoo, CA (SA), member of the SAICA and is an international accounting (IFRS) and audit (ISA) technical specialist at PKF International Limited. He also a member of PKF's International Professional Standards Committee (IPSC), Assurance Strategy Group and Risk Advisory Group.

James Dougherty, MAcc, CPA, CGMA is an audit partner at JLK Rosenberger LLP, who recently moved with the firm to their Dallas, Texas office. James has specialists skills for single audits under Uniform Guidance, insurance statutory accounting principles (SAP) and is a qualified peer reviewer. He is also a member of the AICPA, CalCPA, Texas Society of CPAs and Insurance Accounting and Systems Association (IASA).

Darshan Shah, FCCA, CPA (K), CPA (U), ACA, is a partner with PKF East Africa and the Head of Audit and Assurance for the Eastern Africa PKF member firms. He also heads the technical training function across East Africa.

Minette van der Merwe, CA (SA), is PKF South Africa's IFRS technical expert responsible for the interpretation and application of IFRS within the Southern African region.

Ramanarayanan J, FCA, Cert. in IFRS (ICAEW), is a partner in PKF Sridhar & Santhanam LLP, Chartered Accountants, India. He has been part of the technical team of the firm engaged in transition to Ind AS (the converged IFRS Standards) and the ongoing implementation of new and revised standards.

1 INTRODUCTION TO INTERNATIONAL FINANCIAL REPORTING STANDARDS

INTRODUCTION

The mission of the IFRS Foundation and the International Accounting Standards Board (IASB) is to develop International Financial Reporting Standards (IFRS) that bring transparency, accountability and efficiency to financial markets around the world. They seek to serve the public interest by fostering trust, growth and long-term stability in the global economy.

The driver for the convergence of historically dissimilar financial reporting standards has been mainly to facilitate the free flow of capital so that, for example, investors in the US would become more willing to finance business in, say, China or the Czech Republic. Access to financial statements which are written in the same "language" would help to eliminate a major impediment to investor confidence, sometimes referred to as "accounting risk," which adds to the more tangible risks of making such cross-border investments. Additionally, permission to list a company's equity or debt securities on an exchange has generally been conditional on making filings with national regulatory authorities. These regulators tend to insist either on conformity with local Generally Accepted Accounting Practice (GAAP) or on a formal reconciliation to local GAAP. These procedures are tedious and time-consuming, and the human resources and technical knowledge to carry them out are not always widely available, leading many would-be registrants to forgo the opportunity of broadening their investor bases and potentially lowering their costs of capital.

There were once scores of unique sets of financial reporting standards among the more developed nations ("national GAAP"). The year 2005 saw the beginning of a new era in the global conduct of business, and the fulfilment of a 30-year effort to create the financial reporting rules for a worldwide capital market. During that year's financial reporting cycle, the 27 European Union (EU) member states plus many other countries, including Australia, New Zealand and South Africa, adopted IFRS.

This easing of US registration requirements for foreign companies seeking to enjoy the benefits of listing their equity or debt securities in the US led understandably to a call by domestic companies to permit them also to choose freely between financial reporting under US GAAP and IFRS. By late 2008 the SEC appeared to have begun the process of acceptance, first for the largest companies in those industries having (worldwide) the preponderance of IFRS adopters, and later for all publicly held companies. However, a new SEC chair took office in 2009, expressing a concern that the move to IFRS, if it were to occur, should perhaps take place more slowly than had previously been indicated.

It had been highly probable that non-publicly held US entities would have remained restricted to US GAAP for the foreseeable future. However, the American Institute of Certified Public Accountants (AICPA), which oversees the private-sector auditing profession's standards in the US, amended its rules in 2008 to fully recognise IASB as an accounting standard-setting body (giving it equal status with the Financial Accounting Standards Board (FASB)), meaning that auditors and other service providers in the US could now issue opinions (or provide other levels of assurance, as specified under pertinent guidelines). This change, coupled with the promulgation by IASB of a long-sought standard providing simplified financial reporting rules for privately held entities (described later in this chapter), might be seen as increasing the likelihood that a more broadly-based move to IFRS will occur in the US over the coming years.

The historic 2002 Norwalk Agreement—embodied in a Memorandum of Understanding (MoU) between the US standard setter, FASB, and the IASB—called for "convergence" of the respective sets of standards, and indeed since that time, a number of revisions of either US GAAP or IFRS have already taken place to implement this commitment.

Despite this commitment by the Boards, certain projects such as financial instruments (impairment and hedge accounting), revenue recognition, leases and insurance contracts were deferred due to their complexity and the difficulty in reaching consensus views. The converged standard on revenue recognition, IFRS 15, was finally published in May 2014, although both Boards subsequently deferred its effective date to annual periods beginning on or after January 1, 2018. The standard on leasing, IFRS 16, was published in January 2016, bringing to completion the work of the Boards on the MoU projects. Details of these and other projects of the standard setters are included in a separate section in each relevant chapter of this book.

Despite the progress towards convergence described above, the SEC dealt a blow to hopes of future alignment in its strategic plan published in February 2014. The document states that the SEC "will consider, among other things, whether a single set of high-quality global accounting standards is achievable," which is a significant reduction in its previously expressed commitment to a single set of global standards. This leaves IFRS and US GAAP as the two comprehensive financial reporting frameworks in the world, with IFRS gaining more and more momentum.

The completed MoU with FASB (and with other international organisations and jurisdictional authorities) has been replaced by a MoU with the Accounting Standards Advisory Forum (ASAF). The ASAF is an advisory group to the IASB, which was set up in 2013. It consists of national standard setters and regional bodies with an interest in financial reporting. Its objective is to provide an advisory forum where members can constructively contribute towards the achievement of the IASB's goal of developing globally accepted high-quality accounting standards. FASB's involvement with the IASB is now through ASAF.

THE CURRENT STRUCTURE

The formal structure put in place in 2000 has the IFRS Foundation, a Delaware corporation, as its keystone (this was previously known as the IASC Foundation). The Trustees of the IFRS Foundation have both the responsibility to raise funds needed to finance standard setting, and the responsibility of appointing members to the IASB, the IFRS Interpretations Committee (IFRIC) and the IFRS Advisory Council. The structure was amended to incorporate the IFRS Foundation Monitoring Board in 2009, renaming and incorporating the SME Implementation Group in 2010 as follows:

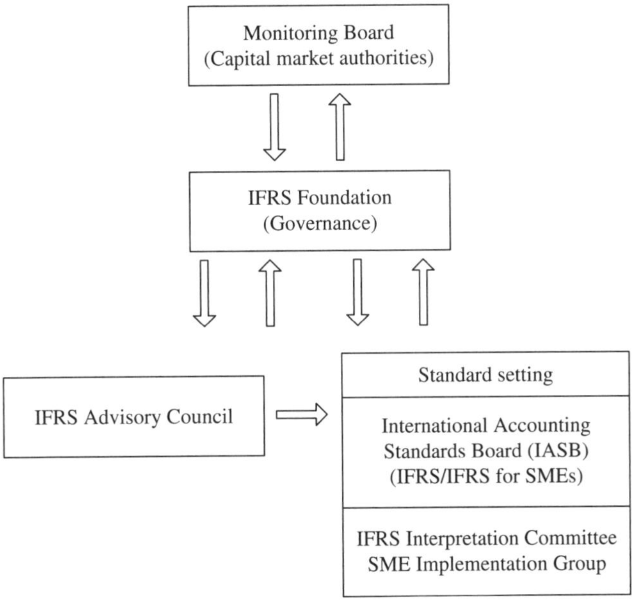

The Monitoring Board is responsible for ensuring that the Trustees of the IFRS Foundation discharge their duties as defined by the IFRS Foundation Constitution and for approving the appointment or reappointment of Trustees. The Monitoring Board consists of the Board and the Growth and Emerging Markets Committees of the IOSCO, the EC, the Financial Services Agency of Japan (JFSA), the SEC, the Brazilian Securities Commission (CVM), the Financial Services Commission of Korea (FSC) and Ministry of Finance of the People's Republic of China (China MOF). The Basel Committee on Banking Supervision participates as an observer.

The IFRS Foundation is governed by trustees and reports to the Monitoring Board. The IFRS Foundation has fundraising responsibilities and oversees the standard-setting work, the IFRS structure and strategy. It is also responsible for a five-yearly, formal, public review of the Constitution.

The IFRS Advisory Council is the formal advisory body to the IASB and the Trustees of the IFRS Foundation. Members consist of user groups, preparers, financial analysts, academics, auditors, regulators, professional accounting bodies and investor groups.

The IASB is an independent body that is solely responsible for establishing IFRS, including the IFRS for small and medium-sized enterprises (SMEs). The IASB also approves new interpretations.

The IFRS Interpretations Committee (the Interpretations Committee) is a committee comprised partly of technical partners in audit firms but also includes preparers and users. The Interpretations Committee's function is to answer technical queries from constituents about how to interpret IFRS—in effect, filling in the cracks between different requirements. It also proposes modifications to standards to the IASB, in response to perceived operational difficulties or the need to improve consistency. The Interpretations Committee liaises with the US Emerging Issues Task Force and similar bodies and standard setters to preserve convergence at the level of interpretation.

Working relationships are set up with local standard setters who have adopted or converged with IFRS, or are in the process of adopting or converging with IFRS.

PROCESS OF IFRS STANDARD SETTING

The IASB has a formal due process, which is currently set out in the *IFRS Foundation Due Process Handbook* issued in February 2013 by the Due Process Oversight Committee (DPOC), and updated in June 2016 to include the final IFRS Taxonomy due process.

The DPOC is responsible for:

1. reviewing regularly, and in a timely manner, together with the IASB and the IFRS Foundation staff, the due process activities of the standard-setting activities of the IASB;
2. reviewing, and proposing updates to, the *Due Process Handbook* that relates to the development and review of Standards, Interpretations and the IFRS Taxonomy so as to ensure that the IASB procedures are best practice;
3. reviewing the composition of the IASB's consultative groups to ensure an appropriate balance of perspectives and monitoring the effectiveness of those groups;
4. responding to correspondence from third parties about due process matters, in collaboration with the Director for Trustee Activities and the technical staff;
5. monitoring the effectiveness of the IFRS Advisory Council ("Advisory Council"), the Interpretations Committee and other bodies of the IFRS Foundation relevant to its standard-setting activities; and
6. making recommendations to the Trustees about constitutional changes related to the composition of committees that are integral to due process, as appropriate.

As a minimum, a proposed standard should be exposed for comment, and these comments should be reviewed before issuance of a final standard, with debates open to the public. However, this formal process is rounded out in practice, with wider consultation taking place on an informal basis.

The IASB's agenda is determined in various ways. Suggestions are made by the Trustees, the IFRS Advisory Council, liaison standard setters, the international accounting firms and others. These are debated by IASB and tentative conclusions are discussed with the various consultative bodies. Long-range projects are first put on the research agenda, which means that preliminary work is being done on collecting information about the problem and potential solutions. Projects can also arrive on the current agenda outside that route.

Once a project reaches the current agenda, the formal process is that the staff (a group of about 20 technical staff permanently employed by the IASB) drafts papers which are then discussed by IASB in open meetings. Following that debate, the staff rewrites the paper, or writes a new paper, which is then debated at a subsequent meeting. In theory at least, there is an internal process where the staff proposes solutions, and IASB either accepts or rejects them. In practice, the process is more involved: sometimes (especially for projects such as financial instruments) individual Board members are delegated special responsibility for the project, and they discuss the problems regularly with the relevant staff, helping to build the papers that come to the Board. Equally, Board members may write or speak directly to the staff outside of the formal meeting process to indicate concerns about one matter or another.

The due process comprises six stages: (1) setting the agenda; (2) project planning; (3) developing and publishing a Discussion Paper; (4) developing and publishing an Exposure Draft; (5) developing and publishing the IFRS; and (6) procedures after an IFRS is issued. The process also includes discussion of Staff Papers outlining the principal issues and analysis of comments received on Discussion Papers and Exposure Drafts. A pre-ballot draft is normally subject to external review. A near-final draft is also posted on the limited access website. If all outstanding matters are resolved, the final ballot is applied.

Final ballots on the standard are carried out in secret, but otherwise the process is quite open, with outsiders able to consult project summaries on the IASB website and attend Board meetings if they wish. Of course, the informal exchanges between staff and Board on a day-to-day basis are not visible to the public, nor are the meetings where IASB takes strategic and administrative decisions.

The basic due process can be modified in different circumstances. The Board may decide not to issue Discussion Papers or to reissue Discussion Papers and Exposure Drafts.

The IASB also has regular public meetings with the Capital Markets Advisory Committee (CMAC) and the Global Preparers Forum (GPF), among others. Special groups are set up from time to time. An example was the Financial Crisis Advisory Group, which was set up to consider how improvements in financial reporting could help enhance investor confidence in financial markets in the wake of the financial crisis of 2008. Formal working groups are established for certain major projects to provide additional practical input and expertise. Apart from these formal consultative processes, IASB also carries out field trials of some standards (examples of this include performance reporting and insurance), where volunteer preparers apply the proposed new standards. The IASB may also hold some form of public consultation during the process, such as roundtable discussions. The IASB engages closely with stakeholders around the world such as investors, analysts, regulators, business leaders, accounting standard setters and the accountancy profession.

The revised *IFRS Foundation Due Process Handbook* has an introduction section dealing with oversight, which identifies the responsibilities of the DPOC. The work of the IASB is divided into development and maintenance projects. Developments are comprehensive projects such as major changes and new IFRS Standards. Maintenance consists of narrow scope amendments. A research programme is also described that should form the development base for comprehensive projects. Each phase of a major project should also include an effects analysis detailing the likely cost and benefits of the project.

APPENDIX A: CURRENT INTERNATIONAL FINANCIAL REPORTING STANDARDS (IAS/IFRS) AND INTERPRETATIONS (SIC/IFRIC)

IFRS 1	First-Time Adoption of IFRS
IFRS 2	Share-Based Payment
IFRS 3	Business Combinations

IFRS 4	Insurance Contracts
IFRS 5	Non-current Assets Held for Sale and Discontinued Operations
IFRS 6	Exploration for and Evaluation of Mineral Resources
IFRS 7	Financial Instruments: Disclosures
IFRS 8	Operating Segments
IFRS 9	Financial Instruments (effective for accounting periods commencing on or after January 1, 2018 and will supersede IAS 39 and IFRIC 9)
IFRS 10	Consolidated Financial Statements
IFRS 11	Joint Arrangements
IFRS 12	Disclosure of Interest in Other Entities
IFRS 13	Fair Value Measurement
IFRS 14	Regulatory Deferral Accounts
IFRS 15	Revenue from Contracts with Customers (effective for accounting periods commencing on or after January 1, 2018 and will supersede IAS 11, IAS 18, IFRIC 13, IFRIC 15, IFRIC 18 and SIC 31)
IFRS 16	Leases (effective for accounting periods commencing on or after January 1, 2019 and will supersede IAS 17, IFRIC 4, SIC 15 and SIC 27)
IFRS 17	Insurance Contracts (effective for accounting periods commencing on or after January 1, 2022 and will supersede IFRS 4, IFRIC 4 and SIC 15)
IAS 1	Presentation of Financial Statements
IAS 2	Inventories
IAS 7	Statement of Cash Flows
IAS 8	Accounting Policies, Changes in Accounting Estimates and Errors
IAS 10	Events after the Reporting Period
IAS 11	Construction Contracts (replaced by IFRS 15)
IAS 12	Income Taxes
IAS 16	Property, Plant and Equipment
IAS 17	Leases
IAS 18	Revenue (replaced by IFRS 15)
IAS 19	Employee Benefits
IAS 20	Accounting for Government Grants and Disclosure of Government Assistance
IAS 21	The Effects of Changes in Foreign Exchange Rates
IAS 23	Borrowing Costs
IAS 24	Related-Party Disclosure
IAS 26	Accounting and Reporting by Retirement Benefit Plans
IAS 27	Separate Financial Statements
IAS 28	Investments in Associates and Joint Ventures
IAS 29	Financial Reporting in Hyperinflationary Economies
IAS 32	Financial Instruments: Presentation
IAS 33	Earnings per Share
IAS 34	Interim Financial Reporting
IAS 36	Impairment of Assets
IAS 37	Provisions, Contingent Liabilities and Contingent Assets
IAS 38	Intangible Assets
IAS 39	Financial Instruments: Recognition and Measurement (replaced by IFRS 9)
IAS 40	Investment Property
IAS 41	Agriculture
IFRIC 1	Changes in Existing Decommissioning, Restoration and Similar Liabilities
IFRIC 2	Members' Shares in Co-operative Entities and Similar Instruments
IFRIC 4	Determining Whether an Arrangement Contains a Lease

IFRIC 5	Rights to Interests Arising from Decommissioning, Restoration and Environmental Rehabilitation Funds
IFRIC 6	Liabilities Arising from Participating in a Specific Market—Waste Electrical and Electronic Equipment
IFRIC 7	Applying the Restatement Approach under IAS 29, *Financial Reporting in Hyperinflationary Economies*
IFRIC 9	Reassessment of Embedded Derivatives (replaced by IFRS 9)
IFRIC 10	Interim Financial Reporting and Impairment
IFRIC 12	Service Concession Arrangements
IFRIC 13	Customer Loyalty Programmes (replaced by IFRS 15)
IFRIC 14	IAS 19—*The Limit on a Defined Benefit Asset, Minimum Funding Requirements and their Interaction*
IFRIC 15	Agreements for the Construction of Real Estate (replaced by IFRS 15)
IFRIC 16	Hedges of a Net Investment in a Foreign Operation
IFRIC 17	Distributions of Non-cash Assets to Owners
IFRIC 18	Transfer of Assets from Customers (replaced by IFRS 15)
IFRIC 19	Extinguishing Financial Liabilities with Equity Instruments
IFRIC 20	Stripping Costs in the Production Phase of a Surface Mine
IFRIC 21	Levies
IFRIC 22	Foreign Currency Transactions and Advance Consideration
IFRIC 23	Uncertainty over Income Tax Treatments
SIC 7	Introduction of the Euro
SIC 10	Government Assistance—No Specific Relation to Operating Activities
SIC 15	Operating Leases—Incentives
SIC 25	Income Taxes—Changes in the Tax Status of an Enterprise or its Shareholders
SIC 27	Evaluating the Substance of Transactions involving the Legal Form of a Lease
SIC 29	Disclosure—Service Concession Arrangements
SIC 31	Revenue—Barter Transactions involving Advertising Services (replaced by IFRS 15)
SIC 32	Intangible Assets—Web Site Costs

APPENDIX B: IFRS FOR SMES

A long-standing debate among professional accountants, users and preparers—between those advocating some form of simplified financial reporting standards for smaller or non-publicly responsible entities (however they are defined), and those arguing that all reporting entities purporting to adhere to officially mandated accounting standards should do so with absolute faithfulness—was resolved on July 9, 2009 with the publication of the *International Financial Reporting Standard (IFRS) for Small and Medium-Sized Entities (IFRS for SMEs)*. Notwithstanding the name, it is actually intended as an optional, somewhat simplified and choice-limited comprehensive financial reporting standard for enterprises not having public accountability. Many of the recognition and measurement principles in full IFRS have been simplified, disclosures significantly reduced and topics not relevant to SMEs omitted from the IFRS for SMEs. The IASB carried out a comprehensive review of the *IFRS for SMEs* which it completed in May 2015 resulting in limited amendments to the standard. A complete revised version of the standard was issued in December 2015 and is effective from January 1, 2017. The IASB expects that revisions to the standard will be limited to once every three years.

The *IFRS for SMEs* is not immediately updated for any changes to full IFRS but, as noted above, the IASB issued amendments in the first half of 2015 and then anticipates updating the standard every three years thereafter.

Definition of SMEs

The *IFRS for SMEs* is intended for entities that do not have public accountability. An entity has public accountability—and therefore would not be permitted to use the *IFRS for SMEs*—if it meets either of the following conditions: (1) it has issued debt or equity securities in a public market; or (2) it holds assets in a fiduciary capacity, as one of its primary businesses, for a broad group of outsiders. The latter category of entity would include most banks, insurance companies, securities brokers/dealers, pension funds, mutual funds and investment banks. The standard does not impose a size test in defining SMEs, notwithstanding its name.

The standard also states that it is intended for entities which publish financial statements for external users, as with IFRS and US GAAP. In other words, the standard is not intended to govern internal or managerial reporting, although there is nothing to prevent such reporting from fully conforming to such standards.

A subsidiary of an entity that employs full IFRS, or an entity that is part of a consolidated entity that reports in compliance with IFRS, may report, on a stand-alone basis, in accordance with the *IFRS for SMEs*, if the financial statements are so identified, and if the subsidiary does not have public accountability itself. If this is done, the standard must be fully complied with, which could mean that the subsidiary's stand-alone financial statements would differ from how they are presented within the parent's consolidated financial statements; for example, in the subsidiary's financial statements prepared in accordance with the *IFRS for SMEs*, borrowing costs incurred in connection with the construction of long-lived assets would be expensed as incurred, but those same borrowing costs would be capitalised in the consolidated financial statements, since IAS 23 as most recently revised no longer provides the option of immediate expensing. In the authors' view, this would not be optimal financial reporting, and the goals of consistency and comparability would be better served if the stand-alone financial statements of the subsidiary were also based on full IFRS.

IFRS for SMEs is a Complete, Self-Contained Set of Requirements

The *IFRS for SMEs* is a complete and comprehensive standard, and accordingly contains much or most of the vital guidance provided by full IFRS. For example, it defines the qualities that are needed for IFRS-compliant financial reporting (reliability, understandability, et al.), the elements of financial statements (assets, liabilities, et al.), the required minimum captions in the required full set of financial statements, the mandate for comparative reporting and so on. There is no need for an entity reporting under this standard to refer elsewhere (other than for guidance in IAS 39, discussed below), and indeed it would be improper to do so.

An entity having no public accountability, which elects to report in conformity with the *IFRS for SMEs*, must make an "explicit and unreserved" declaration to that effect in the notes to the financial statements. As with a representation that the financial statements comply with full IFRS, if this representation is made, the entity must comply fully with all relevant requirements in the standard(s).

Many options under full IFRS remain under the *IFRS for SMEs*. For example, a single statement of comprehensive income may be presented, with profit or loss being an intermediate step in the derivation of the period's comprehensive income or loss, or alternatively a separate statement of income can be displayed, with profit or loss (the "bottom line" in that statement) then being the opening item in the separate statement of comprehensive income. Likewise, most of the mandates under full IFRS, such as the requirement to consolidate special-purpose entities that are controlled by the reporting entity, also exist under the *IFRS for SMEs*.

Modifications of Full IFRS Made in the IFRS for SMEs

Compared to full IFRS, the aggregate length of the standard, in terms of number of words, has been reduced by more than 90%. This was achieved by removing topics deemed not to be generally relevant to SMEs, by eliminating certain choices of accounting treatments and by simplifying methods for recognition and measurement. These three sets of modifications to the content of full IFRS, which are discussed below, respond both to the perceived needs of users of SMEs' financial statements and to cost-benefit concerns. According to the IASB, the set of standards in the *IFRS for SMEs* will be suitable for a typical enterprise having 50 employees and will also be valid for so-called micro-entities having only a single or a few employees. However, no size limits are stipulated in the standard, and thus even very large entities could conceivably elect to apply the *IFRS for SMEs*, assuming they have no public accountability as defined in the standard, and that no objections are raised by their various other stakeholders, such as lenders, customers, vendors or joint venture partners.

Omitted topics. Certain topics covered in the full IFRS were viewed as not being relevant to typical SMEs (e.g., rules pertaining to transactions that were thought to be unlikely to occur in an SME context), and have accordingly been omitted from the standard. This leaves open the question of whether SMEs could optionally seek expanded guidance in the full IFRS. Originally, when the Exposure Draft of the *IFRS for SMEs* was released, cross-references to the full IFRS were retained, so that SMEs would not be precluded from applying any of the financial reporting standards and methods found in IFRS, essentially making the *IFRS for SMEs* standard entirely optional on a component-by-component basis. However, in the final *IFRS for SMEs* standard all of these cross-references have been removed, with the exception of a reference to IAS 39, *Financial Instruments: Recognition and Measurement*, thus making the *IFRS for SMEs* a fully stand-alone document, not to be used in conjunction with the full IFRS. An entity that would qualify for use of the *IFRS for SMEs* must therefore make a decision to use full IFRS or the *IFRS for SMEs* exclusively.

Topics addressed in full IFRS, which are entirely omitted from the *IFRS for SME*s, are as follows:

- Earnings per share;
- Interim reporting;
- Segment reporting;
- Special accounting for assets held for sale;
- Insurance (since, because of public accountability, such entities would be precluded from using *IFRS for SMEs* in any event).

Thus, for example, if a reporting entity concluded that its stakeholders wanted presentation of segment reporting information, and the entity's management wished to provide that to them, it would elect to prepare financial statements in conformity with the full set of IFRS, rather than under the *IFRS for SMEs*.

Only the simpler option included. Where full IFRS provide an accounting policy choice, generally only the simpler option is included in *IFRS for SMEs*. SMEs will not be permitted to employ the other option(s) provided by the full IFRS, as had been envisioned by the Exposure Draft that preceded the standard, as all cross-references to the full IFRS have been eliminated.

The simpler options selected for inclusion in *IFRS for SMEs* are as follows, with the excluded alternatives noted:

- For investment property, measurement is driven by circumstances rather than a choice between the cost and fair value models, both of which are permitted under IAS 40, *Investment Property*. Under the provisions of the *IFRS for SMEs*, if the fair value of investment property can be measured reliably without undue cost or effort, the fair value model must be used. Otherwise, the cost method is required.
- Use of the cost-amortisation-impairment model for intangible assets is required; the revaluation model set out in IAS 38, *Intangible Assets*, is not allowed.
- Immediate expensing of borrowing costs is required; the capitalisation model stipulated under revised IAS 23 is not deemed appropriate for SMEs.
- Jointly controlled entities cannot be accounted for under the proportionate consolidation method under the *IFRS for SMEs* but can be under full IFRS as they presently exist. The *IFRS for SMEs* does permit the use of the fair value-through-earnings method as well as the equity method, and even the cost method can be used when it is not possible to obtain price or value data.
- Entities electing to employ the *IFRS for SMEs* are required to expense development costs as they are incurred, together with all research costs. Full IFRS necessitates making a distinction between research and development costs, with the former expensed and the latter capitalised and then amortised over an appropriate period receiving economic benefits.

It should be noted that the Exposure Draft that preceded the original version of the *IFRS for SMEs* would have required that the direct method for the presentation of operating cash flows be used, to the exclusion of the less desirable, but vastly more popular, indirect method. The final standard has retreated from this position and permits both methods, so it includes necessary guidance on application of the indirect method, which was absent from the draft.

All references to full IFRS found in the original draft of the standard have been eliminated, except for the reference to IAS 39, which may be used, optionally, by entities reporting under the *IFRS for SMEs*. The general expectation is that few reporting entities will opt to do this, since the enormous complexity of that standard was a primary impetus to the development of the streamlined *IFRS for SMEs*.

It is inevitable that some financial accounting or reporting situations will arise for which the *IFRS for SMEs* itself will not provide complete guidance. The standard provides a hierarchy, of sorts, of additional literature upon which reliance could be placed, in the absence of definitive rules contained in the *IFRS for SMEs*. First, the requirements and guidance that are set out for highly similar or closely related circumstances would be consulted within the *IFRS for SMEs*. Secondly, the *Concepts and Pervasive Principles* section (Section 1.2) of the standard would be consulted, in the hope that definitions, recognition criteria and measurement concepts (e.g., for assets, revenues) would provide the preparer with sufficient guidance to reason out a valid solution. Thirdly and lastly, full IFRS is identified explicitly as a source of instruction. Although reference to US (or other) GAAP is not suggested as a tactic, since full IFRS permits preparers to consider the requirements of national GAAP, if based on a framework similar to full IFRS, this omission may not indicate exclusion as such.

Recognition and measurement simplifications. For the purposes of the *IFRS for SMEs*, IASB has made significant simplifications to the recognition and measurement principles included in full IFRS. Examples of the simplifications to the recognition and measurement principles found in full IFRS are as follows:

1. *Financial instruments*:

   a. *Classification of financial instruments*. Only two categories for financial assets (cost or amortised cost, and fair value through profit or loss) are provided, rather than the four found in full IFRS. Because the available-for-sale and held-to-maturity classifications under IAS 39 are not available, there will be no need to deal with all of the "intent-driven" held-to-maturity rules, or related "tainting" concerns, with no need for an option to recognise changes in value of available-for-sale securities in current profit or loss instead of as an item of other comprehensive income.

      (1) The *IFRS for SMEs* requires an amortised cost model for most debt instruments, using the effective interest rate as at initial recognition. The effective rate should consider all contractual terms, such as prepayment options. Investments in non-convertible and non-puttable preference shares and non-puttable ordinary shares that are publicly traded or whose fair value can otherwise be measured reliably are to be measured at fair value with changes in value reported in current earnings. Most other basic financial instruments are to be reported at cost less any impairment recognised. Impairment or uncollectability must always be assessed, and, if identified, recognised immediately in profit or loss; recoveries to the extent of losses previously taken are also recognised in profit or loss.

      (2) For more complex financial instruments (such as derivatives), fair value through profit or loss is generally the applicable measurement method, with cost less impairment being prescribed for those instruments (such as equity instruments lacking an objectively determinable fair value) for which fair value cannot be ascertained.

      (3) Assets which would generally not meet the criteria as being basic financial instruments include (a) asset-backed securities, such as collateralised mortgage obligations, repurchase agreements and securitised packages of receivables; (b) options, rights, warrants, futures contracts, forward contracts and interest rate swaps that can be settled in cash or by exchanging another financial instrument; (c) financial instruments that qualify and are designated as hedging instruments in accordance with the requirements in the standard; (d) commitments to make a loan to another entity; and (e) commitments to receive a loan if the commitment can be net settled in cash. Such instruments would include (a) an investment in another entity's equity instruments other than non-convertible preference shares and

non-puttable ordinary and preference shares; (b) an interest rate swap, which returns a cash flow that is positive or negative, or a forward commitment to purchase a commodity or financial instrument, which is capable of being cash settled and which, on settlement, could have positive or negative cash flow; (c) options and forward contracts, because returns to the holder are not fixed; (d) investments in convertible debt, because the return to the holder can vary with the price of the issuer's equity shares rather than just with market interest rates; and (e) a loan receivable from a third party that gives the third party the right or obligation to prepay if the applicable taxation or accounting requirements change.

b. *Derecognition*. In general, the principle to be applied is that, if the transferor retains any significant risks or rewards of ownership, derecognition is not permitted, although if full control over the asset is transferred, derecognition is valid even if some very limited risks or rewards are retained. The complex "passthrough testing" and "control retention testing" of IAS 39 can thus be omitted, unless full IAS 39 is elected for by the reporting entity. For financial liabilities, derecognition is permitted only when the obligation is discharged, cancelled or expires.
c. *Simplified hedge accounting*. Much more simplified hedge accounting and less strict requirements for periodic recognition and measurement of hedge effectiveness are specified than those set out in IAS 39.
d. *Embedded derivatives*. No separate accounting for embedded derivatives is required.

2. *Goodwill impairment*: An indicator approach has been adopted to supersede the mandatory annual impairment calculations in IFRS 3, *Business Combinations*. Additionally, goodwill and other indefinite-lived assets are considered to have finite lives, thus reducing the difficulty of assessing impairment.
3. *All research and development costs are expensed as incurred* (IAS 38 requires capitalisation after commercial viability has been assessed).
4. *The cost method or fair value through profit or loss of accounting for associates and joint ventures may be used* (rather than the equity method or proportionate consolidation).
5. *Simplified accounting for deferred taxes*: The "temporary difference approach" for recognition of deferred taxes under IAS 12, *Income Taxes*, is allowed with a minor modification. Current and deferred taxes are required to be measured initially at the rate applicable to undistributed profits, with adjustment in subsequent periods if the profits are distributed.
6. *Less use of fair value for agriculture* (being required only if fair value is readily determinable without undue cost or effort).
7. *Share-based payment*: Equity-settled share-based payments should always be recognised as an expense and the expense should be measured on the basis of observable market prices, if available. When there is a choice of settlement, the entity should account for the transaction as a cash-settled transaction, except under certain circumstances.
8. *Finance leases*: A simplified measurement of a lessee's rights and obligations is prescribed.
9. *First-time adoption*: Less prior period data would have to be restated than under IFRS 1, *First-time Adoption of International Financial Reporting Standards*. An impracticability exemption has also been included.

Because the default measurement of financial instruments would be fair value through profit and loss under the *IFRS for SMEs*, some SMEs may actually be required to apply more fair value measurements than do entities reporting under full IFRS.

Disclosure Requirements Under the IFRS for SMEs

There are certain reductions in disclosure requirements under the *IFRS for SMEs* compared to full IFRS, but these are relatively minor and alone would not drive a decision to adopt the standard. Furthermore, key stakeholders, such as banks, often prescribe supplemental disclosures (e.g., major contracts, compensation agreements), which exceed what is required under IFRS, and this would be likely to continue to be true under the *IFRS for SMEs*.

Maintenance of the IFRS for SMEs

SMEs have expressed concerns not only over the complexity of IFRS, but also about the frequency of changes to standards. To respond to these issues, IASB intends to update the *IFRS for SMEs* approximately once every three years via an "omnibus" standard, with the expectation that any new requirements would not have mandatory application dates sooner than one year from issuance. Users are thus assured of having a moderately stable platform of requirements.

Implications of the IFRS for SMEs

The *IFRS for SMEs* is a significant development, which appears to be having a real impact on the future accounting and auditing standards issued by organisations participating in the standard-setting process.

On March 6, 2007, the FASB and the AICPA announced that the newly established Private Company Financial Reporting Committee (PCFRC) will address the financial reporting needs of private companies and of the users of their financial statements. The primary objective of PCFRC will be to help the FASB determine whether and where there should be specific differences in prospective and existing accounting standards for private companies.

In many continental European countries, a close link exists between the statutory financial statements and the results reported for income tax purposes. The successful implementation of SME Standards will require breaking the traditional bond between the financial statements and the income tax return, and may well trigger a need to amend company laws.

Since it is imperative that international convergence of accounting standards be accompanied by convergence of audit standards, differential accounting for SMEs will affect regulators such as the Public Company Accounting Oversight Board (PCAOB) and the SEC. The *IFRS for SMEs* may be a welcome relief for auditors as it will decrease the inherent risk that results from the numerous choices and wide-ranging judgement required by management when utilising the full version of IFRS. The ultimate success of the *IFRS for SMEs* will depend on the extent to which users, preparers and their auditors believe the standard meets their needs.

Application of the IFRS for SMEs

The application of the *IFRS for SMEs* is not covered in this publication. However, there is a detailed accounting manual available, which addresses the requirements, application and interpretation of the standard—*Applying IFRS for SMEs* (available from Wiley).

2 CONCEPTUAL FRAMEWORK

INTRODUCTION

In March 2018, having considered feedback on the Exposure Draft, the IASB completed the project with the issue of its revised *Conceptual Framework for Financial Reporting* (the 2018 framework).

The IASB and IFRS Interpretations Committee started using the 2018 framework in developing and revising standards and interpretations immediately after it was issued. To assist transition from the 2010 framework for preparers of financial statements who develop accounting policies by reference to the conceptual framework, the IASB has set a general effective date for the 2018 framework of accounting periods commencing on or after January 1, 2020, although earlier use is permitted.

The first part of this chapter deals with the 2018 framework. As the 2010 framework remains available to preparers of financial statements for a short period of time, its contents are covered in the second part of this chapter.

CONCEPTUAL FRAMEWORK FOR FINANCIAL REPORTING 2018

Structure

The 2018 framework consists of an introduction setting the status and purpose of the framework, and eight chapters as follows:

1. **The Objective of General-Purpose Financial Reporting:** this chapter is largely unchanged from the 2010 framework, although the IASB has clarified why information used in assessing stewardship is needed to achieve the objective of financial reporting;

2. **Qualitative Characteristics of Useful Financial Information:** this chapter is largely unchanged from the 2010 framework, although the IASB has clarified the roles of prudence, measurement uncertainty and substance over form in assessing whether information is useful;
3. **Financial Statements and the Reporting Entity:** this is a new chapter, which provides guidance on determining the appropriate boundary of a reporting entity;
4. **The Elements of Financial Statements:** the definitions of assets and liabilities have been refined and, following on from this, the definitions of income and expenses have been updated;
5. **Recognition and Derecognition:** the previous recognition criteria have been revised to refer explicitly to the qualitative characteristics of useful information. New guidance on derecognition has been provided;
6. **Measurement:** this chapter has been expanded significantly to describe the information which measurement bases provide and explanations of the factors to be considered when selecting a measurement basis;
7. **Presentation and Disclosure:** this is a new chapter, which sets out concepts that describe how information should be presented and disclosed in financial statements; and
8. **Concepts of Capital and Capital Maintenance:** the material in this chapter has been carried forward unchanged from the 2010 framework, into which it was transferred unchanged from the IASC's 1989 framework.

Status and Purpose

The 2018 framework describes the objective of, and the concepts for, general-purpose financial reporting.

The purpose of the 2018 framework is to:

a. assist the IASB to develop standards which are based on consistent concepts;
b. assist preparers to develop consistent accounting policies when no standard applies to a particular transaction or other event; and
c. assist all parties to understand and interpret the standards.

The 2018 framework is not a standard, and nothing in the framework overrides any standard or any requirement which the standards contain.

The main aim is therefore to help the IASB in preparing new standards and reviewing existing standards. The conceptual framework also helps national standard setters, preparers, auditors, users and others interested in IFRS in achieving their objectives. The conceptual framework is, however, not itself regarded as an IFRS and therefore cannot override any IFRS although there might be potential conflicts. The IASB believes that over time any such conflicts will be eliminated.

1. The Objective of General-Purpose Financial Reporting

The objective of general-purpose financial reporting is defined in the 2018 framework as follows:

> To provide financial information about the reporting entity that is useful to existing and potential investors, lenders and other creditors in making decisions relating to providing resources to the entity.

The decisions to be made concern:

a. buying, selling or holding equity and debt instruments;
b. providing or settling loans and other forms of credit; or
c. exercising rights to vote on, or otherwise influence, management's actions that affect the use of the entity's economic resources.

Since investors, lenders and other creditors are generally not in a position to have the necessary information issued directly to them they have to rely on general-purpose financial reports to make decisions. They are therefore identified as the primary users of general-purpose financial reports.

The framework recognises that users need to evaluate the prospects for future net cash inflows to an entity. To assess these net inflows, information is needed of an entity's resources, claims to those resources and the ability of management and the governing board to discharge their responsibility to use the resources. Assessing stewardship is thus included in the ability of users to assess the net cash flows of an entity.

It is noted that general-purpose financial reports do not provide information regarding the value of a reporting entity but assist in making such valuations.

General-purpose financial reports provide information about the financial position of an entity, its resources and claims against those resources. The entity's financial position is affected by the economic resources which the entity controls, its financial structure, its liquidity and solvency and its capacity to adapt to changes in the environment in which it operates. Information is provided about the strengths and weaknesses of an entity and its ability to acquire finance.

Changes in an entity's economic resources and claims are a result of an entity's financial performance and are derived from other transactions such as issuing debt and equity instruments.

Financial performance is assessed both through the process of accrual accounting and changes in cash flows. Accrual accounting depicts the effects of transactions and other events and circumstances on a reporting entity's economic resources and claims in the period in which those effects occur, even if the resultant cash payments and receipts arise in a different period. Information about the cash flows which occur during a period assists users in assessing the entity's ability to generate future net cash flows. Accrual accounting and reporting of cash flows both help users to understand the return on the resources of an entity and how well management has discharged its stewardship responsibilities.

Changes in economic resources and claims may also occur for reasons other than financial performance. For example, debt or equity instruments may be issued, resulting in cash inflows. Information about these types of changes is necessary to provide users with a complete understanding of why economic resources and claims have changed, and the implications of those changes for future financial performance.

Information about how efficiently and effectively the reporting entity's management has discharged its responsibilities in relation to the entity's economic resources helps users to assess management's stewardship of those resources. This can assist users in assessing management's future stewardship of the entity's resources.

2. Qualitative Characteristics of Useful Financial Information

The qualitative characteristics identify the information which is most useful in financial reporting. Financial reporting includes information in financial statements and financial information that is provided by other means. The qualitative characteristics are divided into fundamental qualitative characteristics and enhancing qualitative characteristics.

The fundamental qualitative characteristics are relevance and faithful representation. Financial information is useful if it possesses these characteristics.

The enhancing qualitative characteristics are comparability, verifiability, timeliness and understandability. The usefulness of financial information is enhanced if it possesses these characteristics.

No hierarchy of applying the qualitative characteristics is determined. The application is, however, a process. The fundamental characteristics are applied by following a three-step process. First, it is necessary to identify the economic phenomenon which has a potential to be useful. Secondly, the type of information regarding the phenomenon that is most relevant that could be faithfully represented should be identified. Finally, it should be determined whether the information is available and could be faithfully represented.

It may be necessary to make a trade-off between relevance and faithful representation to meet the objective of financial reporting, which is to provide useful information about economic phenomena. It is possible that the most relevant information about an economic phenomenon could be a highly uncertain estimate. Measurement uncertainty can sometimes be so high that it may be questionable whether the estimate would provide a sufficiently faithful representation of the economic phenomenon. In such a case, it would be necessary to determine whether the most useful information would be provided by that estimate accompanied by a detailed description of the estimate and an explanation of the uncertainties which accompany it, or whether it would be more useful to provide a less relevant estimate which nonetheless was subject to lower measurement uncertainty.

Once the process described above has been followed, the enhancing characteristics are applied to confirm or enhance the quality of the information.

The fundamental qualitative characteristics are explained as follows:

Relevant financial information can make a difference in decision making. Information can make a difference if it has predictive value, confirmatory value or both. Financial information has predictive value if it can be used as an input in the process to predict future outcomes and has confirmatory value if it confirms or changes previous evaluations. Materiality is included in relevance. Information is material if omitting it or misstating it could influence the decisions of users.

Faithful representation is achieved when information is complete, neutral and free from error. A complete depiction includes all information needed to understand the economic phenomena under consideration, including any necessary descriptions and explanations. A neutral depiction is one which is without bias in the selection or presentation of financial information. Neutrality is supported by the exercise of prudence, which means that assets and income are not overstated, and liabilities and expenses are not understated. (Equally, prudence does not allow for the understatement of assets or income, or the overstatement of liabilities or expenses.) "Free from error" means that there are no errors or omissions in the description of the phenomena and in the process applied (although this does not require that information be perfectly accurate in all respects). The framework acknowledges that in many instances it may be necessary to include estimates in financial information.

The enhancing qualitative characteristics are explained as follows:

Comparability enables users to identify similarities in, and differences between, items. Information about a reporting entity is more useful if it can be compared with similar information about other entities and with similar information about the same entity for another period or another date. *Consistency* (the use of the same methods for the same items, either from period to period within the same entity or in a single period across entities) aids comparability, although it is not the same as comparability.

Verifiability helps to assure users that information represents faithfully the economic phenomena which it purports to represent. It implies that knowledgeable and independent observers could reach a consensus (but not necessarily absolute agreement) that the information does represent faithfully the economic phenomena it purports to represent without material error or bias, or that an appropriate recognition or measurement method has been applied without material error or bias. It means that independent observations would yield essentially the same measure or conclusions.

Timeliness means that the information is provided to users in time to be capable of influencing their decisions. Generally, the older the information is, the less useful it may be to the users.

Understandability is classifying, characterising and presenting information clearly and concisely. Understandability enables users who have a reasonable knowledge of business, economic and financial activities and financial reporting, and who apply reasonable diligence to comprehend the information, to gain insights into the reporting entity's financial position and results of operations, as intended.

The cost constraint is the only constraint included regarding the information provided in useful financial reports. At issue is whether the benefits of providing information exceed the cost of providing and using the information. In developing standards, the IASB considers information about the expected benefits and costs of those benefits which will result. Presumably this would constrain the imposition of certain new requirements, although this is a relative concept, and as information technology continues to evolve and the cost of preparing and distributing financial and other information declines, this constraint conceivably may be relaxed.

3. Financial Statements and the Reporting Entity

This chapter discusses the role of general-purpose financial statements (which are a particular form of general-purpose financial report) and the concept of the reporting entity.

The chapter sets out that general-purpose financial statements consist of a statement of financial position (recognising assets, liabilities and equity), a statement of financial performance which may be a single statement or two statements (recognising income and expenses), and other statements and notes which present information about recognised elements (assets, liabilities, equity, income and expenses), unrecognised elements, cash flows, contributions from and distributions to equity holders, and methods, assumptions and judgements used in estimating the amounts presented or disclosed.

Financial statements are prepared for a specified period of time (the reporting period) and provide information about assets and liabilities (whether recognised or unrecognised) which existed at the end of the reporting period or during it, and income and expenses for the reporting period. Comparative information for at least one preceding reporting period should also be provided.

Information about possible future transactions and other events should be provided if it is useful to users of the financial statements, although information about management's expectations and strategies for the entity is not typically included in the financial statements.

Financial statements are usually prepared on the assumption that the entity is a going concern and will continue to operate for the foreseeable future, although where a decision has been made that the entity will cease trading or enter liquidation, or there is no alternative to such a course of action, a different basis may need to be applied.

In describing the role of financial statements, the 2018 framework states that financial statements are prepared from the perspective of the entity as a whole, instead of from the viewpoint of any particular group of investors, lenders or other creditors.

The framework describes a reporting entity as an entity which is required, or chooses, to prepare general-purpose financial statements. It notes that a reporting entity is not necessarily a legal entity, and could comprise a portion of an entity, or two or more entities.

The framework discusses the boundary of a reporting entity and notes that, in situations where one entity (a parent) has control of another entity (a subsidiary), the boundary of the reporting entity could encompass the parent and any subsidiaries (resulting in consolidated financial statements) or the parent alone (resulting in unconsolidated financial statements). If the reporting entity comprises two or more entities which are not linked by a parent–subsidiary relationship, the reporting entity's financial statements are referred to as "combined financial statements."

Where a reporting entity is not a legal entity and does not comprise only legal entities linked by a parent-subsidiary relationship, determining the appropriate boundary may be difficult. In such cases, the boundary needs to be set in such a way that the financial statements provide the relevant financial information needed by users, and faithfully represent the economic activities of the entity. The boundary should not contain an arbitrary or incomplete set of economic activities, and a description should be provided of how the boundary has been determined.

Where a parent–subsidiary relationship exists, the framework suggests that consolidated financial statements are usually more likely than unconsolidated financial statements to provide useful information to users, but that unconsolidated financial statements may also provide useful information because claims against the parent are typically not enforceable against subsidiaries and in some jurisdictions (for instance, under the UK's Companies Act 2006) the amounts that can legally be distributed to the parent's equity holders depend on the distributable reserves of the parent.

4. The Elements of Financial Statements

This chapter deals with the elements of financial statements, including assets, liabilities, equity, income and expenses. The 2018 framework notes that financial statements provide information about the financial effects of transactions and other events by grouping them into broad classes—the elements of financial statements. The elements are linked to the economic resources and claims, and changes in those economic resources and claims, which are dealt with in Chapter 1 of the 2018 framework.

An *asset* is defined as a present economic resource controlled by the entity as a result of past events. An economic resource is defined as a right that has the potential to produce economic benefits.

A *liability* is defined as a present obligation of the entity to transfer an economic resource as a result of past events.

Equity is defined as the residual interest in the assets of the entity after deducting all its liabilities.

Income is defined as increases in assets, or decreases in liabilities, that result in increases in equity, other than those relating to contributions from holders of equity claims.

Expenses are defined as decreases in assets, or increases in liabilities, that result in decreases in equity, other than those relating to distributions to holders of equity claims.

The 2018 framework also identifies other changes in resources and claims, being either contributions from, and distributions to, holders of equity claims, or exchanges of assets or liabilities that do not result in increases or decreases in equity (for example, acquiring an asset for cash).

As with the earlier frameworks the 2018 framework continues to define income and expenses in terms of changes in assets and liabilities but also notes that important decisions on matters such as recognition and measurement are driven by considering the nature of the resulting information about both financial performance and financial position.

In developing the 2018 framework, the IASB has not addressed the problems which arise in classifying instruments with characteristics of both equity and liabilities. It is considering these matters in its project on financial instruments with the characteristics of equity. The outcomes of that project will assist the IASB in deciding whether it should add a project on amending standards, the conceptual framework or both to its active agenda.

Assets. In relation to the definition of an asset, the chapter discusses three fundamental aspects:

a. rights;
b. the potential to produce economic benefits; and
c. control.

Rights having the potential to produce economic benefits may take many forms, including those corresponding to an obligation of another party (for example, the right to receive cash, goods or services, or the right to exchange economic resources with another party on favourable terms) and those which do not correspond to an obligation of another party (for example, the right to use property, plant and equipment, or intellectual property).

However, not all of an entity's rights are assets of the entity—for an asset to exist, the rights must both have the potential to produce economic benefits to the entity beyond those available to all other parties and be controlled by the entity.

For the potential to produce economic benefits to exist, it need not be certain—or even likely—that the right will produce economic benefits. It is only necessary that the right already exists and that there is at least one circumstance where it would produce economic benefits for the entity beyond those available to all other parties. However, a low probability that economic benefits will be produced may affect the decision on whether to recognise the asset in the financial statements, how it is measured, and what other information is given.

Control links an economic resource to an entity. Control exists if the entity has the present ability to direct the use of the economic resource and obtain the economic benefits that may flow from it. This includes being able to prevent other parties from directing and obtaining in this way. If one party controls an economic resource, then no other party does so. Control usually arises from an ability to enforce legal rights, although this is not always the case. Control could also arise if one party has information or know-how which is not available to any other party and is capable of being kept secret. For control to exist, any future economic benefits from the relevant economic resource must flow directly or indirectly to the entity, and not to another party. However, this does not mean that the entity will be able to ensure that the resource will produce any economic benefits in any circumstances.

Liabilities. In relation to the definition of a liability, the chapter notes that three criteria must all be satisfied:

a. the entity has an obligation;
b. the obligation is to transfer an economic resource; and
c. the obligation is a present obligation that exists as a result of past events.

An obligation is a duty or responsibility that an entity has no practical ability to avoid. An obligation is always owed to another party or parties, but it is not necessary to know the identity of the party or parties to whom the obligation is owed. Many obligations arise from legal commitments (such as contracts or legislative requirements) but an entity may also have obligations (often referred to as "constructive obligations") arising from its customary practices, published policies or specific statements if it has no practical ability to avoid acting in accordance with those practices, policies or statements. An obligation will not exist in any case where there is only an intention on the entity's part to make a transfer of an economic resource, or a high probability that such a transfer will take place, rather than a practically unavoidable requirement upon the entity to make the transfer.

The obligation must have the potential to require the entity to transfer an economic resource to another party or parties. Such transfers include, for example, the payment of cash, the delivery of goods or provision of services, or the exchange of economic resources on unfavourable terms. There need not be certainty that the transfer will take place, only that the obligation exists and that, in at least one circumstance, the entity would be required to transfer an economic resource. For example, the transfer may only become necessary if some specified uncertain future event occurs. However, if the probability of the transfer of an economic resource is low this may affect decisions as to whether the liability is recognised, or simply disclosed, and how it is measured.

For a liability to exist, the obligation must be a present obligation which exists as a result of past events. This will only be the case if the entity has already obtained economic benefits or taken an action, and as a consequence the entity may or will have to transfer an economic resource that it would not otherwise have had to transfer. For example, the entity may have obtained goods and services for which it will later have to make payment, or it may be operating a particular business or in a particular market. The enactment of new legislation may lead to a present obligation, but only where an entity has obtained economic benefits or taken action to which the legislation applies and may or will as a result have to transfer an economic resource which it would not otherwise have had to transfer—the enactment of the legislation itself does not give rise to an obligation. In addition, present obligations do not arise from executory contracts—those where neither party has yet undertaken any of its contractual requirements. For example, under an employment contract the entity may be required to pay an employee a salary for services which the employee will provide. No present obligation to pay the salary arises until the entity has received the employee's services. Until then, the entity has a combined right and obligation to exchange future salary for future employee services.

Unit of account. The chapter defines the unit of account as the right or the group of rights, the obligation or the group of obligations, or the group of rights and obligations, to which recognition criteria and measurement concepts are applied. The unit of account is selected to provide useful information, which means that information provided about an asset or liability and any related income and expenses must be relevant and must faithfully represent the substance of the transaction or other event from which they have arisen. In determining the appropriate unit of account, it is necessary to consider whether the benefits arising from selecting that unit of account justify the costs of providing and using that information.

Units of account which may be used include:

a. an individual right or individual obligation;
b. all rights, all obligations, or all rights and all obligations, arising from a single source, for example a contract;
c. a subgroup of those rights and obligations, for example a subgroup of rights over an item of property, plant and equipment for which the useful life and pattern of consumption differ from those of the other rights over the item;
d. a group of rights and/or obligations arising from a portfolio of similar items;
e. a group of rights and/or obligations arising from a portfolio of dissimilar items, for example a portfolio of assets and liabilities to be disposed of in a single transaction; and
f. a risk exposure within a portfolio of items—if such a portfolio is subject to a common risk, some aspects of accounting for that portfolio could focus on the aggregate exposure to risk within that portfolio.

Substance of contractual rights and contractual obligations. Financial statements are required to report the substance of the rights and obligations for an entity which arise from a contract to which it is a party. Often, this substance is clear from the legal form of the terms of the contract, but in some cases, it is necessary to analyse the legal terms further to identify the substance of the obligation.

All terms of the contract—whether explicit or implicit—are considered in this analysis, unless the terms have no substance (for example, if they bind neither of the parties, or result in rights which neither party will have the practical ability to exercise under any circumstances).

Where a group or series of contracts are put in place to achieve an overall commercial effect, careful analysis will be necessary to identify the appropriate unit of account, dependent upon the nature of the overall commercial effect. For example, it may be necessary to treat the rights and obligations arising from the group or series of contracts as a single unit of account. On the other hand, if a single contract creates two or more sets of rights and obligations that could have been created through two or more separate contracts, faithful representation may require each set of rights and obligations to be accounted for as though it arose from a separate contract.

Definition of equity. The chapter notes that equity claims are claims on the residual interest in the assets of the entity after deducting all of its liabilities. In other words, equity claims do not meet the definition of a liability. Equity claims fall into different classes, such as ordinary shares and preference shares, which may confer different rights, for example to the receipt of dividends. Business activities are often undertaken through non-corporate entities such as sole proprietorships, partnerships, trusts or government undertakings. The legal frameworks applying to such entities may differ from those which govern corporate entities, but the definition of equity for the purposes of the 2018 framework remains the same in all cases.

Definitions of income and expenses. As already noted, income is defined as increases in assets, or decreases in liabilities, that result in increases in equity, other than those relating to contributions from holders of equity claims. Expenses are decreases in assets, or increases in liabilities, that result in decreases in equity, other than those relating to distributions to holders of equity claims.

The chapter emphasises that the definitions of income and expenses mean that contributions from holders of equity claims are not income, and distributions to holders of equity claims are not expenses. Income and expenses arise from financial performance. Users of financial statements need information about both an entity's financial position and its financial performance. Therefore, despite income and expenses being defined in terms of changes in assets and liabilities, information about income and expenses is equally important as information about assets and liabilities.

5. Recognition and Derecognition

Recognition. Recognition is the process of capturing for inclusion in the statement of financial position or the statement(s) of financial performance an item that meets the definition of one of the elements of financial statements—an asset, a liability, equity, income or expenses. An item so recognised is represented in one of the statements by words and a monetary amount, which may be aggregated with other items, and included in one or more of the totals in that statement. The amount at which an item is included in the statement of financial position is referred to as its "carrying amount."

The 2018 framework sets out a recognition process which is based on the linkage between the elements of financial statements, the statement of financial position and the statement(s) of financial performance. This linkage arises from the fact that, in the statement of financial position at the beginning and end of the reporting period, total assets minus total liabilities equal total equity, and recognised changes during the reporting period comprise income minus expenses (recognised in the statement(s) of financial performance, and contributions from holders of equity claims minus distributions to holders of equity claims). Recognition of one item (or a change in its carrying amount) requires the recognition or derecognition (or a change in the carrying amount(s)) of one or more other items. For example, income is recognised in connection with the initial recognition of an asset or the derecognition of a liability. An expense is recognised in connection with the initial recognition of a liability or the derecognition of an asset.

To be recognised in the statement of financial position, an asset, liability or equity must meet the relevant definition. Similarly, only items which meet the definitions of income or expenses will be recognised in the statement(s) of financial position. However, it should be noted that not all items which meet the definitions will necessarily be recognised. Items meeting the definitions are recognised only if such recognition provides users of financial statements with relevant information about the asset or liability and about any income, expenses or changes in equity, a faithful representation of the asset or liability and of any income, expenses or changes in equity, and information which results in benefits which exceed the cost of providing that information.

Certain circumstances are identified in which recognition of an asset or liability may not provide relevant information to the users of the financial statements. For example, it may be uncertain whether an asset exists or whether an inflow of economic benefits will result from that asset. Similarly, it may be uncertain whether a liability exists or whether an outflow of economic benefits will result. However, there is no clear-cut rule as to whether an item should be recognised under these circumstances and a judgement will need to be made. Even if the item is not recognised it may still be necessary to provide an explanation of the uncertainties associated with it.

Even if recognition of an asset or liability would provide relevant information, it may not provide a faithful representation of that asset or liability and any associated income, expenses or changes in equity. This may be the case if the level of measurement uncertainty inherent in an estimate of the value of the asset or liability is particularly high, although it should be noted that even a high level of measurement uncertainty does not necessarily prevent an estimate from providing useful information. Measurement uncertainty may be especially high in situations where the only way of estimating that measure of the asset is by using cash flow-based techniques and the range of outcomes is exceptionally wide and the probability of each outcome exceptionally difficult to estimate, or the measure is exceptionally sensitive to small changes in estimates of the probability of each possible outcome, or measurement of the asset or liability requires exceptionally difficult or subjective allocations of cash flows which do not relate solely to the asset or liability being measured.

Even in such situations, the framework sets out that the most useful information may be provided by recognising the asset or liability at the amount given by the uncertain estimate, accompanied by a description of the estimate and the uncertainties that surround it. If such information would not provide a sufficiently faithful representation, the most useful information may be provided by a different measure (accompanied by appropriate information and explanations) which is less relevant but subject to lower measurement uncertainty. Only in limited circumstances would the asset or liability not be recognised. Even then, it may still be necessary to include explanatory information about the asset or liability.

Derecognition. Derecognition is the removal of all or part of an asset or liability from an entity's statement of financial position. For an asset, derecognition normally occurs when the entity loses control of all or part of a recognised asset. For a liability, derecognition normally occurs when the entity no longer has a present obligation for all or part of the recognised liability.

The requirements for derecognition set out in the 2018 framework aim to achieve faithful representation both of any assets and liabilities retained after the transaction or other event which led to derecognition (including any item acquired, incurred or created as part of the transaction or other event), and the change in the entity's assets or liabilities as a result of that transaction or other event. Any assets or liabilities which have expired or been consumed, collected, fulfilled or transferred (referred to in the 2018 framework as the "transferred component") will be derecognised, with the associated recognition of any resultant income and expenses. Any assets or liabilities which are retained following the transaction or event (referred to as the "retained component") will continue to be recognised, becoming a separate unit of account from the transferred component—no income or expenses will be recognised on the retained component as a result of the derecognition of the transferred component, unless the transaction or event has caused the measurement basis of the retained component to be amended. Where necessary to achieve a faithful representation, the retained component will be presented separately in the statement of financial position, any income and expenses arising on the derecognition of the transferred component will be presented separately in the statement(s) of financial position, and appropriate explanatory information will be given.

Most decisions about derecognition are straightforward, but complexities can arise, especially where the aims referred to above conflict with each other. The 2018 framework provides detailed guidance on such situations.

In situations where an entity appears to have transferred an asset or liability but the item in fact remains an asset or liability of the entity (for example, legal title to an asset has been transferred but the entity retains significant exposure to variations in the amount of economic benefit which may arise from the asset, or the entity has transferred an asset to a party which holds the asset as agent for the entity) derecognition may not be appropriate because it may not provide a faithful representation of the assets or liabilities retained after the transfer, or of the change in the assets or liabilities of the entity which the transfer has brought about. In such cases, it may be appropriate to continue to recognise the transferred component, with no income or expenses being recognised on either the transferred component or any retained component, any proceeds received or paid being treated as a loan received or advanced, and the transferred component being presented separately in the statement of financial position with an explanation that the entity no longer has any rights or obligations arising from the transferred component. It may also be necessary to provide information about any income or expenses arising from the transferred component after the transfer.

The 2018 framework notes that questions about derecognition often arise when a contract is modified in a way which reduces or eliminates existing rights or obligations. When this occurs, it is necessary to consider which unit of account will provide users of the financial statements with the most useful information about the assets and liabilities retained after the modification, and about how the modification changed the assets and liabilities. If the contract modification only eliminates existing rights or obligations, then the approach described in the paragraph above is followed to determine whether to derecognise those rights or obligations. If the modification only adds new rights or obligations then it will be necessary to decide whether to treat the new rights and obligations as a separate asset or liability, or as part of the same unit of account as the existing rights or obligations. If the modification both eliminates existing rights and obligations, and creates new rights or obligations, both the separate and combined effects of the modification need to be considered. If the substance of the modification is that the old asset or liability has been replaced with a new asset or liability, it may be necessary to derecognise the old asset or liability and recognise the new one.

6. Measurement

Elements recognised in financial statements are quantified in monetary terms. This necessitates the selection of a measurement basis by which to determine the amount to be applied to each element. The most appropriate measurement basis to be applied to any element depends on consideration of the qualitative characteristics of useful financial information relating to that element, and the cost constraint. When selecting a measurement basis, it is important to consider the nature of the information which the measurement basis will produce in both the statement of financial position and the statement(s) of financial performance. The 2018 framework describes several possible measurement bases and notes that standards issued by the IASB may need to describe how to implement whichever measurement basis (or bases) they require.

Measurement bases. Measurement bases are categorised as either historic cost or current values. Four measurement bases are described in the 2018 framework, being historical cost, fair value, value in use (for assets) or fulfilment value (for liabilities), and current cost, alongside a discussion of the information which each basis provides.

Historical cost. The historical cost measure provides financial information about assets, liabilities and their related income and expenses derived essentially from the price of the transaction or other event which gave rise to them. Changes in value of the asset or liability over time are not reflected, except to the extent that an asset has become impaired or a liability has become onerous. The historical cost of an asset when it is acquired or created is the value of the cost incurred in acquiring or creating the asset. This will comprise the consideration paid to acquire the asset plus transaction costs. The historical cost of a liability when it is incurred or taken on is the value of the consideration received to incur or take on the liability minus transaction costs.

If an asset is acquired or created, or a liability incurred or taken on, as a result of an event that is not a transaction on market terms, any cost that it is possible to identify may not provide relevant information about the asset or liability. It may then be necessary to use a current value as the deemed cost at initial recognition, and subsequently treat that deemed cost as the historical cost.

Following initial recognition, the historical cost of an asset is updated over time to take account of consumption of the asset (depreciation or amortisation), payments received that extinguish part or all of the asset, the effect of part or all of the asset becoming unrecoverable (impairment), and the accrual of interest to reflect any financing component of the asset.

Financial assets and liabilities may be measured at historic cost by the application of the amortised cost method. This reflects estimates of future cash flows discounted at a rate determined at initial recognition. Where a financial instrument carries a variable rate of interest, the discount rate is updated to reflect changes in the variable rate. The amortised cost of the financial asset or liability is updated over time to reflect changes such as the accrual of interest, the impairment of a financial asset, and receipts and payments.

Where an asset has been acquired in a recent transaction on market terms, it may be expected that the asset will provide sufficient economic benefit to the entity to recover its cost. Similarly, where a liability has been incurred or taken on in a recent transaction on market terms, it may be expected that the value of the obligation to transfer economic resources to fulfil the liability will be no more than the value of the consideration received minus transaction costs. The measurement of an asset or liability at historical cost in these cases provides relevant information about the asset or liability and the price of the transaction from which it arose.

As the historical cost of an asset is reduced to reflect the consumption of an asset or its impairment, the amount expected to be recovered from the asset is at least as great as its carrying amount. Similarly, because the historical cost of a liability is increased when it becomes onerous, the value of the obligation to transfer economic resources needed to fulfil the liability is no more than the carrying amount of the liability.

Information about margin can be obtained from historical cost measurement, because the expense arising from the sale of an asset is recognised at the same time as the related income (the proceeds of sale). The same holds in respect of the fulfilment of all or part of a liability, where the relevant income is measured as the consideration received for the part fulfilled and is recognised at the same time as the expense incurred in fulfilment.

Information derived about margin in this way may have predictive value, because it can be used to assess the entity's prospects of future net cash flows. Such information may also have confirmatory value, as it may confirm (or otherwise) users' past estimates of cash flows or of margins.

Fair value. Fair value is defined in the 2018 framework as the price that would be received to sell an asset, or paid to transfer a liability, in an orderly transaction between market participants at the measurement date. It reflects the perspective of participants in a market to which the entity has access.

Fair value can sometimes be determined directly by observing prices in an active market. In other cases, it must be determined indirectly using measurement techniques such as cash flow forecasting, which reflect estimates of future cash flows, possible variations in the amount or timing of those cash flows caused by inherent uncertainty, the time value of money, the price for bearing the inherent uncertainty (in other words, the risk premium or discount), and other factors which market participants would take into account, such as liquidity.

The fair value of an asset or liability is not affected by transaction costs incurred when the asset is acquired, or the liability incurred or taken on. Similarly, it does not reflect the transaction costs which would be incurred on the ultimate disposal of the asset or on the transfer or settlement of the liability.

Information provided by fair value measurement of assets and liabilities may have predictive value, because fair value represents market participants' current expectations about the amount, timing and uncertainty of future cash flows. Such information may also have confirmatory value by providing feedback about previous expectations. Changes in fair value can have a number of different causes, and identifying the effect of each cause may provide useful information.

Income and expenses which reflect market participants' current expectations may have predictive value, because these amounts can be used as inputs in predicting future income and expenses. They may also assist users in assessing management's stewardship of the entity's economic resources.

Value in use (of assets) and fulfilment value (of liabilities). Value in use is defined in the 2018 framework as the present value of the cash flows, or other economic benefits, that an entity expects to derive from the use of an asset and from its ultimate disposal. Fulfilment value is the present value of the cash, or other economic resources, that an entity expects to be obliged to transfer as it fulfils a liability, including any amounts that the entity expects to be obliged to transfer to other parties besides the liability counterparty to enable it to fulfil the liability.

Because value in use and fulfilment value are based on future cash flows, they do not include transaction costs incurred on acquiring an asset or taking on a liability. However, they do include the present value of any transaction costs the entity expects to incur in ultimately disposing of the asset or fulfilling the liability.

Value in use and fulfilment value are based on entity-specific assumptions, rather than assumptions made by market participants. However, the framework notes that often there is little difference between assumptions made by the entity and those which would be made by market participants.

Value in use and fulfilment value cannot be observed directly and hence are always derived indirectly via cash flow-based measurement techniques, reflecting the same factors as described above for the indirect derivation of fair value.

The value in use of an asset provides information about the cash flows estimated to arise from the use of an asset and, ultimately, its disposal, adjusted to present value. This may have predictive value because it can be used as an input to an assessment of the prospects for future cash flows.

The fulfilment value of a liability provides information about the estimated cash flows needed to fulfil a liability, adjusted to present value. This information may have predictive value.

When estimates of value in use and fulfilment value are updated, the updated amounts may have confirmatory value, because they provide feedback at the accuracy or otherwise of the previous estimates.

Current cost. The current cost of an asset is the cost of an equivalent asset at the measurement date. It includes the consideration that would be paid at the measurement date plus the transaction costs that would be incurred at that date. The current cost of a liability is the consideration that would be received for an equivalent liability at the measurement date minus the transaction costs that would be incurred at that date.

Current cost can sometimes be observed directly (for example, if there is an active market in assets of similar age and condition to the asset in question) but where this is not possible (for example, markets deal only in new assets) it would be necessary to derive current cost indirectly by adjusting the price of a new asset to reflect the age and condition of the asset in question.

Similarly to historical cost, current cost provides information about the cost of an asset consumed or about income from the fulfilment of liabilities. Such information can be used to calculate current margins and to predict future margins. In this respect, current cost has the advantage over historical cost in that current cost reflects prices in force at the time of consumption or fulfilment. Where price changes are significant, margins based on current cost may be more useful in predicting future margins than those based on historical cost.

Selection of a measurement basis. Guidance is provided on factors to consider when selecting a measurement basis. It is noted that for the information provided by a particular measurement basis to be useful to the users of the financial statements, it must be relevant, and it must faithfully represent what it purports to represent. Cost is recognised as a constraint on the selection of a measurement basis, as it is with all other areas of financial reporting. The enhancing qualitative characteristics of comparability, verifiability and understandability are also recognised as having implications for the selection of a measurement basis.

Relevance. The relevance of the information provided by a particular measurement basis is affected by the characteristics of the asset or liability being measured, and the contribution of the asset or liability to future cash flows.

Characteristics of the asset or liability being measured. Where the value of an asset or liability is susceptible to market factors or other risks, its historical cost might differ significantly from its current value. Historical cost may therefore not provide relevant information to users of the financial statements if they attach importance to changes in value. For example, historical cost is not an appropriate measurement basis for derivative financial instruments.

In addition, under the historical cost basis, changes in value are not reported at the time of change, but only upon an event such as disposal, impairment or fulfilment. This could lead to an incorrect conclusion by the users of the financial statements that all of the income and expenses recognised at the time of disposal, impairment or fulfilment arose at that point, rather than at the time when the change in value actually occurred.

Where assets or liabilities are measured at fair value, changes in value arise partly from changes in the expectations of market participants and their attitude to risk. The recognition of such changes in value in financial statements may not provide useful information if the entity's intention is to use the assets within its business or fulfil any liabilities itself, rather than selling or transferring them respectively.

Contribution to future cash flows. When an entity's business activity involves the use of several economic resources which produce cash flows indirectly, by being used in combination to produce and market goods or services to customers, historical cost or current cost measurement are likely to provide relevant information about the activity. As described in the sections on historical cost and current cost above, these measurement bases lend themselves to the reporting of margin, which may be the most relevant information to users of the financial statements of entities involved in this type of activity.

Conversely, for assets and liabilities which produce cash flows directly, such as assets which can be sold independently and without significant economic penalty such as disruption to the business, a measurement basis founded upon current value, such as fair value, or value in use (for assets), or fulfilment value (for liabilities), is likely to provide the most relevant information.

Faithful representation. Whether a measurement basis can provide a faithful representation is affected by measurement inconsistency and measurement uncertainty.

Measurement inconsistency. For assets and liabilities which are related in some way, the use of different measurement bases can create measurement inconsistency (or accounting mismatch). Financial statements containing measurement inconsistencies may not faithfully represent some aspects of the entity's financial position and financial performance. Using the same measurement basis for related assets and liabilities may therefore provide users of the financial statements with information which is more useful than if differing measurement bases were used, especially where the cash flows from one asset or liability are directly linked to the cash flows from another asset or liability.

Measurement uncertainty. Measurement uncertainty arises where a measure cannot be determined directly from observation of prices in an active market and must be estimated. Although measures need not be perfectly accurate for a faithful representation to be provided, in some cases the level of measurement uncertainty associated with an estimate may be so high that it would be preferable to select a different measurement basis which would also result in relevant information.

Enhancing qualitative characteristics. The enhancing qualitative characteristics of comparability, understandability and verifiability are relevant to the selection of a measurement basis.

Comparability. Consistent use of the same measurement basis for the same items, either from reporting period to reporting period within the same entity, or for the same reporting period across entities, can make financial statements more comparable.

Understandability. Understandability may be lost as a result of a change in measurement basis. However, there may be a trade-off in terms of an increase in the relevance of the information which the new measurement basis provides. In general, understandability will decline as the number of measurement bases used within a particular set of financial statements increases. Again, however, any loss of understandability may be countered to a degree by an increase in other factors contributing to the usefulness of the information provided.

Verifiability. Verifiability increases where measurement bases are used whose inputs can be independently corroborated either directly, for example by reference to prices in an active market, or indirectly, for example by checking the inputs to a model.

Specific implications of the enhancing qualitative characteristics for particular measurement bases are as follows:

Historical cost. In general, it is straightforward to measure historical cost, and the concept is usually well understood and the measures it produces simple to verify. However, the estimation of the consumption of assets and the measurement of impairment losses or onerous liabilities can be complex and subjective, reducing understandability and verifiability. In addition, identical assets and liabilities which were initially recognised at different times under historical cost may be reported at different amounts, reducing comparability.

Fair value. Because fair value is determined from the point of view of market participants, rather than of the entity, and, as a current value, is unaffected by the date of acquisition of the asset or incurring of the liability, in principle it will be measured at the same amount by entities which have access to the same markets. This will aid comparability. Where fair values are determined directly by observing active markets, the measurement process is simple and easy to understand, in addition to providing measurements which are verifiable. On the other hand, where fair values cannot be measured directly and need to be derived via valuation techniques, the inputs and valuation process may be complex and subjective, reducing comparability, understandability and verifiability.

Value in use (of assets) and fulfilment value (of liabilities). Value in use and fulfilment value always need to be derived via valuation techniques, meaning that comparability, understandability and verifiability may be impaired for the same reasons set out above in relation to fair value. In addition, value in use cannot be determined in a meaningful way for an individual asset used in combination with other assets. In such a case, value in use is determined for the group of assets and then needs to be allocated to individual assets. This process can be subjective and arbitrary, which serves to reduce verifiability. This tends to indicate that value in use is not usually a suitable measurement basis for regular revaluations of assets, but it may be appropriate for occasional remeasurements, for instance where a possible impairment is identified, and it is necessary to determine if the carrying value of an asset is recoverable.

Current cost. Where a current cost basis is used, identical assets or liabilities which are acquired or incurred at different times will be reported in the financial statements at the same amount. This aids comparability. However, the determination of current cost can be a complex, subjective and costly process. An active market may not exist for items of an identical age and condition to those possessed by the entity, meaning that the active market value of new items may need to be adjusted appropriately. It may not even be possible to obtain the price of an identical new asset if these are no longer available due, for example, to advances in technology. In addition, it may be necessary to split current costs changes between the current cost of consumption and the effect of changes in prices, introducing further arbitrary assumptions which may be complex. These aspects may further diminish the verifiability and understandability of current cost measures.

Factors specific to initial measurement. The 2018 framework notes that, where an asset is acquired, or a liability incurred as a result of a transaction on market terms, historical cost will usually be close to fair value, assuming that transaction costs are not significant. Nonetheless, the framework notes that it is important to state the measurement basis which is being applied. In addition, it will usually be appropriate to apply the same measurement basis at initial recognition as will be used for subsequent measurement.

Where initial recognition of an asset or liability occurs as a result of an event which is not a transaction on market terms (for example, as a result of a related party transaction, or where an asset is granted or donated free of charge, or where a liability is imposed by legislation or a court judgement), the framework notes that recognising the asset or liability at its historical cost (which may be zero) may not provide a faithful representation of the entity's assets and liabilities, or the associated income and expenses. In such cases, it may be appropriate to recognise the asset or liability at a deemed cost, with any difference between that amount and any consideration which is given or received being recognised as income or expenses at the time of initial recognition. Careful analysis of such items is needed to ensure that any assets, liabilities and contributions from or distributions to holders of equity claims are recognised, and sufficient explanation is given to achieve a faithful representation of the entity's financial position and financial performance is given.

More than one measurement basis. Situations where more than one measurement basis is needed to provide information about an asset, liability, income or expense are discussed and it is noted that, usually, the most understandable way to provide such information is to use one measurement basis in both the statement of financial position and the statement(s) of financial performance, and to use the other measurement basis for disclosure only. However, in some cases more relevant information may be provided by using a current value measurement basis in the statement of financial position and a different measurement basis to determine the related income or expenses in the statement of profit and loss.

Measurement of equity. The 2018 framework notes that the carrying amount of equity is not measured directly. Instead, it equals the total of the carrying amounts of all recognised assets less the total of the carrying amounts of all recognised liabilities. Because general-purpose financial statements are not intended to show an entity's value, the total carrying amount of equity will not usually equal the aggregate market value of equity claims on the entity, or the amount that could be obtained by selling the entity as a whole on a going concern basis, or the amount that could be obtained by selling all of the entity's assets and settling all of its liabilities.

Despite the fact that total equity is not measured directly, it may be appropriate for certain classes or components of equity to be measured in this way. However, since total equity is already derived as a residual, there will always be at least one class of equity and one component of equity which cannot be measured directly.

Although total equity and each individual class and component of equity are usually positive, it is not impossible for any of these items to be negative in certain circumstances.

Cash flow-based measurement techniques. The 2018 framework provides some commentary on cash flow-based measurement techniques, which may be applied where a measure cannot be observed directly. The framework notes that such techniques are not measurement bases in themselves, but techniques used in applying the selected measurement basis. When using such techniques, it is therefore necessary to identify the measurement basis being applied, and the extent to which the technique reflects the factors applicable to that measurement basis.

Cash flow-based measurement techniques can also be used in applying a modified measurement basis, for example the fulfilment value of a liability modified to exclude the possibility that an entity may fail to fulfil a liability. This may result in information which is more relevant to the users of the financial statements, or that may be less costly to produce or to understand. On the other hand, it is also possible for modified measurement bases to be more difficult for users to understand.

The framework discusses outcome uncertainty and states that this arises from uncertainty about the amount or timing of future cash flows. Such uncertainties are important characteristics of assets and liabilities and need to be taken into consideration in selecting a single amount from the range of possible cash flows. The amount selected for the estimate is usually located in the central part of the range and may be determined by calculating the probability-weighted average (or expected value), the statistical median or the statistical mode. This estimate depends on estimates of future cash flows and possible variations in their amounts or timing but does not take account of any risk premium or discount. In addition to determining the estimate to be recognised in the financial statements in this way, it may be necessary to provide users with information about the range of possible outcomes.

7. Presentation and Disclosure

The 2018 framework discusses presentation and disclosure as communication tools, sets out presentation and disclosure objectives and principles, and deals with classification and aggregation.

Presentation and disclosure as communication tools. The 2018 framework notes that an entity communicates information about its assets, liabilities, equity, income and expenses by presenting and disclosing information in its financial statements. Effective communication in this way makes the information more relevant and contributes to a faithful representation of the entity's assets, liabilities, equity, income and expenses. Effective communication is achieved by focusing on presentation and disclosure objectives and principles rather than rules, classifying information in a way which groups similar items and separates dissimilar items, and aggregating information in such a way that it is not obscured either by unnecessary detail or excessive aggregation. In making a decision on presentation and disclosure, account is taken of whether the benefits provided to users by presenting or disclosing particular information are likely to justify the costs of providing and using that information.

Presentation and disclosure objectives and principles. The 2018 framework states that when the IASB develops presentation and disclosure requirements in standards, it is necessary to achieve a balance between giving entities the flexibility to provide relevant information that faithfully represents the entity's assets, liabilities, equity, income and expenses, and requiring information which is comparable, both from period to period for reporting entities and in a single period across entities.

The framework notes that the inclusion of presentation and disclosure objectives in the IASB's standards supports effective communication, because such objectives assist entities in identifying useful information and deciding how to communicate it in the most effective manner.

The framework also states that entity-specific information is more useful than standardised descriptions (or "boiler-plate"), and duplication of information in different parts of the financial statements is usually unnecessary and can reduce understandability.

Classification. Classification is the sorting of assets, liabilities, equity, income and expenses on the basis of shared characteristics for presentation and disclosure purposes. Such characteristics include, but are not limited to, the nature of the item, its role within the entity's business activities, and how it is measured. Dissimilar items should not be classified together, as this may obscure relevant information, reduce understandability and comparability and may not provide a faithful representation of what it purports to represent.

In general, classification is applied to the unit of account selected for an asset or liability. However, if it would result in the provision of more useful information, it may be appropriate to separate an asset or liability into components which have different characteristics and to classify those components separately. For example, an asset or liability may be separated into current and non-current components, and these components presented accordingly.

Offsetting (the grouping into a single net amount in the statement of financial position of an asset and a liability which have been measured as separate units of account) is usually not appropriate as it classifies dissimilar items together. However, it should be noted that offsetting differs from treating a set of rights and obligations as a single unit of account.

Where equity claims have different characteristics, it may be appropriate to classify them separately. In addition, it may be appropriate to classify components of equity separately if they are subject to particular legal, regulatory or other requirements. For example, in some country's entities are only permitted to make distributions to holders of equity claims if they have sufficient distributable reserves (e.g., under the UK Companies Act 2006), and separate presentation of such reserves may provide useful information.

In relation to information about financial performance, the 2018 framework does not prescribe a single-statement or dual-statement structure for the statement of financial performance. It refers to the statement (or section) of profit and loss as the primary source of information about an entity's financial performance for the period and requires a total (or subtotal) for profit or loss to be provided. Profit or loss is not defined, but it is stated that, in principle, all income and expenses for the period are included in the statement of profit or loss. However, the IASB may decide in exceptional circumstances that income or expenses arising from a change in the current value of an asset or liability are to be included outside the statement (or section) of profit and loss, in other comprehensive income, when to do so would result in the statement of profit or loss providing more relevant information, or providing a more faithful representation of the entity's financial performance for the period.

Items of income or expenses included in other comprehensive income in one period will be reclassified into the statement of profit or loss in some future period (i.e., be recycled), if doing so will enhance the relevance of the information included in the statement of profit or loss for that future period, or provide a more faithful representation of the entity's financial performance for that future period. This treatment may not be adopted if, for example, there is no clear basis for identifying the period in which that reclassification would enhance the relevance of the information in the statement of profit or loss, or the amount that should be reclassified.

Aggregation. The 2018 framework states that aggregation is the adding together of assets, liabilities, equity, income and expenses that have shared characteristics and are included in the same classification. Aggregation makes information more useful by summarising a large volume of detail. However, it also conceals some of that detail. There is a trade-off between ensuring that relevant information is not obscured either by excessive insignificant detail or by excessive aggregation. Different levels of aggregation may be appropriate in different parts of the financial statements. For example, the statement of financial position and the statement(s) of financial performance may provide information in a more summarised form than the notes to the financial statements, in which more detail is provided.

8. Concepts of Capital and Capital Maintenance

The material in this chapter has been carried forward unchanged from the 2010 framework, into which it was transferred unchanged from the IASC's 1989 framework. In developing the 2018 framework, the IASB decided that updating the discussion of capital and capital maintenance was not feasible and could have delayed the development of the 2018 framework significantly. On the other hand, the IASB decided that it would be inappropriate for the 2018 framework to exclude a discussion of capital and capital maintenance altogether. The IASB has stated that it may revisit these concepts in the future if it considers it necessary.

Concepts of capital. Two concepts of capital are identified. The most common concept is the financial concept, under which capital is synonymous with the net assets or equity of the entity. Under the alternative concept—the physical concept of capital—capital is regarded as the productive capacity of the entity based on, for example, units of output per day. Selection of the appropriate concept should be based on the needs of the users of the financial statements.

Concepts of capital maintenance and the determination of profit. The two concepts of capital maintenance described above give rise to two corresponding concepts of capital maintenance.

Under financial capital maintenance, a profit is only earned if the monetary amount of the entity's net assets at the end of the reporting period exceeds the monetary amount of its net assets at the beginning of that period, after excluding any distributions to and contributions from owners (in other words, holders of equity claims) during the period. Financial capital maintenance can be measured either in nominal monetary units or units of constant purchasing power.

Under physical capital maintenance, a profit is only earned if the physical productive capacity of the entity (or the resources or funds needed to achieve that capacity) at the end of the reporting period exceeds the physical productive capacity at the beginning of the period, after excluding any distributions to and contributions from owners.

The concept of capital maintenance links the concept of capital and the concept of profit because it defines how profit is measured. Profit is the residual following the deduction of expenses from income. If expenses exceed income, then the result is a loss.

Under the financial capital maintenance concept, selection of an appropriate measurement basis depends upon the type of financial capital which the entity is seeking to maintain, for example invested money or invested purchasing power. The physical capital maintenance concept requires the application of the current cost measurement basis.

HIERARCHY OF STANDARDS

The conceptual framework is used by IASB members and staff in their debate, and they expect that those commenting on Exposure Drafts for new or revised standards will articulate their arguments in terms of the conceptual framework. However, the conceptual framework is not normally intended to be used directly by preparers and auditors in determining their accounting methods. In the 2003 revision of IAS 8 the IASB introduced a hierarchy of accounting rules that should be followed by preparers in seeking solutions to accounting problems. This hierarchy says that the most authoritative guidance is IFRS, and the preparer should seek guidance as follows:

1. IAS/IFRS and SIC/IFRIC Interpretations, when these specifically apply to a transaction or condition.
2. In the absence of such a directly applicable standard, judgement is to be used to develop and apply an accounting policy, which conforms to the definitions, recognition criteria and measurement concepts for assets, liabilities, income and expenses set out in the conceptual framework.
3. If this is not possible, the preparer should then look to recent pronouncements of other standard setters which use a similar conceptual framework to develop their standards, as well as other accounting literature and industry practices, which do not conflict with guidance in IFRS dealing with the same or similar circumstances or with the definitions set out in the conceptual framework.

IFRS PRACTICE STATEMENT 1—MANAGEMENT COMMENTARY

Nature and Scope

IFRS Practice Statement *Management Commentary* was issued in December 2010 and is prospectively applicable. The Practice Statement provides a broad, non-binding framework for the presentation of narrative reporting to accompany financial statements prepared in accordance with IFRS. It is therefore not an IFRS standard, and local authorities may voluntarily choose to implement the Practice Statement. However, it is foreseen that many countries will not implement the Practice Statement and will implement the developments regarding integrated reporting instead. Furthermore, many local authorities have similar local guidance.

Management commentary is a narrative report, which provides the context within which the financial position, financial performance and cash flows of an entity need to be interpreted. Management can also explain its objectives and strategies applied to fulfil those objectives. Management commentary falls within the scope of financial reporting, and thus the conceptual framework, and should be read in conjunction with the conceptual framework. The Practice Statement provides the principles, elements and qualitative characteristics of decision-useful information regarding management commentary, and therefore assists management in presenting management commentary.

Management needs to identify the extent of applying the Practice Statement. Full compliance can only be claimed if an entity complies with all the requirements. In applying the Practice Statement, management must consider the needs of the primary users of the financial statements. The primary users are similar to the 2010 conceptual framework: existing and potential investors, lenders and other creditors.

Principles

Management commentary is based on the principles of providing management's view and supplementing and complementing information presented in the financial statements.

Management commentary should include forward-looking information and information possessing the qualitative characteristics described in the conceptual framework. Management commentary should present management's perspective and should be derived from the information important to management decision making.

Supplementary and complementary information explains the amounts provided in financial statements and the conditions and events forming that information. It includes all information that is important in understanding the financial statements.

Regarding forward-looking information, it must provide management's perspective regarding the entity's direction. It does not predict the future, but rather focuses on the entity's objectives and strategies to achieve those objectives. Forward-looking information is provided regarding uncertainties, trends and factors, which could influence an entity's revenue, performance, liquidity and capital resources. Forward-looking information is provided through both narrative descriptions and quantitative data and must include disclosures of the assumptions used.

Qualitative Characteristics

The conceptual framework fundamental qualitative characteristics of relevance and faithful representation are applied, and the enhancing qualitative characteristics of comparability, verifiability, timeliness and understandability should be maximised. Management should include all information that is material to its management commentary.

Presentation

The presentation of management commentary should be clear and straightforward. Management commentary should be consistent with the related financial statements, avoid duplication and avoid generic disclosure. To assist in assessing the performance of an entity, management commentary should include the entity's risk exposures, the risk strategies and how effective the strategies are, how resources recognised could affect the financial performance and how non-financial information affects the financial statements.

Elements

The following main elements should be included:

- Nature of business;
- Management's objectives and strategies to achieve the objectives;
- The most significant sources, risks and relationships;
- The results of the entity's operations and prospects; and
- The critical performance measures and indicators used by management to assess the performance against objectives.

A description of the business to understand the entity and its environment is the starting point of management commentary. It includes information about the entity's industry, its market and competition, the legal, regulatory and macroeconomic environment, its main projects, services, business processes and distribution channels, structure and how it creates value.

Objectives and strategies, and changes thereof, must be disclosed in a way which enables users to understand the priorities of the entity and the resources used to achieve them. This includes performance indicators and the time frame over which success is measured.

Relationships between objectives, strategies, management actions and executive remuneration are also helpful.

A clear description of the most important resources, risks and relationships which affect the entity's value and how they are managed is needed. This includes analysis of financial and non-financial resources, capital structure, financial needs, liquidity and cash flows and human and intellectual capital. Risk disclosure includes principal risk exposures, changes therein, uncertainties, means of mitigating risks and effectiveness of risk strategies. Risk disclosures could be divided into principal strategic, commercial, operational and financial risks. Significant relationships with stakeholders, which are value driven and managed, should also be disclosed.

A clear description of financial and non-financial performances and prospects should be included. A description of performance and progress during the year helps to predict the future by identifying the main trends and factors affecting the business. Comparison of performance, liquidity and financial position with previous years is essential.

Performance measures and indicators (financial and non-financial) used by management should be disclosed and the reasons why they change over time. This increases the comparability of management commentary over time.

US GAAP COMPARISON

The FASB Concept Statements are herein referred to as the FASB Framework. The FASB Framework consists of different concept statements. Chapters 1 and 2 of the new IASB joint framework have also been included in the FASB Concept Statement No. 8 (or CON 8). Both frameworks focus on the asset and liability approach and define assets and liabilities similarly. The IASB Framework only defines two elements of changes in assets and liabilities, namely income and expenses. The FASB Framework identifies more elements such as investments by owners, distributions to owners and other comprehensive income, and subdivides comprehensive income into revenue, expenses, gains and losses. The FASB Framework does not identify probability as a recognition criterion but includes relevance as a recognition criterion. The FASB Framework separates measurement in (1) a selection of the monetary unit and (2) choice of attribute. Both frameworks provide a list of measurement attributes but provide no guideline on when each should be applied. Neither framework has an adequate concept of the reporting entity.

The FASB does have an active project on the definition of a non-public entity. The goal of the project is to re-examine the definition of a non-public entity and a public entity in the FASB Accounting Standards Codification. The FASB issued Accounting Standards Update in December 2013 that defines a public entity to fulfil Phase 1 of this project. When complete, entities that are not defined as public entities will be within the scope of the *Private Company Decision-Making Framework: A Guide for Evaluating Financial Accounting and Reporting for Private Companies*. Phase 2 is under way.

While the FASB's conceptual framework project continues, it is no longer a joint project with the IASB. The IASB has pursued advancement of the conceptual framework through the ASAF meetings. The FASB participates in those meetings as a representative of the US.

The FASB has held several meetings over the years on a project entitled Disclosure Framework—Board's Decision Process. The objective and primary focus of the Disclosure Framework project is to improve the effectiveness of disclosures in notes to financial statements by clearly communicating the information that is most important to users of each entity's financial statements. It is anticipated that the result will be a lower volume of disclosures, although that is not a primary goal. The final draft of FASB Concepts Statement No. 8, Conceptual Framework for Financial Reporting—Chapter 8, Notes to Financial Statements was issued in August 2018.

In a discussion with the FASB's senior project manager in the summer of 2019 it was learned that, "We have three separate projects on the FASB's agenda to revise the conceptual framework. First, we are working on revised definitions of elements (Concepts Statement No. 6). Second, the Board is working on measurement concepts (Concepts Statement No. 5). And finally, the Board is working on concepts for presentation. The Board issued an exposure draft in 2016 addressing presentation concepts . . . [yet it] has put that project on hold until it reconsiders the definitions of revenue, expenses, gains and losses in its elements project. The decisions made in the elements and measurement projects [will] still need to be exposed."

Regarding the IFRS Practice Statement *Management Commentary*, the US SEC maintains regulations that specify the form and content of management commentary as well as other disclosures.

With respect to going concern US GAAP, an entity's management should evaluate whether there are conditions or events, considered in the aggregate, that raise substantial doubt about the entity's ability to continue as a going concern within one year after the date that the financial statements are issued (or within one year after the date that the financial statements are available to be issued when applicable). Additionally, management is required to consider plans that are in place to mitigate the risks of an entity's ability to continue as a going concern. If management concludes it is not able to continue as a going concern, it must make specific disclosures. Prior to 2017, US GAAP provided no guidance to management on assessing and disclosing doubts about the ability of the entity to continue as a going concern; however, US auditing and public company regulations did provide such guidance.

3 PRESENTATION OF FINANCIAL STATEMENTS

INTRODUCTION

As set out in IASB's *Conceptual Framework for Financial Reporting 2018*, the objective of general-purpose financial reporting is to provide financial information about the reporting entity which is useful to existing and potential investors, lenders and other creditors in making decisions about providing resources to the entity. Although financial statements prepared for this purpose meet the needs of these specific users, they do not provide all the information which the users may need to make economic decisions since they largely portray the financial effects of past events and do not necessarily provide non-financial information.

In the past, many considered the lack of guidance on the presentation of the financial statements under IFRS to be a significant impediment to the achievement of comparability among financial statements. Users previously expressed concerns that information in financial statements was highly aggregated and inconsistently presented, making it difficult to fully understand the relationship between the financial statements and the financial results and position of the reporting entity.

The revised IAS 1 presented in this chapter resulted from the IASB's deliberations on Phase A of the Financial Statement Presentation project and brings IAS 1 largely into line with the corresponding US standard—Statement of Financial Accounting Standards 130

(FAS 130), *Reporting Comprehensive Income* (codified in ASC 220). The FASB decided that it would not publish a separate standard on this phase of the project but will expose issues pertinent to this and the next phase together in the future. The revised IAS 1 was effective for annual periods beginning on or after January 1, 2009.

In June 2011, the IASB issued an amendment to IAS 1 titled *Presentation of Items of Other Comprehensive Income*, which took effect for annual periods beginning on or after July 1, 2012. The amendment improves the consistency and clarity of items recorded in other comprehensive income. Components of other comprehensive income are grouped together on the basis of whether they are subsequently reclassified to profit or loss or not. The Board highlighted the importance of presenting profit or loss and other comprehensive income together and with equal prominence. The name of the statement of comprehensive income is changed to statement of profit or loss and other comprehensive income.

In December 2014, the IASB issued *Disclosure Initiative (Amendments to IAS 1)*, which made a number of amendments to IAS 1. In relation to materiality, the amendments clarify first that information should not be obscured by aggregating or by providing immaterial information, secondly that materiality considerations apply to all parts of the financial statements, and thirdly that even when a standard requires a specific disclosure, materiality considerations do apply. In relation to the Statement of Financial Position and Statement of Profit or Loss and Other Comprehensive Income, the amendments first introduce a clarification that the list of line items to be presented in these statements can be disaggregated and aggregated as relevant and provide additional guidance on subtotals in these statements, and secondly clarify that an entity's share of other comprehensive income of equity-accounted associates and joint ventures should be presented in aggregate as single line items based on whether or not it will subsequently be reclassified to profit or loss. In relation to the notes to the financial statements, the amendments add additional examples of possible ways of ordering the notes to clarify that understandability and comparability should be considered when determining the order of the notes, and to demonstrate that the notes need not be presented in the order so far listed in IAS 1. The IASB also removed guidance and examples with regard to the identification of significant accounting policies that were perceived as being potentially unhelpful.

In October 2018, IAS 1 (and consequently IAS 8) was amended by clarifying the definition of material and how materiality should be applied. This has ensured a consistency of the definition of materiality across all International Financial Reporting Standards.

IAS 1 is discussed in this chapter, while the structure and content of the financial statements are discussed in Chapter 4 (Statement of Financial Position), Chapter 5 (Statements of Profit or Loss and Other Comprehensive Income, and Changes in Equity) and Chapter 6 (Statement of Cash Flows).

Sources of IFRS

Conceptual Framework for Financial Reporting 2010

IAS 1, 7, 8, 10, 12, 18, 24, 27, 33, 34 — *IFRS* 5, 8

SCOPE

IAS 1, *Presentation of Financial Statements*, is applicable to all general-purpose financial statements prepared and presented in accordance with IFRS. IAS 1 is applicable both to consolidated and separate financial statements but is not applicable to the structure and content of interim financial statements (see Chapter 34). The general features of IAS 1 are, however, applicable to interim financial statements.

IAS 1 is developed for profit-orientated entities. Entities with not-for-profit activities or public sector entities may apply the standard, provided that appropriate adjustments are made to particular line items in the financial statements. Entities whose share capital is not classified as equity (such as mutual funds) may also apply IAS 1 provided that the member's interest is appropriately disclosed.

DEFINITIONS OF TERMS

General-purpose financial statements. The financial statements intended to meet the needs of users who are not in a position to require an entity to prepare reports tailored to their particular information needs.

Impracticable. Applying a requirement is impracticable when the entity cannot apply it after making every reasonable effort to do so.

International Financial Reporting Standards (IFRS). Standards and Interpretations issued by the International Accounting Standards Board (IASB), which comprise:

1. International Financial Reporting Standards;
2. International Accounting Standards (issued by the former International Accounting Standards Committee (IASC));
3. Interpretations developed by the International Financial Reporting Interpretations Committee (IFRIC); and
4. Interpretations developed by the former Standing Interpretations Committee (SIC).

Material. Information is considered material if omitting, misstating or obscuring it could reasonably be expected to influence the decisions of primary users of financial statements.

Notes. Information provided in addition to that presented in the financial statements, which comprise a summary of significant accounting policies and other explanatory information, including narrative descriptions or disaggregation of items presented in those statements as well as information about items which do not qualify for recognition in those statements.

Other comprehensive income. Items of income and expense (including reclassification adjustments) which are not recognised in profit or loss as required or permitted by other IFRS or Interpretations. The components of other comprehensive income include:

1. Changes in revaluation surplus (IAS 16 and IAS 38);
2. Remeasurements of defined benefit plans (IAS 19);
3. Gains and losses arising from translating the financial statements of a foreign operation (IAS 21);

4. Gains and losses on remeasuring of investments in equity instruments designated and financial assets measured at fair value through other comprehensive income (IFRS 9); and
5. The effective portion of gains and losses on hedging instruments in a cash flow hedge (IFRS 9).

Owners. Holders of instruments classified as equity.

Profit or loss. The total of income less expenses, excluding the components of other comprehensive income.

Reclassification adjustments. Amounts reclassified to profit or loss in the current period which were recognised in other comprehensive income in the current or previous periods.

Total comprehensive income. The change in equity during a period resulting from transactions and other events, other than those changes resulting from transactions with owners in their capacity as owners. It comprises all components of "profit or loss" and of "other comprehensive income."

FINANCIAL STATEMENTS

Financial statements are a central feature of financial reporting—a principal means through which an entity communicates its financial information to external parties. The IASB's *Conceptual Framework* (see Chapter 2) describes the basic concepts by which financial statements are prepared. It does so by defining the objective of financial statements; identifying the qualitative characteristics which make information in financial statements useful; and defining the basic elements of financial statements and the concepts for recognising and measuring them in financial statements.

The elements of financial statements are the broad classifications and groupings which convey the substantive financial effects of transactions and events on the reporting entity. To be included in the financial statements, an event or transaction must meet definitional, recognition and measurement requirements, all of which are set out in the *Conceptual Framework*.

How an entity presents information in its financial statements, for example how assets, liabilities, equity, revenues, expenses, gains, losses and cash flows should be grouped into line items and categories and which subtotals and totals should be presented, is of great importance in communicating financial information to those who use that information to make decisions (e.g., capital providers).

Objective

IAS 1 prescribes the basis for presentation of general-purpose financial statements to ensure comparability both with the entity's financial statements of previous periods and with the financial statements of other entities. It sets out overall requirements for the presentation of financial statements, guidelines for their structure and minimum requirements for their content. In revising IAS 1, the IASB's main objective was to aggregate information in the financial statements based on shared characteristics. Other sources of guidance on financial statement presentation can be found in IAS 7, 8, 10, 12, 24, 27 and 34, and IFRS 5, 8, 15 and 16.

Purpose of Financial Statements

IAS 1 refers to financial statements as "a structured representation of the financial position and financial performance of an entity" and goes on to explain that the objective of financial statements is to provide information about an entity's financial position, its financial performance and its cash flows, which is then utilised by a wide spectrum of end users in making economic decisions. In addition, financial statements show the results of management's stewardship of the resources entrusted to it. All this information is communicated through a complete set of financial statements which provide information about an entity's:

1. Assets;
2. Liabilities;
3. Equity;
4. Income and expenses, including gains and losses;
5. Contributions by and distributions to owners in their capacity as owners; and
6. Cash flows.

All this information, and other information presented in the notes, helps users of financial statements to predict the entity's future cash flows and their timing and certainty.

GENERAL FEATURES

Fair Presentation and Compliance with IFRS

In accordance with IFRS, financial statements should present fairly the financial position, financial performance and cash flows of an entity. Fair presentation means faithful representation of the effects of transactions, other events and conditions in accordance with the definitions and recognition criteria for assets, liabilities, income and expenses set out in the *Conceptual Framework*. As stated in IAS 1, the application of IFRS, with additional disclosure when necessary, should result in financial statements achieving fair presentation. Financial statements should depict financial information without bias for selection or disclosure. However, in extremely rare circumstances where management concludes that compliance with a requirement in an IFRS would be so misleading that it would conflict with the objective of financial statements as set out in the *Conceptual Framework*, the entity can depart from that requirement if the relevant regulatory framework requires, or otherwise does not prohibit, such a departure, and the entity discloses all of the following:

1. Management has concluded that the financial statements present fairly the entity's financial position, financial performance and cash flows;
2. The entity has complied with all applicable IFRS, except that it has departed from a requirement to achieve fair presentation;
3. The title of the IFRS from which the entity has departed, the nature of the departure, including the treatment that the IFRS would require, the reason why that treatment would be so misleading in the circumstances that it would conflict with the objective of financial statements set out in the *Conceptual Framework* and the treatment adopted; and
4. For each period presented, the financial effect of the departure on each item in the financial statements which would have been reported in complying with the requirement.

When an entity has departed from a requirement of an IFRS in a prior period, and that departure affects the amounts recognised in the current period, it shall make the disclosures set out in 3. and 4. above.

The standard notes that deliberately departing from IFRS might not be permissible in some jurisdictions, in which case the entity should comply with the standard in question and disclose in the notes that it believes this to be misleading and show the adjustments which would be necessary to avoid this distorted result. In extremely rare circumstances where management concludes that compliance with a requirement in an IFRS would be so misleading that it would conflict with the objective of financial statements as set out in the *Conceptual Framework*, but the relevant regulatory framework prohibits departure from the requirement, to the maximum extent possible the entity is required to reduce the perceived misleading aspects of compliance by disclosing all of the following:

1. The title of the IFRS in question, the nature of the requirement and the reason why management has concluded that complying with that requirement is so misleading in the circumstances that it conflicts with the objective of financial statements as set out in the *Conceptual Framework*; and
2. For each period presented, the adjustments to each item in the financial statements which management has concluded would be necessary to achieve fair presentation.

When assessing whether complying with a specific requirement in an IFRS would be so misleading that it would conflict with the objective of financial statements as set out in the *Conceptual Framework*, management should consider the following:

1. Why the objective of financial statements is not achieved in the circumstances; and
2. How the entity's circumstances differ from those of other entities which comply with the requirement. If other entities in similar circumstances comply with the requirement, there is a rebuttable presumption that the entity's compliance with the requirement would not be so misleading that it would conflict with the objective of financial statements as set out in the *Conceptual Framework*.

An entity presenting financial statements in accordance with IFRS must include an explicit and unreserved statement of compliance with all the requirements of IFRS in the notes.

Going concern

When preparing financial statements, management makes an assessment regarding the entity's ability to continue in operation for the foreseeable future, i.e., as a going concern. Financial statements should be prepared on a going concern basis unless management either intends to liquidate the entity or to cease trading or has no realistic alternative but to do so. If the result of the assessment casts significant doubt upon the entity's ability to continue as a going concern, management is required to disclose that fact, together with the basis on which it prepared the financial statements and the reason why the entity is not regarded as a going concern. When the financial statements are prepared on the going concern basis it is not necessary to disclose this basis.

Most accounting methods are based on this going concern assumption. For example, the cost principle would be of limited usefulness if we assume potential liquidation of the entity. Using a liquidation approach, fixed assets would be valued at net realisable value (sale price less cost to sell) rather than at amortised cost. The concept of depreciation, amortisation and depletion is justifiable and appropriate only if it is reasonable to assume that the entity will continue to operate for the foreseeable future.

Accrual basis of accounting

Financial statements, except for the statement of cash flows, are to be prepared using the accrual basis of accounting. Under the accrual basis of accounting, an entity recognises the elements of the financial statements (items such as assets, liabilities, income and expenses) when they meet the definition and recognition criteria for those elements in the *Conceptual Framework*. Consequently, transactions and events are recognised when they occur, and they are recorded in the accounting records and presented in the financial statements in the periods when they occur (and not when cash is received or paid). For example, revenues are recognised when earned and expenses are recognised when incurred, without regard to the time of receipt or payment of cash.

Materiality and aggregation

An entity should present separately each material class of similar items as well as present separately material items of a dissimilar nature or function. If a line item is not individually material, it is aggregated with other items either in the financial statements or in the notes. An item which is not considered sufficiently material to justify separate presentation in the financial statements may warrant separate presentation in the notes. It is not necessary for an entity to provide a specific disclosure required by an IFRS if the information is not material.

In general, an item presented in the financial statements is material—and therefore is also relevant—if its omission or misstatement would influence or change the economic decisions of users made on the basis of the financial statements. Materiality depends on the relative size and nature of the item or error, judged in the particular circumstances. For example, preparers and auditors sometimes adopt the rule of thumb that anything under 5% of total assets or net income is considered immaterial. Although the US SEC indicated that a company may use this percentage for an initial assessment of materiality, other factors—quantitative as well as qualitative—must also be considered. For example, the fact that an environmental law (or indeed any law) has been broken could be significant in principle, even if the amount involved is small.

Financial statements are the result of processing, aggregating and classifying many transactions or other events based on their nature or function, and presenting condensed and classified data which are comprised within individual line items. If a line item is not individually material, it can be aggregated either in the financial statements or in the notes (for example, disaggregating total revenues into wholesale revenues and retail revenues), but only to the extent that this will enhance the usefulness of the information in predicting the entity's future cash flows. An entity should disaggregate similar items which are measured on different bases and present them on separate lines; for example, an entity should not aggregate investments in debt securities measured at amortised cost and investments in debt securities measured at fair value.

IFRS Practice Statement 2 *Making Materiality Judgements* was issued in September 2017 for application from September 14, 2017. It provides non-mandatory guidance on making materiality judgements for entities preparing general-purpose financial statements in accordance with IFRS.

The practice statement notes that information is material if omitting it or misstating it could influence decisions that users make on the basis of financial information about a specific reporting entity. In other words, materiality is an entity-specific aspect of relevance based on the nature or magnitude, or both, of the items to which the information relates in the context of an individual entity's financial report.

The need for judgements about materiality is pervasive in the preparation of financial statements. Such judgements apply when making decisions about recognition, measurement, presentation and disclosure. The entity is only required to apply IFRS requirements in these areas when their effect is material.

In making materiality judgements, the entity should consider its own specific circumstances and how the information presented in the financial statements serves the needs of the primary users (defined as existing and potential investors, lenders and other creditors). It is necessary for the entity to consider the types of decisions made by the primary users, and what information they need to make those decisions. This in turn leads to consideration of what information is available to primary users from sources other than the financial statements.

The practice statement suggests a four-step process for making materiality judgements:

1. Identify information that has the potential to be material.
2. Assess whether the information identified in step 1. is, in fact, material.
3. Organise the information within the draft financial statements in a way that communicates the information clearly and concisely to primary users.
4. Review the draft financial statements to determine whether all material information has been identified and materiality considered from a wide perspective and in aggregate, on the basis of the complete set of financial statements.

Identifying information which is potentially material involves considering the requirements of relevant IFRS standards alongside the common information needs of the primary users.

Assessing what is material is judged on the basis of both quantitative and qualitative factors. From the quantitative point of view, this involves considering the size of the impact of transactions, other events or conditions against measures of the entity's financial position, financial performance and cash flows. Qualitative factors are characteristics of transactions, other events or conditions which, if present, make information more likely to influence the decisions of primary users. In judging whether particular items of information are material, it is often necessary to take several factors, both quantitative and qualitative, into account.

Organising information requires classifying, characterising and presenting it clearly and concisely to make it understandable. There is a trade-off between the need to ensure that all material information is included while avoiding unnecessary detail which would hinder understandability.

Finally, a review is necessary to determine whether information is material both individually and in combination with other information included in the financial statements. An item of information which appears to be individually immaterial may nonetheless be material in conjunction with other items presented in the financial statements.

Offsetting

Assets and liabilities, or income and expenses, may not be offset against each other, unless required or permitted by an IFRS. Offsetting in the statement of comprehensive income (or statement of profit or loss, if presented separately) or statement of financial position is allowed in rare circumstances when it more accurately reflects the substance of the transaction or other event. For example, IAS 37 allows warranty expenditure to be netted against the related reimbursement under a supplier's warranty agreement. There are other examples when IFRS "require or permit" offsetting; for example, in IFRS 15 the amount of revenue is reduced by any trade discounts or volume rebates the entity allows. An entity undertakes, in the course of its ordinary activities, other transactions that do not generate revenue but are incidental to the main revenue-generating activities. An entity presents the results of such transactions, when this presentation reflects the substance of the transaction or other event, by netting any income with related expenses arising on the same transaction (see Chapter 20). In addition, an entity can present on a net basis certain gains and losses arising from a group of similar transactions, for example foreign exchange gains and losses or gains and losses on financial instruments held for trading (unless material).

In general, the IASB's position is that offsetting detracts from the ability of users both to understand the transactions and other events and conditions that have occurred, and to assess the entity's future cash flows. However, procedures such as the reduction of accounts receivable by an expected credit loss allowance, or of property, plant and equipment by the accumulated depreciation, are acts which reduce these assets to the appropriate valuation amounts and are not in fact offsetting assets and liabilities.

Frequency of reporting

An entity should present a complete set of financial statements (including comparative information) at least annually. If the reporting period changes such that the financial statements are for a period longer or shorter than one year, the entity should disclose the reason for the longer or shorter period and the fact that the amounts presented are not entirely comparable.

There is a presumption that financial statements will be presented annually, as a minimum. The most common time period for the preparation of financial statements is one year. However, if for practical reasons some entities prefer to report, for example, for a 52-week period, IAS 1 does not preclude this practice.

Comparative information

Unless IFRS permit or require otherwise, comparative information of the previous period should be disclosed for all amounts presented in the current period's financial statements. Comparative narrative and descriptive information should be included when it is relevant to an understanding of the current period's financial statements. As a minimum, two statements of financial position, as well as two statements of comprehensive income, changes in equity, cash flows and related notes, should be presented.

Comparability is the quality of information which enables users to compare the financial statements of an entity through time (i.e., across periods), to identify trends in its financial position and performance, as well as across entities. Comparability should not be confused with uniformity; for information to be comparable, similar elements must look alike and dissimilar elements must look different, and users should be able to identify similarities in and differences between two sets of economic phenomena.

In addition, users must be aware of the accounting policies applied in the preparation of the financial statements as well as any changes in those policies and the effects of such changes. Consequently, an entity is required to include a statement of financial position as at the beginning of the preceding period whenever an entity retrospectively applies an accounting policy, or makes a retrospective restatement of items in its financial statements, or when it reclassifies items in its financial statements. In those limited circumstances, an entity is required to present, as a minimum, three statements of financial position and related notes, as at:

1. The end of the current period;
2. The end of the preceding period (which is the same as the beginning of the current period); and
3. The beginning of the preceding period.

When the entity changes the presentation or classification of items in its financial statements, the entity should reclassify the comparative amounts, unless reclassification is impracticable. In reclassifying comparative amounts, the required disclosure includes:

1. The nature of the reclassification;
2. The amount of each item or class of items that is reclassified; and
3. The reason for the reclassification.

In situations where it is impracticable to reclassify comparative amounts, an entity should disclose:

1. The reason for not reclassifying those amounts; and
2. The nature of the adjustments that would have been made if the amounts had been reclassified.

It should be noted that IAS 8, *Accounting Policies, Changes in Accounting Estimates and Errors*, sets out the adjustments to comparative information needed if changes constitute a change in accounting policy or correction of an error (see Chapter 7).

Note, however, that in circumstances where no accounting policy change is being adopted retrospectively, and no restatement (to correct an error) is being applied retrospectively, the statement of financial position as at the *beginning* of the preceding period included is not required to be presented. Nonetheless, there is no prohibition on doing so.

In May 2012, the IASB issued the Annual Improvements to IFRSs 2009–2011 Cycle of Changes. The Annual Improvements Project provides the vehicle to make non-urgent but necessary changes which are not part of any other project. The amendment made in the Annual Improvements Project clarified that a statement of financial position as at the beginning of the earliest comparative preceding period is required when an entity applies an accounting policy retrospectively or makes a retrospective restatement of items or reclassifies items in its financial statements. Related notes should accompany current and prior year statements of financial position but notes in respect of the opening statement of financial position need not be presented. However, where an entity voluntarily elects to provide an additional statement of financial position, *all* supporting notes for the items included in the statements of financial position must be presented regardless of any changes. The changes were effective for periods beginning on or after January 1, 2013, with early application being permitted.

The related footnote disclosures must also be presented on a comparative basis, except for items of disclosure which would not be meaningful, or might even be confusing, if set out in such a manner. Although there is no official guidance on this issue, certain details, such as schedules of debt maturities as at the end of the preceding reporting period, would seemingly be of little interest to users of the current statements and would largely be redundant when presented alongside information provided for the more recent year-end. Accordingly, such details are often omitted from comparative financial statements. Most other disclosures, however, continue to be meaningful and should be presented for all years for which basic financial statements are displayed.

To increase the usefulness of financial statements, many companies include in their annual reports five- or 10-year summaries of condensed financial information. This is not required by IFRS. These comparative statements allow investment analysts and other interested readers to perform comparative analysis of pertinent information. The presentation of comparative financial statements in annual reports enhances the usefulness of such reports and brings out more clearly the nature and trends of current changes affecting the entity.

Such presentation emphasises the fact that financial statements for a series of periods convey far more understanding than those for a single period and that the accounts for one period are simply an instalment of an essentially continuous history.

Consistency of presentation

The presentation and classification of items in the financial statements should be consistent from one period to the next. A change in presentation and classification of items in the financial statements may be required when there is a significant change in the nature of the entity's operations, another presentation or classification is more appropriate (having considered the criteria of IAS 8), or when an IFRS requires a change in presentation. When making such changes in presentation, an entity should reclassify its comparative information and present adequate disclosures (see *Comparative information* above). Consistency refers to the use of the same accounting policies and procedures, either from period to period within an entity or in a single period across entities. Comparability is the goal and consistency is a means of achieving that goal.

STRUCTURE AND CONTENT

Complete Set of Financial Statements

IAS 1 defines a complete set of financial statements as comprising the following:

1. A *statement of financial position* as at the reporting date (the end of the reporting period). The previous version of IAS 1 used the title "balance sheet" and this may still be applied;
2. A *statement of profit or loss and other comprehensive income* for the period (the name "statement of comprehensive income" may still be used):
    a. Components of *profit or loss* may be presented either as part of a single statement of profit or loss and other comprehensive income or in a separate income statement.
    b. A single statement of comprehensive income for the reporting period is preferred and presents all items of income and expense reported in *profit or loss* (a subtotal in the statement of comprehensive income) as well as items of *other comprehensive income* recognised during the reporting period.
    c. However, a separate statement of profit or loss and a separate statement of comprehensive income (two separate statements—dual presentation) may be presented. Under this method of presentation, the statement of comprehensive income should begin with profit or loss and then report items of other comprehensive income.

3. A *statement of changes in equity* for the reporting period;
4. A *statement of cash flows* for the reporting period (the previous version of IAS 1 used the title "cash flow statement," which may still be used);
5. Notes, comprising a summary of significant accounting policies and other explanatory information, including comparative information in respect of the preceding period; and
6. A statement of financial position as at the beginning of the preceding period when the reporting entity applies an accounting policy retrospectively or makes a retrospective restatement of items in its financial statements, or when it reclassifies items in its financial statements. This requirement is part of the revised IAS 1. (Refer also to *Comparative information* above.)

Financial statements, except for cash flow information, are to be prepared using the accrual basis of accounting. Illustrative examples of the format of the statements of financial position, comprehensive income and changes in equity based on the guidance provided in the appendix to IAS 1 have been provided at the end of this chapter.

The standard provides the structure and content of financial statements and minimum requirements for disclosure on the face of the relevant financial statement or in the notes. These topics are dealt with in the next three chapters (Chapters 4, 5 and 6).

Notes

In accordance with IAS 1, the notes should: (1) present information about the basis of preparation of the financial statements and the specific accounting policies used; (2) disclose the information required by IFRS which is not presented elsewhere in the financial statements; and (3) provide information which is not presented elsewhere in the financial statements but is relevant to an understanding of any of them.

An entity should present notes in a systematic manner and should cross-reference each item in the statements of financial position and of profit or loss and other comprehensive income, or in the separate statement of profit or loss (if presented), and in the statements of changes in equity and of cash flows, to any related information in the notes.

An entity should normally present notes in the following order, to help users to understand the financial statements and to compare them with financial statements of other entities:

1. Statement of compliance with IFRS;
2. Summary of significant accounting policies applied;
3. Supporting information for items presented in the financial statements in the order in which each financial statement and each line item is presented; and
4. Other disclosures, including contingent liabilities and unrecognised contractual commitments; and non-financial disclosures (e.g., the entity's financial risk management objectives and policies).

Statement of compliance with IFRS

IAS 1 requires an entity whose financial statements comply with IFRS to make an explicit and unreserved statement of such compliance in the notes. Financial statements should not be described as complying with IFRS unless they comply with all of the requirements of IFRS.

An entity might refer to IFRS in describing the basis on which its financial statements are prepared without making this explicit and unreserved statement of compliance with IFRS. For example, the EU mandated a carve-out of the financial instruments standard and other jurisdictions have carved out or altered other IFRS standards. In some cases, these differences may significantly affect the reported financial performance and financial position of the entity. This information should be disclosed in the notes.

Accounting policies

The policy note should begin with a clear statement of the nature of the comprehensive basis of accounting used. A reporting entity may only claim to follow IFRS if it complies with every single IFRS in force as at the reporting date. The EU made certain amendments to IFRS when endorsing them (a carve-out from IAS 39), and those EU companies following these directives cannot claim to follow IFRS, and instead will have to acknowledge compliance with IFRS as endorsed by the EU.

Financial statements should include clear and concise disclosure of all significant accounting policies that have been used in the preparation of those financial statements. Management must also indicate the judgements that it has made in the process of applying the accounting policies that have the most significant effect on the amounts recognised. The entity must also disclose the key assumptions about the future and any other sources of estimation uncertainty which have a significant risk of causing a subsequent material adjustment to need to be made to the carrying amounts of assets and liabilities.

IAS 1 requires an entity to disclose in the summary of significant accounting policies:

1. The measurement basis (or bases) used in preparing the financial statements; and
2. The other accounting policies applied that are relevant to an understanding of the financial statements.

Measurement bases may include historical cost, current cost, net realisable value, fair value or recoverable amount. Other accounting policies should be disclosed if they could assist users in understanding how transactions, other events and conditions are reported in the financial statements.

In addition, an entity should disclose the judgements which management has made in the process of applying the entity's accounting policies and which have the most significant effect on the amounts recognised in the financial statements. Examples of such judgements are when management makes decisions on whether lease transactions transfer substantially all the significant risks and rewards of ownership of financial assets to another party or whether, in substance, particular sales of goods are financing arrangements and therefore do not give rise to revenue.

Determining the carrying amounts of some assets and liabilities requires estimation of the effects of uncertain future events on those assets and liabilities at the end of the reporting period. This is likely to be necessary in measuring, for example, the recoverable values of different classes of property, plant and equipment, or the future outcome of litigation in progress. The reporting entity should disclose information about the assumptions it makes regarding the future and other major sources of estimation uncertainty at the end of the reporting period, which have a significant risk of resulting in a material adjustment to the carrying amount of assets and liabilities within the next financial year. The notes to the financial statements should include the nature and the carrying amount of those assets and liabilities at the end of the period.

Financial statement users must be made aware of the accounting policies used by reporting entities so that they can better understand the financial statements and make comparisons with the financial statements of others. The policy disclosures should identify and describe the accounting principles followed by the entity and methods of applying those principles which materially affect the determination of financial position, results of operations or changes in cash flows. IAS 1 requires that disclosure of these policies be an integral part of the financial statements.

IAS 8 (as discussed in Chapter 7) sets out criteria for making accounting policy choices. Policies should be relevant to the needs of users and should be reliable (representationally faithful, reflecting economic substance, neutral, prudent and complete).

Fairness exception under IAS 1

Accounting standard setters have commonly recognised the fact that even full compliance with promulgated financial reporting principles may, on rare occasions, still not result in financial statements which are accurate, truthful or fair. Therefore many, but not all, standard-setting bodies have provided some form of exception whereby the higher demand of having fair presentation of the entity's financial position and results of operations may be met, even if doing so might require a technical departure from the codified body of GAAP.

In the US, this provision has historically been found in the profession's ethics literature (the "Rule 203 exception"), but under various other national GAAP there was commonly found a "true and fair view" requirement which captured this objective. Under revised IAS 1, an approach essentially identical to the true and fair view requirement (which is codified in the EU's Fourth Directive) has been formalised as well. The rule under IFRS should be narrowly construed, with only the most exceptional situations dealt with by permitting departures from IFRS to achieve appropriate financial reporting objectives.

This matter has been addressed in greater detail above. In the authors' view, having such a fairness exception is vital for the goal of ensuring accurate and useful financial reporting under IFRS. However, extreme caution must be applied in reaching any decision to depart from the formal requirements of IFRS, for example because these exceptions may not have been transposed into any relevant stock exchange regulations.

Other disclosures required by IAS 1

The reporting entity is required to provide details of any dividends proposed or declared before the financial statements were authorised for issue but not charged to equity. It should also indicate the amount of any cumulative preference dividends not recognised in the statement of changes in equity.

If not otherwise disclosed within the financial statements, the following items should be reported in the notes:

1. The domicile and legal form of the entity, its country of incorporation and the address of the registered office (or principal place of business, if different);
2. A description of the nature of the reporting entity's operations and its principal activities;
3. The name of the parent entity and the ultimate parent of the group; and
4. If it is a limited life entity, information regarding the length of its life.

These disclosures (which have been modelled on those set out by the Fourth and Seventh EU Directives) are of relevance given the multinational character of many entities reporting in accordance with IFRS.

FUTURE DEVELOPMENTS

The IASB has included several projects in the disclosure initiative that might impact IAS 1. The IASB is in the process of drafting clarifications to the definition of materiality and application of materiality in preparing financial statements. Regarding accounting policies disclosures, guidance and examples is developed to explain and demonstrate the application of the "four-step materiality process" of IFRS Practice Statement 2 Making Materiality Judgements. A future exposure draft is expected. Guidance is developed to help the IASB in drafting disclosure requirements in IFRS standards and to perform targeted standards-level reviews of disclosure requirements. The IASB plans to publish a summary of the research findings of the Principles of Disclosure research project in due course.

ILLUSTRATIVE FINANCIAL STATEMENTS

IAS 1 sets out the format and content of individual financial statements, and minimum requirements for disclosure in the statements of financial position, comprehensive income and changes in equity, as well as other information which may be presented either in the financial statements or in the notes. The illustrative financial statements, prepared based on the guidance provided in the appendix to IAS 1, are presented below. According to the IASB, each entity may change the content, sequencing and format of presentation and the descriptions used for line items to achieve fair presentation in that entity's particular circumstances. For example, the illustrative statement of financial position presents non-current assets followed by current assets, and presents equity followed by non-current liabilities and then by current liabilities (i.e., the most liquid items being presented last), but many entities are used to reversing this sequencing (i.e., the most liquid items being presented first).

The illustrative financial statements show the presentation of comprehensive income in two separate statements—the statement of profit or loss presented separately, followed by the statement of comprehensive income beginning with profit or loss and then reporting items of other comprehensive income. All expenses in the statement of profit or loss are classified by nature. Alternatively, a single statement of profit or loss and comprehensive income could be presented, displaying all items of profit and loss as well as other comprehensive income items in one statement. In addition, expenses could be classified by function instead of by nature.

These examples do not illustrate a complete set of financial statements, which would also include a statement of cash flows, a summary of significant accounting policies and other explanatory information.

Exemplum Reporting PLC
Statement of Financial Position as at December 31, 20XX

	20XX	*20XX-1*
	€	€
Assets		
Non-current assets:		
Property, plant and equipment	X	X
Investment property	X	X
Goodwill	X	X
Other intangible assets	X	X

Investments in associates and joint ventures	X	X
Deferred income tax assets	X	X
Financial assets	X	X
	X	X
Current assets:		
Inventories	X	X
Trade receivables	X	X
Other current assets	X	X
Other financial assets	X	X
Cash and cash equivalents	X	X
Non-current assets held for sale	X	X
	X	X
Liabilities		
Current liabilities:		
Trade and other payables	X	X
Current borrowings	X	X
Current portion of long-term borrowings	X	X
Current tax payable	X	X
Finance lease liabilities	X	X
Current provisions	X	X
Liabilities of a disposal group classified as held-for-sale	X	X
Net current assets		
Non-current liabilities:		
Non-current borrowings	X	X
Deferred tax	X	X
Finance lease liabilities	X	X
Non-current provisions	X	X
Retirement benefit obligations	X	X
Net assets		
Equity attributable to equity holders of the parent		
Ordinary shares	X	X
Share premium	X	X
Translation reserve	X	X
Fair value reserve	X	X
Retained earnings	X	X
Equity attributable to owners of the parent	X	X
Non-controlling interest	X	X
Total equity		

The financial statements were approved and authorised for issue by the board and were signed on its behalf on [date]:

Director Signature

Director Name

Exemplum Reporting PLC
Statement of Profit or Loss
For the Year Ended December 31, 20XX
(Presentation of comprehensive income in two statements and classification of expenses within profit by nature)

	20XX	*20XX-1*
	€	€
Continuing operations		
Revenue	X	X
Other income	X	X
Changes in inventories of finished goods and work in progress	X	X
Work performed by the group and capitalised	X	X
Raw material and consumables used	X	X
Employee benefits expense	X	X
Depreciation and amortisation expense	X	X
Impairment of property, plant and equipment	X	X
Other expenses	X	X
Operating profit	X	X
Investment income	X	X
Finance costs	X	X
Share of profit of associates and joint ventures[1]	X	X
Gain recognised on disposal of interest in former associate	X	X
Profit before tax	X	X
Income tax expense	X	X
Profit for the year from continuing operations	X	X
Profit for the year from discontinued operations	X	X
PROFIT FOR THE YEAR		
Attributable to:		
Equity holders of the parent	X	X
Non-controlling interest	X	X
	X	X
Earnings per share		
From continuing operations		
Basic (cents per share)	X	X
Diluted (cents per share)	X	X
From continuing and discontinued operations		
Basic (cents per share)	X	X
Diluted (cents per share)	X	X

[1] *Share of associates' and joint ventures' profit attributable to owners, after tax and non-controlling interests in the associates.*

Exemplum Reporting PLC
Statement of Profit or Loss and Other Comprehensive Income[2]
For the Year Ended December 31, 20XX
(Presentation of comprehensive income in two statements)

	20XX	*20XX-1*
	€	€
PROFIT FOR THE YEAR	X	X
Other comprehensive income:		
Items that will not be reclassified to profit or loss		
Remeasurement of defined benefit pension plans	X	X
Gains on revaluation of property (if revaluation model is used)	X	X
Share of comprehensive income of associates and joint ventures	X	X
	X	X
Items that may be reclassified subsequently to profit or loss		
Exchange differences on translating foreign operations	X	X
Income tax relating to recyclable components of other comprehensive income	X	X
	X	X
Other comprehensive income for the year, net of tax		
Total comprehensive income for the year		
Total comprehensive income attributable to:		
Equity holders of the parent	X	X
Non-controlling interest	X	X

[2] *The income tax relating to each component of other comprehensive income is disclosed in the notes.*

Exemplum Reporting PLC
Disclosure of Components of Other Comprehensive Income[3]
Notes
Year Ended December 31, 20XX

	20XX		*20XX-1*	
	€		€	
Other comprehensive income				
Exchange differences on translating foreign operations[4]		X		X
Investments recognised in equity:				
Gains arising during the year	X		X	
Cash flow hedges:				
Gains (losses) arising during the year	X		X	
Less: Reclassification adjustments for gains (losses) included in profit or loss	X		X	
Less: Adjustments for amounts transferred to initial carrying amount of hedged items	X	X	X	X
Gains on property revaluation		X		X

Remeasurement of net defined benefit liability	X	X
Share of other comprehensive income of associates	X	X
Other comprehensive income	X	X
Income tax relating to components of other comprehensive income[5]	X	X
Other comprehensive income for the year	X	X

[3] *When an entity chooses an aggregated presentation in the statement of comprehensive income, the amounts for reclassification adjustments and current year gain or loss are presented in the notes.*

[4] *There was no disposal of a foreign operation and therefore there is no reclassification adjustment for the years presented.*

[5] *The income tax relating to each component of other comprehensive income is disclosed in the notes.*

Exemplum Reporting PLC
Disclosure of Tax Effects Relating to Each Component of Other Comprehensive Income (in Notes)
Year Ended December 31, 20XX

	20XX			20XX-1		
	€ *Before-tax amount*	€ *Tax (expense) benefit*	€ *Net-of-tax amount*	€ *Before-tax amount*	€ *Tax (expense) benefit*	€ *Net-of-tax amount*
Exchange differences on translating foreign operations	X	X	X	X	X	X
Investment in equity instruments	X	X	X	X	X	X
Cash flow hedges	X	X	X	X	X	X
Gains on property revaluation	X	X	X	X	X	X
Remeasurement of the net defined benefit liability	X	X	X	X	X	X
Share of other comprehensive income of associates	X	X	X	X	X	X
Other comprehensive income	X	X	X	X	X	X

Exemplum Reporting PLC
Statement of Changes in Equity
For the Year Ended December 31, 20XX

	Ordinary shares	Share premium	Translation reserve	Fair value reserve	Revalua-tion reserve	Retained earnings	Total	Non-controlling interest	Total equity
	€	€	€	€	€	€	€	€	€
Balance at January 1, 20XX-1	X	X	X	X	–	X	X	X	X
Changes in equity for 20XX-1									
Profit for the year	–	–	–	–	–	X	X	X	X
Exchange differences on translating foreign operations	–	–	X	–	–	–	X	X	X
Gain on revaluation of property (if revaluation model is used)	–	–	–	–	X	–	X	X	X
Available for sale financial assets	–	–	–	X	–	–	X	X	X
Actuarial gains/losses on defined benefit plans	–	–	–	–	–	X	X	–	X
Share of comprehensive income of associates	–	–	–	X	–	–	X	–	X
Total comprehensive income for the year	–	–	X	X	–	X	X	X	X
Dividends	–	–	–	–	–	X	X	X	X
Issue of share capital	X	X	–	–	–	–	X	–	X
Balance at December 31, 20XX-1	X	X	X	X	X	X	X	X	X
Balance at January 1, 20XX	X	–	–	–	–	–	X	–	X
Changes in equity for 20XX									
Profit for the year	–	–	–	–	–	X	X	X	X
Exchange differences on translating foreign operations	–	–	X	–	–	–	X	X	X
Gain on revaluation of property (if revaluation model is used)	–	–	–	–	X	–	X	X	X
Available for sale financial assets	–	–	–	X	–	–	X	X	X
Actuarial gains/losses on defined benefit plans	–	–	–	–	–	X	X	–	X
Share of comprehensive income of associates	–	–	–	X	–	–	X	–	X
Total comprehensive income for the year	–	–	X	X	–	X	X	X	X
Dividends	–	–	–	–	–	X	X	X	X
Issue of share capital	X	X	–	–	–	–	X	–	X
Balance at December 31, 20XX	X	X	X	X	X	X	X	X	X

US GAAP COMPARISON

FASB Statement of Financial Accounting Concepts No. 6 Elements of Financial Statements (CON6), which are a basis for US financial reporting and accounting standards, can be viewed online at www.fasb.org and contains the definitions of assets, liabilities and the like which are similar to the IAS definitions. US GAAP Codification has a complete section which is entitled "Presentation", which is the 200's section of the codification and discusses the balance sheet, statements of shareholder equity, income, comprehensive income, cash flows and notes to the financial statements, yet no specific examples as shown above are provided. Nevertheless, presentation of financial statements is similar to IAS examples. The format and content for public companies are prescribed by presentation requirements in the respective standards and by SEC rules.

In respect of the use of the going concern assumption, while US GAAP (as amended by Accounting Standards Update (ASU) 2014-15 for annual periods ending after December 15, 2016) is an attempt at convergence and now requires management to evaluate and disclose uncertainties about an entity's ability to continue as a going concern, some differences with IFRS remain. In particular, the assessment period under US GAAP is one year after the date that the financial statements are issued; and US GAAP sets out detailed guidance on the liquidation basis of accounting.

4 STATEMENT OF FINANCIAL POSITION

INTRODUCTION

The statement of financial position (or the balance sheet) is a statement that presents an entity's assets, liabilities and equity (or net assets) at a given point in time (i.e., as at a specific date). During the early era of financial reporting standard setting, throughout the nineteenth century and first half of the twentieth century, the emphasis of legislation was almost entirely on the statement of financial position but by the mid-twentieth century owners were asking for more and more information about operating performance, leading to presentations of an increasingly complex income statement (or the profit and loss).

Since the two financial statements, are linked together because of double entry book-keeping conventions, they cannot easily serve differing objectives. The stock markets look primarily at earnings expectations, which are largely based on historic performance, as measured by the income statement. If earnings measurement drives financial reporting, this means that, of necessity, the statement of financial position carries the residuals of the earnings measurement process. For example, assets such as motor vehicles with service potential that is used up over several accounting periods will have their costs allocated to these periods through the depreciation process, with the statement of financial position left to report a residual of that allocation process, which may or may not reflect the value of those assets at the end of the reporting period. However, if reporting were truly driven by the statement of financial position, the reporting entity would value the vehicles at the end of each reporting period—for example, by reference to their replacement costs in current condition—and the change in statement of financial position values from one year to another would be reflected in the statement of comprehensive income.

By the 1960s many national GAAP standards were being designed to favour the income statement over the balance sheet, but the pendulum began to swing back to a balance sheet-oriented strategy when standard setters—first the FASB in the US and later others, including the International Accounting Standards Committee, predecessor of the current IASB—developed conceptual frameworks intended to serve as the fundamental theory of financial reporting. Undertaking that exercise had the result of causing accounting theory to revert to its original purpose—namely, to measure economic activity—and implicitly to adopt the definition of income as the change in wealth from period to period. With this in mind, measurement of that wealth, as captured in the balance sheet, became more central to efforts to develop new standards.

In practice, IFRS as currently written are a mixture of both approaches, depending on the transaction being recognised, measured and reported. This mixed attribute approach is partially a legacy of earlier financial reporting rule making, but also reflects the practical difficulties of value measurement for many categories of assets and liabilities. For example, many financial instruments are remeasured at the end of each reporting period, whereas property, plant and equipment are normally held at original cost and are depreciated systematically over estimated useful lives, subject to further adjustment for impairment, as necessary.

Nonetheless, while existing requirements are not entirely consistent regarding financial statement primacy, both the IASB and the FASB, when developing new accounting standards, are now formally committed to a statement of financial position (balance sheet) oriented approach. The IASB's *Conceptual Framework* is expressed in terms of measuring assets and liabilities, and reportedly the two standard-setting bodies and their respective staff analyse transactions affected by proposed standards from the perspective of whether they increase or diminish the assets and liabilities of the entity. Overall, the IASB sees financial reporting as being based on the measuring of assets and liabilities, and has the overall goal of requiring the reporting of all changes to those elements (other than those which are a result of transactions with owners, such as the payment of dividends) in a statement of comprehensive income.

The focus on earnings in the capital markets does not mean that the statement of financial position is irrelevant; clearly the financial structure of the company is an important aspect of the company's risk profile, which in turn is important to evaluating the potential return on an investment from the perspective of a current or potential shareholder. Lenders have an even greater interest in the entity's financial structure. This is why companies sometimes go to great lengths to keep some transactions off the statement of financial position, for example by using special-purpose entities and other complex financing structures. IAS 32 considers that any instrument that gives rise to a right to claim assets from an entity is a liability.

IAS 1 states that "each material class of similar items" should be presented separately in the financial statements. In addition, "items of dissimilar nature or function" should be presented separately, unless they are immaterial. The standard expresses a preference for a presentation based on the current/non-current distinction, but allows a presentation by liquidity if that is more reliable and relevant. An asset or liability is current if it is part of the reporting entity's normal operating cycle (e.g., customer receivables) or if it is expected to be realised or settled within 12 months after the end of the reporting period. Only one of these conditions needs to be satisfied—so, for example, inventory that remains on hand for two years should still be classified as current, while long-term liabilities should be reclassified as current for the final year before settlement. IAS 1 includes a sample of illustrative financial statement structure in its *Guidance on Implementing IAS 1*, but use of this format is optional.

Sources of IFRS	
IAS 1, 8, 10, 24, 32, 36, 38, 40, 41	*IFRS* 5, 6, 7

SCOPE

This chapter discusses the format and content of the statement of financial position by incorporating guidance from the *Conceptual Framework*, IAS 1 and other standards.

DEFINITIONS OF TERMS

The IASB's *Conceptual Framework* describes the basic concepts by which financial statements are prepared. It does so by defining the objective of financial statements; identifying the qualitative characteristics that make information in financial statements useful; and defining the basic elements of financial statements and the concepts for recognising and measuring them in financial statements.

The elements of financial statements are the broad classifications and groupings which convey the substantive financial effects of transactions and events on the reporting entity. To be included in the financial statements, an event or transaction must meet definitional, recognition and measurement requirements, all of which are set out in the *Conceptual Framework*.

The elements of a statement of financial position are:

> **An asset** *is a present economic resource controlled by the entity as a result of past events. (An economic resource is a right that has the potential to produce economic benefits.)*

The following three characteristics must be present for an item to qualify as an asset:

1. The item must provide potential economic benefit, which enables it to deliver future net cash inflows.
2. The entity is able to receive the benefit and restrict other entities' access to that benefit.
3. The event which provides the entity with the right to the benefit has occurred.

In addition, the asset must be capable of being measured reliably. The *Conceptual Framework* states that reliable measurement means that the number must be free from material error and bias and can be depended upon by users to give faithful representation. In the Basis for Conclusions of IFRS 2, the IASB notes that the use of estimates is permitted, and that there may be a trade-off between the characteristics of being free from material error and possessing representational faithfulness.

Assets have features which help to identify them in that they are exchangeable, legally enforceable and have future economic benefit potential. It is this potential which eventually brings cash into the entity and which underlies the concept of an asset.

A liability *is a present obligation of the entity to transfer an economic resource as a result of past events.*

The following three characteristics must be present for an item to qualify as a liability:

1. A liability requires that the entity settle a present obligation by the probable future transfer of an asset on demand or when a specified event occurs or at a particular date.
2. The obligation is to transfer an economic resource.
3. The event that obligates the entity has occurred.

Liabilities are similarly recognised subject to the constraint that they must be able to be measured reliably.

Liabilities usually result from transactions which enable entities to obtain resources. Other liabilities may arise from non-reciprocal transfers, such as the declaration of dividends to the owners of the entity or the pledge of assets to charitable organisations.

An entity may involuntarily incur a liability. A liability may be imposed on the entity by government or by the court system in the form of taxes, fines or levies. A liability may arise from price changes or interest rate changes. Liabilities may be legally enforceable or they may be equitable obligations, which arise from social, ethical or moral requirements. Liabilities continue in existence until the entity is no longer responsible for discharging them.

The diagram which follows, which is taken from one of the statements produced from the conceptual framework project by the US standard setter, the FASB, identifies the three classes of events which affect an entity, and shows the relationship between assets and liabilities, on the one hand, and comprehensive income, on the other.

Equity *is the residual interest in the assets of the entity after deducting all of its liabilities.*

In a business enterprise, the equity is the ownership interest. Equity arises from the ownership relationship and is the basis for distributions of earnings to the owners. Distributions of entity assets to owners are voluntary. Equity is increased by owners' investments and comprehensive income and is reduced by distributions to owners.

In practice, the distinction between equity and liabilities may be difficult to determine. Securities such as convertible debt and certain types of preference shares may have characteristics of both equity (residual ownership interest) and liabilities (non-discretionary future sacrifices). Equity, aside from exchanges with owners, is a residual of the asset/liability recognition model.

Statement of financial position: *a statement of financial position (balance sheet) presents an entity's assets, liabilities and equity as at a specific date.*

GENERAL CONCEPTS, STRUCTURE AND CONTENT

General Concepts

Under IFRS, assets and liabilities are recorded at cost or fair value at inception in the financial statements, which for assets and liabilities arising from arm's-length transactions will generally be equal to negotiated prices. Subsequent measurement is under the historical cost principle or fair value, depending on the requirements of the relevant standard and available accounting policy choices made by the entity. IAS 36, *Impairment of Assets*, requires assets to be reduced in value if their carrying value exceeds the higher of fair value or value in use (expected future cash flows from the asset). IFRS 9, *Financial Instruments*, IAS 40, *Investment Property*, and IAS 41, *Agriculture*, all include some element of subsequent measurement at fair value. Where assets are classified as held-for-sale, they are carried at the lower of their carrying amount or fair value less selling costs (IFRS 5).

Historical exchange prices, and the amortised cost amounts which are later presented, are sometimes cited as being useful because these amounts are objectively determined and capable of being verified independently. However, critics point out that, other than at transaction date, historical cost does not result in presenting, in the statement of financial position, numbers which are comparable between companies so, while they are reliable, they may not be relevant for decision-making purposes. This captures the fundamental conflict regarding accounting information: absolutely reliable or objective information may not be sufficiently relevant to current decision making.

Structure and Content

The titles commonly given to the primary financial statement which presents the state of an entity's financial affairs include the "statement of financial position" or "balance sheet." The revised IAS 1 changed the title of the "balance sheet" to the "statement of financial position," the title used throughout this publication. The IASB concluded that "statement of financial position" better reflects the function of the statement and is consistent with the *Conceptual Framework*. In addition, the title "balance sheet" simply reflected the convention that double entry bookkeeping requires all debits to equal all credits, and did not identify the content or purpose of the statement. According to the IASB, the term "financial position" was a well-known and accepted term, and had already been used in audit opinions internationally for more than 20 years to describe what the "balance sheet" presents.

The three elements which are always to be displayed in the heading of a statement of financial position are:

1. The name of the entity whose financial position is being presented;
2. The title of the statement; and
3. The date of the statement.

The entity's name should appear exactly as written in the legal document which created it (e.g., the certificate of incorporation, partnership agreement, etc.). The title should also clearly reflect the legal status of the entity as a corporation, partnership, sole proprietorship or division of some other entity.

The statement of financial position presents a "snapshot" of the resources (assets) and claims to resources (liabilities and equity) as at a specific date. The last day of a month is normally used as the statement date (in jurisdictions where a choice is allowed) unless the entity uses a fiscal reporting period always ending on a particular day of the week, such as a Friday or Sunday (e.g., the last Friday in December, or the Sunday falling closest to December 31). In these cases, the statement of financial position can be dated accordingly (e.g., December 26, October 1, etc.). In all cases, the implication is that the statement of financial position captures the pertinent amounts as at the close of business on the date noted.

Statements of financial position should generally be uniform in appearance from one period to the next, as indeed should all of the entity's financial statements. The form, terminology, captions and pattern of combining insignificant items should be consistent. The goal is to enhance usefulness by maintaining a consistent manner of presentation unless there are good reasons to change these and the changes are duly reported.

IAS 1 does not prescribe the sequence or format in which items should be presented in the statement of financial position. Thus, for example, in a standard classified statement of financial position, non-current assets may be presented before or after current assets, and within the current assets, cash can be presented as the first or the last line item. However, the standard stipulates the following list of minimum line items, which are sufficiently different in nature or function to justify separate presentation in the statement:

1. Property, plant and equipment;
2. Investment property;
3. Intangible assets;
4. Financial assets (excluding amounts shown under items 5, 8 and 9);
5. groups of contracts witihin the scope of IFRS 17;
6. Investments accounted for using the equity method;
7. Biological assets (within the scope of IAS 41);
8. Inventories;
9. Trade and other receivables;
10. Cash and cash equivalents;
11. The total of assets classified as held-for-sale and assets included in disposal groups classified as held-for-sale in accordance with IFRS 5, *Non-current Assets Held for Sale and Discontinued Operations*;
12. Trade and other payables;
13. Provisions;
14. Financial liabilities (excluding amounts shown under items 11 and 12);
15. Liabilities and assets for current tax, as defined in IAS 12, *Income Taxes*;
16. Deferred tax liabilities and deferred tax assets, as defined in IAS 12;
17. Liabilities included in disposal groups classified as held-for-sale in accordance with IFRS 5;
18. Non-controlling interests, presented within equity; and
19. Issued capital and reserves attributable to owners of the parent.

The format of the statement of financial position as illustrated by the appendix to IAS 1 is along the following lines:

Exemplum Reporting PLC
Consolidated Statement of Financial Position as at December 31, 20XX

	20XX	20XX-1
	€	€
Assets		
Non-current assets:	X	X
Property, plant and equipment	X	X
Investment property	X	X
Goodwill	X	X
Other intangible assets	X	X
Investments in associates and joint ventures	X	X
Deferred income tax assets	X	X
Financial assets	X	X
Current assets:	X	X
Inventories	X	X
Trade receivables	X	X
Other current assets	X	X
Other financial assets	X	X
Cash and cash equivalents	X	X
	X	X
Non-current assets held for sale	X	X
	X	X
Liabilities		
Current liabilities:		
Trade and other payables	X	X
Current borrowings	X	X
Current portion of long-term borrowings	X	X
Current tax payable	X	X
Finance lease liabilities	X	X
Current provisions	X	X
	X	X
Liabilities of a disposal group classified as held-for-sale	X	X
Net current assets	X	X
Non-current liabilities:		
Non-current borrowings	X	X
Deferred tax	X	X
Finance lease liabilities	X	X
Non-current provisions	X	X
Retirement benefit obligations	X	X
	X	X
Net assets	X	X
Equity applicable to equity holders of the parent		
Ordinary shares	X	X
Share premium	X	X
Translation reserve	X	X
Fair value reserve	X	X
Retained earnings	X	X
Equity attributable to owners of the parent	X	X
Non-controlling interest	X	X
Total equity	X	X

CLASSIFICATION OF ASSETS

Assets, liabilities and equity are presented separately in the statement of financial position. In accordance with IAS 1, companies should make a distinction between current and non-current assets and liabilities, except when a presentation based on liquidity provides information that is more reliable or relevant. As a practical matter, the liquidity exception is primarily invoked by banks and some other financial organisations, for which fixed investments (e.g., in property and equipment) are dwarfed by financial instruments and other assets and liabilities.

Current Assets

An asset should be classified as a current asset when it satisfies any one of the following:

1. It is expected to be realised in, or is held for sale or consumption in, the normal course of the entity's operating cycle;
2. It is held primarily for trading purposes;
3. It is expected to be realised within 12 months of the end of the reporting period;
4. It is cash or a cash equivalent asset, which is not restricted in its use.

If a current asset category includes items that will have a life of more than 12 months, the amount that falls into the next financial year should be disclosed in the notes. All other assets should be classified as non-current assets if a classified statement of financial position is to be presented in the financial statements.

Thus, current assets include cash, cash equivalents and other assets that are expected to be realised in cash, or sold or consumed during one normal operating cycle of the business. The operating cycle of an entity is the time between the acquisition of materials entering into a process and their realisation in cash or an instrument which is readily convertible into cash. Inventories and trade receivables should still be classified as current assets in a classified statement of financial position even if these assets are not expected to be realised within 12 months from the end of the reporting period. However, marketable securities could only be classified as current assets if they were expected to be realised (sold, redeemed or to mature) within 12 months after the end of the reporting period, even though most would deem marketable securities to be more liquid than inventories and possibly even more liquid than receivables. Management intention takes priority over liquidity potential. The following items would be classified as current assets:

1. *Inventories* held either for sale in the ordinary course of business or in the process of production for such sale, or in the form of materials or supplies to be consumed in the production process or in the rendering of services (IAS 2). The basis of valuation and the method of pricing, which is limited to FIFO or weighted-average cost, should be disclosed.

Inventories—at the lower of cost (FIFO) or net realisable value	X

   In the case of a manufacturing concern, raw materials, work in process and finished goods should be disclosed separately on the statement of financial position or in the footnotes.

Inventories	**20XX**	**20XX-1**
	€	**€**
Finished goods	X	X
Work in process	X	X
Raw materials	X	X
Total	XX	XX

2. *Receivables*, including accounts and notes receivable, receivables from affiliate companies and officer and employee receivables. The term accounts receivable represents amounts due from customers arising from transactions in the ordinary course of business. Allowances due to expected lack of collectability and any amounts discounted or pledged should be stated clearly. If material, the receivables should be analysed into their component parts. The receivables section may be presented as follows:

Receivables			**20XX**	**20XX-1**
			€	**€**
Customer accounts	X			X
Customer notes/commercial paper	X	X		X
Less allowance for expected credit loss		(X)		(X)
			X	X
Due from associated companies			X	X
Due from officers and employees			X	X
Total			X	X

3. *Prepaid expenses*: these are assets created by the prepayment of cash or the incurrence of a liability. They expire and become expenses with the passage of time, use or events (e.g., prepaid rent, prepaid insurance and deferred taxes). This item is frequently aggregated with others on the face of the statement of financial position with details relegated to the notes, since it is often not a material amount.
4. *Trading financial assets*: assets which are acquired principally for the purpose of generating a profit from short-term fluctuations in price or dealer's margin. Trading financial assets should be classified as fair value through profit or loss. Trading assets include debt and equity securities and loans and receivables acquired by the entity with the intention of making a short-term profit. Derivative financial assets are always deemed held-for-trading unless they are designated as effective hedging instruments.
5. *Cash* and cash equivalents, including cash in hand, consisting of coins, notes and undeposited cheques; money orders and drafts; and deposits in banks. Anything accepted by a bank for deposit would be considered cash. Cash must be available for withdrawal on demand; thus, assets such as certificates of deposit would not be considered cash because of the time restrictions on withdrawal. Also, to be classified as a current asset, cash must be available for current use. According to IAS 1, cash which is restricted in use and whose restrictions will not expire within the operating cycle, or cash restricted for a non-current use, would not be included in current

assets. According to IAS 7, cash equivalents include short-term, highly liquid investments, which are (1) readily convertible to known amounts of cash, and (2) so near their maturity (original maturities of three months or less) that they present negligible risk of changes in value arising from changes in interest rates. Treasury bills, commercial paper and money market funds are all examples of cash equivalents.

Non-Current Assets

IAS 1 uses the term "non-current" to include tangible, intangible, operating and financial assets of a long-term nature. It does not prohibit the use of alternative descriptions, as long as the meaning is clear. Non-current assets include:

- Financial assets;
- Investment property;
- Property, plant and equipment;
- Intangible assets;
- Assets held for sale; and
- Miscellaneous other assets.

Other Assets

An all-inclusive heading for amounts which do not fit neatly into any of the other asset categories (e.g., long-term deferred expenses, which will not be consumed within one operating cycle, and deferred tax assets).

CLASSIFICATION OF LIABILITIES

Liabilities are normally displayed in the statement of financial position in the order of due dates for payment.

Current Liabilities

According to IAS 1, a liability should be classified as a current liability when:

1. It is expected to be settled in the normal course of business within the entity's operating cycle;
2. It is due to be settled within 12 months of the date of the statement of financial position;
3. It is held primarily for the purpose of being traded; or
4. The entity does not have an unconditional right to defer settlement beyond 12 months. Note that the terms of a liability that could at the option of the counterparty result in its settlement by the issue of equity instruments do not affect its classification.

All other liabilities should be classified as non-current liabilities. Obligations which are due on demand or are callable at any time by the lender are classified as current regardless of the present intent of the entity or of the lender concerning early demand for repayment. Current liabilities also include:

1. Obligations arising from the acquisition of goods and services entering into the entity's normal operating cycle (e.g., accounts payable, short-term notes payable, wages payable, taxes payable and other miscellaneous payables);

2. Collections of money in advance for the future delivery of goods or performance of services, such as rent received in advance and unearned subscription revenues;
3. Other obligations maturing within the current operating cycle, such as the current maturity of bonds and long-term notes.

Certain liabilities, such as trade payables and accruals for operating costs, which form part of the working capital used in the normal operating cycle of the business, are to be classified as current liabilities even if they are due to be settled more than 12 months from the date of the statement of financial position.

Other current liabilities which are not settled as part of the operating cycle, but which are due for settlement within 12 months of the date of the statement of financial position, such as dividends payable and the current portion of long-term debt, should also be classified as current liabilities. However, interest-bearing liabilities which provide the financing for working capital on a long-term basis and are not scheduled for settlement within 12 months should not be classified as current liabilities.

IAS 1 provides another exception to the general rule that a liability due to be repaid within 12 months from the end of the reporting period should be classified as a current liability. If the original term was for a period longer than 12 months and the entity intended to refinance the obligation on a long-term basis prior to the date of the statement of financial position, and that intention is supported by an agreement to refinance, or to reschedule payments, which is completed before the financial statements are approved, then the debt is to be reclassified as non-current as at the date of the statement of financial position.

However, an entity would continue to classify as current liabilities its long-term financial liabilities when they are due to be settled within 12 months, if an agreement to refinance on a long-term basis was made after the date of the statement of financial position. Similarly, if long-term debt becomes callable as a result of a breach of a loan covenant, and no agreement with the lender to provide a grace period of more than 12 months has been concluded by the date of the statement of financial position, the debt must be classified as current.

The distinction between current and non-current liquid assets generally rests upon both the ability and the intent of the entity to realise or not to realise cash for the assets within the traditional one-year time frame. Intent is not of similar significance with regard to the classification of liabilities, however, because the creditor has the legal right to demand satisfaction of a currently due obligation, and even an expression of intent not to exercise that right does not diminish the entity's burden should there be a change in the creditor's intention. Thus, whereas an entity can control its use of current assets, it is limited by its contractual obligations with regard to current liabilities and, accordingly, accounting for current liabilities (subject to the two exceptions noted above) is based on legal terms, not expressions of intent.

Non-Current Liabilities

Non-current liabilities are obligations which are not expected to be settled within the current operating cycle, including:

1. Obligations arising as part of the long-term capital structure of the entity, such as the issuance of bonds, long-term notes and lease obligations;
2. Obligations arising out of the normal course of operations, such as pension obligations, decommissioning provisions and deferred taxes; and

3. Contingent obligations involving uncertainty as to possible expenses or losses. These are resolved by the occurrence or non-occurrence of one or more future events which confirm the amount payable, the payee and/or the date payable. Contingent obligations include such items as product warranties (see the section on provisions below).

For all long-term liabilities, the maturity date, nature of obligation, rate of interest and description of any security pledged to support the agreement should be clearly shown. Also, in the case of bonds and long-term notes, any premium or discount should be reported separately as an addition to or subtraction from the par (or face) value of the bond or note. Long-term obligations which contain certain covenants, which must be adhered to, are classified as current liabilities if any of those covenants have been violated and the lender has the right to demand payment. Unless the lender expressly waives that right or the conditions causing the default are corrected, the obligation is current.

Offsetting Assets and Liabilities

In general, assets and liabilities may not be offset against each other. However, the reduction of accounts receivable by the allowance for expected credit losses, or of property, plant and equipment by the accumulated depreciation, are procedures that reduce these assets by the appropriate valuation amounts and are not in fact the offsetting of assets and liabilities.

Only where there is an actual right of setoff is the offsetting of assets and liabilities a proper presentation. This right of setoff exists only when all of the following conditions are met:

1. Each of the two parties owes the other determinable amounts (although they may be in different currencies and bear different rates of interest);
2. The entity has the right to set off against the amount owed by the other party;
3. The entity intends to offset; and
4. The right of setoff is legally enforceable.

The laws of certain countries, including some bankruptcy laws, may impose restrictions or prohibitions against the right of setoff. Furthermore, when maturities differ, only the party with the nearest maturity can offset because the party with the longer maturity must settle in the manner determined by the earlier maturity party.

The question of setoff is sometimes significant for financial institutions which buy and sell financial instruments, often repackaging them as part of the process. IFRS 9 provides detailed rules for determining when derecognition is appropriate and when financial assets and financial liabilities must be retained on the statement of financial position.

CLASSIFICATION OF SHAREHOLDERS' EQUITY

Shareholders' equity represents the interests of the owners in the net assets of a corporation. It shows the cumulative net results of past transactions and other events affecting the entity since its inception.

Share Capital

This consists of the par or nominal value of preference and ordinary shares. The number of shares authorised, the number issued and the number outstanding should be clearly shown. For preference share capital, the preference features must also be stated, as the following example illustrates:

6% cumulative preference shares, €100 par value, callable at €115, 15,000 shares authorised, 10,000 shares issued and outstanding	€1,000,000
Ordinary shares, €10 par value per share, 2,000,000 shares authorised, 1,500,000 shares issued and outstanding	€15,000,000

Preference share capital that is redeemable at the option of the holder should not be treated as a part of equity—rather, it should be reported as a liability. IAS 32 makes it clear that substance prevails over form in the case of compound financial instruments; any instrument which includes a contractual obligation for the entity to deliver cash is considered to be a liability.

Retained Earnings

This represents the accumulated earnings since the inception of the entity, less any earnings distributed to owners in the form of dividends. In some jurisdictions, notably in continental Europe, the law requires that a portion of retained earnings, equivalent to a small proportion of share capital, be set aside as a legal reserve. Historically, this was intended to limit dividend distributions by young or ailing businesses. This practice is expected to wane, and in any event is not congruent with financial reporting in accordance with IFRS and with the distinction made between equity and liabilities.

Also included in the equity section of the statement of financial position is treasury stock representing issued shares that have been reacquired by the issuer in jurisdictions where the purchase of the entity's own shares and holding in treasury is permitted by law. These shares are generally stated at their cost of acquisition as a reduction of shareholders' equity.

Finally, some elements of comprehensive income, the components of other comprehensive income, are reported in equity. These components of other comprehensive income include net changes in the fair values of financial assets classified at fair value through other comprehensive income, unrealised gains or losses on translations of the financial statements of subsidiaries denominated in a foreign currency, net changes in revaluation surplus, actuarial gains and losses on defined benefit plans, and the effective portion of gains and losses on hedging instruments in a cash flow hedge. In accordance with the revised IAS 1, net changes in all items of other comprehensive income should be reported in a new statement called the "statement of profit or loss and other comprehensive income," and accumulated balances in these items are reported in equity. (For a detailed discussion of the statement of profit or loss and other comprehensive income, refer to Chapter 5.)

Non-controlling interests should be shown separately from owners' equity of the parent company in group accounts (i.e., consolidated financial statements), but are included in the overall equity section.

Disclosure of Share Capital

An entity is required to disclose information which enables the users of its financial statements to evaluate the entity's objectives, policies and processes for managing capital.

This information should include a description of what the entity manages as capital, and the nature of externally imposed capital requirements, if there are any, as well as how those requirements are incorporated into the management of capital. Additionally, summary quantitative data about what the entity manages as capital should be provided as well as any changes in the components of capital and methods of managing capital from the previous period. The consequences of non-compliance with externally imposed capital requirements should also be included in the notes. All these disclosures are based on the information provided internally to key management personnel.

An entity should also present either in the statement of financial position or in the statement of changes in equity, or in the notes, disclosures about each class of share capital as well as about the nature and purpose of each reserve within equity. Information about share capital should include the number of shares authorised and issued (fully paid or not fully paid); par value per share or that shares have no par value; the rights, preferences and restrictions attached to each class of share capital; shares in the entity held by the entity (treasury shares) or by its subsidiaries or associates; and shares reserved for issue under options and contracts (including terms and amounts).

FUTURE DEVELOPMENTS

The IASB is exploring targeted improvements to the structure and content of the primary financial statements, with a focus on the statement(s) of financial performance. It will continue its discussions during 2018. No decision has yet been taken on whether to publish a Discussion Paper or an Exposure Draft.

US GAAP COMPARISON

Comparative statements are generally accepted but not required by US GAAP. The SEC requires balance sheets for two years. The balance sheet is usually presented in order of liquidity from most or current to least or non-current. This is usually the opposite of the order found under IFRS. US GAAP contains captions for long-term assets and long-term liabilities. The SEC calls for display of a total for current assets and a total for current liabilities, where appropriate, and public companies must comply with the detailed layout requirements of Regulation S-X.

Non-current debt that matures within one year can be classified as non-current if the entity has the intent and ability to refinance the obligation on a long-term basis. Evidence of intent includes:

- Entering into a refinancing agreement for a term of greater than one year, completed before the financial statements are issued or available to be issued, or
- Issuing long-term debt or equity with the purpose of refinancing the short-term debt before the financial statements are issued or available to be issued.

Debt for which there has been a covenant violation may be classified as non-current, if there is a lender agreement to waive the right to demand repayment for more than one year and that agreement exists before the financial statements are issued or available to be issued.

Current portions of deferred tax assets and liabilities must be shown as current. The term "reserve" is discouraged in US GAAP.

5 STATEMENTS OF PROFIT OR LOSS AND OTHER COMPREHENSIVE INCOME, AND CHANGES IN EQUITY

INTRODUCTION

The IASB's *Conceptual Framework* emphasises the importance of information about the performance of an entity, which is useful to assess potential changes in the economic resources that are likely to be controlled in the future, predict future cash flows and form judgements about the effectiveness with which the entity might employ additional resources. For a period of time from mid-2004, the IASB and FASB collaboratively pursued projects on *Financial Statement Presentation* (originally entitled *Performance Reporting*), which resulted in fundamental changes to the format and content of what is commonly referred to as the income statement (or the profit or loss account). This joint effort was bifurcated. The first phase of the project addressed what constituted a complete set of financial statements and a requirement to present comparative financial statements (absent from US GAAP) and culminated in the issuance of revised IAS 1 in 2007, effective in 2009.

IAS 1, *Presentation of Financial Statements*, as revised in 2007, brings IAS 1 largely into line with the US standard—Statement of Financial Accounting Standards 130, *Reporting Comprehensive Income* (now in Accounting Standards Codification [ASC] 220 *Income Statement—Reporting on Comprehensive Income)*. The standard requires all non-owner changes in equity (i.e., comprehensive income items) to be presented either in one statement of comprehensive income or else in two statements, a separate income statement and a statement of comprehensive income. Components of comprehensive income are not permitted to be presented in the statement of changes in equity as a combined statement of income and comprehensive income became mandatory (or at least preferable); this represented a triumph of the *all-inclusive concept* of performance reporting. While this approach has been officially endorsed by world standard setters for many decades, in fact many standards issued over the years have deviated from adherence to this principle. While IAS 1 encourages the presentation of comprehensive income in a single statement, with net income being an intermediate caption, it remains acceptable to instead report in a two-statement format, with a separate income statement and a separate statement of comprehensive income. The statement of comprehensive income will report all non-owner changes in equity separately from owner changes in equity (investments by or distributions to owners).

IAS 1 in its current incarnation thus marks a notable return to an all-inclusive concept of performance reporting, which had been eroded in earlier decades as items such as gains and losses on financial instruments measured at fair value through other comprehensive income and defined benefit plan actuarial gains or losses became reportable directly in the equity section of the statement of financial position—a practice which generated understandable confusion regarding the contents of the reporting entity's "real" results of operations.

Concepts of performance and measures of income have changed over the years, and current reporting still largely focuses on *realised* income and expense. However, *unrealised* gains and losses also reflect real economic transactions and events and are of great interest to decision makers. Under current IFRS, some of these unrealised gains and losses are *recognised*, while others are *unrecognised*. Both the reporting entities themselves and the financial analyst community go to great lengths to identify those elements within reported income which are likely to continue into the future, since expected earnings and cash flows of future periods are the main drivers of share prices.

IFRS rules for the presentation of income are based on a so-called "mixed attribute model." They therefore reflect a mixture of traditional realised income reporting, accompanied by fair value measures applied to unrealised gains and losses meeting certain criteria. So, for example, financial instruments are accounted for differently from property, plant and equipment. Moreover, unrealised gains and losses arising from the translation of the foreign currency-denominated financial statements of foreign subsidiaries do not flow through the income statement. IAS 1 requires that all owner changes in equity should be reported separately from non-owner changes (deriving from performance) in a separate *statement of changes in equity*.

The traditional income statement has been known by many titles. IFRS refer now to this statement as the statement of profit or loss, which reports all items entering into the determination of periodic earnings but excluding other comprehensive income items which are reported in the other comprehensive income section of the statement of profit or loss and other comprehensive income.

For many years, the income statement had been widely perceived by investors, creditors, management and other interested parties as the single most important part of an entity's basic financial statements. In fact, beginning in the mid-twentieth century, accounting theory development was largely driven by the desire to present a meaningful income statement, even to the extent that the balance sheet sometimes became the repository for balances of various accounts, such as deferred charges and credits, which could scarcely meet any reasonable definitions of assets or liabilities. This was done largely to serve the needs of investors, who are commonly thought to use the past income of a business as the most important input to their predictions of entities' future earnings and cash flows, which in turn form the basis for their estimates of future share prices and dividends.

Creditors look to the statement of profit or loss for insight into the borrower's ability to generate the future cash flows needed to pay interest and eventually to repay the principal amounts of the obligations. Even in the instance of secured debt, creditors do not look primarily to the statement of financial position (balance sheet), inasmuch as the seizure and liquidation of collateral is never the preferred route to recovery of the lender's investment. Rather, generation of cash flows from operations—which is generally closely correlated to income—is seen as the primary source for debt service.

Management, then, must be concerned with the statement of profit or loss by virtue of the importance placed on it by investors and creditors. In many large corporations, senior management receive substantial bonuses relating either to profit targets or share price performance. Consequently, management sometimes devote considerable efforts to massaging what appears in the income statement, to present the most encouraging view of the reporting entity's future prospects. This means that standard setters need to bear in mind the possibilities for abuse afforded by the requirements which they put in place. Indeed, many of the requirements have been imposed in response to previous financial reporting abuses.

The importance placed on income measurement has, as is well known, influenced behaviour by some management personnel, who have sought to manipulate results to, for instance, meet market observers' earnings estimates. The motivation for this improper behaviour is readily understandable when one observes that recent markets have severely punished companies which missed earnings estimates by as little as a penny per share. One very popular vehicle for earnings management has centred around revenue recognition. Historically, certain revenue recognition situations, such as that involving prepaid service revenue, have lacked specific financial reporting rules or have been highly subject to interpretation, opening the door to aggressive accounting by some entities. While in many businesses the revenue-earning cycle is simple and straightforward and therefore difficult to manipulate, there are many other situations where it is a matter of interpretation as to when the revenue has actually been earned. Examples have included recognition by lessors of lease income from long-term equipment rental contracts, which were bundled with supplies and maintenance agreements, and accruals of earnings on long-term construction contracts or software development projects having multiple deliverables.

The information provided by the statement of profit or loss, relating to individual items of income and expense, as well as to the relationships between and among these items (such as the amounts reported as gross margin or profit before interest and taxes), facilitates financial analysis, especially that relating to the reporting entity's historical and possible future profitability. Even with the ascendancy of the statement of financial position as the premier financial statement, financial statement users will always devote considerable attention to the statement of profit or loss.

Further to the 2007 revisions to IAS 1, in 2011 and 2012 the IASB made additional amendments. In June 2011, the IASB issued an amendment to IAS 1 titled *Presentation of Items of Other Comprehensive Income*, which became effective for accounting periods beginning on or after July 1, 2012. The amendment improves the consistency and clarity of items recorded in other comprehensive income. Other comprehensive income is grouped together on the basis of whether or not items are subsequently reclassified to profit or loss. The Board highlighted the importance of presenting profit or loss and other comprehensive income together and with equal prominence. The name of the *statement of comprehensive income* is changed to *statement of profit or loss and other comprehensive income*.

In May 2012, the IASB issued "Annual Improvements 2009–2011 cycle," a collection of amendments to IFRS in response to issues addressed during the 2009–2011 cycle. The IASB became aware of a diversity of views as to the requirements for comparative information when an entity provides individual financial statements beyond the minimum comparative information requirements of IAS 1 and thus issued these amendments to IAS 1 to clarify the requirements for comparative information. These amendments became effective for periods beginning on or after January 1, 2013.

Sources of IFRS		
	Conceptual Framework for Financial Reporting 2010	
IAS 1, 14, 16, 19, 21, 36, 37, 38, 39, 40	*IFRS* 1, 5, 15	*SIC* 29

FUTURE DEVELOPMENTS

The IASB is exploring targeted improvements to the structure and content of the primary financial statements, with a focus on the statement(s) of financial performance. The board plans to publish an exposure draft at the end of 2019 as a new JFRS rather than as amendments to IAS 1.

SCOPE

This chapter focuses on key income measurement issues and on matters of comprehensive income, statement presentation and disclosure. It also explains and illustrates the presentation of the *statement of profit or loss and other comprehensive income* and the *statement of changes in equity*. The chapter incorporates information from the *Conceptual Framework for Financial Reporting 2018*, IAS 1, and other standards.

DEFINITIONS OF TERMS

Elements of Financial Statements

Expenses. *Decreases in assets, or increases in liabilities, that result in decreases in equity, other than those relating to distributions to holders of equity claims*. The term *expenses* is broad enough to include *losses* as well as normal categories of expenses; thus, IFRS differs from the corresponding US GAAP standard (as defined in CON 6), which deems losses to be a separate and distinct element to be accounted for, denoting decreases in equity from peripheral or incidental transactions.

Income. *Increases in assets, or decreases in liabilities, that result in increases in equity, other than those relating to contributions from holders of equity claims*. The IASB's *Conceptual Framework* clarifies that this definition of income encompasses both revenue and gains.

As with expenses and losses, the corresponding US accounting standard holds that revenues and gains constitute two separate elements of financial reporting, with gains denoting increases in equity from peripheral or incidental transactions (as defined in CON 6).

Other comprehensive income. *Items of income and expense (including reclassification adjustments) that are not recognised in profit or loss as required or permitted by other IFRS.* The components of other comprehensive income include (1) changes in revaluation surplus (IAS 16 and 38); (2) actuarial gains and losses on defined benefit plans (IAS 19); (3) translation gains and losses (IAS 21); (4) gains and losses on remeasuring of equity instrument financial assets (IFRS 9); and (5) the effective portion of gains and losses on hedging instruments in a cash flow hedge (IFRS 9).

Profit or loss. The total of income less expenses, excluding the components of other comprehensive income.

Reclassification adjustments. Amounts reclassified to profit or loss in the current period that were recognised in other comprehensive income in the current or preceding periods.

Statement of changes in equity. As prescribed by IAS 1, an entity should present, as a separate financial statement, a statement of changes in equity showing:

1. Total comprehensive income for the period (reporting separately amounts attributable to owners of the parent and to non-controlling interest);
2. For each component of equity, the effect of retrospective application or retrospective restatement recognised in accordance with IAS 8;
3. The amounts of transactions with owners in their capacity as owners, showing separately contributions by and distributions to owners; and
4. A reconciliation for each component of equity (each class of share capital and each reserve) between the carrying amounts at the beginning and the end of the period, separately disclosing each movement.

Statement of profit or loss and other comprehensive income. The statement of profit or loss and other comprehensive income presents all components of "profit or loss" and "other comprehensive income" in a single statement, with net income being an intermediate caption. IAS 1 alternatively permits the use of a two-statement format, with a separate statement of profit or loss and a separate statement of comprehensive income.

Total comprehensive income. The change in equity (net assets) of an entity during a period from transactions and other events and circumstances from non-owner sources. It includes all changes in net assets during a period, except those resulting from investments by owners and distributions to owners. It comprises all components of "profit or loss" and "other comprehensive income" presented in the statement of comprehensive income.

Other Terminology

Additional comparative information. Narrative and descriptive comparative information in addition to the minimum comparative information required by IFRS.

Component of an entity. In the context of discontinued operations, IFRS 5 currently defines a component of an entity as operations and cash flows that can be clearly distinguished, operationally and for financial reporting purposes, from the rest of the entity—a cash-generating unit, or group of cash-generating units.

Discontinued operations. IFRS 5 defines a "discontinued operation" as a component of an enterprise that has been disposed of, or is classified as held-for-sale, and:

1. Represents a separate major line of business or geographical area of operations;
2. Is part of a single coordinated disposal plan;
3. Is a subsidiary acquired exclusively with a view to resale.

Minimum comparative information. Narrative and descriptive information in respect of the preceding period for all amounts reported in the current period's financial statements where it is relevant to an understanding of the current period's financial statements.

Net assets. Net assets are total assets minus total liabilities (which is thus equivalent to owners' equity).

Operating segment. A component of an entity: (1) that engages in business activities from which it may earn revenues and incur expenses (including revenues and expenses relating to transactions with other components of the same entity); (2) whose operating results are regularly reviewed by the entity's chief operating decision maker to make decisions about resources to be allocated to the segment and assess its performance; and (3) for which discrete financial information is available.

Realisation. The process of converting non-cash resources and rights into money, or more precisely the sale of an asset for cash or claims to cash.

Recognition. The process of capturing for inclusion in the statement of financial position or the statement(s) of financial performance an item that meets the definition of one of the elements of financial statements—an asset, a liability, equity, income or expenses. Recognition involves depicting the item in one of those statements—either alone or in aggregation with other items—in words and by a monetary amount and including that amount in one or more totals in that statement.

CONCEPTS OF INCOME

Economists have generally employed a wealth maintenance concept of income. Under this concept, income is the maximum amount that can be consumed during a period and still leave the entity with the same amount of wealth at the end of the period as existed at the beginning. Wealth is determined with reference to the current market values of the net productive assets at the beginning and end of the period. Therefore, the economists' definition of income would fully incorporate market value changes (both increases and decreases in wealth) in the determination of periodic income and this would correspond to measuring assets and liabilities at fair value, with the net of all the changes in net assets equating to comprehensive income.

Accountants, on the other hand, have traditionally defined income by reference to specific transactions which give rise to recognisable elements of revenue and expense during a reporting period. The events which produce reportable items of revenue and expense comprise a subset of economic events which determine economic income. Many changes in the market values of wealth components are deliberately excluded from the measurement of accounting income but are included in the measurement of economic income, although those exclusions have grown fewer as the use of fair values in financial reporting has been more widely embraced in recent years.

This can be seen in IFRS 9, where the changes in market value of some financial instruments are recognised, and in IAS 41, where the change in value of biological assets is recognised even though not realised.

RECOGNITION AND MEASUREMENT

Income

According to the IASB's *Conceptual Framework*:

Income is increases in assets, or decreases in liabilities, that result in increases in equity, other than those relating to contributions from holders of equity claims.

The definition of income encompasses both revenue and gains, and revenue arises in the course of ordinary activities of an enterprise and is referred to by different names, such as sales, fees, interest, dividends, royalties, and rent.

IFRS 15 is the standard which deals with accounting for revenue. IFRS 15, *Revenue from Contracts with Customers*, states that revenue is income arising in the course of an entity's ordinary activities.

IFRS 15 requires that when (or as) a performance obligation is satisfied; an entity shall recognise as revenue the amount of the transaction price that is allocated to that performance obligation and goes on to set out detailed requirements for determining the transaction price. IFRS 15 and revenue recognition are discussed in detail in Chapter 20.

Expenses

According to the IASB's *Conceptual Framework*:

Expenses are decreases in assets, or incurrences in liabilities, that result in decreases in equity, other than those relating to distributions to holders of equity claims.

Expenses are expired costs, or items that were assets but are no longer assets because they have no future value. Costs such as materials and direct labour consumed in the manufacturing process are relatively easy to identify with the related revenue elements. These cost elements are included in inventory and expensed as cost of sales when the product is sold and revenue from the sale is recognised. This is associating cause and effect.

Some costs are more closely associated with specific accounting periods. In the absence of a cause and effect relationship, the asset's cost should be allocated to the benefiting accounting periods in a systematic and rational manner. This form of expense recognition involves assumptions about the expected length of benefit and the relationship between benefit and cost of each period. Depreciation of fixed assets, amortisation of intangibles and allocation of rent and insurance are examples of costs which would be recognised by the use of a systematic and rational method.

All other costs are normally expensed in the period in which they are incurred. This would include those costs for which no clear-cut future benefits can be identified, costs that were recorded as assets in prior periods but for which no remaining future benefits can be identified and those other elements of administrative or general expense for which no rational allocation scheme can be devised. The general approach is first to attempt to match costs with the related revenues. Next, a method of systematic and rational allocation should be attempted. If neither of these measurement principles is beneficial, the cost should be immediately expensed.

Gains and Losses

The *Conceptual Framework* defines the term *expenses* broadly enough to include losses. IFRS include no definition of gains and losses that enables them to be separated from income and expenses. Traditionally, gains and losses are thought by accountants to arise from sales and purchases outside the regular business trading of the company, such as on disposals of non-current assets which are no longer required. IAS 1 used to include an extraordinary category for display of items that were clearly distinct from ordinary activities. The IASB removed this category in its 2003 Improvements Project, concluding that these items arose from the normal business risks faced by an entity and that it is the nature or function of a transaction or other event, rather than its frequency, which should determine its presentation within the statement of comprehensive income.

Gains and losses represent increases and decreases in economic benefits and as such are no different in nature from income and expenses. Hence, they are not regarded as separate elements in IASB's *Conceptual Framework*. Characteristics of gains and losses include the following:

1. They result from peripheral transactions and circumstances that may be beyond an entity's control.
2. They may be classified according to sources or as operating and non-operating.

STATEMENT OF PROFIT OR LOSS AND OTHER COMPREHENSIVE INCOME

IAS 1 states that comprehensive income is the change in the entity's net assets over the course of the reporting period arising from non-owner sources. An entity has the option of presenting comprehensive income in a period either in one statement (the single-statement approach) or in two statements (the two-statement approach). The IASB initially intended to mandate the single-statement approach for the statement of comprehensive income, but during discussions with constituents, many of them were opposed to the concept of a single statement, stating that it could result in undue focus on the "bottom line" of the statement. Consequently, the IASB decided that presentation in a single statement was not as important as its fundamental decision that all non-owner changes in equity should be presented separately from owner changes in equity. Nonetheless, the IASB has indicated that it prefers a one-statement approach. If an entity presents the components of profit or loss in a separate statement, this separate statement of profit or loss (income statement) forms part of a complete set of financial statements and should be displayed immediately before the statement of comprehensive income.

Although IAS 1 uses the terms "profit or loss," "other comprehensive income" and "total comprehensive income," an entity may use other terms to describe the totals, as long as the meaning is clear. For example, an entity may use the term "net income" to describe profit or loss.

Comprehensive income comprises all components of "profit or loss" and of "other comprehensive income."

Total comprehensive income for the period reported in a statement of profit or loss and other comprehensive income is the total of all items of income and expense recognised during the period (including the components of profit or loss and other comprehensive income).

Other comprehensive income is the total of income less expenses (including reclassification adjustments) that are not recognised in profit or loss as required or permitted by other IFRS or Interpretations.

The statement of profit or loss and other comprehensive income must in addition to the information given in the profit and loss and other comprehensive income sections disclose the following totals:

1. Profit or loss;
2. Total other comprehensive income;
3. Comprehensive income for the year (total of 1. and 2.).

IAS 1 stipulates that, in addition to items required by other IFRS, the profit and loss section of the statement of profit or loss and other comprehensive income must include line items which present the following amounts for the period (if they are pertinent to the entity's operations for the period in question):

1. Revenue;
2. Finance costs;
3. Share of the profit or loss of associates and joint ventures accounted for by the equity method;
4. Tax expense;
5. A single amount for the total of discontinued operations.

In addition, an entity should disclose the following items on the face of the statement of profit or loss and other comprehensive income as allocations:

1. Profit or loss for the period attributable to:
   a. Non-controlling interest; and
   b. Owners of the parent.
2. Total comprehensive income for the period attributable to:
   a. Non-controlling interest; and
   b. Owners of the parent.

Items 1–5 listed above and disclosure of profit or loss attributable to non-controlling interest and owners of the parent (listed in 1.) can be presented on the face of a separate statement of profit or loss (income statement).

The foregoing items represent the barest acceptable minimum of detail in the statement of comprehensive income. The standard states that additional line items, headings and subtotals should be presented on the face of the statement when this is relevant to an understanding of the entity's financial performance. This requirement cannot be dealt with by incorporating the items into the notes to the financial statements. When items of income or expense are material, disclosures identifying their nature and amount are required in the statement of comprehensive income or in the notes.

PRESENTATION IN THE PROFIT OR LOSS SECTION

In accordance with IAS 1, if an entity presents the components of profit or loss in a separate statement of profit or loss, this separate statement should be displayed immediately before the statement of comprehensive income. The following also needs to be disclosed.

Statement Title

The legal name of the entity must be used to identify the financial statements and the correct title used to distinguish the statement from other information presented in the annual report.

Reporting Period

The period covered by the statement of profit or loss must be clearly identified, such as "Year ended December 31, 2017" or "Six months ended September 30, 2017." Income statements are normally presented annually (i.e., for a period of 12 months or a year). However, in some jurisdictions they may be required at quarterly or six-monthly intervals, and in exceptional circumstances (such as a newly acquired subsidiary aligning its accounting dates with those of its new parent), companies may need to prepare a statement of profit or loss for periods in excess of one year or for shorter periods as well. IAS 1 requires that when financial statements are presented for periods other than a year, the following additional disclosures should be made:

1. The reason for presenting the statement of profit or loss (and other financial statements, such as the statement of cash flows, statement of changes in equity and notes) for a period other than one year; and
2. The fact that the comparative information presented (in the statement of profit or loss, statement of changes in equity, statement of cash flows and notes) is not entirely comparable.

Entities whose operations form a natural cycle may have a reporting period that ends on a specific day of the week (e.g., the last Friday of the month). Certain entities (typically retail enterprises) may prepare income statements for a fiscal period of 52 or 53 weeks instead of a year (thus, to always end on a day such as Sunday, on which no business is transacted, so that inventory may be taken). These entities should clearly state that the income statement has been presented, for instance "for the fifty-two-week period ended March 25, 2016." IAS 1 notes that it is unlikely that financial statements presented in this way would be materially different from those which would be presented for a full year.

So that the presentation and classification of items in the statement of profit or loss are consistent from period to period, items of income and expenses should be uniform with respect to both appearance and categories from one time period through to the next. If a decision is made to change classification schemes, the comparative prior period financial statements should be restated to conform and thus to maintain comparability between the two periods being presented together. Disclosure must be made of this reclassification, since the earlier period financial statements being presented currently will differ in appearance from those nominally same statements presented in the earlier year.

Comparative Information

The issue of the "Annual Improvements 2009–2011 cycle" in May 2012 clarified the requirements for comparative information. These requirements state that, as a minimum, comparative figures regarding the previous reporting period should be included. The requirements apply for both the profit or loss section and the other comprehensive income section.

Classification of Expenses

An example of the income statement (profit or loss) classification by the "nature of expense" method is shown below:

Exemplum Reporting PLC
Statement of Profit or Loss
For the Year Ended December 31, 20XX
(Classification of expense by nature)

	€	€
Revenue		X
Other income		X
Changes in inventories of finished goods and work in progress	X	
Work performed by the entity and capitalised	X	
Raw material and consumables used	X	
Employee benefits expense	X	
Depreciation and amortisation expense	X	
Impairment of property, plant and equipment	X	
Other expenses	X	
Total expenses		X
Operating profit		X

An example of the income statement (profit or loss) classification by the "function of expense" method is as follows:

Statement of Profit or Loss
For the Year Ended December 31, 20XX
(Classification of expense by function)

	€
Revenue	X
Cost of sales	X
Gross profit	X
Other income	X
Distribution costs	X
Administrative expenses	X
Other expenses	X
Operating profit	X

Under the "function of expense" method an entity should report, at a minimum, its cost of sales separately from other expenses. This method can provide more relevant information to the users of the financial statements than the classification under the "nature of expense" method but allocating costs to functions may require arbitrary allocations based on judgement.

IAS 1 furthermore stipulates that if a reporting entity discloses expenses by function, it must also provide information on the nature of the expenses, including depreciation and amortisation and staff costs (salaries and wages). The standard does not provide detailed guidance on this requirement, but entities need only provide a note indicating the nature of the allocations made to comply with the requirement.

IFRS 5 governs the presentation and disclosures pertaining to discontinued operations. This is discussed later in this chapter. While IAS 1 does not require the inclusion of subsidiary schedules to support major captions in the statement of income, it is commonly found that detailed schedules of line items are included in full sets of financial statements. These will be illustrated in the following section to provide a more expansive discussion of the meaning of certain major sections of the statement of income.

Companies typically show their regular trading operations first and then present any items to which they wish to direct users' attention.

1. *Sales or other operating revenues* are charges to customers for the goods and/or services provided to them during the period. This section of the statement of income should include information about discounts, allowances and returns to determine net sales or net revenues.
2. *Cost of goods sold* is the cost of the inventory items sold during the period. In the case of a merchandising entity, net purchases (purchases less discounts, returns and allowances plus freight-in) are added to the beginning inventory to obtain the cost of goods available for sale. From the cost of goods available-for-sale amount, the ending inventory is deducted to compute cost of goods sold.

   A manufacturing enterprise computes the cost of goods sold in a slightly different way. Cost of goods manufactured would be added to the beginning inventory to arrive at cost of goods available for sale. The ending finished goods inventory is then deducted from the cost of goods available for sale to determine the cost of goods sold. Cost of goods manufactured is computed by adding to raw materials on hand at the beginning of the period the raw materials purchased during the period and all other costs of production, such as labour and direct overheads, thereby yielding the cost of goods placed in production during the period. When adjusted for changes in work in process during the period and for raw materials on hand at the end of the period, this results in the cost of goods produced.
3. *Operating expenses* are primary recurring costs associated with central operations, other than cost of goods sold, which are incurred to generate sales. Operating expenses are normally classified into the following two categories:

   a. Distribution costs (or selling expenses);
   b. General and administrative expenses.

   Distribution costs are those expenses related directly to the entity's efforts to generate sales (e.g., sales salaries, commissions, advertising, delivery expenses, depreciation of store furniture and equipment, and store supplies). General and administrative expenses are expenses related to the general administration of the company's operations (e.g., officers and office salaries, office supplies, depreciation of office furniture and fixtures, telephone, postage, accounting and legal services, and business licences and fees).

4. *Other revenues and expenses* are incidental revenues and expenses not related to the central operations of the company (e.g., rental income from letting parts of premises not needed for company operations).
5. *Separate disclosure items* are items which are of such size, nature or incidence that their disclosure becomes important to explain the performance of the enterprise for the period. Examples of items that, if material, would require such disclosure are as follows:

    a. Write-downs of inventories to net realisable value, or of property, plant and equipment to recoverable amounts, and subsequent reversals of such write-downs;
    b. Costs of restructuring the activities of an enterprise and any subsequent reversals of such provisions;
    c. Costs of litigation settlements;
    d. Other reversals of provisions.

6. *Income tax expense.* The total of taxes payable and deferred taxation adjustments for the period covered by the income statement.
7. *Discontinued operations.* IFRS 5 was issued by the IASB as part of its convergence programme with US GAAP.

IFRS 5 created a new "held-for-sale" category of asset into which assets, or "disposal groups" of assets and liabilities that are to be sold, are classified. Such assets or groups of assets are to be valued at the lower of carrying value and fair value less any selling costs. Any resulting write-down appears, net of tax, as part of the caption "discontinued operations" in the statement of income.

The other component of this line is the post-tax profit or loss on discontinued operations. A discontinued operation is defined as a component of an entity that has either been disposed of or has been classified as held-for-sale. It must also:

- Be a separate major line of business or geographical area of operations;
- Be a part of a single coordinated plan for disposal; or
- Be a subsidiary acquired exclusively with a view to resale.

The two elements of the single line in the statement of income have to be analysed in the notes, breaking down the related income tax expense between the two, as well as showing the components of revenue, expense and pre-tax profit of the discontinued items.

For the asset or disposal group to be classified as held-for-sale, and its related earnings to be classified as discontinued, IFRS 5 says that the sale must be highly probable, the asset must be saleable in its current condition, and the sale price must be reasonable in relation to its fair value. The appropriate level of management in the group must be committed to a plan to sell the asset and an active programme must have been embarked upon. Sale should be expected within one year of classification and the standard sets out stringent conditions for any extension of this, which are based on elements outside the control of the entity.

Where an operation meets the criteria for classification as discontinued but will be abandoned within one year rather than be sold, it should also be included in discontinued operations. Assets or disposal groups categorised as held-for-sale are not depreciated further.

Example of schedule of cost of goods sold

Exemplum Reporting PLC
Schedule of Cost of Goods Sold
For the Year Ended December 31, 20XX

	€	€	€
Beginning inventory			X
Add: Purchases		X	
Freight-in		X	
Cost of purchases		X	
Less: Purchase discounts	X		
Purchase returns and allowances	X	(X)	
Net purchases			X
Cost of goods available for sale			X
Less: Ending inventory			(X)
Cost of goods sold			X

Example of schedules of cost of goods manufactured and sold

Exemplum Reporting PLC
Schedule of Cost of Goods Manufactured
For the Year Ended December 31, 20XX

	€	€
Direct materials inventory, January 1	X	
Purchases of materials (including freight-in and deducting purchase discounts)	X	
Total direct materials available	X	
Direct materials inventory, December 31	(X)	
Direct materials used		X
Direct labour		X
Factory overhead:		
Depreciation of factory equipment	X	
Utilities	X	
Indirect factory labour	X	
Indirect materials	X	
Other overhead items	X	X
Manufacturing cost incurred in 2015		X
Add: Work in process, January 1		X
Less: Work in process, December 31		(X)
Cost of goods manufactured		X

Exemplum Reporting PLC
Schedule of Cost of Goods Sold
For the Year Ended December 31, 20XX

	€
Finished goods inventory, January 1	X
Add: Cost of goods manufactured	X
Cost of goods available for sale	X
Less: Finished goods inventory, December 31	(X)
Cost of goods sold	X

Example of disclosure of discontinued operations under IFRS 5

Exemplum Reporting PLC
Statement of Income
For the Year Ended December 31, 20XX

	20XX	20XX-1
	€	€
Continuing operations (segments X and Y):		
Revenue	X	X
Operating expenses	(X)	(X)
Pre-tax profit from operating activities	X	X
Interest expense	(X)	(X)
Profit before tax	X	X
Income tax expense	(X)	(X)
Profit after taxes	X	X
Discontinuing operations (segment Z):		
Discontinued operations (note)	(X)	X
Total enterprise:		
Profit (loss) attributable to owners	X	X
The relevant note is as follows:		
Discontinued operations		
Revenue	X	X
Operating expenses	(X)	(X)
Provision for end-of-service benefits	(X)	–
Interest expense	(X)	(X)
Pre-tax profit	X	X
Income tax	(X)	(X)
Discontinued earnings	X	X
Impairment loss	(X)	(X)
Income tax	X	X
Write-down of assets	(X)	(X)
Discontinued operations, net	(X)	(X)

Aggregating Items

Aggregation of items should not serve to conceal significant information, as would the netting of revenues against expenses, or the combining of other elements, which are individually of interest to readers, such as bad debts and depreciation. The categories "other" or "miscellaneous expense" should contain, at most, an immaterial total amount of aggregated, individually insignificant elements. Once this total approach, for example 10% of total expenses (or whatever the relevant materiality threshold may be), some other aggregations, together with appropriate explanatory titles, should be selected.

Information is material if its omission, misstatement or non-disclosure could influence the economic decisions of users taken on the basis of the financial statements. Materiality depends on the size of the item judged in the particular circumstances of its omission. But it is often forgotten that materiality is also linked with understandability and the level of precision with which the financial statements are to be presented. For instance, the financial statements are often rendered more understandable by rounding information to the nearest thousand currency units (e.g., euros). This serves to alleviate the danger of loading the financial statements with unnecessary detail. However, it should be borne in mind that the use of the level of precision which makes presentation possible in the nearest thousands of currency units is acceptable only as long as the threshold of materiality is not surpassed.

Offsetting Items of Income and Expense

Materiality also plays a role in the matter of allowing or disallowing the offsetting of items of income and expense. IAS 1 addresses this issue and prescribes rules in this area. According to IAS 1, assets and liabilities or income and expenses may not be offset against each other, unless required or permitted by an IFRS. Usually, when more than one event occurs in a given reporting period, losses and gains on disposal of non-current assets or foreign exchange gains and losses are seen reported on a net basis, because they are not material individually (compared to other items in the income statement). However, if they were material individually, they would need to be disclosed separately according to the requirements of IAS 1.

However, the reduction of accounts receivable by the allowance for expected credit losses, or of property, plant and equipment by the accumulated depreciation, are procedures that reduce these assets by the appropriate valuation amounts and are not in fact the offsetting of assets and liabilities.

Views differ as to the treatment of disposal gains and losses arising from the routine replacement of non-current assets. Some experts believe that these should be separately disclosed as a disposal transaction, whereas others point out that if the depreciation schedule is estimated correctly, there should be no disposal gain or loss. Consequently, any difference between carrying value and disposal proceeds is akin to an adjustment to previous depreciation and should logically flow through the income statement in the same caption where the depreciation was originally reported. Here again, the issue comes down to one of materiality: does it affect users' ability to make economic decisions?

IAS 1 further clarifies that when items of income or expense are offset, the entity should nevertheless consider, based on materiality, the need to disclose the gross amounts in the notes to the financial statements. The standard gives the following examples of transactions that are incidental to the main revenue-generating activities of an enterprise and whose results when presented by offsetting or reporting on a net basis, such as netting any gains with related expenses, reflect the substance of the transaction:

1. Gains or losses on the disposal of non-current assets, including investments and operating assets, are reported by deducting from the proceeds on disposal the carrying amounts of the asset and related selling expenses;
2. Expenditure related to a provision that is reimbursed under a contractual arrangement with a third party may be netted against the related reimbursement.

OTHER COMPREHENSIVE INCOME

Under IAS 1, "other comprehensive income" (OCI) includes items of income and expense (including reclassification adjustments) that are not recognised in profit or loss as may be required or permitted by other IFRS. The components of OCI include (1) changes in revaluation surplus (IAS 16 and IAS 38); (2) actuarial gains and losses on defined benefit plans (IAS 19); (3) translation gains and losses of foreign operations (IAS 21); (4) gains and losses on remeasuring equity investment financial assets (IFRS 9); and (5) the effective portion of gains and losses on hedging instruments in a cash flow hedge (IFRS 9).

The other comprehensive income and an entity's share of other comprehensive income of any associate must be classified between those that:

1. Will not be reclassified subsequently to profit or loss; and
2. Will be reclassified subsequently to profit or loss.

The amount of income tax relating to each component of OCI, including reclassification adjustments, should be disclosed either on the face of the statement of comprehensive income or in the notes.

Components of OCI can be presented in one of two ways:

1. Net of related tax effects; or
2. Before related tax effects with one amount shown for the aggregate amount of income tax relating to those components.

Other IFRS specify whether and when amounts previously recognised in OCI are reclassified to profit or loss. The purpose of this requirement is to avoid double counting of OCI items in total comprehensive income when those items are reclassified to profit or loss in accordance with other IFRS. Under IFRS, some items of OCI are subject to recycling while other items are not (under US GAAP, such items are always recycled). For example, gains realised on the disposal of a foreign operation are included in profit or loss of the current period. These amounts may have been recognised in OCI as unrealised foreign currency translation gains in the current or previous periods. Those unrealised gains must be deducted from OCI in the period in which the realised gains are included in profit or loss to avoid double counting them. In the same manner, for instance, unrealised gains or losses on equity instrument investment financial assets should not include realised gains or losses from the sale of the financial assets during the current period, which are reported in profit or loss. Reclassification adjustments arise, for example, on the following components:

- On disposal of a foreign operation (IAS 21);
- On derecognition or transfer of the financial assets (IFRS 9); and
- When a hedged forecast transaction affects profit or loss (IAS 39).

Reclassification adjustments *do not* arise on the following components, which are recognised in OCI, but are not reclassified to profit or loss in subsequent periods:

- On changes in revaluation surplus (IAS 16; IAS 38);
- On changes in actuarial gains or losses on defined benefit plans (IAS 19).

In accordance with IAS 16 and IAS 38, changes in revaluation surpluses may be transferred to retained earnings in subsequent periods when the asset is sold or when it is derecognised. Actuarial gains and losses are reported in retained earnings in the period during which they are recognised as OCI (IAS 19).

Reclassification Adjustments: An Example

When a financial asset is held in a business model with the objective of collecting the contractual cash flows and selling the financial assets and the cash flows represent solely payments of principal or interest, the financial asset is measured at fair value through other comprehensive income.

When a sale of the financial asset occurs, a reclassification adjustment is necessary to ensure that gains and losses are not double counted. To illustrate, assume that Exemplum Reporting PLC has the following two financial assets classified at fair value through other comprehensive income (FVTOCI), on which interest is monthly settled as due, in its portfolio at the end of 20XX-1, its first year of operations:

Financial asset	*Cost*	*Fair value*	*Unrealised holding gain (loss)*
	€	€	€
Loan A	105,000	125,000	20,000
Loan B	260,000	300,000	40,000
Total value of portfolio	365,000	425,000	60,000
Previous (accumulated) fair value adjustment balance			0
Fair value adjustment (Dr)			60,000

Exemplum Reporting PLC reports net income of €650,000 in 20XX-1 and presents a statement of profit or loss and other comprehensive income as follows:

Exemplum Reporting PLC
Statement of Profit or Loss and Other Comprehensive Income
For the Year Ended December 31, 20XX-1

	€
Profit or loss	650,000
Other comprehensive income	
Holding gains on financial asset	60,000
Comprehensive income	710,000

During 20XX, Exemplum Reporting PLC sold 50% of Loan B for €150,000 and realised a gain on the sale of €20,000 (150,000–130,000). At the end of 20XX, Exemplum Reporting PLC reports its FVTOCI securities as follows:

Investments	*Cost*	*Fair value*	*Unrealised holding gain (loss)*
	€	€	€
Loan A	105,000	130,000	25,000
Loan B	130,000	160,000	30,000
Total value of portfolio	235,000	290,000	55,000
Previous (accumulated) fair value adjustment balance			(60,000)
Fair value adjustment (Dr)			(5,000)

Exemplum Reporting PLC should report an unrealised holding loss of €(5,000) in comprehensive income in 20XX and a realised gain of €20,000 on the sale of Loan B. Exemplum Reporting PLC reports net profit of €830,000 in 20XX and presents the components of holding gains (losses) as follows:

Exemplum Reporting PLC
Statement of Profit or Loss and Other Comprehensive Income
For the Year Ended December 31, 20XX

	€	€
Net income (includes 20,000 realised gain on Loan B)		830,000
Other comprehensive income		
Total holding gains	15,000	
Less: Reclassification adjustment for gains previously included in comprehensive income	(20,000)	(25,000)
Comprehensive income		805,000

In 20XX-1, Exemplum Reporting PLC included the unrealised gain on Loan B in comprehensive income. In 20XX, Exemplum Reporting PLC sold the stock and reported the realised gain on sale in profit, which increased comprehensive income again. To prevent double counting of this gain of €20,000, Exemplum Reporting PLC makes a reclassification adjustment to eliminate the realised gain from the computation of comprehensive income in 20XX.

An entity may display reclassification adjustments on the face of the financial statement in which it reports comprehensive income or disclose them in the notes to the financial statements. The IASB's view is that separate presentation of reclassification adjustments is essential to inform users clearly of those amounts that are included as income and expenses in two different periods—as income or expenses in other comprehensive income in previous periods and as income or expenses in profit or loss (net income) in the current period.

STATEMENT OF CHANGES IN EQUITY

Equity (owners', partners' or shareholders') represents the interest of the owners in the net assets of an entity and shows the cumulative net results of past transactions and other events affecting the entity since its inception. The statement of changes in equity reflects the increases and decreases in the net assets of an entity during the period. In accordance with IAS 1, all changes in equity from transactions with owners are to be presented separately from non-owner changes in equity.

IAS 1 requires an entity to present a statement of changes in equity, including the following components on the face of the statement:

1. Total comprehensive income for the period, segregating amounts attributable to owners and to non-controlling interest;
2. The effects of retrospective application or retrospective restatement in accordance with IAS 8, separately for each component of equity;
3. Contributions from and distributions to owners; and
4. A reconciliation between the carrying amount at the beginning and the end of the period, separately disclosing each change, for each component of equity.

The amount of dividends recognised as distributions to equity holders during the period and the related amount per share should be presented either on the face of the statement of changes in equity or in the notes.

According to IAS 1, except for changes resulting from transactions with owners (such as equity contributions, reacquisitions of the entity's own equity instruments, dividends and costs related to these transactions with owners), the change in equity during the period represents the total amount of income and expense (including gains and losses) arising from activities other than those with owners.

The following should be disclosed, either in the statement of financial position or the statement of changes in equity, or in the notes:

1. For each class of share capital:
   - Number of shares authorised;
   - Number of shares issued and fully paid, and issued but not fully paid;
   - Par value per share, or that the shares have no par value;
   - Recognition of the number of shares outstanding at the beginning and at the end of the periods;
   - Any rights, preferences and restrictions attached;
   - Shares in the entity held by the entity or its subsidiaries; and
   - Shares reserved for issue under options and contracts for the sale of shares, including terms and amounts.
2. A description of the nature and purpose of each reserve within equity.

US GAAP COMPARISON

US GAAP encourages but does not require comparative statements. The SEC requires income statements for three years. US Securities and Exchange Commission (SEC) registrants are generally required to present expenses based on function, but there is no such requirement within US GAAP. The US GAAP income statement is presented in basically the same order as IFRS income statements, with differences in presentation and captions resulting in some differences.

Previously, US GAAP included an income statement caption entitled "Extraordinary Items" for items both infrequent and unusual. In 2015, the concept of extraordinary item was removed, bringing US GAAP in line with IFRS, which does not allow for any extraordinary items. There are no GAAP requirements that address specific performance measures, such as operating profit. However, the SEC requires the presentation of certain headings and subtotals. Also, public companies cannot disclose non-GAAP measures in the financial statements or accompanying notes.

Discontinued operations under US GAAP (ASC 205-20 *Discontinued operations*) are components entities (reportable segment, operating segment, reporting unit, subsidiary or an asset group) held for sale or disposed of, for which there will be no significant continuing cash flows or involvement with the disposed component.

In the measurement of gains or losses from derecognition of non-financial assets, US GAAP (as amended by ASU 2017-05) *Other Income—Gains and Losses from the Derecognition of Nonfinancial Assets (Subtopic 610-20)*) has the concept of an in-substance non-financial asset, which is a financial asset, including a contract of assets disposal where the fair value of non-financial assets represents substantially all of the fair value of the assets which is to be disposed.

6 STATEMENT OF CASH FLOWS

INTRODUCTION

IAS 7, *Cash Flow Statements*, became effective in 1994. IAS 7 had originally required reporting entities to prepare a statement of changes in financial position (commonly referred to as a funds flow statement) as part of a complete set of financial statements. The IASB has amended the title of IAS 7 from *Cash Flow Statements* to *Statement of Cash Flows* (the title used in the US) as a consequence of the latest revision of IAS 1, *Presentation of Financial Statements*, itself a result of the IASB and FASB deliberations on the first phase of the Financial Statement Presentation project. The statement of cash flows is now universally accepted and required under most national GAAP as well as IFRS. While there are some variations in terms of presentation (most of which pertain to the sections in which certain captions appear), the approach is highly similar across all current sets of standards.

The purpose of the statement of cash flows is to provide information about the operating cash receipts and cash payments of an entity during a period, as well as providing insight into its various investing and financing activities. It is a vitally important financial statement, because the ultimate concern of investors is the reporting entity's ability to generate cash flows which will support payments (typically but not necessarily in the form of dividends) to the shareholders. More specifically, the statement of cash flows should help investors and creditors to assess:

1. The ability to generate future positive cash flows;
2. The ability to meet obligations and pay dividends;
3. Reasons for differences between profit or loss and cash receipts and payments;
4. Both cash and non-cash aspects of entities' investing and financing transactions.

Source of IFRS
IAS 7

SCOPE

The statement of cash flows is prepared in accordance with the requirements of IAS 7 and must be presented as an integral part of the financial statements in the form of a separate statement.

DEFINITIONS OF TERMS

Cash. Cash on hand and demand deposits with banks or other financial institutions.

Cash equivalents. Short-term highly liquid investments that are readily convertible to known amounts of cash and which are subject to an insignificant risk of changes in value. Treasury bills, commercial paper, and money market funds are all examples of cash equivalents.

Direct method. A method that derives the net cash provided by or used in operating activities from major components of operating cash receipts and payments.

Financing activities. The transactions and other events that cause changes in the size and composition of an entity's contributed equity and borrowings.

Indirect (reconciliation) method. A method that derives the net cash provided by or used in operating activities by adjusting profit (loss) for the effects of transactions of a non-cash nature, any deferrals or accruals of past or future operating cash receipts or payments, and items of income or expense associated with investing or financing activities.

Investing activities. The acquisition and disposal of long-term assets and other investments not included in cash equivalents. An amendment to IAS 7 effective for annual periods beginning on or after January 1, 2010 states explicitly that only expenditures that result in a recognised asset in the statement of financial position are eligible for classification as investing activities. Examples of expenditures that in certain instances do not result in the recognition of assets are exploration and evaluation activities. In addition, expenditures on advertising and promotional activities, staff training and research and development could raise such an issue.

Operating activities. The transactions and other events not classified as financing or investing activities. In general, operating activities are principal revenue-producing activities of an entity that are brought into the determination of profit or loss, including the sale of goods and the rendering of services.

BACKGROUND

Benefits of Statement of Cash Flows

The perceived benefits of presenting the statement of cash flows in conjunction with the statement of financial position and the statement of profit or loss and comprehensive income have been highlighted by IAS 7 to be as follows:

1. It provides an insight into the financial structure of the entity (including its liquidity and solvency) and its ability to affect the amounts and timing of cash flows to adapt to changing circumstances and opportunities.

   The statement of cash flows discloses important information about the cash flows from operating, investing and financing activities, information that is not available or as clearly discernible in either the statement of financial position or the statement of profit or loss and comprehensive income. The additional disclosures, which are either recommended by IAS 7 (such as those relating to undrawn borrowing facilities or cash flows that represent increases in operating capacity) or required to be disclosed by the standard (such as that about cash held by the entity but not available for use), provide a wealth of information for the informed user of financial statements. Taken together, the statement of cash flows coupled with these required or recommended disclosures provide the user with vastly more insight into the entity's performance and position, and its probable future results, than would the statement of financial position and statement of profit or loss and comprehensive income alone.
2. It provides additional information to the users of financial statements for evaluating changes in assets, liabilities and equity of an entity. When comparative statements of financial position are presented, users are given information about the entity's assets and liabilities at the end of each of the financial periods reported upon. Where the statement of cash flows is not presented as an integral part of the financial statements, it would be necessary for users of comparative financial statements either to speculate about how and why certain amounts reported in the statement of financial position changed from one period to another, or to compute (at least for the latest year presented) approximations of these items for themselves.

   At best, however, such a do-it-yourself approach would derive the net changes (the increase or decrease) in the individual assets and liabilities and attribute these to normally related accounts in the statement of profit or loss and comprehensive income. (For example, the net change in accounts receivable from the beginning to the end of the year would be used to convert reported sales to cash-basis sales or cash collected from customers.)

   While basic changes in the statement of financial position can be used to infer cash flow implications, this is not universally the case. More complex combinations of events (such as the acquisition of another entity, along with its accounts receivable, which would be an increase in that asset which was not related to sales to customers by the reporting entity during the period) would not immediately be comprehensible and might lead to incorrect interpretations of the data unless a statement of actual cash flows were presented.

3. It enhances the comparability of reporting of operating performance by different entities because it eliminates the effects of using different accounting treatments for the same transactions and events.

   There was considerable debate even as early as the 1960s and 1970s over accounting standardisation, which led to the emergence of cash flow accounting. The principal argument in support of cash flow accounting by its earliest proponents was that it avoids the difficult-to-understand and sometimes seemingly arbitrary allocations inherent in accrual accounting. For example, cash flows provided by or used in operating activities are derived, under the indirect method, by adjusting profit (or loss) for items such as depreciation and amortisation, which might have been computed by different entities using different accounting methods. Thus, accounting standardisation will be achieved by converting the accrual-basis profit or loss to cash-basis profit or loss, and the resultant figures will become comparable across entities.
4. It serves as an indicator of the amount, timing and certainty of future cash flows. Furthermore, if an entity has a system in place to project its future cash flows, the statement of cash flows could be used as a touchstone to evaluate the accuracy of past projections of those future cash flows. This benefit is elucidated by the standard as follows:

   a. The statement of cash flows is useful in comparing past assessments of future cash flows against current year's cash flow information; and
   b. It is of value in appraising the relationship between profitability and net cash flows, and in assessing the impact of changing prices.

Exclusion of Non-Cash Transactions

The statement of cash flows, as its name implies, includes only actual inflows and outflows of cash and cash equivalents. Accordingly, it excludes all transactions that do not directly affect cash receipts and payments. However, IAS 7 does require that the effects of transactions not resulting in receipts or payments of cash be disclosed elsewhere in the financial statements. The reason for not including non-cash transactions in the statement of cash flows and placing them elsewhere in the financial statements (e.g., the notes) is that it preserves the statement's primary focus on cash flows from operating, investing and financing activities. It is thus important that the users of financial statements fully appreciate what this financial statement does—and does not—attempt to portray.

Components of Cash and Cash Equivalents

Cash and cash equivalents include unrestricted cash (meaning cash actually on hand, or bank balances whose immediate use is determined by management), other demand deposits and short-term investments whose maturities at the date of acquisition by the entity were three months or less. Equity investments do not qualify as cash equivalents unless they fit the definition above of short-term maturities of three months or less, which would rarely, if ever, be true. Preference shares carrying mandatory redemption features, if acquired within three months of their predetermined redemption date, would meet the criteria above since they are, in substance, cash equivalents. These are very infrequently encountered circumstances, however.

Bank borrowings are normally considered as financing activities. However, in some countries, bank overdrafts play an integral part in the entity's cash management and, as such, overdrafts are to be included as a component of cash equivalents if the following conditions are met:

1. The bank overdraft is repayable on demand; and
2. The bank balance often fluctuates from positive to negative (overdraft).

Statutory (or reserve) deposits by banks (i.e., those held with the central bank for regulatory compliance purposes) are often included in the same position as cash in the statement of financial position. The financial statement treatment of these deposits is subject to some controversy in certain countries, which becomes fairly evident from scrutiny of published financial statements of banks, as these deposits are variously considered to be either a cash equivalent or an operating asset. If the latter, changes in amount would be presented in the operating activities section of the statement of cash flows, and the item could not then be combined with cash in the statement of financial position. Since the appendix to IAS 7, which illustrates the application of the standard to statements of cash flows of financial institutions, does not include statutory deposits with the central bank as a cash equivalent, the authors have concluded that there is little logic to support the alternative presentation of this item as a cash equivalent. Given the fact that deposits with central banks are more or less permanent (and in fact would be more likely to increase over time than to be diminished, given a going concern assumption about the reporting financial institution) the presumption must be that these are not cash equivalents in normal practice.

PRESENTATION

Classifications in the Statement of Cash Flows

The statement of cash flows prepared in accordance with IAS 7 requires classification into the following three categories:

1. *Operating activities*, which can be presented under the (IFRS-preferred) direct method or the indirect method, include all transactions that are not investing and financing activities. In general, cash flows arising from transactions and other events that enter into the determination of profit or loss are operating cash flows. Operating activities are principal revenue-producing activities of an entity and include delivering or producing goods for sale and providing services.
2. *Investing activities* include the acquisition and disposal of property, plant and equipment and other long-term assets and debt and equity instruments of other entities that are not considered cash equivalents or held for dealing or trading purposes. Investing activities include cash advances and collections on loans made to other parties (other than advances and loans of a financial institution).
3. *Financing activities* include obtaining resources from and returning resources to the owners. Also included are obtaining resources through borrowings (short term or long term) and repayments of the amounts borrowed.

The following are examples of the statement of cash flows classification under the provisions of IAS 7:

	Operating	*Investing*	*Financing*
Cash inflows	• Receipts from sale of goods or rendering of services • Sale of loans, debt or equity instruments carried in trading portfolio • Returns on loans (interest) • Returns on equity securities (dividends)	• Principal collections from loans and sales of other entities' debt instruments • Sale of equity instruments* of other entities and returns of investment in those instruments • Sale of plant and equipment	• Proceeds from issuing share capital • Proceeds from issuing debt (short term or long term) • Not-for-profits' donor-restricted cash, which is limited to long-term purposes
Cash outflows	• Payments to suppliers for goods and services • Payments to or on behalf of employees • Payments of taxes • Payments of interest • Purchase of loans, debt or equity instruments carried in trading portfolio	• Loans made and acquisition of other entities' debt instruments • Purchase of equity instruments* of other entities • Purchase of plant and equipment	• Payment of dividends • Repurchase of entity's own shares • Repayment of debt principal, including capital lease obligations

**Unless held for trading purposes or considered to be cash equivalents.*

Non-cash investing and financing activities should, according to IAS 7, be disclosed in the notes to the financial statements ("elsewhere" is the term used by the standard to identify this), but are not intended to be included in the statement of cash flows itself. Examples of significant non-cash financing and investing activities might include:

1. Acquiring an asset through a finance lease;
2. Conversion of debt to equity;
3. Exchange of non-cash assets or liabilities for other non-cash assets or liabilities;
4. Issuance of stock to acquire assets.

Basic example of a classified statement of cash flows

Exemplum Reporting PLC
Statement of Cash Flows
For the Year Ended December 31, 20XX

	€
Cash flows from operating activities:	
Cash receipts from customers	X
Cash paid to suppliers and employees	(X)
Cash generated from operations	X
Interest paid	(X)
Income taxes paid	(X)
Net cash from/(used in) operating activities	X

Cash flows from investing activities:	
Acquisition of subsidiaries, net of cash acquired	X
Purchase of property, plant and equipment	(X)
Proceeds from the sale of equipment	X
Interest received	X
Dividends received	X
Net cash from/(used in) investing activities	X
Cash flows from financing activities:	
Proceeds from the issue of share capital	X
Proceeds from long-term borrowings	X
Dividends paid	(X)
Net cash from/(used in) financing activities	X
Net increase in cash and cash equivalents	X
Cash and cash equivalents at beginning of period	X
Effects of foreign exchange rate changes on the balance of cash held in foreign currencies	X
Cash and cash equivalents at end of period	X
Footnote: Disclosure of non-cash investing and financing activities	
Note X: Supplemental statement of cash flows information	
Significant non-cash investing and financing transactions:	
Conversion of bonds into ordinary shares	X
Property acquired under finance leases	X
	X

Reporting Cash Flows from Operating Activities

Direct vs. indirect methods

The operating activities section of the statement of cash flows can be presented under the direct or the indirect method. However, IFRS has expressed a preference for the direct method of presenting net cash from operating activities. For their part, most preparers of financial statements have chosen overwhelmingly to ignore the recommendation of the standard setter, preferring by a very large margin to use the indirect method rather than the recommended direct method.

The *direct method* shows the items which affected cash flow and the magnitude of those cash flows. Cash received from, and cash paid to, specific sources (such as customers and suppliers) are presented, as opposed to the indirect method's conversion of accrual-basis profit (or loss) to cash flow information by means of a series of add-backs and deductions. Entities using the direct method are required by IAS 7 to report the following major classes of gross cash receipts and gross cash payments:

1. Cash collected from customers;
2. Interest and dividends received[1];
3. Cash paid to employees and other suppliers;
4. Interest paid[2];
5. Income taxes paid;
6. Other operating cash receipts and payments.

[1] *Alternatively, interest and dividends received may be classified as investing cash flows rather than as operating cash flows because they are returns on investments.*

[2] *Alternatively, IAS 7 permits interest paid to be classified as a financing cash flow, because this is the cost of obtaining financing.*

Given the availability of alternative modes of presentation of interest and dividends received, and of interest paid, it is particularly critical that the policy adopted be followed consistently. Since the face of the statement of cash flows will in almost all cases make it clear which approach has been selected, it is not usually necessary to spell this out in the accounting policy note to the financial statements, although there is nothing to prevent this if it would be helpful to do so.

An important advantage of the direct method is that it assists the user's understanding of the relationships between the entity's profit or loss and its cash flows. For example, payments of expenses are shown as cash disbursements and are deducted from cash receipts. In this way, the user is able to recognise the cash receipts and cash payments for the period. Formulae for conversion of various statement of profit or loss and comprehensive income amounts for the direct method presentation from the accrual basis to the cash basis are summarised below.

Accrual basis	*Additions*	*Deductions*	*Cash basis*
Net sales	+ Beginning AR	− Ending AR; AR written off	= Cash received from customers
Cost of goods sold	+ Ending inventory; beginning AP	− Depreciation* and amortisation*; beginning inventory; Ending AP	= Cash paid to suppliers
Operating expenses	+ Ending prepaid expenses; beginning accrued expenses	− Depreciation and amortisation; beginning prepaid expenses; ending accrued expenses payable; bad debts expense	= Cash paid for operating expenses

**Applies to a manufacturing entity only.*
AR = accounts receivable.
AP = accounts payable.

From the foregoing, it can be appreciated that the amounts to be included in the operating section of the statement of cash flows, when the direct approach is utilised, are derived amounts which must be computed, although the computations are not necessarily onerous. They are not generally amounts which exist as account balances simply to be looked up and then placed in the statement. The extra effort needed to prepare the direct method operating cash flow data is at least part of the reason why this method is distinctly unpopular with preparers.

The *indirect method* (sometimes referred to as the reconciliation method) is the most widely used means of presentation of cash from operating activities, primarily because it is easier to prepare. It focuses on the differences between net operating results and cash flows. The indirect format begins with the amount of profit or loss for the year, which can be obtained directly from the statement of profit or loss and comprehensive income. Revenue and expense items not affecting cash are added or deducted to arrive at net cash provided by operating activities. For example, depreciation and amortisation would be added back because these expenses reduce profit or loss but do not arise from cash movements.

The statement of cash flows prepared using the indirect method emphasises changes in the components of most current asset and current liability accounts. Changes in inventory, accounts receivable, and other current accounts are used to determine the cash flow from operating activities. Although most of these adjustments are obvious (most preparers simply relate each current asset or current liability on the statement of financial position to a single caption in the statement of comprehensive income), some changes require more careful analysis. For example, it is important to compute cash collected from sales by relating sales revenue to both the change in accounts receivable and the change in the related doubtful debt allowance account.

As another example of possible complexity in computing the cash from operating activities, the change in short-term borrowings resulting from the purchase of equipment would not be included, since it is not related to operating activities. Instead, these short-term borrowings would be classified as a financing activity. Other adjustments under the indirect method include changes in the account balances of deferred income taxes, non-controlling interest, unrealised foreign currency gains or losses, and the profit or loss from investments under the equity method.

IAS 7 offers yet another alternative way of presenting the cash flows from operating activities. This could be referred to as the *modified indirect method.* Under this variant of the indirect method, the starting point is not profit or loss but rather revenues and expenses as reported in the statement of comprehensive income. In essence, this approach is virtually the same as the regular indirect method, with two more details: revenues and expenses for the period.

The following summary, simply an expanded statement of financial position equation, may facilitate an understanding of the adjustments to profit or loss necessary for converting accrual-basis profit or loss to cash-basis profit or loss when using the indirect method.

	Current assets*	–	***Fixed assets***	=	***Current liabilities***	+	***Long-term liabilities***	+	***Profit or loss***	***Accrual profit adjustment to convert to cash flow***
1.	Increase			=					Increase	Decrease
2.	Decrease			=					Decrease	Increase
3.				=	Increase				Decrease	Increase
4.				=	Decrease				Increase	Decrease

**Other than cash and cash equivalents.*

For example, using row 1 in the above chart, a credit sale would increase accounts receivable and accrual-basis profit but would not affect cash. Therefore, its effect must be removed from the accrual profit to convert to cash profit. The last column indicates that the increase in a current asset balance must be deducted from profit to obtain cash flow.

Similarly, an increase in a current liability, row 3, must be added to profit to obtain cash flows (e.g., accrued wages are in the statement of profit or loss and comprehensive income as an expense, but they do not require cash; the increase in wages payable must be added back to remove this non-cash flow expense from accrual-basis profit).

The major drawback to the indirect method involves the user's difficulty in comprehending the information presented. This method does not show from where the cash was received or to where the cash was paid. Only adjustments to accrual-basis profit or loss are shown. In some cases, the adjustments can be confusing. For instance, the sale of equipment resulting in an accrual-basis loss would require that the loss be added to profit to arrive at net cash from operating activities. (The loss was deducted in the computation of profit or loss, but because the sale will be shown as an investing activity, the loss must be added back to profit or loss.)

Although the indirect method is more commonly used in practice, the IASB encourages entities to use the direct method. As pointed out by IAS 7, a distinct advantage of the direct method is that it provides information that may be useful in estimating or projecting future cash flows, a benefit that is clearly not achieved when the indirect method is utilised instead. Both the direct and indirect methods are presented below.

Direct method

	€
Cash flows from operating activities:	
Cash received from sale of goods	X
Cash dividends received*	X
Cash provided by operating activities	X
Cash paid to suppliers	(X)
Cash paid for operating expenses	(X)
Cash paid for income taxes*	(X)
Cash disbursed for operating activities	(X)
Net cash flows from operating activities	X

**Alternatively, could be classified as investing cash flow.*

Indirect method

Cash flows from operating activities:	
Profit before income taxes	X
Adjustments for:	
Depreciation	X
Unrealised loss on foreign exchange	X
Interest expense	X
Operating profit before working capital changes:	X
Increase in accounts receivable	(X)
Decrease in inventories	X
Increase in accounts payable	X
Cash generated from operations	X
Interest paid	(X)
Income taxes paid**	(X)
Net cash flows from operating activities	X

***Taxes paid are usually classified as operating activities. However, when it is practical to identify the tax cash flow with an individual transaction that gives rise to cash flows that are classified as investing or financing activities, then the tax cash flow is classified as an investing or financing activity as appropriate.*

OTHER REQUIREMENTS

Gross vs. Net Basis

The emphasis in the statement of cash flows is on gross cash receipts and cash payments. For instance, reporting the net change in bonds payable would obscure the financing activities of the entity by not disclosing separately cash inflows from issuing bonds and cash outflows from retiring bonds.

IAS 7 specifies two exceptions where netting of cash flows is allowed. First, items with quick turnovers, large amounts and short maturities may be presented as net cash flows. Secondly, cash receipts and payments on behalf of customers when the cash flows reflect the activities of the customers rather than those of the entity may also be reported on a net rather than a gross basis.

Foreign Currency Cash Flows

Foreign operations must prepare a separate statement of cash flows and translate the statement to the reporting currency using the exchange rate in effect at the time of the cash flow (a weighted-average exchange rate may be used if the result is substantially the same). This translated statement is then used in the preparation of the consolidated statement of cash flows. Non-cash exchange gains and losses recognised in the statement of profit or loss and other comprehensive income should be reported as a separate item when reconciling profit or loss and operating activities. For a more detailed discussion about the effects of exchange rates on the statement of cash flows, see Chapter 23.

Cash Flow per Share

There is no requirement under IFRS to disclose cash flow per share in the financial statements of an entity, unlike the requirement to report earnings per share. In fact, cash flow per share is a somewhat disreputable concept, since it was sometimes touted in an earlier era as being indicative of an entity's "real" performance, when of course it is not a meaningful alternative to earnings per share because, for example, entities that are self-liquidating by selling productive assets can generate very positive total cash flows, and hence cash flows per share, while decimating the potential for future earnings. Since, unlike a comprehensive statement of cash flows, cash flow per share cannot reveal the components of cash flow (operating, investing and financing), its usage could be misleading.

While cash flow per share is not well regarded (it is specifically prohibited under US GAAP), it should be noted that in recent years a growing number of entities have resorted to displaying a wide range of pro forma amounts, some of which roughly correspond to cash-based measures of operating performance. These non-IFRS categories should be viewed with great caution, both because they convey the message that IFRS-based measures of performance are somehow less meaningful, and also because there are no standard definitions of the non-IFRS measures, opening the door to possible manipulation.

Net Reporting by Financial Institutions

IAS 7 permits financial institutions to report cash flows arising from certain activities on a net basis. These activities, and the related conditions under which net reporting would be acceptable, are as follows:

1. Cash receipts and payments on behalf of customers when the cash flows reflect the activities of the customers rather than those of the bank, such as the acceptance and repayment of demand deposits;
2. Cash flows relating to deposits with fixed maturity dates;
3. Placements and withdrawals of deposits from other financial institutions; and
4. Cash advances and loans to banks' customers and repayments thereon.

Reporting Futures, Forward Contracts, Options and Swaps

IAS 7 stipulates that cash payments for and cash receipts from futures contracts, forward contracts, option contracts and swap contracts are normally classified as investing activities, except:

1. When such contracts are held for dealing or trading purposes and thus represent operating activities; or
2. When the payments or receipts are considered by the entity as financing activities and are reported accordingly.

Further, when a contract is accounted for as a hedge of an identifiable position, the cash flows of the contract are classified in the same manner as the cash flows of the position being hedged.

Reporting Extraordinary Items in the Statement of Cash Flows

IFRS long ago eliminated the categorisation of gains or losses as being extraordinary in character, so this no longer impacts the presentation of the statement of cash flows under IFRS.

Reconciliation of Cash and Cash Equivalents

An entity should disclose the components of cash and cash equivalents and should present a reconciliation of the difference, if any, between the amounts reported in the statement of cash flows and equivalent items reported in the statement of financial position.

Acquisitions and Disposals of Subsidiaries and Other Business Units

IAS 7 requires that the aggregate cash flows from acquisitions and disposals of subsidiaries or other business units should be presented separately as part of the investing activities section of the statement of cash flows. The following disclosures are also prescribed by IAS 7 in respect of both acquisitions and disposals:

1. The total consideration paid or received;
2. The portion thereof discharged by cash and cash equivalents;
3. The amount of cash and cash equivalents in the subsidiary or business unit acquired or disposed of; and
4. The amount of assets and liabilities (other than cash and cash equivalents) acquired or disposed of, summarised by major category.

DISCLOSURE AND EXAMPLES

Other Disclosures Required or Recommended by IAS 7

Certain additional information may be relevant to the users of financial statements in gaining an insight into the liquidity or solvency of an entity. With this objective in mind, IAS 7 sets out other disclosures which are required or, in some cases, recommended.

1. *Required disclosure*—The amount of significant cash and cash equivalent balances held by an entity which are not available for use by the group should be disclosed along with a commentary by management.
2. *Recommended disclosures*—The disclosures which are recommended are as follows:

    a. The amount of undrawn borrowing facilities, indicating restrictions on their use, if any;
    b. The aggregate amount of cash flows that are attributable to the increase in operating capacity separately from those cash flows that are required to maintain operating capacity; and

c. The amount of the cash flows arising from the operating, investing and financing activities of each reportable segment determined in accordance with IFRS 8. (See Chapter 28.)

The above disclosures recommended by IAS 7, although difficult to present, are useful in enabling the users of financial statements to better understand the entity's financial position.

Changes in Liabilities Arising from Financing Activities

An entity shall provide disclosures that enable users of financial statements to evaluate changes in liabilities arising from financing activities, including both changes arising from cash flows and non-cash changes.

To the extent necessary to satisfy the requirement above, an entity shall disclose the following changes in liabilities arising from financing activities:

1. Changes from financing cash flows;
2. Changes arising from obtaining or losing control of subsidiaries or other businesses;
3. The effect of changes in foreign exchange rates;
4. Changes in fair values; and
5. Other changes.

Liabilities arising from financing activities are liabilities for which cash flows were, or future cash flows will be, classified in the statement of cash flows as cash flows from financing activities. In addition, the disclosure requirement also applies to changes in financial assets (for example, assets that hedge liabilities arising from financing activities) if cash flows from those financial assets were, or future cash flows will be, included in cash flows from financing activities.

One way to fulfil this disclosure requirement is by providing a reconciliation between the opening and closing balances in the statement of financial position for liabilities arising from financing activities. Where an entity discloses such a reconciliation, it shall provide sufficient information to enable users of the financial statements to link items included in the reconciliation to the statement of financial position and the statement of cash flows.

If an entity provides the disclosure required in combination with disclosures of changes in other assets and liabilities, it shall disclose the changes in liabilities arising from financing activities separately from changes in those other assets and liabilities.

This example illustrates one possible way of providing the disclosures required. The example shows only current period amounts. Corresponding amounts for the preceding period are required to be presented in accordance with IAS 1, *Presentation of Financial Statements*.

			Non-cash changes			
	20XX-1	**Cash flows**	**Acquisitions**	**Foreign exchange movement**	**Fair value changes**	**20XX**
Long-term loans	10,000	(5,175)	–	–	–	4,825
Short-term loans	12,000	(1,500)	–	2,000	–	12,500
Lease liabilities	4,000	(800)	1,500	–	–	4,700
Total liabilities from financing activities	26,000	(7,475)	1,500	2,500	–	22,025

Basic example of preparation of the statement of cash flows under IAS 7 using a worksheet approach

Using the following financial information for Exemplum Reporting PLC, preparation and presentation of the statement of cash flows according to the requirements of IAS 7 are illustrated. (Note that all figures in this example are in thousands of euros.)

Exemplum Reporting PLC
Statements of Financial Position
December 31, 20XX and 20XX-1

	20XX	**20XX-1**
	€	**€**
Assets		
Cash and cash equivalents	3,000	1,000
Accounts receivable	5,000	2,500
Inventory	2,000	1,500
Prepaid expenses	1,000	1,500
Due from associates	19,000	19,000
Property, plant and equipment, at cost	12,000	22,500
Accumulated depreciation	(5,000)	(6,500)
Property, plant and equipment, net	7,000	16,000
Total assets	37,000	42,000
Liabilities		
Accounts payable	5,000	12,500
Income taxes payable	2,000	1,000
Deferred taxes payable	3,000	2,000
Total liabilities	10,000	15,500
Shareholders' equity		
Share capital	6,500	6,500
Retained earnings	20,500	20,000
Total shareholders' equity	27,000	26,500
Total liabilities and shareholders' equity	37,000	42,000

Exemplum Reporting PLC
Statement of Profit or Loss and Comprehensive Income
For the Year Ended December 31, 20XX

	€
Sales	30,000
Cost of sales	(10,000)
Gross profit	20,000
Administrative and selling expenses	(2,000)
Interest expense	(2,000)
Depreciation of property, plant and equipment	(2,000)
Audit fees	(500)
Investment income	3,000
Profit before taxation	16,500
Taxes on income	(4,000)
Profit	12,500

The following additional information is relevant to the preparation of the statement of cash flows:

1. Equipment with a net book value of €7,500 and original cost of €10,500 was sold for €7,500.
2. All sales made by the company are credit sales.
3. The company received cash dividends (from investments) amounting to €3,000, recorded as income in the statement of comprehensive income for the year ended December 31, 20XX.
4. The company declared and paid dividends of €12,000 to its shareholders.
5. Interest expense for the year 20XX was €2,000, which was fully paid during the year. All administration and selling expenses incurred were paid during the year 20XX.
6. Income tax expense for the year 20XX was provided at €4,000, out of which the company paid €2,000 during 20XX as an estimate.

A worksheet can be prepared to ease the development of the statement of cash flows, as follows:

Cash Flow Worksheet

	20XX	*20XX-1*	*Change*	*Operating*	*Investing*	*Financing*	**Cash and** *equivalents*
	€	€	€	€	€	€	€
Cash and equivalents	3,000	1,000	2,000				2,000
Accounts receivable	5,000	2,500	2,500	(2,500)			
Inventories	2,000	1,500	500	(500)			
Prepaid expenses	1,000	1,500	(500)	500			
Due from associates	19,000	19,000	0				
Property, plant and equipment	7,000	16,500	(9,500)	2,000	7,500		
Accounts payable	5,000	12,500	7,500	(7,000)			
Income taxes payable	2,000	1,000	1,000	1,000			
Deferred taxes payable	3,000	2,000	1,000	1,000			
Share capital	6,500	6,500	0				
Retained earnings	20,500	20,500	500	9,500	3,000	(12,000)	–
				3,500	10,500	(12,000)	2,000

Exemplum Reporting PLC
Statement of Cash Flows
For the Year Ended December 31, 20XX
(Direct method)

	€	€
Cash flows from operating activities		
Cash receipts from customers	27,500	
Cash paid to suppliers and employees	(20,000)	
Cash generated from operations	7,500	
Interest paid	(2,000)	
Income taxes paid	(2,000)	
Net cash flows from operating activities		3,500

Cash flows from investing activities		
Proceeds from the sale of equipment	7,500	
Dividends received	3,000	
Net cash flows from investing activities		10,500
Cash flows from financing activities		
Dividends paid	(12,000)	
Net cash flows used in financing activities		(12,000)
Net increase in cash and cash equivalents		2,000
Cash and cash equivalents, beginning of year		1,000
Cash and cash equivalents, end of year		3,000

Details of the computations of amounts shown in the statement of cash flows are as follows:

	€	€
Cash received from customers during the year		
Credit sales	30,000	
Plus: Accounts receivable, beginning of year	2,500	
Less: Accounts receivable, end of year	(5,000)	
Cash received from customers during the year		27,500
Cash paid to suppliers and employees		
Cost of sales	10,000	
Less: Inventory, beginning of year	(1,500)	
Plus: Inventory, end of year	2,000	
Plus: Accounts payable, beginning of year	12,500	
Less: Accounts payable, end of year	(5,000)	
Plus: Administrative and selling expenses paid	2,000	
Cash paid to suppliers and employees during the year		20,000
Interest paid equals interest expense charged to profit or loss (per additional information)		2,000
Income taxes paid during the year		
Tax expense during the year (comprising current and deferred portions)	4,000	
Plus: Beginning income taxes payable	1,000	
Plus: Beginning deferred taxes payable	2,000	
Less: Ending income taxes payable	(2,000)	
Less: Ending deferred taxes payable	(3,000)	
Cash paid toward income taxes		2,000
Proceeds from sale of equipment (per additional information)		7,500
Dividends received during 2014 (per additional information)		3,000
Dividends paid during 2014 (per additional information)		12,000

Exemplum Reporting PLC
Statement of Cash Flows
For the Year Ended December 31, 20XX
(Indirect method)

	€	€
Cash flows from operating activities		
Profit before taxation	16,500	
Adjustments for:		
Depreciation of property, plant and equipment	2,000	
Decrease in prepaid expenses	500	
Investment income	(3,000)	

Interest expense	2,000	
Increase in accounts receivable	(2,500)	
Increase in inventories	(500)	
Decrease in accounts payable	(7,500)	
Cash generated from operations	7,500	
Interest paid	(2,000)	
Income taxes paid	(2,000)	
Net cash from operating activities		3,500
Cash flows from investing activities		
Proceeds from sale of equipment	7,500	
Dividends received	3,000	
Net cash from investing activities		10,500
Cash flows from financing activities		
Dividends paid	(12,000)	
Net cash used in financing activities		(12,000)
Net increase in cash and cash equivalents		2,000
Cash and cash equivalents, beginning of year		1,000
Cash and cash equivalents, end of year		3,000

CONSOLIDATED STATEMENT OF CASH FLOWS

A consolidated statement of cash flows must be presented when a complete set of consolidated financial statements is issued. The consolidated statement of cash flows would be the last statement to be prepared, as the information to prepare it will come from the other consolidated statements (consolidated statement of financial position, statement of profit or loss and comprehensive income and statement of changes in equity). The preparation of these other consolidated statements is discussed in Chapter 14.

The preparation of a consolidated statement of cash flows involves the same analysis and procedures as the statement for an individual entity, with a few additional items. The direct or indirect method of presentation may be used. When the indirect method is used, the additional non-cash transactions relating to any business combination, such as the differential amortisation at group level, must also be reversed. Furthermore, all transfers to subsidiaries must be eliminated, as they do not represent a cash inflow or outflow of the consolidated entity.

All unrealised intragroup profits should have been eliminated in preparation of the other statements; thus, no additional entry of this sort should be required. Any profit allocated to non-controlling parties would need to be added back, as it would have been eliminated in computing consolidated profit but does not represent a true cash outflow. Finally, any dividend payments should be recorded as cash outflows in the financing activities section.

In preparing the operating activities section of the statement by the indirect method following a purchase business combination, the changes in assets and liabilities related to operations since acquisition should be derived by comparing the consolidated statement of financial position as at the date of acquisition with the year-end consolidated statement of financial position. These changes will be combined with those for the acquiring company up to the date of acquisition as adjustments to profit. The effects due to the acquisition of these assets and liabilities are reported under investing activities.

US GAAP COMPARISON

Under US GAAP, bank overdrafts are classified as financing activities.

Under US GAAP, dividends received and interest paid or received are always included in operating cash flows. Dividends paid are always classified as financing activities.

Taxes paid are generally classified as operating cash flows, with specific rules for tax benefits associated with share-based compensation arrangements.

Under US GAAP, cash equivalents are short-term, highly liquid investments that are readily convertible to known amounts of cash and so near their maturity that they present insignificant risk of changes in value because of changes in interest rates. Generally, only investments with original maturities of three months or less qualify under that definition.

Not all investments that qualify are required to be treated as cash equivalents. An entity shall establish a policy concerning which short-term, highly liquid investments that satisfy the definition of cash equivalents are treated as cash equivalents.

If a derivative instrument includes an other-than-insignificant financing element at inception, all cash inflows and outflows of the derivative instrument shall be considered cash flows from financing activities by the borrower.

US GAAP provides specific guidance about the cash flow classification of cash payments for debt prepayment or extinguishment costs, proceeds received from the settlement of insurance claims, proceeds received from the settlement of corporate-owned life insurance policies, including bank-owned life insurance policies, beneficial interests in securitisation transactions, cash payments for the settlement of a zero-coupon debt instrument, contingent consideration payments made after a business combination and distributions received from an equity method investee.

Unlike IFRSs, US GAAP does not have specific guidance requiring that cash payments to manufacture or acquire assets held for rental to others and subsequently held for sale are cash flows from operating activities and that the cash receipts from rents and subsequent sales also are cash flows from operating activities.

Also, US GAAP, as amended by ASU Update 2016-18, set out specific requirements on the presentation of changes in restricted cash and restricted cash equivalents on the statement of cash flows, in that they are included in total cash, cash equivalents and restricted cash beginning and ending on the statement of cash flows where restricted cash exits on the balance sheet. ASU Update 2016-18 is now effective and part of ASC No. 230 *Statement of Cash Flows*.

7 ACCOUNTING POLICIES, CHANGES IN ACCOUNTING ESTIMATES AND ERRORS

INTRODUCTION

It is self-evident that a true picture of an entity's performance only emerges after a series of financial periods' results have been reported and reviewed. The information set out in an entity's financial statements over a period of years must, accordingly, be comparable if it is to be of value to the users of those statements. Users of financial statements usually seek to identify trends in the entity's financial position, performance and cash flows by studying and analysing the information contained in those statements. Thus, it is imperative that, to the maximum extent possible, the same accounting policies be applied from year to year in the preparation of financial statements, and that any necessary departures from this rule be clearly disclosed. This fundamental prerequisite is the basis for the IFRS requirement for restatement of prior periods' financial statements for corrections of accounting errors and retrospective application of new accounting policies.

Financial statements are impacted by the choices made from among different, acceptable accounting principles and methodologies. Companies select those accounting principles and methods which they believe best depict, in their financial statements, the economic reality of their financial position, results of operations and changes in financial position. While the IASB has made great progress in narrowing the range of acceptable alternative accounting for given economic events and transactions (e.g., the elimination of LIFO inventory costing), there still remain choices, which can impair the ability to compare one entity's position and results with another (e.g., first-in, first-out (FIFO) versus weighted-average (WA) inventory costing; or cost versus revaluation basis of accounting for property, plant and equipment and for intangible assets).

Lack of comparability among entities and within a given entity over time can result because of changes in the assumptions and estimates underlying the application of the accounting principles and methods, from changes in the details of acceptable principles made by a promulgating authority, such as an accounting standard-setting body, and for numerous other reasons. While there is no preventing these various factors from causing changes to occur, it is important that changes be made only when they result in improved financial reporting, or when necessitated by the imposition of new financial reporting requirements. Whatever the reason for introducing change, and hence the risk of non-comparability, to the financial reporting process, adequate disclosures must be made to achieve transparency in financial reporting so that users of the financial statements are able to comprehend the effects and compensate for them in performing financial analysis.

IAS 8 deals with accounting changes (i.e., changes in accounting estimates and changes in accounting policies) and also addresses the accounting for the correction of errors. A principal objective of IAS 8 is to prescribe accounting treatments and financial statement disclosures which will enhance comparability, both within an entity over successive years and with the financial statements of other entities.

Even though the correction of an error in financial statements issued previously is not considered an accounting change, it is discussed by IAS 8 and is therefore covered in this chapter.

In the preparation of financial statements there is an underlying presumption that an accounting policy, once adopted, should not be changed, but rather be uniformly applied in accounting for events and transactions of a similar type. This consistent application of accounting policies enhances the decision usefulness of the financial statements. The presumption that an entity should not change an accounting policy may be overcome only if the reporting entity can justify the use of an alternative acceptable accounting policy on the basis that it is preferable under the circumstances.

The IASB's *Improvements Project* resulted in significant changes being made to IAS 8. It now requires retrospective application of voluntary changes in accounting policies and retrospective restatement to correct prior period errors with the earliest reported retained earnings balance being adjusted for any effects of a voluntary change in an accounting policy or of a correction of an error on earlier years. The only exception to this rule occurs when retrospective application or restatement would be impracticable to accomplish, and this has intentionally been made a difficult criterion to satisfy. The revised standard removed the permitted alternative in the previous version of IAS 8 (1) to include in profit or loss for the current period the adjustment resulting from changing an accounting policy or correcting a prior period error, and (2) to present unchanged comparative information from financial statements of prior periods.

The *Improvements Project* also resulted in some reorganisation of materials in the standards, specifically relocating certain guidance between IAS 1 and IAS 8. As revised, certain presentational issues were moved to IAS 1, while guidance on accounting policies, previously found in IAS 1, was moved to IAS 8. In addition, included in revised IAS 8 is a hierarchy of criteria to be applied in the selection of accounting policies.

As amended, IAS 8 incorporates the material formerly found in SIC 18, *Consistency—Alternative Methods*, which requires that an entity select and apply its accounting policies for a period consistently for similar transactions, other events and conditions, unless a standard or an interpretation specifically requires or permits categorisation of items for which different policies may be appropriate, in which case an appropriate accounting policy shall be selected and applied consistently to each category. Simply stated, the expectation is that, in the absence of changes in promulgated standards, or changes in the character of the transactions being accounted for, the reporting entity will continue to use accounting policies from one period to the next without change and use them for all transactions and events within a given class or category without exception.

When IFRS are revised or new standards are developed, they are often issued a year or more prior to the date set for mandatory application. Disclosure of future changes in accounting policies must be made when the reporting entity has yet to implement a new standard that has been issued but that has not yet come into effect. In addition, disclosure of the planned date of adoption is now required, along with an estimate of the effect of the change on the entity's financial position, except if making such an estimate would incur undue cost or effort.

Sources of IFRS
IAS 1, *IAS* 8

SCOPE

IAS 8 is applied in the selection of accounting policies and in accounting for changes in accounting policies, changes in estimates and corrections of prior year errors. This chapter addresses the criteria for selecting and changing accounting policies, together with the accounting treatment and disclosure of changes in accounting policies, changes in accounting estimates and corrections of errors in accordance with IAS 8.

DEFINITIONS OF TERMS

Accounting policies. Specific principles, bases, conventions, rules and practices adopted by an entity in preparing and presenting financial statements. Management is required to adopt accounting policies that result in a fair, full and complete presentation of the financial position, performance and cash flows of the reporting entity.

Change in accounting estimate. An adjustment of the carrying amount of an asset or liability, or related expense, resulting from reassessing the present status of, and expected future benefits and obligations associated with, that asset or liability. Prospective application applies to changes in estimates resulting from new information or new developments (which, therefore, are not corrections of errors). The use of reasonable estimates is an essential part of the financial statement preparation process and does not undermine their reliability.

Change in accounting policy. A change in accounting policy that either (1) is required by an IFRS or (2) is a change that results in the financial statements providing faithfully represented and more relevant information about the effects of transactions, other events or conditions on the entity's financial position, financial performance or cash flows.

Impracticable. Applying a requirement is impracticable when the entity cannot apply it after making every reasonable effort to do so. For management to assert that it is impracticable to apply a change in an accounting policy retrospectively or to make a retrospective restatement to correct an error, one or more of the following conditions must be present: (1) after making every reasonable effort the effect of the retrospective application or restatement is not determinable; (2) the retrospective application or restatement requires assumptions regarding what management's intent would have been in that period; or (3) the retrospective application or retrospective restatement requires significant estimates of amounts and it is impossible to develop objective information that would have been available at the time the original financial statements for the prior period (or periods) were authorised for issue to provide evidence of circumstances which existed at that time regarding the amounts to be measured, recognised and/or disclosed by retrospective application.

International Financial Reporting Standards (IFRS). Standards and Interpretations adopted by the International Accounting Standards Board (IASB). They comprise International Financial Reporting Standards (IFRS), International Accounting Standards (IAS), and Interpretations developed by the International Financial Reporting Interpretations Committee (IFRIC) or the former Standing Interpretations Committee (SIC).

Material. Omissions or misstatements of items are material if they could, individually or collectively, influence the economic decisions that users make on the basis of the financial statements. Materiality depends on the size and nature of the omission or misstatement judged in the surrounding circumstances.

Prior period errors. Omissions from, and misstatements in, the entity's financial statements for one or more prior periods arising from a failure to use, or misuse of, reliable information that (1) was available when financial statements for those periods were authorised for issue, and (2) could reasonably be expected to have been obtained and taken into account in the preparation and presentation of those financial statements. Such errors include the effects of mathematical mistakes, mistakes in applying accounting principles, oversight or misuse of available facts, use of unacceptable GAAP and fraud.

Prospective application. The method of reporting a change in accounting policy and of recognising the effect of a change in an accounting estimate, respectively, by (1) applying the new accounting policy to transactions, other events and conditions occurring after the date as at which the policy is changed, and (2) recognising and disclosing the effect of the change in the accounting estimate in the current and future periods affected by the change.

Retrospective application. Applying a new accounting policy to past transactions, other events and conditions as if that policy has always been applied.

Retrospective restatement. Correcting the recognition, measurement and disclosure of amounts of elements of financial statements as if a prior period error had never occurred.

IMPORTANCE OF COMPARABILITY AND CONSISTENCY IN FINANCIAL REPORTING

Accounting principles—whether various IFRS or national GAAP—have long held that an important objective of financial reporting is to encourage comparability among financial statements produced by essentially similar entities. This is necessary to facilitate informed economic decision making by investors, creditors, regulatory agencies, vendors, customers, prospective employees, joint venturers and others. While full comparability will not be achieved as long as alternative principles of accounting and reporting for like transactions and events remain available, a driving force in developing new accounting standards has been to enhance comparability. The IASB strives to remove alternatives within IFRS.

An important implication of comparability is that users be informed about the accounting policies that were employed in the preparation of the financial statements, any changes in those policies and the effects of such changes. While historically some accountants opposed the focus on comparability, on the grounds that uniformity of accounting removes the element of judgement needed to produce the most faithful representation of an individual entity's financial position and performance, others have expressed concern that overemphasis on comparability might be an impediment to the development of improved accounting methods. Increasingly, however, the paramount importance of comparability is being recognised, to which the ongoing convergence efforts strongly attest.

The *Conceptual Framework for Financial Reporting 2018* lists *comparability* as one of the enhancing qualitative characteristics of accounting information (also included as such characteristics are *verifiability*, *timeliness* and *understandability*), which are complementary to the fundamental qualitative characteristics: *relevance* and *faithful representation*. Comparability is explained as follows:

> **Comparability** *enables users to identify and understand similarities in, and differences among, items.*

In addition, comparability should not be confused with uniformity; for information to be comparable, similar elements must look alike and dissimilar elements must look different. The quality of consistency enhances the decision usefulness of financial statements to users by facilitating analysis and the understanding of comparative accounting data.

Strict adherence to IFRS or any other set of standards obviously helps in achieving comparability, since a common accounting language is employed by all reporting parties. According to IAS 1:

> *The presentation and classification of items in the financial statements should be retained from one period to the next unless it is apparent that, following a significant change in the nature of the entity's operations or a review of its financial statements, another presentation or classification would be more appropriate with regard to the criteria for the selection and application of accounting policies in IAS 8; or an IFRS requires a change in presentation.*

It is, however, inappropriate for an entity to continue accounting for transactions in the same manner if the policies adopted lack the qualitative characteristics of relevance and faithful representation. Thus, if more relevant and/or faithfully representational accounting policy alternatives exist, it is better for the entity to change its methods of accounting for defined classes of transactions with, of course, adequate disclosure of both the nature of the change and of its effects.

ACCOUNTING POLICY

In accordance with IAS 1, the reporting entity's management is responsible for selecting and applying accounting policies which:

1. Present fairly financial position, results of operations and cash flows of an entity, as required by IFRS;
2. Present information in a manner that provides relevant, reliable, comparable and understandable information;
3. Provide additional disclosures where necessary to enable users to understand the impact of particular transactions, other events and conditions on the entity's financial position and performance.

Under IFRS, management is required to disclose, in the notes to the financial statements, a description of all significant accounting policies of the reporting entity. In theory, if only one method of accounting for a type of transaction is acceptable, it is not necessary to cite it explicitly in the accounting policies note, although many entities do routinely identify all accounting policies affecting the major financial statement captions.

The "summary of significant accounting policies" is customarily, but not necessarily, the first note disclosure included in the financial statements.

SELECTING ACCOUNTING POLICIES

IAS 8 has established a hierarchy of accounting guidance for selecting accounting policies in accordance with IFRS. This is comparable to the "hierarchy of GAAP" established under US auditing standards many years ago (which was superseded by guidance in the FASB Accounting Standards Codification) and provides a logical ordering of authority for those instances when competing and possibly conflicting guidance exists. Given the relative paucity of authoritative guidance under IFRS (which is a "principles-based" standard, vs "rules-based" standards found in US GAAP), heavy reliance is placed on reasoning by analogy from the existing standards and from materials found in various non-authoritative sources.

According to IAS 8, when selecting accounting policies with regard to an item in the financial statements, authoritative sources of such policies are included *only* in IFRS, comprising International Financial Reporting Standards, International Accounting Standards (IAS) and Interpretations developed by the International Financial Reporting Standards Interpretations Committee (IFRIC) or the former Standing Interpretations Committee (SIC). IFRS also provide guidance to assist management in applying their requirements. *Improvements to IFRS*, published in May 2008, clarified that only guidance which is an integral part of IFRS is mandatory. Guidance which is not an integral part of IFRS does not provide requirements for financial statements.

When there is *not* any IFRS standard or Interpretation which specifically applies to an item in the financial statements, transaction, other event or condition, management must use judgement in developing and applying an accounting policy. This should result in information which is both:

1. Relevant to the decision-making needs of users; and
2. Reliable in the sense that the resulting financial statements:
   a. Will represent faithfully the financial position, performance and cash flows of the entity;
   b. Will reflect the economic substance of transactions, other events and conditions, and not merely their legal form;
   c. Are neutral (i.e., free from bias);
   d. Are prudent; and
   e. Are complete in all material respects.

In making this judgement, management must give consideration to the following sources, listed in descending order of significance:

1. The requirements in IFRS and in Interpretations dealing with similar and related issues; and
2. The definitions, recognition criteria and measurement concepts for assets, liabilities, income and expenses set out in the *Conceptual Framework*.

Note that when developing a policy where IFRS does not provide guidance, IAS 8 also states that an entity may consider the most recent pronouncements of other standard-setting bodies that use a similar conceptual framework to develop accounting standards, other accounting literature and accepted industry practices, to the extent that these do not conflict with the sources detailed in the preceding paragraph. In practice, this means that many IFRS reporters will look to US GAAP guidance where IFRS does not provide guidance.

CHANGES IN ACCOUNTING POLICIES

A change in an accounting policy means that a reporting entity has exchanged one accounting principle for another. According to IAS 8, the term *accounting policy* includes the accounting principles, bases, conventions, rules and practices used. For example, a change in inventory costing from "WA" to "FIFO" would be a change in accounting policy. Other examples of accounting policy options in IFRS include cost versus revaluation basis of accounting for property, plant and equipment and for intangible assets (IAS 16, IAS 38); cost versus fair value basis of accounting for investment property (IAS 40); and fair value versus proportionate share of the value of net assets acquired for valuing a non-controlling interest in business combinations (IFRS 3). Changes in accounting policy are permitted if:

1. The change is required by a standard or an interpretation; or
2. The change will result in a more relevant and reliable presentation of events or transactions in the financial statements of the entity.

IAS 8 does not regard the following as changes in accounting policies:

1. The adoption of an accounting policy for events or transactions that differ in substance from previously occurring events or transactions; and
2. The adoption of a new accounting policy to account for events or transactions that did not occur previously or that were immaterial in prior periods.

The provisions of IAS 8 are not applicable to the initial adoption of a policy to carry assets at revalued amounts, although such adoption is indeed a change in accounting policy. Rather, this is to be dealt with as a revaluation in accordance with IAS 16 or IAS 38, as appropriate under the circumstances.

Applying Changes in Accounting Policies

Generally, IAS 8 provides that a change in an accounting policy should be reflected in financial statements by retrospective application to all prior periods presented as if that policy had always been applied, unless it is impracticable to do so. When a change in an accounting policy is made consequent to the enactment of a new IFRS, it is to be accounted for in accordance with any transitional provisions set out in that standard.

An entity should account for a change in accounting policy as follows:

1. In general, initial application of an IFRS should be accounted for in accordance with the specific transitional provisions, if any, in that IFRS.
2. Initial application of an IFRS that does not include specific transitional provisions applying to that change should be applied *retrospectively*.
3. Voluntary changes in accounting policy should be applied *retrospectively*.

Retrospective Application

In accordance with IAS 8, retrospective application of a new accounting policy involves (1) adjusting the opening balance of each affected component of equity for the earliest prior period presented, and (2) presenting other comparative amounts disclosed for each prior period as if the new accounting policy had always been applied.

Retrospective application to a prior period is required if it is practicable to determine the effect of the correction on the amounts in both the opening as well as the closing statements of financial position for that period. Adjustments are made to the opening balance of each affected component of equity, usually to retained earnings.

In accordance with IAS 1 (Revised), whenever an entity applies an accounting policy retrospectively, makes a retrospective restatement of items in its financial statements or reclassifies items in its financial statements in accordance with IAS 8, a third statement of financial position is required to be presented as part of the minimum comparative information. The periods required to be presented are as at the end of the current period, the end of the preceding period and the beginning of the preceding period.

The date of that opening statement of financial position should be as at the beginning of the preceding period regardless of whether an entity's financial statements present comparative information for any additional periods presented voluntarily.

For example, assume that a change is adopted in 20XX and comparative 20XX-1 and 20XX-2 financial statements are to be presented with the 20XX financial statements. The change in accounting policy also affects previously reported financial positions and financial performance, but these are not to be presented in the current financial report. Therefore, since other components of equity are not affected, the cumulative adjustment (i.e., the cumulative amount of expense or income which would have been recognised in years prior to 20XX-2) as at the beginning of 20XX-2 is made to opening retained earnings in 20XX-2.

Retrospective application is accomplished by the following steps.

At the beginning of the preceding period presented in the financial statements:

Step 1—Adjust the carrying amounts of assets and liabilities for the cumulative effect of changing to the new accounting principle on periods prior to those presented in the financial statements.

Step 2—Offset the effect of the adjustment in Step 1 (if any) by adjusting the opening balance of each affected component of equity (usually opening balance of retained earnings).

For each individual prior period that is presented in the financial statements:

Step 3—Adjust the financial statements for the effects of applying the new accounting policy to that specific period.

Example of retrospective application of a new accounting policy

Exemplum is a manufacturing business. During the 20XX financial year, the directors reviewed Exemplum's accounting policies and identified inventories as an area where it could change the current accounting policy to better reflect the actual economic substance of its business.

The directors decide to change the valuation method used for raw material from the WA cost method to the FIFO method.

The value of the inventories is as follows:

	Weighted-average	*FIFO*
	€	€
December 31, 20XX-1	160,000	140,000
December 31, 20XX	190,000	160,000

Exemplum was unable to obtain figures as at January 1, 20XX-1 for inventory in terms of FIFO as it was determined to be impracticable. Ignore any income tax effects.

The changes in the closing carrying amounts of inventories due to the change in the accounting policy are calculated as follows:

	Weighted-average	*FIFO*	*Decrease in values*
	€	€	€
December 31, 20XX-1	160,000	140,000	(20,000)
December 31, 20XX	190,000	160,000	(30,000)

Due to the change in the accounting policy, the carrying values of inventories decreased at the beginning of the period by €20,000 and the end of the period by €30,000 (i.e., the period ended December 31, 20XX-1). The effect of this decrease is an increase in the cost of sales of €10,000 (€30,000–€20,000) for the period ended December 31, 20XX-2.

Journals		
December 31, 20XX	€	€
Cost of sales (P/L)	10,000	
Retained earnings—opening balance (Equity)	20,000	
Inventories (SFP)		30,000

Accounting for the retrospective application of the new accounting policy.

NOTE: Had the figures for January 20XX-1 been available, then the comparative statement of comprehensive income would also have been restated retrospectively for the change in accounting policy.

It is important to note that, in presenting the previously issued financial statements, the caption "as adjusted" is included in the column heading.

Indirect effects. Changing accounting policies sometimes results in indirect effects from legal or contractual obligations of the reporting entity, such as profit sharing or royalty arrangements that contain monetary formulae based on amounts in the financial statements. For example, if an entity had an incentive compensation plan that required it to contribute 15% of its pre-tax income to a pool to be distributed to its employees, the adoption of a new accounting policy could potentially require the entity to provide additional contributions to the pool computed.

Contracts and agreements are often silent regarding how such a change might affect amounts that were computed (and distributed) in prior years.

IAS 8 specifies that irrespective of whether the indirect effects arise from an explicit requirement in the agreement or are discretionary, if incurred they are to be recognised in the period in which the reporting entity makes the accounting change, which is 20XX in the example above.

Impracticability Exception

Comparative information presented for a particular prior period need not be restated if doing so is *impracticable*. IAS 8 includes a definition of "impracticability" (see Definitions of Terms in this chapter) and guidance on its interpretation.

The standard states that applying a requirement is impracticable when the entity cannot apply it after making every reasonable effort to do so. For management to assert that it is impracticable to retrospectively apply the new accounting principle, one or more of the following conditions must be present:

1. Management has made every reasonable effort to determine the retrospective adjustment and is unable to do so because the effects of retrospective application are not determinable (e.g., where the information is not available because it was not captured at the time).
2. If it were to apply the new accounting policy retrospectively, management would be required to make assumptions regarding its intent in a prior period that would not be able to be independently substantiated.
3. If it were to apply the new accounting policy retrospectively, management would be required to make significant estimates of amounts for which it is impossible to develop objective information that would have been available at the time the original financial statements for the prior period (or periods) were issued to provide evidence of circumstances that existed at that time regarding the amounts to be measured, recognised and/or disclosed by retrospective application.

Inability to determine period-specific effects. If management is able to determine the adjustment to the opening balance of each affected component of equity as at the beginning of the earliest period for which retrospective application is practicable, but is unable to determine the period-specific effects of the change on all of the prior periods presented in the financial statements, IAS 8 requires the following steps to adopt the new accounting principle:

1. Adjust the carrying amounts of the assets and liabilities for the cumulative effect of applying the new accounting principle at the beginning of the earliest period presented for which it is practicable to make the computation, which may be the current period.
2. Any offsetting adjustment required by applying Step 1 is made to each affected component of equity (usually to beginning retained earnings) of that period.

Inability to determine effects on any prior periods. If it is impracticable to determine the effects of adoption of the new accounting principle on any prior periods, the new principle is applied prospectively as of the earliest date that it is practicable to do so. One example could be when management of a reporting entity decides to change its inventory costing assumption from FIFO to WA, as illustrated in the following example:

Example of change from FIFO to the WA method

During 20XX Exemplum decided to change the inventory costing formula from FIFO to WA. The inventory values are as listed below using both FIFO and WA methods. Sales for the year were €15,000,000 and the company's total purchases were €11,000,000. Other expenses were

€1,200,000 for the year. The company had €1,000,000 ordinary shares outstanding throughout the year.

Inventory values	*FIFO*	*WA*	*Difference*
	€	€	€
December 31, 20XX-1, base year	2,000,000	2,000,000	–
December 31, 20XX	4,000,000	1,800,000	2,200,000
Variation	2,000,000	(2,000,000)	2,200,000

The computations for 20XX-1 would be as follows:

	FIFO	*WA*	*Difference*
Sales	15,000,000	15,000,000	–
Cost of goods sold, beginning inventory	2,000,000	2,000,000	–
Purchases	11,000,000	11,000,000	–
Goods available for sale	13,000,000	13,000,000	–
Ending inventory	4,000,000	1,800,000	2,200,000
	9,000,000	11,200,000	(2,200,000)
Gross profit	6,000,000	3,800,000	2,200,000
Other expenses	1,200,000	1,200,000	–
Net income	4,800,000	2,600,000	2,200,000

The following is an example of the required disclosure in this circumstance.

Note A: Change in Method of Accounting for Inventories

During 20XX, management changed the company's method of accounting for all of its inventories from FIFO to WA. The change was made because management believes that the WA method provides a better matching of costs and revenues. In addition, with the adoption of WA, the company's inventory pricing method is consistent with the method predominant in the industry. The change and its effect on net income (000 omitted except for per share amounts) and earnings per share for 20XX-1 are as follows:

	Profit or loss	*Earnings per share*
Profit or loss before the change	€4,800	€4.80
Reduction of net income due to the change	€2,200	€2.20
Profit or loss as adjusted	€2,600	€2.60

Management has not retrospectively applied this change to prior years' financial statements because beginning inventory on January 1, 20XX using WA is the same as the amount reported on a FIFO basis at December 31, 20XX-1. As a result of this change, the current period's financial statements are not comparable with those of any prior periods. The FIFO cost of inventories exceeds the carrying amount valued using WA by €2,200,000 at December 31, 20XX.

Changes in Amortisation Method

Tangible or intangible long-lived assets are subject to depreciation or amortisation, respectively, as set out in IAS 16 and IAS 38. Changes in methods of amortisation may be implemented to more appropriately recognise amortisation or depreciation as an asset's future economic benefits are consumed. For example, the straight-line method of amortisation may be substituted for an accelerated method when it becomes clear that the straight-line method more accurately reports the consumption of the asset's utility to the reporting entity.

While a change in amortisation method would appear to be a change in accounting policy and thus subject to the requirements of IAS 8 as revised, in fact special accounting for this change is mandated by IAS 16 and IAS 38.

Under IAS 16, which governs accounting for property, plant and equipment (long-lived tangible assets), a change in the depreciation method is a change in the technique used to apply the entity's accounting policy to recognise depreciation as an asset's future economic benefits are consumed. Therefore, it is deemed to be a change in an accounting estimate, to be accounted for as described below. Similar guidance is found in IAS 38, pertaining to intangible assets. These standards are discussed in greater detail in Chapters 9 and 11.

The foregoing exception applies when a change is made to the method of amortising or depreciating existing assets. A different result will be obtained when only newly acquired assets are to be affected by the new procedures.

When a company adopts a different method of amortisation for newly acquired identifiable long-lived assets, and uses that method for all new assets of the same class without changing the method used previously for existing assets of the same class, this is to be accounted for as a change in accounting policy. No adjustment is required to comparative financial statements, nor is any cumulative adjustment to be made to retained earnings at the beginning of the current or any earlier period, since the change in principle is being applied prospectively only. In these cases, a description of the nature of the method changed and the effect on profit or loss and related per share amounts should be disclosed in the period of the change.

In the absence of any specific transitional provisions in a standard, a change in an accounting policy is to be applied retrospectively in accordance with the requirements set out in IAS 8 for voluntary changes in accounting policy, as described below.

When applying the transitional provisions of a standard has an effect on the current period or any prior period presented, the reporting entity is required to disclose:

1. The fact that the change in accounting policy has been made in accordance with the transitional provisions of the standard, with a description of those provisions;
2. The amount of the adjustment for the current period and for each prior period presented (in accordance with IAS 1);
3. The amount of the adjustment relating to periods prior to those included in the comparative information; and
4. The fact that the comparative financial information has been restated, or that restatement for a particular prior period has not been made because it was impracticable.

If the application of the transitional provisions set out in a standard may be expected to have an effect on future periods, the reporting entity is required to disclose the fact that the change in an accounting policy is made in accordance with the prescribed transitional provisions, with a description of those provisions affecting future periods.

Although the "impracticability" provision of revised IAS 8 may appear to suggest that restatement of prior periods' results could easily be avoided by preparers of financial statements, this is not an accurately drawn implication of these rules. The objective of IFRS in general, and of revised IAS 8 in particular, is to enhance the inter-period comparability of information, since doing so will assist users in making economic decisions, particularly by allowing the assessment of trends in financial information for predictive purposes. There is accordingly a general presumption that the benefits derived from restating comparative information will exceed the resulting cost or effort of doing so—and that the reporting entity would make every reasonable effort to restate comparative amounts for each prior period presented.

In circumstances where restatement is deemed impracticable, the reporting entity will disclose the reason for not restating the comparative amounts.

In certain circumstances, a new standard may be promulgated with a delayed effective date. This is done, for example, when the new requirements are complex and IASB wishes to give adequate time for preparers and auditors to master the new requirements. If, as at a financial reporting date, the reporting entity has not elected for early adoption of the standard, it must disclose (1) the nature of the future change or changes in accounting policy; (2) the date by which adoption of the standard is required; (3) the date by which it plans to adopt the standard; and (4) either (a) an estimate of the effect that the change(s) will have on its financial position, or (b) if such an estimate cannot be made without undue cost or effort, a statement to that effect. For an updated list of standards which are currently issued and not yet effective, reference should be made to the IASB's website at www.ifrs.org.

CHANGES IN ACCOUNTING ESTIMATES

The preparation of financial statements requires frequent use of estimates—for such items as asset service lives, residual values, fair values of financial assets or financial liabilities, likely collectability of accounts receivable, inventory obsolescence, accrual of warranty costs, provision for pension costs and so on. These future conditions and events and their effects cannot be identified with certainty; therefore, changes in estimates will be highly likely to occur as new information and more experience is obtained. IAS 8 requires that changes in estimates be *recognised prospectively* by including them in profit or loss in:

1. The period of change if the change affects that period only; or
2. The period of change and future periods if the change affects both.

For example, on January 1, 20XX, a machine purchased for €10,000 was originally estimated to have a 10-year useful life and a salvage value of €1,000. On January 1, 20XX+5 (five years later), the asset is expected to last another 10 years and have a salvage value of €800. As a result, both the current period (the year ending December 31, 20XX+5) and subsequent periods are affected by the change. Annual depreciation expense over the estimated remaining useful life is computed as follows:

Original cost	€10,000
Less estimated salvage (residual) value	(1,000)
Depreciable amount	9,000
Accumulated depreciation, based on original assumptions (10-year life)	
20XX	900
20XX+1	900
20XX+2	900

20XX+3	900
20XX+4	900
	4,500
Carrying value at 1/1/20XX+5	5,500
Revised estimate of salvage value	(800)
Depreciable amount	4,700
Remaining useful life at 1/1/20XX+5	10 years
	470 depreciation per year
Effect on 2016 net income	470 − 900 = 430 increase

The annual depreciation charge over the remaining life would be computed as follows:

$$\frac{\text{Book value of asset} - \text{Residual value}}{\text{Remaining useful life}} = \frac{€5,500 - €800}{10 \text{ years}} = 470/\text{year}$$

An impairment affecting the cost recovery of an asset should not be handled as a change in accounting estimate but instead should be treated as a loss of the period (see the discussion in Chapter 13).

In some situations, it may be difficult to distinguish between changes in accounting policy and changes in accounting estimates. For example, a company may change from deferring and amortising a cost to recording it as an expense as incurred because the future benefits of the cost have become doubtful. In this instance, the company is changing its accounting principle (from deferral to immediate recognition) because of its change in the estimate of the future utility of a particular cost incurred currently.

According to IAS 8, when it is difficult to distinguish a change in an accounting policy from a change in an accounting estimate, the change is treated as a change in an accounting estimate.

CORRECTION OF ERRORS

Although good internal control and the exercise of due care should serve to minimise the number of financial reporting errors that occur, these safeguards cannot be expected to eliminate errors in the financial statements completely. As a result, it was necessary for the accounting profession to develop standards which would ensure uniform treatment of accounting for error corrections.

IAS 8 deals with accounting for error corrections. Under earlier versions of the standard, so-called "fundamental errors" could be accounted for in accordance with either benchmark or allowed alternative approaches to effecting corrections. The IASB's *Improvements Project* resulted in the elimination of the concept of fundamental errors, and also the elimination of what had formerly been the allowed alternative treatment. Under revised IAS 8, therefore, the only permitted treatment is "retrospective restatement" as a prior period adjustment (subject to an exception when doing so is impracticable, as described below). Prior periods must be restated to report financial position and financial performance as they would have been reported had the error never arisen.

There is a clear distinction between errors and changes in accounting estimates. Estimates by their nature are approximations which may need revision as additional information becomes known. For example, when a gain or loss is ultimately recognised on the outcome of a contingency which previously could not be estimated reliably, this does not constitute the correction of an error and cannot be dealt with by restatement. However, if the estimated amount of the contingency had been miscomputed from data available when the financial statements were prepared, at least some portion of the variance between the accrual and the ultimate outcome might reasonably be deemed an error. An error arises only where information available, which should have been taken into account, was ignored or misinterpreted.

Errors are defined by revised IAS 8 as omissions from and other misstatements of the entity's financial statements for one or more prior periods which are discovered in the current period and relate to reliable information which (1) was available when those prior period financial statements were prepared, and (2) could reasonably be expected to have been obtained and taken into account in the original preparation and presentation of those financial statements. Errors include the effects of mathematical mistakes, mistakes in applying accounting policies, oversights or misinterpretations of facts and the effects of financial reporting fraud.

IAS 8 specifies that, when correcting an error in prior period financial statements, the term "restatement" is to be used. That term is exclusively reserved for this purpose so as to effectively communicate to users of the financial statements the reason for a particular change in previously issued financial statements.

An entity should correct material prior period errors retrospectively in the first set of financial statements authorised for issue after their discovery by (1) "restating the comparative amounts for the prior periods presented in which the error occurred or (2) if the error occurred before the earliest prior period presented (beginning of the preceding period), restating the opening balances of assets, liabilities and equity for the earliest prior period presented."

Restatement consists of the following steps:

Step 1—Adjust the carrying amounts of assets and liabilities at the beginning of the first period presented (beginning of the preceding period) in the financial statements for the amount of the correction on periods prior to those presented in the financial statements.

Step 2—Offset the amount of the adjustment in Step 1 (if any) by adjusting the opening balance of retained earnings (or other components of equity or net assets, as applicable to the reporting entity) for that period.

Step 3—Adjust the financial statements of each individual prior period presented for the effects of correcting the error on that specific period (referred to as the period-specific effects of the error).

Example of the correction of a material error

Assume that Exemplum had overstated its depreciation expense by €50,000 in 20XX-2 and €40,000 in 20XX-1, both due to mathematical mistakes. The errors affected both the financial statements and the income tax returns in 20XX-2 and 20XX-1 and are discovered in 20XX. For this example, assume that only one comparative statement of financial position is given (note that the amendments to IAS 1 would require two comparative years to be given where there is a restatement as a result of an error).

Exemplum's statements of financial position and statements of comprehensive income and retained earnings as at and for the year ended December 31, 20XX-1, prior to the restatement, were as follows:

Exemplum
Statement of Comprehensive Income and Retained Earnings
Prior to Restatement
Year Ended December 31, 20XX-1

	20XX-1
	€
Sales	2,000,000
Cost of sales	
Depreciation	750,000
Other	390,000
	1,140,000
Gross profit	860,000
Selling, general and administrative expenses	450,000
Income from operations	410,000
Other income (expense)	10,000
Income before income taxes	420,000
Income taxes	168,000
Profit or loss	252,000
Retained earnings, beginning of year	6,463,000
Dividends	(1,200,000)
Retained earnings, end of year	5,515,000

Exemplum
Statement of Financial Position
Prior to Restatement
December 31, 20XX-1

	20XX-1
	€
Assets	
Current assets	540,000
Property and equipment cost	3,500,000
Accumulated depreciation and amortisation	(430,000)
	3,070,000
Total assets	5,610,000
Liabilities and stockholders' equity	
Income taxes payable	–
Other current liabilities	12,000
Total current liabilities	12,000
Non-current liabilities	70,000
Total liabilities	82,000
Shareholders' equity	
Ordinary share	13,000
Retained earnings	5,515,000
Total shareholders' equity	5,528,000
Total liabilities and shareholders' equity	5,610,000

The following steps are followed to restate Exemplum's prior period financial statements:

Step 1 - Adjust the carrying amounts of assets and liabilities at the beginning of the first period presented (beginning of the preceding period) in the financial statements for the cumulative effect of correcting the error on periods prior to those presented in the financial statements.

The first period presented in the financial statements is 20XX-1. At the beginning of that year, €50,000 of the mistakes had been made and reflected on both the income tax return and financial statements. Assuming a flat 40% income tax rate and ignoring the effects of penalties and interest that would be assessed on the amended income tax returns, the following adjustment would be made to assets and liabilities at January 1, 20XX-1:

Decrease in accumulated depreciation	€50,000
Increase in income taxes payable	(20,000)
	30,000

Step 2 - Offset the effect of the adjustment in Step 1 by adjusting the opening balance of retained earnings (or other components of equity or net assets, as applicable to the reporting entity) for that period.

Retained earnings at the beginning of 20XX-1 will increase by €30,000 as the offsetting entry resulting from Step 1.

Step 3 - Adjust the financial statements of each individual prior period presented for the effects of correcting the error on that specific period (referred to as the period-specific effects of the error).

The 20XX-1 prior period financial statements will be corrected for the period-specific effects of the restatement as follows:

Decrease in depreciation expense and accumulated depreciation	€40,000
Increase in income tax expense and income taxes payable	(16,000)
Increase 20XX-2 profit or loss	24,000

The restated financial statements are presented below.

Exemplum
Statement of Comprehensive Income and Retained Earnings
As Restated Year Ended December 31, 20XX-1

	20XX-1
	Restated
	€
Sales	2,000,000
Cost of sales	
Depreciation	710,000
Other	390,000
	1,100,000
Gross profit	900,000
Selling, general and administrative expenses	450,000
Income from operations	450,000
Other income (expense)	10,000

Income before income taxes	460,000
Income taxes	184,000
Profit or loss	276,000
Retained earnings, beginning of year, as originally reported	6,463,000
Restatement to reflect correction of depreciation (Note X)	30,000
Retained earnings, beginning of year, as restated	6,493,000
Dividends	(1,200,000)
Retained earnings, end of year	5,569,000

Exemplum
Statements of Financial Position
As Restated
Year Ended December 31, 20XX-1

	20XX-1 *Restated* €
Assets	
Current assets	2,540,000
Property and equipment cost	3,500,000
Accumulated depreciation and amortisation	(340,000)
	3,160,000
Total assets	5,700,000
Liabilities and shareholders' equity	
Income taxes payable	36,000
Other current liabilities	12,000
Total current liabilities	48,000
Non-current liabilities	70,000
Total liabilities	118,000
Shareholders' equity	
Ordinary share	13,000
Retained earnings	5,569,000
Total shareholders' equity	5,582,000
Total liabilities and shareholders' equity	5,700,000

When restating previously issued financial statements, management is to disclose:

1. The fact that the financial statements have been restated;
2. The nature of the error;
3. The effect of the restatement on each line item in the financial statements; and
4. The cumulative effect of the restatement on retained earnings (or other applicable components of equity or net assets).

These disclosures need not be repeated in subsequent periods.

The correction of an error in the financial statements of a prior period discovered subsequent to their issuance is reported as a prior period adjustment in the financial statements of the subsequent period. In some cases, however, this situation necessitates the recall or withdrawal of the previously issued financial statements and their revision and reissuance.

Impracticability Exception

IAS 8 stipulates that the amount of the correction of an error is to be accounted for retrospectively. As with changes in accounting policies, comparative information presented for a particular period need not be restated, if restating the information is impracticable. As a result, when it is impracticable to determine the cumulative effect, at the beginning of the current period, of an error, on all prior periods, the entity changes the comparative information as if the error had been corrected prospectively from the earliest date practicable.

However, because the value ascribed to truly comparable data is high, this exception is not to be viewed as an invitation not to restate comparative periods' financial statements to remove the effects of most errors. The standard sets out what constitutes impracticability, as discussed earlier in this chapter, and this should be strictly interpreted. When comparative information for a particular prior period is not restated, the opening balance of retained earnings for the next period must be restated for the amount of the correction before the beginning of that period.

In practice, the major criterion for determining whether or not to report the correction of the error is the materiality of the correction. There are many factors to be considered in determining the materiality of the error correction. Materiality should be considered for each correction individually as well as for all corrections in total. If the correction is determined to have a material effect on profit or loss, or the trend of earnings, it should be disclosed in accordance with the requirements set out in the preceding paragraph.

The prior period adjustment should be presented in the financial statements as follows:

Retained earnings, January 1, 20XX-1, as reported previously	X
Correction of error (description) in prior period(s) (net of xx tax)	X
Adjusted balance of retained earnings at January 1, 20XX-1	X
Profit or loss for the year	X
Retained earnings December 31, 20XX-1	X

In comparative statements, prior period adjustments should also be shown as adjustments to the beginning balances in the retained earnings statements. The amount of the adjustment on the earliest statement shall be the amount of the correction on periods prior to the earliest period presented. The later retained earnings statements presented should also show a prior period adjustment for the amount of the correction as of the beginning of the period being reported on.

Because it is to be handled retrospectively, the correction of an error—which by definition relates to one or more prior periods—is excluded from the determination of profit or loss for the period in which the error is discovered. The financial statements are presented as if the error had never occurred, by correcting the error in the comparative information for the prior period(s) in which the error occurred, unless impracticable. The amount of the correction relating to errors that occurred in periods prior to those presented in comparative information in the financial statements is adjusted against the opening balance of retained earnings of the earliest prior period presented. This treatment is entirely analogous to that now prescribed for changes in accounting policies.

When an accounting error is being corrected, the reporting entity is to disclose the following:

1. The nature of the error;
2. The amount of the correction for each prior period presented;
3. The amount of the correction relating to periods prior to those presented in comparative information; and
4. That comparative information has been restated, or that the restatement for a particular prior period has not been made because it would require undue cost or effort.

FUTURE DEVELOPMENTS

The IASB is undertaking a project to clarify the distinction between a change in accounting policy and a change in an accounting estimate by making those two definitions more distinct and concise. Additional guidance and examples will also be included to demonstrate how accounting policies and accounting estimates relate to each other and to decide whether a change in valuation technique or a change in estimation technique is a change in an accounting estimate. An Exposure Draft was published March 2018.

US GAAP COMPARISON

Under US GAAP, the FASB Accounting Standards Codification (ASC) is the single source of authoritative literature; nevertheless, there is no single standard that addresses accounting policies in US GAAP similar to IAS 8. However, similar to IFRS, accounting policies must be in accordance with existing US GAAP and be applied consistently. Changes in accounting policy must be based on either a change required by an Accounting Standards Update, or a substantive argument that the new policy is superior to the current due to improved representational faithfulness as found in ASC 250, *Accounting Changes and Error Corrections (ASC 250)*.

As noted in ASC 250 errors and changes in accounting policies are applied retrospectively for all the periods presented in a set of financial statements. The effect of errors and changes that occurred prior to the earliest period presented is included in the opening balances of equity for the earliest period presented. The description of the change or error would also be disclosed, and the financial statement line item effected.

ASC 250-10-45-9 states that if it is impracticable to determine the financial effects of changes in accounting principles in prior periods, the effect is presented for the most recent period that is practicable. Reasons why it is impracticable are disclosed. Retrospective application of a new accounting policy, however, includes only direct effects and associated tax effects. Indirect effects (e.g., change in incentive pay accrual as a result of the application) are not included in prior periods, but in the current period, if and when those effects are realised.

Similar to IFRS, policies need not be applied to items that are immaterial. Materiality is defined in US GAAP very similarly to IFRS, which is the inclusion or omission of information from financial statements that would affect the decisions of users. The concept includes changes in the trend of earnings or other measures that otherwise would be considered material. The threshold for materiality for errors for interim financial statements is made on the relevant measure (i.e., income) for the year. However, errors that are material to the quarter must be disclosed.

One significant difference from IFRS is that the FASB Concepts Statements, the equivalent of the IFRS Framework, do not establish accounting standards or disclosure practices for particular items.

Under US GAAP, the accounting policies for subsidiaries do not need to be uniform; however, such variation in accounting policies should be appropriately disclosed in consolidated financial statements.

LIFO inventory is allowed under US GAAP and changes from LIFO to FIFO and FIFO to LIFO are addressed in ASC 250.

8 INVENTORIES

INTRODUCTION

The accounting for inventories is a major consideration for many entities because of its significance on both the statement of profit or loss (cost of goods sold) and the statement of financial position (inventories). Inventories are defined by IAS 2 as assets that are:

> *. . . held for sale in the ordinary course of business; in the process of production for such sale; or in the form of materials or supplies to be consumed in the production process or in the rendering of services.*

This standard applies to all inventories, except:

a. Financial instruments (IFRS 9, *Financial Instruments*); and
b. Biological assets related to agricultural activity and agricultural produce at the point of harvest (IAS 41, *Agriculture*).

This standard does not apply to the measurement of inventories held by:

a. Producers of agricultural and forest products, agricultural produce after harvest and minerals and mineral products that are measured at net realisable value;
b. Commodity broker-traders who measure their inventories at fair value less costs to sell.

The requirements of IAS 2 in respect of recognition, disclosure and presentation, however, continue to apply for such inventories.

The complexity of accounting for inventories arises from several factors:

1. The high volume of activity (or turnover) in the account;
2. The various cost flow alternatives that are acceptable; and
3. The classification of inventories.

There are two types of entities for which the accounting for inventories must be considered. The merchandising entity (generally, a retailer or wholesaler) has a single inventory account, usually entitled *merchandise inventory*. These are goods on hand that are purchased for resale. The other type of entity is the manufacturer, which generally has three types of inventories: (1) raw materials, (2) work in progress and (3) finished goods. *Raw materials inventory* represents goods purchased that will act as inputs in the production process leading to the finished product. *Work in progress* consists of the goods entered into production but not yet completed. *Finished goods inventory* is the completed product that is on hand awaiting sale.

In the case of either type of entity the same basic questions need to be resolved:

1. At what point in time should the items be included in inventory (ownership)?
2. What costs incurred should be included in the valuation of inventories?
3. What cost flow assumption should be used?
4. At what value should inventories be reported (net realisable value)?
5. What happens when inventories are purchased on deferred terms?
6. What are the disclosure requirements?

Sources of IFRS
IAS 2, 8, 18, 34, 41

DEFINITIONS OF TERMS

Absorption (full) costing. Inclusion of all manufacturing costs (fixed and variable) in the cost of finished goods inventory.

By-products. Goods that result as an ancillary product from the production of a primary good; often having minor value when compared to the value of the principal product(s).

Commodity broker-traders. Those who buy or sell commodities for others or on their own account.

Consignments. Marketing method in which the consignor ships goods to the consignee, who acts as an agent for the consignor in selling the goods. The inventory remains the property of the consignor until sold by the consignee.

Cost. The sum of all costs of purchase, costs of conversion and other costs incurred in bringing the inventories to their present location and condition.

Direct (variable) costing. Inclusion of only variable manufacturing costs in the cost of ending finished goods inventory. While often used for management (internal) reporting, this method is not deemed acceptable for financial reporting purposes.

Finished goods. Completed but unsold products produced by a manufacturing firm.

First-In, First-Out (FIFO). Cost flow assumption; the first goods purchased or produced are assumed to be the first goods sold.

Goods in transit. Goods being shipped from seller to buyer at year-end.

Inventories. Assets held for sale in the normal course of business, or which are in the process of production for such sale, or are in the form of materials or supplies to be consumed in the production process or in the rendering of services.

Joint products. Two or more products produced jointly, where neither is viewed as being more important; in some cases, additional production steps are applied to one or more joint products after a split-off point.

Last-In, First-Out (LIFO). Cost flow assumption; the last goods purchased or produced are assumed to be the first goods sold.

Markdown. Decrease below original retail price. A markdown cancellation is an increase (not above original retail price) in retail price after a markdown.

Mark-up. Increase above original purchase price. A mark-up cancellation is a decrease (not below original purchase price) in retail price after a mark-up.

Net realisable value. Estimated selling price in the ordinary course of business less the estimated costs of completion and the estimated costs necessary to make the sale.

Periodic inventory system. Inventory system where quantities are determined only periodically by physical count.

Perpetual inventory system. Inventory system where up-to-date records of inventory quantities are kept.

Raw materials. For a manufacturing firm, materials on hand awaiting entry into the production process.

Retail method. Inventory costing method that uses a cost ratio to reduce ending inventory (valued at retail) to cost. Cost of inventory determined by reducing the sales value of inventories by the appropriate percentage gross margin.

Specific identification. Inventory system where the seller identifies which specific items have been sold and which ones remain in the closing inventories.

Standard costs. Predetermined unit costs, which are acceptable for financial reporting purposes if adjusted periodically to reflect current conditions.

Weighted-average. Periodic inventory costing method/cost flow assumption where ending inventory and cost of goods sold are priced at the weighted-average cost of all items available-for-sale.

Work in progress. For a manufacturing firm, the inventories of partially completed products.

RECOGNITION AND MEASUREMENT

Basic Concept of Inventory Costing

IAS 2 establishes that the lower of cost and net realisable value should be the basis for the valuation of inventories. In contrast to IFRS dealing with property, plant and equipment (IAS 16) or investment property (IAS 40), there is no option for revaluing inventories to current replacement cost or other measures of fair value, presumably due to the far shorter period of time over which such assets are held, thereby limiting the cumulative impact of inflation or other economic factors on reported amounts. However, note measurement exceptions in application of IAS 2 discussed above.

The cost of inventory items that are ordinarily interchangeable, and goods or services produced and segregated for specific projects, are generally assigned carrying amounts by using the specific identification method. For most goods, however, specific identification is not a practical alternative. In cases where there are a large number of items of inventory and where the turnover is rapid, the standard prescribes two inventory costing formulas, namely the First-In, First-Out (FIFO) and the weighted-average methods. A third alternative, the Last-In First-Out (LIFO) costing method, was designated as being unacceptable.

FIFO and weighted-average cost are the only acceptable cost flow assumptions under IFRS. Either method can be used to assign cost of inventories, but once selected an entity must apply that cost flow assumption consistently (unless the change to the other method can be justified under the criteria set forth by IAS 8). Furthermore, an entity is constrained from applying different cost formulas to inventories having similar nature and use to the entity. On the other hand, for inventories having different natures or uses, different cost formulas may be justified. Mere difference in location, however, cannot be used to justify applying different costing methods to otherwise similar inventories. Note that where a change in cost formula is made, this is likely to represent a change in accounting policy rather than a change in accounting estimate and will therefore need to be retrospectively applied under the requirements of IAS 8.

Ownership of Goods

Inventory can only be an asset of the reporting entity if it is an economic resource of the entity at the date of the statement of financial position. In general, an entity should record purchases and sales of inventory when legal title passes. Although strict adherence to this rule may not appear to be important in daily transactions, proper inventory cut-off at the end of an accounting period is crucial for the correct determination of the periodic results of operations. To obtain an accurate measurement of inventory and cost of goods sold in the financial statements (which will be based upon inventory quantities), it is necessary to determine when title passes.

The most common error made for inventories is to assume that title is synonymous with possession of goods on hand. This may be incorrect in that:

1. The goods on hand may not be owned; and
2. Goods that are not on hand may be owned.

Situations which are more likely to cause confusion about proper ownership are:

1. Goods in transit;
2. Consignment sales;
3. Product financing arrangements; and
4. Sales made with the buyer having generous or unusual right of return.

Goods in transit

At the end of the reporting period, any *goods in transit* from seller to buyer may properly be includable in one, and only one, of those parties' inventories, based on the terms and conditions of the sale. Under traditional legal and accounting interpretation, goods are included in the inventory of the party financially responsible for transportation costs. This responsibility may be indicated by shipping terms such as FOB, which is used in overland shipping contracts, and by FAS, CIF, C&F and ex-ship, which are used in maritime transport contracts.

The term *FOB* stands for "free on board." If goods are shipped *FOB destination*, transportation costs are paid by the seller and title does not generally pass until the carrier delivers the goods to the buyer; thus, these goods are part of the seller's inventory while in transit.

If goods are shipped *FOB shipping point*, transportation costs are paid by the buyer and title generally passes when the carrier takes possession; thus, these goods are part of the buyer's inventory while in transit. The terms *FOB destination* and *FOB shipping point* often indicate a specific location at which title to the goods is transferred, such as FOB Milan. This means that the seller would most likely retain title and risk of loss until the goods are delivered to a common carrier in Milan who will act as an agent for the buyer.

A seller who ships *FAS* (free alongside) must bear all expense and risk involved in delivering the goods to the dock next to (alongside) the vessel on which they are to be shipped. The buyer bears the cost of loading and of shipment; thus, title generally passes when the carrier takes possession of the goods.

In a *CIF* (cost, insurance and freight) contract, the buyer agrees to pay in a lump sum the cost of the goods, insurance costs and freight charges. In a C&F contract, the buyer promises to pay a lump sum that includes the cost of the goods and all freight charges. In either case, the seller must deliver the goods to the carrier and pay the costs of loading; thus, both title and risk of loss generally pass to the buyer upon delivery of the goods to the carrier.

A seller who delivers goods *ex-ship* normally bears all expense and risk until the goods are unloaded, at which time both title and risk of loss pass to the buyer.

The above examples give an indication of the most likely point of transfer of risks and rewards; the actual contractual arrangements between a given buyer and a given seller can vary widely and may point towards a different stage at which ownership passes. The accounting treatment must in all cases strive to mirror the substance of the legal terms established between the parties.

Examples of accounting for goods in transit

Example 1

Company J ships a truckload of merchandise in December 20XX to Customer K, which is located 2,000 miles away. The truckload of merchandise arrives at Customer K in January 20XX+1. Between December 20XX and January 20XX+1, the truckload of merchandise is goods in transit. The goods in transit require special attention if either of the companies issue financial statements as of December 20XX. The merchandise is the inventory of one of the two companies, but the merchandise is not physically present at either company. One of the two companies must include the cost of the goods in transit to the cost of the inventory that it has in its possession.

The terms of the sale will indicate which company should include the goods in transit as its inventory as of December 20XX. If the terms are FOB shipping point, and there are no peculiar/unusual contractual conditions, the seller (Company J) will record a sale in 20XX and receivable and will derecognise the goods in transit from its inventory. On December 31, 20XX, Customer K is the owner of the goods in transit and will need to record a liability for the purchase, a trade payable, and must recognise the goods in transit to the cost of the inventory which is in its possession.

If the terms of the sale are FOB destination, and there are no other peculiar/unusual contractual conditions, Company J will not have a sale and receivable until January 20XX+1. This means Company J must continue to include the cost of the goods in transit in its inventory at December 31, 20XX. (Customer K will not have a purchase, trade payable or inventory of these goods until January 20XX+1.)

Example 2

Vartan Gyroscope Company is located in Veracruz, Mexico, and obtains precision jewelled bearings from a supplier in Switzerland. The standard delivery terms are FAS a container ship in the harbour in Nice, France, so that Vartan takes legal title to the delivery once possession of the goods is taken by the carrier's dockside employees for the purpose of loading the goods on board the ship. When the supplier delivers goods with an invoiced value of €1,200,000 to the wharf, it e-mails an advance shipping notice (ASN) and invoice to Vartan via an electronic data interchange (EDI) transaction, itemising the contents of the delivery. Vartan's computer system receives the EDI transmission, notes the FAS terms in the supplier file, and therefore automatically logs it into the company computer system with the following entry:

Inventories	€1,200,000	
Accounts payable		€1,200,000

The goods are assigned an "In Transit" location code in Vartan's perpetual inventory system. When the precision jewelled bearings delivery eventually arrives at Vartan's receiving dock, the receiving staff records a change in inventory location code from "In Transit" to a code designating a physical location within the warehouse.

Vartan's secondary precision jewelled bearings supplier is located in Vancouver, British Columbia, and ships overland using FOB destination Veracruz terms, so the supplier retains title until the shipment arrives at Vartan's location. This supplier also issues an advance shipping notice by EDI to inform Vartan of the estimated arrival date, but in this case Vartan's computer system notes the FOB Veracruz terms, and makes no entry to record the transaction until the goods arrive at Vartan's receiving dock.

Consignment sales

There are specifically defined situations where the party holding the goods is doing so as an agent for the true owner. In *consignments*, the consignor (seller) ships goods to the consignee (buyer), who acts as the agent of the consignor in trying to sell the goods. In some consignments, the consignee receives a commission; in other arrangements, the consignee "purchases" the goods simultaneously with the sale of the goods to the final customer. Goods out on consignment are properly included in the inventory of the consignor and excluded from the inventory of the consignee. Disclosure may be required of the consignee, however, since common financial analytical ratios, such as days' sales in inventory or inventory/turnover, may appear distorted unless the financial statement users are informed. However, IFRS does not explicitly address this.

Examples of a consignment arrangement

Example 1

A company (Manufacturer) which produces Product A wants to attract a new customer B. Customer B is interested in Product A but doesn't want to invest cash in inventory and negotiates an inventory consignment arrangement with Manufacturer. Manufacturer will initially ship 100 tons of Product A to Customer B's warehouse and will replenish this inventory as Customer B uses the product. Customer B will not take title to the product until the product is consumed by Customer B. The selling price for one ton of Product A is set at €100. Manufacturer's cost of one ton of Product A is €60.

At the beginning of November 20XX, Manufacturer ships 100 tons of Product A to Customer B. The following journal entry is recorded by Manufacturer:

Account Titles	Debit	Credit
Inventory (consignments)	€6,000	
Finished goods inventory		€6,000

The consignment inventory amount was determined as €60 × 100 tons = €6,000.

Note: no journal entries are made by Customer B except for entries in an inventory system to track how much consigned inventory was received and consumed.

During November 20XX, Customer B uses 70 tons of Product A and notifies Manufacturer about this consumption by sending an account statement. Manufacturer uses the account statement to issue an invoice to Customer B and records the sale of 70 tons along with the related cost of goods sold:

Account Titles	Debit	Credit
Accounts receivable	€7,000	
Sales		€7,000

The sales amount was determined as €100 × 70 tons = €7,000.

Account Titles	Debit	Credit
Cost of Goods Sold	€4,200	
Inventory (consignments)		€4,200

The cost of goods sold amount was determined as €60 × 70 tons = €4,200.

At the end of November 20XX or beginning of December 20XX, Manufacturer ships 70 tons of Product A to replenish the stock at Customer B's warehouse and makes the following journal entry:

Account Titles	Debit	Credit
Inventory (consignments)	€4,200	
Finished goods inventory		€4,200

Example 2

The Random Gadget Company ships a consignment of its cordless phones to a retail outlet of the Consumer Products Corporation. Random Gadget's cost of the consigned goods is €3,700, and it shifts the inventory cost into a separate inventory account to track the physical location of the goods. The entry is as follows:

Consignment out inventory	€3,700	
Finished goods inventory		€3,700

A third-party shipping company ships the cordless phones from Random Gadget Company to Consumer Products Corporation. Upon receipt of an invoice for this €550 shipping expense, Random Gadget Company charges the cost to consignment inventory with the following entry:

Consignment out inventory	€550	
Accounts payable		€550

To record the cost of shipping goods from the factory to Consumer Products Corporation.

Consumer Products Corporation sells half the consigned inventory during the month for €3,250 in credit card payments, and earns a 22% commission on these sales, totalling €715. According to the consignment arrangement, Random Gadget Company must also reimburse Consumer Products Corporation for the 2% credit card processing fee, which is €65 (€3,250 × 2%). The results of this sale are summarised as follows:

Sales price to Consumer Products Corporation customer earned on behalf of Random Gadget		€3,250
Less: Amounts due to Consumer Products Corporation in accordance with arrangement 22% sales commission	€715	
Reimbursement for credit card processing fee	€65	(€780)
Due to Random Gadget Company		€2,470

Upon receipt of the monthly sales report from Consumer Products Corporation, Random Gadget Company records the following entries:

Accounts receivable	€2,470	
Cost of goods sold	€65	
Commission expense	€715	
Sales		€3,250

To record the sale made by Consumer Products Corporation acting as agent of Random Gadget Company, the commission earned by Consumer Products Corporation and the credit card fee reimbursement to Consumer Products Corporation in connection with the sale.

Cost of goods sold	€2,125	
Consignment out inventory		€2,125

To transfer the related inventory cost to cost of goods sold, including half the original inventory cost and half the cost of the shipment to Consumer Products Corporation [(€3,700 + €550 = €4,250) × ½ = €2,125].

Right to return purchases

A related inventory accounting issue that deserves special consideration arises when the buyer is granted an exceptional right to return the merchandise acquired. This is not meant to address the normal sales terms found throughout commercial transactions (e.g., where the buyer can return goods, whether found to be defective or not, within a short time after delivery, such as five days). Rather, this connotes situations where the return privileges are well in excess of standard practice, to place doubt on the accuracy of the purported sale transaction itself.

In terms of IFRS 15 an entity needs to determine whether it has transferred control of the asset, i.e., when the performance obligation has been satisfied. IFRS 15 provides special guidance for sales with a right of return, consignment arrangement and bill-and-hold arrangement (refer to Chapter 20). Revenue needs to be reduced with any products expected to be returned.

Accounting for Inventories

The major objectives of accounting for inventories are the matching of appropriate costs against revenues to arrive at the correct gross profit and the accurate representation of inventories on hand as assets of the reporting entity at the end of the reporting period.

The accounting for inventories is done under either a periodic or a perpetual system. In a *periodic inventory system*, the inventory quantity is determined periodically by a physical count. Next, a cost formula is applied to the quantity so determined to calculate the cost of ending inventory. Cost of goods sold is computed by adding beginning inventory and net purchases (or cost of goods manufactured) and subtracting ending inventory.

Alternatively, a *perpetual inventory system* keeps a running total of the quantity (and possibly the cost) of inventory on hand by recording all sales and purchases as they occur. When inventory is purchased, the inventory account (rather than purchases) is debited. When inventory is sold, the cost of goods sold and reduction of inventory are recorded. Periodic physical counts are necessary only to verify the perpetual records and to satisfy the tax regulations in some jurisdictions (tax regulations may require that a physical inventory count be undertaken at least annually).

Valuation of Inventories

According to IAS 2, the primary basis of accounting for inventories is cost. *Cost* is defined as the sum of all costs of purchase, costs of conversion and other costs incurred in bringing the inventories to their present location and condition.

For raw materials and merchandise inventory that are purchased outright and not intended for further conversion, the identification of cost is relatively straightforward. The cost of these purchased inventories will include all expenditures incurred in bringing the goods to the point of sale and putting them in a saleable condition. These costs include the purchase price, import duties and other taxes which are not recoverable by the entity from a taxing authority, e.g., VAT, Goods and Services Tax, transportation costs, insurance and handling costs. Trade discounts, rebates and other such items are to be deducted in determining inventory costs; failure to do so would result in valuing inventories at amounts in excess of true historical costs. Exchange differences arising directly on the recent acquisition of inventories invoiced in a foreign currency are not permitted to be included in the costs of purchase of inventories.

The impact of interest costs as they relate to the valuation of inventories (IAS 23) is discussed in Chapter 10. IAS 23 requires capitalisation of financing costs incurred during the manufacture, acquisition or construction of qualifying assets. However, borrowing costs will generally not be capitalised in connection with inventory acquisitions, since the period required to get the goods ready for sale will generally not be significant. On the other hand, when a lengthy production process is required to prepare the goods for sale, the provisions of IAS 23 would be applicable, and a portion of borrowing costs would become part of the cost of inventory. In practice, such situations are rare, and IAS 23 allows an exemption for inventories that are manufactured, or otherwise produced, in large quantities on a repetitive basis.

Conversion costs for manufactured goods should include all costs that are directly associated with the units produced, such as labour and overhead. The allocation of overhead costs, however, must be systematic and rational, and in the case of fixed overhead costs (i.e., those which do not vary directly with level of production) the allocation process should be based on normal production levels. In periods of unusually low levels of production, a portion of fixed overhead costs must accordingly be charged directly to operations and not taken into inventory.

Costs other than material and conversion costs are capitalised only to the extent they are necessary to bring the goods to their present condition and location. Examples might include certain design costs and other types of preproduction expenditures if intended to benefit specific classes of customers. On the other hand, all research costs and most development costs (per IAS 38, as discussed in Chapter 11) would typically *not* become part of inventory costs. Also generally excluded from inventory would be such costs as administrative overheads (which do not contribute to bringing the inventories to their present location and condition), selling expenses, abnormal cost of wasted materials, non-production labour or other expenditures, and storage costs (unless necessary in the production process), which must be treated as period costs and expensed in the Income Statement. Included in overhead, and thus allocable to inventory, would be such categories as repairs, maintenance, utilities, rent, indirect labour, production supervisory wages, indirect materials and supplies, quality control and inspection and the cost of small tools not capitalised.

Example of recording raw material or component parts cost

Accurate Laser-Guided Farm Implements, Inc. purchases lasers, a component that it uses in manufacturing its signature product. The company typically receives delivery of all its component parts and uses them in manufacturing its finished products during the autumn and early winter, and then sells its stock of finished goods in the late winter and spring. The supplier invoice for a January delivery of lasers includes the following line items:

Lasers	€5,043
Shipping and handling	€125
Shipping insurance	€48
Sales tax	€193
Total	€5,409

As Accurate is using the lasers as components in a product that it resells, it will not pay the sales tax. However, both the shipping and handling charge and the shipping insurance are required for ongoing product manufacturing, and so are included in the following entry to record receipt of the goods:

Inventory—components	€5,216	
Accounts payable		€5,216

To record purchase of lasers and related costs (€5,043 + €125 + €48).

On February 1, Accurate purchases a €5,000, two-month shipping insurance (known as "inland marine") policy that applies to all incoming supplier deliveries for the remainder of the winter production season, allowing it to refuse shipping insurance charges on individual deliveries. Since the policy insures all inbound components deliveries (not just lasers) it is too time-consuming to charge the cost of this policy to individual components deliveries using specific identification; the controller can estimate a flat charge per delivery based on the number of expected deliveries during the two-month term of the insurance policy as follows:

€5,000 insurance premium ÷ 200 expected deliveries during the policy term = €25 per delivery and then charge each delivery with €25 as follows:

Inventory—components	€25	
Prepaid insurance		€25

To allocate cost of inland marine coverage to inbound insured components shipments.

In this case, however, the controller determined that shipments are expected to occur evenly during the two-month policy period and therefore will simply make a monthly standard journal entry as follows:

Inventory—components	€2,500	
Prepaid insurance		€2,500

To amortise premium on inland marine policy using the straight-line method.

Note that the controller must be careful, under either scenario, to ensure that perpetual inventory records appropriately track unit costs of components to include the cost of shipping insurance. Failure to do so would result in an understatement of the cost of raw materials inventory on hand at the end of any accounting period.

Joint products and by-products

In some production processes, more than one product is produced simultaneously. Typically, if each product has significant value, they are referred to as *joint products*; if only one has substantial value, the others are known as *by-products*. Under IAS 2, when the costs of each jointly produced good cannot be clearly determined, a rational allocation among them is required. Generally, such allocation is made by reference to the relative values of the jointly produced goods, as measured by ultimate selling prices. Often, after a period of joint production, the goods are split off and separately incur additional costs before being completed and ready for sale. The allocation of joint costs should take into account the additional individual product costs yet to be incurred after the point at which joint production ceases.

By-products are products that have limited value when measured with reference to the primary good being produced. IAS 2 suggests that by-products be valued at net realisable value, with the costs allocated to by-products thereby being deducted from the cost pool which is allocated to the sole or several principal products.

For example, products A and B have the same processes performed on them up to the split-off point. The total cost incurred to this point is €80,000. This cost can be assigned to products A and B using their relative sales value at the split-off point. If A could be sold for €60,000 and B for €40,000, the total sales value is €100,000. The cost would be assigned based on each product's relative sales value. Thus, A would be assigned a cost of €48,000 (60,000/100,000 × 80,000) and B a cost of €32,000 (40,000/100,000 × 80,000).

If inventory is exchanged with another entity for similar goods, the acquired items are recorded at the recorded or book value of the items given up.

In some jurisdictions, the categories of costs that are includable in inventories for tax purposes may differ from those that are permitted for financial reporting purposes under IFRS. To the extent that differential tax and financial reporting is possible (i.e., that there is no statutory requirement that the taxation rules constrain financial reporting) deferred taxation must be considered. This is discussed more fully in Chapter 26.

Direct costing

The generally accepted method of allocating fixed overhead to both ending inventories and cost of goods sold is commonly known as *(full) absorption costing*. IAS 2 requires that absorption costing be employed. However, often for managerial decision-making purposes an alternative to absorption costing, known as *variable or direct costing*, is utilised. Direct costing requires classifying only direct materials, direct labour and variable overheads related to production as inventory costs. All fixed costs are accounted for as period costs. The virtue of direct costing is that under this accounting strategy there will be a predictable, linear effect on marginal contribution from each unit of sales revenue, which can be useful in planning and controlling the business operation.

However, such a costing method does not result in inventory that includes all costs of production, and therefore this is deemed not to be in accordance with IAS 2. If an entity uses direct costing for internal budgeting or other purposes, adjustments must be made to develop alternative information for financial reporting purposes.

Differences in inventory costing between IFRS and tax requirements

In certain tax jurisdictions, there may be requirements to include or exclude certain overhead cost elements which are handled differently under IFRS for financial reporting purposes. For example, in the US the tax code requires elements of overhead to be allocated to inventories, while IFRS demands that these be expensed as period costs. Another common area of difference in the US is the permission of LIFO as a basis of inventory valuation for tax purposes, which as discussed above is not permitted under IFRS. Since tax laws do not dictate IFRS, the appropriate response to such a circumstance is to treat these as temporary differences, which will create the need for inter-period income tax allocation under IAS 12. Deferred tax accounting is fully discussed in Chapter 26.

METHODS OF INVENTORY

Specific Identification

The theoretical basis for valuing inventories and cost of goods sold requires assigning the production and/or acquisition costs to the specific goods to which they relate. For example, the cost of ending inventory for an entity in its first year, during which it produced 10 items (e.g., exclusive single-family homes), might be the actual production cost of the first, sixth and eighth unit produced if those are the actual units still on hand at the date of the statement of financial position. The costs of the other homes would be included in that year's profit or loss as cost of goods sold. This method of inventory valuation is usually referred to as *specific identification*.

Specific identification is generally not a practical technique, as the product will generally lose its separate identity as it passes through the production and sales process. Its use is limited to those situations where there are small inventory quantities, typically having high unit value and a low turnover rate. Under IAS 2, specific identification must be employed to cost inventories that are not ordinarily interchangeable, and goods and services produced and segregated for specific projects. For inventories meeting either of these criteria, the specific identification method is mandatory and alternative methods cannot be used.

Because of the limited applicability of specific identification, it is more likely to be the case that certain assumptions regarding the cost flows associated with inventory will need to be made. One of accounting's peculiarities is that these cost flows may or may not reflect the physical flow of inventory. Over the years, much attention has been given to both the flow of physical goods and the assumed flow of costs associated with those goods. In most jurisdictions, it has long been recognised that the flow of costs need not mirror the actual flow of the goods with which those costs are associated. For example, a key provision in an early US accounting standard stated that:

> *. . . cost for inventory purposes shall be determined under any one of several assumptions as to the flow of cost factors; the major objective in selecting a method should be to choose the one which, under the circumstances, most clearly reflects periodic income.*

Under the current IAS 2, there are two acceptable cost flow assumptions. These are: (1) the FIFO method and (2) the weighted-average method. There are variations of each of these cost flow assumptions that are sometimes used in practice, but if an entity presents its financial statements under IFRS it has to be careful not to apply a variant of these cost flow assumptions that would represent a deviation from the requirements of IAS 2. Furthermore, in certain jurisdictions, other costing methods, such as the LIFO method and the base stock method, continue to be permitted.

First-In, First-Out

The FIFO method of inventory valuation assumes that the first goods purchased will be the first goods to be used or sold, regardless of the actual physical flow. This method is thought to parallel most closely the physical flow of the units for most industries having moderate to rapid turnover of goods. The strength of this cost flow assumption lies in the inventory amount reported in the statement of financial position. Because the earliest goods purchased are the first ones removed from the inventory account, the remaining balance is composed of items acquired closer to period end, at more recent costs. This yields results similar to those obtained under current cost accounting in the statement of financial position, and helps in achieving the goal of reporting assets at amounts approximating current values.

However, the FIFO method does not necessarily reflect the most accurate or decision-relevant income figure when viewed from the perspective of underlying economic performance, as older historical costs are being matched against current revenues. Depending on the rate of inventory turnover and the speed with which general and specific prices are changing, this mismatch could potentially have a material distorting effect on reported income. At the extreme, if reported earnings are fully distributed to owners as dividends, the entity could be left without sufficient resources to replenish its inventory stocks due to the impact of changing prices. (This problem is not limited to inventory costing; depreciation based on old costs of plant assets also may understate the true economic cost of capital asset consumption and serve to support dividend distributions that leave the entity unable to replace plant assets at current prices.)

The following example illustrates the basic principles involved in the application of FIFO:

	Units available	*Units sold*	*Actual unit cost*	*Actual total cost*
Beginning inventory	100	–	€2.10	€210
Sale	–	75	–	–
Purchase	150	–	€2.80	€420
Sale	–	100	–	–
Purchase	50	–	€3.00	€150
Total	300	175		€780

Given these data, the cost of goods sold, and the ending inventory balance are determined as follows:

	Units	*Unit cost*	*Total cost*
Cost of goods sold	100	€2.10	€210
	75	€2.80	€210
	175		€420
Ending inventory	50	€3.00	€150
	75	€2.80	€210
	125		€360

Notice that the total of the units in cost of goods sold and ending inventory, as well as the sum of their total costs, is equal to the goods available-for-sale and their respective total costs.

The unique characteristic of the FIFO method is that it provides the same results under either the periodic or perpetual system. This will not be the case for any other costing method.

Weighted-Average Cost

The other acceptable method of inventory valuation under revised IAS 2 involves averaging and is commonly referred to as the weighted-average cost method. The cost of goods available-for-sale (beginning inventory and net purchases) is divided by the units available-for-sale to obtain a weighted-average unit cost. Ending inventory and cost of goods sold are then priced at this average cost. For example, assume the following data:

	Units available	*Units sold*	*Actual unit cost*	*Actual total cost*
Beginning inventory	100	–	€2.10	€210
Sale	–	75	–	–
Purchase	150	–	€2.80	€420
Sale	–	100	–	–
Purchase	50	–	€3.00	€150
Total	300	175		€780

The weighted-average cost is €780/300, or €2.60. Ending inventory is 125 units at €2.60, or €325; cost of goods sold is 175 units at €2.60, or €455.

When the weighted-average assumption is applied to a perpetual inventory system, the average cost is recomputed after each purchase. This process is referred to as a moving average. Sales are costed at the most recent average. This combination is called the moving-average method and is applied below to the same data used in the weighted-average example above.

	Units on hand	*Purchases in euro*	*Sales in euro*	*Total cost*	*Inventory unit cost*
Beginning inventory	100	–	–	€210.00	€2.10
Sale (75 units @ €2.10)	25	–	€157.50	€52.50	€2.10
Purchase (150 units, €420)	175	€420.00	–	€472.50	€2.70
Sale (100 units @ €2.70)	75	–	€270.00	€202.50	€2.70
Purchase (50 units, €150)	125	€150.00	–	€352.50	€2.82

Cost of goods sold is 75 units at €2.10 and 100 units at €2.70, or a total of €427.50.

Net Realisable Value

As stated in IAS 2:

Net realisable value is the estimated selling price in the ordinary course of business less the estimated costs of completion and the estimated costs necessary to make the sale.

The utility of an item of inventory is limited to the amount to be realised from its ultimate sale; where the item's recorded cost exceeds this amount, IFRS requires that a loss be recognised for the difference. The logic for this requirement is twofold: first, assets (in particular, current assets such as inventory) should not be reported at amounts that exceed net realisable value; and second, any decline in value in a period should be reported in that period's results of operations to achieve proper matching with current period's revenues. Were the inventory to be carried forward at an amount in excess of net realisable value, the loss would be recognised on the ultimate sale in a subsequent period. This would mean that a loss incurred in one period, when the value decline occurred, would have been deferred to a different period, which would clearly be inconsistent with several key accounting concepts.

IAS 2 states that estimates of net realisable value should be applied on an item-by-item basis in most instances, although it makes an exception for those situations where there are groups of related products or similar items that can be properly valued in the aggregate. As a general principle, item-by-item comparisons of cost to net realisable value are required, preventing unrealised "gains" on some items (i.e., where the net realisable values exceed historical costs) to offset the unrealised losses on other items, thereby reducing the net loss to be recognised. Since recognition of unrealised gains in profit or loss is generally prohibited under IFRS, revaluation of inventory declines on a grouped basis would be an indirect or "backdoor" mechanism to recognise gains that should not be given such recognition. Accordingly, the basic requirement is to apply the tests on an individual item basis.

Recoveries of previously recognised losses

IAS 2 stipulates that a new assessment of net realisable value should be made in each subsequent period; when the reason for a previous write-down no longer exists (i.e., when net realisable value has improved), it should be reversed. Since the write-down was taken to profit or loss, the reversal should also be reflected in profit or loss. As under prior rules, the amount to be restored to the carrying value will be limited to the amount of the previous impairment recognised.

It should be noted that net realisable value is not the same as fair value. Net realisable value is the net amount an entity expects to receive from the sale of inventories and is therefore an entity-specific measure. Fair value is a wider market-based valuation that is defined in more detail under IFRS 13.

Other Valuation Methods

Techniques for measurement of cost of inventories, such as the retail method or the standard cost method, may be used for convenience if the results approximate cost and where the application of the above methods is not practical.

Retail method

IAS 2 recognises that the retail method is often used in the retail industry for measuring inventories of large numbers of rapidly changing items with similar margins for which it is impractical to use other costing methods.

The cost of inventory is determined by reducing the sales value of the inventory by the appropriate percentage gross margin. The percentage takes into consideration inventory that has been marked down to below its original selling price. An average percentage for each retail department is often used.

Standard costs

Standard costs are predetermined unit costs used by many manufacturing firms for planning and control purposes. Standard costing is often useful for management (internal) reporting under some conditions. The use of standard costs in financial reporting is acceptable if adjustments are made periodically to reflect current conditions and if its use approximates one of the recognised cost flow assumptions. If appropriate, standard costs are incorporated into the accounts, and materials, work in progress and finished goods inventories are all carried on this basis of accounting.

Inventories valued at fair value less costs to sell. In the case of commodity broker-traders' inventories, IAS 2 permits that these inventories can be valued at fair value less costs to sell. While allowing this exceptional treatment for inventories of commodity broker-traders, IAS 2 makes it mandatory that in such cases the fair value changes should be reported in the profit and loss account for the period of change.

Disclosure Requirements

IAS 2 sets forth certain disclosure requirements relative to inventory accounting methods employed by the reporting entity. According to this standard, the following must be disclosed:

1. The accounting policies adopted in measuring inventories, including the costing methods (e.g., FIFO or weighted-average) employed.

2. The total carrying amount of inventories and the carrying amount in classifications appropriate to the entity.
3. The carrying amount of inventories carried at fair value less costs to sell (inventories of commodity broker-traders).
4. The amount of inventories recognised as an expense during the period.
5. The amount of any write-down of inventories recognised as an expense in the period.
6. The amount of any reversal of any previous write-down that is recognised in profit or loss for the period.
7. The circumstances or events that led to the reversal of a write-down of inventories to net realisable value.
8. The carrying amount of inventories pledged as security for liabilities.

The type of information to be provided concerning inventories held in different classifications is somewhat flexible, but traditional classifications, such as raw materials, work in progress, finished goods and supplies, should normally be employed. In the case of service providers, inventories (which are really similar to unbilled receivables) can be described as work in progress.

In addition to the foregoing, the financial statements should disclose either the cost of inventories recognised as an expense during the period (i.e., reported as cost of sales or included in other expense categories), or the operating costs, applicable to revenues, recognised as an expense during the period, categorised by their respective natures.

Costs of inventories recognised as expense include, in addition to the costs inventoried previously and attaching to goods sold currently, the excess overhead costs charged to expense for the period because, under the standard, they could not be deferred to future periods.

EXAMPLES OF FINANCIAL STATEMENT DISCLOSURES

Exemplum Reporting PLC
Financial Statements
For the year ended December 31, 20XX

IAS 2 p36 p37

Inventories

	20XX	20XX-1
Raw materials	**X**	X
Work in progress	**X**	X
Finished goods	**X**	X
	X	X

Inventories to the value of €X are carried at net realisable value. Inventory written-down during the year amounted to €X (20XX-1: €X).

Inventory with a carrying amount of €X (20XX-1: €X) has been pledged as security for liabilities. The holder of the security does not have the right to sell or re-pledge the inventory in the absence of default. IFRS 7 p14

A prior year write-down of inventories amounting to €X was reversed in the year under review. This was as a result of a change in market conditions which resulted in an increased demand for the product. IAS 2 p36(g)

US GAAP COMPARISON

Accounting for inventory under US GAAP is mainly found under Topic 330 *Inventory* of FASB Accounting Standard Codification and is essentially the same except for inherent differences in measurement of costs (i.e., fair value where applicable, capitalised interest where applicable). The LIFO cost method is permitted under US GAAP. This cost method is used primarily for oil and gas companies to minimise taxable income. The US Tax Code contains a concept called book-tax conformity that would prohibit deductions under LIFO if it is not the primary cost model.

US GAAP measures all inventories at the lower of cost or net realisable value. Net realisable value is the estimated selling price less predictable costs of completion, disposal and transportation. US GAAP requires inventory with costs determined by a method other than the LIFO or retail method to be measured at the lower of cost or net realisable value and in line with IFRS when inventory cost is determined using either the FIFO or average cost methods. However, inventory with costs determined by the LIFO or retail method are measured at the lower of cost and market value under US GAAP.

US GAAP does not permit write-backs of previously recognised write-downs to net realisable value. The written-down value is the new basis. Permanent markdowns do not affect the ratios used in applying the retail inventory method. Permanent markdowns are added to the inventory after the ratio is calculated. US GAAP does not require recognition in interim periods of inventory losses from market declines that reasonably can be expected to be restored in the fiscal year.

Unlike IAS 2, US GAAP does not require that an entity use the same formula for all inventories of a similar nature and with a similar use to the entity.

9 PROPERTY, PLANT AND EQUIPMENT

INTRODUCTION

Long-lived tangible and intangible assets (which include property, plant and equipment as well as development costs, various intellectual property intangibles and goodwill) hold the promise of providing economic benefits to an entity for a period greater than that covered by the current year's financial statements. Accordingly, these assets must be capitalised rather than immediately expensed, and their costs must be allocated over the expected periods of benefit for the reporting entity. IFRS for long-lived assets address matters such as the determination of the amounts at which to initially record the acquisitions of such assets, the amounts at which to present these assets at subsequent reporting dates and the appropriate method(s) by which to allocate the assets' costs to future periods. Under current IFRS, the standard allows for a choice between historical cost and revaluation of long-lived assets.

Long-lived non-financial assets are primarily operational in character (i.e., actively used in the business rather than being held as passive investments), and they may be classified into two basic types: tangible and intangible. *Tangible assets*, which are the subject of the present chapter, have physical substance. *Intangible assets*, on the other hand, have no physical substance. The value of an intangible asset is a function of the rights or privileges that its ownership conveys to the business entity. Intangible assets, which are explored at length in Chapter 11, can be further categorised as being either (1) identifiable, or (2) unidentifiable (i.e., goodwill), and further subcategorised as being finite-life assets and indefinite-life assets.

Long-lived assets are sometimes acquired in non-monetary transactions, either in exchanges of assets between the entity and another business organisation, or else when assets are given as capital contributions by shareholders to the entity. IAS 16 requires such transactions to be measured at fair value, unless they lack commercial substance.

It is increasingly the case that assets are acquired or constructed with an attendant obligation to dismantle, restore the environment or otherwise clean up after the end of the assets' useful lives. Decommissioning costs have to be estimated at initial recognition of the asset and recognised, in most instances, as additional asset cost and as a provision, thus causing the costs to be spread over the useful lives of the assets via depreciation charges.

Measurement and presentation of long-lived assets subsequent to acquisition or construction involves both systematic allocation of cost to accounting periods and possible special write-downs. Concerning cost allocation to periods of use, IFRS requires a "components approach" to depreciation. Thus, significant elements of an asset (in the case of a building, such components as the main structure, roofing, heating plant and elevators, for instance) are to be separated from the cost paid for the asset and amortised over their various appropriate useful lives.

When there is any diminution in the value of a long-lived asset, IAS 36, *Impairment of Assets*, should be applied in determining what, if any, impairment should be recognised.

This Standard shall be applied in accounting for property, plant and equipment except when another Standard requires or permits a different accounting treatment.

Property, plant and equipment specifically exclude the following:

- Property, plant and equipment classified as held for sale (refer to Chapter 13).
- Biological assets related to agriculture activities, other than bearer plants (refer to Chapter 31).
- Recognition and measurement of exploration and evaluation assets (refer to Chapter 32).
- Mineral rights and mineral reserves such as oil, nature gas and similar non-generative resources (refer to Chapter 32).

Sources of IFRS		
IFRS 5, 8	*IAS* 16, 36, 37	*IFRIC* 1, 17

DEFINITIONS OF TERMS

Bearer plant. This is a living plant which has all of the following characteristics: it is used to supply or produce agricultural products; it will provide output for a period greater than one year and for which the possibility of it being sold as agricultural produce is remote.

Carrying amount. Carrying amount of property, plant and equipment is the amount at which an asset is recognised after deducting any accumulated depreciation and accumulated impairment losses.

Cost. Amount of cash or cash equivalent paid or the fair value of the other consideration given to acquire an asset at the time of its acquisition or construction or, where applicable, the amount attributed to that asset when initially recognised in accordance with the specific requirements of other IFRS standards (e.g., IFRS 2, *Share-Based Payment*).

Depreciable amount. Cost of an asset or the other amount that has been substituted for cost, less the residual value.

Depreciation. The process of allocating the depreciable amount (cost less residual value) of an asset over its useful life.

Fair value. The price that would be received to sell an asset or paid to transfer a liability in an orderly transaction between market participants at the measurement date (see Chapter 25).

Impairment loss. The excess of the carrying amount of an asset over its recoverable amount.

Property, plant and equipment. Tangible assets that are used in the production or supply of goods or services, for rental to others or for administrative purposes and that will benefit the entity during more than one accounting period. Also referred to as fixed assets.

Recoverable amount. The greater of an asset's fair value less costs to sell or its value in use.

Residual value. Estimated amount that an entity would currently obtain from disposal of the asset, net of estimated costs of disposal, if the asset were already of the age and in the condition expected at the end of its useful life.

Useful life. Period over which an asset is expected to be available for use by an entity, or the number of production or similar units expected to be obtained from the asset by an entity.

RECOGNITION AND MEASUREMENT

An item of property, plant and equipment should be recognised as an asset only if two conditions are met: (1) it is probable that future economic benefits associated with the item will flow to the entity, and (2) the cost of the item can be determined reliably. Spare parts and servicing equipment are usually carried as inventory and expensed as consumed. However, major spare parts and standby equipment may be used during more than one period, thereby being similar to other items of property, plant and equipment. The 2011 Improvements Project amended IAS 16 to clarify that major spare parts and standby equipment are recognised as property, plant and equipment if they meet the definition of property, plant and equipment, failing which they are recognised as inventories under IAS 2, *Inventories*.

There are four concerns to be addressed in accounting for long-lived assets:

1. The amount at which the assets should be recorded initially on acquisition;
2. How value changes subsequent to acquisition should be reflected in the financial statements, including questions of both value increases and possible decreases due to impairments;
3. The rate at which the assets' recorded value should be allocated as an expense to future periods; and
4. The recording of the ultimate disposal of the assets.

Initial measurement

The standard has not prescribed any specific unit of measure to recognise property, plant and equipment. Thus, judgement may be applied in determining what constitutes an item of property, plant and equipment. At times, disaggregation of an item (as in componentisation) may be appropriate and at times aggregation of individually insignificant items such as mould, dies and tools may be appropriate, to apply the recognition criteria to the aggregate value.

All costs required to bring an asset into working condition should be recorded as part of the cost of the asset. Elements of such costs include:

1. Its purchase price, including legal and brokerage fees, import duties and non-refundable purchase taxes, after deducting trade discounts and rebates;
2. Any directly attributable costs incurred to bring the asset to the location and operating condition as expected by management, including the costs of site preparation, delivery and handling, installation, set-up and testing; and
3. Estimated costs of dismantling and removing the item and restoring the site.

Government grants may be reduced to arrive at the carrying amount of the asset, in accordance with IAS 20, *Accounting for Government Grants and Disclosure of Government Assistance.*

These costs are capitalised and are not to be expensed in the period in which they are incurred, as they are deemed to add value to the asset and were necessary expenditures in acquiring the asset.

The costs required to bring acquired assets to the place where they are to be used includes such ancillary costs as testing and calibrating, where relevant. IAS 16 aims to draw a distinction between the costs of getting the asset to the state in which it is in a condition to be exploited (which are to be included in the asset's carrying amount) and costs associated with the start-up operations, such as staff training, downtime between completion of the asset and the start of its exploitation, losses incurred through running at below normal capacity, etc., which are considered to be operating expenses. Any revenues that are earned from the asset during the installation process are netted off against the costs incurred in preparing the asset for use. As an example, the standard cites the sales of samples produced during this procedure.

IAS 16 distinguishes the situation described in the preceding paragraph from other situations where incidental operations unrelated to the asset may occur before or during the construction or development activities. For example, it notes that income may be earned through using a building site as a car parking lot until construction begins. Because incidental operations such as this are not necessary to bring the asset to the location and working condition necessary for it to be capable of operating in the manner intended by management, the income and related expenses of incidental operations are to be recognised in current earnings and included in their respective classifications of income and expense in profit or loss. These are not to be presented net, as in the earlier example of machine testing costs and sample sales revenues.

Administrative costs, as well as other types of overhead costs, are not normally allocated to fixed asset acquisitions, despite the fact that some costs, such as the salaries of the personnel who evaluate assets for proposed acquisitions, are in fact incurred as part of the acquisition process. As a general principle, administrative costs are expensed in the period incurred, based on the perception that these costs are fixed and would not be avoided in the absence of asset acquisitions. On the other hand, truly incremental costs, such as a consulting fee or commission paid to an agent hired specifically to assist in the acquisition, may be treated as part of the initial amount to be recognised as the asset cost.

While interest costs incurred during the construction of certain *qualifying* assets must be added to the cost of the asset under IAS 23, *Borrowing Costs* (see Chapter 10), if an asset is purchased on deferred payment terms, the interest cost, whether made explicit or imputed, is *not* part of the cost of the asset. Accordingly, such costs must be expensed currently as interest charges. If the purchase price for the asset incorporates a deferred payment scheme, only the cash equivalent price should be capitalised as the initial carrying amount of the asset. If the cash equivalent price is not explicitly stated, the deferred payment amount should be reduced to present value by the application of an appropriate discount rate. This would normally be best approximated by use of the entity's incremental borrowing cost for debt having a maturity similar to the deferred payment term, taking into account the risks relating to the asset under question that a financier would necessarily take into account.

Decommissioning cost included in initial measurement

The elements of cost to be incorporated in the initial recognition of an asset are to include the estimated costs of its eventual dismantlement ("decommissioning costs"). That is, the cost of the asset is "grossed up" for these estimated terminal costs, with the offsetting credit being posted to a liability account. It is important to stress that recognition of a liability can only be effected when all the criteria set forth in IAS 37, *Provisions, Contingent Liabilities and Contingent Assets*, for the recognition of provisions are met. These stipulate that a provision is to be recognised only when:

1. The reporting entity has a present obligation, whether legal or constructive, as a result of a *past* event;
2. It is *probable* that an outflow of resources embodying economic benefits will be required to settle the obligation; and
3. A reliable estimate can be made of the amount of the obligation.

For example, assume that it was necessary to secure a government licence to construct a particular asset, such as a power generating plant, and a condition of the licence is that at the end of the expected life of the property the owner would dismantle it, remove any debris and restore the land to its previous condition. These conditions would qualify as a present obligation resulting from a past event (the construction of the plant), which will probably result in a future outflow of resources. The cost of such future activities, while perhaps challenging to estimate due to the long-time horizon involved and the possible intervening evolution of technology, can normally be accomplished with a requisite degree of accuracy. Per IAS 37, a best estimate is to be made of the future costs, which is then to be discounted to present value. This present value is to be recognised as an additional cost of acquiring the asset.

The cost of dismantlement and similar legal or constructive obligations do not extend to operating costs to be incurred in the future, since those would not qualify as "present obligations." The precise mechanism for making these computations is addressed in Chapter 18.

If estimated costs of dismantlement, removal and restoration are included in the cost of the asset, the effect will be to allocate this cost over the life of the asset through the depreciation process. Each period the discounting of the provision should be "unwound," such that interest cost is accreted each period. If this is done, at the expected date on which the expenditure is to be incurred the provision will be appropriately stated. The increase in the carrying amount of the provision should be reported as interest expense or a similar financing cost.

Examples of decommissioning or similar costs to be recognised at acquisition

Example 1—Leased premises. In accordance with the terms of a lease, the lessee is obligated to remove its specialised machinery from the leased premises prior to vacating those premises, or to compensate the lessor accordingly. The lease imposes a contractual obligation on the lessee to remove the asset at the end of the asset's useful life or upon vacating the premises, and therefore in this situation an asset (i.e., deferred cost) and liability should be recognised. If the lease is a finance lease, it is added to the asset cost; if an operating lease (less likely), a deferred charge would be reported.

Example 2—Owned premises. The same machinery described in Example 1 is installed in a factory that the entity owns. At the end of the useful life of the machinery, the entity will either incur costs to dismantle and remove the asset or will leave it idle in place. If the entity chooses to do nothing (i.e., not remove the equipment), this would adversely affect the fair value of the premises should the entity choose to sell the premises on an "as is" basis. Conceptually, to apply the matching principle in a manner consistent with Example 1, the cost of asset retirement should be recognised systematically and rationally over the productive life of the asset and not in the period of retirement. However, in this example there is no *legal obligation* on the part of the owner of the factory and equipment to retire the asset and, thus, a cost would *not* be recognised at inception for this possible future loss of value.

Example 3—Promissory estoppel. Assume the same facts as in Example 2. In this case, however, the owner of the property sold to a third party an option to purchase the factory, exercisable at the end of five years. In offering the option to the third party, the owner verbally represented that the factory would be completely vacant at the end of the five-year option period and that all machinery, furniture and fixtures would be removed from the premises. The property owner would reasonably expect that the purchaser of the option relied to the purchaser's detriment (as evidenced by the financial sacrifice of consideration made in exchange for the option) on the representation that the factory would be vacant. While the legal status of such a promise may vary depending on local custom and law, in general this is a constructive obligation and should be recognised as a decommissioning cost and related liability.

Example of timing of recognition of decommissioning cost

Teradactyl Corporation owns and operates a chemical company. At its premises, it maintains underground tanks used to store various types of chemicals. The tanks were installed when Teradactyl Corporation purchased its facilities seven years prior. On February 1, 20XX, the legislature of the nation passed a law that requires removal of such tanks when they are no longer being used. Since the law imposes a legal obligation on Teradactyl Corporation, upon enactment, recognition of a decommissioning obligation would be required.

Example of ongoing additions to the decommissioning obligation

Jermyn Manufacturing Corporation operates a factory. As part of its normal operations it stores production by-products and uses cleaning solvents on site in a reservoir specifically designed for that purpose. The reservoir and surrounding land, all owned by Jermyn Manufacturing

Corporation, are contaminated with these chemicals. On February 1, 20XX, the legislature of the nation enacted a law that requires cleanup and disposal of hazardous waste from existing production processes upon retirement of the facility. Upon the enactment of the law, immediate recognition would be required for the decommissioning obligation associated with the contamination that had already occurred. In addition, liabilities will continue to be recognised over the remaining life of the facility as additional contamination occurs.

Changes in decommissioning costs

IFRIC 1 addresses the accounting treatment to be followed where a provision for reinstatement and dismantling costs has been created when an asset was acquired. The Interpretation requires that where estimates of future costs are revised, these should be applied prospectively only, and there is no adjustment to past years' depreciation. IFRIC 1 is addressed in Chapter 18 of this publication.

Initial recognition of self-constructed assets

Essentially the same principles that have been established for recognition of the cost of purchased assets also apply to self-constructed assets. Bearer plants, which from January 1, 2016 are included in the scope of IAS 16, are accounted for in the same manner as self-constructed assets until the point where they are capable of being used in the manner intended by the entity.

All costs that must be incurred to complete the construction of the asset can be added to the amount to be recognised initially, subject only to the constraint that if these costs exceed the recoverable amount (as discussed fully later in this chapter), the excess must be expensed as an impairment loss. This rule is necessary to avoid the "gold-plated hammer syndrome," whereby a misguided or unfortunate asset construction project incurs excessive costs that then find their way into the statement of financial position, consequently overstating the entity's current net worth and distorting future periods' earnings. Of course, internal (intragroup) profits cannot be allocated to construction costs. The standard specifies that "abnormal amounts" of wasted material, labour or other resources may not be added to the cost of the asset.

Self-constructed assets should include, in addition to the range of costs discussed earlier, the cost of borrowed funds used during the period of construction. Capitalisation of borrowing costs, as set forth by IAS 23, is discussed in Chapter 10.

Exchanges of assets

IAS 16 discusses the accounting to be applied to those situations in which assets are exchanged for other similar or dissimilar assets, with or without the additional consideration of monetary assets. This topic is addressed later in this chapter under the heading "Nonmonetary (Exchange) Transactions."

Costs incurred subsequent to purchase or self-construction

Costs that are incurred subsequent to the purchase or construction of the long-lived asset, such as those for repairs, maintenance or betterments, may involve an adjustment to the carrying amount, or may be expensed, depending on the precise facts and circumstances.

To qualify for capitalisation, the costs must meet the recognition criteria of an asset. For example, modifications to the asset made to extend its useful life (measured either in years or in units of potential production) or to increase its capacity (e.g., as measured by units of output per hour) would be capitalised. Similarly, if the expenditure results in an improved quality of output or permits a reduction in other cost inputs (e.g., would result in labour savings), it is a candidate for capitalisation. Where a modification involves changing part of the asset (e.g., substituting a stronger power source), the cost of the part that is removed should be derecognised (treated as a disposal).

For example, roofs of commercial buildings, linings of blast furnaces used for steel making and engines of commercial aircraft all need to be replaced or overhauled before the related buildings, furnaces or aircraft themselves are replaced. If componentised depreciation was properly employed, the roofs, linings and engines were being depreciated over their respectively shorter useful lives, and when the replacements or overhauls are performed, on average, these will have been fully depreciated. To the extent that undepreciated costs of these components remain, they would have to be removed from the account (i.e., charged to expense in the period of replacement or overhaul) as the newly incurred replacement or overhaul costs are added to the asset accounts, to avoid having, for financial reporting purposes, "two roofs on one building."

It can usually be assumed that ordinary maintenance and repair expenditures will occur on a rateable basis over the life of the asset and should be charged to expenses as incurred. Thus, if the purpose of the expenditure is either to maintain the productive capacity anticipated when the asset was acquired or constructed, or to restore it to that level, the costs are not subject to capitalisation.

A partial exception is encountered if an asset is acquired in a condition that necessitates that certain expenditures be incurred to put it into the appropriate state for its intended use. For example, a deteriorated building may be purchased with the intention that it be restored and then utilised as a factory or office facility. In such cases, costs that otherwise would be categorised as ordinary maintenance items might be subject to capitalisation. Once the restoration is completed, further expenditures of a similar type would be viewed as being ordinary repairs or maintenance, and thus expensed as incurred.

However, costs associated with required inspections (e.g., of aircraft) could be capitalised and depreciated. These costs would be amortised over the expected period of benefit (i.e., the estimated time to the next inspection). As with the cost of physical assets, removal of any undepreciated costs of previous inspections would be required. The capitalised inspection cost would have to be treated as a separate component of the asset.

Depreciation of property, plant and equipment

The costs of property, plant and equipment are allocated through depreciation to the periods that will have benefited from the use of the asset. Whatever method of depreciation is chosen, it must result in the systematic and rational allocation of the depreciable amount of the asset (initial cost less residual value) over the asset's expected useful life. The determination of the useful life must take a number of factors into consideration. These factors include technological change, normal deterioration, actual physical use and legal or other limitations on the ability to use the property. The method of depreciation is based on whether the useful life is determined as a function of time or as a function of actual physical usage.

IAS 16 states that, although land normally has an unlimited useful life and is not to be depreciated, where the cost of the land includes estimated dismantlement or restoration costs, these are to be depreciated over the period of benefits obtained by incurring those costs. In some cases, the land itself may have a limited useful life, in which case it is to be depreciated in a manner that reflects the benefits to be derived from it.

IAS 16 requires that depreciation of an asset commences when it is available to use, i.e., when it is in the location and condition necessary for it to be capable of operating in the manner intended by management. Depreciation of an asset ceases at the earlier date of when the asset is derecognised and when the asset is classified as held for sale.

Since, under the historical cost convention, depreciation accounting is intended as a strategy for cost allocation, it does not reflect changes in the market value of the asset being depreciated (except in some cases where the impairment rules have been applied in that way—as discussed below). Thus, with the exception of land, which has indefinite useful life, all tangible property, plant and equipment must be depreciated, even if (as sometimes occurs, particularly in periods of general price inflation) their nominal or real values increase. Furthermore, if the recorded amount of the asset is allocated over a period of time (as opposed to actual use), it should be the expected period of usefulness to the entity, not the physical or economic life of the asset itself that governs. Thus, concerns such as technological obsolescence, as well as normal wear and tear, must be addressed in the initial determination of the period over which to allocate the asset cost. The reporting entity's strategy for repairs and maintenance will also affect this computation, since the same physical asset might have a longer or shorter useful life in the hands of differing owners, depending on the care with which it is intended to be maintained.

Similarly, the same asset may have a longer or shorter useful life, depending on its intended use. A particular building, for example, may have a 50-year expected life as a facility for storing goods or for use in light manufacturing, but as a showroom would have a shorter period of usefulness, due to the anticipated disinclination of customers to shop at entities housed in older premises. Again, it is not physical life, but useful life, that should govern.

Compound assets, such as buildings containing such disparate components as heating plant, roofs and other structural elements, are most commonly recorded in several separate accounts to facilitate the process of depreciating the different elements over varying periods. Thus, a heating plant may have an expected useful life of 20 years, the roof a life of 15 years and the basic structure itself a life of 40 years. Maintaining separate ledger accounts eases the calculation of periodic depreciation in such situations, although for financial reporting purposes a greater degree of aggregation is usual.

IAS 16 requires a component approach for depreciation, where, as described above, each significant component of a composite asset with different useful lives or different patterns of depreciation is accounted for separately for the purpose of depreciation and accounting for subsequent expenditure (including replacement and renewal). Thus, rather than recording a newly acquired or existing office building as a single asset, it is recorded as a building shell, a heating plant, a roof and perhaps other discrete mechanical components, subject to a materiality threshold. Allocation of cost over useful lives, instead of being based on a weighted-average of the varying components' lives, is based on separate estimated lives for each component.

The depreciation is usually charged to the statement of profit and loss. However, there could be exceptions wherein such depreciation costs are included in the cost of another asset, if the depreciation was incurred in the construction of another asset in which the future economic benefit of such use is embodied. In such cases, the depreciation could be added to the cost and carrying value of such property, plant and equipment. It is also provided under IAS 2, *Inventories*, and IAS 38, *Intangible Assets*, for depreciation to be added to the cost of the inventory manufactured or cost of the intangible, if it meets the requirements of these standards.

IAS 16 states that the depreciation method should reflect the pattern in which the asset's future economic benefits are expected to be consumed by the entity, and that appropriateness of the method should be reviewed at least annually in case there has been a change in the expected pattern. Beyond that, the standard leaves the choice of method to the entity, even though it does cite straight-line, diminishing balance and units of production as possible depreciation methods.

A depreciation method that is based on revenues that are generated by activities including the use of an asset are not appropriate, as revenue generally reflects factors other than the consumption of the economic benefits inherent within an asset.

Depreciation Methods Based on Time

1. *Straight-line*—Depreciation expense is incurred evenly over the life of the asset. The periodic charge for depreciation is given as:

$$\frac{\text{Cost or amount substituted for cost less residual value}}{\text{Estimated useful life of asset}}$$

2. *Accelerated methods*—Depreciation expense is higher in the early years of the asset's useful life and lower in the later years. IAS 16 only mentions one accelerated method, the diminishing balance method, but other methods have been employed in various national GAAP under earlier or contemporary accounting standards.

   a. Diminishing balance—the depreciation rate is applied to the net carrying amount of the asset, resulting in a diminishing annual charge. There are various ways to compute the percentage to be applied. The formula below provides a mathematically correct allocation over useful life:

$$\text{Rate}\ \% = \left(1\sqrt[n]{\text{Residual value}}\right)\times 100$$

   where n is the expected useful life in years. However, companies generally use approximations or conventions influenced by tax practice, such as a multiple of the straight-line rate times the net carrying amount at the beginning of the year:

$$\text{Straight-line rate} = \frac{1}{\text{Estimated useful life}}$$

   b. Double-declining balance depreciation (if salvage value is to be recognised, stop when carrying amount = estimated salvage value):

$$\text{Depreciation} = 2 \times \text{Straight-line rate} \times \text{Carrying amount at beginning of year}$$

Another method to accomplish a diminishing charge for depreciation is the sum-of-the-years' digits method, which is commonly employed in the US and certain other venues.

c. Sum-of-the years' digits (SYD) depreciation = (Cost less salvage value) × Applicable fraction

$$\text{where applicable fraction} = \frac{\text{Number of years of estimated life remaining as of the beginning of the year}}{\text{SYD}}$$

$$\text{and SYD} = \frac{n(n+1)}{2} \text{ and } n = \text{estimated useful life.}$$

Example

An asset having a useful economic life of 5 years and no salvage value would have 5/15 (= 1/3) of its cost allocated to year 1, 4/15 to year 2 and so on.

In practice, unless there are tax reasons to employ accelerated methods, large companies tend to use straight-line depreciation. This has the merit that it is simple to apply, and where a company has a large pool of similar assets, some of which are replaced each year, the aggregate annual depreciation charge is likely to be the same, irrespective of the method chosen (consider a trucking company that has 10 trucks, each costing €200,000, one of which is replaced each year: the aggregate annual depreciation charge will be €200,000 under any mathematically accurate depreciation method).

Partial-year depreciation

Although IAS 16 is silent on the matter, when an asset is either acquired or disposed of during the year, the full year depreciation calculation should be prorated between the accounting periods involved. This is necessary to achieve proper matching. However, if individual assets in a relatively homogeneous group are regularly acquired and disposed of, one of several conventions can be adopted, as follows:

1. Record a full year's depreciation in the year of acquisition and none in the year of disposal.
2. Record one-half year's depreciation in the year of acquisition and one-half year's depreciation in the year of disposal.

Example of partial-year depreciation

Assume the following: Taj Mahal Milling Co., a calendar-year entity, acquired a machine on June 1, 20XX that cost €40,000 with an estimated useful life of four years and a €2,500 salvage value. The depreciation expense for each full year of the asset's life is calculated as follows:

	Straight-line	Double-declining balance	*Sum-of-years'* digits
Year 1	€37,500* ÷ 4 = €9,375	50% × €40,000 = €20,000	4/10 × €37,500* = €15,000
Year 2	€9,375	50% × €20,000 = €10,000	3/10 × €37,500 = €11,250
Year 3	€9,375	50% × €10,000 = €5,000	2/10 × €37,500 = €7,500
Year 4	€9,375	50% × €5,000 = €2,500	1/10 × €37,500 = €3,750

*€40,000–€2,500.

Because the first full year of the asset's life does not coincide with the company's fiscal year, the amounts shown above must be prorated as follows:

	Straight-line	Double-declining balance	*Sum-of-years'* digits
20XX	7/12 × 9,375 = €5,469	7/12 × €20,000 = €11,667	7/12 × €15,000 = €8,750
20XX+1	€9,375	5/12 × €20,000 = €8,333	5/12 × €15,000 = €6,250
		7/12 × €10,000 = €5,833	7/12 × €11,250 = €6,563
		Carrying amount = €14,166	Carrying amount = €18,438
20XX+2	€9,375	5/12 × €10,000 = €4,167	5/12 × €11,250 = €4,687
		7/12 × €5,000 = €2,917	7/12 × €7,500 = €4,375
		Carrying amount = €7,084	Carrying amount = €9,375
20XX+3	€9,375	5/12 × €5,000 = €2,083	5/12 × €7,500 = €3,125
		7/12 × €2,500 = €1,458	7/12 × €3,750 = €2,188
		Carrying amount = €3,541	Carrying amount = €4,063
20XX+4	5/12 × 9,375 = €3,906	5/12 × €2,500 = €1,042	5/12 × €3,750 = €1,562
	Carrying amount = €2,500	Carrying amount = €2,500	Carrying amount = €2,500

Depreciation method based on actual physical use—units of production method

Depreciation may also be based on the number of units produced by the asset in a given year. IAS 16 identifies this as the units of production method, but it is also known as the sum of the units approach. It is best suited to those assets, such as machinery, that have an expected life that is most rationally defined in terms of productive output; in periods of reduced production (such as economic recession) the machinery is used less, thus extending the number of years it is likely to remain in service. This method has the merit that the annual depreciation expense fluctuates with the contribution made by the asset each year. Furthermore, if the depreciation finds its way into the cost of finished goods, the unit cost in periods of reduced production would be exaggerated and could even exceed net realisable value unless the units of production approach to depreciation was taken.

$$\text{Depreciation rate} = \frac{\text{Cost less residual value}}{\text{Estimated number of units to be produced by the asset over its estimated useful life}}$$

Units of production depreciation = Depreciation rate × Number of units produced during the period.

Residual value

Most depreciation methods discussed above require that depreciation is applied not to the full cost of the asset, but to the "depreciable amount"; that is, the historical cost or amount substituted therefor (i.e., fair value) less the estimated residual value of the asset. As IAS 16 points out, residual value is often not material and in practice is frequently ignored, but it may impact upon some assets, particularly when the entity disposes of them early in their life (e.g., rental vehicles) or where the residual value is so high as to negate any requirement for depreciation (some hotel companies, for example, claim that they have to maintain their premises to such a high standard that their residual value under historical cost is higher than the original cost of the asset).

Under IAS 16, residual value is defined as the estimated amount that an entity would currently obtain from disposal of the asset, after deducting the estimated costs of disposal, if the asset were already of the age and in the condition expected at the end of its useful life. The residual value is, like all aspects of the depreciation method, subject to at least annual review.

If the revaluation method of measuring property, plant and equipment is chosen, residual value must be assessed anew at the date of each revaluation of the asset. This is accomplished by using data on realisable values for similar assets, ending their respective useful lives at the time of the revaluation, after having been used for purposes similar to the asset being valued. Again, no consideration can be paid to anticipated inflation, and expected future values are not to be discounted to present values to give recognition to the time value of money.

Useful lives

Useful life is affected by such things as the entity's practices regarding repairs and maintenance of its assets, as well as the pace of technological change and the market demand for goods produced and sold by the entity using the assets as productive inputs. Useful life is also affected by the usage pattern of the asset, such as the number of shifts the asset is put to use in the operations and at times the useful life determined considering this may require a relook when, say, originally the useful life was determined based on single shift operation and now the company's operations have become double or triple shift and is likely to continue at such pace in the future. If it is determined, when reviewing the depreciation method, that the estimated life is greater or less than previously believed, the change is treated as a change in accounting estimate, not as a correction of an accounting error. Accordingly, no restatement is to be made to previously reported depreciation; rather, the change is accounted for strictly on a prospective basis, being reflected in the period of change and subsequent periods.

Example of estimating useful life

An asset with a cost of €100,000 was originally estimated to have a productive life of 10 years. The straight-line method is used, and there was no residual value anticipated. After two years, management revises its estimate of useful life to a total of six years. Since the net carrying amount of the asset is €80,000 after two years (= €100,000 × 8/10), and the remaining expected life is four years (two of the six revised total years having already elapsed), depreciation in years three to six will be €20,000 (= €80,000/4) each.

Tax methods

The methods of computing depreciation discussed in the foregoing sections relate only to financial reporting under IFRS. Tax laws in the different nations of the world vary widely in terms of the acceptability of depreciation methods, and it is not possible to address all these. However, to the extent that depreciation allowable for income tax reporting purposes differs from that required or permitted for financial statement purposes, deferred income taxes would have to be computed. Deferred tax is discussed in Chapter 26.

Leasehold improvements

Leasehold improvements are improvements to property not owned by the party making these investments. For example, a lessee of office space may invest its funds to install partitions or to combine several suites by removing certain interior walls. Due to the nature of these physical changes to the property (done with the lessor's permission, of course), the lessee cannot remove or undo these changes and must abandon them upon termination of the lease, if the lessee does not remain in the facility.

A frequently encountered issue with respect to leasehold improvements relates to determination of the period over which they are to be amortised. Normally, the cost of long-lived assets is charged to expense over the estimated useful lives of the assets. However, the right to use a leasehold improvement expires when the related lease expires, irrespective of whether the improvement has any remaining useful life. Thus, the appropriate useful life for a leasehold improvement is the lesser of the useful life of the improvement or the term of the underlying lease.

Some leases contain a fixed, non-cancellable term and additional renewal options. When considering the term of the lease for the purposes of depreciating leasehold improvements, normally only the initial fixed non-cancellable term is included. There are, however, exceptions to this general rule. If a renewal option is a bargain renewal option, which means that it is probable at the inception of the lease that it will be exercised, the option period should be included in the lease term for purposes of determining the amortisable life of the leasehold improvements. Additionally, under the definition of the lease term there are other situations where it is probable that an option to renew for an additional period would be exercised. These situations include periods for which failure to renew the lease imposes a penalty on the lessee in such amount that a renewal appears, at the inception of the lease, to be reasonably assured. Other situations of this kind arise when an otherwise excludable renewal period precedes a provision for a bargain purchase of the leased asset or when, during periods covered by ordinary renewal options, the lessee has guaranteed the lessor's debt on the leased property.

Example

Mojo Corporation occupies a warehouse under a five-year operating lease commencing January 1, 20XX, and expiring December 31, 20XX+4. The lease contains three successive options to renew the lease for additional five-year periods. The options are not bargain renewals as they call for fixed rentals at the prevailing fair market rents that will be in effect at the time of exercise. When the initial calculation was made to determine whether the lease is an operating lease or a finance lease, only the initial non-cancellable term of five years was included in the calculation. Consequently, for the purpose of determining the depreciable life of any leasehold improvements made by Mojo Corporation, only the initial five-year term is used. If Mojo Corporation decides, at the beginning of year four of the lease, to make a substantial amount of leasehold improvements to the leased property, it could be argued that it would now be probable that Mojo would exercise one or more of the renewal periods, since not doing so would impose the substantial financial penalty for abandoning expensive leasehold improvements.

Revaluation of Property, Plant and Equipment

IAS 16 provides for two acceptable alternative approaches to accounting for long-lived tangible assets. The first of these is the historical cost method, under which acquisition or construction cost is used for initial recognition, subject to depreciation over the expected useful life and to possible write-down in the event of a permanent impairment in value. In many jurisdictions this is the only method allowed by statute, but a number of jurisdictions, particularly those with significant rates of inflation, do permit either full or selective revaluation and IAS 16 acknowledges this by also allowing what it calls the "revaluation model." Under the revaluation model, after initial recognition as an asset, an item of property, plant and equipment whose fair value can be measured reliably should be carried at a revalued amount, being its fair value at the date of the revaluation less any subsequent accumulated depreciation and subsequent accumulated impairment losses.

The logic of recognising revaluations relates to both the statement of financial position and the measure of periodic performance provided by the statement of profit or loss and other comprehensive income. Due to the effects of inflation (which even if quite moderate when measured on an annual basis can compound dramatically during the lengthy period over which property, plant and equipment remain in use) the statement of financial position can become a virtually meaningless agglomeration of dissimilar costs.

Furthermore, if the depreciation charge to income is determined by reference to historical costs of assets acquired in much earlier periods, profits will be overstated, and will not reflect the cost of maintaining the entity's asset base. Under these circumstances, a nominally profitable entity might find that it has self-liquidated and is unable to continue in existence, at least not with the same level of productive capacity, without new debt or equity infusions. IAS 29, *Financial Reporting in Hyperinflationary Economies*, addresses adjustments to depreciation under conditions of hyperinflation.

Under the revaluation model the frequency of revaluations depends upon the changes in fair values of the items being revalued and, consequently, when the fair value of a revalued asset differs materially from its carrying amount, a further revaluation is required.

Fair value

As the basis for the revaluation method, the standard stipulates that it is fair value (defined as the price that would be received to sell an asset or paid to transfer a liability in an orderly transaction between market participants at the measurement date) that is to be used in any such revaluations. Furthermore, the standard requires that, once an entity undertakes revaluations, they must continue to be made with sufficient regularity that the carrying amounts in any subsequent statements of financial position are not materially at variance with the then-current fair values. In other words, if the reporting entity adopts the revaluation method, it cannot report obsolete fair values in the statements of financial position that contain previous years' comparative data, since that would not only obviate the purpose of the allowed treatment but would actually make it impossible for the user to meaningfully interpret the financial statements. Accordingly, the IASB recommends that a class of assets should be revalued on a rolling basis provided revaluation of the class of assets is completed within a short period and provided the revaluations are kept up to date.

Fair value is usually determined by appraisers, using market-based evidence. Market values can also be used for machinery and equipment, but since such items often do not have readily determinable market values, particularly if intended for specialised applications, they may instead be valued at depreciated replacement cost. Fair value is determined in terms of IFRS 13, *Fair Value Measurements*. The standard is presented in further detail in Chapter 25.

Example of depreciated replacement cost as a valuation approach

An asset acquired January 1, 20XX, at a cost of €40,000 was expected to have a useful life of 10 years. After three years, on January 1, 20XX+3, it is appraised as having a gross replacement cost of €50,000. The depreciated replacement cost would be 7/10 × €50,000, or €35,000. This compares with a carrying amount of €28,000 at that same date. Mechanically, to accomplish a revaluation at January 1, 20XX+3, the asset should be written up by €10,000 (i.e., from €40,000 to €50,000 gross cost) and the accumulated depreciation should be proportionally written up by €3,000 (from €12,000 to €15,000). Under IAS 16, the net amount of the revaluation adjustment, €7,000, would be credited to other comprehensive income and accumulated in equity as a revaluation surplus.

A recent amendment to IAS 16 has clarified that the gross value is restated (either by reference to market data or proportionally to the change in carrying amount) and that accumulated depreciation is the difference between the new gross amount and the new carrying amount.

An alternative accounting procedure is also permitted by the standard, under which the accumulated depreciation at the date of the revaluation is written off against the gross carrying amount of the asset. In the foregoing example, this would mean that the €12,000 of accumulated depreciation at January 1, 20XX+3, immediately prior to the revaluation, would be credited to the gross asset amount, €40,000, thereby reducing it to €28,000. Then the asset account would be adjusted to reflect the valuation of €35,000 by increasing the asset account by €7,000 (= €35,000–€28,000), with the offset to other comprehensive income (and accumulated in the revaluation surplus in shareholders' equity). In terms of total assets reported in the statement of financial position, this has exactly the same effect as the first method.

Revaluation applied to all assets in the class

IAS 16 requires that if any assets are revalued, all other assets in those groupings or categories must also be revalued. This is necessary to prevent the presentation in a statement of financial position that contains an unintelligible and possibly misleading mix of historical costs and fair values, and to preclude selective revaluation designed to maximise reported net assets. Coupled with the requirement that revaluations take place with sufficient frequency to approximate fair values at the end of each reporting period, this preserves the integrity of the financial reporting process. In fact, given that a statement of financial position prepared under the historical cost method will, in fact, contain non-comparable values for similar assets (due to assets having been acquired at varying times, at differing price levels), the revaluation approach has the possibility of providing more consistent financial reporting. Offsetting this potential improvement, at least somewhat, is the greater subjectivity inherent in the use of fair values, providing an example of the conceptual framework's trade-off between relevance and reliability.

Revaluation adjustments

In general, revaluation adjustments increasing an asset's carrying amount are recognised in other comprehensive income and accumulated in equity as *revaluation surplus*. However, the increase should be recognised in profit or loss to the extent that it reverses a revaluation decrease (impairment) of the same asset previously recognised in profit or loss. If a revalued asset is subsequently found to be impaired, the impairment loss is recognised in other comprehensive income only to the extent that the impairment loss does not exceed the amount in the revaluation surplus for the same asset. Such an impairment loss on a revalued asset is first offset against the revaluation surplus for that asset, and only when that has been exhausted is it recognised in profit or loss.

Revaluation adjustments decreasing an asset's carrying amount, in general, are recognised in profit or loss. However, the decrease should be recognised in other comprehensive income to the extent of any credit balance existing in the revaluation surplus in respect of that asset. The decrease recognised in other comprehensive income reduces the amount accumulated in equity in the revaluation surplus account.

Under the provisions of IAS 16, the amount credited to revaluation surplus can either be transferred directly to retained earnings (but *not* through profit or loss!) as the asset is being depreciated, or it can be held in the revaluation surplus account until such time as the asset is disposed of or retired from service. Any transfer to retained earnings is limited to the amount equal to the difference between depreciation based on the revalued carrying amount of the asset and depreciation based on the asset's original cost. In addition, revaluation surplus may be transferred directly to retained earnings when the asset is derecognised. This would involve transferring the whole of the surplus when the asset is retired or disposed of.

Initial revaluation

Under the revaluation model in IAS 16, at the date of initial revaluation of an item of property, plant and equipment, revaluation adjustments are accounted for as follows:

1. Increases in an asset's carrying amount are credited to other comprehensive income (gain on revaluation); and
2. Decreases in an asset's carrying amount are charged to profit or loss as this is deemed to be an impairment recognised on the related asset.

Example—Initial revaluation

Assume Henan Corporation acquired a plot of land with a cost of €100,000. After one year the land is appraised as having a current fair value of €110,000. The journal entry to increase the carrying amount of the land to its fair value is as follows:

Land	€10,000	
Other comprehensive income—gain on revaluation		€10,000

At the end of the fiscal period, the increase in the carrying amount of the land is accumulated in the "revaluation surplus" in the shareholders' equity section of the statement of financial position.

Subsequent revaluation

In accordance with IAS 16, in subsequent periods, revaluation adjustments are accounted for as follows:

1. Increases in an asset's carrying amount (upward revaluation) should be recognised as income in profit or loss to the extent of the amount of any previous impairment loss recognised, and any excess should be credited to equity through other comprehensive income;
2. Decreases in an asset's carrying amount (downward revaluation) should be charged to other comprehensive income to the extent of any previous revaluation surplus, and any excess should be debited to profit or loss as an impairment loss.

Example—Subsequent revaluation

In the following year, Henan Corporation determines that the fair value of the land is no longer €110,000. Assuming the fair value decreased to €95,000, the following journal entry is made to record downward revaluation:

Other comprehensive income—loss on revaluation	€10,000	
Impairment loss—land (expense)	€5,000	
Land		€15,000

Methods of adjusting accumulated depreciation at the date of revaluation

When an item of property, plant and equipment is revalued, any accumulated depreciation at the date of the revaluation is treated in one of the following ways:

1. Restate accumulated depreciation to reflect the difference between the change in the gross carrying amount of the asset and the revalued amount (so that the carrying amount of the asset after revaluation equals its revalued amount); or
2. Eliminate the accumulated depreciation against the gross carrying amount of the assct.

Example—Accumulated depreciation

Konin Corporation owns buildings with a cost of €200,000 and estimated useful life of five years. Accordingly, depreciation of €40,000 per year is anticipated. After two years, Konin obtains market information suggesting that a current fair value of the buildings is €300,000 and decides to write the buildings up to a fair value of €300,000. There are two approaches to apply the revaluation model in IAS 16: the asset and accumulated depreciation can be "grossed up" to reflect the new fair value information, or the asset can be restated on a "net" basis. These two approaches are illustrated below. For both illustrations, the net carrying amount (carrying amount or depreciated cost) immediately prior to the revaluation is €120,000 [€200,000 – (2 × €40,000)]. The net upward revaluation is given by the difference between fair value and net carrying amount, or €300,000 – €120,000 = €180,000.

Option 1(a). Applying the *"gross-up" approach*; since the fair value after two years of the five-year useful life have already elapsed is found to be €300,000, the gross fair value (gross carrying amount) calculated proportionally is 5/3 × €300,000 = €500,000. To have the net carrying amount equal to the fair value after two years, the balance in accumulated depreciation needs to be €200,000. Consequently, the buildings and accumulated depreciation accounts need to be restated upward as follows: buildings up €300,000 (€500,000 – €200,000) and accumulated depreciation €120,000 (€200,000 – €80,000). Alternatively, this revaluation could be accomplished by restating the buildings account and the accumulated depreciation account so that the ratio of net carrying amount to gross carrying amount is 60% (€120,000/€200,000) and the net carrying amount is €300,000. New gross carrying amount is calculated €300,000/.60 = x; x = €500,000.

The following journal entry and table illustrate the restatement of the accounts:

Buildings	€300,000	
Accumulated depreciation		€120,000
Other comprehensive income—gain on revaluation	€180,000	

	Original cost	Revaluation	Total	%
Gross carrying amount	€200,000	+€300,000	= €500,000	100
Accumulated depreciation	€80,000	+€120,000	= €200,000	40
Net carrying amount	€120,000	+€180,000	= €300,000	60

After the revaluation, the carrying amount of the buildings is €300,000 (= €500,000 – 200,000) and the ratio of net carrying amount to gross carrying amount is 60% (= €300,000/€500,000). This method is often used when an asset is revalued by means of applying an index to determine its depreciated replacement cost.

Option 1(b). Applying the "gross-up" approach where the gross fair value had separately been valued at €450,000 then both the Buildings and Accumulated depreciation entry would be reduced by €50,000 from the example above.

Buildings	€250,000	
Accumulated depreciation		€70,000
Other comprehensive income—gain on revaluation		€180,000

Option 2. Applying the "netting" approach, Konin would eliminate accumulated depreciation of €80,000 and then increase the building account by €180,000 so the net carrying amount is €300,000 (= €200,000 – €80,000 + €180,000):

Accumulated depreciation	€80,000	
Buildings		€80,000
Buildings	€180,000	
Other comprehensive income—gain on revaluation		€180,000

This method is often used for buildings. In terms of total assets reported in the statement of financial position, option 2 has exactly the same effect as option 1.

However, many users of financial statements, including credit grantors and prospective investors, pay heed to the ratio of net property and equipment as a fraction of the related gross amounts. This is done to assess the relative age of the entity's productive assets and, indirectly, to estimate the timing and amounts of cash needed for asset replacements. There is a significant diminution of information under the second method. Accordingly, the first approach described above, preserving the relationship between gross and net asset amounts after the revaluation, is recommended as the preferable alternative if the goal is meaningful financial reporting.

Deferred tax effects of revaluations

Chapter 26 describes how the tax effects of temporary differences must be provided for. Where assets are depreciated over longer lives for financial reporting purposes than for tax reporting purposes, a deferred tax liability will be created in the early years and then drawn down in later years. Generally speaking, the deferred tax provided will be measured by the expected future tax rate applied to the temporary difference at the time it reverses; unless future tax rate changes have already been enacted, the current rate structure is used as an unbiased estimator of those future effects.

In the case of revaluation of assets, it may be that taxing authorities will not permit the higher revalued amounts to be depreciated for purposes of computing tax liabilities. Instead, only the actual cost incurred can be used to offset tax obligations. On the other hand, since revaluations reflect a holding gain, this gain would be taxable if realised. Accordingly, a deferred tax liability is still required to be recognised, even though it does not relate to temporary differences arising from periodic depreciation charges.

SIC 21 confirmed that measurement of the deferred tax effects relating to the revaluation of non-depreciable assets must be made with reference to the tax consequences that would follow from recovery of the carrying amount of that asset through an eventual sale. This is necessary because the asset will not be depreciated, and hence no part of its carrying amount is considered to be recovered through use. As a practical matter this means that if there are differential capital gain and ordinary income tax rates, deferred taxes will be computed with reference to the former. This guidance of SIC 21 has now been incorporated into IAS 12 as part of a December 2010 amendment, which became effective for annual periods commencing on or after January 1, 2012. SIC 21 was consequently withdrawn with effect from that date.

DERECOGNITION

An entity should derecognise an item of property, plant and equipment (1) on disposal, or (2) when no future economic benefits are expected from its use or disposal. In such cases an asset is removed from the statement of financial position. In the case of property, plant and equipment, both the asset and the related contra asset, accumulated depreciation, should be eliminated. The difference between the net carrying amount and any proceeds received will be recognised immediately as a gain or loss arising on derecognition, through the statement of profit and loss, except where IFRS 16 requires otherwise on a sale and leaseback transaction.

If the revaluation method of accounting has been employed, and the asset and the related accumulated depreciation account have been adjusted upward, if the asset is subsequently disposed of before it has been fully depreciated, the gain or loss computed will be identical to what would have been determined had the historical cost method of accounting been used. The reason is that, at any point in time, the net amount of the revaluation (i.e., the step-up in the asset less the unamortised balance in the step-up in accumulated depreciation) will be offset exactly by the remaining balance in the revaluation surplus account. Elimination of the asset, contra asset, and revaluation surplus accounts will balance precisely, and there will be no gain or loss on this aspect of the disposition transaction. The gain or loss will be determined exclusively by the discrepancy between the net carrying amount, based on historical cost, and the proceeds from the disposition. Thus, the accounting outcome is identical under cost and revaluation methods.

In the case of assets (or disposal groups) identified as "held for sale," depreciation will cease once such determination is effected and the amount will be derecognised from Property, Plant and Equipment and accounted separately under "Assets Held for Sale."

In case of an entity which in its normal course routinely sells items of property, plant and equipment that it has held for rental to others once they are ceased from being rented and is considered as held for sale, such items could be transferred to inventories at their carrying value and be considered as inventory to be thereafter, on sale, recognised as revenue in accordance with IFRS 15, *Revenue from contracts with Customers*.

Example of accounting for asset disposal

On January 1, 20XX, Zara Corp. acquired a machine at a cost of €12,000; it had an estimated life of six years, no residual value and was expected to provide a level pattern of utility to the entity. Thus, straight-line depreciation in the amount of €2,000 was charged to operations. At the end of four years, the asset was sold for €5,000. Accounting was done on a historical cost basis. The entries to record depreciation and to report the ultimate disposal on January 1, 20XX+4, are as follows:

1/1/20XX Machinery	€12,000	
Cash, etc.		€12,000
12/31/20XX Depreciation expense	€2,000	
Accumulated depreciation		€2,000
12/31/20XX+1 Depreciation expense	€2,000	
Accumulated depreciation		€2,000
12/31/20XX+2 Depreciation expense	€2,000	
Accumulated depreciation		€2,000
12/31/20XX+3 Depreciation expense	€2,000	
Accumulated depreciation		€2,000
1/1/20XX+4 Cash	€5,000	
Accumulated depreciation	€8,000	
Machinery		€12,000
Gain on asset disposal		€1,000

Now assume the same facts as above, but that the revaluation method is used. At the beginning of year four (20XX+3) the asset is revalued at a gross replacement cost of €15,000, which is the equivalent of a depreciated replacement cost of €7,500 (€15,000 × 3/6). A year later it is sold for €5,000. The entries are as follows (note in particular that the remaining revaluation surplus is transferred directly to retained earnings):

1/1/20XX	Machinery	€12,000	
	Cash, etc.		€12,000
12/31/20XX	Depreciation expense	€2,000	
	Accumulated depreciation		€2,000
12/31/20XX+1	Depreciation expense	€2,000	
	Accumulated depreciation		€2,000
12/31/20XX+2	Depreciation expense	€2,000	
	Accumulated depreciation		€2,000

1/1/20XX+3	Machinery	€3,000	
	Accumulated depreciation		€1,500
	Other comprehensive income—revaluation surplus		€1,500
12/31/20XX+3	Depreciation expense	€2,500	
	Accumulated depreciation		€2,500
	Revaluation surplus	€500	
	Retained earnings		€500
1/1/20XX+4	Cash	€5,000	
	Accumulated depreciation	€10,000	
	Revaluation surplus	€1,000	
	Machinery		€15,000
	Retained earnings		€1,000

DISCLOSURES

The disclosures required under IAS 16 for property, plant and equipment, and under IAS 38 for intangibles, are similar. Furthermore, IAS 36 requires extensive disclosures when assets are impaired or when formerly recognised impairments are being reversed. The requirements that pertain to property, plant and equipment are as follows:

For each class of tangible asset, disclosure is required of:

1. The measurement basis used (cost or revaluation approaches).
2. The depreciation method(s) used.
3. Useful lives or depreciation rates used.
4. The gross carrying amounts and accumulated depreciation at the beginning and at the end of the period.
5. A reconciliation of the carrying amount from the beginning to the end of the period, showing additions, disposals and/or assets included in disposal groups or classified as held for sale, acquisitions by means of business combinations, increases or decreases resulting from revaluations, reductions to recognised impairments, depreciation, the net effect of translation of foreign entities' financial statements and any other material items.

In addition, the financial statements should also disclose the following facts:

1. Any restrictions on titles and any assets pledged as security for debt.
2. The accounting policy regarding restoration costs for items of property, plant and equipment.
3. The expenditures made for property, plant and equipment, including any construction in progress.
4. The amount of outstanding commitments for property, plant and equipment acquisitions.
5. The amount received from any third parties as compensation for any impaired, lost or given-up asset. This is only applicable if the amount received was not separately disclosed in the statement of comprehensive income.

Example of reconciliation of asset carrying amounts

Date	*Gross cost*	*Accumulated depreciation*	*Net carrying amount*
1/1/15	€4,500,000	€2,000,000	€2,500,000
Acquisitions	€3,000,000	–	€3,000,000
Disposals	(€400,000)	(€340,000)	(€60,000)
Impairment		€600,000	(€600,000)
Depreciation	–	€200,000	(€200,000)
31/12/15	€7,100,000	€2,460,000	€4,640,000

Non-Monetary (Exchange) Transactions

Businesses sometimes engage in non-monetary exchange transactions, where tangible or intangible assets are exchanged for other assets, without a cash transaction or with only a small amount of cash "settle-up." These exchanges can involve productive assets such as machinery and equipment, which are not held for sale under normal circumstances, or inventory items, which are intended for sale to customers.

IAS 16 provides guidance on the accounting for non-monetary exchanges of tangible assets. It requires that the cost of an item of property, plant and equipment acquired in exchange for a similar asset is to be measured at fair value, provided that the transaction has commercial substance. The concept of a purely "book value" exchange, formerly employed, is now prohibited under most circumstances.

Commercial substance is defined as the event or transaction causing the cash flows of the entity to change. That is, if the expected cash flows after the exchange differ from what would have been expected without this occurring, the exchange has commercial substance and is to be accounted for at fair value. In assessing whether this has occurred, the entity has to consider if the amount, timing and uncertainty of the cash flows from the new asset are different from the one given up, or if the entity-specific portion of the company's operations will be different. If either of these is significant, then the transaction has commercial substance.

If the transaction does not have commercial substance, or the fair value of neither the asset received nor the asset given up can be measured reliably, then the asset acquired is valued at the carrying amount of the asset given up. Such situations are expected to be rare.

If there is a settle-up paid or received in cash or a cash equivalent, this is often referred to as boot; that term will be used in the following example.

Example of an exchange involving dissimilar assets and no boot

Assume the following:

1. Jamok, Inc. exchanges an automobile with a carrying amount of €2,500 with Springsteen & Co. for a tooling machine with a fair market value of €3,200.
2. No boot is exchanged in the transaction.
3. The fair value of the automobile is not readily determinable.

In this case, Jamok, Inc. has recognised a gain of €700 (= €3,200 – €2,500) on the exchange, and the gain should be included in the determination of net income. The entry to record the transaction would be as follows:

Machine	€3,200	
Automobile		€2,500
Gain on exchange of automobile		€700

Non-reciprocal transfers

In a non-reciprocal transfer, one party gives or receives property without the other party doing the opposite. Often these involve an entity and the owners of the entity. Examples of non-reciprocal transfers with owners include dividends paid-in-kind, non-monetary assets exchanged for common stock, split-ups and spin-offs. An example of a non-reciprocal transaction with parties other than the owners is a donation of property either by or to the entity.

The accounting for most non-reciprocal transfers should be based on the fair market value of the asset given (or received, if the fair value of the non-monetary asset is both objectively measurable and would be clearly recognisable under IFRS). The same principle also applies to distributions of non-cash assets (e.g., items of property, plant and equipment, businesses as defined in IFRS 3, ownership interest in another entity, or disposal groups as defined in IFRS 5); and also, to distributions that give owners a choice of receiving either non-cash assets or a cash alternative. IFRIC 17 was issued in January 2009 to address the accounting that should be followed in such situations and provides that the assets involved must be measured at their fair value and any gains or losses taken to profit or loss. The Interpretation also provides guidance on the measurement of the dividend payable in that the dividend payable is measured at the fair value of the assets to be distributed. If the entity gives its owners a choice of receiving either a non-cash asset or a cash alternative, the entity should estimate the dividend payable by considering both the fair value of each alternative and the associated probability of owners selecting each alternative. At the end of each reporting period and at the date of settlement, the entity is required to review and adjust the carrying amount of the dividend payable, with any changes in the carrying amount of the dividend payable recognised in equity as adjustments to the amount of the distribution.

This approach differs from the previous approach, which permitted the recording of transactions that resulted in the distribution of non-monetary assets to owners of an entity in a spin-off or other form of reorganisation or liquidation being accounted for based on their recorded amount.

Example of accounting for a non-reciprocal transfer

Assume the following:

1. Salaam distributed property with a carrying amount of €10,000 to its shareholder as a dividend during the current year.
2. The property had a fair market value of €17,000 at the date of the transfer.

The transaction is to be valued at the fair market value of the property transferred, and any gain or loss on the transaction is to be recognised. Thus, Salaam should recognise a gain of

€7,000 (= €17,000 – €10,000) in the determination of the current period's profit or loss. The entry to record the transaction would be as follows:

Dividend paid	€17,000	
Property		€10,000
Gain on transfer of property		€7,000

Transfers of Assets from Customers

IFRIC 18, *Transfers of Assets from Customers*, has been replaced by IFRS 15. The IFRS does not refer specifically to the phrase "transfer of assets from clients"; however, included in the measurement provisions, specifically the paragraphs relating to determination of the transaction price, there is section on how to treat non-cash considerations received.

IFRS 15 requires that when a customer contributes goods or services to facilitate the entity fulfilling its contractual obligations, the entity must consider whether it assumes control of these goods or services. If the entity does gain control of these goods or services, the standard then says that these goods or services can be accounted for as non-cash consideration received. The value of this consideration, the transaction price, is then measured at the fair value of the non-cash consideration (i.e., goods or services provided by the customer). Based on the simple double entry accounting system one must then infer that the resulting asset should be measured at the fair value of the non-cash consideration.

One will need to be sure that the items received meet the definition of an item of Property, Plant and Equipment (PPE) before they recognise the item as PPE. In situations where the fair value of the non-cash consideration is not estimated reasonably, the measurement of consideration in determining revenue recognition related to the receipt of the non-cash consideration, and whether or not there is a need to raise deferred revenue, one will need to take into account the revenue recognition principles of IFRS 15; these are dealt with in Chapter 20 of this book.

EXAMPLES OF FINANCIAL STATEMENT DISCLOSURES

Exemplum Reporting PLC
Financial Statements
For the year ended December 31, 20XX

Summary of significant accounting policies

2.5 Property, plant and equipment

All property, plant and equipment assets are stated at cost less accumulated depreciation.	IAS 16 p30
Depreciation of property, plant and equipment is provided to write off the cost, less residual value, on a straight-line basis over the estimated useful life: • Buildings—50 years • Computer equipment—3 years • Motor vehicles—5 years.	IAS 16 p73
Residual values, remaining useful lives and depreciation methods are reviewed annually and adjusted if appropriate.	IAS 16 p51
Gains or losses on disposal are included in profit or loss.	IAS 16 p68

2.16 Discontinued operations and non-current assets held for sale	
The results of discontinued operations are to be presented separately in the statement of comprehensive income.	IFRS 5 p1
Non-current assets (or disposal group) classified as held for sale are measured at the lower of carrying amount and fair value less costs to sell.	IFRS 5 p15
Non-current assets (or disposal group) are classified as held for sale if their carrying amount will be recovered through a sale transaction rather than through continuing use.	IFRS 5 p6
This is the case when the asset (or disposal group) is available for immediate sale in its present condition subject only to terms that are usual and customary for sales of such assets (or disposal groups) and the sale is considered to be highly probable.	IFRS 5 p7
A sale is considered to be highly probable if the appropriate level of management is committed to a plan to sell the asset (or disposal group), and an active programme to locate a buyer and complete the plan has been initiated. Further, the asset (or disposal group) has been actively marketed for sale at a price that is reasonable in relation to its current fair value. In addition, the sale is expected to qualify for recognition as a completed sale within one year from the date that it is classified as held for sale.	IFRS 5 p8
3. Accounting estimates and judgements	
The estimates and judgements that have a significant risk of causing a material adjustment to the carrying amounts of assets and liabilities within the next financial year are as follows:	IAS 1 p122 p125
3.1 Key sources of estimation uncertainty	
Useful lives of items of property, plant and equipment	IAS 1 p129
The group reviews the estimated useful lives of property, plant and equipment at the end of each reporting period. During the current year, the directors determined that the useful lives of certain items of equipment should be shortened, due to developments in technology.	
The financial effect of this reassessment is to increase the consolidated depreciation expense in the current year and for the next three years, by the following amounts:	
20XX €X	
20XX+1 €X	
20XX+2 €X	
20XX+3 €X	

15. Property, Plant and Equipment

Group	**Land and Buildings**	**Plant and Machinery**	**Furniture and Fittings**	**Total**	**IAS 16 p73**
Cost	€	€	€	€	
Opening cost at January 1, 20XX-1	X	X	X	X	
Additions	X	X	X	X	
Exchange differences	X	X	X	X	
Classified as held for sale					

Disposals	X	X	X	X
Acquired through business combination	X	X	X	X
Opening cost at January 1, 20XX	X	X	X	X
Additions	X	X	X	X
Exchange differences	X	X	X	X
Classified as held for sale				
Disposals	X	X	X	X
Acquired through business combination	X	X	X	X
Closing cost at December 31, 20XX	**X**	**X**	**X**	**X**
Accumulated depreciation/impairment				
Opening balance at January 1, 20XX-1	X	X	X	X
Depreciation	X	X	X	X
Disposals	X	X	X	X
Exchange differences	X	X	X	X
Impairment loss	X	X	X	X
Opening balance at January 1, 20XX	X	X	X	X
Depreciation	X	X	X	X
Disposals	X	X	X	X
Exchange differences	X	X	X	X
Impairment loss	X	X	X	X
Impairment reversal	X	X	X	X
Closing balance at December 31, 20XX	**X**	**X**	**X**	**X**
Opening carrying value at January 1, 20XX-1	X	X	X	X
Opening carrying value at January 1, 20XX	X	X	X	X
Closing carrying value at December 31, 20XX	X	X	X	X

Plant and machinery includes the following amounts where the group is a lessee under a finance lease: IAS 17 p31(a)

	20XX	20XX-1
	€	€
Cost—capitalised finance leases	**X**	X
Accumulated depreciation	**X**	X
Net book value	**X**	X

In determining the valuations for land and buildings, the valuer refers to current market conditions including recent sales transactions of similar properties—assuming the highest and best use of the properties.

For plant and machinery, current replacement cost adjusted for the depreciation factor of the existing assets is used. There has been no change in the valuation technique used during the year compared to prior periods.

The fair valuation of property, plant and equipment is considered to represent a level 3 valuation based on significant non-observable inputs being the location and condition of the assets and replacement costs for plant and machinery.

Management does not expect there to be a material sensitivity to the fair values arising from the non-observable inputs.

There were no transfers between level 1, 2 and 3 fair values during the year.

The table above presents the changes in the carrying value of the property, plant and equipment arising from these fair valuation assessments.

US GAAP COMPARISON

US GAAP and IFRS are very similar with regard to property, plant and equipment. Generally, expenditures that qualify for capitalisation under IFRS are also eligible under US GAAP as recorded in FASB ASC 360 *Property, Plant and Equipment*.

Initial measurement can differ for internally constructed assets. US GAAP permits only eligible interest to be capitalised, whereas IFRS includes other borrowing costs. There are also some differences regarding what borrowings are included to compute a capitalisation rate. For costs connected to a specific asset, borrowing costs equal the weighted-average of accumulated expenditures times the borrowing ratc.

Component accounting is not prescribed under US GAAP, but neither is it prohibited, and it is not common. This disparity can result in a different "mix" of depreciation and maintenance expense on the income statement. Only major upgrades to PPE are capitalised under US GAAP, whereas the replacement of a component under IFRS is characterised as accelerated depreciation and additional capital expenditures. Consequently, the classification of expenditures on the statement of cash flows can differ.

Most oil and gas companies use US GAAP for exploration assets since there is no substantial IFRS for the oil and gas industry. IFRS 6 permits entities to disregard the hierarchy of application prescribed in IAS 8 and use another standard (usually US GAAP) immediately.

The accounting for asset retirement obligations assets is largely the same but the difference in the discount rate used to measure the fair value of the liability creates an inherent difference in the carrying cost. US GAAP uses a credit-adjusted, risk-free rate adjusted for the entity's credit risk to discount the obligation. IFRS uses the time value of money rate adjusted for specific risks of the liability. Also, assets and obligations are not adjusted for period-to-period changes in the discount. The discount rate applied to each upward revision of an accrual, termed "layers" in US GAAP, remains with that layer through increases and decreases.

US GAAP requires a two-step method approach to impairment measuring. If the asset fails the first step (future undiscounted cash flows exceed the carrying amount), the second step requires an impairment loss calculated as the excess of carrying amount over fair value.

US GAAP does not permit revaluations (or write-up) of property, plant and equipment or mineral resources once they have been written down, however the depreciation or amortisation may be required.

10 BORROWING COSTS

INTRODUCTION

The core principle of the standard is that borrowing costs that are directly attributable to the acquisition, construction or production of a qualifying asset form part of the cost of that asset, i.e. such costs are capitalised. All other borrowing costs are recognised as an expense.

The standard specifically excludes qualifying assets measured at fair value, for example biological assets and inventories which are produced in large quantities on a repetitive basis. The thought behind these exclusions was as follows:

The determination of fair value, as defined under Chapter 25 and thus the measurement of the asset, is not affected by the amount of borrowing costs incurred. Thus, there is no need for specific requirements for accounting for the borrowing cost; they are simply treated as all other borrowing costs. The excluding of inventories produced in large quantities on a repetitive basis was an acknowledgement that it would be difficult for preparers to collect the information required to monitor and allocate the borrowing costs to inventory items produced in such a manner. The Board determined that the cost would outweigh the benefit of the information provided to the users and thus excluded such inventories from the scope.

Source of IFRS
IAS 23

DEFINITIONS OF TERMS

Borrowing costs. Interest and other costs that an entity incurs in connection with the borrowing of funds. Borrowing costs that are directly attributable to the acquisition, construction or production of qualifying assets may be eligible for capitalisation as part of the cost of the asset. Borrowing costs may include interest expense calculated using the effective interest method (IFRS 9), ancillary costs in connection with the arrangement of borrowings, finance charges in respect of finance leases (IFRS 16) or exchange differences arising from foreign currency borrowings to the extent that they relate to an adjustment of interest costs.

Carrying amount (book value) – the value reported for an asset or liability in the statement of financial position. For assets e.g. property, plant and equipment this is reflective measurement models under IAS 16 i.e. historical cost or revaluation. Carrying amount is often different from market value because depreciation is a cost allocation rather than a means of valuation.

Qualifying asset. An asset that necessarily requires a substantial period of time to get ready for its intended use or sale. Qualifying assets depending on the circumstances can be inventories, plant and equipment, power generation facilities, intangibles, investment properties and bearer plants, unless the assets are accounted for at fair value.

Financial assets or inventories produced over a very short period of time in a repetitive process are *not* qualifying assets. Assets that are acquired and that are already in the condition for their intended use or sale are not qualifying assets. The standard does not define "substantial," and a benchmark of 12 months or more is often used, but a shorter period might be justified as well.

The standard does not require the capitalisation of borrowing costs for inventories that are manufactured in large quantities on a repetitive basis. Interest capitalisation is permitted so long as the production process takes a "substantial period of time." The choice to capitalise borrowing costs on those inventories is an accounting policy choice.

An intangible asset that takes a "substantial period of time" to be developed for its intended use or sale is a "qualifying asset." Similar treatment would apply for an internally generated intangible asset in the development phase when it takes a "substantial period of time" to complete. The interest capitalisation is applied only if the costs relating to the underlying asset have themselves been capitalised.

It is for the management to assess whether an asset, at the date of acquisition, is "ready for its intended use or sale." The asset might be a qualifying asset, depending on how management intends to use it. For example, when an acquired asset can only be used in combination with a larger group of fixed assets or was acquired specifically for the construction of one specific qualifying asset, the assessment of whether the acquired asset is a qualifying asset is made on a combined basis.

The following would not comprise qualifying assets:

1. Assets that are already in use or ready for use;
2. Assets that are not being used and are not awaiting activities to get them ready for use; and
3. When assets are acquired with grants and gifts restricted by the donor to the extent that funds are available from those grants and gifts.

RECOGNITION AND MEASUREMENT

Capitalisation of Borrowing Costs

IAS 23 provides that a reporting entity should capitalise borrowing costs as defined that are directly attributable to the acquisition, construction or production of a qualifying asset as part of the initial carrying amount of that asset, and that all other borrowing costs should be recognised as an expense in the period in which the entity incurs them. IAS 23 provides answers for the following questions:

- From when should capitalisation of the borrowing costs start?
- How much should we capitalise?

- When do we suspend capitalisation?
- When do we cease capitalising borrowing costs?

When do we start capitalising?

Capitalisation of borrowing costs commences when the entity meets all of the following conditions:

1. Expenditures for the asset are being incurred;
2. Borrowing costs are being incurred; and
3. Activities that are necessary to prepare the asset for its intended use or sale are in progress.

As long as these conditions continue, borrowing costs must be capitalised. Expenditures incurred for the asset include only those that have resulted in payments of cash, transfers of other assets or the assumption of interest-bearing liabilities, and are reduced by any progress payments and grants received for that asset.

Necessary activities are interpreted in a very broad manner. They start with the planning process and continue until the qualifying asset is substantially complete and ready to function as intended. These activities may include technical and administrative work prior to actual commencement of physical work, such as obtaining permits and approvals, and may continue after physical work has ceased. Brief, normal interruptions do not stop the capitalisation of interest costs. However, if the entity intentionally suspends or delays the activities for some reason, interest costs should not be capitalised from the point of suspension or delay until substantial activities in regard to the asset resume.

If the asset is completed in a piecemeal fashion, the capitalisation of interest costs stops for each part as it becomes ready to function as intended. An asset that must be entirely complete before the parts can be used as intended can continue to capitalise interest costs until the total asset becomes ready to function.

How much should we capitalise?

Borrowing costs eligible for capitalisation are those that are directly attributable to the acquisition, construction or production of a qualifying asset which would have been avoided if the expenditure on the qualifying asset had not been made. They include actual borrowing costs incurred less any investment income on the temporary investment of excess/available borrowings.

In determining the amount of borrowing costs eligible for capitalisation the standard makes reference to borrowing costs which result from funds borrowed *specifically* for the purpose of purchasing or producing the qualifying asset (*specific borrowings*) as opposed to situations where an entity uses funds it has borrowed *generally* (to be used as necessary and not specifically borrowed with the qualifying asset in mind) to fund the acquisition or production of the qualifying asset (*general borrowings*).

Specific borrowings. The determination of eligible borrowing costs in instances where specific borrowings are utilised is a very simple exercise. In these situations, one simply has to calculate the actual borrowing costs incurred during the period on those specific borrowings. If the full amount of the borrowing is not used immediately in the acquisition of the qualifying asset, any investment income earned on the unutilised borrowings must be subtracted from the borrowing costs to be capitalised. Thus, the following formula could be used to summarise the above:

Eligible *specific* borrowing cost = *Actual borrowing costs* incurred (on the *specific* borrowings) – *Investment income* (earned on temporary investment of surplus *specific* borrowings)

An entity does not need to make an actual investment for the excess borrowings available/ not yet used. Any interest earned on a current account would also need to be deducted from the amount capitalised.

General borrowings. For *general* borrowings, the calculation of the eligible borrowing costs may be more complex. The amount of borrowing costs eligible for capitalisation, in these instances, is determined by applying a capitalisation rate to the expenditures on that asset. The capitalisation rate is the weighted-average of the borrowing costs applicable to the borrowings of the entity that are outstanding during the period, other than borrowings made specifically for the purpose of obtaining a qualifying asset (i.e., the weighted-average borrowing cost applicable to *general* borrowings). The amount of borrowing costs capitalised during a period cannot exceed the amount of borrowing costs incurred.

The selection of borrowings to be used in the calculation of the weighted-average of rates requires judgement. In resolving this problem the best criterion to use is the identification and determination of that portion of interest that could have been avoided if the qualifying assets had not been acquired.

The base (which should be used to multiply the weighted-average rate by) is the average amount of accumulated net capital expenditures incurred for qualifying assets during the relevant reporting period. Capitalised costs and expenditures are not synonymous terms. Theoretically, a capitalised cost financed by a trade payable for which no interest is recognised is not a capital expenditure to which the capitalisation rate should be applied. Reasonable approximations of net capital expenditures are acceptable, however, and capitalised costs are generally used in place of capital expenditures unless there is a material difference.

If the average capitalised expenditures exceed the specific new borrowings for the timeframe involved, the *excess* expenditures amount should be multiplied by the weighted-average of rates and not by the rate associated with the specific debt. This requirement more accurately reflects the interest cost that is actually incurred by the entity in bringing the long-lived asset to a properly functioning condition and location.

The interest being paid on the underlying debt may be either simple or subject to compounding. Simple interest is computed on the principal alone, whereas compound interest is computed on principal and on any accumulated interest that has not been paid. Compounding may be yearly, monthly or daily. Most long-lived assets will be acquired with debt having interest compounded, and that feature should be considered when computing the amount of interest to be capitalised.

The total amount of interest actually incurred by the entity during the relevant time frame is the ceiling for the amount of interest cost capitalised. Thus, the amount capitalised cannot exceed the amount actually incurred during the period. The interest incurred is a gross amount and is netted against interest earned except in rare cases.

Example of accounting for capitalised interest costs

Assume the following:

1. On January 1, 20XX, Gemini Corp. contracted Leo Company to construct a building for €20,000,000 on land that Gemini had purchased years earlier.
2. Gemini Corp. was to make five payments in 20XX, with the last payment scheduled for the date of completion.
3. The building was completed on December 31, 20XX.
4. Gemini Corp. made the following payments during 20XX:

January 1, 20XX	€2,000,000
March 31, 20XX	€4,000,000
June 30, 20XX	€6,100,000
September 30, 20XX	€4,400,000
December 31, 20XX	€3,500,000
	€20,000,000

Gemini Corp. had the following debt outstanding at December 31, 20XX:

a. A 12%, 4-year note dated 1/1/20XX-3 with interest compounded quarterly. Both principal and interest due 12/31/20XX+1 (relates specifically to building project)	€8,500,000
b. A 10%, 10-year note dated 13/31/20XX-8 with simple interest and interest payable annually on December 31	€6,000,000
c. A 12%, 5-year note dated 13/31/20XX-6 with simple interest and interest payable annually on December 31	€7,000,000

The amount of interest to be capitalised during 20XX is computed as follows:

Average accumulated expenditures

Date	Expenditure	Capitalisation period*	Average accumulated expenditures
1/1/20XX	€2,000,000	12/12	€2,000,000
3/31/20XX	€4,000,000	9/12	€3,000,000
6/30/20XX	€6,100,000	6/12	€3,050,000
9/30/20XX	€4,400,000	3/12	€1,100,000
12/31/20XX	€3,500,000	0/12	–
	€20,000,000		€9,150,000

**The number of months between the date when expenditures were made and the date on which interest capitalisation stops (December 31, 20XX).*

Potential interest cost to be capitalised

Specific borrowings		
(€8,500,000 × 1.12) – €8,500,000*	=	€1,020,000
General borrowings	=	€72,020
€650,000 × 0.1108**		
€9,150,000		€1,092,020

**The principal, €8,500,000, is multiplied by the factor for the future amount of €1 for 4 periods at 3% to determine the amount of principal and interest due in 20XX.*
***Weighted-average interest rate.*

Weighted-average interest rate (general borrowings)

	Principal	*Interest*
10%, 10-year note	€6,000,000	€600,000
12%, 5-year note	€7,000,000	€840,000
	€13,000,000	€1,440,000

$$\frac{\text{Total interest}}{\text{Total principal}} = \frac{€1,440,000}{€13,000,000} = 11.08\%$$

The actual interest is

12%, 4-year note [(€8,500,000 × 1.12551) − €8,500,000]	=	€1,020,000
10%, 10-year note (€6,000,000 × 10%)	=	€600,000
12%, 5-year note (€7,000,000 × 12%)	=	€840,000
Total interest		€2,460,000

The interest cost to be capitalised is the lesser of €1,092,020 (avoidable interest) or €2,460,000 (actual interest). The remaining €1,367,980 (= €2,460,000 − €1,092,020) must be expensed.

When do we suspend capitalisation?

The capitalisation of borrowing costs must be temporarily suspended during extended periods during which there is no activity to prepare the asset for its intended use. As a practical matter, unless the break in activity is significant, it is usually ignored. Also, if delays are normal and to be expected given the nature of the construction project (such as a suspension of building construction during the winter months), this would have been anticipated as a cost and would not warrant even a temporary suspension of borrowing cost capitalisation.

If the entity intentionally suspends or delays the activities for some reason, interest costs should not be capitalised from the point of suspension or delay until substantial activities in regard to the asset resume.

When do we cease capitalising borrowing costs?

Capitalisation of borrowing costs would cease when all the activities to prepare the asset are completed. This would occur when the asset is ready for its intended use or for sale to a customer. The fact that routine minor administrative matters still need to be attended to would not mean that the asset had not been completed.

Costs in excess of recoverable amounts

When the carrying amount or the expected ultimate cost of the qualifying asset, including capitalised interest cost, exceeds its recoverable amount (if property, plant or equipment) or net realisable value (if an item is held for resale), it will be necessary to record an adjustment to write down the carrying amount of the asset to its recoverable amount/net realisable value. Any excess interest cost is thus an impairment to be recognised immediately in expenses.

In the case of property, plant and equipment, a later write-up may occur due to the use of the allowed alternative (i.e., revaluation) treatment, recognising revaluation gains, in which case, as described earlier, recovery of a previously recognised loss will be credited to profit or loss.

Disclosure requirements

With respect to an entity's accounting for borrowing costs, the financial statements must disclose:

1. The amount of borrowing costs capitalised during the period; and
2. The capitalisation rate used to determine the amount of borrowing costs eligible for capitalisation.

As noted, this rate will be the weighted-average of rates on all borrowings included in an allocation pool or the actual rate on specific debt identified with a given asset acquisition or construction project.

Annual Improvements to IFRS Standards 2015–2017 Cycle

If any specific borrowing remains outstanding after the related asset is ready for its intended use or sale, that borrowing becomes part of the funds that an entity borrows generally when calculating the capitalisation rate on general borrowings.

US GAAP COMPARISON

Qualifying assets are those that normally take an extended period of time to prepare for their intended uses. While IAS 23 does not give further insight into the limitations of this definition, FASB ASC 835-20, *Capitalization of Interest*, provides certain insights that may prove germane to this matter. In general, interest capitalisation has been applied to those asset acquisition and construction situations in which:

1. Assets are being constructed for an entity's own use or for which deposit or progress payments are made;
2. Assets are produced as discrete projects that are intended for lease or sale (i.e., real estate development or ships); or
3. Investments are being made that are accounted for by the equity method, where the investee is using funds to acquire qualifying assets for its principal operations which have not yet begun.

Generally, routine inventories and land not undergoing preparation for intended use are not qualifying assets. When land is in the process of being developed, it is a qualifying asset. If land is being developed for lots, the capitalised interest cost is added to the cost of the land. The related borrowing costs are then matched against revenues when the lots are sold. If, on the other hand, the land is being developed for a building, the capitalised interest cost should instead be added to the cost of the building. The interest cost is then matched against future revenues as the building is depreciated.

US GAAP and IFRS are nearly identical about capitalised interest. Both have essentially the same definition of eligible assets, when the capitalisation can begin and when it ends. However, there are also some differences regarding what borrowings are included to compute a capitalisation rate, and costs do not include exchange rate differences. US GAAP does not require that all borrowings be included in the determination of the weighted-average capitalisation rate. Only a reasonable measure of cost for financing the acquisition must be capitalised. A reasonable interest cost is the interest incurred that otherwise would have been avoided if not for constructing the eligible asset.

Except for tax-exempt borrowings, US GAAP does not permit offsetting of interest income against interest expense to determine the amount to capitalise. The interest income can only be that which was earned on the tax-exempt borrowing. US GAAP does not permit capitalisation of interest for inventories that are routinely manufactured or otherwise produced in large quantities on a repetitive basis (ASC 835-20-15-6[g]).

11 INTANGIBLE ASSETS

INTRODUCTION

Non-current assets are those that will provide economic benefits to an entity for a number of future periods. Accounting standards regarding long-lived assets involve determination of the appropriate cost at which to record the assets initially, the amount at which to measure the assets at subsequent reporting dates, and the appropriate method(s) to be used to allocate the cost over the periods being benefited, if that is appropriate.

Non-current non-financial assets may be classified into two basic types: tangible and intangible. Tangible assets have physical substance, while intangible assets either have no physical substance, or have a value that is not conveyed by what physical substance they do have. For example, the value of gaming software is not reasonably measured by the cost of the DVDs on which these are contained.

The value of an intangible asset is a function of the rights or privileges that its ownership conveys to the business entity.

The recognition and measurement of intangibles such as brand names are problematic because many brands are internally generated, over a number of years, and there is little or no historical cost to be recognised under IFRS or most national GAAP standards.

As an example: the Dell brand does not appear on Dell's statement of financial position, nor does the Nestlé brand appear on Nestlé's statement of financial position. Exceptions to this are constructions where brand names are being transferred within large corporate clients outside the group structure, and consequently will be recognised and recorded as long-lived assets. In these situations it is particularly important to determine whether the long-lived assets are internally generated or not.

Concepts, designs, sales networks, brands and processes are all important elements of what enables one company to succeed while another fails, but the theoretical support for representing them on the statement of financial position is at an early stage of development. For that matter, few companies even attempt to monitor such values for internal management purposes, so it is hardly surprising that the external reporting is still evolving.

We can draw a distinction between internally generated intangibles which are difficult to measure and thus to recognise in the statement of financial position, such as research and development assets and brands, and those that are purchased externally by an entity and therefore have a purchase price. While an intangible can certainly be bought individually, most intangibles arise from acquisitions of other companies, where a bundle of assets and liabilities is acquired.

In this area of activity, we can further distinguish between identifiable intangibles and unidentifiable ones.

Identifiable intangibles include patents, copyrights, brand names, customer lists, trade names and other specific rights that typically can be conveyed by an owner without necessarily also transferring related physical assets. Goodwill, on the other hand, is a residual which incorporates all the intangibles that cannot be reliably measured separately, and is often analysed as containing both these and benefits that the acquiring entity expected to gain from the synergies or other efficiencies arising from a business combination and cannot normally be transferred to a new owner without also selling the other assets and/or the operations of the business.

Accounting for goodwill is addressed in IFRS 3, *Business Combinations*, and is discussed in Chapter 15 in this publication, in the context of business combinations. In this chapter we will address the recognition and measurement criteria for identifiable intangibles. This includes the criteria for separability and treatment of internally generated intangibles, such as research and development costs.

The subsequent measurement of intangibles depends upon whether they are considered to have indefinite economic value or a finite useful life. The standard on impairment of assets (IAS 36) pertains to both tangible and intangible long-lived assets. This chapter will consider the implications of this standard for the accounting for intangible, separately identifiable assets.

	Sources of IFRS	
IFRS 3	*IAS* 23, 36, 38	*SIC* 32

SCOPE

IAS 38 applies to all reporting entities. It prescribes the accounting treatment for intangible assets, including development costs, but does not address intangible assets covered by other IFRS.

DEFINITIONS OF TERMS

Active market. A market in which all the following conditions exist:

1. The items traded in the market are homogeneous;
2. Willing buyers and sellers can normally be found at any time; and
3. Prices are available to the public.

Amortisation. Systematic allocation of the depreciable amount of an intangible asset on a systematic basis over its useful life.

Asset. A resource that is:

1. Controlled by an entity as a result of past events; and
2. From which future economic benefits are expected to flow to the entity.

Carrying amount. The amount at which an asset is recognised in the statement of financial position, net of any accumulated amortisation and accumulated impairment losses thereon.

Cash-generating unit. The smallest identifiable group of assets that generates cash inflows from continuing use, largely independent of the cash inflows associated with other assets or groups of assets.

Corporate assets. Assets, excluding goodwill, that contribute to future cash flows of both the cash-generating unit under review for impairment and other cash-generating units.

Cost. Amount of cash or cash equivalent paid or the fair value of other considerations given to acquire an asset at the time of its acquisition or construction or, where applicable, the amount attributed to that asset when initially recognised in accordance with the specific requirements of other IFRS (e.g., IFRS 2, *Share-Based Payment*).

Depreciable amount. Cost of an asset or the other amount that has been substituted for cost, less the residual value of the asset.

Development. The application of research findings or other knowledge to a plan or design for the production of new or substantially improved materials, devices, products, processes, systems or services prior to commencement of commercial production or use. This should be distinguished from *research*, which must be expensed whereas development costs are capitalised.

Fair value. The price that would be received to sell an asset or paid to transfer a liability in an orderly transaction between market participants at the measurement date.

Goodwill. An intangible asset representing the future economic benefits arising from other assets acquired in a business combination that are not individually identified and separately recognised.

Impairment loss. The excess of the carrying amount of an asset over its recoverable amount.

Intangible assets. Identifiable non-monetary assets without physical substance.

Monetary assets. Money held and assets to be received in fixed or determinable amounts of money. Examples are cash, accounts receivable and notes receivable.

Net selling price. The amount that could be realised from the sale of an asset by means of an arm's-length transaction, less costs of disposal.

Non-monetary transactions. Exchanges and non-reciprocal transfers that involve little or no monetary assets or liabilities.

Non-reciprocal transfer. Transfer of assets or services in one direction, either from an entity to its owners or another entity, or from owners or another entity to the entity. An entity's reacquisition of its outstanding stock is a non-reciprocal transfer.

Recoverable amount. The greater of an asset's or a cash-generating unit's fair value less costs to sell and its value in use.

Research. The original and planned investigation undertaken with the prospect of gaining new scientific or technical knowledge and understanding. This should be distinguished from development, since the latter is capitalised whereas research costs must be expensed.

Residual value. Estimated amount that an entity would currently obtain from disposal of the asset, net of estimated costs of disposal, if the asset were already of the age and in the condition expected at the end of its useful life.

Useful life. Period over which an asset is expected to be available for use by an entity; or the number of production or similar units expected to be obtained from the asset by an entity.

Value in use. Present value of the cash flows an entity expects to arise from the continuing use of an asset and from its disposal at the end of its useful life.

RECOGNITION AND MEASUREMENT

Over the years, the role of intangible assets has grown ever more important for the operations and prosperity of many types of businesses, as the "knowledge-based" economy becomes more dominant.

IFRS first addressed accounting for intangibles in a thorough way with IAS 38, which was promulgated in 1998. Research and development costs had earlier been addressed by IAS 9 (issued in 1978) and goodwill arising from a business combination was dealt with by IAS 22 (issued in 1983).

IAS 38 is the first comprehensive standard on intangibles and it superseded IAS 9. It established recognition criteria, measurement bases and disclosure requirements for intangible assets. The standard also stipulates that impairment testing for intangible assets (as specified by IAS 36) is to be undertaken on a regular basis. This is to ensure that only assets having *recoverable values* will be capitalised and carried forward to future periods as assets of the business.

IAS 38 was modified in 2004 to acknowledge that intangible assets could have indefinite useful lives. It had been the intent, when developing IAS 38, to stipulate that intangibles should have a maximum life of 20 years, but when this standard was finally approved, it included a rebuttable presumption that an intangible would have a life of no more than 20 years. The most recent amendment to IAS 38 removed the rebuttable presumption as to maximum economic life. IAS 38 now includes a list of intangibles that should normally be given separate recognition, and not merely grouped with goodwill, which is to denote only the unidentified intangible asset acquired in a business combination.

During the amendment project on clarification of acceptable methods of depreciation and amortisation in 2014, some changes came into place effectively as of January 1, 2016. Changes were made to clarify when the use of a revenue-based amortisation method is appropriate.

Nature of Intangible Assets

Identifiable intangible assets include patents, copyrights, licences, customer lists, brand names, import quotas, computer software, marketing rights and specialised know-how. These items have in common the fact that there is little or no tangible substance to them, and they have a useful life of greater than one year. In many but not all cases, the asset is separable; that is, it could be sold or otherwise disposed of without simultaneously disposing of or diminishing the value of other assets held.

Intangible assets are, by definition, assets that have no physical substance. However, there may be instances where intangibles also have some physical form. For example:

- There may be tangible evidence of an asset's existence, such as a certificate indicating that a patent had been granted, but this does not constitute the asset itself;
- Some intangible assets may be contained in or on a physical substance such as a USB stick or compact disc (in the case of computer software); and
- Identifiable assets that result from research and development activities are intangible assets because the tangible prototype or model is secondary to the knowledge that is the primary outcome of those activities.

In the case of assets that have both tangible and intangible elements, there may be uncertainty about whether classification should be as tangible or intangible assets. For example, the IASB has deliberately not specified whether mineral exploration and evaluation assets should be considered as tangible or intangible, but rather in IFRS 6 (see Chapter 32) has established a requirement that a reporting entity consistently account for exploration and evaluation assets as either tangible or intangible.

As a rule of thumb, an asset that has both tangible and intangible elements should be classified as an intangible asset or a tangible asset based on the relative dominance or comparative significance of the tangible or the intangible components of the asset. For instance, computer software that is not an integral part of the related hardware equipment is treated as software (i.e., as an intangible asset). Conversely, certain computer software, such as the operating system, that is essential and an integral part of a computer, is treated as part of the hardware equipment (i.e., as property, plant and equipment as opposed to an intangible asset).

Recognition Criteria

Identifiable intangible assets have much in common with tangible long-lived assets (property, plant and equipment), and the accounting for them is accordingly very similar. Recognition depends on whether the *Framework* definition of an asset is satisfied. The key criteria for determining whether intangible assets are to be recognised are:

1. Whether the intangible asset can be identified separately from other aspects of the business entity;
2. Whether the use of the intangible asset is controlled by the entity as a result of its past actions and events;
3. Whether future economic benefits can be expected to flow to the entity; and
4. Whether the cost of the asset can be measured reliably.

Identifiability

IAS 38 states that an intangible meets the identifiability requirement if:

1. It is separable (i.e., is capable of being separated or divided from the entity and sold, transferred, licensed, rented or exchanged, either individually or together with a related contract, asset or liability); *or*
2. It arises from contractual or other legal rights, regardless of whether those rights are transferable or separable from the entity or from other rights and obligations.

The nature of intangibles is such that, as discussed above, many are not recognised at the time that they come into being. The costs of creating many intangibles are typically expensed year by year (e.g., as research costs or other period expenses) before an asset has been created. The cost of internal intangible asset development cannot be capitalised retrospectively, and this means that such assets remain off the statement of financial position until and unless the entity is acquired by another entity. The acquiring entity must allocate the acquisition price over the bundle of assets and liabilities acquired, irrespective of whether those assets and liabilities had been recognised in the acquired company's statement of financial position. For that reason, the notion of identifiability is significant in enabling an allocation of the cost of a business combination to be made.

In a business acquisition, it is preferred that as many individual assets be recognised as possible, because the residual amount of unallocated acquisition cost is treated as goodwill, which provides less transparency to investors and other financial statement users. Furthermore, since goodwill is not subject to amortisation, and its continued recognition—notwithstanding the impairment testing provision—can be indirectly justified by the creation of internally generated goodwill, improperly combining identifiable intangibles with goodwill can have long-term effects on the representational faithfulness of the entity's financial statements.

Inasmuch as the IASB advocates the recognition of the individual assets that may have been acquired in a business combination, it did acknowledge in the 2009 Improvements Project the difficulty that reporters may face in separating the intangible assets acquired. In this regard, the standard was amended to consider that an intangible asset acquired in a business combination might be separable, but only together with a related contract or liability. In such cases, the acquirer recognises the intangible asset separately from goodwill but together with the related item. The acquirer may recognise a group of complementary intangible assets as a single asset provided the individual assets in the group have similar useful lives. For example, the terms "brand" and "brand name" are often used as synonyms for trademarks and other marks. However, the former are general marketing terms that are typically used to refer to a group of complementary assets such as a trademark (or service mark) and its related trade name, formulas, recipes and technological expertise.

Control

The provisions of IAS 38 require that an entity should be in a position to control the use of any intangible asset that is to be presented in the entity's statement of financial position. Control implies the power to both obtain future economic benefits from the asset as well as restrict others' access to those benefits. Normally, entities register patents, copyrights, etc. to ensure control over these intangible assets, although entities often have to engage in litigation to preserve that control.

A patent provides the registered owner (or licensee) the exclusive right to use the underlying product or process without any interference or infringement from others. In contrast with these, intangible assets arising from technical knowledge of staff, customer loyalty, long-term training benefits, etc., will have difficulty meeting this recognition criteria despite expected future economic benefits to be derived from them. This is because the entity would find it impossible to fully control these resources or to prevent others from controlling them.

For instance, even if an entity expends considerable resources on training that will supposedly increase staff skills, the economic benefits from skilled staff cannot be controlled, since trained employees could leave their current employment and move on in their career to other employers. Hence, staff training expenditures, no matter how material in amount, do not qualify as an intangible asset.

Future economic benefits

Generally, an asset is recognised only if it is *probable* that future economic benefits specifically associated therewith will flow to the reporting entity, and the cost of the asset can be *measured reliably*. Traditionally, the probability issue acts as an on-off switch. If the future cash flow is *more likely than not* to occur, the item is recognised, but if the cash flow is less likely to occur, nothing is recognised. However, under IFRS 3, *Business Combinations*, where an intangible asset is acquired as part of a business combination, it is valued at fair value, and the fair value computation is affected by the probability that the future cash flow will occur. Under the fair value approach, the recorded amount is determined as the present value of the cash flow, adjusted for the likelihood of receiving it, as well as for the time value of money. Under IFRS 3 the probability criteria are always considered satisfied for intangible assets that are acquired separately or in a business combination.

The future economic benefits envisaged by the standard may take the form of revenue from the sale of products or services, cost savings or other benefits resulting from the use of the intangible asset by the entity. A good example of other benefits resulting from the use of the intangible asset is the use by an entity of a secret formula (which the entity has protected legally) that leads to reduced levels of competition in the marketplace, thus enhancing the prospects for substantial and profitable future sales and reduced expenditures on such matters as product development and advertising.

Measurement of the Cost of Intangibles

The conditions under which the intangible asset has been acquired will determine the measurement of its cost.

The cost of an intangible asset acquired separately is determined in a manner largely analogous to that for tangible long-lived assets as described in Chapter 9. Thus, the cost of a separately acquired intangible asset includes:

1. Its purchase price, including legal and brokerage fees, import duties and non-refundable purchase taxes, after deducting trade discounts and rebates; and
2. Any directly attributable costs incurred to prepare the asset for its intended use. Directly attributable costs would include costs of employee benefits arising directly from bringing the asset to its intended use, professional fees incurred in bringing the asset to its working condition, and costs of testing whether the asset is functioning properly.

As with tangible assets, capitalisation of costs ceases at the point when the intangible asset is ready to be placed in service in the manner intended by management. Any costs incurred in using or redeploying intangible assets are accordingly excluded from the cost of those assets. Thus, any costs incurred while the asset is capable of being used in the manner intended by management, but while it has yet to be placed into service, would be expensed, not capitalised. Similarly, initial operating losses, such as those incurred while demand for the asset's productive outputs is being developed, cannot be capitalised. Examples of expenditures that are not part of the cost of an intangible asset include costs of introducing a new product or service, costs of conducting business in a new location or with a new class of customers, and administration and other general overhead costs. On the other hand, further costs incurred for the purpose of improving the asset's level of performance would qualify for capitalisation. In all these particulars, guidance under IAS 38 mirrors that under IAS 16.

According to IAS 38, the cost of an intangible asset acquired as part of a business combination is its fair value as at the date of acquisition. If the intangible asset is separable or arises from contractual or other legal rights sufficient information exists to measure reliably the fair value of the asset. If the intangible asset has no active market, then fair value is determined based on the amount that the entity would have paid for the asset in an arm's-length transaction at the date of acquisition. If the fair value of an intangible asset acquired as part of a business combination cannot be measured reliably, then that asset is not separately recognised, but rather is included in goodwill. This fallback position is to be used only when direct identification of the intangible asset's value cannot be accomplished.

If payment for an intangible asset is deferred beyond normal credit terms, its cost is the cash price equivalent. The difference between this amount and the total payments is recognised as financing cost over the period of credit unless it is capitalised in accordance with IAS 23 (see Chapter 10).

Intangibles acquired through an exchange of assets

In other situations, intangible assets may be acquired in exchange or *partly in exchange for other dissimilar intangible* or other assets. The same *commercial substance* rules under IAS 16 apply under IAS 38. If the exchange will affect the future cash flows of the entity, then it has commercial substance, the acquired asset is recognised at its fair value and the asset given up is also measured at fair value. Any difference between carrying amount of the asset(s) given up and those acquired will be given recognition as a gain or loss. However, if there is no commercial substance to the exchange, or the fair values cannot be measured reliably, then the value used is that of the asset given up.

Internally generated goodwill is not recognised as an intangible asset because it fails to meet recognition criteria, including:

- Reliable measurement of cost;
- An identity separate from other resources; and
- Control by the reporting entity.

In practice, accountants are often confronted with the reporting entity's desire to recognise internally generated goodwill based on the premise that at a certain point in time the market value of an entity exceeds the carrying amount of its identifiable net assets. However, IAS 38 categorically states that such differences cannot be considered to represent the cost of intangible assets *controlled by the entity*, and hence could not meet the criteria for recognition (i.e., capitalisation) of such an asset in the accounts of the entity. Nonetheless, standard setters are concerned that when an entity tests a cash-generating unit for impairment, internally generated goodwill cannot be separated from acquired goodwill, and that it forms a cushion against impairment of acquired goodwill. In other words, when an entity has properly recognised goodwill (i.e., that acquired in a business combination), implicitly there is the likelihood that internally generated goodwill may well achieve recognition in later periods, to the extent that this offsets the impairment of goodwill

Intangibles acquired at little or no cost by means of government grants

If the intangible is acquired without cost or by payment of nominal consideration, as by means of a government grant (e.g., when the government grants the right to operate a radio station) or similar means, and assuming the historical cost treatment is being utilised to account for these assets, obviously there will be little or no amount reflected as an asset. If the asset is important to the reporting entity's operations, however, it must be adequately disclosed in the notes to the financial statements.

If the revaluation method of accounting for the asset is used, as permitted under IAS 38, the fair value should be determined by reference to an active market. However, given the probable lack of an active market, since government grants are virtually never transferable, it is unlikely that this situation will be encountered. If an active market does not exist for this type of intangible asset, the entity must recognise the asset at cost. Cost would include those that are directly attributable to preparing the asset for its intended use. Government grants are addressed in Chapter 21.

Internally Generated Intangibles other than Goodwill

In many instances, intangibles are generated internally by an entity, rather than being acquired via a business combination or some other acquisitions. Because of the nature of intangibles, the measurement of the cost (i.e., the initial amounts at which these could be recognised as assets) is constrained by the fact that many of the costs have already been expensed by the time the entity is able to determine that an asset has indeed been created. For example, when launching a new magazine, an entity may have to operate the magazine at a loss in its early years, expensing large promotional and other costs which all flow through the income statement before such time as the magazine can be determined to have become established, and have branding that might be taken to represent an intangible asset. At the point the brand is determined to be an asset, all the costs of creating it have already been expensed, and no retrospective adjustment is allowed to create a recognised asset.

IAS 38 provides that internally generated intangible assets are to be capitalised and amortised over the projected period of economic utility, provided that certain criteria are met.

Expenditures pertaining to the creation of intangible assets are to be classified alternatively as being indicative of, or analogous to, either research activity or development activity.

- Costs incurred in the *research* phase are expensed immediately; and
- If costs incurred in the *development* phase meet the recognition criteria for an intangible asset, such costs should be capitalised. However, once costs have been expensed during the development phase, they cannot later be capitalised.

In practice, distinguishing research-like expenditures from development-like expenditures might not be easily accomplished. This would be especially true in the case of intangibles for which the measurement of economic benefits cannot be accomplished in anything approximating a direct manner. Assets such as brand names, mastheads and customer lists can prove quite resistant to such direct observation of value (although in many industries there are rules of thumb, such as the notion that a customer list in the securities brokerage business is worth $1,500 per name, implying the amount of promotional costs a purchaser of a customer list could avoid incurring itself).

Thus, entities may incur certain expenditures to enhance brand names, such as engaging in image-advertising campaigns, but these costs will also have ancillary benefits, such as promoting specific products that are being sold currently, and possibly even enhancing employee morale and performance. While it may be argued that the expenditures create or add to an intangible asset, as a practical matter it would be difficult to determine what portion of the expenditures relate to which achievement, and to ascertain how much, if any, of the cost may be capitalised as part of brand names. Thus, it is considered to be unlikely that threshold criteria for recognition can be met in such a case. For this reason, IAS 38 has specifically disallowed the capitalisation of internally generated assets like brands, mastheads, publishing titles, customer lists and items similar in substance to these.

Apart from the prohibited items, however, IAS 38 permits recognition of internally created intangible assets to the extent the expenditures can be attributed to the development phase of a research and development programme. Thus, internally developed patents, copyrights, trademarks, franchises and other assets will be recognised at the cost of creation, exclusive of costs which would be analogous to research, as further explained in the following paragraphs. The Basis for Conclusions to IAS 38 notes that "some view these requirements and guidance as being too restrictive and arbitrary" and that they reflect the standard setter's interpretation of the recognition criteria but agree that they reflect the fact that it is difficult in practice to determine whether there is an internally generated asset separate from internally generated goodwill.

When an internally generated intangible asset meets the recognition criteria, the cost is determined using the same principles as for an acquired tangible asset. Thus, cost comprises all costs directly attributable to creating, producing and preparing the asset for its intended use. IAS 38 closely mirrors IAS 16 with regard to elements of cost that may be considered as part of the asset, and the need to recognise the cash equivalent price when the acquisition transaction provides for deferred payment terms. As with self-constructed tangible assets, elements of profit must be eliminated from amounts capitalised, but incremental administrative and other overhead costs can be allocated to the intangible and included in the asset's cost provided these can be directly attributed to preparing the asset for use. Initial operating losses, on the other hand, cannot be deferred by being added to the cost of the intangible, but rather must be expensed as incurred.

The standard takes this view based on the premise that an entity cannot demonstrate that the expenditure incurred in the research phase will generate probable future economic benefits, and consequently that an intangible asset has been created (therefore, such expenditure should be expensed). Examples of research activities include activities aimed at obtaining new knowledge; the search for, evaluation and final selection of applications of research findings; and the search for and formulation of alternatives for new and improved systems, etc.

The standard recognises that the development stage is further advanced towards ultimate commercial exploitation of the product or service being created than is the research stage. It acknowledges that an entity can possibly, in certain cases, identify an intangible asset and demonstrate that this asset will probably generate future economic benefits for the organisation. Accordingly, IAS 38 allows recognition of an intangible asset during the development phase, provided the entity can demonstrate all of the following:

- Technical feasibility of completing the intangible asset so that it will be available for use or sale;
- Its intention to complete the intangible asset and either use it or sell it;
- Its ability to use or sell the intangible asset;
- The mechanism by which the intangible will generate probable future economic benefits;
- The availability of adequate technical, financial and other resources to complete the development and to use or sell the intangible asset; and
- The entity's ability to reliably measure the expenditure attributable to the intangible asset during its development.

Examples of development activities include: the design and testing of preproduction prototypes or models; design of tools, jigs, moulds and dies, including new technology; design, construction and operation of a pilot plant which is not otherwise commercially feasible; and design and testing of a preferred alternative for new and improved devices, products, processes, systems or services.

Recognition of internally generated computer software costs

The recognition of computer software costs poses several questions:

1. In the case of a company developing software programs for sale, should the costs incurred in developing the software be expensed, or should the costs be capitalised and amortised?
2. Is the treatment for developing software programs different if the program is to be used for in-house applications only?
3. In the case of purchased software, should the cost of the software be capitalised as a tangible asset or as an intangible asset, or should it be expensed fully and immediately?

In view of IAS 38's provisions the position can be clarified as follows:

1. In the case of a software-developing company, the costs incurred in the development of software programs are research and development costs. Accordingly, all expenses incurred in the research phase would be expensed. That is, all expenses incurred before *technological feasibility* for the product has been established should be expensed. The reporting entity would have to demonstrate both technological feasibility and a probability of its commercial success. Technological feasibility would be established if the entity has completed a detailed program design or working model. The entity should have completed the planning, designing, coding and testing activities and established that the product can be successfully produced. Apart from being capable of production, the entity should demonstrate that it has the intention and ability to use or sell the program. Action taken to obtain control over the program in the form of copyrights or patents would support capitalisation of these costs. At this stage, the software program would be able to meet the criteria of identifiability, control and future economic benefits, and can thus be capitalised and amortised as an intangible asset.

2. In the case of software internally developed for in-house use—for example, a computerised payroll program developed by the reporting entity itself—the accounting approach would be different. While the program developed may have some utility to the entity itself, it would be difficult to demonstrate how the program would generate future economic benefits to the entity. Also, in the absence of any legal rights to control the program or to prevent others from using it, the recognition criteria would not be met. Furthermore, the cost proposed to be capitalised should be recoverable. In view of the impairment test prescribed by the standard, the carrying amount of the asset may not be recoverable and would accordingly have to be adjusted. Considering the above facts, such costs may need to be expensed.
3. In the case of purchased software, the treatment could differ and would need to be evaluated on a case-by-case basis. Software purchased for sale would be treated as inventory. However, software held for licensing or rental to others should be recognised as an intangible asset. On the other hand, cost of software purchased by an entity for its own use, and which is integral to the hardware (because without that software the equipment cannot operate), would be treated as part of the cost of the hardware and capitalised as property, plant and equipment. Thus, the cost of an operating system purchased for an in-house computer, or cost of software purchased for a computer-controlled machine tool, is treated as part of the related hardware.

The costs of other software programs should be treated as intangible assets (as opposed to being capitalised along with the related hardware), as they are not an integral part of the hardware. For example, the cost of payroll or inventory software (purchased) may be treated as an intangible asset provided it meets the capitalisation criteria under IAS 38. In practice, the conservative approach would be to expense such costs as they are incurred, since their ability to generate future economic benefits will always be questionable. If the costs are capitalised, useful lives should be conservatively estimated (i.e., kept brief) because of the well-known risk of technological obsolescence.

Example of software developed for internal use

The Hy-Tech Services Corporation employs researchers based in countries around the world. Employee time is the basis upon which charges to many customers are made. The geographically dispersed nature of its operations makes it extremely difficult for the payroll staff to collect time records, so the management team authorises the design of an in-house, web-based timekeeping system. The project team incurs the following costs:

Cost type	*Charged to expense*	*Capitalised*
Concept design	2,500	
Evaluation of design alternatives	3,700	
Determination of required technology	8,100	
Final selection of alternatives	1,400	
Software design		€28,000
Software coding		42,000

Quality assurance testing		30,000
Data conversion costs	3,900	
Training	14,000	
Overhead allocation	6,900	
General and administrative costs	11,200	
Ongoing maintenance costs	6,000	
Totals	€57,700	€100,000

Thus, the total capitalised cost of this development project is €100,000. The estimated useful life of the timekeeping system is five years. As soon as all testing is completed, Hy-Tech's controller begins amortising using a monthly charge of €1,666.67. The calculation is as follows:

$$€100,000 \text{ capitalised cost} \div 60 \text{ months} = €1,666.67 \text{ amortisation charge}$$

Once operational, management elects to construct another module for the system that issues an e-mail reminder for employees to complete their timesheets. This represents significant added functionality, so the design cost can be capitalised. The following costs are incurred:

Labour type	Labour cost	Payroll taxes	Benefits	Total cost
Software developers	11,000	842	1,870	13,712
Quality assurance testers	7,000	536	1,190	8,726
Totals	€18,000	€1,378	€3,060	€22,438

The full €22,438 amount of these costs can be capitalised. By the time this additional work is completed, the original system has been in operation for one year, thereby reducing the amortisation period for the new module to four years. The calculation of the monthly straight-line amortisation follows:

$$€22,438 \text{ capitalised cost} \div 48 \text{ months} = €467.46 \text{ amortisation charge}$$

The Hy-Tech management then authorises the development of an additional module that allows employees to enter time data into the system from their cell phones using text messaging. Despite successfully passing through the concept design stage, the development team cannot resolve interface problems on a timely basis. Management elects to shut down the development project, requiring all of the €13,000 of programming and testing costs to be expensed in the current period.

Costs Not Satisfying the IAS 38 Recognition Criteria

The standard has specifically provided that expenditures incurred for non-financial intangible assets should be recognised as an expense unless:

1. It relates to an intangible asset dealt with in another IFRS;
2. The cost forms part of the cost of an intangible asset that meets the recognition criteria prescribed by IAS 38; or
3. It is acquired in a business combination and cannot be recognised as an identifiable intangible asset. In this case, this expenditure should form part of the amount attributable to goodwill as at the date of acquisition.

As a consequence of applying the above criteria, the following costs are expensed as they are incurred:

- Research costs;
- Pre-opening costs for a new facility or business, and plant start-up costs incurred during a period prior to full-scale production or operation, unless these costs are capitalised as part of the cost of an item of property, plant and equipment;
- Organisation costs such as legal and secretarial costs, which are typically incurred in establishing a legal entity;
- Training costs involved in operating a business or a product line;
- Advertising and related costs;
- Relocation, restructuring and other costs involved in organising a business or product line;
- Customer lists, brands, mastheads and publishing titles that are internally generated.

In some country's entities have previously been allowed to defer and amortise set-up costs and pre-operating costs on the premise that benefits from them flow to the entity over future periods as well. IAS 38 does not condone this view.

The criteria for recognition of intangible assets as provided in IAS 38 are rather stringent, and many entities will find that expenditures either to acquire or to develop intangible assets will fail the test for capitalisation. In such instances, all these costs must be expensed as period costs when incurred. Furthermore, once expensed, these costs cannot be resurrected and capitalised in a later period, even if the conditions for such treatment are later met. This is not meant, however, to preclude correction of an error made in an earlier period if the conditions for capitalisation were met but interpreted incorrectly by the reporting entity at that time.

Example of development cost capitalisation

Assume that Creative Incorporated incurs substantial research and development costs for the invention of new products, many of which are brought to market successfully. In particular, Creative has incurred costs during 20XX amounting to €750,000, relative to a new manufacturing process. Of these costs, €600,000 was incurred prior to December 1, 20XX. As of December 31, the viability of the new process was still not known, although testing had been conducted on December 1. In fact, results were not conclusively known until February 15, 20XX+1, after another €75,000 in costs was incurred post-January 1. Creative's financial statements for 20XX were issued February 10, 20XX+1, and the full €750,000 in research and development costs was expensed, since it was not yet known whether a portion of these qualified as development costs under IAS 38. When it is learned that feasibility had, in fact, been shown as of December 1, Creative's management asks to restore the €150,000 of post-December 1 costs as a development asset. Under IAS 38 this is prohibited. However, the 20XX+1 costs (€75,000 thus far) would qualify for capitalisation, in all likelihood, based on the facts known.

Improvements to IFRS published by the IASB in May 2008 included two amendments to IAS 38. One improvement clarifies that certain expenditures are recognised as an expense when the entity either has access to the goods or has received the services. Examples of expenditures that are recognised as an expense when incurred include research costs, expenditure on start-up activities, training activities, advertising and promotional activities, and on relocating or reorganising part or all of an entity. Advertising and promotional activities now specifically include mail-order catalogues. Logically, these expenditures have difficult-to-measure future economic benefits (e.g., advertising), or are not controlled by the reporting entity (e.g., training), and therefore do not meet the threshold conditions for recognition as assets. For some entities, this amendment may result in expenditures being recognised as an expense earlier than in the past.

In addition, a second improvement to IAS 38 removed the reference to the use of anything other than the straight-line method of amortisation being rare, and makes it clear that entities may use the unit of production method of amortisation even if it results in a lower amount of accumulated amortisation than does the straight-line method. This would specifically apply to some service concession arrangements, where an intangible asset for the right to charge users for public service is created. Consequently, entities will have more flexibility as to the method of amortisation of intangible assets and will need to evaluate a pattern of future benefits arising from those assets when selecting the method.

Example: Revenue-based amortisation

A company that is involved in the extraction of high-value diamonds has a contract to extract diamonds as follows: there are no limitations on the duration or kilograms which can be extracted, there are also no limitations on the extraction value of the diamonds; however, the contract will expire after the company reaches its sales goal of €800 million. The contract in this situation is therefore highly dependent on the revenues so that a revenue-based amortisation method could be appropriate. There are no other factors that have an impact on the revenues gained with the contract.

Subsequently Incurred Costs

Under the provisions of IAS 38, the capitalisation of any subsequent costs incurred on recognised intangible assets is subject to the same recognition criteria as initial costs. In practice, capitalisation of subsequent expenditure is often difficult to justify. This is because the nature of an intangible asset is such that, in many cases, it is not possible to determine whether subsequent costs are likely to enhance the specific economic benefits that will flow to the entity from those assets. Provided they meet the recognition criteria for intangible assets, any subsequent expenditure on an intangible after its purchase or its completion should be capitalised along with its cost. The following example should help to illustrate this point better.

Example of subsequent costs

An entity is developing a new product. Costs incurred by the R&D department in 20XX-1 on the "research phase" amounted to €200,000. In 20XX, technical and commercial feasibility of the product was established. Costs incurred in 20XX were €20,000 personnel costs and €15,000 legal fees to register the patent. In 20XX, the entity incurred €30,000 to successfully defend a legal suit to protect the patent. The entity would account for these costs as follows:

- Research and development costs incurred in 20XX-1, amounting to €200,000, should be expensed, as they do not meet the recognition criteria for intangible assets. The costs do not result in an identifiable asset capable of generating future economic benefits.

- Personnel and legal costs incurred in 20XX, amounting to €35,000, would be capitalised as patents. The company has established technical and commercial feasibility of the product, as well as obtained control over the use of the asset. The standard specifically prohibits the reinstatement of costs previously recognised as an expense. Thus, €200,000, recognised as an expense in the previous financial statements, cannot be reinstated and capitalised.
- Legal costs of €30,000 incurred in 20XX to defend the entity in a patent lawsuit should be expensed. These could be considered as expenses incurred to maintain the asset at its originally assessed standard of performance and would not meet the recognition criteria.
- Alternatively, if the entity were to lose the patent lawsuit, then the useful life and the recoverable amount of the intangible asset would be in question. The entity would be required to provide for any impairment loss, and in all probability even to fully write off the intangible asset. What is required must be determined by the facts of the specific situation.

Measurement Subsequent to Initial Recognition

IAS 38 acknowledges the validity of two alternative measurement bases: the cost model and the revaluation model. This is entirely comparable to what is prescribed under IAS 16 relative to property, plant and equipment.

Cost model

After initial recognition, an intangible asset should be carried at its cost less any accumulated amortisation and any accumulated impairment losses.

Revaluation model

As with tangible assets, the standard for intangibles permits revaluation subsequent to original acquisition, with the asset being written up to fair value. Inasmuch as most of the particulars of IAS 38 follow IAS 16 to the letter, and were described in detail in Chapter 9, these will not be repeated here. The unique features of IAS 38 are as follows:

1. If the intangibles were not initially recognised (i.e., they were expensed rather than capitalised) it would not be possible to later recognise them at fair value.
2. Deriving fair value by applying a present value concept to projected cash flows (a technique that can be used in the case of tangible assets under IAS 16) is deemed to be too unreliable in the realm of intangibles, primarily because it would tend to commingle the impact of identifiable assets and goodwill. Accordingly, fair value of an intangible asset should *only* be determined by reference to an active market in that type of intangible asset. Active markets providing meaningful data are not expected to exist for such unique assets as patents and trademarks, and thus it is presumed that revaluation will not be applied to these types of assets in the normal course of business. As a consequence, the standard effectively restricts revaluation of intangible assets to freely tradable intangible assets.

As with the rules pertaining to property, plant and equipment under IAS 16, if some intangible assets in a given class are subjected to revaluation, all the assets in that class should be consistently accounted for unless fair value information is not or ceases to be available. Also, in common with the requirements for tangible fixed assets, IAS 38 requires that revaluations be recognised in other comprehensive income and accumulated in equity in the revaluation surplus account for that asset, except to the extent that previous impairments had been recognised by a charge against profit or loss, in which case the recovery would also be recognised in profit or loss. If recovery is recognised in profit or loss, any revaluation above what the carrying amount would have been in the absence of the impairment is to be recognised in other comprehensive income.

A recent amendment to IAS 38 has clarified that the gross value is restated (either by reference to market data or proportionally to the change in carrying amount) and that accumulated depreciation is the difference between the new gross amount and the new carrying amount.

Example of revaluation of intangible assets

A patent right is acquired on July 1, 20XX-1, for €250,000; while it has a legal life of 15 years, due to rapidly changing technology, management estimates a useful life of only five years. Straight-line amortisation will be used. At January 1, 20XX, management is uncertain that the process can actually be made economically feasible and decides to write down the patent to an estimated market value of €75,000. Amortisation will be taken over three years from that point. On January 1, 20XX+2, having perfected the related production process, the asset is now appraised at a depreciated replacement cost of €300,000. Furthermore, the estimated useful life is now believed to be six more years. The entries to reflect these events are as follows:

7/1/20XX-1	Patent	€250,000	
	Cash, etc.		€250,000
12/31/20XX-1	Amortisation expense	€25,000	
	Patent		€25,000
1/1/20XX	Loss from asset impairment	€150,000	
	Patent		€150,000
12/31/20XX	Amortisation expense	€25,000	
	Patent		€25,000
12/31/20XX+1	Amortisation expense	€25,000	
	Patent		€25,000
1/1/20XX+2	Patent	€275,000	
	Gain on asset value recovery		€100,000
	Other comprehensive income		€175,000

Certain of the entries in the foregoing example will be explained further. The entry at year-end 20XX-1 is to record amortisation based on original cost, since there had been no revaluations through that time; only a half-year amortisation is provided [(€250,000/5) × 1/2]. On January 1, 20XX, the impairment is recorded by writing down the asset to the estimated value of €75,000, which necessitates a €150,000 charge against profit (carrying amount, €225,000, less fair value, €75,000).

In 20XX and 20XX+1, amortisation must be provided on the new lower value recorded at the beginning of 20XX; furthermore, since the new estimated life was three years from January 20XX, annual amortisation will be €25,000.

As of January 1, 20XX+2, the carrying amount of the patent is €25,000; had the January 20XX revaluation not been made, the carrying amount would have been €125,000 (€250,000 original cost, less two-and-one-half years' amortisation versus an original estimated life of five years). The new appraised value is €300,000, which will fully recover the earlier write-down and add even more asset value than the originally recognised cost. Under the guidance of IAS 38, the recovery of €100,000 that had been charged to expense should be recognised as profit; the excess will be recognised in other comprehensive income and increases the revaluation surplus for the asset in equity.

Development costs as a special case

Development costs pose a special problem in terms of the application of the revaluation method under IAS 38. In general, it will not be possible to obtain fair value data from active markets, as is required by IAS 38. Accordingly, the expectation is that the cost method will be almost universally applied for development costs.

If, however, it is determined that fair value information derived from active markets is indeed available, and the entity desires to apply the revaluation method of accounting to development costs, then it will be necessary to perform revaluations on a regular basis, such that at any reporting date the carrying amounts are not materially different from the current fair values. From a mechanical perspective, the adjustment to fair value can be accomplished either by "grossing up" the cost and the accumulated amortisation accounts proportionally, or by netting the accumulated amortisation, prior to revaluation, against the asset account and then restating the asset to the net fair value as of the revaluation date. In either case, the net effect of the upward revaluation will be recognised in other comprehensive income and accumulated in equity; the only exception would be when an upward revaluation is in effect a reversal of a previously recognised impairment which was reported as a charge against profit or a revaluation decrease (reversal or a yet earlier upward adjustment) which was reflected in profit or loss.

The accounting for revaluations is illustrated below.

Example of accounting for revaluation of development cost

Assume Breakthrough, Inc. has accumulated development costs that meet the criteria for capitalisation at December 31, 20XX, amounting to €39,000. It is estimated that the useful life of this intangible asset will be six years; accordingly, amortisation of €6,500 per year is anticipated. Breakthrough uses the allowed alternative method of accounting for its long-lived tangible and intangible assets. At December 31, 20XX+2, it obtains market information regarding the then-current fair value of this intangible asset, which suggests a current fair value of these development costs is €40,000; the estimated useful life, however, has not changed. There are two ways to apply IAS 38: the asset and accumulated amortisation can be "grossed up" to reflect the new fair value information, or the asset can be restated on a "net" basis. These are both illustrated below. For both illustrations, the carrying amount (amortised cost) immediately prior to the revaluation is €39,000 − (2 × €6,500) = €26,000. The net upward revaluation is given by the difference between fair value and carrying amount, or €40,000 − €26,000 = €14,000.

If the "gross up" method is used: Since the fair value after two years of the six-year useful life have already elapsed is found to be €40,000, the gross fair value must be 6/4 × €40,000 = €60,000. The entries to record this would be as follows:

Development cost (asset)	€21,000	
Accumulated amortisation—development cost		€7,000
Other comprehensive income		€14,000

If the "netting" method is used: Under this variant, the accumulated amortisation as of the date of the revaluation is eliminated against the asset account, which is then adjusted to reflect the net fair value.

Accumulated amortisation—development cost	€13,000	
Development cost (asset)		€13,000
Development cost (asset)	€14,000	
Other comprehensive income—revaluation surplus		€14,000

The existing balance in other comprehensive income is closed at the end of the year and its balance accumulated in equity in the revaluation surplus account.

Amortisation Period

IAS 38 requires the entity to determine whether an intangible has a finite or indefinite useful life. An indefinite future life means that there is no foreseeable limit on the period during which the asset is expected to generate net cash inflows. For the entity, the standard lists a number of factors to be taken into account:

1. The expected usage by the entity;
2. Typical product life cycles for the asset;
3. Technical, technological, commercial or other types of obsolescence;
4. The stability of the industry in which the asset operates;
5. Expected actions by competitors, or potential competitors;
6. The level of maintenance expenditures required to generate the future economic benefits, and the company's ability and intention to reach such a level;
7. The period of control over the asset and legal or similar limits on the use of the asset (such as lease expiry dates);
8. Whether the useful life of the asset is dependent on the useful life of other assets of the company.

Assets having a finite useful life must be amortised over that useful life, and this may be done in any of the usual ways (pro rata over time, over units of production, etc.). If control over the future economic benefits from an intangible asset is achieved through legal rights for a finite period, then the useful life of the intangible asset should not exceed the period of legal rights, unless the legal rights are renewable, and the renewal is a virtual certainty. Thus, as a practical matter, the shorter legal life will set the upper limit for an amortisation period in most cases.

The amortisation method used should reflect the pattern in which the economic benefits of the asset are consumed by the entity. Amortisation should commence when the asset is available for use and the amortisation charge for each period should be recognised as an expense unless it is included in the carrying amount of another asset (e.g., inventory). Intangible assets may be amortised by the same systematic methods that are used to depreciate property, plant and equipment. Thus, IAS 38 permits straight-line, diminishing balance, and units of production methods. The method used should reflect the expected pattern of the consumption of expected future economic benefits.

IAS 38 was amended effective January 1, 2016 to confirm that depreciation methods based on revenues that are generated by activities, including the use of an asset, are not appropriate, as revenue generally reflects factors other than the consumption of the economic benefits inherent within an asset. There is a rebuttable presumption that amortisation methods based on generated revenues are inappropriate. Such revenues are not only dependent on the use of the intangible asset but also dependent on other factors such as the activity itself, other inputs and processes, selling activities and changes in sales volumes and prices.

Basing amortisation on revenues is only allowed in two very limited circumstances:

1. In the situation that intangible fixed assets are a measure of revenue, i.e., when a limit is made in a contract referring to time or units.

   Example: Company ABC is allowed for six months to extract rubies from a certain designated area due to specific environmental legislation. In this situation it is determined in a contract that there is a limited period in which the company may extract the rubies and as a result, intangible fixed assets may be amortised with revenues as a basis.
2. Or the revenue and the realisation of economic benefits resulting from the intangible fixed asset are highly correlated and as such revenue is not dependent on other factors, inputs and processes or activities.

IAS 38 offers several examples of how useful life of intangibles is to be assessed. These include the following types of assets:

Customer lists

Care is urged to ensure that amortisation is only over the expected useful life of the acquired list, ignoring the extended life that may be created as the acquirer adds to the list by virtue of its own efforts and costs, after acquisition. In many instances the initial, purchased list will erode in value rather quickly, since contacts become obsolete as customers migrate to other vendors, leave business and so forth. These assets must be constantly refreshed, and that will involve expenditures by the acquirer of the original list (and whether those costs justify capitalisation and amortisation is a separate issue).

For example, the acquired list might have a useful economic life of only two years (i.e., without additional expenditures, the value will be fully consumed over that time horizon). Two years would be the amortisation period, therefore.

Patents

While a patent has a legal economic life (depending on jurisdiction of issuance) of as long as several decades, realistically, due to evolving technology and end-product obsolescence or changing customer tastes and preferences, the useful life may be much less. IAS 38 offers an example of a patent having a 15-year remaining life and a firm offer to acquire by a third party in five years, at a fixed fraction of the original acquirer's cost. In such a situation (which is probably unusual, however), amortisation of the fraction not to be recovered in the subsequent sale, over a five-year period, would be appropriate.

In other situations, it would be necessary to estimate the economic life of the patent and amortise the entire cost, in the absence of any firmly established residual value, over that period. It should be noted that there is increasing activity involving the monetising of intellectual property values, including via the packaging of groups of patents and transferring them to special-purpose entities which then license them to third-party licensees. This shows promise of becoming an important way for patent holders to reap greater benefits from existing pools of patents held by them but is in its infancy at this time and future success cannot be reliably predicted. Amortisation of existing acquired patents or other intellectual property (intangible assets) should not be based on highly speculative values that might be obtained from such arrangements.

Additionally, whatever lives are assigned to patents for amortisation purposes, these should regularly be reconsidered. As necessary, changes in useful lives should be implemented, which would be changes in estimate affecting current and future periods' amortisation only, unless an accounting error had previously been made.

Copyrights

In many jurisdictions, copyrights now have very lengthy terms, but for most materials so protected the actual useful lives will be very much shorter, sometimes only a year or two.

Renewable licence rights

In many situations, the entity may acquire licence rights, such as broadcasting of radio or television signals, which technically expire after a fixed term, but which are essentially renewable with little or no cost incurred as long as minimum performance criteria are met. If there is adequate evidence to demonstrate that this description is accurate and that the reporting entity has indeed been able, previously, to successfully accomplish this, then the intangible will be deemed to have an indefinite life and not be subjected to periodic amortisation. However, this makes it more vital that impairment be regularly reviewed, since even if control of the rights remains with the reporting entity, changes in technology or consumer demand may serve to diminish the value of that asset. If impaired, a charge against earnings must be recognised, with the remaining unimpaired cost (if any) continuing to be recognised as an indefinite life intangible.

Similar actions would be warranted in the case of airline route authority. If readily renewable, without limitation, provided that minimal regulations are complied with (such as maintaining airport terminal space in a prescribed manner), the standard suggests that this be treated as an indefinite-life intangible. Annual impairment testing would be required, as with all indefinite-life intangibles (more often if there is any indication of impairment).

IAS 38 notes that a change in the governmental licensing regime may require a change in how these are accounted for. It cites an example of a change that ends perfunctory renewal and substitutes public auctions for the rights at each renewal date. In such an instance, the reporting entity can no longer presume to have any right to continue after expiration of the current licence and must amortise its cost over the remaining term.

Residual Value

Tangible assets often have a positive residual value before considering the disposal costs because tangible assets can generally be sold, at least for scrap, or possibly can be transferred to another user that has less need for or ability to afford new assets of that type. Intangibles, on the other hand, often have little or no residual worth. Accordingly, IAS 38 requires that a zero residual value be presumed unless an accurate measure of residual value is possible. Thus, the residual value is presumed to be zero *unless*:

- There is a commitment by a third party to acquire the asset at the end of its useful life; *or*

- There is an active market for that type of intangible asset, and residual value can be measured reliably by reference to that market and it is probable that such a market will exist at the end of the useful life.

IAS 38 specifies that the residual value of an intangible asset is the estimated net amount that the reporting entity currently expects to obtain from disposal of the asset at the end of its useful life, after deducting the estimated costs of disposal, if the asset were of the age and in the condition expected at the end of its estimated useful life. Changes in estimated selling prices or other variables that occur over the expected period of use of the asset are not to be included in the estimated residual value, since this would result in the recognition of projected future holding gains over the life of the asset (via reduced amortisation that would be the consequence of a higher estimated residual value).

Residual value is to be assessed at the end of each reporting period. Any change to the estimated residual, other than that resulting from impairment (accounted for under IAS 36), is to be accounted for prospectively by varying future periodic amortisation. Similarly, any change in amortisation method (e.g., from accelerated to straight-line), based on an updated understanding of the pattern of future usage and economic benefits to be reaped therefrom, is dealt with as a change in estimate, again to be reflected only through changes in future periodic charges for amortisation.

Periodic review of useful life assumptions and amortisation methods employed

As for tangible assets accounted for in conformity with IAS 16, the standard on intangibles requires that the amortisation period be reconsidered at the end of each reporting period, and that the method of amortisation also be reviewed at similar intervals. There is the expectation that due to their nature, intangibles are more likely to require revisions to one or both of these judgements. In either case, a change would be accounted for as a change in estimate, affecting current and future periods' reported earnings but not requiring restatement of previously reported periods.

Intangibles being accounted for as having an indefinite life must furthermore be reassessed periodically, as management plans and expectations almost inevitably vary over time. For example, a trademarked product, despite having wide consumer recognition and acceptance, can become irrelevant as tastes and preferences alter, and a limited horizon, perhaps a very short one, may emerge with little warning. Business history is littered with formerly valuable franchises that, for whatever reason—including management missteps—become valueless.

Impairment Losses

Where an asset is determined to have an indefinite useful life, the entity must conduct impairment tests annually, as well as whenever there is an indication that the intangible may be impaired. Furthermore, the presumption that the asset has an indefinite life must also be reviewed.

The impairment of intangible assets other than goodwill (such as patents, copyrights, trade names, customer lists and franchise rights) should be considered in precisely the same way that long-lived tangible assets are dealt with. The impairment loss under IAS 36 is the amount by which carrying amount exceeds recoverable amount. Carrying amount must be compared to recoverable amount (the greater of fair value less costs to sell or value in use) when there are indications that an impairment may have been suffered. Net selling price is the price of an asset in an active market less disposal costs, and value in use is the present value of estimated future cash flows expected to arise from the continuing use of an asset and from its disposal.

IAS 36 permits reversals of impairment losses on assets other than goodwill under defined conditions. The effects of impairment recognitions and reversals will be reflected in profit or loss, if the intangible assets in question are being accounted for in accordance with the cost method.

On the other hand, if the revaluation method of accounting for intangible assets is followed (use of which is possible only if strict criteria are met), impairments will normally be recognised in other comprehensive income to the extent that revaluation surplus exists, and only to the extent that the loss exceeds previously recognised valuation surplus will the impairment loss be reported as a charge in profit or loss. Recoveries are handled consistent with the method by which impairments were reported, in a manner entirely analogous to the explanation in Chapter 9 dealing with impairments of property, plant and equipment.

Unlike other intangible assets that are individually identifiable, goodwill is amorphous and cannot exist, from a financial reporting perspective, apart from the tangible and identifiable intangible assets with which it was acquired and remains associated. Thus, a direct evaluation of the recoverable amount of goodwill is not actually feasible.

Improvements to IFRS issued in 2009 amended the requirements for allocating goodwill to cash-generating units as described in IAS 36, since the definition of operating segments introduced in IFRS 8 affects the determination of the largest unit permitted for goodwill impairment testing in IAS 36. For the purpose of impairment testing, goodwill acquired in a business combination should, from the acquisition date, be allocated to each of the acquirer's cash-generating units (or groups of cash-generating units) that is expected to benefit from synergies resulting from combination, irrespective of whether other assets or liabilities are allocated to this unit (or units).

Each cash-generating unit should:

1. Represent the lowest level of the entity at which management monitors goodwill (which should be the same as the lowest level of operating segments at which the chief operating decision maker regularly reviews operating results in accordance with IFRS 8); and
2. Not be larger than the operating segment, as defined in IFRS 8, before any permitted aggregation.

Derecognition of Intangible Assets

An intangible asset should be derecognised (1) on disposal, or (2) when no future economic benefits are expected from its use or disposal. With regard to questions of accounting for the disposals of assets, the guidance of IAS 38 is consistent with that of IAS 16. A gain or loss arising from the derecognition of an intangible asset, determined as the difference between its carrying amount and the net disposal proceeds, is recognised in profit or loss (unless IAS 17 requires otherwise on a sale and leaseback) when the asset is derecognised. The 2004 amendment to IAS 38 observes that a disposal of an intangible asset may be effected either by a sale of the asset or by entering into a finance lease. The determination of the date of disposal of the intangible asset is made by applying the criteria in IAS 18 for recognising revenue from the sale of goods, or IAS 17 in the case of disposal by a sale and leaseback. As for other similar transactions, the consideration receivable on disposal of an intangible asset is to be recognised initially at fair value. If payment for such an intangible asset is deferred, the consideration received is recognised initially at the cash price equivalent, with any difference between the nominal amount of the consideration and the cash price equivalent to be recognised as interest revenue under IAS 18, using the effective yield method.

Website Development and Operating Costs

Websites have become integral to doing business and may be designed either for external or internal access. Those designed for external access are developed and maintained for the purposes of promotion and advertising of an entity's products and services to their potential consumers. On the other hand, those developed for internal access may be used for displaying company policies and storing customer details.

With substantial costs being incurred by many entities for website development and maintenance, the need for accounting guidance became evident. SIC 32, issued in 2002, concluded that such costs represent an internally generated intangible asset that is subject to the requirements of IAS 38, and that such costs should be recognised if, and only if, an entity can satisfy the requirements set forth in IAS 38. Therefore, website costs have been likened to "development phase" (as opposed to "research phase") costs.

Thus, the stringent qualifying conditions applicable to the development phase, such as "ability to generate future economic benefits," have to be met if such costs are to be recognised as an intangible asset. If an entity is not able to demonstrate how a website developed solely or primarily for promoting and advertising its own products and services will generate probable future economic benefits, all expenditure on developing such a website should be recognised as an expense when incurred.

Any internal expenditure on development and operation of the website should be accounted for in accordance with IAS 38. Comprehensive additional guidance is provided in the Appendix to SIC 32 and is summarised below:

1. Planning stage expenditures, such as undertaking feasibility studies, defining hardware and software specifications, evaluating alternative products and suppliers, and selecting preferences, should be expensed;
2. Application and infrastructure development costs pertaining to acquisition of tangible assets, such as purchasing and developing hardware, should be dealt with in accordance with IAS 16;
3. Other application and infrastructure development costs, such as obtaining a domain name, developing operating software, developing code for the application, installing developed applications on the Web server and stress testing, should be expensed when incurred unless the conditions prescribed by IAS 38 are met;
4. Graphical design development costs, such as designing the appearance of Web pages, should be expensed when incurred unless recognition criteria prescribed by IAS 38 are met;
5. Content development costs, such as expenses incurred for creating, purchasing, preparing and uploading information onto the website, to the extent that these costs are incurred to advertise and promote an entity's own products or services, should be expensed immediately, consistent with how other advertising and related costs are to be accounted for under IFRS. Thus, these costs are not deferred, even until first displayed on the website, but are expensed when incurred;

6. Operating costs, such as updating graphics and revising content, adding new functions, registering the website with search engines, backing up data, reviewing security access and analysing usage of the website should be expensed when incurred, unless in rare circumstances these costs meet the criteria prescribed in IAS 38, in which case such expenditure is capitalised as a cost of the website; and
7. Other costs, such as selling and administrative overhead (excluding expenditure which can be directly attributed to preparation of website for use), initial operating losses and inefficiencies incurred before the website achieves its planned operating status, and training costs of employees to operate the website, should all be expensed as incurred as required under IFRS.

DISCLOSURES

The disclosure requirements set out in IAS 38 for intangible assets and those imposed by IAS 16 for property, plant and equipment are very similar, and both demand extensive details to be disclosed in the financial statement footnotes. Another marked similarity is the exemption from disclosing "comparative information" with respect to the reconciliation of carrying amounts at the beginning and end of the period. While this may be misconstrued as a departure from the well-known principle of presenting all numerical information in comparative form, it is worth noting that it is in line with the provisions of IAS 1. IAS 1 categorically states that "unless a Standard permit or requires otherwise, comparative information should be disclosed in respect of the previous period for all numerical information in the financial statements. . . ."

For each class of intangible assets (distinguishing between internally generated and other intangible assets), disclosure is required of:

1. Whether the useful lives are indefinite or finite and if finite, the useful lives or amortisation rates used;
2. The amortisation method(s) used;
3. The gross carrying amount and accumulated amortisation (including accumulated impairment losses) at both the beginning and end of the period;
4. A reconciliation of the carrying amount at the beginning and end of the period showing additions (analysed between those acquired separately and those acquired in a business combination), assets classified as held-for-sale, retirements, disposals, acquisitions by means of business combinations, increases or decreases resulting from revaluations, reductions to recognise impairments, amounts written back to recognise recoveries of prior impairments, amortisation during the period, the net effect of translation of foreign entities' financial statements, and any other material items; and
5. The line item in the statement of comprehensive income (or statement of profit or loss, if presented separately) in which the amortisation charge of intangible assets is included.

The standard explains the concept of "class of intangible assets" as a "grouping of assets of similar nature and use in an entity's operations." Examples of intangible assets that could be reported as separate classes are:

1. Brand names;
2. Licences and franchises;

3. Mastheads and publishing titles;
4. Computer software;
5. Copyrights, patents and other industrial property rights, service and operating right;
6. Recipes, formulae, models, designs and prototypes; and
7. Intangible assets under development.

The above list is only illustrative in nature. Intangible assets may be combined (or disaggregated) to report larger classes (or smaller classes) of intangible assets if this results in more relevant information for financial statement users.

In addition, the financial statements should disclose the following:

1. For any asset assessed as having an indefinite useful life, the carrying amount of the asset and the reasons for considering that it has an indefinite life and the significant factors used to determine this;
2. The nature, carrying amount and remaining amortisation period of any individual intangible asset that is material to the financial statements of the entity as a whole;
3. For intangible assets acquired by way of a government grant and initially recognised at fair value, the fair value initially recognised, their carrying amount and whether they are carried under the cost or revaluation method for subsequent measurement;
4. The existence and carrying amounts of intangibles with any restrictions on title and the carrying amounts pledged as security for debt; and
5. The amount of outstanding commitments for the acquisition of intangible assets.

Where intangibles are carried using the revaluation model, the entity must disclose the effective date of the revaluation, the carrying amount of the assets, and what their carrying amount would have been under the cost model, the amount of revaluation surplus applicable to the assets and the significant assumptions used in measuring fair value.

The financial statements should also disclose the aggregate amount of research and development expenditure recognised as an expense during the period. The entity is encouraged but not required to disclose any fully amortised assets still in use and any significant assets in use but not recognised because they did not meet the IAS 38 recognition criteria.

EXAMPLE OF FINANCIAL STATEMENT DISCLOSURE

Exemplum Reporting PLC
Financial Statements
For the Year Ended December 31, 20XX

17. Goodwill

Cost	
Opening cost at January 1, 20XX-1	X
Recognised on acquisition of a subsidiary	X
Derecognised on disposal of subsidiary	X
Opening balance at January 1, 20XX	X
Recognised on acquisition of a subsidiary	X
Derecognised on disposal of a subsidiary	X
Closing balance at December 31, 20XX	X
Accumulated impairment	

Opening balance at January 1, 20XX-1	X
Impairment loss	X
Opening balance at January 1, 20XX	X
Impairment loss	X
Closing balance at December 31, 20XX	X
Opening carrying value at January 1, 20XX-1	X
Opening carrying value at January 1, 20XX	X
Closing carrying value at December 31, 20XX	X

The events and circumstances that led to the recognition of the impairment loss was the disposal of a chain of retail stores in the United Kingdom. No other class of assets was impaired other than goodwill.

[Describe the cash-generating units/individual intangible assets of the group and which operating segment they belong to (if any), and whether any impairment losses were recognised or reversed during the period.]

The aggregation of assets for identifying the cash-generating unit has not changed since the prior year.

The recoverable amount of a cash-generating unit is its value in use. In calculating the value in use of the impaired reportable segment the group used a discount rate of X% (20XX-1: X%).

The carrying amount of goodwill allocated to each reportable segment is as follows:

20XX

	Manufacture	**Retail**	**Distribution**	**Total**
Home country	X	X	X	X
Other countries	X	X	X	X

20XX-1

	Manufacture	**Retail**	**Distribution**	**Total**
Home country	X	X	X	X
Other countries	X	X	X	X

Management has based its cash flow projections on cash flow forecasts covering a five-year period. Cash flows after the five-year period have been extrapolated based on the estimated growth rates disclosed below. These growth rates do not exceed the long-term average growth rate for the industry or market in which the group operates. Other key assumptions used in the cash flow projections are as follows:

	Manufacture	**Retail**	**Distribution**
Growth rates		X	X
Discount rates		X	X
Gross profit margins		X	X

Management has based their assumptions on past experience and external sources of information, such as industry sector reports and market expectations.

18. Other intangible assets

	Development Costs	Patents and Trademarks	Total
Group cost			
Opening cost at January 1, 20XX-1	X	X	X
Additions	X	X	X
Exchange differences	X	X	X
Disposals	X	X	X
Acquired through business combination	X	X	X
Opening cost at January 1, 20XX	X	X	X
Additions	X	X	X
Exchange differences	X	X	X
Disposals	X	X	X
Acquired through business combination	X	X	X
Closing cost at December 31, 20XX	X	X	X
Accumulated depreciation/impairment			
Opening balance at January 1, 20XX-1			
Amortisation	X	X	X
Disposals	X	X	X
Exchange differences	X	X	X
Impairment loss	X	X	X
Opening balance at January 1, 20XX	X	X	X
Amortisation	X	X	X
Disposals	X	X	X
Exchange differences	X	X	X
Impairment loss	X	X	X
Impairment reversal	X	X	X
Closing balance at December 31, 20XX	X	X	X
Opening carrying value at January 1, 20XX-1	X	X	X
Opening carrying value at January 1, 20XX	X	X	X
Closing carrying value at December 31, 20XX	X	X	X

The group has a material patent with a carrying amount of £X and a remaining amortisation period of X years.

	20XX	20XX-1
Intangible assets pledged as security for liabilities (as disclosed in note X)	**X**	X

US GAAP COMPARISON

Internally generated intangible assets are not recognised under US GAAP with the exception of some website development costs. The underlying reason is that these assets do not have objectively measurable values.

Development costs for software developed for external use are capitalised once the entity establishes technological feasibility.

Certain costs related to internal-use software can qualify for capitalisation after the completion of the preliminary project stage and when appropriate management has authorised and commits to funding the software project and it is probable that the project will be completed, and the software will be used as intended. Capitalisation is required to cease no later than the time that the project is substantially complete and is ready for use.

The entity can make a policy choice to expense advertising as incurred or when the advertising takes place for the first time. If specific criteria are met, direct response advertising may be capitalised.

US GAAP requires impairment loss to be measured as the excess of the carrying amount over the asset's fair value. Impairment loss results in a new cost basis, and impairment loss cannot be reversed for assets to be held and used. Revaluation is not permitted for goodwill and other indefinite-life intangible assets. For specific examples of accounting for intangible assets see FASB ASC 350, *Intangibles—Goodwill and Other*, or more specifically ASC 350-30-55, *Implementation Guidance and Illustrations*, which discusses defensible intangible assets, acquired customer lists, acquired patents and other meaningful examples.

12 INVESTMENT PROPERTY

INTRODUCTION

IAS 40 is not a specialised industry standard. IAS 40 applies to the accounting treatment for investment property and related disclosure requirements. Determining whether a property is investment property depends on the use of the property and the type of entity that holds the property. Investment properties are initially measured at cost and, with some exceptions, may be subsequently measured using a cost model or fair value model, with changes in the fair value under the fair value model being recognised in profit or loss.

An investment in property (land and/or buildings) held with the intention of earning rental income or for capital appreciation (or both) is described as an investment property. An investment property is capable of generating cash flows independently of other assets held by the entity. Investment property is sometimes referred to as being a "passive" investment, to distinguish it from actively managed property such as plant assets, the use of which is integrated with the rest of the entity's operations. This characteristic is what distinguishes investment property from owner-occupied property, which is property held by the entity or by the lessee as right-of-use asset in its business (i.e., for use in production or supply of goods or services or for administrative purposes).

Revised IAS 40, effective in 2005, for the first-time permitted property interests held in the form of operating leases to be classified and accounted for as investment property. This may be done if:

1. The other elements of the definition of investment property (see below) are met;
2. The operating lease is accounted for as if it were a finance lease in accordance with IFRS 16, *Leases* (that is, it is capitalised);
3. The lessee uses the fair value model set out in IAS 40 for the asset recognised.

This classification option to report the lessee's property interest as investment property is available on a property-by-property basis.

On the other hand, IAS 40 requires that all investment property should be consistently accounted for using either the fair value or cost model. Given these requirements, it is held that once the investment alternative is selected for one leased property, all property classified as investment property must be accounted for consistently on a fair value basis.

IFRS 16, issued in January 2016, amended the scope of IAS 40 by defining investment property to include both owned investment property and property held by a lessee as a right-of-use asset.

DEFINITIONS OF TERMS

The following terms are used in IAS 40 with the meaning specified:

Carrying amount. The amount at which an asset is recognised in the statement of financial position.

Cost. The amount of cash or cash equivalents paid or the fair value of other consideration given to acquire an asset at the time of its acquisition or construction or, where applicable, the amount attributed to that asset when initially recognised in accordance with the specific requirements of other IFRS.

Fair value. The price that would be received to sell an asset or paid to transfer a liability in an orderly transaction between market participants at the measurement date (IFRS 13).

Investment property. Property (land or a building, or part of a building, or both) held (by the owner or by the lessee as a right-of-use asset) to earn rental income or for capital appreciation purposes or both, rather than for:

- Use in the production or supply of goods or services or for administrative purposes;
- Sale in the ordinary course of business.

Owner-occupied property. Property held (by the owner, i.e., the entity itself or by a lessee as a right-of-use asset) for use in the production or supply of goods or services or for administrative purposes.

IDENTIFICATION

The best way to understand what investment property constitutes is to look at examples of investments that are considered by the standard as investment properties, and contrast these with those investments that do not qualify for this categorisation.

According to the standard, examples of investment property are:

- Land held for long-term capital appreciation as opposed to short-term purposes like land held for sale in the ordinary course of business;
- Land held for a currently undetermined future use;
- A building owned by the reporting entity (or a right-of-use asset relating to a building held by the reporting entity) and leased out under one or more operating leases;
- A vacant building held by an entity to be leased out under one or more operating leases;
- Property under construction or being developed for future use as investment property.

The following are examples of items that are not investment property and are therefore outside the scope of the standard:

- Property employed in the business (i.e., held for use in production or supply of goods or services or for administrative purposes, the accounting for which is governed by IAS 16);
- Owner-occupied property (IAS 16), including property held for future use as owner-occupied property, property held for future development and subsequent use as owner-occupied property, property occupied by employees (whether the employees pay rent at market rates) and owner-occupied property awaiting disposal;
- Property being constructed or developed on behalf of third parties, the accounting of which is outlined in IAS 11;
- Property held for sale in the ordinary course of business or in the process of construction or development for such sale, the accounting for which is specified by IAS 2;
- Property that is leased to another entity under a finance lease.

Example: Entity X built a residential property with the intention of selling it. In the past, X has regularly developed property and then sold it immediately after completion. To increase the chances of a sale, X chooses to let some of the flats as soon as they are ready for occupation. The tenants move into the property before completion. How has X mapped the property on the balance sheet?

Henceforth, X classifies the property as inventory. This corresponds to X's core business and its strategy regarding property. These undertakings are carried out with the intention of increasing the chances of selling the property and not for the long-term generation of rental income. The property is also not held for the purpose of capital appreciation.

X's intention to sell the property under construction immediately after completion in the ordinary course of business has not changed. Consequently, the property under construction does not fulfil the definition of an investment property (IAS 40.9(a)).

Apportioning Property between Investment Property and Owner-Occupied Property

In many cases it will be clear what constitutes investment property as opposed to owner-occupied property, but in other instances making this distinction might be less obvious. Certain properties are not held entirely for rental purposes or for capital appreciation purposes. For example, portions of these properties might be used by the entity for manufacturing or for administrative purposes. If these portions, earmarked for different purposes, could be sold, or leased under a finance lease, separately, then the entity is required to account for them separately (dual-use property). However, if the portions cannot be sold, or leased under a finance lease, separately, the property would be deemed as investment property only if an insignificant portion is held by the entity for business use. An example would include that of a shopping mall, in which the landlord maintains an office for the purposes of managing and administering the commercial building, which is rented to tenants.

When ancillary services are provided by the entity and these ancillary services are a relatively insignificant component of the arrangement, as when the owner of a residential building provides maintenance and security services to the tenants, the entity treats such an investment as investment property. An example is when the owner of an office building provides security and maintenance services to the lessees who occupy the building.

On the other hand, if the service provided is a comparatively significant component of the arrangement, then the investment would be considered as an owner-occupied property. For instance, an entity that owns and operates a hotel and provides services to the guests of the hotel would be unable to argue that it is an investment property in the context of IAS 40. Rather, such an investment would be classified as an owner-occupied property.

Judgement is therefore required in determining whether a property qualifies as investment property. It is so important a factor that if an entity develops criteria for determining when to classify a property as an investment property, it is required by this standard to disclose these criteria in the context of difficult or controversial classifications.

Property Leased to a Subsidiary or a Parent Company

Property leased to a subsidiary or its parent company is considered an investment property from the perspective of the entity in its separate financial statements. However, for the purposes of consolidated financial statements, from the perspective of the group, it will not qualify as an investment property, since it is an owner-occupied property when viewed from the group perspective (which includes both the lessor and the lessee). This will necessitate the processing of appropriate adjustments to account for the difference in classification when preparing the consolidated accounts.

Interrelationship between IFRS 3 and IAS 40

The standard was amended through annual improvements to the IFRS 2011–2013 cycle to clarify the relationship between IFRS 3 and IAS 40. It states that IAS 40 assists preparers to distinguish between investment property and owner-occupied property rather than to determine whether the acquisition of an investment property is a business combination in accordance with IFRS 3 (see Chapter 15). The amendment is effective for annual periods beginning on or after July 1, 2014. Early application to individual acquisitions of investment property was allowed if, and only if, the information necessary to apply the amendment was available.

RECOGNITION AND MEASUREMENT

Recognition

Investment property is recognised as an asset when, and only when, it becomes probable that the entity will enjoy the future economic benefits which are attributable to it, and when the costs of the investment property can be reliably measured.

These recognition criteria are applied to all investment property costs (costs incurred initially to acquire an investment property and subsequent costs to add or to replace a part of an investment property) when the costs are incurred.

In general, this will occur when the property is first acquired or constructed by the reporting entity. In unusual circumstances where it would be concluded that the owner's likelihood of receipt of the economic benefits would be less than probable, the costs incurred would not qualify for capitalisation and would consequently have to be expensed.

Initial measurement will be at cost, which is usually equivalent to fair value, if the acquisition was the result of an arm's-length exchange transaction. Included in the purchase cost will be such directly attributable expenditure as legal fees and property transfer taxes, if incurred in the transaction.

IAS 40 does not provide explicit guidance on measuring cost for a self-constructed investment property. However, IAS 16 provides that the cost of a self-constructed asset is determined using the same principles as for an acquired asset. If an entity makes similar assets for sale in the normal course of business, the cost of the asset is usually the same as the cost of constructing an asset for sale (inventory), which would therefore include overhead charges which can be allocated on a reasonable and consistent basis to the construction activities. To the extent that the acquisition cost includes an interest charge, if the payment is deferred, the amount to be recognised as an investment asset should not include the interest charges, unless the asset meets the definition of a qualifying asset under IAS 23, which requires borrowing costs to be capitalised.

Furthermore, start-up costs (unless they are essential in bringing the property to its working condition), initial operating losses (incurred prior to the investment property achieving planned level of occupancy) or abnormal amounts of wasted material, labour or other resources (in construction or development) do not constitute part of the capitalised cost of an investment property.

If an investment property is acquired in exchange for equity instruments of the reporting entity, the cost of the investment property is the fair value of the equity instruments issued, although the fair value of the investment property received is used to measure its cost if it is more clearly evident than the fair value of the equity instruments issued.

The initial cost of an investment property held by a lessee as a right-of-use asset shall be accounted for by applying IFRS 16, *Leases* (IFRS 16.23). The asset is recognised at cost comprising:

- The present value of the minimum lease payments with equivalent amount recognised as a liability;
- Any lease payments made on or before the lease commencement date reduced by lease incentives received if any;
- Any initial direct costs incurred; and
- Estimated cost of asset dismantling and site restoration.

An entity applying IFRS 16 and its related amendments to this standard for the first time shall apply the transition requirements in Appendix C of IFRS 16 to the investment property held as right-of-use asset as follows:

- No adjustments required for leases where the underlying asset is of low value;
- No adjustments required for leases already accounted in the past as investment property using the fair value model in IAS 40;
- Measure the right-of-use asset at fair value on transition date for leases previously accounted for as operating leases applying IAS 17 and that will be accounted on transition as investment property using the fair value model under IAS 40.

Subsequent expenditures

In some instances, there may be further expenditure incurred on the investment property after the date of initial recognition. Consistent with similar situations arising in connection with property, plant and equipment (dealt with under IAS 16), if the costs meet the recognition criteria discussed above, then those costs may be added to the carrying amount of the investment property. Costs of the day-to-day servicing of an investment property (essentially repairs and maintenance) would not ordinarily meet the recognition criteria and would therefore be recognised in profit or loss as period costs when incurred. Costs of day-to-day servicing would include the cost of labour and consumables and may include the cost of minor parts.

Sometimes, the appropriate accounting treatment for subsequent expenditure would depend upon the circumstances that were considered in the initial measurement and recognition of the investment property. For example, if a property (e.g., an office building) is acquired for investment purposes in a condition that makes it incumbent upon the entity to perform significant renovations thereafter, then such renovation costs (which would constitute subsequent expenditures) will be added to the carrying amount of the investment property when incurred later.

Fair value vs. cost model

Analogous to the financial reporting of property, plant and equipment under IAS 16, IAS 40 provides that investment property may be reported at either fair value (fair value model) or at depreciated cost less accumulated impairment (cost model). The cost model is the benchmark treatment prescribed by IAS 16 for owner-occupied assets. However, the fair value approach under IAS 40 more closely resembles that used for financial instruments than it does the allowed alternative (revaluation) method for owner-occupied assets. Also, under IAS 40 if the cost method is used, fair value information must nonetheless be determined and disclosed. IAS 40 notes that it is highly unlikely for a change from a fair value model to a cost model to occur. And if a lessee applies the fair value model for its investment property, it shall apply the same model for its right-of-use assets as well.

Fair value model

When investment property is carried at fair value, at each subsequent financial reporting date the carrying amount must be adjusted to the then-current fair value, with the adjustment being reported in the profit or loss for the period in which it arises. When choosing the fair value model all of the investment property must be measured at fair value, except when there is an inability to measure fair value reliably (see below). The inclusion of the value adjustments in earnings—in contrast to the revaluation approach under IAS 16, whereby adjustments are generally reported in other comprehensive income—is a reflection of the different roles played by plant or owner-occupied assets and by other investment property. The former are used, or consumed, in the operation of the business, which is often centred upon the production of goods and services for sale to customers. The latter are held for possible appreciation in value, and hence those value changes are highly germane to the assessment of periodic operating performance. With this distinction in mind, the decision was made not only to permit fair value reporting, but to require value changes to be included in profit or loss.

IAS 40 represents the first time that fair value accounting was embraced as an accounting model for non-financial assets. This has been a matter of great controversy, and to address the many concerns voiced during the exposure draft stage, the IASB added more guidance on the subject to the final standard. However, with the issue of IFRS 13, *Fair Value Measurements*, in 2011, much of the fair value guidance in IAS 40 has been superseded by that of IFRS 13 (see Chapter 25).

Entities are alerted to the possibility of double counting in determining the fair value of certain types of investment property. For instance, when an office building is leased on a furnished basis, the fair value of office furniture and fixtures is generally included in the fair value of the investment property (in this case the office buildings). The apparent rationale is that the rental income relates to the furnished office building; when fair values of furniture and fixtures are included along with the fair value of the investment property, the entity does not recognise them as separate assets.

Inability to measure fair value reliably

There is a rebuttable presumption that, if an entity acquires or constructs property that will qualify as investment property under this standard, it will be able to assess the fair value reliably on an ongoing basis. In rare circumstances, however, when an entity acquires for the first time an investment property (or when an existing property first qualifies to be classified as investment property when there has been a change of use), there may be clear evidence that the fair value of the investment property cannot reliably be determined on a continuous basis. This arises when, and only when, the market for comparable properties is inactive and alternative reliable measurement of fair value is not available.

Under such exceptional circumstances, the standard stipulates that the entity should measure that investment property using the cost model in IAS 16 until the disposal of the investment property, even if comparable market transactions become less frequent or market prices become less readily available. According to IAS 40, the residual value of such investment property measured under the cost model in IAS 16 should be presumed to be zero. The standard further states that, under the exceptional circumstances explained above, in the case of an entity that uses the fair value model, the entity should measure the other investment properties held by it at fair values. In other words, notwithstanding the fact that one of the investment properties, due to exceptional circumstances, is being carried under the cost model IAS 16, an entity that uses the fair value model should continue carrying the other investment properties at fair values. While this results in a mixed measure of the aggregate investment property, it underlines the perceived importance of the fair value method.

Example: Can a company opt for the fair value model for an investment property under construction, while all other completed investment properties are valued using the acquisition cost model?

No. The company drawing up its balance sheet must choose between using the fair value model (valuation using the fair value) or the acquisition cost model (valuation using the amortised acquisition or construction costs). This decision is only to be made once and is to be applied consistently to all investment properties. This also includes investment properties under construction (IAS 40.33). As such, it is not permitted to value investment properties under construction using the fair value model and all other investment properties under the acquisition cost model. However, in very rare cases, it may be that the company drawing up its balance sheet opts to use the fair value model; however, the only investment property in the portfolio to date has been valued using the acquisition cost model in accordance with IAS 16, as the fair value of the property cannot be reliably ascertained (IAS 40.53). In this case, the company drawing up its balance sheet must value the investment property under construction using the acquisition cost model despite using the fair value model for its other investment properties (IAS 40.54).

Cost model

After initial recognition, investment property is accounted for in accordance with the cost model as set out in IAS 16, *Property, Plant and Equipment*—cost less accumulated depreciation and less accumulated impairment losses—apart from those that meet the criteria to be classified as held-for-sale (or are included in a disposal group held for sale) in accordance with IFRS 5, *Non-current Assets Held for Sale and Discontinued Operations*, and those that meet the criteria to be classified as right-to-use assets in accordance with IFRS 16, *Leases*.

Transfers to or from investment property

Transfers to or from investment property should be made only when there is demonstrated "change in use" as contemplated by the standard. IAS 40 presents a non-exhaustive list of examples, where a change in use takes place when there is a transfer:

- From investment property to owner-occupied property, when owner-occupation commences;
- From investment property to inventories, on commencement of development with a view to sale;
- From an owner-occupied property to investment property, when owner-occupation ends; or
- From inventories to investment property, when an operating lease to a third party commences.

A change in management's intentions for the use of a property by itself does not constitute evidence of a change in use.

In the case of an entity that employs the cost model, transfers between investment property, owner-occupied property and inventories do not change the carrying amount of the property transferred and thus do not change the cost of that property for measurement or disclosure purposes.

When the investment property is carried under the fair value model, vastly different results follow as far as recognition and measurement is concerned. These are explained below:

1. **Transfers from (or to) investment property to (or from) owner-occupied property (in the case of investment property carried under the fair value model)**

   In some instances, property that at first is appropriately classified as investment property under IAS 40 may later become property, plant and equipment as defined under IAS 16. For example, a building is obtained and leased to unrelated parties, but at a later date the entity expands its own operations to the extent that it now chooses to utilise the building formerly held as a passive investment for its own purposes, such as for the corporate executive offices. The amount reflected in the accounting records as the fair value of the property as of the date of change in status would become the cost basis for subsequent accounting purposes. Previously recognised changes in value, if any, would not be reversed.

   Similarly, if property first classified as owner-occupied property and treated as property, plant and equipment under the benchmark treatment of IAS 16 or treated as right-of-use asset under IFRS 16 is later redeployed as investment property, it is to be measured at fair value at the date of the change in its usage. If the value is lower than the carrying amount (i.e., if there is a previously unrecognised decline in its fair value) then this will be reflected in profit or loss in the period of redeployment as an investment property. On the other hand, if there has been an unrecognised increase in value, the accounting will depend on whether this is a reversal of a previously recognised impairment.

If the increase is a reversal of a decline in value, the increase should be recognised in profit or loss; the amount so reported, however, should not exceed the amount needed to restore the carrying amount to what it would have been, net of depreciation, had the earlier impairment not occurred. If, on the other hand, there was no previously recognised impairment which the current value increase is effectively reversing (or, to the extent that the current increase exceeds the earlier decline), then the increase should be recognised in other comprehensive income. If the investment property is later disposed of, any surplus in equity should be transferred to retained earnings without being recognised through profit or loss.

2. **Transfers from inventories to investment property (in the case of investment property carried under the fair value model)**

   It may also happen that property originally classified as inventories, originally held for sale in the normal course of the business, is later redeployed as investment property. When reclassified, the initial carrying amount should be fair value as of that date. Any difference between the fair value and the carrying amount of the property at the date of transfer would be reported in profit or loss. This is consistent with the treatment of sales of inventories.

   Example: Can a property under construction classified as inventory be reclassified as an investment property if the disposal plans no longer exist?

   No. A property under construction that has been classified as inventory to date is not to be reclassified solely on the basis of its intended use being changed. This requires, for example, an operating lease agreement to be commenced (IAS 40.57(d)).

3. **Transfers from investment property to inventories**

   IAS 40 requires an investment property to be transferred to inventories only when there is a change of use evidenced by commencement of development with a view to sale. When an investment property carried at fair value is transferred to inventories, the property's deemed cost for subsequent accounting in accordance with IAS 2, *Inventories*, is its fair value at the date of change in use.

   When the entity determines that property held as investment property is to be sold, that property should be classified as a non-current asset held for sale in accordance with IFRS 5. It should not be derecognised (eliminated from the statement of financial position) or transferred to inventories. The treatment of non-current assets held for sale is discussed in further detail in Chapter 13. However, in the case of investment property held for sale, these continue to be measured at fair value in accordance with IAS 40 up to the point of sale, unlike, for example, property, plant and equipment, which is measured at the lower of carrying amount or fair value less costs to sell while held for sale.

   Example: Can a property that has previously been classified as an investment property be reclassified as inventory if it is renovated to create disposal through sale?

   Yes, if the renovation is a development that significantly increases the value of the property. This may be the case when a significantly higher rental standard is achieved through renovation or when the lettable area is significantly increased. However, if the renovation only serves to maintain the property at its current level, then in accordance with IAS 40.57(b), there is no development with the aim of sale.

Disposal and retirement of investment property

An investment property should be derecognised (i.e., eliminated from the statement of financial position of the entity) on disposal or when it is permanently withdrawn from use and no future economic benefits are expected from its disposal. The word "disposal" has been used in the standard to mean not only a sale but also the entering into of a finance lease by the entity. In determining the date of disposal of an investment property, the criteria in IFRS 15, *Revenue from Contracts with Customers*, for recognising revenue from the sale of goods should be applied. IFRS 16, *Leases*, applies to a disposal effected by entering into a finance lease and to a sale and leaseback.

Any gains or losses on disposal or retirement of an investment property should be determined as the difference between the net disposal proceeds and the carrying amount of the asset and should be recognised in profit or loss for the period of the retirement or disposal. This is subject to the requirements of IFRS 16 in the case of sale and leaseback transactions.

Compensation from third parties for investment property that was impaired, lost or given up shall be recognised in profit or loss when the compensation becomes receivable.

PRESENTATION AND DISCLOSURE

Presentation

IAS 1, *Presentation of Financial Statements*, requires that, when material, the aggregate carrying amount of the entity's investment property should be presented in the statement of financial position.

Disclosure

IAS 40 stipulates disclosure requirements set out below.

1. **Disclosures applicable to all investment properties (general disclosures)**
    - There is a requirement to disclose whether the entity applies the fair value or the cost model.
    - When classification is difficult, an entity that holds an investment property will need to disclose the criteria used to distinguish investment property from owner-occupied property and from property held for sale in the ordinary course of business.
    - The methods and any significant assumptions that were used in ascertaining the fair values of the investment properties are to be disclosed as well. Such disclosure also includes a statement about whether the determination of fair value was supported by market evidence or relied heavily on other factors (which the entity needs to disclose as well) due to the nature of the property and the absence of comparable market data.

      This disclosure regarding the methods and significant assumptions underlying the determination of fair value is not required for entities that have adopted IFRS 13, *Fair Value Measurement*. Such entities should instead provide the disclosures required under IFRS 13 (see Chapter 25).
    - If investment property has been revalued by an independent appraiser, having recognised and relevant qualifications, and who has recent experience with properties having similar characteristics of location and type, the extent to which

the fair value of investment property (either used in case the fair value model is used or disclosed in case the cost model is used) is based on valuation by such a qualified independent valuation specialist. If there is no such valuation, that fact should be disclosed as well.
- The following should be disclosed in the statement of comprehensive income:
  - The amount of rental income derived from investment property.
  - Direct operating expenses (including repairs and maintenance) arising from investment property that generated rental income during the period.
  - Direct operating expenses (including repairs and maintenance) arising from investment property that did not generate rental income during the period.
  - The cumulative change in fair value recognised in profit and loss on a sale of investment property from a pool of assets in which the cost model is used into a pool in which the fair value model is used.
  - The existence and the amount of any restrictions which may potentially affect the realisability of investment property or the remittance of income and proceeds from disposal to be received.
  - Material contractual obligations to purchase or build investment property or to make repairs, maintenance or improvements thereto.

2. **Disclosures applicable to investment property measured using the fair value model**

In addition to the disclosures outlined above, the standard requires that an entity that uses the fair value model should present a reconciliation of the carrying amounts of the investment property, from the beginning to the end of the reporting period, showing the following:

- Additions, disclosing separately those additions resulting from acquisitions, those resulting from business combinations and those deriving from capitalised expenditures subsequent to the property's initial recognition.
- Assets classified as held-for-sale or included in a disposal group classified as held-for-sale, in accordance with IFRS 5 and other disposals.
- Net gains or losses from fair value adjustments.
- The net exchange differences, if any, arising from the translation of the financial statements of a foreign entity.
- Transfers to and from inventories and owner-occupied property.
- Any other movements.

Comparative reconciliation data for prior periods need not be presented.

Under exceptional circumstances, due to lack of reliable fair value, when an entity measures investment property using the benchmark (cost) treatment under IAS 16, the above reconciliation should disclose amounts separately for that investment property from amounts relating to other investment property. In addition, an entity should disclose:

- A description of such an investment property;
- An explanation of why fair value cannot be reliably measured;

- If possible, the range of estimates within which fair value is highly likely to lie;
- On disposal of such an investment property, the fact that the entity has disposed of investment property not carried at fair value along with its carrying amount at the time of disposal and the amount of gain or loss recognised.

When a valuation obtained for an investment property is adjusted significantly for the purpose of the financial statements (e.g., to avoid double counting of assets or liabilities that are recognised as separate assets and liabilities), the entity is required to present a reconciliation between the valuation obtained and the adjusted valuation included in the financial statements, showing separately the aggregate amount of any recognised lease obligation that has been added back and any other significant adjustments.

3. **Disclosures applicable to investment property measured using the cost model**

In addition to the general disclosure requirements outlined in 1. above, the standard requires that an entity that applies the cost model should disclose:

- The depreciation methods used;
- The useful lives or the depreciation rates used;
- The gross carrying amount and the accumulated depreciation (aggregated with accumulated impairment losses) at the beginning and end of the period;
- A reconciliation of the carrying amount of investment property at the beginning and the end of the period showing the following details:
  - Additions resulting from acquisitions, those resulting from business combinations and those deriving from capitalised expenditures subsequent to the property's initial recognition;
  - Disposals, depreciation, impairment losses recognised and reversed, the net exchange differences, if any, arising from the translation of the financial statements of a foreign entity, transfers to and from inventories and owner-occupied properties, and any other movements.

  Comparative reconciliation data for prior periods need not be presented.
- The fair value of investment property carried under the cost model. In exceptional cases, when the fair value of the investment property cannot be reliably estimated, the entity should instead disclose:
  - A description of such property;
  - An explanation of why fair value cannot be reliably measured;
  - If possible, the range of estimates within which fair value is highly likely to lie.

It is anticipated that in certain cases investment property will be a property leased to others under right-to-use arrangements. In that case, the disclosure requirements set forth in IAS 40 will be applicable despite the arrangement being covered under IFRS 16.

EXAMPLES OF FINANCIAL STATEMENT DISCLOSURES

Exemplum Reporting PLC
Financial Statements
For the Year Ended December 31, 20XX

2. Significant accounting policies

2.6 Investment properties

Investment property comprises non-owner-occupied buildings held to earn rentals and for capital appreciation. — IAS 40 p75

Investment properties are initially recognised at cost, inclusive of transaction costs. Subsequently, investment properties are measured at fair value. Gains and losses arising from changes in the fair value of investment properties are recognised in profit or loss in the period in which they arise.

Investment property is derecognised when disposed of, or when no future economic benefits are expected from the disposal. Any gain or loss arising on derecognition of the property is recognised in profit or loss in the period in which the property is derecognised.

16. Investment property

Fair value model

The fair value of the group's investment properties is determined annually at the reporting date by an independent professionally qualified valuator. — IAS 40 p75

In determining the valuations, the valuator refers to current market conditions and recent sales transactions of similar properties. — IFRS 13 p91

In estimating the fair value of the properties, the highest and best use of the property is their current use. There has been no change in the valuation technique used during the year. — p93

Amounts recognised in profit or loss	**20XX**	**20XX-1**	**IAS 40 p75**
Rental income	X	X	
Direct operating expenses			
On property that generated rental income	X	X	
On property that did not generate rental income	X	X	

Investment properties with a carrying amount of EUR X (20XX-1: EUR X) have been pledged as security for liabilities. The holder of the security does not have the right to sell or re-pledge the investment properties in the absence of default. — IFRS 7 p14

	20XX	**20XX-1**	**IAS 40 p76**
Carrying value at the beginning of the year	X	X	
Fair value changes	X	X	
Exchange differences	X	X	
Additions	X	X	
Carrying value at the end of the year	X	X	

Fair value hierarchy

	Level 1	**Level 2**	**Level 3**	**Fair value**	**IFRS 13 p93**
Rental property units located in X area	–	–	*X*	*X*	

The fair valuation of investment property is considered to represent a level 3 valuation based on significant non-observable inputs being the location and condition of the property, consistent with prior periods. IFRS 13 p93(c)

Management does not expect there to be a material sensitivity to the fair values arising from the non-observable inputs.

There were no transfers between level 1, 2 or 3 fair values during the year.

The table above presents the changes in the carrying value of the investment property arising from these fair valuation assessments.

US GAAP COMPARISON

US GAAP does not separately define investment properties. Property held for investment purposes is treated the same as other property, plant and equipment when being held and used and as held-for-sale under specific criteria. With the release of Leases Topic 842 in US Codified GAAP items related to operating leases above will begin to affect the statement of financial position whereby some aspects of leases are capitalised as property assets and liabilities effective for periods beginning after December 15, 2019 for issuers and December 15, 2021 for all others. Upon implementation of Topic 842, IFRS and US GAAP will be essentially converged on the lease subject in practice.

13 IMPAIRMENT OF ASSETS AND NON-CURRENT ASSETS HELD FOR SALE

INTRODUCTION

This chapter deals both with IAS 36, *Impairment of Assets*, and IFRS 5, *Non-Current Assets Held for Sale and Discontinued Operations*. IAS 36 identifies when the carrying amount of a certain asset needs to be reduced to its recoverable amount. IFRS 5 determines the treatment of non-current assets held for sale and discontinued operations. An impairment exists when the recoverable amount (the higher of fair value less cost to sell and value in use) is less than the carrying amount. This assessment is to be made on an asset-specific basis or on the smallest group of assets for which the entity has identifiable cash flows (the cash-generating unit).

IAS 36 is equally applicable to tangible and intangible assets.

Sources of IFRS	
IFRS 5	*IAS* 36

DEFINITIONS OF TERMS: IMPAIRMENT OF ASSETS

Carrying amount. The amount at which an asset is recognised after deducting any accumulated depreciation (amortisation) and accumulated impairment losses thereon. Carrying amount is often different from market value because depreciation is a cost allocation rather than a means of valuation. For liabilities, the carrying amount is the amount of the liability minus offsets such as any sums already paid or bond discounts.

Cash-generating unit. The smallest identifiable group of assets that generates cash inflows that are largely independent of the cash inflows from other assets or groups of assets.

Corporate assets. Assets other than goodwill that contribute to future cash flows of both the cash-generating unit under review and other cash-generating units.

Cost to sell. The incremental cost directly attributable to a disposal of an asset (or disposal group), excluding finance cost and income tax expenses.

Depreciable amount. The cost of an asset, or other amount substituted for cost in the financial statements, less its residual value.

Depreciation (amortisation). The systematic allocation of the depreciable amount of an asset over its useful life.

Fair value. The price that would be received to sell an asset or paid to transfer a liability in an orderly transaction between market participants at the measurement date.

Impairment loss. The amount by which the carrying amount of an asset or a cash-generating unit exceeds its recoverable amount.

Recoverable amount. The higher of an asset or a cash-generating unit's fair value less costs of disposal and its value in use.

Useful life. Either:

- The period of time over which an asset is expected to be used by the entity; or
- The number of production or similar units expected to be obtained from the asset by the entity.

Value in use. The present value of the future cash flows expected to be derived from an asset or cash-generating unit.

IMPAIRMENT OF ASSETS (IAS 36)

Scope of IAS 36

IAS 36 is applicable to all assets except:

- Inventories (IAS 2);
- Recognised contract assets and assets arising from costs to obtain or fulfil a contract (IFRS 15);
- Deferred tax assets (IAS 12);
- Assets arising from employee benefits (IAS 19);
- Financial assets within the scope of IFRS 9;
- Investment property measured at fair value (IAS 40);
- Biological assets related to agricultural activity measured at fair value less costs to sell (IAS 41);

- Deferred acquisition costs and intangible assets arising from an insurer's contractual right under insurance contracts (IFRS 4); and
- Non-current assets (or disposal groups) classified as held for sale (IFRS 5).

This standard applies to financial assets classified as:

- Subsidiaries, as defined in IFRS 10;
- Associates, as defined in IAS 28; and
- Joint ventures, as defined in IFRS 11.

Principal Requirements of IAS 36

In general, the standard provides the procedures that an entity is required to apply to ensure that its assets are not carried at amounts higher than their recoverable amount. If an asset's carrying amount is more than its recoverable amount (the amount to be recovered through use or sale of the asset), an impairment loss is recognised. IAS 36 requires an entity to assess at the end of each reporting period whether there is any indication that an asset may be impaired. Tests for impairment are only necessary when there is an indication that an asset might be impaired (but are assessed annually for intangible assets having an indefinite useful life, intangible assets not yet available for use and goodwill). When carried out, the test is applied to the smallest group of assets for which the entity has identifiable cash flows, called a "cash-generating unit." The carrying amount of the asset or assets in the cash-generating unit is compared with the recoverable amount, which is the higher of the asset's (or cash-generating unit's) fair value less costs to sell and the present value of the cash flows expected to be generated by using the asset ("value in use"). If the higher of these values is lower than the carrying amount, an impairment loss is recognised for the difference normally in profit or loss.

Identifying Impairments

According to IAS 36, at each financial reporting date the reporting entity should determine whether there are conditions that would indicate that impairments may have occurred. If such indicators are present, the recoverable amount should be estimated.

The standard provides a set of indicators of potential impairment and suggests that these represent a minimum array of factors to be considered. An entity may also identify other indicators. At a minimum, the following external and internal indicators of possible impairments are to be given consideration on an annual basis:

- Asset value declines, beyond the declines expected as a result of the passing of time or normal usage;
- Significant changes with an adverse effect in the technological, market, economic or legal environments in which the entity operates, or the specific market to which the asset is dedicated;
- Increases in the market interest rate or other market-oriented rate of return such that are likely to affect the discount rate used in determining the value in use of an asset and decreasing the recoverable amount materially;
- The carrying amount of the entity's net asset value is more than its market capitalisation;
- Evidence of obsolescence or of physical damage to an asset or group of assets;

- There have been significant internal changes to the entity or its operations adversely affecting the entity, such as assets becoming idle, product discontinuations, restructurings or reductions in the expected remaining useful life of its asset;
- Internal reporting evidence indicating that the economic performance of the asset or group of assets is, or will become, worse than previously expected; and
- For an investment in a subsidiary, joint venture or associate, the investor recognises a dividend from the investment and evidence is available that (1) the carrying amount of the investment in the separate financial statements exceeds the carrying amounts in the consolidated financial statements of the investee's net assets, including associated goodwill; or (2) the dividend exceeds the total comprehensive income of the subsidiary, joint venture or associate in the period the dividend is declared.

The mere fact that one or more of the foregoing indicators suggests that there might be cause for concern about possible asset impairment does not necessarily mean that formal impairment testing must proceed in every instance, although in the absence of a plausible explanation why the signals of possible impairment should not be further considered, the implication would be that some follow-up investigation is needed.

Computing Recoverable Amounts—General Concepts

IAS 36 defines impairment as the excess of carrying amount over recoverable amount and defines recoverable amount as the higher of fair value less costs to sell and value in use. If the one is higher than the carrying amount, the other need not to be calculated. The objective is to recognise an impairment loss when the recoverable amount of an asset (or cash-generating unit) is lower than the carrying value.

Determining Fair Value Less Costs to Sell

The determination of the fair value less costs to sell (i.e., net selling price) of the asset being evaluated might present difficulties when market values are not applicable. IFRS 13, *Fair Value Measurement*, deals specifically with these issues. Refer to Chapter 25 for more detail on how IFRS suggests the fair values are to be determined. Cost to sell represents the incremental cost directly attributable to a disposal of an asset (or disposal group) and specifically excludes finance cost and income tax expenses.

Computing Value in Use

The computation of "value in use" involves a two-step process: first, future cash flows must be estimated; and second, the present value of these cash flows must be calculated by application of an appropriate discount rate.

Projection of future cash flows must be based on reasonable assumptions. Exaggerated revenue growth rates, significant anticipated cost reductions or unreasonable useful lives for plant assets must be avoided if meaningful results are to be obtained. In general, recent experience is a fair guide to the near-term future, but a recent sudden growth spurt should not be extrapolated to more than the very near-term future. For example, if growth over the past five years averaged 5%, but in the latest year equalled 15%, unless the recent rate of growth can be identified with factors that demonstrate it as being sustainable, a future growth rate of 5%, or slightly higher, would be more supportable.

IAS 36 stipulates that steady or declining growth rates must be utilised for periods beyond those covered by the most recent budgets and forecasts. It further states that, barring an ability to demonstrate why a higher rate is appropriate, the growth rate should not exceed the long-term growth rate of the industry in which the entity participates.

The guidance offered by IAS 36 suggests that only normal, recurring cash inflows and outflows from the continuing use of the asset being evaluated should be considered, to which any estimated residual value at the end of the asset's useful life would be added. In determining the cash flows from operations, the company should take into account the effect of the business developments on working capital requirements. These working capital requirements include both assets and liabilities and can be positive and negative. For example, if a growth of revenues is estimated for the coming five years, it can be expected that under normal business circumstances, the receivables increase in a similar direction. The same would be the case for any prepayment of services, for instance in the publishing industry, where many subscriptions are paid up-front.

Non-cash costs, such as depreciation of the asset, obviously must be excluded from this calculation, since, in the case of depreciation, this would in effect double count the very item being measured. Furthermore, projections should always exclude cash flows related to financing the asset—for example, interest and principal repayments on any debt incurred in acquiring the asset—since operating decisions (e.g., keeping or disposing of an asset) are to be evaluated separately from financing decisions (borrowing, leasing, buying with equity capital funds). Also, cash flow projections must relate to the asset in its existing state and in its current use, without regard to possible future enhancements. Income tax effects are also to be disregarded (i.e., the entire analysis should be on a pre-tax basis). An entity should translate the present value of future cash flows estimated in the foreign currency using the spot exchange rate at the date of the value-in-use calculation.

Cash-Generating Units

Under IAS 36, when cash flows cannot be identified with individual assets (as will frequently be the case), assets must be grouped to permit an assessment of future cash flows. The requirement is that this grouping be performed at the lowest level possible, which would be the smallest aggregation of assets for which independent cash flows can be identified. In practice, this unit may be a department, a product line or a factory, for which the output of product and the input of raw materials, labour and overhead can be identified.

Thus, while the precise contribution to overall cash flow made by, say, a given drill press or lathe may be impossible to surmise, the cash inflows and outflows of a department which produces and sells a discrete product line to an identified group of customers can be more readily determined. To comply with IFRS, the extent of aggregation must be the minimum necessary to develop cash flow information for impairment assessment and no greater.

A too-high level of aggregation is prohibited for a very basic reason: doing so could permit some impairments to be concealed by effectively offsetting impairment losses against productivity or profitability gains derived from the expected future use of other assets. IAS 36 requires that cash-generating units be defined consistently from period to period. In addition to being necessary for consistency in financial reporting from period to period, which is an important objective per se, it is also needed to preclude the opportunistic redefining of cash-generating groups affected to minimise or eliminate impairment recognition.

Discount Rate

The other measurement issue in computing value in use comes from identifying the appropriate discount rate to apply to projected future cash flows. The discount rate is comprised of subcomponents. The base component of the discount rate is the current market rate, which should be identical for all impairment testing at any given date. This must be adjusted for the risks specific to the asset, which have not been adjusted in the projected cash flows. The interest rate to apply must reflect current market conditions as of the end of the reporting period.

In practice, this asset class risk adjustment can be built into the cash flows. Appendix A to the standard discusses what it describes as the *traditional approach* to using present value techniques to measure value in use, where forecast cash flows are discounted using a rate that is adjusted for uncertainties. It also describes the *expected cash flow* method, where the forecast cash flows are directly adjusted to reflect uncertainty and then discounted at the market rate. These are alternative approaches and care must be exercised to apply one or the other correctly. Most importantly, risk should not be adjusted for twice in computing the present value of future cash flows.

IAS 36 suggests that identifying the appropriate risk-adjusted cost of capital to employ as a discount rate can be accomplished by reference to the implicit rates in current market transactions (e.g., leasing transactions), or from the weighted-average cost of capital of publicly traded entities operating in the same industry grouping. Such statistics are available for certain industry segments in selected (but not all) markets. The entity's own recent transactions, typically involving leasing or borrowing to buy other non-current assets, will be highly salient information in estimating the appropriate discount rate to use.

When risk-adjusted rates are not available, however, it will become necessary to develop a discount rate from surrogate data. The two steps to this procedure are:

1. To identify the pure time value of money for the requisite time horizon over which the asset will be utilised; and
2. To add an appropriate risk premium to the pure interest factor, which is related to the variability of future cash flows or other, sometimes unidentifiable, factors that market participants would reflect in the pricing.

Regarding the first component, the life of the asset being tested for impairment will be critical; short-term obligations almost always carry a lower rate than intermediate- or long-term ones, although there have been periods when "yield curve inversions" have been dramatic. As to the second element, projected future cash flows having greater variability (which is the technical definition of risk) will be associated with higher risk premiums.

Of these two discount rate components, the latter is likely to prove the more difficult to determine or estimate in practice. IAS 36 provides discussion of the methodology to utilise, and this should be carefully considered before embarking on this procedure. It addresses such factors as country risk, currency risk and pricing risk but also the (il)liquidity of the (group of) asset(s). The latter is also referred to as the small-firm premium.

Corporate Assets

Corporate assets, such as headquarters buildings and shared equipment, which do not themselves generate identifiable cash flows, need to be tested for impairment together with other non-current assets. However, these present a particular problem in practice due to the inability to identify cash flows deriving from the future use of these assets. A failure to test corporate assets for impairment would permit such assets to be carried at amounts that could, under some circumstances, be at variance with requirements under IFRS. It would also permit a reporting entity to deliberately evade the impairment testing requirements by opportunistically defining certain otherwise productive assets as being corporate assets.

To avoid such results, IAS 36 requires that corporate assets be allocated among or assigned to the cash-generating unit or units with which they are most closely associated. For a large and diversified entity, this probably implies that corporate assets will be allocated among most or all of its cash-generating units, perhaps in proportion to annual turnover (revenue). Since ultimately an entity must generate sufficient cash flows to recover its investment in all non-current assets, whether assigned to operating divisions or to administrative groups, there are no circumstances in which corporate assets can be isolated and excluded from impairment testing.

Accounting for Impairments

If the recoverable amount of the cash-generating unit is lower than its carrying amount, an impairment must be recognised. The mechanism for recording an impairment loss depends upon whether the entity is accounting for non-current assets at historical cost subject to depreciation or on the revaluation basis. Impairments computed for assets carried at historical cost will be recognised as charges against current period profit or loss.

Example of assets held for sale

Xebob Corporation (XC) decides on March 28, 20XX to sell three assets that are part of different cash-generating units to the same acquirer. The year-end of XC is March 31, 20XX. The assets are classified as a disposal group in terms of IFRS 5, *Non-current Assets Held for Sale and Discontinued Operations*. The following information is provided on March 31, 20XX:

Asset	*Carrying amount (X)*	*Fair value less cost to sell (Y)*	*Lower of X – Y*
A	€5,600	€5,200	€5,200
B	8,200	8,900	8,200
C	3,500	3,800	3,500
Total	17,300	17,900	16,900

You could assume that the decision to sell was an indication of impairment. The fair value of the whole group was €17,900 on March 31, 20XX. If the assets together do not represent a cash-generating unit they need to be tested for impairment individually. In this group, the assets are independent and therefore do not constitute a cash-generating unit. Therefore, the assets would be tested for impairment individually and an impairment loss of €400 (€5,600 – €5,200) or (€17,300 – €16,900) would be recognised for asset A.

For assets grouped into cash-generating units, it will not be possible to determine which specific assets have suffered impairment losses when the unit as a whole has been found to be impaired, and so IAS 36 prescribes the allocation approach. If the cash-generating unit in question has been allocated any goodwill, any impairment should be allocated fully to goodwill until its carrying amount has been reduced to zero. Any further impairment would be allocated proportionately to all the other assets in that cash-generating unit. In practice, the impairment loss is allocated against the non-monetary assets that are carried, as the carrying amount of monetary assets usually approximates actual values.

If the entity employs the revaluation method of accounting for non-current assets, the impairment adjustment will be treated as the partial reversal of a previous upward revaluation. However, if the entire revaluation account is eliminated due to the recognition of an impairment, any excess impairment should be charged to profit or loss. In other words, the revaluation account cannot contain a net debit balance.

When the calculated impairment is greater than the carrying amount of an asset, a liability (impairment for the asset) can only be created if it is required by another IFRS. After an impairment of an asset, the depreciation needs to be adjusted to reflect the revised carrying amount and residual values. The deferred tax effect of impairment is recognised by comparing the revised carrying amount with the tax base of the asset by applying the guidance in IAS 12, *Income Taxes* (refer to Chapter 26).

Example of accounting for impairment

Xebob Corporation (XC) has one of its (many) departments that performs machining operations on parts that are sold to contractors. A group of machines has an aggregate carrying amount at the end of the latest reporting period (December 31, 20XX) totaling €123,000. It has been determined that this group of machinery constitutes a cash-generating unit for the purposes of applying IAS 36.

Upon analysis, the following facts about future expected cash inflows and outflows become apparent, based on the diminishing productivity expected of the machinery as it ages, and the increasing costs that will be incurred to generate output from the machines:

Year	*Revenues*	*Costs, excluding depreciation*
20XX+1	€75,000	€28,000
20XX+2	80,000	42,000
20XX+34	65,000	55,000
20XX+4	20,000	15,000
Totals	€240,000	€140,000

The fair value of the machinery in this cash-generating unit is determined by reference to used machinery quotation sheets obtained from a prominent dealer. After deducting estimated disposal costs, the fair value less costs to sell is calculated as €84,500.

Value in use is determined with reference to the above-noted expected cash inflows and outflows, discounted at a risk rate of 5%. This yields a present value of about €91,981, as shown below.

Year	*Cash flows*	*PV factors*	*Net PV of cash flows*
20XX+1	€47,000	.95238	€44,761.91
20XX+2	38,000	.90703	34,467.12
20XX+3	10,000	.86384	8,638.38
20XX+4	5,000	.82270	4,113.51
Total			€91,980.91

Since value in use exceeds fair value less costs to sell, value in use is selected to represent the recoverable amount of this cash-generating unit. This is lower than the carrying amount of the group of assets and thus an impairment must be recognised as of the end of 20XX in the amount of €123,000 − €91,981 = €31,019. This will be included in operating expenses (as an impairment caption in the statement of comprehensive income or in the statement of profit or loss, if prepared separately) for 20XX.

Reversals of Impairments under the Historical Cost Method of Accounting

IFRS provides for recognition of reversals of previously recognised impairments. To recognise a recovery of a previously recognised impairment, a process like that which led to the original loss recognition must be followed. This begins with consideration, at the end of each reporting period, of whether there are indicators of possible impairment recoveries, utilising external and internal sources of information. Data relied upon could include that pertaining to material market value increases; changes in the technological, market, economic or legal environment or the market in which the asset is employed; and the occurrence of a favourable change in interest rates or required rates of return on assets which would imply changes in the discount rate used to compute value in use. Also, to be given consideration are data about any changes in the manner in which the asset is employed, as well as evidence that the economic performance of the asset has exceeded expectations and/or is expected to do so in the future.

If one or more of these indicators is present, it will be necessary to compute the recoverable amount of the asset in question or, if appropriate, of the cash-generating unit containing that asset, to determine if the current recoverable amount exceeds the carrying amount of the asset, where it had been previously reduced for impairment.

If that is the case, a recovery can be recognised under IAS 36. The amount of recovery to be recognised is limited, however, to the difference between the current carrying amount and the amount which would have been the current carrying amount had the earlier impairment not been recognised. Note that this means that restoration of the full amount at which the asset was carried at the time of the earlier impairment cannot be made, since time has elapsed between these two events and further depreciation of the asset would have been incurred in the interim.

Example of impairment recovery

To illustrate, assume an asset had a carrying amount of €40,000 at December 31, 20XX-1 based on its original cost of €50,000, less accumulated depreciation representing one-fifth, or two years, of its projected useful life of 10 years which has already elapsed. The carrying amount of €40,000 is after depreciation for 20XX-1 has been computed, but before impairment has been addressed. At that date, a determination was made that the asset's recoverable amount was only €32,000 (assume this was properly computed and that recognition of the impairment was warranted), so that an €8,000 adjustment must be made. For simplicity, assume this was added to accumulated depreciation, so that at December 31, 20XX-1, the asset cost remains €50,000 and accumulated depreciation is stated as €18,000.

At December 31, 20XX, before any adjustments are posted, the carrying amount of this asset is €32,000. Depreciation for 20XX would be €4,000 (= €32,000 carrying amount ÷ 8 years remaining life), which would leave a net carrying amount, after current period depreciation, of €28,000. However, a determination is made that the asset's recoverable amount at this date is €37,000. Before making an adjustment to reverse some or all of the impairment loss previously recognised, the carrying amount at December 31, 20XX, as it would have existed had the impairment not been recognised in 20XX-1, must be computed:

December 31, 20XX-1 pre-impairment carrying amount	€40,000
20XX depreciation based on the above	5,000
Indicated December 31, 20XX carrying value	€35,000

The December 31, 20XX carrying value would have been €40,000 − €5,000 = €35,000; this is the maximum carrying value which can be reflected in the December 31, 20XX statement of financial position. Thus, the full recovery cannot be recognised; instead, the 20XX statement of profit or loss will reflect (net) a *negative* depreciation charge of €35,000 − €32,000 = €3,000, which can be thought of (or recorded) as follows:

Actual December 31, 20XX-1 carrying amount	€32,000
20XX depreciation based on the above	4,000 (a)
Indicated December 31, 20XX carrying amount	**€28,000**
Actual December 31, 20XX carrying amount	**€35,000**
Recovery of previously recognised impairment	€7,000 (b)

Thus, the net effect in 20XX profit or loss is (a) − (b) = €(3,000). The asset cannot be restored to its indicated recoverable amount at December 31, 20XX, amounting to €37,000, as this exceeds the carrying amount that would have existed at this date had the impairment in 20XX-1 never been recognised.

Where a cash-generating unit including goodwill has been impaired, and the impairment has been allocated first to the goodwill and then pro rata to the other assets, *only* the amount allocated to non-goodwill assets can be reversed. The standard specifically prohibits the reversal of impairments to goodwill, on the basis that the goodwill could have been replaced by internally generated goodwill, which cannot be recognised under IFRS.

Reversals of Impairments under the Revaluation Method

Reversals of impairments are accounted for differently if the reporting entity employed the revaluation method of accounting for non-current assets. The basic principle is that the reversal will increase the revaluation reserve; however, any impairment previously recognised in profit or loss since the revaluation reserve was eliminated must first be reversed before a revaluation reserve is created again.

Example of impairment recovery—revaluation method

To illustrate, assume an asset was acquired January 1, 20XX-2, and it had a net carrying amount of €45,000 at December 31, 20XX-1, based on its original cost of €50,000, less accumulated depreciation representing one-fifth, or two years, of its projected useful life of 10 years, which has already elapsed, plus a revaluation write-up of €5,000 net. The increase in carrying amount was recorded a year earlier, based on an appraisal showing the asset's then fair value was €56,250.

At December 31, 20XX, impairment is detected, and the recoverable amount at that date is determined to be €34,000. Had this not occurred, depreciation for 20XX would have been (€45,000 ÷ 8 years remaining life =) €5,625; carrying amount after recording 20XX depreciation would have been (€45,000 − €5,625 =) €39,375. Thus, the impairment loss recognised in 20XX the net amount of the previously recognised valuation increase remaining (i.e., undepreciated) at the end of 20XX, as shown below:

Gross amount of revaluation at December 31, 20XX-2	€6,250
Portion of the above allocable to accumulated depreciation	625
Net revaluation amount at December 31, 20XX-2	5,625
Depreciation taken on appreciation for 20XX-1	625
Net revaluation amount at December 31, 20XX-1	5,000
Depreciation taken on appreciation for 20XX	625
Net revaluation amount at December 31, 20XX, before recognition of impairment	4,375
Impairment recognised as reversal of earlier revaluation	4,375
Net revaluation increase at December 31, 20XX	€0

The remaining €1,000 impairment loss is recognised at December 31, 20XX+1, in profit or loss, since it exceeds the available amount of revaluation surplus.

In 20XX+1 there is a recovery of value that pertains to this asset; at December 31, 20XX+1, it is valued at €36,500. This represents a €2,500 increase in carrying amount from the earlier year's balance, net of accumulated depreciation. The first €1,000 of this recovery in value is credited to profit, since this is the amount of previously recognised impairment that was charged against profit; the remaining €1,500 of recovery is accounted for as other comprehensive income and accumulated in the revaluation surplus in shareholders' equity.

Insurance and Other Recoveries

Impairments of tangible non-current assets resulting from natural or other damages, such as from floods or windstorms, may be insured. IAS 16, *Property, Plant and Equipment*, holds that when property is damaged or lost, impairments and claims for reimbursements should be accounted for separately (i.e., not netted for financial reporting purposes). Impairments are to be accounted for per IAS 36 as discussed above; disposals (of damaged or otherwise impaired assets) should be accounted for consistent with guidance in IAS 16. Compensation from third parties, which are gain contingencies, should be recognised as profit only when the funds become receivable. The cost of replacement items or of restored items is determined in accordance with IAS 16.

Disclosure Requirements

For each class of property, plant and equipment, the amount of impairment losses recognised in profit or loss for each period being reported upon must be stated, with an indication of where in the statement of comprehensive income it has been presented. For each class of asset, the amount of any reversals of previously recognised impairment must also be stipulated, again with an identification of where in the statement of comprehensive income that this has been presented. If any impairment losses were recognised in other comprehensive income and in revaluation surplus in equity (i.e., as a reversal of a previously recognised upward revaluation), this must be disclosed. Finally, any reversals of impairment losses that were recognised in other comprehensive income and in equity must be stated.

If the reporting entity is reporting financial information by segment (in accordance with IFRS 8, *Operating Segments*, as discussed in more detail in Chapter 28), the amounts of impairments and of reversals of impairments, recognised in profit or loss and in other comprehensive income during the year for each reportable segment, must also be stated. Note that the segment disclosures pertaining to impairments need not be categorised by asset class, and the location of the charge or credit in the statement of profit or loss need not be stated (but will be understood from the disclosures relating to the primary financial statements themselves).

IAS 36 further provides that if an impairment loss for an individual asset or group of assets categorised as a cash-generating unit is either recognised or reversed during the period, in an amount that is material to the financial statements taken as a whole, disclosures should be made of the following:

- The events or circumstances that caused the loss or recovery of loss;
- The amount of the impairment loss recognised or reversed;
- If for an individual asset, the nature of the asset and the reportable segment to which it belongs, as defined under IFRS 8;
- If for a cash-generating unit, a description of that unit (e.g., defined as a product line, a plant, geographical area, etc.), the amount of impairment recognised or reversed by class of asset and by reportable segment based on the primary format, and, if the unit's composition has changed since the previous estimate of the unit's recoverable amount, a description of the reasons for such changes;
- Whether fair value less costs to sell or value in use was employed to compute the recoverable amount;
- If recoverable amount is fair value less costs to sell, the basis used to determine it (e.g., whether by reference to active market prices or otherwise) and the fair value hierarchy in which the fair value measure falls, which additional disclosure for Levels 2 and 3, including the valuation method and key assumptions used; and
- If the recoverable amount is value in use, the discount rate(s) used in the current and prior period's estimate.

Furthermore, when impairments recognised or reversed in the current period are material in the aggregate, the reporting entity should provide a description of the main classes of assets affected by impairment losses or reversals of losses, as well as the main events and circumstances that caused recognition of losses or reversals. This information is not required to the extent that the disclosures above are given for individual assets or cash-generating units.

EXAMPLES OF FINANCIAL STATEMENT DISCLOSURES

Exemplum Reporting PLC
Financial Statements
For the Year Ended December 31, 20XX

Accounting policy: Impairment of non-financial assets
The group assesses annually whether there is any indication that any of its assets have been impaired. If such indication exists, the asset's recoverable amount is estimated and compared to its carrying value. Where it is impossible to estimate the recoverable amount of an individual asset, the company estimates the recoverable amount of the smallest cash-generating unit to which the asset is allocated.

If the recoverable amount of an asset (or cash-generating unit) is estimated to be less than its carrying amount an impairment loss is recognised immediately in profit or loss, unless the asset is carried at a revalued amount, in which case the impairment loss is recognised as revaluation decrease.

For goodwill, intangible assets that have an indefinite life and intangible assets not yet available for use, the recoverable amount is estimated annually and at the end of each reporting period if there is an indication of impairment.

Note: Goodwill and impairment		IFRS 3 B67
Cost		
Opening cost at January 1, 20XX-1	X	
Recognised on acquisition of a subsidiary	X	
Derecognised on disposal of a subsidiary	X	
Opening cost at January 1, 20XX	X	
Recognised on acquisition of a subsidiary	X	
Derecognised on disposal of a subsidiary	X	
Closing cost at December 31, 20XX	X	
Goodwill and impairment		IFRS 3 B67
Cost		
Opening cost at January 1, 20XX-1	X	
Recognised on acquisition of a subsidiary	X	
Derecognised on disposal of a subsidiary	X	
Opening cost at January 1, 20XX	X	
Recognised on acquisition of a subsidiary	X	
Derecognised on disposal of a subsidiary	X	
Closing cost at December 31, 20XX	X	
Accumulated impairment		
Opening balance at January 1, 20XX-1	X	
Impairment loss	X	
Opening balance at January 1, 20XX	X	
Impairment loss	X	
Closing balance at December 31, 20XX	X	
Opening carrying value at January 1, 20XX-1	X	
Opening carrying value at January 1, 20XX	X	
Closing carrying value at December 31, 20XX	X	

The events and circumstances that led to the recognition of the impairment loss was the disposal of a chain of retail stores in the United Kingdom. No other class of assets was impaired other than goodwill. IAS 36 p130 (a), (d)

(Describe the cash generating units/individual intangible assets of the group and which operating segment they belong to (if any), and whether any impairment losses were recognised or reversed during the period.) IAS 36 p130 (a), (d)

The aggregation of assets for identifying the cash-generating unit has not changed since the prior year. IAS 36 p130(d)

The recoverable amount of a cash-generating unit is its value in use. In calculating the value in use of the impaired reportable segment the group used a discount rate of X% (20XX-1: X%). IAS 36 p130 (e).(g)

The carrying amount of goodwill allocated to each reportable segment is as follows:

20XX

	Manufacture	**Retail**	**Distribution**	**Total**
Home country	X	X	X	X
Other countries	X	X	X	X

20XX-1

	Manufacture	**Retail**	**Distribution**	**Total**
Home country	X	X	X	X
Other countries	X	X	X	X

Management has based its cash flow projections on cash flow forecasts covering a five-year period. Cash flows after the five-year period have been extrapolated based on the estimated growth rates disclosed below. These growth rates do not exceed the long-term average growth rate for the industry or market in which the group operates. Other key assumptions used in the cash flow projections are as follows: IAS 36 p134(d)

	Manufacture	**Retail**	**Distribution**
Growth rates	X	X	X
Discount rates	X	X	X
Gross profit margins	X	X	X

Management has based its assumptions on past experience and external sources of information, such as industry sector reports and market expectations. IAS 36 p134(d)

DEFINITIONS OF TERMS: NON-CURRENT ASSETS HELD FOR SALE

Cash-generating unit. The smallest identifiable group of assets that generates cash inflows that are largely independent of the cash inflows from other assets or groups of assets.

Component of an entity. Operations and cash flows that can be clearly distinguished, operationally and for financial reporting purposes, from the rest of the entity.

Costs to sell. The incremental costs directly attributed to a disposal of an asset (or disposal group), excluding finance costs and income tax expense.

Current asset. An entity shall classify an asset as current when:

1. It expects to realise the asset, or intends to sell or consume it, in its normal operating cycle;
2. It holds the asset primarily for the purpose of trading;
3. It expects to realise the asset within 12 months after the reporting period; or
4. The asset is cash or a cash equivalent (as defined in IAS 7, *Statement of Cash Flows*) unless the asset is restricted from being exchanged or used to settle a liability for at least 12 months after the reporting period.

Discontinued operation. A component of an entity that either has been disposed of or is classified as held for sale and:

1. Represents a major line of business or geographical area of operations;
2. Is part of a single coordinated plan to dispose of a separate major line of business or geographical area of operations; or
3. Is a subsidiary acquired exclusively with a view to re-sale?

Disposal group. A group of assets to be disposed of, by sale or otherwise, together as a group in a single transaction, and liabilities directly associated with those assets that will be transferred in the transaction. The group includes goodwill acquired in a business combination if the group is a cash-generating unit to which goodwill has been allocated in accordance with the requirements of IAS 36 or if it is an operation within such a cash-generating unit.

Fair value. The price that would be received to sell an asset or paid to transfer a liability in an orderly transaction between market participants at the measurement date.

Firm purchase commitment. An agreement with an unrelated party, binding on both parties and usually legally enforceable, that (1) specifies all significant terms, including the price and timing of the transactions, and (2) includes a disincentive for non-performance that is sufficiently large to make performance highly probable.

Highly probable. Significantly more likely than probable.

Non-current asset. An asset not meeting the definition of a current asset.

Probable. More likely than not.

Recoverable amount. The higher of an asset's fair value less costs to sell and its value in use.

Value in use. The present value of the future cash flows expected to be derived from an asset or cash-generating unit.

NON-CURRENT ASSETS HELD FOR SALE

As part of its ongoing efforts to converge IFRS with US GAAP, the IASB issued IFRS 5, *Non-current Assets Held for Sale and Discontinued Operations*. This introduced new and substantially revised guidance for accounting for non-current tangible (and other) assets that have been identified for disposal, as well as new requirements for the presentation and disclosure of discontinued operations.

IFRS 5 states that where management has decided to sell an asset, or disposal group, these should be classified in the statement of financial position as "held for sale" and should be measured at the lower of carrying amount or fair value less cost to sell. After reclassification, these assets will no longer be subject to systematic depreciation. The measurement basis for non-current assets classified as held for sale is to be applied to the group as a whole, and any resulting impairment loss will reduce the carrying amount of the non-current assets in the disposal group.

Assets and liabilities which are to be disposed of together in a single transaction are to be treated as a *disposal group*. In accordance with the standard, a disposal group is a group of assets (and liabilities directly associated with those assets) to be disposed of, by sale or otherwise, together as a group in a single transaction. Goodwill acquired in a business combination is included in the disposal group if this group is a cash-generating unit to which goodwill has been allocated in accordance with IAS 36 or if it is an operation within such a cash-generating unit.

IFRIC 17, *Distributions of Non-cash Assets to Owners*, provides guidance on the appropriate accounting treatment when an entity distributes assets other than cash as dividends to its shareholders. As part of the issuance of IFRIC 17, IFRS 5 was amended to include non-cash assets held for distribution to owners as part of IFRS 5 and should be treated in accordance with IFRS 5's classification, presentation and measurement requirements. Whether or not a non-cash asset is classified as "held for distribution to owners" is determined using the principles in IFRS 5 detailed below.

Held-for-sale Classification

The reporting entity would classify a non-current asset (or disposal group) as held for sale if its carrying amount will be recovered principally through a sale transaction rather than through continuing use. The criteria are as follows:

- For an asset or disposal group to be classified as held for sale the asset (or asset group) must be *available for immediate sale* in its present condition and its sale must be *highly probable*.
- In addition, the asset (or disposal group) must be currently being *marketed actively* at a price that is reasonable in relation to its current fair value.
- The sale should be *completed, or expected to be so, within 12 months* from the date of the classification. IFRS 5 does, however, allow for some exceptions to this principle, which are discussed below.
- The actions required to complete the *planned sale will have been made*, and it is unlikely that the plan will be significantly changed.
- For the sale to be *highly probable*, management must be committed to selling the asset and must be actively looking for a buyer.
- In the case that the sale may not be completed within 12 months, the asset could still be classified as held for sale if the delay is caused by events beyond the entity's control and the entity remains committed to selling the asset.

Extension of the period beyond 12 months is allowable in the following situations:

- The reporting entity has committed itself to sell an asset, and it expects that others may impose conditions on the transfer of the asset that could not be completed until after a firm purchase commitment has been made, and a firm purchase commitment is highly probable within a year.

- A firm purchase commitment is made but a buyer unexpectedly imposes conditions on the transfer of the asset held for sale; timely actions are being taken to respond to the conditions, and a favourable resolution is anticipated.
- During the one-year period, unforeseen circumstances arise that were considered unlikely, and the asset is not sold. Necessary action to respond to the change in circumstances should be taken. The asset should be actively marketed at a reasonable price and the other criteria set out for the asset to be classified as held for sale should have been met.

Occasionally companies acquire non-current assets exclusively with a view to disposal. In these cases, the non-current asset will be classified as held for sale at the date of the acquisition only if it is anticipated that it will be sold within the one-year period and it is highly probably that the held-for-sale criteria will be met within a short period of the acquisition date. This period normally will be no more than three months. Exchanges of non-current assets between companies can be treated as held for sale when such an exchange has commercial substance in accordance with IAS 16.

If the criteria for classifying a non-current asset as held for sale occur *after* the reporting date, the non-current asset should *not* be presented as held for sale. Nonetheless, certain information should be disclosed about these non-current assets.

Operations that are expected to be wound down or abandoned do not meet the definition of held for sale. However, a disposal group that is to be abandoned may meet the definition of a discontinued activity. *Abandonment* means that the non-current asset (disposal group) will be used to the end of its economic life, or the non-current asset (disposal group) will be closed rather than sold. The reasoning behind this is that the carrying amount of the non-current asset will be recovered principally through continued usage. A non-current asset that has been temporarily taken out of use or service cannot be classified as being abandoned.

Measurement of Non-Current Assets Held for Sale

Assets that are classified as being held for disposal are measured differently and presented separately from other non-current assets. In accordance with IFRS 5, the following general principles would apply in measuring non-current assets that are held for sale:

- Just before an asset is initially classified as held for sale, it should be measured in accordance with the applicable IFRS.
- When non-current assets or disposal groups are classified as held for sale, they are measured at the *lower of the carrying amount and fair value less costs to sell.*
- When the sale is expected to occur in more than a year's time, the entity should measure the cost to sell at its present value. Any increase in the present value of the cost to sell that arises from the passage of time should be shown in profit and loss as finance cost.
- Any impairment loss is recognised in profit or loss on any initial or subsequent write-down of the asset or disposal group to fair value less cost to sell.
- Any subsequent increases in fair value less cost to sell of an asset can be recognised in profit or loss to the extent that it is *not in excess of the cumulative impairment loss* that has been recognised in accordance with IFRS 5 (or previously in accordance with IAS 36).

- Any impairment loss recognised for a disposal group should be applied in the order set out in IAS 36.
- Non-current assets or disposal groups classified as held for sale should not be depreciated.

The standard stipulates that, for assets not previously revalued (under IAS 16), any recorded decrease in carrying amount (to fair value less cost to sell or value in use) would be an impairment loss taken as a charge against income. Subsequent changes in fair value would also be recognised, but not increased in excess of impairment losses previously recognised.

For an asset that is carried at a revalued amount (as permitted under IAS 16), revaluation under that standard will have to be effected immediately before it is reclassified as held for sale under IFRS 5, with any impairment loss recognised in accordance with IAS 16 and IAS 36. Subsequent increases or decreases in estimated fair value less costs to sell the asset will be recognised in profit or loss.

A disposal group, as defined under IFRS 5, may include some assets, which are accounted for by the revaluation model. For such disposal groups subsequent increases in fair value are to be recognised, but only to the extent that the carrying amounts of the non-current assets in the group, after the increase has been allocated, do not exceed their respective fair values less cost to sell. The increase recognised would continue to be treated as a revaluation increase under IAS 16.

Finally, IFRS 5 states that non-current assets classified as held for sale are not to be depreciated. The constraints on classifying an asset as held for sale are, in part, intended to prevent entities from employing such reclassification as a means of avoiding depreciation. Even after classification as held for sale, however, interest and other costs associated with the asset are still recognised as expenses as required under IFRS.

Measurement of non-current assets held for distribution to owners. Assets that are classified as being held for distribution to owners are measured differently and presented separately from other non-current assets. An entity shall measure a non-current asset (or disposal group) classified as held for distribution to owners at the lower of its carrying amount and fair value less costs to distribute.

Change of Plans

If the asset held for sale or held for distribution to owners is not later disposed of or distributed, it is to be reclassified to the operating asset category it is properly assignable to. The amount to be initially recognised upon such reclassification would be the lower of:

1. The asset's carrying amount before the asset (or disposal group) was classified as held for sale, adjusted for any depreciation or amortisation that would have been recognised during the interim had the asset (disposal group) not been classified as held for sale; and
2. The *recoverable amount* at the date of the subsequent decision not to sell.

If the asset is part of a cash-generating unit (as defined under IAS 36), its recoverable amount will be defined as the carrying amount that would have been recognised after the allocation of any impairment loss incurred from that same cash-generating unit.

Under the foregoing circumstance, the reporting entity would include, as part of income from continuing operations in the period in which the criteria for classification as held for sale or held for distribution to owners are no longer met, any required adjustment to the carrying amount of a non-current asset that ceases to be classified as held for sale or held for distribution to owners. That adjustment would be presented in income from continuing operations. It is not an adjustment to prior period results of operations under any circumstances.

If an individual asset or liability is removed from a disposal group classified as held for sale or held for distribution to owners, the remaining assets and liabilities of the disposal group still to be sold will continue to be measured as a group only if the group meets the criteria for categorisation as held for sale or held for distribution to owners. In other circumstances, the remaining non-current assets of the group that individually meet the criteria to be classified as held for sale or held for distribution to owners will need to be measured individually at the lower of their carrying amounts or fair values less costs to sell at that date.

If an entity reclassifies an asset (or disposal group) directly from being held for sale to being held for distribution to owners, or directly from being held for distribution to owners to being held for sale, then the change in classification is considered a continuation of the original plan of disposal. The guidance above for a change will not apply. The entity shall, however, apply the classification, presentation and measurement requirements in IFRS 5 that are applicable to the changed method of disposal. Any reduction or increase in the fair value less costs to sell/costs to distribute of the non-current asset (or disposal group) shall be recognised by following the normal measurement guidance for non-current assets held for sale or held for distribution to owners. The date of the original classification will not be changed. This does not preclude the application of the conditions for an extension of the period required to complete a sale or a distribution to owners.

Presentation and Disclosure

IFRS 5 specifies that non-current assets classified as held for sale and the assets of a disposal group classified as held for sale must be presented separately from other assets in the statement of financial position. The liabilities of a disposal group classified as held for sale are also presented separately from other liabilities in the statement of financial position.

Several disclosures are required, including a description of the non-current assets of a disposal group, a description of the facts and circumstances of the sale, and the expected manner and timing of that disposal. Any gain or loss recognised for impairment or any subsequent increase in the fair value less costs to sell should also be shown in the applicable segment in which the non-current assets or disposal group is presented in accordance with IFRS 8 (Chapter 28).

The disclosure requirements in other IFRS do not apply to such assets (or disposal groups) unless those IFRS require:

1. Specific disclosures in respect of non-current assets (or disposal groups) classified as held for sale or discontinued operations; or
2. Disclosures about measurement of assets and liabilities within a disposal group that are not within the scope of the measurement requirement of IFRS 5 and such disclosures are not already provided in the other notes to the financial statements.

IFRS 5 also provides that where additional disclosures about non-current assets (or disposal groups) classified as held for sale or discontinued operations are necessary to comply with the general requirements of IAS 1, then such disclosures must still be made.

DISCONTINUED OPERATIONS

Presentation and Disclosure

IFRS 5 requires an entity to present and disclose information that enables users of the financial statements to evaluate the financial effects of discontinued operations. A *discontinued operation* is a part of an entity that has either been disposed of or is classified as held for sale and meets the following requirements:

1. Represents a separate major line of business or geographical area of operations;
2. Is part of a single coordinated plan to dispose of a separate major line of business or geographical area of operations; or
3. Is a subsidiary acquired exclusively with a view to resale.

An entity should present in the statement of comprehensive income a single amount comprising the total of:

- The after-tax profit or loss of discontinued operations; and
- The after-tax gain or loss recognised on the measurement to fair value less costs to sell (or on the disposal) of the assets or disposal groups classified as discontinued operations.

IFRS 5 requires detailed disclosure of revenue, expenses, pre-tax profit or loss, and the related income tax expense, either in the notes or on the face of the statement of comprehensive income. If this information is presented on the face of the statement of comprehensive income (or separate statement of profit or loss if the two-statement alternative is used), the information should be separately disclosed from information relating to continuing operations. Regarding the presentation in the statement of cash flows, the net cash flows attributable to the operating, investing and financing activities of the discontinued operation should be shown separately on the face of the statement or disclosed in the notes.

Any disclosures should cover both the current and all prior periods that have been shown in the financial statements. Retrospective classification as a discontinued operation, where the criteria are met after the statement of financial position date, is prohibited by IFRS. In addition, adjustments made in the current accounting period to amounts that have previously been disclosed as discontinued operations from prior periods must be separately disclosed. If an entity ceases to classify a component as held for sale, the results of that element must be reclassified and included in the results from continuing operations.

EXAMPLES OF FINANCIAL STATEMENT DISCLOSURES

Exemplum Reporting PLC
Financial Statements
For the Year Ended December 31, 20XX

Profit for the period from continuing operations		**X**	X	IAS 1 p82 IFRS 5 p33
Profit for the year from discontinued operations	12	**X**	X	
PROFIT FOR THE YEAR		**X**	X	

Earnings per share				
From continuing operations				
Basic (cents per share)	13	X	X	IAS 33 p66
Diluted (cents per share)	13	X	X	
From continuing and discontinued operations				
Basic (cents per share)	13	X	X	IAS 33 p68
Diluted (cents per share)	13	X	X	

12. Discontinued operations
12.1 Analysis of the statement of comprehensive income result:
In May 20XX the management committed to dispose of the packaging division. The sale is expected to be concluded in February 20XX, and no further loss is expected on the disposal of the assets involved. The packaging division fell within the distribution reporting segment.

	20XX	20XX-1	
Analysis of cash flow movements			IFRS 5 p33(c)
Operating cash flows	X	–	
Investing cash flows	X	–	
Financing cash flows	X	–	
Total cash flows	X	X	

Analysis of statement of comprehensive income result	**20XX**	20XX-1	IFRS 5 p33(c)
Revenue	X	X	
Expenses	X	X	
Loss before tax of discontinued operations	X	X	
Income tax expense	X	X	
Loss after tax of discontinued operations	X	X	
Pre-tax loss recognised on the measurement to fair value	X	–	
Income tax expenses	X	–	
After-tax loss recognised on the measurement to fair value	X	–	
Loss for the year from discontinued operations	X	X	

12.2 Analysis of assets and liabilities:

Cumulative income or expense recognised directly in other comprehensive income:	**20XX**	20XX-1	IFRS 5 p38
Foreign exchange translation adjustments	X	–	
	X	–	

Analysis of assets and liabilities	**20XX**	20XX-1	IFRS 5 p38
Property, plant and equipment	**X**	–	
Goodwill	**X**	–	
Inventory	**X**	–	
Other current assets	**X**	–	
Other current liabilities	**X**	–	
Current provisions	**X**	–	
	X	–	

US GAAP COMPARISON

Under US GAAP impairment does not have a particular standard or section. The most prominent ACS sections containing impairment matters are ASC 350, *Intangibles—Goodwill and Other*, and ASC 360, *Property, Plant and Equipment*.

For impairment for assets under US GAAP the definition is similar in that the carrying value is greater than its fair value. An entity has the option first to assess qualitative factors to determine whether the existence of events and circumstances indicates that it is more likely than not that the indefinite-lived intangible or long-lived asset is impaired. If, after assessing the totality of events and circumstances, an entity concludes that it is more likely than not that the indefinite-lived intangible or long-lived asset is not impaired, then the entity is not required to take further action. If it is determined that it is likely that the long-lived asset is impaired, then the entity must proceed to the quantitative step which is generally an undiscounted cash flow analysis. An entity may skip the qualitative assessment and proceed with the quantitative steps.

The first quantitative step is to compare the undiscounted future cash flows, termed the recoverable amount, of the assets being tested to the carrying value. If the recoverable amount is less than the carrying value, the second step is taken, resulting in a write-down of the excess of the fair value of the asset over the carrying value. Impairments once recorded may not be reversed.

The previous differences between IFRS and US GAAP in the definition, and hence the accounting, of discontinued operations were largely removed by ASU No. 2014-08, *Presentation of Financial Statement* (Topic 205), and *Property, Plant and Equipment Topic* (Topic 360), which are more particularly identified in ASC 205-20-45-1E.

ASU 2017-04, *Intangibles—Goodwill and Other* (Topic 350), eliminated step 2 from the goodwill impairment test under US GAAP, resulting in guidance that more closely aligns with the requirements in IFRS regarding goodwill impairment.

For **assets measured at amortized cost**, ASU No. 2016-13, *Financial Instruments—Credit Losses (Topic 326): Measurement of Credit Losses on Financial Instruments* (ASU 2016-13) eliminates the "probable" initial recognition threshold. Simply said, this provides users useful decision-making information on expected losses from financial instruments. Under this standard the current impairment methodology for incurred losses in current GAAP is replaced with a methodology that uses a broader range of supportable and reasonable information to inform estimates of credit loss.

ASU 2016-13 also applies to **available-for-sale** debt securities whereas entities will be required to provide an allowance for credit losses on available-for-sale debt securities rather than a permanent write-down. Troubled debt restructurings this update changes the impairment recognized on the restructuring – using the expected credit loss model eliminating the discounted cash flow methodology. This update is effective for public entities for fiscal years beginning after December 15, 2019 and all others December 15, 2020.

14 CONSOLIDATIONS, JOINT ARRANGEMENTS, ASSOCIATES AND SEPARATE FINANCIAL STATEMENTS

INTRODUCTION

IFRS 10, *Consolidated Financial Statements*, establishes principles for the presentation and preparation of consolidated financial statements when an entity controls one or more other entities, and introduces a single model for identifying control to replace the previous concepts of control contained within the former IAS 27 and SIC-12. IFRS 11, *Joint Arrangements*, establishes principles for the financial reporting by parties to a joint arrangement. The option to proportionately consolidate joint ventures that was previously available to jointly controlled entities under IAS 31 has been eliminated. IFRS 12, *Disclosure of Interest in Other Entities*, combines, enhances and replaces the disclosure requirements for subsidiaries, joint arrangements, associates and unconsolidated structured entities. IAS 27 (revised) deals with the presentation of separate financial statements. IAS 28 (revised) identifies associates and deals with equity accounting for both associates and joint ventures.

DEFINITIONS OF TERMS

Associate. An entity over which an investor has significant influence.

Consolidated financial statements. Financial statements of a group in which the assets, liabilities, equity, income, expenses and cash flows of the parent and its subsidiaries are presented as those of a single economic entity.

Control of an investee. An investor controls an investee when the investor is exposed, or has rights, to variable returns from its involvement with the investee and has the ability to affect those returns through its power over the investee.

Decision maker. An entity with decision-making rights that is either a principal or an agent of the principal.

Equity method. A method of accounting whereby the investment is initially recorded at cost and adjusted thereafter for the post-acquisition change in the investor's share of the investee's net assets. The investor's profit or loss includes its share of the investee's profit or loss and the investor's other comprehensive income includes its share of the investee's other comprehensive income.

Group. A parent and its subsidiaries.

Income from a structured entity. Includes, but is not limited to, recurring and non-recurring fees, interest, dividends, gains or losses on the remeasurement or derecognition of interest in structured entities and gain and losses from the transfer of assets and liabilities to the structured entity.

Interest in another entity. An interest in another entity refers to contractual and non-contractual involvement that exposes an entity to variability of returns from the performance of the other entity.

Investment entity. An entity that obtains funds from one or more investors for the purpose of providing those investor(s) with investment management services; commits to its investor(s) that its business purpose is to invest funds solely for returns from capital appreciation, investment income or both; and measures and evaluates the performance of substantially all of its investments on a fair value basis.

Joint arrangement. An arrangement of which two or more parties have joint control.

Joint control. The contractually agreed sharing of control of an arrangement, which exists only when decisions about the relevant activities require the unanimous consent of the parties sharing control.

Joint operation. A joint arrangement whereby the parties that have joint control of the arrangement have rights to the assets, and obligations for the liabilities, relating to the arrangement.

Joint operator. A party to a joint operation that has joint control of the operation.

Joint venture. A joint arrangement whereby the parties that have joint control of the arrangement have rights to the net assets of the arrangement.

Joint venturer. A party to a joint venture that has joint control of the joint venture.

Non-controlling interest. Equity in a subsidiary not attributable, directly or indirectly, to the parent.

Parent. An entity that controls one or more entities.

Party to a joint arrangement. An entity that participates in a joint arrangement, regardless of whether that entity has joint control of the arrangement.

Power. Existing rights that give the current ability to direct the relevant activities.

Protective rights. Rights designed to protect the interest of the party holding those rights without giving that party power over the entity to which those rights relate.

Relevant activities. Activities of the investee that significantly affect the investee's returns.

Removal rights. Rights to deprive the decision maker of its decision-making power.

Separate financial statements. Financial statements presented by an entity in which the entity could elect to account for its investment in subsidiaries, joint ventures and associates either at cost, in accordance with IFRS 9, *Financial Instruments*, or using the equity method as described in IAS 28, *Investments in Associates and Joint Ventures*.

Separate vehicle. A separately identifiable financial structure, including separate legal entities or entities recognised by statute, regardless of whether those entities have a legal personality.

Significant influence. The power to participate in the financial and operating policy decisions of the investee but it is not control or joint control of those policies.

Structured entity. An entity that has been designed so that voting or similar rights are not the dominant factor in deciding who controls the entity, such as when any voting rights relate to administrative tasks only and the relevant activities are directed by means of contractual arrangements.

Subsidiary. An entity that is controlled by another entity.

CONSOLIDATED FINANCIAL STATEMENTS

Scope

IAS 27 defines control as "the power to govern the financial and operating policies of an entity so as to obtain benefits from its activities," whereas SIC-12 considered both benefits and risks in its assessment of control of special-purpose entities. This subtle but important difference in concepts led to inconsistent application of the principles in practice. IFRS 10 provides a revised definition of control and establishes control as the basis for consolidation, so that a single control model can be applied to all entities.

IFRS 10 sets out related guidance to apply the principle of control to identify whether an investor controls an investee and therefore must consolidate the investee. IFRS 10 also sets out the accounting requirements for the preparation of consolidated financial statements.

IFRS 10 requires that an entity that is a parent must present consolidated financial statements that include all subsidiaries of the parent. Only three exceptions to this rule are available. First, a parent need not present consolidated financial statements if all the following criteria are met:

- The parent itself is a wholly owned subsidiary or it is a partially-owned subsidiary of another entity and all of its owners, including those not normally entitled to vote, have been informed about, and do not object to, the parent not presenting consolidated financial statements;
- Its debt and equity instruments are not traded in a public market;
- It did not file, nor is it in the process of filing, its financial statements with a securities exchange commission or other regulatory organisation for the purpose of issuing any class of its instruments in a public market; and
- Its ultimate or intermediate parent produces consolidated financial statements that are available for public use and comply with IFRS.

Secondly, post-employment benefit plans or other long-term employee benefits plans to which IAS 19, *Employee Benefits*, apply are also excluded from the scope of IFRS 10.

Thirdly, an investment entity need not present consolidated financial statements if it is required to measure those subsidiaries at fair value through profit or loss in accordance with IFRS 9, *Financial Instruments*. Investment entities are discussed later in this chapter.

Identification of a subsidiary

Under IFRS 10 an investor shall determine if it is a parent by assessing whether it controls the investee. A subsidiary is defined as "an entity that is controlled by another entity" (IFRS 10 App A). An investor controls an investee when the investor is exposed, or has rights, to variable returns from its involvement with the investee and has the ability to affect those returns through its power over the investee. The definition contains three requirements that must be present for control to exist:

- Power over the investee;
- Exposure, or rights, to variable returns; and
- The ability to use the power over the investee to affect the amount of returns.

The three requirements are interrelated. The ability to use power to affect the returns creates a link between the first two requirements. Only when the power could be used to affect the returns is the definition of control met. An investor must assess all facts and circumstances to determine whether it controls an entity. Appendix B to IFRS 10 contains the following factors that investors should use to determine if they control a subsidiary:

(1) the purpose and design of the investee;

(2) what the relevant activities are;

(3) how decisions about those activities are made;

(4) whether the rights of the investors give it the current ability to direct the relevant activities;

(5) whether the investor is exposed, or has the rights to variable returns from its involvement with the investee; and

(6) whether the investor has the ability to use its power over the investee to affect the amount of the investor's return.

These facts and circumstances should be continuously monitored, and if there are any changes to the facts or circumstances, control should be reassessed.

Power

Regarding the first requirement, an investor has power over an investee when the investor has existing rights that give it the current ability to direct the relevant activities that significantly affect the investee's returns. Returns will only be affected if the investor can control the activities that generate the returns.

Examples of activities that could, depending on the circumstances, be principal activities include: the purchase and sale of goods or services, the selection, acquisition or sale of assets, research and development for new products or procedures, and the establishment of finance structures or the procurement of funds. If two or more investors currently have the ability to manage the principal activities and these activities take place at different times, the investors must determine which of them has the ability to manage those activities that have the greatest effect on these returns.

Example of more than one investor

Two investors agree to form an entity to develop and market a new product. The one investor has unilateral decision-making power regarding the research and development of the product and the other has unilateral decision-making power regarding the manufacture and sale of the product.

To determine whether one or any of the investors controls the entity, the ability to direct the relevant activities must be assessed. This is achieved by first clarifying which activities are actually classified as relevant. If all activities—i.e., development as well as production and marketing—are relevant, each investor must determine whether he has the ability to direct the activities that most significantly affect the entity's returns.

Power arises from rights, and could arise in any of the following circumstances:

1. Rights in the form of voting rights (or potential voting rights) of an investee;
2. Rights to appoint, reassign or remove members of an investee's key management personnel who have the ability to direct the relevant activities;
3. Rights to appoint or remove another entity that directs the relevant activities;
4. Rights to direct the investee to enter into, or veto any changes to, transactions for the benefit of the investor; and
5. Other rights that give the holder the ability to direct the relevant activaties.

The lower one moves down this hierarchy, the more complex the assessment becomes. In the assessment, all the rights of others must be considered. An investor assessing whether he has decision-making power is only assessing substantive rights. Consequently, an investor that only holds protective rights does not have the power to direct the activities. A right is substantive when the holder has the practical ability to exercise the right. This requires judgement, taking into account all facts and circumstances. The following factors can be used in the assessment:

- Whether there are barriers (economic or otherwise) that prevent the holder from exercising the rights.
- Financial penalties and incentives that would prevent (or deter) the holder from exercising the rights.
- Terms and conditions that make it unlikely that the rights would be exercised.
- The absence of an explicit, reasonable mechanism in the founding documents of an investee or in the applicable laws or regulations that would allow the holder to exercise the rights.
- The inability of the holder of the rights to obtain the information necessary to exercise the rights.
- Operational barriers or incentives that would prevent the holder from exercising the rights.
- Legal or regulatory requirements that prevent the holder from exercising the rights.

Usually the substantive rights need to be exercisable when the decision regarding the direction of the relevant activities needs to be made. Rights may, however, also be of a substantial nature even if they cannot be exercised at present. An example for rights which are currently not exercisable but are even then substantive is shown later in this chapter.

Majority of voting rights

Control is presumed if the majority of voting rights is held, unless other factors indicate that the majority of voting rights does not create control. Holding the majority of voting rights normally results in control if:

- The relevant activities are directed by the vote of the majority holder; or
- The holder of the majority of voting rights may appoint the majority of members of the governing body that directs the activities (for example, the board of directors).

For a majority of voting rights to result in control, those rights must be substantive. If another party, which is not an agent, has existing rights that provide the other party with the ability to direct the operating activities, the majority of voting rights presumption is rebutted. The test is to determine who has power over the activities.

Example of majority of voting rights

Investor B has a 51% interest in an investment vehicle (T). B is only a passive investor and is not involved in the decision-making process.

Since investor B is passive, the rights of others must be considered to determine if they have power to direct the activities. In the absence of other facts and circumstances, the assumption is that B will exercise his voting rights to prevent resolutions being adopted that are not in his interests. As such, B currently has the power to direct relevant activities, even though he may not have exercised that power in the past. B must therefore consolidate T.

Less than a majority of voting rights

Control could also exist when a party has less than a majority of voting rights. The following are examples of instances where control could exist even though less than a majority of voting rights is held:

- A contractual arrangement between the investor and other parties that provides the investor with a right to direct the relevant activities.
- Rights arising from other contractual arrangements. Other decision-making rights together with voting rights might provide the party with the right to direct the relevant activities.
- The extent of the investor's voting rights. Although an investor may not hold the majority of the voting rights, the rights that are held could be so significant as to give it power to have the practical ability to direct the relevant activities unilaterally. This is referred to as de facto control.
- The investor may hold potential voting rights that are substantive. Potential voting rights are rights to obtain voting rights of an investee, such as convertible instruments and options. To be substantive, potential voting rights need to be exercisable when decisions about the direction of the relevant activities need to be made. Usually they must be presently exercisable to be classified as substantial, although sometimes rights may be substantial even if they cannot be exercised at present. Example: An investor is the contracting partner in a forward contract for the acquisition of a majority holding in the associate company. The settlement value of the forward contract is due within 25 days. The existing shareholders cannot change the company's current policy with regard to its principal activities because extraordinary general meetings cannot be held in less than 30 days, at which time the forward contract will already have been fulfilled. By virtue of his possession of the forward contract, the investor is in a position to make decisions on the management of those principal activities. The investor's forward contract is a substantive right that gives him the ability to manage those principal activities now, before the forward contract is fulfilled.

Any combination of the above scenarios could result in an investor having control of an investee. In assessing de facto control, the size of the investor's holdings relative to size and dispersion of other investors is considered, together with the other considerations listed above.

Examples of less than a majority of voting rights

Example 1: Investor A holds 45% of an entity's voting rights and no other investor holds more than 3%. De facto control might be present if no other consideration indicates that investor A has control, because the absolute size of his stake and the relative size of the other shareholdings indicate that A holds a sufficiently dominant share of the voting rights.

Example 2: Investor B holds 48% of an entity's voting rights and the other two investors hold 28% and 24%, respectively. Beyond that, no other agreements exist that might influence the adoption of resolutions. The size of the other investors' rights indicates that investor B does not hold de facto control. The other two investors only need to join forces to prevent investor B from directing the relevant activities of the joint venture.

Exposure, or rights, to variable returns from an investee

An investor is exposed, or has rights to, variable returns when the investor's returns from the involvement have the potential to vary as a result of the investor's performance, whether negative or positive. Variable returns can arise in various forms, for example:

- Dividends or other distributions of economic benefits from an investee and changes in the value of the investment.
- Remuneration for servicing an investee's assets or liabilities, fees and exposure to loss from providing credit or liquidity support, residual interests in the investee's assets and liabilities on liquidation of that investee, tax benefits, and access to future liquidity that an investor has from its involvement with an investee.
- Returns that are not available to other interest holders. For example, combining operating functions to achieve economies of scale, cost savings, sourcing scarce products, gaining access to proprietary knowledge or limiting some operations or assets to enhance the value of the investor's other assets.

Link between power and returns

An investor controls an investee if the investor not only has power over the investee and exposure or rights to variable returns from its involvement with the investee, but also has the ability to use its power to affect the investor's return from its involvement with the investee. Therefore, it is important to determine whether the investor is acting as an agent or the principal. If the investor acts as an agent, the investor does not control the investee. The investor will have been delegated power on behalf of another party or parties. An agent is a party primarily engaged to act on behalf or for the benefit of another party or partics (the principal). A decision maker must consider the overall relationship between itself; the investee being managed and other parties involved with the investee, and in particular the following factors to determine whether the decision maker is acting as an agent or principal:

- The scope of the decision-making authority. This is directly linked to the activities the decision maker can control. The scope is evaluated by considering
  (1) the activities that are permitted according to the decision-making agreement(s) and specified by law, and
  (2) the discretion that the decision maker has when making decisions about those activities.
  If, for example, a decision maker has a significant share in shaping the associate company (in determining the extent of decision-making authorities, for example), this may indicate that he has the opportunity and incentive to acquire rights that confer on the decision maker the ability to manage its principal activities.
- The rights held by other parties. Substantive removal or other rights may indicate that the person is only acting as an agent, since these rights could remove the power. Rights of others might restrict the decision-making power or discretion.

- Remuneration to which the decision maker is entitled in accordance with any remuneration agreement(s). In making this assessment, it is necessary to consider whether the remuneration is commensurate with the service rendered and whether the remuneration contract is based on similar arm's-length transactions. A full arm's-length remuneration contract in which the decision maker is compensated for services rendered would ordinarily indicate that the decision maker is acting as an agent.
- The decision maker's exposure to variability of returns from other interests that it holds in the investee. Holding an interest in an entity with variable returns might indicate that the decision maker is a principal. Based on the last two criteria, the more variable the returns are in relation to determining remuneration, the more likely that the decision maker is a principal.

Example of a fund manager

A decision maker founds, markets and manages a fund offering investment opportunities to a number of investors. The decision maker (fund manager) must make decisions in the interests of all investors and in accordance with the contracts that are most important to the fund. Nonetheless, the fund manager has a great deal of discretion where his decisions are concerned. For his services he receives a fee at the normal market level of 1% of assets under management plus 20% of the gains made by the fund once a specified level is reached. The fee is in reasonable proportion to the services provided.

Although the fund manager must make decisions in the interests of all investors, he enjoys wide decision-making authority in the management of the fund's principal activities. The fund manager receives fixed and variable fees at standard market levels. In addition, his remuneration has the effect of aligning the interests of fund managers and those of other investors in a rise in the fund's value. However, this imposes no risk arising from fluctuating returns from fund activities of such a magnitude that the remuneration, when viewed in isolation, might be seen as an indicator that the fund manager is the principal.

Other arrangements

Control can also exist through other contractual arrangements. This would usually be the case with structured entities. A structured entity is an entity that has been designed so that voting or similar rights are not the dominant factor in deciding who controls the entity, such as when any voting rights relate to administrative tasks only and the relevant activities are directed by means of contractual arrangements. The assessment of control in such instances is based on the normal principles discussed above as well as an assessment of the special arrangements and the size of the exposure regarding the variability in returns. In assessing the purpose and design of the structured entity, the risk that was created and passed on to the parties to the arrangement is considered to establish the party's exposure to some or all of the risks. A large exposure to variability in returns might also indicate that the party has power over the entity. Such risk and returns are, however, on their own not conclusive. All facts and circumstances must be considered.

The involvement of the parties and decisions made at the inception of the arrangement are considered to determine whether the transaction terms and features provide the investor with rights that are sufficient to create control. Both explicit and implicit decision-making rights embedded in the contractual arrangement that are closely linked to the investor must be considered. Further contractual rights such as call rights, put rights and liquidation rights are also considered.

Consolidation Procedures

Consolidated financial statements shall present fairly the financial position, financial performance and cash flows of the group. IFRS 10 contains only a little guidance on the preparation of consolidated financial statements. A parent shall prepare consolidated financial statements using uniform accounting policies for like transactions and other events in similar circumstances. Consolidation begins from the date the investor obtains control and ceases when the investor loses control.

Intercompany transactions and balances

In preparing consolidated financial statements an entity combines the items presented in the financial statements line by line, adding together like items of assets, liabilities, equity, income and expenses. To present financial information about the group as that of a single economic entity, the following procedures are followed:

- Like items of assets, liabilities, equity, income, expenses and cash flows of the parent are combined with those of the subsidiary.
- The carrying amount of the parent's investment in each subsidiary is eliminated (offset) against the parent's portion of equity of each subsidiary.
- Intragroup assets and liabilities, equity, income, expenses and cash flows relating to transactions of the entities in the group are eliminated. For example, a parent may sell merchandise to its subsidiary, at cost or with a profit margin added, before the subsidiary ultimately sells the merchandise to unrelated parties in arm's-length transactions. Furthermore, any balances due to or from members of the consolidated group at the end of the reporting period must also be eliminated. If assets have been transferred among the entities in the controlled group at amounts in excess of the transferor's cost, and they have not yet been further transferred to outside parties (e.g., inventories) or not yet consumed (e.g., plant assets subject to depreciation) by the end of the reporting period, the amount of profit not yet realised through an arm's-length transaction must be eliminated.
- Requirements of IAS 12, *Income Taxes*, shall be applied to the temporary differences that arise from the elimination of profits and losses resulting from intragroup transactions.

Non-controlling interests

When less than 100% of the shares of the acquired entity are owned by the acquirer, a complication arises in the preparation of consolidated statements, and a non-controlling interest must be determined and presented. According to IFRS 10, non-controlling interests must be presented in the consolidated statement of financial position within equity, separately from the equity of controlling interests (the owners of the parent). If a company holds non-controlling interests in several subsidiaries, the various non-controlling interests can be reported within a single position. This method complies with the economic unit concept that is employed in the world of Anglo-Saxon accounting. The profit or loss and each component of other comprehensive income to the owners of the parent and to the non-controlling interests must be attributed separately. This applies even if this allocation brings about a situation in which the non-controlling interests post or will in future post a negative equity balance. Not even the non-existence of an additional-funding obligation on the part of the non-controlling interests makes any difference to this allocation. In this event a negative share of the non-controlling interests must consequently be reported within equity.

The control concept of IFRS 10 and the economic unit concept can jointly lead to a situation where a parent company, even though it has a minority holding in an entity, controls the relevant activities of the subsidiary—by virtue of other agreements, for example—and hence also controls the subsidiary itself. Since shares in the equity and the profit or loss are determined on the basis of ownership interest (for which see below), this leads to a situation in which consolidation includes 100% of an entity's assets and liabilities while the majority of the equity must be allocated to non-controlling interests. In these cases IFRS 12 requires the disclosure of the nature of the relationship between a parent and a subsidiary when less than 50% of voting rights are owned.

Measurement of non-controlling interests: According to IFRS 3, entities have the choice to measure the non-controlling interests at either fair value or at its proportionate share in the recognised amounts of the acquiree's identifiable net assets. This choice can be made on a transaction-by-transaction basis. It is not required for entities to make an accounting policy choice. In the subsequent periods, the non-controlling interest is not remeasured to fair value. But, the share of the profit or loss and each component of other comprehensive income is allocated to non-controlling interests as described above.

Profit or loss and each component of other comprehensive income must be allocated to the owners of the parent and non-controlling interest. The total comprehensive income must also be allocated, even if this results in non-controlling interest having a deficit balance.

Non-controlling interests in the net assets consist of (1) the amount recognised at the date of the original business combination (calculated in accordance with IFRS 3), and (2) the non-controlling interests' share of changes in equity (net assets) of the subsidiary since the date of combination.

Changes in the proportion of non-controlling interests

Changes in a parent's interest in a subsidiary that do not result in the parent losing control are equity transactions and result in transfers to and from the owner's equity to non-controlling interest. The difference between the amount by which the non-controlling interest is adjusted and the fair value of the consideration paid or received is recognised directly in equity attributable to the parent.

Example of recognising changes in the level of the parent's controlling ownership interest

Konin Corporation (KC) owns a 75% interest in Donna Corporation (DC). KC decided to acquire an additional 10% interest in DC from the non-controlling shareholders in exchange for cash of €100,000. DC has net assets of €800,000. KC accounts for this transaction in the consolidated financial statements as follows:

Equity—Non-controlling interest	80,000	
Equity—Controlling interest	20,000	
Cash		100,000

Uniformity of accounting policies

There is a presumption that all the members of the consolidated group should use the same accounting principles to account for similar events and transactions. However, in many cases this will not occur, as, for example, when a subsidiary is acquired that uses cost for investment property while the parent has long employed the fair value method. IFRS 10 requires that the policies of the combining entities should be uniform and therefore appropriate adjustments should be made in the consolidated accounts. When a subsidiary of a corporate group is acquired and different accounting policies exist, the principles of IAS 8 permit the subsidiary to alter its accounting policy to that of the group in its individual financial statements. Alternatively, the subsidiary may retain its previous principles in its individual financial statements. In this event the group should make appropriate adjustments in the consolidated accounts.

Measurement

Income and expenses of the subsidiary are included in the consolidated financial statements from the date control is obtained until the date when control is lost. The income and expenses are based on the amounts of assets and liabilities recognised at the acquisition date. The depreciation charges entered in the consolidated income statement after the date of acquisition, for example, are based on the fair value of the associated depreciable assets reported in the consolidated financial statements on the date of acquisition.

Reporting date

A practical consideration in preparing consolidated financial statements is to have information on all constituent entities current as of the parent's year-end. If a subsidiary has a different reporting date, the subsidiary prepares additional financial information as of the date of the consolidated financial statements to enable the parent to consolidate the subsidiary, unless it is impracticable to do so.

If it is impracticable, the subsidiary is consolidated using the most recent financial statements of the subsidiary adjusted for the effect of significant transactions or events that occur between the date of those financial statements and the date of the consolidated financial statements. The difference between the date of the subsidiary's financial statements and the consolidated financial statements is limited to three months and must be applied consistently from period to period. Of course, if this option is elected, the process of eliminating intercompany transaction and balances may become a bit more complicated, since reciprocal accounts (e.g., sales and cost of sales) will be out of balance for any events occurring after the earlier fiscal year-end but before the later one.

Ownership interest

In the preparation of consolidated financial statements there is usually a question mark over the share of the profit or loss or changes in the equity of the subsidiary that the parent company must take into account in the preparation of its own consolidated financial statements if, for example, potential voting rights or non-controlling interests exist. IFRS 10 determines that the proportion of profit or loss and changes in equity allocated to the parent and non-controlling interests in preparing consolidated financial statements is determined solely on the basis of existing ownership interests, unless an entity has, in substance, an existing ownership interest as a result of a transaction that currently gives the entity access to the return associated with an ownership interest.

Example

X has a 70% holding in Y and a 20% holding in Z. Y, in its turn, has a 35% holding in Z. Solution: X controls Y and thus also Z, because X directly and indirectly holds 55% of Z's shares. Y's holding in Z must be allocated in full to X, as X controls Y. Y and Z must consequently be included in X's consolidated financial statements. X's share of Z's profit or loss or changes in equity is 44.5% (20% + (70% of 35%)). X consequently allocates 55.5% of its subsidiary Z to non-controlling interests.

Indirect interest

If a parent company has an indirect holding, the treatment of the non-controlling interests is more complicated than in a single-tiered group. Furthermore, the amount of potential goodwill to be reported is contentious. The non-controlling interests in the parent company's consolidated financial statements are calculated by multiplying the fractions applying to the various tiers of the group. The calculation for the purposes of consolidation can be carried out either in a single step, or first at the level of the indirect holding, then at that of the parent company with a corresponding adjustment of the indirect holding (multi-tier consolidation).

Example

Parent company P holds 85% of the equity of its subsidiary S1 (€400). S1 holds 75% of the equity of second-tier subsidiary S2 (€100).

From P's viewpoint the non-controlling interest in S1 must be taken into account first: 15% of €400 = €60. The indirect holding of non-controlling shareholder S1 in S2 is determined by multiplication: 15% of 75% of €100 = €11.25. Finally, the non-controlling shareholder's direct holding in S2 is included: 25% of €100 = €25. A non-controlling interest total of €96.25 must therefore be reported in P's consolidated financial statements.

If goodwill was revealed in the first consolidation of S2 in S1 in the revaluation process, the question arises as to the level of goodwill that must be included in P's consolidated financial statements.

Example

Modified example: S2 was also found to have goodwill of €30 (in S1's subgroup financial statements). S2's equity is thus €130. The interests of non-controlling shareholders in S2 remains unchanged at €25, as goodwill is basically only allocated to the acquirer (S1).

The treatment of goodwill at the level of P is contentious. On the one hand it is contended that here, too, goodwill should be reported at €30, and that the non-controlling interest is accordingly €4.5 higher (€30 × 15%). This is argued on the grounds that non-controlling shareholders in S1 were part of the S2 acquisition transaction.

The second view is based on net assets from the viewpoint of the group. This holds that P holds only 85% of the goodwill and may thus report only €25.5, while the remaining €4.5 are offset against the non-controlling interest, restoring this to the amount in the original example.

We prefer the second view, because this reflects the goodwill commercially acquired by the group shareholders at its correct level. Also this does not result in any blending with the full goodwill method as in the first view.

If the full goodwill method is applied as per IFRS 3, accounting is ambiguous. At the level of S1, goodwill of €40 is detected (full goodwill = €30 (S1 goodwill)/75%). Of this, €10 are allocated to S2's non-controlling shareholders and €4.5 to those of S1. In total, non-controlling interests of €110.75 (equity share of €96.25 plus €14.5 as a share of goodwill) must be reported in P's consolidated financial statements.

Subsidiaries to be disposed of or acquired with a view to resale

Subsidiaries that were acquired with a view to resale or are to be sold, where these meet the definition of an asset held for sale in accordance with IFRS 5, are not excluded from the consolidation. They must continue to be consolidated, and furthermore their results, assets and liabilities must be reported separately. These subsidiaries are presented in a single amount in the statement of comprehensive income comprising the total of:

- The post-tax profit or loss of discontinued operations; and
- The post-tax gain or loss recognised on the measurement to fair value less costs to sell or on the disposal of the assets or disposal group(s) constituting the discontinued operation.

The assets of the subsidiaries classified as held for sale must be separately presented from other assets in the statement of financial position. The same is true for the liabilities of the subsidiaries classified as held for sale.

The provisions of IFRS 5 are dealt with in detail in Chapter 13.

Example—Cement manufacturer A purchases competitor C

German cement manufacturer A purchases a Belgian competitor C. The EU Commission approves the transaction on condition that A sells its German subsidiary Y. A has consented to this condition.

Y, therefore, fulfils all of the prerequisites of IFRS 5 at that time. Y is balanced at the time of purchase and evaluated in accordance with IFRS 5.

Y is shown on the consolidated balance sheet under two positions ("Non-current assets classified as held for sale" and "Liabilities directly associated with non-current assets classified as held for sale"). As Y also constitutes a discontinued operation in accordance with IFRS 5, the profits of C are shown separately in the profit and loss account ("Profit for the year—discontinued operations").

Changes in ownership interest resulting in loss of control

If a parent company ceases to have a controlling financial interest in a subsidiary, the parent is required to deconsolidate the subsidiary as of the date on which its control ceased. Examples of situations that can result in a parent being required to deconsolidate a subsidiary include:

a. Sale by the parent of all or a portion of its ownership interest in the subsidiary resulting in the parent no longer holding a controlling financial interest.
b. Expiration of a contract that granted control of the subsidiary to the parent.
c. Issuance by the subsidiary of shares that reduces the ownership interest of the parent to a level not representing a controlling financial interest.
d. Loss of control of the subsidiary by the parent because the subsidiary becomes subject to control by a governmental body, court, administrator or regulator.

Should the parent's loss of controlling financial interest occur through two or more transactions, management of the former parent is to consider whether the transactions should be accounted for as a single transaction. In evaluating whether to combine the transactions, management of the former parent is to consider all of the terms and conditions of the transactions as well as their economic impact. The presence of one or more of the following indicators may lead to management concluding that it should account for multiple transactions as a single transaction:

a. The transactions are entered into simultaneously or in contemplation of one another.
b. The transactions form a single transaction designed to achieve an overall commercial effect.
c. The occurrence of one transaction depends on the occurrence of at least one other transaction.
d. One transaction, when considered on its own merits, does not make economic sense, but when considered together with the other transaction or transactions would be considered economically justifiable.

Obviously, this determination requires the exercise of sound judgement and attention to economic substance over legal form.

When control of a subsidiary is lost and a non-controlling interest is retained, consistent with the approach applied in step acquisitions, the parent should measure that retained interest at fair value and recognise, in profit or loss, a gain or loss on disposal of the controlling interest. The gain or loss is measured as follows:

FVCR	=	Fair value of consideration received, if any
FVNIR	=	Fair value of any non-controlling investment retained by the former parent at the derecognition date (the date control is lost)
DISTRoS	=	Any distribution of shares of the subsidiary to owners
CVNI	=	Carrying value of the non-controlling interest in the former subsidiary on the derecognition date, including any accumulated other comprehensive income attributable to the non-controlling interest
CVAL	=	Carrying value of the former subsidiary's assets (including goodwill) and liabilities at the derecognition date

(FVCR + FVNIR + DISTRoS + CVNI) − CVAL = Gain (Loss)

Example of accounting for the parent's loss of control of a subsidiary

Konin Corporation (KC) owns an 85% interest in Donna Corporation (DC). On January 1, 20XX, KC decided to sell a 50% interest in DC to a third party in exchange for cash of €600,000. At the disposal date the total fair value of DC amounts to €1,000,000. Furthermore, in KC's consolidated financial statements the carrying value of DC's net assets is €1,000,000 and the carrying value of the non-controlling interest in DC (including the non-controlling interest's share of accumulated other comprehensive income) is €100,000. As a result of this transaction, KC loses control of DC but retains a 35% interest in the former subsidiary, valued at €350,000 on that date. The gain or loss on the disposal of 50% interest in DC is calculated as follows:

Cash received	€600,000
Fair value of retained non-controlling interest	€350,000
Carrying value of DC's non-controlling interest	€100,000
	€1,050,000
Less: Carrying value of DC's net assets	€1,000,000
Gain on disposal	€50,000

If a parent loses control of a subsidiary, it must recognise all amounts that were previously reported for the relevant subsidiary in other comprehensive income. Recognition takes place on the same basis as would have been prescribed by the parent company for a direct disposal of the corresponding assets or liabilities. Example: Subsidiary X is sold by parent company A. The previous consolidated balance sheet contained other comprehensive income reserves pursuant to IFRS 9 and actuarial losses pursuant to IAS 19 resulting from subsidiary X. At the time of the loss of control of X, A must reclassify the reserve to profit or loss, and leave the remeasurements of the net defined benefit liability (asset) recognised in other comprehensive income under IAS 19 in the consolidated equity of A. This is because, under IAS 19.122, remeasurements shall not be reclassified to profit or loss in a subsequent period, and under IFRS 9 the reserve must be reclassified on the sale of the securities.

If a parent loses control of a subsidiary (which does not constitute a business as defined in IFRS 3) as a result of sale of interest in the subsidiary to its associate or joint venture, then the gain or loss resulting from such transaction is recognised in profit or loss only to the extent of gain attributable to unrelated interest in the associate or joint venture. Example: Entire interest in subsidiary X is sold by parent company A to its associate B wherein A holds 20% interest. In such case, the gain from sale of interest in subsidiary is recognised in profit or loss only to the extent of 80% (100% – 20%, being unrelated interest) and the balance 20% of gain is adjusted against the carrying amount of the investment in the associate. *(Note: Effective date for complying with this requirement yet to be determined by the IASB; however, earlier application is permitted.)*

Investment Entities

Investment Entities require a parent that is an investment entity to measure its investments in particular subsidiaries at fair value through profit or loss in accordance with IFRS 9 instead of consolidating those subsidiaries in its consolidated and separate financial statements. However, as an exception to this requirement, if a subsidiary provides investment-related services or activities to the investment entity, it should be consolidated.

A parent of an investment entity has to consolidate all entities that it controls, even those subsidiaries who are controlled by an investment entity, unless the parent itself is an investment entity.

Example: Vehicle manufacturer X is the parent company of investment entity B. B has holdings in various companies that are not active in the automotive sector. Whereas X is not an investment entity pursuant to IFRS 10, B is classed as an investment entity pursuant to IFRS 10. For the purposes of this example it should be assumed that both X and B must prepare consolidated financial statements. Solution: Since B is an investment entity, it must report companies in which it holds a controlling interest at fair value through profit or loss. X, conversely, must fully consolidate all its subsidiaries, including B.

Definition

IFRS 10 requires a parent to determine whether it is an investment entity. An investment entity is defined as an entity that:

a. Obtains funds from one or more investors for the purpose of providing those investors with investment management services;
b. Commits to its investors that its business purpose is to invest funds solely for returns from capital appreciation, investment income or both; and
c. Measures and evaluates the performance of substantially all of its investments on a fair value basis.

The standard explains that an investment entity will usually display the following typical characteristics, which entities should consider in determining whether the definition is met:

a. It will have more than one investment;
b. It will have more than one investor;
c. It will have investors that are not related parties of the entity; and
d. It will have ownership interests in the form of equity or similar interests.

Although these typical characteristics are not essential factors in determining whether an entity qualifies to be classified as an investment entity, the standard does require an investment entity that does not have all of these typical characteristics to provide additional disclosure regarding the judgement made in arriving at the conclusion that it is in fact an investment entity.

Investment management services

From the point of view of the IASB, one of the essential activities of an investment entity is that it obtains funds from investors to provide those investors with investment management services. Even though detailed guidance is not given about the first criteria of the definition, the IASB notes that this provision differentiates investment entities from other entities.

Business purpose

The purpose of an investment entity should be to invest solely for capital appreciation, investment income (such as dividends, interest or rental income) or both. This would typically be evident in documents such as the entity's offering memorandum, publications distributed by the entity and other corporate or partnership documents. Further evidence may include the manner in which the entity presents itself to other parties (such as potential investors or potential investees).

Example of business purpose

Investo's offering memorandum describes its business purpose to be ". . . the undertaking of investment activities for the purpose of earning investment income and capital appreciation." However, its practice thus far has been to jointly develop, produce or market products with its investees. Notwithstanding its stated business purpose, Investo's actual business purpose is inconsistent with the business purpose of an investment entity, because the entity will earn returns from the development, production or marketing activity as well as from its investments.

An investment entity may provide investment-related services (for example, investment advisory services, investment management, investment support and administrative services), either directly or through a subsidiary, to third parties as well as to its investors, even if those activities are substantial to the entity. However, such services should not be offered to investees, unless they are undertaken to maximise the entity's investment return. In addition, if these services to investees represent a separate substantial business activity or a separate substantial source of income to the entity, it would not be able to classify itself as an investment entity in the context of IFRS 10.

Exit strategies

A common characteristic of investment entities is that they would not plan to hold investments indefinitely. The standard requires an investment entity to have an exit strategy documenting how the entity plans to realise capital appreciation from substantially all of its equity investments and non-financial asset investments. An investment entity would also be required to have an exit strategy for any debt instruments that have the potential to be held indefinitely, for example perpetual debt investments. Although it is not necessary to document specific exit strategies for each individual investment, an investment entity should at least be able to identify different potential strategies for different types or portfolios of investments, including a substantive time frame for exiting the investments. For the purposes of this assessment, it would not be sufficient to consider exit mechanisms that are only put in place for default events, such as breach of contract or non-performance.

Examples of exit strategies for private equity securities could include:

- An initial public offering;
- A private placement;
- A trade sale of a business;
- Distributions (to investors) of ownership interests in investees; and
- Sales of assets (including the sale of an investee's assets followed by a liquidation of the investee).

Example of exit strategies for publicly trade equity securities could include:

- Selling the investment in a private placement or in a public market.

Example of exit strategies for real estate investments include:

- Sale of the real estate through specialised property dealers or the open market.

Earnings from investments

An entity would not be investing solely for capital appreciation, investment income or both, if the entity or another member of the group to which the entity belongs obtains, or has the objective of obtaining, other benefits from the entity's investments that are not available to other parties that are not related to the investee.

Examples of benefits which would usually result in disqualification from investment entity status include:

a. The acquisition, use, exchange or exploitation of the processes, assets or technology of an investee;
b. Joint arrangements or other agreements between the entity or another group member and an investee to develop, produce, market or provide products or services;
c. Financial guarantees or assets provided by an investee to serve as collateral for borrowing arrangements of the entity or another group member;
d. An option held by a related party of the entity to purchase, from that entity or another group member, an ownership interest in an investee of the entity; and
e. Transactions between the entity or another group member and an investee that:
    i. Are on terms that are unavailable to entities that are not related parties of either the entity, another group member or the investee;
    ii. Are not at fair value; or
    iii. Represent a substantial portion of the investee's or the entity's business activity, including business activities of other group entities.

Example—Biotechnology Fund (based on IFRS 10 para IE 7, example 2)

Select Biotechnology Fund was formed by Pharma Ltd to invest in pharmaceuticals start-up companies for capital appreciation. Pharma Ltd holds an 80% interest in Select Biotechnology Fund and controls Select Biotechnology Fund; the other 20% ownership interest in Select Biotechnology Fund is owned by 10 unrelated investors. Pharma Ltd holds options to acquire investments held by Select Biotechnology Fund, at fair value, which would be exercised if the certain medical trials of pharmaceuticals products developed by investees would benefit the operations of Pharma Ltd. No plans for exiting the investments have been identified by Select Biotechnology Fund. Select Biotechnology Fund is managed by an investment adviser that acts as agent for the investors in Select Biotechnology Fund.

Can Select Biotechnology Fund be considered as an investment company? Although Select Biotechnology Fund has the business purpose to invest for capital appreciation and it provides investment management services to its investor, Select Biotechnology Fund is not an investment entity for two reasons: (1) Pharma Ltd, the parent of Select Biotechnology Fund, holds options to acquire investments in investees held by Select Biotechnology Fund if the assets developed by the investees would benefit the operations of Pharma Ltd. This provides a benefit in addition to capital appreciation or investment income; and (2) the investment plans of Select Biotechnology Fund do not include exit strategies for its investments, which are equity investments. The options held by Pharma Ltd are not controlled by Select Biotechnology Fund and do not constitute an exit strategy.

Fair value measurement

An essential element of the definition of an investment entity is that it measures and evaluates the performance of substantially all of its investments on a fair value basis. An investment entity would ordinarily be expected to provide investors with fair value information and measure substantially all of its investments at fair value in its financial statements whenever fair value is required or permitted in accordance with IFRS standards. Investment entities would typically also report fair value information internally to the entity's key management personnel (as defined in IAS 24, *Related Party Disclosures*), who use fair value as the primary measurement attribute to evaluate the performance of substantially all of its investments and to make investment decisions. Areas where fair value would be expected to feature as the accounting policy of choice for accounting for investments include:

- Electing to account for any investment property using the fair value model in IAS 40, *Investment Property*;
- Electing the exemption from applying the equity method in IAS 28 for investments in associates and joint ventures; and
- Measuring financial assets at fair value using the requirements in IFRS 9.

These choices would be expected for all investment assets, but an investment entity would not be expected to measure any non-investment assets at fair value. Thus, there would be no requirement for non-investment assets (such as property, plant and equipment, or intangible assets) or liabilities to be measured at fair value.

In determining whether it meets the definition of an investment entity the following typical characteristics could be used. The absence of any of these characteristics may indicate that an entity does not meet the definition of an investment entity. If an entity does not meet one or more of the typical characteristics, additional judgement is necessary in determining whether an entity is an investment entity.

More than one investment

An investment entity typically holds several investments to diversify risk and maximise returns. An investment entity may hold a portfolio of investments directly or indirectly, for example by holding a single investment in another investment entity that itself holds several investments. There may be times when the entity holds a single investment. However, holding a single investment does not necessarily prevent an entity from meeting the definition of an investment entity. For example, an investment entity may hold only a single investment when the entity is in its start-up period or has not yet made other investments to replace those it has disposed of. In some cases, an investment entity may be established to pool investors' funds to invest in a single investment when that investment is unobtainable by individual investors (for example, when the required minimum investment is too high for an individual investor). In such a situation, the entity with a single investment could still meet the definition of an investment entity, but these circumstances would have to be explained in the judgements applied by management.

More than one investor

An investment entity would typically have several investors who pool their funds to gain access to investment management services and investment opportunities that they might not have had access to individually. Having several investors would make it less likely that the entity, or other members of the group containing the entity, would obtain benefits other than capital appreciation or investment income. Alternatively, an investment entity may be formed by, or for, a single investor that represents or supports the interests of a wider group of investors (for example, a pension fund, government investment fund or family trust). The standard also explains that the entity's investors would typically be unrelated to one another, again making it less likely that there would be any other benefits to investors besides capital appreciation or investment income.

Unrelated investors

An investment entity normally has various investors who are not related to the company or to other members of the company. The existence of unrelated parties is an indication that the companies or members of the company derive advantages from the investment mostly through increases in value or capital returns. Even if the investors are related to one another, however, the possibility of qualifying the company as an investment entity exists. An investment entity may, for example, set up a separate parallel fund for a group of its employees to reward them.

Change in status

Since the determination of investment entity status is dependent on an assessment of the relevant facts and circumstances at a point in time, an entity's status may change over time. If facts and circumstances indicate changes to one or more of the three elements that qualify an entity to be an investment entity, a parent needs to reassess whether it is an investment entity. If an entity's status changes due to a change in circumstances, the effects of the change are accounted for prospectively.

When an entity that was previously classified as an investment entity ceases to be an investment entity, it applies IFRS 3 to any subsidiary that was previously measured at fair value through profit or loss. The date of the change of status is the deemed acquisition date for the purposes of applying the acquisition method, and the fair value of the subsidiary at the deemed acquisition date represents the transferred deemed consideration when measuring any goodwill or gain from a bargain purchase that arises from the deemed acquisition. The entity consolidates its subsidiaries with effect from the deemed acquisition date until control is lost.

If an entity becomes an investment entity, it deconsolidates its subsidiaries at the date of the change in status. The deconsolidation of subsidiaries is accounted for as though the investment entity has lost control of those subsidiaries at that date, and any difference between the fair value of the retained investment and the net asset value of the former subsidiary is recognised in profit or loss.

EXAMPLES OF FINANCIAL STATEMENT DISCLOSURES

Exemplum Reporting PLC
Financial Statements
For the Year Ended December 31, 20XX

19. Investment in subsidiaries

Composition of the group

Name	Country of incorporation	Proportion of ownership interest		Proportion owned by subsidiary companies		Principal activities	Wholly or non-wholly owned subsidiary	IFRS 12 p10, p4, B4, B5, B6
		20XX	20XX-1	20XX	20XX-1			
Subsidiary A	UK	48%	48%	–	–	Distribution of widgets	Non-wholly	
Subsidiary B	UK	90%	100%			Manufacturing of widgets	Non-wholly	
Subsidiary C	France	–	–	90%	90%	Retail of widgets	Non-wholly	
Company A	UK	100%	100%	–	–	Manufacturing of widgets	Wholly	
Company B	France	100%	100%	–	–	Distribution of widgets	Wholly	

Details of non-wholly owned subsidiaries that have material non-controlling interests

Name of subsidiary	Proportion of ownership interest held by non-controlling interest		Profit or loss allocated to non-controlling interest		Accumulated non-controlling interests		IFRS 12 p10, p12, B11
	20XX	20XX-1	20XX	20XX-1	20XX	20XX-1	
Subsidiary A (a)	52%	52%	X	X	X	X	
Subsidiary B	10%	0%	X	–	X	–	
Subsidiary C	10%	10%	X	X	X	X	
Total					X	X	

(a) The group owns 48% equity shares of Subsidiary A. The remaining 52% is widely held by thousands of unrelated shareholders. An assessment of control was performed by the group based on whether the group has the practical ability to direct the relevant activities unilaterally and it was concluded that the group had a dominant voting interest to direct the relevant activities of Subsidiary A and it would take a number of vote holders to outvote the group, therefore the group has control over Subsidiary A and Subsidiary A is consolidated in these financial statements. IFRS 12 p9

Summarised financial information

Summarised financial information in respect of each of the group's subsidiaries that has material non-controlling interests is set out below. The summarised financial information below represents amounts before intragroup eliminations. IFRS 12 p12, B10, B11

	Subsidiary A		**Subsidiary B**		**Subsidiary C**	
	20XX	**20XX-1**	**20XX**	**20XX-1**	**20XX**	**20XX-1**
Current assets	X	X	X	–	X	X
Non-current assets	X	X	X	–	X	X
Current liabilities	(X)	(X)	(X)	–	(X)	(X)
Non-current liabilities	(X)	(X)	(X)	–	(X)	(X)
Equity attributable to owners of the company	X	X	X	–	X	X
Non-controlling interests	X	X	X	–	X	X
Revenue	X	X	X	–	X	X
Expenses	(X)	(X)	(X)	–	(X)	(X)
Profit or loss for the year	X	X	X	–	X	X
Profit or loss attributable to owners of the company	X	X	X	–	X	X
Profit or loss attributable to the non-controlling interests	X	X	X	–	X	X
Profit or loss for the year	X	X	X	–	X	X
Other comprehensive income attributable to owners of the company	X	X	X	–	X	X
Other comprehensive income to the non-controlling interests	X	X	X	–	X	X
Other comprehensive income for the year	X	X	X	–	X	X
Total comprehensive income attributable to owners of the company	X	X	X	–	X	X
Total comprehensive income to the non-controlling interests	X	X	X	–	X	X
Total comprehensive income for the year	X	X	X	–	X	X
Dividends paid to non-controlling interests	–	–	–	–	–	–
Net cash in/(out) flow from operating activities	X	X	X	–	X	X

Net cash in/(out) flow from investing activities	(X)	X	X	–	(X)	X
Net cash in/(out) flow from financing activities	(X)	X	(X)	–	(X)	(X)
Net cash in/(out) flow	X	X	X	–	X	X

Change in the group's ownership interest in a subsidiary IFRS 12 p18

10% of the group's interest in Subsidiary B was disposed of during the year, reducing its continuing interest to 90%. The difference between the consideration received of X and the increase in the non-controlling interest of X has been credited to retained earnings.

Significant restrictions IFRS 12 p13

There are no significant restrictions on the company's or subsidiary's ability to access or use the assets and settle the liabilities of the group.

Financial support IFRS 12 p14, p15, p16, p17

The group has not given any financial support to a consolidated structured entity.

JOINT ARRANGEMENTS

Scope

IFRS 11, *Joint Arrangements*, deals with financial reporting by parties to a joint arrangement. IFRS 11 replaced IAS 31, *Interest in Joint Ventures*, and SIC 13, *Jointly Controlled Entities—Non-monetary Contributions by Venturers*, and sets principles for the accounting for all joint arrangements. Joint arrangements are classified in two types: joint operations and joint ventures. The party to a joint arrangement must determine the type of joint arrangement it is involved in by assessing its rights and obligations created by the arrangement.

Joint Arrangements

A joint arrangement is defined as an arrangement of which two or more parties have joint control and has two characteristics:

(1) the parties must be bound by contractual arrangement, and

(2) the contractual arrangement must give two or more of the parties' joint control over the arrangement.

Therefore, not all parties need to have joint control. IFRS 11 distinguishes between parties that have joint control and parties that participate in the joint arrangement but do not have joint control. Judgement is applied to assess whether parties have joint control by considering all the facts and circumstances. If the facts and circumstances change, joint control must be reassessed.

Enforceable contractual arrangements are normally created through a written contract or other documented discussions between the parties. However, statutory mechanisms (articles of association, charters, bylaws and similar mechanisms) can also create enforceable arrangements on their own or in conjunction with the written documentation. The contractual arrangement normally deals with activities such as:

- The purpose, activity or duration of the arrangement;
- How members of the board of directors or other governing body are appointed;
- The decision-making process;
- The capital or other contributions required; and
- How parties share assets, liabilities, revenue, expenditure or the profit or loss.

Joint control is defined as the contractually agreed sharing of control of an arrangement, which exists only when decisions about the relevant activities require the unanimous consent of the parties sharing control. The parties must assess whether the contractual arrangement gives them control collectively. Parties control the arrangement collectively when they must act together to direct the activities that significantly affect the returns of the arrangement (the relevant activities). The collective control could be created by all the parties or a group of parties.

Even if collective control is established, joint control exists only when decisions about the relevant activities require the unanimous consent of all the parties that control the arrangement collectively. This can either be explicitly agreed or implicit in the arrangement. For instance, two parties may each hold 50% of the voting rights, but the arrangement states that more than 50% of the voting rights are needed to make decisions about the relevant activities. Because the parties must agree to make decisions, joint control is implied.

When the minimum required proportion of rights required to make decisions can be achieved by different combinations of parties agreeing, joint control is normally not established.

The requirement of unanimous consent means that any party with joint control can prevent any of the other parties from making unilateral decisions about the relevant activities. However, clauses on the resolving of disputes, such as arbitration, do not prevent the arrangement from being a joint arrangement.

Identifying a joint arrangement is based on answering the following two questions positively:

1. Does the arrangement give all the parties, or a group of parties, control of the arrangement collectively?
2. Do decisions about the relevant activities require the unanimous consent of all the parties, or of a group of parties, that collectively control the arrangement?

Types of Joint Arrangement

Joint arrangements are classified as either joint operations or joint ventures. A joint operation is defined as a joint arrangement whereby the parties that have joint control of the arrangement have rights to the assets, and obligations for the liabilities, relating to the arrangement. A joint venture is defined as a joint arrangement whereby the parties that have joint control of the arrangement have rights to the net assets of the arrangement.

The classification is thus dependent on the rights and obligations of the parties to the arrangements:

Type	*Rights and obligations*
Joint operation	Rights to the assets, and obligations for the liabilities, relating to the arrangement
Joint venture	Rights to the net assets of the arrangement

A joint operator has rights and obligations directly in the assets and liabilities, while a joint venturer has rights in the net assets.

Judgement is applied in assessing whether a joint arrangement is a joint operation or a joint venture. Rights and obligations are assessed by considering the structure and legal form, the terms agreed by the parties and other facts and circumstances. The joint arrangement could be structured through a separate vehicle. IFRS 11 specifically states that a joint arrangement that is not structured through a separate vehicle is a joint operation. This is because no rights and obligations in the net assets are created.

If a joint arrangement is structured through a separate vehicle, an assessment must be made to establish whether it is a joint operation or a joint venture, based on the rights and obligations created. A separate vehicle does not automatically indicate a right in the net assets. Specifically, in the case of a separate vehicle, the assessment is based on the legal form, the terms of the contractual arrangement and other relevant facts and circumstances.

The legal form could create a separate vehicle that is considered in its own right. The separate vehicle holds the assets and liabilities and not the parties to the arrangement. By implication, the parties have only indirect rights in the net assets, which indicates a joint venture. In contrast, the legal form will create a joint operation, when the legal form does not create a separation between the parties and the separate vehicle.

However, when a separation is created between the parties and the separate vehicle, a joint venture is not automatically assumed. The terms of the contractual arrangement and, if relevant, other factors and circumstances can override the assessment of the rights and obligations conferred upon the parties by the legal form. The contractual arrangement could be used to reverse or modify the rights and obligations conferred by the legal form of the separate vehicle. When the contractual arrangement specifies that the parties have rights to the assets and obligations for the liabilities, the arrangement is a joint operation and other facts and circumstances do not need to be considered. IFRS 11 includes the examples set out in the table below to identify when the contractual arrangements created a joint operation or joint venture.

Examples of classification based on the contractual agreement

Joint operation

The parties to the joint arrangement share all liabilities, obligations, costs and expenses in a specific proportion.

The parties are liable for claims raised by third parties.

The allocation of the revenue and expenses is based on the relative performance of each party. In this case, the allocations of revenue and expenses differ from the interest in the net assets, if any.

Joint venture
The joint arrangement is liable for the debts and obligations of the arrangement.
The parties to the joint arrangement are liable to the arrangement only to the extent of their respective investments in the arrangement.
The parties to the joint arrangement are liable to the arrangement only to their respective obligation to contribute any unpaid or any additional capital to the arrangement.
Creditors of the joint arrangement do not have rights or recourse against any party with respect to debts or obligations of the arrangement.
Each party's shares in the profit and loss relating to the activities of the arrangement is established.

Other facts and circumstances are assessed to classify the joint arrangement when the terms of the arrangement are not conclusive. IFRS 11 provides one situation when other facts and circumstances override the legal form and contractual arrangement. When the activities of the arrangement are designed to provide output mainly to the joint parties and the arrangement is limited in its ability to sell to third parties, it is an indication that the joint parties have rights to substantially all the economic benefits of the arrangement. The effect of such an arrangement is that the liabilities incurred by the arrangement are, in substance, settled by the cash flows received from the joint parties for their share of the output. Since the joint parties are substantially the only contributor to the cash of the joint arrangement, they indirectly assume responsibility for the liabilities.

A joint arrangement through a separate vehicle is not automatically a joint venture. Only if the answers to all three of the questions identified below are negative would the separate vehicle be classified as a joint venture.

Assessment Questions

1. Does the legal form of the separate vehicle give the parties rights to the assets, and obligations for the liabilities, relating to the arrangement?
2. Do the terms of the contractual arrangement specify that the parties have rights to the assets, and obligations for the liabilities, relating to the arrangement?
3. Have the parties designed the arrangement so that:
   - Its activities primarily aim to provide the parties with an output (i.e., the parties have rights to substantially all the economic benefits of the assets held in the separate vehicle); and
   - It depends on the parties on a continuous basis for settling the liabilities relating to the activity conducted through the arrangement?

Accounting for Joint Operations

Basic principles

The principle established in IFRS 11 is that joint operations should be accounted for by following the contractual arrangement established between the parties to the joint arrangement. In its own financial statements, a joint operator will account in accordance with IFRS 11 for the following:

- Its assets, including its share of any assets held jointly;
- Its liabilities, including its share of any liabilities incurred jointly;

- Its revenue from the sale of its share of the output arising from the joint operation;
- Its share of the revenue from the sale of the output by the joint operation; and
- Its expenses, including its share of any expense incurred jointly.

It is clear that in a joint operation, a joint operator could either have an interest in the assets or incur the liabilities or expenses, directly as its own assets, liabilities and expenses, or the joint operator could have a shared interest. If a shared interest exists, the terms of the contractual arrangement will determine each operator's share. Once a joint operator's direct or shared interest in the assets, liabilities, income and expenses is determined, the joint operator accounts for them by following the IFRS applicable in each instance.

Special guidelines are also provided for transactions, such as the sale, contribution or purchase of assets between the entity of the joint operator and the joint operations. The joint operator only recognises gains and losses resulting from sales and contributions to the joint operation to the extent of other parties' interest in the joint operations. Therefore, if a joint operator has a 40% interest in the joint operation it will only recognise 60% of the profit or losses on the transactions attributable to the other joint operators. The logic is that a portion of the profit has in fact been realised. As a further example, if venturers A, B and C jointly control joint operation D (each having a 1/3 interest), and A sells equipment having a book value of €40,000 to the operation for €100,000, only 2/3 of the apparent gain of €60,000 or €40,000 may be realised. However, if the transaction provides evidence of an impairment or reduction in the net realisable value of the assets sold or contributed, the joint operator must recognise the loss fully.

Similarly, if joint operators purchase assets from the joint operation, it may not recognise its share of gains and losses until the assets are resold to other parties. Again, if such transaction provides evidence of an impairment or reduction in the net realisable value of the assets purchased, the joint operator must recognise its full share of the losses.

A party to an arrangement that is a joint operation that does not have joint control, but has rights to the assets and obligations for the liabilities of the joint operation, accounts for its interest by following the principle established in IFRS 11. However, if the participating party does not have rights to the assets and obligations for the liabilities, it accounts for its interest in the joint operation by applying the applicable IFRS.

Accounting for acquisitions of interests in joint operations in which the activity constitutes a business

In May 2014 the IASB issued the amendments to IFRS 11 "Accounting for Acquisitions of Interests in Joint Operations" ruling the accounting for acquisitions of interests in joint operations in which the activity constitutes a business. Those amendments, which are explained below, shall be applied prospectively in annual periods beginning on or after January 1, 2016. The IASB had noted that it was unclear how acquisitions of interests in joint operations, in which the activities constitute a business, were to be reported and thus the need for the amendment to IFRS 11. When an entity acquires an interest in a joint operation that constitutes a business, as defined in IFRS 3, it shall apply, to the extent of its share in the assets and liabilities in a joint operation, all of the principles on business combinations accounting in accordance with IFRS 3, and any other IFRS that do not conflict with the guidance in IFRS 11 and disclose the information that is required in those IFRS in relation to business combinations. This applies to the acquisition of both the initial interest and additional interests in a joint operation in which the activity of the joint operation constitutes a business. According to IFRS 11, the principles on business combinations accounting that do not conflict with the guidance in IFRS 11 include but are not limited to:

- Measuring identifiable assets and liabilities at fair value, other than items for which exceptions are given in IFRS 3 and other IFRS;
- Recognising acquisition-related costs as expenses in the periods in which the costs are incurred and the services are received, with the exception that the costs to issue debt or equity securities are recognised in accordance with IAS 32 and IFRS 9;
- Recognising deferred tax assets and deferred tax liabilities that arise from the initial recognition of assets or liabilities, except for deferred tax liabilities that arise from the initial recognition of goodwill, as required by IFRS 3 and IAS 12 for business combinations;
- Recognising the excess of the consideration transferred over the net of the acquisition-date amounts of the identifiable assets acquired and the liabilities assumed, if any, as goodwill; and
- Testing for impairment a cash-generating unit to which goodwill has been allocated at least annually, and whenever there is an indication that the unit may be impaired, as required by IAS 36 for goodwill acquired in a business combination.

These principles also apply to the formation of a joint operation if, and only if, an existing business, as defined in IFRS 3, is contributed to the joint operation on its formation by one of the parties that participate in the joint operation. However, these principles do not apply to the formation of a joint operation if all of the parties that participate in the joint operation only contribute assets or groups of assets that do not constitute businesses to the joint operation on its formation. These principles also do not apply on the acquisition of an interest in a joint operation when the parties sharing joint control, including the entity acquiring the interest in the joint operation, are under the common control of the same ultimate parent. A joint operator might increase its interest in a joint operation in which the activity of the joint operation constitutes a business, as defined in IFRS 3, by acquiring an additional interest in the joint operation. In such cases, previously held interests in the joint operation are not remeasured if the joint operator retains joint control.

Example (based on IFRS 11 IE 53; example 7)

Entities A, B and C have joint control of joint operation X whose activity constitutes a business, as defined in IFRS 3. Entity D acquires company A's 40% ownership interest in joint operation X at a cost of €500,000 and incurs acquisition-related costs of €70,000.

The contractual arrangement between the counterparties that entity D joined as part of the acquisition stipulates that entity D's shares in several assets and liabilities vary from its ownership interest in joint operation X. The following table sets out entity D's share in the assets and liabilities related to joint operation X as established in the contractual arrangement between the counterparties:

Entity D's share in the assets and liabilities related to joint operation X	
Property, plant and equipment	52%
Intangible assets (excluding goodwill)	89%
Accounts receivable	38%

Inventory	42%
Retirement benefit obligations	17%
Accounts payable	45%
Contingent liabilities	49%

Entity D recognises in its financial statements its share of the assets and liabilities resulting from the contractual arrangement. It applies the principles on business combinations accounting in IFRS 3 and other IFRS for identifying, recognising, measuring and classifying the assets acquired, and the liabilities assumed, on the acquisition of the interest in joint operation X. This is because entity D acquired an interest in a joint operation in which the activity constitutes a business. However, entity D does not apply the principles on business combinations accounting in IFRS 3 and other IFRS that conflict with the guidance in IFRS 11.

Consequently, in accordance with IFRS 11, entity D recognises, and therefore measures, in relation to its interest in joint operation X, only its share in each of the assets that are jointly held and in each of the liabilities that are incurred jointly, as stated in the contractual arrangement. Entity D does not include in its assets and liabilities the shares of the other parties in joint operation X. Due to IFRS 3, entity D has to measure the identifiable assets acquired and the liabilities assumed at their acquisition-date fair values with limited exceptions; for example, deferred tax assets and deferred tax liabilities are not measured at fair value but are measured in accordance with IAS 12. Such measurement does not conflict with this IFRS and thus those requirements apply.

Consequently, entity D determines the fair value, or other measure specified in IFRS 3, of its share in the identifiable assets and liabilities related to joint operation X. The following table sets out the fair value or other measure specified by IFRS 3 of entity D's shares in the identifiable assets and liabilities related to joint operation X:

Fair value or other measure specified by IFRS 3 for Company X's shares in the identifiable assets and liabilities of joint operation	**€**
Property, plant and equipment	145,000
Intangible assets (excluding goodwill)	83,000
Accounts receivable	78,000
Inventory	60,000
Retirement benefit obligations	(18,000)
Accounts payable	(55,000)
Contingent liabilities	(60,000)
Deferred tax liability	(45,000)
Net assets	188,000

In accordance with IFRS 3, the excess of the consideration transferred over the amount allocated to entity D's shares in the net identifiable assets is recognised as goodwill:

Consideration transferred	€500,000
Company E's shares in the identifiable assets and liabilities relating to its interest in the joint operation	€188,000
Goodwill	€312,000

Acquisition-related costs of €70,000 are not considered to be part of the consideration transferred for the interest in the joint operation. In accordance with IFRS 3.53 they are recognised as expenses in profit or loss in the period that the costs are incurred and the services are received.

Accounting for Joint Ventures

A joint venturer recognises its interest in a joint venture as an investment by applying the equity method of accounting as described in IAS 28, *Investment in Associates and Joint Ventures*. The proportionate consolidation method of accounting that was previously permitted for jointly controlled entities under IAS 31 is no longer available to joint ventures. Any participating party in the joint venture that does not have joint control accounts for its interest by applying IFRS 9, unless it has significant influence over the joint venture. If the participating party has significant influence, it too will apply equity accounting in accordance with IAS 28. And if the participating party obtains joint control at a subsequent date, then, in such cases, previously held interests in the joint operations are not remeasured.

Separate Financial Statements

The accounting for a joint operation in the consolidated and separate financial statements is the same. A party that participates in a joint operation that does not have joint control must also apply the same principles as discussed above to account for its interest.

Equity accounting is not only applied in the consolidated financial statements of the joint venture. In the separate financial statements, IAS 27, *Separate Financial Statements*, does also allow the application of equity accounting. This will be detailed further on in this chapter.

ASSOCIATES

Identification of an Associate

An associate is an entity over which an investor has significant influence. Significant influence is the power to participate in the financial and operating policy decisions of the investee but is not in control or joint control of those policies.

In defining the concept of significant influence, there was recognition that the actual determination of the existence of significant influence could be difficult and that, to facilitate such recognition, there might be a need to set out a bright line against which significant influence would be measured. To this end, a somewhat arbitrary, refutable presumption of such influence was set at a 20% (direct or indirect) voting power in the investee. This has been held out as the de facto standard on assessing significant influence, and thus an investor accounts for such an investment as an associate unless it can prove otherwise. If the investor holds less than 20% voting power, it is presumed that significant influence is not applicable, unless such influence can be clearly demonstrated. Specifically, a substantial or majority ownership from another party does not preclude significant influence.

No top bright line (such as 50%) is set to identify significant influence. In difficult situations control must first be considered. The reason is that control could be achieved with a voting power of less than 50%. If control is not applicable and the voting power is above 20%, significant influence is assumed, unless it can be demonstrated otherwise.

In assessing significant influence, all facts and circumstances are assessed, including the term of exercise of potential voting rights and any other contractual arrangements. The following factors are indicators of significant influence:

- Representation on the board of directors or equivalent governing body;
- Participation in policy-making process, including decisions about dividends and other distributions;
- Material transactions between parties;
- Interchange of managerial personnel; and
- Provision of essential technical information.

Only the existence and effect of potential voting rights that are currently exercisable or convertible are considered in the assessment. Potential voting rights exist in the form of options, warrants, convertible shares or a contractual arrangement to acquire additional shares. In making the assessment, all facts and circumstances, such as the terms of exercise and other contractual arrangements that affect potential rights, must be considered. Potential voting rights held by others must also be considered. Intentions of management and the financial ability to exercise or convert are, however, not considered.

Accounting for an Associate

An entity recognises its interest in an associate by applying the equity method of IAS 28, *Investment in Associates and Joint Ventures*, except if an exception is applicable.

EQUITY METHOD OF ACCOUNTING

Scope and Application

The equity method of accounting is applied to investments in associates and joint ventures. The cost method for accounting for associates would simply not reflect the economic reality of the investor's interest in an entity whose operations were indicative, in part at least, of the reporting entity's (i.e., the investor's) management decisions and operational skills. Thus, the clearly demonstrable need to reflect substance, rather than mere form, made the development of the equity method highly desirable. This is in keeping with the thinking that is currently driving IFRS that all activities that have a potential impact on the financial position and performance of an entity must be reported, including those that are deemed to be off-balance-sheet-type transactions.

The equity method is applied to an investment in a joint venture since the investor has an interest in the net assets of the joint venture. The investor has no direct interest in the underlying assets or liabilities of the venture and can therefore not recognise such assets or liabilities.

An exception is applicable to investments in associates or joint ventures held (directly or indirectly) by a venture capital organisation or a mutual fund, unit trust or similar entity, including unit-link insurance funds. Such entities may elect to measure the investment at fair value through profit and loss in accordance with IFRS 9. When those investments are measured at fair value, changes in fair value are included in profit or loss in the period of the change. This election may also be applied to a portion of investment in associates or joint ventures held indirectly through such exempted entities. The other portion of the investment in the associate or joint venture should still be equity accounted.

IFRS 5 is applied to an investment (or a portion) in an associate or joint venture that meets the requirements to be classified as held for sale (see Chapter 13). The portion of the investment that is not classified as held for sale must still be equity accounted until disposal of the held-for-sale portion takes place. After the disposal, the remaining portion must be reassessed to determine whether it is still an investment in associate or joint venture, and if not, recorded in terms of IFRS 9.

Specifically, an entity that has control over a subsidiary and is exempt from consolidating the subsidiary because its ultimate or intermediate parent does prepare financial statements is not required to apply the equity method.

The Equity Method

Basic principles

The equity method permits an entity (the investor) controlling a certain share of the voting interest in another entity (the investee) to incorporate its pro rata share of the investee's operating results into its profit or loss. However, rather than include its share of each component of the investee's revenues, expenses, assets and liabilities into its financial statements, the investor will only include its share of the investee's profit or loss as a separate line item in its statement of profit or loss and comprehensive income. Similarly, only a single line in the investor's statement of financial position is presented, but this reflects, to a degree, the investor's share in each of the investee's assets and liabilities.

Initially under the equity method the investment in the associate or joint venture is recognised at cost, and the carrying amount is increased or decreased to include the investor's share of the profit or loss of the investee after the acquisition date. The investor's share of the profit or loss is recognised in the investor's profit and loss. The carrying amount is also adjusted for the investor's share of other comprehensive income, and the contra entry is recognised in other comprehensive income. Distributions received from the investee reduce the carrying amount of the investment.

When determining the entity's share in the associate or joint venture, potential voting rights or other derivatives containing potential voting rights are ignored. The entity's share is solely based on the existing ownership interest. However, if an entity has, in substance, existing ownership because a transaction currently gives it access to the returns associated with an ownership interest, this right to returns is taken into account to determine the entity's share in profits. Such instruments that are included in the determination of the entity's share in the associate or joint venture are specifically excluded from IFRS 9, even if they meet the definition of a derivative.

Many of the procedures applicable to equity accounting are similar to the consolidation procedures discussed above.

Example of a simple case ignoring deferred taxes

Assume the following information:

On January 2, 20XX, Regency Corporation (the investor) acquired 40% of Elixir Company's (the investee) voting shares on the open market for €100,000. Unless demonstrated otherwise, it is assumed that Regency Corporation can exercise significant influence over Elixir Company's operating and financing policies. On January 2, Elixir's shareholders' equity is comprised of the following accounts:

Shares, par €1,100,000 shares authorised, 50,000 shares issued and outstanding	€50,000
Additional paid-capital/Share premium	150,000
Retained earnings	50,000
Total shareholders' equity	€250,000

Note that the cost of Elixir Company common shares was equal to 40% of the book value of Elixir's net assets. Assume also that there is no difference between the book value and the fair value of Elixir Company's assets and liabilities. Accordingly, the balance in the investment account in Regency's records represents exactly 40% of Elixir's shareholders' equity (net assets). Assume further that Elixir Company reported a 20XX net profit of €30,000 and paid cash dividends of €10,000. Its shareholders' equity at year-end would be as follows:

Shares, par €1,100,000 shares authorised, 50,000 shares issued and outstanding	€50,000
Additional paid-in capital/Share premium	150,000
Retained earnings	70,000
Total shareholders' equity	€270,000

Regency Corporation would record its share of the increase in Elixir Company's net assets during 20XX as follows:

Investment in Elixir Company	12,000	
Equity in Elixir profit or loss (€30,000 × 40%)		12,000

Recognise the investment

Cash	4,000	
Investment in Elixir Company (€10,000 × 40%)		4,000

Recognise the dividend

When Regency's statement of financial position is prepared at December 31, 20XX, the balance reported in the investment account would be €108,000 (= €100,000 + €12,000 − €4,000). This amount represents 40% of the book value of Elixir's net assets at the end of the year (40% × €270,000). Note also that, according to IAS 1.82 and IFRS 12.B16, the equity in Elixir's profit or loss is reported as one amount in Regency's profit or loss separately (e.g., net income from associates).

Accounting at acquisition

The principles regarding the acquisition of business combinations (Chapter 15) are also adopted in the acquisition of associates and joint ventures.

The equity method starts from the date an associate or joint venture is acquired. On the acquisition date, any positive difference between the cost of the investment and the entity's share of the net fair value of the investee's identifiable assets and liabilities is identified as goodwill and included in the carrying amount of the investment. Amortisation of the goodwill is not allowed. Any excess of the entity's share of the net fair value of the investee's identifiable assets and liabilities over the cost of the investment is recognised as income and included in the entity's share of the associate's or joint venture's profit or loss for the year.

Adjustments are made to the entity's share of profit and losses of the associate or joint venture after acquisition to account for the effect of the fair value on acquisition, such as adjusted depreciation.

Example of a complex case ignoring deferred taxes

Assume again that Regency Corporation acquired 40% of Elixir Company's shares on January 2, 20XX, but that the price paid was €140,000. Elixir Company's assets and liabilities at that date had the following book and fair values:

	Book value	*Fair value*
Cash	€10,000	€10,000
Accounts receivable (net)	40,000	40,000
Inventories (FIFO cost)	80,000	90,000
Land	50,000	40,000
Plant and equipment (net of accumulated depreciation)	140,000	220,000
Total assets	**€320,000**	**€400,000**
Liabilities	(70,000)	(70,000)
Net assets (shareholders' equity)	**€250,000**	**€330,000**

The first order of business is the calculation of the differential, as follows:

Regency's cost for 40% of Elixir's ordinary share	€140,000
Book value of 40% of Elixir's net assets (€250,000 × 40%)	(100,000)
Total differential	**€40,000**

Next, the €40,000 is allocated to those individual assets and liabilities for which fair value differs from book value. In the example, the differential is allocated to inventories, land and plant and equipment, as follows:

Item	*Book value*	*Fair value*	*Difference debit (credit)*	*40% of difference debit (credit)*
Inventories	€80,000	€90,000	€10,000	€4,000
Land	50,000	40,000	(10,000)	(4,000)
Plant and equipment	140,000	220,000	80,000	32,000
Differential allocated				**€32,000**

The difference between the allocated differential of €32,000 and the total differential of €40,000 is essentially identical to goodwill of €8,000. As shown by the following computation, goodwill represents the excess of the cost of the investment over the fair value of the net assets acquired.

Regency's cost for 40% of Elixir's ordinary share	€140,000
40% of Elixir's net assets (€330,000 × 40%)	(132,000)
Excess of cost over fair value (goodwill)	**€8,000**

At this point it is important to note that the allocation of the differential is not recorded formally by either Regency Corporation or Elixir Company. Furthermore, Regency does not remove the differential from the investment account and allocate it to the respective assets, since the use of the equity method does not involve the recording of individual assets and liabilities. Regency leaves the differential of €40,000 in the investment account, as part of the balance of €140,000 at January 2, 20XX. Accordingly, information pertaining to the allocation of the differential is maintained by the investor, but this information is outside the formal accounting system, which is comprised of journal entries and account balances.

After the differential has been allocated, the amortisation pattern is developed. To develop the pattern in this example, assume that Elixir's plant and equipment have 10 years of useful life remaining and that Elixir depreciates its property, plant and equipment on a straight-line basis. Under the provisions of IFRS 3, Regency may not amortise the unallocated differential, which is akin to goodwill, but must consider its possible impairment whenever IFRS 9 indicates that the investment may be impaired. Regency would prepare the following amortisation schedule:

			Amortisation		
Item	*Differential debit (credit)*	*Useful life*	*20XX-1*	*20XX*	*20XX+1*
Inventories (FIFO)	€4,000	Sold in 20XX-1	€4,000	€ –	€ –
Land	(4,000)	Indefinite	–	–	–
Plant and equipment (net)	32,000	10 years	3,200	3,200	3,200
Goodwill	8,000	N/A	–	–	–
Totals	**€40,000**		**€7,200**	**€3,200**	**€3,200**

Note that the entire differential allocated to inventories is amortised in 20XX because the cost flow assumption used by Elixir is FIFO. If Elixir had been using weighted-average costing instead of FIFO, amortisation might have been computed on a different basis. Note also that the differential allocated to Elixir's land is not amortised, because land is not a depreciable asset. Goodwill likewise is not subject to amortisation.

The amortisation of the differential, to the extent required under IFRS, is recorded formally in the accounting system of Regency Corporation. Recording the amortisation adjusts the equity in Elixir's income that Regency recorded based on Elixir's statement of comprehensive income. Elixir's income must be adjusted because it is based on Elixir's book values, not on the cost that Regency incurred to acquire Elixir. Regency would make the following entries in 20XX, assuming that Elixir reported profit of €30,000 and paid cash dividends of €10,000:

1. Investment in Elixir	12,000	
Equity in Elixir income (€30,000 × 40%)		12,000
2. Equity in Elixir income (amortisation of differential)	7,200	
Investment in Elixir		7,200
3. Cash	4,000	
Investment in Elixir (€10,000 × 40%)		4,000

The balance in the investment account on Regency's records at the end of 20XX is €140,800 [= €140,000 + €12,000 − (€7,200 + €4,000)], and Elixir's shareholders' equity, as shown previously, is €270,000. The investment account balance of €140,800 is not equal to 40% of €270,000. However, this difference can easily be explained, as follows:

Balance in investment account at December 31, 20XX		€140,800
40% of Elixir's net assets at December 31, 20XX		108,000
Difference at December 31, 20XX		**€32,800**
Differential at January 2, 20XX	€40,000	
Differential amortised during 20XX	(7,200)	
Unamortised differential at December 31, 20XX		**€32,800**

As the years go by, the balance in the investment account will come closer and closer to representing 40% of the book value of Elixir's net assets. After 20 years, the remaining difference between these two amounts would be attributed to the original differential allocated to land (a €4,000 credit) and the amount similar to goodwill (€8,000), unless written off due to impairment. This €4,000 difference on the land would remain until Elixir sold it.

To illustrate how the sale of land would affect equity-method procedures, assume that Elixir sold the land in the year 20XX+34 for €80,000. Since Elixir's cost for the land was €50,000, it would report a gain of €30,000, of which €12,000 (= €30,000 × 40%) would be recorded by Regency, when it records its 40% share of Elixir's reported profit, ignoring income taxes. However, from Regency's viewpoint, the gain on sale of land should have been €40,000 (€80,000 − €40,000) because the cost of the land from Regency's perspective was €40,000 at January 2, 20XX. Therefore, besides the €12,000 share of the gain recorded above, Regency should record an additional €4,000 gain [(= €40,000 − €30,000) × 40%] by debiting the investment account and crediting the equity in Elixir income account. This €4,000 debit to the investment account will negate the €4,000 differential allocated to land on January 2, 20XX, since the original differential was a credit (the fair value of the land was €10,000 less than its book value).

Intercompany transactions between investor and investee

Transactions between the investor and the investee may require that the investor make certain adjustments when it records its share of the investee earnings. In terms of the concept that governs realisation of transactions, profits can be recognised by an entity only when realised through a sale to outside (unrelated) parties in arm's-length transactions (sales and purchases). Similar problems can arise when sales of property, plant and equipment between the parties occur. In all cases, there is no need for any adjustment when the transfers are made at carrying amounts (i.e., without either party recognising a profit or loss in its separate accounting records).

In preparing consolidated financial statements, all intercompany (parent-subsidiary) transactions are eliminated. However, when the equity method is used to account for investments, only the profit component of intercompany (investor-investee) transactions is eliminated. This is because the equity method does not result in the combining of all statement of comprehensive income accounts (such as sales and cost of sales) and therefore will not cause the financial statements to contain redundancies. In contrast, consolidated statements would include redundancies if the gross amounts of all intercompany transactions were not eliminated.

Only the percentage held by the investor is eliminated and this applies to unrealised profits and losses arising from both "upstream" and "downstream" transactions (i.e., sales from investee to investor, and from investor to investee), which should be eliminated to the extent of the investor's interest in the investee.

Elimination of the investor's interest in the investee, rather than the entire unrealised profit on the transaction, is based on the logic that in an investor-investee situation, the investor does not have control (as would be the case with a subsidiary), and thus the non-owned percentage of profit is effectively realised through an arm's-length transaction. For purposes of determining the percentage interest in unrealised profit or loss to be eliminated, a group's interest in an associate is the aggregate of the holdings in that associate by the parent and its subsidiaries (excluding any interests held by non-controlling interests of subsidiaries).

Any holdings of the group's other associates (i.e., equity-method investees) or joint ventures are ignored for the purpose of applying the equity method. When an associate has subsidiaries, associates or joint ventures, the profits or losses and net assets taken into account in applying the equity method are those recognised in the associate's consolidated financial statements (including the associate's share of the profits or losses and net assets of its associates and joint ventures), after any adjustments necessary to give effect to the investor's accounting policies.

Example of accounting for intercompany transactions

Continue with the same information from the previous example and also assume that Elixir Company sold inventory to Regency Corporation in 20XX for €2,000 profit. Thirty percent of this inventory remains unsold by Regency at the end of 20XX-1. Elixir's net profit for 20XX, including the gross profit on the inventory sold to Regency, is €20,000; Elixir's income tax rate is 34%. Regency should make the following journal entries for 20XX (ignoring deferred taxes):

1.	Investment in Elixir	€8,000	
	Equity in Elixir income (€20,000 × 40%)		€8,000
2.	Equity in Elixir income (amortisation of differential)	3,600	
	Investment in Elixir		3,600
3.	Equity in Elixir income	158	
	Investment in Elixir (€2,000 × 30% × 66% × 40%)		158

The amount in the last entry needs further elaboration. Since 30% of the inventory remains unsold, only €600 (€2,000 × 30%) of the intercompany profit is unrealised at year-end. This profit, net of income taxes, is €396 (€300 × 66%). Regency's share of this profit, €158 (€396 × 40%), is included in the first (€8,000) entry recorded. Accordingly, the third entry is needed to adjust or correct the equity in the reported net income of the investee.

Eliminating entries for intercompany profits on property, plant and equipment are similar to those in the examples above. However, intercompany profit is realised only as the assets are depreciated by the purchasing entity. In other words, if an investor buys or sells property, plant and equipment from or to an investee at a price above book value, the gain would only be realised piecemeal over the asset's remaining depreciable life. Accordingly, in the year of sale the pro rata share (based on the investor's percentage ownership interest in the investee, regardless of whether the sale is upstream or downstream) of the unrealised portion of the intercompany profit would have to be eliminated. In each subsequent year during the asset's life, the pro rata share of the gain realised in the period would be added to income from the investee.

Example of eliminating intercompany profit on property, plant and equipment

Assume that Radnor Co., which owns 25% of Empanada Co., sold to Empanada an item of property, plant and equipment having a five-year remaining life, at a gain of €100,000. Radnor Co. expects to remain in the 34% marginal tax bracket. The sale occurred at the end of 20XX-1; Empanada Co. will use straight-line depreciation to amortise the asset over the years 20XX through 20XX+4.

The entries related to the foregoing are:

	20XX-1		
1.	Gain on sale of property, plant and equipment	€25,000	
	Deferred gain		€25,000

To defer the unrealised portion of the gain.

2.	Deferred tax benefit	€8,500	
	Income tax expense		€8,500

Tax effect of gain deferral.

Alternatively, the 20XX-1 events could have been reported by this single entry.

Equity in Empanada income	€16,500	
Investment in Empanada Co.		€16,500

20XX through 20XX+4 (each year).

1.	Deferred gain	€5,000	
	Gain on sale of property, plant and equipment		€5,000

To amortise deferred gain.

2.	Income tax expense	€1,700	
	Deferred tax benefit		€1,700

Tax effect of gain realisation.

The alternative treatment would be:

Investment in Empanada Co.	€3,300	
Equity in Empanada income		€3,300

In the example above, the tax currently paid by Radnor Co. (34% × €25,000 taxable gain on the transaction) is recorded as a deferred tax benefit in 20XX-1 since taxes will not be due on the book gain recognised in the years 20XX through 20XX+4. Under provisions of IAS 12, deferred tax benefits should be recorded to reflect the tax effects of all deductible temporary differences. Unless Radnor Co. could demonstrate that future taxable amounts arising from existing temporary differences exist, this deferred tax benefit might be offset by an equivalent valuation allowance in Radnor Co.'s statement of financial position at year-end 20XX-1, because of the doubt that it will ever be realised. Thus, the deferred tax benefit might not be recognisable, net of the valuation allowance, for financial reporting purposes unless other temporary differences not specified in the example provided future taxable amounts to offset the net deductible effect of the deferred gain.

NOTE: The deferred tax impact of an item of income for book purposes in excess of tax is the same as a deduction for tax purposes in excess of book.

This is discussed more fully in Chapter 26. When downstream transactions provide evidence of a reduction in the net realisable value of assets to be sold or contributed, or of an impairment loss, the investor must recognise the full loss. Similarly, when upstream transactions provide evidence of a reduction in the net realisable value of the asset to be purchased, or of an impairment loss, the investor shall recognise its share in those losses.

Contribution of non-monetary assets

If an investee makes a contribution of non-monetary assets that do not constitute a business, as defined in IFRS 3, to an associate or joint venture in exchange for an equity interest, the fair value of the asset is in principle capitalised as part of the investment. However, fair value gains and losses are only recognised by the investor to the extent of the unrelated investors' interest in the associate or joint venture. Any fair value profit or loss regarding the investee's share in the associate or joint venture is not recognised.

Accounting for Changes in Ownership Interest

This section covers the accounting issues that arise when the investor either sells some or all of its equity or acquires additional equity in the investee. The consequence of these actions could involve discontinuation of the equity method of accounting, or resumption of the use of that method.

Loss of significant influence

Significant influence is lost when an investee loses the power to participate in the financial and operating policy decisions of the investee. The loss of significant influence does not always occur with a change in absolute or relative ownership levels. The associate may for instance be subjected to the control of a government, court, administrator or regulator. Contractual arrangements could also change significant influence.

Discontinuing the equity method

The equity method is discontinued from the date when the investment ceases to be an associate or joint venture. Different situations may arise. If the investment changes to a subsidiary, IFRS 3, *Business Combinations*, is applied for the initial recognition of the subsidiary (Chapter 15).

If the retained interest becomes a financial instrument (not classified as a subsidiary, joint arrangement or associate) the retained interest should be measured at fair value and the fair value change recognised in profit or loss. The fair value on the date of discontinuance of the equity method becomes the initial recognition value of the financial instrument. The profit or loss is the difference between:

- The fair value of the retained interest and any proceeds from the sale of a part of the interest; and
- The carrying value of the investment on the date the equity method is discontinued.

When the equity method is discontinued, any equity share of the associate or joint venture recognised in other comprehensive income must be removed by regarding this as part of the sale of the transaction. The effect is that the gain and loss previously recognised in other comprehensive income is reclassified (as a reclassification adjustment) to profit or loss.

If an associate changes to a joint venture or a joint venture changes to an associate, the equity method is continued without any remeasurement of the retained interest.

If the interest in an associate or joint venture is reduced, but the equity method is still applied, a profit and loss is calculated on the portion sold as the difference between the proceeds received and the carrying value of the portion sold. Any proportionate profit or loss recognised in other comprehensive income that relates to the portion of the investment sold must also be reclassified to profit or loss.

Example of accounting for a discontinuance of the equity method

Assume that Plato Corp. owns 10,000 ordinary shares (30%) of Xenia Co. for which it paid €250,000 ten years ago. On July 1, 20XX, Plato sells 5,000 Xenia shares for €375,000. The balance in the investment in Xenia Co. account at January 1, 20XX was €600,000. Assume that all the original differential between cost and book value has been amortised. To calculate the gain (loss) on the sale of 5,000 shares, it is necessary first to adjust the investment account so that it is current as of the date of sale. Assuming that the investee reported net profit of €100,000 for the six months ended June 30, 20XX, the investor should record the following entries:

1.	Investment in Xenia Co.	€30,000	
	Equity in Xenia income (€100,000 × 30%)		€30,000
2.	Income tax expense	2,040	
	Deferred tax liability (€30,000 × 20% × 34%)		2,040

The gain on sale can now be computed, as follows:

Proceeds on sale of 5,000 shares	€375,000
Book value of the 5,000 shares (€630,000 × 50%)	315,000
Gain from sale of investment in Xenia Co.	€60,000

Two entries will be needed to reflect the sale: one to record the proceeds, the reduction in the investment account, and the gain (or loss); the other to record the tax effects thereof. Recall that the investor must have computed the deferred tax effect of the undistributed earnings of the investee that it had recorded each year, on the basis that those earnings either would eventually be paid as dividends or would be realised as capital gains. When those dividends are ultimately received or when the investment is disposed of, the deferred tax liability recorded previously must be amortised.

The gains (losses) from sales of investee equity instruments should be reported in the investor's profit or loss as a separate line item after the line of its share of those joint ventures or associated profit or loss from continuing operations.

Acquisition of an associate in stages

An entity may hold an investment in another entity's ordinary share that is below the level that would create a presumption of significant influence, which it later increases so that the threshold for application of the equity method is exceeded. The guidance of IAS 28 would suggest that when the equity method is first applied, the difference between the carrying amount of the investment and the fair value of the underlying net identifiable assets must be computed (as described earlier in the chapter). Even though IFRS 9's fair value provisions were being applied, there will likely be a difference between the fair value of the passive investment (gauged by market prices for publicly-traded instruments) and the fair value of the investee's underlying net assets (which are driven by the ability to generate cash flows, etc.). Thus, when the equity method accounting threshold is first exceeded for a formerly passively held investment, determination of the "goodwill-like" component of the investment will typically be necessary.

Increasing a stake in an associate while continuing the equity method

When an entity increases its stake in an existing associate continuing to have significant influence but not gaining control, the cost of acquiring the additional stake (including any directly attributable costs) is added to the carrying value of the associate. Goodwill that arises from the purchase of the additional stake is calculated based on the fair value information at the date of the acquisition of the additional stake. The previously held interest may not be stepped up because the status of the investment has not changed. The same applies, for example, when existing stakes are reduced, thus resulting in an increased stake in an existing associate (e.g., where the investee purchases treasury shares from outside shareholders (i.e., owners other than the reporting entity)).

Dilution losses

A stake in an associate or joint venture may decrease, for example, following a capital increase on the part of the investee in which the investor does not take part. This constitutes a partial disposal of an entity's interest in an associate. Investor accounting for investee capital transactions that dilute the share of the investor's investment is not addressed by IAS 28. Although due to IFRS 10.B96, changes in the proportion held by non-controlling interests shall be recognised directly in equity, we feel that this principle is not applicable in this instance as the investor only accounts for his stake in the investee in his equity accounting and has not entered into a transaction with the associate. Accounting adjustments such as these therefore do not constitute transactions with owners, and any profit or loss must be recognised in the income statement.

Example of accounting for an investee capital transaction

Assume that Roger Corp. purchases, on February 1, 20XX, 30% (2,000 shares) of Energetic Corp.'s outstanding shares for €1,000,000. The carrying amount held by Roger Corp. in Energetic Corp. is €1,000,000, including goodwill and fair value adjustments in respect of the identified assets and liabilities of Energetic Corp. On March 1, 20XX, Energetic Corp. raises its equity by €1,000,000 by means of a cash capital increase. Roger Corp. does not take part in this capital increase. As a result, the stake held by Roger Corp. in Energetic Corp. drops to 23%.

The loss suffered by Roger Corp. is calculated as follows:

Dilution of original stake (€1,000,000/30% × 7%) = €233,333
Stake in increased assets following cash capital increase (€1,000,000 × 23%) = €230,000
Loss €3,333

EXAMPLES OF FINANCIAL STATEMENT DISCLOSURES

Exemplum Reporting PLC
Financial Statements
For the Year Ended December 31, 20XX

20. Investments accounted for using the equity method

Name	**Country of incorporation**	**Proportion of ownership interest**		**Proportion owned by associates and joint venture**		**Principal activities**	**IFRS 12 p20, p21**
		20XX	**20XX-1**	**20XX**	**20XX-1**		
Associate A **(a)**	UK	16%	16%	–	–	Marketing of widgets	
Associate B **(b)**	UK	–	–	32%	32%	Property holding	
Joint Venture C	UK	33.3%	33.3%	–	–	Distribution	

(a) Associate A is an associate of the group even though the group only owns 16% interest in Associate A. Significant influence arises by virtue of the groups' contractual right to appoint three out of the seven board of directors of Associate A. IFRS 12 p9

(b) Associate B has a year end of November 30. This reporting date was established when the company was incorporated. The reporting date cannot change as it is not permitted by the government in the UK. IFRS 12 p21, p22

Associate A's financial statements for the year ended November 30, 20XX have been used and appropriate adjustments have been made for the effects of any significant transactions that occurred between Associate A's year end and the group's year end. This was necessary so as to apply the equity method of accounting. IFRS 13 p97

Based on the quoted market price available on the UK stock exchange as at December 31, 20XX, the fair value of the group's interest in Associate A was €X.

Impairment of the Value of Equity-Method Investments

An entity applies IFRS 9, *Financial Instruments*, to determine if any investment in an associate or joint venture is impaired. IFRS 9 is also used to determine if other interests in the associate or joint venture should be impaired. Since goodwill is included in the carrying value of the investment, it is not separately assessed for impairment. The total value of the investment is assessed in terms of IFRS 9 and the goodwill portion is not assessed in terms of IAS 36, *Impairment of Assets* (see Chapter 13). However, if IFRS 9 indicates that an impairment is applicable, the total carrying value of the investment is compared to its recoverable amount (higher of value in use or fair value) determined in terms of IAS 36. Specifically, the impairment loss is not allocated to any individual asset, including goodwill. Instead, the total investment is impaired.

A reversal of an impairment loss is only applied when the recoverable amount of the investment increases. In determining the value in use, an entity should consider:

1. Its share of the present value of the estimated future cash flows expected to be generated by the investee as a whole, including the cash flows from the operations of the investee and the proceeds on the ultimate disposal of the investment; or
2. The present value of the estimated future cash flows that are expected to arise from dividends to be received from the investment and from its ultimate disposal.

Under appropriate assumptions (given a perfectly functioning capital market), both methods give the same result.

Other Requirements of IAS 28

Separate financial statements

IAS 28 provides that in the separate financials of the investor, the investment in the associate or joint venture may be carried at either cost, in terms of IFRS 9, or using the equity method as described in IAS 27. This is an accounting policy choice that the investor must make and apply consistently across each category of investments.

Consistency of accounting policies

Financial statements should be prepared using uniform accounting policies. If the accounting policies of the associate or joint venture differ from the reporting entity, adjustments should be made to the financial statements of the associate or joint venture to conform to those of the reporting entity.

Coterminous year-end dates

The most recent available financial statements of the associate or joint venture are used to apply the equity method. If the reporting dates of the entity and the associate or joint venture differ, financial statements on the reporting date of the entity are prepared for the associate or joint venture, unless it is impracticable to do so. If the reporting dates differ, adjustments are required for the effect of significant transactions that occur between the dates. IAS 28 requires that a reporting date difference of no more than three months is permissible. The length of the reporting period and difference in reporting dates must be applied consistently from year to year.

Treatment of cumulative preferred shares

If an associate has outstanding cumulative preferred shares, held by parties other than the investor that are classified as equity, the investor computes its share of the profits or losses after deducting dividends due to the preferred shareholders, whether or not declared.

Treatment of long-term interests in an associate/joint venture

If an entity has long-term interests in an associate/joint venture to which the equity method is not applied, then such long-term interests shall be recognised and measured initially in accordance with IFRS 9 without taking into account the adjustments that are required to be made in accordance with IAS 28. For instance, a long-term loan to an associate, which forms part of the net investment in the associate and for which the equity method cannot be applied, shall be first measured as per the requirements of IFRS 9 before recognising any impairment adjustments for share of losses of associate against such loan as explained below.

Share of losses exceeding the interest

If an entity's share of losses exceeds its interest in the associate or joint venture, the recognition of its share of future losses is discontinued. The interest in the associate or joint venture is the carrying amount of the equity accounted investment and other long-term interests that are regarded as part of the entity's net investment in the associate or joint venture. Long-term items for which settlement is neither planned nor likely to occur are deemed to be an extension of the investment. Losses incurred after the investment in the associate or joint venture is reduced to zero are applied to other interests in reverse order of seniority (i.e., priority in liquidation).

If the entity's interest is reduced to zero, any further losses are only recognised as a liability to the extent that the entity has incurred legal or constructive obligations or made payments on behalf of the associate or joint venture. If the associate or joint venture is again profitable, the entity only resumes recognising its share of profits after the share of losses not recognised are eliminated.

SEPARATE FINANCIAL STATEMENTS

IAS 27, *Separate Financial Statements*, addresses issues related to accounting for investments in subsidiaries, joint ventures and associates when the entity elects or is required by local regulations to prepare separate financial statements in accordance with IFRS. Separate financial statements are financial statements that are presented in addition to consolidated financial statements and financial statements of companies without subsidiaries, but which have investments in associates or joint ventures which are required by IAS 28 to be accounted by applying the equity method. Individual financial statements prepared by companies that do not have subsidiaries, associates or joint ventures are not separate financial statements. However, entities that are exempted from preparing consolidated financial statements or from applying equity accounting may present separate financial statements as their only financial statements. In addition, an investment entity that is required to apply the exception to consolidation for all of its subsidiaries by measuring these at fair value presents separate financial statements as its only financial statements.

An entity preparing its separate financial statements may account for investments in subsidiaries, joint ventures and associates either:

1. At cost; or
2. In accordance with IFRS 9; or
3. Using the equity method as described in IAS 28.

The possibility of using the equity method in separate financial statements was introduced by the amendments to IAS 27 ("Equity Method in Separate Financial Statements") in August 2014. An entity shall apply those amendments for annual periods beginning on or after January 1, 2016 retrospectively in accordance with IAS 8. Earlier application is permitted. If this option is chosen by the entity, it shall be disclosed.

The same accounting should be applied for each category of investments presented in the separate financial statements. Investments accounted for at cost or using the equity method and classified as held for sale (or included in a disposal group that is classified as held for sale) are accounted for in accordance with IFRS 5, *Non-current Assets Held for Sale and Discontinued Operations* (measured at fair value less costs to sell). Investments accounted for at fair value in accordance with IFRS 9 are excluded from IFRS 5's measurement requirements. Consequently, an entity should continue to account for such investments in accordance with IFRS 9 even if they meet the held-for-sale criteria in IFRS 5. If an entity that is a venture capital or similar organisation elects to account for its investments in associates and joint ventures at fair value in its consolidated financial statements, it must also use fair value in its individual financial statements.

An entity should recognise a dividend from a subsidiary, jointly controlled entity, or associate in profit or loss in its separate financial statements when it has the right to receive the dividend. The dividend is recorded in the profit or loss unless the equity method has been used. In this case the dividend has to be reduced from the carrying amount of the investment.

Special guidance is provided to determine cost in certain reorganisations if the cost option is applied in the separate financial statements. The new parent, in such circumstances, shall measure cost at the carrying amount of its share of the equity items shown in the separate financial statements of the original parent at the date of the reorganisation. The guidance is applicable when a new entity is established meeting the following requirements:

1. The new parent obtains control of the original parent (or other entity) by issuing equity instruments in exchange for existing equity instruments.
2. The assets and liabilities of the new group and the original group (or entity) are the same before and after the reorganisation.
3. The owners of the original parent (or other entity) before the reorganisation maintain the same absolute and relative interest in the net assets of the group before and after the reorganisation.

Investment Entities

Although investment entities present separate financial statements as their only financial statements, the cost option is not available to investment entities, since these would have to measure their investments at fair value through profit or loss. When an entity ceases to be an investment entity, it is required to consolidate any subsidiaries under IFRS 10. Should it continue to present separate financial statements in addition to consolidated financial statements, the cost option or the equity method will become available to it as with any other entity, subject to the requirements discussed above. The date of the change of status shall be the deemed acquisition date. The fair value of any subsidiary at the date of change in status becomes the deemed consideration of the subsidiary in the separate financial statements, when accounting for the investments in accordance with the options shown above. If an entity becomes an investment entity, the difference between the previous carrying amount of the subsidiary and its fair value at the date of the change of status of the entity is recognised as a gain or loss in profit or loss. The cumulative amount of any gain or loss previously recognised in other comprehensive income in respect of those subsidiaries must be treated as if the investment entity had disposed of those subsidiaries at the date of change in status.

Disclosure in Separate Financial Statements

All applicable IFRS are applied in the separate financial statements. Additionally, when a parent (because of the exemption in IFRS 10) elects not to prepare consolidated financial statements and instead prepares separate financial statements, the following should be disclosed in those separate financial statements:

- The fact that the financial statements are separate financial statements; that the exemption from consolidation has been used; the name and principal place of business (and country of incorporation if different) of the entity whose consolidated financial statements that comply with IFRS have been produced for public use; and the address where those consolidated financial statements are obtainable;
- A list of significant investments in subsidiaries, jointly controlled entities and associates, including the name, principal place of business (and country of incorporation if different), proportion of ownership interest and, if different, proportion of voting rights; and
- A description of the method used to account for the foregoing investments.

When a parent (other than a parent covered by the above-mentioned exemption) or an investor with joint control of, or significant influence over, an investee prepares separate financial statements, the parent or investor is required to identify the financial statements prepared in accordance with IFRS 10, IFRS 11 or IAS 28 to which they relate. The parent or investor must also disclose the following in its separate financial statements:

- The fact that the statements are separate financial statements and the reasons why those statements are prepared if not required by law;
- A list of significant investments in subsidiaries, jointly controlled entities and associates, including the name, principal place of business (and country of incorporation if different), proportion of ownership interest and, if different, proportion of voting rights; and
- A description of the method used to account for the foregoing investments.

DISCLOSURE REQUIREMENTS

IFRS 12, *Disclosure of Interest in Other Entities*, combines the disclosure about an entity's interest in subsidiaries, joint arrangements, associates and unconsolidated "structured entities" in one standard. IFRS 12 does not apply to employee benefit plans, separate financial statements (except in relation to unconsolidated structured entities), participants in joint ventures that do not share in joint control, and investments accounted for in accordance with IFRS 9, except for interests in associates, joint ventures or unconsolidated structured entities measured at fair value.

IFRS 12 specifically provides disclosure requirements for structured entities that are not consolidated to identify the nature and risk associated with them. A structured entity is an entity that has been designated so the voting or similar rights are not the dominant factor in deciding who controls the entity, such as when any voting rights relate to administrative tasks only and the relevant activities are directed by means of contractual arrangements. The main features or attributes of structured entities could include:

- Restricted activities;
- A narrow and well-defined objective;
- Insufficient equity to finance its activities without subordinated financial support; and
- Financing in the form of multiple contractually linked instruments to investors that creates concentration of credit risks and other risks.

The disclosures in IFRS 12 are presented as a series of objectives, with detailed guidance on satisfying those objectives. The objectives are listed below, and entities need to consider the level of detail needed to meet these objectives. For annual periods beginning on or after January 1, 2017, the amendments to IFRS 12 clarify that the disclosure requirements in the standard, except for those in paragraphs B10–B16, apply to an entity's interests listed in paragraph IFRS 5 that are classified as held for sale, as held for distribution or as discontinued operations in accordance with IFRS 5.

Main Objective

The objective of IFRS 12 is to require the disclosure of information that enables users of financial statements to evaluate:

- The nature of, and risks associated with, its interests in other entities; and
- The effects of those interests on its financial position, financial performance and cash flows.

Where the disclosures required by IFRS 12, together with the disclosures required by other IFRS, do not meet the above objectives, an entity is required to disclose whatever additional information is necessary to meet the objectives.

Significant Judgements and Assumptions

An entity discloses information about significant judgements and assumptions it has made (and changes in those judgements and assumptions) in determining whether:

- It controls another entity;
- It has joint control of an arrangement or significant influence over another entity;
- It has a joint arrangement (i.e., joint operation or joint venture which has been structured through a separate vehicle); or
- It meets the definition of an investment entity, if applicable.

Interests in Subsidiaries

An entity must disclose information that enables users of its consolidated financial statements to:

- Understand the composition of the group;
- Understand the interest that non-controlling interests have in the group's activities and cash flows;

- Evaluate the nature and extent of significant restrictions on its ability to access or use assets, and settle liabilities, of the group;
- Evaluate the nature of, and changes in, the risks associated with its interests in consolidated structured entities;
- Evaluate the consequences of changes in its ownership interest in a subsidiary that do not result in a loss of control; and
- Evaluate the consequences of losing control of a subsidiary during the reporting period.

Interests in Joint Arrangements and Associates

An entity must disclose information that enables users of its financial statements to evaluate:

- The nature, extent and financial effects of its interests in joint arrangements and associates, including the nature and effects of its contractual relationship with the other investors with joint control of, or significant influence over, joint arrangements and associates; and
- The nature of, and changes in, the risks associated with its interests in joint ventures and associates.

Interests in Unconsolidated Structured Entities

An entity must disclose information that enables users of its financial statements to:

- Understand the nature and extent of its interests in unconsolidated structured entities; and
- Evaluate the nature of, and changes in, the risks associated with its interests in unconsolidated structured entities.

Investment Entities

An investment entity that measures all its subsidiaries at fair value should provide the IFRS 12 disclosures related to investment entities.

An investment entity is required to disclose information about significant judgements and assumptions it has made in determining that it is an investment entity. If the investment entity does not have one or more of the typical characteristics of an investment entity, it must disclose its reasons for concluding that it is nevertheless an investment entity. In addition, an investment entity is required to disclose the following information, in addition to any disclosures required by other standards (such as IFRS 7 or IAS 24):

- The effects of changes in investment entity status;
- The composition of the group;
- The nature and extent of any significant restrictions;
- Any current commitments or intentions to provide financial or other support to an unconsolidated subsidiary;
- Details of any sponsorship of unconsolidated subsidiaries; and
- Terms of any contractual arrangements to provide support to unconsolidated subsidiaries.

US GAAP COMPARISON

Although the IFRS 10 consolidation project was a joint project with the FASB, the FASB delayed their changes to consolidation and later issued ASU No. 2015-02 Consolidation (Topic 810) and have since issued two more ASUs, ASU 2016-17 – *Interests Held through Related Parties That Are Under Common Control* and ASU 2018 *Targeted Improvements to Related Party Guidance for Variable Interest Entities, October 2018*. ASU 2015-02 and 2016-17 are currently effective as part of the codified US GAAP. ASC 810 Consolidation uses two determining models for controlling financial interest which is based upon an entity being evaluated as a voting interest entity or a variable interest entity (VIE). IFRS 10 as discussed above surrounds the principle of control as being the basis for concluding to consolidate entities. US GAAP provides direction for determining if "fees paid to a decision maker are a variable interest and when the decision maker is the primary beneficiary." Both the size of the compensation and the decision maker's scope of authority are both found in IFRS and US GAAP, yet they might not be considered similarly in understanding if there exists a variable interest or who is the primary beneficiary using US GAAP. Also, US GAAP does not have a "principal versus agent analysis" as is included in IFRS; instead the evaluation is included when determining the controlling financial interest. Finally, there are a number of similarities and key differences that may create different conclusions regarding consolidation for IFRS vs. US GAAP.

Changes introduced by IFRS 11 and IFRS 12 are not incorporated into US GAAP. The basic consolidation and equity accounting principles, however, remain the same.

US GAAP requires preparation of consolidated financial statements, with certain industry-specific exceptions. US GAAP also contains certain quantitative thresholds regarding investment at risk for stakeholders that impact requirements to consolidate entities. Certain leases with a company whose primary purpose is to lease property back to a company under certain circumstances must be consolidated. US GAAP permits different reporting dates for the parent and subsidiary up to three months, but only if the use of the same reporting date is impracticable. The effects of significant events between the dates must be disclosed. US GAAP does not require uniform accounting policies within the group.

Under US GAAP, consolidation of entities is based on a controlling financial interest model, which includes a VIE model and, if the VIE model is not applicable, a voting interest model. Under the VIE model, a reporting entity has a controlling financial interest in a VIE if it has the power to direct the activities of the VIE that most significantly impact the VIE's economic performance and the obligation to absorb losses or the rights to receive benefits from the VIE. According to the voting interest model, a controlling financial interest generally exists if a reporting entity has continuing power to govern the financial and operating policies of an entity. In assessing control, substantive kick-out rights are sometimes viewed differently under US GAAP. Under US GAAP the concept of "de facto control" does not exist.

Under US GAAP, like IFRS, control of a VIE is evaluated on a continuous basis; however, under US GAAP, control of a non-VIE is reassessed only when there is a change in the voting interest of the investee. However, with the issuance of ASU 2018-17 a private company (reporting entity) has the choice to not to apply VIE guidance to those "legal entities under common control (including common control leasing arrangements)" given that the legal entities involved are not public companies (issuers). Additionally, amendments for figuring out whether a "decision-making fee" represents a variable interest requires an entity that is reporting to take consideration the indirect interests held through "related parties under common control on a proportional basis" instead as if it were an equivalent of a direct interest in its entirety (as currently required in GAAP). This becomes effective for public companies for years beginning after December 15, 2020 and for all others December 15, 2021.

In a business combination, US GAAP requires non-controlling interest (NCI) to be recorded at fair market value, whereas under IFRS there is an option to record NCI at its proportionate interest in the net assets or at fair market value.

In the case of the loss of control, under US GAAP, all amounts recognised in accumulated non-controlling interest are reclassified. Push-down accounting is required in certain circumstances for public companies and is optional for private companies under US GAAP. Push-down accounting is not allowable under IFRS.

For equity-method investments under US GAAP, potential voting rights are not considered when determining significant influence. Entities have the option to account for equity-method investees at fair value. If fair value is not elected, and significant influence exists, the equity method of accounting is required. Uniform accounting policies between investor and investee are not required.

Under US GAAP, the carrying amount of an equity-method investee is written down only if the impairment can be deemed as "other than temporary." US GAAP provides specific guidelines on changes in the status of an equity-method investee.

Under US GAAP, there is no definition of a "joint arrangement" and of a "joint operation." Unlike IFRS the definition of a "joint venture" refers to a jointly controlled activity. Joint ventures defined as in accordance with IFRS are generally accounted under US GAAP using the equity method of accounting, unless the fair value option is elected. Proportionate consolidation is permitted in limited circumstances to account for interests in unincorporated entities where it is an established practice in a particular industry.

Under US GAAP, unlike IFRS, which only permits fair value accounting of an investment company investee if the parent is itself an investment company, investments in investment entities are always accounted for at fair value if the investee meets the characteristics of an investment company. These characteristics are very similar to IFRS. This is because the FASB and IASB undertook a joint project in 2011 to more closely align the accounting for investment entities.

Under US GAAP, unlike IFRS, there is no topic that deals with the disclosure of an entity's interests in other entities like IFRS 12 does. The disclosure requirements related to the composition of the group and the interests of non-controlling interests in the group's activities and cash flows are not as extensive as under IFRS.

US GAAP does not require disclosure of an entity's interest in joint arrangements. On the other hand, disclosures are required about an entity's involvement with both consolidated and unconsolidated VIE and disclosures required by investment companies in respect of an investee are more extensive than under IFRS.

15 BUSINESS COMBINATIONS

INTRODUCTION

Background

Under IFRS 3 entities have a choice for each business combination entered into to measure non-controlling interest in the acquiree either at its full fair value or at its proportionate share of the acquiree's identifiable net assets. This choice will result in either recognising goodwill relating to 100% of the business (applying the full fair value option and allocating implied goodwill to non-controlling interest) or recognising goodwill relating only to the percentage interest acquired.

All business combinations are accounted for as an acquisition. The assets acquired and liabilities assumed are recorded in the acquirer's books at their respective fair values using *acquisition accounting*. Goodwill is measured initially as the difference between (1) the acquisition-date fair value of the consideration transferred plus the fair value of any non-controlling interest in the acquiree, plus the fair value of the acquirer's previously held equity interest in the acquiree, if any; and (2) the acquisition-date fair values (or other amounts recognised in accordance with IFRS 3) of the identifiable assets acquired and liabilities assumed. Goodwill can arise only in the context of a business combination and cannot arise from purchases of an asset or group of assets.

The core principles adopted in IFRS 3 are that an acquirer of a business recognises assets acquired and liabilities assumed at their acquisition-date fair values and discloses additional information that enables users to evaluate the nature and financial effects of the acquisition. While fair values of many assets and liabilities can readily be determined (and in an arm's-length transaction should be known to the parties), certain recognition and measurement problems do inevitably arise. Among these are the value of contingent consideration (for example, earn-outs) promised to former owners of the acquired entity, and the determination as to whether certain expenses that arise by virtue of the transaction, such as those pertaining to elimination of duplicate facilities, should be treated as part of the transaction or as an element of post-acquisition accounting.

This chapter addresses in detail the application of the acquisition method of accounting for business combinations and, to a lesser extent, the accounting for goodwill. Chapter 11 presents the detailed accounting for all intangible assets, including goodwill. This chapter addresses the two allowed options of measuring non-controlling interest in the acquiree under IFRS 3:

1. The option to measure a non-controlling interest at its fair value and to allocate implied goodwill to the non-controlling interest; and
2. The option to measure the non-controlling interest at its proportionate share of the acquiree's identifiable net assets.

The major accounting issues affecting business combinations and the preparation of consolidated or combined financial statements are:

1. The proper recognition and measurement of the assets and liabilities of the combining entities;
2. The accounting for goodwill or gain from a bargain purchase (negative goodwill);
3. The elimination of intercompany balances and transactions in the preparation of consolidated financial statements; and
4. The manner of reporting the non-controlling interest.

The IFRS 10 standard is discussed in further detail within Chapter 14. The accounting for the assets and liabilities of entities acquired in a business combination is largely dependent on the fair values assigned to them at the transaction date. IFRS 13, *Fair Value Measurement*, establishes clear and consistent guidance for the measurement of fair value and also addressing valuation issues that arise in inactive markets. The fair value concepts and procedures are discussed in greater detail within Chapter 25.

Sources of IFRS			
IFRS 3, 10, 13	*IAS* 27, 36, 37, 38	*SIC* 32	*IFRIC* 5, 10

DEFINITIONS OF TERMS

Acquiree. One or more businesses in which an acquirer obtains control in a business combination.

Acquirer. An entity that obtains control over the acquiree. When the acquiree is a special-purpose entity (SPE), the creator or sponsor of the SPE (or the entity on whose behalf the SPE was created) may be deemed to be the acquirer.

Acquisition. A business combination in which one entity (the acquirer) obtains control over the net assets and operations of another (the acquiree) in exchange for the transfer of assets, incurrence of liability or issuance of equity.

Acquisition date. The date on which control of the acquiree is obtained by the acquirer.

Acquisition method. The method of accounting for each business combination under IFRS. Applying the acquisition method requires:

1. Identifying the acquirer;
2. Determining the acquisition date;
3. Recognising and measuring the identifiable assets acquired, the liabilities assumed and any non-controlling interest in the acquiree; and
4. Recognising and measuring goodwill or a gain from a bargain purchase.

Acquisition-related costs. Costs incurred by an acquirer to enter into a business combination.

Bargain purchase. A business combination in which the net of the acquisition-date fair value of the identifiable assets acquired, and the liabilities assumed, measured in accordance with IFRS 3, exceeds the aggregate of the acquisition-date fair value of the consideration transferred, plus the amount of any non-controlling interest in the acquiree, plus the acquisition-date fair value of the acquirer's previously held equity interest in the acquiree.

Business. An integrated set of assets and activities capable of being conducted and managed for the purpose of providing goods or services to customers, generating investment income (such as dividends or interest) or generating other income from ordinary activities. A development stage enterprise is not precluded from qualifying as a business under this definition, and the guidance that accompanies it is provided in IFRS 3 (Appendix B).

Business combination. A transaction or other event that results in an acquirer obtaining control over one or more businesses. Transactions that are sometimes referred to as "true mergers" or "mergers of equals" are also considered to be business combinations with an acquirer and one or more acquirees.

Closing date. The day on which an acquirer legally transfers consideration, acquires the assets and assumes the liabilities of an acquiree.

Consideration transferred. The acquirer measures the consideration transferred in a business combination in exchange for the acquiree (or control of the acquiree) at fair value, which is calculated as the aggregate of the acquisition-date fair values of the assets transferred, liabilities incurred to former owners of the acquiree and the equity interests issued by the acquirer. The acquisition-date fair value of contingent consideration should also be recognised as part of the consideration transferred in exchange for the acquiree. Acquisition-related costs are expenses recognised when incurred in profit or loss.

Contingency. An existing, unresolved condition, situation or set of circumstances that will eventually be resolved by the occurrence or non-occurrence of one or more future events. A potential gain or loss to the reporting entity can result from the contingency's resolution.

Contingent consideration. An acquirer's obligation to transfer additional assets or equity interests to the acquiree's former owners if specified future events occur or conditions are met. The contingent obligation is incurred as part of a business combination to obtain control of an acquiree. Contingent consideration might also arise when the terms of the business combination provide a requirement that the acquiree's former owners return previously transferred assets or equity interests to the acquirer under certain specified conditions.

Equity interests. For the purposes of IFRS 3, the term *equity interests* is used broadly to mean ownership interests (or instruments evidencing rights of ownership) of investor-owned entities. In a mutual entity, equity interests means instruments evidencing ownership, membership or participation rights.

Fair value. The amount for which an asset could be exchanged, or a liability settled in an orderly transaction between market participants at the measurement date.

Gain from a bargain purchase. In a business combination resulting in a bargain purchase, the difference between:

1. The acquisition-date fair value of the consideration transferred plus the amount of any non-controlling interest in the acquiree plus the acquisition-date fair value of the acquirer's previously held equity interest in the acquiree; and
2. The acquisition-date fair values (or other amounts measured in accordance with IFRS 3) of the identifiable assets acquired and liabilities assumed.

A gain from a bargain purchase is recognised when (2) exceeds (1). After the acquirer's reassessment of whether all the assets acquired and all the liabilities assumed have been correctly identified, the resulting gain from a bargain purchase is recognised in profit or loss on the acquisition date. A gain from a bargain purchase is also referred to in accounting literature as negative goodwill.

Goodwill. An intangible asset acquired in a business combination representing the future economic benefits expected to be derived from the business combination that are not allocated to other individually identifiable and separately recognisable assets acquired. Goodwill is initially measured as the difference between:

1. The acquisition-date fair value of the consideration transferred plus the amount of any non-controlling interest in the acquiree plus the acquisition-date fair value of the acquirer's previously held equity interest in the acquiree; and

2. The acquisition-date fair values (or other amounts measured in accordance with IFRS 3) of the identifiable assets acquired and liabilities assumed.

Goodwill is recognised when (1) exceeds (2). After initial recognition, goodwill is measured at cost less any accumulated impairment losses. Entities have a choice for each business combination to measure non-controlling interest in the acquiree either at its fair value (and recognising goodwill relating to 100% of the business) or at its proportionate share of the acquiree's net assets.

Identifiable asset. An asset is identifiable if it either:

1. Is separable from the entity that holds it; or
2. Represents a legal and/or contractual right.

An asset is considered separable if it is capable of being separated or divided from the entity that holds it for the purpose of the asset's sale, transfer, licence, rental, or exchange, by itself or together with a related contract, or other identifiable asset or liability, irrespective of whether management of the entity intends to do so. A legal and/or contractual right is considered identifiable irrespective of whether it is transferable or separable from the entity or from other rights and obligations.

Intangible asset. An identifiable non-monetary asset that lacks physical substance.

Market participants. Buyers and sellers in the principal or most advantageous market for an asset or liability who are:

1. Independent of the reporting entity (i.e., they are not related parties);
2. Knowledgeable to the extent that they have a reasonable understanding about the asset or liability and the transaction based on all available information, including information that is obtainable through the performance of usual and customary due diligence efforts;
3. Able to buy or sell the asset or liability;
4. Willing to enter into a transaction for the asset or liability (i.e., they are not under duress that would force or compel them to enter into the transaction).

Mutual entity. An entity that is not investor-owned, organised for the purpose of providing dividends, reduced costs or other economic benefits directly to its owners, members or participants. Examples of mutual entities include mutual insurance companies, credit unions and co-operative entities.

Non-controlling interest. The equity (net assets) in a subsidiary not directly or indirectly attributable to its parent. Non-controlling interests were formerly referred to in accounting literature as minority interests.

Owners. For the purposes of IFRS 3, the term *owners* is used broadly to include holders of equity interests (ownership interests) in investor-owned or mutual entities. Owners include parties referred to as shareholders, partners, proprietors, members or participants.

Parent. An entity that has one or more subsidiaries.

Reverse acquisition. An acquisition when one entity, nominally the acquirer, issues so many shares to the former owners of the target entity that they become the majority owners of the successor entity.

Subsidiary. An entity, including an unincorporated entity such as a partnership that is controlled by another entity (known as the parent).

BUSINESS COMBINATIONS AND CONSOLIDATIONS

Objectives

The overriding objective of IFRS 3 is to improve the relevance, representational faithfulness, transparency and comparability of information provided in financial statements about business combinations and their effects on the reporting entity by establishing principles and requirements with respect to how an acquirer, in its consolidated financial statements:

1. Recognises and measures identifiable assets acquired, liabilities assumed and the non-controlling interest in the acquiree, if any;
2. Recognises and measures acquired goodwill or a gain from a bargain purchase;
3. Determines the nature and extent of disclosures sufficient to enable the reader to evaluate the nature of the business combination and its financial effects on the consolidated reporting entity;
4. Accounts for and reports non-controlling interests in subsidiaries; and
5. Deconsolidates a subsidiary when it ceases to hold a controlling interest in it.

Scope

Transactions or other events that meet the definition of a business combination are subject to IFRS 3. Excluded from the scope of these standards, however, are:

1. Formation of a joint venture/arrangement;
2. Acquisition of an asset or group of assets that does not represent a business; and
3. Combinations between entities or businesses under common control.

The requirements of this Standard do not apply to the acquisition by an investment entity, as defined in IFRS 10 Consolidated Financial Statements, of an investment in a subsidiary that is required to be measured at fair value through profit or loss.

BUSINESS COMBINATIONS

IFRS 3 establishes the fair value principle for accounting for business combinations. The fair value principle means that, upon obtaining control of the subsidiary, the exchange transaction is measured at fair value. All assets, liabilities and equity (except equity acquired by the controlling interest) of the acquired entity are measured at fair value. IFRS 3 includes several exceptions to this principle.

Determining Fair Value

Accounting for acquisitions requires the determination of the fair value for each of the acquired entity's identifiable tangible and intangible assets and for each of its liabilities at the date of combination (except for assets which are to be resold and which are to be accounted for at fair value less costs to sell under IFRS 5; and for those items to which limited exceptions to recognition and measurement principles apply). IFRS 3 provides illustrative examples of how to treat certain assets, particularly intangibles, but provides no general guidance on determining fair value. IFRS 13, *Fair Value Measurement*, which defines the term *fair value* and sets out in a single standard a framework for measuring fair value and the related disclosures. IFRS 13 is discussed in further detail within Chapter 25.

Transactions and Events Accounted for as Business Combinations

A business combination results from the occurrence of a transaction or other event that results in an acquirer obtaining control of one or more businesses. This can occur in many different ways that include the following examples individually or in some cases in combination:

1. Transfer of cash, cash equivalents or other assets, including the transfer of assets of another business of the acquirer;
2. Incurring liabilities;
3. Issuance of equity instruments;
4. Providing more than one type of consideration; or
5. By contract alone without the transfer of consideration, such as when:
   a. An acquiree business repurchases enough of its own shares to cause one of its existing investors (the acquirer) to obtain control over it;
   b. There is a lapse of minority veto rights that had previously prevented the acquirer from controlling an acquiree in which it held a majority voting interest; or
   c. An acquirer and acquiree contractually agree to combine their businesses without a transfer of consideration between them.

Qualifying as a Business

Under IFRS 3, to be considered a business, an integrated group of activities and assets must be *capable* of being conducted and managed for the purpose of providing goods or services to customers, generating investment income (such as dividends or interest) or generating other income from ordinary activities.. The word *capable* was added to emphasise the fact that the definition does not preclude a development stage enterprise from qualifying as a business. The business definition was amended for accounting periods commencing on or after 1 January 2020 through a post-implementation review of the standard, aiming to address the practical difficulties experienced in identifying businesses. The definition and related guidance elaborate further that a business consists of inputs and processes applied to those inputs that have the ability to create outputs. While outputs are usually present in a business, they are not required to qualify as a business as long as there is the *ability* to create them.

An input is an economic resource that creates or has the ability to create outputs when one or more processes are applied to it. Examples of inputs include property, plant and equipment, intangible rights to use property, plant and equipment, intellectual property or other intangible assets and access to markets in which to hire employees or purchase materials.

A process is a system, protocol, convention or rule with the ability to create outputs when applied to one or more inputs. Processes are usually documented; however, an organised workforce with the requisite skills and experience may apply processes necessary to create outputs by following established rules and conventions. In evaluating whether an activity is a process, functions such as accounting, billing, payroll and other administrative systems do not meet the definition. Thus, processes are the types of activities that an entity engages in to produce the products and/or services that it provides to the marketplace rather than the internal activities it follows in operating its business.

An output is simply the by-product resulting from applying processes to inputs. An output provides, or has the ability to provide, a return to the investors, members, participants or other owners.

To assist preparers, a concentration test has been added to IFRS 3. An entity can elect to adopt the test on each transaction or event. The concentration test, when met, will result in the set of activities or assets not meeting the definition of a business. No further assessment is required. The concentration test is met if substantially all of the fair value of the gross assets acquired is concentrated in a single identifiable or asset or group of similar identifiable assets. Further guidance on the application of the concentration test is included within Appendix B, including examples of what does not constitute a group of similar identifiable assets. IFRS 3 does not include any additional commentary on the meaning of "substantially all" as this phrase is used in several standards already.

If the concentration test has not been adopted, when analysing a transaction or event to determine whether it is a business combination, it is not necessary that the acquirer retain, post-combination, all of the inputs or processes used by the seller in operating the business. If market participants could, for example, acquire the business in an arm's-length transaction and continue to produce outputs by integrating the business with their own inputs and processes, then that subset of remaining inputs and processes still meets the definition of a business from the standpoint of the acquirer.

The guidance in IFRS 3 provides additional flexibility by providing that it is not necessary that a business have liabilities, although that situation is expected to be rare. The broad scope of the term "capable of" requires judgement in determining whether an acquired set of activities and assets constitutes a business, to be accounted for by applying the acquisition method.

As discussed previously, development stage enterprises are not precluded from the criteria for being deemed a business. This is true even if they do not yet produce outputs. If there are no outputs being produced, the acquirer is to determine whether the enterprise constitutes a business by considering whether it:

1. Has started its planned principal activities;
2. Has hired employees;
3. Has obtained intellectual property;
4. Has obtained other inputs;
5. Has implemented processes that could be applied to its inputs;
6. Is pursuing a plan to produce outputs;
7. Will have the ability to obtain access to customers that will purchase the outputs.

It is important to note, however, that not all of these factors need to be present for a given set of development stage activities and assets to qualify as a business. The relevant question to ask is whether a market participant would be capable of conducting or managing the set of activities and assets as a business irrespective of whether the seller did so, or the acquirer intends to do so.

Finally, IFRS 3 acknowledged the circular logic of asserting that, in the absence of evidence to the contrary, if goodwill is included in a set of assets and activities, it can be presumed to be a business. The circularity arises from the fact that, to apply IFRS to determine whether to initially recognise goodwill, the accountant would be required to first determine whether there had, in fact, been an acquisition of a business. Otherwise, it would not be permitted to recognise goodwill. It is not necessary, however, that goodwill be present to consider a set of assets and activities to be a business.

Techniques for Structuring Business Combinations

A business combination can be structured in a number of different ways that satisfy the acquirer's strategic, operational, legal, tax and risk management objectives. Some of the more frequently used structures are:

1. One or more businesses become subsidiaries of the acquirer. As subsidiaries, they continue to operate as separate legal entities.
2. The net assets of one or more businesses are legally merged into the acquirer. In this case, the acquiree entity ceases to exist (in legal vernacular, this is referred to as a statutory merger and normally the transaction is subject to approval by a majority of the outstanding voting shares of the acquiree).
3. The owners of the acquiree transfer their equity interests to the acquirer entity or to the owners of the acquirer entity in exchange for equity interests in the acquirer.
4. All of the combining entities transfer their net assets, or their owners transfer their equity interests into a new entity formed for the purpose of the transaction. This is sometimes referred to as a roll-up or put-together transaction.
5. A former owner or group of former owners of one of the combining entities obtains control of the combined entities collectively.
6. An acquirer might hold a non-controlling equity interest in an entity and subsequently purchase additional equity interests sufficient to give it control over the investee. These transactions are referred to as step acquisitions or business combinations achieved in stages.

Accounting for Business Combinations under the Acquisition Method

The acquirer is to account for a business combination using the acquisition method. This term represents an expansion of the now-outdated term "purchase method." The change in terminology was made to emphasise that a business combination can occur even when a purchase transaction is not involved.

The following steps are required to apply the acquisition method:

1. Identify the acquirer;
2. Determine the acquisition date;
3. Identify assets and liabilities requiring separate accounting;
4. Identifying assets and liabilities that require acquisition date classification or designation;
5. Recognise and measure the identifiable tangible and intangible assets acquired and liabilities assumed;
6. Recognise and measure any non-controlling interest in the acquiree;
7. Measure the consideration transferred; and
8. Recognise and measure goodwill or, if the business combination results in a bargain purchase, recognise a gain from the bargain purchase.

Step 1—Identify the acquirer

IFRS 3 strongly emphasises the concept that every business combination has an acquirer. In the "basis for conclusions" that accompanies IFRS 3, the IASB asserts that:

"true mergers" or "mergers of equals" in which none of the combining entities obtain control of the others are so rare as to be virtually non-existent.[1]

The provisions of IFRS 10, *Consolidated Financial Statements*, should be used to identify the acquirer—the entity that obtains *control* of the acquiree. The acquirer is the combining entity that obtains control of the other combining entities.

While IFRS 10 provides that, in general, control is presumed to exist when the parent owns, directly or indirectly, a majority of the voting power of another entity, this is not an absolute rule to be applied in all cases. In fact, IFRS 10 explicitly provides that in exceptional circumstances, it can be clearly demonstrated that majority ownership does not constitute control, but rather that the minority ownership may constitute control (refer to Chapter 14). Exceptions to the general majority ownership rule include, but are not limited to, the following situations:

1. An entity that is in legal re-organisation or bankruptcy;
2. An entity subject to uncertainties due to government-imposed restrictions, such as foreign exchange restrictions or controls, whose severity casts doubt on the majority owner's ability to control the entity; or
3. If the acquiree is an SPE, the creator or sponsor of the SPE is always considered to be the acquirer. Accounting for SPEs is discussed later in this chapter.

If applying the guidance in IFRS 10 does not clearly indicate the party that is the acquirer, IFRS 3 provides factors to consider in making that determination under different facts and circumstances.

1. *Relative size*—Generally, the acquirer is the entity whose relative size is significantly larger than that of the other entity or entities. Size can be compared by using measures such as assets, revenues or net profit.
2. *Initiator of the transaction*—When more than two entities are involved, another factor to consider (besides relative size) is which of the entities initiated the transaction.
3. *Roll-ups or put-together transactions*—When a new entity is formed to issue equity interests to effect a business combination, one of the pre-existing entities is to be identified as the acquirer. If, instead, a newly formed entity transfers cash or other assets, or incurs liabilities as consideration to effect a business combination, that new entity may be considered to be the acquirer.
4. *Non-equity consideration*—In business combinations accomplished primarily by the transfer of cash or other assets, or by incurring liabilities, the entity that transfers the cash or other assets, or incurs the liabilities, is usually the acquirer.
5. *Exchange of equity interests*—In business combinations that are accomplished primarily by the exchange of equity interests, the entity that issues its equity interests is generally considered to be the acquirer. One notable exception that occurs frequently in practice is often referred to as a reverse acquisition, discussed in detail later in this chapter. In a reverse acquisition, the entity issuing equity interests is legally the acquirer, but for accounting purposes is considered the acquiree. There are, however, other factors that should be considered in identifying the acquirer when equity interests are exchanged. These include:

---

[1] *IFRS 3, paragraph BC35.*

a. *Relative voting rights in the combined entity after the business combination*—Generally, the acquirer is the entity whose owners, as a group, retain or obtain the largest portion of the voting rights in the consolidated entity. This determination must take into consideration the existence of any unusual or special voting arrangements as well as any options, warrants or convertible securities.
b. *The existence of a large minority voting interest in the combined entity in the event no other owner or organised group of owners possesses a significant voting interest*—Generally, the acquirer is the entity whose owner or organised group of owners holds the largest minority voting interest in the combined entity.
c. *The composition of the governing body of the combined entity*—Generally, the acquirer is the entity whose owners have the ability to elect, appoint or remove a majority of members of the governing body of the combined entity.
d. *The composition of the senior management of the combined entity*—Generally, the acquirer is the entity whose former management dominates the management of the combined entity.
e. *Terms of the equity exchange*—Generally, the acquirer is the entity that pays a premium over the pre-combination fair value of the equity interests of the other entity or entities.

Step 2—Determine the acquisition date

The acquisition date is that date on which the acquirer obtains control of the acquiree. As discussed previously, this concept of control is not always evidenced by ownership of voting rights.

The general rule is that the acquisition date is the date on which the acquirer legally transfers consideration, acquires the assets and assumes the liabilities of the acquiree. This date, in a relatively straightforward transaction, is referred to as the closing date. Not all transactions are that straightforward, however. All pertinent facts and circumstances are to be considered in determining the acquisition date and this includes the meeting of any significant condition's precedent. The parties to a business combination might, for example, execute a contract that entitles the acquirer to the rights and obligates the acquirer with respect to the obligations of the acquiree prior to the actual closing date. Thus, in evaluating economic substance over legal form, the acquirer will have contractually acquired the target on the date it executed the contract.

Example of acquisition date preceding closing date

In 20XX, Henan Corporation (HC), a China-based holding company, purchased more than 20 wine brands and specified distribution assets from a French company. In its annual report, HC disclosed that the acquired assets were transferred to a subsidiary of the seller, in which HC received, in connection with the transaction, economic rights (these were structured as "tracker shares" in the holding subsidiary of the seller) with respect to the acquired assets prior to their actual legal transfer to the company. In addition, HC obtained the contractual right to manage the acquired assets prior to their legal transfer to HC, resulting in the acquirer obtaining control of the acquiree on the date before the closing date. Among the reasons HC cited for entering into these arrangements was their commercial desire to obtain the economic benefits associated with owning and operating the acquired assets as soon as possible after funding the purchase price for them.

Until the assets were legally transferred to HC, the transaction was accounted for under IFRS 10 and consequently HC's interests in the tracker shares of the seller's subsidiary were consolidated since HC was considered the sponsor of that subsidiary. The seller's residual interest in the holding subsidiary was reported in the consolidated financial statements of HC as a non-controlling interest.

Step 3—Identify assets and liabilities requiring separate accounting

IFRS 3 provides a basic recognition principle that, as of the acquisition date, the acquirer is to recognise, separately from goodwill, the fair values of all identifiable assets acquired (whether tangible or intangible), the liabilities assumed, and, if applicable, any non-controlling interest (previously referred to as "minority interest") in the acquiree.

In applying the recognition principle to a business combination, the acquirer may recognise assets and liabilities that had not been recognised by the acquiree in its pre-combination financial statements, but which meet the definitions of assets and liabilities in the *Conceptual Framework for Financial Reporting* at the acquisition date. IFRS 3 continues to permit recognition of acquired intangibles (e.g., patents, customer lists) that would not be granted recognition if they were internally developed.

The pronouncement elaborates on the basic principle by providing that recognition is subject to the following conditions:

1. At the acquisition date, the identifiable assets acquired and liabilities assumed must meet the definitions of assets and liabilities as set forth in the *Conceptual Framework for Financial Reporting*;[2] and
2. The assets and liabilities recognised must be part of the exchange transaction between the acquirer and the acquiree (or the acquiree's former owners) and not part of a separate transaction or transactions.

Restructuring or exit activities. Frequently, in a business combination, the acquirer's plans include the future exit of one or more of the activities of the acquiree or the termination or relocation of employees of the acquiree. Since these exit activities are discretionary on the part of the acquirer and the acquirer is not obligated to incur the associated costs, the costs do not meet the definition of a liability and are not recognised at the acquisition date. Rather, the costs will be recognised in post-combination financial statements in accordance with other IFRS.

Boundaries of the exchange transaction. Pre-existing relationships and arrangements often exist between the acquirer and acquiree prior to beginning negotiations to enter into a business combination. Furthermore, while conducting the negotiations, the parties may enter into separate business arrangements. In either case, the acquirer is responsible for identifying amounts that are not part of the exchange for the acquiree. Recognition under the acquisition method is only given to the consideration transferred for the acquiree and the assets acquired, and liabilities assumed in exchange for that consideration. Other transactions outside the scope of the business combination are to be recognised by applying other relevant IFRS.

The acquirer is to analyse the business combination transaction and other transactions with the acquiree and its former owners to identify the components that comprise the transaction in which the acquirer obtained control over the acquiree. This distinction is

---

[2] *An asset is defined as "a present economic resource controlled by the entity as a result of past events". A liability is defined as "A present obligation of the entity to transfer an economic resource as a result of past events".*

important to ensure that each component is accounted for according to its economic substance, irrespective of its legal form.

The imposition of this condition was based on an observation that, upon becoming involved in negotiations for a business combination, the parties may exhibit characteristics of related parties. In so doing, they may be willing to execute agreements designed *primarily* for the benefit of the acquirer of the combined entity that might be designed to achieve a desired financial reporting outcome after the business combination has been consummated. The imposition of this condition is expected to curb such abuses.

In analysing a transaction to determine inclusion or exclusion from a business combination, consideration should be given to which of the parties will reap its benefits. If a pre-combination transaction is entered into by the acquirer, or on behalf of the acquirer, or *primarily* to benefit the acquirer (or to benefit the to-be-combined entity as a whole) rather than for the benefit of the acquiree or its former owners, the transaction most likely would be considered to be a "separate transaction" outside the boundaries of the business combination and for which the acquisition method would not apply.

The acquirer is to consider the following factors, which the IASB states "are neither mutually exclusive nor individually conclusive" in determining whether a transaction is a part of the exchange transaction or recognised separately:

1. *Purpose of the transaction*—Typically, there are many parties involved in the management, ownership, operation and financing of the various entities involved in a business combination transaction. Of course, there are the acquirer and acquiree entities, but there are also owners, directors, management and various parties acting as agents representing their respective interests. Understanding the motivations of the parties in entering into a particular transaction potentially provides insight into whether or not the transaction is a part of the business combination or a separate transaction.
2. *Initiator of the transaction*—Identifying the party that initiated the transaction may provide insight into whether or not it should be recognised separately from the business combination. IASB believes that if the transaction was initiated by the acquirer, it would be less likely to be part of the business combination and, conversely, if it were initiated by the acquiree or its former owners, it would be more likely to be part of the business combination.
3. *Timing of the transaction*—Examining the timing of the transaction may provide insight into whether, for example, the transaction was executed in contemplation of the future business combination to provide benefits to the acquirer or the post-combination entity. IASB believes that transactions that take place during the negotiation of the terms of a business combination may be entered into in contemplation of the eventual combination for the purpose of providing future economic benefits *primarily* to the acquirer of the to-be-combined entity and, therefore, should be accounted for separately.

IFRS 3 provides the following pair of presumptions after analysing the economic benefits of a pre-combination transaction:

Primarily for the benefit of	*Transaction likely to be*
Acquirer or combined entity	Separate transaction
Acquiree or its former owners	Part of the business combination

IFRS 3 provides three examples of separate transactions that are *not* to be included in applying the acquisition method:

1. A settlement of a pre-existing relationship between acquirer and acquiree;
2. Compensation to employees or former owners of the acquiree for future services; and
3. Reimbursement to the acquiree or its former owners for paying the acquirer's acquisition-related costs.

The section entitled "Determining what is part of the business combination transaction," later in this chapter, will discuss related application guidance for these transactions that are separate from the business combination (i.e., not part of the exchange for the acquiree).

Acquisition-related costs are, under IFRS 3, generally expensed through profit or loss at the time the services are received, which will generally be prior to, or at, the date of the acquisition. This is consistent with the now-prevalent view that such costs do not increase the *value* of the assets acquired, and thus should not be capitalised.

Step 4—Identify assets and liabilities that require acquisition date classification or designation

To facilitate the combined entity's future application of IFRS in its post-combination financial statements, management is required to make decisions on the acquisition date relative to the classification or designation of certain items. These decisions are to be based on the contractual terms, economic and other conditions, and the acquirer's operating and accounting policies as they exist *on the acquisition date*. Examples include, but are not limited to, the following:

1. Classification of particular financial assets and liabilities as measured at fair value through profit or loss or at amortised cost, or as a financial asset measured at fair value through other comprehensive income in accordance with IFRS 9, *Financial Instruments*;
2. Designation of a derivative instrument as a hedging instrument in accordance with IFRS 9; and
3. Assessment of whether an embedded derivative should be separated from a host contract in accordance with IFRS 9 (which is a matter of "classification" as this IFRS uses that term).

In applying Step 5, specific exceptions are provided for lease contracts and insurance contracts: classification of a lease contract as either an operating lease or a finance lease in accordance withIFRS 16, *Leases*, and classification of a contract as an insurance contract in accordance with IFRS 17, *Insurance Contracts*. Generally, these contracts are to be classified by reference to the contractual terms and other factors that were applicable *at their inception* rather than at the acquisition date. If, however, the contracts were modified subsequent to their inception and those modifications would change their classification at that date, then the accounting for the contracts will be determined by the modification date facts and circumstances. The modification date could be the same as the acquisition date.

Step 5—Recognise and measure the identifiable tangible and intangible assets acquired and liabilities assumed

In general, the measurement principle is that an acquirer measures the identifiable tangible and intangible assets acquired, and the liabilities assumed, at their fair values on the acquisition date. IFRS 3 provides the acquirer with a choice of two methods to measure non-controlling interests arising in a business combination:

1. To measure the non-controlling interest at fair value (recognising the acquired business at fair value); or
2. To measure the non-controlling interest at the non-controlling interest's share of the acquiree's net assets.

Exceptions to the recognition and/or measurement principles. IFRS 3 provides certain exceptions to its general principles for recognising assets acquired and liabilities assumed at their acquisition date fair values. These can be summarised as follows:

Nature of exception	*Recognition*	*Measurement*
Contingent liabilities	x	
Income taxes	x	x
Employee benefits	x	x
Indemnification assets	x	x
Reacquired rights		x
Share-based payment awards		x
Assets held for sale		x

Exceptions to the Recognition Principle

Contingent liabilities of the acquiree. In accordance with IAS 37, *Provisions, Contingent Liabilities and Contingent Assets*, a contingent liability is defined as:

1. A possible obligation that arises from past events and whose existence will be confirmed only by the occurrence or non-occurrence of one or more uncertain future events not wholly within the control of the entity; or
2. A present obligation that arises from past events but is not recognised because:
   a. It is not probable that an outflow of resources embodying economic benefits will be required to settle the obligation; or
   b. The amount of the obligation cannot be measured with sufficient reliability.

Under IFRS 3 the acquirer recognises as of the acquisition date a contingent liability assumed in a business combination if it is a present obligation that arises from past events and its fair value can be measured reliably, regardless of the probability of cash flow arising.

Exceptions to both the Recognition and Measurement Principles

Income taxes. The basic principle that applies to income tax accounting in a business combination (carried forward without change by IFRS 3) is that the acquirer is to recognise in accordance with IAS 12, *Income Taxes*, as of the acquisition date, deferred income tax assets or liabilities for the future effects of temporary differences and carryforwards of the acquiree that either:

1. Exist on the acquisition date; *or*
2. Are generated by the acquisition itself.

However, IAS 12 has been amended to accommodate the new business combinations framework and, consequently, management must carefully assess the reasons for changes in the deferred tax benefits during the measurement period. As a result of these amendments, deferred tax benefits that do not meet the recognition criteria at the date of acquisition are subsequently recognised as follows:

- Acquired deferred tax benefits recognised within the measurement period (within one year after the acquisition date) that result from new information regarding the facts and circumstances existing at the acquisition date are accounted for as a reduction of goodwill related to this acquisition. If goodwill is reduced to zero, any remaining portion of the adjustment is recorded as a gain from a bargain purchase.
- All other acquired deferred tax benefits realised are recognised in profit or loss (or outside profit or loss if otherwise required by IAS 12).

In addition, IAS 12 has been amended to require any tax benefits arising from the difference between the income tax basis and IFRS carrying amount of goodwill to be accounted for as any other temporary difference at the date of acquisition.

Employee benefits. Liabilities (and assets, if applicable), associated with acquiree employee benefit arrangements are to be recognised and measured in accordance with IAS 19, *Employee Benefits*. Any amendments to a plan (and their related income tax effects) that are made as a result of business combination are treated as a post-combination event and recognised in the acquirer's post-combination financial statements in the periods in which the changes occur.

Indemnification assets. Indemnification provisions are usually included in the voluminous closing documents necessary to effect a business combination. Indemnifications are contractual terms designed to fully or partially protect the acquirer from the potential adverse effects of an unfavourable future resolution of a contingency or uncertainty that exists at the acquisition date (e.g., legal or environmental liabilities, or uncertain tax positions). Frequently the indemnification is structured to protect the acquirer by limiting the maximum amount of post-combination loss that the acquirer would bear in the event of an adverse outcome. A contractual indemnification provision results in the acquirer obtaining, as a part of the acquisition, an indemnification asset and simultaneously assuming a contingent liability of the acquiree.

Exceptions to the Measurement Principle

Reacquired rights. An acquirer and acquiree may have engaged in pre-acquisition business transactions such as leases, licences, franchises, trade name or technology that resulted in the acquiree paying consideration to the acquirer to use tangible and/or intangible assets of the acquirer in the acquiree's business. The acquisition results in the acquirer reacquiring that right. The acquirer measures the value of a reacquired right recognised as an intangible asset. If the terms of the contract giving rise to a reacquired right are favourable or unfavourable compared with current terms and prices for the same or similar items, a settlement gain or loss will be recognised in profit or loss.

The IFRS accounting requirements after acquisition, on subsequently measuring and accounting for reacquired rights, contingent liabilities and indemnification assets, are discussed later in this chapter in the section entitled "Post-combination measurement and accounting."

Share-based payment awards. In connection with a business combination, the acquirer often replaces the acquiree's share-based payment awards with the acquirer's own share-based payment awards. Obviously, there are many valid business reasons for the exchange, not the least of which is ensuring smooth transition and integration as well as retention of valued employees. The acquirer measures a liability, or an equity instrument related to share-based payment transactions of the acquiree or the replacement of an acquiree's share-based payment awards with the acquirer's share-based awards in accordance with IFRS 2, *Share-Based Payment*, at the acquisition date.

Assets held for sale. Assets classified as held-for-sale individually or as part of a disposal group are to be measured at acquisition date fair value less cost to sell, consistent with IFRS 5, *Non-current Assets Held for Sale and Discontinued Operations* (discussed in detail within Chapter 9). In determining fair value less cost to sell, it is important to differentiate costs to sell from expected future losses associated with the operation of the long-lived asset or disposal group to which it belongs.

In post-acquisition periods, long-lived assets classified as held for sale are not to be depreciated or amortised. If the assets are part of a disposal group (discussed within Chapter 9), interest and other expenses related to the liabilities included in the disposal group continue to be accrued.

Costs to sell are defined as the incremental direct costs necessary to transact a sale. To qualify as costs to sell, the costs must result directly from the sale transaction, incurring them needs to be considered essential to the transaction, and the cost would not have been incurred by the entity in the absence of a decision to sell the assets. Examples of costs to sell include brokerage commissions, legal fees, title transfer fees and closing costs necessary to effect the transfer of legal title.

Costs to sell are expressly not permitted to include any future losses that are expected to result from operating the assets (or disposal group) while it is classified as held for sale. If the expected timing of the sale exceeds one year from the end of the reporting period, which is permitted in limited situations by paragraph B1 of IFRS 5, the costs to sell are to be discounted to their present value.

Should a loss be recognised in subsequent periods due to a decline in the fair value less cost to sell, such losses may be restored by future periods' gains only to the extent to which the losses have been recognised cumulatively from the date the asset (or disposal group) was classified as held for sale.

IFRS guidance on recognising and measuring the identifiable assets acquired and liabilities assumed is discussed later in this chapter.

Step 6—Recognise and measure any non-controlling interest in the acquiree

The term "non-controlling interest" replaces the term "minority interest" in referring to that portion of the acquiree, if any, not controlled by the parent subsequent to the acquisition. IFRS 3 provides the acquirer with a choice of two methods to measure non-controlling interests at the acquisition date arising in a business combination:

1. To measure the non-controlling interest at *fair value* (also recognising the acquired business at fair value); or

2. To measure the non-controlling interest at the present ownership instruments' share in the recognised amounts of the acquiree's identifiable net assets (under this approach the only difference is that, in contrast to the approach of measuring the non-controlling interest at fair value, no portion of imputed goodwill is allocated to the non-controlling interest).

The second choice is only available for present ownership interest that entitles the holder to a proportionate share of the entity's net assets in the event of liquidation. All other components of non-controlling interest are measured at the acquisition date fair value unless required otherwise by IFRS.

The choice of the method to measure the non-controlling interest should be made separately for each business combination rather than as an accounting policy. In making this election, management must carefully consider all factors, since the two methods may result in significantly different amounts of goodwill recognised, as well as different accounting for any changes in the ownership interest in a subsidiary. One important factor would be the entity's future intent to acquire non-controlling interest, because of the potential effects on equity when the outstanding non-controlling interest is acquired. Any subsequent acquisition of the outstanding non-controlling interest under IFRS 3 would not result in additional goodwill being recognised, since such a transaction would be considered as taking place between shareholders.

Measuring non-controlling interest at fair value. IFRS 3 allows the non-controlling interest in the acquiree to be measured at fair value at the acquisition date, determined based on market prices for equity shares not held by the acquirer, or, if not available, by using a valuation technique. If the acquirer is not acquiring all of the shares in the acquiree and there is an active market for the remaining outstanding shares in the acquiree, the acquirer may be able to use the market price to measure the fair value of the non-controlling interest. Otherwise, the acquirer would measure fair value using other valuation techniques. Under this approach, recognised goodwill represents all of the goodwill of the acquired business, not just the acquirer's share.

In applying the appropriate valuation technique to determine the fair value of the non-controlling interest, it is likely that there will be a difference in the fair value per share of the non-controlling interest and the fair value per share of the controlling interest (the acquirer's interest in the acquiree). This difference is likely to be the inclusion of a control premium in the per-share fair value of the controlling interest or, similarly, what has been referred to as a "non-controlling interest discount" applicable to the non-controlling shares. Obviously, an investor would be unwilling to pay the same amount per share for equity shares in an entity that did not convey control of that entity as it would pay for shares that did convey control. For this reason, the amount of consideration transferred by an acquirer is not usually indicative of the fair value of the non-controlling interest, since the consideration transferred by the acquirer often includes a control premium.

Example of measuring non-controlling interest at fair value

Konin Corporation (KC) acquires a 75% interest in Bartovia Corporation (BC), in exchange for cash of €360,000. BC has 25% of its shares traded on an exchange; KC acquired the 60,000 non-publicly traded shares outstanding, at €6 per share. The fair value of BC's identifiable net assets is €300,000; the shares of BC at the acquisition date are traded at €5 per share.

Under the full fair value approach, the non-controlling interest is measured based on the trading price of the shares of entity BC at the date control is obtained by KC (€5 per share) and a value of €100,000 is assigned to the 25% non-controlling interest, indicating that KC has paid a control premium of €60,000 (€360,000 – [€5 × 60,000]):

$$\text{Equity} - \text{Non-controlling interest in net assets}\,(€5 \times 20{,}000) = €100{,}000$$

It is important to note from this analysis that, from the perspective of the acquirer, the computation of the acquisition-date fair value of the non-controlling interest in the acquiree is not computed by simply multiplying the same fair value per share that the acquirer paid for its controlling interest. Such a calculation would have yielded a different result:

$$\text{Equity} - \text{Non-controlling interest in net assets}\,(€6 \times 20{,}000) = €120{,}000$$

If this method had been used, the non-controlling interest would be overvalued by €20,000 (the difference between €120,000 and €100,000).

Under the fair value approach to measure non-controlling interest, the acquired business will be recognised at fair value, with the controlling share of total goodwill assigned to the controlling interest and the non-controlling share allocated to the non-controlling interest.

Measuring non-controlling interest at its share of the identifiable net assets of the acquiree, calculated in accordance with IFRS 3. Under this approach, non-controlling interest is measured as the non-controlling interest's proportionate interest in the value of the identifiable assets and liabilities of the acquiree, determined under current requirements of IFRS 3.

Example of measuring non-controlling interest at share of net assets of the acquiree

Konin Corporation (KC) acquires a 75% interest in Bartovia Corporation (BC), in exchange for cash of €360,000. BC has 25% of its shares traded on an exchange; KC acquired the 60,000 non-publicly traded shares outstanding, at €6 per share. The fair value of BC's identifiable net assets is €300,000; the shares of entity BC at the acquisition date are traded at €5 per share. The consideration transferred indicates that KC has paid a control premium of €60,000 (€360,000 – [€5 × 60,000]).

Since KC elects to measure non-controlling interest in BC at its share of the acquiree's net assets, a value of €75,000 is assigned to the 25% non-controlling interest:

$$\text{Equity} - \text{Non-controlling interest in net assets}\,(€300{,}000 \times 25\%) = €75{,}000$$

Under this approach to measure non-controlling interest, goodwill recognised will represent only the acquirer's share.

IFRS 10 requires that the non-controlling interest is to be classified in the consolidated statement of financial position within the equity section, separately from the equity of the parent company, and clearly identified with a caption such as "non-controlling interest in subsidiaries." Should there be non-controlling interests attributable to more than one consolidated subsidiary, the amounts may be aggregated in the consolidated statement of financial position.

Only equity-classified instruments issued by the subsidiary may be classified as equity in this manner. If, for example, the subsidiary had issued a financial instrument that, under applicable IFRS, was classified as a liability in the subsidiary's financial statements, that instrument would not be classified as a non-controlling interest since it does not represent an ownership interest.

Step 7—Measure the consideration transferred

In general, consideration transferred by the acquiree is measured at its acquisition-date fair value. Examples of consideration that could be transferred include cash, other assets, a business, a subsidiary of the acquirer, contingent consideration, ordinary or preference equity instruments, options, warrants and member interests of mutual entities. The aggregate consideration transferred is the sum of the following elements measured at the acquisition date:

1. The fair value of the assets transferred by the acquirer;
2. The fair value of the liabilities incurred by the acquirer to the former owners of the acquiree; and
3. The fair value of the equity interests issued by the acquirer subject to the measurement exceptions discussed earlier in this chapter for the portion, if applicable, of acquirer share-based payment awards exchanged for awards held by employees of the acquiree that is included in consideration transferred.

To the extent the acquirer transfers consideration in the form of assets or liabilities with carrying amounts that differ from their fair values at the acquisition date, the acquirer is to remeasure them at fair value and recognise a gain or loss on the acquisition date. If, however, the transferred assets or liabilities remain within the consolidated entity post-combination, with the acquirer retaining control of them, no gain or loss is recognised, and the assets or liabilities are measured at their carrying amounts to the acquirer immediately prior to the acquisition date. This situation can occur, for example, when the acquirer transfers assets or liabilities to the entity being acquired rather than to its former owners.

The structure of the transaction may involve the exchange of equity interests between the acquirer and either the acquiree or the acquiree's former owners. If the acquisition-date fair value of the acquiree's equity interests is more reliably measurable than the equity interests of the acquirer, the fair value of the acquiree's equity interests is to be used to measure the consideration transferred.

When a business combination is effected without transferring consideration—for example, by contract alone—the acquisition method of accounting also applies. Examples of such combinations include:

- The acquiree repurchases a sufficient number of its own shares for an existing investor (the acquirer) to obtain control;
- Minority veto rights lapse that kept the acquirer, holding the majority voting rights, from controlling an acquiree;
- The acquirer and acquiree agree to combine their businesses by contract alone (e.g., a stapling arrangement or dual-listed corporation).

In a business combination achieved by contract alone, the entities involved are not under common control and the combination does not involve one of the combining entities obtaining an ownership interest in another combining entity. Consequently, there is a 100% non-controlling interest in the acquiree's net assets since the acquirer must contribute the fair value of the acquiree's assets and liabilities to the owners of the acquiree. Depending on the option elected to measure non-controlling interest (at fair value or share of the acquiree's net assets), this may result in recognising goodwill allocated only to the non-controlling interest or recognising no goodwill at all.

Contingent consideration. In many business combinations, the acquisition price is not completely fixed at the time of the exchange but is instead dependent on the outcome of future events. There are two major types of contingent future events that might commonly be used to modify the acquisition price: the performance of the acquired entity (acquiree) and the market value of the consideration initially given for the acquisition.

The most frequently encountered contingency involves the post-acquisition performance of the acquired entity or operations. The contractual agreement dealing with this is often referred to as an "earn-out" provision. It typically calls for additional payments to be made to the former owners of the acquiree if defined revenue or earnings thresholds are met or exceeded. These may extend for several years after the acquisition date and may define varying thresholds for different years. For example, if the acquiree during its final pre-transaction year generated revenues of €4 million, there might be additional sums due if the acquired operations produced €4.5 million or greater revenues in year one after the acquisition, €5 million or greater in year two and €6 million in year three. Care will have to be taken to ensure that compensation for post-acquisition services is excluded from the calculation of contingent consideration. Additional guidance is discussed later in this chapter.

Contingent consideration arrangements in connection with business combinations can be structured in many different ways and can result in the recognition of either assets or liabilities under IFRS 3. An acquirer may agree to transfer (or receive) cash, additional equity instruments or other assets to (or from) former owners of an acquiree after the acquisition date, if certain specified events occur in the future. In either case, according to IFRS 3 the acquirer is to include contingent assets and liabilities as part of the consideration transferred, measured at acquisition-date fair value. Contingent consideration can only be recognised when the contingency is probable and can be reliably measured. If the contingent consideration includes a future payment obligation, that obligation is to be classified as either a liability or equity under the provisions of:

- Paragraph 11 of IAS 32, *Financial Instruments: Presentation*; or
- Other applicable IFRS.

The acquirer is to carefully consider information obtained subsequent to the acquisition-date measurement of contingent consideration. Additional information obtained during the measurement period that relates to the facts and circumstances that existed at the acquisition date result in measurement period adjustments to the recognised amount of contingent consideration and a corresponding adjustment to goodwill or gain from bargain purchase. The IFRS accounting requirements on subsequently measuring and accounting for contingent consideration in the post-combination periods are discussed later in this chapter in the section entitled "Post-combination measurement and accounting."

Step 8—Recognise and measure goodwill or gain from a bargain purchase

The last step in applying the acquisition method is the measurement of goodwill or a gain from a bargain purchase. Goodwill represents an intangible that is not specifically identifiable. It results from situations when the amount the acquirer is willing to pay to obtain its controlling interest exceeds the aggregate recognised values of the net assets acquired, measured following the principles of IFRS 3. It arises largely from the synergies and economies of scale expected from combining the operations of the acquirer and acquiree. Goodwill's elusive nature as an unidentifiable, residual asset means that it cannot be measured directly but rather can only be measured by reference to the other amounts measured as a part of the business combination. In accordance with IFRS 3, management must select, for each acquisition, the option to measure the non-controlling interest, and consequently the amount recognised as goodwill (or gain on a bargain purchase) will depend on whether non-controlling interest is measured at fair value (option 1) or at the non-controlling interest's share of the acquiree's net assets (option 2).

GW	=	Goodwill.
GBP	=	Gain from a bargain purchase.
NI	=	Non-controlling interest in the acquiree, if any, measured at fair value (option 1) or as the non-controlling interest's share of the acquiree's net assets (option 2).
CT	=	Consideration transferred, generally measured at acquisition-date fair value.
PE	=	Fair value of the acquirer's previously held interest in the acquiree if the acquisition was achieved in stages. This includes any investment in a joint venture/ arrangement which is now controlled.
NA	=	Net assets acquired—consisting of the acquisition-date fair values (or other amounts recognised under the requirements of IFRS 3[R] as described in the chapter) of the identifiable assets acquired and liabilities assumed.
GW (or GBP)	=	(CT + NI + PE) – NA

Thus, when application of the formula yields an excess of the acquisition-date fair value of the consideration transferred plus the amount of any non-controlling interest and plus fair value of the acquirer's previously held equity interest over the net assets acquired, this means that the acquirer has paid a premium for the acquisition and that premium is characterised as goodwill.

When the opposite is true, that is, when the formula yields a negative result, a gain from a bargain purchase (sometimes referred to as negative goodwill) is recognised, since the acquirer has, in fact, obtained a bargain purchase as the value the acquirer obtained in the exchange exceeded the fair value of what it surrendered.

In a business combination in which no consideration is transferred, the acquirer is to use one or more valuation techniques to measure the acquisition-date fair value of its equity interest in the acquiree and substitute that measurement in the formula for CT, "the consideration transferred." The techniques selected require the availability of sufficient data to properly apply them and are to be appropriate for the circumstances. If more than one technique is used, management of the acquirer is to evaluate the results of applying the techniques, including the extent of data available and how relevant and reliable the inputs (assumptions) used are. Guidance on the use of valuation techniques is provided in the standard, IFRS 13, *Fair Value Measurement*, presented in Chapter 25.

Example of recognising goodwill—non-controlling interest measured at the non-controlling interest's proportionate share of the acquiree's net assets

Konin Corporation (KC) acquires a 75% interest in Donna Corporation (DC), in exchange for cash of €350,000. DC has 25% of its shares traded on an exchange; KC acquired the 60,000 non-publicly traded shares outstanding. The fair value of DC's identifiable net assets is €300,000; the shares of DC at the acquisition date are traded at €5 per share. The consideration transferred indicates that KC has paid a control premium of €50,000 (€350,000 − [€5 × 60,000]).

Management chooses the option to measure non-controlling interest at its share of the acquiree's net assets and a value assigned to the non-controlling interest is €75,000 (€300,000 × 25%).

The amount of goodwill recognised is €125,000. This is calculated by:

Consideration exchanged—Cash	350,000
Equity—Non-controlling interest (25% × €300,000)	75,000
	425,000
Less net assets acquired at fair value	(300,000)
Goodwill	125,000

No goodwill is assigned to the non-controlling interest. The acquirer (KC) would record its acquisition of DC in its consolidated financial statement as follows:

Identifiable net assets acquired, at fair value	300,000	
Goodwill (€425,000 – €300,000)	125,000	
Equity—Non-controlling interest		75,000
Cash		350,000

Under the approach to measure non-controlling interest at the proportionate share of the acquiree's net assets, goodwill recognised €125,000 (€350,000 + €75,000 − €300,000) represents only the acquirer's share of the goodwill.

Example of recognising goodwill—non-controlling interest measured at fair value

Konin Corporation (KC) acquires a 75% interest in Danube Corporation (DC), in exchange for cash of €350,000. DC has 25% of its shares traded on an exchange; KC acquired the 60,000 non-publicly traded shares outstanding. The fair value of DC's identifiable net assets is €300,000; the shares of DC at the acquisition date are traded at €5 per share. The consideration transferred indicates that KC has paid a control premium of €50,000 (€350,000 − [€5 × 60,000]).

Management chooses the option to measure non-controlling interest at fair value and a value of €100,000 (€5 × 20,000 non-controlling interest shares) is assigned to the 25% non-controlling interest.

Goodwill on the acquisition is calculated by:

Consideration exchanged—Cash	350,000
Equity—Non-controlling interest (€5 × 20,000 shares)	100,000
	450,000
Less net assets acquired at fair value	(300,000)
Goodwill	150,000

The amount of goodwill accruing to the controlling interest is €125,000, which is equal to the consideration transferred, €350,000, for the controlling interest minus the controlling interest's share in the fair value of the identifiable net assets acquired, €225,000 (€300,000 × 75%). The amount of goodwill accruing to the non-controlling interest is €25,000 (€150,000 total goodwill less €125,000 allocated to the controlling interest). The acquirer (KC) would record its acquisition of DC in its consolidated financial statements as follows:

Identifiable net assets acquired, at fair value	300,000	
Goodwill (€450,000 − €300,000)	150,000	
Equity—Non-controlling interest		100,000
Cash		350,000

Under the approach to measure non-controlling interest at fair value, the acquired business is recognised at €450,000 (€350,000 + 100,000) fair value and full goodwill (€150,000 = €450,000 − €300,000) is recognised. The amount of goodwill associated with the controlling interest is €125,000 (€350,000 − (€300,000 × 75%)), and the amount of goodwill associated with non-controlling interest is €25,000 (€150,000 − €125,000).

Bargain purchases. A bargain purchase occurs when the value of net assets acquired is in excess of the acquisition-date fair value of the consideration transferred plus the amount of any non-controlling interest and plus fair value of the acquirer's previously held equity interest. While not common, this can happen, as, for example, in a business combination that is a forced sale, when the seller is acting under compulsion.

Under IFRS 3, when a bargain purchase occurs, a gain on acquisition is recognised in profit or loss at the acquisition date, as part of income from continuing operations.

Before recognising a gain on a bargain purchase, IASB prescribed a verification protocol for management to follow given the complexity of the computation involved. If the computation initially yields a bargain purchase, acquirer's management should perform the following procedures before recognising a gain on the bargain purchase:

1. Perform a completeness review of the identifiable tangible and intangible assets acquired and liabilities assumed to reassess whether all such items have been correctly identified. If any omissions are found, recognise the assets and liabilities that had been omitted.
2. Perform a review of the procedures used to measure all of the following items. The objective of the review is to ensure that the acquisition-date measurements appropriately considered all available information available at the acquisition date relating to:

    a. Identifiable assets acquired;
    b. Liabilities assumed;
    c. Consideration transferred;
    d. Non-controlling interest in the acquiree, if applicable; and
    e. Acquirer's previously held equity interest in the acquiree for a business combination achieved in stages.

Example of a bargain purchase

On January 1, 20XX, Konin Corporation (KC) acquires 75% of the equity interests of Laska Corporation (LC), a private entity, in exchange for cash of €250,000. The former owners of LC were forced to sell their investments within a short period of time and unable to market LC to multiple potential buyers in the marketplace. The management of KC initially measures at the acquisition date in accordance with IFRS 3 the separately recognisable identifiable assets acquired at €500,000 and liabilities at €100,000. KC engages an independent valuation specialist who determines that the fair value of the 25% non-controlling interest in LC is €110,000.

Since the amount of LC's identifiable net assets (€400,000 calculated as €500,000 − €100,000) exceeds the fair value of the consideration transferred (€250,000) plus the fair value of the non-controlling interest (€110,000), the acquisition initially results in a bargain purchase. In accordance with the requirements of IFRS 3, KC must perform a review to ensure whether all assets, liabilities, consideration transferred and non-controlling interest have been correctly measured. KC concludes that the procedures and resulting measures are correct.

The acquirer (KC) recognises the gain on its acquisition of the 75% interest as follows:

Consideration exchanged—Cash	250,000
Equity—Non-controlling interest at fair value	110,000
	360,000
Less net assets acquired at fair value	(400,000)
Gain on bargain purchase	(40,000)

The acquirer (KC) would record its acquisition of LC in its consolidated financial statements as follows:

Identifiable net assets acquired	400,000	
Cash		250,000
Gain on the bargain purchase		40,000
Equity—Non-controlling interest in LC		110,000

If the acquirer (KC) elects to measure the non-controlling interest in LC on the basis of its proportionate interest in the identifiable net assets of the acquiree, the recognised amount of the non-controlling interest would be €100,000 (€400,000 × 25%); the gain on the bargain purchase would be €50,000 (€400,000 − [€250,000 + €100,000]).

Measurement period. More frequently than not, management of the acquirer does not obtain all of the relevant information needed to complete the acquisition-date measurements in time for the issuance of the first set of interim or annual financial statements subsequent to the business combination. If the initial accounting for the business combination has not been completed by that time, the acquirer is to report provisional amounts in the consolidated financial statements for any items for which the accounting is incomplete.

IFRS 3 provides for a "measurement period" during which any adjustments to the provisional amounts recognised at the acquisition date are to be retrospectively adjusted to reflect new information that management obtains regarding facts and circumstances existing as of the acquisition date. Information that has a bearing on this determination must not relate to post-acquisition events or circumstances. The information is to be analysed to determine whether, if it had been known at the acquisition date, it would have affected the measurement of the amounts recognised as of that date.

In evaluating whether new information obtained is suitable for the purpose of adjusting provisional amounts, management of the acquirer is to consider all relevant factors. Critical in this evaluation is the determination of whether the information relates to facts and circumstances as they existed at the acquisition date, or the information results from events occurring after the acquisition date. Relevant factors include:

1. The timing of the receipt of the additional information; *and*
2. Whether management of the acquirer can identify a reason that a change is warranted to the provisional amounts.

Obviously, information received shortly after the acquisition date has a higher likelihood of relevance to acquisition-date circumstances than information received months later. However, the measurement period should not exceed one year from the acquisition date.

Example of consideration of new information obtained during the measurement period

Konin Corporation (KC) acquired Automotive Industries, Inc. (AI) on September 30, 20XX-1. KC hired independent valuation specialists to determine valuation for an asset group acquired in the combination, but the valuation was not complete by the time KC authorised for issue its 20XX-1 consolidated financial statements. As a result, KC assigned a provisional fair value of €40 million to an asset group acquired, consisting of a factory and related machinery that manufactures engines used in large trucks and sport utility vehicles.

As of the acquisition date, the average cost of gasoline in the markets served by the customers of AI was €4.30 per gallon. For the first six months subsequent to the acquisition, the per-gallon price of gasoline was relatively stable and only fluctuated slightly up or down on any given day. Upon further analysis, management was able to determine that, during that six-month period, the production levels of the asset group and related order backlog did not vary substantially from the acquisition date.

In April 20XX, however, due to an accident on April 3, 20XX, at a large refinery, the average cost per gallon skyrocketed to more than €6.00. As a result of this huge spike in the price of fuel, AI's largest customers either cancelled orders or sharply curtailed the number of engines they had previously ordered.

Scenario 1: On March 31, 20XX, management of KC received the independent valuation, which estimated the assets' acquisition-date fair value as €30 million. Given the fact that management was unable to identify any changes that occurred during the measurement period that would have accounted for a change in the acquisition-date fair value of the asset group, management determines that it will retrospectively reduce the provisional fair value assigned to the asset group to €30 million.

In its financial statements for the year ended December 31, 20XX, KC retrospectively adjusted the 20XX-1 prior year information as follows:

1. The carrying amount of assets is decreased by €10,600,000. That adjustment is measured as the fair value adjustment at the acquisition date of €10,000,000 plus the reduced depreciation that would have been recognised if the asset's fair value at the acquisition date had been recognised from that date (€600,000 for three months' depreciation).
2. The carrying amount of goodwill as of December 31, 20XX-1 is increased by €10,000,000.
3. Depreciation expense for 20XX-1 is decreased by €600,000.

Scenario 2: KC has not received the independent valuation of assets until May 20XX. On April 15, 20XX, management of KC signed a sales agreement with Jonan International (JI) to sell the asset group for €30 million. Given the intervening events that affected the price of fuel and the demand for AI's products, management determines that the €10 million decline in the fair value of the asset group from the provisional fair value it was originally assigned resulted from those intervening changes and, consequently, does not adjust the provisional fair value assigned to the asset group at the acquisition date.

In addition to adjustments to provisional amounts recognised, the acquirer may determine during the measurement period that it omitted recognition of additional assets or liabilities that existed at the acquisition date. During the measurement period, any such assets or liabilities identified are also to be recognised and measured on a retrospective basis.

In determining adjustments to the provisional amounts assigned to assets and liabilities, management should be alert for interrelationships between recognised assets and liabilities. For example, new information that management obtains that results in an adjustment to the provisional amount assigned to a liability for which the acquiree carries insurance could also result in an adjustment, in whole or in part, to a provisional amount recognised as an asset representing the claim receivable from the insurance carrier. In addition, as discussed in this chapter and Chapter 26, changes in provisional amounts assigned to assets and liabilities frequently will also affect temporary differences between the items' income tax basis and IFRS carrying amount, which in turn will affect the computation of deferred income tax assets and liabilities.

Adjustments to the provisional amounts that are made during the measurement period are recognised retrospectively as if the accounting for the business combination had actually been completed as of the acquisition date. This will result in the revision of comparative information included in the financial statements for prior periods, including any necessary adjustments to depreciation, amortisation or other effects on profit or loss or other comprehensive income related to the adjustments. The measurement period ends on the *earlier* of:

1. The date management of the acquirer receives the information it seeks regarding facts and circumstances as they existed at the acquisition date or learns that it will be unable to obtain any additional information; *or*
2. One year after the acquisition date.

After the end of the measurement period, the only revisions that are permitted to be made to the initial acquisition-date accounting for the business combination are restatements for corrections of prior period errors in accordance with IAS 8, *Accounting Policies, Changes in Accounting Estimates and Errors*, discussed in detail within Chapter 7.

Acquisition-related costs

Acquisition-related costs, under IFRS 3, are generally to be charged as an expense in the period in which the costs are incurred and the related services received. Examples of these costs include:

Accounting fees	Internal acquisitions department costs
Advisory fees	Legal fees
Consulting fees	Other professional fees
Finder's fees	Valuation fees

Acquisition-related costs are not part of the fair value exchange between the buyer and the seller for the acquired business, they are accounted for separately as operating costs in the period in which services are received. This may significantly affect the operating results reported for the period of any acquisition.

IFRS 3 makes an exception to the general rule of charging acquisition-related costs against profit with respect to costs to register and issue equity or debt securities. These costs are to be recognised in accordance with IAS 32 and IFRS 9. Share issuance costs are normally charged against the gross proceeds of the issuance (see Chapter 16). Debt issuance costs are treated as a reduction of the amount borrowed or as an expense of the period in which they are incurred; however, some reporting entities have treated these costs as deferred charges and amortised them against profit during the term of the debt (see Chapter 24).

Post-combination measurement and accounting

In general, in accordance with IFRS 3 in post-combination periods, an acquirer should measure and account for assets acquired, liabilities assumed or incurred, and equity instruments issued in a business combination on a basis consistent with other applicable IFRS for those items, which include:

- IAS 38 prescribes the accounting for identifiable intangible assets acquired in a business combination;
- IAS 36 provides guidance on recognising impairment losses;
- IFRS 17 prescribes accounting for an insurance contract acquired in a business combination;
- IAS 12 prescribes the post-combination accounting for deferred tax assets and liabilities acquired in a business combination;
- IFRS 16 provides guidance on leases;
- IFRS 2 provides guidance on subsequent measurement and accounting for share-based payment awards; and
- IAS 27 prescribes accounting for changes in a parent's ownership interest in a subsidiary after control is obtained.

IFRS 3 provides special guidance on accounting for the following items arising in a business combination:

1. Reacquired rights;
2. Contingent liabilities recognised as of the acquisition date;
3. Indemnification assets; and
4. Contingent consideration.

After acquisition, a *reacquired right* recognised as an intangible asset is amortised over the remaining contractual term, without taking into consideration potential renewal periods. If an acquirer subsequently sells a reacquired right to a third party, the carrying amount of the right should be included in calculating the gain or loss on the sale.

In post-combination periods, until the liability is settled, cancelled or expires, the acquirer measures a *contingent liability* recognised as of the acquisition date at the higher of:

1. The amount that would be recognised by applying the requirements of IAS 37; and
2. The amount initially recognised, less any cumulative amount of income recognised in accordance with IFRS 15, *Revenue from Contracts with Customers*.

This requirement would not apply to contracts accounted for under the provisions of IFRS 9. In accordance with this standard, the financial liability is to be measured at fair value at each reporting date, with changes in value recognised either in profit or loss or in other comprehensive income in accordance with IFRS 9.

At each reporting date subsequent to the acquisition date, the acquirer should measure an *indemnification asset* recognised as part of the business combination using the same basis as the indemnified item, subject to any limitations imposed contractually on the amount of the indemnification. If an indemnification asset is not subsequently measured at fair value (because to do so would be inconsistent with the basis used to measure the indemnified item), management is to assess the recoverability of the asset. Any changes in the measurement of the asset (and the related liability) are recognised in profit or loss.

The acquirer needs to carefully consider information obtained subsequent to the acquisition-date measurement of *contingent consideration*. Some changes in the fair value of contingent consideration result from additional information obtained during the measurement period that relates to the facts and circumstances that existed at the acquisition date. Such changes are measurement period adjustments to the recognised amount of contingent consideration and a corresponding adjustment to goodwill or gain from bargain purchase. However, changes that result from events occurring after the acquisition date, such as meeting a specified earnings target, reaching a specified share price, or reaching an agreed-upon milestone on a research and development (R&D) project, do not constitute measurement period adjustments, and no longer result in changes to goodwill.

Contingent consideration, which is classified as an asset or liability, is remeasured at fair value at each reporting date. All changes in fair value are recognised in profit or loss in accordance with IFRS 9. Contingent consideration which is classified as equity is not remeasured.

The potential impact of post-acquisition remeasurements on subsequent profit or loss as well as on debt covenants or management remuneration should be analysed at the date of acquisition.

IFRS guidance on recognising and measuring reacquired rights, contingent liabilities and indemnification assets on the acquisition date was discussed earlier in this chapter in the paragraph entitled "Accounting for Business Combinations under the Acquisition Method, Steps 3, 4 and 5—Classify or designate the identifiable assets acquired and liabilities assumed"; and guidance on contingent consideration in "Step 7—Measure the consideration transferred."

DISCLOSURE REQUIREMENTS

The acquirer should disclose information that enables users of its financial statements to evaluate:

- The nature as well as financial effect of a business combination that occurs either: (1) during the current period, or (2) after the end of the reporting period but before the financial statements are authorised for issue;
- The financial effects of adjustments recognised in the current reporting period that relate to business combinations that occurred during: (1) the current period, or (2) previous reporting periods.

Recognising and Measuring the Identifiable Assets Acquired and Liabilities Assumed

The following guidance is to be followed in applying the recognition and measurement principles (subject to certain specified exceptions).

Assets with uncertain cash flows (valuation allowances). Since fair value measurements consider the effects of uncertainty regarding the amounts and timing of future cash flows, the acquirer measures receivables, including loans, at their acquisition-date fair values. A separate valuation allowance is not recognised for assets subject to such uncertainties (e.g., acquired receivables, including loans). This may be a departure from current practice, especially for entities operating in the financial services industry.

Assets in which the acquiree is the lessee. For businesses adopting IFRS 16, the acquirer recognises a right-to-use asset and a lease liability for leases in which the acquiree is the lessee. The acquirer is not required to recognise a right-to-use asset and lease liability for:

- Leases for which the lease term ends within 12 months of the acquisition date; or
- Leases for which the underlying asset is of low value.

The acquirer shall measure the lease liability at the present value of the remaining lease payments as if the acquired lease were a new lease at the acquisition date. The right-to-use asset is recognised at the same value as the lease liability, adjusted to reflect favourable or unfavourable terms of the lease when compared with market terms.

Assets the acquirer plans to leave idle or to use in a way that is different from the way other market participants would use them. If the acquirer intends, for competitive or other business reasons, to idle an acquired asset (for example, an R&D intangible asset) or use it in a manner that is different from the manner in which other market participants would use it, the acquirer is still required to initially measure the asset at fair value determined in accordance with its use by other market participants.

Identifiable intangibles to be recognised separately from goodwill. Intangible assets acquired in a business combination are to be recognised separately from goodwill if they meet either of the two criteria to be considered *identifiable*. These criteria are:

1. *Separability criterion*—The intangible asset is capable of being separated or divided from the entity that holds it, and sold, transferred, licensed, rented or exchanged, regardless of the acquirer's intent to do so. An intangible asset meets this criterion even if its transfer would not be alone, but instead would be accompanied or bundled with a related contract, other identifiable asset or a liability.
2. *Legal/contractual criterion*—The intangible asset results from contractual or other legal rights. An intangible asset meets this criterion even if the rights are not transferable or separable from the acquiree or from other rights and obligations of the acquiree.

IFRS 3's illustrative examples include a lengthy, though not exhaustive, listing of intangible assets that the IASB believes have characteristics that meet one of these two criteria (legal/contractual or separability). A logical approach in practice would be for the acquirer to first consider whether the intangibles specifically included on the IASB list are applicable to the particular acquiree and then to consider whether there may be other unlisted intangibles included in the acquisition that meet one or both of the criteria for separate recognition.

IFRS 3 organises groups of identifiable intangibles into categories related to or based on:

1. Marketing;
2. Customers or clients;
3. Artistic works;
4. Contractual;
5. Technological.

These categorisations are somewhat arbitrary. Consequently, some of the items listed could fall into more than one of the categories. Examples of identifiable intangibles included in each of the categories are as follows:

Marketing-Related Intangible Assets

1. *Trademarks, service marks, trade names, collective marks, certification marks*. A trademark represents the right to use a name, word, logo or symbol that differentiates a product from products of other entities. A service mark is the equivalent of a trademark for a service offering instead of a product. A collective mark is used to identify products or services offered by members affiliated with each other. A

certification mark is used to designate a particular attribute of a product or service such as its geographic source (e.g., Colombian coffee or Italian olive oil) or the standards under which it was produced (e.g., ISO 9000 Certified).

2. *Trade dress*. The overall appearance and image (unique colour, shape or package design) of a product.
3. *Newspaper mastheads*. The unique appearance of the title page of a newspaper or other periodical.
4. *Internet domain names*. The unique name that identifies an address on the Internet. Domain names must be registered with an Internet registry and are renewable.
5. *Non-competition agreements*. Rights to assurances that companies or individuals will refrain from conducting similar businesses or selling to specific customers for an agreed-upon period of time.

Customer-Related Intangible Assets

1. *Customer lists*. Names, contact information, order histories and other information about a company's customers that a third party, such as a competitor or a telemarketing firm, would want to use in its own business.
2. *Order or production backlogs*. Unfilled sales orders for goods and services in amounts that exceed the quantity of finished goods and work-in-process on hand for filling the orders.
3. *Customer contracts and related customer relationships*. When a company's relationships with its customers arise primarily through contracts and are of value to buyers who can "step into the shoes" of the sellers and assume their remaining rights and duties under the contracts, and which hold the promise that the customers will place future orders with the entity or relationships between entities and their customers for which:
   a. The entities have information about the customers and have regular contact with the customers; and
   b. The customers have the ability to make direct contact with the entity.
4. *Non-contractual customer relationships*. Customer relationships that arise through means such as regular contacts by sales or service representatives, the value of which is derived from the prospect of the customers placing future orders with the entity.

Artistic-Related Intangible Assets

1. Plays, operas, ballets.
2. Books, magazines, newspapers and other literary works.
3. Musical works such as compositions, song lyrics and advertising jingles.
4. Pictures and photographs.
5. Video and audiovisual material, including motion pictures or films, music videos and television programmes.

Contract-Based Intangible Assets

1. *Licence, royalty, standstill agreements*. Licence agreements represent the right, on the part of the licensee, to access or use property that is owned by the licensor for a specified period of time at an agreed-upon price. A royalty agreement entitles its holder to a contractually agreed-upon portion of the income earned from the sale or licence of a work covered by patent or copyright. A standstill agreement conveys

assurances that a company or individual will refrain from engaging in certain activities for specified periods of time.

2. *Advertising, construction, management, service or supply contracts.* For example, a contract with a newspaper, broadcaster or Internet site to provide specified advertising services to the acquiree.
3. *Lease agreements (irrespective of whether the acquiree is the lessee or lessor).* A contract granting use or occupation of property during a specified period in exchange for a specified rent.
4. *Construction permits.* Rights to build a specified structure at a specified location.
5. *Construction contracts.* Rights to become the contractor responsible for completing a construction project and benefit from the profits it produces, subject to the remaining obligations associated with performance (including any past-due payments to suppliers and/or subcontractors).
6. *Construction management, service or supply contracts.* Rights to manage a construction project for a fee, procure specified services at a specified fee or purchase specified products at contractually agreed-upon prices.
7. *Broadcast rights.* Legal permission to transmit electronic signals using specified bandwidth in the radio frequency spectrum, granted by the operation of communication laws.
8. *Franchise rights.* Legal rights to engage in a trade-named business, to sell a trademarked good or to sell a service-marked service in a particular geographic area.
9. *Operating rights.* Permits to operate in a certain manner, such as those granted to a carrier to transport specified commodities.
10. *Use rights, such as drilling, water, air, timber cutting and route authorities.* Permits to use specified land, property or air space in a particular manner, such as the right to cut timber, expel emissions or to land airplanes at specified gates at an airport.
11. *Servicing contracts.* The contractual right to service a loan. Servicing entails activities such as collecting principal and interest payments from the borrower, maintaining escrow accounts, paying taxes and insurance premiums when due, and pursuing collection of delinquent payments.
12. *Employment contract.* A contract that is beneficial from the perspective of the employer because of favourable market-related terms.

Technology-Based Intangible Assets

1. *Patented or copyrighted software.* Computer software source code, program specifications, procedures and associated documentation that is legally protected by patent or copyright.
2. *Computer software and mask works.* Software permanently stored on a read-only memory chip as a series of stencils or integrated circuitry. Mask works may be provided statutory protection in some countries.
3. *Unpatented technology.* Access to knowledge about the proprietary processes and workflows followed by the acquiree to accomplish desired business results.
4. *Databases, including title plants.* Databases are collections of information generally stored digitally in an organised manner. A database can be protected by copyright (e.g., the database contained on the CD-ROM version of this publication). Many databases, however, represent information accumulated as a natural by-product of

a company conducting its normal operating activities. Examples of these databases are plentiful and include title plants, scientific data and credit histories. Title plants represent historical records with respect to real estate parcels in a specified geographic location.

5. *Trade secrets*. Trade secrets are proprietary, confidential information, such as a formula, process or recipe.

One commonly cited intangible asset deliberately omitted by the IASB from its list of identifiable intangibles is an "assembled workforce." IASB decided that the replacement cost technique that is often used to measure the fair value of an assembled workforce does not faithfully represent the fair value of the intellectual capital acquired. It was thus decided that an exception to the recognition criteria would be made, and that the fair value of an acquired assembled workforce would remain part of goodwill.

R&D assets. IFRS 3 requires the acquirer to recognise and measure all tangible and intangible assets used in R&D activities acquired individually or in a group of assets as part of the business combination. This prescribed treatment is to be followed even if the assets are judged to have no alternative future use. These assets are to be measured at their acquisition-date fair values. Fair value measurements are to be made based on the assumptions that would be made by market participants in pricing the asset. Assets that the acquirer does not intend to use or intends to use in a manner that is different from the manner in which other market participants would use them are, nevertheless, required to be measured at fair value.

Intangible R&D assets. Upon initial recognition, the *intangible* R&D assets are to be classified as indefinite-life assets until the related R&D efforts are either completed or abandoned. In the reporting periods during which the R&D intangible assets are classified as indefinite-life, they are not to be amortised. Instead, they are to be tested for impairment in the same manner as other indefinite-life intangibles. Upon completion or abandonment of the related R&D efforts, management is to determine the remaining useful life of the intangibles and amortise them accordingly. In applying these requirements, assets that are temporarily idled are not to be considered abandoned.

Tangible R&D assets. Tangible R&D assets acquired in a business combination are to be accounted for according to their nature (e.g., supplies, inventory, depreciable assets, etc.).

Determining what is part of the business combination transaction

Transactions entered into by or on behalf of the acquirer or primarily for the benefit of the acquirer or the combined entity, rather than primarily for the benefit of the acquiree (or its former owners), before the combination, are likely to be separate transactions, not accounted for under the acquisition method. In applying the acquisition method to account for a business combination, the acquirer must recognise only the consideration transferred for the acquiree and the assets acquired and liabilities assumed in the exchange for the acquiree. IFRS 3 provides the following examples of separate transactions that are not to be included in applying the acquisition method:

1. A transaction that in effect settles pre-existing relationships between the acquirer and acquiree;
2. A transaction that remunerates employees or former owners of the acquiree for future services; and

3. A transaction that reimburses the acquiree or its former owners for paying the acquirer's acquisition-related costs.

The amount of the gain or loss measured as a result of settling a pre-existing relationship will, of course, depend on whether the acquirer had previously recognised related assets or liabilities with respect to that relationship.

Example of settlement of pre-existing contractual supplier relationship: contract unfavourable to acquirer

Konin Corporation (KC) and Banham Corporation (BC) are parties to a three-year supply contract that contains the following provisions:

1. KC is required to annually purchase 3,000 flat-panel displays from BC at a fixed price of €400 per unit for an aggregate purchase price of €1,200,000 for each of the three years.
2. KC is required to pay BC the annual €1,200,000 irrespective of whether it takes delivery of all 3,000 units and the required payment is non-refundable.
3. The contract contains a penalty provision that would permit KC to cancel it at the end of the second year for a lump-sum payment of €500,000.
4. In each of the first two years of the contract, KC took delivery of the full 3,000 units.

At December 31, 20XX-1, the supply contract was unfavourable to KC because KC was able to purchase flat-panel displays with similar specifications and of similar quality from another supplier for €350 per unit. Therefore, KC accrued a loss of €150,000 (3,000 units remaining under the firm purchase commitment × €50 loss per unit).

On January 1, 20XX, KC acquires BC for €30 million, which reflects the fair value of BC based on what other marketplace participants would be willing to pay. On the acquisition date, the €30 million fair value of BC includes €750,000 related to the contract with KC that consists of:

Identifiable intangibles	€600,000	Representing the remaining year of the contract, at prevailing market prices
Favourable pricing	€150,000	Representing the portion of the contract price that is favourable to BC and unfavourable to KC
	€750,000	

BC has no other identifiable assets or liabilities related to the supply contract with KC. KC would compute its gain or loss on settlement of this pre-existing relationship as follows:

1.	Amount of unfavourableness to acquirer (KC) at acquisition date	€150,000
2.	Lump-sum settlement amount available to KC through the cancellation provision	500,000
3.	Lesser of 1. or 2.	150,000
4.	Amount by which 1. exceeds 2.	N/A

KC had already recognised an unrealised loss on the firm purchase commitment as of December 31, 20XX, upon its acquisition of BC, its loss of €150,000 from recognising the lesser of 1. and 2. above would be offset by the elimination of the liability for the unrealised loss on the firm purchase commitment of the same amount of €150,000. Thus, under these circumstances, KC would have neither a gain nor a loss on the settlement of its pre-existing relationship with BC. The entries to record these events are not considered part of the business combination accounting. It is important to note that, from the perspective of KC, when it applies the acquisition method to record the business combination, it will characterise the €600,000 "at-market" component of the contract as part of goodwill and not as identifiable intangibles. This is the case because of the obvious fallacy of KC recognising customer-relationship intangible assets that represent a relationship with itself.

Example of settlement of pre-existing contractual supplier relationship: contract favourable to acquirer

Using the same facts as the KC/BC example above, assume that, instead of the contract being favourable to the acquirer KC, it was unfavourable to BC in the amount of €150,000 and that there was a cancellation provision in the contract that would permit BC to pay a penalty after year two of €100,000 to cancel the remainder of the contract.

On the acquisition date, the €30 million fair value of BC under this scenario would include €450,000 related to the contract with KC that consists of:

Identifiable intangibles	€600,000	Representing the remaining year of the contract at prevailing market prices
Unfavourable pricing	(€150,000)	Representing the portion of the contract price that is unfavourable to BC and favourable to KC
	€450,000	

Under these changed assumptions, KC would not have incurred or recorded an unrealised loss on the firm purchase commitment with BC since the contract terms were favourable to KC. The determination of KC's gain or loss would be as follows:

1.	Amount of favourability to acquirer (KC) at acquisition date	€150,000
2.	Lump-sum settlement amount available to BC through cancellation provision	€100,000
3.	Lesser of 1. or 2.	€100,000
4.	Amount by which 1. exceeds 2.	€50,000

Under this scenario, unless BC believed that the market would change in the near term, it would be economically advantageous, in the absence of a business combination, for BC to settle the remaining contract at the acquisition date by paying the €100,000 penalty because BC would be able to sell the remaining 3,000 units covered by the contract for an aggregate price of €150,000 more than it was committed to sell those units to KC.

At the acquisition date, KC would record a gain of €100,000 to settle its pre-existing relationship with BC. The entry to record the gain is not considered part of the business combination accounting.

In addition, however, since 2. is less than 1., the €50,000 difference is included in the accounting for the business combination, since economically, in post-combination periods, the combined entity will not benefit from that portion of the acquisition date favourability of the contract.

As was the case in the first example, the portion of the purchase price allocated to the contract in the business combination accounting would be accounted for as goodwill for the same reason.

Contingent payments to employees or former owners of the acquiree. The acquirer is to assess whether arrangements to make contingent payments to employees or selling owners of the acquiree represent contingent consideration that is part of the business combination transaction or represents compensation for future services and a separate transaction to be excluded from the application of the acquisition method to the business combination.

In general, the acquirer is to consider the reasons why the terms of the acquisition include the payment provision, the party that initiated the arrangement and when (at what stage of the negotiations) the arrangement was entered into by the parties. When those considerations do not provide clarity regarding whether the transaction is separate from the business combination, the acquirer considers the following indicators:

1. *Post-combination employment*—Consideration is to be given to the terms under which the selling owners will be providing services as key employees of the combined entity. The terms may be evidenced by a formal employment contract, by provisions included in the acquisition documents, or by other documents. If the arrangement provides that the contingent payments are automatically forfeited upon termination of employment, the consideration is to be characterised as compensation for post-combination services. If, instead, the contingent payments are not affected by termination of employment, this would be an indicator that the contingent payments represent additional consideration that is part of the business combination transaction and not compensation for services.
2. *Duration of post-combination employment*—If the employee is contractually bound to remain employed for a period that equals or exceeds the period during which the contingent payments are due, this may be an indicator that the contingent payments represent compensation for services.
3. *Amount of compensation*—If the amount of the employee's compensation that is not contingent is considered to be reasonable in relation to other key employees of the combined entity, this may indicate that the contingent amounts represent additional consideration and not compensation for services.
4. *Differential between amounts paid to employees and selling owners who do not become employees of the combined entity*—If, on a per-share basis, the contingent payments due to former owners of the acquiree that did not become employees are lower than the contingent payments due to the former owners that did become employees of the combined entity, this may indicate that the incremental amounts paid to the employees are compensation.
5. *Extent of ownership*—The relative ownership percentages (e.g., number of shares, units, percentage of membership interest) owned by the selling owners who remain employees of the combined entity serve as an indicator of how to characterise the substance of the contingent consideration. If, for example, the former owners of substantially all of the ownership interests in the acquiree are continuing to serve as key employees of the combined entity, this may be an indicator that the contingent payment arrangement is substantively a profit-sharing vehicle designed with the intent of providing compensation for services to be performed post-combination. Conversely, if the former owners that remained employed by the combined entity collectively owned only a nominal ownership interest in the acquiree and all of the former owners received the same amount of contingent basis on a per-share basis, this may be an indicator that the contingent payments represent additional consideration. In considering the applicability of this indicator, care must be exercised to closely examine the effects, if any, of transactions, ownership interests and employment relationships, pre-combination and post-combination, with respect to parties related to the selling owners of the acquiree.

6. *Relationship of contingent arrangements to the valuation approach used*—The payment terms negotiated in many business combinations provide that the amount of the acquisition date transfer of consideration from acquirer to acquiree (or the acquiree's former owners) is computed near the lower end of a range of valuation estimates the acquirer used in valuing the acquiree. Furthermore, the formula for determining future contingent payments is derived from or related to that valuation approach. When this is the case, it may be an indicator that the contingent payments represent additional consideration. Conversely, if the formula for determining future contingent payments more closely resembles prior profit-sharing arrangements, this may be an indicator that the substance of the contingent payment arrangement is to provide compensation for services.
7. *Formula prescribed for determining contingent consideration*—Analysing the formula to be used to determine the contingent consideration may provide insight into the substance of the arrangement. Contingent payments that are determined on the basis of a multiple of earnings may be indicative of being, in substance, contingent consideration that is part of the business combination transaction. Alternatively, contingent consideration that is determined as a pre-specified percentage of earnings would be more suggestive of a routine profit-sharing arrangement for the purposes of providing additional compensation to employees for post-combination services rendered.
8. *Other considerations*—Given the complexity of a business combination transaction and the sheer number and girth of the legal documents necessary to effect it, the financial statements preparer is charged with the daunting, but unavoidable, task of performing a comprehensive review of the terms of all the associated agreements. These can take the form of non-compete agreements, consulting agreements, leases, guarantees, indemnifications and, of course, the formal agreement to combine the businesses. Particular attention should be paid to the applicable income tax treatment afforded to the contingent payments. The income tax treatment of these payments may be an indicator that tax avoidance was a primary motivator in characterising them in the manner that they are structured. An acquirer might, for example, simultaneous to a business combination, execute a property lease with one of the key owners of the acquiree. If the lease payments were below market, some or all of the contingent payments to that key owner/lessor under the provisions of the other legal agreements might, in substance, be making up the shortfall in the lease and thus should be re-characterised as lease payments and accounted for separately from the business combination in the combined entity's post-combination financial statements. If this were not the case, and the lease payments were reflective of the market, this would be an indicator pointing to a greater likelihood that the contingent payment arrangements actually did represent contingent consideration associated with the business combination transaction.

Example of contingent payments to employees

Henan Corporation (HC) hired a new accounting director in charge of the conversion to IFRS under a five-year contract. The terms of the contract stated that HC will pay the director €1 million annually if HC is acquired before the expiration of this contract, up to the maximum amount of €5 million. After four years, Konin Corporation (KC) acquires HC. Since the director was still working for HC at the acquisition date, he will receive €1 million payment under the contract.

In this example, the contract for the employment of the accounting director was entered into long before the negotiations of the business combination were initiated, and the purpose of the contract was to receive the services of the director. Therefore, there is no evidence that this contract was primarily entered into to provide benefits to KC or the combined entity. As a result, the liability for the payment of €1 million is included in the application of the acquisition method.

Alternatively, HC might enter into the contract at the recommendation of KC, as part of the negotiations for the business combination, with the intent to provide severance pay to the director. Therefore, the contract may primarily benefit KC and the combined entity rather than HC or its former owners. Consequently, the acquirer KC must account for the liability of €1 million to the director since the payment is considered a separate transaction, excluded from the application of the acquisition method to this business combination.

Replacement awards—Acquirer share-based payment awards exchanged for acquiree awards held by its employees. In connection with a business combination, the acquirer often awards share options or other share-based payments (i.e., replacement awards) to the employees of the acquiree in exchange for the employees' acquiree awards. Obviously, there are many valid business reasons for the exchange, not the least of which is ensuring smooth transition and integration, retention and motivation of valued employees, and maintaining controlling interests in the acquiree.

IFRS 3 provides guidance on determining whether equity instruments (for example, share-based payments awards) issued in a business combination are part of the consideration transferred in exchange for control of the acquiree (and accounted for in accordance with IFRS 3[R]) or are in return for continued service in the post-combination periods (and accounted for under IFRS 2, *Share-Based Payment*, as a modification of a plan).

Acquirer not obligated to exchange. Accounting for the replacement awards under IFRS 3 is dependent on whether the acquirer is obligated to replace the acquiree awards. The acquirer is obligated to replace the acquiree awards if the acquiree or its employees can enforce replacement through rights obtained from the terms of the acquisition agreement, the acquiree awards or applicable laws or regulations.

If the acquirer is not obligated to replace the acquiree awards, all of the market-based measure of the replacement awards is recognised as remuneration cost in the post-combination financial statements.

Goodwill and Gain from a Bargain Purchase

Goodwill

Goodwill represents the difference between the acquisition-date fair value of the consideration transferred plus the amount of any non-controlling interest in the acquiree plus the acquisition-date fair value of the acquirer's previously held equity interest in the acquiree and the acquisition-date fair values of the identifiable assets acquired and liabilities assumed. It is presumed that when an acquiring entity pays such a premium price for the acquiree, it sees value that transcends the worth of the tangible assets and the identifiable intangibles, or else the deal would not have been consummated on such terms. Goodwill arising from acquisitions often consists largely of the synergies and economies of scale expected from combining the operations of the acquirer and acquiree. Goodwill must be recognised as an asset.

The balance in the goodwill account should be reviewed at the end of each reporting period to determine whether the asset has suffered any impairment. If goodwill is no longer deemed probable of being fully recovered through the profitable operations of the acquired business, it should be partially written down or fully written off. Any write-off of goodwill must be charged to profit or loss. Once written down, goodwill cannot later be restored as an asset, reflecting the concern that the independent measurement of goodwill is not possible and the acquired goodwill may, in the post-acquisition periods, be replaced by internally generated goodwill, which is not to be recognised.

It should be noted that in acquisitions of less than 100% of the equity interests, IFRS 3 provides the acquirer with a choice of two options to measure non-controlling interests arising in a business combination:

1. To measure the non-controlling interest at *fair value* (also recognising the acquired business at fair value); or
2. To measure the non-controlling interest at the non-controlling interest's share of the value of net assets acquired.

Under the fair value approach to measure non-controlling interest, the acquired business will be recognised at fair value, with the controlling share of total goodwill assigned to the controlling interest and the non-controlling share allocated to the non-controlling interest. Under the second approach to measure non-controlling interest, while the net identifiable assets attributable to the non-controlling interest are written up to the fair values implied by the acquisition transaction, goodwill will not be imputed for the non-controlling share.

Example of acquisition transaction—goodwill

Oman Heating Corp. acquired 100% of the equity interests of Euro Boiler Manufacturing Co. on January 2, 20XX, in exchange for cash of €15 million and the balance represented by a long-term note to former Euro shareholders. As of January 2, 20XX, immediately prior to the transaction, Euro's statement of financial position is as follows, with both book and fair values indicated (in thousands of €):

	Book value	*Fair value*		*Book value*	*Fair value*
	€	€		€	€
Cash	1,000	1,000	Current liabilities	26,200	26,200
Accounts receivable, net	12,200	12,000	Long-term debt	46,000	41,500
Inventory	8,500	9,750	Guarantee of debt	–	75
Other current assets	500	500			
Property, plant and equipment, net	38,500	52,400			
Customers list	–	1,400			
Patents	2,400	3,900			
In-process research and development (IPR&D)	–	8,600	Shareholders' equity (deficit)	(9,100)	21,775
Totals	**€63,100**	**€89,550**		**€63,100**	**€89,550**

The fair value of inventory exceeded the corresponding book value because Euro Boiler had been using LIFO for many years to cost its inventory, prior to revised IAS 2's prohibiting this method, and actual replacement cost was therefore somewhat higher than carrying value at the date of the acquisition. The long-term debt's fair value was slightly lower than carrying value (cost) because the debt carries a fixed interest rate and the market rates have risen since the debt was incurred. Consequently, Euro Boiler benefits economically by having future debt service requirements which are less onerous than they would be if it were to borrow at current rates.

Conversely, of course, the fair value of the lender's note receivable has declined since it now represents a loan payable at less than market rates. Finally, the fair values of Euro Boiler's receivables have also declined from their carrying amount, due to both the higher market rates of interest and to the greater risk of non-collectibility because of the change in ownership. The higher interest rates impact the valuation in two ways: (1) when computing the discounted present value of the amounts to be received, the higher interest rate reduces the computed present value, and (2) the higher interest rates may serve as an incentive for customers to delay payments to Euro rather than borrow the money to repay the receivables, with that delay resulting in cash flows being received later than anticipated thus causing the present value to decline.

Euro Boiler's customer list has been appraised at €1.4 million and is a major reason for the company's acquisition by Oman Heating. Having been internally developed over many years, the customer list is not recorded as an asset by Euro, however. The patents have been amortised down to €62.4 million in Euro Boiler's accounting records, consistent with IFRS, but an appraisal finds that on a fair value basis the value is somewhat higher.

Similarly, property, plant and equipment has been depreciated to a book value of €38.5 million but has been appraised at a sound value (that is, replacement cost new adjusted for the fraction of the useful life already elapsed) of €52.4 million.

A key asset being acquired by Oman Heating, albeit one not formally recognised by Euro Boiler, is the IPR&D, which pertains to activities undertaken over a period of several years aimed at making significant process and product improvements which would enhance Euro Boiler's market position and will be captured by the new combined operations. It has been determined that duplicating the benefits of this ongoing R&D work would cost Oman Heating €8.6 million. The strong motivation to make this acquisition, and to pay a substantial premium over book value, is based on Euro Boiler's customer list and its IPR&D. Euro Boiler has previously expensed all R&D costs incurred, as required under IFRS, since it conservatively believed that these costs were in the nature of research, rather than development.

Euro Boiler had guaranteed a €1.5 million bank debt of a former affiliated entity, but this was an "off-the-books" event since guarantees issued between corporations under common control were commonly deemed exempt from recognition. The actual contingent obligation has been appraised as having a fair value (considering both the amount and likelihood of having to honour the commitment) of €75,000.

Thus, although Euro Boiler's statement of financial position reflects a shareholders' deficit (including share capital issued and outstanding, and accumulated deficit) of €9.1 million, the value of the acquisition, including the IPR&D, is much higher. The preliminary computation of goodwill is as follows:

Consideration transferred		€32,000,000
Net working capital	(€2,950,000)	
Property, plant and equipment	€52,400,000	
Customer list	€1,400,000	
Patents	€3,900,000	
IPR&D	€8,600,000	

Guarantee of indebtedness of others	(€75,000)	
Long-term debt	(€41,500,000)	€21,775,000
Goodwill		€10,225,000

Under IFRS 3, the fair value allocated to IPR&D must be expensed unless it is separately identifiable, is a resource that is controlled, is a probable source of future economic benefits and has a reliably measurable fair value. Oman Heating determines that €1,800,000 of the cost of IPR&D meets all these criteria and supports capitalisation. All other assets and liabilities are recorded by Oman Heating at the allocated fair values, with the excess consideration transferred being assigned to goodwill. The entry to record the acquisition (for preparation of consolidated financial statements, for example) is as follows:

Cash	€1,000,000	
Accounts receivable, net	€12,000,000	
Inventory	€9,750,000	
Other current assets	€500,000	
Property, plant and equipment	€52,400,000	
Customer list	€1,400,000	
Patents	€3,900,000	
Development costs capitalised	€1,800,000	
R&D expense	€6,800,000	
Goodwill	€10,225,000	
Current liabilities		€26,200,000
Guarantee of indebtedness of others		€75,000
Long-term debt		€41,500,000
Notes payable to former shareholders		€17,000,000
Cash		€15,000,000

Note that, while the foregoing example is for a share acquisition, an asset and liability acquisition would be accounted for in the exact same manner. Also, since the debt is recorded at fair value, which will often differ from face (maturity) value, the differential (premium or discount) must be amortised using the effective yield method from acquisition date to the maturity date of the debt, and thus there will be differences between actual payments of interest and the amounts recognised in profit or loss as interest expense. Finally, note that property, plant and equipment is recorded "net"—that is, the allocated fair value becomes the "cost" of these assets; accumulated depreciation previously recorded in the accounting records of the acquired entity does not carry forward to the post-acquisition financial statements of the consolidated entity.

Deferred income tax—fair value adjustments

IFRS 3 will require an acquirer to account for temporary differences between the fair value of the acquiree's assets and liabilities and their tax base. The fair value of an acquiree's net assets are often higher than the depreciated historic cost adopted in the acquiree's own financial statements, and additional liability is recorded in the consolidated financial statements, increasing goodwill. The deferred tax asset or liability should be calculated using tax rates enacted or substantially enacted at the end of the reporting period.

Example of deferred tax

Continuing with the previous example, the tax rate which is substantially enacted at the end of Oman Holding Corp.'s reporting period is 20%. The deferred tax liability which will be recognised on temporary differences as part of the business combination is:

	Book value	Fair value	Difference
	€	€	€
Cash	1,000,000	1,000,000	
Accounts receivable, net	12,200,000	12,000,000	(200,000)
Inventory	8,500,000	9,750,000	1,250,000
Other current assets	500,000	500,000	
Property, plant and equipment	38,500,000	52,400,000	13,900,000
Customer list	–	1,400,000	1,400,000
Patents	2,400,000	3,900,000	1,500,000
Development costs capitalised	–	1,800,000	1,800,000
R&D expense	–	–	–
Current liabilities	(26,200,000)	(26,200,000)	–
Guarantee of indebtedness of others	–	(75,000)	(75,000)
Long-term debt	(46,000,000)	(41,500,000)	4,500,000
	(9,100,000)	14,975,000	24,075 000
Deferred tax liability @ 20%			€4,815,000

The R&D expense is assumed to be a permanent difference.

The entry to record the acquisition will be:

Cash	€1,000,000	
Accounts receivable, net	€12,000,000	
Inventory	€9,750,000	
Other current assets	€500,000	
Property, plant and equipment	€52,400,000	
Customer list	€1,400,000	
Patents	€3,900,000	
Development costs capitalised	€1,800,000	
R&D expense	€6,800,000	
Goodwill	€15,040,000	
Current liabilities		€26,200,000
Guarantee of indebtedness of others		€75,000
Long-term debt		€41,500,000
Deferred tax liability		€4,815,000
Notes payable to former shareholders		€17,000,000
Cash		€15,000,000

Impairment of goodwill

Assume that an entity acquires another entity and that goodwill arises from this acquisition. Also assume that, for purposes of impairment, it is determined that the acquired business comprises seven discrete cash-generating units. A cash-generating unit is the smallest level of identifiable group of assets that generates cash inflows that are largely independent of the cash inflows from other assets or groups of assets (not larger than an operating segment). The goodwill recorded on the acquisition must be allocated to some or all of those seven cash-generating units. If it is the case that the goodwill is associated with only some of the seven cash-generating units, the goodwill recognised in the statement of financial position should be allocated to only those assets or groups of assets.

Three steps are required for goodwill impairment testing. First, the recoverable amount of a *cash-generating unit* which is the higher of the cash-generating unit's fair value less costs to sell (net selling price) and its value in use, which is the present value of the estimated future cash flows expected to be derived from the cash-generating unit, must be determined. Secondly, the recoverable amount of the cash-generating unit is compared to its carrying value. If the recoverable value exceeds the carrying value, then there is no goodwill impairment, and the third testing step is not required.

IAS 36 requires that if the recoverable amount is less than the carrying value, an impairment write-down must be made. In this third step in goodwill impairment testing, the recoverable value of the cash-generating unit as of the testing date is allocated to its assets (including intangible assets) and liabilities, with the remainder (if any) being assigned to goodwill. If the amount of goodwill resulting from this calculation is less than the carrying amount of goodwill, then the difference is impaired goodwill and must be charged to expense in the current period.

An impairment loss is first absorbed by goodwill, and only when goodwill has been eliminated entirely is any further impairment loss credited to other assets in the group (on a pro rata basis, unless it is possible to measure the recoverable amounts of the individual assets). This is perhaps somewhat arbitrary, but it is also logical, since the excess earnings power represented by goodwill must be deemed to have been lost if the recoverable amount of the cash-generating unit is less than its carrying amount. It is also a conservative approach and will diminish or eliminate the display of that often misunderstood and always suspiciously viewed asset, goodwill, before the carrying values of identifiable intangible and tangible assets are adjusted.

Reversal of previously recognised impairment of goodwill

In general, under IFRS, reversal of an impairment identified with a cash-generating unit is permitted. However, due to the special character of this asset, IAS 36 has imposed a requirement that reversals may not be recognised for previous write-downs in goodwill. Thus, a later recovery in the value of the cash-generating unit will be allocated to assets other than goodwill. (The adjustments to those assets cannot be for amounts greater than would be needed to restore them to the carrying amounts at which they would be currently stated had the earlier impairment not been recognised—i.e., at the former carrying values less the depreciation that would have been recorded during the intervening period.)

IFRIC 10, *Interim Financial Reporting and Impairment*, addresses conflicts between the requirements of IAS 34, *Interim Financial Reporting*, and those in other standards on the recognition and reversal in the financial statements of impairment losses on goodwill and certain financial assets. In conformity with IFRIC 10, any impairment losses recognised in an interim financial statement must not be reversed in subsequent interim or annual financial statements.

Gain from a bargain purchase

In certain business combinations, the consideration transferred is less than the fair value of the net assets acquired. These are often identified as being "bargain purchase" transactions. This difference has traditionally (if illogically) been referred to as "negative goodwill." IFRS 3 suggests that, since arm's-length business acquisition transactions will usually favour neither party, the likelihood of the acquirer obtaining a bargain is considered remote. According to this standard, apparent instances of bargain purchases giving rise to a gain from a bargain purchase are more often the result of a measurement error (i.e., where the fair values assigned to assets and liabilities were incorrect to some extent) or of a failure to recognise a contingent or actual liability (such as for employee severance payments). However, a gain from a bargain purchase can also derive from the risk of future losses, recognised by both parties and incorporated into the transaction price. (One such example was the case of the sale by BMW of its Rover car division to a consortium for €1. It did indeed suffer subsequent losses and eventually failed.)

IFRS 3 requires that, before a gain from a bargain purchase is recognised, the allocation of fair values is to be revisited, and that all liabilities—including contingencies—are to be reviewed; the consolidation transferred is reviewed and for a business combination achieved in stages, the acquirer's previously held interest in the acquiree is also revisited. After this is completed, if indeed the fair values of identifiable assets acquired net of all liabilities assumed exceeds the total consideration transferred, then a gain from a bargain purchase will be acknowledged. The accounting treatment of negative goodwill has passed through a number of evolutionary stages beginning with the original IAS 22, which was later twice revised with major changes to the prescribed accounting treatment of negative goodwill.

Under IFRS 3, a gain from a bargain purchase is taken immediately into profit. Essentially, this is regarded, for financial reporting purposes, as a gain realised upon the acquisition transaction and accounted for accordingly.

Example of acquisition transaction—gain from a bargain purchase

Hoegedorn Corp. acquires, on March 4, 20XX, all of the outstanding ordinary shares of Gemutlicheit Co. in exchange for cash of €800,000. A formerly successful entity, Gemutlicheit had recently suffered from declining sales and demands for repayment of its outstanding bank debt, which were threatening its continued existence. Hoegedorn management perceived an opportunity to make a favourable purchase of a company operating in a related line of business, and accordingly made this modest offer, which was accepted by the shareholders of Gemutlicheit, the acquiree. Gemutlicheit's statement of financial position at the date of acquisition is as follows, with both book and fair values indicated (in thousands of €):

	Book value	*Fair value*		*Book value*	*Fair value*
	€	€		€	€
Cash	800	800	Current liabilities	2,875	2,875
Accounts receivable, net	3,600	3,400	Long-term debt	11,155	11,155
Inventory	1,850	1,800			
Property, plant and equipment	6,800	7,200			
Net operating loss carryforwards	=	2,400	Shareholders' equity (deficit)	(980)	1,570
Totals	**€13,050**	**€15,600**		**€13,050**	**€15,600**

Gemutlicheit had provided a valuation allowance for the deferred income tax asset attributable to the net operating loss carryforward tax benefit, since recurring and increasing losses made it probable that these benefits would not be realised, consistent with IFRS (IAS 12). Hoegedorn Corp., which is highly profitable, is in the same line of business, and intends to continue Gemutlicheit's operation, expects to be able to realise these benefits and therefore will have no valuation allowance against this asset.

Thus, although Gemutlicheit's statement of financial position reflects a shareholders' deficit (including share capital and accumulated deficit in retained earnings) of €980,000, the value of the acquisition is much higher, and furthermore the acquirer is able to negotiate a bargain purchase. The preliminary computation of the gain on a bargain purchase is as follows:

Net working capital	€3,125,000	
Property, plant and equipment	€7,200,000	
Net operating loss carryforward	€2,400,000	
Long-term debt	(€11,155,000)	€1,570,000
Consideration transferred		€800,000
Gain from bargain purchase		€770,000

IFRS 3 requires that a gain from a bargain purchase be taken into profit or loss immediately, after first verifying that all acquired or assumed liabilities, including contingencies, have been fully accounted for, and that assets acquired were not overstated. In the present example, these matters were reviewed, and the amounts shown above were fully supported.

The entry to record the acquisition is therefore as follows:

Cash	€800,000	
Accounts receivable, net	€3,400,000	
Inventory	€1,800,000	
Property, plant and equipment	€7,200,000	
Deferred income tax asset	€2,400,000	
Current liabilities		€2,875,000
Long-term debt		€11,155,000
Cash		€800,000
Gain from bargain purchase		€770,000

Business combinations achieved in stages (step acquisitions)

A step acquisition is a business combination in which the acquirer held an equity interest in the acquiree prior to the acquisition date on which it obtained control. In some instances, control over another entity is not achieved in a single transaction, but rather after a series of transactions. For example, one entity may acquire a 25% interest in another entity, followed by another 20% some time later, and then followed by another 10% at yet a later date. The last step gives the acquirer a 55% interest and, thus, control. The accounting issue is to determine at what point in time the business combination took place and how to measure the acquisition.

IFRS 3 requires the acquirer to remeasure its previous holdings of the acquiree's equity at acquisition-date fair value. Any gain or loss on remeasurement is recognised in profit or loss on that date.

Example of a step acquisition

On December 31, 20XX-1, Konin Corporation (KC) owns 5% of the 30,000 outstanding voting common shares of Henan Corporation (HC). On KC's December 31, 20XX-1 statement of financial position, it classified its investment in HC as fair value through other comprehensive income. On March 31, 20XX, KC acquired additional equity shares in HC sufficient to provide KC with a controlling interest in HC and, thus, become HC's parent company.

The following table summarises KC's initial holdings in HC, the subsequent increase in those holdings and the computation of the gain on remeasurement at the acquisition date of March 31, 20XX:

			Per share		*Aggregate investment*		*Unrealised appreciation included in accumulated other comprehensive income*
Date	*# of shares*	*Percent interest*	*Cost*	*Fair value*	*Cost*	*Fair value*	
12/31/20XX-1	1,500	5%	€10	€16	€$15,000	€24,000	**€9,000**
3/31/20XX	21,000	70%	€20	€20	€420,000	€420,000	
	22,500	**75%**					

Computation of gain (loss) on remeasurement at acquisition date:

Fair value per share on 3/31/20XX	€20
Number of pre-acquisition shares	× 1,500
Aggregate fair value of pre-acquisition shares on 3/31/20XX	€30,000
Carrying amount of pre-acquisition shares on 3/31/20XX	€24,000
Appreciation attributable to the 1st quarter of 20XX	€6,000
Pre-20XX appreciation reclassified from accumulated OCI	€9,000
Gain on remeasurement of HC stock on 3/31/20XX	€15,000

If the acquirer had previously recognised changes in the carrying value of its equity interest in the acquiree in other comprehensive income (e.g., because the investment was classified as fair value with changes in fair value classified through other comprehensive income), that amount is to be reclassified and included in the computation of the acquisition date gain or loss from remeasurement.

Footnote Disclosure: Acquisitions

IFRS 3 provides an illustrative example of footnote disclosures about acquisitions which an acquirer should present in the financial statements.

Example of a footnote acquisition

Footnote XX: **Acquisitions.** On March 30, 20XX-1, Konin Corporation (KC) acquired 10% of the outstanding ordinary shares of Henan Corporation (HC). On September 30, 20XX, KC acquired 65% of the outstanding ordinary shares of HC and obtained control of HC. HC is the provider of electrical distribution products and as a result of the acquisition, KC is expected to be the leading provider of energy sufficiency solutions in Central and Eastern Europe.

The goodwill of €2,500 arising from the acquisition consists largely of the synergies and economies of scale expected from combining the operations of KC and HC. None of the goodwill recognised is expected to be deductible for income tax purposes.

The following information summarises the consideration paid for HC and the fair values of the assets acquired and liabilities assumed, recognised at the acquisition date, as well as the acquisition date fair value of the non-controlling interest in HC.

Consideration (at September 30, 20XX)

	€
Cash	5,000
Equity instruments (65,000 ordinary shares of KC)	6,500
Contingent consideration	1,000
Total consideration transferred	12,500
Fair value of KC's equity interest in HC held before the business combination	2,000
Total value of investment	14,500
Acquisition-related costs (included in selling, general and administrative expenses in KC's statement of comprehensive income for the year ended December 31, 20XX)	1,100

Recognised amounts of identifiable assets acquired and liabilities assumed

	€
Financial assets	4,000
Inventory	3,000
Property, plant and equipment	9,000
Identifiable intangible assets	2,500
Total assets	18,500
Financial liabilities	(3,500)
Contingent liability	(1,000)
Total identifiable net assets	14,000
Non-controlling interest in HC	(3,500)
Goodwill	4,000
Total value of investment	14,500

The fair value of the 65,000 ordinary shares issued as part of the consideration paid for HC (€6,500) was determined on the basis of the acquisition-date closing market price of KC's ordinary shares.

The contingent consideration arrangement requires KC to pay the former owners of HC 4% of the revenues of HC in excess of €25,000 for 20XX, up to a maximum amount of €2,000 (undiscounted). The potential undiscounted amount of all future payments that KC could be required to make under the contingent consideration arrangement is between €0 and €2,000. The fair value of the contingent consideration arrangement (€1,000) was estimated by applying the income approach. The fair value estimates are based on an assumed discount rate range of 15–20% and assumed probability-adjusted revenues in HC of €20,000–€30,000. As of December 31, 20XX, the amount recognised for the contingent consideration and the range of outcomes and assumptions used to develop the estimates have not changed.

The fair value of the financial assets acquired includes receivables from industrial control services provided to a new customer. The gross amount due under the contracts is €2,100 of which €250 is expected to be uncollectible.

The fair value of the acquired identifiable intangible assets (licences) of €2,500 is based on a receipt of the final valuations for those assets.

A contingent liability of €1,000 has been recognised for expected future services to satisfy warranty claims on industrial control products sold by HC during the last four years. It is expected that the majority of this expenditure will be incurred in 20XX+1 and that all will be incurred by the end of 20XX+2. The estimate of potential undiscounted amount of all future payments that HC could be required to make under the warranty claims is between €750 and €1,250. As of December 31, 20XX, there has been no change since September 30, 20XX, in the amount estimated for the liability or any change in the range of outcomes or assumptions used to develop the estimates.

The fair value of the non-controlling interest in HC, an unlisted company, was estimated by applying a market approach and an income approach. The fair value estimates are based on:

1. An assumed discount rate range of 15–20%;
2. An assumed terminal value based on a range of terminal EBITDA multiples between three and five times (or, if appropriate, based on long-term sustainable growth rates ranging from 3 to 6%);
3. Assumed financial multiples of companies deemed to be similar to HC; and
4. Assumed adjustments because of the lack of control or lack of marketability that market participants would consider when estimating the fair value of the non-controlling interest in HC.

KC recognised a gain of €500 as a result of measuring at fair value its 15% equity interest in HC held before the business combination. The gain is included in other income in KC's statement of comprehensive income for the year ending December 31, 20XX.

The revenue included in the consolidated statement of comprehensive income since September 30, 20XX, contributed by HC was €5,550 and profit of €1,100 was generated over the same period. HC reported revenue of €20,200 and profit of €3,910 for 20XX.

EXAMPLES OF FINANCIAL STATEMENT DISCLOSURES

Exemplum Reporting PLC
Financial Statements
For the Year Ended December 31, 20XX

25 Business combinations
25.1 Subsidiaries acquired

20XX	Principal activity	Date of acquisition	Proportion of shares acquired	Consideration transferred
Company A	Manufacturing	February 1, 20XX	100%	X
Company B	Distribution	April 1, 20XX	100%	X
				X

Company A was acquired to expand the production capabilities of the group to enable it to supply to rapidly expanding markets. The acquisition of Company B has significantly improved the distribution network of the group in France and its neighbouring countries.

Goodwill represents the value of the synergies arising from the economies of scale achievable in the enlarged group. These synergistic benefits were the primary reason for entering into the business combinations. The total amount of goodwill that is expected to be deductible for tax purposes is €X. The amount of the new subsidiaries' profits or losses since the acquisition date included in the group profit or loss for the period is €X.

25.2 Consideration transferred

	Company A	Company B
	€	€
Cash	X	X
Deferred consideration (payable in cash)	X	X
Contingent consideration arrangement (a)	X	X
Equity issued	X	X
	X	X

(a) The agreement requires the group to pay the vendors an additional amount of €XX, if the profit of Company A exceeds €X in the year following acquisition. The average profit for the last three years amounted to €X. The directors are of the opinion that the profit will exceed the target set.

Other costs relating to the acquisition of the subsidiaries have not been included in the consideration and have been recognised as an expense. This expense is included in administration expenses.

25.3 Assets acquired and liabilities assumed at the date of acquisition

	Company A	Company B
	€	€
Current assets	X	X
Cash and cash equivalents	X	X
Trade and other receivables	X	X
Inventories	X	X
Plant and equipment	X	X
Trade and other payables	X	X
Contingent liabilities	X	X
	X	X

The initial accounting for the acquisition of Company B has only been provisionally determined at the end of the reporting period. At the date of finalisation of these financial statements, the necessary market valuations and other calculations had not been finalised and they have therefore only been provisionally determined based on the directors' best estimates. IFRS 3 B67(a)

25.4 Non-controlling interest

- The non-controlling interests of Company A and Company B at the date of acquisition were measured at the fair value of these interests. This fair value was estimated by applying a discounted income approach, and amounted to €X. Key assumptions made and inputs used were: IFRS 3 B64(0)

    - discount rate 14%;
    - sustainable growth rates 4%.

25.5 Impact of acquisitions on the results of the group

The contribution to net profit of the group was €X by Company A and €X by Company B, respectively. Group revenue includes €X from the operations of Company A and €X from Company B.	IFRS 3 B64
If these businesses were acquired at the beginning of the reporting period, group revenue would have been €X, and profit for the year from continuing operations would have been €X. The directors of the group consider these results to be representative of the performance of the combined group, annualised, and provide a reference point for comparison against periods in the future.	IFRS 3 p61

The abovementioned "annualised" contributions were calculated from actual results of the companies and adjusted for the following:

- Depreciation of plant and equipment acquired based on the fair values determined rather than the carrying amounts recognised in the pre-acquisition financial statements; and
- Borrowing costs were adjusted to align with group credit ratings and debt/equity position of the group after the business combination.

FUTURE DEVELOPMENTS

- A discussion paper is expected to be released during the first half of 2020 on Accounting for Business Combinations under Common Control. These transactions are outside the scope of IFRS 3 and differences in practice have emerged.

US GAAP COMPARISON

IFRS and US GAAP contain similar requirements for accounting for business combinations. However, IFRS and US GAAP differ with respect to certain business combination recognition and measurement requirements.

Combinations of entities under common control. US GAAP requires that such combinations be accounted for under a carryover basis. IFRS does not provide guidance.

Contingencies. If the fair value of a contingent liability cannot be determined reliably, US GAAP requires that the contingency is recognised as an acquisition per ASC 450, *Contingencies*; IFRS requires that the contingency not be recognised. Also, IFRS does not permit the recognition of contingent assets acquired in a business combination, whereas US GAAP requires recognition of contingent assets acquired at fair value.

Definition of a business. Prior to the adoption of ASU 2017-01, *Clarifying the Definition of a Business*, IFRS and US GAAP were similar. US GAAP when adopted for public businesses for 2018 and 2019 for all other entities has a focus on revenue-generating activities to align with the description of inputs and outputs in ASC 606, *Revenue Recognition*. There is a new concept of a threshold test where, if the threshold is not met, it is not a business; there is no such test in IFRS. The threshold test has to do with an acquired entity measurement which means that if a single or group of assets represents substantially all of "the gross assets acquired" then it is not a business. The concept of "substantially all" is not in IFRS.

Goodwill. Like IFRS, under US GAAP goodwill is recognised only upon the acquisition of a business and is not amortised but tested annually for impairment. Because goodwill is pushed down under IFRS to an operating segment or one level below (cash-generating units are not recognised under US GAAP), the grouping of cash flows used to test for impairment is almost always larger for US GAAP.

Under US GAAP, private companies may make an accounting policy election to apply an accounting alternative for goodwill amortisation and impairment testing. The accounting alternative applies to recognised goodwill arising from business combinations as discussed and from the application of the equity method of accounting, as well as excess reorganisation value recognised by entities that adopt fresh-start reporting in a reorganisation.

Recent ASUs address changes such as leases which are to be considered assets and liabilities where before non-capital (operating) leases were left out of the calculation and takes effect concurrently with the adoption of the new lease standard. Also, private companies and not-for-profit entities are able to amortise goodwill over a period not to exceed 10 years which is currently effective upon issuance of ASU 2019-06 Intangibles-Goodwill and Other (Topic 350), Business Combinations (Topic 805), and Not-for-Profit Entities (Topic 958).

Measurement period adjustments. US GAAP requires measurement period adjustments to be made in the current reporting period rather than by adjusting the comparatives (ASC 805-25-10-17).

Non-controlling interests. US GAAP requires that non-controlling interests be measured at fair value. IFRS give entities the option, on a transaction-by-transaction basis, to measure non-controlling interests at fair value or at the non-controlling interest's proportionate share of the fair value of the identifiable net assets, exclusive of goodwill.

Pushdown accounting. When an acquirer obtains control of an entity, the acquired entity may irrevocably elect the application of pushdown accounting in its own (separate) financial statements.

Additionally, ASU 2016-13 Financial Instruments – Credit Losses (Topic) 360 removes the higher threshold of "probable" incurred loss impairment and allows for the recording of credit losses in an allowance method using developing losses using forecasted developments. Purchased credit deteriorated (PCD) assets the credit loss is added to the purchase price initially and then carried at amortised cost.

16 SHAREHOLDERS' EQUITY

INTRODUCTION

The *Framework* defines equity as the residual interest in the assets of an entity after deducting all its liabilities. Shareholders' equity is comprised of all capital contributed to the entity (including share premium, also referred to as capital paid-in in excess of par value) plus retained earnings (which represents the entity's cumulative earnings, less all distributions that have been made therefrom).

IAS 1 suggests that shareholders' interests be categorised into three broad subdivisions: issued share capital, retained earnings (accumulated profits or losses) and other components of equity (reserves). Depending on jurisdiction, issued share capital may need to be further categorised as par or stated capital and as additional contributed capital/share premium. This standard also sets forth requirements for disclosures about the details of share capital for corporations and the various capital accounts of other types of entities, such as partnerships.

Equity represents an interest in the net assets (i.e., assets less liabilities) of the entity. It is, however, not a claim on those assets in the sense that liabilities are. Upon the liquidation of the business, an obligation arises for the entity to distribute any remaining assets to the shareholders, but only after all liabilities are first settled.

Earnings are not generated by transactions in an entity's own equity (for example, by the issuance, reacquisition or reissuance of its common or preferred shares). Depending on the laws of the jurisdiction of incorporation, distributions to shareholders may be subject to various limitations, such as to the amount of retained (accounting basis) earnings. In other cases, limitations may be based on values not presented in the financial statements, such as the future liquidity and net solvency of the entity as determined on a market value basis; in such instances, IFRS-based financial statements will not provide information needed for making such determination.

A major objective of the accounting for shareholders' equity is the adequate disclosure of the sources from which the capital was derived. For this reason, a number of different contributed capital accounts may be presented in the statement of financial position. The rights of each class of shareholder must also be disclosed. Where shares are reserved for future issuance, such as under the terms of share option plans, this fact must also be made known. Share option plans will be addressed within Chapter 17.

A special situation arises in connection with co-operatives, which are member-owned organisations having capital which exhibits certain characteristics of debt, since it is not permanent in nature. IFRIC 2 addresses the accounting for members' shares in co-operatives. It holds that where a member of a co-operative has a contractual right to request redemption of shares, this does not necessarily require the shares to be classified as a liability. Members' shares are to be classified as equity if the entity has an unconditional right to refuse redemption, or if national law prohibits redemption. On the other hand, if the law prohibits redemption only conditionally (for example, if minimum capital requirements are not maintained), this does not alter the general rule that co-operative shares are to be deemed a liability, not equity, of the entity.

	Sources of IFRS	
IFRS 2	*IAS* 1, 8, 32	*IFRIC* 2, 17

DEFINITIONS OF TERMS

Equity instrument. A contract that evidences a residual interest in the assets of an entity after deducting all of its liabilities.

Equity instrument granted. The right (conditional or unconditional) to an equity instrument of the entity conferred by the entity on another party, under a share-based payment arrangement.

Equity-settled share-based payment transaction. A share-based payment transaction in which the entity receives goods or services:

1. As consideration for its own equity instruments (including shares or share options); or
2. Where it has no obligation to settle the transaction with the supplier in cash or other assets.

Fair value. The price that would be received to sell an asset or paid to transfer a liability in an orderly transaction between market participants at the measurement date.

Measurement date. The date at which the fair value of the equity instruments granted is measured for the purposes of IFRS 2. For transactions with employees and others providing similar services, the measurement date is the grant date. For transactions with parties other than employees (and those providing similar services), the measurement date is the date the entity obtains the goods or the counterparty renders the service.

Puttable financial instruments. Shares which the holders can "put" (sell) back to the issuing entity; that is, the holders can require that the entity repurchases the shares at defined amounts that can include fair value.

RECOGNITION AND MEASUREMENT

The IASB defines equity as the resulting net difference between total assets and total liabilities. Therefore, no recognition requirements for equity have been included in the IFRS.

The IASB has dealt primarily with presentation and disclosure requirements relating to shareholders' equity and are yet to fully address and resolve matters pertaining to the recognition and measurement of the various components of shareholders' equity. The issuance of IFRS 2, which thoroughly addresses the accounting for share-based payments, was a major step forward in this respect. It should be noted that in many jurisdictions, company law sets out specific requirements as regards accounting for equity, which may limit the application of IFRS.

IFRS do not always address all particular scenarios that may exist in practice, and in light of this, it provides in IAS 8 that in the absence of a standard, the preparer should refer to the *Framework* and thereafter to national GAAP based on the same conceptual framework. In the following discussion, therefore, certain guidance under US GAAP will be invoked where IFRS is silent regarding the accounting for specific types of transactions involving the entity's shareholders' equity. Since this is a rapidly evolving area, care should be taken to verify the current status of relevant developments.

PRESENTATION AND DISCLOSURE

Equity includes reserves such as statutory or legal reserves, general reserves and contingency reserves and revaluation surplus. IAS 1 categorises shareholders' interests into three broad subdivisions:

- Issued share capital;
- Retained earnings (accumulated profits or losses); and
- Other components of equity (reserves).

This standard also sets forth requirements for disclosures about the details of share capital for corporations and of the various capital accounts of other types of entities.

Types of Shares

Ownership interest in an entity is made up of ordinary (common) shares and, optionally, preferred (preference) shares. The ordinary shares represent the residual risk-taking ownership of the corporation after the satisfaction of all claims of creditors and senior classes of equity. It is important that the actual common ownership be accurately identified, since the computation of earnings per share (described in Chapter 27) requires that the ultimate residual ownership class be properly associated with that calculation, regardless of what the various equity classes are nominally called.

Preferred shareholders are owners who have certain rights that are superior to those of common shareholders. These rights will pertain either to the earnings or the assets of the entity. Preferences as to earnings exist when the preferred shareholders have a stipulated dividend rate (expressed either as a euro amount or as a percentage of the preferred share's par or stated value). Preferences as to assets exist when the preferred shares have a stipulated liquidation value. If a corporation were to liquidate, the preferred holders would be paid a specific amount before the ordinary shareholders would have a right to participate in any of the proceeds.

In practice, preferred shares are more likely to have preferences as to earnings than as to assets. Some classes of preferred shares may have both preferential rights, although this is rarely encountered. Preferred shares may also have the following features:

- Participation in earnings beyond the stipulated dividend rate;
- A cumulative feature, affording the preferred shareholders the protection that their dividends in arrears, if any, will be fully satisfied before the ordinary shareholders participate in any earnings distribution; and
- Convertibility or callability by the entity.

Whatever preferences exist must be disclosed adequately in the financial statements, either in the statement of financial position or in the notes.

In exchange for the preferences, the preferred shareholders' rights or privileges are limited. For instance, the right to vote may be limited to ordinary shareholders. The most important right denied to the preferred shareholders, however, is the right to participate without limitation in the earnings of the corporation. Thus, if the corporation has exceedingly large earnings for a particular period, these earnings would accrue to the benefit of the ordinary shareholders. This is true even if the preferred shares are participating (itself a fairly uncommon feature) because even participating preferred shares usually have some upper limitation placed on the degree of participation. For example, preferred shares may have a 5% cumulative dividend with a further 3% participation right, so in any one year the limit would be an 8% return to the preferred shareholders (plus, if applicable, the 5% per year prior year dividends not paid).

Occasionally, several classes of share capital will be categorised as ordinary (e.g., Class A ordinary, Class B ordinary, etc.). Since there can be only one class of shares that constitutes the true residual risk-taking equity interest in a corporation, it is clear that the other classes, even though described as ordinary shares, must in fact have some preferential status. Not uncommonly, these preferences relate to voting rights, as when a control group holds ordinary shares with "super voting" rights (e.g., 10 votes per share). The rights and responsibilities of each class of shareholder, even if described as ordinary, must be fully disclosed in the financial statements.

Presentation and Disclosures Relating to Share Capital

The number of shares authorised, issued and outstanding. It is required that a company disclose information relating to the number of shares authorised, issued and outstanding. Authorised share capital is defined as the maximum number of shares that a company is permitted to issue, according to its articles of association, its charter or its bylaws. The number of shares issued and outstanding could vary, based on the fact that a company could have acquired its own shares and is holding them as treasury shares (discussed below under reacquired shares).

Capital not yet paid in (or unpaid capital). In an initial public offering, subscribers may be asked initially to pay in only a portion of the par value, with the balance due in instalments, which are known as calls. Thus, it is possible that at the end of the reporting period a certain portion of the share capital has not yet been paid in. The amount not yet collected must be shown as a contra (i.e., a deduction) in the equity section, since that portion of the subscribed capital has yet to be issued. For example, while the gross amount of the share subscription increases capital, if the due date of the final call falls on February 7, 20XX+1, following the accounting year-end of December 31, 20XX, the amount of capital not yet paid in should be shown as a deduction from shareholders' equity. In this manner, only the net amount of capital received as of the end of the reporting period will be properly included in shareholders' equity, averting an overstatement of the entity's actual equity.

IAS 1 requires that a distinction be made between shares that have been issued and fully paid, on the one hand, and those that have been issued but not fully paid, on the other hand. The number of shares outstanding at the beginning and at the end of each period presented must also be reconciled.

Par value per share. This is also generally referred to as legal value, nominal value or face value per share. The par value of shares is specified in the corporate charter or bylaws and referred to in other documents, such as the share application and prospectus. Par value is the smallest unit of share capital that can be acquired unless the prospectus permits fractional shares (which is very unusual for commercial entities). In certain jurisdictions, it is also permitted for corporations to issue no-par shares (i.e., shares that are not given any par value). In such cases, again depending on local corporation laws, sometimes a stated value is determined by the board of directors, which is then accorded effectively the same treatment as par value. IAS 1 requires disclosure of par values or of the fact that the shares were issued without par values. If the shares do not have a par value, this must be stated.

Movements in share capital accounts during the year. This information is usually disclosed in the financial statements or the footnotes to the financial statements, generally in a tabular or statement format, although in some circumstances merely set forth in a narrative. Reporting entities must present a statement showing that changes in all the equity accounts (including issued capital, retained earnings and reserves transactions with owners in their capacity as owners) are reported in the statement of changes in equity, while all changes other than those resulting from transactions with owners are to be reported in the statement of comprehensive income. The statement of changes in equity highlights the changes during the period in the various components of shareholders' equity. It also serves the purpose of reconciling the beginning and the ending balances of shareholders' equity, as shown in the statement of financial position.

Rights, preferences and restrictions with respect to the distribution of dividends and to the repayment of capital. When there is more than one class of share capital having varying rights, adequate disclosure of the rights, preferences and restrictions attached to each such class of share capital will enhance understandability of the information provided by the financial statements.

Cumulative preference dividends in arrears. If an entity has preferred shares outstanding and does not pay cumulative dividends on the preference shares annually when due, it will be required by statute to pay such arrears in later years, before any distributions can be made on common (ordinary) shares. Although practice varies, most preference shares are cumulative in nature. Preference shares that do not have this feature are called non-cumulative preference shares.

Treasury shares. Shares that are issued but then reacquired by a company are referred to as treasury shares. The entity's ability to reacquire shares may be limited by its corporate charter or by covenants in its loan and/or preferred share agreements (for example, it may be restricted from doing so as long as bonded debt remains outstanding) or by local legislation. In those jurisdictions where company law permits the repurchase of shares, such shares, on acquisition by the company or its consolidated subsidiary, become legally available for reissue or resale without further authorisation.

Shares outstanding refers to shares other than those held as treasury shares. That is, treasury shares do not reduce the number of shares issued but affect the number of shares outstanding. It is to be noted that certain countries prohibit companies from purchasing their own shares, since to do so is considered as a reduction of share capital that can be achieved only with the express consent of the shareholders in an extraordinary general meeting, and then only under certain defined conditions.

IAS 1 requires that shares in the entity held in its treasury or by its subsidiaries be identified for each category of share capital and be deducted from contributed capital. IAS 32 states that the treasury share acquisition transaction is to be reported in the statement of changes in equity. When later resold, any difference between acquisition cost and ultimate proceeds represents a change in equity and is therefore not to be considered a gain or loss to be reported in the statement of comprehensive income. Accounting for treasury shares is discussed in further detail later in this chapter.

IAS 32 also specifies that the costs associated with equity transactions are to be accounted for as reductions of equity if the corresponding transaction was a share issuance, or as increases in the contra equity account when incurred in connection with treasury share reacquisitions. Relevant costs are limited to incremental costs directly associated with the transactions. If the issuance involves a compound instrument, the issuance costs should be associated with the liability and equity components, respectively, using a rational and consistent basis of allocation.

Shares reserved for future issuance under options and sales contracts, including the terms and amounts. Companies may issue share options that grant the holder of these options rights to a specified number of shares at a certain price. Share options have become a popular means of employee remuneration, and often the top echelon of management is offered this non-cash perquisite as a major part of their remuneration packages. The options grant the holder the right to acquire shares over a defined time horizon for a fixed price, which may equal fair value at the grant date or, less commonly, at a price lower than fair value. Granting options usually is not legal unless the entity has enough authorised but unissued shares to satisfy the holders' demands, if made, although in some instances this can be done, with management thus becoming bound to the reacquisition of enough shares in the market (or by other means) to enable it to honour these new share option commitments. If a company has shares reserved for future issuance under option plans or sales contracts, it is necessary to disclose the number of shares, including terms and amounts, so reserved. These reserved shares are not available for sale or distribution to others during the terms of the unexercised options.

IAS 32 deals with situations in which entity obligations are to be settled in cash or in equity securities, depending on the outcome of contingencies not under the issuer's control. In general, these should be classed as liabilities, unless the part that could require settlement in cash is not genuine, or settlement by cash or distribution of other assets is available only in the event of the liquidation of the issuer. If the option holder can demand cash, the obligation is a liability, not equity.

The accounting for share options, which was introduced by IFRS 2, is dealt within Chapter 17. As will be seen, it presents many intriguing and complex issues.

Presentation and Disclosures Relating to Other Equity

Capital contributed in excess of par value. This is the amount received on the issuance of shares that is the excess over the par value. It is called "additional contributed capital" in the US, while in many other jurisdictions it is referred to as "share premium." Essentially the same accounting would be required if a stated value is used in lieu of par value, where permitted.

Revaluation reserve. When a company carries property, plant and equipment or intangible assets under the revaluation model, as is permitted by IAS 16 and IAS 38 (revaluation to fair value), the difference between the cost (net of accumulated depreciation) and the fair value is recognised in other comprehensive income and accumulated in equity.

IAS 1 requires that movements of this revaluation reserve during the reporting period (year or interim period) be disclosed in the other comprehensive income section of the statement of comprehensive income. Increases in an asset's carrying value are recognised in other comprehensive income and accumulated in equity. Decreases are recognised in other comprehensive income only to the extent of any credit balance existing in the revaluation reserve in respect of that asset and additional decreases are taken to profit or loss. Also, restrictions as to any distributions of this reserve to shareholders should be disclosed. Note that in some jurisdictions the directors may be empowered to make distributions in excess of recorded book capital, and this often will require a determination of fair values.

Reserves. Reserves include capital reserves as well as revenue reserves. Also, statutory reserves and voluntary reserves are included under this category. Finally, special reserves, including contingency reserves, are included herein. The use of general reserves and statutory reserves, once common or even required under company laws in many jurisdictions, is now in decline.

Statutory reserves (or legal reserves, as they are called in some jurisdictions) are created based on the requirements of the law or the statute under which the company is incorporated. For instance, many corporate statutes in Middle Eastern countries require that companies set aside 10% of their net income for the year as a "statutory reserve," with such appropriations to continue until the balance in this reserve account equals 50% of the company's equity capital. The intent is to provide an extra "cushion" of protection to creditors, such that even significant losses incurred in later periods will not reduce the entity's actual net worth below zero, which would, were it to occur, threaten creditors' ability for repayment of liabilities.

Sometimes a company's articles, charter or bylaws may require that each year the company set aside a certain percentage of its net profit (income) by way of a contingency or general reserve. Unlike statutory or legal reserves, contingency reserves are based on the provisions of corporate bylaws. The use of general reserves is not consistent with IFRS.

The standard requires that movements in these reserves during the reporting period be disclosed, along with the nature and purpose of each reserve presented within shareholders' equity.

Retained earnings. By definition, retained earnings represent an entity's accumulated profits (or losses) less any distributions that have been made therefrom. However, based on provisions contained in IFRS, other adjustments are also made to the amount of retained earnings. IAS 8 requires the following to be shown as adjustments to retained earnings:

1. Correction of accounting errors that relate to prior periods should be reported by adjusting the opening balance of retained earnings. Comparative information should be restated, unless it is impracticable to do so.
2. The adjustment resulting from a change in accounting policy that is to be applied retrospectively should be reported as an adjustment to the opening balance of retained earnings. Comparative information should be restated unless it is impracticable to do so.

Disclosure of dividends proposed but not formally approved is required by IAS 1. Dividends declared after the end of the reporting period, but prior to the issuance of the financial statements, must be disclosed but cannot be formally recognised via a charge against retained earnings. Also, the amount of any cumulative preference dividends not recognised as charges against accumulated profits must be disclosed (i.e., arrears), either parenthetically or in the footnotes.

IAS 1 mandates that an entity should present in a statement of changes in equity the amount of total comprehensive income for the period, showing separately the total amounts attributable to owners of the parent (controlling interest) and to the non-controlling interest. Comprehensive income includes all components of what was formerly denoted as "profit or loss" and of "other recognised income and expense." The latter category will henceforth be known as "other comprehensive income." This topic is covered in more detail in a separate discussion within Chapter 5.

CLASSIFICATION BETWEEN LIABILITIES AND EQUITY

A longstanding challenge under IFRS has been to discern between instruments that are liabilities and those that truly represent permanent equity in an entity. This has been made more difficult as various hybrid instruments have been created over recent decades. IAS 32 requires that the issuer of a financial instrument should classify the instrument, or its components, as a liability or as equity, according to the substance of the contractual arrangement on initial recognition.

The standard defines a financial liability as a contractual obligation:

1. To deliver cash or another financial asset to another entity; or
2. To exchange financial instruments with another entity under conditions that are potentially unfavourable.

An equity instrument, on the other hand, has been defined by the standard as any contract that evidences a residual interest in the assets of an entity after deducting all its liabilities.

A special situation arises in connection with co-operatives, which are member-owned organisations having capital which exhibits certain characteristics of debt, since it is not permanent in nature. IFRIC 2 addresses the accounting for members' shares in co-operatives. This is further elaborated in the paragraph "Members' Shares in Co-operative Entities."

IASB also considered the special case of shares which are puttable to the entity for a proportion of the fair value of the entity. Under then-existing IFRS, when this right was held by the shareholder, redemption could be demanded, and accordingly the shares were to be classified as a liability and to be measured at fair value. This created what was viewed by many as an anomalous situation whereby a successful entity using historical cost would have a liability that increases every year and leaves the reporting entity with, potentially, no equity at all in its statement of financial position. The logic was that, since the equity in the business would not be truly permanent in nature and would represent a claim on the assets of the entity, it would not be properly displayed as a liability—although clearly this must be adequately explained to users of the financial statements.

In responding to the foregoing concern, the IASB issued the Amendment to IAS 32, "Financial Instruments: Presentation," and IAS 1, "Presentation of Financial Statements, Puttable Financial Instruments and Obligations Arising on Liquidation," which requires that financial instruments that are puttable at fair value, as well as obligations to deliver to another entity a pro rata share of the net assets of the entity upon its liquidation, should be classified as equity. Under prior practice these instruments were classified as financial liabilities.

Puttable Shares

A puttable financial instrument includes a contractual obligation for the issuer to repurchase or redeem that instrument for cash or another financial asset on exercise of the put. Certain puttable shares, which were classified as liabilities in the statement of financial position under a previous version of IAS 32, are now required to be presented as equity if strict conditions are met. The purpose is to avoid anomalous results when residual equity interests, which would be entitled to a pro rata share of the entity's net assets upon liquidation, are puttable throughout the life of the entity at fair value.

The conditions that must be met should limit the application of this exception to the general and fundamental rule that instruments that obligate the entity to the payment of cash must be reported as liabilities. The conditions that must be met which allow the puttable shares to be classified as an equity instrument are:

- The instruments' holders are entitled to their pro rata share of the entity's net assets upon the liquidation of the entity.
- The instrument is in the class of instruments that is most subordinate (i.e., is among the residual equity interests in the entity) and all instruments in that class have identical features.
- The instrument has no other features that would require classification as a liability.
- The total expected cash flows attributable to the instrument, over its life, are based substantially on profit or loss, or changes in recognised net assets, or changes in the fair value of recognised or unrecognised net assets.
- There must be no other instruments outstanding that have equivalent terms that would effectively restrict or fix the residual returns to these instrument holders.

This results in equity classification of puttable shares having the foregoing characteristics, whether the shares are puttable throughout the instrument's life at fair value or only upon liquidation. Puttable instruments not meeting the criteria must be presented as liabilities.

IAS 1 requires the following expanded disclosures in circumstances when puttable instruments are included in equity. These disclosures include:

- Summary quantitative data about the amount classified as equity;
- The entity's objectives, policies and processes for managing the obligation to repurchase or redeem such instruments, including changes therein;
- The expected cash outflow on redemption or repurchase; and
- Information on the means of determining such cash outflows.

Compound Financial Instruments

Increasingly, entities issue financial instruments that exhibit attributes of both equity and liabilities. IAS 32 stipulates that an entity that issues such financial instruments, which are technically known as compound instruments, should classify the component parts of the financial instrument separately as equity or liability as appropriate. (For a detailed discussion on financial instruments, refer to Chapter 24.) In terms of IAS 32, the full fair value of the liability component(s) must be reported as liabilities, and only the residual value, at issuance, should be included as equity.

SHARE ISSUANCES AND RELATED MATTERS

Additional Guidance Relative to Share Issuances and Related Matters

IFRS provides only minimal guidance regarding the actual accounting for share-based transactions, including the issuance of shares of various classes of equity instruments. In the following paragraphs suggestions are made concerning the accounting for such transactions, which are within the spirit of IFRS, although largely drawn from other authoritative sources. This is done to provide guidance which conforms to the requirements under IAS 8 (hierarchy of professional standards), and to illustrate a wide array of actual transactions that often need to be accounted for.

Accounting for the issuance of shares

The accounting for the sale of shares by a corporation depends on whether the share capital has a par or stated value. If there is a par or stated value, the amount of the proceeds representing the aggregate par or stated value is credited to the ordinary or preferred share capital account. The aggregate par or stated value is generally defined as legal capital not subject to distribution to shareholders. Proceeds in excess of par or stated value are credited to an additional contributed capital account or share premium. The additional contributed capital represents the amount in excess of the legal capital that may, under certain defined conditions, be distributed to shareholders. A corporation selling shares below par value credits the share capital account for the par value and debits an offsetting discount account for the difference between par value and the amount actually received.

If there is a discount on the original issue of share capital, it serves to notify the actual and potential creditors of the contingent liability of those investors. As a practical matter, corporations avoided this problem by reducing par values to an arbitrarily low amount. This reduction in par eliminated the chance that shares would be sold for amounts below par. Where corporation laws make no distinction between par value and amounts in excess of par, the entire proceeds from the sale of shares may be credited to the ordinary share capital account without distinction between the share capital and the additional contributed capital accounts. The following entries illustrate these concepts:

Facts:	A corporation sells 100,000 shares of €5 par ordinary share for €8 per share cash		
	Cash	€800,000	
	Ordinary share capital		€500,000
	Additional contributed capital/share premium		300,000
Facts:	A corporation sells 100,000 shares of no-par ordinary share for €8 per share cash		
	Cash	€800,000	
	Ordinary share capital		€800,000

Preferred shares will often be assigned a par value because in many cases the preferential dividend rate is defined as a percentage of par value (e.g., 5%, €25 par value preferred share will have a required annual dividend of €1.25). The dividend can also be defined as a euro amount per year, thereby obviating the need for par values.

Share capital issued for services

If the shares in a corporation are issued in exchange for services or property rather than for cash, the transaction should be reflected at the fair value of the property or services received. If this information is not readily available, the transaction should be recorded at the fair value of the shares that were issued. Where necessary, appraisals should be obtained to properly reflect the transaction. As a final resort, a valuation by the board of directors of the shares issued can be utilised. Shares issued to employees as compensation for services rendered should be accounted for at the fair value of the shares issued. (See discussion of IFRS 2 within Chapter 17.)

Occasionally, particularly for start-up operations having limited working capital, the controlling owners may directly compensate certain vendors or employees. If shares are given by a major shareholder directly to an employee for services performed for the entity, this exchange should be accounted for as a capital contribution to the company by the major shareholder and as compensation expense incurred by the company. Only when accounted for in this manner will there be conformity with the general principle that all costs incurred by an entity, including compensation, should be reflected in its financial statements.

Issuance of share units

In certain instances, ordinary and preferred shares may be issued to investors as a unit (e.g., a unit of one share of preferred and two ordinary shares can be sold as a package). Where both of the classes of shares are publicly traded, the proceeds from a unit offering should be allocated in proportion to the relative market values of the securities. If only one of the securities is publicly traded, the proceeds should be allocated to the one that is publicly traded based on its known market value. Any excess is allocated to the other. Where the market value of neither security is known, appraisal information might be used. The imputed fair value of one class of security, particularly the preferred shares, can be based on the stipulated dividend rate. In this case, the amount of proceeds remaining after the imputing of a value of the preferred shares would be allocated to the ordinary shares.

The foregoing procedures would also apply if a unit offering were made of an equity and a non-equity security such as convertible debentures, or of shares and rights to purchase additional shares for a fixed time period.

Share subscriptions

Occasionally, particularly in the case of a newly organised corporation, a contract is entered into between the corporation and prospective investors, whereby the latter agree to purchase specified numbers of shares to be paid for over some instalment period. These share subscriptions are not the same as actual share issuances, and the accounting differs accordingly. In some cases, laws of the jurisdiction of incorporation will govern how subscriptions have to be accounted for (for example, when pro rata voting rights and dividend rights accompany partially paid subscriptions).

The amount of share subscriptions receivable by a corporation is sometimes treated as an asset in the statement of financial position and is categorised as current or non-current in accordance with the terms of payment. However, most subscriptions receivable are shown as a reduction of shareholders' equity in the same manner as treasury shares. Since subscribed shares do not have the rights and responsibilities of actual outstanding shares, the credit is made to a share subscribed account instead of to the share capital accounts.

If the ordinary shares have par or stated value, the ordinary shares subscribed account is credited for the aggregate par or stated value of the shares subscribed. The excess over this amount is credited to additional contributed capital or share premium. No distinction is made between additional contributed capital relating to shares already issued and shares subscribed for. This treatment follows from the distinction between legal capital and additional contributed capital. Where there is no par or stated value, the entire amount of the ordinary shares subscribed is credited to the shares subscribed account.

As the amount due from the prospective shareholders is collected, the share subscriptions receivable account is credited, and the proceeds are debited to the cash account. Actual issuance of the shares, however, must await the complete payment of the share subscription. Accordingly, the debit to ordinary shares subscribed is not made until the subscribed shares are fully paid for and the shares are issued.

The following journal entries illustrate these concepts:

1. 10,000 preferred shares of €50 par are subscribed at a price of €65 each; a 10% down payment is received.

Cash	€65,000	
Share subscriptions receivable	585,000	
Preferred share subscribed		€500,000
Additional contributed capital/share premium		150,000

2. 2,000 shares of no-par ordinary shares are subscribed at a price of €85 each, with one-half received in cash.

Cash	€85,000	
Share subscriptions receivable	85,000	
Ordinary shares subscribed		€170,000

3. All preferred subscriptions are paid, and one-half of the remaining ordinary subscriptions are collected in full and subscribed shares are issued.

Cash [€585,000 + (€85,000 × 0.50)]	€627,500	
Shares subscriptions receivable		€627,500
Preferred shares subscribed	500,000	
Preferred shares issued		500,000
Ordinary shares subscribed	127,500	
Ordinary shares issued (€170,000 × 0.75)		127,500

When the company experiences a default by the subscriber, the accounting will follow the provisions of the jurisdiction in which the entity is incorporated. In some of these, the subscriber is entitled to a proportionate number of shares based on the amount already paid on the subscriptions, sometimes reduced by the cost incurred by the entity in selling the remaining defaulted shares to other shareholders. In other jurisdictions, the subscriber forfeits the entire investment on default. In this case the amount already received is credited to an additional contributed capital account that describes its source.

Distinguishing additional contributed capital from the par or stated value of the shares

For largely historical reasons, entities sometimes issue share capital having par or stated value, which may be only a nominal value, such as €1 or even €0.01. The actual share issuance will be at a much higher (market-driven) amount, and the excess of the issuance price over the par or stated value might be assigned to a separate equity account referred to as premium on capital (ordinary) shares or additional contributed (paid-in) capital. Generally, but not universally, the distinction between ordinary shares and additional contributed capital has little legal import, but may be maintained for financial reporting purposes nonetheless.

Additional contributed capital represents all capital contributed to an entity other than that defined as par or stated value. Additional contributed capital can arise from proceeds received from the sale of ordinary and preferred shares in excess of their par or stated values. It can also arise from transactions relating to the following:

1. Sale of shares previously issued and subsequently reacquired by the entity (treasury shares).
2. Retirement of previously outstanding shares.
3. Payment of share dividends in a manner that justifies the dividend being recorded at the market value of the shares distributed.
4. Lapse of share purchase warrants or the forfeiture of share subscriptions, if these result in the retaining by the entity of any partial proceeds received prior to forfeiture.
5. Warrants that are detachable from bonds.
6. Conversion of convertible bonds.
7. Other gains on the entity's own shares, such as that which results from certain share option plans.

When the amounts are material, the sources of additional contributed capital should be described in the financial statements.

Examples of various transactions giving rise to (or reducing) additional contributed capital accounts are set forth below.

Examples of additional contributed capital transactions

Alta Vena Company issues 2,000 shares of ordinary shares having a par value of €1, for a total price of €8,000. The following entry records the transaction:

Cash	€8,000	
Ordinary shares		€2,000
Additional contributed capital/share premium		6,000

Alta Vena Company buys back 2,000 shares of its own ordinary share for €10,000 and then sells these shares to investors for €15,000. The following entries record the buyback and sale transactions, respectively:

Treasury shares	€10,000	
Cash		€10,000
Cash	15,000	
Treasury shares		10,000
Additional contributed capital/share premium		5,000

Alta Vena Company buys back 2,000 shares of its own €1 par value ordinary shares (which it had originally sold for €8,000) for €9,000 and retires the shares, which it records with the following entry (assuming there are no national requirements for capital maintenance):

Ordinary shares	€2,000	
Additional contributed capital/share premium	6,000	
Retained earnings	1,000	
Cash		€9,000

Alta Vena Company issues a small share dividend of 5,000 ordinary shares at the market price of €8 per share. Each share has a par value of €1. The following entry records the transaction:

Retained earnings	€40,000	
Ordinary shares		€5,000
Additional contributed capital/share premium		35,000

Alta Vena Company previously has recorded €1,000 of share options outstanding as part of a compensation agreement. The options expire a year later, resulting in the following entry:

Share options outstanding	€1,000	
Retained earnings		€1,000

Alta Vena's bondholders convert a €1,000 bond with an unamortised premium of €40 and a market value of €1,016 into 127 shares of €1 par ordinary share whose market value is €8 per share. This results in the following entry:

Bonds payable	€1,000	
Premium on bonds payable	40	
Ordinary shares		€127
Additional contributed capital—warrants		913

Donated capital

Donated capital can result from an outright gift to the entity (for example, a major shareholder donates land or other assets to the company in a non-reciprocal transfer) or may result when services are provided to the entity. Such a transaction may be treated as a capital contribution in the books of the receiving entity as it is received from a shareholder, the argument being that it is a capital injection from the shareholder. The dangling "credit" when recognising a below market-interest rate or interest-free long-term loan from a related party is commonly recorded as donated capital.

Compound and Convertible Equity Instruments

Entities sometimes issue preferred shares which are convertible into ordinary shares. Where the preferred shares are non-redeemable, the accounting for both the preferred and ordinary shares is similar as they both represent equity in the issuer. The treatment of convertible preferred shares at its issuance is no different from that of non-convertible preferred shares. When it is converted, the book value approach is used to account for the conversion. Use of the market value approach would entail a gain or loss for which there is no theoretical justification, since the total amount of contributed capital does not change when the share capital is converted. When the preferred shares are converted, the "Preferred shares" and related "Additional contributed capital—preferred shares" accounts are debited for their original values when purchased, and "Ordinary shares" and "Additional contributed capital—ordinary shares" (if an excess over par or stated value exists) are credited. If the book value of the preferred shares is less than the total par value of the ordinary shares being issued, retained earnings is charged for the difference. This charge is supported by the rationale that the preferred shareholders are offered an additional return to facilitate their conversion to ordinary share. Some jurisdictions require that this excess instead reduces additional contributed capital from other sources.

On the other hand, the issuance of debt that is convertible into equity (almost always into ordinary shares) does trigger accounting complexities. Under IAS 32, it is necessary for the issuer of non-derivative financial instruments to ascertain whether it contains both liability and equity components. If the instrument does contain both elements (for example, debentures convertible into ordinary shares), these components must be separated and accounted for according to their respective natures.

In the case of convertible debt, the instrument is viewed as being constituted of both an unconditional promise to pay (a liability) and an option granting the holder the right, but not the obligation, to obtain the issuer's shares under a fixed conversion ratio arrangement. (Under the provisions of IAS 32, unless the number of shares that can be obtained on conversion is fixed, the conversion option is not an equity instrument.) This option, at issuance date, is an equity instrument and must be accounted for as such by the issuer, whether subsequently exercised or not.

The amount allocated to equity is the residual derived by deducting the fair value of the liability component (typically, by discounting to present value the future principal and interest payments on the debt by the relevant interest rate) from the total proceeds of issuance. It would not be acceptable to derive the amount to be allocated to debt as a residual, on the other hand. This is a conservative rule that effectively maximises the allocation to debt and minimises the allocation to equity.

Retained Earnings

Accounting traditionally has clearly distinguished between equity contributed by owners (including donations from owners) and that resulting from the operating results of the reporting entity, consisting mainly of accumulated earnings since the entity's inception less amounts distributed to shareholders (i.e., dividends). Equity in each of these two categories is generically distinct from the other, and financial statement users need to be informed of the composition of shareholders' equity so that, for example, the cumulative profitability of the entity can be accurately gauged.

Legal capital (the defined aggregate par or stated value of the issued shares), additional contributed capital and donated capital collectively represent the contributed capital of the entity. The other major source of capital is retained earnings, which represents the accumulated amount of earnings of the entity from the date of inception (or from the date of reorganisation) less the cumulative amount of distributions made to shareholders and other charges to retained earnings (e.g., from treasury share transactions). The distributions to shareholders generally take the form of dividend payments, but may take other forms as well, such as the reacquisition of shares for amounts in excess of the original issuance proceeds. The key events impacting retained earnings are:

- Dividends;
- Certain sales of shares held in the treasury at amounts below acquisition cost;
- Certain share retirements at amounts in excess of book value;
- Prior period adjustments;
- In consolidated financial statements, changes in ownership stake of the non-controlling interests which do not result in a loss of control of the subsidiary; and
- Recapitalisations and reorganisations.

Examples of retained earnings transactions

Baking Bread Co. declares a dividend of €84,000, which it records with the following entry:

Retained earnings	€84,000	
Dividends payable		€84,000

Baking Bread acquires 3,000 shares of its own €1 par value ordinary shares for €15,000 and then resells them for €12,000. The following entries record the buyback and sale transactions, respectively, assuming the use of the cost method of accounting for treasury shares:

Treasury shares	€15,000	
Cash		€15,000
Cash	12,000	
Retained earnings	3,000	
Treasury shares		15,000

Baking Bread buys back 12,000 shares of its own €1 par value ordinary shares (which it had originally sold for €60,000) for €70,000 and retires the shares, which it records with the following entry (assuming there are no national requirements for capital maintenance):

Ordinary shares	€12,000	
Additional contributed capital	48,000	
Retained earnings	10,000	
Cash		€70,000

Baking Bread's accountant makes a mathematical mistake in calculating depreciation, requiring a prior period reduction of €30,000 to the accumulated depreciation account and corresponding increases in its income tax payable and retained earnings accounts. Baking Bread's income tax rate is 35%. It records this transaction with the following entry:

Accumulated depreciation	€30,000	
Income taxes payable		€10,500
Retained earnings		19,500

An important rule relating to retained earnings is that transactions in an entity's own shares can result in a reduction of retained earnings (i.e., a deficiency on such transactions can be charged to retained earnings) but cannot result in an increase in retained earnings (any excesses on such transactions are credited to contributed capital, never to retained earnings).

If a series of operating losses have been incurred or distributions to shareholders in excess of accumulated earnings have been made and if there is a debit balance in retained earnings, the account is generally referred to as accumulated deficit.

Dividends and Distributions

Cash dividends

Dividends represent the pro rata distribution of earnings to the owners of the entity. The amount and the allocation between the preferred and ordinary shareholders is a function of the stipulated preferential dividend rate, the presence or absence of (1) a participation feature, (2) a cumulative feature and (3) arrears on the preferred shares, and the wishes of the board of directors. Dividends, even preferred share dividends where a cumulative feature exists, do not accrue. Depending on the jurisdiction, one may find that dividends become a liability of the entity only when they are declared by the board of directors or when shareholders vote to accept a dividend.

Traditionally, entities were not allowed to declare dividends in excess of the amount of retained earnings. Alternatively, an entity could pay dividends out of retained earnings and additional contributed capital but could not exceed the total of these categories (i.e., they could not impair legal capital by the payment of dividends). Local company law obviously dictates, directly or by implication, the accounting to be applied in many of these situations. For example, in some jurisdictions, entities can declare and pay dividends in excess of the book amount of retained earnings if the directors conclude that, after the payment of such dividends, the fair value of the entity's net assets will still be a positive amount. Thus, directors can declare dividends out of unrealised appreciation, which, in certain industries, can be a significant source of dividends beyond the realised and recognised accumulated earnings of the entity. This action, however, represents a major departure from traditional practice and demands both careful consideration and adequate disclosure.

Four important dividend dates are:

1. The declaration date;
2. The approval date;
3. The record date; and
4. The payment date.

The declaration date or approval date (depending on the jurisdiction) governs the incurrence of a legal liability by the entity. The approval date is the date when the shareholders of the entity vote on whether or not to accept the dividend declared. This date governs the incurrence of a legal liability by the entity. In some jurisdictions, the applicable legislation stipulates that an entity does not incur an obligation to pay a dividend until such time as the shareholders' vote to accept a dividend payment.

The record date refers to that point in time when a determination is made as to which specific registered shareholders will receive dividends and in what amounts.

Finally, the payment date relates to the date when the distribution of the dividend takes place.

These concepts are illustrated in the following example:

Example of payment of dividends

On April 1, the directors of River Corp. declare a €0.75 per share quarterly dividend on River Corp.'s 650,000 outstanding ordinary shares. The shareholders vote and approve the dividend on May 1. The dividend is payable May 25 to shareholders on the record on May 15.

May 1	Retained earnings (or dividends)	€487,500	
	Dividends payable		€487,500
May 15	No entry passed		
May 25	Dividends payable	487,500	
	Cash		487,500

If a dividends account is used, it is closed directly to retained earnings at year-end.

Dividends may be made in the form of cash, property or scrip. Cash dividends are either a given currency amount per share, such as euros, or a percentage of par or stated value. Property dividends consist of the distribution of any assets other than cash (e.g., inventory or equipment). Finally, scrip dividends are either promissory notes due at some time in the future, sometimes bearing interest until final payment is made; or are the issuance of additional shares made in lieu of a cash dividend. In such a scenario, shareholders are often able to choose whether to receive a cash dividend or shares in settlement of the dividend due to them.

Occasionally, what appear to be disproportionate dividend distributions are paid to some but not all of the owners of closely held entities. Such transactions need to be analysed carefully. In some cases, these may actually represent compensation paid to the recipients. In other instances, these may be a true dividend paid to all shareholders on a pro rata basis, to which certain shareholders have waived their rights. If the former, the distribution should not be accounted for as a dividend but as compensation or some other expense category and included in the statement of comprehensive income. If the latter, the dividend should be grossed up to reflect payment on a proportional basis to all the shareholders, with an offsetting capital contribution to the company recognised as having been effectively made by those to whom payments were not made.

Upon occasion, dividends may be paid by distributing assets other than cash. For example, a merchandising firm may distribute merchandise to shareholders in lieu of cash, although this makes it more difficult to assure absolute proportionality. When, say, inventory is used to distribute earnings to shareholders, the accounting is similar to that shown above, except inventory is credited rather than cash. IFRIC 17, *Distributions of Non-cash Assets to Owners*, addresses the accounting relating to the distribution of such assets to shareholders. IFRIC 17 works on the assumption that the fair value of the assets to be distributed can be determined and it is on this basis that the accounting then follows. For example, if inventory carried at a cost of €100,000, and having a fair value of €125,000, is distributed to shareholders as a dividend, the entity would record a profit of €25,000 on realisation of the inventory and a dividend payment of €125,000.

Liquidating dividends

Liquidating dividends are not distributions of earnings, but rather a return of capital to the investing shareholders. A liquidating dividend is normally recorded by the declarer through charging additional contributed capital rather than retained earnings. The exact accounting for a liquidating dividend is affected by the laws where the business is incorporated, and these laws vary among jurisdictions. There will often be tax implications of liquidating dividend payments, which must also be considered.

Taxation impact

Any income tax relating to distributions to holders of an equity instrument and to transaction costs of an equity transaction should be accounted for in accordance with IAS 12, *Income Taxes* (see Chapter 26). Tax consequences of a dividend, such as a secondary tax on companies or a withholding tax on distributions, should be accounted for under IAS 12 and not as part of the equity distribution.

Accounting for Treasury Share Transactions

The term treasury share refers to the entity's shares that were issued but subsequently reacquired and are being held ("in the company's treasury") without having been cancelled. An entity may buy back its own shares, subject to laws of the jurisdiction of incorporation, for possibly many different and legitimate business purposes, such as to have on hand for later share-based payments to employees or vendors, or to decrease the "float" of shares outstanding—which may be done to provide upward pressure on the quoted price of the share or increase the earnings per share by decreasing the number of outstanding shares.

IFRS addresses treasury shares and sets as a general principle that "earnings" cannot be created by transactions in an entity's own shares, and thus the proper accounting would be to report these as capital transactions only.

Treasury shares do not reduce the number of shares issued but do reduce the number of shares outstanding, as well as total shareholders' equity. These shares are not eligible to receive cash dividends. Treasury shares are not an asset. Reacquired shares that are awaiting delivery to satisfy a liability created by the firm's compensation plan or reacquired shares that are held in a profit-sharing trust may still be considered outstanding and, thus, may not be considered treasury shares. The terms and conditions of the compensation plan would need to be considered in the light of IFRS 10, *Consolidated Financial Statements*, which is addressed in Chapter 15.

Members' Shares in Co-operative Entities

Certain organisations are dubbed membership organisations or co-operatives. These are often entities providing services to a group having common membership or interests, such as labour unions or university faculty and staff. Credit unions (a form of savings and loan association) are a common example of this form of organisation. Other co-operatives may serve as marketing vehicles, as in the case of farmers' co-ops, or as buying organisations, as in co-operatives formed by merchants in certain types of businesses, generally to gain economies of scale and market power to compete with larger merchant chains. Generally, these types of organisations will refund or rebate profits to the members in proportion to the amount of business transacted over a time period, such as a year.

Ownership in co-operatives is represented by shares. Members' shares in co-operative entities have some characteristics of equity, but also, often, characteristics of debt, since they are not permanent equity which cannot be withdrawn. Members' shares typically give the holder the right to request redemption for cash, although that right may be subject to certain limitations or restrictions, imposed by law or by the terms of the membership agreement. IFRIC 2, *Members' Shares in Co-operative Entities and Similar Instruments*, gives guidance on how those redemption terms should be evaluated in determining whether the shares should be classified as financial liabilities or as equity.

Under IFRIC 2, shares for which the member has the right to request redemption are normally liabilities. Even when the intent is to leave in the equity interest for a long period, such as until the member ceases business operations, this does not qualify as true equity as defined in the *Framework*. However, the shares qualify as equity if:

- The co-operative entity has an unconditional right to refuse redemption; or
- Local law, regulation, or the entity's governing charter imposes prohibitions on redemption.

However, the mere existence of law, regulation or charter provisions that would prohibit redemption only if conditions (such as liquidity constraints) are met, or are not met, does not result in members' shares being treated as equity.

FUTURE DEVELOPMENTS

In June 2018 the IASB issued a Discussion Paper *Financial Instruments with Characteristics of Equity* to provide a clearer rationale for the classification of financial instruments as either a liability or equity. The rationale for classifying a financial instrument as a liability is based on two separate features. The first is that the instrument contains an unavoidable contractual obligation to transfer cash or another financial instrument at a specific time other than liquidation (the time feature). The second is an unavoidable contractual obligation for an amount independent from the entity's available economic resources (the amount feature). In September 2019, the IASB tentatively decided that the issues can be addressed by clarifying some of the principles in IAS 32. At the time of writing, no indicative date has been released for the clarifications.

EXAMPLES OF FINANCIAL STATEMENT DISCLOSURES

Exemplum Reporting PLC
Financial Statements
For the Year Ended December 31, 20XX

26. Share capital and reserves

26.1 Ordinary shares

	20XX	**20XX-1**
Authorised	X	X
X million ordinary shares of €X each	X	X

Issued and fully paid for	X	X
X million ordinary shares of €X each	X	X
Reconciliation of the number of shares outstanding		
Opening balance	X	X
Shares issued	X	X
Shares repurchased	(X)	(X)
Closing balance	X	X

All fully paid-up shares have a par value of €X and entitle the holder to one vote and equal rights to dividends declared.

26.2 Disclosure of components of other comprehensive income

The available for sale movement in other comprehensive income comprises arising gains recognised during the year of €X (20XX-1: €X) less amounts recycled through profit or loss of €X (20XX-1: €X).

26.3 Disclosure of tax effects relating to each component of other comprehensive income

	20XX			20XX-1		
	Before Tax amount	**Tax (expense)/ benefit**	**Net-of-tax amount**	**Before tax amount**	**Tax (expense)/ benefit**	**Net-of-tax amount**
Exchange differences in translating foreign operations	X	X	X	X	X	X
Equity instrument financial assets	X	X	X	X	X	X
Actuarial gains or losses on defined benefit pension plan	X	X	X	X	X	X
Share of other comprehensive income of associates	X	X	X	X	X	X
Other comprehensive income	X	X	X	X	X	X

26.4 Disclosure of the nature and purpose of reserves in equity

Cash flow reserve	The cash flow reserve is used to record the effective portion of the cumulative net change in the fair value of cash flow hedging instruments related to hedged transactions that have not yet occurred. The items generating these foreign exchange movements are in designated cash flow hedge relationships.

Financial instrument fair value reserve	The reserve is used to record the cumulative fair value gains and losses on financial instruments classified at fair value through other comprehensive income. The cumulative gains and losses are recycled to the income statement on disposal of the assets.
Translation reserve	The translation reserve is used to record cumulative translation differences on the assets and liabilities of foreign operations. The cumulative translation differences are recycled to the income statement on disposal of the foreign operation.
Treasury reserve	This reserve relates to shares held by an independently managed employee share ownership trust (ESOT) and treasury shares held by the company. The shares held by the ESOT were purchased to satisfy outstanding employee share options and potential awards under the Long-Term Incentive Plan and other incentive schemes.

US GAAP COMPARISON

There are differences in terminology between IFRS and US GAAP. For example, US GAAP does not use the terms "reserve" or "surplus," rather it uses "retained earnings" or "accumulated deficit." US GAAP uses the Accumulated Other Comprehensive Income account. FASB Concept Statement 6 (CON6) defines comprehensive income as "the change in equity of a business enterprise during a period from transactions and other events and circumstances from nonowner sources. It includes all changes in equity during a period except those resulting from investments by owners and distributions to owners." Items included in other comprehensive income include gains or losses on investments, net of the related deferred tax impacts, foreign currency translation adjustments, pension adjustments and the like.

IFRS reports "revaluation surplus" for increases or decreases in property, plant and equipment; mineral resources; intangible assets, etc. US GAAP does not report unrealised gains on those items in the financial statements.

Preference shares (i.e., preferred stock), under US GAAP, are presented in equity and not with liabilities, unless such shares are mandatorily redeemable.

Additionally, US GAAP allows presentation in the notes to the financial statements of the changes in shareholders' equity whereas IFRS requires a separate statement.

17 SHARE-BASED PAYMENT

INTRODUCTION

The IASB's *Conceptual Framework* defines equity as the residual interest in the assets of an entity after deducting all its liabilities. Shareholders' equity comprises all capital contributed to the entity (including share premium, also referred to as capital paid-in in excess of par value) plus retained earnings (which represents the entity's cumulative earnings, less all distributions that have been made therefrom).

In the past, the matter of share-based payments (e.g., share option plans and other arrangements whereby employees or others, such as vendors, are compensated via issuance of shares) has received significant attention. The IASB introduced a comprehensive standard, IFRS 2, *Share-based Payment*, which requires a fair value-based measurement of all such arrangements.

A major objective of the accounting for shareholders' equity is the adequate disclosure of the sources from which the capital was derived. The appropriate accounting treatment is dealt with in Chapter 16. Where shares are reserved for future issuance, such as under the terms of share option plans, this fact must also be made known. The accounting for this is addressed in this chapter.

Source of IFRS
IFRS 2

SCOPE

IFRS 2 applies to the accounting for *all* share-based payment transactions, including:

- Equity-settled share-based payment transactions;
- Cash-settled share-based payment transactions; and
- Cash-settled *or* equity-settled share-based payment transactions (when the entity has a choice to settle the transaction in cash (or other assets) or by issuing equity instruments).

The standard may also apply in the absence of specifically identifiable goods and services but when other circumstances indicate that goods or services have been (or will be) received.

Furthermore—and very importantly—IFRS 2 applies to all entities (both publicly and privately held). Also, a subsidiary using its parent's or another subsidiary's equity as consideration for goods or services is within the scope of the standard. However, an entity should *not* apply the standard to transactions in which the entity acquires goods as part of the net assets acquired in a business combination (such transactions are within the scope of IFRS 3). In such cases, it is important to distinguish share-based payments related to the acquisition from those related to employee services. Also, IFRS 2 does not apply to share-based payment contracts within the scope of IAS 32 and IFRS 9.

IFRS 2 was amended in 2013 to provide for changes to the definition of vesting condition and market condition and separate definitions were also introduced for "performance condition" and "service condition." The changes were applied for grant dates on or after July 1, 2014.

The definition of "fair value" used in IFRS 2 differs in some respects from that in IFRS 13, *Fair Value Measurement*. Thus, when applying IFRS 2 the "local" definition of "fair value" is utilised rather than the IFRS 13 definition.

DEFINITIONS OF TERMS

Cash-settled share-based payment transaction. A share-based payment transaction in which the entity acquires goods or services by incurring a liability to transfer cash or other assets to the supplier of those goods or services for amounts that are based on the price (or value) of equity instruments (including shares or shares options) of the entity or another group entity.

Employees and others providing similar services. Individuals who render personal services to the entity and meet one of the following additional criteria:

a. The individuals are regarded as employees for legal or tax purposes;
b. The individuals work for the entity under its direction in the same way as individuals who are regarded as employees for legal or tax purposes; or
c. The services rendered are similar to those rendered by employees.

For example, the term encompasses all management personnel, i.e., those persons having authority and responsibility for planning, directing and controlling the activities of the entity, including non-executive directors.

Equity instrument. A contract that evidences a residual interest in the assets of an entity after deducting all of its liabilities. (A liability is defined in the *Conceptual Framework* as a present obligation of the entity to transfer an economic resource as a result of past events.)

Equity instrument granted. The right (conditional or unconditional) to an equity instrument of the entity conferred by the entity on another party.

Equity-settled share-based payment transaction. A share-based payment transaction in which the entity:

a. Receives goods or services as consideration for its own equity instruments (including shares or share options); or
b. Receives goods or services but has no obligation to settle the transaction with the supplier.

Fair value. The amount for which an asset could be exchanged, a liability settled, or an equity instrument granted could be exchanged, between knowledgeable, willing parties in an arm's-length transaction.

Grant date. The date at which the entity and another party (including an employee) agree to a share-based payment arrangement, being when the entity and the counterparty have a shared understanding of the terms and conditions of the arrangement. At grant date, the entity confers on the counterparty the right to cash, other assets or equity instruments of the entity, provided the specified vesting conditions, if any, are met. If that agreement is subject to an approval process (for example, by shareholders), grant date is the date when that approval is obtained.

Intrinsic value. The difference between the fair value of the shares to which the counterparty has the (conditional or unconditional) right to subscribe or which it has the right to receive, and the price (if any) the counterparty is (or will be) required to pay for those shares. For example, a share option with an exercise price of €15, on a share with a fair value of €20, has an intrinsic value of €5.

Market condition. A performance condition upon which the exercise price, vesting or exercisability of an equity instrument depends that is related to the market price (or value) of the entity's equity instruments (or the equity instruments of another entity in the same group), such as:

a. Attaining a specified share price or a specified amount of intrinsic value of a share option; or
b. Achieving a specified target that is based on the market price (or value) of the entity's equity instruments (or the equity instruments of another entity in the same group) relative to an index of market prices of equity instruments of other entities.

A market condition requires the counterparty to complete a specified period of service (i.e., a service condition); the service requirement can be explicit or implicit.

Measurement date. The date at which the fair value of the equity instruments granted is measured for the purposes of IFRS 2. For transactions with employees and others providing similar services, the measurement date is the grant date. For transactions with parties other than employees (and those providing similar services), the measurement date is the date the entity obtains the goods or the counterparty renders service.

Performance condition. A vesting condition that requires:

a. The counterparty to complete a specified period of service (i.e., a service condition); the service requirement can be explicit or implicit; and
b. Specified performance target(s) to be met while the counterparty is rendering the service required in (a).

The period of achieving the performance target(s):

a. Shall not extend beyond the end of the service period; and
b. May start before the service period on the condition that the commencement date of the performance target is not substantially before the commencement of the service period.

A performance target is defined by reference to:

a. The entity's own operations (or activities) or the operations or activities of another entity in the same group (i.e., a non-market condition); or
b. The price (or value) of the entity's equity instruments or the equity instruments of another entity in the same group (including shares and share options) (i.e., a market condition).

A performance target might relate either to the performance of the entity as a whole or to some part of the entity (or part of the group), such as a division or an individual employee.

Puttable financial instruments. Shares which the holders can "put" back to the issuing entity; that is, the holders can require that the entity repurchases the shares at defined amounts that can include fair value.

Reload feature. A feature that provides for an automatic grant of additional share options whenever the option holder exercises previously granted options using the entity's shares, rather than cash, to satisfy the exercise price.

Reload option. A new share option granted when a share is used to satisfy the exercise price of a previous share option.

Service condition. A vesting condition that requires the counterparty to complete a specified period of service during which services are provided to the entity. If the counterparty, regardless of the reason, ceases to provide service during the vesting period, it has failed to satisfy the condition. A service condition does not require a performance target to be met.

Share-based payment arrangement. An agreement between the entity (including its shareholder or another group entity) and another party (including an employee) to enter into a share-based payment transaction, which entitles the other party to receive:

a. Cash or other assets of the entity for amounts that are based on the price (or value) of equity instruments (including shares or shares options) of the entity or another group entity; or
b. Equity instruments (including shares or share options) of the entity or another group entity provided the specified vesting conditions, if any, are met.

Share-based payment transaction. A transaction in which the entity:

a. Receives goods or services from the supplier of those goods or services (including an employee) in a share-based arrangement; or
b. Incurs an obligation to settle the transaction with the supplier in a share-based payment arrangement when another group entity receives those goods or services.

Share option. A contract that gives the holder the right, but not the obligation, to subscribe to the entity's shares at a fixed or determinable price for a specified period of time.

Vest. To become an entitlement. Under a share-based payment arrangement, a counterparty's right to receive cash, other assets or equity instruments of the entity vests when the counterparty's entitlement is no longer conditional on the satisfaction of any vesting conditions.

Vesting condition. A condition that determines whether the entity receives the services that entitle the counterparty to receive cash, other assets or equity instruments of the entity, under a share-based payment arrangement. A vesting condition is either a service condition or a performance condition. (A non-vesting condition is not specifically defined in the standard. Accordingly, any condition which a vesting condition is not would be a non-vesting condition.)

Vesting period. The period during which all the specified vesting conditions of a share-based payment arrangement are to be satisfied.

OVERVIEW

In accordance with IFRS 2, a share-based payment is a transaction in which the entity receives goods or services as consideration for its equity instruments or acquires goods or services by incurring liabilities for amounts that are based on the price (or value) of the entity's shares (or other equity instruments of the entity). The concept of share-based payments is broad and includes not only employee share options but also share appreciation rights, employee share ownership plans, employee share purchase plans, share option plans and other share arrangements. The accounting approach for a share-based payment depends on whether the transaction is settled by the issuance of:

1. Equity instruments;
2. Cash; or
3. Equity and cash.

The general principle is that all share-based payment transactions should be recognised in the financial statements at fair value, with an asset or expense recognised when the goods or services are received. Depending on the type of share-based payment, fair value may be determined based on the value of goods or services received, or by the value of the shares or rights to shares given up. In accordance with IFRS, the following rules should be followed:

- If the equity-settled share-based payment is for goods or services (other than from employees and others providing similar services), the equity-settled share-based payment should be measured by reference to the fair value of goods and services received;
- If the equity-settled share-based payment is to employees (or those similar to employees), the transaction should be measured by reference to the fair value of the equity instruments granted at the date of grant;
- For cash-settled share-based payments, the fair value should be determined at each reporting date; and
- If the share-based payment can be settled in cash or in equity, then the equity component should be measured at the grant date only, but the cash component is measured at each reporting date.

In general, then, transactions in which goods or services are received as consideration for equity instruments of the entity are to be measured at the fair value of the goods or services received by the reporting entity. However, if their value cannot be readily determined (as the standard suggests is the case for employee services) they are to be measured with reference to the fair value of the equity instruments granted.

In the case of transactions with parties other than employees, there is a rebuttable presumption that the fair value of the goods or services received is more readily determinable than is the value of the shares granted. This follows logically from the fact that, in arm's-length transactions, it should be the case that the value which the entity has received would be readily apparent (whether merchandise, plant assets, personal services, etc.) and that such data would not take undue effort to gather and utilise. Arguments to the contrary raise basic questions about managerial performance and corporate governance and can rarely be given much credence.

Additional guidance is also provided in the standard with regard to situations in which the entity cannot identify specifically some or all of the goods or services received. If the identifiable consideration received (if any) appears to be less than the fair value of the equity instruments granted or liability incurred, typically this situation indicates that other consideration (i.e., unidentifiable goods or services) has also been (or will be) received. The entity should measure the unidentifiable goods or services received (or to be received) at the grant date as the difference between the fair value of the share-based payment given or promised and the fair value of any identifiable goods or services received (or to be received). However, for cash-settled transactions, the liability is remeasured at each reporting date until it is settled.

Given the added challenge of estimating fair value for non-traded shares, this was a major point of contention among those responding to the initial draft standard. Realistically, entities granting share-based compensation to executives and other employees almost always have a sense of the value being transferred, for otherwise these bargained transactions would not make business sense, nor would they satisfy the demands or expectations of the recipients.

Where payment is made or promised in the reporting entity's shares only, the value is determined using a fair value technique that computes the cost at the date of the transaction, which is not subsequently revised, except for revised terms which increase the amount of fair value to be transferred to the recipients. In contrast, for cash-settled transactions, the liability should be remeasured at each reporting date until it is settled.

For transactions measured at the fair value of the equity instruments granted (such as compensation transactions with employees), fair value is estimated at the grant date. A point of contention here has often been whether the grant date or exercise date is the more appropriate reference point, but the logic of the former is that the economic decision, and the employee's contractual commitment, were made at the grant date, and the timing of subsequent exercise (or, in some cases, forfeiture) is not indicative of the bargained-for value of the transaction. The grant date is when the employee accepts the commitment, not when the offer is first made. Accordingly, IFRS 2 requires the use of the grant date to ascertain the fair value to be associated with the transaction.

When share capital is issued immediately, measurement is not generally difficult. For example, if 100 shares having a fair (market) value of €33 per share are given outright to an employee, the compensation cost is simply computed as €3,300. Since the grant vests immediately (no future service is demanded from the recipient), the expense is immediately reported.

The more problematic situation is when employees (or others) are granted *options* to later acquire shares that permit exercise over a defined time horizon. The holders' ability to wait and later assess the desirability of exercising the options has value—and the lengthier the period until the options expire, the more likely the underlying shares will increase in value, and thus the greater is the value of the option. Even if the underlying shares are publicly traded, the value of the options will be subject to some debate. Only when the options themselves are traded (which is rarely the case with employee share options, which are restricted to the grantees themselves) will fair value be directly determinable by observation. If market options on the entity's shares do trade, the value will likely exceed that to be attributed to non-tradable employee share options, even if they have nominally similar terms (exercise dates, prices, etc.).

The standard holds that, to estimate the fair value of a share option in the likely instance where an observable market price for that option does not exist, an *option pricing model* should be used. IFRS 2 does not specify which particular model should be used. The entity must disclose the model used, the inputs to that model, and various other information bearing on how fair value was computed. In practice, these models are all fairly sophisticated and complicated (although commercially available software promises to ease the computational complexities) and a number of the variables have inherently subjective aspects.

One issue that has to be dealt with involves the tax treatment of options, which varies across jurisdictions. In most instances, the tax treatment will not comply with the fair value measurement mandated under IFRS 2, and thus there will be a need for specific guidance as to the accounting for the tax effects of granting the options and of the ultimate exercise of those options, if they are not forfeited by the option holders. This is described later in this discussion.

In respect of the appropriate tax treatment of share-based payments, the *Basis for Conclusions* of IFRS 2 notes that in jurisdictions where a tax deduction is given, the measurement of the tax deduction does not always coincide with that of the accounting deduction. Where the tax deduction is in excess of the expense reported in the statement of profit or loss and other comprehensive income, the excess is taken directly to equity.

RECOGNITION AND MEASUREMENT

The entity recognises the goods or services received or acquired in a share-based payment transaction when ownership of the goods passes, or when the services have been rendered. A corresponding increase in equity is recognised if the goods or services were received in a transaction that was settled through the issuance of shares, or as an increase in liabilities if the goods or services were acquired in a cash-settled share-based payment transaction. If the goods or services acquired do not meet the qualification criteria for recognition as an asset, the transaction should be recognised as an expense.

Example—Construction services settled by issuing shares

A contractor has been appointed to complete alterations to buildings owned by Bangkok. The contract price is fixed at €2,200,000. After completion of specific milestones, the work is certified by independent controllers. On receipt of a certificate, 50% of the amount certified is payable in cash, and the balance by issuing shares at their market value to settle the remaining 50% balance. The shares have a nominal value of €5. On March 31, 20XX, Bangkok received a certificate of €2,200,000 when the fair value of the shares was €40. The number of shares to be issued is 27,500 shares [(€2,200,000 × 50%)/€40].

Journal
March 31, 20XX

Building under construction	€2,200,000	
Bank		€1,100,000
Share capital (Equity)		137,500
Share premium (Equity)		962,500

Recognition of payments in respect of the expansion of the building.

$$(27{,}500 \times \text{€s5})\ and\ (27{,}500 \times \text{€}35)$$

Recognition When There are Vesting Conditions

In certain instances, equity instruments which vest immediately are granted to employees; as such, these instruments immediately accrue to the employees. In essence, this means that the employees are not required to provide any additional service to the entity or meet any performance condition before they are unconditionally entitled to those equity instruments. In the absence of facts that contradict this position, the entity is required to recognise the associated employee cost in full, with a corresponding increase in equity. It is presumed that the services rendered by the employee as consideration for the equity instruments have already been received by the grant date.

With equity instruments that do not vest until the employee completes a specified period of service or meets a specified performance condition, the entity assumes that the services rendered by the employee, as consideration for those equity instruments, will only be received in the future. As such, the entity accounts for those services as they are rendered over the vesting period with a corresponding increase in equity.

Example—Vesting condition (service condition)

The eight directors of San Francisco each received an option at January 1, 20XX to take up 100 €1 shares in San Francisco for a purchase consideration of €30 per share after the completion of a two-year service period. San Francisco obtained the services of a valuation expert who calculated the fair value of the share options provided to the directors to be €15 on January 1, 20XX.

The benefits do not vest immediately since the benefits have a two-year vesting period. The transaction should be accounted for as an equity-settled share-based payment in the accounting records.

The transaction is a share-based payment transaction with an employee and should be measured at the fair value of the equity instruments (options) at the grant date. This value should not be adjusted over the life of the share-based payment transaction.

Calculation for 20XX
8 directors × 100 options each × €15 fair value of options at grant date × ½ completed service period = €6,000

Journal
December 31, 20XX

Employment cost (P/L)	€6,000	
Equity reserve (Equity)		€6,000

Accounting for the 20XX share-based payments to directors.

EQUITY-SETTLED SHARE-BASED PAYMENTS

Goods and Services

An entity is required to measure the goods or services received (debit) and the corresponding increase in equity (credit) based on the fair value of the goods or services received. In some instances, the fair value of the goods or services received cannot be estimated reliably, and in such a situation the entity should measure the value of the goods or services and the related increase in equity based on the fair value of the equity instruments granted. Fair value is determined as of the date when the entity obtains the goods or the service is rendered.

Employees

In respect of transactions with employees and other providers of similar services, the entity should determine the fair value of the services based on the fair value of the instruments issued. The presumption in such an instance is that one cannot reliably estimate the fair value of the services received.

The value of the instruments is determined at the grant date of such instruments. All market conditions and non-vesting conditions must be considered when the fair value of the instrument is calculated on the grant date with no subsequent adjustment for a different outcome. Service and non-market performance conditions must be considered when the number of shares that is expected to vest is estimated.

Service Conditions

A service condition is when a grant of shares or share options to an employee is conditional on the employee remaining in the entity's employment for a specified period of time. Service conditions are considered in determining the fair value of the shares or share options at the grant date. At each measurement date, the estimate of the number of equity instruments should be revised to equal the amount that will actually be issued to the employees or other parties. At the vesting date, the actual number of shares that vest is taken into consideration in the final estimation.

Example—Vesting service conditions

On January 1, 20XX, Lisbon grants 20 share options to each of its 100 employees. Each grant is subject to the condition that the employees must work for another two years. Lisbon estimates that 80% of the employees will fulfil the condition to stay for two years. During 20XX, 10 employees left, and Lisbon still estimated that 20% of the original employees will leave over the two-year period. During 20XX+1, another 15 employees left before the maturity date. The fair value of each option is estimated to be €10 at the grant date.

Journals

December 31, 20XX	**€**	**€**
Employment cost (P/L)	8,000	
Equity reserve (Equity)		8,000

Accounting for the 20XX share-based payment employment cost. (20 options × 100 employees × 80% (estimated) × €10 × ½ years)

December 31, 20XX+1		
Employment cost (P/L)	7,000	

Equity reserve (Equity)		7,000
Accounting for the 20XX+1 share-based payment employment cost. [(20 options × 75 employees (actual) × €10) = 15,000 − 8,000 (previously recognised) = 7,000]		

Market and Non-Market Performance Conditions

Market and non-market performance conditions may be included in the share-based transaction. An example of a market performance condition is a specified increase in the entity's credit rating. Market conditions are included in the estimation of the fair value on the grant date.

Example—Market performance conditions

At January 1, 20XX, Boston grants a senior executive 1,000 share options with no service conditions. The share options are exercisable on December 31, 20XX. The share options may only be exercised on December 31, 20XX, if the credit rating of Boston increases from BB to BB+ during 20XX.

Boston applied a binomial option pricing model to estimate the fair value of the options at the grant date to be €20.

The credit rating condition is a market condition and is considered in the valuation on the grant date.

Since no further vesting conditions are included, the share-based transaction is recognised at the grant date.

Journals		
January 1, 20XX		
Employment cost (P/L)	20,000	
Equity reserve (Equity)		20,000
Accounting for the 20XX employment cost. (1,000 shares × €20)		

A non-market performance condition is, for example, an entity achieving a specified growth in revenue. Non-market conditions are taken into account in determining the quantity of the instruments that will be issued and not in the fair value of the instrument on the grant date.

Example—Non-market performance conditions

On January 1, 20XX, Calgary grants 40 shares to 200 employees subject to the condition that the employees remain in the employment of the entity for the vesting period. The shares will vest on December 31, 20XX, if the earnings of the entity increase by 10%, and on December 31, 20XX+1, if the earnings increase by an average of 8% per year over the two years. The shares had a fair value of €25 at the grant date.

On December 31, 20XX, the earnings only increased by 9%, 30 employees left and Calgary expects that another 20 employees will leave during the 20XX+1 financial period. Calgary expects that the vesting conditions will be met during the 20XX+1 financial period.

On December 31, 20XX+1, the vesting conditions are met since the earnings increased by 10% during 20XX+1. Fifteen employees left employment during the 20XX+1 financial period before the shares vested.

Journals	**€**	**€**
20XX		
Employment cost (P/L)	75,000	
Equity reserve (Equity)		75,000

Accounting for the 20XX share-based payment employment cost. (40 shares × 150 (200 − 30 − 20) employees (expected) × €25 × 1/2 years)

20XX+1

Employment cost (P/L)	80,000	
Equity reserve (Equity)		80,000

Accounting for the 20XX+1 share-based payment employment cost. (40 shares × 155 (200-30-15) employees (actual) × €25) = 155,000 − 75,000 (previously recognised) = 80,000

A summary of the conditions can be categorised as depicted in the Implementation Guide to the Standard as shown below:

Summary of conditions that determine whether a counterparty receives an equity instrument granted

	Vesting conditions			Non-vesting conditions		
	Service conditions	Performance conditions				
		Performance conditions that are market conditions	Other performance conditions	Neither the entity nor the counterparty can choose whether the condition is met	Counterparty can choose whether to meet the condition	Entity can choose whether to meet the condition
Example conditions	Requirement to remain in service for three years	Target based on the market price of the entity's equity instruments	Target based on a successful initial public offering with a specified service requirement	Target based on a commodity index	Paying contributions towards the exercise price of a share-based payment	Continuation of the plan by the entity
Include in grant date fair value?	No	Yes	No	Yes	Yes	Yes[(a)]
Accounting treatment if the condition is not met after the grant date and during the vesting period	Forfeiture. The entity revises the expense to reflect the best available estimate of the number of equity instruments expected to vest	No change to accounting. The entity continues to recognise the expense over the remainder of the vesting period	Forfeiture. The entity revises the expense to reflect the best available estimate of the number of equity instruments expected to vest	No change to accounting. The entity continues to recognise the expense over the remainder of the vesting period	Cancellation. The entity recognises immediately the amount of the expense that would otherwise have been recognised over the remainder of the vesting period	Cancellation. The entity recognises immediately the amount of the expense that would otherwise have been recognised over the remainder of the vesting period

	(para graph 19)	(para graph 21)	(para graph 19)	(para graph 21A)	(para graph 28A)	(para graph 28A)
(a) In the calculation of the fair value of share-based payment, the probability of continuation of the plan by the entity is assumed to be 100 per cent.						

Measurement of Fair Value

If the fair value of the goods or services received cannot be measured reliably, the fair value of the shares, share options or equity-settled share appreciation rights must be determined using the three-tier measurement hierarchy included in Figure 17.1.

Observable market price of the equity instruments granted is only used if such a price is available. This is unlikely to be applicable where an entity is not listed on a stock exchange. In the absence of observable market prices, observable market data may be used, such as:

- A recent transaction in the entity's shares.
- A recent independent fair valuation of the entity or its principal assets.

If the value of shares cannot be measured by an observable market price, or reliable measurement under level two is impractical, the shares are measured indirectly by using a valuation method. A valuation method uses, to the greatest extent practicable, market data that can be externally verified to arrive at a value at which the equity instruments under consideration would be exchanged at the grant date between knowledgeable willing parties. Similarly, share options and share appreciation rights are valued under level three of the hierarchy by using an option pricing model. This would, in effect, be a directors' valuation, and as such the directors should apply their judgement in determining the amount. The valuation method should, however, comply with generally accepted methodologies for valuing equity instruments.

For a detailed example of calculating fair value for employee share options, see Appendix B of IFRS 2 and the Appendix of this chapter.

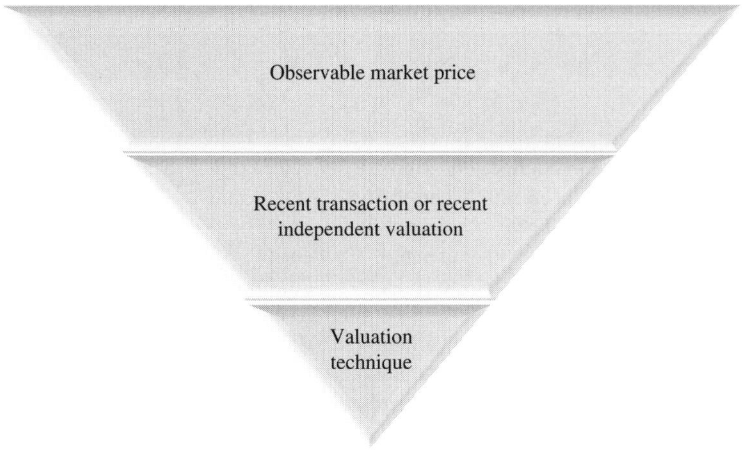

Figure 17.1 Fair value hierarchy

Modifications and Cancellations to the Terms and Conditions

Changes in the economic conditions or circumstances of the entity may sometimes make an entity change the vesting conditions that are attached to employee share ownership schemes. The entity may modify the vesting conditions in a manner that is beneficial to the employee (for example, by reducing the exercise price of an option, or reducing the vesting period, or by modifying or eliminating a performance condition). Modification to vesting conditions is only considered if it is beneficial to the employees.

Such changes should be taken into account in accounting for the share-based payment transaction as illustrated in Figure 17.2.

If the Modification Increases the Fair Value

If the modification to the scheme increases the fair value of the equity instruments granted, or the number of equity instruments granted, the entity should account for the incremental total fair value equity instruments granted as a share-based payment expense. The incremental fair value is the difference between the fair value of the modified equity instrument and the original equity instrument on the date of the modification. The balance of the original equity instruments granted is recognised over the remainder of the original vesting period.

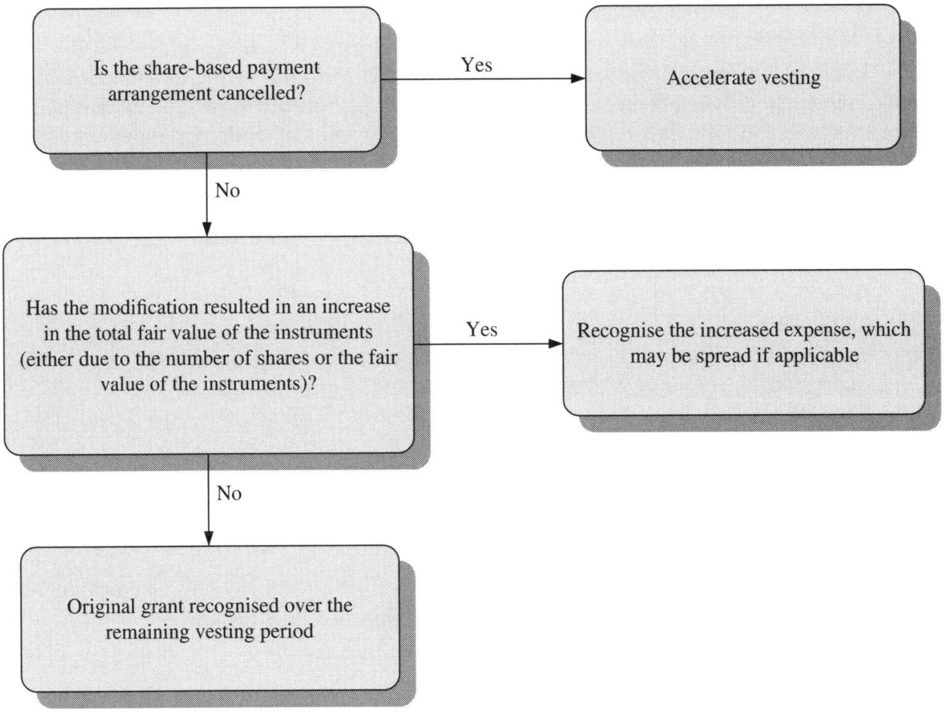

Figure 17.2 Modifications and cancellations to the terms and conditions

Example—Modification of a share-based payment transaction

The 10 directors of Brno received options on January 1, 20XX, to take up 100 €1 shares in Brno for a purchase consideration of €20 per share after the completion of a two-year service period. Brno obtained the services of a valuation expert who calculated the fair value of the share options provided to the directors to be €11 on January 1, 20XX.

The amount recognised as a share-based expense during 20XX amounted to:

$$\left(100 \text{ options} \times 10 \text{ employees} \times €11 \times 1/2 \text{ years}\right) = €5{,}500$$

On January 1, 20XX+1, the share price of Brno shares decreased to €18. The directors expressed concern that their options carried no value, and requested that the entity decrease the consideration price to be paid to €15. The entity decreased the purchase consideration from €20 to €15; a valuation expert calculated the fair value of the €20 share option to be €2 and a €15 share option to be €8 as at January 1, 20XX. All the directors exercised their options on December 31, 20XX+1.

Calculation	
Original issue	**€**
Total benefit	11,000
(10 directors × 100 options each × €11)	
Previously recognised	5,500
Amount still to be recognised	5,500
Modification	

Since the incremental fair value is positive (€8 – €2), the value of the modification based on the incremental fair value is included in the share-based payment expense. The value is €6,000 [10 directors × 100 options each × (€8 – €2) incremental fair value of options at modification date × 1/1 completed service period].

Current year expense

€11,000 (original issue) + €6,000 (modification) – €5,500 (prior year) = €11,500

Journals

December 31, 20XX+1	**€**	**€**
Employment cost (P/L)	11,500	
Equity reserve (Equity)		11,500
Accounting for the 20XX+1 employment cost.		
Bank (SFP)	15,000	
(10 directors × 100 shares × €15)		
Equity reserve (Equity)	17,000	
[€5,500 (20X1) + €11,500 (20XX+1)]		
Share capital (Equity)		1,000
(10 directors × 100 Brno shares)		
Share premium (Equity)		31,000
Accounting for the issue of the share capital to honour the shares issued.		

If the Modification Decreases the Fair Value

If the modification reduces the total fair value of the share-based payment arrangement, or the terms are changed in such a way that the arrangement is no longer for the benefit of the employee, the entity is still required to account for the services received as consideration for the equity instruments granted as if that modification had not occurred.

No changes are therefore made to the accounting for the share-based payment arrangement. Therefore, in the above example, only the €11,000 expense relating to the original issue would be recognised over the vesting period.

Cancellations and Settlements

Where an entity cancels or settles an equity-settled share-based payment award, it accounts for such cancellation or settlement as an acceleration of vesting. The entity, therefore, recognises immediately in profit or loss the amount that otherwise would have been recognised for services received over the remainder of the vesting period.

Example—Vesting service conditions

On January 1, 20XX, Baghdad grants 30 share options to each of its 200 employees. Each grant is subject to the condition that the employees must work for Baghdad for another three years. The fair value of each option is estimated to be €10 at the grant date. Baghdad estimates that 80% of the employees will fulfil the condition to stay for three years. Based on the estimation, the following was recognised during the 20XX financial period:

Employment cost (P/L)	€16,000	
Equity reserve (Equity)		€16,000

Accounting for the 20XX employment cost.
(30 options × 200 employees × 80% (estimated) × €10 × 1/3 years)

During 20XX+1 the share-based transaction was cancelled because the options are out of the money.

The vesting period is accelerated and any outstanding balance is recognised.

Employment cost (P/L)	€32,000	
Equity reserve (Equity)		€32,000

Accounting for the 20XX+1 employment cost.
(30 options × 200 employees × 80% × €10) = 48,000 − 16,000 = 32,000

Employee share options with graded vesting characteristics and service conditions

Under IFRS 2, the compensation expense for share options with graded vesting characteristics and service conditions must be made on an accelerated attribution basis. IFRS does not permit the straight-line method for attribution of the compensation cost of share options with service conditions and graded vesting characteristics. A graded vesting plan assigns the share options to the period in which they vest. This is because IFRS 2 views each tranche of vesting as a separate grant for which services have been provided since the date of the original grant.

The mandatory use of the accelerated amortisation method for share options with graded vesting features results in a higher compensation cost in the earlier years of the vesting period as shown in the example below.

Example—Vesting service conditions

1,000 share options are granted to 100 employees at a grant date fair value of €10 per option, which gives a total share option grant value of €1,000,000. The share option plan provides for a graded vesting of these 1,000 share options, in four equal tranches over a four-year period (or

25%) at each anniversary of the grant. Ignore forfeiture rates for this example. Under the accelerated attribution method, the compensation cost for each of the four years is as follows:

	Year 1	*Year 2*	*Year 3*	*Year 4*
First year vesting 25%	€250,000			
Second year vesting 25%	125,000	€125,000		
Third year vesting 25%	83,333	83,333	€83,333	
Fourth year vesting 25%	62,500	62,500	62,500	€62,500
Total compensation cost for each of the years	520,833	270,833	145,833	62,500

Accordingly, options which vest in Year 2 are deemed to have a two-year vesting period and the ones which vest in Year 3 have a three-year vesting period. The accelerated attribution method shows that the compensation cost for graded options is highly front loaded from the year of grant. The straight-line method of attribution followed under US GAAP would have resulted in a share option compensation expense of only €250,000 in Year 1 compared to €520,833 under IFRS.

CASH-SETTLED SHARE-BASED PAYMENTS

Generally, when goods and services are provided, the seller of the goods and services is paid in cash and the transaction ends. In some cases, the seller expects that the value of the buyer's entity will increase substantially because of the unique nature of or value added by the goods and services provided. In such cases, the seller might prefer to receive a share in the appreciation of the buyer's value and thus structures the "price and payment" to incorporate payment by way of shares in the buyer's entity. Such arrangements amount to a share-based payment. If the buyer does not want to dilute its shareholding, but still wants to pass on a portion of the appreciation to the seller, they could enter into a cash-settled share-based payment. In other words, the cash amount ultimately paid is based on the value of the shares of the buyer.

By the nature of such settlement, these transactions are long term (beyond 12 months). For instance, if they are cash settled immediately or within the financial year, the same accounting entries would be made as for any other cash transaction and recognised as such. However, the objective in cash-settled share-based transactions is to benefit from the potential increase in value of the buyer entity. Therefore, in such transactions an entity should recognise the goods or services either as assets or expenses as the case may be and simultaneously recognise a liability incurred at the fair value of the liability. Until the liability is settled, the entity shall remeasure the fair value of the liability at the end of each reporting period and at the date of settlement. Any changes in fair value of the liability shall be recognised in profit or loss for the period.

In case of services rendered in exchange for share appreciation rights, it may vest immediately or after fulfilment of service conditions.

For example, employees may receive share appreciation rights as part of their remuneration package. In some instances these share appreciation rights vest immediately, and the employees are not required to complete a specified period of service to become entitled to the cash payment. In these instances, the entity shall immediately recognise the services received and a liability to pay for those services.

If the share appreciation rights do not vest until the employees have completed a specified period of service, the entity shall recognise the services received and the corresponding liability as the employees render services over the period required.

Measurement

Fair value of the liability is measured (initially and at each subsequent reporting period) by applying an option pricing model, taking into account the terms and conditions on which the share appreciation rights were granted and the extent to which the services required have been rendered. If the contract also includes services, then the extent of service provided shall also be considered.

Treatment of Vesting and Non-Vesting Conditions

A cash-settled share-based payment transaction might be conditional upon satisfying specified vesting conditions as below:

- *Performance conditions*—Such as the entity achieving a specified growth in profit or a specified increase in the entity's share price.
- *Market conditions*—Such as attaining a specified share price or a specified amount of intrinsic value of a share option and the like.

If the vesting conditions are performance based, then while estimating the fair value of liability, the value is not changed, but the number of awards of "rights" included in the measurement is adjusted.

The following steps will be useful in this regard:

- Recognise an amount for the goods or services received during the vesting period.
- That amount shall be based on the best available estimate of the number of awards that are expected to vest.
- Revise that estimate, if necessary, if subsequent information indicates that the number of awards that are expected to vest differs from previous estimates.
- On the vesting date, finally revise the estimate to equal the number of awards that ultimately vested.

If the vesting conditions are market based, then the fair value is changed based on the market price every time the estimate is remeasured and at the end of the reporting date and at final settlement.

Share-Based Payment Transactions with a Net Settlement Feature for Withholding Tax Obligations

The tax laws or regulations in some countries may require the payee to withhold an associated tax at the time of payment and pay such money directly to the tax authorities on behalf of the recipient. Simply because a payment is made by way of shares (share-based payment) may not remove such withholding tax obligations. The entity that makes a share-based payment may well still have the obligation to withhold tax and pay it to government.

To fulfil this obligation, and using the example of a share-based payment to employees, the terms of the share-based payment arrangement may permit or require the entity to withhold the number of equity instruments equal to the monetary value of the employee's tax obligation from the total number of equity instruments that otherwise would have been issued to the employee or other sellers of goods and services upon exercise (or vesting) of the share-based payment. This arrangement is called the "net settlement feature."

The payment made shall be accounted for as a deduction from equity for the shares withheld, except to the extent that the payment exceeds the fair value at the net settlement date of the equity instruments withheld. Any excess is to be recorded as an expense. In spite of the fact that payment to the tax authorities will involve a cash payment, transactions with "net settlement features" shall be classified in their entirety as an equity-settled share-based payment transaction if they would have been so classified in the absence of the net settlement feature.

The entity shall disclose an estimate of the amount that it expects to transfer to the tax authority to settle the employee's (or other sellers') tax obligation when it is necessary to inform users about the future cash flow effects associated with the share-based payment arrangement.

Classification in its entirety as equity-settled share-based payment is allowed only where the net settlement is because of a tax obligation. It does not apply to:

a. A share-based payment arrangement with a net settlement feature for which there is no obligation on the entity under tax laws or regulations to withhold an amount for an employee's tax obligation associated with that share-based payment; or
b. Any equity instruments that the entity withholds in excess of the employee's tax obligation associated with the share-based payment (i.e., the entity withheld an amount of shares that exceeds the monetary value of the employee's tax obligation). Such excess shares withheld shall be accounted for as a cash-settled share-based payment when this amount is paid in cash (or other assets) to the employee.

Modifications to the Terms and Conditions of a Cash-Settled Share-Based Payment

IFRS 2 did not originally specifically address situations where a cash-settled share-based payment changes to an equity-settled share-based payment because of modifications of the terms and conditions. The IASB subsequently introduced the following clarifications.

On such modifications, the original liability recognised in respect of the cash-settled share-based payment is derecognised and the equity-settled share-based payment is recognised at the modification date fair value to the extent services have been rendered up to the modification date.

Any difference between the carrying amount of the liability as at the modification date and the amount recognised in equity at the same date would be recognised in profit and loss immediately. Guidance on the above is set out in paragraphs B44A–B44C in Appendix B to IFRS 2.

Example—Cash-settled share-based payment

At January 1, 20XX, Casablanca grants a cash-settled share-based payment transaction to 100 employees. In terms of the transaction, each employee is entitled to receive the increase of the independent value of the 10 shares of Casablanca above €20, in cash, after a vesting period of two years' service.

On January 1, 20XX, it was expected that 90% of the employees will still be in service on the vesting date. The actual number of employees in service on December 31, 20XX+1, was 88.

The independent expert valued the right attached to one share as follows:

December 31, 20XX	€6
December 31, 20XX+1	€9

The full liability was settled on December 31, 20XX+1.

Journals		
December 31, 20XX	**€**	**€**
Employment cost (P/L)	2,700	
Share-based payment liability (SFP)		2,700
Accounting for the 20XX share-based payment employment cost. (10 shares × 100 employees × 90% × €6 × 1/2 years)		
December 31, 20XX+1		
Employment cost (P/L)	5,220	
Share-based payment liability (SFP)		5,220
Accounting for the 20XX+1 employment cost. [10 shares × 88 employees (actual) × €9] = 7,920 − 2,700 = 5,220		

SHARE-BASED PAYMENT TRANSACTIONS WITH CASH ALTERNATIVES

Some share-based payment agreements give the parties a choice of settling the transaction in cash or through the transfer of equity instruments. Where such a choice exists, the transaction is accounted for as a cash-settled share-based payment transaction unless either of the following criteria is met:

- There has been a past practice of settling obligations by issuing equity instruments (which can be demonstrated).
- The choice has no commercial substance because the cash settlement amount bears no relationship to, and is likely to be lower in value than, the fair value of the equity instrument. As such, the likelihood of the settlement taking place in cash is, at best, very remote.

If either of these two criteria is met, then the entity can account for the transaction as an equity-settled share-based payment transaction.

Example—Settlement alternatives

On January 1, 20XX, Brighton grants 1,000 shares to a senior executive, subject to a service condition of two years. Each share has a fair value of €25 at the grant date. The executive can choose to receive the 1,000 shares, or cash equal to the value of 1,000 shares, on the vesting date. The fair value of the shares is:

December 31, 20XX	€27
December 31, 20XX+1	€31

The transaction is recorded as a cash-settled share-based payment because the executive has a choice of settlement.

December 31, 20XX	**€**	**€**
Employment cost (P/L)	13,500	
Share-based payment liability (SFP)		13,500
Accounting for the 20XX employment cost. (1,000 shares × €27 × 1/2 years)		
December 31, 20XX+1		

Employment cost (P/L)	17,500	
Share-based payment liability (SFP)		17,500
Accounting for the 20XX+1 employment cost. [(1,000 shares × €31) = 31,000 − 13,500 = 17,500]		

SHARE-BASED TRANSACTIONS AMONG GROUP ENTITIES

The 2009 amendments to IFRS 2 incorporated the guidance contained previously in IFRIC 11 (and IFRIC 11, *Group and Treasury Share Transactions*, accordingly, was withdrawn). For share-based transactions among group entities, in its separate or individual financial statements, the entity receiving the goods or services should measure the expense as either an *equity-settled* or *cash-settled* share-based transaction by assessing:

1. The nature of the awards granted; and
2. Its own rights and obligations.

The entity receiving goods or services may recognise a different amount than the amount recognised by the consolidated group or by another group entity settling the share-based payment transaction.

The entity should measure the expense as an *equity-settled* share-based payment transaction (and remeasure this expense only for changes in vesting conditions) when:

1. The awards granted are its own equity instruments; or
2. The entity has no obligation to settle the share-based payment transaction.

In all other cases, the expense should be measured as a *cash-settled* share-based payment transaction. Consequently, the entity should recognise the transaction as an *equity-settled* share-based transaction *only* if it is to be settled in the entity's own equity instruments (in all other circumstances the transaction is a *cash-settled* share-based payment transaction). In group transactions based on repayment arrangements that require the payment of the equity instruments to the suppliers of goods or services, the entity receiving goods or services should recognise the share-based payment expense regardless of repayment arrangements.

For example, there are various circumstances whereby a parent entity's equity shares are granted to employees of its subsidiaries. One common situation occurs where the parent is publicly traded but its subsidiaries are not (e.g., where the subsidiaries are wholly owned by the parent company), and thus the parent company's shares are the only "currency" that can be used in share-based payments to employees. If the arrangement is accounted for as an equity-settled transaction in the consolidated (group) financial statements of the parent company, the subsidiary is to measure the services under the equity-settled share-based payment transaction. A capital contribution by the parent is also recognised by the subsidiary in such situations.

Furthermore, if the employee transfers from one subsidiary to another, each is to measure compensation expense by reference to the fair value of the equity instruments at the date the rights were granted by the parent, allocated according to the relative portion of the vesting period the employee works for each subsidiary. There is no remeasurement associated with the transfer between entities. If a vesting condition other than a market condition (defined by IFRS 2, Appendix A) is not met and the share-based compensation is forfeited, each subsidiary adjusts previously recognised compensation cost to remove cumulative compensation cost from each of the subsidiaries.

On the other hand, if the subsidiary grants rights to its parent company's shares to the subsidiary's employees, that entity accounts for this as a cash-settled transaction. This means the obligation is reported as a liability and adjusted to fair value at each reporting date.

In group transactions based on repayment arrangements that require the payment of the equity instruments to the suppliers of goods or services, the entity receiving goods or services should recognise the share-based payment expense regardless of repayment arrangements.

Example—Parent company granting stock options to the employees of its subsidiary

On January 1, 20XX, P&Co (the parent company) grants 10,000 shares to senior executives of S&Co (the subsidiary company), subject to a service condition of two years in the subsidiary. Each option has a fair value of €25 at the grant date. At the grant date, S&Co estimates that 75% of the employees will complete the two-year service period. This estimate does not change during the vesting period. At the end of the vesting period, 80% of the employees complete the required two years of service. P&Co does not require S&Co to pay for the shares.

The transactions are recorded in the books of S&Co as follows:

20XX	€	€
Employment cost (P/L)	93,750	
Equity (contribution from P&Co)		93,750
Accounting for the 20XX employment cost. (10,000 shares × 75% × €25 × 1/2 years)		
20XX+1		
Employment cost (P/L)	106,250	
Share-based payment liability (SFP)		106,250
Accounting for the 20XX+1 employment cost. [(10,000 shares × 80% × €25) − 93,750]		

DISCLOSURE

IFRS 2 imposes extensive disclosure requirements, calling for an analysis of share-based payments made during the year, of their impact on earnings and financial position, and of the basis upon which fair values were measured. An entity should disclose information enabling users of the financial statements to understand the nature and extent of share-based payment transactions that occurred during the period.

Each type of share-based payment transaction that existed during the year must be described, giving vesting requirements, the maximum term of the options and the method of settlement (but entities that have several "substantially similar" schemes may aggregate this information). The movement (i.e., changes) within each scheme must be analysed, including the number of share options and the weighted-average exercise price for the following:

- Outstanding at the beginning of the year;
- Granted during the year;
- Forfeited during the year;
- Exercised during the year (plus the weighted-average share price at the time of exercise);
- Expired during the year;

- Outstanding at the end of the period (plus the range of exercise prices and the weighted-average remaining contractual life);
- Exercisable at the end of the period.

The entity must disclose the total expense recognised in the statement of profit or loss and other comprehensive income arising from share-based payment transactions, and a subtotal of that part which was settled by the issue of equity. Where the entity has liabilities arising from share-based payment transactions, the total amount at the end of the period must be separately disclosed, as must be the total intrinsic value of those options that had vested.

The fair value methodology disclosures apply to new instruments issued during the reporting period, or old instruments modified in that time. Regarding share options, the entity must disclose the weighted-average fair value, plus details of how the fair value was measured. These will include the option pricing model used, the weighted-average share price, the exercise price, expected volatility, option life, expected dividends, the risk-free interest rate and any other inputs. The measurement of expected volatility must be explained, as must be the manner in which any other features of the option were incorporated in the measurement.

Where a modification of an existing arrangement has taken place, the entity should provide an explanation of the modifications, and disclose the incremental fair value and the basis on which that was measured (as above).

Where a share-based payment was made to a non-employee, such as a vendor, the entity should confirm that fair value was determined directly by reference to the market price for the goods or services.

If equity instruments *other than share options* were granted during the period, the number and weighted-average fair value of these should be disclosed together with the basis for measuring fair value, and if this was not market value, then how it was measured. The disclosure should cover how expected dividends were incorporated into the value and what other features were incorporated into the measurement.

Financial Statement Presentation under IFRS

The following is an illustration of the treatment of equity that may be required in the financial statements.

EXAMPLES OF FINANCIAL STATEMENT DISCLOSURES

Exemplum Reporting PLC
Financial Statements
For the Year Ended December 31, 20XX

xx. Share-based payments

[A description of each type of share-based payment arrangement that existed at any time during the period, including the general terms and conditions of each arrangement, such as vesting requirements, the maximum term of options granted and the method of settlement (e.g., whether in cash or equity)].	IFRS 2 p44 p45

	20XX Options	**Weighted-average exercise price**	**20XX-1 Options**	**Weighted-average exercise price**	IFRS 2 p44, p45
Outstanding at the beginning of the period	X	X	X	X	
Granted during the period	X	X	X	X	
Forfeited during the period	X	X	X	X	
Exercised during the period	X	X	X	X	
Expired during the period	X	X	X	X	
Outstanding at the end of the period	X	X	X	X	
Exercisable at the end of the period	X	X	X	X	

The weighted average share price of share options exercised during the period at the date of exercise was €X. IFRS 2 p44, p45

Share options outstanding at December 31, 20XX had a weighted average exercise price of €X and a weighted average remaining contractual life of X years. IFRS 2 p44, p45

[Disclose information that enables users of the financial statements to understand how the fair value of the goods or services received, or the fair value of the equity instruments granted, during the period was determined.] IFRS 2 p46

The fair value of the share-based payment instruments were determined by the Black–Scholes–Merton model. The effect of non-transferability has been taken into account by adjusting the expected life of the instruments. Volatility was calculated based on the share price volatility over a similar period preceding the grant date. IFRS 2 p51

Inputs into the model	X
Grant date share price	X
Exercise price	X
Expected volatility	X%
Option life	X years
Dividend yield	X%
Risk-free interest rate	X%

	20XX	**20XX-1**	**IFRS 2 p51**
Total expense recognised from share-based payment transactions	**X**	X	
Equity-settled share-based payment expense	**X**	X	
Share-based payment liability	**X**	X	
Intrinsic value of liabilities arising from vested rights	**X**	X	

US GAAP COMPARISON

Stock Compensation is found in Topic 718 under US GAAP Codification. ASU No. 2018-07 Compensation-Stock Compensation (Topic 718) amends the way that non-employee stock compensation is accounted for under US GAAP. Historically, fair value of the stock was used, now the compensation is calculated similarly using the grant date to be consistent with employee-based compensation and evidence of the completion of the service or delivery of the product which is consistent with the new revenue recognition standard. This "applies to all share-based payment transactions in which a grantor acquires goods or services to be used or consumed in a grantor's own operations by issuing share-based payment awards" and is effective for years beginning after December 15, 2018 for public entities and December 15, 2019 for all other entities.

APPENDIX: EMPLOYEE SHARE OPTIONS VALUATION EXAMPLE UNDER IFRS

An entity should expense the value of share options granted to an employee over the period during which the employee is earning the option—that is, the period until the option vests (becomes unconditional). If the options vest (become exercisable) immediately, the employee receiving the grant cannot be compelled to perform future services, and accordingly the fair value of the options is compensation in the period of the grant. More commonly, however, there will be a period (several years, typically) of future services required before the options may be exercised; in those cases, compensation is to be recognised over that vesting period. There are two practical difficulties with this:

1. Estimating the value of the share options granted (true even if vesting is immediate); and
2. Allowing for the fact that not all options initially granted will ultimately vest or, if they vest, be exercised by the holders.

IFRS 2 requires that where directly observable market prices are not available (which is virtually always the case for employee share options, since they cannot normally be sold), the entity must estimate fair value using a valuation technique that is "consistent with generally accepted valuation methodologies for pricing financial instruments, and shall incorporate all factors and assumptions that knowledgeable, willing market participants would consider in setting the price." No specific valuation method is endorsed by the standard, however.

Appendix B of the standard notes that all acceptable option pricing models take into account:

- The exercise price of the option;
- The current market price of the share;
- The expected volatility of the share price;
- The dividends expected to be paid on the shares;
- The risk-free interest rate; and
- The life of the option.

In essence, the grant date value of the share option is the current market price of the share, less the present value of the exercise price, less the dividends that will not be received during the vesting period, adjusted for the expected volatility. The time value of money, as is well understood, arises because the holder of an option is not required to pay the exercise price until the exercise date. Instead, the holder of the option can invest his funds elsewhere, while waiting to exercise the option. According to IFRS 2, the time value of money component is determined by reference to the rate of return available on *risk-free* securities. If the share pays a *dividend* or is expected to pay a dividend during the life of the option, the value to the holder of the option from delaying payment of the exercise price is only the excess (if any) of the return available on a risk-free security over the return available from exercising the option today and owning the shares. The time value of money component for a dividend-paying share equals the discounted present value of the expected interest income that could be earned less the discounted present value of the expected dividends that will be forgone during the expected life of the option.

The time value associated with *volatility* represents the ability of the holder to profit from appreciation of the underlying shares while being exposed to the loss of only the option premium, and not the full current value of the shares. A more volatile share has a higher probability of big increases or decreases in price, compared with one having lower volatility. As a result, an option on a highly volatile share has a higher probability of a big payoff than an option on a less volatile share, and so has a higher value relating to the volatility fair value component. The longer the option term, the more likely, for any given degree of volatility, that the share price will appreciate before option expiration, making exercise attractive. Greater volatility, and a longer term, each contribute to the value of the option.

Volatility is the measure of the amount by which a share's price fluctuates during a period. It is expressed as a percentage because it relates share price fluctuations during a period to the share's price at the beginning of the period. Expected annualised volatility is the predicted amount that is the input to the option pricing model. This is calculated largely from the share's historical price fluctuations.

To illustrate this basic concept, assume that the present market price of the underlying shares is €20 per share, and the option plan grants the recipient the right to purchase shares at today's market price at any time during the next five years. If a risk-free rate, such as that available on government treasury notes having maturities of five years is 5%, then the present value of the future payment of €20 is €15.67 {= [€20 ÷ $(1.05)^5$]}, which suggests that the option has a value of (€20 − €15.67 =) €4.33 per share before considering the value of lost dividends. If the shares are expected to pay a dividend of €0.40 per share per year, the present value of the dividend stream that the option holder will forgo until exercise five years hence is about €1.64, discounting again at 5%. Therefore, the *net* value of the option being granted, assuming it is expected to be held to the expiration date before being exercised, is (€4.33 − €1.64 =) €2.69 per share. (Although the foregoing computation was based on the full five-year life of the option, the actual requirement is to use the *expected term* of the option, which may be shorter.)

Commercial software is readily available to carry out these calculations. However, accountants must understand the theory underlying these matters so that the software can be appropriately employed, and the results verified. Independent auditors, of course, have additional challenges in verifying the financial statement impacts of share-based compensation plans.

Estimating volatility does, however, involve special problems for unlisted or newly listed companies, since the estimate is usually based on an observation of past market movements, which are not available for such entities. The *Basis for Conclusions* says that IASB decided that, nonetheless, an estimate of volatility should still be made. Appendix B of IFRS 2 states that newly listed entities should compute actual volatility for whatever period this information is available and should also consider volatility in the prices of shares of other companies operating in the same industry. Unlisted entities should consider the volatility of prices of listed entities in the same industry, or, where valuing them on the basis of a model, such as net earnings, should use the volatility of the earnings.

IASB considered the effect of the *non-transferability* on the value of the option. The standard option pricing models (such as Black–Scholes) were developed to value traded options and do not take into account any effect on value of non-transferability. It came to the view that non-transferability generally led to the option being exercised early, and that this should be reflected in the expected term of the option, rather than by any explicit adjustment for non-transferability itself.

The likelihood of the option vesting is a function of the vesting conditions. IASB concluded that these conditions should not be factored into the value of the option, but should be reflected in calculating the number of options to be expensed. For example, if an entity granted options to 500 employees, the likelihood that only 350 would satisfy the vesting conditions should be used to determine the number of options expensed, and this should be subsequently adjusted in the light of actual experience as it unfolds.

Employee Share Options: Valuation Models

IFRS 2 fully imposes a fair value approach to measuring the effect of share options granted to employees. It recognises that directly observable prices for employee options are not likely to exist, and thus that valuation models will have to be employed in almost all instances. The standard discusses the relative strengths of two types of approaches: the venerable Black-Scholes (now called Black–Scholes–Merton, or BSM) option pricing model, designed specifically to price publicly traded European-style options (exercisable only at the expiration date) and subject to criticism as to possible inapplicability to non-marketable American-style options; and the mathematically more challenging but more flexible lattice models, such as the binomial. IFRS 2 does not dictate choice of model and acknowledges that the Black-Scholes model may be validly applied in many situations.

To provide a more detailed examination of these two major types of options valuation approaches, several examples are presented below.

Both valuation models (hereinafter referred to as BSM and binomial) must take into account the following factors, at a minimum:

1. Exercise price of the option.
2. Expected term of the option, taking into account several things, including the contractual term of the option, vesting requirements and post-vesting employee termination behaviours.
3. Current price of the underlying share.
4. Expected volatility of the price of the underlying share.
5. Expected dividends on the underlying share.
6. Risk-free interest rate(s) for the expected term of the option.

In practice, there are likely to be ranges of reasonable estimates for expected volatility, dividends and option term. The closed form models, of which BSM is the most widely regarded, are predicated on a set of assumptions that remain invariant over the full term of the option. For example, the expected dividend on the shares on which options are issued must be a fixed amount each period over the full term of the option. In the real world, of course, the condition of invariability is almost never satisfied. For this reason, current thinking is that a lattice model, of which the binomial model is an example, would be preferred. Lattice models explicitly identify nodes, such as the anniversaries of the grant date, at each of which new parameter values can be specified (e.g., expected dividends can be independently defined each period).

Other features that may affect the value of the option include changes in the issuer's credit risk, if the value of the awards contains cash settlement features (i.e., if they are liability instruments), and contingent features that could cause either a loss of equity shares earned or reduced realised gains from sale of equity instruments earned, such as a "clawback" feature (for example, where an employee who terminates the employment relationship and begins to work for a competitor is required to transfer to the issuing entity shares granted and earned under a share-based payment arrangement).

Before presenting specific examples of accounting for share options, simple examples of calculating the fair value of options using both the BSM and the binomial methods are provided. First, an example of the BSM, closed-form model is provided.

BSM actually computes the theoretical value of a "European" call option, where exercise can occur only at the expiration date. "American" options, which describes most employee share options, can be exercised at any time until expiration. The value of an American-style option on dividend-paying shares is generally greater than a European-style option, since pre-exercise, the holder does not have a right to receive dividends that are paid on the shares. (For non-dividend-paying shares, the values of American and European options will tend to converge.) BSM ignores dividends, but this is readily dealt with, as shown below, by deducting from the computed option value the present value of the expected dividend stream over the option holding period.

BSM also is predicated on constant volatility over the option term, which available evidence suggests may not be a wholly accurate description of share price behaviour. On the other hand, the reporting entity would find it very difficult, if not impossible, to compute differing volatilities for each node in the lattice model described later in this section, lacking a factual basis for presuming that volatility would increase or decrease in specific future periods.

The BSM model is:

$$C = SN(d_1) - K_e\left({}^{-n}N(d_2)\right)$$

where:

C	=	Theoretical call premium
S	=	Current share price
t	=	Time until option expiration
K	=	Option striking price
r	=	Risk-free interest rate
N	=	Cumulative standard normal distribution
e	=	Exponential term (2.7183)
d_1	=	$\dfrac{\ln(S/K)+\left(r+s^2/2\right)^t}{Svvt}$
d_2	=	$d_2 = d_1 - s$
s	=	Standard deviation of share returns
$1n$	=	Natural logarithm

The BSM valuation is illustrated with the following assumed facts; note that dividends are ignored in the initial calculation but will be addressed once the theoretical value is computed. Also note that volatility is defined in terms of the variability of the entity's share price, measured by the standard deviation of prices over the past three years, which is used as a surrogate for expected volatility over the next 12 months.

Example—Determining the fair value of options using the BSM model

BSM is a closed-form model, meaning that it solves for an option price from an equation. It computes a theoretical call price based on five parameters—the current share price, the option exercise price, the expected volatility of the share price, the time until option expiration and the short-term risk-free interest rate. Of these, expected volatility is the most difficult to ascertain. Volatility is generally computed as the standard deviation of recent historical returns on the shares. In the following example, the shares are currently selling at €40 and the standard deviation of prices (daily closing prices can be used, among other possible choices) over the past several years was €6.50, thus yielding an estimated volatility of €6.50/€40 = 16.25%.

Assume the following facts:

S	=	€40
T	=	2 years
K	=	€45
R	=	3% annual rate
S	=	Standard deviation of percentage returns = 16.25% (based on €6.50 standard deviation of share price compared to current €40 price)

From the foregoing data, all of which is known information (the volatility, s, is computed or assumed, as discussed above) the factors d_1 and d_2 can be computed. The cumulative standard normal variates (N) of these values must then be determined (using a table or formula), following which the BSM option value is calculated, *before the effect of dividends*. In this example, the computed amounts are:

$$N(d_1) = 0.2758$$
$$N(d_2) = 0.2048$$

With these assumptions the value of the share options is approximately €2.35. This is derived from the BSM as follows:

$$\begin{aligned} C &= SN(d_1) - Ke^{(-rt)}N(d_2) \\ &= 40(.2758) - 45(.942)(.2048) \\ &= 11.03 - 8.68 \\ &= 2.35 \end{aligned}$$

The forgone two-year stream of dividends, which in this example are projected to be €0.50 annually, have a present value of €0.96. Therefore, the net value of this option is €1.39 (= €2.35 − 0.96).

Example—Determining the fair value of options using the binomial model

In contrast to the BSM, the binomial model is an open form inductive model. It allows for multiple (theoretically, unlimited) branches of possible outcomes on a "tree" of possible price movements and induces the option's price. As compared to the BSM approach, this relaxes the constraint on exercise timing. It can be assumed that exercise occurs at any point in the option period, and past experience may guide the reporting entity to make certain such assumptions (e.g., that one-half of the options will be exercised when the market price of the shares reaches 150% of the strike price). It also allows for varying dividends from period to period.

It is assumed that the common (Cox, Ross and Rubinstein) binomial model will be used in practice. To keep this preliminary example relatively simple to focus on the concepts involved, a single-step binomial model is provided here for illustrative purposes. Assume an option is granted of a €20 share that will expire in one year. The option exercise price equals the share price of €20. Also, assume there is a 50% chance that the price will jump 20% over the year and a 50% chance the shares will drop 20%, and that no other outcomes are possible. The risk-free interest rate is 4%. With these assumptions there are three basic calculations:

1. Plot the two possible future share prices.
2. Translate these share prices into future options values.
3. Discount these future values into a single present value.

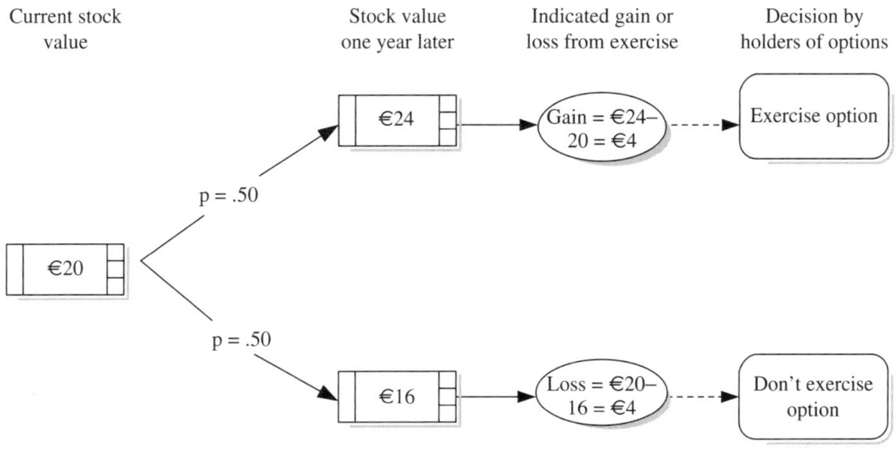

In this case, the option will only have value if the share price increases, and otherwise the option would expire worthless and unexercised. In this simplistic example, there is only a 50% chance of the option having a value of (€4 ÷ 1.04 =) €3.84, and therefore the option is worth (€3.84 × .50 =) €1.92 at grant date.

The foregoing was a simplistic single-period, two-outcome model. A more complicated and realistic binomial model extends this single-period model into a randomised walk of many steps or intervals. In theory, the time to expiration can be broken into a large number of ever-smaller time intervals, such as months, weeks or days. The advantage is that the parameter values (volatility, etc.) can then be varied with greater precision from one period to the next (assuming, or course, that there is a factual basis for these estimates). Calculating the binomial model then involves the same three calculation steps. First, the possible future share prices are determined for each branch, using the volatility input and time to expiration (which grows shorter with each successive node in the model). This permits computation of terminal values for each branch of the tree. Secondly, future share prices are translated into option values at each node of the tree. Thirdly, these future option values are discounted and added to produce a single present value of the option, taking into account the probabilities of each series of price moves in the model.

Example—Multiperiod option valuation using the binomial model

Consider the following example of a two-period binomial model. Again, certain simplifying assumptions will be made so that a manual calculation can be illustrated (in general, computer programs will be necessary to compute option values). Eager Corp. grants 10,000 options to its employees at a time when the market price of shares is €40. The options expire in two years; expected dividends on the shares will be €0.50 per year; and the risk-free rate is currently 3%, which is not expected to change over the two-year horizon. The option exercise price is €43.

The entity's past experience suggests that, after one year (of the two-year term) elapses, if the market price of the share exceeds the option exercise price, one-half of the options will be exercised by the holders. The other holders will wait another year to decide. If at the end of the second year—without regard to what the share value was at the end of the first year—the market value exceeds the exercise price, all the remaining options will be exercised. The workforce has been unusually stable, and it is not anticipated that option holders will cease employment before the end of the option period.

The share price moves randomly from period to period. Based on recent experience, it is anticipated that in each period the shares may increase by €5, stay the same or decrease by €5, with equal probability, versus the price at the period year-end. Thus, since the price is €40 at grant date, one year hence it might be €45, €40 or €35. The price at the end of the second year will follow the same pattern, based on the price when the first year ends.

Logically, holders will rather exercise their options than see them expire, as long as there is gain to be realised. Since dividends are not paid on options, holders have a motive to exercise earlier than the expiration date, which explains why historically one-half the options are exercised after one year elapses, as long as the market price exceeds the exercise price at that date, even though the exercising holders risk future market declines.

The binomial model formulation requires that each sequence of events and actions be explained. This gives rise to the commonly seen decision tree representation. In this simple example, following the grant of the options, one of three possible events occurs: the share price rises €5 over the next year, or it remains constant, or it falls by €5. Since these outcomes have equal a priori probabilities, $p = 1/3$ is assigned to each outcome of this first-year event. If the price does rise, one-half of the option holders will exercise at the end of the first year, to reap the economic gain and capture the second year's dividend. The other holders will forgo this immediate gain and wait to see what the share price does in the second year before making an exercise decision.

If the share price in the first year either remains flat or falls by €5, no option holders are expected to exercise. However, there remains the opportunity to exercise after the second-year elapses, if the share price recovers. Of course, holding the options for the second year means that no dividends will be received.

The cost of the options granted by Eager Corp., measured by fair value using the binomial model approach, is computed by the sum of the probability-weighted outcomes, discounted to present value using the risk-free rate. In this example, the rate is expected to remain at 3% per year throughout the option period, but it could be independently specified for each period—another advantage the binomial model has over the more rigid BSM. The sum of these present value computations measures the cost of compensation incorporated in the option grant, regardless of what pattern of exercise ultimately is revealed, since at the grant date, using the available information about share price volatility, expected dividends, exercise behaviour and the risk-free rate, this best measures the value of what was promised to the employees.

The following graphic offers a visual representation of the model, although in practice it is not necessary to prepare such a document. The actual calculations can be made by computer program, but to illustrate the application of the binomial model, the computation will be presented explicitly here. There are four possible scenarios under which, in this example, holders will exercise the options, and thus the options will have value. All other scenarios (combinations of share price movements over the two-year horizon) will cause the holders to allow the options to expire unexercised.

First, if the share price goes to €45 in the first year, one-half of the holders will exercise at that point, paying the exercise price of €43 per share. This results in a gain of €2 (= €45 − €43) per share. However, having waited until the first year-end, considering the dividend of €0.50 per, the net economic gain is only €1.50 (= €2.00 − €0.50) per share. As this occurs after one year, the present value is only €1.50 × 1.03^{-1} = €1.46 per share. When this is weighted by the probability of this outcome (given that the share price rise to €45 in the first year has only a 1/3 probability of happening and given further that only one-half of the option holders would elect to exercise under such conditions), the actual expected value of this outcome is [(1/3)(1/2)(€1.46) =] €0.24. More formally,

$$\left[(1/3)(1/2)(€2.00-€0.50)\right]\times 1.03^{-1}=€0.2427$$

The second potentially favourable outcome to holders would be if the share price rises to €45 the first year and then either rises another €5 the second year or holds steady at €45 during the second year. In either event, the option holders who did not exercise after the first year's share price rise will all exercise at the end of the second year, before the options expire. If the price goes to €50 the second year, the holders will reap a gross gain of €7 (= €50 − €43) per share; if it remains constant at €45, the gross gain is only €2 per share. In either case, dividends in both years one and two will have been forgone. To calculate the compensation cost associated with these branches of the model, the first-year dividend lost must be discounted for one year, and the gross gain and the second-year dividend must be discounted for two years. Also, the probabilities of the entire sequence of events must be used, taking into account the likelihood of the first year's share price rise, the proclivity of holders to wait for a second year to elapse and the likelihood of a second-year price rise or price stability. These computations are shown below.

For the outcome if the share price rises again:

$$\left[(1/3)(1/2)(1/3)\right]\left\{\left[\left(€7.00\times 1.03^{-2}\right]\left[\left(€0.50\right)\times 1.03^{-1}\right]-\left[€0.50\times 1.03^{-2}\right]\right\}$$

$$=\left[0.05544\right]\left\{€6.59-€0.48-€0.47\right\}=€0.31276$$

For the outcome if the share price remains stable:

$$\left[(1/3)(1/2)(1/3)\right]\left\{\left[\left(€2.00\times 1.03^{-2}\right]\left(€2.00\times 1.03^{-2}\right]-\left[\left(€0.50\right)\times 1.03^{-1}\right]-\left[€0.50\times 1.03^{-2}\right]\right\}$$

$$=\left[0.05544\right]\left\{€1.88-€0.48-€0.47\right\}=€0.05147$$

The final favourable outcome for holders would occur if the share price holds constant at €40 the first year but rises to €45 the second year, making exercise the right decision. Note that none of the holders would exercise after the first year given that the price, €40, was below exercise price. The calculation for this sequence of events is as follows:

$$[(1/3)(1/3)]\{[(€2.00\times 1.03^{-2}]-[(€0.50)\times 1.03^{-1}]-[€0.50\times 1.03^{-2}]\}$$

$$=[0.01111]\{-1.88-€0.48-€0.47\}=€0.10295$$

Summing these values yields €0.709879 (€0.2427 + €0.31276 + €0.05147 + €0.10295), which is the expected value per option granted. When this per-unit value is then multiplied by the number of options granted, 10,000, the total compensation cost to be recognised, €7,098.79, is derived. This would be attributed over the required service period, which is illustrated later in this section. (In the facts of this example, no vesting requirements were specified; in such cases, the employees would not have to provide future service to earn the right to the options, and the entire cost would be recognised upon grant.)

A big advantage of the binomial model is that it can value an option that is exercisable before the end of its term (i.e., an American-style option). This is the form that employee share-based compensation arrangements normally take. IASB appears to recognise the virtues of the binomial type of model, because it can incorporate the unique features of employee share options. Two key features that should generally be incorporated into the binomial model are vesting restrictions and early exercise. Doing so, however, requires that the reporting entity will have had previous experience with employee behaviours (e.g., gained with past employee option programmes) that would provide it with a basis for making estimates of future behaviour. In some instances, there will be no obvious bases upon which such assumptions can be developed.

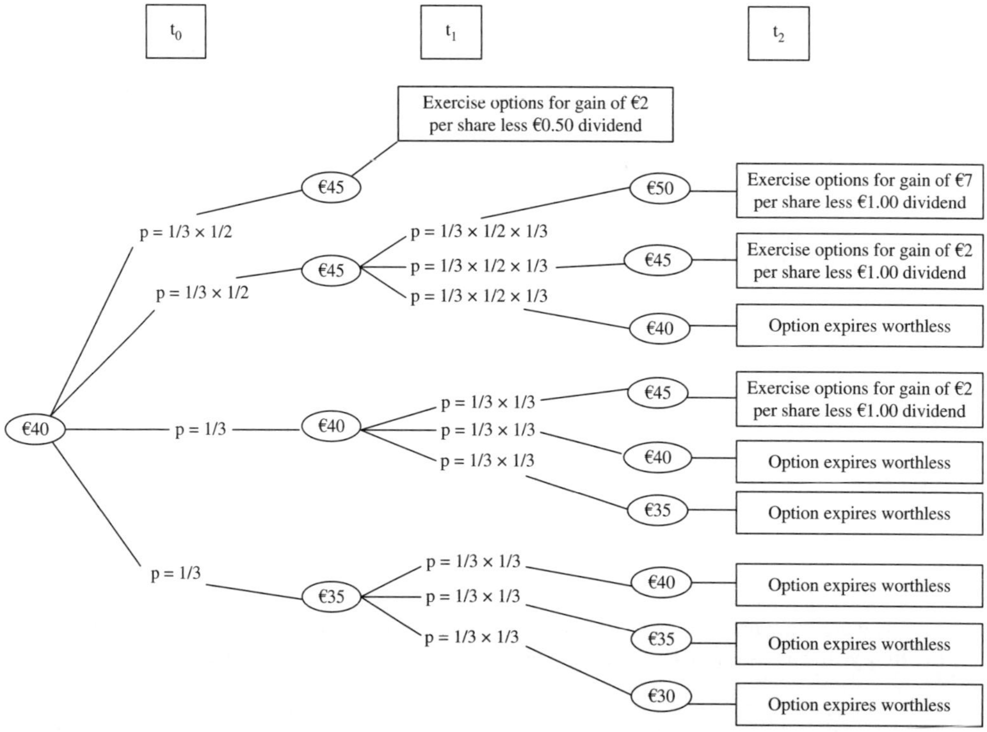

The binomial model permits the specification of more assumptions than does the BSM, which has generated the perception that the binomial model will more readily be manipulated so as to result in lower option values, and hence lower compensation costs, when contrasted to the BSM. But this is not necessarily the case: switching from BSM to the binomial model can increase, maintain or decrease the option's value. Having the ability to specify additional parameters, however, does probably give management greater flexibility and, accordingly, will present additional challenges for the auditors who must attest to the financial statement effects of management's specification of these variables.

18 CURRENT LIABILITIES, PROVISIONS, CONTINGENCIES AND EVENTS AFTER THE REPORTING PERIOD

INTRODUCTION

Accounting for all of a reporting entity's liabilities is clearly necessary to accurately convey its financial position to investors, creditors and other stakeholders. Different kinds of liabilities have differing implications: *short-term trade payables* indicate a near-term outflow, while *long-term debt* covers a wide range of periods, and *provisions* have yet other significance to those performing financial analysis. At the same time, a company with a long operating cycle will have operating liabilities that stretch for more than a year ahead, and some long-term debt may call for repayment within one year, so the distinction is not so clear, and presentation in the statement of financial position is an issue. Transparency of disclosure will also be a consideration beyond mere questions of current or non-current classification.

Historically, it has long been recognised that prudence would normally necessitate the recognition of uncertain liabilities, while uncertain assets were not to be recognised. IAS 37, the key standard on provisions, addresses the boundaries of recognition.

The recognition and measurement of provisions can have a major impact on the way in which the financial position of an entity is viewed. IAS 37 addresses so-called "onerous contracts" which require a company to take into current earnings the entire cost of fulfilling contracts that continue into the future under defined conditions. This can be a very sensitive issue for a company experiencing trading difficulties.

Another sensitive issue is the accounting for decommissioning or similar asset retirement costs, which increasingly are becoming a burden for companies engaged in mineral extraction and manufacturing, but also potentially for those engaged in agriculture and other industry segments. Where historically it was assumed that these costs were future events to be recognised in later periods, it is now clear that these are costs of asset ownership and operation that need to be reflected over the productive lives of the assets, and that the estimated costs are to be recognised as a formal obligation of the reporting entity.

The reporting entity's financial position may also be affected by events, both favourable and unfavourable, which occur between the end of the reporting period and the date when the financial statements are authorised for issue. Under IAS 10, such events require either formal recognition in the financial statements or only disclosure, depending on the character and timing of the event in question, which are referred to as "adjusting" and "non-adjusting," respectively.

In practice, there may be some ambiguity as to when the financial statements are actually "authorised for issuance." For this reason, the standard recognises that the process involved in authorising the financial statements for issue will vary and may be dependent upon the reporting entity's management structure, statutory requirements and the procedures prescribed for the preparation and finalisation of the financial statements. Thus, IAS 10 illustrates in detail the principles governing the determination of the financial statements' authorisation date, which date is required to be disclosed.

	Sources of IFRS	
IAS 1, 10, 37	*IFRS* 9	*IFRIC* 1, 6, 21

DEFINITIONS OF TERMS

Adjusting events after the reporting period. Those events after the reporting period that provide evidence of conditions that existed at the end of the reporting period and require that the financial statements be adjusted.

Authorisation date. The date when the financial statements would be considered legally authorised for issue.

Constructive obligation. An obligation resulting from an entity's actions such that the entity:

a. By an established pattern of past practice, published policies or a sufficiently specific current statement, has indicated to other parties that it will accept certain responsibilities; and

b. As a result, has created a valid expectation on the part of those other parties that it will discharge those responsibilities.

Contingent asset. A possible asset that arises from past events and whose existence will be confirmed only by the occurrence or non-occurrence of one or more uncertain future events not wholly within the control of the reporting entity.

Contingent liability. An obligation that is either:

a. A possible obligation that arises from past events and whose existence will be confirmed only on the occurrence or non-occurrence of one or more uncertain future events which are not wholly within the control of the reporting entity; or
b. A present obligation arising from past events, which is not recognised either because it is not probable that an outflow of resources will be required to settle the obligation, or where the amount of the obligation cannot be measured with sufficient reliability.

Current liability. A liability of the entity which:

a. The entity expects to settle in its normal operating cycle; or
b. The entity holds primarily for the purpose of trading; or
c. Is due to be settled within 12 months after the reporting period; or
d. Does not allow the entity an unconditional right to defer settlement thereof for at least 12 months after the reporting period.

Events after the reporting period. Events, favourable and unfavourable, that occur between the end of the entity's reporting period and the date the financial statements are authorised for issue that would necessitate either adjusting the financial statements or disclosure. These include adjusting events and non-adjusting events.

Legal obligation. An obligation that derives from the explicit or implicit terms of a contract, or from legislation or other operation of law.

Levy. An outflow of resources embodying economic benefits that are imposed by governments on entities in accordance with legislation (i.e., laws and/or regulations), other than:

a. Outflows of resources that are within the scope of other standards (such as income taxes that are within the scope of IAS 12, *Income Taxes*); and
b. Fines or other penalties that are imposed for breaches of the legislation.

Liability. A present obligation of the entity arising from past events, the settlement of which is expected to result in an outflow from the entity of resources embodying economic benefits.

Non-adjusting events after the reporting period. Those events after the reporting period that provide evidence of conditions that arose *after* the end of the reporting period and which thus would *not* necessitate adjusting financial statements. Instead, if significant, these would require disclosure.

Obligating event. An event that creates a legal or constructive obligation that results in an entity having no realistic alternative but to settle that obligation.

Onerous contract. A contract in which the unavoidable costs of meeting the obligations under the contract exceed the economic benefits expected to be received therefrom.

Operating cycle. The operating cycle of an entity is the time between the acquisition of assets for processing and their realisation in cash or cash equivalents. When the entity's normal operating cycle is not clearly identifiable, it is assumed to be 12 months.

Provision. A liability of uncertain timing or amount.

Restructuring. A programme that is planned and controlled by management and which materially changes either the scope of business undertaken by the entity or the manner in which it is conducted.

RECOGNITION AND MEASUREMENT

Current Liabilities

Classification

IAS 1 requires that the reporting entity must present current and non-current assets, and current and non-current liabilities, as separate classifications on the face of its statement of financial position, except when a liquidity presentation provides more relevant and reliable information. In those exceptional instances, all assets and liabilities are to be presented broadly in order of liquidity. Whether classified or employing the order of liquidity approach, for any asset or liability reported as a discrete line item that combines amounts expected to be realised or settled within no more than 12 months after the reporting period and more than 12 months after the reporting period, the reporting entity must disclose the amount expected to be recovered or settled after more than 12 months.

IAS 1 also makes explicit reference to the requirements imposed by IAS 32 concerning financial assets and financial liabilities. Since such common items in the statement of financial position as trade and other receivables and payables are within the definition of financial instruments, information about maturity dates is already required under IFRS. While most trade payables and accrued liabilities will be due within 30 to 90 days, and thus are understood by all financial statement readers to be current, this requirement would necessitate additional disclosure, either in the statement of financial position or in the footnotes thereto, when this assumption is not warranted.

The other purpose of presenting a classified statement of financial position is to highlight those assets and obligations that are "continuously circulating" in the phraseology of IAS 1. That is, the goal is to identify specifically resources and commitments that are consumed or settled in the normal course of the operating cycle. In some types of businesses, such as certain construction entities, the normal operating cycle may exceed one year. Thus, some assets or liabilities might fail to be incorporated into a definition based on the first goal of reporting, providing insight into liquidity, but be included in one that meets the second goal.

As a compromise, if a classified statement of financial position is indeed being presented, the convention for financial reporting purposes is to consider assets and liabilities current if they will be realised and settled within one year or one operating cycle, whichever is longer. Since this may vary in practice from one reporting entity to another, however, it is important for users to read the accounting policies set out in the notes to the financial statements. The classification criterion should be set out there, particularly if it is other than the "one-year threshold" rule most commonly employed.

Nature of current liabilities

Current liabilities are generally perceived to be those that are payable within 12 months of the reporting date. The convention has long been to use one year after the reporting period as the threshold for categorisation as current, subject to the operating cycle issue for liabilities linked to operations. Examples of liabilities which are not expected to be settled in the normal course of the operating cycle but which, if due within 12 months would be deemed current, are current portions of long-term debt and bank overdrafts, dividends declared and payable, and various non-trade payables.

Current liabilities would almost always include not only obligations that are due on demand (typically including bank lines of credit, other demand notes payable and certain overdue obligations for which forbearance has been granted on a day-to-day basis), but also the currently scheduled payments on longer-term obligations, such as instalment agreements. Also included in this group would be trade credit and accrued expenses, and deferred revenues and advances from customers for which services are to be provided or products delivered within one year. If certain conditions are met (described below), short-term obligations that are intended to be refinanced may be excluded from current liabilities. An amendment to IAS 1, effective January 1, 2009, clarified that terms of a liability that could, at the option of the counterparty, result in its settlement by the issue of equity instruments do not affect its classification. For example, if a liability to be settled in full in cash after five years also allows the lender to demand settlement in shares of the borrower at any point prior to the settlement date, that liability will be classified as non-current.

Like all liabilities, current liabilities may be known with certainty as to amount, due date and payee, as is most commonly the case. However, one or more of these elements may be unknown or subject to estimation. Consistent with basic principles of accrual accounting, however, the lack of specific information on, say, the amount owed will not serve to justify a failure to record and report on such obligations. The former commonly used term "estimated liabilities" has been superseded in IAS 37 by the term "provisions." Provisions and contingent liabilities are discussed in detail later in this chapter.

Offsetting current assets against related current liabilities

IAS 1 states that current liabilities are not to be reduced by the deduction of a current asset (or vice versa) unless required or permitted by another IFRS. In practice, there are few circumstances that would meet this requirement; certain financial instruments (to the extent permitted by IAS 32) are the most commonly encountered exceptions. As an almost universal rule, therefore, assets and liabilities must be shown "gross," even where the same counterparties are present (e.g., amounts due from and amounts owed to another entity).

Types of liabilities

Current obligations can be divided into those where:

1. Both the amount and the payee are known;
2. The payee is known but the amount may have to be estimated;
3. The payee is unknown and the amount may have to be estimated; and
4. The liability has been incurred due to a loss contingency.

These types of liabilities are discussed in the following sections.

Amount and Payee Known

Accounts payable arise primarily from the acquisition of materials and supplies to be used in the production of goods or in conjunction with providing services. Payables that arise from transactions with suppliers in the normal course of business, which customarily are due in no more than one year, may be stated at their face amount rather than at the present value of the required future cash flows if the effect of discounting is immaterial.

Notes payable are more formalised obligations that may arise from the acquisition of materials and supplies used in operations or from the use of short-term credit to purchase capital assets. Monetary obligations, other than those due currently, should be presented at the present value of future payments, thus giving explicit recognition to the time value of money. Discounting, however, is only required where the impact of the discounting would be material on the financial statements. In many cases, the discounting of short-term obligations would not be material. (Note that if the obligations are interest-bearing at a reasonable rate determined at inception, discounting is not an issue.)

Dividends payable become a liability of the entity when a dividend has been approved. However, jurisdictions vary as to how this is interpreted. Under most continental European company law, only the shareholders in a general meeting can approve a dividend, and so the function of the directors is to propose a dividend, which itself does not give rise to a liability. In other jurisdictions, the decision of the board of directors would trigger recognition of a liability. Since declared dividends are usually paid within a short period of time after the declaration date, they are classified as current liabilities, should a statement of financial position be prepared at a date between the two events.

Unearned revenues or advances result from customer prepayments for either performance of services or delivery of product. They may be required by the selling entity as a condition of the sale or may be made by the buyer as a means of guaranteeing that the seller will perform the desired service or deliver the product. Unearned revenues and advances should be classified as current liabilities at the end of the reporting period if the services are to be performed or the products are to be delivered within one year or the operating cycle, whichever is longer.

Returnable deposits may be received to cover possible future damage to property. Many utility companies require security deposits. A deposit may be required for the use of a reusable container. Refundable deposits are classified as current liabilities if the entity expects to refund them during the current operating cycle or within one year, whichever is longer.

Accrued liabilities have their origin in the end-of-period adjustment process required by accrual accounting. They represent economic obligations, even when the legal or contractual commitment to pay has not yet been triggered. Commonly accrued liabilities include wages and salaries payable, interest payable, rent payable and taxes payable.

Agency liabilities result from the legal obligation of the entity to act as the collection agent for employee or customer taxes owed to various federal, state or local government units. Examples of agency liabilities include value-added tax, sales taxes, income taxes withheld from employee salaries and employee social security contributions, where mandated by law. In addition to agency liabilities, an employer may have a current obligation for unemployment taxes. Payroll taxes typically are not legal liabilities until the associated payroll is actually paid, but in keeping with the concept of accrual accounting, if the payroll has been accrued, the associated payroll taxes should be as well.

Obligations that are, by their terms, due on demand or will become due on demand within one year (or the operating cycle, if longer) from the end of the reporting period, even if liquidation is not expected to occur within that period, must be classified as current liabilities.

However, when the reporting entity breaches an undertaking or covenant under a long-term loan agreement, thereby causing the liability to become due and payable on demand, it must be classified as current at the end of the reporting period, even if the lender has agreed, after the end of the reporting period and before the authorisation of the financial statements for issue, not to demand payment as a consequence of the breach (i.e., to give forbearance to the borrower).

On the other hand, if the lender has granted an extension before the end of the reporting period (extending for at least one year from the end of the reporting period), then non-current classification would be warranted. Similarly, if the lender has agreed by the end of the reporting period to provide a grace period within which the entity can rectify a breach of an undertaking or covenant under a long-term loan agreement and during that time the lender cannot demand immediate repayment, the liability is to be classified as non-current if it is due for settlement, without that breach of an undertaking or covenant, at least 12 months after the reporting period *and either*:

1. The entity rectifies the breach within the period of grace; *or*
2. When the financial statements are authorised for issue, the grace period is incomplete, and it is probable that the breach will indeed be rectified.

Failure to rectify the breach confirms that current classification of the liability was warranted, and the financial statements would be adjusted to conform to that fact.

Short-term obligations expected to be refinanced

Long-term financial liabilities within 12 months of maturity are current liabilities in a classified statement of financial position. In some cases, the reporting entity has plans or intentions to refinance the debt (to "roll it over") and thus does not expect its maturity to cause it to deploy its working capital. Under provisions of IAS 1, this debt must be shown as current when due to be settled within 12 months of the end of the reporting period, notwithstanding that its original term was for a period of more than 12 months; and that an agreement to refinance, or to reschedule payments, on a long-term basis is completed after the reporting period and before the financial statements are authorised for issuance.

However, if the reporting entity has the ability, unilaterally, to refinance or "roll over" the debt for at least 12 months after the end of the reporting period, under the terms of an existing loan facility, it is classified as non-current, even if it is otherwise due to be repaid within 12 months of the end of the reporting period, if a "rollover" is the entity's intent. This differs from the situation in which refinancing or "rolling over" the obligation is not at the discretion of the entity (as when there is no agreement to refinance), in which case the potential to refinance (which is no more than the borrowers hope in such instance) is not considered and the obligation is classified as current.

Example of short-term obligations to be refinanced

The Marrakech Warehousing Company has obtained a €3,500,000 bridge loan to assist it in completing a new warehouse. All construction is completed by the end of the reporting period, after which Marrakech has the following three choices for refinancing the bridge loan:

- Enter into a 30-year fixed-rate mortgage for €3,400,000 at 7% interest, leaving Marrakech with a €100,000 obligation to fulfil from short-term funds. Under this scenario, Marrakech reports as current debt the €100,000, as well as the €50,000 portion of the mortgage due within one year, with the remainder of the mortgage itemised as long-term debt. The presentation follows:

Current liabilities	€
Short-term notes	100,000
Current portion of long-term debt	50,000
Non-current liabilities	
7% mortgage note due in full by 20XX+30	3,350,000

- Pay off the bridge loan with Marrakech's existing variable rate line of credit (LOC), which expires in two years. The maximum amount of the LOC is 80% of Marrakech's accounts receivable. Over the two-year remaining term of the LOC, the lowest level of qualifying accounts receivable is expected to be €2,700,000. Thus, only €2,700,000 of the debt can be classified as long-term, while €800,000 is classified as a short-term obligation. The presentation follows:

Current liabilities	€
Short-term note—variable rate line of credit	800,000
Non-current liabilities	
Variable rate line of credit due in 20XX+2	2,700,000

- Obtain a loan bearing interest at 10% from Marrakech's owner, with a balloon payment due in five years. Under the terms of this arrangement, the owner can withdraw up to €1,500,000 of funding at any time, even though €3,500,000 is currently available to Marrakech. Under this approach, €1,500,000 is callable, and therefore must be classified as a short-term obligation. The remainder is classified as long-term debt. The presentation follows:

Current liabilities	€
Short-term note—majority stockholder	1,500,000
Non-current liabilities	
10% balloon note payable to majority stockholder, due in 20XX+5	2,000,000

Long-term debt subject to demand for repayment

A lender may have the right to demand immediate or significantly accelerated repayment, or such acceleration rights vest with the lender upon the occurrence of certain events. For example, long-term (and even many short-term) debt agreements typically contain covenants, which effectively are negative or affirmative restrictions on the borrower as to undertaking further borrowings, paying dividends, maintaining specified levels of working capital and so forth. If a covenant is breached by the borrower, the lender will typically have the right to call the debt immediately, or to otherwise accelerate repayment.

In other cases, the lender will have certain rights under a "subjective acceleration clause" inserted into the loan agreement, giving it the right to demand repayment if it perceives that its risk position has deteriorated as a result of changes in the borrower's business operations, liquidity or other sometimes vaguely defined factors. Obviously, this gives the lender great power and subjects the borrower to the real possibility that the nominally long-term debt will, in fact, be short-term.

IAS 1 addresses the matter of breach of loan covenants but does not address the less common phenomenon of subjective acceleration clauses in loan agreements. As to the former, it provides that continued classification of the debt as non-current, when one or more of the stipulated default circumstances has occurred, is contingent upon meeting two conditions. First, the lender has agreed, prior to approval of the financial statements, not to demand payment as a consequence of the breach (giving what is known as a debt compliance waiver); and secondly, that it is considered not probable that further breaches will occur within 12 months of the end of the reporting period. If one or both of these cannot be met, the debt must be reclassified to current status if a classified statement of financial position is, as is generally required under IAS 1, to be presented.

Logic suggests that the existence of subjective acceleration clauses convert nominally long-term debt into currently payable debt as the entity does not have an unconditional right to defer payment for 12 months from year-end. Such debt should be shown as current, with sufficient disclosure to inform the reader that the debt could effectively be "rolled over" until the nominal maturity date, at the sole discretion of the lender.

Payee Known but Amount May Need to Be Estimated

Provisions

Under IAS 37, *Provisions, Contingent Liabilities and Contingent Assets*, those liabilities for which amount, or timing of expenditure is uncertain are deemed to be provisions.

First and foremost, with the issuance of IFRS 15 applicable to entities from January 1, 2018, there are key impacts on IAS 37 as detailed hereunder:

- Type of provision, contingent liability and contingent asset arising from IFRS 15, *Revenue from Contracts with Customers*, shall be dealt with as detailed therein and not under IAS 37;
- However, as IFRS 15 does not deal specifically with contracts with customers that are, or have become, onerous, the same will continue to be dealt with under IAS 37.

Another significant change has been brought about with the issuance of IFRS 16 applicable to entities from January 1, 2019. The key implication is detailed here:

- Where IFRS 16, *Leases*, deals with any types of provisions these provisions are then excluded from the scope of IAS 37. This is unless the lease becomes onerous before the commencement date of the lease in terms of IFRS 16, in which case any provision or contingent liability is then included back into the scope of IAS 37.
- IAS 37 requirements will apply to short-term leases and leases for which the underlying asset is of a low value accounted for in accordance with paragraph 6 of IFRS 16.

IAS 37 provides a comprehensive definition of the term "provision." It mandates, in a clear-cut manner, that a provision should be recognised *only* if:

- The entity has a present obligation (legal or constructive) as a result of a past event;
- It is probable that an outflow of resources embodying economic benefits will be required to settle the obligation; and
- A reliable estimate can be made of the amount of the obligation.

Thus, a whole range of vaguely defined reserves found in financial statements in days past are clearly not permitted under IFRS. This includes the oft-manipulated restructuring reserves commonly created during the business combination process. Now, unless there is a *present obligation* as of the purchase combination date, such reserves cannot be established—in most instances, any future restructuring costs will be recognised after the merger event and charged against the successor entity's earnings.

Many other previously employed reserves are likewise barred by the strict conditions set out in IAS 37. However, the mere need to estimate the amount to be reflected in the provision is not evidence of a failure to qualify for recognition. If an actual obligation exists, despite one or more factors making the amount less than precisely known, recognition is required.

IAS 37 offers in-depth guidance on the topic of provisions. Each of the key words in the definition of the term "provision" is explained in detail by the standard. Explanations and clarifications offered by the standard are summarised below:

- *Present obligation.* The standard states that in almost all cases it will be clear when a present obligation exists. The notion of an obligation in the standard includes not only a legal obligation (e.g., deriving from a contract or legislation) but also a constructive obligation. It explains that a constructive obligation exists when the entity from an established pattern of past practice or stated policy has created a valid expectation that it will accept certain responsibilities.
- *Past event.* There must be some past event which has triggered the present obligation—for example, an accidental oil spillage. An accounting provision cannot be created in anticipation of a future event. The entity must also have no realistic alternative to settling the obligation caused by the event. In other words, if the entity can avoid the expenditure through its own actions, a provision cannot be recognised (e.g., planned future maintenance on a plant).
- *Probable outflow of resources embodying economic benefits.* For a provision to qualify for recognition it is essential that it is not only a present obligation of the reporting entity, but also it should be probable that an outflow of resources embodying benefits used to settle the obligation will in fact result. For the purposes of this standard, probable is defined as "more likely than not." A footnote to the standard states that this interpretation of the term "probable" does not necessarily apply to other IFRS. The use of terms such as probable, significant or impracticable creates problems of interpretation, both within a given set of standards (e.g., IFRS) and across different sets.
- *Reliable estimate of the obligation.* The standard recognises that using estimates is common in the preparation of financial statements and suggests that by using a range of possible outcomes, an entity will usually be able to make an estimate of the obligation that is sufficiently reliable to use in recognising a provision. Where no reliable estimate can be made, though, no liability is recognised.

Other salient features of provisions explained by the standard include the following:

1. *Best estimate.* For all estimated liabilities that are included within the definition of provisions, the amount to be recorded and presented in the statement of financial position should be the *best estimate*, at the end of the reporting period, of the amount of expenditure that will be required to settle the obligation. This is often referred to as the "expected value" of the obligation, which may be operationally

defined as the amount the entity would pay, currently, to either settle the actual obligation or provide consideration to a third party to assume it (e.g., as a single occurrence insurance premium). For estimated liabilities comprised of large numbers of relatively small, similar items, weighting by probability of occurrence can be used to compute the aggregate expected value; this is often used to compute accrued warranty reserves, for example. For those estimated liabilities consisting of only a few (or a single) discrete obligations, the most likely outcome may be used to measure the liability when there is a range of outcomes having roughly similar probabilities; but if possible outcomes include amounts much greater (and lesser) than the most likely, it may be necessary to accrue a larger or lesser amount if there is a significant chance that the larger or lower obligation will have to be settled, even if that is not the most likely outcome as such.

The concept of "expected value" can be best explained through an example:

> Good Samaritan Inc. provides warranty for the machines sold by it, where customers are entitled to refunds if they return defective machines with valid proof of purchase. Good Samaritan Inc. estimates that if all machines sold and still in warranty had major defects, total replacement costs would equal €1,000,000; if all those machines suffered from minor defects, the total repair costs would be €500,000. Good Samaritan's past experience, however, suggests that only 10% of the machines sold will have major defects, and that another 30% will have minor defects. Based on this information, the expected value of the product warranty costs to be accrued at year-end would be computed as follows:

Expected value of the cost of refunds

Resulting from major defects	€1,000,000 × 0.10	=	€100,000
Resulting from minor defects	€500,000 × 0.30	=	150,000
No defects	€0 × 0.60	=	0
	Total	=	€250,000

2. *Risks and uncertainties*. The "risks and uncertainties" surrounding events and circumstances should be taken into account in arriving at the best estimate of a provision. However, as pointedly noted by the standard, uncertainty should not be used to justify the creation of excessive provisions or a deliberate overstatement of liabilities.
3. *Discounting*. The standard also addresses the use of present values or discounting (i.e., recording the estimated liability at present value, after taking into account the time value of money). While the entire subject of present value measurement in accounting has been widely debated, in practice there is a notable lack of consistency (with some standards requiring it, others prohibiting it and many others remaining silent on the issue). IAS 37 has stood firm on the subject of present value measurement and requires the use of discounting when the effect would be material, but it can be ignored if immaterial in effect. Thus, provisions estimated to be due farther into the future will have more need to be discounted than those due currently. As a practical matter, all but trivial provisions should be discounted unless the timing is unknown (which makes discounting a computational impossibility).

   IAS 37 clarifies that the discount rate applied should be consistent with the estimation of cash flows (i.e., if cash flows are projected in nominal terms). That is, if the estimated amount expected to be paid out reflects whatever price inflation is anticipated to occur between the end of the reporting period and the date of ultimate settlement of the estimated obligation, then a nominal discount rate should be used. If future cash outflows are projected in real terms, net of any price inflation, then a real interest rate should be applied. In either case, past experience must be used to ascertain likely timing of future cash flows, since discounting cannot otherwise be performed.

4. *Future events.* Future events that may affect the amount required to settle an obligation should be reflected in the provision amount where there is sufficient objective evidence that such future events will in fact occur. For example, if an entity believes that the cost of cleaning up a plant site at the end of its useful life will be reduced by future changes in technology, the amount recognised as a provision for cleanup costs should reflect a reasonable estimate of cost reduction resulting from any anticipated technological changes. However, in many instances making such estimates will not be possible.
5. *Decommissioning provisions.* IFRIC 1 mandates that changes in decommissioning provisions should be recognised prospectively (i.e., by amending future depreciation charges). More clarity is provided elsewhere in this chapter under the relevant paragraph.
6. *Disposal proceeds.* Gains from expected disposals of assets should not be taken into account in arriving at the amount of the provision (even if the expected disposal is closely linked to the event giving rise to the provision).
7. *Reimbursements.* Reimbursements by other parties should be taken into account when computing the provision, only if it is virtually certain that the reimbursement will be received. The reimbursement should be treated as a separate asset on the statement of financial position, and not netted against the estimated liability. However, in the statement of comprehensive income the provision may be presented net of the amount recognised as a reimbursement. In the authors' observation, recognition of such contingent assets would be very rare in practice due to the longtime horizons and concerns about the viability of the parties promising to make reimbursement payments over the long term.
8. *Changes in provisions.* Changes in provisions should be considered at the end of each reporting period, and provisions should be adjusted to reflect the current best estimate. If upon review it appears that it is no longer probable that an outflow of resources embodying economic benefits will be required to settle the obligation, then the provision should be reversed through current period profit or loss as a change in estimate.
9. *Use of provisions recognised.* Use of a provision is to be restricted to the purpose for which it was recognised originally. A reserve for plant dismantling, for example, cannot be used to absorb environmental pollution claims or warranty payments. If an expenditure is set against a provision that was originally recognised for another purpose, that would camouflage the impact of the two different events, distorting income performance and possibly constituting financial reporting fraud.
10. *Future operating losses.* Provisions for future operating losses cannot be recognised. This is explicitly proscribed by the standard, since future operating losses do not meet the definition of a liability at the end of the reporting period (as defined in the standard) and the general recognition criteria set out in the standard.
11. *Onerous contracts.* Present obligations under *onerous contracts* should be recognised and measured as a provision. In respect of leases, with the introduction of IFRS 16,

only lease contracts which have become onerous before the commencement date of the lease shall be covered by the scope of IAS 37. The standard introduces the concept of onerous contracts, which it defines as contracts under which the unavoidable costs of satisfying the obligations exceed the economic benefits expected. Executory contracts that are not onerous do not fall within the scope of this standard. In other words, the expected negative implications of such contracts (executory contracts which are not onerous) cannot be recognised as a provision.

The standard mandates that unavoidable costs under a contract represent the "least net costs of exiting from the contract." Such unavoidable costs should be measured at the *lower* of:

- The cost of fulfilling the contract; *or*
- Any compensation or penalties arising from failure to fulfil the contract.

12. *Restructuring provisions*. Provisions for restructuring costs are recognised only when the general recognition criteria for provisions are met. A constructive obligation to restructure arises only when an entity has a *detailed formal plan* for the restructuring, which identifies at least the following:

    - The business or the part of the business concerned;
    - Principal locations affected;
    - Approximate number of employees that would need to be compensated for termination resulting from the restructuring (along with their function and location);
    - Expenditure that would be required to carry out the restructuring; and
    - Information as to when the plan is to be implemented.

Furthermore, the recognition criteria also require that the entity should have raised a valid expectation among those affected by the restructuring that it will, in fact, carry out the restructuring by starting to implement that plan or announcing its main features to those affected by it. Thus, until all the conditions mentioned above are satisfied, a restructuring provision cannot be made based upon the concept of constructive obligation. In practice, given the strict criteria of IAS 37, restructuring costs are more likely to become recognisable when actually incurred in a subsequent period.

Only *direct* expenditures arising from restructuring should be provided for. Such direct expenditures should be both necessarily incurred for the restructuring *and* not associated with the ongoing activities of the entity. Thus, a provision for restructuring would not include costs like: cost of retraining or relocating the entity's current staff members or costs of marketing or investments in new systems and distribution networks (such expenditures are in fact categorically disallowed by the standard, as they are considered to be expenses relating to the future conduct of the business of the entity, and thus are not liabilities relating to the restructuring programme). Also, identifiable future operating losses up to the date of an actual restructuring are not to be included in the provision for a restructuring (unless they relate to an onerous contract). Furthermore, in keeping with the general measurement principles relating to provisions outlined in the standard, the specific guidance in IAS 37 relating to restructuring prohibits taking into account any gains on expected disposal of assets in measuring a restructuring provision, even if the sale of the assets is envisaged as part of the restructuring.

A management decision or a board resolution to restructure taken before the end of the reporting period does not automatically give rise to a constructive obligation at the end of the reporting period unless the entity has, before the end of the reporting period: either started to implement the restructuring plan, or announced the main features of the restructuring plan to those affected by it in a sufficiently specific manner that a valid expectation is raised in them (i.e., that the entity will in fact carry out the restructuring and that benefits will be paid to them).

Examples of events that may fall within the definition of restructuring are:

- A fundamental reorganisation of an entity that has a material effect on the nature and focus of the entity's operations;
- Drastic changes in the management structure—for example, making all functional units autonomous;
- Removing the business to a more strategic location or place by relocating the headquarters from one country or region to another; and
- The sale or termination of a line of business (if certain other conditions are satisfied, such that a restructuring could be considered a discontinued operation under IFRS 5).

DISCLOSURES

Disclosures mandated by the standard for provisions are the following:

- For each class of provision, the carrying amount at the beginning and the end of the period, additional provisions made during the period, amounts used during the period, unused amounts reversed during the period and the increase during the period in the discounted amount arising from the passage of time and the effect of change in discount rate (comparative information is not required).
- For each class of provision, a brief description of the nature of the obligation and the expected timing of any resulting outflows of economic benefits, an indication of the uncertainties regarding the amount or timing of those outflows (including, where necessary to provide adequate information, disclosure of major assumptions made concerning future events), and the amount of any expected reimbursement, stating the amount of the asset that has been recognised for that expected reimbursement.
- In extremely rare circumstances, if the above disclosures as envisaged by the standard are expected to seriously prejudice the position of the reporting entity in a dispute with third parties on the subject matter of the provision, then the standard takes a lenient view and allows the reporting entity to disclose the general nature of the dispute together with the fact that, and reason why, the information has not been disclosed. This is to satisfy the concerns of those who believe that mere disclosure of certain provisions will encourage potential claimants to assert themselves, thus becoming a "self-fulfilling prophecy."

For the purposes of making the above disclosures, it may be essential to group or aggregate provisions. The standard also offers guidance on how to determine which provisions may be aggregated to form a class. In determining this, the nature of the items should be sufficiently similar for them to be aggregated together and reported as a class. For example, while it may be appropriate to aggregate into a single class all provisions relating to warranties of different products, it may not be appropriate to group and present, as a single class, amounts relating to normal warranties and amounts that are subject to legal proceedings.

Example footnote illustrating disclosures required under IAS 37 with respect to provisions

Model Disclosure
Provisions

	Environmental costs	Restructuring costs	Decommissioning costs	Total	IAS 37 p84
Balance at January 1, 20XX	X	X	X	X	
Additional provision	X	X	X	X	
Amounts used	X	X	X	X	
Unused amounts reversed	X	X	X	X	
Unwinding of the discount	X	X	X	X	
Balance at December 31, 20XX	**X**	**X**	**X**	**X**	
Non-current provisions	X	X	X	X	IAS 1 p60
Current provisions	X	X	X	X	

Provision for environmental costs. Statutory decontamination costs relating to old chemical manufacturing sites are determined based on periodic assessments undertaken by environmental specialists employed by the company and verified by independent experts.

Provision for restructuring costs. Restructuring provisions arise from a fundamental reorganisation of the company's operations and management structure.

Provision for decommissioning costs. Provision is made for estimated decommissioning costs relating to oilfields operated by the company based on engineering estimates and independent experts' reports.

PRACTICAL EXAMPLES

The following paragraphs provide examples of provisions that would need to be recognised, based on the rules laid down by the standard. It also discusses common provisions and the accounting treatment that is often applied to these particular items.

Dry-Docking Costs

In some countries, it is required by law, for the purposes of obtaining a certificate of seaworthiness, that ships must periodically (e.g., every three to five years) undergo extensive repairs and incur maintenance costs that are customarily referred to as "dry-docking costs." Depending on the type of vessel and its remaining useful life, such costs could be significant in amount. Before IAS 37 came into effect, some argued that dry-docking costs should be periodically accrued (in anticipation) and amortised over a period of time such that the amount is spread over the period commencing from the date of accrual to the date of payment. Using this approach, if every three years a vessel has to be dry-docked at a cost of €5 million, then such costs could be recognised as a provision at the beginning of each triennial period and amortised over the following three years.

Under the requirements set out by IAS 37, provisions for future dry-docking expenditures cannot be accrued, since these future costs are not contractual in nature and can be avoided (e.g., by disposing of the vessel prior to its next overhaul). In general, such costs are to be expensed when incurred. However, consistent with IAS 16, if a separate component of the asset cost was recognised at inception (e.g., at acquisition of the vessel) and depreciated over its (shorter) useful life, then the cost associated with the subsequent dry-docking can likewise be capitalised as a separate asset component and depreciated over the interval until the next expected dry-docking. While the presumption is that this asset component would be included in the property and equipment accounts, in practice, some entities record major inspection or overhaul costs as a deferred charge (a non-current prepaid expense account) and amortise them over the expected period of benefit, which has the same impact on total assets and periodic results of operations.

Unlawful Environmental Damage

Cleanup costs and penalties resulting from unlawful environmental damage (e.g., an oil spill by a tanker ship which contaminates the water near the seaport) would need to be provided for in those countries which have laws requiring cleanup, since it would lead to an outflow of resources embodying economic benefits in settlement regardless of the future actions of the entity.

In case the entity which has caused the environmental damage operates in a country that has not yet enacted legislation requiring cleanup, in some cases a provision may still be required based on the principle of constructive obligation (as opposed to a legal obligation). This may be possible if the entity has a widely publicised environmental policy in which it undertakes to clean up all contamination that it causes, and the entity has a clean track record of honouring its published environmental policy. The reason a provision would be needed under the second situation is that the recognition criteria have been met—that is, there is a present obligation resulting from a past obligating event (the oil spill) and the conduct of the entity has created a valid expectation on the part of those affected by it that the entity will clean up the contamination (a constructive obligation) and the outflow of resources embodying economic benefits is probable.

The issue of determining what constitutes an "obligating event" under IAS 37 has been addressed, in a highly particularised setting, by IFRIC 6, *Liabilities Arising from Participating in a Specific Market—Waste Electrical and Electronic Equipment*. This was in response to a European Union Directive on Waste Electrical and Electronic Equipment (WE&EE), which regulates the collection, treatment, recovery and environmentally sound disposal of waste equipment. Such items contain toxic metals and other materials and have become a concern in recent years, due to the large quantities (e.g., obsolete computers) of goods being dumped by household and business consumers.

The EU Directive deals only with private household WE&EE sold before August 13, 2005 ("historical household equipment"). Assuming enactment of legislation by member states, it is to be mandated that the cost of waste management for this historical household equipment will be borne by the producers of that type of equipment, with levies being assessed on them in proportion to their market shares. This will be done with reference to those manufacturers that are in the market during a period to be specified in the applicable legislation of each EU member state (the "measurement period").

The accounting issue is simply this: what is the obligating event that creates the liabilities for these producers of the defined historical household equipment, which of course all has already been sold by the producers in months and years gone by. IFRIC 6 concludes that it is participation in the market during the measurement period that will be the obligating event, rather than the earlier event (manufacture of the equipment) or a later event (incurrence of costs in the performance of waste management activities). Accordingly, initial recognition of the liability will occur when the measurement period occurs.

While IFRIC 6 was promulgated in response to a specific, and unusual, situation, it does illustrate well how significant making such determinations (the obligating event, in this instance) can be with regard to presentation in the financial statements.

Onerous Contracts

An entity has contracted to obtain forex advisory services for a period of 5 years from an advisory firm with a committed payment for all the five years, with the option to cancel the contract only by paying a significant portion of the professional fee for the balance period. Three months into the contract, the company's business model changes with the result that there is no forex exposure to the company. However, the forex advisory contract can be cancelled only at a significant cost. This is a case of an onerous contract wherein the unavoidable costs of meeting the obligations under the contract exceed the economic benefits under it. A provision is thus required to be made for the best estimate of unavoidable payments under the contract.

Decommissioning Costs

An oil company installed an oil refinery on leased land. The installation was completed before the end of the reporting period. Upon expiration of the lease contract, seven years hence, the refinery will have to be relocated to another strategic location that would ensure uninterrupted supply of crude oil. The estimated relocation or decommissioning costs would need to be recognised at the end of the reporting period. Accordingly, a provision should be recognised for the present value of the estimated decommissioning costs which will arise after seven years.

In 2004, the IASB's committee dealing with implementation issues (IFRIC) issued a final interpretation, IFRIC 1, *Changes in Decommissioning, Restoration and Similar Liabilities*, which provides further guidance on this topic. Specifically, this interpretation specifies how the following matters would be accounted for:

1. Changes in the estimated outflows of resources embodying economic benefits (e.g., cash flows) required to settle the obligation;
2. Changes in current market assessments of the discount rate as defined in IAS 37 (i.e., including changes in both the time value of money and the risks specific to the liability); and
3. Increases that reflect the passage of time (also referred to as the unwinding of the discount, or as accretion of the estimated liability amount).

The interpretation holds that, regarding changes in either the estimated future cash flows or in the assessed discount rate, these would be added to (or deducted from) the related asset to the extent the change relates to the portion of the asset that will be depreciated in future periods. These charges or credits will thereafter be reflected in periodic results of operations over future periods. Thus, no prior period adjustments will be permitted in respect to such changes in estimates, consistent with IAS 8.

Regarding accretion of the discount over the asset's useful life, so that the liability for decommissioning costs reaches full value at the date of decommissioning, the interpretation holds that this must be included in current income, presumably as a finance charge. Importantly, the interpretation states that this cannot be capitalised as part of the asset cost.

Example of adjustment for changes in discount rate

To illustrate the accounting for this change, assume an oil refinery was recorded inclusive of an estimated removal cost, at present value, of €2,333,000. Now assume that, after two years have elapsed, the relevant discount rate is assessed at 6%. There have been no changes in the estimated ultimate removal costs, which are still expected to total €4,000,000. The accreted recorded liability value at this date is €2,722,000, but given the new discount rate, it needs to be adjusted to €2,989,000, for an increase of €267,000 as of the beginning of the third year. The provision account must be credited by this amount, as shown in the journal entry below.

The asset account and accumulated depreciation must also be adjusted for this change in discount rate. Under the proposed requirement, this would be done by recomputing the amount that would have been capitalised, using the initial discount rate for the first two years, followed by the new discount rate over the remaining five years (note that the new rate is not imposed on the period already elapsed, because the rate originally used was correct during those earlier periods). If the €4,000,000 future value were discounted for five years at 6% and two years at 8%, the adjusted initial present value would have been €2,563,000, instead of the €2,333,000 actually recorded. To adjust for this, the asset must be increased by (€2,563,000 − €2,333,000 =) €230,000.

Had the revised present value of the removal costs been capitalised, €732,286 (= €2,563,000 × 2/7) would have been depreciated to date, instead of the €666,571 (= €2,333,000 × 2/7) that was in fact recorded, for a net difference in accumulated depreciation of €65,715. This amount must be credited to the contra asset account:

Asset	€230,000	
Expense	€102,715	
Accumulated depreciation		€65,715
Decommissioning liability		€267,000

The remaining part of the entry above, a debit to expense totalling €102,715, is the net effect of the increase in the net book value of the asset (€230,000 − €65,715 =) €164,285, offset by the increased provision, €267,000, which is an expense of the period.

Bonus payments may require estimation since the amount of the bonus payment may be affected by the amount of income taxes currently payable.

Compensated absences refer to paid vacation, paid holidays and paid sick leave. IAS 19 addresses this issue and requires that an employer should accrue a liability for employees' compensation of future absences if the employees' right to receive compensation for future absences is attributable to employee services already rendered, the right vests or accumulates, ultimate payment of the compensation is probable, and the amount of the payment can be reasonably estimated.

If an employer is required to compensate an employee for unused vacation, holidays or sick days, even if employment is terminated, the employee's right to this compensation is said to vest. Accrual of a liability for non-vesting rights depends on whether the unused rights expire at the end of the year in which they were earned or accumulated and are carried forward to succeeding years. If the rights expire, a liability for future absences should not be accrued at year-end because the benefits to be paid in subsequent years would not be attributable to employee services rendered in prior years. If unused rights accumulate and increase the benefits otherwise available in subsequent years, a liability should be accrued at year-end to the extent that it is probable that employees will be paid in subsequent years for the increased benefits attributable to the accumulated rights, and the amount can reasonably be estimated.

Pay for employee leaves of absence that represent time off for past services should be considered compensation subject to accrual. Pay for employee leaves of absence that will provide future benefits and that are not attributable to past services rendered would not be subject to accrual. Although in theory such accruals should be based on expected future rates of pay, as a practical matter these are often computed on current pay rates that may not materially differ and have the advantage of being known. Also, if the payments are to be made some time in the future, discounting of the accrual amounts would seemingly be appropriate, but again this may not often be done for practical considerations.

Similar arguments can be made to support the accrual of an obligation for post-employment benefits other than pensions if employees' rights accumulate or vest, payment is probable, and the amount can be reasonably estimated. If these benefits do not vest or accumulate, these would be deemed to be contingent liabilities. Contingent liabilities are discussed in IAS 37 and are considered later in this chapter.

Levies

In May 2013, IFRIC issued a new interpretation, IFRIC 21, dealing with levies imposed by a government (or similar body) on an entity. The interpretation addresses the timing of recognition of such a levy that would be within the scope of IAS 37. The interpretation does not apply to liabilities in the scope of other standards, such as IAS 12, *Income Taxes*, nor does it apply to liabilities arising from commercial transactions between government and an entity. The interpretation also explicitly scopes out liabilities arising from emissions trading schemes, presumably since the emissions trading scheme project is still incomplete. The interpretation addresses six specific issues relating to the timing and recognition of levies but does not address measurement of the liability arising from the levy. Once the levy meets the recognition criteria, measurement thereof is the same as for any other liability within the scope of IAS 37.

The first issue deals with identification of the obligating event. The interpretation concludes that the obligating event that gives rise to a liability to pay a levy is the activity that triggers the payment of the levy, as identified by the relevant legislation.

The second issue clarifies that, although an entity may be compelled to continue to operate in a future period from an economic perspective, an entity may claim to have a constructive obligation to pay a levy that will only be triggered by operating in a future period.

The third issue follows on from the second by confirming that an entity that asserts that it is a going concern does not have a present obligation to pay a levy that will only be triggered by operating in a future period.

The fourth issue deals with the timing of recognition of the liability—if the obligating event that gives rise to the levy occurs over a period of time (i.e., if the activity that triggers the payment of the levy, as identified by the legislation, occurs over a period of time), the levy would likewise be recognised as a liability over time. By implication then, if the obligating event occurs at a singular point in time, then the liability is also only recognised when that event occurs, which is consistent with the conclusion reached in issue one.

Some levies may only be payable once a minimum threshold of economic activity has been reached, such as a minimum level of sales during a particular period. The fifth issue reiterates that the previous principles established in the first four issues of the interpretation apply in such cases as well. As a result, a levy will be recognised as a liability only when the minimum threshold (the obligating event) has been reached.

The sixth and last issue addresses those entities that publish interim financial statements. The same principles that are applied in an entity's annual results must be applied to the interim results. This means that if the obligating event has not yet occurred as of the end of the reporting period, no liability may be recognised. The entity may also not recognise a liability for a levy in anticipation of the obligating event being reached by the end of the reporting period.

Any amounts that an entity may have prepaid in respect of a levy must be presented as an asset if the entity does not yet have a present obligation to pay the levy.

Example of accounting for levy payable only after a threshold

To illustrate the accounting for such a levy, assume that a particular levy is applicable if an entity's turnover is in excess of €75,000 in a financial year. In an entity which does not have such turnover per annum at the inception of the year, this leads to the question as to whether the provision should be estimated upfront or not. So long as the obligating event is not reached as of a given date, an estimate of whether such obligating event would be reached by year-end is not required and no levy provision is mandated.

Payee Unknown and the Amount May Have to Be Estimated

The following are further examples of estimated liabilities, which also will fall within the definition of provisions under IAS 37.

Premiums are usually offered by an entity to increase product sales. They may require the purchaser to return a specified number of box tops, wrappers or other proofs of purchase. They may or may not require the payment of a cash amount. If the premium offer terminates at the end of the current period but has not been accounted for completely if it extends into the next accounting period, a current liability for the estimated number of redemptions expected in the future period will have to be recorded. If the premium offer extends for more than one accounting period, the estimated liability must be divided into a current portion and a long-term portion.

Product warranties providing for repair or replacement of defective products may be sold separately or may be included in the sale price of the product. If the warranty extends into the next accounting period, a current liability for the estimated amount of warranty expense anticipated for the next period must be recorded. If the warranty spans more than the next period, the estimated liability must be partitioned into a current and long-term portion.

Example of product warranty expense accrual

The River Rocks Corporation manufactures washing machines. It sold washing machines to the value of €900,000 during its most recent month of operations. Based on its historical warranty claims experience, it provides for an estimated warranty expense of 2% of revenues with the following entry:

Warranty expense	€18,000	
Provision for warranty claims		€18,000

During the following month, River Rocks incurs €10,000 of actual labour and €4,500 of actual materials expenses to repair warranty claims, which it charges to the warranty claims provision with the following entry:

Provision for warranty claims	€14,500	
Labour expense		€10,000
Materials expense		4,500

River Rocks also sells three-year extended warranties on its washing machines that begin once the initial one-year manufacturer's warranty is completed. For one month, it sells extended warranties to the value of €54,000, which it records with the following entry:

Cash	€54,000	
Unearned warranty revenue		€54,000

This liability remains unaltered for one year from the purchase date, during the period of normal warranty coverage, after which the extended warranty servicing period begins. River Rocks recognises the warranty revenue on a straight-line basis over the 36 months of the warranty period, considering that it is not material and hence not discounted, using the following entry each month:

Unearned warranty revenue	€1,500	
Warranty revenue		€1,500

Contingent Liabilities

IAS 37 defines a contingent liability as an obligation that is either:

- A *possible* obligation arising from past events, the outcome of which will be confirmed only on the occurrence or non-occurrence of one or more uncertain future events which are not wholly within the control of the reporting entity; *or*
- A *present* obligation arising from past events, which is not recognised either because it is not probable that an outflow of resources will be required to settle an obligation, or the amount of the obligation cannot be measured with sufficient reliability.

Under IAS 37, the reporting entity does not recognise a contingent liability in its statement of financial position. Instead, it should disclose in the notes to the financial statements the following information:

1. An estimate of its financial effect;
2. An indication of the uncertainties relating to the amount or timing of any outflow; and
3. The possibility of any reimbursement.

Disclosure of this information is not required if the possibility of any outflow in settlement is remote, or if it is impracticable to do so.

Contingent liabilities may develop in a way not initially anticipated. Thus, it is imperative that they be reassessed continually to determine whether an outflow of resources embodying economic benefits has become probable. If the outflow of future economic benefits becomes probable, then a provision is required to be recognised in the financial statements of the period in which the change in such a probability occurs (except in extremely rare cases, when no reliable estimate can be made of the amount needed to be recognised as a provision).

Contingent liabilities must be distinguished from provisions, although both involve uncertainties that will be resolved by future events. However, an estimate exists because of uncertainty about the amount of an event requiring an acknowledged accounting recognition. The event is known, and the effect is known, but the amount itself is uncertain.

In a contingency, whether there will be an impairment of an asset or the occurrence of a liability is the uncertainty that will be resolved in the future. The amount is also usually uncertain, although that is not an essential characteristic defining the contingency.

Assessing the likelihood of contingent events

It is tempting to express quantitatively the likelihood of the occurrence of contingent events (e.g., an 80% probability), but this exaggerates the degree of precision possible in the estimation process. For this reason, accounting standards have not been written to require quantification of the likelihood of contingent outcomes. Rather, qualitative descriptions, ranging along the continuum from remote to probable, have historically been prescribed.

IAS 37 sets the threshold for accrual at "more likely than not," which most experts have defined as being a probability of very slightly over a 50% likelihood. Thus, if there is even a hint that the obligation is more likely to exist than not to exist, it will need to be formally recognised if an amount can be reasonably estimated for it. The impact will be both to make it much less ambiguous when a contingency should be recorded and to force recognition of far more of these obligations at earlier dates than are being given recognition at present.

When a loss is probable, and no estimate is possible, these facts should be disclosed in the current period. The accrual of the loss should be made in the period in which the amount of the loss can be estimated. This accrual of a loss in future periods is a change in estimate. It is *not* to be presented as a prior period adjustment.

Remote contingent losses

With the exception of certain remote contingencies for which disclosures have traditionally been given, contingent losses that are deemed remote in terms of likelihood of occurrence are not accrued or disclosed in the financial statements. For example, every business risks loss by fire, explosion, government expropriation or guarantees made in the ordinary course of business. These are all contingencies (though not necessarily contingent liabilities) because of the uncertainty surrounding whether the future event confirming the loss will or will not take place. The risk of asset expropriation exists, but this has become less common an occurrence in recent decades and, in any event, would be limited to less developed or politically unstable nations. Unless there is specific information about the expectation of such occurrences, which would thus raise the item to the possible category in any event, thereby making it subject to disclosure, these are not normally discussed in the financial statements.

Litigation

The most difficult area of contingencies accounting involves litigation. In some nations, there is a great deal of commercial and other litigation, some of which exposes reporting entities to risks of incurring very material losses. Accountants must generally rely on attorneys' assessments concerning the likelihood of such events. Unless the attorney indicates that the risk of loss is remote or slight, or that the impact of any loss that does occur would be immaterial to the company, the accountant will require that the entity add explanatory material to the financial statements regarding the contingency. In cases where judgements have been entered against the entity, or where the attorney gives a range of expected losses or other amounts, certain accruals of loss contingencies for at least the minimum point of the range must be made. Similarly, if the reporting entity has made an offer in settlement of unresolved litigation, that offer would normally be deemed the lower end of the range of possible loss and, thus, subject for accrual. In most cases, however, an estimate of the contingency is unknown, and the contingency is reflected only in footnotes.

Example of illustrative footnotes—contingent liabilities

1. A former plant manager of the establishment has filed a claim related to injuries sustained by him during an accident in the factory. The former employee is claiming approximately €3.5 million as damages for permanent disability, alleging that the establishment had violated a safety regulation. At the end of the reporting period, no provision has been made for this claim, as management intends to vigorously defend these allegations and believes the payment of any penalty is not probable.
2. Based on allegations made by a competitor, the company is currently the subject of a government investigation relating to antitrust matters. If the company is ultimately accused of violations of the country's antitrust laws, fines could be assessed. Penalties would include sharing of previously earned profits with a competitor on all contracts entered into from inception. The competitor has indicated to the governmental agency investigating the company that the company has made excessive profits ranging from €50 million to €75 million by resorting to restrictive trade practices that are prohibited by the law of the country. No provision for any penalties or other damages has been made at the end of the reporting period since the company's legal counsel is confident that these allegations will not be sustained in a court of law.

Financial Guarantee Contracts

Guarantees are commonly encountered in the commercial world; these can range from guarantees of bank loans made as accommodations to business associates to negotiated arrangements made to facilitate sales of the entity's goods or services.

IFRS provides guidance on the accounting for all financial guarantees—those which are in effect insurance, the accounting for which is therefore to be guided by the provisions of IFRS 4, and those which are not akin to insurance and which are to be accounted for consistent with IFRS 9.

Contingent Assets

According to IAS 37, a contingent asset is a possible asset that arises from past events and whose existence will be confirmed only by the occurrence or non-occurrence of one or more uncertain future events that are not wholly within the control of the reporting entity.

Contingent assets usually arise from unplanned or unexpected events that give rise to the possibility of an inflow of economic benefits to the entity. An example of a contingent asset is a claim against an insurance company that the entity is pursuing legally.

Contingent assets should not be recognised; instead, they should be disclosed if the inflow of the economic benefits is probable. As with contingent liabilities, contingent assets need to be continually assessed to ensure that developments are properly reflected in the financial statements. For instance, if it becomes virtually certain that the inflow of economic benefits will arise, the asset and the related income should be recognised in the financial statements of the period in which the change occurs. If, however, the inflow of economic benefits has become probable (instead of virtually certain), then it should be disclosed as a contingent asset.

Example of illustrative footnotes—gain contingency/contingent asset

1. During the current year, a trial court found that a major multinational company had infringed on certain patents and trademarks owned by the company. The court awarded €100 million in damages for these alleged violations by the defendant. In accordance with the court order, the defendant will also be required to pay interest on the award amount and legal costs as well. Should the defendant appeal to an appellate court, the verdict of the trial court could be reduced or the amount of the damages could be reduced. Therefore, at the end of the reporting period, the company has not recognised the award amount in the accompanying financial statements since it is not virtually certain of the verdict of the appellate court.
2. In June 20XX, the company settled its longtime copyright infringement and trade secrets lawsuit with a competitor. Under the terms of the settlement, the competitor paid the company €2.5 million, which was received in full and final settlement in October 20XX, and the parties have dismissed all remaining litigation. For the year ended December 31, 20XX, the company recognised the amount received in settlement as "other income," which is included in the accompanying financial statements.

Disclosures Prescribed by IAS 37 for Contingent Liabilities and Contingent Assets

An entity should disclose, for each class of contingent liability at the end of the reporting period, a brief description of the nature of the contingent liability and, where practicable, an estimate of its financial effect measured in the same manner as provisions, an indication of the uncertainties relating to the amount or timing of any outflow and the possibility of any reimbursement.

In aggregating contingent liabilities to form a class, it is essential to consider whether the items are sufficiently similar in nature such that they could be presented as a single class.

In the case of contingent assets where an inflow of economic benefits is probable, an entity should disclose a brief description of the nature of the contingent assets at the end of the reporting period and, where practicable, an estimate of their financial effect, measured using the same principles as provisions.

Where any of the above information is not disclosed because it is not practical to do so, that fact should be disclosed. In extremely rare circumstances, if the above disclosures as envisaged by the standard are expected to seriously prejudice the position of the entity in a dispute with third parties on the subject matter of the contingencies, then the standard takes a lenient view and allows the entity to disclose the general nature of the dispute, together with the fact that, and reason why, the information has not been disclosed.

Disclosure example

BP
December 31, 2014
(millions of US dollars)

Part of Note 1: Significant estimate or judgement: provisions

The group holds provisions for the future decommissioning of oil and natural gas production facilities and pipelines at the end of their economic lives.

The largest decommissioning obligations facing BP relate to the plugging and abandonment of wells and the removal and disposal of oil and natural gas platforms and pipelines around the world. Most of these decommissioning events are many years in the future and the precise requirements that will have to be met when the removal event occurs are uncertain. Decommissioning technologies and costs are constantly changing, as well as political, environmental, safety and public expectations. BP believes that the impact of any reasonably foreseeable change to these provisions on the group's results of operations, financial position or liquidity will not be material. If oil and natural gas production facilities and pipelines are sold to third parties and the subsequent owner is unable to meet their decommissioning obligations, judgement must be used to determine whether BP is then responsible for decommissioning, and if so the extent of that responsibility. Consequently, the timing and amounts of future cash flows are subject to significant uncertainty. Any changes in the expected future costs are reflected in both the provision and the asset.

Decommissioning provisions associated with downstream and petrochemicals facilities are generally not recognised, as the potential obligations cannot be measured, given their indeterminate settlement dates. The group performs periodic reviews of its downstream and petrochemicals long-lived assets for any changes in facts and circumstances that might require the recognition of a decommissioning provision.

The provision for environmental liabilities is estimated based on current legal and constructive requirements, technology, price levels and expected plans for remediation. Actual costs and cash outflows can differ from estimates because of changes in laws and regulations, public expectations, prices, discovery and analysis of site conditions and changes in clean-up technology.

Other provisions and liabilities are recognised in the period when it becomes probable that there will be a future outflow of funds resulting from past operations or events and the amount of cash outflow can be reliably estimated. The timing of recognition and quantification of the liability require the application of judgement to existing facts and circumstances, which can be subject to change. Since the cash outflows can take place many years in the future, the carrying amounts of provisions and liabilities are reviewed regularly and adjusted to take account of changing facts and circumstances.

The timing and amount of future expenditures are reviewed annually, together with the interest rate used in discounting the cash flows. The interest rate used to determine the balance sheet obligation at the end of 2014 was a real rate of 0.75% (2013 1.0%), which was based on long-dated US government bonds.

Provisions and contingent liabilities relating to the Gulf of Mexico oil spill are discussed in Note 2. Information about the group's other provisions is provided in Note 21. As further described in Note 21, the group is subject to claims and actions. The facts and circumstances relating to particular cases are evaluated regularly in determining whether it is probable that there will be a future outflow of funds and, once established, whether a provision relating to a specific litigation should be established or revised. Accordingly, significant management judgement relating to provisions and contingent liabilities is required, since the outcome of litigation is difficult to predict.

(The extract from Note 2 is not presented and can be referred to from their Annual Report available online.)

21. Provisions

						$ million
	Decommissioning	**Environmental**[a]	**Litigation and claims**	**Clean Water Act penalties**	**Other**	**Total**
At January 1, 2014	17,205	3,454	4,911	3,510	2,880	31,960
Exchange adjustments	(489)	(18)	(12)	–	(122)	(641)
Acquisitions	8	–	–	–	13	21
New or increased provisions	2,216	561	1,290	–	1,101	5,168
Write-back of unused provisions	(60)	(92)	(27)	–	(252)	(431)
Unwinding of discount	202	19	12	–	24	257
Change in discount rate	778	21	14	–	9	822
Utilisation	(682)	(1,098)	(1,449)	–	(565)	(3,794)
Deletions	(458)	–	–	–	(6)	(464)
At December 31, 2014	18,720	2,847	4,739	3,510	3,082	32,898
Of which – current	836	927	1,420	–	635	3,818
– non-current	17,884	1,920	3,319	3,510	2,447	29,080
Of which – Gulf of Mexico oil spill[b]	–	1,141	3,954	3,510	–	8,605

[a]*Spill response provisions are now included within environmental provisions as they are no longer individually significant.*
[b]*Further information on the financial impacts of the Gulf of Mexico oil spill is provided in Note 2.*

The decommissioning provision comprises the future cost of decommissioning oil and natural gas wells, facilities and related pipelines. The environmental provision includes provisions for costs related to the control, abatement, cleanup or elimination of environmental pollution relating to soil, groundwater, surface water and sediment contamination. The litigation and claims category includes provisions for matters related to, for example, commercial disputes, product liability and allegations of exposures of third parties to toxic substances. Included within the other category at December 31, 2014 are provisions for deferred employee compensation of $553 million (2013 $602 million).

For information on significant estimates and judgements made in relation to provisions, including those for the Gulf of Mexico oil spill, see Provisions, contingencies and reimbursement assets within Note 1.

REPORTING EVENTS OCCURRING AFTER THE REPORTING PERIOD

The issue addressed by IAS 10 is to what extent anything that happens between the end of the entity's reporting period and the date the financial statements are authorised for issue should be reflected in those financial statements. The standard distinguishes between events that provide information about the state of the entity existing at the end of the reporting period and those that concern the next financial period. A secondary issue is the cutoff point beyond which the financial statements are considered to be finalised.

Authorisation Date

The determination of the authorisation date (i.e., the date when the financial statements could be considered legally authorised for issuance, generally by action of the board of directors of the reporting entity) is critical to the concept of events after the reporting period. It serves as the cutoff point after the reporting period, up to which the events after the reporting period are to be examined to ascertain whether such events qualify for the treatment prescribed by IAS 10. This standard explains the concept through the use of illustrations.

The general principles that need to be considered in determining the authorisation date of the financial statements are set out below:

- When an entity is required to submit its financial statements to its shareholders for approval after they have already been issued, the authorisation date in this case would mean the date of original issuance and not the date when they are approved by the shareholders; and
- When an entity is required to issue its financial statements to a supervisory board made up wholly of non-executives, authorisation date would mean the date on which management authorises them for issue to the supervisory board.

Consider the following examples:

1. The preparation of the financial statements of Xanadu Corp. for the reporting period ended December 31, 20XX, was completed by the management on February 15, 20XX+1. The draft financial statements were considered at the meeting of the board of directors held on February 18, 20XX+1, on which date the Board approved them and authorised them for issuance. The annual general meeting (AGM) was held on March 28, 20XX+1, after allowing for printing and the requisite notice period mandated by the corporate statute. At the AGM the shareholders approved the financial statements. The approved financial statements were filed by the corporation with the Company Law Board (the statutory body of the country that regulates corporations) on April 6, 20XX+1.

   Given these facts, the date of authorisation of the financial statements of Xanadu Corp. for the year ended December 31, 20XX, is February 18, 20XX+1, the date when the Board approved them and authorised them for issue (and not the date they were approved in the AGM by the shareholders). Thus, all post-reporting period events between December 31, 20XX, and February 18, 20XX+1, need to be considered by Xanadu Corp. for the purposes of evaluating whether or not they are to be accounted or reported under IAS 10.
2. Suppose in the above cited case the management of Xanadu Corp. was required to issue the financial statements to a supervisory board (consisting solely of non-executives, including representatives of a trade union). The management of Xanadu Corp. had issued the draft financial statements to the supervisory board on February 16, 20XX+1. The supervisory board approved them on February 17, 20XX+1, and the shareholders approved them in the AGM held on March 28, 20XX+1. The approved financial statements were filed with the Company Law Board on April 6, 20XX+1.

In this case the date of authorisation of financial statements would be February 16, 20XX+1, the date the draft financial statements were issued to the supervisory board. Thus, all post-reporting period events between December 31, 20XX, and February 16, 20XX+1, need to be considered by Xanadu Corp. for the purposes of evaluating whether or not they are to be accounted for or reported under IAS 10.

Adjusting and Non-Adjusting Events (After the Reporting Period)

Two types of events after the reporting period are distinguished by the standard. These are, respectively, "adjusting events after the reporting period" and "non-adjusting events after the reporting period." Adjusting events are those post-reporting period events that provide evidence of conditions that actually existed at the end of the reporting period, albeit they were not known at the time. Financial statements should be adjusted to reflect adjusting events after the reporting period.

Examples of *adjusting events*, given by the standard, are the following:

1. Resolution after the reporting period of a court case that confirms a present obligation requiring either an adjustment to an existing provision or recognition of a provision instead of mere disclosure of a contingent liability;
2. Receipt of information after the reporting period indicating that an asset was impaired or that a previous impairment loss needs to be adjusted. For instance, the bankruptcy of a customer subsequent to the end of the reporting period usually confirms that the customer was credit impaired at the end of the reporting period, and the disposal of inventories after the reporting period provides evidence (not always conclusive, however) about their net realisable value at the date of the statement of financial position;
3. The determination after the reporting period of the cost of assets purchased, or the proceeds from assets disposed of, before the reporting date;
4. The determination subsequent to the end of the reporting period of the amount of profit sharing or bonus payments, where there was a present legal or constructive obligation at the reporting date to make the payments as a result of events before that date; and
5. The discovery of frauds or errors, after the reporting period, that show that the financial statements were incorrect at the reporting date before the adjustment.

Commonly encountered situations of adjusting events are illustrated below:

- During the year 20XX Taj Corp. was sued by a competitor for €10 million for infringement of a trademark. Based on the advice of the company's legal counsel, Taj accrued the sum of €5 million as a provision in its financial statements for the year ended December 31, 20XX. Subsequent to the date of the statement of financial position, on February 15, 20XX+1, the Supreme Court decided in favour of the party alleging infringement of the trademark and ordered the defendant to pay the aggrieved party a sum of €7 million. The financial statements were prepared by the company's management on January 31, 20XX+1, and approved by the Board on February 20, 20XX+1. Taj Corp. should adjust the provision by €2 million to reflect the award decreed by the Supreme Court (assumed to be the final appellate authority on the matter in this example) to be paid by Taj Corp. to its competitor. Had the judgement of the Supreme Court been delivered on February 25, 20XX+1, or later, this post-reporting period event would have occurred after the cutoff point (i.e., the date the financial statements were authorised for original issuance). If so, adjustment of financial statements would not have been required.

- Penn Corp. carries its inventory at the lower of cost and net realisable value. At December 31, 20XX, the cost of inventory, determined under the FIFO method, as reported in its financial statements for the year then ended, was €5 million. Due to severe recession and other negative economic trends in the market, the inventory could not be sold during the entire month of January 20XX+1. On February 10, 20XX+1, Penn Corp. entered into an agreement to sell the entire inventory to a competitor for €4 million. Presuming the financial statements were authorised for issuance on February 15, 20XX+1, the company should recognise a write-down of €1 million in the financial statements for the year ended December 31, 20XX, provided that this was determined to be an indicator of the value at year-end.

In contrast with the foregoing, *non-adjusting events* are those post-reporting period events that are indicative of conditions that arose after the reporting period. Financial statements should not be adjusted to reflect non-adjusting events after the end of the reporting period. An example of a non-adjusting event is a decline in the market value of investments between the date of the statement of financial position and the date when the financial statements are authorised for issue. Since the fall in the market value of investments after the reporting period is not indicative of their market value at the date of the statement of financial position (instead it reflects circumstances that arose subsequent to the end of the reporting period) the fall in market value need not, and should not, be recognised in the financial statements at the date of the statement of financial position.

Not all non-adjusting events are significant enough to require disclosure, however. The revised standard gives examples of non-adjusting events that would impair the ability of the users of financial statements to make proper evaluations or decisions if not disclosed. Where non-adjusting events after the reporting period are of such significance, disclosure should be made for each such significant category of non-adjusting event, of the nature of the event and an estimate of its financial effect or a statement that such an estimate cannot be made. Examples given by the standard of such significant non-adjusting post-reporting period events are the following:

1. A major business combination or disposing of a major subsidiary;
2. Announcing a plan to discontinue an operation;
3. Major purchases and disposals of assets or expropriation of major assets by government;
4. The destruction of a major production plant by fire;
5. Announcing or commencing the implementation of a major restructuring;
6. Abnormally large changes in asset prices or foreign exchange rates;
7. Significant changes in tax rates and enacted tax laws;

8. Entering into significant commitments or contingent liabilities; and
9. Major litigation arising from events occurring after the reporting period.

Dividends Proposed or Declared After the Reporting Period

Dividends on equity instruments proposed or declared after the reporting period should not be recognised as a liability at the end of the reporting period. In other words, such declaration is a non-adjusting subsequent event. While at one-time IFRS did permit accrual of post-balance sheet dividend declarations, this has not been permissible for quite some time. Furthermore, the revisions made to IAS 10 as part of the IASB's Improvements Project in late 2003 (which became effective 2005) also eliminated the display of post-reporting period dividends as a separate component of equity, as was formerly permitted. Footnote disclosure is, on the other hand, required unless immaterial.

A further clarification has been added by the 2008 *Improvements*, a collection of major and minor changes made in 2008. It states that, if dividends are declared (i.e., the dividends are appropriately authorised and no longer at the discretion of the entity) after the reporting period but before the financial statements are authorised for issue, the dividends are not recognised as a liability at the end of the reporting period, for the very simple reason that *no obligation existed at that time*. This rudimentary expansion of the language of IAS 10 was deemed necessary because it had been asserted that a *constructive obligation* could exist under certain circumstances, making formal accrual of a dividend liability warranted. The *Improvements* language makes it clear that this is never the case.

Going Concern Considerations

Deterioration in an entity's financial position after the end of the reporting period could cast substantial doubts about an entity's ability to continue as a going concern. IAS 10 requires that an entity should not prepare its financial statements on a going concern basis if management determines after the end of the reporting period that it either intends to liquidate the entity or cease trading, or that it has no realistic alternative but to do so. IAS 10 notes that disclosures prescribed by IAS 1 under such circumstances should also be complied with.

Disclosure Requirements

The following disclosures are mandated by IAS 10:

1. The date when the financial statements were authorised for issue and who gave that authorisation. If the entity's owners have the power to amend the financial statements after issuance, this fact should be disclosed;
2. If information is received after the reporting period about conditions that existed at the date of the statement of financial position, disclosures that relate to those conditions should be updated in the light of the new information; and
3. Where non-adjusting events after the reporting period are of such significance that non-disclosure would affect the ability of the users of financial statements to make proper evaluations and decisions, disclosure should be made for each such significant category of non-adjusting event, of the nature of the event and an estimate of its financial effect or a statement that such an estimate cannot be made.

EXAMPLES OF FINANCIAL STATEMENT DISCLOSURES

Exemplum Reporting PLC
Financial Statements
For the Year Ended December 31, 20XX

35.1 Flood damage

A widget manufacturing factory was severely damaged in a flash flood on January 17, 20XX. The value of the factory and its contents were insured in full and claims put forward to the insurers are being processed. The group was, however, not insured for the loss of business due to factory downtime. The loss of business is estimated to result in financial losses of €X. IAS 10 p21

35.2 Acquisition of a subsidiary

After the reporting period but before the financial statements were authorised for issue the group acquired 100% of the share capital of Subsidiary D Ltd. The fair value of assets acquired and liabilities assumed on the acquisition date of February 1, 20XX+1 were as follows: IFRS 3 Pb64

	€
Cash	X
Inventories	X
Trade receivables	X
Property, plant and equipment	X
Trade payables	X
Long-term debt	X
Total net assets	X
Goodwill	X
Total fair value of consideration paid	X
Less: Fair value of shares issued	X
Cash	X
Less: Cash of Subsidiary D Ltd	X
Cash flow on acquisition net of cash acquired	X

Goodwill represents the value of the synergies arising from the vertical integration of the group's operations. These synergistic benefits were the primary reason for entering into the business combination. The total amount of goodwill that is expected to be deductible for tax purposes is €X.

US GAAP COMPARISON

There are substantial differences between US GAAP and IFRS, the first of which is US GAAP does not use the term "provisions"; the term "accrual" is used instead.

Under US GAAP, constructive obligations are only recognised for environmental obligations, decommissioning obligations, post-retirement benefits and legal disputes. Discount rates used to measure provisions at present value are a risk-adjusted risk-free rate that reflects the entity's credit standing.

To recognise a contingency under US GAAP, a loss must be "probable," meaning "likely to occur" and no percentage is assigned. Under IFRS, "probable" is interpreted as more likely than not, which refers to a probability of greater than 50%. In this scenario IFRS is more likely to have recorded the liability sooner in IFRS than under US GAAP.

When a range of estimates is available for a provision, the minimum amount is accrued under US GAAP when other estimates are equally probable, including zero. IFRS uses the single most likely estimate to measure a provision.

Under US GAAP, joint and several liability arrangements for which the total amount of the obligation is fixed at the reporting date are recognised as the sum of the amount the reporting entity agreed to pay on the basis of its arrangement among its co-obligors and any additional amount the reporting entity expects to pay on behalf of its co-obligors. However, this measurement attribute does not apply if the obligations are addressed within existing US GAAP.

Onerous contracts are not recognised as provisions. The effects are recognised upon settlement of the obligation. Exit costs are provided for only when a detailed plan is in place and recipients of severance have agreed to the terms. Costs for which employees are required to work are recognised as the work is performed. There are no provisions that allow for accrual of general costs to wind down a business under US GAAP.

Asset retirement obligations (AROs) are largely the same, but the difference in the discount rate used to measure the obligations creates an inherent difference in the carrying value. To discount the obligation, US GAAP uses a risk-free rate adjusted for the entity's credit risk. IFRS uses the time value of money rate adjusted for specific risks of the liability. Also, period-to-period changes in the discount rate do not affect an accrual that has not changed. The discount rate applied to each increment of an accrual, termed "layers" in US GAAP, remains within that layer. Also, AROs are not recognised under GAAP unless there is a present legal obligation and the fair value of the obligation can be reasonably estimated.

Under US GAAP, provisions may be discounted when the liability's amount and timing are fixed or reliably determinable or when the obligation is at fair value. The discount rate depends on the nature of the accrual.

Regarding restructuring costs, under US GAAP, once management has committed to a restructuring plan, each type of cost is examined to determine when it should be recognised. Involuntary employee terminations costs under a one-time benefit arrangement are expensed over the future service period. If no future service is required, the costs are expensed immediately. Other exit costs are expensed when incurred.

Current updates are concurrent with the new leasing standards which pull the lease liability obligations as part of the liabilities which are similar to IFRS.

19 EMPLOYEE BENEFITS

INTRODUCTION

The prescribed rules for the accounting for employee benefits under IFRS have evolved markedly over the past 25 years. The current standard, IAS 19, was last subjected to a major revision in 1998, with further limited amendments made in 2000, 2002, 2004 and 2008, and yet further amendments made in 2011 and in November 2013. IAS 19 provides broad guidance, applicable to all employee benefits, not merely to pension plans.

The objective of employee benefit accounting is primarily the appropriate determination of periodic cost. Under IAS 19, only one basic method, the "projected unit credit" variation on the *accrued benefit valuation* method, is permitted for the periodic determination of this cost.

IAS 19 identifies and provides accounting direction for four categories of employee benefits: short-term benefits such as wages, bonuses and emoluments such as medical care; post-employment benefits such as pensions and other post-retirement benefits; other long-term benefits such as sabbatical leave; and termination benefits. Another major category of employee compensation, share-based compensation arrangements, is dealt with in terms of IFRS 2, which is addressed in detail in Chapter 17.

Pension plans traditionally have existed in two basic varieties: defined contribution and defined benefit. The accounting for the latter is comparatively more complex. Defined benefit plan accounting in particular remains a controversial subject because of the heavy impact that various management assumptions have on expense determination.

IAS 19 also establishes requirements for disclosures to be made by employers when defined contribution or defined benefit pension plans are settled, curtailed or terminated.

IAS 19 defines all post-employment benefits other than defined contribution plans as defined benefit plans and, thus, all the accounting complexities of defined benefit pension plans would apply. These difficulties may be exacerbated, in the case of post-retirement health care plans, by the need to project the future escalation in health care costs over a rather lengthy time horizon, which is a famously difficult exercise to undertake.

In July 2007, IFRIC 14 was issued, addressing the problems that arise from the interaction between the limitation on defined benefit plan asset recognition by employers/plan sponsors under IAS 19 and the statutory minimum funding requirements that exist under some jurisdictions. An amendment to IFRIC 14 was issued in November 2009 to correct an unintended consequence of that interpretation, which caused certain reporting entities, under some circumstances, to be prevented from recognising as an asset some prepayments for minimum funding contributions.

Sources of IFRS	
IAS 19	*IFRIC* 14

DEFINITIONS OF TERMS

Actuarial gains and losses. Include (1) experience adjustments (the effects of differences between the previous actuarial assumptions and what has actually occurred), and (2) the effects of changes in actuarial assumptions.

Asset ceiling. The present value of any economic benefits available in the form of refunds from the plan or reductions in future contributions to the plan.

Current service cost. The increase in the present value of the defined benefit obligation resulting from services rendered by employees during the period.

Deficit or surplus. The present value of the defined benefit obligations less the fair value of plan assets (if any).

Defined benefit plans. Any post-employment benefit plan other than a defined contribution plan. These are generally retirement benefit plans under which amounts to be paid as retirement benefits are determinable, usually by reference to employees' earnings and/or years of service. The fund (and/or employer) is obligated either legally or constructively to pay the full amount of promised benefits whether or not sufficient assets are held in the fund.

Defined contribution plans. Benefit plans under which amounts to be paid as retirement benefits are determined by the contributions to a fund together with accumulated investment earnings thereon; the plan has no obligation to pay further sums if the amounts available cannot pay all benefits relating to employee services in the current and prior periods.

Employee benefits. All forms of consideration to employees in exchange for services rendered.

Fair value. Amount that an asset could be exchanged for between willing, knowledgeable parties in an arm's-length transaction.

Multi-employer plans. Defined contribution plans or defined benefit plans, other than state plans, that (1) pool the assets contributed by various entities that are not under common control; and (2) use those assets to provide benefits to employees of more than one entity, on the basis that contribution and benefit levels are determined without regard to the identity of the entity that employs the employees concerned.

Net defined benefit liability (asset). Deficit or surplus adjusted for any effect of limiting a net defined benefit asset to the asset ceiling

Net interest on the net defined benefit liability (asset). The change during the period in the net defined benefit liability (asset) that arises from the passage of time.

Other long-term employee benefits. Benefits other than post-employment, termination and stock equity compensation benefits that are not due to be settled within 12 months after the end of the period in which service was rendered.

Past service cost. The change in the present value of the defined benefit obligation for employee services in prior periods, resulting in the current period from the introduction of, or changes to, post-employment benefits or other long-term employee benefits. Past service cost may be either positive (when benefits are introduced or changed so that the present value of the defined benefit obligation increases) or negative (when existing benefits are changed so that the present value of the defined benefit obligation decreases).

Plan assets. The assets held by a long-term employee benefit fund and qualifying insurance policies. Regarding *assets held by a long-term employee benefit fund*, these are assets (other than non-transferable financial instruments issued by the reporting entity) that both:

1. Are held by a fund that is legally separate from the reporting entity and exists solely to pay or fund employee benefits; and
2. Are available to be used only to pay or fund employee benefits, are not available to the reporting entity's own creditors (even in the event of bankruptcy) and cannot be returned to the reporting entity unless either:
    a. The remaining assets of the fund are sufficient to meet all related employee benefit obligations of the plan or the entity; or
    b. The assets are returned to the reporting entity to reimburse it for employee benefits already paid by it.

Regarding the *qualifying insurance policy*, this must be issued by a non-related party if the proceeds of the policy both:

1. Can be used only to pay or fund employee benefits under a defined benefit plan; and
2. Are not available to the reporting entity's own creditors (even in the event of bankruptcy) and cannot be returned to the reporting entity unless either:
    a. The proceeds represent surplus assets that are not needed for the policy to meet all related employee benefit obligations; or

b. The proceeds are returned to the reporting entity to reimburse it for employee benefits already paid by it.

Post-employment benefit plans. Formal or informal arrangements under which an entity provides post-employment benefits for one or more employees.

Post-employment benefits. Employee benefits, other than termination benefits and short-term employee benefits, that are payable after the completion of employment.

Present value of a defined benefit obligation. Present value, without deducting any plan assets, of expected future payments required to settle the obligation resulting from employee service in the current and prior periods.

Remeasurements of the net defined benefit liability (asset). Comprised of:

1. Actuarial gains and losses;
2. The return on plan assets, excluding amounts included in net interest on the net defined benefit liability (asset); and
3. Any change in the effect of the asset ceiling, excluding amounts included in net interest on the net defined benefit liability (asset).

Return on plan assets. Interest, dividends and other revenues derived from plan assets, together with realised and unrealised gains or losses on the plan assets, less administrative costs (other than those included in the actuarial assumptions used to measure the defined benefit obligation), including taxes payable by the plan.

Service costs. Comprised of:

1. *Current service cost.* The increase in the present value of the defined benefit obligation resulting from services rendered by employees during the period;
2. *Past service cost.* The change in the present value of the defined benefit obligation for employee service in prior periods, resulting from a plan amendment (the introduction or withdrawal of, or changes to, a defined benefit plan) or a curtailment (a significant reduction by the entity in the number of employees covered by a plan); and
3. Any gain or loss on *settlement*.

Settlement. A transaction that eliminates all further legal or constructive obligations for part or all of the benefits provided under a defined benefit plan, other than a payment of benefits to, or on behalf of, employees that is set out in the terms of the plan and included in the actuarial assumptions.

Short-term employee benefits. Benefits, other than termination and equity compensation benefits, that are due to be settled within 12 months after the end of the period in which the employees rendered the related service.

Termination benefits. Employee benefits payable as a result of the entity's termination of employment before normal retirement or the employee's acceptance of early retirement inducements.

BACKGROUND

Importance of Pension and Other Benefit Plan Accounting

For a variety of cultural, economic and political reasons, the existence of private pension plans has increased tremendously over the past 40 years, and these arrangements are the most common and desired of the assorted "fringe benefits" offered by employers in many nations. Under the laws of some nations, employers may be required to have such programmes in place for their permanent employees. For many entities, pension costs have become a very material component of the total compensation paid to employees. Unlike for wages and other fringe benefits, the timing of the payment of cash to either the plan's administrators or to the plan beneficiaries can vary substantially from the underlying economic event (that is, the plans are not always fully funded on a current basis). This creates the possibility of misleading financial statement representation of the true costs of conducting business, unless a valid accrual method is employed. For this reason, and also because of the complexity of these arrangements and the impact they have on the welfare of the workers, accounting for the cost of pension plans and similar schemes (post-retirement benefits other than pensions, etc.) has received a great deal of attention from national and international standards setters.

Basic Objectives of Accounting for Pension and Other Benefit Plan Costs

Need for pension accounting rules

The principal objectives of pension accounting are to measure the compensation cost associated with employees' benefits and to recognise that cost over the employees' respective service periods. The relevant standard, IAS 19, is concerned only with the accounting aspects of pensions (and other benefit plans). The funding of pension benefits is considered to be a financial management and legal concern, and accordingly is not addressed by this pronouncement.

When an entity provides benefits, the amounts of which can be estimated in advance, to its retired employees and their beneficiaries, the arrangement is deemed to be a pension plan. The typical plan is written, and the amounts of future benefits can be determined by reference to the plan documents. However, the plan and its provisions can also be implied from unwritten but established past practices. Plans may be unfunded, insured, trust fund, defined contribution and defined benefit plans, and deferred compensation contracts, if equivalent. Independent (i.e., not employer-sponsored) deferred profit-sharing plans and pension payments which are made to selected employees on a case-by-case basis are not considered pension plans.

The establishment of a pension plan represents a long-term financial commitment to employees. Although some entities manage their own plans, this commitment usually takes the form of contributions that are made to an independent trustee or, in some countries, to a governmental agency. These contributions are used by the trustee to acquire plan assets of various kinds, although the available types of investments may be restricted by governmental regulations in certain jurisdictions. Plan assets are used to generate a financial return, which typically consists of earned interest and/or appreciation in asset values.

The earnings from the plan assets (and occasionally the proceeds from their liquidation) provide the trustee with cash to pay the benefits to which the employees become entitled at the date of their retirements. These benefits in turn are defined by the terms of the pension plan, which is known as the plan's benefit formula. In the case of defined benefit plans, the benefit formula incorporates many factors, including the employee's current and future compensation, service longevity, age and so on. The benefit formula is the best indicator of the plan's obligations at any point in time. It is used as the basis for determining the pension cost to be recognised each fiscal year.

BASIC PRINCIPLES OF IAS 19

Applicability: Pension Plans

IAS 19 is applicable to both defined contribution and defined benefit pension plans. The accounting for *defined contribution* plans is normally straightforward, with the objective of matching the cost of the programme with the periods in which the employees earn their benefits. Since contributions are formula-driven (e.g., as a percentage of wages paid), typically the payments to the plan will be made currently; if they do not occur by the end of the reporting period, an accrual will be recognised for any unpaid current contribution liability. Once made or accrued, the employer has no further obligation for the value of the assets held by the plan or for the sufficiency of fund assets for payment of the benefits, absent any violation of the terms of the agreement by the employer. Employees thus suffer or benefit from the performance of the assets in which the contributions made on their behalf were invested; often the employees themselves are charged with responsibility for selecting those investments.

IAS 19 requires that disclosure be made of the amount of expense recognised in connection with a defined contribution pension plan. If not explicitly identified in the statement of profit or loss, this should therefore be disclosed in the notes to the financial statements.

Compared to defined contribution plans, the accounting for *defined benefit* plans is vastly more complex, because the employer (sponsor) is responsible not merely for the current contribution to be made to the plan on behalf of participants, but additionally for the sufficiency of the assets in the plan for the ultimate payments of benefits promised to the participants. Thus, the current contribution is at best a partial satisfaction of its obligation, and the amount of actual cost incurred is not measured by this alone. The measurement of pension cost under a defined benefit plan necessarily involves the expertise of actuaries—persons who are qualified to estimate the numbers of employees who will survive (both as employees, in the case of vesting requirements which some of them may not yet have met, and as living persons who will be present to receive the promised retirement benefits), the salary levels at which they will retire (if these are incorporated into the benefit formula, as is commonly the case), their expected life expectancy (since benefits are typically payable for life) and other factors which will influence the amount of resources needed to satisfy the employer's promises. Accounting for defined benefit plans is described at length in the following pages.

Applicability: Other Employee Benefit Plans

IAS 19 explicitly applies not merely to pension plans, but also three other categories of employee and post-employment benefits. These are:

1. *Short-term employee benefits*, which include normal wages and salaries as well as compensated absences, profit sharing and bonuses, and such non-monetary fringe benefits as health insurance, housing subsidies and employer-provided automobiles, to the extent these are granted to current (not retired) employees.
2. *Other long-term employee benefits*, such as long-term (sabbatical) leave, long-term disability benefits and, if payable after 12 months beyond the end of the reporting period, profit sharing and bonus arrangements and deferred compensation.
3. *Termination benefits*, which are payments to be made upon termination of employment under defined circumstances, generally when employees are induced to leave employment before normal retirement age.

Each of the foregoing categories of employee benefits will be explained later in this chapter.

IAS 19 also addresses post-employment benefits *other than pensions*, such as retiree medical plan coverage, as part of its requirements for pension plans, since these are essentially similar in nature. These are also discussed further later in this chapter.

IAS 19 considers all plans other than those explicitly structured as defined contribution plans to be defined benefit plans. Unless the employer's obligation is strictly limited to the amount of contribution currently due, typically driven by a formula based on entity performance or by employee wages or salaries, the obligations to the employees (and the amount of recognisable expense) will have to be estimated in accordance with actuarial principles.

Cost Recognition Distinguished from Funding Practices

Although it is arguably a sound management practice to fund retirement benefit plans on a current basis, in some jurisdictions the requirement to do this is either limited or absent entirely. Furthermore, in some jurisdictions the currently available tax deduction for contributions to pension plans may be limited, reducing the incentive to make such contributions until such time as the funds are actually needed for making payouts to retirees. Since the objective of periodic financial reporting is to match costs and revenues properly on a current basis, the pattern of funding is obviously not always going to be a useful guide to proper accounting for pension costs.

POST-EMPLOYMENT BENEFIT PLANS

General Discussion

Absent specific information to the contrary, it is assumed that a company will continue to provide retirement benefits well into the future. The accounting for the plan's costs should be reflected in the financial statements and these amounts should not be discretionary. All pension costs—with the exception noted below—should be charged against income. No amounts should be charged directly to retained earnings. The principal focus of IAS 19 is on the allocation of cost to the periods being benefited, which are the periods in which the covered employees provide service to the reporting entity.

Periodic Measurement of Cost for Defined Contribution Plans

Under the terms of a defined contribution plan, the employer will be obligated for fixed or determinable contributions in each period, often computed as a percentage of the wage and salary base paid to the covered employees during the period. For one example, contributions might be set at 4% of each employee's wages and salaries, up to €50,000 wages per annum. Generally, the contributions must actually be made by a specific date, such as 90 days after the end of the reporting entity's fiscal year, consistent with local law. The expense must be accrued for accounting purposes in the year the cost is incurred, whether the contribution is made currently or not.

IAS 19 requires that contributions payable to a defined contribution plan be accrued currently, even if not paid by year-end. If the amount is due over a period extending more than one year from the end of the reporting period, the long-term portion should be discounted at the rate applicable to high quality long-term corporate bonds. For currencies, where a deep market for high-quality corporate bonds is not available, the market yields applicable to government bonds of the appropriate term consistent with the estimated term of the obligation denominated in the respective currencies are used as the alternative discount rate.

Past service costs arise when a plan is amended retroactively, so that additional attribution for benefits is given to services rendered in past years. The expense related to past service cost is recognised in income when the related plan amendment, curtailment or settlement occurs.

Periodic Measurement of Cost for Defined Benefit Plans

Defined benefit plans present a far greater challenge to accountants than do defined contribution plans, since the amount of expense to be recognised currently will need to be determined on an actuarial basis. Under current IFRS, only the accrued benefit valuation method may be used to measure defined benefit plan pension cost. Furthermore, only a single variant of the accrued benefit method—the "projected unit credit" method—is permitted.

Net periodic pension cost will consist of the sum of the following components:

1. Service costs:
   a. Current service costs.
   b. Past service costs.
   c. Gain or loss on settlement.
2. Net interest cost for the current period on the net defined benefit liability (asset).
3. Remeasurement of the net defined benefit liability (asset):
   a. Actuarial gains and losses. Return on plan assets, excluding amounts included in net interest on;
   b. The net defined benefit liability (asset); and
   c. Any change in the effect of the asset ceiling, excluding amounts included in net interest on the net defined benefit liability (asset).

Disclosures required by IAS 19 effectively require that these cost components be displayed in the notes to the financial statements.

Current Service Cost

Current service cost must be determined by an actuarial valuation and will be affected by assumptions such as expected turnover of staff, average retirement age, the plan's vesting schedule and life expectancy after retirement. The probable progression of wages over the employees' remaining working lives will also have to be taken into consideration if retirement benefits will be affected by levels of compensation in later years, as will be true in the case of career-average and final pay plans, among others.

It is worth stressing this last point: when pension arrangements call for benefits to be based on the employees' ultimate salary levels, experience will show that those benefits will increase, and any computation based on current salary levels will surely understate the actual economic commitment to the future retirees. Accordingly, IFRS requires that, for such plans, future salary progression must be considered in determining current period pension costs. While future salary progression (where appropriate to the plan's benefit formula) must be incorporated (via estimated wage increase rates), current pension cost is a function of the services provided by the employee in the reporting period, emphatically not including services to be provided in later periods.

Under IAS 19, service cost is based on the present value of the defined benefit obligation, and is attributed to periods of service without regard to conditional requirements under the plan calling for further service. Thus, vesting is not taken into account in the sense that there is no justification for non-accrual prior to vesting. However, in the actuarial determination of pension cost, the statistical probability of employees leaving employment prior to vesting must be taken into account.

Interest on the Accrued Benefit Obligation

As noted, since the actuarial determination of current period cost is the present value of the future pension benefits to be paid to retirees by virtue of their service in the current period, the longer the time until the expected retirement date, the lower will be the service cost recognised. However, over time this accrued cost must be further increased, until at the employees' respective retirement dates the full amounts of the promised payments have been accreted. In this regard, the accrued pension liability is much like a sinking fund that grows from contributions plus the earnings thereon.

While service cost and interest are often the major components of expense recognised in connection with defined benefit plans, there are other important elements of benefit cost to be accounted for. IAS 19 identifies the expected return on plan assets, actuarial gains and losses, past service costs and the effects of any curtailments or settlements as categories to be explicitly addressed in the disclosure of the details of annual pension cost for defined benefit plans. These will be discussed in the following sections in turn.

The Expected Return on Plan Assets

IAS 19 has adopted the approach that since pension plan assets are intended as long-term investments, the random and perhaps sizeable fluctuations from period to period should not be allowed to excessively distort the operating results reported by the sponsoring entity. This standard identifies the expected return rather than the actual return on plan assets as the salient component of pension cost, with the difference between actual and expected return being an *actuarial gain or loss* to be dealt with as described below. Expected return for a given period is determined at the same rate that the discount rate applied to determine the defined benefit pension obligation.

The IAS 19 amendment adopted in 2000 also added certain new requirements which relate to recognition and measurement of the right of reimbursement of all or part of the expenditure to settle a defined benefit obligation. It established that only when it is virtually certain that another party will reimburse some or all of the expenditure required to settle a defined benefit obligation, the sponsoring entity would recognise its right to reimbursement as a separate asset, which would be measured at fair value. In all other respects, however, the asset (amount due from the pension plan) is to be treated in the same way as plan assets. In the statement of profit or loss and other comprehensive income or separate income statement presented, defined benefit plan expense may be presented net of the reimbursement receivable recognised.

After the amendment in 2000, qualifying insurance policies are to be included in plan assets, arguably because those plans have similar economic effects to funds whose assets qualify as plan assets under the revised definition.

Actuarial Gains and Losses

Changes in the amount of the actuarially determined defined benefit pension obligation, and differences in the actual versus the expected return on plan assets, as well as demographic changes (e.g., composition of the workforce, changes in life expectancy, etc.) contribute to actuarial (or "experience") gains and losses and are immediately recognised in other comprehensive income, without deferral or any off-balance-sheet treatment previously permitted under the "corridor approach."

Past Service Costs

Past service costs refer to increases in the amount of a defined benefit liability that results from the initial adoption of a plan, or from a change or amendment to an existing plan which increases the benefits promised to the participants with respect to previous service rendered. Less commonly, a plan amendment could reduce the benefits for past services, if local laws permit this. Employers will amend plans for a variety of reasons, including competitive factors in the employment marketplace, but often it is done with the hope and expectation that it will engender goodwill among the workers and thus increase future productivity. For this reason, it is sometimes the case that these added benefits will not vest immediately, but rather must be earned over some defined time period.

IAS 19 requires immediate recognition of past service costs when they occur as a result of a plan amendment, curtailment or settlement as the case may be.

Settlements occur when the entity enters into a transaction which effectively transfers the obligation to another entity, such as an insurance company, so that the sponsor has no legal or constructive obligation to fund any benefit shortfall. Merely acquiring insurance which is intended to cover the benefit payments does not constitute a settlement, since a funding mechanism does not relieve the underlying obligation.

With the issuance of an amendment to IAS 19 in February 2018, which is required to be applied to all amendments, curtailments or settlements to a plan occurring on or after the beginning of the first annual reporting period that begins on or after January 1, 2019, there is a change in the basis of application to determine past service cost and computation of current service cost and net interest for the period after such amendment, curtailment or settlement. The amendments require an entity to use updated assumptions to determine current service cost and net interest for the period after a plan amendment, curtailment or settlement. Earlier application is permitted but in case of such early application is to be disclosed.

Transition Adjustment

Where an entity has to change its accounting policy to bring these accounting requirements into effect it shall do so on a fully retroactive basis. However, an entity need not adjust the carrying amount of assets outside the scope of IAS 19 for changes in employee benefit costs that were included in the carrying amount before the date of initial application. The date of initial application is the beginning of the earliest prior period presented in the first financial statements in which the entity adopts this standard.

EMPLOYER'S LIABILITY AND ASSETS

IAS 19 requires that a defined benefit liability or asset be included in the sponsor's statement of financial position when certain conditions are met. Specifically, under the provisions of IAS 19, the amount recognised as a defined benefit liability in the employer's statement of financial position is the net total of:

1. The present value of the defined benefit obligation at the end of the reporting period;
2. The fair value of plan assets at the end of the reporting period.

If this amount nets to a negative sum, it represents the defined benefit asset to be reported in the employer's statement of financial position. However, the amount of asset that can be displayed, per IAS 19, is subject to a *ceiling requirement*.

The asset ceiling defined in IAS 19 is the lower of:

1. The amount computed in the preceding paragraph; or
2. The total of the present value of any economic benefits available in the form of refunds from the plan, or reductions in future contributions to the plan, determined using the discount rate, which in turn determines the present value of the defined benefit liability obligation.

The amendment in February 2018 clarified the effect of plan amendment, curtailment or settlement on the requirements regarding the asset ceiling. It clarifies that when a plan amendment or curtailment occurs the current service cost and net interest for the remainder of an annual period are calculated using updated assumptions.

MINIMUM FUNDING REQUIREMENT

IFRIC 14: IAS 19—The Limit on a Defined Benefit Asset, Minimum Funding Requirements and Their Interaction

In July 2007, IFRIC issued Interpretation 14 to provide guidance on the limitation on asset recognition and the statutory minimum funding requirements. IFRIC 14 was amended in November 2009, effective for annual periods beginning on or after January 1, 2011. The amendment is applicable to limited circumstances where an entity is subject to minimum funding requirements and makes an early payment of contributions to cover the funding requirements. The benefit of such an early payment is regarded as an asset.

According to IASB, the interaction of this limit and minimum funding requirement has two possible effects:

1. The minimum funding requirement may restrict the economic benefits available as a reduction in future contributions; and
2. The limit may make the minimum funding requirement onerous because contributions payable under the requirement for services already received may not be available once they have been paid, either as a refund or as a reduction in future contributions.

In some jurisdictions, there are statutory (or contractual) minimum funding requirements that require sponsors to make future contributions. This is an increasingly common phenomenon, given the public's growing awareness that many defined benefit plans have been underfunded, raising concerns that retirees will find insufficient assets to pay their benefits after, for example, the plan sponsor has ceased operations or been sold. The question raised was whether those requirements should limit the amount of plan assets the employer may report in its statement of financial position in those situations where application of IAS 19 would otherwise permit asset recognition, as discussed in the preceding paragraphs. In other words, the problem was that the IAS 19-based asset might not be available to the entity (and thus not be an asset of the reporting entity) in certain situations where future minimum funding requirements exist.

IFRIC 14 addresses the extent to which the economic benefit, via refund or reduction in future contributions, is constrained by contractual or statutory minimum funding obligations. It also addresses the calculation of the available benefits under such circumstances, as well as the effect of the minimum funding requirement on the measurement of defined benefit plan asset or liability.

IFRIC 14 addresses the following issues:

1. When refunds or reductions in future contributions should be regarded as "available to the employer";
2. The effect of a minimum funding requirement on the economic benefit available as a reduction in future contributions; and
3. When a minimum funding requirement may give rise to a liability.

Economic Benefit Available as a Refund

IFRIC 14 specifies that the availability of a refund of a surplus or a reduction in future contributions would be determined in accordance with the terms and conditions of the plan and any statutory requirements in its jurisdiction. An economic benefit, in the form of a refund of surplus or a reduction in future contributions, would be deemed available (and hence an asset of the sponsor) if it will be realisable at some point during the life of the plan or when the plan liabilities are finally settled. Most importantly, an economic benefit, in the form of a refund from the plan or reduction in future contributions, may still be deemed available even if it is not realisable immediately at the end of the reporting period, as long as the refunds from the plan will be realisable during the life of a plan or at final settlement.

In cases where the question to be resolved is the amount of asset that is deemed to be an economic benefit to be received via a refund, this is to be measured as the amount that will be refunded to the entity *either*:

1. During the life of the plan, without assuming that the plan liabilities have to be settled to get the refund (e.g., in some jurisdictions, the entity may have a contractual right to a refund during the life of the plan, irrespective of whether the plan liability is settled); *or*
2. Assuming the gradual settlement of the plan liabilities over time until all members have left the plan; *or*
3. Assuming the full settlement of the plan liabilities in a single event (i.e., as a plan termination and settlement).

The amount of the economic benefit is to be determined on the basis of the approach that is the *most advantageous* to the entity. It is thus to be measured as the amount of the surplus (i.e., the fair value of the plan assets less the present value of the defined benefit obligation) that, at the end of the reporting period, the reporting entity has a right to receive as a refund after all the associated costs (such as taxes other than those on income) are paid.

If the refund is calculated using the approach in 3. above, then the costs associated with the settlement of the plan liabilities and making the refund are to be taken into account. These could include professional fees to be paid by the plan, as well as the costs of any insurance premiums that might be required to secure the liability upon plan settlement.

Since under IAS 19 the surplus at the end of the reporting period is measured at present value, even if the refund is realisable only at a future date no further adjustment will need to be made for the time value of money.

The Economic Benefit Available as a Contribution Reduction

When there is no minimum funding requirement for contributions relating to future service, the economic benefit available as a reduction in future contributions is the future service cost to the entity for each period over the shorter of the expected life of the plan and the expected life of the entity. The future service cost to the entity excludes amounts borne by employees.

An entity shall determine the future service costs using assumptions consistent with those used to determine the defined benefit obligation and with the situation that exists at the end of the reporting period as determined by IAS 19. Therefore, an entity shall assume no change to the benefits to be provided by a plan in the future until the plan is amended and shall assume a stable workforce in the future unless the entity makes a reduction in the number of employees covered by the plan. In the latter case, the assumption about the future workforce shall include the reduction.

The Effect of a Minimum Funding Requirement on the Economic Benefit Available as a Reduction in Future Contributions

In cases where there is a minimum funding requirement, the question to be resolved is the amount of asset that is deemed to be an economic benefit to be received via a future contribution reduction using IAS 19 assumptions applicable at the end of the reporting period. The amount is the sum of:

1. Any amount that reduces future minimum funding requirement contributions for future service because the entity made a prepayment; and
2. The estimated future service cost in each period (excluding any part of the total cost that is borne by employees); *less*
3. Any future minimum funding requirement contribution that would be required for future service in those periods if no prepayment as described in 1. is applicable.

Any expected changes in the future minimum funding contributions as a result of the entity paying the minimum contributions due would be reflected in the measurement of the available contribution reduction. However, no allowance could be made for expected changes in the terms and conditions of the minimum funding requirement that are not substantively enacted at the end of the reporting period. Any allowances for expected future changes in the demographic profile of the workforce would have to be consistent with the assumptions underlying the calculation of the present value of the defined benefit obligation itself at the end of the reporting period.

If the future minimum funding requirement contribution for future service exceeds the future IAS 19 service cost in any given period, the excess would be used to reduce the amount of the economic benefit available as a future contribution reduction. The amount of the total asset available as a reduction in future contributions (point 2. above) can never be less than zero.

When a Minimum Funding Requirement May Give Rise to a Liability

If an entity has a statutory or contractual obligation under a minimum funding requirement to pay additional contributions to cover an existing shortfall on the minimum funding requirements in respect of services already received by the end of the reporting period, the entity would have to ascertain whether the contributions payable will be available as a refund or reduction in future contributions after they are paid into the plan. To the extent that the contributions payable will not be available once paid into the plan, the reporting entity would be required to recognise a liability. The liability would reduce the defined benefit asset or increase the defined benefit liability when the obligation arises, so that no gain or loss results when the contributions are later paid.

The adjustment to the defined benefit asset or liability in respect of the minimum funding requirement, and any subsequent remeasurement of that adjustment, would be recognised immediately in other comprehensive income as a remeasurement.

IFRIC 14 provides a number of examples illustrating how to calculate the economic benefit available or not available when an entity has a certain funding level on the minimum funding requirement.

OTHER PENSION CONSIDERATIONS

Multiple and Multi-Employer Plans

If an entity has more than one plan, IAS 19 provisions should be applied separately to each plan. Offsets or eliminations are not allowed unless there clearly is the right to use the assets in one plan to pay the benefits of another plan.

Participation in a multi-employer plan (to which two or more unrelated employers contribute) requires that the contribution for the period be recognised as net pension cost and that any contributions due and unpaid be recognised as a liability. Assets in this type of plan are usually commingled and are not segregated or restricted. A board of trustees usually administers these plans, and multi-employer plans are generally subject to a collective bargaining agreement. If there is a withdrawal from this type of plan and if an arising obligation is either probable or reasonably possible, the provisions of IFRS that address contingencies (IAS 37) apply.

Some plans are, in substance, a pooling or aggregation of single employer plans and are ordinarily without collective bargaining agreements. Contributions are usually based on a selected benefit formula. These plans are not considered multi-employer plans, and the accounting is based on the respective interest in the plan.

Example of disclosure on multi-employer scheme in annual report

ASM International NV

In significant accounting policies

Pension plans and similar commitments

The Company has retirement plans covering substantially all employees. The principal plans are defined contribution plans, except for the plans of the Company's operations in the Netherlands and Japan. The Company's employees in the Netherlands participate in a multi-employer defined benefit plan. Payments to defined contribution plans and the multi-employer plan are recognised as an expense in the consolidated statement of profit and loss and other comprehensive income as they fall due. The Company accounts for the multi-employer plan as if it were a defined contribution plan since the manager of the plan is not able to provide the Company with the required Company-specific information to enable the Company to account for the plan as a defined benefit plan.

The Company's employees in Japan participate in defined benefit plans. Pension costs in respect of this defined benefit plan are determined using the projected unit credit method. These costs primarily represent the increase in the actuarial present value of the obligation for pension benefits based on employee service during the year and the interest on this obligation in respect of employee service in previous years, net of the expected return on plan assets.

For the defined benefit plan of Japan the Company recognises in its consolidated balance sheet an asset or a liability for the plan's overfunded status or underfunded status, respectively. Actuarial gains and losses are recognised in income when incurred. Reference is made to Note 17.

Note 17

Pension plans

The Company has retirement plans covering substantially all employees. The principal plans are defined contribution plans, except for the plans of the Company's operations in the Netherlands and Japan.

Multi-employer plan

The Company's employees in the Netherlands, approximately 143 employees, participate in a multi-employer union plan, "Pensioenfonds van de Metalektro" ("PME") determined in accordance with the collective bargaining agreements effective for the industry in which ASMI operates. This collective bargaining agreement has no expiration date. This multi-employer union plan covers approximately 1,260 companies and 145,000 contributing members. ASMI's contribution to the multi-employer union plan is less than 5% of the total contribution to the plan as per the annual report for the year ended December 31, 20XX. The plan monitors its risks on a global basis, not by company or employee, and is subject to regulation by Dutch governmental authorities. By law (the Dutch Pension Act), a multi-employer union plan must be monitored against specific criteria, including the coverage ratio of the plan assets to its obligations. This coverage ratio must exceed 104.3% for the total plan. Every company participating in a Dutch multi-employer union plan contributes a premium calculated as a percentage of its total pensionable salaries, with each company subject to the same percentage contribution rate. The premium can fluctuate yearly based on the coverage ratio of the multi-employer union plan. The pension rights of each employee are based upon the employee's average salary during employment.

ASMI's net periodic pension cost for this multi-employer union plan for any period is the amount of the required contribution for that period. A contingent liability may arise from, for example, possible actuarial losses relating to other participating entities because each entity that participates in a multi-employer union plan shares in the actuarial risks of every other participating entity or any responsibility under the terms of a plan to finance any shortfall in the plan if other entities cease to participate.

The coverage ratio of the multi-employer union plan decreased to 102% as of December 31, 20XX+1 (December 31, 20XX: 103.4%). Because of the low coverage ratio, PME prepared and executed a so-called "Recovery plan" which was approved by De Nederlandsche Bank, the Dutch central bank, which is the supervisor of all pension companies in the Netherlands. Due to the low coverage ratio and according to the obligation of the "Recovery plan" the pension premium percentage is 23.6% in 201XX+1 (20XX: 24.1%). The coverage ratio is calculated by dividing the plan assets by the total sum of pension liabilities and is based on actual market interest.

The Company accounts for the multi-employer plan as if it were a defined contribution plan as the manager of the plan, PME, stated that its internal administrative systems do not enable PME to provide the Company with the required Company-specific information to account for the plan as a defined benefit plan. The Company's net periodic pension cost for the multi-employer plan for a fiscal period is equal to the required contribution for that period.

A contingent liability may arise from, for example, possible actuarial losses relating to other participating companies because each company that participates in a multi-employer plan shares in the actuarial risks of other participating companies or any responsibility under the terms of a plan to finance any shortfall in the plan if other companies cease to participate. The plan thus exposes the participating companies to actuarial risks associated with current and former employees of other companies with the result that no consistent and reliable basis for allocating the pension obligation, plan assets and cost to individual companies participating in the plan exists.

Business Combinations

When an entity that sponsors a single employer-defined benefit plan is acquired and must therefore be accounted for under the provisions of IFRS 3*, Business Combinations*, the purchaser should assign part of the purchase price to an asset if plan assets exceed the projected benefit obligation, or to a liability if the projected benefit obligation exceeds plan assets. The projected benefit obligation should include the effect of any expected plan curtailment or termination. This assignment eliminates any existing unrecognised components, and any future differences between contributions and net pension cost will affect the asset or liability recognised when the purchase took place.

Contributions from Employees or Third Parties

The November 2013 amendment, applicable for accounting periods starting on or after July 1, 2014, requires contributions from employees or third parties, set out in the formal terms of the plan, to be first determined as to whether they reduce the cost of benefit to the entity or are in the nature of reimbursement rights. In the case of reimbursement rights, it is to be dealt with as explained in other sections in this chapter.

In respect of those which are in the nature of reducing the cost of benefit to the entity:

a. Reduce service cost, if they are linked to service; or
b. Affect remeasurements of the net defined benefit liability (asset) if they are not linked to service (for instance, a contribution to reduce a deficit arising from losses on plan assets or from actuarial losses).

Where contributions from employees and third parties are linked to service, they reduce the service cost:

a. If the contribution is dependent on the number of years of service, then it shall be attributed to the periods of service using the same attribution method as applied to the gross benefit. Changes in such contributions result in:
   i. Current and past service costs (where those changes are not set out in the formal terms of a plan and do not arise from a constructive obligation); or
   ii. Actuarial gains and losses (where those changes are set out in the formal terms of a plan or arise from a constructive obligation).

b. If the contribution is independent of the number of years' service (such as a fixed percentage of employee's salary, a fixed amount throughout the period, an amount linked to the age of the employee, etc.), then the entity is to recognise such contributions as a reduction in the service cost in the period when related services are rendered.

DISCLOSURES FOR POST-EMPLOYMENT BENEFIT PLANS

For defined contribution plans, IAS 19 requires only that the amount of expense included in current period earnings be disclosed. Good practice would suggest that disclosure be made of the general description of each plan, identifying the employee groups covered and of any other significant matters related to retirement benefits that affect comparability with the previous period reported on.

For defined benefit plans, as would be expected, much more expansive disclosures are mandated. These include:

1. A general description of each plan identifying the employee groups covered.
2. The accounting policy regarding recognition of actuarial gains or losses.
3. A reconciliation of the plan-related assets and liabilities recognised in the statement of financial position, showing at the minimum:
    a. The present value of wholly unfunded defined benefit obligations.
    b. The present value (gross, before deducting plan assets) of wholly or partly funded obligations.
    c. The fair value of plan assets.
    d. Any amount not recognised as an asset because of the limitation to the present value of economic benefits from refunds and future contribution reductions.
    e. The amounts which are recognised in the statement of financial position.
4. The amount of plan assets represented by each category of the reporting entity's own financial instruments or by property which is occupied by, or other assets used by, the entity itself.
5. A reconciliation of movements (i.e., changes) during the reporting period in the net asset or liability reported in the statement of financial position.
6. The amount of, and location in profit or loss of, the reported amounts of current service cost, net interest cost (income), remeasurements, past service cost, and effect of any curtailment or settlement.
7. The actual return earned on plan assets for the reporting period.
8. The principal actuarial assumptions used, including (if relevant) the discount rates, expected rates of return on plan assets, expected rates of salary increases or other index or variable specified in the pension arrangement, medical cost trend rates and any other material actuarial assumptions utilised in computing benefit costs for the period. The actuarial assumptions are to be explicitly stated in absolute terms, not merely as references to other indices.
9. A sensitivity analysis on the significant actuarial assumptions.
10. A description of the risks and characteristics of the defined benefit plans.

Amounts presented in the sponsor's statement of financial position cannot be offset (presented on a net basis) unless legal rights of offset exist. Furthermore, even with a legal right to offset (which itself would be a rarity), unless the intent is to settle on a net basis, such presentation would not be acceptable. Thus, a sponsor having two plans, one being in a net asset position, and another in a net liability position, cannot net these in most instances.

EXAMPLES OF FINANCIAL STATEMENT DISCLOSURES

Exemplum Reporting PLC
Financial Statements
For the Year Ended December 31, 20XX

30. Employee benefit schemes

The group pension arrangements are operated through a defined contribution scheme and a group defined benefit scheme.

Defined contribution schemes

	20XX	20XX-1	
Amount recognised as an expense	X	X	IAS 19 p53

Defined benefit schemes

The Exemplum Reporting Pension is a final salary pension plan operating for qualifying employees of the group. The plan is governed by the employment laws of (Country). The level of benefits provided depends on members' length of service and salary at retirement age. The fund is governed by a Board of Trustees which comprise an equal number of employee and employer representatives. The Board is responsible for the investment strategy with regard to the assets of the fund. The pension plan is exposed to (X Country's) inflation, interest rate risk, investment risk, salary risk and changes in the life expectancy for pensioners. IAS 19 p138 p139

The amounts recognised in the statement of financial position are as follows: IAS 19 p10

	Defined benefit pension plans	
	20XX	20XX-1 (Restated)
Present value of funded obligations	X	X
Fair value of plan assets	X	X
Funded status	X	X
Present value of unfunded obligations	X	X
Impact of minimum funding requirement or asset ceiling	X	X
Liability arising from defined benefit obligation	**X**	**X**
	X	X
Amounts in the statement of financial position		
Liabilities	X	X
Assets	X	X
Net liability	**X**	**X**

The amounts recognised in profit or loss are as follows: IAS 19 p120 p135

	Defined benefit pension plans	
	20XX	20XX-1 (Restated)
Current service cost	X	X
Past service cost	X	X
Net interest expense	X	X

Subtotal included in profit or loss	X	X
Remeasurement gains or losses		
Return on plan assets (excluding amounts included in net interest expense)	X	X
Actuarial changes arising from:		
Changes in demographic assumptions	X	X
Changes in financial assumptions	X	X
Experience adjustments	X	X
Adjustments for restrictions of the defined benefit asset	X	X
Subtotal included in other comprehensive income	X	X
Total	**X**	**X**

Of the expense for the year, €X (20XX-1: €X) has been included in cost of sales and administrative expense. The remeasurement of the net defined benefit liability is included in other comprehensive income.

IAS 19 p141

Changes in the present value of the defined benefit obligation are as follows:

	Defined benefit pension plans	
	20XX	20XX-1
(Restated)		
Opening defined benefit obligation	X	X
Service cost	X	X
Interest cost	X	X
Actuarial losses (gains) arising from:		
Changes in demographic assumptions	X	X
Changes in financial assumptions	X	X
Experience adjustments	X	X
Losses (gains) on curtailments	X	X
Liabilities extinguished on settlements	X	X
Liabilities assumed in a business combination		
Exchange differences on foreign plans	X	X
Benefits paid	X	X
Closing defined benefit obligation	X	X

Changes in the fair value of plan assets are as follows: IAS 19 p141

	Defined benefit pension plans	
	20XX	20XX-1
(Restated)		
Opening fair value of plan assets	X	X
Interest income	X	X
Remeasurement gains/(losses): Return on plan assets (excluding amounts included in net interest expense)	X	X
Assets distributed on settlements	X	X
Contributions by employer	X	X
Assets acquired in a business combination	X	X
Exchange differences on foreign plans	X	X
Benefits paid	X	X
Closing fair value of plan assets	**X**	**X**

The fair value of the plan assets at the end of the reporting period for each category is as follows:

	20XX	20XX-1	IAS 19 p142
Cash and cash equivalents	X	X	
Equity investments by industry type			
Manufacturing industry	X	X	
Financial institutions	X	X	
Debt investments by issuer's credit rating			
AAA	X	X	
BB and lower	X	X	
Property investments by geographic location			
Country A	X	X	
Country B	X	X	
Derivatives	X	X	
Other	X	X	
Total	**X**	**X**	

The fair value of the above is based on quoted market prices in active markets. IAS 19 p143

The pension plan assets include ordinary shares issued by Exemplum Reporting PLC with a fair value of €X (20XX-1: €X). Plan assets also include property occupied by Exemplum Reporting PLC with a fair value of €X (20XX-1: €X). Principal assumptions used for the purposes of the actuarial valuations at the statement of financial position date (expressed as weighted averages): IAS 19 p144

	20XX	20XX-1
Discount rate at December 31	X%	X%
Expected return on plan assets at December 31	X%	X%
Future salary increases	X%	X%
Future pension increases	X%	X%
Proportion of employees opting for early retirement	X%	X%

Investigations have been carried out within the past three years into the mortality experience of the group's schemes. These investigations concluded that the current mortality assumptions include sufficient allowance for future improvements in mortality rates. The assumed life expectations on retirement at age 65 are: IAS 19 p144

	20XX	20XX-1
Retiring today:		
Males	X	X
Females	X	X
Retiring in 20 years:		
Males	X	X
Females	X	X

A sensitivity analysis of the defined benefit obligation to changes in the weighted principal assumptions is shown below: IAS 19 p145

	Increase in assumption		**Decrease in assumption**	
	Percentage or years	Impact on defined benefit obligation	Percentage or years	Impact on defined benefit obligation
Discount rate	X%	X	X%	X
Salary growth rate	X%	X	X%	X
Pension growth rate	X%	X	X%	X
Life expectancy of male pensioners	X years	X	X years	X
Life expectancy of female pensioners	X years	X	X years	X

The above sensitivity analysis is based on reasonably possible changes in the principal assumptions occurring at the end of the reporting period, while holding all other assumptions constant. In practice it is unlikely that the change in assumptions would occur in isolation, as some of the assumptions may be correlated.

When calculating the sensitivity of the defined benefit obligation, the present value of the defined benefit obligation has been calculated using the project unit credit method at the end of the reporting period, which is consistent with the calculation of the defined benefit obligation liability recognised in the statement of financial position.

There was no change in the methods and assumptions used in preparing the sensitivity analysis compared to prior years.

Each year a review of the asset-liability matching strategy and investment risk management policy is performed. Contribution policies are based on the results of this review. The aim is to have a portfolio mix of x% equity, x% property and x% debt instruments. IAS 19 p146

There has been no change in the process used to manage its risks from prior years.

Funding levels are monitored on an annual basis and the current agreed contribution rate is fixed at x% of pensionable salary. The funding requirements are based on an actuarial valuation. IAS 19 p147

The group expects to contribute €X to its defined benefit pension plans in 20XX.

The weighted-average duration of the defined benefit plan obligation at the end of the reporting period is X years (20XX-1: X years).

OTHER EMPLOYEE BENEFITS

Short-Term Employee Benefits

According to IAS 19, short-term benefits are those falling due within 12 months from the end of the period in which the employees render their services. These include wages and salaries, as well as short-term compensated absences (vacations, annual holiday, paid sick days, etc.), profit sharing and bonuses if due within 12 months after the end of the period in which these were earned, and such non-monetary benefits as health insurance and housing or automobiles. The standard requires that these be reported as incurred. Since they are accrued currently, no actuarial assumptions or computations are needed and, since they are due currently, discounting is not to be applied.

Compensated absences may provide some accounting complexities, if they accumulate and vest with the employees. Accumulated benefits can be carried forward to later periods when not fully consumed currently; for example, when employees are granted two weeks' leave per year, but can carry forward to later years an amount equal to no more than six weeks, the compensated absence benefit can be said to be subject to limited accumulation. Depending on the programme, accumulation rights may be limited or unlimited; and, furthermore, the usage of benefits may be defined to occur on a LIFO basis, which in conjunction with limited accumulation rights further limits the amount of benefits which employees are likely to use, if not fully used in the period earned.

The cost of compensated absences should be accrued in the periods earned. In some cases it will be understood that the amounts of compensated absences to which employees are contractually entitled will exceed the amount that they are likely to actually utilise. In such circumstances, the accrual should be based on the *expected* usage, based on past experience and, if relevant, changes in the plan's provisions since the last reporting period.

Example of compensated absences

Consider an entity with 500 workers, each of whom earns two weeks' annual leave, with a carryforward option limited to a maximum of six weeks, to be carried forward no longer than four years. Also, this employer imposes a last in first out (LIFO) basis on any usages of annual leave (e.g., a worker with two weeks' carryforward and two weeks earned currently, taking a three-week leave, will be deemed to have consumed the two currently earned weeks plus one of the carryforward weeks, thereby increasing the risk of ultimately losing the older carried-forward compensated absence time). Based on past experience, 80% of the workers will take no more than two weeks' leave in any year, while the other 20% take an average of four extra days. At the end of the year, each worker has an average of five days' carryforward of compensated absences. The amount accrued should be the cost equivalent of $[(.80 \times 0 \text{ days}) + (.20 \times 4 \text{ days})] \times 500$ workers = 400 days' leave.

Other Post-Retirement Benefits

Other post-retirement benefits include medical care and other benefits offered to retirees partially or entirely at the expense of the former employer. These are essentially defined benefit plans very much like defined benefit pension plans. Like the pension plans, these require the services of a qualified actuary to estimate the true cost of the promises made currently for benefits to be delivered in the future. As with pensions, a variety of determinants, including the age composition, life expectancies and other demographic factors pertaining to the present and future retiree groups, and the course of future inflation of medical care (or other covered) costs (coupled with predicted utilisation factors), need to be projected to compute current period costs. Developing these projections requires the skills and training of actuaries; the projected pattern of future medical costs has been particularly difficult to achieve with anything approaching accuracy. Unlike most defined benefit pension plans, other post-retirement benefit plans are more commonly funded on a pay-as-you-go basis, which does not alter the accounting but does eliminate earnings on plan assets as a cost offset.

Other Long-Term Employee Benefits

These are defined by IAS 19 as including any benefits other than post-employment benefits (pensions, retiree medical care, etc.), termination benefits and equity compensation plans. Examples would include sabbatical leave, "jubilee" or other long-service benefits, long-term profit-sharing payments and deferred compensation arrangements. Executive deferred compensation plans have become common in nations where these are tax-advantaged (i.e., not taxed to the employee until paid), and these give rise to deferred tax accounting issues as well as measurement and reporting questions, as benefit plans. In general, measurement will be less complex than for defined benefit pension or other post-retirement benefits, although some actuarial measures may be needed.

IAS 19 requires that past service cost (resulting from the granting of enhanced benefits to participants on a retroactive basis) must be reported in profit or loss in the period in which these are granted or occur.

For liability measurement purposes, IAS 19 stipulates that the present value of the obligation be presented in the statement of financial position, less the fair value of any assets that have been set aside for settlement thereof. The long-term corporate bond rate is used here, as with defined benefit pension obligations, to discount the expected future payments to present value. As to expense recognition, the same cost elements as are set forth for pension plan expense should be included, with the exceptions that, as noted, actuarial gains and losses and past service cost must be recognised immediately, not amortised over a defined time horizon.

Termination Benefits

Termination benefits are to be recognised at the earlier of when the entity can no longer withdraw the offer of those benefits, and when the entity recognises costs for a restructuring that is within the scope of IAS 37.

Since termination benefits do not confer any future economic benefits on the employing entity, these must be expensed immediately.

US GAAP COMPARISON

ASC 710, *Compensation—General*, ASC 712, *Compensation—Nonretirement Postemployment Benefits*, and ASC 715, *Compensation—Retirement Benefits*, are the main sources of US GAAP for employee benefits other than share-based payments. Differences exist related to defined benefit plans. US GAAP employs different actuarial methods, depending on the characteristics of the plan's benefit formula.

Under US GAAP, as a result of an election by the entity, actuarial gains and losses are recognised in net income as they occur or deferred through a "corridor" approach, that is, if the gain or loss exceeds 10% of obligation or asset. Past service costs are initially deferred in other comprehensive income and subsequently recognised in net income, amortised over average remaining service period of active employees or average remaining life expectancy of inactive participants.

The calculation of the expected return on plan assets is based on the expected long-term rate of return on plan assets and the market-related value of the plan assets.

Under US GAAP, anticipating changes in the law that would affect variables such as state medical or social security benefits is expressly prohibited. Differences also exist related to termination benefits. US GAAP differentiates between special termination benefits (which are offered for a short time in exchange for employees' voluntary termination of service) and contractual termination benefits.

Special termination benefits are expensed when employees accept, and the amount can be reasonably estimated; Contractual termination benefits are recognised when it is probable that the specified event that will trigger termination will occur, employees will accept, and the amount is reasonably estimable. However, if there is a time short time frame offered as an incentive for early termination, the loss shall not be recognised when the offer is made as there is still uncertainty as to the amount being reasonably estimable.

US GAAP requires that non-retirement post-employment benefits provided to former or inactive employees, their beneficiaries and covered dependants are accounted for consistent with compensated absences if certain criteria are met. Otherwise, a loss is accrued if it is probable and reasonably estimable.

US GAAP contains no explicit guidance on whether to discount post-employment liabilities and at what rate.

Under US GAAP (as amended by ASU 2017-07, *Compensation—Retirement Benefits (Topic 715) Improving the Presentation of Net Periodic Pension Cost and Net Periodic Postretirement Benefit Cost*, March 2017) the service cost component is the only component of defined benefit cost that is eligible to be capitalised as part of the cost of inventory or other assets.

20 REVENUE FROM CONTRACTS WITH CUSTOMERS

INTRODUCTION

IFRS 15, *Revenue from Contracts with Customers*, issued on May 28, 2014, replaced IAS 18, *Revenue*, and IAS 11, *Construction Contracts*, effective for annual periods beginning on or after January 1, 2018, to create a comprehensive standard which provides a single revenue recognition model that can be applied consistently across various industries, geographical regions and transactions. IFRS 15 also supersedes IFRIC 13, *Customer Loyalty Programmes*, IFRIC 15, *Agreements for the Construction of Real Estate*, IFRIC 18, *Transfers of Assets from Customers*, and SIC-31, *Revenue—Barter Transactions Involving Advertising Services*.

The objective of IFRS 15 is to establish principles to report useful information to users of financial statements about the nature, amount, timing and uncertainty of revenue and cash flows arising from a contract with a customer. To meet this objective, the core principle of IFRS 15 is that an entity should recognise revenue to depict the transfer of promised goods or services to the customer in an amount that reflects the consideration to which the entity expects to be entitled in exchange for those goods or services. The transfer of goods and services is based on the concept of control derived from the definition of an asset in the IASB's *Framework*.

The contract determines the agreement between parties and therefore revenue recognition is derived from the enforceable rights and obligations agreed upon. IFRS 15 entails interpretation and judgement to be applied and requires management to document their basis and rationale for such interpretations and judgements. Revenue recognition is based on the terms of the contract and all relevant facts and circumstances such as created practices. The guidance in IFRS 15, including the use of the practical expedients, should be applied consistently to contracts with similar characteristics and in similar circumstances.

Sources of IFRS	
IASB's *Framework for Preparation and Presentation of Financial Statements*	
IFRS 15	*IFRIC* 12

DEFINITIONS OF TERMS

Contract. An agreement between two or more parties that creates enforceable rights and obligations.

Contract asset. An entity's right to consideration in exchange for goods or right is conditioned on something other than the passage of time (for example, the entity's future performance).

Contract liability. An entity's obligation to transfer goods or services to a customer for which the entity has received consideration (or the amount is due) from the customer.

Customer. A party that has contracted with an entity to obtain goods or services that are an output of the entity's ordinary activities in exchange for consideration.

Income. Increases in economic benefits during the accounting period in the form of inflows or enhancements of assets or decreases of liabilities that result in an increase in equity, other than those relating to contributions from equity participants.

Performance obligation. A promise in a contract with a customer to transfer to the customer either:

- A good or service (or a bundle of goods or services) that is distinct; or
- A series of distinct goods or services that are substantially the same and that have the same pattern of transfer to the customer.

Revenue. Income arising in the course of an entity's ordinary activities.

Stand-alone selling price (of a good or service). The price at which an entity would sell a promised good or service separately to a customer.

Transaction price (for a contract with a customer). The amount of consideration to which an entity expects to be entitled in exchange for transferring promised goods or services to a customer, excluding amounts collected on behalf of third parties.

SCOPE

Revenue is defined as income arising in the course of an entity's ordinary activities. Therefore, IFRS 15 in principle applies to income deriving from the ordinary activities of an entity.

IFRS 15 applies to all contracts with customers except leases, insurance contracts, financial instruments, guarantees and certain non-monetary exchanges. Dividend income and interest income previously included in IAS 18 is in the scope of the financial instrument standards (refer to Chapter 24). The sale of non-monetary financial assets, such as property, plant and equipment, real estate or intangible assets, will also be subject to some of the requirements of IFRS 15.

A contract with a customer may be partially within the scope of IFRS 15 and within the scope of another IFRS standard. If the other IFRS standards specify how to separate and/or initially measure components of the contract, then that IFRS standard is applied first. The transaction price for the purposes of IFRS 15 is then reduced by the amounts measured under the other IFRS standard(s). However, if the other IFRS standard(s) does not provide such guidance, then IFRS 15 will be applied to the whole contract.

IFRS 15 only applies if the counterparty to the contract is a customer. A customer is defined as a party that has contracted with an entity to obtain goods or services that are an output of the entity's ordinary activities in exchange for consideration. For instance, counterparties' partners that share risks or do activities together would not be regarded as customers for the purpose of IFRS 15. In such a case they share benefits and an output of ordinary activities is not provided to the customer.

IFRS 15 also deals with the incremental cost of obtaining a contract and cost incurred to fulfil a contract, which are not dealt with in other IFRS standards.

THE REVENUE MODEL

The Core Principle and Steps

IFRS 15 introduces a revenue model in which the core principle is that revenue is recognised to depict the transfer of promised goods or services to the customer in an amount that reflects the consideration expected to be entitled in exchange for those goods or services. To recognise revenue, five steps should be applied at contract inception, which do not need to be applied in sequence:

- Step 1: Identify the contract with customers
- Step 2: Identify the performance obligations in the contract
- Step 3: Determine the transaction price
- Step 4: Allocate the transaction price
- Step 5: Recognise revenue when a performance obligation is satisfied

The revenue model is applied to each individual contract. However, as a practical expedient, a portfolio approach is permitted for contracts with similar characteristics provided it is reasonably expected that the impact on the financial statements will not be materially different from applying this model to the individual contracts.

Step 1: Identify the contract with customers

A contract is defined as an agreement between two or more parties that creates enforceable rights and obligations. The object of identifying a contract with customers is to establish the enforceable rights and obligations. Therefore, IFRS 15 only applies to valid contracts that meet specified criteria. This step also identifies when contracts should be combined and recorded as one contract and provides guidance for the accounting for contract modifications.

Identifying the contract. IFRS 15 clarifies that a contract can be oral, written or implied by business practice. A contract with a customer will be regarded as a valid contract in the scope of IFRS 15 when *all the following* criteria are met:

1. The parties to the contract have approved the contract;
2. Each party's rights in relation to the goods or services to be transferred can be identified;
3. The payment terms and conditions for the goods or services to be transferred can be identified;
4. The contract has commercial substance; and
5. The collection of an amount of consideration to which the entity is entitled in exchange for the goods or services is probable.

The criteria are assessed at contract inception and should not be re-assessed unless an indication of a significant change in facts or circumstances is evident. If a contract does not meet the above criteria, revenue is not recognised and going forward the contract is re-assessed to determine when the criteria are subsequently met to trigger the recognition of revenue.

The collectability criterion will normally not create problems in practice if an entity has proper credit control procedures to assess the credit status of customers. However, in the case of, for instance, state-owned entities that apply IFRS, this criterion could be problematic if the state-owned entities are required to provide services by law even if it is probable that the customers will not be able to settle their accounts.

IFRS 15 states that the enforceability of the rights and obligations in a contract is a matter of law, which could be applied and interpreted differently across legal jurisdictions. Business practice and procedures could also differ within an entity. These business practice and procedures should also be considered to determine whether and when an agreement with a customer creates enforceable rights and obligations. The duration of a contract should also be established to determine the period over which the contract creates enforceable rights and obligations.

Specifically, a contract does not exist if all parties to the contract have a unilateral enforceable right to terminate the contract without compensating other parties.

No transaction is recognised for a wholly underperformed contract. A contract is regarded to be wholly underperformed and regarded as an executory contract if both the following are present:

1. Promised goods or services are not transferred to the customer.
2. No consideration is received or receivable in exchange for the promised goods or services.

When a contract with a customer does not meet the criteria to identify a valid contract and consideration is received from the customer, revenue shall only be recognised for the consideration received when *either of the following* events happens:

1. No remaining obligations to transfer goods or services to the customer exist and substantially all of the consideration promised by the customer has been received and is non-refundable; or
2. The contract has been terminated and the consideration received from the customer is non-refundable.

The consideration received for invalid contracts shall be recognised as a liability until one of the events above happens or the contract becomes a valid contract. The liability is measured at the amount received. Normally the liability recognised represents the obligation to either transfer goods or services in the future or to refund the consideration received.

Example of collectability of consideration

A real estate developer (RED) enters into a contract with a customer for the sale of a building for €1 million. The customer intends to open a restaurant in the building. The building is located in an area where new restaurants face high levels of competition and the customer has little experience in the restaurant industry.

The customer pays a non-refundable deposit of €50,000 at inception of the contract and enters into a long-term financing agreement with the RED for the remaining 95% of the promised consideration. The financing arrangement is provided on a non-recourse basis, which means that if the customer defaults, the RED can repossess the building, but cannot seek further compensation from the customer, even if the collateral does not cover the full value of the amount owed. The RED's cost of the building is €600,000. The customer obtains control of the building at contract inception.

The criteria of a valid contract are not met because it is **not probable** that the RED will collect the consideration to which it is entitled in exchange for the transfer of the building. In reaching this conclusion, the RED observes that the customer's ability and intention to pay may be in doubt because of the restaurant business facing significant risks being high competition in the industry and the customer's limited experience, and additionally the customer lacks other income or assets. Revenue recognition is deferred and the non-refundable deposit of €50,000 is recognised as a contract liability since the RED has not received substantially all of the consideration and it has not terminated the contract.

Combination of contracts. Contracts are normally assessed separately. Contracts are, however, combined and treated as a single contract for the purpose of IFRS 15 if they are entered into at or near the same time with the same customer (or related parties of the customer) *in any one of the following cases*:

1. The contracts are negotiated as a package with a single commercial objective.
2. The amount of consideration to be paid in one contract depends on the price or performance of the other contract.
3. The goods or services promised in the contracts (or some goods or services promised in each of the contracts) are a single performance obligation.

Contract modifications. A contract modification is regarded as a change in the scope or price (or both) in a contract that is approved by the parties of the contract. A contract modification therefore either creates new or changes the existing enforceable rights and obligations in the contract. A contract modification should also be approved by the parties either in writing, by oral agreement or implied by customary business practices.

A contract modification must be distinguished from a variable consideration (discussed under Step 3). A variable consideration is an uncertainty in the price of an existing contract that will only be resolved when the future uncertainty is clarified. Judgement is needed to distinguish between modifications and variable consideration.

When a modification is not approved by the parties to the contract, IFRS 15 is applied to the existing contract until the contract modification is approved. All relevant facts and circumstances, including the terms of the contract and other available evidence, should also be considered to determine whether a valid contract modification exists and is enforceable.

A contract modification may, however, exist although a dispute arises about the scope or price of the modification or the parties have approved a change in the scope of the contract but has not yet determined the corresponding change in price. If the parties to a contract have approved a change in the scope of the contract but have not yet determined the corresponding change in price, the change in the transaction price shall be estimated by applying the guidance in step 3 regarding the estimation of variable consideration and constraining estimates of variable consideration.

To determine the accounting treatment of contract modifications, an assessment is made to determine whether the modification is a separate contract or a change in an existing contract. A contract modification is accounted for as a separate contract when *both the following* conditions are met:

1. An addition of promised goods or services exists that is distinct (as discussed in step 2) and increases the scope of the contract; and
2. The price increase of the additional goods or services reflects the stand-alone selling prices of the additional goods or services, with appropriate adjustments to reflect the circumstances of the particular contract.

If the above conditions are not met, the contract modification is treated as a change of the existing contract. Changes of existing contracts are accounted for either prospectively or retrospectively. The accounting treatment depends on whether the remaining goods or services to be delivered after the modification are distinct from those delivered before the modification. This assessment will result in the contract being treated in one of the following three ways:

1. The contract modification is treated as a termination of the existing contract and the creation of a new contract, if the remaining goods or services are distinct from the goods or services transferred on or before the date of the contract modification. The amount of consideration to be allocated to the remaining performance obligations is then the sum of:
   a. The portion of the transaction price of the contract before modification not yet recognised as revenue.
   b. The additional consideration promised as part of the contract modification.
2. The contract modification is treated as part of the existing contract if the remaining goods or services are not distinct. The modification is then treated on a cumulative catch-up basis. Under the cumulative catch-up basis, the effect of the contract modification on both the total transaction price and the measure of progress towards completion are recognised as an adjustment to revenue at the date of the contract modification.
3. When the remaining goods or services are a combination of creating a new contract and adjusting an existing contract, the effects of the modification on the unsatisfied (including partially unsatisfied) performance obligations are separated by following the principles of both options 1 and 2 above. IFRS 15 does not specifically state how the separation between the creation of a new contract and the adjustment of an existing contract (cumulative catch-up basis) should be done and a logical application of the principles is needed.

Example of a contract modification

Entity X promises to sell 120 products to a customer for €12,000 (€100 per product). The products are transferred to the customer over a six-month period. Entity X transfers control of each product at a point in time. After Entity X has transferred control of 60 products to the customer, the contract is modified to require the delivery of an additional 30 products (a total of 150 identical products) to the customer. The additional 30 products were not included in the initial contract.

Case A: Additional products for a price that reflects the stand-alone selling price

When the contract is modified, the price of the contract modification for the additional 30 products is an additional €2,850 or €95 per product. The pricing for the additional products reflects the stand-alone selling price of the products at the time of the contract modification and the additional products are distinct from the original products.

The contract modification for the additional 30 products is, in effect, a new and separate contract for future products that does not affect the accounting for the existing contract. Entity X recognises revenue of €100 per product for the 120 products in the original contract and €95 per product for the 30 products in the new contract.

Case B: Additional products for a price that does not reflect the stand-alone selling price

During the process of negotiating the purchase of an additional 30 products, the parties initially agree on a price of €80 per product. However, the customer discovers that the initial 60 products transferred to the customer contained minor defects that were unique to those delivered products. Entity X promises a partial credit of €15 per product to compensate the customer for the poor quality of those products. The entity and the customer agree to incorporate the credit of €900 (€15 credit × 60 products) into the price that the entity charges for the additional 30 products. Consequently, the contract modification specifies that the price of the additional 30 products is €1,500 or €50 per product. That price comprises the agreed-upon price for the additional 30 products of €2,400, or €80 per product, less the credit of €900.

At the time of modification, Entity X recognises the €900 as a reduction of the transaction price and therefore as a reduction of revenue for the initial 60 products transferred. In accounting for the sale of the additional 30 products, the entity determines that the negotiated price of €80 per product does not reflect the stand-alone selling price of the additional products. Consequently, the contract modification does not meet the conditions to be accounted for as a separate contract. Because the remaining products to be delivered are distinct from those already transferred, Entity X accounts for the modification as a termination of the original contract and the creation of a new contract.

As a result, the amount recognised as revenue for each of the remaining products is a blended price of €93.33 {[(€100 × 60 products not yet transferred under the original contract) + (€80 × 30 products to be transferred under the contract modification)] ÷ 90 remaining products}.

Step 2: Identify the performance obligations in the contract

At contract inception, goods or services promised in a contract are identified as separate performance obligations when the goods or services are distinct. However, to make IFRS 15 more practical, a series of distinct goods or services is also identified as a performance obligation when the goods or services are substantially the same and have the same pattern of transfer to the customer.

A contract with a customer normally explicitly states the goods or services that are promised to be transferred to a customer. However, the performance obligations identified in a contract are not limited to the goods or services that are explicitly stated in that contract. Promises implied by customary business practices, published policies or specific statements are also included if those promises create a valid expectation that goods or services will be transferred to the customer.

Performance obligations only include activities in a contract that transfers goods and services to the customer. Administrative tasks to fulfil or set up a contract will therefore not be separate performance obligations. IFRS 15 includes the following examples of promised goods and services:

1. Sale of goods produced by an entity.
2. Resale of goods purchased.
3. Resale of rights to goods or services such as tickets.
4. Services performed.
5. A stand-ready service to provide goods or services such as insurance contracts.
6. Making goods or services available for a customer to be used.
7. Acting as an agent for another party to transfer goods and services.
8. Granting rights to goods or services linked to original good and services.

9. Constructing, manufacturing or developing an asset on behalf of a customer.
10. Granting licences.
11. Granting options to purchase additional goods or services.

Distinct performance obligations

A contract includes promises to transfer goods or services to a customer. If those goods or services are distinct, the performance obligation is accounted for separately. A good or service is regarded as distinct if the *following two criteria are met*:

1. The customer can benefit from the good or service on its own or together with other readily available resources; and
2. The promise to transfer the good or service to the customer is separately identifiable from other promises in the contract, which means that the promised goods and services are distinct in contents of the contract.

A customer is regarded as benefiting from a good or service if the good or service could be used, consumed or sold for an amount that is greater than scrap value or otherwise held to generate economic benefits. A customer could benefit from goods and services on its own or in conjunction with other readily available resources. A readily available resource is a good or service that is sold separately or a resource that the customer has already obtained from the entity or from other transactions or events.

Separately identifiable is assessed, within the context of the contract, by determining whether each of the goods or services is transferred individually or alternatively transferred as a combined item or items to which the promised goods or services are inputs. The following *factors* identify whether goods and services are not separately identifiable:

1. A significant service of integrating the good or service with other goods or services promised in the contract is provided and therefore a combined output is provided.
2. The good or service does significantly modify or customise another good or service promised in the contract (or is modified or customised by other goods and services).
3. The good or service is highly interdependent on or highly interrelated with other goods or services promised in the contract.

The effect of the factors is that each good and service is significantly affected by the other goods and services.

Example of determining whether goods or services are distinct

An entity, a software developer, enters into a contract with a customer to transfer:

1. A software licence.
2. An installation service (includes changing the web screen for each user).
3. Software updates.
4. Technical support for two years.

The entity sells the above separately. The installation service is routinely performed by other entities and does not significantly modify the software. The software remains functional without the updates and the technical support.

Are the goods or services promised to the customer distinct in terms of IFRS 15?

The software is delivered before the other goods or services and remains functional without the updates and the technical support; therefore, the entity concludes that the customer can benefit from each of the goods and services either on their own or together with the other goods and services that are readily available.

The promise to transfer each good and service to the customer is separately identifiable from each other. In particular, the installation service does not significantly modify or customise the software itself and, as such, the software and the installation service are separate outputs promised by the entity instead of inputs used to produce a combined output.

Based on the assessment, four performance obligations in the contract have been identified for all four of the above goods or services.

When promised goods or services are not distinct, they are combined until a bundle of goods or services is identified that is distinct. This could result in an entity combining all the goods or services promised in a contract as a single performance obligation.

A series of distinct goods and services

This option is included to limit the overidentification of separate performance obligations in a contract when the goods and services are substantially the same and have the same pattern of transfer to the customer. IFRS 15 determines that a series of distinct goods or services has the same pattern of transfer to the customer *if both of the following criteria* are met:

1. Each distinct good or service in the series of goods and services is regarded to be a performance obligation satisfied over time; and
2. The same method would be used to measure the progress to completion of each distinct good or service in the series to the customer.

Step 3: Determine the transaction price

The transaction price is the amount of consideration that an entity expects to be entitled to in exchange for transferring promised goods or services to a customer. The transaction price excludes amounts collected on behalf of others. In determining the transaction price, the terms of the contract and past customary business practices are considered. Furthermore, it is assumed that the goods and services will be transferred as promised and that the contract will not be cancelled, renewed or modified.

The amount of consideration could be a fixed or variable amount and could be paid in cash or otherwise. If the consideration is not fixed the amount of consideration should be estimated limited to a specific constraint for variable consideration. In determining the transaction price, the nature, timing and amount of consideration are also considered, including the possible existence of a significant financing component in the contract.

At the end of each reporting period the estimated transaction price is reconsidered and updated with circumstances present at the end of the reporting period and changes in circumstances during the reporting period.

Variable consideration

Variable amounts in a contract are estimated to determine the amount entitled under the contract, including consideration contingent on the occurrence of a future uncertain event. A variable consideration is, however, not included in the transaction price if the uncertainty regarding the amount is too uncertain (refer to constraining estimates of variable consideration below).

Variable fees arise when an entity provides goods or services for a consideration that varies based on the occurrence or non-occurrence of a future event. The timing of recognition of variable fees may now change and need to be recognised sooner as a result of IFRS 15. Revenues for industries like construction, asset management, technology, life sciences, entertainment and media and engineering may have a significant portion of revenue that is made up of variable fees, such as performance bonuses and other forms of contingent consideration.

Per the previous IFRS standards, such industries had to delay revenue recognition for variable fees until they were earned, received or the contingency resolved. Based on the new standard, revenue may be recognised earlier if an entity can point to experience with similar arrangements. As a result of this, a new process may need to be established to estimate these variable amounts each year.

The consideration promised could vary because of discounts, rebates, refunds, credits, price concessions, incentives, performance bonuses, penalties or other similar items, including consideration contingent on the occurrence or non-occurrence of a future event such as right of return options or performance bonuses. Right of return is specifically discussed later under specific transaction. Variability could be explicitly stated in the contract, or could result from customary business practices, published policies, specific statements or other facts and circumstances that a price concession will be granted.

The amount of variable consideration is estimated by using the *following two methods* depending on which method better predicts the amount of consideration entitled to:

1. The expected value: the sum of probability-weighted amounts in a range of possible consideration amounts. This method could be used to estimate the amount of variable consideration for contracts with similar characteristics.
2. The most likely amount: the single most likely amount in a range of possible outcomes. This method could be used to estimate the amount of variable consideration if only two possible outcomes exist.

The method chosen should be applied consistently throughout the contract. All information (historical, current and forecast) that is reasonably available, including a reasonable number of possible consideration amounts, should be considered. These considerations are normally based on information used by management during bidding and establishing prices for promised goods or services.

Constraining estimates of variable consideration

IFRS 15 deals with the uncertainty relating to variable consideration by limiting the amount of variable consideration that can be recognised. Specifically, variable consideration is only included in the transaction price if, and to the extent that, it is highly probable that its inclusion will not result in a significant revenue reversal in the future when the uncertainty has been subsequently resolved.

Both the likelihood and the magnitude of the revenue reversal should be considered in assessing the constraint. IFRS 15 identifies the *following factors* that could increase both the likelihood and the magnitude of a revenue reversal:

1. The amount of consideration is highly susceptible to factors outside the entity's influence, such as volatility in a market, the judgement or actions of third parties, weather conditions and a high risk of obsolescence.

2. The uncertainty about the amount of consideration is not expected to be resolved for a long period of time.
3. The experience (or other evidence) with similar types of contracts is limited or has limited predictive value.
4. A practice exists of either offering a broad range of price concessions or changing the payment terms and conditions of similar contracts in similar circumstances.
5. The contract has a large number and broad range of possible consideration amounts.

Example of a volume discount incentive

Big Bed enters into a contract with a customer to sell beds for €400 per bed on January 1, 20XX. If the customer purchases more than 1,000 beds in a calendar year, the contract states that the price per unit is retrospectively reduced to €380 per unit. As a result of this the consideration in the contract is variable.

As at March 31, 20XX, Big Bed sells 80 beds to the customer, therefore Big Bed estimates that the customer's purchase will not exceed the 1,000-bed threshold required for the volume discount in the calendar year.

When considering the requirements of IFRS 15 and the significant experience Big Bed has with this product and the entity's purchasing pattern, it was concluded that it is highly probable that a significant reversal in the cumulative amount of revenue recognised (original sale price of €400 per bed) will not occur when the uncertainty is resolved (i.e., when the total amount of purchases is known). Consequently, the entity recognises revenue of €32,000 (80 beds × €400) for the first quarter ended March 31, 20XX.

At the beginning of June 20XX, the customer acquires another company and at the end of the second quarter, June 30, 20XX, Big Bed sells an additional 500 beds to the customer. In light of the new fact, Big Bed estimates that the customer's purchases will exceed the 1,000-bed threshold for the calendar year and therefore it would have to retrospectively reduce the price per unit.

Big Bed therefore recognises revenue of €188,400 for the quarter ended June 30, 20XX. The amount is calculated from €190,000 (500 beds × €380) less the change in transaction price of €1,600 (80 beds sold as at March 31, 20XX × €20 price reduction) for the reduction of the beds sold in the first quarter.

The existence of a significant financing component in the contract

An adjustment for the time value of money is made to a transaction price for significant effects of financing. As a practical expedient, a finance component need not be identified when the period between the transfer of promised goods or services and the payment therefor is expected to be less than 12 months.

Time value of money plays an important role in IFRS 15. This is especially prevalent when a contract contains explicitly or implicitly a significant financing component as the transaction price will be affected. As a result, operational challenges associated with measuring the time value of money might be faced. In addition, judgement will play a role in deciding what is considered to be significant.

The objective of adjusting the amount of consideration for a significant financing component is to recognise revenue at an amount that reflects the cash price on the date of transfer. Therefore, all facts and circumstances are considered to assess whether a contract contains a significant financing component. Specifically, the *following are considered* to identify a significant financing component:

1. The difference between the identified consideration and the cash selling price of the promised goods or services.
2. The combined effect of both the expected period between the transfer of promised goods or services and the payment therefor, and the prevailing interest rates in the relevant market.

IFRS 15 identifies that a significant financing component *would not exist in the following cases*:

1. The goods or services are paid in advance and the timing of the transfer of those goods or services is at the discretion of the customer.
2. A substantial amount of the consideration is variable, and the amount or timing of that consideration varies based on the occurrence or non-occurrence of a future event that is not substantially within the control of the customer or the entity.
3. The difference between the promised consideration and the cash selling price arises for reasons other than the provision of financing and the difference between those amounts is proportional to the reason for the difference. An example is a construction contract where a deposit is paid upfront to protect the risk of non-performance by the customer.

The discount rate is determined at contract inception and not updated for changes in interest rates or other circumstances. The discount rate should reflect the applicable discount rate between the entity and other customers in a separate financing transaction. Such a rate reflects the credit characteristics of the customer receiving the finance and considers any collateral or security and assets transferred in the contract. The rate might also be determined by identifying the rate that discounts the contract payments to the normal cash price.

In the statement of comprehensive income, the effect of financing is presented separately from revenue from contracts with customers. Interest revenue or interest expense is recognised only if a related contract asset or liability is recognised for unpaid amounts.

Non-cash consideration

Non-cash consideration is measured at fair value. However, when the fair value cannot reasonably be estimated, the non-cash consideration is measured indirectly by reference to the stand-alone selling price of the goods or services provided. Non-cash consideration could be variable regarding the form of the consideration (such as share payments) or for other reasons such as performance measures. In the latter case the requirements for variable consideration and any possible uncertainty constraint (discussed above) need to be considered.

When a customer contributes goods or services (such as materials, equipment or labour) to facilitate the fulfilment of the contract, an assessment is made whether the entity obtains control of the contributed goods or services. If control is obtained, the contributed goods and services are accounted for as non-cash consideration received from the customer.

Consideration payable to a customer

Sometimes consideration might be payable to a customer. Consideration payable to a customer might also include credit or other items (such as a coupon or voucher) that can be applied against amounts owed to the customer. This could also include other parties that purchase the entity's goods or services from the customer.

Such consideration payable to a customer is normally regarded as a reduction of the transaction price and resultant revenue, unless the payment to the customer is for a distinct good or service transferred from the customer. The requirements for variable consideration and any constraint are also applicable to consideration payable to a customer.

When the consideration payable to a customer is for a distinct good or service from the customer it is regarded as a normal purchase transaction. Any excess of the consideration payable to the customer over the fair value of the distinct good or service is accounted for as a reduction of the original transaction price. However, if the fair value of the good or service received from the customer cannot be reasonably estimated, the full amount is regarded as a reduction of the transaction price.

Any reduction in the transaction price as a result of a consideration payable to a customer is recognised when the latter of the following events occurs:

1. Revenue is recognised for the transfer of the related goods or services to the customer.
2. Payment is made or promised to the customer.

Changes in the transaction price

The basic principle is that a change in the transaction price after contract inception is allocated to performance obligations on the same basis as at contract inception. The transaction price is therefore not reallocated to subsequent changes in stand-alone selling prices. This is regarded as a change in accounting estimates that is recognised when the change happens.

A change in the transaction price is allocated to some of the performance obligations or a series of distinct goods or services based on the guidance, discussed in step 4, to allocating variable consideration to some performance obligations.

A change in the transaction price from a contract modification is accounted for as a contract modification discussed in step 1. However, for a change in the transaction price that occurs after a contract modification, the issue is whether the modification would be accounted for as a separate contract or not. If the modification is accounted for as a separate contract, any change in the transaction that refers to an amount of variable consideration, promised before the modification, is allocated to the performance obligation identified in the contract before the modification. If the modification is not accounted for as a separate contract, the change in the transaction price is allocated to the performance obligations identified in the modified contract.

Step 4: Allocate the transaction price

The objective in IFRS 15 is that the transaction price is allocated to each performance obligation in an amount that depicts the amount of consideration expected to be entitled to in exchange for transferring the promised goods or services to the customer. The requirements also specify when an entity allocates variable consideration to only some of the performance obligations in a contract.

Allocation based on stand-alone selling prices

The transaction price is allocated to different performance obligations in the contract by reference to their relative stand-alone selling prices. If a stand-alone selling price is not directly observable, it needs to be estimated.

The stand-alone selling price is the price at which an entity would sell a promised good or service separately to a customer. The best evidence of a stand-alone selling price is the observable price used in similar circumstances to similar customers. Alternatively, a contractually stated price or a list price for goods and services may be an indication of the stand-alone selling price.

When estimating a stand-alone selling price, all information is considered that is reasonably available to the entity. In doing so, the use of observable inputs is maximised. Estimation methods are applied consistently in similar circumstances.

Suitable methods for estimating the stand-alone selling price might include the following:

1. *Adjusted market approach*: Evaluate the market in which the goods or services are sold and estimate the price that a customer in that market would be willing to pay for those goods or services. This approach might also include using prices of competitors for similar goods or services and adjusting those prices as necessary to reflect the entity's costs and margins.
2. *Expected cost plus a margin approach*: Forecast the expected costs of satisfying a performance obligation and adding an appropriate margin for that good or service.
3. *Residual approach*: Estimate the stand-alone selling price by reference to the total transaction price less the sum of the observable stand-alone selling prices of other goods or services promised in the contract.

The use of the residual approach is limited to cases of uncertainty. Therefore, the residual approach may only be used in any of the following cases:

1. The same good or service is sold to different customers for a broad range of amounts resulting in the selling price being highly variable and the stand-alone selling price not being determinable from past transactions or other observable evidence.
2. The selling price is not established for that good or service that has not previously been sold on a stand-alone basis.

In highly variable and uncertain cases the methods may be combined for a contract to estimate the stand-alone selling prices for different performance obligations depending on the uncertainty and variability. However, the objective of depicting the expected amount of consideration should still be achieved.

Allocation of a discount

Sometimes the transaction price may include a discount. A discount is granted for a bundle of goods or services if the sum of the stand-alone selling prices of the promised goods or services in the contract exceeds the promised consideration in a contract. Normally the overall discount is allocated between the performance obligations in a contract on a relative stand-alone selling price basis. However, in some circumstances it may be appropriate to allocate the discount to certain performance obligations in the contract when there is observable evidence that the discount relates to specific performance obligations in the contract.

Example of allocating a trade discount in a phone transaction

An entity typically sells a phone, a 24-month service contract and 24-month phone insurance together as a package for €25 per month. The entity also sells the phone, the 24-month contract and the 24-month phone insurance independently at €408, €15 per month for 24 months and €4 per month for 24 months, respectively. Lastly, the entity also sells the phone and the 24-month phone insurance as a package for €480.

Under previous IAS 18, the entity is required to measure revenue for each good and service at "the fair value of the consideration received or receivable taking into account the amount of any trade discounts and volume rebates allowed by the entity"—but no guidance is given as to how the trade discount should be allocated. It is thus the practice of the entity to apply the entire discount of €264 [(€15 × 24) + (€4 × 24) + €408 – (€25 × 24)] to the purchase of the phone thus recognising only €144 at the start of the bundled contract with the remainder recognised over the period of the contract.

Under IFRS 15 the discount should be allocated to all the performance obligations in the contract unless the entity has observable evidence that the discount relates to certain performance obligations in the contract:

1. Determine if any portion of the discount relates specifically to one or more performance obligations—in this case €24 [(€4 × 24) + (€408 − €480)] relates specifically to the phone and the insurance as they are regularly sold together at this discount. This would result in an initial fair value for these two components of €389 for the phone and €91 for the insurance, by allocating the discount proportionally (ignoring for this example decimal places) [€480/€504 × component amount].
2. The remaining discount of €240 should then be split proportionally among the phone (€389), the 24-month contract (€360) and the 24-month insurance (€91).

A discount is allocated to only specific performance obligations in the contract if all of the following criteria are met:

1. Each distinct good or service in the contract is sold regularly on a stand-alone basis.
2. A bundle (or bundles) of some of those distinct goods or services is also regularly sold on a stand-alone basis at a discount.
3. The discount attributable to each bundle of goods or services is substantially the same as the discount in the contract and provides observable evidence of the performance obligation(s) to which the discount belongs.

The discount is allocated to certain performance obligations in the contract before using the residual approach to estimate the stand-alone selling price of any good or service.

Example of allocating a discount to one or more performance obligations

A fashion outlet named Fashionable regularly sells scarves, shoes and handbags individually, thereby establishing stand-alone selling prices. In addition, Fashionable regularly sells shoes and handbags together for €60. Fashionable enters into a contract with a customer to sell all three products in exchange for €100. Fashionable will satisfy the performance obligations for each of the products at different points in time.

The contract includes a discount of €40 on the overall transaction. This discount will be allocated proportionately to all three obligations when allocating the transaction price using the relative stand-alone selling price method. However, because Fashionable regularly sells shoes and handbags together for €60 and scarves for €40, it has evidence that the entire discount should be allocated to the promises to transfer shoes and handbags.

If Fashionable transfers control of the shoes and handbags at the same point in time, then Fashionable could as a practical matter account for the transfer of those products as a single performance obligation. That is, the entity could allocate €60 of the transaction price to the single obligation and recognise revenue of €60 when shoes and handbags are simultaneously transferred to the customer.

If the contract requires Fashionable to transfer the control of the shoes and handbags at different points in time, then the amount of €60 is individually allocated to the products based on their stand-alone selling price as follows:

Shoes	=	€33 (€55 ÷ €100 [total stand-alone selling price] × €60)
Handbag	=	€27 (€45 ÷ €100 [total stand-alone selling price] × €60)
Total	=	€60

Allocation of variable consideration

Variable consideration that is promised in a contract may be attributable to the entire contract or to a specific part of the contract. A variable amount is allocated to a specific part of a contract if the terms of a variable payment relate specifically to the satisfaction of specific performance obligation. The allocation of the variable must also meet the objective of depicting the amount of consideration expected to be entitled to for transferring the promised goods or services to the customer.

Example of allocating a price concession

A software supplier typically sells 10,000 copies of its program to retailers at an initial price of €40 per copy. Due to the nature of the industry (fast moving with software quickly becoming out of date) the contract includes a price concession whereby the retailer will receive a refund of €10 per unsold copy at a certain specified date.

Under IAS 18 the supplier only recognises the revenue for this transaction on the specified date—this is due to the requirement that "the amount of revenue can be measured reliably." The supplier is only able to reliably measure the revenue from the date it knows how many copies are unsold on this date.

Under IFRS 15 the supplier is allowed to recognise variable income to the extent that it is not constrained (or to the extent that it is highly probable that a significant reversal in the amount of cumulative revenue recognised will not occur) and gives guidance on how this estimate may be made. The supplier thus assesses its historical data and determines that historically it pays refunds based on non-sales of between 0% and 20% of the initial purchase volume.

The supplier thus determines it should initially recognise €385,000 [(10,000 × 85% × CU40) + (10,000 × 15% × €30)] as it has assessed that 15% is the level at which no significant reversal of revenue is expected.

Step 5: Recognise revenue when performance obligations are satisfied

Based on the principle of control, revenue is recognised when an entity's performance obligation is satisfied by transferring a promised good or service to a customer. A performance obligation could either be satisfied over time or at a point in time. The assessment of over time or at a point in time must be done at contract inception for each performance obligation by first assessing the application of over time. If the performance obligation is not satisfied over time it defaults to point in time.

Benefits are transferred to a customer. IFRS 15 assumes that the control of an asset is transferred even if the benefit is immediately consumed. Control of an asset means having the ability to direct the use of and obtain substantially all of the remaining benefits from the asset. Control also includes the ability to prevent others from directing the use of and obtaining the benefits. The benefits of an asset are the potential cash flows (inflows or savings in outflows) that can be obtained directly or indirectly in many ways, such as by:

1. Using the asset to produce goods or provide services.
2. Using the asset to enhance the value of other assets.
3. Using the asset to settle liabilities or reduce expenses.
4. Selling or exchanging the asset.
5. Pledging the asset to secure a loan.
6. Holding the asset.

When evaluating whether a customer obtains control of an asset any agreement to repurchase the asset should be considered (refer to specific transactions discussed later).

Performance obligations satisfied over time

IFRS 15 determines that revenue is recognised over time *if one of the following three criteria is met*:

1. The customer simultaneously receives and consumes the benefit provided by the entity as the entity performs; or
2. The entity's performance creates or enhances an asset that the customer controls as the asset is created or enhanced; or
3. The entity's performance does not create an asset with an alternative use to the entity and the entity has an enforceable right to payment for the performance completed to date.

Criterion 1: Simultaneous receipt and consumption of benefits. The assessment of whether a customer simultaneously receives and consumes a benefit is regarded as a "pure service." This assessment might be easy in some cases, such as a cleaning service, but could be more difficult in other cases. To overcome any difficulty, IFRS 15 requires that a performance obligation is regarded as a "pure service" satisfied over time if another entity would not need to substantially reperform the work the entity has completed to date if that other entity were to fulfil the remaining performance obligation to the customer.

In the assessment whether another entity would not need to substantially reperform the work completed to date, any contractual restrictions or practical limitations are ignored. Furthermore, the other entity fulfilling the remainder of the performance obligation must not have the benefit of any asset presently controlled and remained controlled by the original entity.

Criterion 2: Customer controls the asset as it is created or enhanced. In determining whether a customer controls an asset as it is created or enhanced, the requirements of control are assessed. The asset created or enhanced could be either tangible or intangible.

If the customer controls the asset, the customer could protect others from using the asset and therefore indirectly receive the benefits the asset has created or enhanced. In certain instances, such as a construction contract that is fulfilled on the premises of the customer, it could be easy to determine that the customer can restrict others from using the asset as it is created or enhanced. However, if the work in progress is not done at the premises of the customer it could be more difficult to establish whether the customer controls the asset. To overcome such uncertainty, IFRS 15 includes the third "over time" criterion discussed below.

Criterion 3: Entity's performance does not create an asset with an alternative use. The criterion is based on two requirements *that both must be present*:

1. The performance does not create an asset with an alternative use to the entity; and
2. An enforceable right to payment exists for the performance completed to date.

The first assessment is whether an asset has an alternative use at contract inception. After contract inception, the assessment of the alternative use of an asset is not updated unless the parties to the contract approve a contract modification that substantively changes the performance obligation.

The rationale for including the alternative use requirement is the assumption that an asset is specifically created for the customer if the entity cannot readily direct that asset for another use. In assessing the alternative use requirement, the effects of contractual restrictions and practical limitations on the ability to readily direct that asset for another use should be considered. The possibility of the contract with the customer being terminated is not a relevant consideration in assessing whether the entity would be able to readily direct the asset for another use.

A contractual restriction on the ability to direct an asset for another use must be substantive for the asset not to have an alternative use to the entity. A contractual restriction is regarded to be substantive if a customer could enforce its rights to the promised asset if the asset is directed for another use. In contrast, a contractual restriction is not regarded to be substantive *if both*:

1. The asset is largely interchangeable with another asset without breaching the contract; and
2. Significant cost will not be incurred to interchange the asset.

A practical limitation on the ability to direct an asset for another use exists if significant economic losses would be incurred to direct the asset for another use. A significant economic loss would be incurred if the cost to rework the asset for alternative sale is significant or the asset could only be sold at a significant loss. Examples provided by IFRS 15 that could create significant economic losses are design specifications unique to a customer or activities located in remote areas.

The second requirement, the right to payment for performance completed to date, represents an entitlement to compensation for performance completed to date if the customer or another party terminates the contract for reasons other than the failure to perform as promised. The compensation should be an amount that approximates the selling price of the goods or services transferred to date, being a recovery of the costs incurred to date plus a reasonable profit margin. A reasonable profit margin need not be equal to the profit margin expected if the contract was fulfilled as promised, but should compensate for either of the following:

1. The expected profit margin in the contract that reasonably reflects the extent of the performance to date; or
2. If the contract-specific margin is higher than the return usually generated from similar contracts, a reasonable return on the cost of capital for similar contracts.

IFRS 15 clarifies that the right to payment for performance completed to date need not be a present unconditional right to payment. An unconditional right to payment may only be created if agreed-upon milestones are reached or upon complete satisfaction of the performance obligation. Therefore, consideration is made whether an enforceable right to demand or retain payment for performance completed to date exists if the contract were terminated early.

In certain contracts a customer may have a right to terminate the contract only at specified times during the life of the contract or the customer might not have any right to terminate the contract. If a customer terminates the contract prematurely, the contract (or other laws) might entitle the entity to continue to transfer to the customer the goods or services promised in the contract and require the customer to pay the consideration promised in exchange for those goods or services. The IASB clarifies that the entity has a right to payment for performance completed to date because the entity has a right to continue to perform its obligations in accordance with the contract and to require the customer to perform its obligations, which include payment for the promised consideration.

In assessing the existence and enforceability of a right to payment for performance completed to date the contractual terms as well as any legislation or legal precedent that could supplement or override those contractual terms are considered, including an assessment of whether:

1. Legislation, administrative practice or legal precedent confers a right to payment for performance to date even though that right is not specified in the contract.
2. Relevant legal precedent indicates that similar rights to payment for performance completed to date in similar contracts have no binding legal effect.
3. Customary business practices of choosing not to enforce a right to payment has resulted in the right being rendered unenforceable in that legal environment.

IFRS 15 also clarifies that the payment schedule specified in a contract does not necessarily indicate whether an enforceable right to payment for performance completed to date exists. The payment schedule in a contract normally specifies the timing and amount of consideration that is payable by a customer but might not necessarily provide evidence of the entity's right to payment for performance completed to date.

Example of construction and sale of flats

An entity's normal business is the construction and sale of flats, simplexes and/or duplexes in residential housing developments. Its standard contract contains clauses that stipulate in event of default that a deposit of 10% of the contract value and the dwelling itself will be retained.

Under IFRS 15 these contracts would be recognised at a point in time as the contract does not satisfy the requirements for recognition over time, namely:

1. The customer simultaneously receives and consumes the benefits provided by the entity's performance as the entity performs (the customer does not take possession of the dwelling until it is completed at which stage legal title is passed).
2. The entity's performance creates or enhances an asset (for example, work in progress) that the customer controls as the asset is created or enhanced (the customer does not control the asset until legal title passes).
3. The entity's performance does not create an asset with an alternative use to the entity (this is met as contractually the entity has to sell the asset to the customer unless the customer defaults) and the entity has an enforceable right to payment for performance completed to date (this is not met as the entity can only claim the 10% deposit for the work completed to date).

Measuring progress towards complete satisfaction of a performance obligation

If a performance obligation is satisfied over time, an entity should select an appropriate measure of progress to recognise revenue over time. The objective of measuring progress is to depict the performance satisfied in transferring goods or services to a customer.

A single method of measuring progress is applied for each performance obligation satisfied over time and the method should be applied consistently to similar performance obligations in similar circumstances. Progress towards completion should be remeasured at the end of each reporting period. Such changes to an entity's measure of progress shall be accounted for as a change in accounting estimate in accordance with IAS 8.

Determining the appropriate method for measuring progress considers the nature of the good or service promised in the contract. Both input and output methods may be used to measure progress to completion.

Output methods. Output methods recognise revenue based on a direct measurement of the value to the customer of the goods or services transferred to date relative to the remaining goods or services promised under the contract. Output methods include methods such as surveys of performance completed to date, appraisals of results achieved, milestones reached, time elapsed and units produced, or units delivered.

The output method selected should faithfully depict the performance towards complete satisfaction of the performance obligation. Work in progress or finished goods controlled by the customer should be included in the measurement of the output delivered.

A practical expedient exists for using invoiced amounts if the amounts correspond directly with the value to the customer of the entity's performance completed to date. An example is service contracts where fixed amounts are billed for each hour of service or unit delivered.

If the output used to measure progress to completion is not directly observable and therefore cannot be applied without undue cost, an input method is used.

Input methods. Input methods recognise revenue based on efforts or inputs to the satisfaction of a performance obligation relative to the total expected inputs to satisfy the performance obligation. Examples of inputs are resources consumed, labour hours used, costs incurred, time elapsed or machine hours used. For practical reasons revenue might be recognised on a straight-line basis if the efforts or inputs are incurred evenly throughout the performance period.

An issue with input methods is that there may not be a direct relationship between inputs and the transfer of control of goods or services to a customer. Specifically excluded from an input method are efforts that do not depict the entity's performance in transferring control of goods or services to the customer. When using a cost-based input method, adjustments to the measure of progress may be required for:

1. Costs incurred that do not contribute to the progress of performance. Therefore, significant inefficiencies in performance not reflected in the price of the contract should be excluded, such as unexpected wasted materials or labour incurred.
2. Costs incurred that are not proportionate to the progress of completion. Therefore, cost of goods used to satisfy a performance obligation may only be used if at contract inception it is expected *that all of the following conditions would be present*:

    a. The good is not distinct.
    b. The customer is expected to obtain control of the good significantly before receiving services related to the good.

c. The cost of the transferred good is significant relative to the total expected costs to completely satisfy the performance obligation.
d. The good is procured from a third party without being significantly involved in designing and manufacturing the good.

Reasonable measures of progress. Revenue is only recognised based on performance obligation satisfied over time only if a reasonable measure of progress towards complete satisfaction of the performance obligation could be made. A reasonable measure would not be made if reliable information to apply an appropriate method of measuring progress is not available. This could especially be applicable at the early stage of a contract. If, however, the costs are recoverable, revenue is only recognised to the extent of the costs incurred until a reasonable measure of progress could be made.

Performance obligations satisfied at a point in time

If a performance obligation is not satisfied over time, the performance obligation is by default satisfied at a point in time. To determine the point in time when revenue should be recognised, the requirements of control are considered. The control requirements are that the customer has (1) obtained the ability to direct the use of the asset and (2) obtained substantially all of the remaining benefits from the asset. Control is also present when the customer could restrict others from using the asset.

Factors which may indicate that control is passed to the customer at a point in time are:

1. *The present right to payment for the asset exists*: A present right of payment for an asset might indicate that the performance obligation is completed and therefore control is transferred by implication.
2. *The customer has legal title to the asset*: Legal title may indicate which party controls that asset and therefore could restrict the access of others to those benefits. An asset could still be transferred if legal title is retained solely for protection against failure of customer payment.
3. *Physical possession of the asset is transferred*: Physical possession of an asset may indicate control is being transferred. However, in repurchase and consignment arrangements, physical possession might not result in the transfer of control.
4. *The customer has the significant risks and rewards of ownership of the asset*: The transfer of significant risks and rewards of ownership of an asset may indicate that the customer has obtained control. However, additional performance obligations such as maintenance services must be assessed separately.
5. *The customer has accepted the asset*: Acceptance of an asset by a customer may indicate that control is transferred if the customer obtained the ability to direct the use of the asset and obtain substantially all of the remaining benefits from the asset.

Customer acceptance. IFRS 15 clarifies that customer assessment clauses should be assessed to determine when control is obtained by the customer. Such clauses normally allow the customer to cancel the contract or may require further work if the customer is not satisfied. Acceptance of an asset may indicate that the customer is satisfied with the assets and therefore has obtained control of the asset.

Customer acceptance is regarded to be a formality when it can objectively determine that the agreed-upon specifications in the contract are met. This assessment can be based on previous experience with contracts for similar goods or services. When the customer acceptance is a formality, revenue can be recognised before customer acceptance. Then a consideration is made whether there are any remaining performance obligations, such as installation of equipment, which should be recognised separately.

In contrast, if the customer acceptance is not a formality, revenue could not be recognised until acceptance by the customer. A product could also be delivered to a customer for trial or evaluation purposes without payment of any consideration until the trial period ends. Then revenue recognition is deferred until the customer either accepts the product or the trial period ends.

CONTRACT COST

Incremental Costs of Obtaining a Contract

Incremental costs of obtaining a contract with a customer are recognised as an asset only when it is expected that the cost will be recovered through the contract. Incremental costs are costs incurred to obtain a contract that would not have been incurred if the contract had not been successfully obtained. A practical expedient, however, exists, allowing the incremental costs of obtaining a contract to be expensed if the amortisation period would be one year or less.

Costs to obtain a contract that would have been incurred regardless of whether the contract was obtained or not are expensed, unless those costs are explicitly chargeable to a customer.

Example of incremental costs of obtaining a contract

A consulting services entity wins a competition bid to provide consulting services to a new customer. The following costs were incurred by the entity to obtain the contract:

	€
External legal fees for due diligence	15,000
Travel costs to deliver the proposal	25,000
Commissions paid to sales employees	10,000
Total costs incurred	50,000

In accordance with IFRS 15, the entity recognises an asset for the €10,000 (commission) incremental costs of obtaining the contract because the entity expects to recover those costs through future fees for consulting services. The entity also pays discretionary annual bonuses to sales employees based on annual sales targets, overall profitability and individual performance. Taking into account IFRS 15, the entity does not recognise an asset for the bonuses paid because they are not incremental to obtaining a contract. The bonus amounts are discretionary and are based on other factors, including the overall profitability of the entity and the individuals' performance, therefore they are not directly attributable to identifiable contracts.

The legal fees and travel costs would have been incurred whether the bid was won or not, therefore those costs are recognised as expenses when incurred, unless they are within the scope of another standard, in which case the relevant provisions of that standard apply.

Costs to fulfil a contract

Costs incurred to fulfil a contract are in the scope of IFRS 15 if it is not in the scope of another IFRS standard (such as IAS 2 or IAS 16). If not in the scope of IFRS 15, the other IFRS standard is applied. Fulfilment costs in the scope of IFRS 15 are recognised as an asset only *if all the following criteria are met*:

1. The costs relate directly to a contract or to an anticipated contract that can specifically be identified.
2. The costs generate or enhance resources that will be used in satisfying performance obligations in the future.
3. The costs are expected to be recovered.

Examples of costs that may be incurred to fulfil a contract are direct labour, direct materials, allocation of overheads that relate directly to the contract, costs that are explicitly chargeable to the customer under the contract and other costs that are incurred because of entering into the contract.

The following costs are, however, expenses as incurred:

1. General and administrative costs.
2. Costs of wasted materials, labour or other resources to fulfil the contract that were not reflected in the price of the contract.
3. Costs that relate to past performance being satisfied performance obligations or partially satisfied performance obligations.
4. Costs which cannot be distinguished whether they relate to satisfied or unsatisfied performance obligations.

Amortisation

A contract asset recognised is amortised on a systematic basis consistent with the transfer to the customer of the goods or services to which the asset relates. The amortisation is updated to reflect significant changes in the expected timing of transfer to the customer of the goods or services. Such a change is regarded as a change in accounting estimate in accordance with IAS 8.

Impairment

An impairment loss is recognised in profit or loss to the extent that the carrying amount of a contract asset recognised exceeds:

1. The remaining amount of consideration expected to be received in exchange for the goods or services; *less*
2. The costs that relate directly to providing those goods or services that have not been recognised already as an expense.

The remaining expected amount of consideration is determined by using the principles for determining the transaction price in step 3 of the revenue recognition process, excluding the requirements on constraining estimates of variable consideration. The amount is further adjusted to reflect the effects of the customer's credit risk.

A step approach is followed before an impairment loss is recognised for a contract asset, and any impairment loss is recognised for assets related to the contract that are recognised in accordance with another IFRS standard. After applying the impairment test, the resulting carrying amount of the asset is included in the carrying amount of the cash-generating unit to which it belongs for the purpose of applying IAS 36 (refer to Chapter 13).

Any later reversal of an impairment loss is recognised in profit or loss when the impairment conditions no longer exist or have improved. The new increased carrying amount of the contract asset shall not exceed the amount that would have been determined (net of amortisation) if no impairment loss had been recognised previously.

PRESENTATION

Statement of Financial Position

Balances on a revenue contract are presented in the statement of financial position as a contract asset or contract liability. A contract liability normally represents prepayments on a contract, such a revenue being received in advance. The contract liability represents the obligation to transfer goods or services to a customer. A contract liability is also recognised when a right to an amount of consideration exists that is unconditional (a receivable), before the entity transfers a good or service to the customer. Then a contract liability and a receivable are recognised.

A contract asset is recognised for transfer of goods and services that are still conditional and separately receivable for unconditional rights. Contract assets are assessed for impairment in terms of IFRS 9. An impairment of a contract asset shall be measured, presented and disclosed on the same basis as a financial asset that is within the scope of IFRS 9.

A receivable is the right to consideration that is unconditional. A right to consideration is unconditional if only the passage of time is required before payment of that consideration is due. A receivable is recognised for a present right even though that amount may be subject to refund in the future (refer to specific transactions discussed later). A receivable is accounted for in accordance with IFRS 9. Upon initial recognition of a receivable from a revenue contract any difference between the measurement of the receivable and the corresponding amount of revenue recognised is recognised as an expense.

IFRS 15 uses the terms "contract asset" and "contract liability" but does not prohibit an entity from using alternative descriptions. If alternative descriptions for contract assets are used, sufficient information should be disclosed for a user of the financial statements to distinguish between receivables and contract assets.

DISCLOSURE

The disclosure objective of IFRS 15 is that sufficient information should be disclosed to enable users of financial statements to understand the nature, amount, timing and uncertainty of revenue and cash flows arising from contracts with customers. To achieve this, both qualitative and quantitative information are disclosed.

The level of detail necessary to satisfy the disclosure objective and how much emphasis to place on each of the various requirements require judgements. Disclosure is aggregated or disaggregated so that useful information is not obscured by either the inclusion of a large amount of insignificant detail or the aggregation of items that have substantially different characteristics. Disclosure required by IFRS 15 is not provided if the information is provided by another IFRS standard.

Revenue recognised shall be disaggregated into categories that depict how the nature, amount, timing and uncertainty of revenue and cash flows are affected by economic factors. The disaggregation is based on facts and circumstances applicable to the entity and disclosures for other purposes, including *all of the following*:

1. Disclosures presented outside the financial statements, such as earnings releases, annual reports or investor presentations.
2. Information regularly reviewed by the chief operating decision maker for evaluating the financial performance of operating segments.
3. Other information that is used by the entity or users of the financial statements to evaluate the entity's financial performance or make resource allocation decisions.

Examples of categories that might be appropriate are:

a. Type of good or service.
b. Geographical region (country or region).
c. Market or type of customer (governmental or non-governmental).
d. Type of contract (fixed-price and time-and-materials contracts).
e. Contract duration (short-term or long-term).
f. Timing of transfer of goods or services (point in time or over time).
g. Sales channels (directly or through intermediaries).

The following information should be disclosed in terms of IFRS 15:

1. The *amount of revenue* recognised, including:
    a. The disaggregation of revenue into appropriate categories.
    b. For contract balances:
        i. The opening and closing balances of receivables, contract assets and contract liabilities.
        ii. Revenue recognised in the reporting period that was included in the contract liabilities' opening balance.
        iii. Revenue recognised in the reporting period from performance obligations satisfied in previous periods.
    c. For performance obligations, a description of:
        i. When the company typically satisfies its performance obligations.
        ii. The significant payment terms.
        iii. The nature of the goods or services that the entity has promised to transfer.
        iv. Obligations for returns, refunds and other similar obligations.
        v. Types of warranties and related obligations.
    d. The amount of the transaction price that is allocated to the remaining performance obligations in a contract.

2. The *significant judgements*, and changes in judgements, made in applying IFRS 15, in particular:

   a. The timing of satisfaction of performance obligations.
   b. The transaction price and the amounts allocated to performance obligations.

3. Any assets recognised from the costs to obtain or fulfil a revenue contract, including:

   a. A description of the judgements made in determining the amount of the costs and the amortisation method used for each reporting period.
   b. The closing balances of the assets by the main category of assets.
   c. The amount of amortisation and any impairment losses recognised.

4. Any impairment losses recognised (in accordance with IFRS 9) on any receivables or contract assets from revenue contracts separately from impairment losses from other contracts.
5. Sufficient information to understand the relationship between the disclosure of disaggregated revenue and revenue information that is disclosed for each reportable segment, if applicable.
6. An explanation of how the timing of satisfaction of performance obligations relates to the typical timing of payment and the effect that those factors have on the contract asset and the contract liability balances. The explanation provided may use qualitative information.
7. Significant changes in the contract asset and the contract liability balances during the reporting period. The explanation shall include qualitative and quantitative information. Examples of changes in balances of contract assets and contract liabilities include any of the following:

   a. Changes due to business combination.
   b. Cumulative catch-up adjustments to revenue that affect the corresponding contract asset or contract liability, including adjustments arising from a change in the measure of progress, a change in an estimate of the transaction price (including any changes in the assessment of whether an estimate of variable consideration is constrained) or a contract modification.
   c. Impairment of a contract asset.
   d. A change in the timeframe for a right to consideration to become unconditional (i.e., for a contract asset to be reclassified to a receivable).
   e. A change in the timeframe for a performance obligation to be satisfied (i.e., for the recognition of revenue arising from a contract liability).

8. Information about performance obligations in contracts with customers, including a description of all of the following:

   a. When performance obligations are satisfied, including when performance obligations are satisfied in a bill-and-hold arrangement.
   b. The significant payment terms.
   c. The nature of the goods or services that the entity has promised to transfer, highlighting any performance obligations to arrange for another party (as an agent) to transfer goods or services.

   d. Obligations for returns, refunds and other similar obligations.
   e. Types of warranties and related obligations.

9. Information about remaining performance obligations:
   a. The aggregate amount of the transaction price allocated to the performance obligations that are unsatisfied (or partially unsatisfied) as of the end of the reporting period.
   b. An explanation of when the entity expects to recognise as revenue the amount disclosed, which the entity shall disclose in either of the following ways:
      i. On a quantitative basis using the time bands that would be most appropriate for the duration of the remaining performance obligations.
      ii. By using qualitative information.
10. As a *practical expedient*, the information in point 9 for a performance obligation need not be disclosed if either of the following conditions is met:
    a. The performance obligation is part of a contract that has an original expected duration of one year or less.
    b. The entity recognises revenue from the satisfaction of the performance obligation.
11. A qualitative explanation of whether it is applying the practical expedient and whether any consideration from contracts with customers is not included in the transaction price and therefore not included in the information disclosed in point 9. For example, an estimate of the transaction price would not include any estimated amounts of variable consideration that are constrained.
12. For performance obligations *satisfied over time*:
    a. The methods used to recognise revenue (for example, a description of the output methods or input methods used and how those methods are applied).
    b. An explanation of why the methods used provide a faithful depiction of the transfer of goods or services.
13. For performance obligations satisfied at a *point in time*, the significant judgements made in evaluating when a customer obtains control of promised goods or services.
14. Information about the *methods, inputs and assumptions* used for all of the following:
    a. Determining the transaction price, which includes, but is not limited to, estimating variable consideration, adjusting the consideration for the effects of the time value of money and measuring non-cash consideration.
    b. Assessing whether an estimate of variable consideration is constrained.
    c. Allocating the transaction price, including estimating stand-alone selling prices of promised goods or services and allocating discounts and variable consideration to a specific part of the contract (if applicable).
    d. Measuring obligations for returns, refunds and other similar obligations.
15. The fact that an election is made to use the practical expedient about the existence of a significant financing component or about incremental costs of obtaining a contract.

EXAMPLE OF FINANCIAL STATEMENT DISCLOSURES

Exemplum Reporting PLC
Financial Statements
For the Year Ended December 31, 20XX

Accounting policy: Revenue from contracts with customers

Revenue comprises sales and/or services to external customers (excluding VAT and other sales taxes). Performance obligation for sale of goods is satisfied on delivery of the goods and for services when the services are rendered based on the stage of completion. Contract costs are recognised for incomplete services and amortised when the service is rendered	IFRS 15 (119) (123) (128)

Note to financial statements: Revenue from contracts with customer

	20XX	**20XX-1**	
The group has recognised the following amounts relating to revenue in the statement of profit or loss:			
Revenue from contracts with customers	X	X	IFRS 15
Revenue from other sources	X	X	(113) (a)
Total revenue	X	X	
Revenue from contracts with customers consists of:			
Sale of goods	X	X	(114)
Services	X	X	
Total revenue	X	X	

The total revenue is further disaggregated in the segment report in product lines and geographical areas.	(115)
Revenue recognised of €X in the current year was included in the liability for revenue received in advance in the previous year.	(116) (b)
Significant judgements are applied to determine the stage of completion of services.	(123)
Revenue of €X was recognised in the current year regarding estimation adjustments of such performance obligations satisfied in the previous year.	(116) (c)
A two-month credit term without finance charges is granted for all sales of goods and services.	(117)

The related contact cost asset for services provided changed as follows (could be in a separate note):			
Opening balance	X	X	
Cost transfer to projects	X	X	(116) (a)
Cost transfer to cost of sales	**(X)**	**(X)**	(117)
Closing balance	X	X	(128)

The transaction price allocated to unperformed services at year-end is €X and would be earned within six months after the year-end (a practical expedient of one year may be used not to disclose the information, but then the fact must be disclosed).	(120) (121/122)

SPECIFIC TRANSACTIONS IN IFRS 15

IFRS 15 also clarifies the application of the five-step approach to specific transaction.

Sale with a Right of Return

IFRS 15 clarifies that a sale of a right of return could be any combination of the following:

1. A full or partial refund of any consideration paid.
2. A credit that can be applied against amounts owed.
3. Another product in exchange.

IFRS 15 clarifies that the following should be recorded for a sale or service with a right of return and that no further obligation for the expected return should be created:

1. The expected revenue after deducting the expected products to be returned.
2. A refund liability for the portion expected to be returned.
3. An asset and a corresponding adjustment to cost of sales for the products expected to be recovered.

The asset is presented separately from the refund liability. The asset for the products expected to be recovered is initially measured at the former carrying amount of the product less any expected costs to recover those products and any potential decreases in the value.

The expected consideration is determined by using the principles of determining the transaction price, including assessing for constraining estimates of variable consideration. The revenue amount is subsequently updated at the end of each year with new expectations.

IFRS 15 also specifically clarifies that:

1. Exchanges of one product for another of the same type, quality, condition and price are not considered to be a return.
2. Return of a defective product in exchange for a functioning product is treated as a warranty.

Warranties

Warranties could be provided for both sale and services and could differ across industries and contracts. Warranties could also include services to rectify a default product.

When a warranty is purchased separately it is regarded as a separate distinct performance obligation and recognised separately by allocation of a portion of the total consideration, if not separately identified or negotiated, to the warranty.

Warranties not purchased separately (they are included in standard contracts) are not regarded as a separate performance obligation and treated as a **provision** in terms of IAS 37 (refer to Chapter 18). Warranties could provide a customer with a service in addition to assuring the agreed-upon quality of the product. In assessing the additional service, the following factors are considered:

1. *Whether the warranty is required by law*: Then the law protects the customer from the risk of default products.

2. *The length of the warranty coverage period*: A longer coverage period might be an indication of a separate performance obligation to provide a service in addition to assuring the quality of the product.
3. *The nature of the tasks promised to be performed*: Specific tasks linked to the assurance of the quality of the product, such as a service to return the product, are regarded as part of the warranty and not a separate performance obligation.

Any service included in addition to ensuring the quality of the product is regarded as a separate performance obligation to which a portion of the transaction price should be allocated. In instances where both an assurance-type warranty and a service-type warranty are promised that cannot reasonably be separated, the warranties are treated together as a single performance obligation.

IFRS 15 also clarifies that the *following are not regarded as separate performance obligations* and should also be treated in terms of IAS 37:

1. A law that requires payment of compensation when products cause harm or damage.
2. Promises to indemnify the customer for liabilities and damages arising from claims of patent, copyright, trademark or other infringement by the entity's products.

Principal versus Agent Considerations

IFRS 15 determines that when another party is involved in providing goods or services to a customer an assessment needs to be made as to whether the other party is a principal or an agent. This assessment must be made for each individual good or service promised in a contract that is distinct. The nature of the promise is determined by:

1. Identifying the specified goods or services to be provided to the customer; and
2. Assessing who controls each specified good or service before that good or service is transferred to the customer.

A principal controls the promised good or service before it is transferred to a customer. However, IFRS 15 specifically clarifies that legal title of a product held momentarily before it is transferred to a customer is not in itself an indication of a principal. A principal in a contract may also use another party, such as a subcontractor, to perform performance obligations on its behalf.

When another party is involved, the principal could obtain control in any of the following ways:

1. Acquiring a good or another asset from the other party that it then transfers to the customer.
2. Acquiring a right to a service to be performed by the other party, which gives the entity the ability to direct that party to provide the service to the customer on the entity's behalf.
3. Acquiring a good or service from the other party that it then combines with other goods or services in providing the specified good or service to the customer.

When acting as a principal, revenue is recognised for the gross amount of consideration entitled. In contrast, an agent does not control the specified good or service before that good or service is transferred to the customer. An agent recognises revenue for the amount of any expected fee or commission in exchange for proving the agent functions. The agents fee may be the net amount deducted from the total consideration. IFRS 15 provides the following **indicators** to identify that an entity controls the goods and services before it is transferred to the customer:

1. The entity is primarily responsible for fulfilling the contract.
2. Inventory risk both before and after the goods have been ordered by a customer, during shipping or on return is borne by the entity.
3. The discretion to establishing prices and the benefit of the agent lies primarily with the entity, although the agent might have some discretion.

The application of the indicators depends on the nature of the specified good or service and the terms and conditions of the contract.

IFRS 15 also clarifies that when another entity takes over the performance obligations and contractual rights in the contract so that the entity is no longer obliged to satisfy the performance obligation in the contract, no revenue should be recognised by the entity. Then the entity should consider whether it is an agent and entitled to any revenue.

Customer options for additional goods or services

Customer options for additional goods or services could include sales incentives, customer award credits (or points), contract renewal options or other discounts on future goods or services. The issue is whether the option in the contract creates a separate performance obligation.

The test in IFRS 15 is whether the option creates a material right to the customer, which it would not obtain without entering into that contract. The result of a material right is that the customer effectively pays in advance for future goods or services and therefore a contract liability is created. Revenue for the option could then only be recognised when the future goods or services are transferred or when the option expires.

A material right is not created when the option grants the customer the right to obtain additional goods and services at a price reflecting the stand-alone selling price. Also, IFRS 15 clarifies that a marketing offer granted to the customer is only subject to IFRS 15 when the option is exercised.

When an option creates a material right, a portion of the total consideration is allocated to the material right based on the stand-alone selling price of the option. If the stand-alone selling price for the option is not observable, it should be estimated. The estimation should include any discount the customer is entitled to and adjusted *for both*:

1. Any discount that the customer could receive without exercising the option; and
2. The likelihood that the option will be exercised.

As a practical alternative the stand-alone selling price of the option could be determined by allocating the transaction price to the optional goods and services by reference to the goods and services expected to be provided and the corresponding expected consideration. The practical alternative is normally applicable to contract renewals and can therefore only be used when:

1. The customer has a material right to acquire future goods or services.
2. The goods or services are similar to the original goods or services in the contract.
3. The goods and services are provided in accordance with the terms of the original contract.

Customers' unexercised rights

In this section IFRS 15 clarifies different unexercised rights of customers. If a prepayment is received from a customer, a contract liability is recognised for the prepayment. The contract liability is derecognised and revenue recognised when the related performance obligation(s) is satisfied.

When a customer does not exercise all its rights and a non-refundable contract liability is recognised, a breakage in a contract could occur. An expected breakage in a contract is determined by considering the requirements of constraint estimates of variable consideration, which means that a high probability needs to exist that the breakage identification will not be reversed.

The expected breakage amount identified in the non-refundable contract liability should be recognised as revenue in proportion to the pattern of rights exercised by the customer. However, if the entity does not expect to be entitled to a breakage amount, revenue is only recognised for the expected breakage amount when the likelihood of the customer exercising its remaining rights becomes remote.

Any consideration received for customers' unexercised rights that are required to be remitted to another party is recognised as a liability and not revenue.

Non-refundable upfront fees (and some related costs)

Non-refundable upfront fees could be paid at or near contract inception such as a joining fee at sport clubs. The issue that IFRS 15 clarifies is whether these fees relate to the transfer of any specific promised goods or services and therefore whether revenue could be recognised. An assessment should also be made whether the cost incurred in setting up a contract could be recognised as an asset.

Activities performed by the entity upfront do not always result in a transfer of promised goods and services to the customer. If not, the upfront fee is regarded as a prepayment for future goods and services in the contract. The revenue recognition period recognises that the future goods and services would extend beyond the initial contractual period when the customer has an option to renew the contract and that option provides the customer with a material right.

When the non-refundable upfront fee relates to a specific good or service, an assessment is made whether the good or service relates to a distinct performance obligation to determine whether revenue could be recognised separately upfront.

A non-refundable fee may be charged to compensate an entity for costs incurred in setting up a contract. Such activities are also disregarded when measuring progress if they do not satisfy any performance obligations. That is because the setup costs do not depict the transfer of goods or services to the customer.

Licensing

Entities that license their intellectual property to customers will be greatly affected. Licences allow a customer to use an entity's intellectual property such as trademarks, media and copyrights. The issue is to determine whether the licence that transfers to the customer is over time or at a point in time.

A licence could, either explicitly or implied in the contract, be granted with the transfer of goods and services to a customer. Then an assessment should be made whether a licence is a distinct performance obligation. When the licence granted is not distinct from other promised goods or services, the licence and promised goods and services are regarded together as a single performance obligation which is either satisfied over time or at a point in time. IFRS 15 provides the following examples of licences that are *not distinct*:

1. A licence that forms a component of a tangible good that is integral to the functionality of the good.
2. A licence that the customer can benefit from only in conjunction with a related service. IFRS 15 provides the example of an online service that enables the customer to access content through granting the licence.

When the licence granted is distinct and therefore a separate performance obligation, an assessment is made whether the licence transfers either at a point in time or over time. The nature of the licence, as discussed below, is considered to determine whether the customer is provided with:

1. A right to access the intellectual property as it exists throughout the licence period; or
2. A right to use the intellectual property as it exists at the point in time when the licence is granted.

Determining the nature of the entity's promise

A customer could either obtain the right to access the entity's intellectual property as it exists throughout the licence period, or a right to use the entity's intellectual property as it exists at a point in time when the licence is granted. Revenue would be recognised for a right of access over the licence period and for the right of usage at a point of time when the licence is granted. The right to access an intellectual property is only applicable if the nature of the promise *meets all of the following criteria*:

1. The contract requires, or the customer reasonably expects that activities will be undertaken that significantly affect the intellectual property.
2. The rights granted directly expose the customer to any positive or negative effects of activities undertaken.
3. Those activities do not result in the transfer of a good or a service to the customer as those activities are undertaken.

If the right to access an intellectual property is granted, the entity shall account for the promise to grant a licence as a performance obligation satisfied over time because the customer will simultaneously receive and consume the benefit from the entity's performance of providing access to its intellectual property as access is granted. An example is a brand where different customers may obtain the benefit of the brand and the entity itself builds the name of the brand out (the activities that change the brand).

Factors that may indicate that a customer could reasonably expect that such activities will be undertaken include customary business practices, published policies or specific statements. IFRS 15 clarifies that the existence of a shared economic interest, such as a sales-based royalty, may also indicate that the customer could reasonably expect that such activities will be undertaken. An entity's activities significantly affect the intellectual property to which the customer has rights when either:

1. Those activities are expected to significantly change the form or the functionality of the intellectual property; or
2. The ability of the customer to obtain benefit from the intellectual property is substantially derived from, or dependent upon, those activities, such as the entity maintaining the brand name.

If the above criteria are not met, the customer is regarded as obtaining the use of the intellectual property by default. Then it allows a customer access to the intellectual property when the licence was sold. As a result, the revenue would be recognised when the licence is sold to the customer. The point in time needs to be determined by considering from when the intellectual property can effectively be used.

Intellectual property that has significant stand-alone functionality derives a substantial portion of its benefit from that functionality. Consequently, if the entity's activities do not significantly change the form or functionality of such intellectual property, then the entity's activities will not significantly affect the customer's ability to derive benefit from that intellectual property and would result in a right of usage of the intellectual property.

The following factors are specifically disregarded when making an assessment of right of access or right of usage:

1. Restrictions of time, geographical region or use: these are regarded as attributes of the promised licence.
2. Guarantees provided of a valid patent to intellectual property and that it will defend that patent from unauthorised use: a promise to defend is not regarded as a performance obligation since it protects the value of the patent.

Sales-based or usage-based royalties

The requirement for a sales-based or usage-based royalty applies when the royalty relates only to a licence of intellectual property or when a licence of intellectual property is the predominant item to which the royalty relates (thus significantly more value is given to the licence than to the other goods or services to which the royalty relates). Then, revenue from a sales-based or usage-based royalty shall be recognised at the latest of the following events:

1. The subsequent sale or usage occurs.
2. The performance obligation to which some or all of the sales-based or usage-based royalty has been allocated has been satisfied.

When the requirement above is not met, the requirements on variable consideration apply to the sales-based or usage-based royalty.

Repurchase agreements

A repurchase agreement is a contract in which an asset is sold, which is a promise or option to repurchase the asset. The repurchased asset may represent:

1. The original asset sold.
2. An asset that is substantially the same.
3. Another asset of which the asset that was originally sold is a component.

IFRS 15 identifies three forms of repurchase agreements:

1. An obligation to repurchase the asset (a forward).
2. A right to repurchase the asset (a call option).
3. An obligation to repurchase the asset at the customer's request (a put option).

A forward or a call option

In the case of a forward or a call option to repurchase an asset, control is not regarded to be transferred to the customer because of the limited ability of the customer to direct the use of and obtain substantially all of the remaining benefits from the asset. The contract is therefore treated *as either*:

1. A lease in accordance with IAS 17 (refer to Chapter 22) when the repurchase of the asset is for an amount that is less than the original selling price of the asset; or
2. A financing arrangement when the repurchase of the asset is for an amount that is equal to or more than the original selling price of the asset.

Time value is considered to compare the repurchase price with the selling price.

In the case of a financing arrangement, the asset is not derecognised, but a financial liability is recognised for the consideration received from the customer. The difference between the consideration received from the sale and the consideration to be paid for the repurchase is regarded as interest. When an option is not exercised the liability is derecognised and revenue is recognised.

A put option

In the case of a put option an obligation to repurchase the asset only arises when the customer requests the repurchase. The exercising of the right could result in the customer using the asset for just a time period. Two assessments need to be made by considering the time value of money:

1. If the repurchase price is lower, equal or higher than the original purchase price.
2. When the repurchase price is lower, whether the customer has a significant economic incentive to exercise that right. A significant economic incentive is assessed by considering various factors. These factors include:
   a. The relationship of the repurchase price to the expected market value of the asset at the date of the repurchase. A significant higher repurchase price indicates a significant economic incentive.
   b. The amount of time until the right expires.

Based on these assessments, *four different accounting treatments* are applicable:

1. When the repurchase price is lower than the original selling price and a significant economic incentive to exercise that right exists, the agreement is regarded as a lease in accordance with IAS 17.
2. When the repurchase price is lower than the original selling price and a significant economic incentive to exercise that right does not exist, the agreement is regarded as a sale of a product with a right of return.
3. When the repurchase price of the asset is equal to or greater than the original selling price and is more than the expected market value of the asset, the agreement is effectively a financing arrangement and accounted for as discussed under a forward or put option.
4. When the repurchase price of the asset is equal to or greater than the original selling price and is less than or equal to the expected market value of the asset, and the customer does not have a significant economic incentive to exercise its right, the agreement is also regarded as a sale of a product with a right of return.

Consignment arrangements

When a product is delivered to an intermediary, such as a dealer or a distributor, for sale to end customers, an assessment is made whether the intermediary obtains control of the product. If the intermediary does not obtain control of the product, the product delivered is held in a consignment arrangement. No revenue is recognised if the product is held as a consignment.

IFRS 15 identifies the following *indicators* of a consignment arrangement:

1. The product is still controlled by the entity until a specified event occurs, such as the sale of the product to a customer of the intermediary or until a specified period expires.
2. The entity is able to require the return of the product or transfer the product to a third party, such as another intermediary.
3. The intermediary does not have an unconditional obligation to pay for the product, although the payment of a deposit may be required.

Bill-and-hold arrangements

A bill-and-hold arrangement is a contract under which a customer is billed for a product, but the supplier retains physical possession of the product until it is transferred to the customer.

An assessment needs to be made whether the customer obtains control of that product before it is delivered by reviewing the terms of the agreement. Control would be obtained when the customer has the ability to direct the use of and obtain substantially all of the remaining benefits from the product even though it has decided not to exercise its right to take physical possession of that product. Then the supplier provides custodial services to the customer over the customer's asset.

For the customer to obtain control in a bill-and-hold arrangement, *all of the following criteria must be met*:

1. The reason for the bill-and-hold arrangement must be substantive, such as the customer requesting the arrangement;
2. The product must be identified separately as belonging to the customer;
3. The product must be ready for physical transfer to the customer; and
4. The supplier does not have the ability to use the product or to direct it to other customers.

When revenue is recognised for the sale of a product on a bill-and-hold basis, consideration should be made of other performance obligations to which a portion of the transaction price should be allocated.

OTHER SPECIFIC TRANSACTIONS

Service Concession Arrangements

In many countries, public-to-private service concession arrangements have evolved as a mechanism for providing public services. Under such arrangements, a private entity is used to construct, operate or maintain the infrastructure for public use such as roads, bridges, hospitals, airports, water distribution facilities and energy supply. IFRIC 12, *Service Concession Arrangements*, deals with a private sector entity (an operator) that provides a public service and operates and maintains that infrastructure (operation services) for a specified period of time. This Interpretation applies to service concession arrangements when the infrastructure for public use is constructed or acquired by the operator or given for use by the grantor and (1) the grantor controls what services the operator must provide, to whom and at what price, and (2) the grantor controls any significant residual interest in the existing infrastructure at the end of the term of the service concession arrangement. Since the grantor controls the infrastructure assets within the scope of the Interpretation, these assets are not recognised as property, plant and equipment of the operator.

The operator recognises and measures revenue for the services it performs in accordance with IFRS 15. If more than one service is performed (e.g., construction or upgrade services and operation services) under a single contract or arrangement, the total consideration received, or receivable, is allocated between the different services based on relative fair values of the services provided, when the amounts are separately identifiable. Later maintenance and upgrade services are also subject to IFRS 15. The nature of the consideration the operator receives in exchange for the construction services determines its subsequent accounting treatment.

When the consideration received is a financial asset because the operator has an unconditional contractual right to receive from the grantor cash or other financial asset, the subsequent accounting in accordance with IFRS 9 would apply. In this case the grantor bears the risk (demand risk) that the cash flows generated from the users will not recover the operator's investment. A financial asset is recognised during construction, giving rise to revenues from construction recovered during the period of use of the asset.

An intangible asset is recognised when the consideration the operator receives consists of rights to charge users of the public service, for example a licence to charge users tolls for using roads or bridges, and it is accounted for within the scope of IAS 38. In this case, the operator bears the risk (demand risk) that the cash flows generated from the use of the public service will not recover its investment. The intangible asset received from the grantor in exchange for the construction services is used to generate cash flows from users of the public service. Borrowing cost are only capitalised in terms of IAS 23 under the intangible asset treatment.

Services or assets obtained for no consideration

In situations where a service or an asset is obtained for no consideration from a party who has no investment interest in the entity, the terms and conditions around the asset given must be considered. Where no terms and conditions are imposed, revenue can be recognised immediately. Where terms and conditions are imposed, revenue can only be recognised as the terms and conditions set out are fulfilled.

In these situations, historical cost is not adequate to reflect properly the substance of the transaction, since the historical cost to the corporation would be zero. Accordingly, these events should be reflected at fair value. If long-lived assets are donated to the corporation, they should be recorded at their fair value at the date of donation, and the amount so recorded should be depreciated over the normal useful economic life of such assets. Disclosure will be required in the financial statements of both the assets donated and the conditions required to be met.

Example of donated capital

A board member of the not-for-profit organisation Village Social Services donates land to the organisation that has a fair market value of €1 million. Village Social Services records the donation with the following entry:

Land	€1,000,000	
Revenue—donations		€1,000,000

The same board member donates one year of accounting labour to Village Social Services. The fair value of services rendered is €75,000. Village Social Services records the donation with the following entry:

Salaries—accounting department	€75,000	
Revenue—donations		€75,000

The board member also donates one year of free rent of a local building to Village Social Services. The annual rent in similar facilities is €45,000. Village Social Services records the donation with the following entry:

Rent expense	€45,000	
Revenue—donations		€45,000

Finally, the board member pays off a €100,000 debt owed by Village Social Services. Village Social Services records the donation with the following entry:

Notes payable	€100,000	
Revenue—donations		€100,000

Following the closing of the fiscal period, the effect of all the foregoing donations will be reflected in Village Social Services' retained earnings account.

Note that IFRS explicitly addresses the proper accounting for government grants (see discussion in Chapter 21), which may differ from the foregoing illustrative example, which involved private donations only. Readers should be alert to further developments in this area.

US GAAP COMPARISON

In 2014, the FASB and IASB issued a joint revenue recognition standard. Issued as ASU No. 2014-9 Revenue from Contracts with Customers (Topic 606), which is nearly identical to IFRS 15 except for some transitional matters and matters that are consequences of the inherent differences between IFRS and US GAAP. For public entities, ASU 2014-96 is effective for annual reporting periods beginning after December 15, 2017, including interim periods within that reporting period. For non-public entities, Topic 606 is effective for annual reporting periods beginning after December 15, 2018, with interim periods within annual periods beginning after December 15, 2019. Early application is not permitted. A retrospective adoption of the standard is required.

IASB issued amendments to IFRS 15 in April 2016 and FASB issued corresponding amendments to Topic 606 in April and May. A number of differences between IFRS 15 and Topic 606 arise as a result of these amendments. The basic principle of IFRS 15 and Topic 606 standards being an entity will recognise revenue to show the exchange of promised services or goods to customers at an amount reflecting the consideration the entity anticipates to be entitled to in trade for those services or goods. These accounting standards additionally necessitate full and complete disclosures and alter the way entities convey information in the financial statement notes. The main differences are as follows:

- US GAAP allows an entity to make a policy election to account for shipping and handling activities that occur after the customer has obtained control of a good as an activity to fulfil the promise to transfer the good rather than as an additional promised service.
- While revenue for all licences to symbolic intellectual property is recognised over time under US GAAP, revenue for similar licences under IFRS 15 may be recognised at a point in time if the reporting entity undertakes no activities that significantly affect the ability of the customer to obtain benefit from the intellectual property, although such cases are expected to be relatively rare.
- Under US GAAP, a renewal or extension of a licence will result in revenue recognition at the beginning of the renewal period. Under IFRS, revenue for similar arrangements may result in revenue recognition when the parties agree to the renewal or when the renewal period begins, depending on the facts and circumstances.
- Under US GAAP, an entity may make a policy election to exclude all sales (and other similar) taxes from the measurement of the transaction price. IFRS 15 does not set out a similar permission.

21 GOVERNMENT GRANTS

INTRODUCTION

Government grants or other types of assistance, where provided, are usually intended to encourage entities to embark on activities that they would not have otherwise undertaken. IAS 20, *Accounting for Government Grants and Disclosure of Government Assistance*, addresses selected accounting and reporting issues arising in connection with such grants. *Government assistance*, according to this standard, is action undertaken by a government designed to provide an economic benefit specific to an entity or range of entities qualifying under certain criteria. Examples of such government assistance could include the provision of guarantee facilities to encourage foreign trade or the provision of free training, advice or other resources/incentives (premises and so on). A *government grant*, on the other hand, is government assistance in the form of transfers of resources to an entity in return for past or future compliance with certain conditions relating to the operating activities of the entity (the most common example is provision of monetary amounts to assist with capital purchases or with operating expenditure).

A former gap in the literature, addressing the accounting for service concessions, which occur relatively frequently in Europe, where government assets may be operated by commercial entities, has recently been dealt with by the issuance of IFRIC 12, *Service Concession Arrangements*, which resolved a related series of three draft interpretations. IFRIC 12 is discussed later in this chapter.

IAS 20 provides the authoritative guidance on financial statement presentation for all entities enjoying government grants or assistance, with additional guidance to be found within IAS 41, *Agriculture*, which is restricted to agricultural situations. IAS 20 deals with the accounting treatment and disclosure of government grants and the disclosure requirements of government assistance. Depending on the nature of the assistance given and the associated conditions, government assistance could be of many types, including grants, forgivable loans, and indirect or non-monetary forms of assistance, such as technical advice.

Sources of IFRS	
IAS 20, 41	*SIC* 10, 29 *IFRIC* 12

SCOPE

IAS 20 deals with the accounting treatment and disclosure requirements of grants received by entities from a government. It also mandates disclosure requirements of other forms of government assistance.

The standard specifies certain exclusions. In addition to the four exclusions contained within the definitions of the terms "government grant" and "government assistance," IAS 20 *excludes* the following from the scope of the standard:

1. Special problems arising in reflecting the effects of changing prices on financial statements or similar supplementary information;
2. Government assistance provided in the form of tax benefits (including income tax holidays, investment tax credits, accelerated depreciation allowances and concessions in tax rates);
3. Government participation in the ownership of the entity; and
4. Government grants covered by IAS 41, *Agriculture*.

Items 1. and 2. above are excluded as they are covered by other IAS; IAS 29, *Financial Reporting in Hyperinflationary Economies*, addresses accounting in hyperinflationary conditions, while tax benefits are dealt with by IAS 12.

Income taxes. Government participation in the ownership of the entity has been excluded from the scope of IAS 20, as participation in ownership of an enterprise is normally made in anticipation of a return on the investment, while government assistance is provided with a different economic objective in mind, for example the public interest or public policy. Thus, when the government invests in the equity of an entity (with the intention, for example, of encouraging the entity to undertake a line of business that it would normally not have embarked upon), such government participation in ownership of the entity would *not qualify* as a government grant under this standard.

Government Grants

Government grants are assistance provided by government by means of a transfer of resources (either monetary or non-monetary) to business or other types of entities. To qualify as a government grant, it is a prerequisite the grant should be provided by the government to an entity in return for past or future compliance with conditions relating to the operating activities of the entity.

Prior to the issuance of SIC 10, *Government Assistance—No Specific Relation to Operating Entities*, it was unclear whether the provisions of IAS 20 would apply to government assistance aimed at encouraging or supporting business activities in certain regions or industry sectors, since related conditions may not specifically relate to the operating activities of the entity. Examples of such grants are: government grants which involve transfer of resources to enterprises to operate in a particular area (e.g., an economically less developed area) or a particular industry (e.g., one that due to low profitability may not otherwise be attractive to entrepreneurs). SIC 10 clarified that "the general requirement to operate in certain regions or industry sectors in order to qualify for the government assistance constitutes such a condition in accordance with IAS 20." This confirms that such government assistance does fall within the definition of government grants, and thus the requirements of IAS 20 apply to them as well.

DEFINITIONS OF TERMS

Fair value. The price that would be received to sell an asset or paid to transfer a liability in an orderly transaction between market participants at the measurement date.

Forgivable loans. Those loans which the lender undertakes to waive repayment of under certain prescribed conditions.

Government. For the purposes of IAS 20, the term government refers not only to a government (of a country), as is generally understood, but also to government agencies and similar bodies, whether local, national or international.

Government assistance. Government assistance is action taken by government designed to provide an economic benefit specific to an entity or range of entities qualifying under certain criteria. Government assistance for the purpose of IAS 20 does not include benefits provided only indirectly through action affecting general trading conditions, such as the provision of infrastructure in development areas or the imposition of trading constraints on competitors.

Government grants. A government grant is a form of government assistance that involves the transfer of resources to an entity in return for past or future compliance (by the entity) with certain conditions relating to its operating activities. It excludes:

- Those forms of government assistance that cannot reasonably be valued; and
- Transactions with governments that cannot be distinguished from the normal trading transactions of the enterprise.

Grants related to assets. Those government grants whose primary condition is that an entity qualifying for them should acquire (either purchase, construct or otherwise acquire) a long-term asset or assets are referred to as "grants related to assets." Secondary conditions may also be attached to such a grant. Examples of secondary conditions include specifying the type of long-term assets, location of long-term assets or periods during which the long-term assets are to be acquired or held.

Grants related to income. Government grants, other than those related to assets, are grants related to income.

RECOGNITION OF GOVERNMENT GRANTS

Criteria for Recognition

Government grants are provided in return for past or future compliance with certain defined conditions. Thus, grants should not be recognised until there is *reasonable assurance* that:

1. The entity will comply with the conditions attaching to the grant(s); and
2. The grant(s) will be received.

Certain concerns affecting the application of IAS 20, relating to recognition and treatment of government grants, are addressed in the following paragraphs.

First, the mere receipt of the grant does not provide any assurance that, in fact, the conditions attaching to the grant have been or will be complied with by the enterprise. Both of these conditions are equally important, and the reporting entity should have reasonable assurance with respect to these two conditions before a grant is to be recognised.

Secondly, the term "reasonable assurance" has not been defined by this standard. However, one of the recognition criteria under the IASB's *Framework* is the existence of a "sufficient degree of certainty."

Thirdly, under IAS 20 a forgivable loan from a government is treated as a government grant when there is *reasonable assurance* that the enterprise will meet the terms of forgiveness set forth in the loan agreement. Thus, upon receiving a forgivable loan from a government and furthermore upon fulfilling the criterion of reasonable assurance with respect to meeting the terms of forgiveness of the loan, an enterprise would normally recognise the receipt of a government grant, rather than a loan.

Some have suggested that the grant should be recognised when the loan is forgiven, not when the forgivable loan is received. Under IAS 20, however, it is quite apparent that delayed recognition is not prescribed, but that "a forgivable loan from the government is treated as a grant when there is reasonable assurance that the enterprise will meet the terms for forgiveness of the loan." In the authors' opinion, this unambiguously directs that the recognition of the grant is to be made at the point of time when the forgivable loan is expected to be forgiven, as opposed to the point of time when it is actually forgiven.

Once a grant has been recognised, IAS 20 clarifies that any related contingency would be accounted for in accordance with IAS 37. The conforming amendments as a result of IFRS 9 clarified the accounting treatment of low interest loans received from the government. IAS 20 states that the loan should be recognised and measured in accordance with the requirements of IFRS 9, *Financial Instruments*. The difference between the amount received and the initial carrying amount of the loan as determined in accordance with IFRS 9 is to be accounted for in accordance with IAS 20, *Government Grants*.

Example of application of IAS 20 for below-market loans

Maytag Corp. is encouraged to relocate to Springville Township on July 1, 20XX, by an economic stimulus package that includes a €3,000,000 loan due in equal annual instalments (inclusive of interest) through 20YX. The local government provides this loan at a below-market rate of 3%, which differs markedly from Maytag's own marginal borrowing rate of 6.5%. The present value of the annual payments (€351,000 each), discounted at 6.5%, is €2,528,251. Accordingly, the receipt of the loan on July 1, 20XX, is recorded by the following journal entry:

Cash	€3,000,000	
Loan payable		€2,528,251
Income—government grants		471,749

The discount on the loan payable is amortised over the 10-year term, such that an effective rate of 6.5% on the loan balance will be reported as a finance cost (interest expense) in Maytag's income statements. If the grant was unconditional, it would be taken into income immediately, as suggested by the above journal entry. However, if Maytag has ongoing obligations (such as to remain as an employer in the community throughout the term of the loan), then it should be recognised as deferred income and amortised to income (on a straight-line basis) over the term of the obligation.

Recognition Period

There are two broad approaches to the accounting treatment of government grants that have been discussed by the standard: the "capital approach" and the "income approach." IAS 20 does *not* support the capital approach, which advocates crediting a grant directly to shareholders' equity. Endorsing the income approach, the standard sets forth the rule for recognition of government grants as follows: government grants should be recognised as income, on a systematic and rational basis, over the periods necessary to match them with the related costs. The standard reiterates that government grants should *not* be credited directly to shareholders' interests.

The standard established rules for recognition of grants under different conditions. These are explained through numerical examples below:

1. Grants in recognition of specific costs are recognised as income over the same period as the relevant expense.

Example of a grant received in recognition of specific costs

An enterprise receives a grant of €30 million to defray environmental costs over a period of five years. Environmental costs will be incurred by the enterprise as follows:

Year	Costs
1	€1 million
2	€2 million
3	€3 million
4	€4 million
5	€5 million

Total environment costs will equal €15 million, whereas the grant received is €30 million.

Applying the principle outlined in the standard for recognition of the grant, that is, recognising the grant as income "over the period which matches the costs" and using a "systematic and rational basis" (in this case, a reverse sum-of-the-years' digits amortisation), the total grant would be recognised as follows:

Year	*Grant recognised*
1	€30 * (1/15) = €2 million
2	€30 * (2/15) = €4 million
3	€30 * (3/15) = €6 million
4	€30 * (4/15) = €8 million
5	€30 * (5/15) = €10 million

2. Grants related to depreciable assets are usually recognised as income over the periods and in the proportions in which depreciation on those assets is charged.

Example of a grant relating to a depreciable asset

An enterprise receives a grant of €100 million to purchase a refinery in an economically disadvantaged area. The enterprise has estimated that such a refinery would cost €200 million. The secondary condition attached to the grant is that the enterprise should hire labour locally (i.e., from the economically disadvantaged area where the refinery is located) instead of employing workers from other parts of the country. It should maintain a ratio of 1:1 (local workers: workers from outside) in its labour force for the next five years. The refinery is to be depreciated using the straight-line method over a period of 10 years.

The grant will be recognised over a period of 10 years. In each of the 10 years, the grant will be recognised in proportion to the annual depreciation on the refinery. Thus, €10 million will be recognised as income in each of the 10 years. With regard to the secondary condition of maintenance of the ratio of 1:1 in the labour force, as there is a possibility that some of the loan may need to be repaid, this contingency would need to be disclosed in the notes to the financial statements for the next five years (during which period the condition is in force) in accordance with disclosure requirements of IAS 37.

3. Grants related to non-depreciable assets may also require the fulfilment of certain obligations and would then be recognised as income over periods which bear the cost of meeting the obligations.

Example of a grant with conditions attached relating to a non-depreciable asset

ABN Inc. was granted 1,000 acres of land, on the outskirts of the city, by a local government authority. The condition attached to this grant was that ABN Inc. should clean up this land and lay roads by employing labourers from the village in which the land is located. The government has fixed the minimum wage payable to the workers. The entire operation will take three years and is estimated to cost €60 million. This amount will be spent as follows: €10 million each in the first and second years and €40 million in the third year. The fair value of this land is presently €120 million.

ABN Inc. would need to recognise the fair value of the grant over the period of three years in proportion to the cost of meeting the obligation. Thus, €120 million will be recognised as follows:

Year	Grant recognised
1	€120 * (10/60) = €20 million
2	€120 * (10/60) = €20 million
3	€120 * (40/60) = €80 million

4. Grants are sometimes received as part of a package of financial or fiscal aids to which a number of conditions are attached.

   When different conditions attach to different components of the grant, the terms of the grant would have to be evaluated to determine how the various elements of the grant would be earned by the enterprise. Based on that assessment, the total grant amount would then be apportioned.

Example of a grant received as part of financial aid subject to a number of conditions

An enterprise receives a consolidated grant of €120 million. Two-thirds of the grant is to be utilised to purchase a college building for students from third-world or developing countries. The balance of the grant is for subsidising the tuition costs of those students for four years from the date of the grant.

The grant would first be apportioned as follows:

Grant related to assets (2/3) = €80 million; and
Grant related to income (1/3) = €40 million

The grant related to assets would be recognised in income over the useful life of the college building, for example, 10 years, using a systematic and rational basis. Assuming the college building is depreciated using the straight-line method, this portion of the grant (i.e., €80 million) would be recognised as income over a period of 10 years at €8 million per year.

The grant related to income would be recognised over a period of four years. Assuming that the tuition subsidy will be offered evenly over the period of four years, this portion of the grant (i.e., €40 million) would be taken to income over a period of four years at €10 million per year.

5. A government grant that becomes receivable as compensation for expenses or losses already incurred or for the purpose of giving immediate financial support to the enterprise with no future related costs should be recognised as income of the period in which it becomes receivable.

   Sometimes grants are awarded for the purposes of giving immediate financial support to an enterprise, for example to revive a commercially insolvent business (referred to as "sick unit" in some less-developed countries). Such grants are not given as incentives to invest funds in specified areas or for a specified purpose from which the benefits will be derived over a period in the future. Instead such grants are awarded to compensate an enterprise for losses incurred in the past. Thus, they should be recognised as income in the period in which the enterprise becomes eligible to receive such grants.

Non-Monetary Grants

A government grant may not always be given in cash or cash equivalents. Sometimes a government grant may take the form of a transfer of a non-monetary asset, such as grant of a plot of land or a building in a remote area. In these circumstances the standard prescribes the following optional accounting treatments:

1. To account for both the grant and the asset at the fair value of the non-monetary asset; or
2. To record both the asset and the grant at a "nominal amount."

PRESENTATION AND DISCLOSURE

Presentation of Grants Related to Assets

Presentation on the statement of financial position

Government grants related to assets, including non-monetary grants at fair value, should be presented in the statement of financial position in either of two ways:

1. By setting up the grant as deferred income; or
2. By deducting the grant in arriving at the carrying amount of the asset.

Example of setting up a grant as deferred income or reducing the carrying amount of the asset

Natraj Corp. received a grant related to a factory building which it bought in 20XX. The total amount of the grant was €3 million. Natraj Corp. purchased the building from an industrialist identified by the government. The factory building was located in the slums of the city and was to be repossessed by a government agency from the industrialist, had Natraj Corp. not purchased it from him. The factory building was purchased for €9 million by Natraj Corp. The useful life of the building is not considered to be more than three years mainly because it was not properly maintained by the industrialist.
Under Option 1: Set up the grant as deferred income:

- The grant of €3 million would be set up initially as deferred income in 20XX.
- At the end of 20XX, €1 million would be recognised as income and the balance of €2 million would be carried forward in the statement of financial position.
- At the end of 20XX+1, €1 million would be taken to income and the balance of €1 million would be carried forward in the statement of financial position.
- At the end of 20XX+2, €1 million would be taken to income.

Under Option 2: The grant will be deducted from the carrying amount of the building. The grant of €3 million is deducted from the gross carrying amount of the asset to arrive at the carrying amount of €6 million. The useful life being three years, annual depreciation of €2 million per year is charged to the income statement for the years 20XX, 20XX+1 and 20XX+2.

The effect on the operating results is the same whether the first or the second option is chosen.

Under the second option, the grant is indirectly recognised in income through the reduced depreciation charge of €1 million per year, whereas under the first option, it is taken to income directly.

Presentation in the statement of cash flows

When grants related to assets are received in cash, there is an inflow of cash to be shown under the investing activities section of the statement of cash flows. Furthermore, there would also be an outflow resulting from the purchase of the asset. IAS 20 specifically requires that both these movements should be shown separately and not be offset. The standard further clarifies that such movements should be shown separately regardless of whether the grant is deducted from the related asset for the purposes of the statement of financial position presentation.

Presentation of Grants Related to Comprehensive Income

The standard allows a choice between two presentations:

Option 1: Grant presented as a credit in the statement of profit or loss and comprehensive income, either separately or under a general heading other income.

Option 2: Grant deducted in reporting the related expense.

The standard does not show any bias towards any one option. It acknowledges the reasoning given in support of each approach by its supporters. The standard considers both methods as acceptable. However, it does recommend disclosure of the grant for a proper understanding of the financial statements. The standard recognises that the disclosure of the effect of the grants on any item of income or expense may be appropriate.

Disclosures

The following disclosures are prescribed:

1. The accounting policy adopted for government grants, including the methods of presentation adopted in the financial statements;
2. The nature and extent of government grants recognised in the financial statements and an indication of other forms of government assistance from which the enterprise has directly benefited; and
3. Unfulfilled conditions and other contingencies attaching to government assistance that has been recognised.

OTHER ISSUES

Repayment of Government Grants

When a government grant becomes repayable—for example, due to non-fulfilment of a condition attaching to it—it should be treated as a change in estimate, under IAS 8, *Accounting Policies, Changes in Accounting Estimates and Errors*, and accounted for prospectively (as opposed to retrospectively).

Repayment of a grant related to income should:

1. First be applied against any unamortised deferred income (credit) set up in respect of the grant; and
2. To the extent the repayment exceeds any such deferred income (credit), or in case no deferred credit exists, the repayment should be recognised immediately as an expense.

Repayment of a grant related to an asset should be:

1. Recorded by increasing the carrying amount of the asset or reducing the deferred income balance by the amount repayable; and
2. The cumulative additional depreciation that would have been recognised to date as an expense in the absence of the grant should be recognised immediately as an expense.

When a grant related to an asset becomes repayable, it would become incumbent upon the enterprise to assess whether any impairment in value of the asset (to which the repayable grant relates) has resulted. For example, a bridge is being constructed through funding from a government grant and during the construction period, because of non-fulfilment of the terms of the grant, the grant became repayable. Since the grant was provided to assist in the construction, it is possible that the enterprise may not be in a position to arrange funds to complete the project. In such a circumstance, the asset is impaired and may need to be written down to its recoverable value, in accordance with IAS 36.

Example of repayment of a government grant

During 20XX-2 Trident Corp. invests €1,000,000 in an item of plant, which has an anticipated useful life of five years. Depreciation is recognised on a straight-line basis. In the year of acquisition, Trident Corp. receives a government grant of €250,000 towards the purchase of this plant, which is conditional on certain employment targets being achieved within the next three years (i.e., to the end of 20XX). At the end of 20XX, it is evident that the employment targets will not be achieved and therefore the criterion attached to the receipt of this grant has been failed. The grant becomes repayable and under the two methods of presentation of the grant, the treatment of the repayment is as follows:

Option 1: Grant shown as deferred income

Grant received and credited in 20XX-2 to deferred income	€250,000
Recognised in profit or loss 20XX-2 to 20XX (3 × €50,000)	(€150,000)
Deferred income balance at end of 20XX before repayment of grant	€100,000
Total repayment of grant (Cr bank)	€250,000
Repayment debited to deferred income balance (Dr deferred income)	(€100,000)
Balance of repayment recognised in profit or loss (Dr profit or loss)	€150,000

Note: under this method the repayment does not impact the carrying amount of plant or depreciation expense recognised.

Option 2: Grant deducted from cost of asset

Cost of plant	€1,000,000
Less grant received	(€250,000)
Net cost of equipment	€750,000
Depreciation expense recognised 20XX-2 to 20XX (3 × €150,000)	(€450,000)
Carrying amount of plant at end of 20XX before repayment of grant	€300,000
Add back grant repayable	€250,000
	€550,000
Cumulative additional depreciation to be recognised in profit or loss for 20XX-2 to 20XX (3 × €50,000)	(€150,000)
Carrying amount of equipment at end of 20XX after repayment of grant	€400,000

Impairment of Assets and Government Grants

IAS 36 requires an entity to assess at the end of the reporting period if there are any indications that an asset may be impaired. Chapter 13 provides further guidance on impairment of assets. When an entity has adopted Option 1—Government grants shown as deferred income, and it has impaired the asset related to the grant, the treatment of the deferred grant should be considered.

Assuming all of the grant's conditions have been met, the deferred grant income should be released to match the impairment recognised as an expense. If there are conditions attached to the grant, the entity must carefully consider if the requirements prevent an acceleration of the grant's release. Irrespective of the accounting policy chosen, the entity should reconsider whether the impairment of the asset increases the probability of any potential repayment of the grant.

Government Assistance

Under the provisions of IAS 20, government grants exclude government assistance. Government assistance is defined as action taken by government designed to provide an economic benefit specific to an entity or range of entities qualifying under certain criteria. IAS 20 deals with both accounting and disclosure of government grants and disclosure of government assistance. Government assistance comprises government grants and other forms of government assistance (i.e., those not involving transfer of resources).

Excluded from the government assistance are certain forms of government benefits that cannot reasonably have a value placed on them, such as free technical or other professional advice. Also excluded from government assistance are government benefits that cannot be distinguished from the normal trading transactions of the enterprise. The reason for the second exclusion, although the benefit cannot be disputed, is that any attempt to segregate it would necessarily be arbitrary.

SERVICE CONCESSIONS

Government involvement directly with business is much more common in Europe and elsewhere than in North America, and European adoption of IFRS has created a need to expand the IFRS literature to address a number of such circumstances. The *service concession*, particularly common in France, typically occurs when a commercial entity operates a commercial asset which is owned by, or has to be transferred to, a local, regional or national government organisation. More generally, these arrangements exist when the public is provided with access to major economic or social facilities. The most famous example of this is perhaps the Channel Tunnel, linking England and France. This was built by a commercial entity which has a concession to operate it for a period of years, at the end of which time the asset reverts to the British and French governments. A more mundane example would be companies that erect bus shelters free of charge in municipalities, in return for the right to advertise on them for a period of time.

SIC 29, issued as an interpretation of IAS 1, addressed only disclosures to be made for service concession arrangements. Under SIC 29, both the concession operator and the concession provider are directed to make certain disclosures in the notes to financial statements that purport to conform with IFRS. These disclosures include:

1. A description of the arrangement;
2. The significant terms of the arrangement that might affect the nature, timing or amounts of future cash flows, which could include terms and repricing dates and formulae;
3. The nature and the extent of rights to use specified assets; obligations to provide (or rights to expect) services; obligations to acquire or build property or equipment; options to deliver (or rights to receive) specific assets at the conclusion of the concession period; renewal and termination options; and other rights and obligations, such as for major overhauls of equipment; and
4. Changes to the concession arrangement occurring during the reporting period.

In 2006, the IASB issued IFRIC 12 to deal with the accounting for service concession arrangements. IFRIC 12 sets forth two accounting models and stipulates how revenue is to be recognised.

Service Concession Arrangements

Service concession arrangements are those whereby a government or other body grants contracts for the supply of public services (e.g., roads, energy distribution, prisons or hospitals) to private operators. The Interpretation draws a distinction between two types of service concession arrangements. In one, the operator receives a *financial asset*, specifically an unconditional contractual right to receive cash or another financial asset from the government in return for constructing or upgrading the public sector asset.

In the other, the operator receives an *intangible asset*—a right to charge for use of the public sector asset that it constructs or upgrades. The right to charge users is not an unconditional right to receive cash, because the amounts that might be received are contingent on the extent to which the public uses the service.

IFRIC 12 allows for the possibility that both types of arrangement may exist within a single contract: to the extent that the government has given an unconditional guarantee of payment for the construction of the public sector asset, the operator has a financial asset; to the extent that the operator has to rely on the public using the service to obtain payment, the operator has an intangible asset. The accounting to be applied is governed by the extent to which one or both types of assets are received.

Accounting under the Financial Asset Model

The operator recognises a financial asset to the extent that it has an *unconditional* contractual right to receive cash or another financial asset from, or at the direction of, the grantor for the construction services. The operator has an unconditional right to receive cash if the grantor contractually guarantees to pay the operator:

- Specified or determinable amounts; or
- The shortfall, if any, between amounts received from users of the public service and specified or determinable amounts, even if payment is contingent on the operator ensuring that the infrastructure meets specified quality or efficiency requirements.

Under the provisions of IFRIC 12, the operator measures the financial asset at fair value.

Accounting under the Intangible Asset Model

The operator recognises an intangible asset to the extent that it receives a right (a licence) to charge users of the public service. A right to charge users of the public service is not an unconditional right to receive cash because the amounts are contingent on the extent that the public uses the service.

Under the provisions of IFRIC 12, the operator measures the intangible asset at fair value.

Operating Revenue

The operator of a service concession arrangement recognises and measures revenue in accordance with IFRS 15 for the services it performs. No special revenue recognition principles are to be applied. Thus, the financial asset model would require the use of percentage of completion revenue recognition in most instances, while the intangible asset model would suggest that revenue be recognised as services are performed.

Accounting by the Government (Grantor)

IFRIC 12 does not deal with the accounting to be applied by the government unit that grants service concession arrangements. That is because IFRS are not designed to apply to not-for-profit activities in the private sector or the public sector. International Public Sector Accounting Standards (IPSAS) 32, *Service Concession Arrangements: Grantor*, was released by the International Public Sector Accounting Standards Board.

US GAAP COMPARISON

US GAAP does not actually have specific guidance for grant revenue except that which is specifically called out for not-for-profit entities (NFPs). Other than that, US GAAP does not have guidance for non-NFPs.

22 LEASES

INTRODUCTION

Leasing has long been a popular financing option for the acquisition of business property. During the past few decades, however, the business of leasing has experienced staggering growth, and much of this volume is reported in the statements of financial position. The tremendous popularity of leasing is quite understandable, as it offers great flexibility, often coupled with a range of economic advantages over ownership. Thus, with leasing, a lessee (borrower) is typically able to obtain 100% financing, whereas under a traditional credit purchase arrangement the buyer would generally have to make an initial equity investment. In many jurisdictions, a leasing arrangement offers tax benefits compared to the purchase option. The lessee is protected to an extent from the risk of obsolescence, although the lease terms will vary based on the extent to which the lessor bears this risk. For the lessor, there will be a regular stream of lease payments, which include interests that often will be at rates above commercial lending rates, and, at the end of the lease term, usually some residual value.

The IASB issued a new leases standard which supersedes the previous leases standard. The previous leases standard, IAS 17, focused on identifying when a lease is economically similar to purchasing the asset being leased. When a lease was determined to be economically similar to the purchase of the asset being leased, the lease was classified as a finance lease and reported on the balance sheet. An asset was recognised to bring into account the underlying asset effectively purchased, together with the corresponding liability of the lease. All other leases were classified as operating leases and not reported on the company's balance sheet, i.e., the expense was reported in the income statement as and when incurred.

Various stakeholders reported concerns to both the IASB and FASB about the lack of transparency of information about lease obligations. In response, the IASB and FASB initiated a project to improve the accounting for leases. The absence of information about leases on the balance sheet meant that investors and analysts were not able to properly compare companies that borrow to buy assets with those that lease assets, without making adjustments.

The IASB is of the opinion that IFRS 16 will result in a more faithful representation of a company's assets and liabilities and greater transparency about the company's financial leverage and capital employed.

In essence, the new leases standard requires the lessee to recognise an intangible asset as a result of the right to use the leased asset, with a corresponding liability. This is irrespective of whether the lessee will take ownership of the leased asset or not at the end of the lease period. There are few changes to how lessors should account for leases.

The standard deals with stand-alone leases; however, it does allow entities to apply the requirements of this standard to a portfolio of leases with similar characteristics, provided that the entity has assessed that applying the standard to the portfolio of leases would not differ significantly from applying it to separate leases.

Sources of IFRS
IFRS 16

DEFINITIONS OF TERMS

The following terms are specific to leases:

Commencement date of the lease. The date by which a lessor makes an underlying asset available for use by a lessee.

Economic life. Either the period over which an asset is expected to be economically usable by one or more users or the number of production or similar units expected to be obtained from an asset by one or more users.

Effective date of the modification. The date when both parties agree to a lease modification.

Fair value. For the purpose of applying the lessor accounting requirements, the amount for which an asset could be exchanged, or a liability settled, between knowledgeable, willing parties to an arm's-length transaction.

Finance lease. A lease that substantially transfers all the risks and rewards incidental to ownership of an underlying asset.

Fixed payments. Payments made by a lessee to a lessor for the right to use an underlying asset during the lease term, excluding variable lease payments.

Gross investment in the lease. The sum of:

a. The lease payments receivable by a lessor under a finance lease; and
b. Any unguaranteed residual value accruing to the lessor.

Inception date of the lease. The earlier of the date of a lease agreement and the date of commitment by the parties to the principal terms and conditions of the lease.

Initial direct costs. Incremental costs of obtaining a lease that would not have been incurred if the lease had not been obtained, except for such costs incurred by a manufacturer or dealer lessor in connection with a finance lease.

Interest rate implicit in the lease. The rate of interest that causes the present value (PV) of (a) the lease payments and (b) the unguaranteed residual value to equal the sum of (i) the fair value of the underlying asset and (ii) any initial direct costs of the lessor.

Lease. A contract, or part of a contract, that conveys the right to use an asset (the underlying asset) for a period of time in exchange for consideration.

Lease incentives. Payments made by a lessor to a lessee associated with a lease, or the reimbursement or assumption by a lessor of costs of a lessee.

Lease modification. A change in the scope of a lease, or the consideration for a lease, that was not part of the original terms and conditions of the lease (for example, adding or terminating the right to use one or more underlying assets, or extending or shortening the contractual lease term).

Lease payments. Payments made by a lessee to a lessor relating to the right to use an underlying asset during the lease term, comprising the following:

a. Fixed payments (including in-substance fixed payments), less any lease incentives;
b. Variable lease payments that depend on an index or a rate;
c. The exercise price of a purchase option if the lessee is reasonably certain to exercise that option; and
d. Payments of penalties for terminating the lease, if the lease term reflects the lessee exercising an option to terminate the lease.

For the lessee, lease payments also include amounts expected to be payable by the lessee under residual value guarantees. Lease payments to not include payments allocated to non-lease components of a contract, unless the lessee elects to combine non-lease components with a lease component and to account for them as a single lease component.

For the lessor, lease payments also include any residual value guarantees provided to the lessor by the lessee, a party related to the lessee or a third party unrelated to the lessor that is financially capable of discharging the obligations under the guarantee. Lease payments do not include payments allocated to non-lease components.

Lease term. The non-cancellable period for which a lessee has the right to use an underlying asset, together with both:

a. Periods covered by an option to extend the lease if the lessee is reasonably certain to exercise that option; and
b. Periods covered by an option to terminate the lease if the lessee is reasonably certain not to exercise that option.

Lessee. An entity that obtains the right to use an underlying asset for a period of time in exchange for consideration.

Lessee's incremental borrowing rate. The rate of interest that a lessee would have to pay to borrow over a similar term, and with similar security, the funds necessary to obtain an asset of a similar value to the right-of-use asset in a similar economic environment.

Lessor. An entity that provides the right to use an underlying asset for a period of time in exchange for consideration.

Net investment in the lease. The gross investment in the lease discounted at the interest rate implicit in the lease.

Operating lease. A lease that does not transfer substantially all the risks and rewards incidental to ownership of an underlying asset.

Optional lease payments. Payments to be made by a lessee to a lessor for the right to use an underlying asset during periods covered by an option to extend or terminate a lease that are not included in the lease term.

Period of use. The total period of time that an asset is used to fulfil a contract with a customer (including any non-consecutive periods of time).

Residual guarantee value. A guarantee made to a lessor by a party unrelated to the lessor that the value (or part of the value) of an underlying asset at the end of the lease will be at least a specified amount.

Right-of-use asset. An asset that represents a lessee's right to use an underlying asset for the lease term.

Short-term lease. A lease that, at the commencement date, has a lease term of 12 months or less. A lease that contains a purchase option is not a short-term lease.

Sublease. A transaction for which an underlying asset is re-leased by a lessee ("intermediate lessor") to a third party, and the lease ("head lease") between the head lessor and lessee remains in effect.

Underlying asset. An asset that is the subject of a lease, for which the right to use that asset has been provided to a lessee by a lessor.

Unearned finance income. The difference between:

a. The gross investment in the lease; and
b. The net investment in the lease.

Unguaranteed residual value. That portion of the residual value of the underlying asset, the realisation of which by a lessor is not assured or is guaranteed solely by a party related to the lessor.

Variable lease payments. The portion of payments made by a lessee to a lessor for the right to use an underlying asset during the lease term that varies because of changes in facts or circumstances occurring after the commencement date, other than the passage of time.

CLASSIFICATION OF LEASES

Classification of Leases—Lessee

Identifying a lease

A contract contains, or is, a lease if the contract:

a. conveys the right to control
b. the use of
c. the identified asset
d. for a period of time
e. in exchange for consideration.

In essence, an entity needs to establish whether it has the right to obtain substantially all of the economic benefits from use of the identified asset and the right to direct the use of the identified asset.

The asset is generally specifically identified in the contract. However, care should be taken when determining the identified asset where the asset is not physically distinct. Examples of where an asset is not physically distinct could include the rental of portion of a fibre optic cable, telephone cables etc. This may indicate that the asset is not identifiable in terms of the lease definition unless the agreement represents substantially all of the capacity of the asset and thereby provides the customer right to obtain substantially all of the economic benefits from use of the asset. The classification as a lease also depends on where in the line the lease takes place e.g. end-use customer (refer to the FASB's standard ASC 842).

However, if the supplier has the substantive right to substitute the asset throughout the period of use, the entity does not have the exclusive right to control the use of the identified asset. A supplier's right to substitute an asset is substantive only if both of the following conditions exist:

a. The supplier has the practical ability to substitute alternative assets throughout the period of use; and
b. The supplier would benefit economically from the exercise of its right to substitute the asset.

It is important to note that the above can only be applied if the supplier has the right to substitute the underlying asset throughout the entire period of the contract, i.e., at the discretion of the supplier, and not only at a certain specific point in time. When assessing the above, potential future events are not considered. Generally, if the asset is located at the customer's premises or elsewhere, the costs associated with substitution are generally higher than when located at the supplier's premises and, therefore, are more likely to exceed the benefits associated with substituting the asset. The supplier's right or obligation to substitute the asset for repairs and maintenance, if the asset is not operating properly or if a technical upgrade becomes available does not preclude the customer from having the right to use an identified asset. This would typically be the case where the entity rents office furniture, such as printers and copiers, that is removed from the entity's premises every once in a while, for repairs and maintenance. Accordingly, these types of leases would not fall into the scope of the substitution exemption mentioned above.

The lessee has the right to direct the use of an identified asset throughout the period of use only if:

a. The lessee has the right to direct how and for what purpose the asset is used during the period of use; or
b. The relevant decisions about how and for what purpose the asset is used are predetermined and:
    i. The lessee has the right to operate the asset throughout the period of use, without the supplier having the right to change those operating instructions; or
    ii. The lessee designed the asset in a way that predetermines how and for what purpose the asset will be used throughout the period of use.

Generally, each lease component must be accounted for separately from non-lease components unless the entity chooses to classify the entire contract as one lease component. Each lease component is allocated a stand-alone price, which is based on what the lessor, or similar supplier, would charge an entity for that component separately. If the stand-alone price is not available, the lessee must estimate the stand-alone price, maximising the use of observable information.

The standard allows the lessee to expense leases that have the following characteristics:

a. The underlying asset is of low value; or
b. The lease term is short-term in nature and does not exceed 12 months.

The lease term cannot include any options to extend or purchase the underlying asset. Accordingly, even if the lease term, including the extension or purchase options, is still less than 12 months, this exemption may not be applied.

When assessing whether the underlying asset is of low value, the entity must assess the underlying asset based on its value when it is new, regardless of the actual age of the asset when it is being leased.

While the standard does not define low value, it does provide the entity with two identifying characteristics of low value assets:

a. The lessee can benefit from use of the underlying asset on its own or together with other resources that are readily available to the lessee; and
b. The underlying asset is not highly dependent on, or highly interrelated with, other assets.

Examples provided include tablets, laptops or small items of office furniture and telephones. Entities are therefore required to assess what type of assets are significant to their business and to the financial statements.

Short term leases must be applied consistently to the same class of assets however the low value exemption may be applied on a lease by lease basis. In summary, the following questions should be asked when determining whether a contract contains a lease:

1. Is there an identified asset?
2. Does the customer have the right to obtain substantially all of the economic benefits from use of the asset throughout the period of use?
3. Does the customer have the right to direct how and for what purpose the asset is used throughout the period of use?

If the answer to all three questions is yes, the contract most likely contains a lease.

Example—Identification of a lease in a contract

Mellwood Limited enters into an agreement with Allgear Limited for the use of five trucks for one week to transport cargo from Barcelona to Madrid. Allgear Limited does not have any substitution rights. Only cargo specific in the agreement is permitted to be transported in these trucks for the week. The agreement specifies the maximum distance each truck can be driven. Mellwood Limited is able to choose the details of the journey, such as speed travelled, route, rest stops, etc. within the parameters of the agreement. Mellwood has to return the trucks to Allgear Limited and is not allowed to continue using the trucks after the specific week of use and/or completion of the journey, whichever comes first. The cargo to be transported, timing and location of pick-up and delivery are specified in the agreement. Mellwood Limited is responsible to provide the drivers for the trucks for the trip from Barcelona to Madrid.

Assessment of whether the contract contains a lease

The agreement contains a lease of the trucks as Mellwood Limited has the right to use the trucks for the duration of the specific trip. The trucks have specifically been identified in the agreement and Allgear Limited is not allowed to substitute the trucks.

Mellwood Limited has the right to control the trucks throughout the period of use because:

a. It has the right to obtain substantially all of the economic benefits from use of the trucks over the period of use. It has exclusive use of the trucks throughout the period of use.
b. It has the right to direct the use of the trucks because how and for what purpose the trucks will be used (i.e., the transportation of specified cargo from Barcelona to Madrid within a specified timeframe) is predetermined in the agreement. Mellwood Limited furthermore directs the use of the trucks because it has the right to operate the trucks (for example, speed, route, rest stops) throughout the period of use. It makes all of the decisions about the use of the trucks that can be made during the period of use through its control of the operations of the trucks.

In addition, the agreement is for similar identified assets and will all be used in the same period for the same purpose. As such, Mellwood Limited can account for the use of the trucks as one lease.

However, since the lease term is for less than 12 months, the lease meets the definition of a short-term lease. Mellwood therefore does not need to capitalise a right-to-use asset and corresponding lease liability but can expense the costs associated with the agreement as and when incurred.

Lease term

The lease term is the non-cancellable period of a lease, together with:

a. Periods covered by an option to extend the lease if the lessee is reasonably certain to exercise that option; and
b. Periods covered by an option to terminate the lease if the lessee is reasonably certain not to exercise that option.

The minimum lease term therefore is the non-cancellable period of the lease and the contract is therefore enforceable. A lease is no longer enforceable when the lessee and the lessor have the right to terminate the lease without permission from the other party with no more than an insignificant penalty. It must be noted that both the lessee and the lessor should have the right to terminate the lease; if only one party to the contract has the right to terminate the lease, the termination rights are included in the determination of the lease term. The shorter the non-cancellable period of a lease, the more likely that a lessee will exercise its option to extend the lease and not early terminate the lease. This is generally because the cost of replacing the asset is likely to be higher than the non-cancellable period of the lease.

It is furthermore important to note that the standard only refers to the legally enforceable lease term. The intention of lessees to lease an asset indefinitely (as is typical with related parties) becomes irrelevant if the lease agreement does not specifically state this.

Generally, one entity will own all properties leased by other related entities in the group; the sole purpose of the investment property entity is to lease out its properties to other entities within the group. In addition, these type of lease agreements are typically so-called "gentleman's agreements" for at least one year and are verbally agreed. These agreements are renewed annually. Entities will be required to analyse carefully what the implications are of these agreements as it impacts on the lease term, and subsequent treatment of these leases. In all likelihood, entities will not be able to classify these leases as short-term leases given the annual options to renew.

The lease term includes any rent-free periods provided to the lessee by the lessor.

When determining whether the lessee will extend the lease or early terminate the lease, the standard provides examples of factors to consider:

a. Contractual terms and conditions for the option periods compared to market rates, such as:
    i. Amount of payments for the lease in any optional period;
    ii. Amount of any variable payments for the lease or other contingent payments; and
    iii. Terms and conditions of any options that are exercisable after initial optional periods;
b. Significant leasehold improvements undertaken (or expected to be undertaken) over the term of the contract that are expected to have significant economic benefit for the lessee when the option to extend or terminate the lease, or to purchase the underlying asset, becomes exercisable;
c. Costs relating to the termination of the lease, such as negotiation costs, relocation costs, costs of identifying another underlying asset suitable for the lessee's needs, costs of integrating a new asset into the lessee's operations, or termination penalties and similar costs, including costs associated with returning the underlying asset in a contractually specified condition or to a contractually specified location;
d. Importance of that underlying asset to the lessee's operations; and
e. Conditionality associated with exercising the option (i.e., when the option can be exercised only if one or more conditions are met), and the likelihood that those conditions will exist.

Classification of Leases—Lessor

The lessor must apply the same principles in determining whether a contract contains a lease or not. Once it has been established that a contract does in fact contain a lease, the lessor has the following alternatives in classifying a lease:

1. Operating lease.
2. Finance lease.

Finance leases (which are known as capital leases under the corresponding US GAAP, because such leased property is treated as owned, and accordingly capitalised in the statement of financial position) are those that essentially are alternative means of financing the acquisition of property or of substantially all the service potential represented by the property.

The proper classification of a lease is determined by the circumstances surrounding the leasing transaction. According to IFRS 16, whether a lease is a finance lease or not will have to be judged based on the substance of the transaction, rather than on its mere form. If substantially all of the benefits and risks of ownership will be transferred to the lessee, the lease should be classified as a finance lease; such a lease is normally noncancellable and the lessor is assured (subject to normal credit risk) of recovery of the capital invested plus a reasonable return on its investment. Examples of situations that individually or in combination would normally lead to a lease being classified as a finance lease are as follows:

a. Ownership of the underlying asset is transferred to the lessee by the end of the lease term;
b. The lessee has the option to purchase the underlying asset at a price that is expected to be sufficiently lower than the fair value at the date the option becomes exercisable for it to be reasonably certain, at the inception date, that the option will be exercised;
c. The lease term is for the major part of the underlying asset's economic life, even if title is not transferred;
d. At inception date, the PV of the lease payments amounts to at least substantially all of the fair value of the underlying asset;
e. The underlying asset is of such a specialised nature that only the lessee can use it without major modifications;
f. The lessor's losses associated with the cancellation of the lease by the lessee are borne by the lessee;
g. Gains or losses from the fluctuation in the fair value of the residual accrue to the lessee; or
h. The lessee has the ability to continue the lease for a secondary period at a rent that is substantially lower than market rent.

Thus, under IFRS 16, an evaluation of at least the above eight criteria would be required to properly assess whether there is sufficient evidence to conclude that a given arrangement should be accounted for as a finance lease. Of the eight criteria set forth in the standard, the first five are essentially determinative in nature; that is, meeting any one of these would normally result in concluding that a given arrangement is in fact a finance lease. The final three criteria, however, are more suggestive in nature, and the standard states that these could lead to classification as a finance lease.

Different Types of Finance Leases

Finance leases can have various forms. Some common examples are sales-type, direct financing and leveraged leases.

A lease is classified as a sales-type lease when the criteria set forth above have been met and the lease transaction is structured such that the lessor (generally a manufacturer or dealer) recognises a profit or loss on the transaction in addition to interest revenue. For this to occur, the fair value of the property, or if lower the sum of the PVs of the minimum lease payments and the estimated unguaranteed residual value, must differ from the cost (or carrying value, if different). The essential substance of this transaction is that of a sale, thus its name. Common examples of sales-type leases: (1) when an automobile dealership opts to lease a car to its customers in lieu of making an actual sale, and (2) the re-lease of equipment coming off an expiring lease.

A direct financing lease differs from a sales-type lease in that the lessor does not realise a profit or loss on the transaction other than the interest revenue to be earned over the lease term. In a direct financing lease, the fair value of the property at the inception of the lease is equal to the cost (or carrying value, if the property is not new). This type of lease transaction most often involves entities regularly engaged in financing operations. The lessor (usually a bank or other financial institution) purchases the asset and then leases the asset to the lessee. This mode of transaction is merely a replacement for the conventional lending transaction, where the borrower uses the borrowed funds to purchase the asset.

There are many economic reasons why a lease transaction may be considered. These include:

1. The lessee (borrower) is often able to obtain 100% financing.
2. There may be tax benefits for the lessee, such as the ability to expense the asset over its lease term, instead of over a longer depreciable life.
3. The lessor receives the equivalent of interest as well as an asset with some remaining value at the end of the lease term (unless title transfers as a condition of the lease).
4. The lessee is protected from the risk of obsolescence (although presumably this risk protection is priced into the lease terms).

One specialised form of direct financing lease is a *leveraged lease*. This type is mentioned separately both here and in the following section on how to account for leases because it is to receive a different accounting treatment by a lessor. A leveraged lease meets all the definitional criteria of a direct financing lease but differs because it involves at least three parties: a lessee, a long-term creditor and a lessor (commonly referred to as the equity participant). Other characteristics of a leveraged lease are as follows:

1. The financing provided by the long-term creditor must be without recourse as to the general credit of the lessor, although the creditor may hold recourse with respect to the leased property. The amount of the financing must provide the lessor with substantial leverage in the transaction.
2. The lessor's net investment declines during the early years and rises during the later years of the lease term before its elimination.

RECOGNITION AND MEASUREMENT

Accounting for Leases—Lessee

Initial measurement

At the commencement date of the lease, the lessee shall recognise a right-of-use asset with a corresponding lease liability. It is important to note that no distinction is made as to whether the lease transfers the risks and rewards associated with ownership or not; the lessee has the right to use the asset for a predetermined period in exchange for consideration and as such has an intangible asset.

At the initial recognition date, the entity is first required to measure the lease liability. This lease liability is the PV of the lease payments that are not paid at that date. The lease payments must be discounted using the interest rate implicit in the lease, if that rate can be readily determined. If this rate cannot be used, the entity must use the entity's incremental borrowing rate.

In determining the lease payments, the following must be taken into account:

a. Fixed payments (including in-substance fixed payments) less any lease incentives receivable;
b. Variable lease payments that depend on an index or rate, initially measured using the index or rate as at the commencement date;
c. Amounts expected to be payable by the lessee under residual value guarantees;
d. Exercise price of a purchase option if the lessee is reasonably certain to exercise that option; and
e. Payments of penalties for terminating the lease, if the lease reflects the lessee exercising an option to terminate the lease.

The discount rate that should be used in measuring the liability at initial recognition date should be the rate implicit in the lease, provided that that rate can be readily determined. If that rate cannot be readily determined, the incremental borrowing rate should be used.

The rate used must reflect how the contract is priced. It is accepted that the interest rate implicit in the lease is likely to be similar to the lessee's incremental borrowing rate in many cases. This is because both rates take into account the credit standing of the lessee, the length of the lease, the nature and quality of the collateral provided and the economic environment in which the transaction occurs. However, the interest rate implicit in the lease is generally also affected by a lessor's estimate of the residual value of the underlying asset at the end of the lease and may be affected by taxes and other factors known only to the lessor, such as any initial direct costs of the lessor. Accordingly, it is accepted that the lessee may not be able to determine the interest rate implicit in the lease due to information not being readily available to the lessee as a result of inputs required by the lessor, particularly where the asset has a significant residual value at the end of the lease.

The incremental rate is therefore a lessee-specific rate, taking into account the creditworthiness of the lessee, the terms of the contract, the amount of the funds borrowed, the type of asset leased and the economic environment in which the lessee operates.

The incremental borrowing rate can be determined by using a rate that is readily observable, such as the standard borrowing rate or the property yield, and adjusted for the specific nature of the asset and the terms and conditions contained in the lease.

It is therefore not appropriate to only use the current borrowing rate in the jurisdictional environment in which the lessee operates, even if the lessee has a good credit track record. This rate must be adjusted to reflect the asset used, the period of the contract as well as any specific conditions contained in the contract. Generally, the following rules can be applied when adjusting the discount rate:

a. The better the quality of the security provided, the lower the discount rate;
b. The higher the funds/value of the contract, the higher the discount rate; and
c. The shorter the borrowing term, the lower the discount rate.

It is also important to note that a lessee may not use its weighted average cost of capital as its incremental borrowing cost, as this incorporates all types of funding (including equity), whereas a lease is purely borrowings. It furthermore does not take into account the terms of the contract or the asset being leased. While this rate may be an appropriate starting point in determining the incremental borrowing rate, it must be adjusted for the specific requirements of the lease.

Each rate must be determined based on the inputs specific to each individual lease.

Once the lease liability has been calculated, the right-of-use asset can be calculated, which is as follows:

a. Amount of the initial measurement of the lease liability;
b. Any lease payments made at or before the commencement date, less any lease incentives received;
c. Any initial direct costs incurred by the lessee; and
d. An estimate of costs to be incurred by the lessee in dismantling and removing the underlying asset, restoring the site on which it is located or restoring the underlying asset to the condition required by the terms and conditions contained in the lease, unless those costs are to produce inventories.

Costs relating to the construction or design of an underlying asset must be accounted for in terms of the applicable standard, such as IAS 16, and should not be considered payments for the right to use of the underlying asset. It is also true that any payments made for the right-to-use asset should be included in the cost of the right-to-use asset and not be capitalised under IAS 16. Such payments are still made in terms of the lease contract and as such are payments for a lease, regardless of the timing of these payments.

Example—Initial measurement of the right-to-use asset and lease liability

Organica Limited (lessee) enters into a 10-year lease of a floor of a building, with an option to extend for five years. Lease payments are €50,000 per year during the initial term and €55,000 per year during the optional period, all payable at the beginning of each year. To obtain the lease, Organica Limited incurs initial direct costs of €20,000, of which €15,000 relates to a payment to a former tenant occupying that floor of the building and €5,000 relates to a commission paid to the real estate agent that arranged the lease. As an incentive to Organica Limited for entering into the lease, Plastica Limited agrees to reimburse to Organica Limited the real estate commission of €5,000 and Organica Limited's leasehold improvements of €7,000.

At the commencement date, Organica Limited concludes that it is not reasonably certain to exercise the option to extend the lease and, therefore, determines that the lease term is 10 years.

The interest rate implicit in the lease is not readily determinable. Organica Limited's incremental borrowing rate is 5% per annum, which reflects the fixed rate at which Organica Limited could borrow an amount similar to the value of the right-of-use asset, in the same currency, for a 10-year term, and with similar collateral.

Solution

At the commencement date, Organica Limited makes the lease payment for the first year, incurs initial direct costs, receives lease incentives from Plastica Limited and measures the lease liability at the PV of the remaining nine payments of €50,000, discounted at the interest rate of 5% per annum, which is €355,391. Organica Limited initially recognises assets and liabilities in relation to the lease as follows:

Dr Right-of-use asset	€405,391	
Cr Lease liability		€355,391
Cr Cash (lease payment for first year)		50,000
Dr Right-of-use asset	€20,000	
Cr Cash (initial direct costs)		€20,000
Dr Cash (lease incentive)	€5,000	
Cr Right-of-use asset		€5,000

Subsequent measurement

Subsequently, an entity may measure the right-of-use asset using the following measurement models:

a. Cost model as described in IAS 16, *Property, Plant and Equipment*. Depreciation must be provided over the lease period unless the entity will obtain ownership at the end of the lease period, in which case depreciation must be provided over the useful life of the underlying asset;
b. Fair value model if the entity already applies the fair value model in IAS 40, *Investment Property*, to its investment property and the lease also meets the definition of investment property; or
c. Revaluation model as per IAS 16, *Property, Plant and Equipment*, if the underlying leased asset falls within the class of property, plant and equipment already measured using the revaluation model.

The lease liability must subsequently be measured by:

a. Increasing the carrying amount to reflect interest on the lease liability;
b. Reducing the carrying amount to reflect lease payments made; and
c. Remeasuring the carrying amount to reflect any reassessment or lease modifications or to reflect revised in-substance fixed lease payments.

The interest rate applied in a. above shall be the discount rate used to calculate the initial lease liability.

The lease liability must be remeasured if either the discounting rate changes or the lease payments change. The lease liability will be remeasured using a revised discount rate if:

a. There is a change in the lease term; or
b. There is a change in the assessment of an option to purchase the underlying asset.

The lease liability will be remeasured using the revised lease payments if:

a. There is a change in the amounts expected to be payable under a residual value guarantee;
b. There is a change in future lease payments resulting from a change in an index or rate used to determine those payments.

Once the liability has been remeasured, the right-to-use asset must be adjusted with the change in the liability as well.

Lease modifications

Modifications to lease contracts shall be treated as separate leases only if:

a. The modification increases the scope of the lease by adding the right to use one or more underlying assets; and
b. The consideration for the lease increases by an amount commensurate with the stand-alone price to reflect the circumstances of the particular contract.

If the lease modification is not considered to be a separate lease, the lessee shall at the effective date of the modification:

a. Allocate the consideration in the modified contract to all lease and non-lease components (if applicable) using their stand-alone prices;
b. Determine the amended lease term;
c. Remeasure the lease liability and, in turn, adjust the balance of the right-to-use asset.

Accounting for Leases—Lessor

There are two classifications of leases with which a lessor must be concerned:

1. Operating.
2. Finance.

Operating leases

The operating lease requires a less complex accounting treatment than does a finance lease. The payments received by the lessor are to be recorded as rental income in the period in which the payment is received or becomes receivable. If the rentals vary from a straight-line basis, or if the lease agreement contains a scheduled rent increase over the lease term, the revenue is nonetheless to be recognised on a straight-line basis unless an alternative basis of systematic and rational allocation is more representative of the time pattern of the earning process contained in the lease.

Additionally, if the lease agreement provides for a scheduled increase(s) in contemplation of the lessee's increased (i.e., more intensive) physical use of the leased property, the total amount of rental payments, including the scheduled increase(s), is allocated to revenue over the lease term on a straight-line basis. However, if the scheduled increase(s) is due to additional leased property (e.g., larger space, more machines), recognition should be proportional to the leased property, with the increased rents recognised over the years that the lessee has control over use of the additional leased property.

Under the leasing standard all initial direct costs incurred must be added to the carrying amount of the leased asset and recognised as an expense over the lease term on the same basis as the lease income. Initial direct costs are incurred by lessors in negotiating and arranging an operating lease, and may include commissions, legal fees and those internal costs that are actually incremental (i.e., would not exist if the lease were not being negotiated) and directly attributable to negotiating and arranging the lease.

When negotiating a new or renewed lease, the lessor may provide incentives for the lessee to enter into the agreement. Such incentives include reimbursement of relocation costs, leasehold improvement costs and recognised costs associated with a pre-existing lease commitment of the lessee.

All incentives shall be as an integral part of the net consideration agreed for the use of the leased asset, irrespective of the incentive's nature or form or the timing of the payments.

The lessor shall recognise the aggregate cost of incentives as a reduction of the rental income over the lease term on a straight-line basis unless another systematic approach is more representative of the time pattern over which the benefit of the leased asset is diminished.

Depreciation of leased assets should be on a basis consistent with the lessor's normal depreciation policy for similar assets, and the depreciation expense should be computed on the basis set out in IAS 16.

Any modifications to the original lease contract must be treated as new lease contracts.

Example of straight-lining of lease income

SandStone PLC leases two buildings to Rockwood Limited. The details are as follows:

Lease 1:

3-year lease
Lease payment €100,000 p.a. escalating at inflation
Inflation for years 1–3 is 8%

Lease 2:

3-year lease
Lease payment €100,000 p.a. escalating at 8% p.a. to reflect inflation
Inflation for years 1–3 is −8%

Accounting for Lease 1:

Year 1

Bank	€100,000	
Statement of comprehensive income – lease income		€100,000

Year 2

Bank	€108,000	
Statement of comprehensive income – lease income		€108,000

Year 3

Bank	€116,640	
Statement of comprehensive income – lease income		€116,640

Accounting for Lease 2:

As the escalation is a fixed percentage, and not a contingent amount as per Lease 1 (note that inflation is considered contingent), then the lease income must be straight-lined. Note that the difference between the amount charged to the statement of comprehensive income and the amount received from the lessee should be recognised in the statement of financial provision as an asset.

Total lease payments over lease term:

Year 1	€100,000
Year 2	€108,000
Year 3	€116,640
Total	€324,640
Therefore, the annual charge will be €324,640/3 =	€108,213

Year 1

Bank	€100,000	
Operating lease provision (SoFP)	8,213	
Statement of comprehensive income – lease income		€108,213

Year 2

Bank	€108,000	
Operating lease provision (SoFP)	213	
Statement of comprehensive income – lease income		€108,213

Year 3

Bank	€116,640	
Operating lease provision (SoFP)		€8,426
Statement of comprehensive income – lease income		108,214

Finance leases

The accounting by the lessor for finance leases depends on which variant of finance lease is at issue. In sales-type leases, an initial profit, analogous to that earned by a manufacturer or dealer, is recognised, whereas a direct financing lease does not give rise to an initial recognition of profit.

At initial recognition, the lessor must recognise a receivable in the balance sheet equal to the net investment in the lease.

Sales-type leases

In the accounting for a sales-type lease, it is necessary for the lessor to determine the following amounts:

1. Gross investment.
2. Fair value of the leased asset.
3. Cost.

From these amounts, the remainder of the computations necessary to record and account for the lease transaction can be made. The first objective is to determine the numbers necessary to complete the following entry:

Lease receivable	XX	
Cost of goods sold	XX	
Sales		XX
Inventory		XX
Unearned finance income		XX

The gross investment (lease receivable) of the lessor is equal to the sum of the minimum lease payments (excluding contingent rent and executory costs) from the standpoint of the lessor, plus the unguaranteed residual value accruing to the lessor. The difference between the gross investment and the PV of the two components of gross investment (i.e., minimum lease payments and unguaranteed residual value) is recorded as "unearned finance income" (also referred to as "unearned interest revenue"). The PV is to be computed using the lease term and implicit interest rate (both of which were discussed earlier).

IFRS 16 stipulates that the resulting unearned finance income is to be amortised and recognised into income using the effective rate (or yield) interest method, which will result in a constant periodic rate of return on the "lessor's net investment" (which is computed as the "lessor's gross investment" less the "unearned finance income").

Recall that the fair value of the leased property is by definition equal to the normal selling price of the asset adjusted by any residual amount retained (including any unguaranteed residual value, investment credit, etc.). According to IAS 17, the selling price to be used for a sales-type lease is equal to the fair value of the leased asset, or if lower the sum of the PVs of the minimum lease payment and the estimated unguaranteed residual value accruing to the lessor, discounted at a commercial rate of interest. In other words, the normal selling price less the PV of the unguaranteed residual value is equal to the PV of the minimum lease payment. (Note that this relationship is sometimes used while computing the minimum lease payment when the normal selling price and the residual value are known; this is illustrated in a case study that follows.)

Under IFRS 16, initial direct costs incurred in connection with a sales-type lease (i.e., where the lessor is a manufacturer or dealer) must be expensed as incurred. This is a reasonable requirement, since these costs offset some of the profit recognised at inception, as do other selling expenses. Thus, the costs recognised at the inception of such lease arrangements would include the carrying value of the equipment or other items being leased, as well as incidental costs of negotiating and executing the lease. The profit recognised at inception would be the gross profit on the sale of the leased asset, less all operating costs, including the initial direct costs of creating the lease arrangement.

The estimated unguaranteed residual values used in computing the lessor's gross investment in a lease should be reviewed regularly. In case of a permanent reduction (impairment) in the estimated unguaranteed residual value, the income allocation over the lease term is revised and any reduction with respect to amounts already accrued is recognised immediately.

To attract customers, manufacturer or dealer lessors sometimes quote artificially low rates of interest. This has a direct impact on the recognition of initial profit, which is an integral part of the transaction and is inversely proportional to the finance income to be generated by it. Thus, if finance income is artificially low, this results in recognition of excessive profit from the transaction at the time of the sale. Under such circumstances, the standard requires that the profit recognised at inception, analogous to a cash sale of the leased asset, be restricted to that which would have resulted had a commercial rate of interest been used in the deal. Thus, the substance, not the form, of the transaction should be reflected in the financial statements. The PV of the scheduled lease payments, discounted at the appropriate commercial rate, must be computed to derive the effective selling price of the leased asset under these circumstances.

The difference between the selling price and the amount computed as the cost of goods sold is the gross profit recognised by the lessor on the inception of the lease (sale). Manufacturer or dealer lessors often give an option to their customers of either leasing the asset (with financing provided by them) or buying the asset outright. Thus, a finance lease by a manufacturer or dealer lessor, also referred to as a sales-type lease, generates two types of revenue for the lessor:

1. The gross profit (or loss) on the sale, which is equivalent to the profit (or loss) that would have resulted from an outright sale at normal selling prices, adjusted if necessary, for a non-commercial rate of interest.
2. The finance income or interest earned on the lease receivable to be spread over the lease term based on a pattern reflecting a constant periodic rate of return on either the lessor's net investment outstanding or the net cash investment outstanding in respect of the finance lease.

The application of these points is illustrated in the example below.

Example of accounting for a sales-type lease

XYZ Inc. is a manufacturer of specialised equipment. Many of its customers do not have the necessary funds or financing available for outright purchase. Because of this, XYZ offers a leasing alternative. The data relative to a typical lease are as follows:

1. The non-cancellable fixed portion of the lease term is five years. The lessor has the option to renew the lease for an additional three years at the same rental. The estimated useful life of the asset is 10 years. The lessee guarantees a residual value of €40,000 at the end of five years, but the guarantee lapses if the full three-year renewal period is exercised.
2. The lessor is to receive equal annual payments over the term of the lease. The leased property reverts back to the lessor on termination of the lease.
3. The lease is initiated on January 1, 20XX. Payments are due on December 31 for the duration of the lease term.
4. The cost of the equipment to XYZ Inc. is €100,000. The lessor incurs cost associated with the inception of the lease in the amount of €2,500.
5. The selling price of the equipment for an outright purchase is €150,000.
6. The equipment is expected to have a residual value of €15,000 at the end of five years and €10,000 at the end of eight years.
7. The lessor desires a return of 12% (the implicit rate).

The first step is to calculate the annual payment due to the lessor. Recall that the PV of the minimum lease payments is equal to the selling price adjusted for the PV of the residual amount. The PV is to be computed using the implicit interest rate and the lease term. In this case, the implicit rate is given as 12% and the lease term is eight years (which includes the fixed non-cancellable portion plus the renewal period, since the lessee guarantee terms make renewal virtually inevitable). Thus, the structure of the computation would be as follows:

Normal selling price − PV of residual value = PV of minimum lease payment

Or, in this case,

€150,000	−(0.40388* × €10,000)	= 4.96764** × Minimum lease payment
€145,961.20	÷ 4.96764	= Minimum lease payment
	€29,382.40	= Minimum lease payment

** 0.40388 is the PV of an amount of €1 due in eight periods at a 12% interest rate.*
*** 4.96764 is the PV of an annuity of €1 for eight periods at a 12% interest rate.*

Prior to examining the accounting implications of a lease, we must determine the lease classification. In this example, the lease term is eight years (discussed above), while the estimated useful life of the asset is 10 years; thus, this lease qualifies as something other than an operating lease. Note that the lease also meets the fair market value (FMV) versus PV criterion because the PV of the minimum lease payments of €145,961.20, which is 97% of the FMV [€150,000], could be considered to be equal to substantially all of the fair value of the leased asset. Now it must be determined if this is a sales-type or direct financing lease. To do this, examine the FMV or selling price of the asset and compare it to the cost. Because the two are not equal, we can determine this to be a sales-type lease.

Next, obtain the figures necessary to record the entry on the books of the lessor. The gross investment is the total minimum lease payments plus the unguaranteed residual value, or (€29,382.40 × 8) + €10,000 = €245,059.20

The cost of goods sold is the historical cost of the inventory (€100,000) plus any initial direct costs (€2,500) less the PV of the unguaranteed residual value (€10,000 × 0.40388). Thus, the cost of goods sold amount is €98,461.20 (€100,000 + €2,500 − €4,038.80). Note that the initial direct costs will require a credit entry to some account, usually accounts payable or cash. The inventory account is credited for the carrying value of the asset, in this case €100,000.

The adjusted selling price is equal to the PV of the minimum payments, or €145,961.20. Finally, the unearned finance income is equal to the gross investment (i.e., lease receivable) less the PV of the components making up the gross investment (the minimum lease payment of €29,382.40 and the unguaranteed residual of €10,000). The PV of these items is €150,000 [(€29,382.40 × 4.96764) + (€10,000 × 0.40388)]. Therefore, the entry necessary to record the lease is:

Lease receivable	€245,059.20	
Cost of goods sold	98,461.20	
Inventory		€100,000.00
Sales		145,961.20
Unearned finance income		95,059.20
Accounts payable (initial direct costs)		2,500.00

The next step in accounting for a sales-type lease is to determine proper handling of the payment. Both principal and interest are included in each payment. According to IAS 17, interest is recognised on a basis such that a constant periodic rate of return is earned over the term of the lease. This will require setting up an amortisation schedule as illustrated below.

Date or year ended	*Cash payment*	*Interest*	*Reduction in principal*	*Balance of net investment*
January 1, 20XX				€150,000.00
December 31, 20XX+1	€29,382.40	€18,000.00	€11,382.40	€138,617.00
December 31, 20XX+2	€29,382.40	€16,634.11	€12,748.29	€125,869.31
December 31, 20XX+3	€29,382.40	€15,104.32	€14,278.08	€111,591.23
December 31, 20XX+4	€29,382.40	€13,390.95	€15,991.45	€95,599.78
December 31, 20XX+5	€29,382.40	€11,471.97	€17,910.43	€77,689.35
December 31, 20XX+6	€29,382.40	€9,322.72	€20,059.68	€57,629.67
December 31, 20XX+7	€29,382.40	€6,915.56	€22,466.84	€35,162.83
December 31, 20XX+8	€29,382.40	€4,219.57	€25,162.83	€10,000.00
	€235,059.20	**€95,059.20**	**€140,000.00**	

A few of the columns need to be elaborated on. First, the net investment is the gross investment (lease receivable) less the unearned finance income. Notice that at the end of the lease term, the net investment is equal to the estimated residual value. Also note that the total interest earned over the lease term is equal to the unearned interest (unearned finance income) at the beginning of the lease term.

The entries below illustrate the proper treatment to record the receipt of the lease payment and the amortisation of the unearned finance income in the year ended December 31, 20XX+1.

Cash	€29,382.40	
Lease receivable		€29,382.40
Unearned finance income	€18,000.00	
Interest revenue		€18,000.00

Notice that there is no explicit entry to recognise the principal reduction. This is done automatically when the net investment is reduced by decreasing the lease receivable (gross investment) by €29,382.40 and the unearned finance income account by only €18,000. The €18,000 is 12% (implicit rate) of the net investment. These entries are to be made over the life of the lease.

At the end of the lease term, December 31, 20XX+8, the asset is returned to the lessor and the following entry is required:

Asset	€10,000	
Leased receivable		€10,000

If the estimated residual value has changed during the lease term, the accounting computations would have also changed to reflect this.

Direct financing leases

Another form of finance lease is a direct financing lease. The accounting for a direct financing lease exhibits many similarities to that for a sales-type lease. Of particular importance is that the terminology used is much the same; however, the treatment accorded these items varies greatly. Again, it is best to preface the discussion by determining the objectives in the accounting for a direct financing lease. Once the lease has been classified, it must be recorded. To do this, the following amounts must be determined:

1. Gross investment.
2. Cost.
3. Residual value.

As noted, a direct financing lease generally involves a leasing company or other financial institution and results in only interest revenue being earned by the lessor. This is because the FMV (selling price) and the cost are equal, and therefore no dealer profit is recognised on the actual lease transaction. Note how this is different from a sales-type lease, which involves both a profit on the transaction and interest revenue over the lease term. The reason for this difference is derived from the conceptual nature underlying the purpose of the lease transaction. In a sales-type lease, the manufacturer (distributor, dealer, etc.) is seeking an alternative means to finance the sale of his product, whereas a direct financing lease is a result of the consumer's need to finance an equipment purchase. Because the consumer is unable to obtain conventional financing, he or she turns to a leasing company that will purchase the desired asset and then lease it to the consumer. Here the profit on the transaction remains with the manufacturer while the interest revenue is earned by the leasing company.

Like a sales-type lease, the first objective is to determine the amounts necessary to complete the following entry:

Lease receivable	XXX	
Asset		XXX
Unearned finance income		XXX

The gross investment is still defined as the minimum amount of lease payments (from the standpoint of a lessor) exclusive of any executory costs, plus the unguaranteed residual value. The difference between the gross investment as determined above and the cost (carrying value) of the asset is to be recorded as the unearned finance income because there is no manufacturer's/dealer's profit earned on the transaction. The following entry would be made to record initial direct costs:

Initial direct costs	XXX	
Cash		XXX

Under IFRS 16, the net investment in the lease is defined as the gross investment less the unearned income plus the unamortised initial direct costs related to the lease. Initial direct costs are incremental costs that are directly attributable to negotiating and arranging a lease, except for such costs incurred by manufacturer or dealer lessors. These are to be capitalised and allocated over the lease term.

Employing initial direct cost capitalisation, the unearned lease (i.e., interest) income and the initial direct costs will be amortised to income over the lease term so that a constant periodic rate is earned either on the lessor's net investment outstanding or on the net cash investment outstanding in the finance lease (i.e., the balance of the cash outflows and inflows in respect of the lease, excluding any executory costs that are chargeable to the lessee). Thus, the effect of the initial direct costs is to reduce the implicit interest rate, or yield, to the lessor over the life of the lease.

The lease payments included in the measurement of the net investment in the lease comprise the following payments for the right to use the underlying asset during the lease term that are not received at commencement date:

a. Fixed payments (including in-substance fixed payments) less any lease incentives payable;
b. Variable lease payments that depend on an index or a rate, initially measured using the index or rate as at the commencement date;
c. Any residual value guarantees provided to the lessor by the lessee, a party related to the lessee or a third party unrelated to the lessor that is financially capable of discharging the obligations under the guarantee;
d. Exercise price of a purchase option if the lessee is reasonably certain to exercise the option; and
e. Payments of penalties for terminating the lease, the lease term reflects the lessee exercising an option to terminate the lease.

Subsequently, the lessor must recognise finance income over the lease term, based on a pattern reflecting a constant periodic rate of return on the lessor's net investment in the lease.

An example follows that illustrates the preceding principles.

Example of accounting for a direct financing lease

Emirates Refining needs new equipment to expand its manufacturing operation; however, it does not have sufficient capital to purchase the asset at this time. Because of this, Emirates Refining has employed Consolidated Leasing to purchase the asset. In turn, Emirates will lease the asset from Consolidated. The following information applies to the terms of the lease:

1. A three-year lease is initiated on January 1, 20XX, for equipment costing €131,858, with an expected useful life of five years. FMV at January 1, 20XX, of equipment is €131,858.
2. Three annual payments are due to the lessor beginning December 31, 20XX. The property reverts back to the lessor on termination of the lease.
3. The unguaranteed residual value at the end of year three is estimated to be €10,000.
4. The annual payments are calculated to give the lessor a 10% return (the implicit rate).
5. The lease payments and unguaranteed residual value have a PV equal to €131,858 (FMV of asset) at the stipulated discount rate.

6. The annual payment to the lessor is computed as follows:

PV of residual value	= €10,000 × .7513* = €7,513
PV of lease payments	= Selling price − PV of residual value
	= €131,858 − €7,513 = €124,345
Annual payment	= €124,345 ÷ 2.4869** = €50,000

** 7,513 is the PV of an amount due in three periods at 10%.*
*** 2.4869 is the PV of an ordinary annuity of €1 per period for three periods, at 10% interest.*

7. Initial direct costs of €7,500 are incurred by ABC in the lease transaction.

As with any lease transaction, the first step must be to classify the lease appropriately. In this case, the PV of the lease payments (€124,345) is equal to 94% of the FMV (€131,858), thus it could be considered as equal to substantially all of the FMV of the leased asset. Next, the unearned interest and the net investment in the lease are to be determined.

Gross investment in lease [(3 × €50,000) + €10,000]	€160,000
Cost of leased property	€131,858
Unearned finance income	**€28,142**

The unamortised initial direct costs are to be added to the gross investment in the lease, and the unearned finance income is to be deducted to arrive at the net investment in the lease. The net investment in the lease for this example is determined as follows:

Gross investment in lease	€160,000
Add:	
Unamortised initial direct costs	€7,500
Less:	
Unearned finance income	€28,142
Net investment in lease	**€139,358**

The net investment in the lease (Gross investment – Unearned finance income) has been increased by the amount of initial direct costs. Therefore, the implicit rate is no longer 10%, and the implicit rate must be recomputed, which is the result of performing an internal rate of return calculation. The lease payments are to be €50,000 per annum and a residual value of €10,000 is available at the end of the lease term. In return for these payments (inflows), the lessor is giving up equipment (an outflow) and incurring initial direct costs (also an outflow), with a net investment of €139,358 (€131,858 + €7,500). The way to obtain the new implicit rate is to employ a calculator or computer routine that does this iterative computation automatically:

$$\frac{50,000}{(1+i)}1 + \frac{50,000}{(1+i)}2 + \frac{50,000}{(1+i)}3 + \frac{10,000}{(1+i)}3 = €139,358$$

where: i = implicit rate of interest.

In this case, the implicit rate is equal to 7.008%. Thus, the amortisation table would be set up as follows:

	(a) *Lease* *payments*	*(b)* *Reduction in unearned interest*	*(c)* *PV × Implicit rate (7.008%)*	*(d)* *Reduction in initial direct costs (b – c)*	*(e)* *Reduction in PVI net investment (a – b + d)*	*(f)* *PVI net investment in lease (f)(n + 1) = (f)n – (e)*
At inception						€139,358
20XX	€50,000	€13,186 (1)	€9,766	€3,420	€40,234	€99,124
20XX+1	€50,000	€9,504 (2)	€6,947	€2,557	€43,053	€56,071
20XX+2	€50,000	€5,455 (3)	€3,929	€1,526	€46,071	€10,000
	€150,000	€28,145*	€20,642	€7,503	€129,358	

**Rounded*

(b.1) €131,858 × 10% = €13,186
(b.2) [€131,858 − (€50,000 − 13,186)] × 10% = €9,504
(b.3) [€95,044 − (€50,000 − 9,504)] × 10% = €5,455

Here the interest is computed as 7.008% of the net investment. Note again that the net investment at the end of the lease term is equal to the estimated residual value.

The entry made initially to record the lease is as follows:

Lease receivable** [(€50,000 × 3) + €10,000]	€160,000	
Asset acquired for leasing		€131,858
Unearned lease revenue		€28,142

When the payment (or obligation to pay) of the initial direct costs occurs, the following entry must be made:

Initial direct costs	€7,500	
Cash		€7,500

Using the schedule above, the following entries would be made during each of the indicated years:

	20XX		**20XX+1**		**20XX+2**	
	€		**€**		**€**	
Cash	50,000		50,000		50,000	
Lease receivable**		50,000		50,000		50,000
Unearned finance income	13,186		9,504		5,455	
Initial direct costs		3,420		2,557		1,526
Interest income		9,766		6,947		3,929

Finally, when the asset is returned to the lessor at the end of the lease term, it must be recorded on the books. The necessary entry is as follows:

Property, plant and equipment	€10,000	
Lease receivable		€10,000

***Also commonly referred to as the "gross investment in lease."*

Lease Modifications

Modifications to lease contracts shall be treated as separate leases only if:

a. The modification increases the scope of the lease by adding the right to use one or more underlying assets; and
b. The consideration for the lease increases by an amount commensurate with the stand-alone price to reflect the circumstances of the particular contract.

If the modification is not seen as a new separate lease contract, the lessor must account for the modification to the original lease contract as follows:

a. If the lease would have been classified as an operating lease had the modification been in effect from the commencement date:

    i. Account for the lease modification as a new lease from the effective date of the modification; and
    ii. Measure the carrying amount of the underlying asset as the net investment in the lease immediately before the effective date of the lease modification.

b. Otherwise, apply the requirements of IFRS 9, *Financial Instruments*.

DISCLOSURE REQUIREMENTS UNDER IFRS 16

Lessee Disclosures

1. Right-to-use assets and lease liabilities must be disclosed separately in the statement of financial position, or the notes. If the right-to-use assets and lease liabilities are not disclosed separately:

    a. The right-to-use assets must be included in the same line item as that within which the corresponding underlying assets would be presented if they were owned and disclose which line items include these right-to-use assets; and
    b. Which line items include the lease liabilities.

The above is not applicable to leases meeting the definition of investment property.

2. The interest expense arising from the lease liability must be disclosed separately in the statement of comprehensive income from the depreciation charge for the right-to-use asset.
3. In the statement of cash flows, the lessee must classify:

    a. Cash payments for the principal portion of the lease liability as financing activities;
    b. Cash payments for the interest portion in line with the requirements of IAS 7, *Cash Flow Statements*;
    c. Short-term lease payments, payments for leases of low-value assets and variable lease payments not included in the measurement of the lease liability within operating activities.

4. The following amounts must be disclosed separately for the reporting period:

   a. Depreciation charge for right-of-use assets by class of underlying asset;
   b. Interest expense on lease liabilities;
   c. Expense relating to short-term leases;
   d. Expense relating to leases of low-value assets;
   e. Expense relating to variable lease payments not included in the measurement of the lease liability;
   f. Income from subleasing right-to-use assets;
   g. Total cash outflow for leases;
   h. Additions to right-of-use assets;
   i. Gains or losses arising from sale and leaseback transactions; and
   j. Carrying amount of right-of-use assets at the end of the reporting period by class of underlying asset.

   The above must be presented in a tabular format.

5. Amount of its lease commitments for short-term leases if the portfolio of short-term leases to which it is committed at the end of the reporting period is dissimilar to the portfolio of short-term leases to which the short-term lease expense relates to.
6. Maturity analysis of its lease liabilities as required by IFRS 7, *Financial Instruments: Disclosures*.

Lessor Disclosures

It is important to remember the objective of the disclosures required by IFRS 16, being to disclose information gives a basis for users of the financial statements to assess the effect that leases have on the financial position, financial performance and cash flows of the lessor.

1. **General**

   a. Qualitative and quantitative information about its leasing activities, including but not limited to:

      i. Nature of the lessor's leasing activities; and
      ii. How the lessor manages the risk associated with any rights it retains in underlying assets.

2. **Finance leases**

   a. Selling profit or loss;
   b. Finance income on the net investment in the lease;
   c. Income relating to variable lease payments not included in the measurement of the net investment in the lease;
   d. Qualitative and quantitative explanation of the significant changes in the carrying amount of the net investment in finance leases;
   e. Maturity analysis of the lease payments receivable, showing the undiscounted lease payments to be received on an annual basis for a minimum of each of the first five years and a total for the remaining years;

f. Reconciliation between the undiscounted lease payments to the net investment in the lease. This reconciliation must show:

   i. Unearned finance income; and
   ii. Discounted unguaranteed residual value.

3. **Operating leases**

   For lessors under operating leases, IFRS 16 has prescribed the following expanded disclosures:

   a. The future minimum lease payments under non-cancellable operating leases, in the aggregate and classified into:

      i. Those due in no more than one year;
      ii. Those due in more than one but not more than five years; and
      iii. Those due in more than five years.

   b. In addition to the above, the disclosure requirements relating to the assets recognised by the lessor or lessee required in the respective standards governing the accounting for those assets should be given. These include IAS 16, IAS 38, IAS 40 and IAS 41. These disclosure requirements are detailed in the respective chapters looking at each of these sections.

EXAMPLES OF FINANCIAL STATEMENT DISCLOSURES

Exemplum Reporting PLC
Financial Statements
For the Year Ended December 31, 20XX

2. Accounting policies

2.13 Leases

2.13.1 As lessor

Operating leases

Rental income from operating leases is recognised on a straight-line basis over the term of the relevant lease. Any balloon payments and rent-free periods are taken into account when determining the straight-line charge.

2.13.2 As lessee

At inception of the contract, the company assesses whether the contract contains a lease. A right-of-use asset and corresponding lease liability is recognized at inception of the lease.

Leases of low value assets or short term leases (less than 12 months) are expensed on a straight-line basis over the lease term unless another systematic basis if more representative of the time pattern in which economic benefits from the leased asset are consumed.

The lease liability is initially measured at the present value of the lease payments that are not paid at the commencement date, discounted by the rate implicit in the lease. If this rate cannot readily be determined, the company's incremental borrowing rate is used.

The lease liability is subsequently measured using the effective interest method.

The right-of-use asset comprise the initial measurement of the lease liability, any lease payments made at or before commencement of the contract and any direct initial costs. Subsequently, these assets are measured at cost less accumulated depreciation and impairment.

These assets are depreciated over the shorter of the lease term and its useful live. If the lease transfers ownership at the end of the contract, the asset is depreciated over its useful live.

6. Disclosure of expenses

	20XX	20XX-1
The following amounts were expensed or credited during the year:		
Operating lease expense	**X**	X
Depreciation on right-of-use assets	**X**	0

8. Finance costs

	20XX	20XX-1
Interest expense on lease liabilities	**X**	0

15. Property, plant and equipment

. . .

. . . (continued)

Plant and machinery includes the following amounts where the group is a lessee:

	20XX	20XX-1
Cost—right-of-use assets	**X**	X
Accumulated depreciation	**X**	X
Net book value	**X**	X

24. Notes to the statement of cash flows

24.1 Significant non-cash transactions

During the period the group acquired property, plant and equipment with a total cost of £X of which £Y was acquired by means of leases.

27. Lease liabilities

	20XX	20XX-1
Within one year	X	X
Later than one year and no later than five years	X	X
Later than five years	X	X
	X	X
Future finance charges on leases	X	X
Present value of lease liabilities	X	X
The present value of lease liabilities is analysed as follows:		
Within one year	X	X
Later than one year and no later than five years	X	X
Later than five years	X	X
	X	X

33. Operating lease commitments

As a lessor

The company leases its investment property to various third parties under operating lease agreements. The average lease term was 10 years, with annual escalation set at 2%.

	20XX	20XX-1
Future minimum lease receipts under non-cancellable operating leases:		
Within one year	X	X
From one to five years	X	X
After five years	X	X
	X	X

No contingent rentals were recognised in income.

US GAAP COMPARISON

US GAAP accounting and criteria for leases are very similar. However, US GAAP uses quantitative criteria to classify a lease as either operating or capital. IFRS is based on the substance of the transaction to assess whether a substantial amount of the value or useful life of the asset is conveyed to the lessee.

Third-party guarantees are not included in the minimum lease payments (nor measurement of the obligation and asset). Leases of land and buildings are accounted for together unless land is greater than 25% of the property value.

US GAAP does not contain the direct guidance about identifying an embedded derivative in the lease if the lessee has a stake in the market value of the asset.

IFRS 16, *Leases*, was issued in January 2016 with a mandatory effective date of January 1, 2019. A corresponding Accounting Standards Update 2016-2 *Leases (Topic 842),* also referred to as ASC 842, was released in February 2016, and is effective for fiscal years beginning after December 15, 2018 for public entities and all other entities for years beginning after December 15, 2019.

Although IFRS 16 and ASC 842 was a joint project of IASB and FASB, and many requirements of the two standards are the same, a number of differences remain. The main differences are relating to the lessee accounting since ASC 842 continues to distinguish between finance leases and operating leases, but IFRS 16 requires lessees to account for all leases similarly, except for short-term or low-value leases. Consequently, lessees will account for many leases differently if they are classified as operating leases under ASC 842. While many current differences between IFRS and US GAAP may no longer be relevant when the two new standards become effective in 2019, new differences follow:

1. Accounting model—lessee
    a. US GAAP does not have a lessee recognition and measurement exemption like IFRS 16 has for leases of assets with values of less than $5,000.
2. Accounting model—lessor
    a. US GAAP distinguishes between direct financing and sales-type leases where IFRS 16 leases are either finance or operating leases and IFRS 26 permits at direct financing lease commencement a recognition of selling profit.
    b. US GAAP has guidance where collectability assessed for the purposes of initial recognition and measurement of sales-type leases does whereas IFRS does not have explicit guidance on collectability to satisfy a residual value guarantee.
    c. IFRS 16 applies financial instruments guidance to a model to modifications of sales-type and direct financing leases.
3. Right-of-use asset—investment property
    a. US GAAP investment property is accounted for as held and used or held for sale and not separately defined. IFRS 16 permits alternative measurement means for the right-of-use asset (for example, under IAS 16, *Property, Plant and Equipment*, allow a revalued amount utilising fair value model as prescribed by IAS 40, *Investment Property*).
4. Variable lease payments
    a. US GAAP variable lease payment changes based on an index or rate requires remeasurement of the lease liability only when the lease liability changes for another reason such as a lease term change. Consequently IFRS 16 requires remeasurement when there is a change in the cash flows resulting from a change in the reference index or rate of variable lease payments dependent on an index or a rate when an adjustment to the lease payments is effective.
5. Subleases
    a. US GAAP indicates that when classifying a sublease, the sublessor based on the underlying asset classifies the sublease rather than IFRS 16's right-of-use asset on the head lease.

6. Sale and leaseback transactions

   a. US GAAP includes guidance to determine if the transfer of an asset in a sale and leaseback transaction is a sale, whereas IFRS 16 guidance helps to understand if the seller-lessee has a substantive repurchase option regarding the underlying asset, then no sale has occurred.
   b. US GAAP the seller-lessee recognises gain or loss as adjusted for off-market terms on inception.

7. Private companies

   a. US GAAP allows private companies an accounting policy election to use a risk-free rate to discount each lease liability.

8. Statement of cash flows

   a. US GAAP classifies interest as operating whereas IFRS 16 points to IAS 7, *Statement of Cash Flows*, where interest is allowed to be reported within operating, investing or financing activities.

9. Disclosure

   a. US GAAP is not identical to the qualitative and quantitative disclosure requirements in IFRS 16.

10. Transition

    a. US GAAP allows for early adoption, whereas IFRS 16 requires application of IFRS 15 first or concurrently.

Previous US GAAP & IFRS Differences

Topic 840 *Leases* had basic criteria when looking at leases that was different from IAS 17 *Leases*. US GAAP has a 4 basic lease criteria if the lease was to be considered a capital lease which were:

1. Does the lease contain a bargain purchase option?
2. Does ownership transfer as result of the lease?
3. Does the lease term equal 75% of the useful life of the asset?
4. Does the sum of the minimum lease payments equal 90% or more of the fair value of the property being leased?

IAS 17's focus is on the overall substance the transaction was to transfer the "risk and rewards" that ownership would bring to the lessee.

Under IFRS there is a better chance of capitalising the lease arrangement. In a sales and lease back arrangement, US GAAP would have you defer the gain and amortise it over the life of the lease whereas IFRS would have you capture the gain immediately if resulted in an operating lease. When there are leases involving land and buildings typically US GAAP accounts for those leases as a whole whereas IFRS would have you separate the building and land. Additionally, when accounting for land leases under IFRS the outcome is more frequently recorded as a financing lease.

23 FOREIGN CURRENCY

INTRODUCTION

International trade continues to become more prevalent, and "multinational corporations" (MNC) now comprise not only the international giants which are household names, but also many mid-tier companies. Corporations worldwide are reaching beyond national boundaries and engaging in international trade. International activity by most domestic corporations has increased significantly, which means that transactions are consummated not only with independent foreign entities but also with foreign subsidiaries.

Foreign subsidiaries, associates and branches often handle their accounts and prepare financial statements in the respective currencies of the countries in which they are located. Thus, it is more than likely that an MNC ends up receiving, at year-end, financial statements from various foreign subsidiaries expressed in a number of foreign currencies, such as dollars, euros, pounds, lira, dinars, won, rubles, rand and yen. However, for users of these financial statements to analyse the MNC's foreign involvement, overall financial position and results of operations properly, foreign currency-denominated financial statements must first be expressed in terms that the users can understand. This means that the foreign currency financial statements of the various subsidiaries will have to be translated into the currency of the country where the MNC is registered or has its major operations.

In addition to foreign operations, an entity may have foreign currency transactions (e.g., export and import transactions denominated in the foreign currency). These give rise to other financial reporting implications, which are also addressed in this chapter. Note that even a purely domestic company may have transactions (e.g., with foreign suppliers or customers) denominated in foreign currencies, and these same guidelines will apply in those circumstances as well.

IFRS governing the translation of foreign currency financial statements and the accounting for foreign currency transactions are found primarily in IAS 21, *The Effects of Changes in Foreign Exchange Rates*. IAS 21 applies to:

1. Accounting for foreign currency transactions (e.g., exports, imports and loans) which are denominated in other than the reporting entity's functional currency.
2. Translation of foreign currency financial statements of branches, divisions, subsidiaries and other investees that are incorporated in the financial statements of an entity by consolidation, proportionate consolidation or the equity method of accounting.

DEFINITIONS OF TERMS

Closing rate. This refers to the spot exchange rate (defined below) at the end of the reporting period.

Conversion. The exchange of one currency for another.

Exchange difference. The difference resulting from reporting the same number of units of a foreign currency in the presentation currency at different exchange rates.

Exchange rate. This refers to the ratio for exchange between two currencies.

Fair value. The amount for which an asset could be exchanged, or a liability could be settled, between knowledgeable willing parties in an arm's-length transaction.

Foreign currency. A currency other than the functional currency of the reporting entity (e.g., the Japanese yen is a foreign currency for a euro-reporting entity).

Foreign currency financial statements. Financial statements that employ as the unit of measure a foreign currency that is not the presentation currency of the entity.

Foreign currency transactions. Transactions whose terms are denominated in a foreign currency or require settlement in a foreign currency. Foreign currency transactions arise when an entity:

1. Buys or sells goods or services whose prices are denominated in foreign currency;
2. Borrows or lends funds and the amounts payable or receivable are denominated in foreign currency;
3. Is a party to an unperformed foreign exchange contract; or
4. For other reasons acquires or disposes of assets or incurs or settles liabilities denominated in foreign currency.

Foreign currency translation. The process of expressing in the presentation currency of the entity amounts that are denominated or measured in a different currency.

Foreign entity. When the activities of a foreign operation are not an integral part of those of the reporting entity, such a foreign operation is referred to as a foreign entity.

Foreign operation. A foreign subsidiary, associate, joint venture or branch of the reporting entity whose activities are based or conducted in a country other than the country where the reporting entity is domiciled.

Functional currency. The currency of the primary economic environment in which the entity operates, which thus is the currency in which the reporting entity measures the items in its financial statements, and which may differ from the presentation currency in some instances.

Group. A parent company and all of its subsidiaries.

Monetary items. Money held and assets and liabilities to be received or paid in fixed or determinable amounts of money.

Net investment in a foreign operation. The amount refers to the reporting entity's interest in the net assets of that foreign operation.

Non-monetary items. All items presented in the statement of financial position other than cash, claims to cash and cash obligations.

Presentation currency. The currency in which the reporting entity's financial statements are presented. There is no limitation on the selection of a presentation currency by a reporting entity.

Reporting entity. An entity or group whose financial statements are being referred to. Under this standard, those financial statements reflect (1) the financial statements of one or more foreign operations by consolidation, proportionate consolidation or equity accounting; (2) foreign currency transactions; or (3) both of the foregoing.

Spot exchange rate. The exchange rate for immediate delivery of currencies exchanged.

Transaction date. In the context of recognition of exchange differences from settlement of monetary items arising from foreign currency transactions, transaction date refers to the date at which a foreign currency transaction (e.g., a sale or purchase of merchandise or services the settlement for which will be in a foreign currency) occurs and is recorded in the accounting records.

SCOPE, OBJECTIVES AND DISCUSSION OF DEFINITIONS

The objective of IAS 21 is to prescribe (1) how to include foreign currency transactions and foreign operations in the financial statements of an entity, and (2) how to translate financial statements into a presentation currency. The scope of IAS 21 applies to:

1. Accounting for transactions and balances in foreign currencies, except for those derivative transactions and balances that are within the scope of IFRS 9, *Financial Instruments*. However, those foreign currency derivatives that are not within the scope of IFRS 9 (e.g., some foreign currency derivatives that are embedded in other contracts), and the translation of amounts relating to derivatives from its functional currency to its presentation currency are within the scope of this standard;
2. Translating the financial position and financial results of *foreign operations* that are included in the financial statements of the reporting entity as a result of consolidation or the equity method; and
3. Translating an entity's financial statements into a *presentation currency*.

IAS 21 does not apply to the presentation, in the statement of cash flows, of cash flows arising from transactions in a foreign currency, or to the translation of cash flows of a foreign operation, which are within the scope of IAS 7, *Statement of Cash Flows*.

IAS 21 does not apply also to hedge accounting of foreign currency items, including the hedging of net investment in a foreign operation. These are covered under IFRS 9 and are dealt with in this chapter under the section "Hedging."

Functional Currency

The concept of *functional currency* is key to understanding translation of foreign currency financial statements. Functional currency is defined as being the currency of the primary economic environment in which an entity operates. This is normally, but not necessarily, the currency in which that entity principally generates and expends cash.

In determining the relevant functional currency, an entity would give primary consideration to the following factors:

1. The currency that mainly influences sales prices for goods and services, as well as the currency of the country whose competitive forces and regulations mainly determine the sales prices of the entity's goods and services; and
2. The currency that primarily influences labour, material and other costs of providing those goods or services.

Note that the currency which influences selling prices is often that currency in which sales prices are denominated and settled, while the currency that most influences the various input costs is normally that in which input costs are denominated and settled. There are many situations in which input costs and output prices will be denominated in or influenced by differing currencies (e.g., an entity which manufactures all of its goods in Mexico, using locally sourced labour and materials, but sells all or most of its output in Europe in euro-denominated transactions).

In addition to the foregoing, IAS 21 notes other factors which may provide additional evidence of an entity's functional currency. These may be deemed secondary considerations, and these are:

1. The currency in which funds from financing activities (i.e., from the issuance of debt and equity instruments) are generated; and
2. The currency in which receipts from operating activities are usually retained.

In making a determination of whether the functional currency of a foreign operation (e.g., a subsidiary, branch, associate or joint venture) is the same as that of the reporting entity (parent, investor, etc.), certain additional considerations may also be relevant. These include:

1. Whether the activities of the foreign operation are carried out as an extension of the reporting entity, rather than being executed more or less autonomously;
2. What proportion of the foreign operation's activities is comprised of transactions with the reporting entity;
3. Whether the foreign operation's cash flows directly impact upon the cash flows of the reporting entity, and are available for prompt remittance to the reporting entity; and

4. Whether the foreign operation is largely cash flow independent (i.e., if its own cash flows are sufficient to service its existing and reasonably anticipated debts without the injection of funds by the reporting entity).

Foreign operations are characterised as being adjuncts of the operations of the reporting entity when, for example, the foreign operation only serves to sell goods imported from the reporting entity and in turn remits all sales proceeds to the reporting entity. On the other hand, the foreign operation is seen as being essentially autonomous when it accumulates cash and other monetary items, incurs expenses, generates income and arranges borrowings, all done substantially in its local currency.

In practice, there are many gradations along the continuum between full autonomy and the state of being a mere adjunct to the reporting entity's operations. When there are mixed indications, and thus the identity of the functional currency is not obvious, judgement is required to make this determination. The selection of the functional currency should most faithfully represent the economic effects of the underlying transactions, events and conditions. According to IAS 21, however, priority attention is to be given to the identity of the currency (or currencies) that impact selling prices for outputs of goods and services, and inputs for labour and materials and other costs. The other factors noted above are to be referred to secondarily, when a clear conclusion is not apparent from considering the two primary factors.

Example—Determining functional currency

A US-based company, Majordomo, Inc., has a major subsidiary located in the UK, John Bull Co., which produces and sells goods to customers almost exclusively in the EU. Transactions are effected primarily in euros both for sales and, to a lesser extent, for raw materials purchases. The functional currency is determined to be euros in this instance, given the facts noted. Transactions are to be measured in euros accordingly. For purposes of the John Bull Co.'s stand-alone financial reporting, euro-based financial data will be translated into pounds sterling, using the translation rules set forth in IAS 21. For consolidation of the UK subsidiary into the financial statements of parent entity Majordomo, Inc., translation into US dollars will be required, again using the procedures defined in the standard.

In some cases, the determination of functional currency can be complex and time-consuming. The process is difficult especially if the foreign operation acts as an investment company or holding company within a group and has few external transactions. Management must document the approach followed in the determination of the functional currency for each entity within a group—particularly when factors are mixed and judgement is required.

Once determined, an entity's functional currency will rarely be altered. However, since the entity's functional currency is expected to reflect its most significant underlying transactions, events and conditions, there obviously can be a change in functional currency if there are fundamental changes in those circumstances. For example, if the entity's manufacturing and sales operations are relocated to another country, and inputs are thereafter sourced from that new location, this may justify changing the functional currency for that operation. When there is a change in an entity's functional currency, the entity should apply the translation procedures applicable to the new functional currency *prospectively* from the date of the change.

If the functional currency is the currency of a hyperinflationary economy, as that term is defined under IAS 29, *Financial Reporting in Hyperinflationary Economies*, the entity's financial statements are restated in accordance with the provisions of that standard. IAS 21 stresses that an entity cannot avert such restatement by employing tactics such as adopting an alternate functional currency, such as that of its parent entity. There are currently very few such economies in the world, but this situation of course may change in the future. There are also instances that have been noted where economies have experienced severe hyperinflation and have been unable to restate their financial statements in terms of the procedures required by IAS 29 due to the unavailability of reliable information on restatement factors. The difficulties experienced by reporters in such jurisdictions have been addressed by the IASB, in that IFRS 1, *First-time Adoption of International Financial Reporting Standards*, was amended and now permits the readoption of IFRS by such entities through the application of exceptions and exemptions provided for in this standard.

Monetary and Non-Monetary Items

For purposes of applying IAS 21, it is important to understand the distinction between monetary and non-monetary items. Monetary items are those granting or imposing "a right to receive, or an obligation to deliver, a fixed or determinable number of units of currency." In contrast, non-monetary items are those exhibiting "the absence of a right to receive, or an obligation to deliver, a fixed or determinable number of units of currency." Examples of monetary items include accounts and notes receivable; pensions and other employee benefits to be paid in cash; provisions that are to be settled in cash; and cash dividends that are properly recognised as a liability. Examples of non-monetary items include inventories; amounts prepaid for goods and services (e.g., prepaid insurance); property, plant and equipment; goodwill; other intangible assets; and provisions that are to be settled by the delivery of a non-monetary asset.

FOREIGN CURRENCY TRANSACTIONS

Foreign currency transactions are those denominated in, or requiring settlement in, a foreign currency. These can include such common transactions as those arising from:

1. The purchase or sale of goods or services in transactions where the price is denominated in a foreign currency;
2. The borrowing or lending of funds, where the amounts owed or to be received are denominated in a foreign currency; or
3. Other routine activities such as the acquisition or disposal of assets, or the incurring or settlement of liabilities, if denominated in a foreign currency.

Under the provisions of IAS 21, foreign currency transactions are to be initially recorded in the functional currency by applying to the foreign currency-denominated amounts the spot exchange rate between the functional currency and the foreign currency at the date of the transaction. However, when there are numerous, relatively homogeneous transactions over the course of the reporting period (e.g., year), it is acceptable, and much more practical, to apply an appropriate average exchange rate provided such an average would approximate the spot rates applicable. In the simplest scenario, the simple numerical average (i.e., the midpoint between the beginning and ending exchange rates) could be used. Care must be exercised to ensure that such a simplistic approach is actually meaningful, however.

If exchange rate movements do not occur smoothly throughout the reporting period, or if rates move alternately up and down over the reporting interval, rather than monotonically up or down, then a more carefully constructed, weighted-average exchange rate should be used. Also, if transactions occur in other than a smooth pattern over the period—as might be the case for products characterised by seasonal sales—then a weighted-average exchange rate might be needed if exchange rates have moved materially over the course of the reporting period. For example, if the bulk of revenues is generated in the fourth quarter, the annual average exchange rate would probably not result in an accurately translated statement of comprehensive income.

IFRIC 22, *Foreign Currency Transactions and Advance Consideration*, was issued by the IASB in December 2016. This interpretation was issued to clarify how to determine the transaction date in situations where an advance payment was made or received in a foreign currency and a non-monetary asset/liability was raised (as the case may be) before initial recognition of the related asset/expense or income in IAS 21.

The IFRIC clarified that the transaction date (and thus the spot rate) to be used in recognising the asset/expense or income on derecognition of the advance payment or receipt (non-monetary asset/liability) is the date on which the entity initially recognised the non-monetary assets/liability arising from the advance payment or receipt.

This IFRIC does not apply when the related asset/expense or income is measured on initial recognition at fair value or at the fair value of the consideration paid or received at a date other than the initial recognition of the non-monetary asset/liability arising from the advanced consideration (for example, the IFRIC refers to the measurement of goodwill as described in IFRS 3). Additionally, it is not required that the interpretation is applied to income taxes and insurance contracts (including reinsurance contracts) issued or reinsurance contracts held by the entity.

Example—Continuing need to translate foreign currency denominated events

Continuing the preceding example, the UK-based subsidiary, John Bull Co., which produces and sells goods to customers almost exclusively in the EU, also had sizeable sales to a Swiss company, denominated in Swiss francs. These occurred primarily in the fourth quarter of the year, when the Swiss franc-euro exchange rate was atypically strong. In converting these sales to the functional currency (euros), the average exchange rate in the fourth quarter was deemed to be most relevant.

Subsequent to the date of the underlying transaction, there may be a continuing need to translate the foreign currency-denominated event into the entity's functional currency. For example, a purchase or sale transaction may have given rise to an account payable or an account receivable, which remains unsettled at the next financial reporting date (e.g., the following month-end). According to IAS 21, at each end of the reporting period the foreign currency *monetary* items (such as payables and receivables) are to be translated using the closing rate (i.e., the exchange rate at the date of the statement of financial position).

Example—Exchange differences

If John Bull Co. (from the preceding examples) acquires receivables denominated in a foreign currency, Swiss francs (CHF), in 20XX, these are translated into the functional currency, euros, at the date of the transaction. If the CHF-denominated receivables are still outstanding at year-end, the company will translate those (ignoring any allowance for uncollectables) into euros at the year-end exchange rate. If these remain outstanding at the end of 20XX+1 (again ignoring collectability concerns), these will be translated into euros using the *year-end 20XX+1* exchange rate.

To the extent that exchange rates have changed since the transaction occurred (which will likely happen), exchange differences will have to be recognised by the reporting entity, since the amount due to or from a vendor or customer, denominated in a foreign currency, is now more or less valuable than when the transaction occurred.

Example—Non-Monetary items

Assume now that John Bull Co. acquired the above-noted receivables denominated in Swiss francs in mid-20XX, when the exchange rate of the Swiss franc versus the euro was CHF 1 = €.65. At year-end 20XX, the rate is CHF 1 = €.61, and by year-end 20XX+1, the euro has further strengthened to CHF 1 = €.58. Assume that John Bull acquired CHF 10,000 of receivables in mid-20XX, and all remain outstanding at year-end 20XX+1. (Again, for purposes of this example only, ignore collectability concerns.)

At the date of initial recognition, John Bull records accounts receivable denominated in CHF in the euro equivalent value of €6,500, since the euro is the functional currency. At year-end 20XX these receivables are the equivalent of only €6,100, and as a result a loss of €400, which must be recognised in the company's 20XX profit and loss statement. In effect, by holding CHF-denominated receivables while the Swiss franc declined in value against the euro, John Bull suffered a loss. The Swiss franc further weakens over 20XX+1, so that by year-end 20XX+1 the CHF 10,000 of receivables will be worth only €5,800, for a further loss of €300 in 20XX+1, which again is to be recognised currently in John Bull's profit and loss statement.

Non-monetary items (such as property purchased for the company's foreign operation), on the other hand, are to be translated at historical exchange rates. The actual historical exchange rate to be used, however, depends on whether the non-monetary item is being reported on the historical cost basis, or on a revalued basis, in those instances where the latter method of reporting is permitted under IFRS. If the non-monetary items are measured in terms of historical cost in a foreign currency, then these are to be translated by using the exchange rate at the actual historical date of the transaction. If the item has been restated to a fair value measurement, then it must be translated into the functional currency by applying the exchange rate at the date when the fair value was determined.

Example—Historical cost accounting employed by reporting entity

Assume that John Bull Co. acquired machinery from a Swiss manufacturer, in a transaction denominated in Swiss francs in 20XX, when the CHF-euro exchange rate was CHF 1 = €.65. The price paid was CHF 250,000. For purposes of this example, ignore depreciation. At the transaction date, John Bull Co. records the machinery at €162,500. This same amount will be presented in the year-end 20XX and 20XX+1 statements of financial position. The change in exchange rates subsequent to the transaction date will not be considered, since machinery is a non-monetary asset.

Example—Revaluation accounting employed by reporting entity

Assume again that John Bull Co. acquired machinery from a Swiss manufacturer, in a transaction denominated in Swiss francs in 20XX, when the CHF-euro exchange rate was CHF 1 = €.65. The price paid was CHF 250,000. For purposes of this example, ignore depreciation. At year-end 20XX, John Bull Co. elects to use the allowed alternative method of accounting under IAS 16, and determines that the fair value of the machinery is CHF 285,000. In the entity's year-end statement of financial position, this is reported at the euro equivalent of the revalued amount, using the exchange rate at the revaluation date, or €173,850 (= CHF 285,000 × €.61). This same amount will appear in the 20XX+1 statement of financial position (assuming no further revaluation is undertaken post-20XX).

If a non-monetary asset was acquired in a foreign currency transaction by incurring debt which is to be repaid in the foreign currency (e.g., when a building for the foreign operation was financed locally by commercial debt), subsequent to the actual transaction date the translation of the asset and the related debt will be at differing exchange rates (unless rates remain unchanged, which is not likely to happen). The result will be either a gain or a loss, which reflects the fact that a non-monetary asset was purchased but the burden of the related obligation for future payment will vary as the exchange rates fluctuate over time, until the debt is ultimately settled—in other words, the reporting entity has assumed exchange rate risk. On the other hand, if the debt were obtained in the reporting (parent) entity's home country or were otherwise denominated in the buyer's functional currency, there would be no exchange rate risk and no subsequent gain or loss resulting from such an exposure.

Example—Other Situations

Assume now that John Bull Co. acquired machinery from a Swiss manufacturer, in a transaction denominated in Swiss francs in 20XX, when the CHF-euro exchange rate was CHF 1 = €.65. The price paid was CHF 250,000. For purposes of this example, ignore depreciation. At the transaction date, John Bull Co. records the machinery at €162,500. This same amount will be presented in the year-end 20XX and 20XX+1 statements of financial position. The change in exchange rates subsequent to the transaction date will not be considered, since machinery is a non-monetary asset.

However, the purchase of the machinery was effected by signing a five-year note, payable in Swiss francs. Assume for simplicity the note is not subject to amortisation (i.e., due in full at maturity). The note is recorded, at transaction date, as a liability of €162,500. However, at year-end 20XX, since the euro has strengthened, the obligation is the equivalent of €152,500. As a result, an exchange gain of €10,000 is reported in profit or loss in the current period.

At year-end 20XX+1, this obligation has the euro-equivalent value of €145,000, and thus a further gain of €7,500 is recognised by John Bull Co. for financial reporting purposes.

Had the machinery been acquired for a euro-denominated obligation of €162,500, this valuation would remain in the financial statements until ultimately retired. In this case, the Swiss machinery manufacturer, not the British customer (whose functional currency is the euro), accepted exchange rate risk, and John Bull Co. will report no gain or loss arising from exchange differences.

Other complications can arise when accounting for transactions executed in a foreign currency. IAS 21 identifies circumstances where the carrying amount of an item is determined by comparing two or more amounts, for example when inventory is to be presented at the lower of cost or net realisable value (NRV), consistent with the requirements of IAS 2, *Inventories*. Another cited example pertains to long-lived assets, which must be reviewed for impairment, per IAS 36, *Impairments of Assets*. In situations such as these (i.e., where the asset is non-monetary and is measured in a foreign currency) the carrying amount in terms of functional currency is determined by comparing:

1. The cost or carrying amount, as appropriate, translated at the exchange rate at the date when that amount was determined (i.e., the rate at the date of the transaction for an item measured in terms of historical cost, or the date of revaluation if the item were restated under relevant IFRS); and
2. The NRV or recoverable amount, as appropriate, translated at the exchange rate at the date when *that* value was determined (which would normally be the closing rate at the end of the reporting period).

Note that by comparing translated amounts that are determined using exchange rate ratios as of differing dates, the actual effect of performing the translation will reflect two economic phenomena: namely, the IFRS-driven lower of cost or fair value comparison (or equivalent), and the changing exchange rates. The effect may be that an impairment loss is to be recognised in the functional currency when it would not have been recognised in the foreign currency, or the opposite relationship may hold (and, of course, there could be impairments in either case, albeit for differing amounts).

Example—Impairments

John Bull Co. acquired raw materials inventory from a Swiss manufacturer, in a transaction denominated in Swiss francs in 20XX, when the CHF-euro exchange rate was CHF 1 = €.65. The price paid was CHF 34,000. At year-end, when the exchange rate was CHF 1 = €.61, the NRV of the inventory, which was still on hand, was CHF 32,000. Applying the IAS 21 requirements, it is determined that (1) the purchase price in euros was €22,100 (= CHF 34,000 × €.65), and (2) NRV at the end of the reporting period is €19,520 (= CHF 32,000 × €.61). A lower of cost or realisable value impairment adjustment is reported equal to €2,580 (= €22,100 − €19,520).

TRANSLATION OF FOREIGN CURRENCY FINANCIAL STATEMENTS

IAS 21 adopted the functional currency approach that requires the foreign entity to present all of its transactions in its functional currency. Translation is the process of converting transactions denominated in its functional currency into the investor's presentation currency. If an entity's transactions are denominated in other than its functional currency, the foreign transactions must first be adjusted to their equivalent functional currency value before translating to the presentation currency (if different than the functional currency). Three different situations that can arise in translating foreign currency financial statements are illustrated in the following example:

Example

Foreign entity's local currency	Foreign entity's functional currency	Investor's presentation currency	Translation method	Exchange differences
Euro	Euro	Canadian dollar	Translation to the presentation currency at the closing rate for all assets and liabilities	Other comprehensive income (OCI) and equity
Euro	Canadian dollar	Canadian dollar	Translation to the functional currency (which is also the presentation currency) at the closing rate for all monetary items	Gain (or loss) in profit or loss
Swiss franc	Euro	Canadian dollar	1. Translation to the functional currency (€) 2. Translation to the presentation currency (Can $)	Gain (or loss) in profit or loss OCI and equity

IAS 21 prescribes two sets of requirements when translating foreign currency financial statements. The first of these deals with reporting foreign currency *transactions* by each individual entity, which may also be part of reporting group (e.g., consolidated parent and subsidiaries) in the individual entities' functional currencies or remeasuring the foreign currency financial statements into the functional currency. The second set of requirements is for the translation of entities' financial statements (e.g., those of subsidiaries) from the functional currency into presentation currency (e.g., of the parent). These matters are addressed in the following paragraphs.

Translation of functional currency financial statements into a presentation currency

If the investor's presentation currency (e.g., Canadian dollar) differs from the foreign entity's functional currency (e.g., euro), the foreign entity's financial statements have to be translated into the presentation currency when preparing consolidated financial statements. In accordance with IAS 21, the method used for translation of the foreign currency financial statements from the functional currency into the presentation currency is essentially what is commonly called the *current (closing) rate* method under US GAAP. In general, the translation methods under both IFRS and US GAAP are the same, except for the translation of financial statements in hyperinflationary economies (see Chapter 35).

Under the translation to the presentation currency approach, all assets and liabilities, both monetary and non-monetary, are translated at the closing (end of the reporting period) rate, which simplifies the process compared to all other historically advocated methods. More importantly, this more closely corresponds to the viewpoint of financial statement users, who tend to relate to currency exchange rates in existence at the end of the reporting period rather than to the various specific exchange rates that may have applied in prior months or years.

However, financial statements of preceding years should be translated at the rate(s) appropriately applied when these translations were first performed (i.e., these are *not* to be updated to current closing or average rates). This rule applies because it would cause great confusion to users of financial statements if amounts once reported (when current) were now all restated even though no changes were being made to the underlying data, and, of course, the underlying economic phenomena, now one or more years in the past, cannot have changed since initially reported upon.

The theoretical basis for this translation approach is the "net investment concept," whereby the foreign entity is viewed as a separate entity that the parent invested into, rather than being considered as part of the parent's operations. Information provided about the foreign entity retains the internal relationships and results created in the foreign environments (economic, legal and political) in which the entity operates. This approach works best, of course, when foreign-denominated debt is used to purchase the assets that create foreign-denominated revenues; these assets thus serve as a hedge against the effects caused by changes in the exchange rate on the debt. Any excess (i.e., net) assets will be affected by this foreign exchange risk, and this is the effect that is recognised in the parent company's statement of financial position, as described below.

The following rules should be used in translating the financial statements of a foreign entity:

1. All assets and liabilities in the current year-end statement of financial position, whether monetary or non-monetary, should be translated at the closing rate in effect at the date of that statement of financial position.
2. Income and expense items in each statement of comprehensive income should be translated at the exchange rates at the dates of the transactions, except when the foreign entity reports in a currency of a hyperinflationary economy (as defined in IAS 29), in which case they should be translated at the closing rates.
3. All resulting exchange differences should be recognised in other comprehensive income and reclassified from equity to profit or loss on the disposal of the net investment in a foreign entity.
4. All assets and liabilities in *prior period* statements of financial position, being presented currently (e.g., as comparative information) whether monetary or non-monetary, are translated at the exchange rates (closing rates) in effect at the date of each of the statements of financial position.
5. Income and expense items in *prior period* statements of income, being presented currently (e.g., as comparative information), are translated at the exchange rates as of the dates of the original transactions (or averages, where appropriate).

Under the translation to the presentation currency approach, all assets and liabilities are valued (1) higher, as a result of a direct exchange rate increase, or (2) lower, as a result of a direct rate decrease. Since the liabilities offset a portion of the assets, constituting a natural hedge, only the subsidiary's net assets (assets in excess of liabilities) are exposed to the risk of fluctuations in the currency exchange rates. As a result, the effect of the exchange rate change can be calculated by multiplying the foreign entity's average net assets by the change in the exchange rate.

On the books of the parent, the foreign entity's net asset position is reflected in the parent's investment account. If the equity method is applied, the investment account should be adjusted upward or downward to reflect changes in the exchange rate; if a foreign entity is included in the consolidated financial statements, the investment account is eliminated. (See "Comprehensive example: translation into the presentation currency" later in this chapter.)

Translation (remeasurement) of financial statements into a functional currency

When a foreign entity keeps its books and records in a currency other than its functional currency, translation of foreign currency items presented in the statement of financial position into functional currency (remeasurement) is driven by the distinction between monetary and non-monetary items. Foreign currency monetary items are translated using the closing rate (the spot exchange rate at the end of the reporting period). Foreign currency non-monetary items are translated using the historical exchange rates. There is a presumption that the effect of exchange rate changes on the foreign operation's net assets will directly affect the parent's cash flows, so the exchange rate adjustments are reported in the parent's profit or loss.

For example, branch sales offices or production facilities of a large, integrated operation (e.g., the European field operation of a US corporation, which is principally supplied by the home office, but which occasionally also enters into local currency transactions) would qualify for this treatment. Since the US dollar influences sales prices, most (but not all) of its sales are US dollar denominated, and most of its costs, including merchandise, are the result of US transactions, the application of the previously mentioned criteria would conclude that the functional currency of the European sales office is the US dollar, and translation of foreign currency-denominated assets and liabilities, and transactions would follow the monetary/non-monetary distinction noted above with the effect of exchange rate differences reported in profit or loss.

In general, translation of non-monetary items (inventory, plant assets, etc.) is done by applying the historical exchange rates. The historical rates usually are those in effect when the asset was acquired or (less often) when the non-monetary liability was incurred, but if there was a subsequent revaluation, if this is permitted under IFRS, then using the exchange rate at the date when the fair value was determined.

When a gain or loss on a non-monetary item is recognised in profit or loss (e.g., from applying lower of cost or realisable value for inventory), any exchange component of that gain or loss should be recognised in profit or loss. When, on the other hand, a gain or loss on a non-monetary item is recognised under IFRS in other comprehensive income (e.g., from revaluation of plant assets, or from fair value adjustments made to financial assets classified at fair value through other comprehensive income securities investments), any exchange component of that gain or loss should also be recognised in other comprehensive income.

As a result of conversion into functional currency, if a foreign unit is in a net monetary asset position (monetary assets in excess of monetary liabilities), an increase in the direct exchange rate causes a favourable result (gain) to be reported in profit or loss; if it is in a net monetary liability position (monetary liabilities in excess of monetary assets), it reports an unfavourable result (loss). If a foreign unit is in a net monetary asset position, a decrease in the direct exchange rate causes an unfavourable result (loss) to report, but if it is in a net monetary liability position, a favourable result (gain) is reported.

In cases when an entity keeps its books and records in a currency (e.g., Swiss franc) other than its functional currency (e.g., euro), and other than the presentation currency of the parent (e.g., Canadian dollar), the two-step translation process would be required: (1) translation of the financial statements (e.g., from Swiss franc) into the functional currency (e.g., euro) and (2) translation of the functional currency (e.g., euro) into the reporting currency (e.g., Canadian dollar).

Net investment in a foreign operation

A special rule applies to a net investment in a foreign operation. According to IAS 21, when the reporting entity has a monetary item that is receivable from or payable to a foreign operation for which settlement is neither planned nor likely to occur in the foreseeable future, this is, in substance, a part of the entity's net investment in its foreign operation. This item should be accounted for as follows:

1. Exchange differences arising from translation of monetary items forming part of the net investment in the foreign operation should be reflected in profit or loss in the *separate* financial statements of the reporting entity (investor/parent) and in the separate financial statements of the foreign operation; *but*
2. In the consolidated financial statements, which include the investor/parent and the foreign operation, the exchange difference should be recognised initially in other comprehensive income and reclassified from equity to profit or loss upon disposal of the foreign operation.

Note that when a monetary item is a component of a reporting entity's net investment in a foreign operation and it is denominated in the functional currency of the reporting entity, an exchange difference arises only in the foreign operation's individual financial statements. Conversely, if the item is denominated in the functional currency of the foreign operation, an exchange difference arises only in the reporting entity's separate financial statements.

Consolidation of foreign operations

The most commonly encountered need for translating foreign currency financial statements into the investor entity reporting currency is when the parent entity is preparing consolidated financial statements, and one or more of the subsidiaries have reported in their respective (local) currencies. The same need presents itself if an investee or joint venture's financial information is to be incorporated via the proportionate consolidation or the equity methods of accounting. When consolidating the assets, liabilities, income and expenses of a foreign operation with those of the reporting entity, the general consolidation processes apply, including the elimination of intragroup balances and intragroup transactions. Goodwill and any fair value-based adjustments to the carrying amounts of foreign operation's assets and liabilities should be expressed in the functional currency and translated using the closing rate.

Taxation effect

Gains and losses on foreign currency transactions and exchange differences arising on translating the results and financial position of an entity, including its foreign operations, into a different currency may have tax effects. IAS 12, *Income Taxes*, applies to these tax effects.

Comprehensive example: Translation into the presentation currency

Assume that a US company has a 100%-owned subsidiary in Germany that began operations in 20XX. The subsidiary's operations consist of utilising company-owned space in an office building. This building, which cost €5,000,000, was financed primarily by German banks, although the parent did invest €2,000,000 in the German operation. All revenues and cash expenses are received and paid in euros. The subsidiary also maintains its books and records in euros, its functional currency.

The financial statements of the German subsidiary are to be translated (from the functional currency euros to the presentation currency US dollars) for incorporation into the US parent's financial statements. The subsidiary's statement of financial position at December 31, 20XX, and its combined statement of income and retained earnings for the year ended December 31, 20XX, are presented below in euros.

German Company
Statement of Financial Position
December 31, 20XX (in thousands of €)

Assets		*Liabilities and shareholders' equity*	
Cash	€500	Accounts payable	€300
Note receivable	200	Unearned rent	100
Land	1,000	Mortgage payable	4,000
Building	5,000	Ordinary shares	400
Accumulated depreciation	(100)	Additional paid-in capital	1,600
		Retained earnings	200
Total assets	**€6,600**	Total liabilities and shareholders' equity	**€6,600**

German Company
Combined Statement of Profit or Loss and Retained Earnings
For the Year Ended December 31, 20XX
(in thousands of €)

Revenues	€2,000
Operating expenses (including depreciation expense of €100)	1,700
Profit for the year	300
Add retained earnings, January 1, 20XX-1	–
Deduct dividends	(100)
Retained earnings, December 31, 20XX-1	**€200**

Various *assumed* exchange rates for 20XX are as follows:

€1 = $0.90 at the beginning of 20XX (when the ordinary shares were issued and the land and building were financed through the mortgage)
€1 = $1.05 weighted-average for 20XX
€1 = $1.10 at the date the dividends were declared and the unearned rent was received
€1 = $1.20 closing (December 31, 20XX)

The German company's financial statements must be translated into US dollars in terms of the provisions of IAS 21 (i.e., by the current rate method). This translation process is illustrated below.

German Company
Statement of Financial Position Translation
December 31, 20XX
(in thousands)

	Euros	*Exchange rates*	*US dollars*
Assets			
Cash	€500	1.20	$600
Accounts receivable	200	1.20	240

Land	1,000	1.20	1,200
Building (net)	4,900	1.20	5,880
Total assets	**€6,600**		**$7,920**
Liabilities and shareholders' equity			
Accounts payable	€300	1.20	$360
Unearned rent	100	1.20	120
Mortgage payable	4,000	1.20	4,800
Ordinary shares	400	0.90	360
Additional paid-in capital	1,600	0.90	1,440
		(see combined income and retained earnings statement translation)	
Retained earnings	200		205
Cumulative exchange difference (translation adjustments)	–	–	635
Total liabilities and shareholders' equity	**€6,600**		**$7,920**

German Company
Combined Statement of Profit or Loss and Retained Earnings Translation
For the Year Ended December 31, 20XX
(in thousands)

	Euros	*Exchange rates*	*US dollars*
Revenues	€2,000	1.05	$2,100
Expenses (including €100 depreciation expense)	1,700	1.05	1,785
Profit for the year	300		315
Add retained earnings, January 1	–	–	–
Deduct dividends	(100)	1.10	(110)
Retained earnings, December 31	**€200**		**$205**

German Company
Statement of Cash Flows Translation
For the Year Ended December 31, 20XX
(in thousands)

	Euros	*Exchange rates*	*US dollars*
Operating activities			
Profit for the year	€300	1.05	$315
Adjustments to reconcile net income to net cash provided by operating activities:			
Depreciation	100	1.05	105
Increase in accounts receivable	(200)	1.05	(210)
Increase in accounts payable	300	1.05	315
Increase in unearned rent	100	1.10	110

Net cash provided by operating activities	600		635
Investing activities			
Purchase of land	(1,000)	0.90	(900)
Purchase of building	(5,000)	0.90	(4,500)
Net cash used by investing activities	(6,000)		(5,400)
Financing activities			
Ordinary shares issue	2,000	0.90	1,800
Mortgage payable	4,000	0.90	3,600
Dividends paid	(100)	1.10	(110)
Net cash provided by financing	5,900		5,290
Effect on exchange rate changes on cash	N/A		75
Increase in cash and equivalents	500		600
Cash at beginning of year	–		–
Cash at end of year	**€500**	**1.20**	**$600**

The following points should be noted concerning the translation into the presentation currency:

1. All assets and liabilities are translated using the closing rate at the end of the reporting period (€1 = $1.20). All revenues and expenses should be translated at the rates in effect when these items are recognised during the period. Due to practical considerations, however, weighted-average rates can be used to translate revenues and expenses (€1 = $1.05) only if such weighted-average rates approximate actual rates that were ruling at the time of the transactions.
2. Shareholders' equity accounts are translated by using historical exchange rates. Ordinary shares were issued at the beginning of 20XX-2 when the exchange rate was €1 = $0.90. The translated balance of retained earnings is the result of the weighted-average rate applied to revenues and expenses and the specific rate in effect when the dividends were declared (€1 = $1.10).
3. Cumulative exchange differences (translation adjustments) result from translating all assets and liabilities at the closing (current) rate, while shareholders' equity is translated by using historical and weighted-average rates. The adjustments have no direct effect on cash flows; however, changes in exchange rate will have an indirect effect on sale or liquidation. Prior to this time, the effect is uncertain and remote. Also, the effect is due to the net investment rather than the subsidiary's operations. For these reasons, the translation adjustments balance is reported as "other comprehensive income item" in the statement of comprehensive income and as a separate component in the shareholders' equity section of the US company's consolidated statement of financial position. This balance essentially equates the total debits of the subsidiary (now expressed in US dollars) with the total credits (also in dollars). It may also be determined directly, as shown next, to verify the translation process.
4. The cumulative exchange differences (translation adjustments) credit of $635 is calculated as follows:

Net assets at the beginning of 20XX-2 (after ordinary shares were issued and the land and building were acquired through mortgage financing)	€2,000 (1.20 − 0.90)	= $600 credit
Profit for the year	€300 (1.20 − 1.05)	= 45 credit
Dividends	€100 (1.20 − 1.10)	= 10 debit
Exchange difference (translation adjustment)		**$635 credit**

5. Since the net exchange differences (translation adjustment) balance that appears as a separate component of shareholders' equity is cumulative in nature, the change in this balance during the year should be disclosed in the financial statements. In the illustration, this balance went from zero to $635 at the end of 20XX-1. The analysis of this change was presented previously. The translation adjustment has a credit balance because the German entity was in a net asset position during the period (assets in excess of liabilities) and the spot exchange rate at the end of the period is higher than the exchange rate at the beginning of the period or the average for the period.

In addition to the foregoing transactions, assume that the following occurred during 20XX+1:

German Company
Statement of Financial Position
December 31, 20XX+1
(in thousands of €)

	20XX	*20XX-1*	*Increase/(decrease)*
Assets			
Cash	€1,000	€500	€500
Accounts receivable	–	200	(200)
Land	1,500	1,000	500
Building (net)	4,800	4,900	(100)
Total assets	**€7,300**	**€6,600**	**€700**
Liabilities and shareholders' equity			
Accounts payable	€500	€300	€200
Unearned rent	–	100	(100)
Mortgage payable	4,500	4,000	500
Ordinary shares	400	400	–
Additional paid-in capital	1,600	1,600	–
Retained earnings	300	200	100
Total liabilities and shareholders' equity	**€7,300**	**€6,600**	**€700**

German Company
Combined Statement of Profit or Loss and Retained Earnings
For the Year Ended December 31, 20XX+1
(in thousands of €)

Revenues	€2,200
Operating expenses (including depreciation expense of €100)	1,700
Profit for the year	500
Add: Retained earnings, January 1, 20XX	200
Deduct dividends	(400)
Retained earnings, December 31, 20XX	**€300**

Exchange rates were:

€1 = $1.20 at the beginning of 20XX+1
€1 = $1.16 weighted-average for 20XX+1
€1 = $1.08 closing (December 31, 20XX+1)
€1 = $1.10 when dividends were paid in 20XX and land bought by incurring mortgage

The translation process for 20XX+1 is illustrated below.

German Company
Statement of Financial Position Translation
December 31, 20XX+1
(in thousands)

	Euros	*Exchange rates*	*US dollars*
Assets			
Cash	€1,000	1.08	$1,080
Land	1,500	1.08	1,620
Building	4,800	1.08	5,184
Total assets	**€7,300**		**$7,884**
Liabilities and shareholders' equity			
Accounts payable	€ 500	1.08	$540
Mortgage payable	4,500	1.08	4,860
Ordinary shares	400	0.90	360
Additional paid-in capital	1,600	0.90	1,440
	(see combined income and retained earnings statement translation)		
Retained earnings	300		345
Cumulative translation adjustments	–		339
Total liabilities and shareholders' equity	**€7,300**		**$7,884**

German Company
Combined Statement of Profit or Loss and Retained Earnings Translation
For the Year Ended December 31, 20XX+1
(in thousands)

	Euros	*Exchange rates*	*US dollars*
Revenues	€2,200	1.16	$2,552
Operating expenses (including depreciation of €100)	1,700	1.16	1,972
Profit for the year	500	1.16	580
Add: Retained earnings 1/1/20XX	200	–	205
Less: Dividends	(400)	1.10	(440)
Retained earnings 12/31/20XX	**€300**		**$345**

German Company
Statement of Cash Flows Translation
For the Year Ended December 31, 20XX+1
(in thousands)

	Euros	*Exchange rates*	*US dollars*
Operating activities			
Profit for the year	€500	1.16	$580
Adjustments to reconcile net income to net cash provided by operating activities:			

Depreciation	100	1.16	116
Decrease in accounts receivable	200	1.16	232
Increase in accounts payable	200	1.16	232
Decrease in unearned rent	(100)	1.16	(116)
Net cash provided by operating activities	900		1,044
Investing activities			
Purchase of land	(500)	1.10	(550)
Net cash used in investing activities	(500)		(550)
Financing activities			
Mortgage payable	500	1.10	550
Dividends	(400)	1.10	(440)
Net cash provided by financing activities	100		110
Effect of exchange rate changes on cash	N/A		(124)
Increase in cash and equivalents	500		480
Cash at beginning of year	500		600
Cash at end of year	**€1,000**	1.08	**$1,080**

Using the same mode of analysis that was presented before, the total exchange differences (translation adjustment) attributable to 20XX+1 would be computed as follows:

Net assets at January 1, 20XX	€2,200 (1.08 − 1.20)	=	$264 credit
Net income for 20XX	€500 (1.08 − 1.16)	=	40 credit
Dividends for 20XX	€400 (1.08 − 1.10)	=	8 debit
Total			$296 credit

The balance in the exchange differences (translation adjustment) account at the end of 20XX would be $339 ($635 from 20XX-1 less $296 from 20XX). The balance in this account decreased during 20XX since the German entity was in a net asset position during the period and the spot exchange rate at the end of the period (closing rate) is lower than the exchange rate at the beginning of the period or the average for the period.

Use of the equity method by the US company in accounting for the subsidiary would result in the following journal entries based on the information presented above:

	20XX-1		*20XX*	
Original investment				
Investment in German subsidiary	1,800*		–	
Cash		1,800		–

* [$0.90 × common share of €400 plus additional paid-in capital of €1,600]

**[$1.10 × dividend of €100]*
***[$1.10 × dividend of €400]*

Note that the shareholders' equity of the US company should be the same whether or not the German subsidiary is consolidated. Since the subsidiary does not report the translation adjustments on its financial statements, care should be exercised so that it is not forgotten in application of the equity method.

6. If the US company disposes of its investment in the German subsidiary, the translation adjustments balance becomes part of the gain or loss that results from the transaction and must be eliminated. For example, assume that on January 2, 20XX+1, the US company sells its entire investment for €3,000. The exchange rate at this date is €1 = $1.08. The balance in the investment account at December 31, 20XX+1 is $2,484 as a result of the entries made previously.

	Investment in German subsidiary	
1/1/13	1,800	110
	315	
	635	
1/1/14	2,640	
	580	
		440
		296
12/31/14	2,484	

The following entries would be made to reflect the sale of the investment:

Cash (€3,000 × $1.08)	$3,240	
Investment in German subsidiary		$2,484
Gain from sale of subsidiary		756
Translation adjustments	339	
Gain from sale of subsidiary		339

If the US company had sold a portion of its investment in the German subsidiary, only a proportionate share of the translation adjustments balance (cumulative amount of exchange differences) would have become part of the gain or loss from the transaction. To illustrate, if 80% of the German subsidiary was sold for €2,500 on January 2, 20XX+2, the following journal entries would be made:

Cash (€2,500 × $1.08)	$2,700.00	
Investment in German subsidiary (0.8 × $2,484)		$1,987.20
Gain from sale of subsidiary		712.80
Cumulative exchange difference (translation adjustments) (0.8 × $339)	271.20	
Gain from sale of subsidiary		271.20

GUIDANCE APPLICABLE TO SPECIAL SITUATIONS

Non-controlling interests

When a foreign entity is consolidated, but it is not wholly owned by the reporting entity, there will be non-controlling interest reported in the consolidated statement of financial position. IAS 21 requires that the accumulated exchange differences resulting from translation and attributable to the non-controlling interest be allocated to and reported as non-controlling interest in net assets.

Goodwill and fair value adjustments

Any goodwill arising on the acquisition of a foreign entity and any fair value adjustments to the carrying amounts of assets and liabilities arising on the acquisition of that foreign operation should be treated as assets and liabilities of the foreign operation. Thus, they should be expressed in the functional currency of the foreign operation and translated at the closing rate in accordance with IAS 21.

Exchange differences arising from elimination of intragroup balances

While incorporating the financial statements of a foreign entity into those of the reporting entity, normal consolidation procedures such as elimination of intragroup balances and transactions are undertaken as required by IAS 28 and IFRS 3, 10, 11 and 12.

Different reporting dates

The financial statements of the parent and its subsidiaries used in the preparation of the consolidated financial statements shall have the same reporting date. When the end of the reporting period of the parent is different from that of a subsidiary, the subsidiary prepares, for consolidation purposes, additional financial information as of the same date as the financial statements of the parent to enable the parent to consolidate the financial information of the subsidiary, unless it is impracticable to do so.

If it is "impracticable" to do so, the parent shall consolidate the financial information of the subsidiary using the most recent financial statements of the subsidiary adjusted for the effects of significant transactions or events that occur between the date of those financial statements and the date of the consolidated financial statements. In any case, the difference between the date of the subsidiary's financial statements and that of the consolidated financial statements shall be no more than three months, and the length of the reporting periods and any difference between the dates of the financial statements shall be the same from period to period.

Disposal of a foreign operation

On the disposal of a foreign operation, the cumulative amount of the exchange differences relating to that foreign operation, recognised in other comprehensive income and accumulated in the separate component of equity, shall be reclassified from equity to profit or loss (as a reclassification adjustment) when the gain or loss on disposal is recognised

Disposal has been defined to include a sale, liquidation, repayment of share capital or abandonment of all or part of the entity. Normally, payment of dividends would not constitute a repayment of capital. However, in rare circumstances, it does; for instance, when an entity pays dividends out of capital instead of accumulated profits, as defined in the companies' acts of certain countries, such as the United Kingdom, this would constitute repayment of capital. In such circumstances, obviously, dividends paid would constitute a disposal for the purposes of this standard.

In addition to the disposal of an entity's entire interest in a foreign operation, the following partial disposals are accounted for as disposals:

1. When the partial disposal involves the loss of control of a subsidiary that includes a foreign operation, regardless of whether the entity retains a non-controlling interest in its former subsidiary after the partial disposal; and

2. When the retained interest after the partial disposal of an interest in a joint arrangement or a partial disposal of an interest in an associate that includes a foreign operation is a financial asset that includes a foreign operation.

On disposal of a subsidiary that includes a foreign operation:

1. The cumulative amount of the exchange differences relating to that foreign operation that have been attributed to the non-controlling interests shall be derecognised, but shall not be reclassified to profit or loss;
2. On partial disposal of such a subsidiary the entity shall reattribute the proportionate share of the cumulative amount of the exchange differences recognised in other comprehensive income to the non-controlling interests in that foreign operation. In any other partial disposal of a foreign operation the entity shall reclassify to profit or loss only the proportionate share of the cumulative amount of the exchange differences recognised in other comprehensive income.

Change in functional currency

If there is a change in the functional currency, an entity should apply the translation procedures applicable to the new functional currency prospectively from the date of this change.

Reporting a Foreign Operation's Inventory

Under IAS 21, only a single method can be used for translating functional currency financial statements into the presentation currency. Specifically, the reporting entity is required to translate the assets and liabilities of its foreign operations and foreign entities at the closing (end of the reporting period) rate, and required to translate income and expenses at the exchange rates at the dates of the transactions (or at the average rate for the period, if this offers a reasonable approximation of actual transaction date rates).

As noted previously, sometimes an adjustment may be required to reduce the carrying amount of an asset in the financial statements of the reporting entity even though such an adjustment was not necessary in the separate, foreign currency-based financial statements of the foreign operation. This stipulation of IAS 21 can best be illustrated by the following case study.

Example

Inventory of merchandise owned by a foreign operation of the reporting entity is being carried by the foreign operation at 3,750,000 SR (Saudi riyals) in its statement of financial position. Suppose that the indirect exchange rate fluctuated from 3.75 SR = 1 US dollar at September 15, 20XX, when the merchandise was bought, to 4.25 SR = 1 US dollar at December 31, 20XX (i.e., the end of the reporting period). The translation of this item into the functional currency will necessitate an adjustment to reduce the carrying amount of the inventory to its NRV if this value when translated into the functional currency is lower than the carrying amount translated at the rate prevailing on the date of purchase of the merchandise.

Although the NRV, which in terms of Saudi riyals is 4,000,000 (SR), is higher than the carrying amount in Saudi riyals (i.e., 3,750,000 SR) when translated into the functional currency (i.e., US dollars) at the end of the reporting period, the NRV is lower than the carrying amount (translated into the functional currency at the exchange rate prevailing on the date of acquisition of the merchandise). Thus, on the financial statements of the foreign operation the inventory would not have to be adjusted. However, when the NRV is translated at the closing rate (which is 4.25 SR = 1 US dollar) into the functional currency, it will require the following adjustment:

1. Carrying amount translated at the exchange rate on September 15, 20XX (i.e., the date of acquisition) = SR 3,750,000 ÷ 3.75 = $1,000,000.
2. NRV translated at the closing rate = SR 4,000,000 ÷ 4.25 = $941,176.
3. Adjustment needed = $1,000,000 − $941,176 = $58,824.

Conversely, IAS 21 further stipulates that an adjustment that already exists on the financial statements of the foreign operation may need to be reversed in the financial statements of the reporting entity. To illustrate this point, the facts of the example above are repeated, with some variation, below.

Example

All other factual details remaining the same as the preceding example, it is now assumed that the inventory, which is carried on the books of the foreign operation at SR 3,750,000, instead has an NRV of SR 3,250,000 at year-end. Also assume that the indirect exchange rate fluctuated from 3.75 SR = 1 US dollar at the date of acquisition of the merchandise to 3.00 SR = 1 US dollar at the end of the reporting period.

Since in terms of Saudi riyals, the NRV at the end of the reporting period was lower than the carrying value of the inventory, an adjustment must have been made in the statement of financial position of the foreign operation (in Saudi riyals) to reduce the carrying amount to the lower of cost or NRV. In other words, a contra asset account (i.e., a lower of cost or NRV) representing the difference between the carrying amount (SR 3,750,000) and the NRV (SR 3,250,000) must have been created on the books of the foreign operation.

On translating the financial statements of the foreign operation into the functional currency, however, it is noted that due to the fluctuation of the exchange rates the NRV when converted to the functional currency (SR 3,250,000 ÷ 3.00 = $1,083,333) is no longer lower than the translated carrying value which is to be converted at the exchange rate prevailing on the date of acquisition of the merchandise (SR 3,750,000 ÷ 3.75 = $1,000,000).

Thus, a reversal of the adjustment (for lower of cost or NRV) is required on the financial statements of the reporting entity, upon translation of the financial statements of the foreign operation.

Translation of Foreign Currency Transactions in Further Detail

According to IAS 21, a foreign currency transaction is a transaction that is "denominated in or requires settlement in a foreign currency." Denominated means that the amount to be received or paid is fixed in terms of the number of units of a particular foreign currency, regardless of changes in the exchange rate.

Example

From the viewpoint of a US company, for instance, a foreign currency transaction results when it imports or exports goods or services to a foreign entity or makes a loan involving a foreign entity and agrees to settle the transaction in currency other than the US dollar (the presentation currency of the US company). In these situations, the US company has "crossed currencies" and directly assumes the risk of fluctuating exchange rates of the foreign currency in which the transaction is denominated. This risk may lead to recognition of foreign exchange differences in the profit or loss of the US company. Note that exchange differences can result only when the foreign currency transactions are denominated in a foreign currency.

When a US company imports or exports goods or services and the transaction is to be settled in US dollars, the US company will incur neither gain nor loss because it bears no risk due to exchange rate fluctuations. The following example illustrates the terminology and procedures applicable to the translation of foreign currency transactions.

Assume that a US company, an exporter, sells merchandise to a customer in Germany on December 1, 20XX, for €10,000. Receipt is due on January 31, 20XX+1, and the US company prepares financial statements on December 31, 20XX. At the transaction date (December 1, 20XX), the spot rate for immediate exchange of foreign currencies indicates that €1 is equivalent to $1.18.

To find the US dollar equivalent of this transaction, the foreign currency amount, €10,000, is multiplied by $1.18 to get $11,800. At December 1, 20XX, the foreign currency transaction should be recorded by the US company in the following manner:

Accounts receivable—Germany	$11,800	
Sales		$11,800

The accounts receivable and sales are measured in US dollars at the transaction date using the spot rate at the time of the transaction. While the accounts receivable is measured and reported in US dollars, the receivable is denominated or fixed in euros.

Foreign exchange gains or losses may occur if the spot rate for euros changes between the transaction date and the date of settlement (January 31, 20XX+1). If financial statements are prepared between the transaction date and the settlement date, all receivables and payables that are denominated in a currency different than that in which payment will ultimately be received or paid (the euro) must be restated to reflect the spot rates in existence at the end of the reporting period.

Assume that on December 31, 20XX, the spot rate for euros is €1 = $1.20. This means that the €10,000 is now worth $12,000 and that the accounts receivable denominated in euros should be increased by $200. The following journal entry would be recorded as of December 31, 20XX:

Accounts receivable—Germany	$200	
Foreign currency exchange difference		$200

Note that the sales account, which was credited on the transaction date for $11,800, is not affected by changes in the spot rate. This treatment exemplifies what may be called a two-transaction viewpoint. In other words, making the sale is the result of an operating decision, while bearing the risk of fluctuating spot rates is the result of a financing decision. Therefore, the amount determined as sales revenue at the transaction date should not be altered because of a financing decision to wait until January 31, 20XX+1, for payment of the account.

The risk of a foreign exchange transaction loss can be avoided either by demanding immediate payment on December 1 or by entering into a forward exchange contract to hedge the exposed asset (accounts receivable). The fact that the US company in the example did not act in either of these two ways is reflected by requiring the recognition of foreign currency exchange differences (transaction gains or losses) in its profit or loss (reported as financial or non-operating items) in the period during which the exchange rates changed.

On the settlement date (January 31, 20XX+1), assume that the spot rate is €1 = $1.17. The receipt of €10,000 and their conversion into US dollars would be journalised in the following manner:

Foreign currency	$11,700	
Foreign currency transaction loss	300	
Accounts receivable—Germany		$12,000

The net effect of this foreign currency transaction was to receive $11,700 from a sale that was measured originally at $11,800. This realised net foreign currency transaction loss of $100 is reported on two income statements: a $200 gain in 20XX and a $300 loss in 20XX+1. The reporting of the gain or loss in two income statements causes a temporary difference between pre-tax accounting and taxable income. This results because the transaction loss of $100 is not deductible until 20XX+1 as it concerns an unrealised transaction, the year the transaction was completed or settled. Accordingly, interperiod tax allocation is required for foreign currency transaction gains or losses.

DISCLOSURE

A number of disclosure requirements have been prescribed by IAS 21. Primarily, disclosure is required of the amounts of exchange differences included in profit or loss for the period, exchange differences that are included in the carrying amount of an asset and those that are recognised in other comprehensive income.

When there is a change in classification of a foreign operation, disclosure is required as to the nature of the change, reason for the change and the impact of the change on the current and each of the prior years presented. When the presentation currency is different from the currency of the country of domicile, the reason for this should be disclosed, and in case of any subsequent change in the presentation currency, the reason for making this change should also be disclosed. An entity should also disclose the method selected to translate goodwill and fair value adjustments arising on the acquisition of a foreign entity. Disclosure is encouraged of an entity's foreign currency risk management policy.

The following additional disclosures are required:

- When the functional currency is different from the currency of the country in which the entity is domiciled, the reason for using a different currency;
- The reason for any change in functional currency or presentation currency;
- When financial statements are presented in a currency other than the entity's functional currency, the reason for using a different presentation currency and a description of the method used in the translation process;
- When financial statements are presented in a currency other than the functional currency, an entity should state the fact that the functional currency reflects the economic substance of underlying events and circumstances;
- When financial statements are presented in a currency other than the functional currency, and the functional currency is the currency of a hyperinflationary economy, an entity should disclose the closing exchange rates between functional currency and presentation currency existing at the end of each reporting period presented;
- When additional information not required by IFRS is displayed in financial statements and in a currency other than presentation currency, as a matter of convenience to certain users, an entity should:
  - Clearly identify such information as supplementary information;
  - Disclose the functional currency used to prepare the financial statements and the method of translation used to determine the supplementary information displayed;

- Disclose the fact that the functional currency reflects the economic substance of the underlying events and circumstances of the entity and the supplementary information is displayed in another currency for convenience purposes only; and
- Disclose the currency in which supplementary information is displayed.

HEDGING

Hedging a Net Investment in a Foreign Operation or Foreign Currency Transaction

Hedges of a net investment in a foreign operation

While IAS 21 did not address hedge accounting for foreign currency items other than classification of exchange differences arising on a foreign currency liability accounted for as a hedge of a net investment in a foreign entity, IFRS 9 has established accounting requirements which largely parallel those for cash flow hedges. (Cash flow hedging is discussed in Chapter 24.) Specifically, IFRS 9 states that the portion of the gain or loss on the hedging instrument that is determined to be an effective hedge is to be recognised in other comprehensive income, whereas the ineffective portion of the hedge is to be either recognised immediately in results of operations if the hedging instrument is a derivative instrument, or else reported in other comprehensive income if the instrument is not a derivative.

The gain or loss associated with an effective hedge is reported in other comprehensive income, similar to foreign currency translation gain or loss. In fact, if the hedge is fully effective (which is rarely achieved in practice, however) the hedging gain or loss will be equal in amount and opposite in sign to the translation loss or gain.

In the examples set forth earlier in this chapter, which illustrated the accounting for a foreign (German) operation of a US company, the cumulative translation gain as of year-end 20XX was reported as $635,000. If the US entity had been able to enter into a hedging transaction that was perfectly effective (which would most likely have involved a series of currency forward contracts), the net loss position on the hedging instrument as of that date would have been $635,000. If this were reported in other comprehensive income and accumulated in shareholders' equity, as required under IFRS 9 and IAS 1, it would have served to exactly offset the cumulative translation gain at that point in time.

It should be noted that under the translation methodology prescribed by IAS 21 the ability to precisely hedge the net (accounting) investment in the German subsidiary would have been very remote, since the cumulative translation gain or loss is determined by both the changes in exchange rates since the common share issuances of the subsidiary (which occurred at discrete points in time and thus could conceivably have been hedged), as well as the changes in the various periodic increments or decrements to retained earnings (which having occurred throughout the years of past operations, would involve a complex array of exchange rates, making hedging very difficult to achieve). As a practical matter, hedging the net investment in a foreign subsidiary would serve a very limited economic purpose at best. Such hedging is more often done to avoid the potentially embarrassing impact of changing exchange rates on the reported financial position and financial results of the parent company, which may be important to management, but rarely connotes real economic performance over a longer time horizon.

Notwithstanding the foregoing comments, it is possible for a foreign currency transaction to act as an economic hedge against a parent's net investment in a foreign entity if:

1. The transaction is designated as a hedge.
2. It is effective as a hedge.

Example

To illustrate, assume that a US parent has a wholly owned British subsidiary which has net assets of £2 million. The US parent can borrow £2 million to hedge its net investment in the British subsidiary. Assume further that the British pound is the functional currency and that the £2 million liability is denominated in pounds. Fluctuations in the exchange rate for pounds will have no net effect on the parent company's consolidated statement of financial position because increases (decreases) in the translation adjustments balance due to the translation of the net investment will be offset by decreases (increases) in this balance due to the adjustment of the liability denominated in pounds.

In 2008, the IFRS Interpretations Committee issued IFRIC Interpretation 16, *Hedges of a Net Investment in a Foreign Operation*, which came into effect for annual periods beginning on or after October 1, 2008, with earlier application permitted.

IFRIC 16 clarifies that an entity can hedge (the hedge item) up to 100% of the carrying amount of the net assets (net investment) of the foreign operation in the consolidated financial statements of the parent. In addition, as with other hedge relationships, an exposure to foreign currency risk cannot be hedged twice. This means that if the same foreign currency risk is nominally hedged by more than one parent entity within the group (a direct and an indirect parent entity), only one hedge relationship can qualify for hedge accounting.

IFRS 9 does not require that the operating unit that is exposed to the risk being hedged holds the hedging instrument. IFRIC 16 clarifies that this requirement also applies to the hedge of the net investment in a foreign operation. The functional currency of the entity holding the instrument is irrelevant in determining effectiveness, and any entity within the group, regardless of its functional currency, can hold the hedging instrument.

Hedges of foreign currency transactions

It may be more important for managers to hedge specific foreign currency-denominated transactions, such as merchandise sales or purchases which involve exposure for the time horizon over which the foreign currency-denominated receivable or payable remains outstanding. For example, consider the illustration set forth earlier in this chapter which discussed the sale of merchandise by a US entity to a German customer, denominated in euros, with the receivable being due sometime after the sale. During the period the receivable remains pending, the creditor is at risk for currency exchange rate changes that might occur, leading to exchange rate gains or losses, depending on the direction the rates move. The following discussion sets forth the possible approach that could have been taken (and the accounting therefor) to reduce or eliminate this risk.

Example

In the example, the US company could have entered into a forward exchange contract on December 1, 20XX, to sell €10,000 for a negotiated amount to a foreign exchange broker for future delivery on January 31, 20XX+1. Such a forward contract would be a hedge against the exposed asset position created by having an account receivable denominated in euros. The negotiated rate referred to above is called a futures or forward rate. This instrument would qualify as a derivative under IFRS 9.

In most cases, this futures rate is not identical to the spot rate at the date of the forward contract. The difference between the futures rate and the spot rate at the date of the forward contract is referred to as a discount or premium. Any discount or premium must be amortised over the term of the forward contract, generally on a straight-line basis. The amortisation of discount or premium is reflected in a separate revenue or expense account, not as an addition or subtraction to the foreign currency transaction gain or loss amount. It is important to observe that under this treatment, no net foreign currency transaction gains or losses result if assets and liabilities denominated in foreign currency are completely hedged at the transaction date.

Example

To illustrate a hedge of an exposed asset, consider the following additional information for the German transaction.

On December 1, 20XX, the US company entered into a forward exchange contract to sell €10,000 on January 31, 20XX+1, at $1.14 per euro. The spot rate on December 1 is $1.12 per euro. The journal entries that reflect the sale of goods and the forward exchange contract appear as follows:

Sale transaction entries			*Forward exchange contract entries (futures rate €1 = $1.14)*		
12/1/20xx (spot rate €1 = $1.12)			Due from exchange broker ($)	11,400	
Accounts receivable	11,200		Due to exchange broker (€)		11,200
(€)—Germany					
Sales		11,200	Premium on forward contract		200
12/31/20xx (spot rate €1 = $1.15)			Foreign currency transaction loss	300	
Accounts receivable (€)—Germany	300		Due to exchange broker (€)		300
Foreign currency transaction gain		300	Premium on forward contract	100	
			Financial revenue ($100 = $200/2months)		100

1/31/20xx+1 (spot rate €1 = $1.17)					
Foreign currency	11,700		Due to exchange broker	11,500	
Accounts reccivable (€)—Germany		11,500	Foreign currency transaction loss	200	
			Foreign currency		11,700
Foreign currency transaction gain		200			
			Cash	11,400	
			Due from exchange broker		11,400
			Premium on forward contract	100	
			Financial revenue		100

The following points should be noted from the entries above:

1. The net foreign currency transaction gain or loss is zero. The account "Due from exchange broker" is fixed in terms of US dollars, and this amount is not affected by changes in spot rates between the transaction and settlement dates. The account "Due to exchange broker" is fixed or denominated in euros. The US company owes the exchange broker €10,000, and these must be delivered on January 31, 20XX+1. Because this liability is denominated in euros, its amount is determined by spot rates. Since spot rates change, this liability changes in amount equal to the changes in accounts receivable because both of the amounts are based on the same spot rates. These changes are reflected as foreign currency transaction gains and losses that net out to zero.
2. The premium on forward contract is fixed in terms of US dollars. This amount is amortised to a financial revenue account over the life of the forward contract on a straight-line basis.
3. The net effect of this transaction is that $11,400 was received on January 31, 20XX+1, for a sale originally recorded at $11,200. The $200 difference was taken into income via amortisation.

Currency of Monetary Items Comprising Net Investment in Foreign Operations

Monetary items (whether receivable or payable) between any subsidiary of the group and a foreign operation may form part of the group's investment in that foreign operation. Thus, these monetary items can be denominated in a currency other than the functional currency of either the parent or the foreign operation itself, for exchange differences on these monetary items to be recognised in other comprehensive income and accumulated in a separate component of equity until the disposal of the foreign operation.

Example

Assume the following group structure: Parent, a French company, Eiffel SARL (Group Eiffel), has a functional currency of the euro. Parent company has a 100% direct interest in a US investment company, Freedom, Inc., which has a functional currency of the US dollar. Freedom, in turn, owns a British subsidiary, Royal Ltd. (100% ownership), which has a functional currency of the pound sterling. Freedom lends $100,000 to Royal. The question is whether the loan can be accounted for as part of Group Eiffel's net investment in Royal with any exchange differences recognised in other comprehensive income.

Under provisions of the 2003 version of IAS 21, the $100,000 loan between Freedom and Royal could not be accounted for as part of Group Eiffel's net investment, since the loan was made in a third currency, and not in the functional currency of the parent (the euro) or of the foreign subsidiary (£). As a result, any exchange differences on this loan would be reported in the consolidated profit or loss statement of Group Eiffel.

The results obtained under the 2003 version of IAS 21 struck many as not being entirely logical, and these concerns were dealt with in the 2005 amendment. This allows that exchange differences on loans, such as in the foregoing example, can be recognised in other comprehensive income and in equity in the consolidated statement of financial position of reporting entities such as Group Eiffel. This change in accounting requirements allows many more funding structures to be accounted for as net investments in foreign operations. Thus, the accounting will no longer be dependent upon which of the group's entities conducts a transaction with the foreign operation, nor will it be dependent upon the currency of the monetary items.

EXAMPLES OF FINANCIAL STATEMENT DISCLOSURES

Exemplum Reporting PLC
Financial Statements
For the Year Ended December 31, 20XX

Accounting policy: Foreign currencies
Foreign currency transactions

Transactions in foreign currencies are translated to the respective functional currencies of the entities within the group. Monetary items denominated in foreign currencies are retranslated at the exchange rates applying at the reporting date. Non-monetary items carried at fair value that are denominated in foreign currencies are retranslated at the rates prevailing at the date when the fair value was determined. Non-monetary items that are measured in terms of historical cost in a foreign currency are not retranslated. Exchange differences are recognised in profit or loss in the period in which they arise except for:

- Exchange differences on foreign currency borrowings which are regarded as adjustments to interest costs, where those interest costs qualify for capitalisation to assets under construction;
- Exchange differences on transactions entered into to hedge foreign currency risks (assuming all hedge accounting tests are met); and
- Exchange differences on loans to or form a foreign operation for which settlement is neither planned nor likely to occur and therefore forms part of the net investment in the foreign operation, which are recognised initially in other comprehensive income and reclassified from equity to profit or loss on disposal or partial disposal of the net investment.

Foreign operations

The functional currency of the parent company and the presentation currency of the consolidated financial statements is pounds sterling. The assets and liabilities of the group's foreign operations are translated to pounds sterling using exchange rates at period end. Income and expense items are translated at the average exchange rates for the period, unless exchange rates fluctuated significantly during that period, in which case the exchange rate on transaction date is used. Goodwill acquired in business combinations of a foreign operations are treated as assets and liabilities of that operation and translated at the closing rate.

Exchange differences are recognised in other comprehensive income and accumulated in a separate category of equity.

On the disposal of a foreign operation, the accumulated exchange differences of that operation, which are attributable to the group, are recognised in profit or loss.

US GAAP COMPARISON

There are very few differences between IFRS and US GAAP. The authors are not aware of any differences between IFRS and US GAAP in accounting for foreign currency other than (1) determining the functional currency, and (2) when the foreign subsidiary resides in a highly inflationary country.

- Under US GAAP, the financial statements of a foreign subsidiary, which resides in a highly inflationary economy, are remeasured as if the parent's reporting currency were its functional currency.
- Under US GAAP, a number of indicators must be considered in determining the entity's functional currency. Those indicators are not set up in a hierarchical structure as they are under IFRS.

24 FINANCIAL INSTRUMENTS

INTRODUCTION

Accounting for financial instruments is extremely complex and dealt with by three separate accounting standards as follows:

1. IFRS 9, *Financial Instruments* (replaced IAS 39, *Financial Instruments: Recognition and Measurement*, from January 1, 2018);
2. IFRS 7, *Financial Instruments: Disclosures*;
3. IAS 32, *Financial Instruments: Presentation*.

Introduction to IFRS 9

The International Accounting Standards Board in 2014 completed the final version of its overall response to the 2008 global financial crises leading to the issuance of IFRS 9, *Financial Instruments*, which replaced IAS 39, *Financial Instruments: Recognition and Measurement*, with effect from January 1, 2018.

Because IAS 39 was considered to be complex and difficult to understand, simplifying the requirements of IAS 39 was one of the main objectives of the IASB. IFRS 9 uses an increasingly principle-based model as compared to the rule-based model of IAS 39, thus reducing the complexity revolving around classification, recognition and reclassification of financial instruments. In terms of measurement, IFRS 9 includes a completely overhauled methodology for recognition of impairment losses.

IFRS 9 requires all financial assets to be measured at amortised cost or fair value, depending on their classification by reference to the business model within which they are held and their contractual cash flow characteristics. There is therefore significant importance given to the business model under IFRS 9. There is also equal importance given to the nature of underlying cash flows relating to financial instruments, which also plays a significant part in determining classification.

IFRS 9 retains all of the existing requirements of IAS 39 related to the subsequent measurement of financial liabilities except where the fair value through profit or loss option is adopted, under which gains and losses attributable to changes in own credit risk are recognised in other comprehensive income (rather than in profit or loss). This change will result in increases in own credit risk not resulting in gains recognised within profit or loss.

The incurred loss model under IAS 39 had been criticised for delaying the recognition of credit losses until there was evidence of a trigger event. IAS 39 also had multiple and complex impairment models that were difficult to understand, apply and interpret. The new expected credit loss model for the recognition and measurement of impairment aims to address concerns with upfront recognition of expected credit losses. However, the new approach requires considerable time and effort for the development of suitable historical and forward-looking financial models.

IFRS 9 has been significantly amended in relation to hedge accounting with an aim of having a better reflection in financial statements of how risk management activities are undertaken when hedging financial and non-financial risks. The new hedge accounting requirements are meant to more closely reflect the underlying business model and objectives and thus result in improved accounting for hedging arrangements.

Significant Differences Between IFRS 9 and IAS 39

1. *Scope*: IAS 39 excluded from its scope contracts to buy or sell non-financial items in the entity's expected purchase, sale or usage requirements. IFRS 9 allows an entity to irrevocably designate such contracts as measured at fair value through profit or loss (FVTPL).
2. *Classification of assets*: IFRS 9 has only three classifications for financial assets, being FVTPL, fair value through other comprehensive income (FVTOCI) and amortised cost. Under IAS 39, in addition to FVTPL, there were separate classifications, being loans and receivables, held to maturity and available for sale. There are differing requirements on how the classifications are selected under IFRS 9, including reclassification of items between other comprehensive income and profit or loss depending on whether the instrument is equity or debt in nature. This is covered in more detail under classification later in the chapter.
3. *Impairment*: IFRS 9 includes an expected credit loss model in determining impairment provisions. In addition, IFRS 9 includes requirements for the measurement of expected credit losses on written loan commitments and financial guarantee commitments. IAS 39 was based largely on an incurred credit loss model and did not scope in loan commitments and financial guarantee contracts.

4. *Hedge accounting*: IFRS 9 more closely aligns hedge accounting with the business risk management model. It also has fewer restrictions as compared to IAS 39 in respect of hedging non-financial items, hedging portfolios or groups of items and hedging net positions.

Financial institutions have been significantly impacted by IFRS 9 and particularly in respect of recognition and measurement of credit losses. The insurance industry has also been impacted by the adoption of IFRS 9 for both its financial instruments and insurance contracts where insurance companies have not elected to defer the adoption of IFRS 9. IASB issued IFRS 17, *Insurance Contracts*, on May 18, 2017, which will replace IFRS 4. Under the provisions of IFSR 17, insurance companies that meet certain criterea have the option to defer the implementation of IFRS 9 until the date they adopt IFRS 17.

Non-financial institutions have also been impacted by IFRS 9, the extent of which has been based on the complexity of their business, the extent of use of complex financial instruments and the profile of their receivables book.

Objective

IFRS 9, IFRS 7 and IAS 32 establish principles for the financial reporting of financial assets and financial liabilities that will present relevant and useful information to users of financial statements for their assessment of the amounts, timing and uncertainty of an entity's future cash flows.

Scope

The financial instrument standards apply to all financial instruments with specific scope exclusions as detailed below:

IFRS 9/IFRS 7 AND IAS 32

Scope exclusions	Exceptions (i.e., considered within scope)	Alternate standards
Interests in subsidiaries, associates and joint ventures unless required by the alternate standards.	IFRS 9 includes in its scope derivatives on an interest in a subsidiary, associate or joint venture unless the derivative meets the definition of an equity instrument.	IFRS, 10 *Consolidated Financial Statements* IAS 27, *Separate Financial Statements* IAS 28, *Investments in Associates and Joint Ventures*
Rights and obligations under leases.	Finance lease and operating lease receivables recognised by a lessor are subject to the impairment and derecognition criteria. Lease liabilities recognised by a lessee are subject to the derecognition criteria. Derivatives that are embedded in leases are subject to the embedded derivatives criteria.	IFRS 16, *Leases*
Rights and obligations under employee benefit plans.	N/A	IAS 19, *Employee Benefits*

Insurance contracts.	Financial guarantee contracts (such as guarantees, types of letters of credit, credit default contracts, insurance contracts, etc.), contracts with discretionary participation features and embedded derivatives are subject to the requirements of IFRS 9. The accounting for financial guarantee contracts is dependent on substance rather than legal form, and although such a contract will meet the definition of an insurance contract, it is accounted for in line with IFRS 9. However, if an issuer of financial guarantee contracts has previously asserted explicitly that it regards such contracts as insurance contracts and has used accounting that is applicable to insurance contracts the issuer may elect to apply either this standard or IFRS 4 to such financial guarantee contracts. The issuer may make that election contract by contract, but the election for each contract is irrevocable.	IFRS 4, *Insurance Contracts*
Forward contracts *(where the term of the forward contract does not reasonably exceed a period normally necessary to complete a transaction)* between an acquirer and a selling shareholder for a transaction that meets the definition of a business combination (as defined in IFRS 3).	N/A	IFRS 3, *Business Combinations*
Loan commitments other than those loan commitments that are designated at FVTPL, loan commitments that can be settled net by delivery of cash or another financial instrument (derivative instruments) and commitments to provide a loan at below market interest rate.	An issuer of loan commitments shall apply the impairment requirements of IFRS 9 to loan commitments that are not otherwise within the scope of this standard. All loan commitments are subject to the derecognition requirements of IFRS 9. Also see below loan commitments that are within the scope of IFRS 9.	–
Share-based payments.	Contracts to buy or sell a non-financial item that can be settled net in cash or another financial instrument, or by exchanging financial instruments, as if the contracts were financial instruments, fall under the scope of IFRS 9.	IFRS 2, *Share-based Payments*

Reimbursements of expenditure provisions.	N/A	IAS 37, *Provisions, Contingent Liabilities and Contingent Assets*
Financial instruments that represent rights and obligations within the scope of IFRS 15, *Revenue from Contracts with Customers*, except those which IFRS 15 specifies are accounted for in accordance with IFRS 9.	The impairment requirements of IFRS 9 shall be applied to those rights that IFRS 15 specifies are accounted for in accordance with IFRS 9 for the purposes of recognising impairment gains or losses.	IFRS 15, *Revenue from Contracts with Customers*

The following loan commitments are specifically within the scope of IFRS 9:

1. Loan commitments that are designated as financial liabilities at FVTPL. An entity that has a past practice of selling the assets resulting from its loan commitments shortly after origination is required to apply IFRS 9 to all its loan commitments in the same class.
2. Loan commitments that can be settled net in cash or by delivering or issuing another financial instrument. These loan commitments are derivatives. A loan commitment is not regarded as settled net merely because the loan is paid out in instalments (for example, a mortgage construction loan that is paid out in instalments in line with the progress of construction).
3. Loan commitments to provide a loan at a below-market interest rate.

DEFINITIONS OF TERMS

12 months expected credit loss. This is a portion of the *lifetime expected credit loss* that represents the *expected credit losses* that result from default events on a financial instrument that are possible within 12 months after the reporting date.

Accounts receivable. Amounts due from customers for goods or services which have been provided in the normal course of business operations.

Amortised cost of financial asset or financial liability. The amount at which the financial asset or liability is measured upon initial recognition, minus principal repayments, plus or minus the cumulative amortisation using the *effective interest method* of any difference between that initial amount and the maturity amount, and, for financial assets, adjusted for any *loss allowance*.

Cash. Refers to cash on hand and demand deposits with banks or other financial institutions.

Cash equivalents. Short-term, highly liquid investments that are readily convertible to known amounts of cash which are subject to an insignificant risk of changes in value.

Cash shortfall. The difference between the cash flow due to an entity in line with the contract and the cash flow that the entity expects to receive.

Compound instrument. An issued single financial instrument that contains both liability and equity (e.g., a convertible loan). Under IAS 32 principles, such instruments are split accounted.

Contract assets. Those rights that IFRS 15, *Revenue from Contracts with Customers*, specifies are accounted for in accordance with this standard for the purpose of recognition and measuring impairment gains or losses.

Control. The ability to direct the strategic and financial and operating policies of an entity to obtain benefits from its activities.

Credit adjusted effective interest rate. The rate that exactly discounts the estimated future cash payments or receipts through the expected life of the financial asset to the amortised cost of a financial asset that is a purchased or originated credit-impaired financial asset. When calculating the credit-adjusted effective interest rate, an entity shall estimate the expected cash flows by considering all contractual terms of the financial asset (e.g., prepayments, extension, call and similar options) and expected credit losses. The calculation includes all fees and points paid or received between parties to the contract that are an integral part of the effective interest rate, transaction costs and all other premiums and discounts.

Credit-impaired financial asset. A financial asset is credit impaired at initial recognition when one or more events that have a detrimental impact on the estimated future cash flows of that financial asset have occurred. Evidence that a financial asset is credit impaired include observable data about the following events:

1. Significant financial difficulty of the issuer or the borrower;
2. A breach of contract, e.g., default or past-due event;
3. A lender having granted a concession to the borrower for economic or contractual reasons relating to the borrower's financial difficulty that the lender would not otherwise consider;
4. The probability that the borrower will enter bankruptcy or other financial reorganisation;
5. The disappearance of an active market for the financial asset because of financial difficulties;
6. The purchase of origination of a financial asset at a deep discount that reflects the incurred credit losses; or
7. The impossibility of identifying a single discrete event. Instead, the combined effect of several events may have caused financial assets to become credit impaired.

Credit loss. The difference between all contractual cash flows that are due to an entity in line with the contract and all the cash flows an entity expects to receive (i.e., the present value of all cash shortfalls, discounted at the original *effective interest rate* or *credit-adjusted effective interest rate* for *purchased or originated credit-impaired financial assets*).

Credit risk. The risk that a loss may occur from the failure of one party to a financial instrument to discharge an obligation according to the terms of a contract.

Derecognition. The removal of a previously recognised financial asset or liability from an entity's statement of financial position.

Derivative. A financial instrument or other contract with *all* three of the following features:

1. Its value changes in response to changes in a specified interest rate, security price, commodity price, foreign exchange rate, index of prices or rates, a credit rating or credit index, or other variable, provided in the case of a non-financial variable that the variable is not specific to a party to the contract (sometimes called the "underlying").
2. It requires little or no initial net investment relative to the other types of contracts that have a similar response to changes in market conditions.
3. It is settled at a future date.

Dividends. Profit distribution to holders of equity instruments in proportion to their holdings of a particular class of capital.

Effective interest method. The method that is used in the calculation of the amortised cost of a financial asset or a financial liability and in the allocation and recognition of the interest revenue or interest expense in profit or loss over the relevant period.

Effective interest rate. The rate that exactly discounts estimated future cash flows to the net carrying amount of the financial instrument through the expected life of the instrument (or a shorter period, when appropriate). In calculating the effective rate, the entity should estimate future cash flows after considering all of the contractual terms of the financial instrument but without considering future expected credit losses. Fees, points paid or received between parties to the contract, transaction costs and other premiums and discounts are also included.

Embedded derivative. A component of a hybrid (combined) financial instrument, which also includes a non-derivative host contract, with the effect that some of the cash flows of the combined instrument vary in a way similar to a stand-alone derivative.

Equity instrument. Any contract that evidences a residual interest in the assets of an entity after deducting all its liabilities.

Expected credit losses. The weighted-average of credit losses with the respective risks of a default occurring as the weights.

Fair value. The amount for which an asset could be exchanged, or a liability settled, between knowledgeable and willing parties in an arm's-length transaction.

Financial asset. Any asset that is one of the following:

1. Cash;
2. An equity instrument of another entity;
3. A contractual right:
   a. To receive cash or another financial asset from another entity; or
   b. To exchange financial instruments with another entity under conditions that are potentially favourable.
4. A contract that will be settled in the reporting entity's own equity instruments and is:
   a. A non-derivative for which the entity is, or may be, obligated to receive a variable number of its own equity instruments; or
   b. A derivative that will, or may, be settled other than by the exchange of a fixed amount of cash or another financial asset for a fixed number of the entity's own equity instruments (which excludes puttable financial instruments classified as equity and instruments that are themselves contracts for the future receipt or delivery of the entity's equity instruments).

Financial guarantee contract. A contract that requires the issuer to make specified payments to reimburse the holder for a loss it incurs because a specified debtor fails to make payment when due in accordance with the original or modified terms of a debt instrument.

Financial instrument. Any contract which gives rise to both a financial asset of one entity and a financial liability or equity instrument of another entity.

Financial liability. Any liability which meets either of the following criteria:

1. A contractual obligation:
   a. To deliver cash or another financial asset to another entity; or
   b. To exchange financial instruments with another entity under conditions which are potentially unfavourable to the entity.
2. A contract that will, or may, be settled in the entity's own equity instruments and is:
   a. A non-derivative for which the entity is, or may, be obligated to deliver a variable number of its own equity instruments; or
   b. A derivative that will, or may, be settled other than by the exchange of a fixed amount of cash or another financial asset for a fixed number of the entity's own equity instruments (which excludes puttable financial instruments classified as equity and instruments that are themselves contracts for the future receipt or delivery of the entity's equity instruments).

Financial liability at fair value through profit or loss. A financial liability that meets one of the following conditions:

1. The definition of held for trading;
2. Upon initial recognition, it is designated at fair value through profit or loss;
3. It is a credit derivative that is designated either upon initial recognition or subsequently as at fair value through profit or loss.

Firm commitment. A binding agreement for the exchange of a specified quantity of resource at a specified price on a specified future date or dates.

Forecast transaction. An uncommitted but anticipated future transaction.

Gross carrying amount of a financial asset. The amortised cost of a financial asset, before adjusting for any loss allowance.

Hedge effectiveness. The degree to which changes in the fair value or cash flows of the hedged item that are attributable to a hedged risk are offset by changes in the fair value or cash flows of the hedging instrument.

Hedge ratio. Relationship between the quantity of the hedging instrument and the quantity of the hedged item in terms of their relative weighting.

Hedged item. An asset, liability, firm commitment, highly probable forecast transaction or net investment in a foreign operation that (1) exposes the entity to risk of changes in fair value or future cash flows, and (2) is designated as being hedged.

Hedging. Involves designating one or more hedging instruments such that the change in fair value or cash flows of the hedging instrument is offset, in whole or part, to the change in fair value or cash flows of the hedged item. The objective is to ensure that the gain or loss on the hedging instrument is recognised in profit or loss in the same period that the hedged item affects profit or loss.

Hedging instrument. For hedge accounting purposes, a designated derivative or (for a hedge of the risk of changes in foreign currency exchange rates only) a designated non-derivative financial asset or non-derivative financial liability whose fair value or cash flows are expected to offset changes in the fair value or cash flows of a designated hedged item.

Held for trading. Financial asset or financial liability that:

1. Is acquired or incurred principally for the purpose of selling or repurchasing it in the near term;

2. Upon initial recognition is part of a portfolio of identified financial instruments that are managed together and for which there is evidence of a recent actual pattern of short-term profit-taking; or
3. Is a derivative (except for a derivative that is a financial guarantee contract or a designated and effective hedging instrument).

Impairment gain or loss. Gains or losses that are recognised in profit or loss arising from applying the impairment requirements of IFRS 9.

Lifetime expected credit loss. The expected credit losses that result from all possible default events over the expected life of a financial instrument.

Liquidity risk. The risk that an entity may encounter difficulty in meeting obligations associated with financial liabilities.

Loss allowance. The allowance for expected credit losses on financial assets, lease receivables and *contract* assets, the accumulated impairment amount for financial assets and the provision of expected credit losses on loan commitments and financial guarantee contracts.

Market risk. The risk that the fair value or future cash flows of a financial instrument will fluctuate because of changes in market prices. There are three types of market risk:

1. Currency risk;
2. Interest rate risk; and
3. Other price risk.

Market value. The amount obtainable from a sale, or payable on acquisition, of a financial instrument in an active market.

Marketable equity instruments. Instruments representing actual ownership interest, or the rights to buy or sell such interests that are actively traded or listed on a national securities exchange.

Modification gain or loss. The amount arising from adjusting the gross carrying amount of a financial asset to reflect the renegotiated or modified contractual cash flows. The entity recalculates the gross carrying amount of a financial asset as the present value of the estimated future cash payments or receipts through the expected life of the renegotiated or modified financial asset that are discounted at the financial asset's original effective interest rate (or the original credit-adjusted effective interest rate for purchased or originated credit-impaired financial assets) or when applicable. When estimating the expected cash flows of a financial asset, an entity shall consider all contractual terms of the financial asset (for example, prepayment, call and similar options) but shall not consider the expected credit losses, unless the financial asset is a purchased or originated credit-impaired financial asset, in which case an entity shall also consider the initial expected credit losses that were considered when calculating the original credit-adjusted effective interest rate.

Monetary financial assets and financial liabilities. Financial assets and financial liabilities to be received or paid in fixed or determinable amounts of currency.

Net realisable value. The estimated selling price in the ordinary course of business less the estimated costs of completion and the estimated costs necessary to make the sale.

Other price risk. The fair value or future cash flows of a financial instrument will fluctuate because of changes in market prices (other than those arising from interest rate risk or currency risk), whether those changes are caused by factors specific to the individual financial instrument or its issuer, or factors affecting all similar financial instruments traded in the market.

Past due. A financial asset is past due when a counterparty has failed to make a payment when that payment was contractually due.

Percentage-of-sales method. Procedure for computing the adjustment for uncollectible accounts receivable based on the historical relationship between bad debts and gross credit sales.

Pledging. Process of using an asset as collateral for borrowings. It generally refers to borrowings secured by accounts receivable.

Purchased or originated credit-impaired financial asset. Purchased or originated financial assets that are credit impaired on initial recognition.

Puttable instrument. A financial instrument that gives the holder the right to put the instrument back to the issuer for cash or another financial asset. It can also be automatically put back to the issuer on the occurrence of an uncertain future event or the death or retirement of the instrument holder.

Realised gain (loss). Difference between the cost or adjusted cost of a marketable security and the net selling price realised by the seller, which is to be included in the determination of profit or loss in the period of the sale.

Reclassification date. First day of the first reporting period following the change in business model that results in an entity reclassifying financial assets.

Recourse. Right of the transferee (factor) of accounts receivable to seek recovery for an uncollectible account from the transferor. It is often limited to specific conditions.

Regular-way purchase or sale. A purchase or sale of a financial asset under a contract whose terms require delivery of the asset within the timeframe established generally by regulations or convention in the marketplace concerned.

Repurchase agreement. An agreement to transfer a financial asset to another party in exchange for cash or other considerations, with a concurrent obligation to reacquire the asset at a future date.

Securitisation. The process whereby financial assets are transformed into securities.

Short-term investments. Financial instruments or other assets acquired with excess cash, having ready marketability and intended by management to be liquidated, if necessary, within the current operating cycle.

Trade date. The date at which the entity commits itself to purchase or sell an asset. The trade date refers to:

1. The recognition of an asset to be received and the liability to pay for it on the trade date; and
2. The derecognition of an asset that is sold, recognition of any gain or loss on disposal and the recognition of a receivable from the buyer for payment on the trade date.

Transaction costs. The incremental costs directly attributable to the acquisition or disposal of a financial asset or liability.

RECOGNITION, MEASUREMENT AND DERECOGNITION OF FINANCIAL INSTRUMENTS

Initial Recognition

A financial asset or a financial liability should be recognised in the statement of financial position when, and only when, an entity becomes party to the contractual provisions of the instrument.

An entity recognises all of its contractual rights and obligations under derivatives in its statement of financial position as assets and liabilities, respectively, except for derivatives that prevent a transfer of financial assets from being accounted for as a sale. For example:

1. Unconditional receivables and payables are recognised as assets or liabilities when an entity becomes a party to the contractual agreement and, as a consequence, has a legal right to receive or a legal obligation to pay cash.
2. Assets to be acquired and liabilities to be incurred as a result of a firm commitment to purchase or sell goods or services are generally not recognised until at least one of the parties has performed under the agreement.
3. A forward contract is recognised as an asset or a liability on the commitment date, instead of on the date on which settlement takes place.
4. Option contracts are recognised as assets or liabilities when the holder or writer becomes a party to the contract.
5. Planned future transactions, no matter how likely, are not assets or liabilities because the entity has not become a party to a contract.

If, for the transferor, a transfer of a financial asset does not qualify for derecognition, the transferee is also not able to recognise the transferred asset.

Initial Measurement

Financial instruments can arise from various transactions that can be broken down into two main sources:

1. Trade receivables that originate from revenue transactions that are recognised under the provisions of IFRS 15; and
2. All other financial instruments that are acquired or assumed.

Except for trade receivables, which do not contain a significant financing component, at initial recognition, an entity shall measure a financial asset or financial liability at its fair value plus or minus, in the case of a financial asset or financial liability not at FVTPL, transaction costs that are directly attributable to the acquisition or issue of the financial asset or financial liability.

The initial recognition of trade receivables that arise from transactions under the scope of IFRS 15 are determined by the recognition principles of IFRS 15 and are generally measured at the transaction price where the transaction does not include a significant financing component. In respect of all other financial assets or liabilities, IFRS 9 requires that these be measured at initial recognition at fair value.

Initial Measurement: Transaction Costs

Transaction costs should be included in the initial measurement of financial assets and financial liabilities other than those at FVTPL. For financial assets not measured at FVTPL, transaction costs are added to the fair value at initial recognition. For financial liabilities, transaction costs are deducted from the fair value at initial recognition.

For financial instruments that are measured at amortised cost, transaction costs are subsequently included in the calculation of amortised cost using the effective interest method and, in effect, amortised through profit or loss over the life of the instrument.

For financial instruments that are measured at FVTOCI (other than debt instruments), transaction costs are recognised in other comprehensive income as part of a change in fair value at the next remeasurement date. If the financial asset is measured at FVTOCI as a debt instrument, transaction costs are amortised to profit or loss using the effective interest method over the life of the instrument.

Transaction costs expected to be incurred on subsequent transfer or disposal of a financial instrument are not included in the measurement of the financial instrument.

Transaction costs on financial instruments measured at FVTPL are recognised in profit or loss.

Fair Value on Initial Recognition?

IFRS 9 refers to the definition of fair valuation as specified within IFRS 13, i.e., fair value is the price that would be received to sell an asset or paid to transfer a liability in an orderly transaction between market participants at the measurement date. As a result, measurement of fair value for IFRS 9 purposes is based on a market approach and not on the entity's specific value.

The fair value of a financial instrument at initial recognition is normally the transaction price particularly for financial instruments that are traded on the basis of fair values (i.e., the fair value of the consideration given or received). However, if part of the consideration given or received is for something other than the financial instrument, or where the transaction price is not at true fair value (e.g., transactions between related parties, transactions under duress, etc.), an entity is required to measure the fair value of the financial instrument using the fair valuation techniques and hierarchies as specified within IFRS 13.

For example, the fair value of a long-term loan or receivable that carries no interest can be measured as the present value of all future cash receipts discounted using the prevailing market rate(s) of interest for a similar instrument (similar as to currency, term, type of interest rate and other factors) with a similar credit rating. Any additional amount lent is an expense or a reduction of income unless it qualifies for recognition as some other type of asset.

If an entity originates a loan that bears an off-market interest rate (e.g., 5% when the market rate for similar loans is 8%), and receives an upfront fee as compensation, the entity recognises the loan at its fair value, i.e., net of the fee it receives. Assuming that the upfront fee received is exactly the same as the discounted value differential between the market and contractual rate, the fair value of the debt instrument should in theory equate the amount lent net of the upfront fee.

If an entity determines that the fair value at initial recognition differs from the transaction price, the entity shall account for that instrument at that date as follows:

1. If that fair value is evidenced by a quoted price in an active market for an identical asset or liability (i.e., a level 1 input) or based on a valuation technique that uses only data from observable markets (level 2 input). An entity shall recognise the difference between the fair value at initial recognition and the transaction price as a gain or loss recognised within profit or loss—also referred to as a day 1 profit or loss. However, in some cases, other IFRS may require this gain or loss to be recognised differently. For example, where a gain arises from an interest-free loan received by a subsidiary from a parent, they would ordinarily represent a capital contribution recognised directly within equity.
2. For all other sources of fair value (typically level 3 inputs), the difference between the fair value at initial recognition and the transaction price is deferred. After initial recognition, the entity shall recognise that deferred difference as a gain or loss only to the extent that it arises from a change in a factor (including time) that market

participants would consider when pricing the asset or liability. In this case, it would be expected that the difference would be recognised in profit or loss over the term of the instrument or the period to derecognition.

When an entity uses settlement date accounting for an asset that is subsequently measured at amortised cost, the asset is recognised initially at its fair value on the trade date.

Contracts to buy or sell a non-financial item

Contracts to buy or sell non-financial items are treated as financial instruments if it can be settled net in cash or another financial instrument or by exchanging financial instruments. For example:

1. When the terms of the contract permit either party to settle the transaction as above;
2. When the ability to settle is not explicit (in the terms of the contract) but the entity has a practice of settling similar contracts net in cash or another financial instrument or by exchanging financial instruments (whether with the counterparty, by entering into offsetting contracts or by selling the contract before its exercise or lapse);
3. When, for similar contracts, the entity has a practice of taking delivery of the underlying and selling it within a short period after delivery for the purpose of generating a profit from short-term fluctuations in price or dealer's margin; and
4. When the non-financial item that is the subject of the contract is readily convertible to cash.

However, IFRS 9 shall be applied to such contracts that an entity designates as measured at FVTPL. A contract to buy or sell a non-financial item that can be settled net in cash or another financial instrument, or by exchanging financial instruments, as if the contract was a financial instrument, may be irrevocably designated as measured at FVTPL even if it was entered into for the purpose of the receipt or delivery of a non-financial item in accordance with the entity's expected purchase, sale or usage requirements. This designation is available only at the inception of the contract and only if it eliminates or significantly reduces a recognition inconsistency/accounting mismatch that would otherwise arise from not recognising that contract.

IFRS 9 shall also be applied to a written option to buy or sell a non-financial item that can be settled net in cash or another financial instrument, or by exchanging financial instruments on the basis that such a contract cannot be entered into for the purpose of the receipt or delivery of the non-financial item in accordance with the entity's expected purchase, sale or usage requirements.

Financial Assets

Regular-way purchase or sale of financial assets

A regular-way purchase or sale is a transaction under a contract whose terms require delivery of the asset within the timeframe established generally by regulations or convention in the market place concerned and is recognised and derecognised using trade date accounting or settlement date accounting (which should be consistently applied to purchases and sales of financial assets that are classified in a similar way).

A contract that requires or permits net settlement of the change in the value of the contract is not a regular-way contract. Instead, such a contract is accounted for as a derivative in the period between the trade date and the settlement date.

When settlement date accounting is applied, an entity accounts for any change in the fair value of the asset to be received during the period between the trade date and the settlement date in the same way as it accounts for the acquired assets.

Classification of financial assets

Simplifying the requirements of IAS 39 was one of the objectives of the IASB when it embarked on the financial instruments project and it set out as one of its aims the requirement to reduce the number of categories of financial assets. As a result, IFRS 9 categorises financial assets into just two main categories: amortised cost and fair value (further broken down into FVTPL and FVTOCI). The "available-for-sale" and "held-to-maturity" categories included in IAS 39 do not form part of IFRS 9.

A financial asset shall be classified as subsequently measured at either FVTPL, FVTOCI or amortised cost. An entity can still make an irrevocable decision to designate a financial asset as measured through FVTPL if doing so eliminates or significantly reduces an accounting mismatch.

The classification of a financial asset is based on both the *business model for managing the financial asset* and the *contractual cash flow characteristics* of the financial asset and in summary is as follows:

Classification categories	**What does the category apply to**
FVTPL	This category applies to all financial assets that do not meet the criteria set below for the amortised cost and FVTOCI options, as well as instruments specifically elected to be measured under this category as covered below.
FVTOCI	This category applies to financial assets whose business model is a combination of holding to collect contractual cash flows as well as sell, and whose contractual cash flows are made solely of principal and interest. Note as detailed below that IFRS 9 permits equity instruments to also be categorised within this on election.
Amortised cost	This category applies to financial assets whose business model is to hold to collect contractual cash flows and whose contractual cash flows are made solely of principal and interest.

Classification of Financial Assets—Decision Tree

The business model

Business model refers to how an entity manages its financial assets to generate cash flows, i.e., from collecting contractual cash flows, selling or both and is determined by key management personnel.

A business model is normally determined at a level that reflects how groups of financial assets are managed together to achieve a particular business objective and not at individual instrument level. This level may be an aggregation of financial assets to a suitable degree, which reflects a common business model. For example, an entity may hold a portfolio of investments that it manages to collect contractual cash flows and another portfolio of investments that it manages to trade to realise fair value changes.

In certain circumstances, cash flows are realised in a way that is different from the business model assessed at the time of classification. Such a change does not give rise to a prior period error nor does it change the classification of the remaining financial assets held in that business model (i.e., those assets that the entity recognised in prior periods and still holds) as long as the entity considered all relevant information that was available at the time that it made the business model assessment. However, when an entity assesses the business model for newly originated or newly purchased financial assets, it must consider information about how cash flows were realised in the past, along with all other relevant information.

The assessment of a business model requires a level of judgement and is not determined by a single factor. IFRS 9 requires entities to consider all relevant evidence available at the date of assessment. Suggested evidence includes, but is not limited to:

1. How the performance of the business model and the financial assets held within that business model are evaluated and reported to the entity's key management personnel;
2. The risks that affect the performance of the business model (and the financial assets held within that business model) and, in particular, the way in which those risks are managed; and
3. How managers of the business are compensated (for example, whether the compensation is based on the fair value of the assets managed or on the contractual cash flows collected).

The assessment of a business model is based on scenarios that are reasonably expected to occur and not worst case or stress case scenarios. For example, an expectation to sell a portfolio of investments only during a stress case scenario does not affect the assessment of a business model for those investments.

Cash Flow Characteristics

Cash flow characteristics refers to how an entity collects future cash flows from its financial assets and whether these relate to payments of interest, principal or other gains.

Fair value through profit or loss (FVTPL)

Financial assets that are not held within a business model whose objective is to hold assets to collect contractual cash flows or within a business model whose objective is achieved by both collecting contractual cash flows and selling financial assets are subsequently measured at FVTPL.

Examples include business models whose objectives are to realise cash flows through the sale of financial assets. Contractual cash flows collected during the time an entity holds such a financial asset do not override the objectives of the business model and are not considered to be integral to achieving the objectives of the model.

However, even though an asset could be classified as amortised cost or FVTOCI, an irrevocable decision may be made at initial recognition to designate a financial asset as measured at FVTPL if doing so eliminates or significantly reduces a measurement or recognition inconsistency (accounting mismatch) that would otherwise arise from measuring assets or liabilities or recognising the gains and losses on them on different bases and therefore would provide more relevant information.

The above decision to designate a financial asset an FVTPL is like an accounting policy choice except that it does not require to be applied consistently across similar transactions.

Elimination or reduction of accounting mismatches (also applies to financial liabilities classified as FVTPL) An entity must demonstrate that the designation eliminates or significantly reduces an accounting mismatch. An example of a mismatch occurs when the classification of a financial asset and financial liability in a hedging relationship differs, i.e., one is classified at FVTPL while the other is at amortised cost.

Managing performance of financial instruments and evaluating its performance on a fair value basis The management and evaluation of the performance of a group of financial liabilities or financial assets may be such that measuring that group at FVTPL results in more relevant information—the key here being how the financial instruments are managed and evaluated and not the nature of the instrument.

Documentation of the entity's strategy need not be extensive but should be sufficient to demonstrate compliance with the principle of the standard. Such documentation is not required for each individual item, but may be on a portfolio basis.

Fair Value Through Other Comprehensive Income (FVTOCI)

The FVTOCI category of classification applies when both the following conditions are met:

1. The financial asset is held within the business model whose objective is achieved by both collecting contractual cash flows and selling financial assets; and
2. The contractual term of the financial asset gives rise on specified dates to cash flows that are solely payment of *principle* and *interest* on the principal amount outstanding.

Financial assets which are held to collect both to contractual cash flows and cash flows from sale are subsequently classified as FVTOCI. Models designed to manage liquidity needs and maintain yield profiles are examples of such business models. Such models will involve a greater frequency and value of sales due to this being integral, achieving the business model's objective. There is no prescribed threshold for the frequency and value of sales.

Example of how the objective of business models are achieved

Activity	How is the objective met?
An entity anticipates capital expenditure in a few years. The entity invests its excess cash in short- and long-term financial assets so that it can fund the expenditure when the need arises. Many of the financial assets have contractual lives that exceed the entity's anticipated investment period. The entity will hold financial assets to collect the contractual cash flows and, when an opportunity arises, it will sell financial assets to reinvest the cash in financial assets with a higher return. The managers responsible for the portfolio are remunerated based on the overall return generated by the portfolio.	The objective of the business model is achieved by both collecting contractual cash flows and selling financial assets. The entity will make decisions on an ongoing basis about whether collecting contractual cash flows or selling financial assets will maximise the return on the portfolio until the need arises for the invested cash. In contrast, consider an entity that anticipates a cash outflow in five years to fund capital expenditure and invests excess cash in short-term financial assets. When the investments mature, the entity reinvests the cash in new short-term financial assets. The entity maintains this strategy until the funds are needed, at which time the entity uses the proceeds from the maturing financial assets to fund the capital expenditure. Only sales that are insignificant in value occur before maturity (unless there is an increase in credit risk). The objective of this contrasting business model is to hold financial assets to collect contractual cash flows.

An insurer holds financial assets to fund insurance contract liabilities. The insurer uses the proceeds from the contractual cash flows on the financial assets to settle insurance contract liabilities as they come due. To ensure that the contractual cash flows from the financial assets are sufficient to settle those liabilities, the insurer undertakes significant buying and selling activity on a regular basis to rebalance its portfolio of assets and to meet cash flow needs as they arise.	The objective of the business model is to fund the insurance contract liabilities. To achieve this objective, the entity collects contractual cash flows as they come due and sells financial assets to maintain the desired profile of the asset portfolio. Thus, both collecting contractual cash flows and selling financial assets are integral to achieving the business model's objective.

Amortised Cost

The amortised cost category of classification applies when both the following conditions are met:

1. The financial asset is held within the business model whose objective is to hold financial assets to collect contractual cash flows; and
2. The contractual term of the financial asset gives rise on specified dates to cash flows that are solely payment of *principal* and *interest* on the principal amount outstanding.

Principal is defined as the fair value of the financial asset at initial recognition. Interest consists of consideration for the time value of money, credit risk associated with the principal amount outstanding during a particular period of time and for other basic lending risks and costs, as well as a profit margin.

Business model for assets classified as amortised cost

Financial assets which are held to collect contractual cash flows and those that are managed to realise cash flows by collecting contractual payments over the life of the asset are classified under the amortised cost category. History in relation to the frequency, timing and value of sales needs to be considered when determining whether the business model is that of collecting contractual cash flows.

There are circumstances when financial assets that are held with an aim of collecting contractual cash flows are sold. This in itself does not impact the business model and one must understand the reasons and conditions that existed at the time of a sale. Examples of events that do not impact the business model are sales made due to an increase in credit risk of the instrument.

Cash flow characteristics for assets classified as amortised cost

A determination of whether contractual cash flows from a financial asset are solely payments of principal and interest on principal needs to be made.

Generally, a basic lending arrangement will meet the criteria of having contractual cash flows which are solely payments of principal and interest on principal. This is because in a basic lending arrangement, consideration of *time value of money* and credit risk are the most significant elements of interest. Interest can also include consideration for other basic lending risks such as liquidity risks, costs associated with holding and servicing the financial asset as well as a profit margin. In extreme economic circumstances, interest can be negative if, for example, the holder of a financial asset either explicitly or implicitly pays for the deposit of its money for a particular period of time (and that fee exceeds the consideration that the holder receives for the time value of money, credit risk and other basic lending risks and costs).

Certain arrangements may also include a margin for exposure to other risks (for example, changes in equity prices/commodity prices). Such margins clearly do not give rise to contractual cash flows that are solely related to payments of principal and related interest.

Time value of money is the element of interest that provides consideration for only the passage of time and provides no consideration for other risks or costs. Judgement needs to be applied in assessing whether the time value of money element does not include other risks. In doing so, consideration of various factors such as the currency denomination and tenor of the financial asset needs to be made.

In certain circumstances, the time value of money element could be modified, e.g., interest rate applied monthly but based on a one-year rate or the periodic resetting of interest rate to an average of short- and long-term rates.

The modification should be assessed to determine whether the contractual payments remain that of principal and interest on principal. The assessment of such a modification would be to calculate the difference between contractual (undiscounted) cash flows of the modified and unmodified time value of money elements. If the modification results in undiscounted contractual cash flows being significantly different, the condition of contractual payments that are solely payments of principal and interest on principal is not met and the financial asset cannot be classified as subsequently measured at amortised cost.

Where interest rates are regulated, the regulated interest rate is considered to meet the requirements of the time value of money element provided that it is broadly consistent with the passage of time and does not provide exposure to risks or volatility in contractual cash flows that are inconsistent with a basic lending arrangement.

Changes to contractual terms

Some financial asset arrangements may contain contractual conditions that could change the timing or amount of contractual cash flows (e.g., prepayment or tenor extension options). A determination of whether contractual cash flows from a financial asset are solely payments of principal and interest on principal needs to be made due to the contractual condition, i.e., assess the contractual cash flows that could arise both before, and after, the change in contractual cash flows.

The assessment of the nature of any contingent/trigger event that could change the timing or amount of the contractual cash flows would be required. While the nature of the contingent event in itself is not a determinative factor in assessing whether the contractual cash flows are solely payments of principal and interest, it may be an indicator.

For example, compare a financial instrument with an interest rate that is reset to a higher rate if the debtor misses a particular number of payments to a financial instrument with an interest rate that is reset to a higher rate if a specified equity index reaches a particular level. It is more likely in the former case that the contractual cash flows over the life of the instrument will be solely payments of principal and interest on the principal amount outstanding because of the relationship between missed payments and an increase in credit risk.

IFRS 9 was amended with effect from January 1, 2019 to include *negative compensation* under the concept of *reasonable additional compensation*. Negative compensation comes into play when the party exercising the prepayment receives compensation that is reasonable for doing so and where the fair value of such prepayment options on inception is insignificant. This clarifies the previous concern that negative compensation would not meet the requirements of being solely payments of principal and interest.

Examples of contractual terms that result in contractual cash flows that are solely payments of principal and interest

1. A variable interest rate that consists of consideration for the time value of money, the credit risk associated with the principal amount outstanding during a particular period of time (the consideration for credit risk may be determined at initial recognition only, and so may be fixed) and other basic lending risks and costs, as well as a profit margin;
2. A contractual term that permits the issuer (i.e., the debtor) to prepay a debt instrument or permits the holder (i.e., the creditor) to put a debt instrument back to the issuer before maturity and the prepayment amount substantially represents unpaid amounts of principal and interest on the principal amount outstanding, which may include reasonable additional or negative compensation for the early termination of the contract; and
3. A contractual term that permits the issuer or the holder to extend the contractual term of a debt instrument (i.e., an extension option) and the terms of the extension option result in contractual cash flows during the extension period that are solely payments of principal and interest on the principal amount outstanding, which may include reasonable additional or negative compensation for the extension of the contract.

Despite the above, a financial asset that would otherwise meet the conditions in IFRS 9 but does not do so only as a result of a contractual term that permits (or requires) the issuer to prepay a debt instrument or permits (or requires) the holder to put a debt instrument back to the issuer before maturity is eligible to be measured at amortised cost or FVTOCI if:

1. The entity acquires or originates the financial asset at a premium or discount to the contractual par amount;
2. The prepayment amount substantially represents the contractual par amount and accrued (but unpaid) contractual interest, which may include reasonable additional or negative compensation for the early termination of the contract; and
3. When the entity initially recognises the financial asset, the fair value of the prepayment feature is insignificant.

Based on the guidance above, debt instruments with the following features would normally be construed to be instruments with contractual cash flows that are payments of principal and interest on principal:

- Instruments with a stated maturity date where the interest rate is linked to an unleveraged inflation index of the currency in which the instrument was issued because such a link simply reflects a real interest rate;

- Instruments that have variable interest rates, where the issuer is permitted to select the market interest rate at various reset dates, e.g., three-month LIBOR vs one-month LIBOR as long as the reference period matches the reset dates;
- Instruments that pay variable interest but which also contain a cap (although the cap would need to be separately assessed to determine whether it represents an embedded derivative that needs to be separated from the host); and
- Instruments that are fully secured by collateral—the existence of collateral does not change the fact that the payments represent solely principal and interest on principal.

Instruments that contain conversion options and pay interest at rates that are inverse to market rates will not normally meet the condition of having contractual cash flows that are solely payments of principal and interest on principal.

Subsequent Measurement of Financial Assets

After initial recognition, an entity shall measure a financial asset in accordance with IFRS 9 at:

1. Fair Value Through Profit or Loss (FVTPL);
2. Fair Value Through Other Comprehensive Income (FVTOCI); or
3. Amortised Cost.

The determination of the basis of measurement will be based on the classification of the financial asset as discussed above. An entity shall apply the impairment requirements to financial assets that are measured at amortised cost and to financial assets that are measured at FVTOCI. Impairment is covered in further detail in this chapter.

Investments in Equity Instruments

IFRS 9 requires that investments in equity instruments are measured at fair value. An entity can make an irrevocable election at initial recognition for investments in equity instruments that do not meet the definition of held for trading to be measured at FVTOCI rather than FVTPL. For such equity instruments, changes in fair value are required to be presented within other comprehensive income and reclassifications of amounts previously presented in other comprehensive income to profit or loss are not permitted, even at derecognition. This is an area of significant change from IAS 39, which required that such gains and losses be recycled to profit or loss on derecognition.

Dividends on such equity instruments are recognised within profit or loss unless they represent a recovery of part or all the cost of the investment.

While IFRS 9 no longer contains an option for measurement of investments in unquoted equity instruments at cost, the standard specifies that only *in limited circumstances* may cost be an appropriate estimate of fair value. These circumstances would include the following two scenarios:

- Since the date of acquisition of the instrument, recent reliable information is not available to measure the fair value, and there are no factors that may indicate that cost is no longer an appropriate estimate of fair value; and/or
- Only a wide range of possible fair value measurements is possible, *and* the cost of the instrument is within this determined range.

The application guidance to IFRS 9 specifies the following indicators (which are not exhaustive), which may suggest that cost is *not* representative of fair value (IFRS 9 B5.2.4):

1. A significant change in the performance of the investee compared with budgets, plans or milestones agreed on acquisition.
2. Changes in expectation that the investee's technical product milestones will be achieved.
3. A significant change in the market for the investee's equity or its products or potential products.
4. A significant change in the global economy or the economic environment in which the investee operates.
5. A significant change in the performance of comparable entities, or in the valuations implied by the overall market.
6. Internal matters of the investee such as fraud, commercial disputes, litigation, changes in management or strategy.
7. Evidence from external transactions in the investee's equity, either by the investee (such as a fresh issue of equity), or by transfers of equity instruments between third parties.

In practice, this is a significant area of difference between IAS 39 and IFRS 9. The approach used by a number of entities of carrying such investments at cost is likely to be no longer permitted. In effect, it is going to be extremely rare for such equity investments to be carried at cost as a realistic estimate of fair value.

Reclassification of Financial Assets

Reclassification of financial assets is permitted if, and only if, the objective of the entity's business model for managing those financial assets changes.

Such changes are expected to be very infrequent and are determined by the entity's senior management as a result of external or internal changes and must be significant to the entity's operations and demonstrable to external parties. Accordingly, a change in an entity's business model will occur only when an entity either begins or ceases to perform an activity that is significant to its operations; for example, when the entity has acquired, disposed of or terminated a business line.

IFRS 9 provides the following examples of circumstances that are or are not changes in the business model:

Change in business model:

1. An entity has a portfolio of commercial loans that it holds to sell in the short term. The entity acquires a company that manages commercial loans and has a business model that holds the loans to collect the contractual cash flows. The original portfolio of commercial loans is no longer for sale, and this portfolio is now managed together with the acquired commercial loans. All of the loans are held to collect the contractual cash flows.
2. A financial services firm decides to shut down its retail mortgage business. That business no longer accepts new business and the financial services firm is actively marketing its mortgage loan portfolio for sale.

Not a change in business model:

1. An entity changes its intention for particular financial assets (even in circumstances of significant changes in market conditions), e.g., a particular market for financial assets temporarily disappears or financial assets are transferred between parts of an entity with different business models.
2. If an entity reclassifies financial assets it shall apply the reclassification prospectively from the reclassification date. The entity shall not restate any previously recognised gains, losses (including impairment gains or losses) or interest.
3. IFRS 9's reclassification related measurement requirements are as summarised below:

Initial classification	Revised classification	Notes
Amortised cost	FVTPL	Fair value is measured at the reclassification date. Any gain or loss arising from a difference between the previous amortised cost of the financial asset and fair value is recognised in profit or loss.
FVTPL	Amortised cost	Fair value on reclassification date becomes new gross carrying amount. Effective interest rate determined based on this carrying amount.
Amortised cost	FVTOCI	Fair value measured on reclassification date. No change to recognition of interest income as the original effective interest rate continues to be applied. Also, no changes to measurement of impairment. However, the impairment amount would be recognised within other comprehensive income and not as a reduction from carrying amount.
FVTOCI	Amortised cost	Fair value on reclassification date used for purposes of the transfer; however, cumulative gain or loss previously recognised in other comprehensive income is adjusted against this fair value such that asset reverts to measurement basis that would have always been determined under the amortised cost approach. No change to recognition of interest income as the original effective interest rate continues to be applied. Also, no changes to measurement of impairment. However, the impairment amount would now be recognised as a reduction from carrying amount.
FVTPL	FVTOCI	Continued measurement at fair value with gains or losses subsequently recognised in other comprehensive income.
FVTOCI	FVTPL	Continued measurement at fair value with gains or losses subsequently recognised through profit or loss. However, cumulative gain or loss previously recognised under other comprehensive income is reclassified to profit or loss.

Derecognition of Financial Assets

An entity first needs to determine whether the derecognition principles are applied to part of a financial asset (or group of similar assets) or a financial asset (or group) in its entirety as follows:

1. A financial asset can only be derecognised when, and only when, the rights to the contractual cash flows from a financial asset expire and when an entity transfers (see below) a financial asset.
2. Derecognition requirements are applied to a part of a financial asset if, and only if, the part being considered for derecognition meets one of the following three conditions:
   - The part comprises only specifically identified cash flows from a financial asset (e.g., in the case of an interest rate strip where a counterparty only obtains cash flow rights to interest cash flows); or
   - The part comprises only a fully proportionate (pro rata) share of the cash flows from a financial asset (e.g., where a counterparty obtains rights to a percentage of all cash flows); or
   - The part comprises only a fully proportionate (pro rata) share of specifically identified cash flows from a financial asset (e.g., where a counterparty obtains rights to a percentage of interest cash flows).

Transferring of Financial Assets

A transfer occurs when an entity either transfers its contractual right to receive cash flows or retains the contractual rights to receive cash flows, but takes on an obligation to pass these cash flows to a counterparty under an arrangement that meets *all* of the following three conditions:

1. The entity has no obligation to pass on the amounts to a counterparty unless it collects equivalent amounts for the asset;
2. The entity is prohibited from pledging or selling the asset other than as security to the counterparty; and
3. The entity has an obligation to remit cash flows to the counterparty without any material delay.

At the time of transfer, an entity evaluates the extent to which it retains the risks and rewards of ownership of the financial asset:

1. If the entity transfers substantially all the risks and rewards of ownership of the financial asset, the entity shall derecognise the financial asset and recognise separately as assets or liabilities any rights and obligations created or retained in the transfer. Examples include:
   - An unconditional sale of a financial asset;
   - A sale of a financial asset together with an option to repurchase the financial asset at its fair value at the time of repurchase; and
   - A sale of a financial asset together with a put or call option that is deeply out of the money.

2. If the entity retains substantially all the risks and rewards of ownership of the financial asset, the entity shall continue to recognise the financial asset.
3. If the entity neither transfers nor retains substantially all the risks and rewards of ownership of the financial asset, the entity shall determine whether it has retained control (based on the practical ability to sell the transferred financial asset to a third party in an active market) of the financial asset. In this case:

   - If the entity has not retained control, it shall derecognise the financial asset and recognise separately as assets or liabilities any rights and obligations created or retained in the transfer.
   - If the entity has retained control, it shall continue to recognise the financial asset to the extent of its continuing involvement in the financial asset.

Transferring of Financial Assets that Qualify for Derecognition

Where an entity transfers (a transfer qualifying for derecognition in its entirety) a financial asset and retains the right to service the financial asset for a fee, it shall recognise either a servicing asset or a servicing liability for that servicing contract. In particular:

1. If the fee to be received is not expected to compensate the entity adequately for performing the servicing, a servicing liability for the servicing obligation shall be recognised at its fair value; or
2. If the fee to be received is expected to be more than adequate compensation for the servicing, a servicing asset shall be recognised for the servicing right.

Where an asset is transferred in its entirety, the entity will recognise a new financial asset or assume a new financial liability or service liability at fair value. The difference between the carrying amount at the date of derecognition and the consideration received (including any new asset obtained less any new liability assumed) is recognised in profit or loss.

Where the asset is part of a larger financial asset, the previous carrying amount of the larger financial asset should be allocated between the part that it continues to recognise (i.e., the servicing asset) and the part that has been derecognised based on the relative fair values at the time of transfer. The difference between the carrying amount of the part derecognised at the date of derecognition and the consideration received for the part derecognised (including any new asset obtained less any new liability assumed) is recognised in profit or loss.

Transferring of Financial Assets that do not Qualify for Derecognition

If a transfer does not result in derecognition because the entity has *retained substantially all the risks and rewards* of ownership of the transferred asset, the entity shall continue to recognise the transferred asset in its entirety and shall recognise a financial liability for the consideration received. In subsequent periods, the entity shall recognise any income on the transferred asset and any expense incurred on the financial liability.

The following examples relate to when an entity has *retained substantially all the risks and rewards* of ownership of the transferred asset:

1. A sale and repurchase transaction where the repurchase price is a fixed price or the sale price plus a lender's return;
2. A securities lending agreement;

3. A sale of a financial asset together with a total return swap that transfers the market risk exposure back to the entity;
4. A sale of a financial asset together with a deep in-the-money put or call option (i.e., an option that is so far in the money that it is highly unlikely to go out of the money before expiry); and
5. A sale of short-term receivables in which the entity guarantees to compensate the transferee for credit losses that are likely to occur.

Continuing Involvement in Transferred Financial Assets

If an entity's continuing involvement is in only a part of a financial asset (e.g., when an entity retains an option to repurchase part of a transferred asset, or retains a residual interest that does not result in the retention of substantially all the risks and rewards of ownership and the entity retains control), the entity allocates the previous carrying amount of the financial asset between the part it continues to recognise under continuing involvement and the part it no longer recognises on the basis of the relative fair values of those parts on the date of the transfer. The difference between:

1. The carrying amount (measured at the date of derecognition) allocated to the part that is no longer recognised; and
2. The consideration received for the part no longer recognised shall be recognised in profit or loss.

A simple example of the scenario above is a debt factoring agreement under which a specified percentage of the debt factored is without recourse and the remainder of the debt remains under recourse to the entity.

If a guarantee provided by an entity to pay for default losses on a transferred asset prevents the transferred asset from being derecognised to the extent of the continuing involvement, the transferred asset at the date of the transfer is measured at the lower of:

1. The carrying amount of the asset; and
2. The maximum amount of the consideration received in the transfer that the entity could be required to repay. The associated liability is initially measured at the guarantee amount plus the fair value of the guarantee (which is normally the consideration received for the guarantee). Subsequently, the initial fair value of the guarantee is recognised in profit or loss when the obligation is satisfied (in accordance with the principles of IFRS 15) and the carrying value of the asset is reduced by any loss allowance.

If a transferred asset continues to be recognised, the asset and the associated liability shall not be offset. Similarly, the entity shall not offset any income arising from the transferred asset with any expense incurred on the associated liability.

If a transferor provides non-cash collateral (such as debt or equity instruments) to the transferee, the accounting for the collateral by the transferor and the transferee depends on whether the transferee has the right to sell or repledge the collateral and on whether the transferor has defaulted. The transferor and transferee shall account for the collateral as follows:

1. If the transferee has the right by contract or custom to sell or repledge the collateral, then the transferor shall reclassify that asset in its statement of financial position separately from other assets.

2. If the transferee sells collateral pledged to it, it shall recognise the proceeds from the sale and a liability measured at fair value for its obligation to return the collateral.
3. If the transferor defaults under the terms of the contract and is no longer entitled to redeem the collateral, it shall derecognise the collateral, and the transferee shall recognise the collateral as its asset initially measured at fair value or, if it has already sold the collateral, derecognise its obligation to return the collateral.
4. Except as provided in the third point above, the transferor shall continue to carry the collateral as its asset, and the transferee shall not recognise the collateral as an asset.

FINANCIAL LIABILITIES

Classification of Financial Liabilities

All financial liabilities shall be classified as subsequently measured at *amortised cost*, except for:

1. Financial liabilities designated at FVTPL. Such liabilities, including derivatives that are liabilities, shall be subsequently measured at fair value.
2. Financial liabilities that arise when a transfer of a financial asset does not qualify for derecognition or when the continuing involvement approach applies.
3. Financial guarantee contracts—after initial recognition, an issuer of such a contract shall (unless (1) or (2) applies) subsequently measure it at the higher of:

   a. The amount of the loss allowance (impairment); and
   b. The amount initially recognised less, when appropriate, the cumulative amount of income recognised in accordance with the principles of IFRS 15, *Revenue from Contracts with Customers*.

4. Commitments to provide a loan at a below-market interest rate. An issuer of such a commitment shall (unless (1) applies) subsequently measure it at the higher of:

   a. The amount of the loss allowance (impairment); and
   b. The amount initially recognised less, when appropriate, the cumulative amount of income recognised in accordance with the principles of IFRS 15, *Revenue from Contracts with Customers*.

5. Contingent consideration recognised by an acquirer in a business combination to which IFRS 3, *Business Combinations*, applies. Such contingent consideration shall subsequently be measured at fair value with changes recognised in profit or loss.

In respect of transfers that do not qualify for derecognition, the financial liability associated with continuing involvement is measured in such a way that the net carrying amount of the transferred asset and the associated liability is:

1. The amortised cost of the rights and obligations retained by the entity, if the transferred asset is measured at amortised cost; or
2. Equal to the fair value of the rights and obligations retained by the entity when measured on a standalone basis, if the transferred asset is measured at fair value.

An entity may, at initial recognition, irrevocably designate a financial liability as measured at FVTPL (when a contract contains one or more embedded derivatives and the host is not an asset within the scope of this standard) or when doing so results in more relevant information, because either:

1. It eliminates or significantly reduces a measurement or recognition inconsistency (sometimes referred to as "an accounting mismatch") that would otherwise arise from measuring assets or liabilities or recognising the gains and losses on them on different bases; or
2. A group of financial liabilities or financial assets and financial liabilities is managed and its performance is evaluated on a fair value basis, in accordance with a documented risk management or investment strategy, and information about the group is provided internally on that basis to the entity's key management personnel.

Examples of financial liabilities that are likely to be classified and measured either at amortised cost or at FVTPL

Amortised cost	**FVTPL**
Trade payables	Interest rate swaps (not designated in a hedging relationship)
Loan payables with standard interest rates (such as a benchmark rate plus margin) of the host contract arising from a loan agreement which contains separable embedded derivatives	Commodity futures/option contracts (not designated in a hedging relationship)
Bank borrowings	Foreign exchange future/option contracts (not designated in a hedging relationship)
	Convertible note liability designated at FVTPL
	Contingent consideration payable that arises from one or more business combinations

SUBSEQUENT MEASUREMENT OF FINANCIAL LIABILITIES

After initial recognition, financial liabilities will be subsequently measured using the same principles as set out under classification of financial liabilities that have been covered above. Exceptions include where hedge accounting is applied. See the section Hedge Accounting later in this chapter for guidance in this respect.

Liabilities Designated as at Fair Value Through Profit or Loss and Recognition of Own Credit Risk Related Fair Value Changes

An entity shall present a gain or loss on a financial liability that is designated as at FVTPL as follows:

1. The amount of change in the fair value of the financial liability that is attributable to changes in the own credit risk of the issuer shall be presented in other comprehensive income; and
2. The remaining amount of change in the fair value of the liability shall be presented in profit or loss unless the treatment of the effects of changes in the liability's credit risk described in (1) would create or enlarge an accounting mismatch in profit or loss, in which case the total change is presented in profit or loss.

When an entity designates a financial liability as at FVTPL, it must determine whether presenting the effects of changes in the liability's credit risk in other comprehensive income would create or enlarge an accounting mismatch in profit or loss. An accounting mismatch would be created or enlarged if presenting the effects of changes in the liability's credit risk in other comprehensive income would result in a greater mismatch in profit or loss than if those amounts were presented in profit or loss.

To make that determination, an entity must assess whether it expects that the effects of changes in the liability's credit risk will be offset in profit or loss by a change in the fair value of another financial instrument measured at FVTPL. Such an expectation must be based on an economic relationship between the characteristics of the liability and the characteristics of the other financial instrument.

That determination is made at initial recognition and is not reassessed. For practical purposes, the entity need not enter into all of the assets and liabilities giving rise to an accounting mismatch at exactly the same time. A reasonable delay is permitted provided that any remaining transactions are expected to occur. An entity must apply consistently its methodology for determining whether presenting in other comprehensive income the effects of changes in the liability's credit risk would create or enlarge an accounting mismatch in profit or loss.

However, an entity may use different methodologies when there are different economic relationships between the characteristics of the liabilities designated as at FVTPL and the characteristics of the other financial instruments. IFRS 7 requires an entity to provide qualitative disclosures in the notes to the financial statements about its methodology for making that determination.

Example of a mismatch

An example of a situation where a mismatch would be created is where a bank issues fixed term loans to borrowers. It funds those loans with bonds that are also issued and traded openly, and therefore measured at FVTPL. As part of the loan agreement, the bank permits a borrower to purchase a bond and deliver it to the bank effectively as a prepayment of the debt. The loans represent financial assets of the bank and the bonds represent its financial liability. In the case where the market value of the bonds drops (a decrease in the fair value of the financial liability on the bank's statement of financial position which may be attributed to own credit risk effects), it can be imputed that the fair value of the bank's financial asset (the loans issued) to which these bonds are linked has also reduced. In this case recognising the change in fair value of the liability in other comprehensive income could be seen to create an accounting mismatch.

Own credit risk

IFRS 7 defines credit risk as "the risk that one party to a financial instrument will cause a financial loss for the other party by failing to discharge an obligation." The requirement in IFRS 9 relating to own credit risk on debt instruments relates to the risk that the issuer will fail to perform on that particular liability. It does not necessarily relate to the creditworthiness of the issuer. For example, if an entity issues a collateralised liability and a non-collateralised liability that are otherwise identical, the credit risk of those two liabilities will be different, even though they are issued by the same entity.

The credit risk on the collateralised liability will be less than the credit risk of the non-collateralised liability. The credit risk for a collateralised liability may be close to zero.

For the purposes of applying the requirements above, credit risk is different from asset-specific performance risk. Asset-specific performance risk is not related to the risk that an entity will fail to discharge a particular obligation but instead it is related to the risk that a single asset or a group of assets will perform poorly (or not at all).

Determining the effects of changes in credit risk

For the purposes of applying the requirements above, an entity shall determine the amount of change in the fair value of the financial liability that is attributable to changes in the credit risk of that liability either:

1. As the amount of change in its fair value that is not attributable to changes in market conditions that give rise to market risk; or
2. Using an alternative method the entity believes more faithfully represents the amount of change in the liability's fair value that is attributable to changes in its credit risk.

Changes in market conditions that give rise to market risk include changes in a benchmark interest rate, the price of another entity's financial instrument, a commodity price, a foreign exchange rate or an index of prices or rates.

As with all fair value measurements, an entity's measurement method for determining the portion of the change in the liability's fair value that is attributable to changes in its credit risk must make maximum use of relevant observable inputs and minimum use of unobservable inputs.

Reclassification of Financial Liabilities

An entity shall not reclassify any financial liability.

Derecognition of financial liabilities

Financial liabilities (or part thereof) are derecognised from an entity's statement of financial position only when the liability is extinguished—i.e., when the obligation specified in the contract is discharged or cancelled or expires.

An exchange between a borrower and lender of debt instruments that carry significantly different terms or a substantial modification of the terms of an existing liability are both accounted for as an extinguishment of the original financial liability and the recognition of a new financial liability.

Significantly different terms or a substantial modification of terms are measured as at least a 10% variance (recommended) of discounted present value (based on the original effective interest rate) of cash flows under the new terms (including transactional costs such as fees) and the discounted present value of cash flows of the original financial liability. Transaction costs (fees, etc.) where a financial liability that had a modification is extinguished are recognised as part of the gain or loss on extinguishment. For transaction costs (fees, etc.) where a financial liability that had a modification is not extinguished are adjusted to the carrying value of the financial liability and amortised over the remaining term of the modified liability.

The difference between the carrying value of a financial liability (or part thereof) extinguished and the consideration paid (including value of non-cash consideration) or liabilities assumed is recognised in profit or loss. Where an entity repurchases part of a financial liability, the previous carrying amount of the financial liability is allocated between the part derecognised and the part continued to be recognised based on the relative fair values at the date of repurchase.

Example of accounting for the extinguishment of debt

A 0%, 10-year, €200,000 bond is dated and issued on 1/1/20XX at €98, with the interest payable semi-annually. Associated bond issue costs of €14,000 are incurred. Four years later, on 1/1/20XX+4 the entire bond issue is repurchased at €102 per €100 face value and is retired. The straight-line method of amortisation is used since the result is not materially different from that when the effective interest method is used. The gain or loss on the repurchase is computed as follows:

Reacquisition price [(102/100) × €200,000]		€204,000
Net carrying amount:		
Face value	€200,000	
Unamortised discount [2% × €200,000 × (6/10)]	€(2,400)	
Unamortised issue costs [€14,000 × (6/10)]	€(8,400)	€189,200
Loss on bond repurchase		€14,800

Example of accounting for debt exchange or restructuring with gain recognition

Assume that Debtor Corp. owes Friendly Bank €90,000 on a 5% interest-bearing non-amortising note payable in five years, plus accrued and unpaid interest, due immediately, of €4,500. Friendly Bank agrees to a restructuring to assist Debtor Corp., which is suffering losses and is threatening to declare bankruptcy. The interest rate is reduced to 4%, the principal is reduced to €72,500 and the accrued interest is forgiven outright. Future payments will be on normal terms.

Whether there is recognition of a gain on the restructuring depends on the 10% threshold. The relevant discount rate to be used to compare the present values of the old and the new debt obligations is 5%. The present value of the old debt is simply the principal amount, €90,000, plus the interest due at present, €4,500, for a total of €94,500.

The present value of the replacement debt is the discounted present value of the reduced principal and the reduced future interest payments; the forgiven interest does not affect this. The new principal, €72,500, discounted at 5%, equals €56,806. The stream of future interest payments (€72,500 × .04 = €2,900 annually in arrears), discounted at 5%, equals €12,555. The total present value therefore is €69,361, which is about 27% below the present value of the old debt obligation. Thus, the 10% threshold is exceeded, and a gain will be recognised at the date of the restructuring.

However, given Debtor's current condition, the market rate of interest for its debt would actually be 12%, and since the new obligation must be recorded at fair value, this must be computed. The present value of the reduced principal, €72,500, discounted at 12%, has a present value of €41,138. The stream of future interest payments (€72,500 × .04 = €2,900 annually, in arrears), discounted at 12%, has a present value of €10,454. The total obligation thus has a fair value of €51,592.

The entry to record this event would be:

	DR	CR
Debt obligation (old) payable	90,000	
Interest payable	4,500	
Discount on debt obligation (new)	20,908	
Debt obligation (new) payable		72,500
Gain on debt restructuring		42,908

Note that the new debt obligation is recorded at a net of €51,592, not at the face value of €72,500. The difference, €20,908, is a discount to be amortised to interest expense over the next five years to reflect the actual market rate of 12%, rather than the nominal 4% being charged. Amortisation should be accomplished on the effective yield method.

Example of accounting for debt exchange or restructuring with gain deferral

Assume now that Hopeless Corp. owes Callous Bank €90,000 on a 5% interest-bearing non-amortising note payable in five years, plus accrued and unpaid interest, due immediately, of €4,500. Callous Bank agrees to a restructuring to assist Hopeless Corp., which is also suffering losses and is threatening to declare bankruptcy. However, Callous is only willing to reduce the principal amount from €90,000 to €85,000 and reduce interest to 4.5% from 5%. It is not willing to forgo the currently owed €4,500 interest payment, and furthermore requires that the loan maturity be shortened to three years, from five, to limit its risk. Hopeless agrees to the new terms.

To comply with IFRS 9, the present value of the new debt must be compared to the present value of the old, existing obligation. As in the preceding example, the present value of the old debt is simply the principal amount, €90,000, plus the interest due at present, €4,500, for a total of €94,500.

The present value of the replacement debt is the discounted present value of the reduced principal and the reduced future interest payments, plus the interest using a 5% discount factor (= .86384 for the new three-year term). The discounted present value of the reduced principal is €73,426. The stream of future interest payments (€85,000 × .045 = €3,825 annually in arrears), discounted at 5% (= 2.7231 annuity factor), has a present value of €10,416. The total present value therefore is (€73,426 + €10,416 + €4,500 =) €88,342, which is about 7% below the present value of the old debt obligation. Accordingly, since the 10% threshold is not exceeded, the difference of (€94,500 − €88,342 =) €6,158 is not recognised as a gain at the date of the restructuring, but rather is deferred and amortised over the new three-year term of the restructured loan.

The entry to record this event would be:

	DR	CR
Debt obligation (old) payable	90,000	
Discount on debt obligation (new)	1,158	
Debt obligation (new) payable		85,000
Deferred gain on debt restructuring		6,158

Note that the new debt obligation is recorded at a net of €83,842, not at the face value of €85,000. The difference of €1,158 represents a discount to be amortised to interest expense over the subsequent three years; this will result in an interest expense at the actual market rate of 5%, rather than at the nominal 4.5% rate. Amortisation should be computed on the effective yield method, although if the discrepancy is not material the straight-line method may be employed. The deferred gain, €6,158, will be amortised over the three-year revised term. While the discount amortisation will be added to interest expense, IFRS 9 is silent as to how the amortisation of the deferred gain should be handled. However, by reference to how a gain in excess of the 10% threshold (and thus subject to immediate recognition) would have been reported, it is thought likely that this amortisation should be included in "other income," and should not be offset against interest expense as it does not relate to time value of money related cost.

Presentation of the gain or loss from debt restructurings is not explicitly dealt with under IFRS. However, since IAS 8 was revised, as part of the IASB's Improvements Project to eliminate the presentation of extraordinary items in profit or loss, there is no difficulty in making the appropriate decision. Gain or loss on debt extinguishments should, in the authors' opinion, be displayed as items of "other" income or expense in profit or loss.

EMBEDDED DERIVATIVES

A derivative part of a contract is referred to as an embedded derivative. IFRS 9 defines an embedded derivative as a component of a hybrid contract that also includes a non-derivative host—with the effect that some of the cash flows of the combined instrument vary in a way similar to a stand-alone derivative.

An embedded derivative can cause all or part of the cash flows assigned to a contract to be modified to a specific element, e.g., interest rate, commodity price, foreign exchange rate, credit rating, etc.

If a hybrid contract contains a host that is an asset within the scope of IFRS 9, an entity should apply the requirements for the classification of financial assets to the entire hybrid contract.

Where a hybrid contract contains a host that is not an asset within the scope of IFRS 9, an embedded derivative shall be separated from the host and accounted for as a derivative if, and only if:

1. The economic characteristics and risks of the embedded derivative are not closely related to the economic characteristics and risks of the host;
2. A separate instrument with the same terms as the embedded derivative would meet the definition of a derivative; and
3. The hybrid contract is not measured at fair value with changes in fair value recognised in profit or loss (i.e., a derivative that is embedded in a financial liability at FVTPL is not separated).

When an entity becomes a party to a hybrid contract with a host that is not an asset within the scope of IFRS 9, the standard requires the entity to identify any embedded derivative, assess whether it is required to be separated from the host contract and, for those that are required to be separated, measure the derivatives at fair value at initial recognition and subsequently at FVTPL.

The above assessment is made at the time when the entity first becomes a party to the contract. Any subsequent reassessment is prohibited unless there is a change in the terms of the contract which significantly modifies the cash flows required to service the contract. The subsequent reassessment prohibition does not, however, apply to derivative contracts acquired in:

1. A business combination (as defined in IFRS 3, *Business Combinations*);
2. A combination of entities or businesses under common control; or
3. The formation of a joint venture as defined in IFRS 11, *Joint Arrangements*.

Some examples of embedded derivatives that will need to be accounted for separately from the host contract are as follows:

1. Put or call options in debt instruments where the put or call price is reflective of, or determined with reference to, a basis that is unrelated to the debt instrument;
2. Changes to the term of debt without a reflective change to the interest rate for a similar new term; and
3. Put, call or prepayment options in a debt instrument where the exercise price of such an option does not approximate the amortised cost of the instrument, plus an amount representing forgone interest (i.e., reimburses the lender).

If a host contract has no stated or predetermined maturity and represents a residual interest in the net assets of an entity, then its economic characteristics and risks are those of an equity instrument, and an embedded derivative would need to possess equity characteristics related to the same entity to be regarded as closely related. If the host contract is not an equity instrument and meets the definition of a financial instrument, then its economic characteristics and risks are those of a debt instrument.

If a contract contains one or more embedded derivatives and the host is not an asset within the scope of IFRS 9, an entity may designate the entire hybrid contract as at FVTPL unless:

1. The embedded derivative(s) do(es) not significantly modify the cash flows that otherwise would be required by the contract; or
2. It is clear with little or no analysis when a similar hybrid instrument is first considered that separation of the embedded derivative(s) is prohibited, such as a prepayment option embedded in a loan that permits the holder to prepay the loan for approximately its amortised cost.

Generally, the requirements in respect of separation of embedded derivatives can be complex, or result in less reliable measures, than measuring the entire instrument at FVTPL. For that reason, this IFRS 9 permits the entire hybrid contract to be designated as at FVTPL. However, in the cases set out in (1) and (2) above, designating the entire contract as FVTPL would not be justified because doing so would not reduce complexity or increase reliability.

Generally, multiple embedded derivatives in a single hybrid contract are treated as a single compound embedded derivative. However, embedded derivatives that are classified as equity (see IAS 32, *Financial Instruments: Presentation*) are accounted for separately from those classified as assets or liabilities. In addition, if a hybrid contract has more than one embedded derivative and those derivatives relate to different risk exposures and are readily separable and independent of each other, they are accounted for separately from each other.

If an entity is unable to measure reliably the fair value of a separated embedded derivative on the basis of its terms and conditions, the fair value of the embedded derivative can be derived as the difference between the fair value of the hybrid contract and the fair value of the host. If the entity is unable to measure the fair value of the embedded derivative using this method either at acquisition or at the end of a subsequent financial reporting period, it shall designate the entire hybrid contract as at FVTPL.

FINANCIAL INSTRUMENTS MEASURED AT AMORTISED COST

IFRS 9 requires the effective interest method to be applied to the measurement of all financial instruments that are classified to be measured at amortised cost as well as for determination of interest revenue for debt investments measured at FVTOCI. The effective interest rate method is a method under which interest income or expense is allocated over the relevant period of the financial instrument using the effective interest rate on the financial instrument.

The effective interest rate is the rate that exactly discounts expected future cash payments and receipts over the life of the financial instrument to the initial carrying amount of the financial asset or liability. It requires determination and estimation of all such cash payments that are relevant to the instrument, including fees paid that are an integral part of the interest rate, transaction costs and any other premiums or discounts. Because transaction costs are included within this calculation, the overall effect of applying the effective interest rate is to spread such costs over the life of the instrument.

IFRS 9 requires that interest revenue shall be calculated by using the effective interest method. This shall be calculated by applying the effective interest rate to the gross carrying amount of a financial asset except for:

1. Purchased or originated credit-impaired financial assets. For those financial assets, the entity shall apply the credit-adjusted effective interest rate to the amortised cost of the financial asset from initial recognition;
2. Financial assets that are not purchased or originated credit-impaired financial assets but subsequently have become credit-impaired financial assets. For those financial assets, the entity shall apply the effective interest rate to the amortised cost of the financial asset in subsequent reporting periods.

In applying the effective interest method, an entity identifies fees that are an integral part of the effective interest rate of a financial instrument. The description of fees for financial services may not be indicative of the nature and substance of the services provided. Fees that are an integral part of the effective interest rate of a financial instrument are treated as an adjustment to the effective interest rate, unless the financial instrument is measured at fair value, with the change in fair value being recognised in profit or loss. In those cases, the fees are recognised in profit or loss when the instrument is initially recognised.

Fees that are an integral part of the effective interest rate of a financial instrument include:

1. Origination fees received by the entity relating to the creation or acquisition of a financial asset. Such fees may include compensation for activities such as evaluating the borrower's financial condition, evaluating and recording guarantees, collateral and other security arrangements, negotiating the terms of the instrument, preparing and processing documents and closing the transaction. These fees are an integral part of generating an involvement with the resulting financial instrument.

2. Commitment fees received by the entity to originate a loan when the loan commitment is not measured and it is probable that the entity will enter into a specific lending arrangement. These fees are regarded as compensation for an ongoing involvement with the acquisition of a financial instrument. If the commitment expires without the entity making the loan, the fee is recognised as revenue on expiry.
3. Origination fees paid on issuing financial liabilities measured at amortised cost. These fees are an integral part of generating an involvement with a financial liability. An entity distinguishes fees and costs that are an integral part of the effective interest rate for the financial liability from origination fees and transaction costs relating to the right to provide services, such as investment management services.

Fees that are not an integral part of the effective interest rate of a financial instrument and are accounted for in accordance with IFRS 15 include:

1. Fees charged for servicing a loan;
2. Commitment fees to originate a loan when the loan commitment is not measured and it is unlikely that a specific lending arrangement will be entered into; and
3. Loan syndication fees received by an entity that arranges a loan and retains no part of the loan package for itself (or retains a part at the same effective interest rate for comparable risk as other participants).

Dealing with changes in cash flows subsequent to the initial calculation of the effective interest rate

For floating rate financial assets and floating rate financial liabilities, periodic re-estimation of cash flows to reflect the movements in the market rates of interest alters the effective interest rate. If a floating rate financial asset or a floating rate financial liability is recognised initially at an amount equal to the principal receivable or payable on maturity, re-estimating the future interest payments normally has no significant effect on the carrying amount of the asset or the liability and therefore there is normally no immediate impact on profit or loss of such a change in cash flows.

If an entity revises its estimates of payments or receipts (excluding modifications in accordance with the paragraph above and changes in estimates of expected credit losses), it shall adjust the gross carrying amount of the financial asset or amortised cost of a financial liability (or group of financial instruments) to reflect actual and revised estimated contractual cash flows. The entity recalculates the gross carrying amount of the financial asset or amortised cost of the financial liability as the present value of the estimated future contractual cash flows that are discounted at the financial instrument's original effective interest rate (or credit-adjusted effective interest rate for purchased or originated credit-impaired financial assets). The adjustment is recognised in profit or loss as income or expense.

In some cases, a financial asset is considered credit impaired at initial recognition because the credit risk is very high, and in the case of a purchase it is acquired at a deep discount. An entity is required to include the initial expected credit losses in the estimated cash flows when calculating the credit-adjusted effective interest rate for financial assets that are considered to be purchased or originated credit impaired at initial recognition. However, this does not mean that a credit-adjusted effective interest rate should be applied solely because the financial asset has high credit risk at initial recognition.

Modification of contractual cash flows

When the contractual cash flows of a financial asset are renegotiated or otherwise modified and the renegotiation or modification does not result in the derecognition of that financial asset in accordance with IFRS 9 (i.e., it does not meet the definition of a substantial modification as it does not exceed the 10% threshold), an entity shall recalculate the gross carrying amount of the financial asset and shall recognise a modification gain or loss in profit or loss. The gross carrying amount of the financial asset shall be recalculated as the present value of the renegotiated or modified contractual cash flows that are discounted at the financial asset's original effective interest rate (or credit-adjusted effective interest rate for purchased or originated credit-impaired financial assets). Any costs or fees incurred adjust the carrying amount of the modified financial asset and are amortised over the remaining term of the modified financial asset.

Write-off

An entity shall directly reduce the gross carrying amount of a financial asset when the entity has no reasonable expectations of recovering a financial asset in its entirety or a portion thereof. A write-off constitutes a derecognition event.

Write-offs can relate to a financial asset in its entirety or to a portion of it. For example, an entity plans to enforce the collateral on a financial asset and expects to recover no more than 30% of the financial asset from the collateral. If the entity has no reasonable prospects of recovering any further cash flows from the financial asset, it should write off the remaining 70% of the financial asset.

Write-offs will result in an immediate impact to profit or loss in most cases. In certain cases, however, e.g., where the write-off relates to transactions between parties having a parent/subsidiary relationship, the impact can be either recognised within equity (as a capital contribution) or as a distribution.

FAIR VALUATION GAINS AND LOSSES

A gain or loss on a financial asset or financial liability that is measured at fair value shall be recognised in profit or loss unless:

1. It is part of a hedging relationship;
2. It is an investment in an equity instrument and the entity has elected to present gains and losses on that investment in other comprehensive income;
3. It is a financial liability designated as at FVTPL and the entity is required to present the effects of changes in the liability's credit risk in other comprehensive income; or
4. It is a financial asset measured at FVTOCI.

Dividends are recognised in profit or loss only when:

1. The entity's right to receive payment of the dividend is established;
2. It is probable that the economic benefits associated with the dividend will flow to the entity; and
3. The amount of the dividend can be measured reliably.

Gains or losses on financial assets and financial liabilities that are measured at amortised cost and are not part of a hedging relationship shall be recognised in profit or loss when the financial asset or liability is derecognised through the amortisation process or to recognise impairment gains or losses (for financial assets).

A gain or loss on a financial asset measured at FVTOCI shall be recognised in other comprehensive income, except for impairment gains or losses and foreign exchange gains and losses, until the financial asset is derecognised or reclassified.

Recognition of Foreign Exchange Gains and Losses

An entity applies IAS 21 to financial assets and financial liabilities that are monetary items and denominated in a foreign currency. IAS 21 requires any foreign exchange gains and losses on monetary assets and monetary liabilities to be recognised in profit or loss. An exception is a monetary item that is designated as a hedging instrument in a cash flow hedge, a hedge of a net investment or a fair value hedge of an equity instrument for which an entity has elected to present changes in fair value in other comprehensive income.

For the purpose of recognising foreign exchange gains and losses under IAS 21, a financial asset measured at FVTOCI is treated as a monetary item, with the exception of equity instruments which the entity elects to measure at FVTOCI. Accordingly, such a financial asset is initially treated as an asset measured at amortised cost in the foreign currency. Exchange differences on the amortised cost are recognised in profit or loss and other changes in the fair value are recognised in other comprehensive income.

Financial asset measured at FVTOCI with foreign currency movements IFRS 9 and IAS 21

The cumulative gain or loss that is recognised in other comprehensive income is the difference between the amortised cost of the financial asset and the fair value of the financial asset in the functional currency of the reporting entity. For the purpose of applying IAS 21 the asset is treated as an asset measured at amortised cost in the foreign currency.

To illustrate: on December 31, 20XX, Entity A acquires a bond denominated in a foreign currency (FC) for its fair value of FC1,000. The bond has five years remaining to maturity and a contractual par amount of FC1,250, carries fixed interest of 4.7% that is paid annually (FC1,250 × 4.7% = FC59 per year) and has an effective interest rate of 10%. Entity A classifies the bond as subsequently measured at FVTOCI in accordance with paragraph IFRS 9, and thus recognises gains and losses in other comprehensive income. The entity's functional currency is the euro (€). The exchange rate is FC1 to €1.5 and the carrying amount of the bond is €1,500 (= FC1,000 × 1.5).

Dr Bond	€1.500	
Cr Cash		€1.500

On December 31, 20XX+1, the foreign currency has appreciated and the exchange rate is FC1 to €2. The fair value of the bond is FC1,060 and thus the carrying amount is €2,120 (= FC1,060 × 2). The amortised cost is FC1,041 (= €2,082). In this case, the cumulative gain or loss to be recognised in other comprehensive income and accumulated in equity is the difference between the fair value and the amortised cost on December 31, 20XX+1, i.e., €38 (= €2,120 − €2,082).

Interest received on the bond on December 31, 20XX+1, is FC59 (= €118). Interest revenue determined in accordance with the effective interest method is FC100 (= FC1,000 × 10%). The average exchange rate during the year is FC1 to €1.75. For the purpose of this question, it is assumed that the use of the average exchange rate provides a reliable approximation of the spot rates applicable to the accrual of interest revenue during the year (see paragraph 22 of IAS 21).

Thus, reported interest revenue is €175 (= FC100 × 1.75), including accretion of the initial discount of €72 (= [FC100 − FC59] × 1.75). Accordingly, the exchange difference on the bond that is recognised in profit or loss is €510 (= €2,082 − €1,500 − €72). Also, there is an exchange gain on the interest receivable for the year of €15 (= FC59 × [2.00 − 1.75]).

Dr Bond	€620	
Dr Cash	118	
Cr Interest revenue		€175
Cr Exchange gain		525
Cr Fair value change in other comprehensive income		38

On December 31, 20XX+2, the foreign currency has appreciated further, and the exchange rate is FC1 to €2.50. The fair value of the bond is FC1,070 and thus the carrying amount is €2,675 (= FC1,070 × 2.50). The amortised cost is FC1,086 (= €2,715). The cumulative gain or loss to be accumulated in other comprehensive income is the difference between the fair value and the amortised cost on December 31, 20XX+2, i.e., negative €40 (= €2,675 − €2,715). Thus, the amount recognised in other comprehensive income equals the change in the difference during 20X3 of €78 (= €40 + €38).

Interest received on the bond on December 31, 20XX+2, is FC59 (= €148). Interest revenue determined in accordance with the effective interest method is FC104 (= FC1,041 × 10%). The average exchange rate during the year is FC1 to €2.25. Thus, recognised interest revenue is €234 (= FC104 × 2.25) including accretion of the initial discount of €101 (= [FC104 – FC59] × 2.25). Accordingly, the exchange difference on the bond that is recognised in profit or loss is €532 (= €2,715 − €2,082 − €101). Also, there is an exchange gain on the interest receivable for the year of €15 (= FC59 × [2.50 − 2.25]).

Dr Bond	€555	
Dr Cash	148	
Dr Fair value change in other comprehensive income	78	
Cr Interest revenue		€234
Cr Exchange gain		547

Exchange differences arising on translation of foreign entities

Paragraphs 32 and 48 of IAS 21 state that all exchange differences resulting from translating the financial statements of a foreign operation should be recognised in other comprehensive income until disposal of the net investment. This would include exchange differences arising from financial instruments carried at fair value, which would include both financial assets measured at FVTPL and financial assets that are measured at FVTOCI in accordance with IFRS 9.

IFRS 9 requires that changes in fair value of financial assets measured at FVTPL should be recognised in profit or loss and changes in fair value of financial assets measured at FVTOCI should be recognised in other comprehensive income.

If the foreign operation is a subsidiary whose financial statements are consolidated with those of its parent, in the consolidated financial statements, how are IFRS 9 and paragraph 39 of IAS 21 applied?

IFRS 9 applies in the accounting for financial instruments in the financial statements of a foreign operation and IAS 21 applies in translating the financial statements of a foreign operation for incorporation in the financial statements of the reporting entity. Therefore, the requirements of IFRS 9 would be applied at the subsidiary financial statements level using the functional currency of the subsidiary. IAS 21 would then be applied in recognising gains and losses arising from foreign exchange on consolidation of the subsidiary into the parent company financial statements.

Interaction between the standards

IFRS 9 includes requirements about the measurement of financial assets and financial liabilities and the recognition of gains and losses on remeasurement in profit or loss. IAS 21 includes rules about the reporting of foreign currency items and the recognition of exchange differences in profit or loss. In what order are IAS 21 and IFRS 9 applied?

Statement of financial position

Generally, the measurement of a financial asset or financial liability at fair value or amortised cost is first determined in the foreign currency in which the item is denominated in accordance with IFRS 9. Then, the foreign currency amount is translated into the functional currency using the closing rate or a historical rate in accordance with IAS 21 (paragraph B5.7.2 of IFRS 9). For example, if a monetary financial asset (such as a debt instrument) is measured at amortised cost in accordance with IFRS 9, amortised cost is calculated in the currency of denomination of that financial asset.

Then, the foreign currency amount is recognised using the closing rate in the entity's financial statements (paragraph 23 of IAS 21). That applies regardless of whether a monetary item is measured at amortised cost or fair value in the foreign currency. A non-monetary financial asset (such as an investment in an equity instrument) that is measured at fair value in the foreign currency is translated using the closing rate (paragraph 23(c) of IAS 21).

As an exception, if the financial asset or financial liability is designated as a hedged item in a fair value hedge of the exposure to changes in foreign currency rates under IFRS 9 (or IAS 39 if an entity elects to apply the hedge accounting requirements in IAS 39), the hedged item is remeasured for changes in foreign currency rates even if it would otherwise have been recognised using a historical rate under IAS 21 (paragraph 6.5.8 of IFRS 9), i.e., the foreign currency amount is recognised using the closing rate. This exception applies to non-monetary items that are carried in terms of historical cost in the foreign currency and are hedged against exposure to foreign currency rates (paragraph 23(b) of IAS 21).

IMPAIRMENT OF FINANCIAL INSTRUMENTS

The approach to impairment is probably the most significant area of change under IFRS 9 when compared against IAS 39. IAS 39 in general adopted an approach of recognising impairment losses when an impairment event had occurred. In contrast, IFRS 9 requires impairment losses to be recognised for financial assets measured at amortised cost or FVTOCI on recognition using an expected credit loss model. IFRS 9 also requires the recognition of impairment losses on lease receivables, contract assets, loan commitments and financial guarantees. Under IFRS 9 it is not necessary for an impairment event to have taken place before credit losses are recognised.

In general, it is expected that impairment provisions will increase by varying degrees depending on the nature and quality of financial assets for most reporters. The new requirements for impairment require significant judgement and estimation and for more complex businesses, such as those involved in lending, the development of models that will need to consider historic as well as forward-looking information to be able to reliably measure expected credit losses.

The requirements to recognise expected credit losses on loan commitments and guarantees follow the thinking that under each of these arrangements, the holder of the instrument has a contractual obligation to the issuer and under that contractual obligation is exposed to credit risk, irrespective of the fact that at the reporting date neither has the loan commitment been drawn nor a guarantee event taken place.

IFRS 9 sets out two approaches to the recognition of expected credit losses: a general approach and a simplified approach.

A Simplified Decision Tree

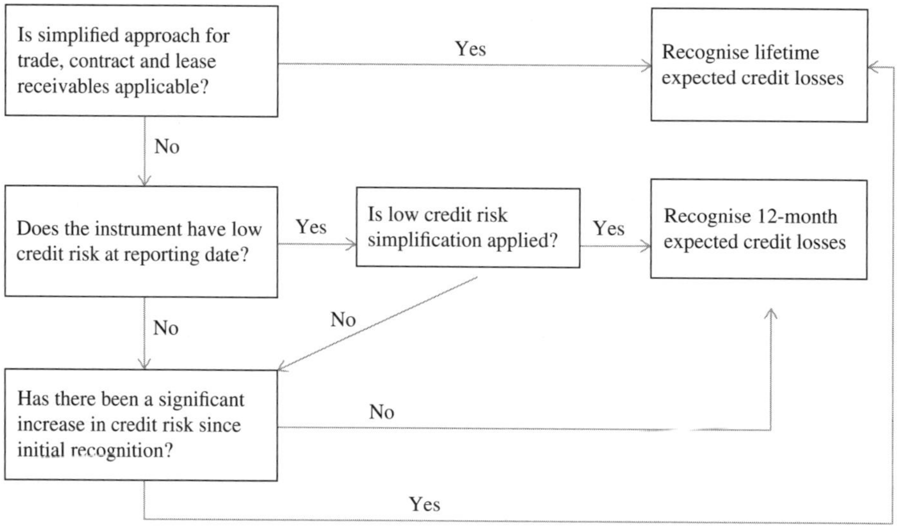

The general approach

Under the general approach to impairment under IFRS 9, impairment loss allowances are recognised at each reporting date as follows:

1. For financial instruments where there has *not* been any significant increase in credit risk since the date of initial recognition, the loss allowance recognised shall represent the 12-month expected credit loss; and
2. For financial instruments where there has been a significant increase in credit risk since initial recognition, a loss allowance for lifetime expected credit losses will be recognised.

Example of the general approach

Bank A issues a loan of €1 million on January 1, 20XX, repayable over three years. It has determined the following probabilities with respect to this loan based on history:

1. The probability of the loan being in default over the three-year term is 3% and the present value of the contractual cash flow over the life of the loan that will not be recovered given the default is €500,000.
2. The probability of the loan being in default over the next 12 months is 1% and the present value of the contractual cash flows due in the next 12 months that will not be recovered given the default is €100,000.
3. The probability of the loan being in default over the next 12 months is 1% and the present value of the contractual cash flows over the life of the loan that will not be recovered given the default is €300,000.

Under the example above, if Bank A was using the approach of recognising 12-month expected credit losses (if there was no significant increase in credit risk), the loss allowance that it would recognise would be under option (3) above and would be measured at 1% of €300,000 = €3,000.

If the credit risk had significantly increased since initial recognition and Bank A was therefore required to measure expected credit losses using the lifetime approach, the loss allowance that it would recognise would be based on option (1) above and would be measured at 3% of €500,000 = €15,000.

The objective of the impairment requirements under the general approach is to recognise lifetime expected credit losses for all financial instruments for which there have been significant increases in credit risk since initial recognition, whether assessed on an individual or collective basis, considering all reasonable and supportable information, including that which is forward looking.

For loan commitments and financial guarantee contracts, the date that the entity becomes a party to the irrevocable commitment shall be the date of initial recognition for the purposes of applying the impairment requirements.

If an entity has measured the loss allowance for a financial instrument at an amount equal to lifetime expected credit losses in the previous reporting period but determines at the current reporting date that there is no longer a significant increase in credit risk from the initial recognition date, the entity shall measure the loss allowance at an amount equal to 12-month expected credit losses at the current reporting date.

In respect of assets classified to be measured at FVTOCI, the loss allowance shall be recognised in other comprehensive income and shall not reduce the carrying amount of the financial asset in the statement of financial position, i.e., the carrying amount of the financial instrument must equate to its fair value, which will be expected to have already factored in any impairment.

Example of debt instrument measured at FVTOCI (IFRS 9 IE78–81)

An entity purchases a debt instrument with a fair value of €1,000 on December 15, 20XX, and measures the debt instrument at FVTOCI. The instrument has an interest rate of 5% over the contractual term of 10 years and has a 5% effective interest rate. At initial recognition, the entity determines that the asset is not purchased or originated credit impaired.

	Debit	Credit
Financial asset—FVOCI	€1,000	
Cash		€1,000
(To recognise the debt instrument measured at its fair value)		

On December 31, 20XX (the reporting date), the fair value of the debt instrument has decreased to €950 because of changes in market interest rates. The entity determines that there has not been a significant increase in credit risk since initial recognition and that expected credit losses should be measured at an amount equal to 12-month expected credit losses, which amounts to €30. For simplicity, journal entries for the receipt of interest revenue are not provided.

	Debit	Credit
Impairment loss (profit or loss)	€30	
Other comprehensive income	20	
Financial asset—FVOCI		€50
(To recognise 12-month expected credit losses and other fair value changes on the debt instrument)		

Disclosure would be provided about the accumulated impairment amount of €30. On January 1, 20XX+1, the entity decides to sell the debt instrument for €950, which is its fair value at that date.

	Debit	Credit
Cash	€950	
Financial asset—FVTOCI		€950
Loss (profit or loss)	€20	
Other comprehensive income		€20
(To derecognise the FVTOCI asset and recycle amounts accumulated in other comprehensive income to profit or loss)		

Determining Significant Increases in Credit Risk Since Initial Recognition

Based on the requirements above, the determination of whether credit risk has increased, and whether that increase is significant, is a critical aspect of applying the general approach to impairment under IFRS 9.

IFRS 9 requires an assessment to be made at each reporting date as to whether the credit risk on a financial instrument has increased significantly since initial recognition. When making the assessment, the change in the risk of a default occurring over the expected life of the financial instrument is used instead of the change in the amount of expected credit losses. To make that assessment, an entity shall compare the risk of a default occurring on the financial instrument as at the reporting date with the risk of a default occurring on the financial instrument as at the date of initial recognition and consider reasonable and supportable information, that is available without undue cost or effort, that is indicative of significant increases in credit risk since initial recognition.

Indicators that are relevant in assessing credit risk include:

1. A change in the internal interest rate, or other pricing, of instruments since the date the instrument was first recognised;
2. A change in other terms of instruments such as conditions and covenants, collateral, etc.;
3. Changes in market interest rates and spreads for similar instruments;
4. Internal and external credit rating scores;
5. Changes in the operations of the borrower, including financial performance and deviation from forecasts and projections;
6. Changes in economic conditions, including regulatory changes that affect the borrower;
7. Changes in the value of collateral;
8. Defaults on other instruments by the same borrower;
9. Changes in the ability or intention of guarantors as well as parent entities of the borrowers that may be instrumental in providing financial support to the borrower; and
10. Past due information, including the rebuttable presumption that has been discussed above.

Lifetime expected credit losses are generally expected to be recognised before a financial instrument becomes past due. Typically, credit risk increases significantly before a financial instrument becomes past due or other lagging borrower-specific factors (for example, a modification or restructuring) are observed. Consequently, when reasonable and supportable information that is more forward looking than past due information is available without undue cost or effort, it must be used to assess changes in credit risk.

IFRS 9 includes a rebuttable presumption that the credit risk on a financial asset has increased significantly since initial recognition when contractual payments are more than 30 days past due. This is irrespective of the way an entity measures significant increases in credit risk. An entity can, however, rebut this presumption based on reasonable and supportable information that is available without undue cost or effort, which demonstrates that the credit risk has not increased significantly since initial recognition even though the contractual payments are more than 30 days past due.

Example of significant increase in credit risk (IFRS 9 IE7–11 adapted)

Company Y has a funding structure that includes a senior secured loan facility with different tranches. Bank X provides a tranche of that loan facility to Company Y. At the time of origination of the loan by Bank X, although Company Y's leverage was relatively high compared with other issuers with similar credit risk, it was expected that Company Y would be able to meet the covenants for the life of the instrument. In addition, the generation of revenue and cash flow was expected to be stable in Company Y's industry over the term of the senior facility. However, there was some business risk related to the ability to grow gross margins within its existing businesses.

At initial recognition, Bank X considers that despite the level of credit risk at initial recognition, the loan is not an originated credit-impaired loan.

After initial recognition, macroeconomic changes have had a negative effect on total sales volume and Company Y has underperformed on its business plan for revenue generation and net cash flow generation. Although spending on inventory has increased, anticipated sales have not materialised. To increase liquidity, Company Y has drawn down more on a separate revolving credit facility, thereby increasing its leverage ratio. Consequently, Company Y is now close to breaching its covenants on the senior secured loan facility with Bank X.

Bank X makes an overall assessment of the credit risk on the loan to Company Y at the reporting date by taking into consideration all reasonable and supportable information that is available without undue cost or effort and that is relevant for assessing the extent of the increase in credit risk since initial recognition. This may include factors such as:

1. Bank X's expectation that the deterioration in the macroeconomic environment may continue soon, which is expected to have a further negative impact on Company Y's ability to generate cash flows and to deleverage.
2. Company Y is closer to breaching its covenants, which may result in a need to restructure the loan or reset the covenants.
3. Bank X's assessment that the trading prices for Company Y's bonds have decreased and that the credit margin on newly originated loans have increased reflecting the increase in credit risk, and that these changes are not explained by changes in the market environment (for example, benchmark interest rates have remained unchanged). A further comparison with the pricing of Company Y's peers shows that reductions in the price of Company Y's bonds and increases in credit margin on its loans have probably been caused by company-specific factors.
4. Bank X has reassessed its internal risk grading of the loan based on the information that it has available to reflect the increase in credit risk.

Bank X determines that there has been a significant increase in credit risk since initial recognition of the loan in accordance with IFRS 9. Consequently, Bank X recognises lifetime expected credit losses on its senior secured loan to Company Y.

Example of no significant increase in credit risk (IFRS 9 IE12–17 adapted)

Company C is the holding company of a group that operates in a cyclical production industry. Bank B provided a loan to Company C. At that time, the prospects for the industry were positive, because of expectations of further increases in global demand. However, input prices were volatile and given the point in the cycle, a potential decrease in sales was anticipated.

In addition, in the past Company C has been focused on external growth, acquiring majority stakes in companies in related sectors. As a result, the group structure is complex and has been subject to change, making it difficult for investors to analyse the expected performance of the group and to forecast the cash that will be available at the holding company level. Even though leverage is at a level that is considered acceptable by Company C's creditors at the time that Bank B originates the loan, its creditors are concerned about Company C's ability to refinance its debt because of the short remaining life until the maturity of the current financing. There is also concern about Company C's ability to continue to service interest using the dividends it receives from its operating subsidiaries.

At the time of the origination of the loan by Bank B, Company C's leverage was in line with that of other customers with similar credit risk and based on projections over the expected life of the loan, the available capacity (i.e., headroom) on its coverage ratios before triggering a default event was high. Bank B applies its own internal rating methods to determine credit risk and allocates a specific internal rating score to its loans. Bank B's internal rating categories are based on historical, current and forward-looking information and reflect the credit risk for the tenor of the loans. On initial recognition, Bank B determines that the loan is subject to considerable credit risk, has speculative elements and that the uncertainties affecting Company C, including the group's uncertain prospects for cash generation, could lead to default. However, Bank B does not consider the loan to be originated credit impaired.

After initial recognition, Company C has announced that three of its five key subsidiaries had a significant reduction in sales volume because of deteriorated market conditions but sales volumes are expected to improve in line with the anticipated cycle for the industry in the following months. The sales of the other two subsidiaries were stable. Company C has also announced a corporate restructure to streamline its operating subsidiaries. This restructuring will increase the flexibility to refinance existing debt and the ability of the operating subsidiaries to pay dividends to Company C.

Despite the expected continuing deterioration in market conditions, Bank B determines that there has not been a significant increase in the credit risk on the loan to Company C since initial recognition. This is demonstrated by factors that include:

1. Although current sale volumes have fallen, this was as anticipated by Bank B at initial recognition. Furthermore, sales volumes are expected to improve in the following months.
2. Given the increased flexibility to refinance the existing debt at the operating subsidiary level and the increased availability of dividends to Company C, Bank B views the corporate restructure as being credit enhancing. This is despite some continued concern about the ability to refinance the existing debt at the holding company level.
3. Bank B's credit risk department, which monitors Company C, has determined that the latest developments are not significant enough to justify a change in its internal credit risk rating.

Therefore, Bank B does not recognise a loss allowance at an amount equal to lifetime expected credit losses on the loan. However, it updates its measurement of the 12-month expected credit losses for the increased risk of a default occurring in the next 12 months and for current expectations of the credit losses that would arise if a default were to occur.

Instruments Determined to Have Low Credit Risk at the Reporting Date

IFRS 9 allows an entity to assume that the credit risk on a financial instrument has not increased significantly since initial recognition if the financial instrument is determined to have low credit risk at the reporting date. Low credit risk applies if the financial instrument has a minimal risk of default, the borrower has a strong capacity to meet its contractual cash flow obligations in the near term and adverse changes in economic and business conditions in the longer term may, but will not necessarily, reduce the ability of the borrower to fulfil its contractual cash flow obligations.

Financial instruments are, however, not considered to have low credit risk when they are regarded as having a minimal risk of loss simply because of the value of collateral, and the financial instrument without that collateral would not be considered low credit risk. Financial instruments are also not considered to have low credit risk simply because they have a lower risk of default than the entity's other financial instruments or relative to the credit risk of the jurisdiction within which an entity operates.

Lifetime expected credit losses are not recognised on a financial instrument simply because it was considered to have low credit risk in the previous reporting period and is not considered to have low credit risk at the reporting date. In such a case, an entity shall determine whether there has been a significant increase in credit risk since initial recognition and thus whether lifetime expected credit losses are required to be recognised.

Collective and Individual Assessment Basis for Determining Significant Increases in Credit Risk

To meet the objective of recognising lifetime expected credit losses for significant increases in credit risk since initial recognition, it may be necessary to perform the assessment of significant increases in credit risk on a collective basis by considering information that is indicative of significant increases in credit risk on, for example, a group or subgroup of financial instruments. This is particularly in cases where an entity does not have reasonable and supportable information that is available without undue cost or effort to measure lifetime expected credit losses on an individual instrument basis. In that case, lifetime expected credit losses shall be recognised on a collective basis that considers comprehensive credit risk information. This comprehensive credit risk information must incorporate not only past due information but also all relevant credit information, including forward-looking macroeconomic information, to approximate the result of recognising lifetime expected credit losses when there has been a significant increase in credit risk since initial recognition on an individual instrument level.

For determining significant increases in credit risk and recognising a loss allowance on a collective basis, an entity can group financial instruments based on shared credit risk characteristics with the objective of facilitating an analysis that is designed to enable significant increases in credit risk to be identified on a timely basis. The entity should not obscure this information by grouping financial instruments with different risk characteristics. Examples of shared credit risk characteristics may include, but are not limited to:

1. Instrument type;
2. Credit risk ratings;
3. Collateral type;
4. Date of initial recognition;
5. Remaining term to maturity;
6. Industry;
7. Geographical location of the borrower; and
8. Value of collateral relative to the financial asset if it has an impact on the probability of a default occurring (for example, non-recourse loans in some jurisdictions or loan-to-value (LTV) ratios).

Example of responsiveness to changes in credit risk (IFRS 9 IE 29–39 adapted)

Bank ABC provides mortgages to finance residential real estate in three different regions. The mortgage loans are originated across a wide range of (LTV) criteria and a wide range of income groups. As part of the mortgage application process, customers are required to provide information such as the industry within which the customer is employed and the post code of the property that serves as collateral on the mortgage.

Bank ABC sets its acceptance criteria based on credit scores. Loans with a credit score above the "acceptance level" are approved because these borrowers can meet contractual payment obligations. When new mortgage loans are originated, Bank ABC uses the credit score to determine the risk of a default occurring as at initial recognition.

At the reporting date Bank ABC determines that economic conditions are expected to deteriorate significantly in all regions. Unemployment levels are expected to increase while the value of residential property is expected to decrease, causing the LTV ratios to increase. Because of the expected deterioration in economic conditions, Bank ABC expects default rates on the mortgage portfolio to increase.

Individual assessment

In Region One, Bank ABC assesses each of its mortgage loans monthly by means of an automated behavioural scoring process. Its scoring models are based on current and historical past due statuses, levels of customer indebtedness, LTV measures, customer behaviour on other financial instruments with Bank ABC, the loan size and the time since the origination of the loan. Bank ABC updates the LTV measures on a regular basis through an automated process that re-estimates property values using recent sales in each post code area and reasonable and supportable forward-looking information that is available without undue cost or effort.

Bank ABC has historical data that indicates a strong correlation between the value of residential property and the default rates for mortgages. That is, when the value of residential property declines, a customer has less economic incentive to make scheduled mortgage repayments, increasing the risk of a default occurring.

Through the impact of the LTV measure in the behavioural scoring model, an increased risk of a default occurring due to an expected decline in residential property value adjusts the behavioural scores. The behavioural score can be adjusted because of expected declines in property value even when the mortgage loan is a bullet loan with the most significant payment obligations at maturity (and beyond the next 12 months). Mortgages with a high LTV ratio are more sensitive to changes in the value of the residential property and Bank ABC can identify significant increases in credit risk since initial recognition on individual customers before a mortgage becomes past due if there has been a deterioration in the behavioural score.

When the increase in credit risk has been significant, a loss allowance at an amount equal to lifetime expected credit losses is recognised. Bank ABC measures the loss allowance by using the LTV measures to estimate the severity of the loss, i.e., the loss given default. The higher the LTV measure, the higher the expected credit losses, all else being equal.

If Bank ABC was unable to update behavioural scores to reflect the expected declines in property prices, it would use reasonable and supportable information that is available without undue cost or effort to undertake a collective assessment to determine the loans on which there has been a significant increase in credit risk since initial recognition and recognise lifetime expected credit losses for those loans.

Collective assessment

In Regions Two and Three, Bank ABC does not have an automated scoring capability. Instead, for credit risk management purposes, Bank ABC tracks the risk of a default occurring by means of past due statuses. It recognises a loss allowance at an amount equal to lifetime expected credit losses for all loans that have a past due status of more than 30 days past due. Although Bank ABC uses past due status information as the only borrower-specific information, it also considers other reasonable and supportable forward-looking information that is available without undue cost or effort to assess whether lifetime expected credit losses should be recognised on loans that are not more than 30 days past due. This is necessary to meet the objective in IFRS 9 of recognising lifetime expected credit losses for all significant increases in credit risk.

Region Two

Region Two includes a mining community that is largely dependent on the export of coal and related products. Bank ABC becomes aware of a significant decline in coal exports and anticipates the closure of several coal mines. Because of the expected increase in the unemployment rate, the risk of a default occurring on mortgage loans to borrowers who are employed by the coal mines is determined to have increased significantly, even if those customers are not past due at the reporting date. Bank ABC therefore segments its mortgage portfolio by the industry within which customers are employed (using the information recorded as part of the mortgage application process) to identify customers that rely on coal mining as the dominant source of employment (i.e., a "bottom-up" approach in which loans are identified based on a common risk characteristic). For those mortgages, Bank ABC recognises a loss allowance at an amount equal to lifetime expected credit losses while it continues to recognise a loss allowance at an amount equal to 12-month expected credit losses for all other mortgages in Region Two.

Newly originated mortgages to borrowers who rely on the coal mines for employment in this community would, however, have a loss allowance at an amount equal to 12-month expected credit losses because they would not have experienced significant increases in credit risk since initial recognition. However, some of these mortgages may experience significant increases in credit risk soon after initial recognition because of the expected closure of the coal mines.

Region Three

In Region Three, Bank ABC anticipates the risk of a default occurring and thus an increase in credit risk, because of an expected increase in interest rates during the expected life of the mortgages. Historically, an increase in interest rates has been a lead indicator of future defaults on mortgages in Region Three—especially when customers do not have a fixed interest rate mortgage. Bank ABC determines that the variable interest rate portfolio of mortgages in Region Three is homogeneous and that unlike for Region Two, it is not possible to identify subportfolios based on shared risk characteristics that represent customers who are expected to have increased significantly in credit risk. However, because of the homogeneous nature of the mortgages in Region Three, Bank ABC determines that an assessment can be made of a proportion of the overall portfolio that has significantly increased in credit risk since initial recognition (i.e., a "top-down" approach can be used).

Based on historical information, Bank ABC estimates that an increase in interest rates of 200 basis points will cause a significant increase in credit risk on 20% of the variable interest rate portfolio. Therefore, because of the anticipated increase in interest rates, Bank ABC determines that the credit risk on 20% of mortgages in Region Three has increased significantly since initial recognition. Accordingly, Bank ABC recognises lifetime expected credit losses on 20% of the variable rate mortgage portfolio and a loss allowance at an amount equal to 12-month expected credit losses for the remainder of the portfolio.

Reasonable and Supportable Forward-Looking Information

If reasonable and supportable forward-looking information is available without undue cost or effort, an entity cannot rely solely on past due information when determining whether credit risk has increased significantly since initial recognition. However, IFRS 9 permits that when information that is more forward looking than past due (either on an individual or a collective basis) is not available without undue cost or effort, an entity may use past due information to determine whether there have been significant increases in credit risk since initial recognition.

For IFRS 9, reasonable and supportable information is that which is reasonably available at the reporting date without undue cost or effort, including information about past events, current conditions and forecasts of future economic conditions. Information that is available for financial reporting purposes is considered to be available without undue cost or effort.

While an entity is not required to undertake an exhaustive search for all possible information, the standard requires an entity to consider the information that is available without undue cost of effort. An entity can use various sources for such data collection, including internal information on past performance, credit ratings, pricing and margins, as well as external information such as that from credit rating agencies as well as wider macroeconomic and regulatory information.

Significant information can also be obtained from a review of the borrower's financial and operational performance as well as forecast information/budgets and historical performance against such forecasts. It should be borne in mind that while the standard recognises the need for and importance of historical information, it requires such historical data to be adjusted to reflect current conditions and forecasts of future conditions.

An entity shall regularly review the methodology and assumptions used for estimating expected credit losses to reduce any differences between estimates and actual credit loss experience.

Modified Financial Assets

If the contractual cash flows on a financial asset have been renegotiated or modified and the financial asset was not derecognised, an entity shall assess whether there has been a significant increase in the credit risk of the financial instrument in accordance by comparing:

1. The risk of a default occurring at the reporting date (based on the modified contractual terms); and
2. The risk of a default occurring at initial recognition (based on the original, unmodified contractual terms).

In cases where the renegotiation or modification of the contractual cash flows of a financial asset leads to the derecognition of the existing financial asset and the subsequent recognition of the modified financial asset, the modified asset is considered a "new" financial asset. This typically means measuring the loss allowance at an amount equal to 12-month expected credit losses on the newly recognised financial asset until the requirements for the recognition of lifetime expected credit losses are met. However, in some circumstances following a modification that results in derecognition of the original financial asset, there may be evidence that the modified financial asset is credit impaired at initial recognition, and thus the financial asset should be recognised as an originated credit-impaired financial asset.

Purchased or Originated Credit-Impaired Financial Assets

Where an entity initially recognises a financial asset that is purchased or originated credit impaired, the entity shall only recognise the cumulative changes in lifetime expected credit losses since initial recognition as a loss allowance for purchased or originated credit-impaired financial assets.

A financial asset is credit impaired on purchase or origination where one or more events that have a detrimental impact on expected future cash flows of that financial asset have occurred at the date of initial recognition. Such events include significant financial difficulty of the issuer/borrower, breach of contract, probability of bankruptcy or other financial reorganisation, disappearance of an active trading market and purchases of the financial asset at a deep discount.

Simplified Approach for Trade Receivables, Contract Assets and Lease Receivables

As an alternative to the general approach, IFRS 9 provides for a simplified approach to the measurement of loss allowances in respect of:

1. Trade receivables or contract assets that result from transactions that are within the scope of IFRS 15, and that:
   - Do not contain a significant financing component in accordance with IFRS 15 (or when the entity applies the practical expedient in accordance with paragraph 63 of IFRS 15); or

- Contain a significant financing component in accordance with IFRS 15, if the entity chooses as its accounting policy to measure the loss allowance at an amount equal to lifetime expected credit losses. That accounting policy shall be applied to all such trade receivables or contract assets but may be applied separately to trade receivables and contract assets.

2. Lease receivables that result from transactions that are within the scope of IFRS 16, if the entity chooses as its accounting policy to measure the loss allowance at an amount equal to lifetime expected credit losses. That accounting policy shall be applied to all lease receivables but may be applied separately to finance and operating lease receivables.

For such assets, IFRS 9 permits the recognition of lifetime expected credit losses from inception. This is a simplified approach in that it does not require the significant estimation and judgement necessary to determine whether there have been changes in credit risk and whether such changes are significant. It does, however, mean that the credit loss allowances recognised under the simplified approach will likely be higher than the credit losses under the general approach for those assets where the credit risk has not significantly increased.

As a practical expedient, IFRS 9 permits the use of a provision matrix for purposes of measuring lifetime expected credit losses for trade receivables.

Example of a provision matrix (adapted from IFRS 9 IE74–77 Example 12)

Company M, a manufacturer, has a portfolio of trade receivables of €30 million in 20XX and operates only in one geographical region. The customer base consists of many small clients and the trade receivables are categorised by common risk characteristics that are representative of the customers' abilities to pay all amounts due in accordance with the contractual terms. The trade receivables do not have a significant financing component in accordance with IFRS 15, *Revenue from Contracts with Customers*. In accordance with the simplified approach under IFRS 9, the loss allowance for such trade receivables is always measured at an amount equal to lifetime expected credit losses.

To determine the expected credit losses for the portfolio, Company M uses a provision matrix. The provision matrix is based on its historical observed default rates over the expected life of the trade receivables and is adjusted for forward-looking estimates. At every reporting date, the historical observed default rates are updated and changes in the forward-looking estimates are analysed. In this case it is forecast that economic conditions will deteriorate over the next year.

On that basis, Company M estimates the following provision matrix:

	Current	**1–30 days past due**	**31–60 days past due**	**61–90 days past due**	**More than 90 days past due**
Default rate	0.3%	1.6%	3.6%	6.6%	10.6%

The trade receivables from the large number of small customers amount to €30 million and are measured using the provision matrix.

	Gross carrying amount	Lifetime expected credit loss allowance (Gross carrying amount × Lifetime expected credit loss rate)
Current	€15,000,000	€45,000
1–30 days past due	€7,500,000	€120,000
31–60 days past due	€4,000,000	€144,000
61–90 days past due	€2,500,000	€165,000
More than 90 days past due	€1,000,000	€106,000
	€30,000,000	€580,000

Measurement of Expected Credit Losses and Applying Probabilities

An entity shall measure expected credit losses of a financial instrument in a way that reflects:

1. An unbiased and probability-weighted amount that is determined by evaluating a range of possible outcomes;
2. The time value of money; and
3. Reasonable and supportable information that is available without undue cost or effort at the reporting date about past events, current conditions and forecasts of future economic conditions.

When measuring expected credit losses, an entity need not necessarily identify every possible scenario. However, it shall consider the risk or probability that a credit loss occurs by reflecting the possibility that a credit loss occurs and the possibility that no credit loss occurs, even if the possibility of a credit loss occurring is very low.

The estimate of expected credit losses should reflect an unbiased and probability-weighted amount that is determined by evaluating a range of possible outcomes. In practice, this may not need to be a complex analysis. In some cases, relatively simple modelling may be sufficient, without the need for a large number of detailed simulations of scenarios. For example, the average credit losses of a large group of financial instruments with shared risk characteristics may be a reasonable estimate of the probability-weighted amount. In other situations, the identification of scenarios that specify the amount and timing of the cash flows for outcomes and the estimated probability of those outcomes will probably be needed. In those situations, the expected credit losses shall reflect at least two outcomes (i.e., the probability of a credit loss and the probability of no credit loss).

The maximum period to consider when measuring expected credit losses is the maximum contractual period (including extension options) over which the entity is exposed to credit risk and not a longer period, even if that longer period is consistent with business practice.

However, some financial instruments include both a loan and an undrawn commitment component and the entity's contractual ability to demand repayment and cancel the undrawn commitment does not limit the entity's exposure to credit losses to the contractual notice period. For such financial instruments, and only those financial instruments, the entity shall measure expected credit losses over the period that the entity is exposed to credit risk and expected credit losses would not be mitigated by credit risk management actions, even if that period extends beyond the maximum contractual period.

Expected credit losses are a probability-weighted estimate of credit losses (i.e., the present value of all cash flow shortfalls) over the expected life of the financial instrument. A cash shortfall is the difference between the cash flows that are due to an entity in accordance with the contract and the cash flows that the entity expects to receive. Because expected credit losses consider the amount and timing of payments, a credit loss arises even if the entity expects to be paid in full but later than when contractually due.

For financial assets, a credit loss is the present value of the difference between:

1. The contractual cash flows that are due to an entity under the contract; and
2. The cash flows that the entity expects to receive.

For undrawn loan commitments, a credit loss is the present value of the difference between:

1. The contractual cash flows that are due to the entity if the holder of the loan commitment draws down the loan; and
2. The cash flows that the entity expects to receive if the loan is drawn down.

For a financial guarantee contract, the entity is required to make payments only in the event of a default by the debtor in accordance with the terms of the instrument that is guaranteed. Accordingly, cash shortfalls are the expected payments to reimburse the holder for a credit loss that it incurs less any amounts that the entity expects to receive from the holder, the debtor or any other party. If the asset is fully guaranteed, the estimation of cash shortfalls for a financial guarantee contract would be consistent with the estimations of cash shortfalls for the asset subject to the guarantee.

For a financial asset that is credit impaired at the reporting date, but that is not a purchased or originated credit-impaired financial asset, an entity shall measure the expected credit losses as the difference between the asset's gross carrying amount and the present value of estimated future cash flows discounted at the financial asset's original effective interest rate. Any adjustment is recognised in profit or loss as an impairment gain or loss.

When measuring a loss allowance for a lease receivable, the cash flows used for determining the expected credit losses should be consistent with the cash flows used in measuring the lease receivable in accordance with IFRS 16, *Leases*.

Impact of Collateral

For the purposes of measuring expected credit losses, the estimate of expected cash shortfalls shall reflect the cash flows expected from collateral and other credit enhancements that are part of the contractual terms and are not recognised separately by the entity. The estimate of expected cash shortfalls on a collateralised financial instrument reflects the amount and timing of cash flows that are expected from foreclosure on the collateral less the costs of obtaining and selling the collateral, irrespective of whether foreclosure is probable (i.e., the estimate of expected cash flows considers the probability of a foreclosure and the cash flows that would result from it).

Consequently, any cash flows that are expected from the realisation of the collateral beyond the contractual maturity of the contract should be included in this analysis. Any collateral obtained because of foreclosure is not recognised as an asset that is separate from the collateralised financial instrument unless it meets the relevant recognition criteria for an asset in this or other standards.

HEDGE ACCOUNTING

The topic of hedging is almost intertwined with the subject of derivatives, since most (but not all) hedging is accomplished using derivatives. In this section, derivatives and derivative financial instruments will be presented first, followed by hedging activities.

Derivatives

As a general principle under IFRS 9, all derivatives are accounted for in the statement of financial position at fair value, irrespective of whether they are used as part of a hedging relationship. Changes in fair value are recognised in profit or loss unless this is part of an effective cash flow hedge of net investment hedge, in which case the change in fair value of the effective portion is recognised in other comprehensive income.

IFRS 9 defines a derivative as a financial instrument or other contract with all three of the following features:

1. Its value changes in response to changes in a specified interest rate, security price, commodity price, foreign exchange rate, index of prices or rates, a credit rating or credit index or other variable, provided in the case of a non-financial variable that the variable is not specific to a party to the contract;
2. It requires little or no initial net investment relative to the other types of contracts that have a similar response to changes in market conditions; and
3. It is settled at a future date.

The definition is important because it is used in determining the classification and measurement of financial instruments. If any financial instrument meets the above definition it is classified as FVTPL unless the instrument is designated as a hedging instrument.

The underlying variable is that variable that will determine the settlement of a derivative (with a notional amount or a payment provision).

Examples of financial instruments that meet the foregoing definition include the following, along with the underlying variable which affects the derivative's value:

Type of contract	**Main pricing—settlement variable (underlying variable)**
Interest rate swap	Interest rates
Currency swap (foreign exchange swap)	Currency rates
Commodity swap	Commodity prices
Equity swap (equity of another entity)	Equity prices
Credit swap	Credit rating, credit index or credit price
Total return swap	Total fair value of the reference asset and interest rates
Purchased or written treasury bond option (call or put)	Interest rates
Purchased or written currency option (call or put)	Currency rates
Purchased or written commodity option (call or put)	Commodity prices

Purchased or written share option (call or put)	Equity prices (equity of another entity)
Interest rate futures linked to government debt (treasury futures)	Interest rates
Currency futures	Currency rates
Commodity futures	Commodity prices
Interest rate forward linked to government debt (treasury forward)	Interest rates
Currency forward	Currency rates
Commodity forward	Commodity prices
Equity forward	Equity prices (equity of another entity)

The issue of what is meant by "little or no net investment" has been explored by the IASB's Implementation Guidance Committee (IGC). IGC's view is that professional judgement will be required in determining what constitutes little or no initial net investment and is to be interpreted on a relative basis. The initial net investment is less than that needed to acquire a primary financial instrument with a similar response to changes in market conditions. This reflects the inherent leverage features typical of derivative agreements compared to the underlying instruments. If, for example, a "deep in the money" call option is purchased (that is, the option's value consists mostly of intrinsic value), a significant premium is paid. If the premium is equal or close to the amount required to invest in the underlying instrument, this would fail the "little initial net investment" criterion.

A margin account is not part of the initial net investment in a derivative instrument. Margin accounts are a form of collateral for the counterparty or clearing house and may take the form of cash, instruments or other specified assets, typically liquid ones. Margin accounts are separate assets that are to be accounted for separately. Accordingly, in determining whether an arrangement qualifies as a derivative, the margin deposit is not a factor in assessing whether the "little or no net investment" criterion has been met.

A financial instrument can qualify as a derivative even if the settlement amount does not vary proportionately. An example of this phenomenon was provided by the IGC.

Example of a derivative transaction

Accurate enters into a contract that requires it to pay Aimless €2 million if the share price of Reference rises by €5 per share or more during a six-month period. Conversely, Accurate will receive from Aimless a payment of €2 million if the share price of Reference declines by €5 or more during that same six-month period. If price changes are within the ±€5 collar range, no payments will be made or received by the parties. This arrangement would qualify as a derivative instrument, the underlying being the price of Reference. IFRS 9 provides that "a derivative could require a fixed payment as a result of some future event that is unrelated to a notional amount."

In some instances, what might first appear to be a normal financial instrument may actually be a derivative.

Example of apparent loans that qualify as a derivative transaction

Aguilar makes a five-year fixed rate loan to Battapaglia, while Battapaglia at the same time makes a five-year variable rate loan for the same amount to Aguilar. There are no transfers of principal at inception of the two loans, since Aguilar and Battapaglia have a netting agreement. While superficially these appear to be two unconditional debt obligations, in fact this meets the definition of a derivative, as there is an underlying variable, no or little initial net investment and future settlement, such that the contractual effect of the loans is the equivalent of an interest rate swap arrangement with no initial net investment. Non-derivative transactions are aggregated and treated as a derivative when the transactions result, in substance, in a derivative.

Indicators of this situation would include:

1. The transactions are entered into at the same time and in contemplation of one another;
2. They have the same counterparty;
3. They relate to the same risk; and
4. There is no apparent economic need or substantive business purpose for structuring the transactions separately that could not also have been accomplished in a single transaction. Note that even in the absence of a netting agreement, the foregoing arrangement would have been deemed to be a derivative.

Another example of this is debt instruments that include options for early settlement (prepayments), puts or calls which allow either party to terminate the contract before maturity. Such options comprise derivatives (embedded derivatives as defined below) which may need to be separately accounted for from the underlying debt instrument (see below for further guidance in this respect).

Identifying whether certain transactions involve derivatives

The definition of derivatives has already been addressed. While seemingly straightforward, the almost limitless and still expanding variety of "engineered" financial products often makes definitive categorisation more difficult than this at first would appear to be.

The IGC illustrates this with examples of two variants on interest rate swaps, both of which involve prepayments. The first of these, a prepaid interest rate swap (fixed rate payment obligation prepaid at inception or subsequently), qualifies as a derivative; the second, a variable rate payment obligation prepaid at inception or subsequently, would not be a derivative. The reasoning is set forth in the next paragraphs, which are adapted from the IGC guidance.

Example of interest rate swap to be accounted for as a derivative

First, consider the "pay-fixed, receive-variable" interest rate swap that the party prepays at inception. Assume enters into a €100 million notional amount five-year pay-fixed, receive-variable interest rate swap with Baltic. The interest rate of the variable part of the swap resets on a quarterly basis to the three-month LIBOR. The interest rate of the fixed part of the swap is 10% per year. Assume prepays its fixed obligation under the swap of €50 million (= €100 million × 10% × 5 years) at inception, discounted using market interest rates, while retaining the right to receive interest payments on the €100 million reset quarterly based on three-month LIBOR over the life of the swap.

The initial net investment in the interest rate swap is significantly less than the notional amount on which the variable payments under the variable leg will be calculated. The contract requires little initial net investment relative to other types of contracts that have a similar response to changes in market conditions, such as a variable rate bond. Therefore, the contract fulfils the "no or little initial net investment" provision of IFRS 9. Even though Assume has no future performance obligation, the ultimate settlement of the contract is at a future date and the value of the contract changes in response to changes in the LIBOR index. Accordingly, the contract is considered to be a derivative contract. The IGC further notes that the fixed rate payment obligation is prepaid subsequent to initial recognition, which would be considered a termination of the old swap and an origination of a new instrument, which would have to be evaluated under IFRS 9.

Now consider the opposite situation, a prepaid pay-variable, receive-fixed interest rate swap, which the IGC concludes is not a derivative. This result obtains because it provides a return on the prepaid (invested) amount comparable to the return on a debt instrument with fixed cash flows.

Example of interest rate swap not to be accounted for as a derivative

Synchronous enters into a €100 million notional amount five-year "pay-variable, receive-fixed" interest rate swap with counterparty Cabot. The variable leg of the swap resets on a quarterly basis to the three-month LIBOR. The fixed interest payments under the swap are calculated as 10% times the swap's notional amount, or €10 million per year. Synchronous prepays its obligation under the variable leg of the swap at inception at current market rates, while retaining the right to receive fixed interest payments of 10% on €100 million per year.

The cash inflows under the contract are equivalent to those of a financial instrument with a fixed annuity stream, since Synchronous knows it will receive €10 million per year over the life of the swap. Therefore, all else being equal, the initial investment in the contract should equal that of other financial instruments that consist of fixed annuities. Thus, the initial net investment in the pay-variable, receive-fixed interest rate swap is equal to the investment required in a non-derivative contract that has a similar response to changes in market conditions. For this reason, the instrument fails the "no or little net investment" criterion of IFRS 9. Therefore, the contract is *not* to be accounted for as a derivative under IFRS 9. By discharging the obligation to pay variable interest rate payments, Synchronous effectively extends an annuity loan to Cabot. In this situation, the instrument is accounted for as a loan originated by the entity unless Synchronous has the intent to sell it immediately or in the short term.

In yet other instances arrangements that technically meet the definition of derivatives are not to be accounted for as such.

Example of derivative not to be settled for cash

National Wire enters into a fixed-price forward contract to purchase two million kilograms of copper. The contract permits National Wire to take physical delivery of the copper at the end of 12 months or to pay or receive a net settlement in cash, based on the change in fair value of copper. While such a contract meets the definition of a derivative, it is not necessarily accounted for as a derivative. The contract is a derivative instrument because there is no initial net investment, the contract is based on the price of an underlying, copper, and it is to be settled at a future date. However, if National Wire intends to settle the contract by taking delivery and has no history of settling in cash, the contract is not accounted for as a derivative under IFRS 9. Instead, it is accounted for as an executory contract for the purchase of inventory.

This follows the provisions under IFRS 9 under which contracts to buy or sell non-financial items will not be within the scope of financial instruments accounting when they were entered into, and continue to be held, for the purpose of the receipt of the non-financial item in accordance with the entity's expected purchase, sale or usage requirements (unless the entity elects to treat such contracts as FVTPL because they eliminate or reduce a financial reporting mismatch).

For example, Autoco enters into forward contracts to purchase steel for use in the manufacturing of motor vehicles. It has established past practice of settling such contracts through actual delivery and subsequent consumption of the steel within its manufacturing process. Such forward contracts will be excluded under the provisions of IFRS 9 discussed above. Just as some seemingly derivative transactions may be accounted for as not involving a derivative instrument, the opposite situation can also occur, where some seemingly non-derivative transactions would be accounted for as being derivatives.

Example of non-financial derivative to be settled for cash

Argyle enters into a forward contract to purchase a commodity or other non-financial asset that contractually is to be settled by taking delivery. Argyle has an established pattern of settling such contracts prior to delivery by contracting with a third party. Argyle settles any market value difference for the contract price directly with the third party. This pattern of settlement prohibits Argyle from qualifying for the exemption based on normal delivery; the contract is accounted for as a derivative. IFRS 9 applies to a contract to purchase a non-financial asset if the contract meets the definition of a derivative and the contract does not qualify for the exemption for delivery in the normal course of business. In this case, Argyle does not expect to take delivery. Under the standard, a pattern of entering into offsetting contracts that effectively accomplishes settlement on a net basis does not qualify for the exemption on the grounds of delivery in the normal course of business.

Forward contracts

Forward contracts to purchase, for example, fixed rate debt instruments (such as mortgages) at fixed prices are to be accounted for as derivatives. They meet the definition of a derivative because there is no or little initial net investment, there is an underlying variable (interest rates) and they will be settled in the future. However, such transactions are to be accounted for as a regular-way transaction, if regular-way delivery is required. "Regular-way" delivery is defined to include contracts for purchases or sales of financial instruments that require delivery in the timeframe generally established by regulation or convention in the marketplace concerned. Regular-way contracts are explicitly defined as not being derivatives.

Future contracts

Future contracts are financial instruments that require delivery of a commodity, for example, an equity instrument or currency, at a specified price agreed to on the contract inception date (exercise price), on a specified future date. Futures are like forward contracts except futures have standardised contract terms and are traded on organised exchanges.

Options

Options are contracts that give the buyer (option holder) the right, but not the obligation, to acquire from or sell to the option seller (option writer) a certain quantity of an underlying financial instrument or other commodity, at a specified price (the strike price) and up to a specified date (the expiration date). An option to buy is referred to as a "call"; an option to sell is referred to as a "put."

Swaps

Interest rate (and currency) swaps have become widely used financial arrangements. Swaps are to be accounted for as derivatives whether an interest rate swap settles gross or net. Regardless of how the arrangement is to be settled, the three key defining characteristics are present in all interest rate swaps:

1. Value changes are in response to changes in an underlying variable (interest rates or an index of rates);
2. There are little or no initial net investments; and
3. Settlements will occur at future dates.

Thus, swaps are always derivatives.

Derivatives that are not based on financial instruments

Not all derivatives involve financial instruments. For example, Corboy owns an office building and enters a put option, with a term of five years, with an investor that permits it to put the building to the investor for €15 million. The current value of the building is €17.5 million. The option, if exercised, may be settled through physical delivery or net cash at Corboy's option. Corboy's accounting depends on Corboy's intent and past practice for settlement. Although the contract meets the definition of a derivative, Corboy does not account for it as a derivative if it intends to settle the contract by delivering the building if it exercises its option and there is no past practice of settling net.

The investor, however, cannot conclude that the option was entered to meet the investor's expected purchase, sale or usage requirements because the investor does not have the ability to require delivery. Therefore, the investor has to account for the contract as a derivative. Regardless of past practices, the investor's intention does not affect whether settlement is by delivery or in cash. The investor has written an option, and a written option in which the holder has the choice of physical delivery or net cash settlement can never satisfy the normal delivery requirement for the exemption for the investor. However, if the contract required physical delivery and the reporting entity had no past practice of settling net in cash, the contract would not be accounted for as a derivative.

Examples of contracts that meet the definition of a derivative

Contract	Payment provision/ notional amount	Underlying condition	Initial investment	Future settlement
A future contract to buy 10 million kilograms of rice at €1 (per kilogram) in one month and the contract is not for physical delivery of rice for use in the ordinary course of business	10 million kilograms of rice	Price of rice	Nil	Yes—one month
A contract to receive €20 million if Spa's share price increases by €0.5 per share, at the end of six months. The initial investment is €1 million	Payment provision	Spa's share price	€1 million	Yes—six months
A forward to buy €100 for $120 in one year	$120 or €100	$/€ exchange rate	Nil	One year

A five-year interest rate cap over €100 million. The cap will pay if LIBOR increases beyond 8%. The premium paid to enter into the arrangement is €1 million	€100 million	LIBOR	€1 million	Yes—if during the five-year period LIBOR exceeds 8%

Objective and Scope of Hedge Accounting

Every entity is exposed to commercial risks from its operations. A number of these risks have an impact on its cash flows or the values of its assets or liabilities and therefore ultimately on profit or loss, or other comprehensive income. To manage these risks, entities enter into derivative and other contracts to hedge them. Hedging is therefore a risk management tool used to manage the entity's risk profile.

The application of IFRS to risk management activities can result in accounting mismatches where gains and losses on a hedging instrument are not recognised in the same period (or in the same place in the financial statements) as gains and losses on the hedged exposure or accounting for the hedging instrument.

The requirement of IFRS 9 is to "represent, in the financial statements, the effect of an entity's risk management activities." IFRS 9 does not mandate the use of hedge accounting and it is therefore voluntary.

The link between the risk management strategy of an entity and the risk management objective is crucial, as a change in a risk management objective without a change in the risk management strategy may affect the application of hedge accounting. This is further illustrated through an example below:

Risk management strategy	**Risk management objective**
Maintain 40% of borrowings in floating interest rates	Designate an interest rate swap as a fair value hedge of a €10 million fixed rate borrowing
Hedge foreign currency risk exposure of up to 85% of revenue forecasts in euros up to nine months	Designate a foreign exchange forward contract to hedge the foreign exchange risk

An entity may choose to designate a hedging relationship between a hedging instrument and a hedged item. For hedging relationships that meet the qualifying criteria described below, an entity shall account for the gains or losses on the hedging instruments and the hedged item in accordance with the provisions of IFRS 9, as explained below.

IFRS 9 recognises three types of hedge accounting, depending on the nature of the risk exposure as follows:

1. A *fair value hedge* is a hedge of the exposure to changes in fair values of a recognised asset or liability or an unrecognised firm commitment, or an identified portion of such an asset, liability or firm commitment (a binding agreement for the exchange of a specified quantity of goods or services at a specified price and date), which is attributed to a particular risk and could affect profit or loss.

2. A *cash flow hedge* is a hedge of the exposure to variability in cash flows that is attributed to a particular risk associated with a recognised asset or liability or a highly probable forecast transaction which could affect profit or loss.
3. A *net investment hedge* is a hedge of a foreign currency exposure to changes in the reporting entity's share in the net assets of that foreign operation.

Derivatives cannot be designated as hedged items and the only exception to this under IFRS 9 is a written option to qualify as a hedging instrument if it is designated as an offset to a purchase option, including one that is embedded in another financial instrument (for example, a written call option used to hedge a callable liability).

Qualifying Criteria for Hedge Accounting

Under IFRS 9, a hedging relationship qualifies for hedge accounting only if all of the following criteria are met:

1. The hedging relationship consists only of eligible hedging instruments and eligible hedged items.
2. At the inception of the hedging relationship, there is formal designation and documentation of the hedging relationship and the entity's risk management objective and strategy for undertaking the hedge. That documentation shall include identification of the hedging instrument, the hedged item, the nature of the risk being hedged and how the entity will assess whether the hedging relationship meets the hedge effectiveness requirements (including its analysis of the sources of hedge ineffectiveness and how it determines the hedge ratio).
3. The hedging relationship meets all the following hedge effectiveness requirements:
    - There is an economic relationship between the hedged item and the hedging instrument;
    - The effect of credit risk does not dominate the value changes that result from that economic relationship; and
    - The hedge ratio of the hedging relationship is the same as that resulting from the quantity of the hedged item that the entity actually hedges and the quantity of the hedging instrument that the entity actually uses to hedge that quantity of the hedged item. However, that designation shall not reflect an imbalance between the weightings of the hedged item and the hedging instrument that would create hedge ineffectiveness (irrespective of whether it is recognised or not) that could result in an accounting outcome that would be inconsistent with the purpose of hedge accounting.

Designation of Hedging Instruments

A qualifying instrument must be designated in its entirety as a hedging instrument. The only exceptions permitted are:

1. Separating the intrinsic value and time value of an option contract and designating as the hedging instrument only the change in intrinsic value of an option and not the change in its time value;

2. Separating the forward element and the spot element of a forward contract and designating as the hedging instrument only the change in the value of the spot element of a forward contract and not the forward element; similarly, the foreign currency basis spread may be separated and excluded from the designation of a financial instrument as the hedging instrument; and
3. A proportion of the entire hedging instrument, such as 50% of the nominal amount, may be designated as the hedging instrument in a hedging relationship. However, a hedging instrument may not be designated for a part of its change in fair value that results from only a portion of the time period during which the hedging instrument remains outstanding.

For hedges other than hedges of foreign currency risk, when an entity designates a non-derivative financial asset or a non-derivative financial liability measured at FVTPL as a hedging instrument, it may only designate the non-derivative financial instrument in its entirety or a proportion of it.

An entity may view in combination, and jointly designate as the hedging instrument, any of the following (including those circumstances in which the risk or risks arising from some hedging instruments offset those arising from others):

1. Derivatives or a proportion of them; and
2. Non-derivatives or a proportion of them.

However, a derivative instrument that combines a written option and a purchased option (for example, an interest rate collar) does not qualify as a hedging instrument if it is, in effect, a net written option at the date of designation (unless it qualifies in accordance with the written options provisions discussed above). Similarly, two or more instruments (or proportions of them) may be jointly designated as the hedging instrument only if, in combination, they are not, in effect, a net written option at the date of designation.

A single hedging instrument may be designated as a hedging instrument of more than one type of risk if there is a specific designation of the hedging instrument and of the different risk positions as hedged items. Those hedged items can be in different hedging relationships.

For hedge accounting purposes, only contracts with a party external to the reporting entity (i.e., external to the group or individual entity that is being reported on) can be designated as hedging instruments.

An entity may designate an item in its entirety or a component of an item as the hedged item in a hedging relationship. An entire item comprises all changes in the cash flows or fair value of an item. A component comprises less than the entire fair value change or cash flow variability of an item. In that case, an entity may designate only the following types of components (including combinations) as hedged items:

1. Only changes in the cash flows or fair value of an item attributable to a specific risk or risks (risk component), provided that, based on an assessment within the context of the particular market structure, the risk component is separately identifiable and reliably measurable. Risk components include a designation of only changes in the cash flows or the fair value of a hedged item above or below a specified price or other variable (a one-sided risk);

2. One or more selected contractual cash flows; or
3. Components of a nominal amount, i.e., a specified part of the amount of an item.

A derivative measured at fair value through profit or loss may be designated as a hedging instrument, except for some written options (see below), derivatives that are embedded in hybrid contracts but that are not separately accounted for and an entity's own equity instruments.

A written option does not qualify as a hedging instrument unless it is designated as an offset to a purchased option, including one that is embedded in another financial instrument (for example, a written call option used to hedge a callable liability).

A non-derivative financial asset or a non-derivative financial liability measured at fair value through profit or loss may be designated as a hedging instrument unless it is a financial liability designated as at fair value through profit or loss for which the amount of its change in fair value that is attributable to changes in the credit risk of that liability is presented in other comprehensive income.

For a hedge of foreign currency risk, the foreign currency risk component of a non-derivative financial asset or a non-derivative financial liability (as determined in accordance with IAS 21) may be designated as a hedging instrument provided that it is not an investment in an equity instrument for which an entity has elected to present changes in fair value in other comprehensive income.

Designation of Hedged Items

To be eligible for designation as a hedged item, a risk component must be a separately identifiable component of the financial or the non-financial item, and the changes in the cash flows or the fair value of the item attributable to changes in that risk component must be reliably measurable.

When identifying what risk components qualify for designation as a hedged item, an entity assesses such risk components within the context of the market structure to which the risk or risks relate and in which the hedging activity takes place. Such a determination requires an evaluation of the relevant facts and circumstances, which differ by risk and market.

When designating risk components as hedged items, an entity considers whether the risk components are explicitly specified in a contract (contractually specified risk components) or whether they are implicit in the fair value or the cash flows of an item of which they are a part (non-contractually specified risk components). Non-contractually specified risk components can relate to items that are not a contract (for example, forecast transactions) or contracts that do not explicitly specify the component (for example, a firm commitment that includes only one single price instead of a pricing formula that references different underlying).

When designating a risk component as a hedged item, the hedge accounting requirements apply to that risk component in the same way as they apply to other hedged items that are not risk components. For example, the qualifying criteria apply, including that the hedging relationship must meet the hedge effectiveness requirements, and any hedge ineffectiveness must be measured and recognised. (See below for measurement of hedge effectiveness.)

An entity can also designate changes only in the cash flows or fair value of a hedged item above or below a specified price or other variable (a "one-sided risk"). The intrinsic value of a purchased option hedging instrument (assuming that it has the same principal terms as the designated risk), but not its time value, reflects a one-sided risk in a hedged item. For example, an entity can designate the variability of future cash flow outcomes resulting from a price increase of a forecast commodity purchase. In such a situation, the entity designates only cash flow losses that result from an increase in the price above the specified level. The hedged risk does not include the time value of a purchased option, because the time value is not a component of the forecast transaction that affects profit or loss.

IFRS 9 includes a rebuttable presumption that unless inflation risk is contractually specified, it is not separately identifiable and reliably measurable and hence cannot be designated as a risk component of a financial instrument. However, in limited cases, it is possible to identify a risk component for inflation risk that is separately identifiable and reliably measurable because of the circumstances of the inflation environment and the relevant debt market.

Components of a Nominal Amount

A component of a nominal amount is a specified part of an item. Examples include:

1. As a monetary value, e.g., first €1 million from a customer from sales volumes;
2. A physical volume, e.g., second sale of 1,000 kilograms of salt.

There are two types of components of nominal amounts that can be designated as the hedged item in a hedging relationship: a component that is a proportion of an entire item or a layer component. The type of component changes the accounting outcome. IFRS 9 requires an entity to designate the component for accounting purposes consistently with its risk management objective.

An example of a component that is a proportion is 50% of the contractual cash flows of a loan.

Relationship Between Components and the Total Cash Flows of an Item

If a component of the cash flows of a financial or a non-financial item is designated as the hedged item, that component must be less than or equal to the total cash flows of the entire item. However, all of the cash flows of the entire item may be designated as the hedged item and hedged for only one particular risk (for example, only for those changes that are attributable to changes in LIBOR or a benchmark commodity price).

For example, in the case of a financial liability whose effective interest rate is below LIBOR, an entity cannot designate:

1. A component of the liability equal to interest at LIBOR (plus the principal amount in case of a fair value hedge); and
2. A negative residual component.

However, in the case of a fixed rate financial liability whose effective interest rate is (for example) 100 basis points below LIBOR, an entity can designate as the hedged item the change in the value of that entire liability (i.e., principal plus interest at LIBOR minus 100 basis points) that is attributable to changes in LIBOR. If a fixed rate financial instrument is hedged some time, after its origination and interest rates have changed in the meantime, the entity can designate a risk component equal to a benchmark rate that is higher than the contractual rate paid on the item. The entity can do so provided that the benchmark rate is less than the effective interest rate calculated on the assumption that the entity had purchased the instrument on the day when it first designates the hedged item.

Example

For example, assume that an entity originates a fixed rate financial asset of €100 that has an effective interest rate of 6% at a time when LIBOR is 4%. It begins to hedge that asset some time later when LIBOR has increased to 8% and the fair value of the asset has decreased to €90. The entity calculates that if it had purchased the asset on the date it first designates the related LIBOR interest rate risk as the hedged item, the effective yield of the asset based on its then fair value of €90 would have been 9.5%. Because LIBOR is less than this effective yield, the entity can designate a LIBOR component of 8% that consists partly of the contractual interest cash flows and partly of the difference between the current fair value (i.e., €90) and the amount repayable on maturity (i.e., €100).

Designation of Financial Items as Hedged Items

As along as the effectiveness can be measured, it is possible to designate only a portion of either the cash flows or fair value of a financial instrument as a hedged item.

When designating the hedged item on the basis of the aggregated exposure, an entity considers the combined effect of the items that constitute the aggregated exposure for the purpose of assessing hedge effectiveness and measuring hedge ineffectiveness. However, the items that constitute the aggregated exposure remain accounted for separately. This means that, for example:

1. Derivatives that are part of an aggregated exposure are recognised as separate assets or liabilities measured at fair value; and
2. If a hedging relationship is designated between the items that constitute the aggregated exposure, the way in which a derivative is included as part of an aggregated exposure must be consistent with the designation of that derivative as the hedging instrument at the level of the aggregated exposure. For example, if an entity excludes the forward element of a derivative from its designation as the hedging instrument for the hedging relationship between the items that constitute the aggregated exposure, it must also exclude the forward element when including that derivative as a hedged item as part of the aggregated exposure. Otherwise, the aggregated exposure shall include a derivative, either in its entirety or a proportion of it.

Example of an aggregated exposure

An entity constructing houses is expecting to purchase steel in 12 months. The steel price is fluctuating and is denominated in euros, which is a foreign currency for the entity. The entity is exposed to two main risks, the steel price risk and the foreign exchange risk.

The entity first decides to hedge the steel price fluctuation risk using a steel futures contract. By doing so, the entity now has a fixed-price steel purchase denominated in a foreign currency and is therefore still exposed to foreign exchange risk.

Three months later, the entity decides to hedge the foreign exchange risk by entering into a foreign exchange forward contract to buy a fixed number of euros in nine months. By doing so, the entity is hedging the aggregated exposure, which is the combination of the original exposure to variability of the steel price and the steel futures contract.

IFRS 9 clarifies the range of eligible hedged items by including aggregated exposures that are a combination of an exposure that could qualify as a hedged item and a derivative.

Consequently, in the scenario above, the entity could designate the foreign exchange forward contract in a cash flow hedge of the combination of the original exposure and the steel futures contract (i.e., the aggregated exposure) without affecting the first hedging relationship. In other words, it would no longer be necessary to discontinue and redesignate the first hedging relationship.

For hedge accounting purposes, only assets, liabilities, firm commitments or highly probable forecast transactions with a party external to the reporting entity can be designated as hedged items. Hedge accounting can be applied to transactions between entities in the same group only in the individual or separate financial statements of those entities and not in the consolidated financial statements of the group, except for the consolidated financial statements of an investment entity, as defined in IFRS 10, where transactions between an investment entity and its subsidiaries measured at fair value through profit or loss will not be eliminated in the consolidated financial statements.

However, as an exception to this, the foreign currency risk of an intragroup monetary item (for example, a payable/receivable between two subsidiaries) may qualify as a hedged item in the consolidated financial statements if it results in an exposure to foreign exchange rate gains or losses that are not fully eliminated on consolidation in accordance with IAS 21, *The Effects of Changes in Foreign Exchange Rates*.

In accordance with IAS 21, foreign exchange rate gains and losses on intragroup monetary items are not fully eliminated on consolidation when the intragroup monetary item is transacted between two group entities that have different functional currencies. In addition, the foreign currency risk of a highly probable forecast intragroup transaction may qualify as a hedged item in consolidated financial statements provided that the transaction is denominated in a currency other than the functional currency of the entity entering into that transaction and the foreign currency risk will affect consolidated profit or loss.

An equity method investment cannot be a hedged item in a fair value hedge. This is because the equity method recognises in profit or loss the investor's share of the investee's profit or loss, instead of changes in the investment's fair value. For a similar reason, an investment in a consolidated subsidiary cannot be a hedged item in a fair value hedge. This is because consolidation recognises in profit or loss the subsidiary's profit or loss, instead of changes in the investment's fair value. A hedge of a net investment in a foreign operation is different because it is a hedge of the foreign currency exposure, not a fair value hedge of the change in the value of the investment.

Hedge Effectiveness

Hedge effectiveness is the extent to which changes in the fair value or the cash flows of the hedging instrument offset changes in the fair value or the cash flows of the hedged item (for example, when the hedged item is a risk component, the relevant change in fair value or cash flows of an item is the one that is attributable to the hedged risk). Hedge ineffectiveness is the extent to which the changes in the fair value or the cash flows of the hedging instrument are greater or less than those on the hedged item.

IFRS requires an entity to assess at the inception of the hedging relationship, and on an ongoing basis, whether a hedging relationship meets the hedge effectiveness requirements. At a minimum, an entity shall perform the ongoing assessment at each reporting date or upon a significant change in the circumstances affecting the hedge effectiveness requirements, whichever comes first. The assessment relates to expectations about hedge effectiveness and is therefore only forward looking.

When designating a hedging relationship on an ongoing basis, IFRS 9 requires an entity to analyse the sources of hedge ineffectiveness that are expected to affect the hedging relationship during its term. This analysis (including any updates arising from rebalancing a hedging relationship) is the basis for the entity's assessment of meeting the hedge effectiveness requirements.

For the avoidance of doubt, the effects of replacing the original counterparty with a clearing counterparty and making the associated changes shall be reflected in the measurement of the hedging instrument and therefore in the assessment of hedge effectiveness and the measurement of hedge effectiveness.

Entities no longer need to perform a retrospective qualitative effectiveness assessment using the 80% to 125% bright lines as was required under IAS 39. A prospective effectiveness assessment is still required as a minimum at each reporting date. Hedge effectives is now based on three assessments. All three assessments need to be met for the hedging relationship to be effective and thus meet the qualifying criteria for hedge accounting. If Assessments 1 and 2 are no longer met, hedge accounting is stopped. However, Assessment 3, the hedging ratio, could be rebalanced to continue hedge accounting.

Assessment 1: Economic relationship between the hedged item and the hedging instrument The requirement that an economic relationship (there needs to be an economic rationale rather than just a chance of an event occurring) exists means that the hedging instrument and the hedged item have values that generally move in the opposite direction because of the same risk, which is the hedged risk. Hence, there must be an expectation that the value of the hedging instrument and the value of the hedged item will systematically change in response to movements in either the same underlying or an underlying that is economically related in such a way that they respond in an analogous way to the risk that is being hedged (for example, Brent and WTI crude oil).

If the underlying is not the same but is economically related, there can be situations in which the values of the hedging instrument and the hedged item move in the same direction, for example because the price differential between the two related underlying changes while the underlying themselves do not move significantly. That is still consistent with an economic relationship between the hedging instrument and the hedged item if the values of the hedging instrument and the hedged item are still expected to typically move in the opposite direction when the underlying moves.

The assessment of whether an economic relationship exists includes an analysis of the possible behaviour of the hedging relationship during its term to ascertain whether it can be expected to meet the risk management objective. The mere existence of a statistical correlation between two variables does not, by itself, support a valid conclusion that an economic relationship exists.

IFRS 9 does not specify a method for assessing whether a hedging relationship meets the hedge effectiveness requirements. However, it gives direction on the methods that capture the relevant characteristics of the hedging relationship, including the sources of hedge ineffectiveness. Depending on those factors, the method can be a qualitative or a quantitative assessment.

For example, when the critical terms (such as the nominal amount, maturity and underlying) of the hedging instrument and the hedged item match or are closely aligned, it might be possible for an entity to conclude on the basis of a qualitative assessment of those critical terms that the hedging instrument and the hedged item have values that will generally move in the opposite direction because of the same risk and hence that an economic relationship exists between the hedged item and the hedging instrument.

The fact that a derivative is in or out of the money when it is designated as a hedging instrument does not in itself mean that a qualitative assessment is inappropriate. It depends on the circumstances whether hedge ineffectiveness arising from that fact could have a magnitude that a qualitative assessment would not adequately capture.

If the critical terms of the hedging instrument and the hedged item are not closely aligned, there is an increased level of uncertainty about the extent of offset. Consequently, the hedge effectiveness during the term of the hedging relationship is more difficult to predict. In such a situation, it might only be possible for an entity to conclude on the basis of a quantitative assessment that an economic relationship exists between the hedged item and the hedging instrument. In some situations, a quantitative assessment might also be needed to assess whether the hedge ratio used for designating the hedging relationship meets the hedge effectiveness requirements. An entity can use the same or different methods for those two different purposes.

If there are changes in circumstances that affect hedge effectiveness, an entity may have to change the method for assessing whether a hedging relationship meets the hedge effectiveness requirements to ensure that the relevant characteristics of the hedging relationship, including the sources of hedge ineffectiveness, are still captured.

An entity's risk management is the main source of information to perform the assessment of whether a hedging relationship meets the hedge effectiveness requirements. This means that the management information (or analysis) used for decision-making purposes can be used as a basis for assessing whether a hedging relationship meets the hedge effectiveness requirements.

An entity's documentation of the hedging relationship includes how it will assess the hedge effectiveness requirements, including the method or methods used. The documentation of the hedging relationship shall be updated for any changes to the methods.

Assessment 2: Credit risk IFRS 9 requires that to achieve hedge accounting, the impact of the changes in credit risk should not be of a magnitude such that it dominates the value changes.

Since the hedge accounting model is based on a general notion of offset between gains and losses on the hedging instrument and the hedged item, hedge effectiveness is determined not only by the economic relationship between those items (i.e., the changes in their underlying) but also by the effect of credit risk on the value of both the hedging instrument and the hedged item. The effect of credit risk means that even if there is an economic relationship between the hedging instrument and the hedged item, the level of offset might become erratic.

This can result from a change in the credit risk of either the hedging instrument or the hedged item that is of such a magnitude that the credit risk dominates the value changes that result from the economic relationship (i.e., the effect of the changes in the underlying). A level of magnitude that gives rise to dominance is one that would result in the loss (or gain) from credit risk frustrating the effect of changes in the underlying on the value of the hedging instrument or the hedged item, even if those changes were significant. Conversely, if during a particular period there is minor change in the underlying, the fact that even small credit risk-related changes in the value of the hedging instrument or the hedged item might affect the value more than the underlying does not create dominance.

An example of credit risk dominating a hedging relationship is when an entity hedges an exposure to commodity price risk using an uncollateralised derivative. If the counterparty to that derivative experiences a severe deterioration in its credit standing, the effect of the changes in the counterparty's credit standing might outweigh the effect of changes in the commodity price on the fair value of the hedging instrument, whereas changes in the value of the hedged item depend largely on the commodity price changes.

Assessment 3: Hedge ratio To meet hedge accounting requirements, where an entity hedges less than 100% of the hedged item, it needs to designate the hedging ratio on the basis of the actual percentage that is hedged. For example, where an entity hedges 75% of an underlying risk, and documents this as such, for hedge accounting purposes 75% will used as the effective hedge ratio. The hedging ratio of 100% could be created by designating only a portion of the hedge item or hedging instrument. Then an ineffective portion need not be determined. The portion of the movement in a hedging instrument, such as a derivative, not designated would then automatically be recognised in profit or loss.

Rebalancing the Hedging Relationship and Changes to the Hedge Ratio

IFRS 9 requires rebalancing in circumstances where the quantities of the hedged item or hedging instrument need to be changed to maintain the hedge ratio (as discussed above) such that the hedging relationship continued to meet the hedge accounting requirements. Rebalancing to maintain this hedge ratio can be achieved by increasing or decreasing the volume of the hedged item or the hedging instrument. Such increases or decreases in quantities do not necessarily require change in contracted quantities of either the hedged item or hedging instrument but relate more to the amounts that are, or are not, designated within the hedging relationship.

Rebalancing refers to the adjustments made to the designated quantities of the hedged item or the hedging instrument of an already existing hedging relationship for the purpose of maintaining a hedge ratio that complies with the hedge effectiveness requirements. Changes to designated quantities of a hedged item or of a hedging instrument for a different purpose do not constitute rebalancing for the purpose of IFRS 9.

Rebalancing is accounted for as a continuation of the hedging relationship (see explanations below). On rebalancing, the hedge ineffectiveness of the hedging relationship is determined and recognised immediately before adjusting the hedging relationship.

Adjusting the hedge ratio allows an entity to respond to changes in the relationship between the hedging instrument and the hedged item that arise from their underlying's or risk variables. For example, a hedging relationship in which the hedging instrument and the hedged item have different but related underlyings changes in response to a change in the relationship between those two underlyings (for example, different but related reference indices, rates or prices). Hence, rebalancing allows the continuation of a hedging relationship in situations in which the relationship between the hedging instrument and the hedged item changes in a way that can be compensated for by adjusting the hedge ratio.

For example, an entity hedges an exposure to Foreign Currency A using a currency derivative that references Foreign Currency B and Foreign Currencies A and B are pegged (i.e., their exchange rate is maintained within a band or at an exchange rate set by a central bank or other authority).

If the exchange rate between Foreign Currency A and Foreign Currency B were changed (i.e., a new band or rate was set), rebalancing the hedging relationship to reflect the new exchange rate would ensure that the hedging relationship would continue to meet the hedge effectiveness requirement for the hedge ratio in the new circumstances. In contrast, if there was a default on the currency derivative, changing the hedge ratio could not ensure that the hedging relationship would continue to meet that hedge effectiveness requirement. Hence, rebalancing does not facilitate the continuation of a hedging relationship in situations in which the relationship between the hedging instrument and the hedged item changes in a way that cannot be compensated for by adjusting the hedge ratio.

Not every change in the extent of offset between the changes in the fair value of the hedging instrument and the hedged item's fair value or cash flows constitutes a change in the relationship between the hedging instrument and the hedged item. An entity analyses the sources of hedge ineffectiveness that it expected to affect the hedging relationship during its term and evaluates whether changes in the extent of offset are:

1. Fluctuations around the hedge ratio, which remains valid (i.e., continues to appropriately reflect the relationship between the hedging instrument and the hedged item); or
2. An indication that the hedge ratio no longer appropriately reflects the relationship between the hedging instrument and the hedged item.

IFRS 9 recognises that an entity performs the evaluation against the hedge effectiveness requirement for the hedge ratio, i.e., to ensure that the hedging relationship does not reflect an imbalance between the weightings of the hedged item and the hedging instrument that would create hedge ineffectiveness (irrespective of whether it is recognised or not) that could result in an accounting outcome that would be inconsistent with the purpose of hedge accounting. Hence, this evaluation requires judgement.

Fluctuation around a constant hedge ratio (and hence the related hedge ineffectiveness) cannot be reduced by adjusting the hedge ratio in response to each outcome. Hence, in such circumstances, the change in the extent of offset is a matter of measuring and recognising hedge ineffectiveness but does not require rebalancing.

Conversely, if changes in the extent of offset indicate that the fluctuation is around a hedge ratio that is different from the hedge ratio that is currently used for that hedging relationship, or that there is a trend leading away from that hedge ratio, hedge ineffectiveness can be reduced by adjusting the hedge ratio, whereas retaining the hedge ratio would increasingly produce hedge ineffectiveness.

Hence, in such circumstances, an entity must evaluate whether the hedging relationship reflects an imbalance between the weightings of the hedged item and the hedging instrument that would create hedge ineffectiveness (irrespective of whether it is recognised or not) that could result in an accounting outcome that would be inconsistent with the purpose of hedge accounting. If the hedge ratio is adjusted, it also affects the measurement and recognition of hedge ineffectiveness because, on rebalancing, the hedge ineffectiveness of the hedging relationship must be determined and recognised immediately before adjusting the hedging relationship.

Rebalancing means that, for hedge accounting purposes, after the start of a hedging relationship an entity adjusts the quantities of the hedging instrument or the hedged item in response to changes in circumstances that affect the hedge ratio of that hedging relationship. Typically, that adjustment should reflect adjustments in the quantities of the hedging instrument and the hedged item that it uses. However, IFRS 9 requires an entity to adjust the hedge ratio that results from the quantities of the hedged item or the hedging instrument that it uses if:

1. The hedge ratio that results from changes to the quantities of the hedging instrument or the hedged item that the entity actually uses would reflect an imbalance that would create hedge ineffectiveness that could result in an accounting outcome that would be inconsistent with the purpose of hedge accounting; or
2. An entity would retain quantities of the hedging instrument and the hedged item that it actually uses, resulting in a hedge ratio that, in new circumstances, would reflect an imbalance that would create hedge ineffectiveness that could result in an accounting outcome that would be inconsistent with the purpose of hedge accounting (i.e., an entity must not create an imbalance by omitting to adjust the hedge ratio).

Rebalancing does not apply if the risk management objective for a hedging relationship has changed. Instead, hedge accounting for that hedging relationship shall be discontinued (even if an entity might designate a new hedging relationship that involves the hedging instrument or hedged item of the previous hedging relationship). If a hedging relationship is rebalanced, the adjustment to the hedge ratio can be effected in different ways:

1. The weighting of the hedged item can be increased (which at the same time reduces the weighting of the hedging instrument) by:
   a. Increasing the volume of the hedged item; or
   b. Decreasing the volume of the hedging instrument.
2. The weighting of the hedging instrument can be increased (which at the same time reduces the weighting of the hedged item) by:
   a. Increasing the volume of the hedging instrument; or
   b. Decreasing the volume of the hedged item.

Changes in volume refer to the quantities that are part of the hedging relationship. Hence, decreases in volumes do not necessarily mean that the items or transactions no longer exist, or are no longer expected to occur, but that they are not part of the hedging relationship. For example, decreasing the volume of the hedging instrument can result in the entity retaining a derivative, but only part of it might remain a hedging instrument of the hedging relationship. This could occur if the rebalancing could be effected only by reducing the volume of the hedging instrument in the hedging relationship, but with the entity retaining the volume that is no longer needed. In that case, the undesignated part of the derivative would be accounted for at FVTPL (unless it was designated as a hedging instrument in a different hedging relationship).

Adjusting the hedge ratio by increasing the volume of the hedged item does not affect how the changes in the fair value of the hedging instrument are measured. The measurement of the changes in the value of the hedged item related to the previously designated volume also remains unaffected.

However, from the date of rebalancing, the changes in the value of the hedged item also include the change in the value of the additional volume of the hedged item. These changes are measured starting from, and by reference to, the date of rebalancing instead of the date on which the hedging relationship was designated.

Example

For example, if an entity originally hedged a volume of 100 tonnes of a commodity at a forward price of €80 (the forward price at inception of the hedging relationship) and added a volume of 10 tonnes on rebalancing when the forward price was €90, the hedged item after rebalancing would comprise two layers: 100 tonnes hedged at €80 and 10 tonnes hedged at €90.

When rebalancing a hedging relationship, an entity shall update its analysis of the sources of hedge ineffectiveness that are expected to affect the hedging relationship during its remaining term and the documentation of the hedging relationship shall be updated accordingly.

Discontinuation of Hedge Accounting

Discontinuing hedge accounting can either affect a hedging relationship in its entirety or only a part of it (in which case hedge accounting continues for the remainder of the hedging relationship).

Discontinuation of hedge accounting applies prospectively from the date on which the qualifying criteria are no longer met. IFRS 9 states that an entity shall not de-designate and thereby discontinue a hedging relationship that:

1. Still meets the risk management objective on the basis of which it qualified for hedge accounting (i.e., the entity still pursues that risk management objective); and
2. Continues to meet all other qualifying criteria (after taking into account any rebalancing of the hedging relationship, if applicable).

The discontinuation of hedge accounting can affect:

1. A hedging relationship in its entirety; or
2. A part of a hedging relationship (which means that hedge accounting continues for the remainder of the hedging relationship).

A hedging relationship is discontinued in its entirety when it ceases to meet the qualifying criteria. For example:

1. The hedging relationship no longer meets the risk management objective on the basis of which it qualified for hedge accounting (i.e., the entity no longer pursues that risk management objective);
2. The hedging instrument or instruments have been sold or terminated (in relation to the entire volume that was part of the hedging relationship); or
3. There is no longer an economic relationship between the hedged item and the hedging instrument or the effect of credit risk starts to dominate the value changes that result from that economic relationship.

A part of a hedging relationship is discontinued (and hedge accounting continues for its remainder) when only a part of the hedging relationship ceases to meet the qualifying criteria. For example:

1. On rebalancing of the hedging relationship, the hedge ratio might be adjusted in such a way that some of the volume of the hedged item is no longer part of the hedging relationship and as a result hedge accounting is discontinued only for the volume of the hedged item that is no longer part of the hedging relationship; or

2. When the occurrence of some of the volume of the hedged item that is (or is a component of) a forecast transaction is no longer highly probable, hedge accounting is discontinued only for the volume of the hedged item whose occurrence is no longer highly probable. However, if an entity has a history of having designated hedges of forecast transactions and having subsequently determined that the forecast transactions are no longer expected to occur, the entity's ability to predict forecast transactions accurately is called into question when predicting similar forecast transactions. This affects the assessment of whether similar forecast transactions are highly probable and hence whether they are eligible as hedged items.

An entity can designate a new hedging relationship that involves the hedging instrument or hedged item of a previous hedging relationship for which hedge accounting was (in part or in its entirety) discontinued. This does not constitute a continuation of a hedging relationship but is a restart. For example:

1. A hedging instrument experiences such a severe credit deterioration that the entity replaces it with a new hedging instrument. This means that the original hedging relationship failed to achieve the risk management objective and is hence discontinued in its entirety. The new hedging instrument is designated as the hedge of the same exposure that was hedged previously and forms a new hedging relationship. Hence, the changes in the fair value or the cash flows of the hedged item are measured starting from, and by reference to, the date of designation of the new hedging relationship instead of the date on which the original hedging relationship was designated.
2. A hedging relationship is discontinued before the end of its term. The hedging instrument in that hedging relationship can be designated as the hedging instrument in another hedging relationship (for example, when adjusting the hedge ratio on rebalancing by increasing the volume of the hedging instrument or when designating a whole new hedging relationship).

Fair Value Hedges

So long as a fair value hedge meets the qualifying criteria as stated above, the hedging relationship shall be accounted for as follows:

1. The gains or losses on the hedging instrument shall be recognised in profit or loss (or other comprehensive income, if the hedging instrument hedges an equity instrument for which an entity has elected to present changes in fair value in other comprehensive income).
2. The hedging gain or loss on the hedged item shall adjust the carrying amount of the hedged item (if applicable) and be recognised in profit or loss. If the hedged item is a financial asset (or a component thereof) that is measured at FVTOCI, the hedging gain or loss on the hedged item shall be recognised in profit or loss. However, if the hedged item is an equity instrument for which an entity has elected to present changes in fair value in other comprehensive income, those amounts shall remain in other comprehensive income. When a hedged item is an unrecognised firm commitment (or a component thereof), the cumulative change in the fair value of the hedged item subsequent to its designation is recognised as an asset or a liability with a corresponding gain or loss recognised in profit or loss.

When a hedged item in a fair value hedge is a firm commitment (or a component thereof) to acquire an asset or assume a liability, the initial carrying amount of the asset or the liability that results from the entity meeting the firm commitment is adjusted to include the cumulative change in the fair value of the hedged item that was recognised in the statement of financial position.

Any adjustment arising from the above recognition principles shall be amortised to profit or loss if the hedged item is a financial instrument (or a component thereof) measured at amortised cost. Amortisation may commence as soon as an adjustment exists and shall begin no later than when the hedged item ceases to be adjusted for hedging gains and losses. The amortisation is based on a recalculated effective interest rate at the date that amortisation begins. In the case of a financial asset (or a component thereof) that is a hedged item and that is measured at FVTOCI, amortisation applies in the same manner but to the amount that represents the cumulative gain or loss previously recognised instead of by adjusting the carrying amount.

Cash Flow Hedges

So long as cash flow hedges meet the qualifying criteria as stated above, the hedging relationship shall be accounted for as follows:

1. The separate component of equity associated with the hedged item (cash flow hedge reserve) is adjusted to the lower of the following (in absolute amounts):
   - The cumulative gain or loss on the hedging instrument from inception of the hedge; and
   - The cumulative change in fair value (net present value) of the hedged item (i.e., the present value of the cumulative change in the hedged expected future cash flows) from inception of the hedge.
2. The portion of the gain or loss on the hedging instrument that is determined to be an effective hedge (i.e., the portion that is offset by the change in the cash flow hedge reserve calculated in accordance with (1)) shall be recognised in other comprehensive income.
3. Any remaining gain or loss on the hedging instrument (or any gain or loss required to balance the change in the cash flow hedge reserve calculated in accordance with (1)) is hedge ineffectiveness that shall be recognised in profit or loss.
4. The amount that has been accumulated in the cash flow hedge reserve in accordance with (1) shall be accounted for as follows:
   - If a hedged forecast transaction subsequently results in the recognition of a non-financial asset or non-financial liability, or a hedged forecast transaction for a non-financial asset or a non-financial liability becomes a firm commitment for which fair value hedge accounting is applied, the entity shall remove that amount from the cash flow hedge reserve and include it directly in the initial cost or other carrying amount of the asset or the liability. This is not a reclassification adjustment (see IAS 1) and hence it does not affect other comprehensive income.
   - For cash flow hedges other than those covered by (1), that amount shall be reclassified from the cash flow hedge reserve to profit or loss as a reclassification adjustment (see IAS 1) in the same period or periods during which the hedged expected future cash flows affect profit or loss (for example, in the periods that interest income or interest expense is recognised or when a forecast sale occurs).

- However, if that amount is a loss and an entity expects that all or a portion of that loss will not be recovered in one or more future periods, it shall immediately reclassify the amount that is not expected to be recovered into profit or loss as a reclassification adjustment (see IAS 1).

When an entity discontinues hedge accounting for a cash flow hedge it shall account for the amount that has been accumulated in the cash flow hedge reserve as follows:

1. If the hedged future cash flows are still expected to occur, that amount shall remain in the cash flow hedge reserve until the future cash flows occur;
2. If the hedged future cash flows are no longer expected to occur, that amount shall be immediately reclassified from the cash flow hedge reserve to profit or loss as a reclassification adjustment (see IAS 1).

Hedges of a Net Investment in a Foreign Operation

Hedges of a net investment in a foreign operation, including a hedge of a monetary item that is accounted for as part of the net investment (see IAS 21), shall be accounted for similarly to cash flow hedges, i.e.:

1. The portion of the gain or loss on the hedging instrument that is determined to be an effective hedge shall be recognised in other comprehensive income; and
2. The ineffective portion shall be recognised in profit or loss.

The cumulative gain or loss on the hedging instrument relating to the effective portion of the hedge that has been accumulated in the foreign currency translation reserve shall be reclassified from equity to profit or loss as a reclassification adjustment (see IAS 1) on the disposal or partial disposal of the foreign operation.

Accounting for the Time Value of Options

The time value of options consists of the intrinsic value and the time value. When using an option for hedging activities, only the intrinsic value is used for offsetting the fair value changes attributable to the hedged risk, unless the hedged item is also an option.

When an entity separates the intrinsic value and time value of an option contract and designates as the hedging instrument only the change in intrinsic value of the option, it shall account for the time value of the option as follows:

1. An entity shall distinguish the time value of options by the type of hedged item that the option hedges:
    - A transaction-related hedged item; or
    - A time period-related hedged item.
2. The change in fair value of the time value of an option that hedges a transaction-related hedged item shall be recognised in other comprehensive income to the extent that it relates to the hedged item and shall be accumulated in a separate component of equity. The cumulative change in fair value arising from the time value of the option that has been accumulated in a separate component of equity (the "amount") shall be accounted for as follows:
    - If the hedged item subsequently results in the recognition of a non-financial asset or a non-financial liability, or a firm commitment for a non-financial asset

or a non-financial liability for which fair value hedge accounting is applied, the entity shall remove the amount from the separate component of equity and include it directly in the initial cost or other carrying amount of the asset or the liability. This is not a reclassification adjustment (refer to IAS 1) and hence does not affect other comprehensive income.
- For hedging relationships other than those covered by (1), the amount shall be reclassified from the separate component of equity to profit or loss as a reclassification adjustment (refer to IAS 1) in the same period or periods during which the hedged expected future cash flows affect profit or loss (for example, when a forecast sale occurs).
- However, if all or a portion of that amount is not expected to be recovered in one or more future periods, the amount that is not expected to be recovered shall be immediately reclassified into profit or loss as a reclassification adjustment (refer to IAS 1).

3. The change in fair value of the time value of an option that hedges a time period-related hedged item shall be recognised in other comprehensive income to the extent that it relates to the hedged item and shall be accumulated in a separate component of equity. The time value at the date of designation of the option as a hedging instrument, to the extent that it relates to the hedged item, shall be amortised on a systematic and rational basis over the period during which the hedge adjustment for the option's intrinsic value could affect profit or loss (or other comprehensive income, if the hedged item is an equity instrument for which an entity has elected to present changes in fair value in other comprehensive income). Hence, in each reporting period, the amortisation amount shall be reclassified from the separate component of equity to profit or loss as a reclassification adjustment (refer to IAS 1). However, if hedge accounting is discontinued for the hedging relationship that includes the change in intrinsic value of the option as the hedging instrument, the net amount (i.e., including cumulative amortisation) that has been accumulated in the separate component of equity shall be immediately reclassified into profit or loss as a reclassification adjustment (refer to IAS 1).

The characteristics of the hedged item, including how and when the hedged item affects profit or loss, also affect the period over which the time value of an option that hedges a time period-related hedged item is amortised, which is consistent with the period over which the option's intrinsic value can affect profit or loss in accordance with hedge accounting. For example, if an interest rate option (a cap) is used to provide protection against increases in the interest expense on a floating rate bond, the time value of that cap is amortised to profit or loss over the same period over which any intrinsic value of the cap would affect profit or loss:

1. If the interest rate option (a cap) hedge increases in its interest rates for the first three years, out of a total life of the floating rate bond of five years, the time value of that interest rate option hedge (the cap) is amortised over the first three years; or
2. If the interest rate option hedge is a forward start option that hedges an increase in interest rates for years two and three, out of a total life of the floating rate bond of five years, the time value of that cap is amortised during years two and three.

The accounting for the time value of options in accordance with the paragraphs above also applies to a combination of a purchased and a written option (one being a put option and one being a call option) that at the date of designation as a hedging instrument has a net nil time value (commonly referred to as a "zero-cost collar"). In that case, an entity shall recognise any changes in time value in other comprehensive income, even though the cumulative change in time value over the total period of the hedging relationship is nil. Hence, if the time value of the option relates to:

1. A transaction-related hedged item, the amount of time value at the end of the hedging relationship that adjusts the hedged item or that is reclassified to profit or loss would be nil;
2. A time period-related hedged item, the amortisation expense related to the time value is nil.

The accounting for the time value of options applies only to the extent that the time value relates to the hedged item (aligned time value). The time value of an option relates to the hedged item if the critical terms of the option (such as the nominal amount, life and underlying) are aligned with the hedged item. Hence, if the critical terms of the option and the hedged item are not fully aligned, an entity shall determine the aligned time value, i.e., how much of the time value included in the premium (actual time value) relates to the hedged item. An entity determines the aligned time value using the valuation of the option that would have critical terms that perfectly match the hedged item.

If the actual time value and the aligned time value differ, an entity shall determine the amount that is accumulated in a separate component of equity as follows:

1. If, at inception of the hedging relationship, the actual time value is higher than the aligned time value, the entity shall:
   - Determine the amount that is accumulated in a separate component of equity on the basis of the aligned time value; and
   - Account for the differences in the fair value changes between the two time values in profit or loss.
2. If, at inception of the hedging relationship, the actual time value is lower than the aligned time value, the entity shall determine the amount that is accumulated in a separate component of equity by reference to the lower of the cumulative change in fair value of:
   - The actual time value; and
   - The aligned time values.

Any remainder of the change in fair value of the actual time value shall be recognised in profit or loss.

Accounting for the Forward Element of Forward Contracts

Forward contracts comprise a spot element and a forward element. IFRS 9 allows an entity to designate only changes in the spot element of the contract in a hedging relationship, under which the changes in the spot element are accounted for in line with the nature of the hedge. When only the spot element is designated, the forward element (which remains undesignated) can be accounted for under one of the following two options, which are choices that are made on a hedge to hedge basis:

- The changes in the forward element can be accounted for in profit or loss; or
- The changes in the forward element that relates to the hedged item can be accounted for in other comprehensive income with subsequent reclassification from equity to profit or loss.

Hedges of a Group of Items

IFRS 9 stipulates that a group of items that constitute a net position is eligible for a hedged item only if:

1. It consists of items (including components of items) that are, individually, eligible hedged items;
2. The items in the group are managed together on a group basis for risk management purposes; and
3. In the case of a cash flow hedge of a group of items whose variabilities in cash flows are not expected to be approximately proportional to the overall variability in cash flows of the group so that offsetting risk positions arise:
    - It is a hedge of foreign currency risk; and
    - The designation of that net position specifies the reporting period in which the forecast transactions are expected to affect profit or loss, as well as their nature and volume.

Example of hedging a group of items

An entity holds a portfolio of shares of Japanese companies that replicates the Market Index (MI). The entity elected to account for the shares at FVTOCI, as allowed by IFRS 9. The entity decides to lock in the current value of the portfolio by entering into corresponding MI futures contracts.

The individual shares would be eligible hedged items if hedged individually. As the objective of the portfolio is to replicate the MI, the entity can also demonstrate that the shares are managed together on a group basis. The entity also assesses the effectiveness criteria for hedge accounting. Consequently, the entity designates the MI futures contracts as the hedging instrument in a hedge of the fair value of the portfolio. As a result, the gains or losses on the MI futures are accounted for in other comprehensive income as well, thus eliminating the accounting mismatch.

Designation of a Component of a Nominal Amount

A component that is a proportion of an eligible group of items is an eligible hedged item if designation is consistent with the entity's risk management objective.

A layer component of an overall group of items (for example, a bottom layer) is eligible for hedge accounting only if:

1. It is separately identifiable and reliably measurable;
2. The risk management objective is to hedge a layer component;

3. The items in the overall group from which the layer is identified are exposed to the same hedged risk (so that the measurement of the hedged layer is not significantly affected by which particular items from the overall group form part of the hedged layer);
4. For a hedge of existing items (for example, an unrecognised firm commitment or a recognised asset) an entity can identify and track the overall group of items from which the hedged layer is defined (so that the entity is able to comply with the requirements for the accounting for qualifying hedging relationships); and
5. Any items in the group that contain prepayment options meet the requirements for components of a nominal amount.

A net position is eligible for hedge accounting only if an entity hedges on a net basis for risk management purposes. Whether an entity hedges in this way is a matter of fact (not merely of assertion or documentation). Hence, an entity cannot apply hedge accounting on a net basis solely to achieve an accounting outcome if that would not reflect its risk management approach. Net position hedging must form part of an established risk management strategy. Normally this would be approved by key management personnel as defined in IAS 24.

Example

For example, Entity A, whose functional currency is its local currency, has a firm commitment to pay €150,000 for advertising expenses in nine months' time and a firm commitment to sell finished goods for €150,000 in 15 months' time. Entity A enters a foreign currency derivative that settles in nine months' time under which it receives €100 and pays €70. Entity A has no other exposures to foreign currency. Entity A does not manage foreign currency risk on a net basis. Hence, Entity A cannot apply hedge accounting for a hedging relationship between the foreign currency derivative and a net position of €100 (consisting of €150,000 of the firm purchase commitment—i.e., advertising services—and €149,900 (of the €150,000) of the firm sale commitment) for a nine-month period.

If Entity A did manage foreign currency risk on a net basis and did not enter the foreign currency derivative (because it increases its foreign currency risk exposure instead of reducing it), then the entity would be in a natural hedged position for nine months. Normally, this hedged position would not be reflected in the financial statements because the transactions are recognised in different reporting periods in the future. The nil net position would be eligible for hedge accounting only if the conditions in the paragraph above are met.

When a group of items that constitute a net position is designated as a hedged item, an entity shall designate the overall group of items that includes the items that can make up the net position. An entity is not permitted to designate a non-specific abstract amount of a net position. For example, an entity has a group of firm sale commitments in nine months' time for €100 and a group of firm purchase commitments in 18 months' time for €120. The entity cannot designate an abstract amount of a net position up to €20. Instead, it must designate a gross amount of purchases and a gross amount of sales that together give rise to the hedged net position. An entity shall designate gross positions that give rise to the net position so that the entity is able to comply with the requirements for the accounting for qualifying hedging relationships.

Layers of Groups of Items Designated as the Hedged Item

A hedging relationship can include layers from several different groups of items. For example, in a hedge of a net position of a group of assets and a group of liabilities, the hedging relationship can comprise, in combination, a layer component of the group of assets and a layer component of the group of liabilities.

Nil net positions

When a hedged item is a group that is a nil net position (i.e., the hedged items among themselves fully offset the risk that is managed on a group basis), an entity is permitted to designate it in a hedging relationship that does not include a hedging instrument, provided that:

1. The hedge is part of a rolling net risk hedging strategy, whereby the entity routinely hedges new positions of the same type as time moves on (for example, when transactions move into the time horizon for which the entity hedges);
2. The hedged net position changes in size over the life of the rolling net risk hedging strategy and the entity uses eligible hedging instruments to hedge the net risk (i.e., when the net position is not nil);
3. Hedge accounting is normally applied to such net positions when the net position is not nil and it is hedged with eligible hedging instruments; and
4. Not applying hedge accounting to the nil net position would give rise to inconsistent accounting outcomes, because the accounting would not recognise the offsetting risk positions that would otherwise be recognised in a hedge of a net position.

EFFECTIVE DATE AND TRANSITION REQUIREMENTS OF IFRS 9

IFRS 9 is effective for annual periods beginning on or after January 1, 2018.

On initial application, entities are required to apply the standard retrospectively except in respect of:

1. Items which have been derecognised by the time of initial application (the date of initial application is the beginning of the reporting period when the entity first applies IFRS 9, which will be January 1, 2018 for non-early adopters);
2. The following areas relating to classification and measurement at the date of initial application:

   - The assessment of the entities' business model is carried out at the date of initial application, and applied retrospectively, irrespective of the actual business models in prior years;
   - Where it is impracticable to assess time value of money elements and the significance of fair values of prepayment features in debt instruments, entities need not take into account the effect of modifications to both the time value of money elements and significance of prepayment features;
   - Fair valuation of hybrid contracts is accounted through an adjustment to opening retained earnings at the date of initial application and not retrospectively.

Entities are required to designate financial assets measured at FVTPL and equity instruments measured at FVTOCI based on facts and circumstances that exist at the date of initial application. This is applied retrospectively.

All revocations and designations of financial assets and liabilities are made based on facts and circumstances that exist at the date of initial application and are applied retrospectively.

The standard reduces the burden for preparers when an entity first adopts IFRS 9 by not requiring a restatement of prior periods. However, comprehensive disclosures are required as of the date of initial application. Where a reporter uses this option, it is required to recognise the differences between the previous carrying amounts and the carrying amount on the date of initial application as a movement in opening retained earnings within equity. For entities desiring a restatement of comparatives, this is permissible but if, and only if, it is possible to do so without the use of hindsight.

Impracticability

Where it is impracticable (refer to IAS 8) to retrospectively apply the effective interest method, the fair value of the financial instrument at the end of each comparative period is presented as the previous carrying value under IAS 39 and is assumed to be the carrying value at the date of initial application.

Where equity instruments were previously measured at cost under IAS 39, and it is impracticable to determine the fair values for comparative periods, the instrument is measured at fair value at the date of initial application and the difference between fair value and the previous carrying value is adjusted in opening retained earnings.

Where entities prepare interim financial reports (refer to IAS 34), retrospective application to previous interim reports are not required, if impracticable.

Impairment

At the date of initial application, reasonable and supportable information that is available without undue cost or effort must be used to determine credit risk at the date of initial recognition of the financial instrument and compare that to the credit risk at the date of initial application of IFRS 9 to determine changes in credit risk.

Impairment of financial instruments for comparative periods needs to be based on the information available at the respective reporting dates without the application of hindsight.

When an entity determines if there has been a significant increase in credit risk since initial recognition, it may:

1. Apply the low credit risk exception (described earlier in the chapter);
2. Apply the rebuttable presumption for contractual payments that are more than 30 days past due if an entity will apply the impairment requirements by identifying significant increases in credit risk since initial recognition for those financial instruments on the basis of past due information.

At the date of initial application, an entity is required to use reasonable and supportable information that is available without *undue cost or effort* to determine the credit risk at the date that a financial instrument was initially recognised (for loan commitments and financial guarantee contracts at the date that the entity became a party to the irrevocable commitment) and compare that to the credit risk at the date of initial application.

An exhaustive search for information is not required when determining if there has been a significant increase in credit risk from the time of initial recognition.

Such information comprises all internal and external information, including portfolio information. An entity with little historical information can use the following sources of information:

1. Information from internal reports and statistics, e.g., that may have been generated when deciding whether to launch a new product;

2. Information about similar products; or
3. Peer group experience for comparable financial instruments.

If it is deemed that undue cost or effort will be required to determine if there has been a significant increase in credit risk, the loss allowance or provision is measured as lifetime expected credit losses, each reporting a date until that financial instrument is derecognised, unless the credit risk of the financial instrument is low credit risk at a reporting date. If the credit risk of a financial instrument is low, an entity may assume that the credit risk on that asset has not increased significantly since initial recognition and may recognise a loss allowance equal to 12 months' expected credit losses.

Classification and Measurement

Business model

The business model in which a financial asset is held is assessed as at the date of initial application. As an exception to retrospective application, the assessment is based on facts and circumstances at the date of initial application. An entity is not required to consider business models that may have applied in previous periods. The resulting classification is then applied retrospectively (irrespective of the entity's business model in prior reporting periods).

On the basis of facts and circumstances at the time of initial application an entity may retrospectively designate:

1. A financial asset as measured at FVTPL; or
2. An investment in an equity instrument as at FVTOCI.

Solely payments of principal and interest on principal

The assessment of whether contractual payments are solely payments of principal and interest on principal is made on the basis of facts and circumstances existing at the time of initial recognition of the financial asset with the two exceptions below:

1. If, at the date of initial application, it is impracticable (as defined in IAS 8) for an entity to assess a *modified time value of money* on the basis of the facts and circumstances that existed at the initial recognition of the financial asset, an entity shall assess the contractual cash flow characteristics of that financial asset on the basis of the facts and circumstances that existed at the initial recognition of the financial asset without taking into account the requirements related to the modification of the time value of money element.
2. If, at the date of initial application, it is impracticable (as defined in IAS 8) for an entity to assess whether the fair value of a *prepayment feature* was insignificant on the basis of the facts and circumstances that existed at the initial recognition of the financial asset, an entity shall assess the contractual cash flow characteristics of that financial asset on the basis of the facts and circumstances that existed at the initial recognition of the financial asset without taking into account the exception for prepayment features.

Hybrid contracts

Where a hybrid contract has been measured at fair value, but the fair value of the hybrid contract had not been measured in comparative reporting periods, the fair value of the hybrid contract in the comparative reporting periods shall be the sum of the fair values of the components (i.e., the non-derivative host and the embedded derivative) at the end of each comparative reporting period if the entity restates prior periods.

If an entity has applied the above then at the date of initial application the entity shall recognise any difference between the fair value of the entire hybrid contract at the date of initial application and the sum of the fair values of the components of the hybrid contract at the date of initial application in the opening retained earnings (or other component of equity, as appropriate) of the reporting period that includes the date of initial application.

Financial liabilities

For financial liabilities, at the date of initial application, an entity:

1. May designate a financial liability as measured at FVTPL if it meets the requirements of IFRS 9 described earlier in the chapter;
2. Shall revoke its previous designation of a financial liability measured at FVTPL if this designation does not satisfy the requirements brought about by IFRS 9; and
3. May revoke its previous designation of a financial liability measured at FVTPL irrespective of the fact that the FVTPL designation satisfies the requirements brought about by IFRS 9. However, an entity cannot revoke the previous FVTPL designation of a financial liability contract that includes an embedded derivative where the entity opted to fair value the entire contract or where groups of financial assets and liabilities are managed on a fair value basis.

Unquoted equity instruments

Equity instruments can be retrospectively designated at FVTOCI at the date of initial application provided they meet the requirements set out earlier in the chapter. The designation is made based on facts and circumstances available at the date of initial application.

Transition for hedge accounting

An entity may choose its accounting policy to continue to apply the hedge accounting principles of IAS 39. If any entity choses this approach, it must apply this to all of its hedge relationships, including IFRIC 16, *Hedges of a Net Foreign Operation*.

To apply hedge accounting under IFSR 9 from the date of initial application of the hedge accounting requirements, all qualifying criteria must be met as at that date.

On initial application of the hedge accounting requirements under IFRS 9, an entity:

1. May start to apply those requirements from the same point in time as it ceases to apply the hedge accounting requirements of IAS 39; and
2. Shall consider the hedge ratio in accordance with IAS 39 as the starting point for rebalancing the hedge ratio of a continuing hedging relationship, if applicable. Any gain or loss from such a rebalancing shall be recognised in profit or loss.

Hedge accounting requirements are prospectively accounted for except:

1. Application of the accounting for the time value of options where the only change in an option's intrinsic value was designated as a hedging instrument in a hedging relationship. This applies only to those hedging relationships that existed at the beginning of the earliest comparative period or were designated thereafter;

2. Application of the accounting for the forward element in forward contracts where only the change in the spot element of a forward contract was designated as a hedging instrument in a hedging relationship.

On application of IFRS 9, hedge relationships should be treated as continuing where they previously met the IAS 39 criteria and continue to meet the IFRS 9 criteria, i.e., the previous hedge relationship is not discontinued on transition.

PRESENTATION OF FINANCIAL INSTRUMENTS UNDER IAS 32

IAS 32 establishes the principles for presenting financial instruments as liabilities or equity and for the offsetting of financial assets and financial liabilities. It deals with classifying financial instruments from the perspective of the issuer into financial assets, financial liabilities and equity instruments (and classification of related interest, dividends, losses and gains).

Distinguishing Liabilities from Equity

Financial instruments of a given issuer may have attributes of both liabilities and equity. A compound instrument is a single financial instrument that contains both a liability and an equity element (e.g., a convertible bond). From a financial reporting perspective, the central issue is whether to account for these "compound" instruments as *either* liabilities or equity *in total*, or to disaggregate them into both liabilities and equity instruments.

Under the provisions of IAS 32, the issuer of a financial instrument must classify it, or its component parts, in accordance with the substance of the respective contractual arrangement and the definitions of a financial liability, financial asset and equity instrument.

A contractual arrangement refers to an agreement between two or more parties that has clear economic consequences that the parties have little, if any, discretion to avoid, usually because the agreement is enforceable by law.

IAS 32 requires that an issuer classifies a financial instrument as equity *only if both* conditions below are met:

1. The instrument includes no contractual obligations:
    - To deliver cash or another financial asset; or
    - To exchange financial assets or financial liabilities with another entity under potentially unfavourable conditions to the issuer; and
2. If the instrument will or may be settled in the issuer's own shares (equity instruments), it is a non-derivative that includes no contractual obligation for the issuer to deliver a variable number of its own shares, or a derivative that will be settled by the issuer exchanging a fixed amount of cash or another financial asset for a fixed number of its own shares. (For this purpose, the issuer's own shares do not include instruments that are themselves contracts for the future receipt or delivery of the issuer's own shares.)

Thus, it is quite clear when the instrument gives rise to an obligation on the part of the issuer to deliver cash or another financial asset or to exchange financial instruments on potentially unfavourable terms, it is to be classified as a liability and not as equity. Mandatorily redeemable preference shares and preference shares issued with put options (options that can be exercised by the holder, potentially requiring the issuer to redeem the shares at agreed-upon prices) must, under this definition, be presented as liabilities.

Example of classification of contracts settled in an entity's own equity instruments

Derivative contract	*Gross physical settlement**	*Net settlement (net cash or net shares)*	*Issuer/counterparty right of gross or net settlement*
Purchased or written call	Equity	Derivative	Derivative
Purchased put	Equity	Derivative	Derivative
Written put	Liability	Derivative	Derivative/Liability
Forward to buy	Liability	Derivative	Derivative/Liability
Forward to sell	Liability	Derivative	Derivative

**Fixed number of shares for fixed amount of cash/financial asset.*

Puttable Financial Instruments

Under IAS 32, puttable financial instruments are presented as equity, only if *all* the following criteria are met:

1. The holder is entitled to a pro rata share of the entity's net assets on liquidation;
2. The instrument is in the class of instruments that is the most subordinate and all instruments in that class have identical features;
3. The instrument has no other characteristics that would meet the definition of a financial liability; and
4. The total expected cash flows attributable to the instrument over its life are based substantially on either:

   - Profit or loss;
   - The change in the recognised net assets; or
   - The change in the fair value of the recognised and unrecognised net assets of the entity (excluding any effects of the instrument itself). Profit or loss or change in recognised net assets for this purpose is as measured in accordance with relevant IFRS.

In addition to the above criteria, the reporting entity is not permitted to have any other instruments or contracts with terms equivalent to (4) above that have the effect of substantially restricting or fixing the residual return to the holders of the puttable financial instruments.

Based on these requirements:

1. Shares that are puttable throughout their lives at fair value, which are also the most subordinate of the instruments issued by the reporting entity, which do not contain any other obligation, and which have only discretionary (i.e., non-fixed) dividends based on profits of the issuer, will be classified as equity.
2. Shares that are puttable at fair value, but which are not the most subordinate class of instrument issued, must be classified as liabilities.
3. Shares that are puttable at fair value only on liquidation, and that are also the most subordinate class of instrument, but which specify a fixed non-discretionary dividend obligation, will be treated as compound financial instruments (that is, as being part equity, part liability).

4. Shares that are puttable at fair value only on liquidation, and that are also part of the most subordinate class of instruments issued, but are entitled to fixed, discretionary dividends, and do not contain any other obligation, are classified as equity and not liabilities.

Instruments are classified as equity from the time that they meet the criteria above. An entity shall reclassify a financial instrument from the date that the instrument ceases to have all the features or meet all the conditions set out above.

Settlement in the Entity's Own Equity Instruments

A contract is not an equity instrument solely because it may result in the receipt or delivery of an entity's own equity instruments. Such contracts will be financial liabilities where the number of equity instruments used as a means of settlement is variable.

IAS 32—Presentation examples

Financial instrument	*Presentation*
Common shares	Equity
Mandatorily redeemable instruments	Liabilities*
Instruments redeemable at the option of the holder	Liabilities*
Puttable instruments	Liabilities*
Obligation to issue shares worth a fixed or determinable amount	Liabilities
Perpetual debt	Liabilities
Instruments with contingent settlement provisions	Liabilities (unless non-substantive provision)
Convertible debt	Potentially compound instrument

**With certain exceptions.*

Interests in Cooperatives

IFRIC 2, *Members' Shares in Cooperative Entities and Similar Instruments*, states that the contractual right of the holder of a financial instrument (including members' shares in cooperative entities) to request redemption does not require that financial instrument to be classified as a financial liability. Rather, the entity must consider all the terms and conditions of the financial instrument in determining its classification as a financial liability or equity, including relevant local laws, regulations and the entity's governing charter in effect at the date of classification.

Members' shares are equity if the entity has an unconditional right to refuse redemption of the members' shares or if redemption is unconditionally prohibited by local law, regulation or the entity's governing charter. However, if redemption is prohibited only if defined conditions—such as liquidity constraints—are met (or are not met), members' shares are not equity.

The unconditional prohibition for redemption may be absolute or partial. Members shares in excess of the prohibition are financial liabilities, unless an unconditional right of refusal to redeem exists.

Convertible Debt Instruments

Bonds are frequently issued with the right to convert them into ordinary shares of the company at the holder's option when certain terms and conditions are met (i.e., a target market price is reached). Convertible debt is used for two reasons. First, when a specific amount of funds is needed, convertible debt often allows fewer shares to be issued (assuming that conversion ultimately occurs) than if the funds were raised by directly issuing the shares. Thus, less dilution is suffered by the other shareholders. Secondly, the conversion feature allows debt to be issued at a lower interest rate and with fewer restrictive covenants than if the debt were issued without it. That is because the bondholders are receiving the benefit of the conversion feature in lieu of higher current interest returns.

This dual nature of debt and equity, however, creates a question as to whether the equity element should receive separate recognition. Support for separate treatment is based on the assumption that this equity element has economic value. Since the convertible feature tends to lower the rate of interest, it can easily be argued that a portion of the proceeds should be allocated to this equity feature. On the other hand, a case can be made that the debt and equity elements are inseparable, and thus that the instrument is either all debt or all equity. IAS 32 defines convertible bonds (among other instruments) as being compound financial instruments, the component parts of which must be classified according to their separate characteristics.

Features of Convertible Debt Instruments

IAS 32 addresses the accounting for compound financial instruments from the perspective of issuers. Convertible debt probably accounts for most of the compound instruments that will be of concern to those responsible for financial reporting. IAS 32 requires the issuer of such a financial instrument to present the liability component and the equity component separately in the statement of financial position. Allocation of proceeds between liability and equity proceeds as follows:

1. Upon initial recognition, the fair value of the liability component of compound (convertible) debt instruments is computed as the present value of the contractual stream of future cash flows, discounted at the rate of interest applied at inception by the market to instruments of comparable credit status and providing substantially the same cash flows, on the same terms, but absent the conversion option. For example, if a 5% interest-bearing convertible bond would have commanded an 8% yield if issued without the conversion feature, the contractual cash flows are to be discounted at 8% to calculate the fair value of the unconditional debt component of the compound instrument.
2. The equity portion of the compound instrument is actually an embedded option to convert the liability into equity of the issuer. The fair value of the option is determined by time value and by the intrinsic value, if there is any. This option has value on initial recognition even when it is out of the money.

The issuance proceeds from convertible debt should be assigned to the components as described above. Convertible debt also has its disadvantages. If the share price increases significantly after the debt is issued, the issuer would have been better off simply by issuing the share. Additionally, if the price of the share does not reach the conversion price, the debt will never be converted (a condition known as overhanging debt).

Classification of Compound Instruments

Compound instruments are those which are sold or acquired jointly, but which provide the holder with more than a single economic interest in the issuing entity. For example, a bond sold with share purchase warrants provides the holder with an unconditional promise to pay (the bond, which carries a rate of interest and a fixed maturity date) plus a right to acquire the issuer's shares (the warrant, which may be for common or preferred shares, at either a fixed price per share or a price based on some formula, such as a price that increases over time). In some cases, one or more of the component parts of the compound instrument may be financial derivatives, as a share purchase warrant would be. In other instances, each element might be a traditional, non-derivative instrument, as would be the case when a debenture is issued with common shares as a unit offering.

The accounting issue that is most obviously associated with compound instruments is how to allocate price or proceeds to the constituent elements. This becomes most important when the compound instrument consists of parts that are both liabilities and equity items. Proper classification of the elements is vital to accurate financial reporting, affecting potentially such matters as debt covenant compliance (if the debt-to-equity ratio, for example, is a covenant to be met by the debtor entity). Under IFRS, there is no mezzanine equity section as is sometimes observed under US GAAP and, for example, redeemable shares, including contingently redeemable shares, are classified as liabilities (exceptions: redeemable only at liquidation, redemption option not genuine or certain puttable instruments representing the most residual interest in the entity).

IAS 32 requires that fair value be ascertained and then allocated to the liability components, with only the residual amount being assigned to equity. This position has been taken to be fully consistent with the definition of equity as instruments that evidence only a residual interest in the assets of an entity, after satisfying all of its liabilities.

If the compound instruments include a derivative element (e.g., a put option), the value of those features, to the extent they are embedded in the compound financial instrument other than the equity component, is included in the liability component.

The sum of the carrying amounts assigned to the liability and equity components on initial recognition is always equal to the fair value that would be ascribed to the instrument as a whole. In other words, there can be no "day one" gains from issuing financial instruments.

Example of accounting by issuer of compound instrument

To illustrate the allocation of proceeds in a compound instrument situation, assume these facts:

- 5,000 convertible bonds are issued by Needy Company on January 1, 20XX. The bonds are due December 31, 20XX+3.
- Issuance price is par (€1,000 per bond); total issuance proceeds are €5,000,000.
- Interest is due in arrears, semi-annually, at a nominal rate of 5%.
- Each (€1,000 face amount) bond is convertible into 150 ordinary shares of Needy Company.
- At issuance date, similar, non-convertible debt must yield 8%.

Required residual value method. The issuer of compound financial instruments must assign full fair value to the portion that is to be classified as a liability, with only the residual value being allocated to the equity component. The computation for the above fact situation would be as follows:

1. Use the reference discount rate, 8%, to compute the market value of straight debt carrying a 5% yield:

PV of €5,000,000 due in four years, discounted at 8%	€3,653,451
PV of semi-annual payments of €125,000 for eight periods, discounted at 8%	841,593
Total	**€4,495,044**

2. Compute the amount allocable to the conversion feature:

Total proceeds from issuance of compound instrument	€5,000,000
Value allocable to debt	4,495,044
Residual value allocable to equity component	**€504,956**

Thus, Needy Company received €4,495,044 in consideration of the actual debt being issued, plus a further €504,956 for the conversion feature, which is a call option on the underlying ordinary share of the issuer. The accounting entry to record this would be:

Cash	5,000,000 Dr	
Discount on bonds payable	504,956 Dr	
Bonds payable		5,000,000 Cr
Paid-in capital—bond conversion option		504,956 Cr

The bond discount would be amortised as additional interest over the term of the debt.

Example of accounting by acquirer of compound instrument

From the perspective of the acquirer, compound financial instruments will often be seen as containing an embedded derivative—for example, a put option or a conversion feature of a debt instrument being held for an investment. This may be required to be valued and accounted for separately (which does not necessarily imply separate presentation in the financial statements, however). In terms of IFRS 9, separate accounting is necessary if, and only if, the economic characteristics and risks of the embedded derivative are not closely related to the host contract; a separate instrument with the same terms would meet the definition of a derivative; and the combined instrument is not to be measured at fair value with changes included in profit or loss (i.e., it is neither held for trading nor subject to the "fair value option" election).

To illustrate the allocation of purchase cost in a compound financial asset situation, assume these facts:

- 500 convertible Needy Company bonds are acquired by Investor Corp. January 1, 20XX. The bonds are due December 31, 20XX+3.
- The purchase price is par (€1,000 per bond); total cost is thus €500,000.
- Interest is due in arrears, semi-annually, at a nominal rate of 5%.
- Each bond is convertible into 150 ordinary shares of the issuer.
- At purchase date, similar, non-convertible debt issued by borrowers having the same credit rating as Needy Company yields 8%.
- At purchase date, Needy Company common shares are trading at €5, and dividends over the next four years are expected to be €0.20 per share per year.

- The relevant risk-free rate on four-year obligations is 4%.
- The historic variability of Needy Company's share price can be indicated by a standard deviation of annual returns of 25%.

In terms of IAS 32, the fair value of the conversion feature should be determined, if possible, and assigned to that embedded derivative. In this example, the popular Black-Scholes-Merton model will be used (but other approaches are also acceptable).

1. Compute the standard deviation of proportionate changes in the fair value of the asset underlying the option multiplied by the square root of the time to expiration of the option:

$$25 \times \sqrt{4} = .25 = -.50$$

2. Compute the ratio of the fair value of the asset underlying the option to the present value of the option exercise price.
   - Since the expected dividend per share is €0.20 per year, the present value of this stream over four years would (at the risk-free rate) be €0.726.
   - The shares are trading at €5.00.
   - Therefore, the value of the underlying optioned asset, stripped of the stream of dividends that a holder of an unexercised option would obviously not receive, is:

$$€5.00 - .726 = €4 / 274 \text{ per share}$$

3. The implicit exercise price is €1,000 ÷ 150 shares = €6.667 per share. This must be discounted at the risk-free rate, 4%, over four years, assuming that conversion takes place at the expiration of the conversion period, as follows:

$$€6.667 \div 1.04^4 = 6.667 \div 1.170 = €5.699$$

4. Therefore, the ratio of the underlying asset, €4.274, to the present value of the exercise price, €5.699, is .750.
5. Reference must now be made to a call option valuation table to assign a fair value to these two computed amounts (the standard deviation of proportionate changes in the fair value of the asset underlying the option multiplied by the square root of the time to expiration of the option, .50, and the ratio of the fair value of the asset underlying the option to the present value of the option exercise price, .750). For this example, assume that the table value is 13.44% (meaning that the fair value of the option is 13.44%) of the fair value of the underlying asset.
6. The valuation of the conversion option, then, is given as:

$$13.44\% \times €4.274 \text{ per share} \times 150 \text{ shares/bond} \times 500 \text{ bonds} = €43,082$$

7. Since the fair value of the options (€43,082) has been determined, this is assigned to the conversion option. The difference between the cost of the hybrid investment, €500,000, and the amount allocated to the conversion feature, €43,082, or €456,918, should be attributed to the debt instrument.
8. The discount on the debt should be amortised, using the effective yield method, over the projected four-year holding period. The effective yield, taking into account the semi-annual interest payments to be received, will be about 7.54%.

If, for some reason, the value of the derivative (the conversion feature in this case) could not be ascertained, the fair value of the debt portion would be computed, and the residual allocated to the derivative. This is illustrated as follows.

9. Use the reference discount rate, 8%, to compute the market value of straight debt carrying a 5% yield:

PV of €500,000 due in four years, discounted at 8%	€365,345
PV of semi-annual payments of €12,500 for eight periods, discounted at 8%	84,159
Total	**€449,504**

10. Compute the residual amount allocable to the conversion feature:

Total proceeds from issuance of compound instrument	€500,000
Value allocable to debt	€449,504
Residual value allocable to embedded derivative	**€50,496**

Debt Instruments Issued with Share Warrants

Warrants are certificates enabling the holder to purchase a stated number of shares at a certain price within a certain period. They are often issued with bonds to enhance the marketability of the bonds and to lower the bond's interest rate.

Detachable warrants are similar to other features, such as the conversion feature discussed earlier, which under IAS 32 make the debt a compound financial instrument and which necessitate that there is an allocation of the original proceeds among the constituent elements using the principles set out above.

Instruments Having Contingent Settlement Provisions

Some financial instruments are issued which have contingent settlement provisions—that is, which may or may not require the issuer/obligor to utilise its resources in subsequent settlement. For example, a note can be issued that will be payable either in cash or in the issuer's shares, depending on whether certain contingent events, such as the share price exceeding a defined target over a defined number of days immediately preceding the maturity date of the note, are met or not. This situation differs from convertible debt, which is exchangeable into the shares of the borrower at the holder's option.

IAS 32 requires that a financial instrument is classified as a financial liability when the manner of settlement depends on the occurrence or non-occurrence of uncertain future events or on the outcome of uncertain circumstances that are beyond the control of *both* the issuer and the holder. Contingent settlement provisions are ignored when they apply only in the event of liquidation of the issuer or are not genuine.

Examples of such contingent conditions would be changes in a stock market index, the consumer price index, a reference interest rate or taxation requirements or the issuer's future revenues, profit or loss or debt to equity ratio. The issuer cannot impact these factors and thus cannot unilaterally avoid settlement as a liability, delivering cash or other assets to resolve the obligation.

Under IAS 32, certain exceptions to the foregoing rule have been established. These exist when:

1. The part of the contingent settlement provision that could require settlement in cash or another financial asset (or otherwise in such a way that it would be a financial liability) is not genuine; or
2. The issuer can be required to settle the obligation in cash or another financial asset (or otherwise to settle it in such a way that it would be a financial liability) only in the event of liquidation of the issuer.

By "not genuine," IAS 32 means that there is no reasonable expectation that settlement in cash or other asset will be triggered. Thus, a contract that requires settlement in cash or a variable number of the entity's own shares only on the occurrence of an event that is extremely rare, highly abnormal and very unlikely to occur is an equity instrument. Similarly, settlement in a fixed number of the entity's own shares may be contractually precluded in circumstances that are outside the control of the entity, but if these circumstances have no genuine possibility of occurring, classification as an equity instrument is appropriate.

If the settlement option is only triggered upon liquidation, this possibility is ignored in classifying the instrument, since the going concern assumption, underlying IFRS-basis financial reporting, presumes ongoing existence rather than liquidation.

Treasury Shares

When an entity reacquires its own equity instruments ("treasury shares"), the consideration paid is deducted from equity. Treasury shares are not treated as assets but are to be deducted from equity. No gain or loss should be recognised in profit or loss on the purchase, sale, issue or cancellation of an entity's own equity instruments since transactions with shareholders do not affect profit or loss. Treasury shares may be acquired and held by the entity or by other members of the consolidated group. Consideration paid or received from transactions with treasury shares should be recognised directly in equity. An entity must disclose the number of treasury shares held either in the statement of financial position or in the notes, in accordance with IAS 1. In addition, disclosures under IAS 24 must be provided if an entity reacquires its own shares from related parties.

Reporting Interest, Dividends, Losses and Gains

IAS 32 establishes that interest, dividends, losses and gains relating to a financial instrument or a component that is a financial liability should be recognised as income or expense in profit or loss. Distributions (dividends) paid on equity instruments issued should be charged directly to equity, and reported in the statement of changes in equity.

Transaction costs of an equity transaction should be accounted for as a deduction from equity. Income tax relating to distributions to holders of an equity instrument and to transaction costs of an equity transaction is accounted for in accordance with IAS 12, *Income Taxes*.

The statement of financial position classification of the instrument drives the statement of comprehensive income classification of the related interest or dividends. For example, if mandatorily redeemable preferred shares have been categorised as debt in the issuer's statement of financial position, dividend payments on those shares must be recognised in profit or loss in the same manner as interest expense. Similarly, gains or losses associated with redemptions or refinancing of financial instruments classed as liabilities would be recognised in profit or loss, while gains or losses on equity instruments are credited or charged to equity directly.

Offsetting Financial Assets and Liabilities

Offsetting financial assets and liabilities is required only when the entity both:

1. Has the legally enforceable right to set off the recognised amounts; and
2. Intends either to settle on a net basis, or to realise the asset and settle the liability simultaneously.

Simultaneous settlement of a financial asset and a financial liability can be presumed only under defined circumstances. The most typical of such cases is when both instruments will be settled through a clearing house functioning for an organised exchange. Other situations may superficially appear to warrant the same accounting treatment but in fact do not give rise to legitimate offsetting. For example, if the entity will exchange cheques with a single counterparty for the settlement of both instruments, it becomes exposed to credit risk for a time, however brief, when it has paid the other party for the amount of the obligation owed to it but has yet to receive the counterparty's funds to settle the amount it is owed by the counterparty. Offsetting would not be warranted in such a context.

Legally enforceable right of setoff means that the right of setoff must be a legal contractual right, not be contingent on a future event and must be legally enforceable in all of the following circumstances:

1. The normal course of business;
2. The event of default; and
3. The event of insolvency or bankruptcy of the entity and all of the counterparties.

The nature and extent of the right of setoff, including any conditions attached to its exercise and whether it would remain in the event of default or insolvency or bankruptcy, may vary from jurisdiction to jurisdiction. As such, it cannot be assumed that the right of setoff is automatically available outside of the normal course of business. For example, bankruptcy or insolvency laws of a jurisdiction may prohibit, or restrict, the right of setoff in some circumstances and this needs to be taken into consideration in assessing whether or not the criteria set out above are met.

The standard sets forth a number of circumstances in which offsetting would *not* be justified. These include:

1. When several different instruments are used to emulate the features of a single type of instrument (which typically would involve a number of different counterparties, thus violating a basic principle of offsetting).
2. When financial assets and financial liabilities arise from instruments having the same primary risk exposure (such as when both are forward contracts) but with different counterparties.
3. When financial assets are pledged as collateral for non-recourse financial liabilities (as the intention is not typically to effect offsetting, but rather to settle the obligation and gain release of the collateral).

4. When financial assets are set aside in a trust for the purpose of discharging a financial obligation, but the assets have not been formally accepted by the creditor (as when a sinking fund is established, or when in-substance defeasance of debt is arranged).
5. When obligations incurred as a consequence of events giving rise to losses are expected to be recovered from a third party by virtue of an insurance claim (again, different counterparties mean that the entity is exposed to credit risk, however slight).

Even the existence of a master netting agreement does not automatically justify the offsetting of financial assets and financial liabilities. Only if both the stipulated conditions (both the right to offset and the intention to do so) are met can this accounting treatment be employed.

DISCLOSURES

Disclosures Required under IFRS 7

IFRS 7 has superseded the disclosure requirements previously found in IAS 32, as well as the financial institution-specific disclosure requirements of IAS 30, which were accordingly withdrawn. Presentation requirements set forth in IAS 32 continue in effect under that standard. IFRS 7 became effective for years beginning in 2007. Some of the amendments to IFRS 7 since 2007 are highlighted below:

1. Improving disclosures about financial instruments issued in March 2009 amended the required disclosures of fair value measurement and liquidity risk;
2. Improvements to IFRS standards issued in May 2010 included amendments to IFRS 7 that mostly clarified and refined certain disclosure requirements. Amendments are effective for financial periods beginning on or after January 1, 2011;
3. Transfer of financial assets issued in October 2010 on transfer of financial assets determining the recognition or derecognition (effective financial periods beginning on or after January 7, 2011);
4. IFRS 13, *Fair Value Measurement*, which transferred all the fair value disclosure from IFRS 7 to IFRS 13 (effective for financial periods beginning on or after January 1, 2013);
5. The amendments to IFRS 7 effective January 1, 2013 required entities to disclose information about rights of offset and related arrangements for financial instruments under an enforceable master netting agreement or similar arrangements irrespective of whether they are offset in the statement of financial position;
6. The latest amendments to IFRS 7 deal with additional disclosure requirements and amendments related to IFRS that are applicable from the same date that an entity applies IFRS 9.

IFRS 7 was made necessary by the increasingly sophisticated (but opaque) methods that reporting entities had begun using to measure and manage their exposure to risks arising from financial instruments. At the same time, new risk management concepts and approaches have gained acceptance. IASB concluded that users of financial statements need information about the reporting entities' exposures to risks and how those risks are being managed.

The principal objectives of this standard are to enable users to evaluate and assess:

1. Significance of financial instruments to an entity's financial position and subsequent performance;
2. Nature and extent of risks arising from financial instruments to which the entity is exposed during the period and at the end of the reporting period, and how the entity manages those risks.

Risk management information can influence the users' assessments of the financial position and performance of reporting entities, as well as of the amount, timing and uncertainty of the respective entity's future cash flows. In short, greater transparency regarding those risks allows users to make more informed judgements about risk and return. This is entirely consistent with the fundamental objective of financial reporting and is consistent with the widely accepted efficient markets hypothesis.

Paragraph 7 of IFRS 7 requires an entity to disclose information that enables users of its financial statements to evaluate the significance of financial instruments for its financial performance and financial position. Therefore, IFRS 7 applies to all risks arising from all financial instruments, with limited exceptions. It furthermore applies to all entities, including those that have only few basic financial instruments (e.g., an entity whose only financial instruments are accounts receivable and payable), as well as those that have many complex financial instruments (e.g., a financial institution, most assets and liabilities of which are financial instruments). Under IFRS 7, the extent of disclosure required depends on the extent of the entity's use of financial instruments and of its exposure to risk.

IFRS 7 sets out the requirements for the disclosure of financial instruments under two broad categories, quantitative disclosures and qualitative disclosures. The quantitative disclosures provide information about the effect of financial instruments on the financial position and financial performance of the entity, whereas the qualitative disclosures provide useful information about how risks relating to financial instruments arise in the entity and how these risks are being managed. The nature of the reporting entity's business and the extent to which it holds financial assets or is obligated by financial liabilities will affect the manner in which such disclosures are presented, and no single method of making such disclosures will be suitable for every entity. The standard therefore adopts an approach that requires the entity to disclose the information required in the form that it is presented internally for use by management and in those areas where management does not prepare the required information it must develop the appropriate disclosures. This approach means that financial instrument disclosures may not be easily comparable between entities.

The risks arising from financial instruments are categorised as follows:

1. *Market risk*, which implies not merely the risk of loss but also the potential for gain, and which is in turn comprised of:
   - *Currency risk*—The risk that the value of an instrument will vary due to changes in currency exchange rates.
   - *Interest rate risk*—The risk that the value of the instrument will fluctuate due to changes in market interest rates. Interest rate risk is the risk associated with holding fixed rate instruments in a changing interest rate environment. As market rates rise, the price of fixed interest rate instruments will decline, and vice versa. This relationship holds in all cases, irrespective of other specific factors, such as changes in perceived creditworthiness of the borrower. However, with certain complex instruments

such as mortgage-backed bonds (a popular form of derivative instrument), where the behaviour of the underlying debtors can be expected to be altered by changes in the interest rate environment (i.e., as market interest rates decline, prepayments by mortgagors increase in frequency, raising reinvestment rate risk to the bondholders and accordingly tempering the otherwise expected upward movement of the bond prices), the inverse relationship will become distorted.

2. *Other price risk*—A broader concept that subsumes interest rate risk; this is the risk that the fair value or future cash flows of a financial instrument will fluctuate due to factors specific to the financial instrument or due to factors that are generally affecting all similar instruments traded in the same markets (e.g., where financial instruments comprise derivative contracts in commodity markets, such price risk will include the risks of changes in the respective commodity prices on international markets).
3. *Credit risk* is related to a loss that may occur from the failure of another party to a financial instrument to discharge an obligation according to the terms of a contract.
4. *Liquidity risk* is the risk that an entity may encounter difficulty in meeting obligations associated with financial liabilities.

Applicability of IFRS 7

IFRS 7 applies to both recognised and unrecognised financial instruments. *Recognised* financial instruments include financial assets and financial liabilities that are within the scope of IFRS 9. *Unrecognised* financial instruments include some financial instruments that, although outside the scope of IFRS 9, are within the scope of this IFRS (such as some loan commitments). The requirements also extend to contracts involving non-financial items if they are subject to IFRS 9.

Under the IFRS 9 related amendments, IFRS 7 also applies to receivables arising from IFRS 15 which IFRS 15 requires to be accounted for under IFRS 9 for the purposes of recognising impairment gains or losses.

Classes of Financial Instruments and Level of Disclosure

Many of the IFRS 7 requirements pertain to grouped data. In such cases, the grouping into classes is to be effected in the manner that is appropriate to the nature of the information disclosed and that takes into account the characteristics of the financial instruments. Importantly, sufficient information must be provided to permit reconciliation to the line items presented in the statement of financial position. Enough detail is required so that users are able to assess the significance of financial instruments to the reporting entity's financial position and results of operations.

IFRS 7 requires that carrying amounts of each of the following categories, as defined in IFRS 9, are to be disclosed either on the face of the statement of financial position or in the notes:

1. Financial assets at FVTPL, showing separately:
   - Those designated as such upon initial recognition; and
   - Those mandatorily classified as FVTPL in accordance with IFRS 9.
2. Financial liabilities at FVTPL, showing separately:
   - Those designated as such upon initial recognition; and
   - Those meeting the definition of held for trading in accordance with IFRS 9.

3. Financial assets measured at amortised cost;
4. Financial liabilities measured at amortised cost;
5. Financial assets measured at FVTOCI, showing separately:
   - Financial assets that are measured at FVTOCI mandatorily under IFRS 9; and
   - Investments in equity instruments designated as FVTOCI at initial recognition under IFRS 9.

Special disclosures apply to those financial assets and liabilities that an entity designates to be classified and accounted for at FVTPL that would otherwise have been measured at FVTOCI or amortised cost as follows:

1. The maximum exposure to credit risk of the loan or receivable (or group thereof) at the reporting date;
2. The amount by which any related credit derivatives or similar instruments mitigate that maximum exposure to credit risk;
3. The amount of change, both during the reporting period and cumulatively, in the fair value of the loan or receivable (or group thereof) that is attributable to changes in the credit risk of the financial asset determined either:
   - As the amount of change in its fair value that is not attributable to changes in market conditions that give rise to market risk; or
   - Using an alternative method the entity believes more faithfully represents the amount of change in its fair value that is attributable to changes in the credit risk of the asset.

   Changes in market conditions that give rise to market risk include changes in an observed (benchmark) interest rate, commodity price, foreign exchange rate or index of prices or rates;
4. The amount of the change in the fair value of any related derivatives or similar instruments that has occurred during the period and cumulatively since the loan or receivable was designated.

If the reporting entity has designated a financial liability to be reported at FVTPL, and is required to present the effects of changes in that liability's credit risk in other comprehensive income, it is to disclose:

1. The amount of change, cumulatively, in the fair value of the financial liability that is attributable to changes in the credit risk of that liability;
2. The difference between the financial liability's carrying amount and the amount the entity would be contractually required to pay at maturity to the holder of the obligation;
3. Any transfers of the cumulative gain or loss within equity during the period, including the reason for such transfers;
4. If a liability is derecognised during the period, the amount (if any) presented in other comprehensive income that was realised at derecognition.

If an entity has designated a financial liability as at FVTPL and is required to present all changes in the fair value of that liability (including the effects of changes in the credit risk of the liability) in profit or loss (to eliminate an accounting mismatch), it shall disclose:

1. The amount of change, during the period and cumulatively, in the fair value of the financial liability that is attributable to changes in the credit risk of that liability; and
2. The difference between the financial liability's carrying amount and the amount the entity would be contractually required to pay at maturity to the holder of the obligation.

The entity shall also disclose:

1. A detailed description of the methods used to comply with the above disclosure requirements, including an explanation of why the method is appropriate;
2. If the entity believes that the disclosure it has given, either in the statement of financial position or in the notes, to comply with the requirements above, does not faithfully represent the change in the fair value of the financial asset or financial liability attributable to changes in its credit risk, the reasons for reaching this conclusion and the factors it believes are relevant;
3. A detailed description of the methodology or methodologies used to determine whether presenting the effects of changes in a liability's credit risk in other comprehensive income would create or enlarge an accounting mismatch in profit or loss. If an entity is required to present the effects of changes in a liability's credit risk in profit or loss, the disclosure must include a detailed description of the economic relationship.

If an entity has designated investments in equity instruments to be measured at FVTOCI, as permitted by IFRS 9, it shall disclose:

1. Which investments in equity instruments have been designated to be measured at FVTOCI;
2. The reasons for using this presentation alternative;
3. The fair value of each such investment at the end of the reporting period;
4. Dividends recognised during the period, showing separately those related to investments derecognised during the reporting period and those related to investments held at the end of the reporting period;
5. Any transfers of the cumulative gain or loss within equity during the period, including the reason for such transfers.

If an entity derecognised investment in equity instruments measured at FVTOCI during the reporting period, it shall disclose:

1. The reasons for disposing of the investments;
2. The fair value of the investments at the date of derecognition;
3. The cumulative gain or loss on disposal.

EXAMPLE OF DISCLOSURES:
Note 3.8 Financial instruments and financial risk management
Sub-note 3.8.1 Categories of financial instruments

20XX

Assets as per balance sheet	Amortised cost	Assets at fair value through profit or loss	Derivatives used for hedging	Assets at fair value through other comprehensive income
Equity investments		X		X
Trade receivables	X			
Other current assets at fair value through profit or loss		X	X	
Cash and cash equivalents	X			
Total	**X**	**X**	**X**	**X**

Liabilities as per balance sheet	Liabilities at fair value through profit or loss	Financial liabilities measured at amortised cost	Derivatives used for hedging
Non-current borrowings		X	
Current borrowings		X	
Current portion of non-current borrowings		X	
Finance lease liability		X	
Total	–	**X**	–

20XX

Assets as per balance sheet	Amortised cost	Assets at fair value through profit or loss	Derivatives used for hedging	Assets at fair value through other comprehensive income
Equity investments		X		X
Trade receivables	X			
Other current assets at fair value through profit or loss		X	X	
Cash and cash equivalents	X			
Total	**X**	**X**	**X**	**X**

Liabilities as per balance sheet	Liabilities at fair value through profit or loss	Financial liabilities measured at amortised cost	Derivatives used for hedging
Non-current borrowings		X	
Current borrowings		X	
Current portion of non-current borrowings		X	
Finance lease liability		X	
Total	–	**X**	–

Disclosures Relating to Reclassifications

An entity shall disclose if, in the current or previous reporting periods, it has reclassified any financial assets in accordance with IFRS 9. For each such event, an entity shall disclose:

1. The date of reclassification;
2. A detailed explanation of the change in business model and a qualitative description of its effect on the entity's financial statements;
3. The amount reclassified into and out of each category.

For each reporting period following reclassification until derecognition, an entity shall disclose for assets reclassified out of the FVTPL category so that they are measured at amortised cost or FVTOCI in accordance with IFRS 9:

1. The effective interest rate determined on the date of reclassification; and
2. The interest revenue recognised.

If, since its last annual reporting date, an entity has reclassified financial assets out of the FVTOCI category so that they are measured at amortised cost or out of the FVTPL category so that they are measured at amortised cost or FVTOCI, it shall disclose:

1. The fair value of the financial assets at the end of the reporting period; and
2. The fair value gain or loss that would have been recognised in profit or loss or other comprehensive income during the reporting period if the financial assets had not been reclassified.

Offsetting Financial Assets and Financial Liabilities

IFRS 7 requires entities to disclose information about rights of offset and related arrangements for financial instruments under an enforceable master netting agreement or similar arrangements irrespective of whether they are offset in the statement of financial position.

The entity shall disclose the information to enable users of its financial statements to evaluate the effect or potential effect of netting arrangements on the entity's financial position. This includes the effect or potential effect of rights of setoff associated with the entity's recognised financial assets and recognised financial liabilities. Some of the quantitative disclosures required are:

1. Gross amounts of those recognised financial assets and recognised financial liabilities.
2. Amounts that are set off in accordance with the criteria in paragraph 42 of IAS 32 when determining the net amounts presented in the statement of financial position.

3. Net amounts presented in the statement of financial position.
4. The amounts subject to enforceable master netting arrangement or a similar agreement that are not otherwise included in paragraph 13c(b) including:
   - Amounts related to recognised financial instruments that do not meet some or all of the offsetting criteria in paragraph 42 of IAS 32;
   - Amounts related to financial collateral (including cash collateral).
5. The net amount after deducting the amounts in (d) from the amounts in (c) above.

The total amount disclosed in accordance with (d) above for an instrument shall be limited to the amount in (c) above for that same instrument. This means that if the amount in (c) is a net financial liability the deducting amount in (d) will not result in it being disclosed as an asset.

The entity shall include a description in the disclosures of the rights of setoff associated with the entity's recognised financial assets and recognised financial liabilities subject to an enforceable master netting arrangement, and a similar agreement that is disclosed in accordance with (d) above, including the nature of those rights.

IFRS 7 paragraph 13E suggests that where disclosures have been made in more than one note, the entity shall cross refer between the notes.

Illustrative examples relating to offsetting disclosures are as below:

FINANCIAL ASSETS SUBJECT TO OFFSETTING, ENFORCEABLE MASTER NETTING ARRANGEMENTS AND SIMILAR AGREEMENTS

Description	**(a) Gross amounts of recognised financial assets**	**(b) Gross amounts of recognised financial liabilities set off in the statement of financial position**	**(c) = (a) – (b) Net amounts of financial assets presented in the statement of financial position**	**(d) Related amounts not set off in the statement of financial position**		**(e) = (c) – (d) Net amount**
				Financial instruments	**Cash collateral received**	
Derivatives	XX	(XX)	XX	(XX)	(XX)	XX
Reverse repurchase, securities borrowing and similar agreements	XX	–	XX	(XX)	–	–
Other financial instruments	–	–	–	–	–	–
Total	XX	(XX)	XX	(XX)	(XX)	XX

FINANCIAL LIABILITIES SUBJECT TO OFFSETTING, ENFORCEABLE MASTER NETTING ARRANGEMENTS AND SIMILAR AGREEMENTS

Description	**(a) Gross amounts of recognised financial assets**	**(b) Gross amounts of recognised financial assets set off in the statement of financial position**	**(c) = (a) – (b) Net amounts of financial liabilities presented in the statement of financial position**	**(d) Related amounts not set off in the statement of financial position**		**(e) = (c) – (d) Net amount**
				Financial instruments	**Cash collateral pledged**	
Derivatives	XX	(XX)	XX	(XX)	(XX)	–
Reverse repurchase, securities lending and similar agreements	XX	–	XX	(XX)	–	–
Other financial instruments	–	–	–	–	–	–
Total	XX	(XX)	XX	(XX)	–	–

NET FINANCIAL ASSETS SUBJECT TO ENFORCEABLE MASTER NETTING ARRANGEMENTS AND SIMILAR AGREEMENTS, BY COUNTERPARTY

Description	**(c) Net amounts of financial assets presented in the statement of financial position**	**(d) Related amounts not set off in the statement of financial position**		**(e) = (c) – (d) Net amounts**
		Financial instruments	**Cash collateral received**	
Counterparty A	XX	–	(XX)	XX
Counterparty B	XX	(XX)	(XX)	–
Counterparty C	XX	(XX)	–	–
Other	–	–	–	–
Total	XX	(XX)	(XX)	XX

Collateral

The reporting entity must disclose the carrying amount of financial assets it has pledged as collateral for liabilities or contingent liabilities, including amounts that have been reclassified in accordance with the provision of IFRS 9 pertaining to rights to repledge, and the terms and conditions relating to its pledge.

Conversely, if the reporting entity holds collateral (of either financial or non-financial assets) and is permitted to sell or repledge the collateral in the absence of default by the owner of the collateral, it must now disclose the fair value of the collateral held and the fair value of any such collateral sold or repledged, whether it has an obligation to return it, and the terms and conditions associated with its use of the collateral.

Loss Allowances for Financial Assets Measured at FVTOCI

The carrying amount of financial assets measured at FVTOCI in accordance with IFRS 9 is not reduced by a loss allowance and an entity shall not present the loss allowance separately in the statement of financial position as a reduction of the carrying amount of the financial asset. However, an entity shall disclose the loss allowance in the notes to the financial statements.

Certain Compound Instruments

If the reporting entity is the issuer of compound instruments, such as convertible debt, having multiple embedded derivatives having interdependent values (such as the conversion feature and a call feature, such that the issuer can effectively force conversion), these matters must be disclosed.

Defaults and Breaches

If the reporting entity is the obligor under loans payable at the date of the statement of financial position, it must disclose:

1. The details of any defaults during the period, involving payment of principal or interest, or into a sinking fund, or of the redemption terms of those loans payable;
2. The carrying amount of the loans payable in default at the reporting date; and
3. Whether the default was remedied, or the terms of the loans payable were renegotiated, before the financial statements were authorised for issue.

Similar disclosures are required for any other breaches of loan agreement terms, if such breaches gave the lender the right to accelerate payment, unless these were remedied, or terms were renegotiated before the reporting date.

Disclosures in the Statements of Comprehensive Income and Changes in Equity

The reporting entity is to disclose the following items of revenue, expense, gains or losses, either on the face of the financial statements or in the notes thereto:

1. Net gain or net losses on:
    - Financial assets or financial liabilities carried at FVTPL, showing separately those incurred on financial assets or financial liabilities designated as such upon initial recognition, and those on financial assets or financial liabilities that are classified as such in accordance with IFRS 9;
    - Financial liabilities carried at amortised cost;

- Financial assets measured at amortised cost;
- Investments in equity instruments designated at FVTOCI; and
- Financial assets measured at FVTOCI under IFRS 9 showing separately the gain or loss recognised in other comprehensive income during the period and the amount reclassified upon derecognition from accumulated other comprehensive income to profit or loss during the period.

2. Total interest income and total interest expense (calculated using the effective interest method) for financial assets that are measured at either amortised cost of FVTOCI or financial liabilities that are not measured at FVTPL.
3. Fee income and expense (other than amounts included in determining the effective interest rate) arising from:
   - Financial assets or financial liabilities that are not carried at FVTPL; and
   - Trust and other fiduciary activities that result in the holding or investing of assets on behalf of individuals, trusts, retirement benefit plans and other institutions.
4. An entity shall disclose an analysis of the gain or loss recognised in the statement of other comprehensive income arising from the derecognition of financial assets measured at amortised cost separating the gains and losses arising from derecognition. Reasons for derecognition of such financial assets shall also be provided.

Example: Gains and losses in respect of financial instruments

	20XX	**20XX-1**
Net gains on financial assets at FVTPL	X	X
Impairment of trade receivables	X	X
Impairment of investments measured at FVTOCI	X	X
Ineffectiveness arising from cash flow hedges	X	X
Ineffectiveness arising from hedges of net investments	X	X

Accounting Policies Disclosure

The reporting entity is to disclose the measurement basis (or bases) used in preparing the financial statements and the other accounting policies used that are relevant to an understanding of the financial statements.

Example: Note 2. Accounting policies

Sub-note 2.8 financial instruments

The group classifies financial instruments, or their component parts, on initial recognition as a financial asset, a financial liability or an equity instrument in accordance with the substance of the contractual arrangement. Financial instruments are recognised when the group becomes a party to the contractual provisions of the instrument.

Financial instruments are recognised initially at fair value plus transactions costs that are directly attributable to the acquisition or issue of the financial instrument, except for financial assets at fair value through profit or loss, which are initially measured at fair value, excluding transaction costs (which are recognised in profit or loss).

Financial assets are derecognised when the rights to receive cash flows from the investments have expired or have been transferred and the group has transferred substantially all risk and rewards of ownership.

Financial assets are classified for measurement purposes into one of the following three categories:

1. Financial assets at amortised cost;
2. Financial assets at fair value through other comprehensive income (FVTOCI); or
3. Financial assets at fair value through profit or loss (FVTPL).

2.8.1 Financial assets measured at amortised cost

Financial assets are measured at amortised cost where they are held within a business model whose objective is to hold the assets to collect contractual cash flows and the contractual cash flows are solely payments of principal and interest.

Such financial assets include trade receivables and cash and cash equivalents. Trade receivables are measured at initial recognition at fair value and are subsequently measured at amortised cost using the effective interest rate method, less provision for impairment. Trade receivables are reduced by appropriate allowances for estimated irrecoverable amounts. Interest on overdue trade receivables is recognised as it accrues.

Cash equivalents comprise short-term, highly liquid investments that are readily convertible into known amounts of cash and which are subject to an insignificant risk of changes in value. An investment with a maturity of three months or less is normally classified as being short term. Bank overdrafts are shown within borrowing in current liabilities.

2.8.2 Financial assets at fair value through other comprehensive income

Financial assets are classified as fair value through other comprehensive income where the asset is held in a business model whose objective is a combination of holding assets to collect contractual cash flows and also selling financial assets and where the contractual cash flows comprise solely of payments of principal and interest. Equity investments that are not held for trading purposes are also classified as fair value through other comprehensive income under specific elections made by the company.

Subsequent to initial recognition, fair value through other comprehensive income financial assets is stated at fair value with fair value changes recognised through other comprehensive income. Fair values are based on prices quoted in an active market if such a market is available. If an active market is not available, the group establishes the fair value of financial instruments by using a valuation technique, usually discounted cash flow analysis. Dividends are recognised in profit or loss when the right to receive payments is established.

2.8.3 Financial assets at fair value through profit or loss

All financial assets other than those classified as amortised cost or fair value through other comprehensive income are classified as fair value through profit or loss. Fair value through profit or loss assets also include financial assets which may meet the business model tests above but which are designated upon initial recognition at fair value through profit or loss. Financial assets at fair value through profit or loss comprise derivative financial instruments, namely interest rate swaps and forward exchange contracts. After initial recognition, financial assets at fair value through profit and loss are stated at fair value. Movements in fair values are recognised in profit or loss, unless they relate to financial assets designated and effective as hedging instruments, in which event the timing of the recognition in profit or loss depends on the nature of the hedging relationship. The group designates certain derivatives as hedging instruments in fair value hedges of recognised assets and liabilities and firm commitments, and in cash flow hedges of highly probable forecast transactions and foreign currency risks relating to firm commitments.

The effective portion of fluctuations in the fair value of interest rate swaps used to hedge interest rate risk and that qualify as fair value hedges is recognised together with finance costs. The ineffective portion of the gain or loss is recognised in other expenses or other income.

Fluctuations in the fair value of forward exchange contracts used to hedge currency risk of future cash flows, and the fair value of foreign currency monetary items on the statement of financial position, are recognised directly in other expenses or other income. This policy has been adopted as the relationship between the forward exchange contracts and the item being hedged does not meet certain conditions to qualify as a hedging relationship.

2.8.4 Financial liabilities

Financial liabilities are classified as measured at amortised cost. Trade payables are initially measured at fair value, and subsequently measured at amortised cost using the effective interest rate method.

Bank overdrafts and interest-bearing borrowings are recognised initially at fair value, net of transaction costs incurred and subsequently measured at amortised cost using the effective interest method.

At the issue date, the fair value of the liability component of a compound instrument is estimated using the market interest rate for a similar non-convertible instrument. This amount is recorded as a liability at amortised cost using the effective interest method until extinguished upon conversion or at the instrument redemption date. The equity component is determined as the difference of the amount of the liability component from the fair value of the instrument. This is recognised in equity, net of income tax effects, and is not subsequently remeasured.

2.8.5 Effective interest method

The effective interest method is a method of calculating the amortised cost of a financial liability and of allocating interest expense over the relevant period. The effective interest rate is the rate that exactly discounts estimated future cash payments through the expected life of the financial liability.

2.8.6 Net investment in foreign operation

The effective portion of fluctuations in the fair value of the hedging instrument used to hedge currency risk of net investments in foreign companies is recognised directly in equity. The ineffective portion of the gain or loss is recognised in profit or loss. The gain or loss deferred in equity, or part thereof, for hedges of net investments in foreign companies is recycled through profit or loss when the interest in, or part of the interest in, the foreign company is disposed of.

2.8.7 Impairment of financial assets

All financial assets measured at amortised cost and at fair value where changes in fair value are reported through other comprehensive income are subject to impairment provisions of IFRS 9. The company applies the simplified approach under IFRS 9 under which lifetime expected credit losses are recognised for its trade receivables. In respect of loans to related parties and other receivables, the company initially recognises 12-month expected credit losses and at each reporting date assesses whether there has been a significant increase in credit risk for such assets since initial recognition, and if so, recognises impairment provisions based on the lifetime expected credit loss model.

2.8.8 Offsetting financial instruments

Financial assets and liabilities are offset, and the net amount reported in the statement of financial position when there is a legally enforceable right to offset the recognised amounts and there is an intention to settle on a net basis or to realise the asset and settle the liability simultaneously.

Hedging Disclosures

Hedge accounting is one of the more complex aspects of financial instruments accounting under IFRS 9, as discussed above in more detail. IFRS 7 requires disclosures about hedge accounting that provide information about:

1. The entity's risk management strategy and how it is applied to manage risk;
2. How the entity's hedging activities may affect the amount, timing and uncertainty of its future cash flows; and
3. The effect that hedge accounting has had on the entity's statement of financial position, statement of comprehensive income and statement of changes in equity.

IFRS 7 requires the following key disclosures in respect of each risk category of risk exposures that the entity decides to hedge. It should be noted that IFRS 7 requires the entity to determine how much detail to disclose, how much emphasis to place on different aspects of the disclosure requirements, the appropriate level of aggregation and disaggregation and whether users of financial statements are likely to need additional explanations to evaluate quantitative information disclosed.

Risk management strategy

The disclosures provided will seek to explain the entity's risk management strategy to provide users with details on how each risk arises, how such risks are managed, including whether the entity hedges an item in entirety for all risks or only a component, and the extent of risk exposures that an entity manages.

The information provided above should include details of hedging instruments used, the way in which the entity determines the economic relationship between the hedged item and the hedging instrument for purposes of assessing hedge effectiveness and how the entity establishes the hedge ratio and what the sources of hedge ineffectiveness are.

The amount, timing and uncertainty of future cash flows

IFRS 7 requires an entity to disclose by risk category quantitative information to allow users of its financial statements to evaluate the terms and conditions of hedging instruments and how they affect the amount, timing and uncertainty of future cash flows of the entity.

To meet the requirement an entity is required to provide a breakdown that discloses:

1. A profile of the timing of the nominal amount of the hedging instrument; and
2. If applicable, the average price or rate (for example, strike or forward prices, etc.) of the hedging instrument.

In situations in which an entity frequently resets (i.e., discontinues and restarts) hedging relationships because both the hedging instrument and the hedged item frequently change (i.e., the entity uses a dynamic process in which both the exposure and the hedging instruments used to manage that exposure do not remain the same for long), IFRS 7 provides relief from detailed instrument-based disclosures and instead requires disclosure of:

1. Information about what the ultimate risk management strategy is in relation to those hedging relationships;
2. A description of how it reflects its risk management strategy by using hedge accounting and designating those hedging relationships; and
3. An indication of how frequently the hedging relationships are discontinued and restarted as part of the entity's process in relation to those hedging relationships.

IFRS 7 also requires disclosure of any sources of hedge ineffectiveness that are expected to affect the hedging relationship over its term. For cash flow hedges, an entity shall disclose a description of any forecast transaction for which hedge accounting had been used in the previous period, but which is no longer expected to occur.

The effects of hedge accounting on financial position and performance

IFRS 7 requires the following disclosures for each type of hedging instrument (i.e., cash flow hedge, fair value hedge and net investment hedge):

1. The carrying amount of the hedging instruments (financial assets separately from financial liabilities);
2. The line item in the statement of financial position that includes the hedging instrument;
3. The change in fair value of the hedging instrument used as the basis for recognising hedge ineffectiveness for the period; and
4. The nominal amounts (including quantities such as tons or cubic metres) of the hedging instruments.

For fair value hedges:
The following disclosure is required for each type of hedged item:

1. The carrying amount of the hedged item recognised in the statement of financial position (presenting assets separately from liabilities);
2. The accumulated amount of fair value hedge adjustments on the hedged item included in the carrying amount of the hedged item recognised in the statement of financial position (presenting assets separately from liabilities);
3. The line item in the statement of financial position that includes the hedged item;
4. The change in value of the hedged item used as the basis for recognising hedge ineffectiveness for the period; and
5. The accumulated amount of fair value hedge adjustments remaining in the statement of financial position for any hedged items that have ceased to be adjusted for hedging gains and losses.

For cash flow hedges and hedges of a net investment in a foreign operation:

1. The change in value of the hedged item used as the basis for recognising hedge ineffectiveness for the period (i.e., for cash flow hedges the change in value used to determine the recognised hedge ineffectiveness in accordance);
2. The balances in the cash flow hedge reserve and the foreign currency translation reserve for continuing hedges that are accounted for; and
3. The balances remaining in the cash flow hedge reserve and the foreign currency translation reserve from any hedging relationships for which hedge accounting is no longer applied.

For fair value hedges:
The following disclosure is required in respect of hedge ineffectiveness:

1. Hedge ineffectiveness—i.e., the difference between the hedging gains or losses of the hedging instrument and the hedged item—recognised in profit or loss (or other comprehensive income for hedges of an equity instrument for which an entity has elected to present changes in fair value in other comprehensive income in accordance with paragraph 5.7.5 of IFRS 9); and

2. The line item in the statement of comprehensive income that includes the recognised hedge ineffectiveness.

For cash flow hedges and hedges of a net investment in a foreign operation:

1. Hedging gains or losses of the reporting period that were recognised in other comprehensive income;
2. Hedge ineffectiveness recognised in profit or loss;
3. The line item in the statement of comprehensive income that includes the recognised hedge ineffectiveness;
4. The amount reclassified from the cash flow hedge reserve or the foreign currency translation reserve into profit or loss as a reclassification adjustment (see IAS 1) (differentiating between amounts for which hedge accounting had previously been used, but for which the hedged future cash flows are no longer expected to occur, and amounts that have been transferred because the hedged item has affected profit or loss);
5. The line item in the statement of comprehensive income that includes the reclassification adjustment (see IAS 1); and
6. For hedges of net positions, the hedging gains or losses recognised in a separate line item in the statement of comprehensive income.

Fair Value Disclosures

IFRS 9 requires that for each class of financial assets and financial liabilities, the reporting entity is to disclose the fair value of that class of assets and liabilities in a way that permits it to be compared with its carrying amount. Grouping by class is required, but offsetting assets and liabilities is generally not permitted (but will conform to statement of financial position presentation).

In instances where the market for a financial instrument is not active, the reporting entity establishes the fair value using a valuation technique. The best evidence of fair value at initial recognition is the transaction price, so there could be a difference between the fair value at initial recognition and the amount that would be determined at that date using the valuation technique. In such a case, disclosure is required by the class of financial instrument of:

1. The entity's accounting policy for recognising that difference in profit or loss to reflect a change in factors (including time) that market participants would consider in setting a price;
2. The aggregate difference yet to be recognised in profit or loss at the beginning and end of the period and a reconciliation of changes in the balance of this difference; and
3. Why the entity concluded that the transaction price was not the best evidence for fair value, including a description of the evidence that supports the fair value.

Disclosures of fair value are not required in these circumstances:

1. When the carrying amount is a reasonable approximation of fair value (e.g., for short-term trade receivables and payables);
2. For an insurance contract containing a discretionary participation feature if the fair value of that feature cannot be measured reliably; or
3. For lease liabilities.

In instances identified in Point 2 immediately above, the reporting entity must disclose information to help users of the financial statements make their own judgements about the extent of possible differences between the carrying amount of those financial assets or financial liabilities and their fair value, including:

1. The fact that fair value information has not been disclosed for these instruments because their fair value cannot be measured reliably;
2. A description of the financial instruments, their carrying amount and an explanation of why fair value cannot be measured reliably;
3. Information about the market for the instruments;
4. Information about whether and how the entity intends to dispose of the financial instruments; and
5. If financial instruments whose fair value previously could not be reliably measured are derecognised, their carrying amount at the time of derecognition and the amount of gain or loss recognised.

Example: Note 3.8. Financial instruments and financial risk management

3.8.2 Classes and fair value of financial instruments Below is a comparison of the carrying value and the fair value of the group's financial instruments, other than those with a carrying value that approximates its fair value.

	20XX		**20XX-1**	
	Carrying value	**Fair value**	**Carrying value**	**Fair value**
Financial assets				
Equity investments	X	X	X	X
Other current assets	X	X	X	X
Other current assets at fair value through profit or loss	X	X	X	X
Cash and cash equivalents	X	X	X	X
Total	**X**	**X**	**X**	**X**
Financial liabilities				
Non-current borrowings	X	X	X	X
Current borrowings/ trade payables	X	X	X	X
Current portion of non-current borrowings	X	X	X	X
Finance lease liability	X	X	X	X
Total	**X**	**X**	**X**	**X**

It is the directors' opinion that the carrying value of trade receivables and trade payables approximates their fair value due to the short-term maturities of these instruments.

3.8.3 Fair value hierarchy and measurements

3.8.3.1 Financial assets and liabilities that are measured at fair value on a recurring basis

	Fair value measurement as at December 31, 20XX			
	Level 1	**Level 2**	**Level 3**	**Total**
Financial assets				
Financial assets at fair value through profit or loss				
Trading derivatives	X	X	X	X
Trading securities	X	X	X	X
Derivatives used for hedging				
Interest rate contracts	X	X	X	X
Financial assets at fair value through other comprehensive income				
Equity investments	X	X	X	X
	Fair value measurement as at December 31, 20XX-1			
	Level 1	**Level 2**	**Level 3**	**Total**
Financial assets				
Financial assets at fair value through profit or loss				
Trading derivatives	X	X	X	X
Trading securities	X	X	X	X
Derivatives used for hedging				
Interest rate contracts	X	X	X	X
Financial assets at fair value through other comprehensive income				
Equity investments	X	X	X	X

Level 1 The fair value of financial instruments traded in an active market is based on quoted market prices at the reporting date. The quoted market price used for financial assets held by the group is the quoted bid price.

Level 2 The fair value of financial instruments not traded in an active market is determined by using valuation techniques. Specific valuation techniques used to value the above financial instruments include:

1. Discounted cash flow analysis using rates currently available for debt on similar terms, credit risk and remaining maturity;
2. Quoted market prices for similar instruments;
3. Price earnings multiple model.

If all significant inputs in the valuation technique used are observable, the instrument is included in level 2, if not the instrument is included in Level 3.

Level 3 Included in Level 3 are holdings in unlisted shares which are measured at fair value, using the price earnings multiple model. The key assumption used by management is a price earnings multiple of X (20XX-1: X) which is not observable from market or related data. Management consider a reasonable possible alternative assumption would result in a decrease/increase of X (20XX-1: decrease/increase of Y) in the value of unlisted investments. This sensitivity represents a change in the price earnings multiple of 10%.

The following table presents the changes in level 3 instruments.

	Financial assets at fair value through profit or loss	**Derivatives used for hedging**	**Financial assets at fair value through other comprehensive income**	**Total**
Opening balance January 1, 20XX	X	X	X	X
Total gains or losses				
In profit or loss	X	X	X	**X**
In other comprehensive income	X	X	X	**X**
Purchases	X	X	X	**X**
Issues	X	X	X	**X**
Settlements	X	X	X	**X**
Transfers out of Level 3	X	X	X	**X**
Closing balance December 31, 20XX	X	X	X	**X**
Total gains or losses for the period included in profit or loss for assets held at the end of the reporting period	X	X	X	**X**
Change in unrealised gains or losses for the period included in profit or loss for assets held at the end of the reporting period	X	X	X	**X**

	Financial assets at fair value through profit or loss	**Derivatives used for hedging**	**Financial assets at fair value through other comprehensive income**	**Total**
Opening balance January 1, 20XX-1	X	X	X	X
Total gains or losses				
In profit or loss	X	X	X	**X**
In other comprehensive income	X	X	X	**X**
Purchases	X	X	X	**X**
Issues	X	X	X	**X**
Settlements	X	X	X	**X**
Transfers out of Level 3	X	X	X	**X**
Closing balance December 31, 20XX-1	X	X	X	**X**

Total gains or losses for the period included in profit or loss for assets held at the end of the reporting period	X	X	X	X
Change in unrealised gains or losses for the period included in profit or loss for assets held at the end of the reporting period	X	X	X	X

3.8.3.2 Financial assets and liabilities that are not measured at fair value on a recurring basis

	Fair value measurement as at December 31, 20XX			
	Level 1	**Level 2**	**Level 3**	**Total**
Financial assets held at amortised cost				
Loans and receivables				
Trade and other receivables	–	X	–	X
Cash and cash equivalents	X	–	–	X
Financial liabilities held at amortised cost			X	X
Bank loans	–	–	X	X
Loans from other entities	–	–	X	X
Trade and other payables	–	X	–	X
Finance lease payables	–	X	–	X

	Fair value measurement as at December 31, 20XX-1			
	Level 1	**Level 2**	**Level 3**	**Total**
Financial assets held at amortised cost				
Loans and receivables				
Trade and other receivables	–	X	–	X
Cash and cash equivalents	X	–	–	X
Financial liabilities held at amortised cost				
Bank loans	–	–	X	X
Loans from other entities	–	–	X	X
Trade and other payables	–	X	–	X
Finance lease payables	–	X	–	X

The fair values of the financial assets and liabilities disclosed under Levels 2 and 3 above have been determined in accordance with generally accepted pricing models based on a discounted cash flow analysis, with the most significant input being the discount rate.

Disclosures About the Nature and Extent of Risks Flowing from Financial Instruments

Reporting entities are required to disclose various information that will enable the users to evaluate the nature and extent of risks the reporting entity is faced with as a consequence of financial instruments it is exposed to at the date of the statement of financial position. Both qualitative and quantitative disclosures are required, as described in the following paragraphs.

Qualitative disclosures

For each type of risk arising from financial instruments, the reporting entity is expected to disclose:

1. The exposures to risk and how they arise;
2. Its objectives, policies and processes for managing the risk and the methods used to measure the risk; and
3. Any changes in 1. or 2. from the previous period.

Quantitative disclosures

For each type of risk arising from financial instruments, the entity must present:

1. Summary quantitative data about its exposure to that risk at the reporting date. This is to be based on the information provided internally to key management personnel of the entity;
2. The disclosures required as set forth below (credit risk, et al.), to the extent not provided in 1., unless the risk is not material;
3. Concentrations of risk, if not apparent from 1. and 2.

If the quantitative data disclosed as of the date of the statement of financial position are not representative of the reporting entity's exposure to risk during the period, it must provide further information that is representative.

Credit Risk Disclosures

IFRS 7 requires credit risk disclosures that enable users of financial statements to understand the effect of credit risk on the amount, timing and uncertainty of future cash flows. To achieve this objective, credit risk disclosures should provide:

1. Information about an entity's credit risk management practices and how they relate to the recognition and measurement of expected credit losses, including the methods, assumptions and information used to measure expected credit losses;
2. Quantitative and qualitative information that allows users of financial statements to evaluate the amounts in the financial statements arising from expected credit losses, including changes in the amount of expected credit losses and the reasons for those changes; and
3. Information about an entity's credit risk exposure (i.e., the credit risk inherent in an entity's financial assets and commitments to extend credit), including significant credit risk concentrations.

To meet the objectives in the paragraph above, an entity shall (except as otherwise specified within the requirements of IFRS 7) consider how much detail to disclose, how much emphasis to place on various aspects of the disclosure requirements, the appropriate level of aggregation or disaggregation and whether users of financial statements need additional explanations to evaluate the quantitative information disclosed.

The credit risk management practices

In disclosing the credit risk management process, IFRS 7 requires specific disclosure of:

1. How an entity determined whether the credit risk of financial instruments has increased significantly since initial recognition, including if and how:
    - Financial instruments are considered to have low credit risk, including the classes of financial instruments to which it applies; and
    - The presumption, that there have been significant increases in credit risk since initial recognition when financial assets are more than 30 days past due, has been rebutted.
2. An entity's definitions of default, including the reasons for selecting those definitions;
3. How the instruments were grouped if expected credit losses were measured on a collective basis;
4. How an entity determined that financial assets are credit-impaired financial assets;
5. An entity's write-off policy, including the indicators that there is no reasonable expectation of recovery and information about the policy for financial assets that are written off but are still subject to enforcement activity; and
6. How the modification of contractual cash flows of financial assets has been applied, including how an entity:
    - Determines whether the credit risk on a financial asset that has been modified while the loss allowance was measured at an amount equal to lifetime expected credit losses has improved to the extent that the loss allowance reverts to being measured at an amount equal to 12-month expected credit losses; and
    - Monitors the extent to which the loss allowance on financial assets meeting the criteria in the bullet point above is subsequently remeasured at an amount equal to lifetime expected credit losses.

Where an entity uses a model, whether simple or complex, to comply with the impairment requirements of IFRS 9, it is required to explain the inputs, assumptions and estimation techniques used therein. Specifically, disclosure is required of:

1. The basis of inputs and assumptions and the estimation techniques used to:
    - Measure the 12-month and lifetime expected credit losses;
    - Determine whether the credit risk of financial instruments has increased significantly since initial recognition; and
    - Determine whether a financial asset is a credit-impaired financial asset.
2. How forward-looking information has been incorporated into the determination of expected credit losses, including the use of macroeconomic information; and
3. Changes in the estimation techniques or significant assumptions made during the reporting period and the reasons for those changes.

Quantitative and qualitative information about amounts arising from expected credit losses

To explain the changes in the loss allowance and the reasons for those changes, an entity shall provide, by class of financial instrument, a reconciliation from the opening balance to the closing balance of the loss allowance, in a table, showing separately the changes during the period for:

1. The loss allowance measured at an amount equal to 12-month expected credit losses;
2. The loss allowance measured at an amount equal to lifetime expected credit losses for:
   - Financial instruments for which credit risk has increased significantly since initial recognition but that are not credit-impaired financial assets;
   - Financial assets that are credit impaired at the reporting date (but that are not purchased or originated credit impaired); and
   - Trade receivables, contract assets or lease receivables for which the loss allowances are measured.
3. Financial assets that are purchased or originated credit impaired. In addition to the reconciliation, an entity shall disclose the total amount of undiscounted expected credit losses at initial recognition on financial assets initially recognised during the reporting period.

To enable users of financial statements to understand the changes in the loss allowance disclosed, an entity shall provide an explanation of how significant changes in the gross carrying number of financial instruments during the period contributed to changes in the loss allowance. The information shall be provided separately for financial instruments that represent the loss allowance and shall include relevant qualitative and quantitative information. Examples of changes in the gross carrying number of financial instruments that contributed to the changes in the loss allowance may include:

1. Changes because of financial instruments originated or acquired during the reporting period;
2. The modification of contractual cash flows on financial assets that do not result in a derecognition of those financial assets in accordance with IFRS 9;
3. Changes because of financial instruments that were derecognised (including those that were written off) during the reporting period; and
4. Changes arising from whether the loss allowance is measured at an amount equal to 12-month or lifetime expected credit losses.

To enable users of financial statements to understand the nature and effect of modifications of contractual cash flows on financial assets that have not resulted in derecognition and the effect of such modifications on the measurement of expected credit losses, an entity shall disclose:

1. The amortised cost before the modification and the net modification gain or loss recognised for financial assets for which the contractual cash flows have been modified during the reporting period while they had a loss allowance measured at an amount equal to lifetime expected credit losses; and
2. The gross carrying amount at the end of the reporting period of financial assets that have been modified since initial recognition at a time when the loss allowance

was measured at an amount equal to lifetime expected credit losses and for which the loss allowance has changed during the reporting period to an amount equal to 12-month expected credit losses.

To enable users of financial statements to understand the effect of collateral and other credit enhancements on the amounts arising from expected credit losses, an entity shall disclose by class of financial instrument:

1. The amount that best represents its maximum exposure to credit risk at the end of the reporting period without taking account of any collateral held or other credit enhancements (e.g., netting agreements that do not qualify for offset in accordance with IAS 32);
2. A narrative description of collateral held as security and other credit enhancements, including:
    - A description of the nature and quality of the collateral held;
    - An explanation of any significant changes in the quality of that collateral or credit enhancements because of deterioration or changes in the collateral policies of the entity during the reporting period; and
    - Information about financial instruments for which an entity has not recognised a loss allowance because of the collateral.
3. Quantitative information about the collateral held as security and other credit enhancements (for example, quantification of the extent to which collateral and other credit enhancements mitigate credit risk) for financial assets that are credit impaired at the reporting date.

An entity shall disclose the contractual amount outstanding on financial assets that were written off during the reporting period and are still subject to enforcement activity.

Credit risk exposure

To enable users of financial statements to assess an entity's credit risk exposure and understand its significant credit risk concentrations, an entity shall disclose, by credit risk rating grades, the gross carrying amount of financial assets and the exposure to credit risk on loan commitments and financial guarantee contracts. This information shall be provided separately for financial instruments:

1. For which the loss allowance is measured at an amount equal to 12-month expected credit losses;
2. For which the loss allowance is measured at an amount equal to lifetime expected credit losses and that are:
    - Financial instruments for which credit risk has increased significantly since initial recognition but that are not credit-impaired financial assets;
    - Financial assets that are credit impaired at the reporting date (but that are not purchased or originated credit impaired); and
    - Trade receivables, contract assets or lease receivables for which the loss allowances are measured in accordance with IFRS 9.
3. That are purchased or originated credit-impaired financial assets.

Collateral and other credit enhancements obtained

When an entity obtains financial or non-financial assets during the period by taking possession of collateral it holds as security or calling on other credit enhancements (e.g., guarantees), and such assets meet the recognition criteria in other IFRS, an entity shall disclose for such assets held at the reporting date:

1. The nature and carrying amount of the assets; and
2. When the assets are not readily convertible into cash, its policies for disposing of such assets or for using them in its operations.

The following illustrative disclosures, as derived from the Implementation Guidance to IFRS 7, illustrates one way of providing information about the changes in the loss allowance and the significant changes in the gross carrying amount of financial assets during the period that contributed to changes in the loss allowance. This example does not illustrate the requirements for financial assets that are purchased or originated credit impaired.

Mortgage loans—loss allowance	**12-month expected credit losses**	**Lifetime expected credit losses (collectively assessed)**	**Lifetime expected credit losses (individually assessed)**	**Credit-impaired financial assets (lifetime expected credit losses)**
€'000				
Loss allowance as at January 1	X	X	X	X
Changes due to financial instruments recognised as at January 1:				
(Transfer to lifetime expected credit losses)	(X)	X	X	–
(Transfer to credit-impaired financial assets)	(X)	–	(X)	X
(Transfer to 12-month expected credit losses)	X	(X)	(X)	–
(Financial assets that have been derecognised during the period)	(X)	(X)	(X)	(X)
New financial assets originated or purchased	X	–	–	–
Write-offs	–	–	(X)	(X)
Changes in models/risk parameters	X	X	X	X
Foreign exchange and other movements	X	X	X	X
Loss allowance as at December 31	X	X	X	X

Significant changes in the gross carrying amount of mortgage loans that contributed to changes in the loss allowance were:

1. The acquisition of the ABC prime mortgage portfolio increased the residential mortgage book by X%, with a corresponding increase in the loss allowance measured on a 12-month basis;
2. The write-off of the XX DEF portfolio following the collapse of the local market reduced the loss allowance for financial assets with objective evidence of impairment by €X;
3. The expected increase in unemployment in Region X caused a net increase in financial assets whose loss allowance is equal to lifetime expected credit losses and caused a net increase of €X in the lifetime expected credit losses allowance.

The significant changes in the gross carrying amount of mortgage loans is further explained below:

Mortgage loans—gross carrying amount	**12-month expected credit losses**	**Lifetime expected credit losses (collectively assessed)**	**Lifetime expected credit losses (individually assessed)**	**Credit-impaired financial assets (lifetime expected credit losses)**
€'000				
Gross carrying amount as at January 1	X	X	X	X
Individual financial assets transferred to lifetime expected credit losses	(X)	–	X	–
Individual financial assets transferred to credit-impaired financial assets	(X)	–	(X)	X
Individual financial assets transferred from credit-impaired financial assets	X	–	X	(X)
Financial assets assessed on collective basis	(X)	X	–	–
New financial assets originated or purchased	X	–	–	–
Write-offs	–	–	(X)	(X)
Financial assets that have been derecognised	(X)	(X)	(X)	(X)
Changes due to modifications that did not result in derecognition	(X)	–	(X)	(X)
Other changes	X	X	X	X
Gross carrying amount as at December 31	X	X	X	X

IFRS 7 requires disclosures about credit risk grades used (both internal and external). However, if information about credit risk rating grades is not available without undue cost or effort and an entity uses past due information to assess whether credit risk has increased significantly since initial recognition, the entity shall provide an analysis by past due status for those financial assets. This is illustrated below using an example also derived from the Implementation Guidance to IFRS 7.

Entity A manufactures cars and provides financing to both dealers and end customers. Entity A discloses its dealer financing and customer financing as separate classes of financial instruments and applies the simplified approach to its trade receivables so that the loss allowance is always measured at an amount equal to lifetime expected credit losses. The following table illustrates the use of a provision matrix as a risk profile disclosure under the simplified approach:

20XX €'000	**Trade receivables days past due**				
Dealer financing: Expected credit loss rate, estimated total gross carrying amount at default	Current 0.10%, €20,777	More than 30 days 2%, €1,416	More than 60 days 5%, €673	More than 90 days 13%, €235	Total €23,101
Lifetime expected credit losses—dealer financing	€21	€28	€34	€31	€114
Customer financing: Expected credit loss rate, estimated total gross carrying amount at default	0.20%, €19,222	3%, €2,010	8%, €301	15%, €154	€21,687
Lifetime expected credit losses— customer financing	€38	€60	€24	€23	€145

Liquidity risk disclosures

The entity is required to disclose:

1. A maturity analysis for non-derivative financial liabilities that shows the remaining contractual maturities;
2. A maturity analysis for derivative financial liabilities. The maturity analysis shall include the remaining contractual maturities for those derivative financial liabilities for which contractual maturities are essential for an understanding of the timing of the cash flows; and
3. A description of how the entity manages the liquidity risk inherent in 1. and 2. above.

Disclosure example: Liquidity risk

The group maintains sufficient cash and marketable securities. Management review cash flow forecasts on a regular basis to determine whether the group has sufficient cash reserves to meet future working capital requirements and to take advantage of business opportunities. The group has further undrawn banking facilities of €X (20XX-1: €X), which can be used as an additional means of easing liquidity risk if considered necessary. The average creditor payment period is X days (20XX-1: X days).

Contractual maturity analysis for financial liabilities

20XX	**Due or due in less than 1 month**	**Due between 1 and 3 months**	**Due between 3 months and 1 year**	**Due between 1 and 5 years**	**Due after 5 years**	**Total**
Financial liabilities	–	–	–	X	X	X
Non-current borrowings	X	X	–	–	–	X
Trade and other payables	–	–	X	–	–	X
Current borrowings	X	X	X	–	–	X
Current portion of non-current borrowings	X	X	X	–	–	X
Finance lease liability	X	X	X	X	X	X
	X	X	X	X	X	X
20XX-1	**Due or due in less than 1 month**	**Due between 1 and 3 months**	**Due between 3 months and 1 year**	**Due between 1 and 5 years**	**Due after 5 years**	**Total**
Financial liabilities						
Non-current borrowings	–	–	–	X	X	X
Trade and other payables	X	X	–	–	–	X
Current portion of non-current borrowings	X	X	X	–	–	X
Finance lease liability	X	X	X	X	X	X
	X	X	X	X	X	X

Market Risk Disclosures

A number of informative disclosures are mandated, as described in the following paragraphs.

Sensitivity analysis:

1. A sensitivity analysis for each type of market risk to which the entity is exposed at the reporting date, showing how profit or loss and equity would have been affected by changes in the relevant risk variable that were reasonably possible at that date;
2. The methods and assumptions used in preparing the sensitivity analysis; and
3. Changes from the previous period in the methods and assumptions used, and the reasons for such changes.

If the reporting entity prepares a sensitivity analysis, such as value-at-risk, that reflects interdependencies between risk variables (e.g., between interest rates and exchange rates) and uses it to manage financial risks, it may use that sensitivity analysis in place of the analysis specified in the preceding paragraph. The entity would also have to disclose:

1. An explanation of the method used in preparing such a sensitivity analysis, and of the main parameters and assumptions underlying the data provided; and
2. An explanation of the objective of the method used and of limitations that may result in the information not fully reflecting the fair value of the assets and liabilities involved.

Disclosure example: Sensitivity analysis

Interest rate exposure and sensitivity analysis:

20XX	**Carrying amount**	**Average interest rate %**	**If interest rates were X% higher**		**If interest rates were X% lower**	
			Net profit	Equity	Net profit	Equity
Financial assets						
Trade receivables	X	X	X	X	X	X
Other financial assets at fair value through profit and loss	X	X	X	X	X	X
Cash and cash equivalents	X	X	X	X	X	X
Financial liability						
Non-current borrowings	X	X	X	X	X	X
Current borrowings	X	X	X	X	X	X
Current portion of non-current borrowings	X	X	X	X	X	X
Finance lease liability	X	X	X	X	X	X

20XX-1	**Carrying amount**	**Average interest rate %**	**If interest rates were X% higher**		**If interest rates were X% lower**	
			Net profit	Equity	Net profit	Equity
Financial assets						
Trade receivables	X	X	X	X	X	X
Other financial assets at fair value through profit and loss	X	X	X	X	X	X
Cash and cash equivalents	X	X	X	X	X	X
Financial liability						
Non-current borrowings	X	X	X	X	X	X
Current borrowings	X	X	X	X	X	X
Current portion of non-current borrowings	X	X	X	X	X	X
Finance lease liability	X	X	X	X	X	X

Other market risk disclosures may also be necessary to fully inform financial statement users. When the sensitivity analyses are unrepresentative of a risk inherent in a financial instrument (e.g., because the year-end exposure does not reflect the actual exposure during the year), the entity is to disclose that fact, together with the reason it believes the sensitivity analyses are unrepresentative.

Disclosure example: Foreign currency risk and equity price risk disclosures

Foreign currency risk

Foreign currency risk refers to the risk that the value of a financial commitment or recognised asset or liability will fluctuate due to changes in foreign currency rates. The group is exposed to foreign currency risk as a result of future transactions, foreign borrowings and investments in foreign companies, denominated in euros.

The group makes use of forward exchange contracts to manage the risk relating to future transactions, in accordance with its risk management policy. The fair value of the forward exchange contracts was €X (20XX-1: €X). Gains on the forward exchange contracts were €X (20XX-1: €X). The future transactions related to the forward exchange contracts are expected to occur within the next three months. No amounts were recognised directly in equity during the period or the prior period as the relationship between the forward exchange contracts and the item being hedged does not meet certain conditions to qualify as a hedging relationship. Changes in the fair values of forward exchange contracts are recognised directly in profit or loss.

The group foreign currency risk exposure from recognised assets and liabilities arises primarily from non-current foreign borrowings (note XX) and investments in foreign companies (note XX) denominated in euros. The group manages the exchange risk on translation of investments in foreign companies with borrowings denominated in the same currency. There is no significant impact on profit or loss from foreign currency movements associated with these assets and liabilities as the effective portion of foreign currency gains or losses arising are recorded through the translation reserve. The net gain of €X (20XX-1: €X) in the translation reserve takes into account the related hedges. The ineffective portion of the gain or loss is recognised in profit or loss and amounted to €€X (20XX-1: €X).

Foreign currency risk sensitivity analysis:

	Profit/loss		**Equity**	
	20XX	**20XX-1**	**20XX**	**20XX-1**
If there was an X% weakening in the sterling/euro exchange rate with all other variables held constant—increase/(decrease)	**X**	X	**X**	X
If there was an X% strengthening in the sterling/euro exchange rate with all other variables held constant—increase/(decrease)	**X**	X	**X**	X

The impact of a chance of X% has been selected as this is considered reasonable given the current level of exchange rates and the volatility observed both on a historical basis and market expectations for future movement. When applied to the sterling/euro exchange rate this would result in a weakened exchange rate of X and a strengthened exchange rate of X. This range is considered reasonable given the historic changes that have been observed. For example, over the last five years, the sterling exchange rate against the euro has traded in the range X to X. The group's sensitivity to exchange rates has not changed significantly from the prior year.

Equity price risk

Investments by the group in available-for-sale financial assets expose the group to equity price risk. This risk is managed by diversifying the group's investment portfolio. There is no impact on profit or loss until the investments are disposed of as fluctuations in fair value for the year of €X (20XX-1: €X) are recorded directly in the fair value reserve. Fluctuations in the fair value of investments are not hedged.

Equity price risk sensitivity analysis:

	Profit/loss		**Equity**	
	20XX	**20XX-1**	**20XX**	**20XX-1**
If there was an X% decrease in equity prices with all other variables held constant—increase/(decrease)	**X**	X	**X**	X
If there was an X% increase in equity prices with all other variables held constant—increase/(decrease)	**X**	X	**X**	X

The impact of a change of X% has been selected as this is considered reasonable given the current level of volatility observed both on a historical basis and market expectations for future movement. The range in equity prices is considered reasonable given the historic changes that have been observed. The group's sensitivity to equity prices has not changed significantly from the prior year.

Disclosures Required on Initial Application of IFRS 9

In the reporting period that includes the date of initial application of IFRS 9, the entity shall disclose the following information for each class of financial assets and financial liabilities as at the date of initial application:

1. The original measurement category and carrying amount determined in accordance with IAS 39 or in accordance with a previous version of IFRS 9 (if the entity's chosen approach to applying IFRS 9 involves more than one date of initial application for different requirements);
2. The new measurement category and carrying amount determined in accordance with IFRS 9;
3. The amount of any financial assets and financial liabilities in the statement of financial position that were previously designated as measured at FVTPL but are no longer so designated, distinguishing between those that IFRS 9 requires an entity to reclassify and those that an entity elects to reclassify at the date of initial application.

Depending on the entity's chosen approach to applying IFRS 9, the transition can involve more than one date of initial application. Therefore, this paragraph may result in disclosure on more than one date of initial application. An entity shall present these quantitative disclosures in a table unless another format is more appropriate.

In the reporting period that includes the date of initial application of IFRS 9, an entity shall disclose qualitative information to enable users to understand:

1. How it applied the classification requirements in IFRS 9 to those financial assets whose classification has changed because of applying IFRS 9;
2. The reasons for any designation or de-designation of financial assets or financial liabilities as measured at FVTPL at the date of initial application.

In the reporting period that an entity first applies the classification and measurement requirements for financial assets in IFRS 9 (i.e., when the entity transitions from IAS 39 to IFRS 9 for financial assets), it shall present the disclosures as set out in the below paragraphs as required by IFRS 9.

An entity shall disclose the changes in the classifications of financial assets and financial liabilities as at the date of initial application of IFRS 9, showing separately:

1. The changes in the carrying amounts on the basis of their measurement categories in accordance with IAS 39 (i.e., not resulting from a change in measurement attribute on transition to IFRS 9); and
2. The changes in the carrying amounts arising from a change in measurement attribute on transition to IFRS 9.

The disclosures above need not be made after the annual reporting period in which the entity initially applies the classification and measurement requirements for financial assets in IFRS 9.

An entity shall disclose the following for financial assets and financial liabilities that have been reclassified so that they are measured at amortised cost and, in the case of financial assets, that have been reclassified out of FVTPL so that they are measured at FVTOCI, as a result of the transition to IFRS 9:

1. The fair value of the financial assets or financial liabilities at the end of the reporting period; and
2. The fair value gain or loss that would have been recognised in profit or loss or other comprehensive income during the reporting period if the financial assets or financial liabilities had not been reclassified.

The disclosures above need not be made after the annual reporting period in which the entity initially applies the classification and measurement requirements for financial assets in IFRS 9.

An entity shall disclose the following for financial assets and financial liabilities that have been reclassified out of the FVTPL category as a result of the transition to IFRS 9:

1. The effective interest rate determined on the date of initial application; and
2. The interest revenue or expense recognised.

If an entity treats the fair value of a financial asset or a financial liability as the new gross carrying amount at the date of initial application, the disclosures above shall be made for each reporting period until derecognition. Otherwise, these disclosures need not be made after the annual reporting period in which the entity initially applies the classification and measurement requirements for financial assets in IFRS 9.

When an entity presents the disclosures, those disclosures must permit reconciliation between:

1. The measurement categories presented in accordance with IAS 39 and IFRS 9; and
2. The class of financial instrument as at the date of initial application.

On the date of initial application, an entity is required to disclose information that would permit the reconciliation of the ending impairment allowances in accordance with IAS 39 and the provisions in accordance with IAS 37 to the opening loss allowances determined in accordance with IFRS 9. For financial assets, this disclosure shall be provided by the related financial assets' measurement categories in accordance with IAS 39 and IFRS 9 and shall show separately the effect of the changes in the measurement category on the loss allowance at that date.

FUTURE DEVELOPMENTS

In June 2018 the IASB issued a Discussion Paper, *Financial Instruments with Characteristics of Equity*, to provide a clearer rationale for the classification of financial instruments as either a liability or equity. The rational for classifying a financial instrument as a liability is based on two separate features. The first is that the instrument contains an unavoidable contractual obligation to transfer cash or another financial instrument at a specific time other than liquidation (the time feature). The second is an unavoidable contractual obligation for an amount independent from the entity's available economic resources (the amount feature). The IASB in its meeting in September 2019 tentatively decided on an approach that addresses practice issues by clarifying some principles in IAS 32.

US GAAP

US GAAP matters relating to financial instruments are imbedded throughout the Codification. Receivables (Topic 310) has some references and investments which is experiencing change (2018 for public entities and 2019 for all other entities) the Topic numbers and guidance is found as follows: Investments – Debt Securities (Topic 320), Investments – Equity Securities (Topic 321), Financial Instruments – Credit Losses (Topic 326) (which is effective for years beginning after December 31, 2019 for public entities and for all others for fiscal years beginning after December 31, 2020), Derivatives and Hedging (Topic 815) – specifically 815-15-25-4 and 815-15-25-5, Fair Value Measurements (Topic 825), Transfers and Servicing (Topic 860).

It should be noted that Topic 326 was an IFRS / FASB collaboration that stemmed out of the 2008 Financial Crisis Advisory Group they formed. The basic premise of this standard was to eliminate the "probable" initial recognition threshold. Simply said, this provides users useful decision-making information on expected losses from financial instruments. Under this standard the current impairment methodology for incurred losses in current GAAP is replaced with a methodology that uses a broader range of supportable and reasonable information to inform estimates of credit loss.

25 FAIR VALUE

INTRODUCTION

Financial statement preparers, users, auditors, standard setters and regulators have long engaged in a debate regarding the relevance, transparency and decision-usefulness of financial statements prepared under IFRS, which is one among the various families of comprehensive financial reporting standards that rely on what has been called the "mixed attribute" model for measuring assets and liabilities. That is, existing IFRS imposes a range of measurement requirements, including both historical (i.e., transaction-based) cost and a variety of approximations to current economic values, for the initial and subsequent reporting of the assets and liabilities that define the reporting entity's financial position and, indirectly, for the periodic determination of its results of operations.

While current fair or market value data have become more readily obtainable, some of these measures do exhibit some degree of volatility, albeit this is typically only a reflection of the turbulence in the markets themselves and is not an artefact of the measurement process. Nonetheless, the ever-expanding use of fair value for accounting measurements, under various national GAAP as well as under IFRS, has attracted its share of critical commentary. The debate has become even more heated due to the recent economic turmoil in credit markets, which more than a few observers have cited as having been exacerbated by required financial reporting of current value-based measures of financial performance.

Although the evidence will ultimately demonstrate that fundamental economic and financial behaviours (such as bank lending decisions) were not, in the main, caused by the mandatory reporting of value changes, the chorus of complaints has caused the standard setters to take certain steps to mollify their critics, including revisiting some of the mechanisms by which fair values have heretofore been assessed. Notwithstanding, both the IASB and FASB have reaffirmed their commitment to the continued use of fair values in financial reporting in appropriate circumstances, while acknowledging the need for more guidance with respect to the determination of fair values.

Most investors and creditors that use financial statements for decision-making purposes argue that reporting financial instruments at historical cost or amortised cost deprives them of important information about the economic impact on the reporting entity of real economic gains and losses associated with changes in the fair values of assets and liabilities that it owns or owes. Many assert that, had they been provided timely fair value information, they might well have made different decisions regarding investing in, lending to or entering into business transactions with the reporting entities.

Others, however, argue that transparent reporting of fair values creates "procyclicality," whereby the reporting of fair values has the effect of directly influencing the economy and potentially causing great harm. These arguments are countered by fair value advocates, who state their belief that the "Lost Decade"—the extended economic malaise that afflicted Japan from 1991 to 2000—was exacerbated by the lack of transparency in its commercial banking system, which allowed its banks to avoid recognising losses on loans of questionable credit quality and diminished, but concealed, values.

Source of IFRS
IFRS 13

SCOPE

IFRS 13, *Fair Value Measurement*, applies when another IFRS requires or permits the use of fair value measurements or disclosures about fair value measurements. To that extent the IFRS does not extend the use of fair value measures in financial reporting but does bring about a more cohesive and comprehensive scope within which the concept of fair values is applied.

Excluded from the measurement and disclosure scope of the IFRS, however, are some "fair value-based" transactions such as:

- Share-based payments within the scope of IFRS 2, *Share-Based Payments*;
- Leasing transactions accounted for in accordance with IFRS 16 *Leases*; and
- Other measurements with similarities to fair value such as net realisable value as it relates to IAS 2, *Inventory*, or value in use in terms of IAS 36, *Impairment of Assets*.

In addition, the disclosure requirements of the IFRS do not apply to disclosures relating to:

- Fair value of plan assets in terms of IAS 19, *Employee Benefits*;
- Retirement benefit plan investments in terms of IAS 26, *Accounting and Reporting by Retirement Benefit Plans*;
- Assets for which the recoverable amount is fair value less costs to sell in terms of IAS 36, *Impairment of Assets*.

NOTE: The fair value measurement framework described in IFRS 13 applies to both initial and subsequent measurement if fair value is required or permitted by other IFRS.

DEFINITIONS OF TERMS

Active market. A market in which transactions for the asset or liability occur with sufficient frequency and volume to provide pricing information on an ongoing basis.

Cost approach. A valuation technique that reflects the amount that would be required currently to replace the service capacity of an asset (sometimes referred to as current replacement cost).

Entry price. The price paid to acquire an asset or received to assume a liability in an exchange transaction.

Exit price. The price that would be received to sell an asset or paid to transfer a liability.

Expected cash flow. The probability-weighted average (i.e., mean of the distribution) of possible future cash flows.

Fair value. The price that would be received to sell an asset or paid to transfer a liability in an orderly transaction between market participants at the measurement date.

Highest and best use. The use of a non-financial asset by market participants that would maximise the value of the asset or the group of assets and liabilities (e.g., a business) within which the asset would be used.

Income approach. Valuation techniques that convert future amounts (e.g., cash flows or income and expenses) to a single current (i.e., discounted) amount. The fair value measurement is determined on the basis of the value indicated by current market expectations about those future amounts.

Inputs. The assumptions that market participants would use when pricing the asset or liability, including assumptions about risk, such as the risk inherent in a particular valuation technique used to measure fair value (such as a pricing model) and the risk inherent in the inputs to the valuation technique. Inputs may be observable or unobservable.

Level 1 inputs. Quoted prices (unadjusted) in active markets for identical assets or liabilities that the entity can access at the measurement date.

Level 2 inputs. Inputs other than quoted prices included within Level 1 that are observable for the asset or liability, either directly (i.e., as prices) or indirectly (i.e., derived from prices).

Level 3 inputs. Unobservable inputs for the asset or liability.

Market approach. A valuation approach that uses prices and other relevant information generated by market transactions involving identical or comparable (i.e., similar) assets, liabilities or a group of assets and liabilities (i.e., a business).

Market-corroborated inputs. Inputs that are derived principally from or corroborated by observable market data by correlation or other means.

Market participants. Buyers and sellers in the principal (or most advantageous) market for an asset or liability that have all of the following characteristics:

1. Independent of each other, i.e., they are not *related parties* as defined in IAS 24, although the price in a related party transaction may be used as an input to a fair value measurement if the entity has evidence that the transaction was entered into at market terms.
2. Knowledgeable and have a reasonable understanding about the asset or liability and the transaction using all available information, including information that might be obtained through due diligence efforts that are usual and customary.
3. Able to enter into a transaction for the asset or liability.
4. Willing to enter into a transaction for the asset or liability (i.e., they are not under duress that would force or compel them to enter into the transaction).

Most advantageous market. The market that maximises the amount that would be received from the sale of the asset or that minimises the amount that would be paid to transfer the liability, after consideration of transaction and transport costs. (Although transaction costs are considered in making a determination of the market that is most advantageous, such costs are not to be factored into the fair value valuation determined by reference to that market.)

Non-performance risk. The risk that the entity will not fulfil an obligation. This includes, but is not limited to, the entity's own credit risk.

Observable inputs. Inputs that are developed on the basis of available market data, such as publicly available information about actual events or transactions, and that reflect the assumptions that market participants would use when pricing the asset or liability.

Orderly transaction. A transaction that assumes exposure to the market for a period before the measurement date to allow for marketing activities that are usual and customary for transactions involving such assets or liabilities; it is not a forced transaction (e.g., a forced liquidation or distress sale).

Principal market. The market with the greatest volume and level of activity for the asset or the liability.

Risk premium. Compensation sought by risk-averse market participants for bearing the uncertainty inherent in the cash flows of an asset or a liability, sometimes referred to as a "risk adjustment."

Transaction costs. The costs to sell an asset or transfer a liability in the principal (or most advantageous) market for the asset or liability that are directly attributable to the disposal of the asset or the transfer of the liability and result directly from and are essential to the transaction, and would not have been incurred had the transaction not occurred (similar to the "costs to sell" in terms of IFRS 5, *Non-current Assets Held for Sale and Discontinued Operations*).

Transport costs. The costs that would be incurred to transport an asset from its current location to its principal or most advantageous market.

Unit of account. The level at which an asset or liability is aggregated or disaggregated in an IFRS for recognition purposes.

Unobservable inputs. Inputs for which market data are not available and that are developed using the best information available about the assumptions that market participants would use when pricing the asset or liability.

FAIR VALUE MEASUREMENT PRINCIPLES AND METHODOLOGIES

In its objectives the IFRS clearly sets out that fair value is a market-based measurement and not an entity-specific measurement. This premise permeates the entire approach to the determination of fair value for assets and liabilities and makes the asset or the liability and the related markets the centre of the approach and not the entity's circumstances at the measurement date. Consequently, fair value is based on the presumption of an orderly transaction between market participants (as defined) at measurement date under current market conditions, from the perspective of a market participant that holds the asset or owes the liability; in other words, it is an exit price.

To the extent possible, fair value should be based on an observable price. However, in many instances such a price may not be available, and the determination of fair value will rely on the use of valuation techniques. Such valuation techniques should have a strong bias towards the use of observable rather than unobservable inputs, as these are considered more objective and more likely to be taken into consideration by market participants.

Although the IFRS has a focus on assets and liabilities, the requirements of the IFRS are equally applicable to the determination of the fair value of an entity's own equity instrument, where required.

The exit price of an asset or liability embodies expectations about the future cash inflows and outflows associated with the asset or liability from the perspective of market participants, at the measurement date. Since an entity generates cash inflows from an asset either by using it or by selling it, even if an entity intends to generate cash inflows from an asset by using it rather than by selling it, an exit price embodies expectations of the cash flows that would arise for a market participant holding the asset.

For a similar reason, a liability gives rise to outflows of cash (or other economic resources) as an entity fulfils the liability over time or when it transfers the liability to another party. Even if an entity intends to fulfil the liability over time, an exit price embodies expectations about cash outflows because a market participant transferee would ultimately be required to fulfil the liability. Accordingly, an exit price is always a relevant definition of fair value for liabilities, regardless of whether an entity intends to fulfil the liability over time or to transfer it to another party that will fulfil it over time.

The level at which this IFRS is to be applied is determined by the unit of account in terms of the relevant IFRS that requires or permits the use of fair value in the first instance, and therefore the level of application is not specifically addressed by this IFRS unless otherwise specified.

It is helpful to break down the measurement process of determining fair value measurement into a series of steps. Although not necessarily performed in a linear manner, the following procedures and decisions need to be applied and made to value an asset or liability at fair value. Each of the steps will be discussed in greater detail:

1. *Identify the item to be valued and the unit of account.* Identify the asset or liability, including the unit of account to be used for the measurement.
2. *Determine the most advantageous market and the relevant market participants.* From the reporting entity's perspective, determine the most advantageous market in which it would sell the asset or transfer the liability. In the absence of evidence to the contrary, the most advantageous market can be considered to be the principal market for the asset or the liability, which is the market with the greatest volume of transactions and level of activity. Once the most advantageous market is identified, it should be easier to determine the characteristics of the market participants. It is not necessary that specifically named individuals or enterprises be identified for this purpose.
3. *Select the valuation premise to be used for asset measurements.* If the item being measured is a non-financial asset, determine the valuation premise to be used by evaluating how market participants would apply the "highest and best use," for example considering the value of the asset on a stand-alone basis or its fair value in conjunction with other related assets and liabilities.
4. *Consider the risk assumptions applicable to liability measurements.* If the item being measured is a liability, identify the key assumptions that market participants would make regarding non-performance risk including, but not limited to, the reporting entity's own credit risk (credit standing).

5. *Identify available inputs.* Identify the key assumptions that market participants would use in pricing the asset or liability, including assumptions about risk. In identifying these assumptions, referred to as "inputs," maximise the inputs that are relevant and observable (i.e., that are based on market data available from sources independent of the reporting entity). In so doing, assess the availability of relevant, reliable market data for each input that significantly affects the valuation, and identify the level of the new fair value input hierarchy in which it is to be categorised.
6. *Select the appropriate valuation technique(s).* Based on the nature of the asset or liability being valued, and the types and reliability of inputs available, determine the appropriate valuation technique or combination of techniques to use in valuing the asset or liability. The three broad categories of techniques are the market approach, the income approach and the cost approach.
7. *Make the measurement.* Measure the asset or liability.
8. *Determine amounts to be recognised and information to be disclosed.* Determine the amounts and information to be recorded, classified and disclosed in interim and annual financial statements.

Item Identification and Unit of Account

In general, the same unit of account at which the asset or liability is aggregated or disaggregated by applying other applicable IFRS is to be used for fair value measurement purposes. The asset or liability measured at fair value might be either a stand-alone asset or liability (e.g., a financial instrument or a non-financial asset) or a group of assets, a group of liabilities or a group of assets and liabilities (e.g., a cash-generating unit or a business). No adjustment may be made to the valuation for a "blockage factor." A blockage factor is an adjustment made to a valuation that takes into account the fact that the investor holds a large quantity (block) of shares relative to the market trading volume in those shares. The prohibition applies even if the quantity held by the reporting entity exceeds the market's normal trading volume—and that, if the reporting entity were, hypothetically, to place an order to sell its entire position in a single transaction, that transaction could affect the quoted price.

The Principal or Most Advantageous Market

IFRS 13 requires the entity performing the valuation to maximise the use of relevant assumptions (inputs) that are observable from market data obtained from sources independent of the reporting entity. In making a fair value measurement, management is to assume that the asset or liability is exchanged in a hypothetical, orderly transaction between market participants at the measurement date.

To characterise the exchange as orderly, it is assumed that the asset or liability will have been exposed to the market for a sufficient period of time prior to the measurement date to enable marketing activities to occur that are usual and customary with respect to transactions involving such assets or liabilities. It is also to be assumed that the transaction is not a forced transaction (e.g., a forced liquidation or distress sale).

The fair value is to be measured by reference to the principal market, or in the absence of a principal market, the most advantageous market. Unless otherwise apparent it is assumed that the principal market is the market in which the entity would normally transact to sell the asset or transfer the liability. An entity, therefore, need not engage in elaborate efforts to identify the principal market. This approach is deemed appropriate and broadly consistent with the concept of the most advantageous market, as it is reasonable that an entity would normally transact in the most advantageous market to which it is has access, taking into consideration *transaction and transport costs*.

Note that the determination of the most advantageous market is made from the perspective of the reporting entity, as the reporting entity needs to have access to the principal market. Thus, different reporting entities engaging in different specialised industries, or with access to different markets, might not have the same most advantageous market for an identical asset or liability. The IFRS provides a typology of markets that potentially exist for assets or liabilities:

1. *Exchange markets*. A market in which closing prices are readily available and generally representative of fair value. Examples of such markets include NYSE, Euronext, Toronto Stock Exchange, London Stock Exchange, Hong Kong Stock Exchange and Johannesburg Securities Exchange among others.
2. *Dealer markets*. A market in which parties (dealers referred to as market makers) stand ready to buy or sell a particular investment for their own account at bid and ask prices that they quote. The bid price is the price the dealer is willing to pay to purchase the investment and the ask price is the price at which the dealer is willing to sell the investment. In these markets, these "bid and ask" prices are typically more readily available than are closing prices characteristic of active exchange markets. By using their own capital to finance and hold an inventory of the items for which they "make a market," these dealers provide the market with liquidity. Dealer markets include over-the-counter markets for which the prices at which transactions have been concluded could be publicly available. Dealer markets exist for financial instruments and non-financial assets such as commodities, equipment and such items.
3. *Brokered market*. These markets use "brokers" or intermediaries to match buyers with sellers. Brokers do not trade for their own account and do not hold an inventory in the security. The broker knows the bid and ask prices of the potential counterparties to the transaction, but the counterparties are unaware of each other's price requirements. Prices of consummated transactions are sometimes available privately or as a matter of public record. Brokered markets include electronic communication networks that match buy and sell orders, as well as commercial and residential real estate markets. In some cases, each of the counterparties is aware of the other's identity, while in other cases, their identities are not disclosed by the broker.
4. *Principal-to-principal market*. A market in which the counterparties negotiate directly and independently without an intermediary. Because no intermediary or exchange is involved, little if any information about these transactions is released to the public.

Example: Principal or most advantageous market

An asset is sold in two different active markets at different prices. An entity enters in transactions in both markets and can access the price in those markets for the asset at the measurement date.

	Market A	Market B
Price	€26	€25
Transaction costs	€3	€1
Transportation costs	€2	€2
Net amount	€21	€22

If Market A is the principal market for the asset (the market with the greatest volume and level of activity for the asset), the fair value of the asset would be measured using the price in Market A less transportation costs (€24).

If neither market is the principal market for the asset, the fair value would be measured using the price in the most advantageous market. To identify the most advantageous market, it is the market that maximises the net amount that would be received to sell the asset after deducting transaction costs and transportation costs from the gross amount. Although the transaction costs are taken into account when determining the most advantageous market, the price used to measure the fair value is not adjusted for these costs.

In the case above this would be Market B, and the fair value of the asset would be €23 (price €25 less transportation costs of €2).

Market Participants

In light of the market-oriented alignment, company-specific assumptions are therefore irrelevant, and the valuation must be based on premises that typical market participants would assume when defining a price in their own commercial interests. As such, the consideration of factors whose impacts would be assessed differently by a typical market participant is crucial, and therefore the company-specific circumstances and assumptions of the reporting company are not decisive.

The hypothetical market participants can be summarised as:

1. Independent of each other (i.e., are unrelated third parties);
2. Knowledgeable (i.e., are sufficiently informed to make an investment decision and are presumed to be as knowledgeable as the reporting entity about the asset or liability);
3. Able to enter into a transaction for the asset or liability;
4. Willing to enter into a transaction for the asset or liability (i.e., they are motivated but not forced or otherwise compelled to do so).

Measurement considerations when transactions are not orderly. In recent years, there have been heightened concerns about the effects of tumultuous or illiquid credit markets. The previously active markets for certain types of securities have become illiquid or less liquid. Questions have arisen regarding whether transactions occurring in less liquid markets with less frequent trades might cause those market transactions to be considered forced or distress sales, thus rendering valuations made using those prices not indicative of the actual fair value of the securities.

The presence of the following factors may indicate that a quoted price is not obtained from a transaction that could be considered orderly and therefore may not be indicative of fair value:

1. There has been a significant decrease in the volume and level of activity for the asset or liability when compared with normal market activity for the asset or liability (or for similar assets or liabilities).
2. There have been few recent transactions.
3. Price quotations are not based on current information about the fair value of an asset or liability.
4. Indices that previously were highly correlated with the fair values of the asset or liability are demonstrably uncorrelated with recent indications of fair value of that asset or liability.
5. There has been a significant increase in implied liquidity risk premiums, yields or performance indicators (such as delinquency rates or loss severities) for observed transactions or quoted prices when compared with the entity's estimate of expected cash flows, considering all available market data about credit and other non-performance risk for the asset or liability.
6. There has been a wide bid–ask spread or significant increase in the bid–ask spread.
7. There has been a significant decline or absence of a market for new issues (i.e., in the primary market) for the asset or liability (or similar assets or liabilities).
8. Little information has been released publicly (e.g., as occurs in a principal-to-principal market).

An entity should evaluate the significance and relevance of the indicators above (together with other pertinent factors) to determine whether, on the basis of the evidence available, a market is not active. If it concludes that a market is not active, it may then also deduce that transactions or quoted prices in that market are not indicative of fair value (e.g., because there may be transactions that are not orderly). Further analysis of the transactions or quoted prices may therefore be needed, and a significant adjustment to the transactions or quoted prices may be necessary to measure fair value.

IFRS 13 does not prescribe a methodology for making significant adjustments to transactions or quoted prices in such circumstances; however, the typology of valuation techniques—the market, income and cost approaches, respectively—applies to these situations equally. Regardless of the valuation technique used, an entity must include any appropriate risk adjustments, including a risk premium reflecting the amount market participants would demand because of the risk (uncertainty) inherent in the cash flows of an asset or liability.

Absent this, the measurement would not faithfully represent fair value. The risk premium should be reflective of an orderly transaction between market participants at the measurement date under current market conditions. If there has been a significant decrease in the volume or level of activity for the asset or liability, a change in valuation technique or the use of multiple valuation techniques may be appropriate. When weighting indications of fair value resulting from the use of multiple valuation techniques (market, income or cost approach), an entity shall consider the reasonableness of the range of fair value measurements. The objective is to determine the point within the range that is most representative of fair value under current market conditions.

Example: Measuring fair value when there has been a significant decrease in the volume or level of activity

Entity A invests in a junior AAA-rated tranche of a residential mortgage-backed security on January 1, 20XX (the issue date of the security). The junior tranche is the second most senior of a total of six tranches. The underlying collateral for the residential mortgage-backed security is unguaranteed non-conforming residential mortgage loans that were issued in the second half of 20XX-2.

At March 31, 20XX+1 (measurement date) the junior tranche is now A rated. This tranche of the residential mortgage-backed securities was previously traded through a brokered market. However, trading volume was infrequent with only a few transactions taking place per month, so Entity A concludes that the volume and level of activity of the junior tranche have significantly decreased. As there is not enough trading activity to support using a market approach, Entity A decides to use an income approach using the discount rate adjustment technique. Entity A uses the contractual cash flows from the residential mortgage-backed security and then estimates a discount rate to discount those contractual cash flows.

Entity A estimates that one indication of the market rate of return that market participants would use is 12% (1.200 basis points), which was estimated as follows:

- 300 basis points: relevant risk-free rate of interest at measurement date.
- + 250 basis points: credit spread over the risk-free rate when the junior tranche was issued.
- + 700 basis points: change in credit spread over the risk-free rate of the junior tranche between January 1, 20XX and the measurement date. This estimate was developed on the basis of the change in the most comparable index available for that time period.
- − 350 basis points adjustment to the index used before. This was estimated by comparing the implied yield from the most recent transactions for the residential mortgage-backed security in June 20XX with the implied yield in the index price in those same dates.
- + 300 basis points adjustment as best estimation for the additional liquidity risk inherent in its security (a cash position) when compared with the index (a synthetic position). This estimate was derived after taking into account liquidity risk premiums implied in recent cash transactions for a range of similar securities.

As an additional indication of the market rate of return, Entity A takes into account two recent indicative quotes (i.e., non-binding quotes) provided by reputable brokers for the junior tranche of the residential mortgage-backed security that imply yields of 15–17%. Entity A is unable to evaluate the valuation technique(s) or inputs used to develop the quotes. However, Entity A is able to confirm that the quotes do not reflect the results of transactions.

Entity A concludes that 13% is the point within the range of indications that is most representative of fair value under current market conditions. Entity A places more weight on the 12% indication as it concludes that its own estimate appropriately incorporated the risks that market participants would use when pricing the asset and the broker quotes were non-binding and did not reflect the results of transactions.

Of most importance, even when a market is not active, the objective of a fair value measurement remains the same—to identify the price that would be received to sell an asset or paid to transfer a liability in a transaction that is orderly and not a forced liquidation or distress sale, between market participants at the measurement date under current market conditions. Therefore, an entity's intention to hold the asset or to settle, or otherwise fulfil, the liability is not relevant when measuring fair value, because fair value is a market-based measurement and not an entity-specific measurement.

Even if a market is not active, it would be inappropriate to conclude that all transactions in that market are not orderly (i.e., that they are forced or distress sales). Circumstances that may suggest that a transaction is not orderly, however, include, *inter alia*, the following:

1. There was not adequate exposure to the market for a period before the measurement date to allow for marketing activities that are usual and customary for transactions involving such assets or liabilities under current market conditions.
2. There was a usual and customary marketing period, but the seller marketed the asset or liability to a single market participant.
3. The seller is in or near bankruptcy or receivership (i.e., distressed) or the seller was required to sell to meet regulatory or legal requirements (i.e., forced).
4. The transaction price is an outlier when compared with other recent transactions for the same or similar asset or liability.

The reporting entity is required to evaluate the circumstances to determine, based on the weight of the evidence then available, whether the transaction is orderly. If it indicates that a transaction is indeed *not* orderly, the reporting entity places little, if any, weight (in comparison with other indications of fair value) on that transaction price when measuring fair value or estimating market risk premiums.

On the other hand, if the evidence indicates that a transaction is in fact orderly, the reporting entity is to consider that transaction price when measuring fair value or estimating market risk premiums. The weight to be placed on that transaction price when compared with other indications of fair value will depend on the facts and circumstances—such as the volume of the transaction, the comparability of the transaction to the asset or liability being measured, and the proximity of the transaction to the measurement date.

IFRS 13 does not preclude the use of quoted prices provided by third parties—such as pricing services or brokers—when the entity has determined that the quoted prices provided by those parties are determined in accordance with the standard. If a market is not active, however, the entity must evaluate whether the quoted prices are based on current information that reflects orderly transactions or a valuation technique that reflects market participant assumptions (including assumptions about risks). In weighting a quoted price as an input to a fair value measurement, however, the entity should place less weight on quotes that do not reflect the result of transactions.

Selection of the Valuation Premise for Asset Measurements

The measurement of the fair value of a non-financial asset is to assume the highest and best use of that asset by market participants. Generally, the highest and best use is the way that market participants would be expected to deploy the asset (or a group of assets and liabilities within which they would use the asset) that would maximise the value of the asset (or group). This highest and best use assumption might differ from the way that the reporting entity is currently using the asset or group of assets or its future plans for using it (them).

At the measurement date, the highest and best use must be physically possible, legally permissible and financially feasible. In this context, *physically possibly* takes into account the physical characteristics of the asset that market participants would consider when pricing the asset (e.g., the location or size of a property). *Legally permissible* takes into account any legal restrictions on the use of the asset that market participants would consider when pricing the asset (e.g., the zoning regulations applicable to a property). *Financially feasible* takes into account whether a use of the asset that is physically possible and legally permissible generates adequate income or cash flows (taking into consideration the costs of converting the asset to that use) to produce an investment return that market participants would require from an investment in that asset put to that use.

Example: Restriction on the sale of an equity instrument

An entity holds an equity instrument (a financial asset) for which sale is contractually restricted for a specified period. The restriction is a characteristic of the instrument and would be transferred to market participants. Thus, fair value would be measured on the basis of the quoted price for an otherwise identical unrestricted equity instrument of the same issuer that trades in a public market, adjusted to reflect the effect of the restriction. The adjustment reflects the amount market participants would demand because of the risk relating to the inability to access a public market for the instrument for the specified period. The adjustment varies depending on:

- The nature and duration of the restriction;
- The extent to which buyers are limited by the restriction; and
- Qualitative and quantitative factors specific to both the instrument and the issuer.

In all cases, the highest and best use is determined from the perspective of market participants, even if the reporting entity intends a different use. The highest and best use of an asset acquired in a business combination might differ from the intended use of the asset by the acquirer. The highest and best use is normally the use for which an asset is currently engaged unless market or other factors indicate otherwise. For example, for competitive or other reasons, the acquirer may intend not to use an acquired asset actively or it may not intend to use the asset in the same way as other market participants. This may particularly be the case for certain acquired intangible assets, for example, an acquired trademark that competes with an entity's own trademark. Nevertheless, the reporting entity is to measure the fair value of the asset assuming its highest and best use by market participants.

Example: Highest and best use versus current use

An entity acquires land in a business combination, which is currently developed for industrial use as a site for a factory. Nearby sites have recently been developed for residential use as sites for high-rise apartment buildings. The entity determines that the land currently used as a site for a factory could be developed as a site for residential use.

The highest and best use of the land would be determined by comparing both of the following:

a. The value of the land as currently developed for industrial use (i.e., the land would be used in combination with other assets, such as the factory, or with other assets and liabilities);
b. The value of the land as a vacant site for residential use, taking into account the costs of demolishing the factory and other costs (including the uncertainty about whether the entity would be able to convert the asset to the alternative use) necessary to convert the land to a vacant site (i.e., the land is to be used by market participants on a stand-alone basis).

The highest and best use of the land would be determined on the basis of the higher of those values.

Where the highest and best use of an asset is determined by its use in conjunction with other assets and liabilities, fair value should be determined on that basis, thereby assuming that the asset would be used with other assets and liabilities and that those assets and liabilities (i.e., its complementary assets and the associated liabilities) would be available to market participants. Consequently, the fair value of all other assets in that group of associated assets and liabilities should be determined on the same basis.

Risk Assumptions when Valuing a Liability

Many accountants, analysts and others find the concept of computing fair value of liabilities and recognising changes in the fair value thereof to be counterintuitive. Consider the case when a reporting entity's own credit standing declines (universally acknowledged as a "bad thing"). A fair value measurement that incorporates the effect of this decline in credit rating would result in a decline in the fair value of the liability and a resultant increase in stockholders' equity (which would be seen as a "good thing"). Nonetheless, the logic of measuring the fair value of liabilities is as valid, and as useful, as it is for assets.

In measuring the fair value of a liability, the evaluator is to assume that the reporting entity's obligation to its creditor (i.e., the counterparty to the obligation) will continue at and after the measurement date (i.e., the obligation will not be repaid or settled prior to its contractual maturity). This being the case, this hypothetical transfer price would most likely represent the price that the current creditor (holder of the debt instrument) could obtain from a marketplace participant willing to purchase the debt instrument in a transaction involving the original creditor assigning its rights to the purchaser. In effect, the hypothetical market participant that purchased the instrument would be in the same position as the current creditor with respect to expected future cash flows (or expected future performance, if the liability is not able to be settled in cash) from the reporting entity.

The evaluator is to further assume that the non-performance risk related to the obligation would be the same before and after the hypothetical transfer occurs. Non-performance risk is the risk that the obligation will not be fulfilled. It is an all-encompassing concept that includes the reporting entity's own credit standing but also includes other risks associated with the non-fulfilment of the obligation. For example, a liability to deliver goods and/or perform services may bear non-performance risk associated with the ability of the debtor to fulfil the obligation in accordance with the timing and specifications of the contract. Furthermore, nonperformance risk increases or decreases as a result of changes in the fair value of credit enhancements associated with the liability (e.g., collateral, credit insurance and/or guarantees).

Example: Non-performance risk

Entity A and Entity B each enter into a contractual obligation to pay an amount of €500 to Entity C in five years. Entity A has a AA credit rating and can borrow at 6% p.a., Entity B has a BBB credit rating and can borrow at 12% p.a. Entity A will receive about €374 in exchange for its promise (the present value of €500 in five years at 6%). Entity B will receive about €284 in exchange for its promise (the present value of €500 in five years at 12%). The fair value of the liability to each entity (i.e., the proceeds) incorporates that entity's credit standing.

As with the valuation of assets, company-specific elements are also ignored when measuring liabilities. Accordingly, valuations do not consider more favourable cost structures, for example for non-financial liabilities, nor credit terms and conditions that may be more or less favourable than the market norm. To meet the objective of a fair value measurement in accordance with IFRS 13, an entity shall maximise the use of relevant observable inputs and minimise the use of unobservable inputs. To meet this requirement even if there is no observable market to provide pricing information about the transfer of a liability, there might be an observable market for such items if they are held by other parties as assets (e.g., a corporate bond).

Liabilities and Equity Instruments Held by Other (Third) Parties as an Asset

When a quoted price for the transfer of an identical or a similar liability or entity's own equity instrument is not available, and the identical item is held by another party as an asset, an entity shall measure the fair value of the liability or equity instrument from the perspective of a market participant that holds the identical item as an asset at the measurement date.

In the case where a third party held the liability or equity instrument, an entity shall measure the fair value as follows:

1. Using the quoted price in an active market for the identical item held by another party as an asset, if that price is available.
2. If that price is not available, using other observable inputs, such as the quoted price in a market that is not active for the identical item held by another party as an asset.
3. If the observable prices in 1. and 2. are not available, using another valuation technique, such as:
    a. An income approach (e.g., a present value technique that takes into account the future cash flows that a market participant would expect to receive from holding the liability or equity instrument as an asset);
    b. A market approach (e.g., using quoted prices for similar liabilities or equity instruments held by other parties as assets).

An entity shall adjust the price of a liability or an entity's own equity instrument held by another party as an asset only if there are factors specific to the asset that are not applicable to the fair value measurement of the liability or equity instrument. Accordingly, adjustments are made such as:

1. The quoted price for the asset relates to a similar (but not identical) liability or equity instrument held by another party as an asset. For example, the liability or equity instrument may have a particular characteristic (e.g., the credit quality of the issuer) that is different from that reflected in the fair value of the similar liability or equity instrument held as an asset.
2. The unit of account for the asset is not the same as for the liability or equity instrument. For example, for liabilities, in some cases the price for an asset reflects a combined price for a package comprising both the amounts due from the issuer and a third-party credit enhancement. If the unit of account for the liability is not for the combined package, the objective is to measure the fair value of the issuer's liability,

not the fair value of the combined package. Thus, in such cases, the entity would adjust the observed price for the asset to exclude the effect of the third-party credit enhancement.

Liabilities and Equity Instruments not Held by Other (Third) Parties as an Asset

There are certain liabilities that are not held by a third party as an asset. An example is a decommissioning liability assumed in a business combination, warranty obligations and many other performance commitments.

In this respect, the accounting entity must determine the fair value of the liabilities or of the equity instrument by applying valuation methods from the perspective of a market participant who must honour the claims to payment from the liability or from the equity instrument.

These valuation techniques can include a present value technique that considers either:

1. Future cash outflows that a market participant would expect to incur in fulfilling the obligation, including the compensation that a market participant would require for taking on the obligation; or
2. The amount that a market participant would receive to enter into or issue an identical liability or equity instrument, using the assumptions that market participants would use when pricing the identical item (e.g., having the same credit characteristics) in the principal (or most advantageous) market for issuing a liability or an equity instrument with the same contractual terms.

When using a present value technique to measure the fair value of a liability that is not held by another party as an asset, an entity shall, among other things, estimate the future cash outflows that market participants would expect to incur in fulfilling the obligation. Those future cash outflows shall include market participants' expectations about the costs of fulfilling the obligation and the compensation that a market participant would require for taking on the obligation. Such compensation includes the return that a market participant would require for the following:

1. Undertaking the activity (i.e., the value of fulfilling the obligation; e.g., by using resources that could be used for other activities); and
2. Assuming the risk associated with the obligation (i.e., a risk premium that reflects the risk that the actual cash outflows might differ from the expected cash outflows).

For example, a non-financial liability does not contain a contractual rate of return and there is no observable market yield for that liability. In some cases, the components of the return that market participants would require will be indistinguishable from one another (e.g., when using the price, a third-party contractor would charge on a fixed-fee basis). In other cases, an entity needs to estimate those components separately (e.g., when using the price, a third-party contractor would charge on a cost-plus basis because the contractor in that case would not bear the risk of future changes in costs).

Non-performance risk in valuing liabilities. The fair value of a liability reflects the effect of *non-performance risk*, which is the risk that an entity will not fulfil an obligation. For valuation purposes, non-performance risk is assumed to be the same before and after the transfer of the liability. This assumption is rational, because market participants would not enter into a transaction that changes the non-performance risk associated with the liability without reflecting that change in the price.

Non-performance risk includes credit risk, the effect of which may differ depending on the nature of the liability. For example, an obligation to deliver cash (a financial liability) is distinct from an obligation to deliver goods or services (a non-financial liability). Also, the terms of credit enhancements related to the liability, if any, would impact valuation.

Liabilities with inseparable third-party credit enhancements. Creditors often impose a requirement, in connection with granting credit to a debtor, that the debtor obtain a guarantee of the indebtedness from a creditworthy third party. Under such an arrangement, should the debtor default on its obligation, the third-party guarantor would become obligated to repay the obligation on behalf of the defaulting debtor and, of course, the debtor would be obligated to repay the guarantor for having satisfied the debt on its behalf.

The issuer of a liability issued with an inseparable third-party credit enhancement that is accounted for separately from the liability shall not include the effect of the credit enhancement in the fair value measurement of the liability. If the credit enhanced is accounted for separately from the liability, the issuer should take into account its own credit standing and not that of the third-party guarantor.

Restriction preventing the transfer of a liability or an entity's own equity instrument. If there are restrictions on the transfer of a liability or equity instrument, which is not an uncommon feature in certain circumstances, that should not be a consideration when measuring the fair value of such an instrument. IFRS 13 takes the view that the effect of such a feature is already included in other inputs to the fair value measurement of such instruments.

Financial liability with a demand feature. The fair value of financial liability with a demand feature is not less than the amount payable on demand, discounted from the first date that the amount could be required to be paid.

Shareholders' equity. IFRS 13 is equally applicable to the entity's equity instruments. These include the entity's own equity instruments, and how these are issued as consideration in the course of a business combination, for example. The valuation procedure adheres to the same regulations that govern the valuation of liabilities. Accordingly, own equity instruments are valued from the perspective of a market participant who holds the instrument as an asset. If such an instrument is not held as an asset by a third party, it is measured using a valuation procedure that reflects the assumptions of the market participant, in line with the regulations governing the valuation of liabilities. One such typical valuation method might be the income approach.

Fair value for net exposures. Where an entity manages a portfolio of financial assets and liabilities with a view to managing net exposures to counterparty risk, including credit and market risks, the standard permits that fair value may be determined for the net long (asset) or short (liability) position. This exception is available only if the entity qualifies for that exception by demonstrating that the net exposure is consistent with how it manages risk and it has elected to measure the financial assets and liabilities at fair value. Fair value would therefore be determined on the basis of what market participants would take into consideration when considering a transaction on the net exposure risks.

The exception does not, however, extend to the presentation of such net exposures in the financial statements, unless otherwise permitted by another IFRS.

IFRS 13 and IFRS 9 have not resulted in the abolition of the option of measuring short-term receivables and payables with no stated interest rate at invoice amount, without discounting them, as long as the effects of not discounting them were not material.

The portfolio exception applies to all contract accounting within the scope of IAS 39, *Financial Instruments: Recognition and Measurement*, or IFRS 9, *Financial Instruments*, regardless of whether the contracts meet the definitions of financial assets or financial liabilities as defined in IAS 32, *Financial Instruments: Presentation.*

Inputs. For the purpose of fair value measurements, inputs are the assumptions that market participants would use in pricing an asset or liability, including assumptions regarding risk. An input is either observable or unobservable. Observable inputs are either directly observable or indirectly observable. An entity is to maximise the use of relevant observable inputs and minimise the use of unobservable inputs.

An entity shall select inputs that are consistent with the characteristics of the asset or liability that market participants would take into account in a transaction for the asset or liability. In some cases, those characteristics result in the application of an adjustment, but adjustments are solely applicable for characteristics of the asset or liability which are consistent with the unit of account that requires or permits the fair value measurement.

An observable input is based on market data obtainable from sources independent of the reporting entity. For an input to be considered relevant, it must be considered determinative of fair value. Examples of markets in which inputs might be observable for some assets and liabilities include exchange markets, dealer markets, broker markets and principal-to-principal markets.

An unobservable input reflects assumptions made by management of the reporting entity with respect to assumptions it believes market participants would use to price an asset or liability based on the best information available under the circumstances.

The standard provides a fair value input hierarchy (see diagram below) to serve as a framework for classifying inputs based on the extent to which they are based on observable data. In some instances, inputs used in a valuation technique may be categorised at different levels across the hierarchy; in such instances the fair value measurement is categorised in the same level as the lowest level of input significant to the measurement of fair value. Determining significance in this context requires the use of judgement. Adjustments to arrive at measurements based on fair value, such as costs to sell when measuring fair value less costs to sell, shall not be taken into account when determining the level of the fair value hierarchy within which a fair value measurement is categorised.

The fair value hierarchy is determined by the predominant input factor with the aim of maximising the use of observable input parameters and keeping non-observable input parameters to the lowest possible minimum. The measurement method (measurement technique) that is applied is dictated by the available data, since the adopted measurement method constitutes the appropriate procedure for the given circumstances, and sufficient data are available to measure the fair value using that method.

Hierarchy of Fair Value Inputs

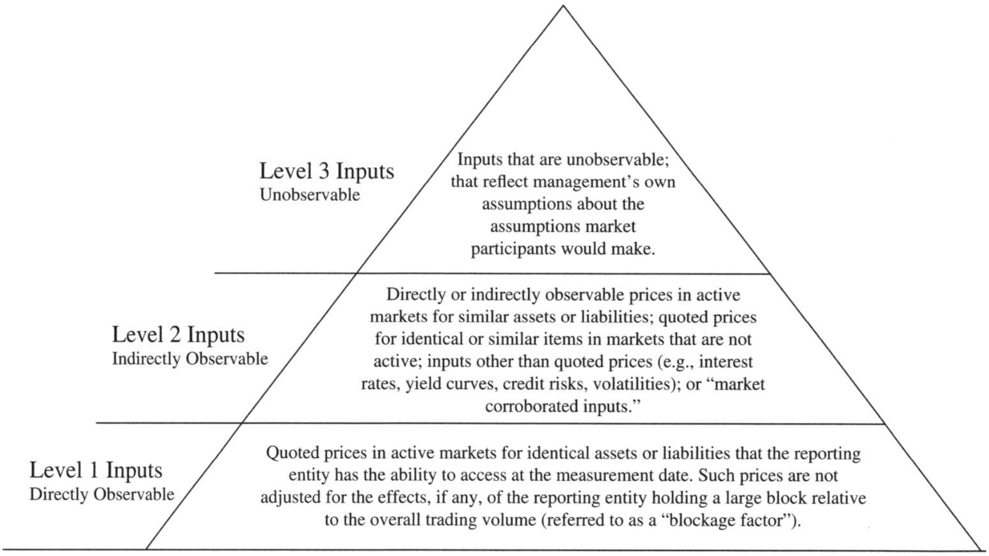

Level 1 inputs are considered the most reliable evidence of fair value and are to be used whenever they are available. These inputs consist of quoted prices in active markets for identical assets or liabilities. The active market must be the principal market for the asset or liability or, in the absence of a principal market, the most advantageous market for the asset or liability in which the reporting entity has the ability to enter into a transaction for the asset or liability at the price in that market at the measurement date. A quoted price in an active market is the most reliable evidence of fair value and should be used without adjustment except in the following circumstances:

1. As a practical expedient where an entity holds a large number of similar but non-identical assets and liabilities that are measured at fair value and a quoted price in an active market is available but not readily accessible for each of those assets or liabilities without difficulty. The entity may use a pricing alternative (e.g., pricing matrix) but the resultant fair value will be categorised as lower than Level 1.
2. When a quoted price in an active market does not reflect fair value at measurement date, for example when there is a significant after-market transaction which takes place after the close of a market but before the measurement date. If an adjustment is made in this regard the resultant fair value will be categorised as lower than Level 1.
3. Where the fair value of a liability or an entity's own equity instrument is determined using the quoted price for the identical asset adjusted for features present in the asset but not the liability. The resultant fair value is categorised as lower than Level 1.

Under no circumstances, however, is management to adjust the quoted price for blockage factors. Blockage adjustments arise when an entity holds a position in a single financial instrument that is traded on an active market that is relatively large in relation to the market's daily trading volume. That is the case even if a market's normal daily trading volume is not sufficient to absorb the quantity held and placing orders to sell the position in a single transaction might affect the quoted price.

Level 2 inputs are inputs for the asset or liability (other than quoted prices within Level 1) that are either directly or indirectly observable. Level 2 inputs are to be considered when quoted prices for the identical asset or liability are not available. If the asset or liability being measured has a contractual term, a Level 2 input must be observable for substantially the entire term. These inputs include:

1. Quoted prices for *similar* assets or liabilities in active markets;
2. Quoted prices for identical or similar assets or liabilities in markets that are *not active*;
3. Inputs other than quoted prices that are observable for the asset or liability (e.g., interest rates and yield curves observable at commonly quoted intervals; implied volatilities; prepayment speeds; loss severities; credit risks; and default rates);
4. Inputs that are derived principally from or corroborated by observable market data that, through correlation or other means, are determined to be relevant to the asset or liability being measured (market-corroborated inputs).

Adjustments made to Level 2 inputs necessary to reflect fair value, if any, will vary depending on an analysis of specific factors associated with the asset or liability being measured. These factors include:

1. Condition;
2. Location;
3. Extent to which the inputs relate to items comparable to the asset or liability;
4. Volume and level of activity in the markets in which the inputs are observed.

Depending on the level of the fair value input hierarchy in which the inputs used to measure the adjustment are classified, an adjustment that is significant to the fair value measurement in its entirety could render the measurement a Level 3 measurement.

Example: Corroborated by observable market data

The assumption is that German pharmaceutical company A's corporate bond interest rates correlate with French pharmaceutical company B's corporate bond interest rates. While A has issued various corporate bonds on the German stock market of a maximum maturity of 15 years, B has also issued various corporate bonds on the French stock market, albeit with a maximum maturity of 14 years. B could derive the yield for a hypothetical 15-year corporate bond from the yield of its own 14-year corporate bond and the correlation between corporate bonds between A and B. In this case, the yield of B's 15-year corporate bond will constitute a Level 2 input factor. If a 15-year corporate bond from B could be extrapolated in a meaningful way solely through significant adjustments to the observable input factors, this would constitute a Level 3 input factor.

Level 3 inputs are unobservable inputs. These are necessary when little, if any, market activity occurs for the asset or liability. Level 3 inputs are to reflect management's own assumptions about the assumptions regarding an exit price that a market participant holding the asset or owing the liability would make, including assumptions about risk. The best information available in the circumstances is to be used to develop the Level 3 inputs. This information might include internal data of the reporting entity. Cost-benefit considerations apply in that management is not required to "undertake all possible efforts" to obtain information about the assumptions that would be made by market participants. Attention is to be paid, however, to information available to management without undue cost and effort and, consequently, management's internal assumptions used to develop unobservable inputs are to be adjusted if such information contradicts those assumptions.

Inputs based on bid and ask prices represent the maximum price at which market participants are willing to buy an asset; quoted ask prices represent the minimum price at which market participants are willing to sell an asset. If available market prices are expressed in terms of bid and ask prices, management is to use the price within the bid–ask spread (the range of values between bid and ask prices) that is most representative of fair value irrespective of where in the fair value hierarchy the input would be classified. The standard permits the use of pricing conventions such as midmarket pricing as a practical alternative for determining fair value measurements within a bid–ask spread.

Valuation techniques. In measuring fair value, management may employ one or more valuation techniques consistent with the market approach, the income approach and/or the cost approach. As previously discussed, the selection of a particular technique (or techniques) to measure fair value is to be based on its appropriateness to the asset or liability being measured and in particular the sufficiency and observability of inputs available.

In certain situations, such as when using Level 1 inputs, use of a single valuation technique will be sufficient. In other situations, such as when valuing a reporting unit, management may need to use multiple valuation techniques. When doing so, the results yielded by applying the various techniques are to be evaluated and appropriately weighted based on judgement as to the reasonableness of the range of results. The objective of the weighting is to determine the point within the range that is most representative of fair value.

If the transaction price is fair value at initial recognition and a valuation technique that uses unobservable inputs will be used to measure fair value in subsequent periods, the valuation technique shall be calibrated so that at initial recognition the result of the valuation technique equals the transaction price. Calibration ensures that the valuation technique reflects current market conditions, and it helps an entity to determine whether an adjustment to the valuation technique is necessary (e.g., there might be a characteristic of the asset or liability that is not captured by the valuation technique).

Management is required to consistently apply the valuation techniques it elects to use to measure fair value. It would be appropriate to change valuation techniques or how they are applied if the change results in fair value measurements that are equally or more representative of fair value. Situations that might give rise to such a change would be when new markets develop, new information becomes available, previously available information ceases to be available or improved techniques are developed. Revisions that result from either a change in valuation technique or a change in the application of a valuation technique are to be accounted for as changes in accounting estimate under IAS 8.

Market approaches valuations use information generated by actual market transactions for identical or comparable assets or liabilities (including a business in its entirety). Market approach techniques often will use market multiples derived from a set of comparable transactions for the asset or liability or similar items. The entity will need to consider both qualitative and quantitative factors in determining the point within the range that is most representative of fair value. An example of a market approach is matrix pricing. This is a mathematical technique used primarily for the purpose of valuing debt securities without relying solely on quoted prices for the specific securities. Matrix pricing uses factors such as the stated interest rate, maturity, credit rating and quoted prices of similar issues to develop the issue's current market yield.

The market approach uses prices and other relevant information generated by market transactions involving identical or comparable (i.e., similar) assets. The following valuation techniques are described under the market approach:

1. Transaction price paid for an identical or a similar instrument of an investee;
2. Comparable company valuation multiples (typically trading or transaction multiples).

Where there has been a recent acquisition of the identical equity instruments in the same entity, that price would be indicative of the fair value of the instrument. For example, if another third party had purchased 5% of the same company recently for €500,000, then it would be reasonable to assume that this would be indicative of a similar holdings value. Note that the investor should assess whether factors or events that have occurred after the purchase date that could affect the fair value of the unquoted equity instrument at measurement date. If so, the value would need to be adjusted for these factors.

If the equity instrument that was recently acquired is *similar* to the unquoted equity instrument being valued, the investor needs to understand, and make adjustments for, any differences between the two equity instruments. These could include economic rights (e.g., dividend rights, priority upon liquidation, etc.) and control rights (i.e., control premium).

Comparable company valuation multiples assume that the value of an unquoted asset can be measured by comparing that investment to a similar investment where market prices are available. There are two main sources of information about the pricing of comparable company peers: quoted prices in exchange markets (for example, the Singapore Exchange or the Frankfurt Stock Exchange) and observable data from transactions such as mergers and acquisitions.

In doing a comparable company valuation (trading multiples or transaction multiples), you would need to ascertain the following:

1. Identify a comparable peer company for which information is available.
2. Select the performance measure that is most relevant to assessing the value for the investee (i.e., earnings, equity book value or revenue). Once selected, derive and analyse possible valuation multiples and select the most appropriate one (e.g., EBIT, EBITA, EBITDA or P/E). Note that this may need to be adjusted for differences between the companies that may impact the multiple being used (e.g., size of the business where revenues are being used).
3. Apply the appropriate valuation multiple to the relevant performance measure of the investee to obtain an indicated fair value of the investee's equity value or the investee's enterprise value.
4. To ensure comparability between the unquoted equity instruments held in the investee and the equity instruments of the comparable company peers, further adjustment may be required to the derived multiple before applying it to reflect the effect of factors such as:

    a. *Non-controlling discount:* for instance, if the multiple is derived from the price in an acquisition involving the acquisition of control, the derived multiple will include the effect of the control premium which must be removed in determining the appropriate multiple for the valuation of your non-controlling investment.

b. *Liquidity effect*: it is accepted that unlisted entities tend to trade at a discount to fair value compared to comparable peer companies which are listed. This discount should be determined and adjusted for.
c. Isolation of *non-core activities*: for the purposes of deriving the value generated by an investee's operating assets and liabilities an investor must remove the non-operating items effect (including any income or expenses they generate) from both the valuation multiple obtained from the comparable company peers (see (b) above.) and from the investee's performance measure.

Income approaches are techniques used to measure fair value based on current market expectations about future amounts (such as cash flows or net income) and discount them to an amount in measurement date dollars. Valuation techniques that follow an income approach include present value techniques, option pricing models, such as the Black–Scholes–Merton model (a closed-form model) and binomial, i.e., a lattice model (an open-form model), which incorporate present value techniques, as well as the multi-period excess earnings method that is used in fair value measurements of certain intangible assets such as in-process research and development.

The income approach is a valuation technique that converts future amounts (e.g., cash flows or income and expenses) to a single current (i.e., discounted) amount. The fair value measurement is determined on the basis of the value indicated by current market expectations about those future amounts. The guide details the following valuation techniques:

Discounted cash flow method

The discounted cash flow method is generally applied by projecting expected cash flows for a discrete period (e.g., three to five years) and then determining a value for the periods thereafter (terminal value) and discounting the projected cash flows to a present value at a rate reflecting the time value of money and the relative risks of the investment.

Dividend discount model

The dividend discount model assumes the price (fair value) of an entity's equity instrument equals the present value of all its expected future dividends in perpetuity. This method is most applicable to entities that are consistent dividend payers.

Constant-growth dividend discount model

The constant-growth dividend discount model is the same as the dividend discount method but applies a simplified assumption of a constant growth rate in dividends. This method is most suitable for mature enterprises with a consistent dividend policy.

Capitalisation method

The capitalisation method applies a rate to an amount that represents a measure of economic income (e.g., free cash flows to firm or free cash flows to equity) to arrive at an estimate of present value. The model is useful as a cross-check when other approaches have been used.

Cost approaches are based on quantifying the amount required to replace an asset's remaining service capacity (i.e., the asset's current replacement cost) from the perspective of a market participant buyer. A valuation technique classified as a cost approach would measure the cost to a market participant (buyer) to acquire or construct a substitute asset of comparable utility, adjusted for obsolescence. Obsolescence adjustments include factors for physical wear and tear, improvements to technology and economic (external) obsolescence. Thus, obsolescence is a broader concept than financial statement depreciation, which simply represents a cost allocation convention and is not intended to be a valuation technique.

Example: Multiple valuation techniques—machine held and used

An entity acquires a machine in a business combination, which will be held and used in its operations. The machine was originally purchased from an outside vendor and was customised by the acquired entity for use in its operations. However, the customisation of the machine was not extensive. The entity determines that sufficient data are available to apply the cost approach and because the customisation was not extensive the market approach. The income approach is not used because the machine does not have a separately identifiable income stream.

a. The market approach is applied using quoted prices for similar machines adjusted for differences between the machine (as customised) and the similar machines. The measurement reflects the price that would be received for the machine in its current condition (used) and location (installed and configured for use). The fair value indicated by that approach ranges from €40,000 to €48,000.
b. The cost approach is applied by estimating the amount that would be required currently to construct a substitute (customised) machine of comparable utility. The estimate takes into account the condition of the machine and the environment in which it operates, including physical wear and tear, improvements in technology, external conditions such as a market decline in the demand for similar machines and installation costs. The fair value indicated by that approach ranges from €40,000 to €52,000.

The entity determines that the higher end of the range indicated by the market approach is most representative of fair value. That determination is made on the basis of the relative subjectivity of the inputs:

- The inputs in the market approach (quoted prices for similar machines) require fewer and less subjective adjustments than the inputs used in the cost approach;
- The range indicated by the market approach overlaps with, but is narrower than, the range indicated by the cost approach;
- There are no known unexplained differences (between the machine and the similar machines) within that range.

Accordingly, the entity determines that the fair value of the machine is €48,000.

Measurement Considerations

Initial recognition. When the reporting entity first acquires an asset or incurs (or assumes) a liability in an exchange transaction, the transaction price represents an entry price, the price paid to acquire the asset and the price received to assume the liability. Fair value measurements are based not on entry prices, but rather on exit prices; the price that would be received to sell the asset or paid to transfer the liability. In some cases (e.g., in a business combination) there is not a transaction price for each individual asset or liability. Likewise, sometimes there is not an exchange transaction for the asset or liability (e.g., when biological assets regenerate).

While entry and exit prices differ conceptually, in many cases they may be nearly identical and can be considered to represent fair value of the asset or liability at initial recognition. This is not always the case, however, and in assessing fair value at initial recognition, management is to consider transaction-specific factors and factors specific to the assets and/or liabilities that are being initially recognised.

Examples of situations where transaction price is not representative of fair value at initial recognition include:

1. Related-party transactions, although the price in a related party transaction may be used as an input into a fair value measurement if the entity has evidence that the transaction was entered into at market terms.
2. Transactions taking place under duress such as a forced or liquidation transaction. Such transactions do not meet the criterion in the definition of fair value that they be representative of an "orderly transaction."
3. Different units of account that apply to the transaction price and the assets/liabilities being measured. This can occur, for example, where the transaction price includes other elements besides the assets/liabilities that are being measured such as unstated rights and privileges that are subject to separate measurement or when the transaction price includes transaction costs (see discussion below).
4. The exchange transaction takes place in a market different from the principal (or most advantageous) market in which the reporting entity would sell the asset or transfer the liability. An example of this situation is when the reporting entity is a securities dealer that enters into transactions in different markets depending on whether the counterparty is a retail customer or another securities dealer.

Transaction costs. Transaction costs are the incremental direct costs that would be incurred to sell an asset or transfer a liability. While, as previously discussed, transaction costs are considered in determining the market that is most advantageous, they are not used to adjust the fair value measurement of the asset or liability being measured.

Transport costs. If an attribute of the asset or liability being measured is its location, the price determined in the principal (or most advantageous) market is to be adjusted for the costs that would be incurred by the reporting entity to transport it to or from that market.

The possible discrepancies between entry and exit values may create so-called "day one gains or losses." If an IFRS requires or permits an entity to measure an asset or liability initially at fair value and the transaction price differs from fair value, the entity recognises the resulting gain or loss in profit or loss unless the IFRS requires otherwise.

FAIR VALUE DISCLOSURE

The IFRS on fair value measurement provides that, for assets and liabilities that are measured at fair value on a recurring or non-recurring basis, the reporting entity is to disclose information that enables users of its financial statements to assess the methods (valuation technique) and inputs used to develop those measurements. For recurring fair value measurements using significant unobservable inputs (Level 3), the entity has to disclose the effect of the measurements on profit or loss or other comprehensive income for the period. To accomplish these objectives, it must (except as noted below) determine how much detail to disclose, how much emphasis to place on different aspects of the disclosure requirements, the extent of aggregation or disaggregation and whether users need any additional (qualitative) information to evaluate the quantitative information disclosed. An entity shall present the quantitative disclosures required in a tabular format unless another format is more appropriate.

The disclosures in the Notes distinguish between recurring or non-recurring fair value measurements. More detailed information must be provided for recurring fair value measurements.

At a minimum, the entity is to disclose the following information for each class of assets and liabilities:

1. The fair value measurement at the end of the reporting period. In addition, for non-recurring fair value measurements, the reasons for the measurement.
2. The level of the fair value hierarchy within which the fair value measurements are categorised in their entirety (Levels 1, 2 or 3).
3. For assets and liabilities held at the reporting date that are measured at fair value on a recurring basis, any significant transfers between Level 1 and Level 2 of the fair value hierarchy and the reasons for those transfers. Transfers into each level are to be disclosed and discussed separately from transfers out of each level. For this purpose, significance is to be judged with respect to profit or loss, and total assets or total liabilities.
4. For recurring and non-recurring fair value measurements categorised within Level 2 and Level 3 of the fair value hierarchy, the methods and the inputs used in the fair value measurement and the information used to develop those inputs. If there has been a change in valuation technique (e.g., changing from a market approach to an income approach), the entity must disclose that change, the reasons for making it and its effect on the fair value measurement. In case entities utilise within Level 3 of the fair value hierarchy quantitative information about the significant unobservable inputs, this quantitative information has to be disclosed.
5. For recurring fair value measurements categorised within Level 3 of the fair value hierarchy, a reconciliation from the opening balances to the closing balances, disclosing separately changes during the period attributable to the following:

   a. Total gains or losses for the period recognised in profit or loss, and a description of where they are presented in the statement of comprehensive income or the separate income statement (if presented);
   b. Total gains or losses for the period recognised in other comprehensive income and a description of where they are presented in the other comprehensive income;
   c. Purchases, sales, issues and settlements (each of those types of change disclosed separately);
   d. Transfers into or out of Level 3 (e.g., transfers attributable to changes in the observability of market data) and the reasons for those transfers. For significant transfers, transfers into Level 3 shall be disclosed and discussed separately from transfers out of Level 3. For this purpose, significance shall be judged with respect to profit or loss, and total assets or total liabilities.

6. The amount of the total gains or losses for the period in 5a. above included in profit or loss that are attributable to gains or losses relating to those assets and liabilities held at the reporting date, and a description of where those gains or losses are presented in the statement of comprehensive income or separate income statement (if presented).

7. For recurring and non-recurring fair value measurements categorised within Level 3, a description must be provided of the valuation processes used by the entity, including the measurement strategy and method, as well as the procedure for analysing changes in the fair value between the periods.
8. For recurring fair value measurements categorised within Level 3 of the fair value hierarchy, narrative description of the sensitivity of the fair value measurement to changes in unobservable inputs (used in valuation) if a change in those inputs to a different amount might result in a significantly higher or lower fair value measurement. If there are interrelationships between unobservable inputs used in the fair value measurement, an entity shall also provide a description of those interrelationships and of how they might magnify or mitigate the effect of changes in the unobservable inputs on the fair value measurement.

   For recurring financial assets and financial liabilities, if changing one or more of the unobservable inputs to reasonably possible alternative assumptions would change fair value significantly, the entity is to state that fact and disclose the effect of those changes. An entity is to disclose how it calculated those changes. For this purpose, significance is to be judged with respect to profit or loss, and total assets or total liabilities, or, when changes in fair value are recognised in other comprehensive income, total equity.
9. For recurring and non-recurring fair value measurements, if the highest and best use of a non-financial asset differs from its current use, an entity shall disclose that fact and why the non-financial asset is being used in a manner that differs from its highest and best use.
10. The appropriate classification of assets and liabilities is determined, on the one hand, on the basis of the properties, attributes and risks attached to the asset or liability, and its respective level in the measurement hierarchy. Since measuring fair value at Level 3 involves a higher degree of uncertainty and subjectivity, the number of classes at this hierarchy level may need to be larger than for Levels 1 or 2. A class of assets or liabilities frequently needs to be broken down into more detail than that which is reflected by the individual items on a statement of financial position.

In addition to the foregoing, for each class of assets and liabilities *not* measured at fair value (recurring and non-recurring) in the statement of financial position, but for which the fair value is disclosed, the reporting entity is to disclose the fair value by the level of the fair value hierarchy, for fair value measurements categorised within Level 2 and Level 3 of the fair value hierarchy, a description of the valuation technique and the inputs used in the fair value measurement as well as reasons for changing the valuation technique. In addition, if an asset's current use differs from its best use, an entity shall disclose that fact and why the non-financial asset is being used in a manner that differs from its highest and best use.

Example: Valuation techniques and inputs

Description	Fair value at 31.12.20X	Valuation technique	Unobservable input	Range (weighted-average)
Other equity securities				
– Healthcare industry	53	Discounted cash flow	Weighted-average cost of capital	7%–16% (12, 1%)
			Long-term revenue growth rate	2%–5% (4, 2%)
			Long-term pre-tax operating margin	3%–20% (10, 3%)
			Discount for lack of marketability	5%–20% (17%)
			Control premium	10%–30% (20%)
		Market comparable companies	EBITDA multiple	10–13 (11, 3)
			Revenue multiple	1, 5–2, 0 (1, 7)
			Discount for lack of marketability	5%–20% (17%)
			Control premium	10%–30% (20%)
– Energy industry	32	Discounted cash flow	Weighted-average cost of capital	8%–12% (11, 1%)
			Long-term revenue growth rate	3%–5, 5% (4, 2%)
			Long-term pre-tax operating margin	7, 5%–13% (9, 2%)
			Discount for lack of marketability	5%–20% (10%)
			Control premium	10%–20% (12%)
		Market comparable companies	EBITDA multiple	6, 5–12 (9, 5)
			Revenue multiple	1, 0–3, 0 (2, 0)
			Discount for lack of marketability	5%–20% (10%)
			Control premium	10%–20% (12%)
Debt securities				
– Residential mortgage-backed securities	125	Discounted cash flow	Constant prepayment rate	3, 5%–5, 5% (4, 5%)
			Probability of default	5%–50% (10%)
			Loss severity	40%–100% (60%)
– Collateralised debt obligations	35	Consensus pricing	Offered quotes	20–45
			Comparability adjustments (%)	−10% – +15% (+5%)

Derivatives				
– Credit contracts	38	Option model	Annualised volatility of credit	10%–20%
			Counterparty credit risk	0, 5%–3, 5%
			Own credit risk	0, 3%–2%
Investment properties				
– Commercial—Asia	31	Discounted cash flow	Long-term net operating income margin	18%–32% (20%)
			Cap rate	0, 08–0, 12 (0, 10)
		Market comparable approach	Price per square metre (USD)	\$3.000–\$7.000 (\$4.500)
– Commercial—Europe	27	Discounted cash flow	Long-term net operating income margin	15%–25% (18%)
			Cap rate	0, 06–0, 10 (0, 08)
		Market comparable approach	Price per square metre (USD)	\$4.000–\$12.000 (\$8.500)

Example: Description about sensitivity to changes in significant unobservable inputs (IFRS 13.IE66)

The significant unobservable inputs used in the fair value measurement of the entity's residential mortgage-backed securities are prepayment rates, probability of default and loss severity in the event of default. Significant increases (decreases) in any of those inputs in isolation would result in a significantly lower (higher) fair value measurement. Generally, a change in the assumption used for the probability of default is accompanied by a directionally similar change in the assumption used for the loss severity and a directionally opposite change in the assumption used for prepayment rates.

FUTURE DEVELOPMENTS

The IASB issued the exposure draft *Post-implementation Review—IFRS 13 Fair Value Measurement* in May 2017. The exposure draft asked questions regarding the implementation of IFRS 13, which may result in future changes in IFRS 13. In December 2018, the results of this were that the standard appears to be working as intended, that it is 1) useful to users of the financial statements 2) there are challenges in implementing especially where professional judgment is required, and those in the fair value industry appear to be resolving these challenges accordingly, 3) costs associated with implementation / application are within expectations.

US GAAP COMPARISON

IFRS 13 mirrors closely the US GAAP fair value measurement standard with some small specific additional expediencies and requirements:

- Under US GAAP, when accounting for alternative investments, a practical expedient allows entities to measure the fair value of certain investments at net asset value.
- Under US GAAP, the fair value measurement of a financial liability with a demand feature (e.g., a demand deposit) is described as the amount payable on demand as of the reporting date.
- Under US GAAP, a quantitative sensitivity analysis is required to be disclosed in the financial statements footnotes for all financial instruments categorised as Level 3 investment.
- If an asset or a liability is measured initially at fair value under US GAAP, any difference between the fair value and the transaction price is recognised at the inception as a gain or loss in earnings unless otherwise specified.

26 INCOME TAXES

INTRODUCTION

Income taxes are an expense incurred in operating most businesses, and as such are to be reflected in the entity's operating results. However, accounting for income taxes is complicated by the fact that, in most jurisdictions, the amounts of revenues and expenses recognised in a given period for taxation purposes will not fully correspond to what is reported in the financial statements. The venerable matching principle (still having some relevance, although it is no longer a central concept underlying financial reporting rules) implies that for financial reporting purposes the amount presented as current period tax expense should bear an appropriate relationship to the amount of pre-tax accounting income being reported. That expense will normally not equal—and may differ markedly from—the amount of the current period's tax payment obligation. The upshot is that deferred income tax assets and/or liabilities must be recognised. These are measured, approximately, as the difference between the amounts currently owed and the amounts recognisable for financial reporting purposes.

The statement of financial position liability method applied in IAS 12 focuses on temporary differences, which are the difference between the carrying value and tax base of all assets and liabilities. Discounting of deferred tax assets and liabilities to present values is not permitted.

Both deferred tax assets and liabilities are measured by reference to expected tax rates, which in general are the enacted, effective rates as of the date of the statement of financial position. IAS 12 has particular criteria to be used for the recognition of the tax effects of temporary differences arising from ownership interests in investees and subsidiaries, and for the accounting related to goodwill arising from business acquisitions. Presentation of deferred tax assets or liabilities as current assets or liabilities is prohibited by the standard, which also establishes extensive financial statement disclosures.

Source of IFRS	
IAS 12	*IFRIC* 23

SCOPE

IAS 12 is applied in the accounting for income taxes. Income taxes include all domestic and foreign taxes which are based on taxable profit, including withholding taxes payable on distributions by the reporting entity. Although IAS 12 does not deal with the accounting of government grants and investment tax credits, it deals with the accounting of temporary differences on such transactions.

DEFINITIONS OF TERMS

Accounting profit. Profit or loss for a period before deducting tax expense.

Current tax. The amount of income taxes payable (recoverable) in respect of the taxable profit (tax loss) for a period.

Deductible temporary differences. Temporary differences that will result in amounts that are deductible in determining future taxable profit (tax loss) when the carrying amount of the asset or liability is recovered or settled.

Deferred tax asset. The amounts of income taxes recoverable in future periods in respect of deductible temporary differences, the carryforward of unused tax losses and the carryforward of unused tax credits.

Deferred tax liability. The amounts of income taxes payable in future periods in respect of taxable temporary differences.

Tax base. The amount attributable to an asset or liability for tax purposes.

Tax expense (tax income). The aggregate amount included in the determination of profit or loss for the period in respect of current tax and deferred tax.

Taxable profit (tax loss). The profit (loss) for a taxable period, determined in accordance with the rules established by the taxation authorities, upon which income taxes are payable (recoverable).

Taxable temporary differences. Temporary differences that will result in taxable amounts in determining taxable profit (tax loss) of future periods when the carrying amount of the asset or liability is recovered or settled.

Temporary differences. Differences between the carrying amount of an asset or liability in the statement of financial position and its tax base.

IDENTIFICATION

Tax expense (income) comprises two components: current tax expense and deferred tax expense. Either of these can be an income (i.e., a credit amount in the statement of profit or loss and other comprehensive income), rather than an expense (a debit), depending on whether there is taxable profit or loss for the period. For convenience, the term "tax expense" will be used to denote either an expense or an income. Current tax expense is easily understood as the tax effect of the entity's reported taxable income or loss for the period, as determined by relevant rules of the various taxing authorities to which it is subject. Deferred tax expense, in general terms, arises as the tax effect of temporary differences occurring during the reporting period.

Using the liability method, the reporting entity's current period total income tax expense cannot be computed directly (except when there are no temporary differences). Rather, it must be calculated as the sum of the two components: current tax expense and deferred tax expense. This total will not, in general, equal the amount that would be derived by applying the current tax rate to pre-tax accounting profit. The reason is that deferred tax expense is defined as the change in the deferred tax asset and liability accounts occurring in the current period, and this change may encompass more than the mere effect of the current tax rate times the net temporary differences arising or being reversed in the present reporting period.

Although the primary objective of income tax accounting is no longer the proper matching of current period revenue and expenses, the once-critical matching principle retains some importance in financial reporting theory. Therefore, the tax effects of items excluded from profit and loss are also excluded from the profit and loss section of the statement of profit or loss and other comprehensive income. For example, the tax effects of items reported in other comprehensive income are likewise reported in other comprehensive income.

The recognition of income tax is based on the liability method. The liability method is statement of financial position-oriented. To understand the application of the liability method as incorporated in IAS 12, the basic recognition and measurement principles in IAS 12 must be understood, including how these recognition and measurement principles are applied to determine the current and deferred tax amounts.

RECOGNITION AND MEASUREMENT OF CURRENT TAX

Recognition of Current Tax

The primary goal of the liability method is to present the estimated actual taxes to be payable in current and future periods as the income tax liability on the statement of financial position. Based on this goal, current tax for the current and prior periods is recognised as a liability to the extent it is unpaid at the end of the reporting period. If the amount paid exceeds the respective current tax recorded, an asset is recognised. The benefit of a tax loss that can be carried back to recover current tax of previous periods must also be recognised as an asset as the benefit is both probable and reliably measurable.

Measurement of Current Tax

Current tax liabilities are measured at the amount expected to be paid to the taxation authorities, using the tax rates (and tax laws) that have been enacted or substantially enacted by the end of the reporting period. Current tax assets are similarly measured at the amount expected to be recovered from the taxation authorities.

RECOGNITION AND MEASUREMENT OF DEFERRED TAX

Recognition of Deferred Tax

The recognition of deferred tax is based on a statement of financial position orientation. Based on this orientation, deferred tax liabilities are recognised for taxable temporary differences and deferred tax assets are recognised for deductible temporary differences, the carryforward of unused tax losses and the carryforward of unused tax credits.

The general principle is that a deferred tax liability is recognised for all taxable temporary differences. Two exceptions are, however, applicable. The first is temporary differences arising from the initial recognition of goodwill and the second is temporary differences arising from the initial recognition of an asset or liability in a transaction which is not a business combination and at the time of the transaction affects neither accounting profit nor taxable profit (tax loss).

Deferred tax assets recognised for deductible temporary difference, the carryforward of unused tax losses and the carryforward of unused tax credits are subject to a probability limitation. Deferred tax is only recognised to the extent that it is probable that taxable profits are available against which the deductible temporary difference could be utilised. An exception, similar to a deferred tax liability, is also applicable to deductible temporary differences arising from the initial recognition of an asset or liability in a transaction which is not a business combination and at the time of the transaction affects neither accounting profit nor taxable profit (tax loss).

Special principles are applicable to the recognition of temporary differences associated with investments in subsidiaries, branches and interest in joint ventures, which is discussed under Specific Transactions.

Measurement of Deferred Tax Assets

Deferred tax assets and deferred tax liabilities are measured at the tax rates that are expected to apply to the period when the assets are realised or the liabilities are settled. The applicable tax rate is based on the tax rate (and tax laws) that have been enacted or substantively enacted by the end of the reporting period.

The computation of the amount of deferred taxes is based on the rate expected to be in effect when the temporary differences reverse. The annual computation is considered a tentative estimate of the liability (or asset) that is subject to change as the statutory tax rate changes or as the taxpayer moves into other tax rate brackets. The measurement of deferred tax liabilities and deferred tax assets reflects the tax consequences that would follow the manner in which management expects, at the end of the reporting period, to recover or settle the carrying amount of its assets and liabilities.

The issue is that both the tax rate and the tax base of an asset or liability can be dependent on the manner in which the entity recovers or settles the asset or liability. An asset can either be recovered through usage or sale, or a combination. IAS 12 clarifies that the tax rate and tax base consistent with the expected manner of recovery or settlement must be used.

Special guidance is applicable to non-depreciable assets measured under the revaluation model and investment properties measured under the fair value model:

- Revalued non-depreciable assets are regarded to be recovered only through sale, since these assets are not depreciated. The tax rate and tax base that should be used is the one that would be applicable if the asset were sold at the end of the reporting period.
- A rebuttable presumption exists that investment properties carried at fair value will be recovered through sale. Deferred tax is thus created as if the entire investment property is recovered through sale at the end of the reporting period.

The presumption regarding investment properties is rebutted if the investment property is depreciated (for example, buildings and leasehold land) and held within a business model whose objective is to consume substantially all the economic benefits embodied in the investment property over time, rather than through sale. The presumption cannot be rebutted for freehold land, which is not depreciable. The rebuttable presumption is also applicable to investment properties measured at fair value in a business combination.

RECOGNITION IN PROFIT OR LOSS

The general principle is that all changes in current and deferred tax are recognised in profit or loss. Two exceptions are applicable. The first relates to transactions recognised in other comprehensive income. The current and deferred tax related to items recognised in other comprehensive income and equity should also be recognised in other comprehensive income and equity.

Secondly, the initial deferred tax recognised on assets and liabilities acquired in a business combination are recognised as an adjustment to goodwill or any gain on a bargain purchase.

CALCULATION OF DEFERRED TAX ASSET OR LIABILITY

While conceptually the application of the liability method is straightforward, in the application of IAS 12 a number of complexities need to be addressed. The following process needs to be followed to calculate and measure deferred tax assets and liabilities:

1. Identification of temporary differences.
2. Identification of exceptions.

3. Identification of unused tax losses or tax credits.
4. Calculation and measurement of deferred tax assets or deferred tax liabilities.
5. Limitations on the recognition of deferred tax assets.

Identification of Temporary Differences

The preponderance of the typical reporting entity's revenue and expense transactions are treated identically for tax and financial reporting purposes. Some transactions and events, however, will have different tax and accounting implications. In many of these cases, the difference relates to the period in which the income or expense will be recognised. Under earlier iterations of IAS 12, the latter differences were referred to as *timing differences* and were said to originate in one period and to reverse in a later period.

The current IAS 12 introduced the concept of *temporary differences*, which is a somewhat more comprehensive concept than that of timing differences. Temporary differences include all the categories of items defined under the earlier concept and add a number of additional items as well. Temporary differences are defined to include *all* differences between the carrying amount and the tax base of assets and liabilities.

Carrying Value	–	Tax Base	=	Temporary Difference

The tax base of an asset or liability is defined as the amount attributable to that asset or liability for tax purposes. The following principles are included in IAS 12 to determine the tax base of assets and liabilities:

Element	**Tax base**
Asset	The amount that would be deductible for tax purposes when the carrying amount of the asset is recovered. If the economic benefits recovered from the asset are not taxable, the tax base of the asset is equal to its carrying amount.
Liability	The carrying amount less any amount that will be deductible for tax purposes in respect of the liability in future periods. In the case of revenue received in advance, the tax base is the carrying amount less any amount of the revenue that will not be taxed in future periods.

The tax base can also be determined for transactions not recognised in the statement of financial position. For example, if an amount is expensed, but the amount is only deductible for tax purposes in the future, the tax base will be equal to the amount deductible in the future. When the tax base of an item is not immediately apparent, the following general principle of IAS 12 must be followed to determine the tax base:

1. Recognise a deferred tax asset when recovery or settlement of the carrying amount will reduce future taxable income; and
2. A deferred tax liability when the recovery or settlement of the carrying amount will increase future taxable income.

Once the tax base is determined the related temporary difference is calculated as the difference between carrying value and the tax base. Temporary differences are divided into taxable and deductible temporary differences. Taxable temporary differences represent a liability and are defined as temporary differences that will result in taxable amounts in determining taxable profits of future periods when the carrying amount of the asset or liability is recovered or settled. Deductible temporary differences represent an asset and are defined as temporary differences that will result in amounts that will be deductible in determining the taxable profits of future periods when the carrying amount of the asset or liability is recovered or settled.

Deductible and taxable temporary differences are thus based on the future taxable effect explained in the following examples:

1. *Revenue recognised for financial reporting purposes before being recognised for tax purposes.* Examples include revenue accounted for by the instalment method for tax purposes but reflected in income currently; certain construction-related revenue recognised on a completed-contract method for tax purposes, but on a percentage-of-completion basis for financial reporting; earnings from investees recognised by the equity method for accounting purposes but taxed only when later distributed as dividends to the investor. These are taxable temporary differences because the amounts are taxable in future periods, which give rise to deferred tax liabilities.
2. *Revenue recognised for tax purposes prior to recognition in the financial statements.* These include certain types of revenue received in advance, such as prepaid rental income and service contract revenue that is taxable when received. Referred to as deductible temporary differences, these items give rise to deferred tax assets.
3. *Expenses that are deductible for tax purposes prior to recognition in the financial statements.* This results when accelerated depreciation methods or shorter useful lives are used for tax purposes, while straight-line depreciation or longer useful economic lives are used for financial reporting; and when there are certain pre-operating costs and certain capitalised interest costs that are deductible currently for tax purposes. These items are taxable temporary differences and give rise to deferred tax liabilities.
4. *Expenses that are reported in the financial statements prior to becoming deductible for tax purposes.* Certain estimated expenses, such as warranty costs, as well as such contingent losses as accruals of litigation expenses, are not tax deductible until the obligation becomes fixed. These are deductible temporary differences, and accordingly give rise to deferred tax assets.

Other examples of temporary differences include:

1. *Reductions in tax-deductible asset bases arising in connection with tax credits.* Under tax provisions in certain jurisdictions, credits are available for certain qualifying investments in plant assets. In some cases, taxpayers are permitted a choice of either full accelerated depreciation coupled with a reduced investment tax credit, or a full investment tax credit coupled with reduced depreciation allowances. If the taxpayer chose the latter option, the asset basis is reduced for tax depreciation, but would still be fully depreciable for financial reporting purposes. Accordingly, this election would be accounted for as a taxable timing difference and give rise to a deferred tax liability.
2. *Increases in the tax bases of assets resulting from the indexing of asset costs for the effects of inflation.* Occasionally, proposed and sometimes enacted by taxing jurisdictions,

such a tax law provision allows taxpaying entities to finance the replacement of depreciable assets through depreciation based on current costs, as computed by the application of indices to the historical costs of the assets being remeasured. This re-evaluation of asset costs gives rise to deductible temporary differences that would be associated with deferred tax benefits.

3. *Certain business combinations accounted for by the acquisition method.* Under certain circumstances, the costs assignable to assets or liabilities acquired in purchase business combinations will differ from their tax bases. The usual scenario under which this arises is when the acquirer must continue to report the predecessor's tax bases for tax purposes, although the price paid was more or less than book value. Such differences may be either taxable or deductible and, accordingly, may give rise to deferred tax liabilities or assets. These are recognised as temporary differences by IAS 12.
4. *Assets that are revalued for financial reporting purposes although the tax bases are not affected.* This is analogous to the matter discussed in point 2. Under certain IFRS (such as IAS 16 and IAS 40), assets may be upwardly adjusted to current fair values (revaluation amounts), although for tax purposes these adjustments are ignored until and unless the assets are disposed of. The discrepancies between the adjusted book carrying values and the tax bases are temporary differences under IAS 12, and deferred taxes are to be provided on these variations. This is required even if there is no intention to dispose of the assets in question, or if, under the salient tax laws, exchanges for other similar assets (or reinvestment of proceeds of sales in similar assets) would effect a postponement of the tax obligation.

Identification of Exemptions

Two exemptions are applicable to the recognition of deferred tax, namely goodwill and initial recognition exception.

Goodwill

No deferred tax liability should be recognised on the initial recognition of goodwill. Although goodwill represents an asset, no deferred tax is considered to arise since goodwill is measured as a residual of the value of net assets acquired in a business combination. The deferred tax recognised on the acquired net assets of the business combination, however, affects the value of goodwill as the residual. IAS 12 also clarifies that no deferred tax effects are applicable to the later impairment of goodwill.

If goodwill or a gain on a bargain purchase is not deductible or taxable, respectively, in a given tax jurisdiction (that is, it is a permanent difference), in theory its tax base is zero, and thus there is a difference between tax and financial reporting bases, to which one would logically expect deferred taxes would be attributed. However, given the residual nature of goodwill or a gain on a bargain purchase, recognition of deferred taxes would in turn create yet more goodwill, and thus more deferred tax, etc. There would be little purpose achieved by loading up the statement of financial position with goodwill and related deferred tax in such circumstances, and the computation itself would be quite challenging. Accordingly, IAS 12 prohibits grossing up goodwill in such a fashion. Similarly, no deferred tax benefit will be computed and presented in connection with the financial reporting recognition of a gain on a bargain purchase.

However, IAS 12 states that if the carrying amount of goodwill under a business combination is less than its tax base, a deferred tax asset should be recognised. This will be in jurisdictions where future tax deductions are available for goodwill. The deferred tax assets will only be recognised to the extent that it is probable that future taxable profits will be available to utilise the deduction.

Initial recognition exemption

No deferred tax liability or asset is recognised on the initial recognition of an asset or liability that is not part of a business combination, and at the time of the transaction affects neither accounting profit nor taxable profits. IAS 12, for example, states that an asset which is not depreciated for tax purposes will be exempt under this initial recognition exemption, provided that any capital gain or loss on the disposal of the asset will also be exempt for tax purposes.

In some tax jurisdictions, the costs of certain assets are never deductible in computing taxable profit. For accounting purposes such assets may be subjected to depreciation or amortisation. Thus, the asset in question has a differing accounting base than tax base and this results in a temporary difference. Similarly, certain liabilities may not be recognised for tax purposes resulting in a temporary difference. While IAS 12 accepts that these represent temporary differences, a decision was made not to permit recognition of deferred tax on these. The reason given is that the new result would be to "gross up" the recorded amount of the asset or liability to offset the recorded deferred tax liability or benefit, and this would make the financial statements "less transparent." It could also be argued that when an asset has, as one of its attributes, non-deductibility for tax purposes, the price paid for this asset would have been affected accordingly, so that any such "gross-up" would cause the asset to be reported at an amount in excess of fair value.

Basic example of initial recognition

Johnson PLC purchases an intangible asset from Peters PLC. Johnson will not be entitled to any tax deductions on the intangible asset. The asset was purchased for €1,000,000.

On day one, the temporary difference would be as follows:

Carrying value	€1,000,000
Tax base	0
Temporary difference	**1,000,000**
Tax rate	20%
Deferred tax	200,000

Without this exemption, the journal entries on day one would be as follows:

Intangible asset	€1,200,000	
Bank		€1,000,000
Deferred tax liability		200,000

As a result, the carrying value of the asset would also now be €1,200,000 and deferred tax would again be calculated to incorporate the increase in the asset's carrying value. This is a circular calculation which would eventually result in a carrying amount much higher than the purchase price. The initial recognition exemption criterion therefore requires no deferred tax to be recognised in this example.

Identification of Unused Tax Losses or Tax Credits

Unused tax losses or unused tax credits must be identified to determine whether deferred tax assets should be recognised in such transactions. Deferred tax assets are recognised for these amounts if they are regarded to be probable.

Calculation and Measurement of Deferred Tax Assets and Liabilities

The procedure to compute the gross deferred tax provision (i.e., before addressing whether the deferred tax asset is likely to be realised and therefore should be recognised) after exempt temporary differences and unused tax losses and tax credits are identified is as follows:

1. Segregate the temporary differences into those that are taxable and those that are deductible. This step is necessary because under IAS 12 only those deferred tax assets that are likely to be realised are recognised, whereas all deferred tax liabilities are recognised in full.
2. Accumulate information about the *deductible* temporary differences, particularly the net operating loss and credit carryforwards that have expiration dates or other types of limitations.
3. Measure the tax effect of aggregate *taxable* temporary differences by applying the appropriate expected tax rates (federal plus any state, local and foreign rates that are applicable under the circumstances).
4. Similarly, measure the tax effects of *deductible* temporary differences, including net operating loss carryforwards.

It should be emphasised that separate computations should be made for each tax jurisdiction, since in assessing the propriety of recording the tax effects of deductible temporary differences it is necessary to consider the entity's ability to absorb deferred tax assets against tax liabilities. Inasmuch as assets receivable from one tax jurisdiction will not reduce taxes payable to another jurisdiction, separate calculations will be needed. Also, for purposes of statement of financial position presentation (discussed below in detail), the offsetting of deferred tax assets and liabilities may be permissible only within jurisdictions, since there may not be a legal right to offset obligations due to and from different taxing authorities. Similarly, separate computations should be made for each taxpaying component of the business. Thus, if a parent company and its subsidiaries are consolidated for financial reporting purposes but file separate tax returns, the reporting entity comprises a number of components, and the tax benefits of any one will be unavailable to reduce the tax obligations of the others.

The principles set forth above are illustrated by the following examples.

Basic example of the computation of deferred tax liability and asset

Assume that Noori Company has pre-tax financial income of €250,000 in 20XX-1, a total of €28,000 of taxable temporary differences and a total of €8,000 of deductible temporary differences. Noori has no operating loss or tax credit carryforwards. The tax rate is a flat (i.e., not graduated) 40%. Also assume that there were no deferred tax liabilities or assets in prior years.

Taxable income is computed as follows:

Pre-tax financial income	€250,000	
Taxable temporary differences	(€28,000)	
Deductible temporary differences	€8,000	
Taxable income	**€230,000**	
The journal entry to record required amounts is:		
Current income tax expense	€92,000	
Deferred tax asset	€3,200	
Income tax expense—deferred	€8,000	
Deferred tax liability		€11,200
Income taxes currently payable		€92,000

Current income tax expense and income taxes currently payable are each computed as taxable income times the current rate (€230,000 × 40%). The deferred tax asset of €3,200 represents 40% of deductible temporary differences of €8,000. The deferred tax liability of €11,200 is calculated as 40% of taxable temporary differences of €28,000. The deferred tax expense of €8,000 is the *net* of the deferred tax liability of €11,200 and the deferred tax asset of €3,200.

In 20XX, Noori Company has pre-tax financial income of €450,000, aggregate taxable and deductible temporary differences are €75,000 and €36,000, respectively, and the tax rate remains a flat 40%. Taxable income is €411,000, computed as pre-tax financial income of €450,000 minus taxable differences of €75,000 plus deductible differences of €36,000. Current income tax expense and income taxes currently payable each are €164,400 (€411,000 × 40%).

Deferred amounts are calculated as follows:

	Deferred tax liability	*Deferred tax asset*	*Deferred tax expense*
Required balance at 12/31/XX			
€75,000 × 40%	€30,000		–
€36,000 × 40%		€14,400	–
Balances at 12/31/XX-1	€11,200	€3,200	–
Adjustment required	**€18,800**	**€11,200**	**€7,600**

The journal entry to record the deferred amounts is:

Deferred tax asset	€11,200	
Income tax expense—deferred	€7,600	
Deferred tax liability		€18,800

Because the *increase* in the liability in 20XX is larger (by €7,600) than the increase in the asset for that year, the result is a deferred tax *expense* for 20XX.

Limitation on the Recognition of Deferred Tax Assets

Although the case for presentation in the financial statements of any amount computed for deferred tax liabilities is clear, it can be argued that deferred tax assets should be included in the statement of financial position only if they are, in fact, very likely to be recovered in future periods. Since recoverability will almost certainly be dependent on the future profitability of the reporting entity, it may become necessary to ascertain the likelihood that the enterprise will be profitable.

Under IAS 12, deferred tax assets resulting from temporary differences, tax loss carryforwards and tax credits carryforwards are to be given recognition only if realisation is deemed to be *probable*. The standard establishes that:

1. It is *probable* that future taxable profit will be available against which a deferred tax asset arising from a deductible temporary difference can be utilised when there are sufficient taxable temporary differences relating to the same taxation authority which will reverse either:
   a. In the same period as the reversal of the deductible temporary difference; or
   b. In periods into which the deferred tax asset can be carried back or forward; or
2. If there are insufficient taxable temporary differences relating to the same taxation authority, it is probable that the enterprise will have taxable profits in the same period as the reversal of the deductible temporary difference or in periods to which the deferred tax can be carried back or forward, or there are tax-planning opportunities available to the enterprise that will create taxable profit in appropriate periods.

When an entity assesses whether taxable profits are probable, it must consider the effect of any tax law restrictions on the sources of taxable profits. A deferred tax asset is then assessed in combination only with other deferred tax assets that are also restricted.

There necessarily will be an element of judgement in making an assessment about how probable the realisation of the deferred tax asset is, for those circumstances in which there is not an existing balance of deferred tax liability equal to or greater than the amount of the deferred tax asset. If it cannot be concluded that realisation is probable, the deferred tax asset is not recognised.

As a practical matter, there are a number of positive and negative factors which may be evaluated in reaching a conclusion as to amount of the deferred tax asset to be recognised. *Positive factors* (those suggesting that the full amount of the deferred tax asset associated with the gross temporary difference should be recorded) might include:

1. Evidence of sufficient future taxable income, exclusive of reversing temporary differences and carryforwards, to realise the benefit of the deferred tax asset.
2. Evidence of sufficient future taxable income arising from the reversals of existing taxable temporary differences (deferred tax liabilities) to realise the benefit of the tax asset.
3. Evidence of sufficient taxable income in prior year(s) available for realisation of an operating loss carryback under existing statutory limitations.
4. Evidence of the existence of prudent, feasible tax planning strategies under management control that, if implemented, would permit the realisation of the tax asset. These are discussed in greater detail below.
5. An excess of appreciated asset values over their tax bases, in an amount sufficient to realise the deferred tax asset. This can be thought of as a subset of the tax strategies idea, since a sale or sale/leaseback of appreciated property is one rather obvious tax-planning strategy to salvage a deferred tax benefit that might otherwise expire unused.

6. A strong earnings history exclusive of the loss that created the deferred tax asset. This would, under many circumstances, suggest that future profitability is likely and therefore that realisation of deferred tax assets is probable.

Although the foregoing may suggest that the reporting entity will be able to realise the benefits of the deductible temporary differences outstanding as of the date of the statement of financial position, certain *negative factors* should also be considered in determining whether realisation of the full amount of the deferred tax benefit is probable under the circumstances. These factors could include:

1. A cumulative recent history of accounting losses. Depending on extent and length of time over which losses were experienced, this could reduce the assessment of likelihood of realisation below the important "probable" threshold.
2. A history of operating losses or of tax operating loss or credit carryforwards that have expired unused.
3. Losses that are anticipated in the near future years, despite a history of profitable operations.

Thus, the process of determining how much of the computed gross deferred tax benefit should be recognised involves the weighing of both positive and negative factors to determine whether, based on the preponderance of available evidence, it is probable that the deferred tax asset will be realised. IAS 12 notes that a history of unused tax losses should be considered "strong evidence" that future taxable profits might prove elusive. In such cases, it would be expected that primary reliance would be placed on the existence of taxable temporary differences that, upon reversal, would provide taxable income to absorb the deferred tax benefits that are candidates for recognition in the financial statements. In the absence of those taxable temporary differences, recognition would be much more difficult.

The estimation of probable future taxable profit may include the recovery of some of an entity's assets for more than their carrying amount if there is sufficient evidence that it is probable that the entity will achieve this. For example, when an asset is measured at fair value, the entity shall consider whether there is sufficient evidence to conclude that it is probable that the entity will recover the asset for more than its carrying amount.

Example

To illustrate this computation in a more specific fact situation, assume the following facts:

1. Malpasa Corporation reports deferred tax under IAS 12. As of the December 31, 20XX statement of financial position, Malpasa has taxable temporary differences of €85,000 relating to depreciation, deductible temporary differences of €12,000 relating to deferred compensation arrangements, a net operating loss carryforward (which arose in 20XX-1) of €40,000 and a capital loss carryover of €10,000. Note that capital losses can only be offset against capital gains (not ordinary income) but may be carried forward until used.
2. Malpasa's expected tax rate for future years is 40% for ordinary income, and 25% for net long-term capital gains.

The first steps are to compute the required balances of the deferred tax asset and liability accounts, without consideration of whether the tax asset would be probable of realisation. The computations would proceed as follows:

Deferred tax liability	
Taxable temporary difference (depreciation)	€85,000
Effective tax rate	×40%
Required balance	**€34,000**
Deferred tax asset	
Deductible temporary differences	€12,000
Deferred compensation	€40,000
Net operating loss	€52,000
Effective tax rate	× 40%
Required balance (a)	**€20,800**
Capital loss	€10,000
Effective tax rate	×25%
Required balance (b)	**€2,500**
Total deferred tax asset	
Ordinary (a)	€20,800
Capital (b)	€2,500
Total required balance	**€23,300**

The next step would be to consider whether realisation of the deferred tax asset is probable. Malpasa management must evaluate both positive and negative evidence to determine this matter. Assume now that management identifies the following factors that may be relevant:

1. Before the net operating loss deduction, Malpasa reported taxable income of €5,000 in 20XX. Management believes that taxable income in future years, apart from net operating loss deductions, should continue at about the same level experienced in 20XX.
2. The taxable temporary differences are not expected to reverse in the foreseeable future.
3. The capital loss arose in connection with a transaction of a type that is unlikely to recur. The company does not generally engage in activities that have the potential to result in capital gains or losses.
4. Management estimates that certain productive assets have a fair value exceeding their respective tax bases by about €30,000. The entire gain, if realised for tax purposes, would be a recapture of depreciation previously taken. Since the current plans call for a substantial upgrading of the company's plant assets, management feels that it could easily accelerate those actions to realise taxable gains, should it be desirable to do so for tax-planning purposes.

Based on the foregoing information, Malpasa Corporation management concludes that a €2,500 adjustment to deferred tax assets is required. The reasoning is as follows:

1. There will be some taxable operating income generated in future years (€5,000 annually, based on the earnings experienced in 20XX), which will absorb a modest portion of the reversal of the deductible temporary difference (€12,000) and net operating loss carryforward (€40,000) existing at year-end 20XX.
2. More important, the feasible tax planning strategy of accelerating the taxable gain relating to appreciated assets (€30,000) would certainly be sufficient, in conjunction with operating income over several years, to permit Malpasa to realise the tax benefits of the deductible temporary difference and net operating loss carryover.

3. However, since capital loss carryovers are only usable to offset future capital gains and Malpasa management is unable to project future realisation of capital gains, the associated tax benefit accrued (€2,500) will probably not be realised, and thus cannot be recognised.

Based on this analysis, deferred tax benefits in the amount of €20,800 should be recognised.

Future temporary differences as a source for taxable profit to offset deductible differences

In some instances, an entity may have deferred tax assets that will be realisable when future tax deductions are taken, but it cannot be concluded that there will be sufficient taxable profits to absorb these future deductions. However, the enterprise can reasonably predict that if it continues as a going concern, it will generate other temporary differences such that taxable (if not book) profits will be created. It has indeed been argued that the going concern assumption underlying much of accounting theory is sufficient rationale for the recognition of deferred tax assets in such circumstances.

However, IAS 12 makes it clear that this is not valid reasoning. The new taxable temporary differences anticipated for future periods will themselves reverse in even later periods; these cannot do "double duty" by also being projected to be available to absorb currently existing deductible temporary differences. Thus, in evaluating whether realisation of currently outstanding deferred tax benefits is probable, it is appropriate to consider the currently outstanding taxable temporary differences, but not taxable temporary differences that are projected to be created in later periods.

Tax-planning opportunities that will help realise deferred tax assets

When an entity has deductible temporary differences and taxable temporary differences pertaining to the same tax jurisdiction, there is a presumption that realisation of the relevant deferred tax assets is probable, since the relevant deferred tax liabilities should be available to offset these. However, before concluding that this is valid, it will be necessary to consider further the *timing* of the two sets of reversals. If the deductible temporary differences will reverse, say, in the very near term, and the taxable differences will not reverse for many years, it is a matter for concern that the tax benefits created by the former occurrence may expire unused prior to the latter event occurring. Thus, when the existence of deferred tax obligations serves as the logical basis for the recognition of deferred tax assets, it is also necessary to consider whether, under pertinent tax regulations, the benefit carryforward period is sufficient to assure that the benefit will not be lost to the reporting enterprise.

For example, if the deductible temporary difference is projected to reverse in two years but the taxable temporary difference is not anticipated to occur for another 10 years, and the tax jurisdiction in question offers only a five-year tax loss carryforward, then (absent other facts suggesting that the tax benefit is probable of realisation) the deferred tax benefit could not be given recognition under IAS 12.

However, the entity might have certain tax-planning opportunities available to it, such that the pattern of taxable profits could be altered to make the deferred tax benefit, which might otherwise be lost, probable of realisation. For example, again depending on the rules of the salient tax jurisdiction, an election might be made to tax interest income on an accrual rather than on a cash received basis, which might accelerate income recognition such that it would be available to offset or absorb the deductible temporary differences. Also, claimed tax deductions might be deferred to later periods, similarly boosting taxable profits in the short term.

More subtly, a reporting entity may have certain assets, such as buildings, which have appreciated in value. It is entirely feasible, in many situations, for an enterprise to take certain steps, such as selling the building to realise the taxable gain thereon and then either leasing back the premises or acquiring another suitable building, to salvage the tax deduction that would otherwise be lost to it due to the expiration of a loss carryforward period. If such a strategy is deemed to be reasonably available, even if the entity does not expect to have to implement it (for example, because it expects other taxable temporary differences to be originated in the interim), it may be used to justify recognition of the deferred tax benefits.

Consider the following example of how an available tax planning strategy might be used to support recognition of a deferred tax asset that otherwise might have to go unrecognised.

Example of the impact of a qualifying tax strategy

Assume that Kirloski Company has a €180,000 operating loss carryforward as of December 31, 20XX-1, scheduled to expire at the end of the following year. Taxable temporary differences of €240,000 exist that are expected to reverse in approximately equal amounts of €80,000 in 20XX, 20XX+1 and 20XX+2. Kirloski Company estimates that taxable income for 20XX (exclusive of the reversal of existing temporary differences and the operating loss carryforward) will be €20,000. Kirloski Company expects to implement a qualifying tax planning strategy that will accelerate the total of €240,000 of taxable temporary differences to 20XX. Expenses to implement the strategy are estimated to approximate €30,000. The applicable expected tax rate is 40%.

In the absence of the tax planning strategy, €100,000 of the operating loss carryforward could be realised in 20XX based on estimated taxable income of €20,000 plus €80,000 of the reversal of taxable temporary differences. Thus, €80,000 would expire unused at the end of 20XX and the net amount of the deferred tax asset at 12/31/XX would be recognised at €40,000, computed as €72,000 (= €180,000 × 40%) minus the valuation allowance of €32,000 (€80,000 × 40%).

However, by implementing the tax planning strategy, the deferred tax asset is calculated as follows:

Taxable income for 20XX

Expected amount without reversal of taxable temporary differences	€20,000
Reversal of taxable temporary differences due to tax planning strategy, net of costs	210,000
	230,000
Operating loss to be carried forward	(180,000)
Operating loss expiring unused at 12/31/XX	€ 0

The deferred tax asset to be recorded at 12/31/15 is €54,000. This is computed as follows:

Full benefit of tax loss carryforward	
€180,000 × 40% =	€72,000
Less: Net-of-tax effect of anticipated expenses related to implementation of the strategy	
€30,000 − (€30,000 × 40%) =	18,000
Net	**€54,000**

Kirloski Company will also recognise a deferred tax liability of €96,000 at the end of 20XX (40% of the taxable temporary differences of €240,000).

Subsequently revised expectations that a deferred tax benefit is recoverable

It may happen that, in a given reporting period, a deferred tax asset is deemed unlikely to be realised and accordingly is not recognised, but in a later reporting period the judgement is made that the amount is in fact recoverable. If this change in expectation occurs, the deferred tax asset previously not recognised will now be recorded. This does not constitute a prior period adjustment because no accounting error occurred. Rather, this is a change in estimate and is to be included in current earnings. Thus, the tax provision in the period when the estimate is revised will be affected.

Similarly, if a deferred tax benefit provision is made in a given reporting period, but later events suggest that the amount is, in whole or in part, not probable of being recovered, the provision should be partially or completely reversed. Again, this adjustment will be included in the tax provision in the period in which the estimate is altered, since it is a change in an accounting estimate. Under either scenario the footnotes to the financial statements will need to provide sufficient information for the users to make meaningful interpretations, since the amount reported as tax expense will seemingly bear an unusual relationship to the reported pre-tax accounting profit for the period.

If the deferred tax provision in a given period is misstated due to a clerical error, such as miscalculation of the effective expected tax rate, this would constitute an accounting error, and this must be accounted for according to IAS 8's provisions; this standard requires restatement of prior period financial statements and does not permit adjusting opening retained earnings for the effect of the error. Errors are thus distinguished from changes in accounting estimate, as the latter are accounted for prospectively, without restatement of prior period financial statements. Correction of accounting errors is discussed in Chapter 7.

Example of determining the extent to which the deferred tax asset is recovered

Assume that Zacharias Corporation has a deductible temporary difference of €60,000 at December 31, 20XX. The applicable tax rate is a flat 40%. Based on available evidence, management of Zacharias Corporation concludes that it is probable that all sources will not result in future taxable income sufficient to realise more than €15,000 (i.e., 25%) of the deductible temporary difference. Also, assume that there were no deferred tax assets in previous years and that prior years' taxable income was inconsequential.

At December 13, 20XX Zacharias Corporation records a deferred tax asset in the amount of €6,000 (= €60,000 × 25% × 40). The journal entry at 12/31/XX is:

Deferred tax asset	€6,000	
Income tax benefit—deferred		€6,000

The deferred income tax benefit of €6,000 represents the tax effect of that portion of the deferred tax asset (25%) that is probable of being realised.

EFFECT OF CHANGED CIRCUMSTANCES

The carrying amount of deferred tax assets or liabilities may change when there is no change in the amount of the related temporary differences. Examples are tax rate or tax law changes, reassessment of the recoverability of deferred tax assets and changes in the expected manner of recovery of an asset. These changes are normally recognised in profit or loss as discussed below.

Uncertainties over Income Tax Treatments

IFRIC 23, *Uncertainty over Income Tax Treatments*, was issued June 2017 to clarify how to apply the recognition and measurement requirements in IAS 12 when there is uncertainty over the income tax treatment. The IFRIC is effective for annual reporting periods beginning on or after January 1, 2019, and earlier application is permitted. The current or deferred tax asset or liability shall still be recognised and measured applying the requirements of IAS 12 regarding, for instance, taxable profit (tax loss), tax bases, unused tax losses, unused tax credits and tax rates.

Clarification of application

Uncertain tax treatments shall be considered separately or together (regarded as a group of uncertain tax treatments) based on which approach better predicts the resolution of the uncertainty by considering the following:

1. How the entity prepares its income tax filings and supports the tax treatments; or
2. How the entity expects the taxation authority to make its examination and resolve issues arising from that examination.

In the assessment it is assumed that a taxation authority will examine amounts it has a right to examine and have full knowledge of all related information when making those examinations. The entity then considers whether it is probable that a taxation authority will accept an uncertain tax treatment or not. When an entity concludes it is probable that the taxation authority will accept an uncertain tax treatment, the uncertainty is treated consistently with the tax treatment used or planned to be used in its income tax filings. However, when the entity concludes it is not probable that the taxation authority will accept an uncertain tax treatment, the entity shall reflect the effect of uncertainty for each uncertain tax treatment by using either of the following methods, depending on which of the two methods the entity expects to better predict the resolution of the uncertainty:

1. The most likely amount: the single most likely amount in a range of possible outcomes. The most likely amount normally predicts the resolution of the uncertainty better if the possible outcomes are binary or are concentrated on one value.
2. The expected value: the sum of the probability-weighted amounts in a range of possible outcomes. The expected value normally predicts the resolution of the uncertainty better if there is a range of possible outcomes that are neither binary nor concentrated on one value.

If an uncertain tax treatment affects both current tax and deferred tax, consistent judgements and estimates should be made for both. These judgements and estimates are reconsidered when the facts and circumstances on which the judgement or estimate was based change or as a result of new information that becomes available. For example, a change in facts and circumstances might change an entity's conclusions about the acceptability of a tax treatment or the entity's estimate of the effect of uncertainty, or both. A particular event might result in the reassessment of a judgement or estimate made for one tax treatment but not another, if those tax treatments are subject to different tax laws.

In making the assessment an entity shall assess the relevance and effect of a change in facts and circumstances or of new information in the context of applicable tax laws by considering, for instance, the following:

1. Examinations or actions by a taxation authority. For example:
   a. Agreement or disagreement by the taxation authority with the tax treatment or a similar tax treatment used by the entity;
   b. Information that the taxation authority has agreed or disagreed with a similar tax treatment used by another entity; and
   c. Information about the amount received or paid to settle a similar tax treatment.
2. Changes in rules established by a taxation authority.
3. The expiry of a taxation authority's right to examine or re-examine a tax treatment.

The absence of agreement or disagreement by a taxation authority with a tax treatment, in isolation, is unlikely to constitute a change in facts and circumstances or new information that affects the judgements and estimates.

Disclosure

IAS 8 is used to reflect the effect of a change in facts and circumstances or of new information as a change in accounting estimate (refer to Chapter 7) and IAS 10 is used to determine whether a change that occurs after the reporting period is an adjusting or non-adjusting event (refer to Chapter 18).

For uncertainty income tax treatments, an entity shall determine whether to disclose:

1. Judgements made in determining the uncertainty in terms of IAS 1 (refer to Chapter 3); and
2. Information about the assumptions and estimates made in determining the uncertainty in terms of IAS 1 (refer to Chapter 3).

If an entity concludes it is probable that a taxation authority will accept an uncertain tax treatment, the entity shall determine whether to disclose the potential effect of the uncertainty as a tax-related contingency.

Effect of Tax Law Changes on Previously Recorded Deferred Tax Assets and Liabilities

The statement of financial position-oriented measurement approach of IAS 12 necessitates the revaluation of the deferred tax asset and liability balances at each year-end. Although IAS 12 does not directly address the question of changes to tax rates or other provisions of the tax law (e.g., deductibility of items), which may be enacted that will affect the recoverability of future deferred tax assets or liabilities, the effect of these changes should be reflected in the year-end deferred tax accounts in the period the changes are enacted. The offsetting adjustments should be made through the current period tax provision.

When revised tax rates are enacted, they may affect not only the unreversed effects of items which were originally reported in the continuing operations section of the statement of income (under revised IAS 1, the income statement section of a combined statement of profit or loss and other comprehensive income), but also the unreversed effects of items first presented as other comprehensive income. Although it might be conceptually superior to report the effects of tax law changes on such unreversed temporary differences in these same statements of profit or loss and other comprehensive income captions, as a practical matter the complexities of identifying the diverse treatments of these originating transactions or events would make such an approach unworkable. Accordingly, remeasurements of the effects of tax law changes should generally be reported in the tax provision associated with continuing operations.

Example of the computation of a deferred tax asset with a change in rates

Assume that the Fanuzzi Company has €80,000 of deductible temporary differences at the end of 20XX, which are expected to result in tax deductions of approximately €40,000 each in 20XX+1 and thereafter. Enacted tax rates are 50% for the years 20XX-4–20XX, and 40% for 20XX+1 and thereafter.

The deferred tax asset is computed at December 31, 20XX, under each of the following independent assumptions:

1. If Fanuzzi Company expects to offset the deductible temporary differences against taxable income in the years 20XX+1 and thereafter, the deferred tax asset is €32,000 (€80,000 × 40%).
2. If Fanuzzi Company expects to realise a tax benefit for the deductible temporary differences of an assessed loss, the deferred tax asset is €40,000 (= €80,000 × 50%).

Changes in tax law may affect rates and may also affect the taxability or deductibility of income or expense items. While the latter type of change occurs infrequently, the impact is similar to the more common tax rate changes.

Example of effect of change in tax law

Leipzig Corporation has, at December 31, 20XX-1, gross receivables of €12,000,000 and an allowance for bad debts in the amount of €600,000. Also assume that expected future taxes will be at a 40% rate. Effective January 1, 20XX, the tax law is revised to eliminate deductions for accrued bad debts, with existing allowances required to be taken into income over three years (a three-year spread). A statement of financial position of Leipzig Corporation prepared on January 1, 20XX would report a deferred tax benefit in the amount of €240,000 (i.e., €600,000 × 40%, which is the tax effect of future deductions to be taken when specific receivables are written off and bad debts are incurred for tax purposes); a current tax liability of €80,000 (one-third of the tax obligation); and a non-current tax liability of €160,000 (two-thirds of the tax obligation). Under the requirements of IAS 12, the deferred tax benefit must be entirely reported as non-current in classified statements of financial position, inasmuch as no deferred tax benefits or obligations can be shown as current.

Reporting the Effect of Tax Status Changes

Changes in the tax status of the reporting entity should be reported in a manner that is entirely analogous to the reporting of enacted tax law changes. When the tax status change becomes effective, the consequent adjustments to deferred tax assets and liabilities are reported in current tax expense as part of the tax provision relating to continuing operations.

The most commonly encountered changes in status are those attendant to an election, where permitted, to be taxed as a partnership or other flow-through enterprise. (This means that the corporation will not be treated as a taxable entity but rather as an enterprise that "flows through" its taxable income to the owners on a current basis. This favourable tax treatment is available to encourage small businesses, and often will be limited to entities having sales revenue under a particular threshold level, or to entities having no more than a maximum number of shareholders.) Enterprises subject to such optional tax treatment may also request that a previous election be terminated. When a previously taxable corporation becomes a non-taxed corporation, the stockholders become personally liable for taxes on the company's earnings, whether the earnings are distributed to them or not (similar to the relationship among a partnership and its partners).

As issued, IAS 12 did not explicitly address the matter of reporting the effects of a change in tax status, although the appropriate treatment was quite obvious given the underlying concepts of that standard. This ambiguity was subsequently resolved by the issuance of SIC 25, which stipulates that in most cases the current and deferred tax consequences of the change in tax status should be included in net profit or loss for the period in which the change in status occurs. The tax effects of a change in status are included in results of operations because a change in a reporting entity's tax status (or that of its shareholders) does not give rise to increases or decreases in the pre-tax amounts recognised directly in equity.

The exception to the foregoing general rule arises in connection with those tax consequences which relate to transactions and events that result, in the same or a different period, in a direct credit or charge to the recognised amount of equity. For example, an event that is recognised directly in equity is a change in the carrying amount of property, plant or equipment revalued under IAS 16. Those tax consequences that relate to change in the recognised amount of equity, in the same or a different period (not included in net profit or loss), should be charged or credited directly to equity.

The most common situation giving rise to a change in tax status would be the election by a corporation, in those jurisdictions where it is permitted to do so, to be taxed as a partnership, trust or other flow-through entity. If a corporation having a net deferred tax liability elects non-taxed status, the deferred taxes will be eliminated through a credit to current period earnings. That is because what had been an obligation of the corporation has been eliminated (by being accepted directly by the shareholders, typically); a debt thus removed constitutes earnings for the formerly obligated party.

Similarly, if a previously non-taxed corporation becomes a taxable entity, the effect is to assume a net tax benefit or obligation for unreversed temporary differences existing at the date the change becomes effective. Accordingly, the financial statements for the period of such a change will report the effects of the event in the current tax provision. If the entity had at that date many taxable temporary differences as yet unreversed, it would report a large tax expense in that period. Conversely, if it had a large quantity of unreversed deductible temporary differences, a substantial deferred tax benefit (if recoverable) would need to be recorded, with a concomitant credit to the current period's tax provision in the statement of comprehensive income. Whether eliminating an existing deferred tax balance or recording an initial deferred tax asset or liability, the income tax note to the financial statements will need to fully explain the nature of the events that transpired.

In some jurisdictions, non-taxed corporation elections are automatically effective when filed. In such a case, if a reporting entity makes an election before the end of the current fiscal year, it is logical that the effects be reported in current year income to become effective at the start of the following period. For example, an election filed in December 20XX-1 would be reported in the 20XX-1 financial statements to become effective at the beginning of the company's next fiscal year, January 1, 20XX. No deferred tax assets or liabilities would appear on the December 31, 20XX-1 statement of financial position, and the tax provision for the year then ended would include the effects of any reversals that had previously been recorded. Practice varies, however, and in some instances the effect of the elimination of the deferred tax assets and liabilities would be reported in the year the election actually becomes effective.

Implications of Changes in Tax Rates and Status Made in Interim Periods

Tax rate changes may occur during an interim reporting period, either because a tax law change mandated a midyear effective date, or because tax law changes were effective at year-end, but the reporting entity has adopted a fiscal year-end other than the natural year (December 31).

The fact that income taxes are assessed annually is the primary reason for concluding that taxes are to be accrued based on an entity's estimated average annual effective tax rate for the full fiscal year. If rate changes have been enacted to take effect later in the fiscal year, the expected effective rate should take into account the rate changes as well as the anticipated pattern of earnings to be experienced over the course of the year. Thus, the rate to be applied to interim period earnings (or losses, as discussed further below) will take into account the expected level of earnings for the entire forthcoming year, as well as the effect of enacted (or substantially enacted) changes in the tax rates to become operative later in the fiscal year. In other words, and as expressed by IAS 34, the estimated average annual rate would "reflect a blend of the progressive tax rate structure expected to be applicable to the full year's earnings enacted or substantially enacted changes in the income tax rates scheduled to take effect later in the financial year."

While the principle espoused by IAS 34 is both clear and logical, a number of practical issues can arise. The standard does address in detail the various computational aspects of an effective interim period tax rate, some of which are summarised in the following paragraphs.

Many modern business entities operate in numerous nations or states and therefore are subject to a multiplicity of taxing jurisdictions. In some instances, the amount of income subject to tax will vary from one jurisdiction to the next, since the tax laws in different jurisdictions will include and exclude disparate items of income or expense from the tax base. For example, interest earned on government-issued bonds may be exempted from tax by the jurisdiction that issued them but be defined as fully taxable by other tax jurisdictions the entity is subject to. To the extent feasible, the appropriate estimated average annual effective tax rate should be separately ascertained for each taxing jurisdiction and applied individually to the interim period pre-tax income of each jurisdiction, so that the most accurate estimate of income taxes can be developed at each interim reporting date. In general, an overall estimated effective tax rate will not be as satisfactory for this purpose as would a more carefully constructed set of estimated rates, since the pattern of taxable and deductible items will fluctuate from one period to the next.

Similarly, if the tax law prescribes different income tax rates for different categories of income, then to the extent practicable, a separate effective tax rate should be applied to each category of interim period pre-tax income. IAS 34, while mandating such detailed rules of computing and applying tax rates across jurisdictions or across categories of income, nonetheless recognised that such a degree of precision may not be achievable in all cases. Thus, IAS 34 allows usage of a weighted-average of rates across jurisdictions or across categories of income provided it is a reasonable approximation of the effect of using more specific rates.

In computing an expected effective tax rate given for a tax jurisdiction, all relevant features of the tax regulations should be taken into account. Jurisdictions may provide for tax credits based on new investment in plant and machinery, relocation of facilities to backward or underdeveloped areas, research and development expenditures, levels of export sales, and so forth, and the expected credits against the tax for the full year should be given consideration in the determination of an expected effective tax rate. Thus, the tax effect of new investment in plant and machinery, when the local taxing body offers an investment credit for qualifying investment in tangible productive assets, will be reflected in those interim periods of the fiscal year in which the new investment occurs (assuming it can be forecast to occur later in a given fiscal year), and not merely in the period in which the new investment occurs. This is consistent with the underlying concept that taxes are strictly an annual phenomenon, but it is at variance with the purely discrete view of interim financial reporting.

IAS 34 notes that, although tax credits and similar modifying elements are to be taken into account in developing the expected effective tax rate to apply to interim earnings, tax benefits that will relate to onetime events are to be reflected from the interim period when those events take place. This is perhaps most likely to be encountered in the context of capital gains taxes incurred in connection with occasional disposals of investments and other capital assets; since it is not feasible to project the timing of such transactions over the course of a year, the tax effects should be recognised only as the underlying events actually do transpire.

While in most cases tax credits are to be handled as suggested in the foregoing paragraphs, in some jurisdictions tax credits, particularly those that relate to export revenue or capital expenditures, are in effect government grants. Accounting for government grants is set forth in IAS 20; in brief, grants are recognised in income over the period necessary to properly match them to the costs which the grants are intended to offset or defray. Thus, compliance with both IAS 20 and IAS 34 would require that tax credits be carefully analysed to identify those which are in substance grants, and that credits are accounted for consistent with their true natures.

When an interim period loss gives rise to a tax loss carryback, it should be fully reflected in that interim period. Similarly, if a loss in an interim period produces a tax loss carryforward, it should be recognised immediately, but only if the criteria set forth in IAS 12 are met. Specifically, it must be deemed probable that the benefits will be realisable before the loss benefits can be given formal recognition in the financial statements. In the case of interim period losses, it may be necessary to assess not only whether the enterprise will be profitable enough in future fiscal years to utilise the tax benefits associated with the loss, but furthermore, whether interim periods later in the same year will provide earnings of sufficient magnitude to absorb the losses of the current period.

IAS 12 provides that changes in expectations regarding the recoverability of benefits related to net operating loss carryforwards should be reflected currently in tax expense. Similarly, if a net operating loss carryforward benefit is not deemed probable of being realised until the interim (or annual) period when it in fact becomes realised, the tax effect will be included in tax expense of that period. Appropriate explanatory material must be included in the notes to the financial statements, even on an interim basis, to provide users with an understanding of the unusual relationship reported between pre-tax accounting income and the provision for income taxes.

SPECIFIC TRANSACTIONS

Income Tax Consequences of Dividends Paid

Dividends are defined in IFRS 9 as "distributions of profits to holders of equity instruments in proportion to their holdings of a particular class of capital." IAS 12 clarifies that the income tax consequences of dividends are recognised when the corresponding liability to pay a dividend is recognised. Therefore, if dividends are declared before the end of the year, but are payable after year-end, the dividends become a legal liability of the reporting entity and taxes should be computed at the appropriate rate on the amount thus declared. If the dividend is declared after year-end but before the financial statements are issued, a liability cannot be recognised on the statement of financial position at year-end, and thus the tax effect related thereto also cannot be recognised. Disclosure would be made, however, of this event after the reporting date.

An entity shall recognise the income tax consequences of dividends in profit or loss, other comprehensive income or equity according to where the entity originally recognised those past transactions or events that create the dividend. The reason is that the income tax consequences of dividends are linked more directly to past transactions or events that generated distributable profits than to distributions to owners.

To illustrate the foregoing, consider the following example:

Amir Corporation operates in a jurisdiction where income taxes are payable at a higher rate on undistributed profits than on distributed earnings. For the year 20XX-1, the company's taxable income is €150,000. Amir also has net taxable temporary differences amounting to €50,000 for the year, thus creating the need for a deferred tax provision. The tax rate on distributed profits is 25%, and the rate on undistributed profits is 40%; the difference is refundable if profits are later distributed. As of the date of the statement of financial position no liability for dividends proposed or declared has been reflected on the statement of financial position. On March 31, 20XX, however, the company distributes dividends of €50,000.

The tax consequences of dividends on undistributed profits, current and deferred taxes for the year 20XX-1, and the recovery of 20XX-1 income taxes when dividends are subsequently declared, would be as follows:

1. Amir Corporation recognises a current tax liability and a current tax expense for 20XX-1 of €150,000 × 40% = €60,000;
2. No asset is recognised for the amount that will be (potentially) recoverable when dividends are distributed;
3. Deferred tax liability and deferred tax expense for 20XX-1 would be €50,000 × 40% = €20,000; and
4. In the following year (20XX) when the company recognises dividends of €50,000, the company will also recognise the recovery of income taxes of €50,000 × (40% − 25%) = €7,500 as a current tax asset and a reduction of the current income tax expense.

The only exception to the foregoing accounting for tax effects of dividends that are subject to differential tax rates arises in the situation of a dividend-paying corporation which is required to withhold taxes on the distribution and remit these to the taxing authorities. In general, withholding tax is offset against the amounts distributed to shareholders, and is later forwarded to the taxing bodies rather than to the shareholders, so that the total amount of the dividend declaration is not altered. However, if the corporation pays the tax in addition to the full amount of the dividend payments to shareholders, some might view this as a tax falling on the corporation and, accordingly, add this to the tax provision reported on the statement of comprehensive income. IAS 12, however, makes it clear that such an amount, if paid or payable to the taxing authorities, is to be charged to equity as part of the dividend declaration if it does not affect income taxes payable or recoverable by the enterprise in the same or a different period.

Finally, IAS 12 provides that disclosure will be required of the potential income tax consequences of dividends. The reporting enterprise should disclose the amounts of the potential income tax consequences that are practically determinable, and whether there are any potential income tax consequences not practically determinable.

Accounting for Business Combinations at the Acquisition Date

When assets and liabilities are valued at fair value, as required under IFRS 3, but the tax base is not adjusted (i.e., there is a carryforward basis for tax purposes), there will be differences between the tax and financial reporting bases of these assets and liabilities, which will constitute temporary differences. Deferred tax assets and liabilities need to be recognised for these differences as an adjustment to goodwill or the bargain purchase gain. The most common example of this is where taxes are calculated at a subsidiary level in a group, and when these items are consolidated into the group accounts, there are consolidation adjustments to the carrying amounts of the assets which result in additional temporary differences at group level.

The limitation on the recognition of deferred tax assets is also applicable to business combinations.

Example of temporary differences in business acquisition

An example, in the context of the business acquisition of Windlass Corp., follows:

1. The income tax rate is a flat 40%.
2. The acquisition of a business is effected at a cost of €500,000.
3. The fair values of assets acquired total €750,000.
4. The carryforward tax bases of assets acquired total €600,000.
5. The fair and carryforward tax bases of the liabilities assumed in the purchase are €250,000.
6. The difference between the tax and fair values of the assets acquired, €150,000, consists of taxable temporary differences of €200,000 and deductible temporary differences of €50,000.
7. There is no doubt as to the realisability of the deductible temporary differences in this case.

Based on the foregoing facts, allocation of the purchase price is as follows:

Gross purchase price	€500,000
Allocation to identifiable assets and (liabilities):	
Assets acquired	€ 750,000
Deferred tax asset (€50,000 × 40%)	€20,000
Liabilities acquired	(€250,000)
Deferred tax liability (€200,000 × 40%)	(€80,000)
Net of the above allocations	€440,000
Goodwill	**€60,000**

Accounting for Business Combinations after the Acquisition

Under the provisions of IAS 12, net deferred tax benefits are not to be carried forward as assets unless the deferred tax assets are deemed *probable* of being recovered. The assessment of this probability was discussed earlier in the chapter.

In the above example (Windlass Corp.), it was specified that all deductible temporary differences were fully recoverable, and therefore the deferred tax benefits associated with those temporary differences were recorded as of the acquisition date. In other situations, there may be substantial doubt concerning recoverability; that is, it may not be probable that the benefits will be realised. Accordingly, under IAS 12, the deferred tax asset would not be recognised at the date of the business acquisition. If so, the allocation of the purchase price would have to reflect that fact, and more of the purchase cost would be allocated to goodwill than would otherwise be the case.

If, at a later date, it is determined that some of or the entire deferred tax asset that was not recognised at the date of the acquisition is, in fact, probable of being ultimately realised, the effect of that re-evaluation will reduce the carrying amount of goodwill. If the carrying amount of goodwill is reduced to nil, any remaining deferred tax asset will be recognised in the tax expense in profit or loss. If a bargain purchase price gain was recognised initially, the deferred tax asset adjustment must be recorded in profit or loss.

Example of revising estimate of tax benefit recoverability in business combination

To illustrate this last concept, assume that a business acquisition occurs on January 1, 20XX-2, and that deferred tax assets of €100,000 are *not* recognised at that time, due to an assessment that recoverability is not probable. The unrecognised tax asset is implicitly allocated to goodwill during the purchase price assignment process. On January 1, 20XX, the likelihood of ultimate recoverability of the tax benefit is reassessed as being probable, with recoverability projected for later years. The balance of goodwill on January 1, 20XX, was €80,000. The entries at that date are as follows:

Deferred tax asset	€100,000	
Goodwill		€80,000
Profit and loss		20,000

A related issue is that the probability of recoverability of a pre-acquisition deferred tax asset of the acquirer could change due to the business combination. For instance, the acquirer has an unrecognised deferred tax loss that would in the future be recoverable from income receivable from the acquired subsidiary. The acquirer recognises the change in the deferred tax asset in the period of the acquisition but cannot include it in the accounting of the business combination, and therefore in the determining of the goodwill or bargain purchase gain of the business combination. This is because the unrecognised deferred tax is not a transaction of the acquiree.

Temporary Differences in Consolidated Financial Statements

Temporary differences in consolidated financial statements are determined by comparing the consolidated carrying values of assets and liabilities with the relevant tax base. The tax base is determined by reference to the applicable tax regime. If the entity is taxed on a group base, the tax base is the group tax base. However, if each entity in the group is taxed separately, the tax base is determined with reference to each individual entity. In the latter case, additional deferred tax can arise that is only recognised in the consolidated financial statements.

Assets Carried at Fair Value

IFRS allows certain assets to be recognised at fair value or at revalued amounts. If the revaluation or adjustment to the fair value affects the taxable profit immediately, the tax base is also adjusted and no deferred tax would be recognised. Examples include derivatives recognised at fair value for both accounting and tax purposes. However, if the revaluation or restatement to fair value does not affect the taxable profit immediately, deferred tax must be created on the revaluation. The tax base of the asset is not adjusted.

The difference between the adjusted carrying value and the tax base is a temporary difference. The normal principles regarding the recovery of the assets through use or sale will be applicable to determine the amount of the related deferred tax. It should be noted that IAS 12 has specific provisions relating to the recognition of deferred tax on revalued assets (under IAS 16) and investment properties at fair value (under IAS 40). For these assets, IAS 12 has a presumption that the assets will be recovered through sale. As a result, any deferred tax raised on the revalued or fair valued assets is done so at the rate applicable on sale. This presumption can be rebutted should the entity be able to prove that it consumes substantially all the asset through use, and that the asset is a depreciable asset, in which case it may use the use rate to calculate the deferred tax.

What this means in practice is that should an entity rebut the presumption, it would need to split the deferred tax into that relating to the land and that relating to the building. The deferred tax on the land will always be raised at the sale rate as it is not a depreciable asset, whereas the deferred tax relating to the building would be raised at the use rate. This split can prove difficult in practice, which is why most entities elect to use the sale rate for all temporary differences arising on revalued and fair valued buildings.

The example below adjusted from IAS 12 illustrates that a temporary difference should be recognised even if the fair value reduces below the carrying value.

Basic example of asset carried at fair value

John PLC purchases for €1,000 a debt instrument at the beginning of 20XX-1 with a nominal value of €1,000 payable on maturity in five years. The interest rate of 2% is payable at the end of each year. The effective interest rate is 2%. The debt instrument is measured at fair value.

At the end of 20XX, the fair value of the debt instrument has decreased to €918 as a result of an increase in market interest rates to 5%. It is probable that John PLC will collect all the contractual cash flows if it continues to hold the debt instrument.

Any gains (losses) on the debt instrument are taxable (deductible) only when realised. The gains (losses) arising on the sale or maturity of the debt instrument are calculated for tax purposes as the difference between the amount collected and the original cost of the debt instrument. Accordingly, the tax base of the debt instrument is its original cost.

The difference between the carrying amount of the debt instrument in John PLC's statement of financial position of €918 and its tax base of €1,000 gives rise to a deductible temporary difference of €82 at the end of 20XX, irrespective of whether John PLC expects to recover the carrying amount of the debt instrument by sale or by use, i.e., by holding it and collecting contractual cash flows, or a combination of both.

This is because deductible temporary differences are differences between the carrying amount of an asset or liability in the statement of financial position and its tax base that will result in amounts that are deductible in determining taxable profit (tax loss) of future periods, when the carrying amount of the asset or liability is recovered or settled. John PLC obtains a deduction equivalent to the tax base of the asset of €1,000 in determining taxable profit (tax loss) either on sale or on maturity.

Tax on Investments in Subsidiaries, Associates and Joint Ventures

In terms of the general rule, deferred tax should also be recognised on investments in subsidiaries, associates and joint ventures similar to other assets. In an important exception to the general rule, IAS 12 provides that when the parent, investor or joint venturer can prevent the taxable event from occurring, deferred taxes are not recognised. Specifically, under IAS 12, two conditions must *both* be satisfied to justify *not* reflecting deferred taxes in connection with the earnings of a subsidiary (a control situation), branches and associates (significant influence) and joint ventures. These are (1) that the parent, investor or venturer is able to control the timing of the reversal of the temporary difference and (2) it is probable that the difference will not reverse in the foreseeable future. Unless *both* conditions are met, the tax effects of these temporary differences must be given recognition.

When a parent company that has the ability to control the dividend and other policies of its subsidiary determines that dividends will not be declared, and thus that the undistributed profit of the subsidiary will not be taxed at the parent company level, no deferred tax liability is to be recognised. If this intention is later altered, the tax effect of this change in estimate would be reflected in the current period's tax provision.

On the other hand, an investor, even one having significant influence, cannot absolutely determine the associate's dividend policy. Accordingly, it has to be presumed that earnings will eventually be distributed and that these will create taxable income at the investor company level. Therefore, deferred tax liability must be provided for the reporting entity's share of all undistributed earnings of its associates for which it is accounting by the equity method, unless there is a binding agreement for the earnings of the investee not to be distributed within the foreseeable future.

In the case of joint ventures there are a wide range of possible relationships between the venturers, and in some cases the reporting entity has the ability to control the payment of dividends. As in the foregoing, if the reporting entity has the ability to exercise this level of control and it is probable that distributions will not be made within the foreseeable future, no deferred tax liability will be reported.

In all these various circumstances, it will be necessary to assess whether distributions within the foreseeable future are probable. The standard does not define "foreseeable future" and thus this will remain a matter of subjective judgement. The criteria of IAS 12, while subjective, are less ambiguous than under the original standard, which permitted non-recognition of deferred tax liability when it was "reasonable to assume that (the associate's) profits will not be distributed."

Example of tax allocation for investee and subsidiary income

To illustrate the application of these concepts, assume that Parent Company owns 30% of the outstanding ordinary shares of an Associate Company and 70% of the ordinary shares of a Subsidiary Company. Additional data for the year 20XX are as follows:

	Associate company	*Subsidiary company*
Net income	€50,000	€100,000
Dividends paid	€20,000	€60,000

How the foregoing data are used to recognise the tax effects of the stated events is discussed below.

Investment in associate company. The investment in the associate company will be equity accounted. The equity income capitalised will be the net income less the dividend received. The investments in the associate will thus increase with €9,000 (30% × (€50,000 − €20,000)). Deferred tax needs to be created on the increase of the investment of €9,000. The increase in the carrying amount could be recovered through dividends or through the ultimate sale of the associate. Dividend income might be taxed at a different rate than the capital gains on the sale of the associate. Assume that only 20% of the dividend is subject to tax of 34% and the capital gains tax rate is also 34%. Based on recovery through dividends the deferred tax will be €612 (20% × 34% × €9,000). Based on the recovery through sale the deferred tax will be €3,060 (34% × €9,000).

Investment in subsidiary company. Normally an investment in a subsidiary company will be recorded at cost in the records of the parent company. No deferred tax will therefore be recognised. However, if the option is followed to fair value the investment, deferred tax must be created using the appropriate rate of recovery of the investment, unless the exception to the general rule applies.

However, in the consolidated financial statements the investment in the subsidiary will be replaced by the assets and liabilities. Therefore, any deferred tax created on the investment in the subsidiary company in the parents' own financial statements should also be reversed.

Tax Effects of Compound Financial Instruments

IAS 32 established the important notion that when financial instruments are compound, the separately identifiable components are to be accounted for according to their distinct natures. For example, when an entity issues convertible debt instruments, those instruments may have characteristics of both debt and equity securities, and accordingly the issuance proceeds should be allocated among those components. (IAS 32 requires that the full fair value of the liability component be recognised, with only the residual allocated to equity, consistent with the concept that equity is only the residual interest in an entity.) A problem arises when the taxing authorities do not agree that a portion of the proceeds should be allocated to a secondary instrument. IAS 12 requires that deferred tax must be created on both the liability and equity component. The deferred tax on the equity component should be recognised directly in equity.

Example of tax effects of a compound financial instrument at issuance

Consider the following scenario. Tamara Corp. issues 6% convertible bonds with a face value of €3,000,000, due in 10 years, with the bonds being convertible into Tamara ordinary shares at the holders' option. Proceeds of the offering amount to €3,200,000, for an effective yield of approximately 5.13% at a time when "straight" debt with similar risks and time to maturity is yielding just less than 6.95% in the market. Since the fair value of the debt component is thus €2.8 million out of the actual proceeds of €3.2 million, the convertibility feature is seemingly worth €400,000 in the financial marketplace. Under revised IAS 32, the full fair value of the liability component must be allocated to it, with only the residual value being attributed to equity.

The entry to record the issuance of the bonds is as follows:

Cash	€3,200,000	
Unamortised debt discount	200,000	
Debt payable		€3,000,000
Equity portion of bond		400,000

Deferred tax is created on both the carrying amount of the equity and liability component.

Example of tax effects of a compound financial instrument in subsequent periods

To illustrate, continue the preceding example and assume that the tax rate is 30%, and for simplicity also assume that the debt discount will be amortised on a straight-line basis over the 10-year term (€200,000 ÷ 10 = €20,000 per year), although in theory amortisation using the "effective yield" method is preferred. The tax effect of the total debt discount is €200,000 × 30% = €60,000. Annual interest expense is €20,000 + (€3,000,000 × 6%) = €200,000. The entries to establish deferred tax liability accounting at inception and to reflect interest accrual and reversal of the deferred tax account are as follows:

At inception (in addition to the entry shown above)

Equity portion of bond	€60,000	
Deferred tax liability		€60,000

Each year thereafter

Interest expense	€200,000	
Interest payable		€180,000
Unamortised debt discount		20,000
Deferred tax liability	€6,000	
Tax expense—deferred		€6,000

Note that the offset to deferred tax liability at inception is a charge to equity, in effect reducing the credit to the portion of the bond recognised in equity of the compound financial instrument to a net-of-tax basis, since allocating a portion of the proceeds to the equity component caused the creation of a non-deductible deferred charge, debt discount. When the deferred charge is later amortised, however, the reversing of the temporary difference leads to a reduction in tax expense to better "match" the higher interest expense reported in the financial statements than on the tax return.

Share-Based Payment Transactions

Share-based payment transactions are similar to other transactions subject to deferred tax if the carrying amount differs from the tax base. For example, the expense for the share options granted as compensations is recognised over the vesting period of the share options. For tax purposes assume the amount is only deducted when the options are granted; the tax base will be the expense recognised in equity that is only deducted for tax in future periods. A deferred tax asset is created for the amount that is deducted in the future.

PRESENTATION AND DISCLOSURE

Presentation

Somewhat surprisingly, IAS 12 stated that should the reporting entity classify its statement of financial position (into current and non-current assets and liabilities), deferred tax assets and liabilities should never be included in the current category. All deferred tax balances are always classified as non-current.

Current tax and deferred tax assets and liabilities may only be offset if specific criteria are met. Current tax assets and current tax liabilities may only be offset if:

- The entity has a legally enforceable right to offset the recognised amounts; and
- The entity intends either to settle on a net basis, or to realise the asset and settle the liability simultaneously.

Current tax assets and current tax liabilities of different entities can also only be offset if the above offsetting rules apply, which would be rare, except if the group is taxed on a consolidated basis.

Deferred tax assets and deferred tax liabilities are only offset if:

- The entity has a legal enforceable right to set off current tax assets and current tax liabilities; and
- The deferred tax asset and deferred tax liabilities relate to income levied by the same tax authority on the same tax entity or different entities which intend either to settle current tax assets and liabilities on a net basis or simultaneously, in each future period when significant deferred tax assets or liabilities are expected to be recovered or settled.

Disclosures

Revised IAS 12 mandated a number of disclosures, including some that had not been required under earlier practice. The purpose of these disclosures is to provide the user with an understanding of the relationship between pre-tax accounting profit and the related tax effects, as well as to aid in predicting future cash inflows or outflows related to tax effects of assets and liabilities already reflected in the statement of financial position. The more recently imposed disclosures were intended to provide greater insight into the relationship between deferred tax assets and liabilities recognised, the related tax expense or benefit recognised in earnings and the underlying natures of the related temporary differences resulting in those items. There is also enhanced disclosure for discontinued operations under IAS 12. Finally, when deferred tax assets are given recognition under defined conditions, there will be disclosure of the nature of the evidence supporting recognition. The specific disclosures are presented in greater detail in the following paragraphs.

Statement of financial position disclosures

A reporting entity is required to disclose the amount of a deferred tax asset and the nature of evidence supporting its recognition, when:

1. Utilisation of the deferred tax asset is dependent on future taxable profits in excess of the profits arising from the reversal of the existing taxable temporary differences; *and*
2. The enterprise has suffered a loss in the same tax jurisdiction to which the deferred tax assets relate in either the current or preceding period.

Statement of profit or loss and other comprehensive income disclosures

IAS 12 places primary emphasis on disclosure of the components of income tax expense or benefit. The following information must be disclosed about the components of tax expense for each year for which a statement of profit or loss and other comprehensive income is presented.

The components of tax expense or benefit may include some or all of the following:

1. Current tax expense or benefit.
2. Any adjustments recognised in the current period for taxes of prior periods.
3. The amount of deferred tax expense or benefit relating to the origination and reversal of temporary differences.
4. The amount of deferred tax expense or benefit relating to changes in tax rates or the imposition of new taxes.
5. The amount of the tax benefit arising from a previously unrecognised tax loss, tax credit or temporary difference of a prior period that is used to reduce current period tax expense.
6. The amount of the tax benefit from a previously unrecognised tax loss, tax credit or temporary difference of a prior period that is used to reduce deferred tax expense.
7. Deferred tax expense arising from the write-down of a deferred tax asset because it is no longer deemed probable of realisation.
8. The amount of tax expense relating to changes in accounting policies and errors that cannot be accounted for retrospectively.

In addition to the foregoing, IAS 12 requires that disclosures be made of the following items which are to be separately stated:

1. The aggregate current and deferred tax relating to items that are charged or credited to equity.
2. The amount of income tax related to each component of other comprehensive income.
3. The relationship between tax expense or benefit and accounting profit or loss either (or both) as:

    a. A numerical reconciliation between tax expense or benefit and the product of accounting profit or loss times the applicable tax rate(s), with disclosure of how the rate(s) was determined; or
    b. A numerical reconciliation between the average effective tax rate and applicable rate, also with disclosure of how the applicable rate was determined.

4. An explanation of changes in the applicable rate vs. the prior reporting period.
5. The amount and date of expiration of unrecognised tax assets relating to deductible temporary differences, tax losses and tax credits.
6. The aggregate amount of any temporary differences relating to investments in subsidiaries, branches and associates and interests in joint ventures for which deferred liabilities have not been recognised.
7. For each type of temporary difference, including unused tax losses and credits, disclosure of:
   c. The amount of the deferred tax assets and liabilities included in each statement of financial position presented; and
   d. The amount of deferred income or expense recognised in the statement of comprehensive income, if not otherwise apparent from changes in the statements of financial position.
8. Disclosure of the tax expense or benefit related to discontinued operations.
9. Amount of income tax consequences of dividends proposed or declared before the authorisation of the financial statement not recognised as a liability.
10. Changes in the pre-acquisition deferred tax assets of the acquirer of a business combination due to the incorporation of the business acquired.
11. Deferred tax assets of a business combination recognised after the acquisition date with a description of the event or change in circumstances.

Disclosure must be made of the amount of deferred tax asset and the evidence supporting its presentation in the statement of financial position, when both these conditions exist: utilisation is dependent upon future profitability beyond that assured by the future reversal of taxable temporary differences, *and* the entity has suffered a loss in either the current period or the preceding period in the jurisdiction to which the deferred tax asset relates.

The nature of potential income tax consequences related to the payments of dividends must also be disclosed.

EXAMPLE OF FINANCIAL STATEMENT DISCLOSURES

Exemplum Reporting PLC
Financial Statements
For the Year Ended December 31, 20XX

Accounting policy note: taxation

Income tax for the period is based on the taxable income for the year. Taxable income differs from profit as reported in the statement of comprehensive income for the period as there are some items which may never be taxable or deductible for tax and other items which may be deductible or taxable in other periods. Income tax for the period is calculated using the current ruling tax rate.

Deferred tax is the future tax consequences of temporary differences between the carrying amounts and tax bases of assets and liabilities shown on the statement of financial position. Deferred tax assets and liabilities are not recognised if they arise in the following situations: the initial recognition of goodwill; or the initial recognition of assets and liabilities that affect neither accounting nor taxable profit. The amount of deferred tax provided is based on the expected manner of recovery or settlement of the carrying amount of assets and liabilities, using tax rates enacted or substantially enacted at the statement of financial position date.

The group does not recognise deferred tax liabilities, or deferred tax assets, on temporary differences associated with investments in subsidiaries, joint ventures and associates where the parent company is able to control the timing of the reversal of the temporary differences and it is not considered probable that the temporary differences will reverse in the foreseeable future. It is the group's policy to reinvest undistributed profits arising in group companies.

A deferred tax asset is recognised only to the extent that it is probable that future taxable profits will be available against which the asset can be utilised. The carrying amount of the deferred tax assets is reviewed at each statement of financial position date and reduced to the extent that it is no longer probable that sufficient taxable profit will be available to allow all or part of the asset to be recovered.

Income tax expense note

	20XX	**20XX-1**	
			IAS 12 p79
UK corporation tax	**X**	X	
Utilisation of assessed losses not previously recognised	**X**	X	
Foreign tax	**X**	X	
	X	X	
Deferred tax			IAS 12 p79
Current year	**X**	X	
Change in tax rate	**X**	X	
Total tax expense	**X**	X	
	X	X	

Corporation tax is calculated at X% (20XX-1: X%) of the estimated assessable profit for the IAS 12 year.			IAS 12 p81
The tax expense for the year can be reconciled to the profit for the year as follows:			IAS 12 p81
	20XX	20XX-1	
Profit before tax	**X**	X	
Tax thereon at X% (20XX-1: X%)	**X**	X	
Share of profit from associates and joint ventures	**X**	X	
Non-deductible expenses	**X**	X	
Utilisation of assessed loss not previously recognised	**X**	X	
Change in tax rate	**X**	X	
Foreign tax expensed at lower rates than (country of domicile) standard rate	**X**	X	
Total tax expense	**X**	X	
	X	X	

(Alternative) The tax rate can be reconciled to the effective tax rate as follows:			IAS 12 p81
	20XX	20XX-1	
	%	%	
Tax rate	**X**	X	
Share of profit from associates and joint ventures	**X**	X	
Non-deductible expenses	**X**	X	
Utilisation of assessed loss not previously recognised	**X**	X	
Change in tax rate	**X**	X	

Foreign tax expensed at lower rates than (country of domicile) standard rate	**X**	X	
	X	X	
Total effective tax rate	**X**	X	
	X	X	

Deferred tax relating to changes in fair value of financial assets classified at FVTOCI €X (20XX-1: €X) has been recognised directly in equity. IAS 12 p81

Deferred tax note

	20XX	20XX-1	IAS 12 p81
Deferred tax assets	**X**	X	
Deferred tax liabilities	**X**	X	
Net deferred tax liability	**X**	X	

Deferred tax assets comprise:			IAS 12 p81
Unused tax losses	**X**	X	
Retirement benefit obligations	**X**	X	
	X	X	

Deferred tax liabilities comprise:			IAS 12 p81
Accelerated capital allowances	**X**	X	
Fair value gains	**X**	X	
	X	X	

At the statement of financial position date the aggregate amount of temporary differences associated with investments in subsidiaries for which deferred tax liabilities have not been recognised was €X (20XX-1: €X). Deferred tax has not been raised in the statement of financial position as the group is in a position to control the timing of the reversal of these temporary differences and it is probable that such differences will not reverse in the foreseeable future. IAS 12 p81

Deferred tax assets	**Unused tax losses**	**Retirement benefit obligations**	**Total**
Balance at January 1, 20XX-1	X	X	X
Recognised in the statement of comprehensive income	X	X	X
Recognised directly in equity	X	X	X
Balance at January 1, 20XX	X	X	X
Recognised in the statement of comprehensive income	X	X	X
Recognised directly in equity	X	X	X
Balance at December 31, 20XX	X	X	X

Deferred income tax assets are recognised to the extent that the realisation of the related tax benefit through future taxable profits is probable. Deferred tax assets of €X (20XX-1: €X) have not been recognised in respect of losses amounting to €X (20XX-1: €X) that can be carried forward against future taxable income. The unrecognised tax credits amounting to €X (20XX-1: €X) will expire in 20XX+2 and 20XX+1, respectively. IAS 12 p81(e)

Deferred tax liabilities	**Capital allowances**	**Fair value gains**	**Total**
Balance at January 1, 20XX-1	X	X	X
Recognised in the statement of comprehensive income	X	–	X
Recognised directly in equity		X	
Balance at January 1, 20XX	X	X	X
Recognised in the statement of comprehensive income	X	–	X
Recognised directly in equity	–	X	–
Balance at December 31, 20XX	**X**	**X**	**X**

FUTURE DEVELOPMENTS

The IASB proposed that the initial deferred tax recognition exception should not be applied to transactions that recognise both an asset and a liability, such as the initial capitalisation of a lease transaction. However, the initial recognition of a deferred tax liability may not exceed the deferred tax asset recognised.

US GAAP COMPARISON

US GAAP and IFRS record deferred taxes using the asset and liability approach. However, there are several differences:

- Under US GAAP, a deferred tax asset is recognised in full and is then reduced by a valuation account if it is more likely than not that all or some of the asset will not be realised. The valuation allowance is revised upward or downward in future periods as the tax rates, probabilities of recovery or characterisation of tax attributes change.
- US GAAP uses the enacted tax rate.
- US GAAP requires entities to assess whether uncertain tax positions will be upheld under audit on the assumption that the tax examiner has access to all relevant information. If the position is more likely than not to be disallowed, potential liabilities must be accrued using a weighted probability method for the amount that has a minimum cumulative probability over 50% of being assessed by the tax jurisdiction in question. Consequently, an accrual for an uncertain tax position may vary significantly between IFRS and US GAAP. Additionally, a roll forward of uncertain tax positions is required. An entity must also disclose a description of tax years that remain subject to examination by major tax jurisdictions. Another disclosure for uncertain tax positions is the total amounts of interest and penalties recognised in the statement of operations and the statement of financial position.
- US GAAP does not require recognition of deferred taxes for investments in a foreign subsidiary or corporate joint venture that is essentially permanent in duration, unless it is apparent that the difference will reverse in the future.
- US GAAP requires deferral of taxes paid on intercompany profits and does not allow the recognition of deferred taxes on temporary differences between the tax bases of assets transferred that remain within the consolidation group.

- When graduated rates are significant elements in an entity's tax calculation, both IFRS and US GAAP require factoring this into the applied rate. US GAAP specifically directs users to use the rate applicable to the average income for the years projected.
- Presentation of income tax expense attributable to operations within a period (e.g., a quarter) is specifically defined under US GAAP to be income from continuing operations multiplied by the effective tax rate. Allocation of remaining income tax expense is then prorated to other elements of comprehensive income (e.g., discontinuing operations, foreign currency translation adjustments in equity). Changes in rates from prior-year tax positions are explicitly to be included in income from continuing operations regardless of the original financial statement characterisation.
- ASU 2016-16 aligns the recognition of income tax consequences for intra-entity transfers of assets other than inventory with IFRS, requiring that an entity should recognise the income tax consequences of an intra-entity transfer of an asset other than inventory when the transfer occurs.

27 EARNINGS PER SHARE

INTRODUCTION

The IFRS governing the calculation and disclosure of earnings per share (EPS) is IAS 33. According to IAS 1, if an entity presents the components of profit or loss in a separate statement of profit or loss, it should present basic and fully diluted EPS (or one EPS measure, if applicable) in that separate statement. The principal goal in these measures is to calculate the interest of potential ordinary shares in the performance of an entity. When the entity's capital structure is simple, EPS is computed by simply dividing profit or loss by the average number of outstanding equity shares. The computation becomes more complicated with the existence of securities that, while not presently equity shares, have the potential of causing additional equity shares to be issued in future, thereby diluting each currently outstanding share's claim to future earnings. Examples of such dilutive securities include convertible preference shares and convertible debt, as well as various options and warrants. It was long recognised that if calculated EPS were to ignore these potentially dilutive securities, there would be a great risk of misleading current shareholders regarding their claim to future earnings of the reporting entity.

Source of IFRS
IAS 33

SCOPE

IAS 33 states that the standard's applicability is both to entities whose ordinary shares or potential ordinary shares are traded in a public market (a domestic or foreign stock exchange or an over-the-counter market, including local and regional markets), and those entities that are in the process of issuing ordinary shares or potential ordinary shares in public securities markets. IAS 33 defines the point in the share issuance process when these requirements become effective as the point when the consideration is receivable.

Some private entities wish to report a statistical measure of performance, and often choose to use EPS. While these entities are not required to issue EPS data, when they elect to do so they must also comply with the requirements of IAS 33.

In situations when both parent company and consolidated financial statements are presented, IAS 33 stipulates that the information called for by this standard need only be presented for consolidated information. The reason for this rule is that users of financial statements of a parent company are interested in the results of operations of the group as a whole, as opposed to the parent company on a stand-alone basis. Of course, nothing prevents the entity from also presenting the parent-only information, including EPS, should it choose to do so. Again, the requirements of IAS 33 would have to be met by those making such an election.

Entities should present both basic EPS and diluted EPS for profit or loss from continuing operations in the statement of profit or loss and other comprehensive income or in the statement of profit or loss, if presented separately, for each class of ordinary shares that has a different right to share in profit or loss for the period. Equal prominence should be given to both the basic EPS and diluted EPS figures for all periods presented.

An entity that reports a discontinued operation shall disclose the basic EPS and diluted EPS for the discontinued operation either in the statement of profit or loss and other comprehensive income or in the notes.

Entities should present basic EPS and diluted EPS even if the amounts disclosed are negative. In other words, the standard mandates disclosure of not just *earnings per share*, but even *loss per share* figures.

DEFINITIONS OF TERMS

A number of terms used in a discussion of earnings per share have special meanings in that context. When used, they are intended to have the meanings given in the following definitions.

Antidilution. An increase in earnings per share or reduction in loss per share, resulting from the assumption that convertible securities are converted, that options or warrants are exercised or that ordinary shares are issued upon the satisfaction of specified conditions.

Contingent share agreement. An agreement in which the issue of shares is dependent on the satisfaction of a specified condition.

Contingently issuable ordinary shares issuance. Ordinary shares issuable for little or no cash or other consideration upon the satisfaction of specified conditions in a contingent share agreement.

Dilution. A reduction in earnings per share or an increase in net loss per share resulting from the assumption that convertible instruments are converted, that options and warrants are exercised or that ordinary shares are issued upon the satisfaction of specified conditions.

Options, warrants and their equivalents. Financial instruments that give the holder the right to purchase ordinary shares.

Ordinary shares. An equity instrument that is subordinate to all other classes of equity instruments. Ordinary shares participate in profit for the period only after other types of shares such as preference shares have participated. An entity may have more than one class of ordinary shares; ordinary shares of the same class have the same rights as dividends.

Potential ordinary shares. A financial instrument or other contract that may entitle its holders to ordinary shares.

Put option (on ordinary shares). Contract which gives the holder the right to sell ordinary shares at a specified price for a given period.

CONCEPTS, RULES AND EXAMPLES

Simple Capital Structure

A simple capital structure may be said to exist either when the capital structure consists solely of ordinary shares or when it includes no potential ordinary shares, which could be in the form of options, warrants or other rights, that on conversion or exercise could, in the aggregate, dilute EPS. Dilutive securities are essentially those that exhibit the rights of debt or other senior security holders (including warrants and options) and which have the potential on their issuance to reduce the EPS.

Computational guidelines

In its simplest form, the EPS calculation is profit or loss divided by the weighted-average number of ordinary shares outstanding. The objective of the EPS calculation is to determine the amount of earnings attributable to each ordinary share. Complexities arise because profit or loss does not necessarily represent the earnings available to the ordinary equity holder, and a simple weighted-average of ordinary shares outstanding does not necessarily reflect the true nature of the situation. Adjustments can take the form of manipulations of the numerator or of the denominator of the formula used to compute EPS, as discussed in the following paragraphs.

Numerator

The numerator is the profit or loss attributable to ordinary equity shareholders of the entity, and, if presented, from continuing operations. Preference share dividends are therefore deducted from profit or loss. If the preference shares are cumulative, the dividend is to be deducted from profit (or added to the loss), whether it is declared or not. If preference shares do not have a cumulative right to dividends and current period dividends have been omitted, such dividends should not be deducted in computing EPS. Cumulative dividends in arrears that are paid currently do not affect the calculation of EPS in the current period, since such dividends have already been considered in prior periods' EPS computations. However, the amount in arrears should be disclosed, as should all of the other effects of the rights given to senior securities on the EPS calculation.

There may be various complications resulting from the existence, issuance or redemption of preferred shares. Thus, if "increasing rate" preferred shares are outstanding—where contractually the dividend rate is lower in early years and higher in later years—the amount of preferred dividends in the early years must be adjusted to accrete the value of later, increased dividends, using an effective yield method akin to that used to amortise bond discount. If a premium is paid to preferred shareholders to retire the shares during the reporting period, this payment is treated as additional preferred dividends paid for purposes of EPS computations. Similarly, if a premium is paid (in cash or in terms of improved conversion terms) to encourage the conversion of convertible preferred shares, that payment (including the fair value of additional ordinary shares granted as an inducement) is included in the preferred dividends paid in the reporting period, thereby reducing earnings allocable to ordinary shares for EPS calculation purposes. Contrariwise, if preferred shares are redeemed at a value lower than carrying (book) amount—admittedly, not a very likely occurrence—that amount is used to reduce earnings available for ordinary equity holders in the period, thereby increasing EPS.

Denominator

The weighted-average number of ordinary shares outstanding is used to calculate the denominator. The difficulty in computing the weighted-average exists because of the effect that various transactions have on the computation of ordinary shares outstanding. Although it is impossible to analyse all the possibilities, the following discussion presents some of the more common transactions affecting the number of ordinary shares outstanding.

If a company reacquires its own shares in countries where it is legally permissible to do so, the number of shares reacquired (referred to as treasury shares) should be excluded from EPS calculations from the date of acquisition. The same computational approach holds for the issuance of ordinary shares during the period. The number of shares newly issued is included in the computation only for the period after their issuance date. The logic for this treatment is that since the consideration for the shares was not available to the reporting entity, and hence could not contribute to the generation of earnings, until the shares were issued, the shares should not be included in the EPS computation prior to issuance. This same logic applies to the reacquired shares because the consideration expended in the repurchase of those shares was no longer available to generate earnings after the reacquisition date.

A share dividend (bonus issue) or a share split does not generate additional resources or consideration, but it does increase the number of shares outstanding. The increase in shares as a result of a share split or dividend, or the decrease in shares as a result of a reverse split, should be given retrospective recognition for all periods presented. Thus, even if a share dividend or split occurs at the end of the period, it is considered effective for the entire period of each (i.e., current and historical) period presented. The reasoning is that a share dividend or split has no effect on the ownership percentage of ordinary shares, and likewise has no impact on the resources available for productive investment by the reporting entity. As such, to show a dilution in the EPS in the period of the split or dividend would erroneously give the impression of a decline in profitability when in fact it was merely an increase in the shares outstanding due to the share dividend or split. Furthermore, financial statement users' frame of reference is the number of shares outstanding at the end of the reporting period, including shares resulting from the split or dividend, and using this in computing all periods' EPS serves to most effectively communicate to them.

Complications also arise when a business combination occurs during the period. In a combination accounted for as an acquisition the shares issued in connection with a business combination are considered issued as of the date of acquisition and the income of the acquired company is included only for the period after acquisition.

IAS 33 recognises that in certain countries it is permissible for ordinary shares to be issued in partly paid form, and the standard accordingly stipulates that partly paid instruments should be included as ordinary share equivalents to the extent to which they carry rights (during the financial reporting year) to participate in dividends in the same manner as fully paid shares.

Furthermore, in the case of contingently issuable shares (i.e., ordinary shares issuable on fulfilment of certain conditions, such as achieving a certain level of profits or sales), IAS 33 requires that such shares be considered outstanding and included in the computation of basic EPS only when all these required conditions have been satisfied.

IAS 33 gives examples of situations where ordinary shares may be issued, or the number of shares outstanding may be reduced, without causing corresponding changes in resources of the corporation. Such examples include bonus issues, a bonus element in other issues such as a rights issue (to existing shareholders), a share split, a reverse share split and a capital reduction without a corresponding refund of capital. In all such cases, the number of ordinary shares outstanding before the event is adjusted, as if the event had occurred at the beginning of the earliest period reported. For instance, in a "5-for-4 bonus issue" the number of shares outstanding prior to the issue is multiplied by a factor of 1.25. These and other situations are summarised in the tabular list that follows.

Weighted-average computation

Transaction	*Effect on weight-average computation*
Ordinary shares outstanding at the beginning of the period	Increase number of shares outstanding by the number of shares
Issuance of ordinary shares during the period	Increase number of shares outstanding by the number of shares issued weighted by the portion of the year the ordinary shares are outstanding
Conversion into ordinary shares	Increase number of shares outstanding by the number of shares converted weighted by the portion of the year shares are outstanding
Company reacquires its shares	Decrease number of shares outstanding by the number of shares reacquired times the portion of the year outstanding
Share dividend or split	Increase number of shares outstanding by the number of shares issued or increased due to the split
Reverse split	Decrease number of shares outstanding by decrease in shares
Acquisition	Increase number of shares outstanding by the number of shares issued weighted by the portion of year since the date of acquisition

Rights offerings are used to raise additional capital from existing shareholders. These involve the granting of rights in proportion to the number of shares owned by each shareholder (e.g., one right for each 100 shares held). The right gives the holder the opportunity to purchase a share at a discounted value, as an inducement to invest further in the entity and in recognition of the fact that, generally, rights offerings are less costly as a means of floating more shares, versus open market transactions which involve fees to brokers. In the case of rights shares, the number of ordinary shares to be used in calculating basic EPS is the number of ordinary shares outstanding prior to the issue, multiplied by the following factor:

$$\frac{\text{Fair value immediately prior to the exercise of the rights}}{\text{Theoretical ex} - \text{rights fair value}}$$

There are several ways to compute the theoretical value of the shares on an ex-rights basis. IAS 33 suggests that this be derived by adding the aggregate fair value of the shares immediately prior to exercise of the rights to the proceeds from the exercise, and dividing the total by the number of shares outstanding after exercise.

To illustrate, consider that the entity currently has 10,000 shares outstanding, with a market value of €15 per share, when it offers each holder rights to acquire one new share at €10 for each four shares held. The theoretical value ex-rights would be given as follows:

$$\frac{(10{,}000 \times €15) + (2{,}500 \times €10)}{12{,}500} = \frac{€175{,}000}{12{,}500} = €14$$

Thus, the ex-rights value of the ordinary shares is €14 each. The foregoing does not characterise all possible complexities arising in the EPS computation; however, most of the others occur under a complex structure which is considered in the following section of this chapter. The illustration below applies the foregoing concepts to a simple capital structure.

Example of EPS computation—Simple capital structure

Assume the following information:

Numerator information		*Denominator information*	
a. Profit from continuing operations	€130,000	a. Ordinary shares outstanding January 1, 20XX	100,000
b. Loss on discontinued operations	30,000	b. Shares issued for cash April 1, 20XX	20,000
c. Profit for the year	100,000	c. Shares issued in 10% share dividend declared in July 20XX	12,000
d. 6% cumulative preference shares, €100 par, 1,000 shares issued and outstanding	100,000	d. Treasury shares purchased October 1, 20XX	10,000

When calculating the numerator, the claims of preference shares should be deducted to arrive at the earnings attributable to ordinary equity holders. In this example, the preference shares are cumulative. Thus, regardless of whether or not the board of directors declares a preference dividend, holders of the preference shares have a claim of €6,000 (1,000 shares × €100 × 6%) against 20XX earnings. Therefore, €6,000 must be deducted from the numerator to arrive at profit or loss attributable to the owners of ordinary shares.

Note that any cumulative preference dividends in arrears are ignored in computing this period's EPS since they would have been incorporated into previous periods' EPS calculations. Also note that this €6,000 would have been deducted for non-cumulative preferred only if a dividend of this amount had been declared during the period. The EPS calculations for the foregoing fact pattern follow:

Earnings per ordinary share

On profit from continuing operations = (€130,000 − €6,000 preference dividends) ÷ Weighted number of ordinary shares outstanding (see below)	= €1.00
On profit for the year = (€130,000 − €30,000 − €6,000) ÷ Weighted number of ordinary shares outstanding (see below)	= €0.76

Only the EPS amounts relating to the parent company from continued operations, in the case of consolidated (group) financial statements, must be provided.

The computation of the denominator is based on the weighted-average number of ordinary shares outstanding. Recall that use of a simple average (e.g., the sum of year-beginning and year-end outstanding shares, divided by two) is not considered appropriate because it fails to accurately give effect to various complexities. The table below illustrates one way of computing the weighted-average number of shares outstanding. Note that, had share issuances occurred mid-month, the weighted-average number of shares would have been based on the number of days elapsing between events.

Item	*Number of shares actually outstanding*	*Fraction of the year outstanding*	*Shares times fraction of the year*
Number of shares as of beginning of the year January 1, 20XX	110,000 [100,000 + 10% (100,000)]	12/12	110,000
Shares issued April 1, 20XX	22,000 [20,000 + 10% (20,000)]	9/12	16,500
Treasury shares purchased October 1, 20XX	(10,000)	3/12	(2,500)
Weighted-average number of ordinary shares outstanding			**124,000**

Recall that the share dividend declared in July is considered to be retroactive to the beginning of the year. Thus, for the period January 1, 20XX through April 1, 20XX, 110,000 shares are considered to be outstanding. When shares are issued, they are included in the weighted-average beginning with the date of issuance. The share dividend applicable to these newly issued shares is also assumed to have existed for the same period. Thus, we can see that of the 12,000-share dividend, 10,000 shares relate to the beginning balance and 2,000 shares to the new issuance (10% of 100,000 and 20,000, respectively). The purchase of the treasury shares requires that these shares be excluded from the calculation for the remainder of the period after their acquisition date. The figure is subtracted from the calculation because the shares were purchased from those outstanding prior to acquisition. To complete the example, we divided the previously derived numerator by the weighted-average number of ordinary shares outstanding to arrive at EPS, which is [(€100,000 − €6,000) ÷ 124,000 =] €0.76.

Reporting a €0.24 loss per share (€30,000 ÷ 124,000) due to the discontinued operations is optional. The numbers computed above for the EPS based on profit for the year are the only presentation required in the statement of profit or loss and other comprehensive income (or separate statement of profit or loss, if presented).

Complex Capital Structure

The computation of EPS under a complex capital structure involves all of the complexities discussed under the simple structure and many more. By definition, a complex capital structure is one that has dilutive potential ordinary shares, which are shares or other instruments that have the potential to be converted or exercised and thereby reduce EPS. The effects of any antidilutive potential ordinary shares (those that would increase EPS) are not to be included in the computation of diluted EPS. Thus, diluted EPS can never provide a more favourable impression of financial performance than the basic EPS.

Note that a complex structure requires dual presentation of both basic EPS and diluted EPS even when the basic EPS is a loss per share. Under the current standard, both basic and diluted EPS must be presented, unless diluted EPS would be antidilutive.

For the purposes of calculating diluted EPS, the profit or loss attributable to ordinary equity holders and the weighted-average number of ordinary shares outstanding should be adjusted for the effects of the dilutive potential ordinary shares. That is, the presumption is that the dilutive securities have been converted or exercised, with ordinary shares being outstanding for the entire period, and with the effects of the dilution removed from earnings (e.g., interest or dividends). In removing the effects of dilutive securities that in fact were outstanding during the period, the associated tax effects must also be eliminated, and all consequent changes—such as employee profit-sharing contributions that are based on reported profit or loss—must similarly be adjusted.

According to IAS 33, the numerator, representing the profit or loss attributable to the ordinary equity holders for the period, should be adjusted by the after-tax effect, if any, of the following items:

1. Interest recognised in the period for the convertible debt which constitutes dilutive potential ordinary shares;
2. Any dividends recognised in the period for the convertible preferred shares which constitute dilutive potential ordinary shares, where those dividends have been deducted in arriving at net profit attributable to ordinary equity holders; and
3. Any other consequential changes in profit or loss that would result from the conversion of the dilutive potential ordinary shares.

For example, the conversion of debentures into ordinary shares will reduce interest expense, which in turn will cause an increase in the profit for the period. This will have a consequential effect on contributions based on the profit figure, for example the employer's contribution to an employee profit-sharing plan. The effect of such consequential changes on profit or loss available for ordinary equity holders should be considered in the computation of the numerator of the diluted EPS ratio.

The denominator, which has the weighted number of ordinary shares, should be adjusted (increased) by the weighted-average number of ordinary shares that would have been outstanding assuming the conversion of all dilutive potential ordinary shares.

Example—Truly Dilutive

To illustrate, consider Chelsea Corporation, which has 100,000 ordinary shares outstanding for the entire period. It also has convertible debentures outstanding, on which interest of €30,000 was paid during the year. The debentures are convertible into 100,000 shares. Profit after tax (effective rate is 30%) amounts to €15,000, which is net of an employee profit-sharing contribution of €10,000, determined as 40% of after-tax income. Basic EPS is €15,000 ÷ 100,000 shares = €0.15. Diluted EPS assumes that the debentures were converted at the beginning of the year, thereby averting €30,000 of interest which, after tax effect, would add €21,000 to net results for the year. Conversion also would add 100,000 shares, for a total of 200,000 shares outstanding. Furthermore, had operating results been boosted by the €21,000 of avoided after-tax interest cost, the employee profit sharing would have increased by €21,000 × 40% = €8,400, producing net results for the year of €15,000 + €21,000 − €8,400 = €27,600. Diluted EPS is thus €27,600 ÷ 200,000 = €0.138. Since this is truly dilutive, IFRS requires presentation of this amount.

Determining Dilution Effects

In the foregoing example, the assumed conversion of the convertible debentures proved to be dilutive. If it had been *antidilutive*, presentation of the (more favourable) diluted EPS would not be permitted under IFRS. To ascertain whether the effect would be dilutive or antidilutive, each potential ordinary share issue (i.e., each convertible debenture, convertible preferred or other issuance outstanding having distinct terms) must be evaluated separately from other potential ordinary share issuances. Since the interactions among potential ordinary share issues might cause diluted EPS to be moderated under certain circumstances, it is important that each issue be considered in the order of decreasing effect on dilution. In other words, the most dilutive of the potential ordinary share issues must be dealt with first, then the next most dilutive, and so on.

Potential ordinary shares are generally deemed to have been outstanding ordinary shares for the entire reporting period. However, if the potential shares were only first issued, or became expired or were otherwise cancelled during the reporting period, then the related ordinary shares are deemed to have been outstanding for only a portion of the reporting period. Similarly, if potential shares are exercised during the period, then for that part of the year the actual shares outstanding are included for purposes of determining basic EPS, and the potential (i.e., unexercised) shares are used in the determination of diluted EPS by deeming these to have been exercised or converted for only that fraction of the year before the exercise occurred.

Options and warrants

The exercise of options and warrants results in proceeds being received by the reporting entity. If actual exercise occurs, of course, the entity has resources which it will, logically, put to productive use, thereby increasing earnings to be enjoyed by ordinary equity holders (both those previously existing and those resulting from exercising their options and warrants). However, the presumed exercise for purposes of diluted EPS computations does not invoke actual resources being received, and earnings are not enhanced as they might have been in the case of actual exercise. If this fact were not dealt with, diluted EPS would be unrealistically depressed since the number of assumed shares would be increased but earnings would reflect the lower, actual level of investment being utilised by the entity.

IFRS prescribes the use of the "treasury share method" to deal with the hypothetical proceeds from the presumed option and warrant exercises. This method assumes that the proceeds from the option and warrant exercises would have been used to repurchase outstanding shares, at the average prevailing market price during the reporting period. This assumed repurchase of shares eliminates the need to speculate as to what productive use the hypothetical proceeds from option and warrant exercise would be put, and also reduces the assumed number of outstanding shares for diluted EPS calculation.

Treasury Share (Stock) Method

Denominator must be increased by net dilution, as follows:

Net dilution = Shares issued – Shares repurchased

where:

Shares issued = Proceeds received/Exercise price

Shares repurchased = Proceeds received/Average market price per share

IAS 33's way of expressing the required use of the "treasury share/stock method" is as follows: "The difference between the number of ordinary shares issued and the number of ordinary shares that would have been issued at the average market price of ordinary shares during the period shall be treated as an issue of ordinary shares for no consideration."

Example

Assume the reporting entity issued 1,000 ordinary shares to option holders who exercised their rights and paid €15,000 to the entity. During the reporting period, the average price of ordinary shares was €25. Using the proceeds of €15,000 to acquire shares at a per share cost of €25 would have resulted in the purchase of 600 shares. Thus, a net of 400 additional shares would be assumed outstanding for the year, at no net consideration to or from the entity.

In all cases where the exercise price is lower than the market price, assumed exercise will be dilutive and some portion of the shares will be deemed issued for no consideration. If the exercise price is greater than the average market price, the exercise should not be assumed since the result of this would be antidilutive.

Convertible instruments

Convertible instruments are assumed to be converted when the effect is dilutive. Convertible preferred shares will be dilutive if the preferred dividend declared (or, if cumulative, accumulated) in the current period is lower than the computed basic EPS. If the contrary situation exists, the impact of assumed conversion would be antidilutive, which is not permitted by IFRS.

Similarly, convertible debt is dilutive, and thus assumed to have been converted, if the after-tax interest, including any discount or premium amortisation, is lower than the computed basic EPS. If the contrary situation exists, the assumption of conversion would be antidilutive, and thus not to be taken into account for diluted EPS computations.

While the term "if converted" is not explicitly employed by IAS 33, the methodology of the if-converted method is used for those securities that are currently sharing in the earnings of the company through the receipt of interest or dividends as senior securities but have the potential for sharing in the earnings as ordinary shares. The if-converted method logically recognises that the convertible security can only share in the earnings of the company as one or the other, not as both. Thus, the dividends or interest less tax effects applicable to the convertible security as a senior security are not recognised in the profit or loss figure used to compute EPS, and the weighted-average number of shares is adjusted to reflect the conversion as of the beginning of the year (or date of issuance, if later). See the example of the if-converted method for illustration of treatment of convertible securities when they are issued during the period and therefore were not outstanding for the entire year.

Example of the if-converted method

Assume a net profit for the year of €50,000 and a weighted-average number of ordinary shares outstanding of 10,000. The following information is provided regarding the capital structure:

1. Convertible debt, 200 bonds each convertible into 40 ordinary shares. The bonds were issued at par (€1,000 per bond). The bonds were outstanding the entire year. The income tax rate is 40%. No bonds were converted during the year.
2. 4% convertible, cumulative preferred shares, par €100, 1,000 shares issued and outstanding. Each preferred share is convertible into two ordinary shares. The preferred shares were issued at par and were outstanding the entire year. No shares were converted during the year.

The first step is to compute the basic EPS, that is, assuming only the issued and outstanding ordinary shares. This figure is simply computed as €4.60 (€50,000 − €4,000 preferred dividends) ÷ (10,000 ordinary shares outstanding). The diluted EPS must be less than this amount for a dual presentation of EPS to be necessary.

To determine the dilutive effect of the preferred shares an assumption (generally referred to as the if-converted method) is made that all of the preferred shares are converted at the earliest date that it could have been during the year. In this example, the date would be January 1. (If the preferred had been first issued during the year, the earliest date conversion could have occurred would have been the issuance date.) The effects of this assumption are twofold: (1) if the preferred is converted, there will be no preferred dividends of €4,000 for the year; and (2) there will be an additional 2,000 ordinary shares outstanding during the year (the conversion rate is 2 for 1 on 1,000 shares of preferred). Diluted EPS is computed, as follows, reflecting these two assumptions:

$$\frac{\text{Net profit for the year}}{\text{Weighted} - \text{average of ordinary shares outstanding} + \text{Shares issued upon conversion of preferred}} = \frac{€50{,}000}{12{,}000 \text{ shares}} = €4.17$$

The convertible preferred is dilutive because it reduced EPS from €4.60 to €4.17. Accordingly, a dual presentation of EPS is required.

In the example, the convertible bonds are also assumed to have been converted at the beginning of the year. Again, the effects of the assumption are twofold: (1) if the bonds are converted, there will be no interest expense of €14,000 (7% × €200,000 face value), the net effect of not having interest expense of €14,000 is €8,400 [(1 − 0.40) × €14,000], and (2) there will be an additional 8,000 shares (200 bonds × 40 shares) of ordinary shares outstanding during the year. Diluted EPS is computed as follows, reflecting the dilutive preferred and the effects noted above for the convertible bonds.

$$\frac{\text{Net profit for the year} + \text{Interest expense}(\text{net of tax})}{\text{Weighted} - \text{average of ordinary shares outstanding} + \text{Shares issued upon conversion of preferred shares and conversion of bonds}} = \frac{€50{,}000 + 8{,}400}{12{,}000} = €2.92$$

The convertible debt is also dilutive, as it reduces EPS from €4.17 to €2.92. Together the convertible bonds and preferred reduced EPS from €4.60 to €2.92.

The complete computation of basic and diluted EPS under IAS 33 is shown in the following table:

	EPS on outstanding ordinary shares (the "benchmark" EPS)		*Basic*		*Diluted*	
Items	*Numerator*	*Denominator*	*Numerator*	*Denominator*	*Numerator*	*Denominator*
Profit for the year	€50,000		€50,000		€50,000	
Preferred dividend	(€4,000)					
Ordinary shares outstanding		10,000 shares		10,000 shares		10,000 shares
Conversion of preferred				2,000		2,000
Conversion of bonds	8,400	8,000				
Totals	€46,000 ÷	10,000 shares	€50,000 ÷	12,000 shares	€58,400 ÷	20,000 shares
EPS		**€4.60**		**€4.17**		**€2.92**

The preceding example was simplified to the extent that none of the convertible securities were, in fact, converted during the year. In most real situations, some or all of the securities may have been converted, and thus actual reported earnings (and basic EPS) would already have reflected the fact that preferred dividends were paid for only part of the year and/or that interest on convertible debt was accrued for only part of the year. These factors would need to be taken into consideration in developing a time-weighted numerator and denominator for the EPS equations.

Contingent Issuances of Ordinary Shares

As for the computation of basic EPS, shares whose issuance is contingent on the occurrence of certain events are considered outstanding and included in the computation of basic EPS only if the stipulated conditions have been met (i.e., the event has occurred). If at the end of the reporting period the triggering event has not occurred, issuance of the contingently issuable shares is not to be assumed for the computation of basic EPS.

Issuances that are dependent on certain conditions being met can be illustrated as follows. Assume that a condition or requirement exists in a contract to increase earnings over a period of time to a certain stipulated level and that, upon attainment of this targeted level of earnings, the issuance of shares is to take place. This is regarded as a contingent issuance of shares for purposes of applying IAS 33. If the condition is met at the end of the reporting period, the effect is included in basic EPS, even if the actual issuance takes place after year-end (e.g., upon delivery of the audited financial statements, per terms of the contingency agreement).

If the condition must be met and then maintained for a subsequent period, such as for a two-year period, then the effect of the contingent issuance is excluded from basic EPS, but is included in diluted EPS. In other words, the contingent shares, which will not be issued until the defined condition is met for two consecutive years, are assumed to be met for diluted EPS computation if the condition is met at the end of the reporting period. Meeting the terms of the contingency for the current period forms the basis for the expectation that the terms may again be met in the subsequent period, which would trigger the issuance of the added shares, causing dilution of EPS.

In some instances, the terms of the contingent issuance arrangement make reference to share prices over a period of time extending beyond the end of the reporting period. In such instances, if issuance is to be assumed for purposes of computing diluted EPS, only the prices or other data through the end of the reporting period should be deemed pertinent to the computation of diluted EPS. Basic EPS is not affected, of course, since the contingent condition is not met at the end of the reporting period.

IAS 33 identifies circumstances in which the issuance of contingent shares is dependent upon meeting both future earnings and future share price threshold levels. Reference must be made to both these conditions, as they exist at the end of the reporting period. If both threshold conditions are met, the effect of the contingently issuable shares is included in the computation of diluted EPS.

The standard also cites circumstances where the contingency does not pertain to market price of ordinary shares or to earnings of the reporting entity. One such example is the achievement of a defined business expansion goal, such as the opening of a targeted number of retail outlets; other examples could be the achievement of a defined level of gross revenues, or development of a certain number of commercial contracts. For purposes of computing diluted EPS, the number of retail outlets, level of revenue, etc., at the end of the reporting period are to be presumed to remain constant until the expiration of the contingency period.

Example

Contingent shares will be issued at year-end 20XX, with 1,000 shares issued for each retail outlet in excess of the number of outlets at the base date, year-end 20XX-1. At year-end 20XX, seven new outlets are open. Diluted EPS should include the assumed issuance of 7,000 additional shares. Basic EPS would not include this, since the contingency period has not ended and no new shares are yet required to be issued.

Contracts Which May Be Settled in Shares or for Cash

Increasingly complex financial instruments have been issued by entities in recent decades. Among these are obligations that can be settled in cash or by the issuance of shares, at the option of the debtor (the reporting entity). Thus, debt may be incurred and later settled, at the entity's option, by increasing the number of its ordinary shares outstanding, thereby diluting EPS but averting the need to disperse its resources for purposes of debt retirement.

Note that this situation differs from convertible debt, discussed above, as it is the debtor, not the debt holder, which has the right to trigger the issuance of shares.

It is to be presumed that the debtor will elect to issue shares to retire this debt, if making that assumption results in a dilution of EPS. This is assumed for the calculation of diluted EPS but is not included in basic EPS.

A similar result obtains when the reporting entity has written (i.e., issued) a call option to creditors, giving them the right to demand shares instead of cash in settlement of an obligation. Again, if dilutive, share issuance is to be presumed for diluted EPS computation purposes.

Written put options

The entity may also write put options giving shareholders the right to demand that the entity repurchase certain outstanding shares. Exercise is to be presumed if the effect is dilutive. According to IAS 33, the effect of this assumed exercise is to be calculated by assuming that the entity will issue enough new shares, at average market price, to raise the proceeds needed to honour the put option terms.

Example

If the entity is potentially required to buy back 25,000 of its currently outstanding shares at €40 each, it must assume that it will raise the required €1,000,000 cash by selling new ordinary shares into the market. If the average market price was €35 during the reporting period, it must be assumed that €1,000,000 ÷ €35 = 28,572 shares would be issued, for a net dilution of about 3,572 net ordinary shares, which is used to compute diluted EPS.

The foregoing guidance does not apply, however, to the situation where the reporting entity holds options, such as call options on its own shares, since it is presumed that the options would only be exercised under conditions where the impact would be antidilutive. That is, the entity only would choose to repurchase its optioned shares if the option price were below market price. Similarly, if the entity held a put contract (giving it the right to sell shares to the option writer) on its own shares, it would only exercise this option if the option price were above market price. In either instance, the effect of assumed exercise would likely be antidilutive.

Sequencing of Dilution Effects

The sequence followed in testing the dilution effects of each of several series of convertible securities may affect the outcome, although this is not always true. It is best to perform the sequential procedures by computing the impact of each issue of potential ordinary shares from the most dilutive to the least dilutive. This rule also applies if convertible securities (for which the if-converted method will be applied) and options (for which the treasury stock approach will be applied) are outstanding simultaneously.

To determine the sequencing of the dilution analysis, it is necessary to use a "trial and error" approach. However, options and warrants should be dealt with first, since these will not affect the numerator of the EPS equation, and thus are most dilutive in their impact. Convertible securities are dealt with subsequently, and these issues will affect both numerator and denominator, with varying dilutive effects.

No antidilution. No assumptions of conversion should be made if the effect would be antidilutive. As in the discussion above, it may be that the sequence in which the different issues or series of convertible or other instruments that are potentially ordinary shares are considered will affect the ultimate computation. The goal in computing diluted EPS is to calculate the maximum dilutive effect. The individual issues of convertible securities, options and other items should be dealt with from the most dilutive to the least dilutive to effect this result.

Presentation and Disclosure Requirements under IAS 33

Entities should disclose amounts used as the numerator in calculating basic EPS and diluted EPS along with a reconciliation of those amounts to profit or loss for the period. Disclosure is also required of the weighted-average number of ordinary shares used as the denominator in calculating basic EPS and diluted EPS along with a reconciliation of these denominators to each other, including instruments (i.e., contingently issuable shares) that could potentially dilute basic EPS in the future, but were not included in the calculation of diluted EPS because they were antidilutive for the period(s) presented.

If an entity chooses to disclose per share amounts using a reported component of the separate statement of profit or loss other than profit or loss for the period attributable to ordinary equity holders, such amounts should be calculated using the weighted-average number of ordinary shares determined in accordance with the requirements of IAS 33; this will ensure comparability of the per share amounts disclosed.

In cases where an entity chooses to disclose the above per share amounts using a reported component of the separate statement of profit or loss, other than profit or loss for the year, a reconciliation is mandated by the standard, which should reconcile the difference between the reported component of profit or loss and profit or loss reported in the statement of profit or loss and comprehensive income or separate statement of profit or loss presented.

When additional disclosure is made by an entity of the above per share amounts, basic and diluted per share amounts should be disclosed with equal prominence (just as basic EPS and diluted EPS figures are given equal prominence).

Entities are encouraged to disclose the terms and conditions of financial instruments or contracts generating potential ordinary shares since such terms and conditions may determine whether or not any potential ordinary shares are dilutive and, if so, the effect on the weighted-average number of shares outstanding and any consequent adjustments to profit or loss attributable to the ordinary equity holders.

If changes (resulting from a bonus issue or share split, etc.) in the number of ordinary or potential ordinary shares occur after the end of the reporting period but before issuance of the financial statements, and the per share calculations reflect such changes in the number of shares, such a fact should be disclosed.

Entities are also encouraged to disclose a description of ordinary share transactions or potential ordinary share transactions other than capitalisation issues and share splits, occurring after the end of the reporting period that are of such importance that non-disclosure would affect the ability of the users of the financial statements to make proper evaluations and decisions.

EXAMPLE OF FINANCIAL STATEMENT DISCLOSURES

Exemplum Reporting PLC
Financial Statements
For the Year Ended December 31, 20XX

Earnings per share

From continuing operations Basic (cents per share) Diluted (cents per share)	13	**XX**	XX
From continuing and discontinued operations Basic (cents per share) Diluted (cents per share)	13	**XX**	XX

13. Earnings per share

	20XX	20XX-1	
Reconciliation of net profit to basic earnings:			
Net profit attributable to equity holders of the parent	X	X	IAS 33
Basic earnings	X	X	
Loss for the period on discontinued operations	**X**	X	
Basic earnings from continued operations	**X**	X	
Reconciliation of basic earnings to diluted earnings:			IAS 33 p70
Basic earnings	**X**	X	
Interest on convertible debentures	X	X	
Diluted earnings	X	X	
Loss for the period on discontinued operations	**X**	X	
Diluted earnings from continued operations	**X**	X	
Reconciliation of basic weighted-average number of ordinary IAS 33 shares to diluted weighted-average number of ordinary shares:	**Number**	Number	IAS 33 p70
Basic weighted-average number of ordinary shares	**X**	X	
Dilutive effect of convertible debentures	**X**	X	
Diluted weighted-average number of ordinary shares	**X**	X	

Share options granted to employees could potentially dilute basic earnings per share in the future but were not included in the calculation of diluted earnings per share as they are anti-dilutive for the period presented. The weighted number of shares used in the calculation of basic and diluted earnings per share is the same for continuing and total earnings per share calculations.

Commentary on notes

Earnings per share

Where there has been any transaction in ordinary or potential ordinary shares after the statement of financial position date that has significantly changed the number of ordinary or potential ordinary shares in issue, a description of such transactions shall be given.	IAS 33 p70(d)
Capitalisation, bonus or share split issues are required to be adjusted retrospectively and therefore the descriptive disclosure mentioned above would not apply to these types of issues. The fact that the per share calculations have been adjusted should be disclosed.	IAS 33 p64

US GAAP COMPARISON

The accounting and presentation under US GAAP for EPS is very similar to IFRS. Entities with simple capital structures, which are entities that have only one class of shares and no other potential equity instruments outstanding, present only basic EPS. Basic EPS is calculated by dividing the earnings available to ordinary shareholders by the average shares outstanding for the period (each quarter). This is done for operating results, net income and discontinued operations. The earnings available to ordinary shareholders for an entity with a simple capital structure can differ if the entity has non-controlling interests.

Entities that have potentially issued shares must also present diluted EPS. The diluted EPS calculation includes the shares that would have been issued if events necessary to issue those shares had occurred (market price trigger). Potential shares include contingent share agreements, convertible debt, convertible preferred stock, options and warrants. For all potentially issued shares, it is assumed in the calculation that the shares were outstanding from either the beginning of the period or the date at which the instruments or agreements were issued.

The number of potentially issued shares that require the holder to convey to the issuer assets in exchange (i.e., options with a strike price) are adjusted for the assumption that the issuer will use those proceeds to purchase outstanding shares (referred to as the treasury stock method). This has the effect of always reducing the number of shares in the calculation. The theoretical number of shares purchased is calculated by dividing the total theoretical proceeds by the average price per share of the securities in the period. Potentially issued shares that require the holder to convey assets to the issuer are only included in the calculation of diluted EPS if the average price per share is above the strike price. This is because it is assumed that a holder would not exercise the option or warrant if it is "out-of-the-money." Companies using the treasury stock method will exclude excess tax benefits since they will no longer be recognised in additional paid-in capital and will be applied prospectively. Note that IAS 33 does not require the income tax effects in the calculation of the treasury stock method of such awards.

Potentially issued shares are only included in diluted EPS if the effect is to reduce EPS (or decrease loss per share) below basic EPS. These shares are called antidilutive. To maximise the dilution, each series or set of potential shares are added to outstanding shares in order of most dilutive to least dilutive. Shares that would be issued that do not require the conveyance of assets from the instrument holder to the issuer would be the most dilutive.

Dividends on preference shares are deducted from earnings to calculate earnings available to ordinary shares.

If an entity has participating shares outstanding that are separate classes of shares that are entitled to different dividends, both the basic and diluted EPS must reflect this. This is referred to in US GAAP as a two-tiered calculation.

Mandatorily convertible instruments are not specifically addressed; however, an entity should consider whether or not the contract is considered participating and, if so, apply the two-class method.

The number of dilutive potential ordinary shares included in the year-to-date period is a weighted-average of the dilutive potential ordinary shares included in each interim computation.

For contracts that are permitted to be settled in either common stock or cash at the entity's option, the presumption that the contract will be settled in ordinary shares if the effect is dilutive can be overcome if the entity has an existing practice or stated policy that provides a reasonable basis to conclude that the contract will be settled partially or wholly in cash.

Instruments that contain embedded conversion features that are contingently convertible or exercisable on the basis of a market price trigger are included in diluted EPS (if dilutive) regardless of whether the market price trigger has been met. ASU 2017-11 *Earnings Per Share (Topic 260) – Distinguishing Liabilities from Equity (Topic 480) – Derivatives and Hedging (Topic 815)* bring in the concept of a **down round** feature in which a non-convertible instrument is treated as a dividend when calculating basic EPS. Which is effective for public entities for years after December 15, 2018 and for all others is effective for years after December 31, 2019.

The presentation of cash flow per share, or similar information, in the financial statements is specifically prohibited.

28 OPERATING SEGMENTS

INTRODUCTION

Segmental information is essential for good management as it enables management to monitor performance within its specific business and geographical regions and to decide how best to allocate resources to segments.

The value of segmental information is not only limited to its application as an internal management tool. It also has an important role in external reporting, since by providing segmental information in financial statements, the entity's management can explain to investors and to the market many of the factors that contribute to the results for the year.

The core principle set out in IFRS 8 requires an entity to disclose information that enables users of the financial statements to evaluate the nature and financial effects of the business activities in which the entity engages and the economic environments in which it operates. This should be considered when an entity forms its judgements about how and what information should be disclosed.

Source of IFRS
IFRS 8

SCOPE

IFRS 8 applies to:

1. The separate or individual financial statements of an entity:
   a. Whose debt or equity instruments are traded in a public market (a domestic or foreign stock exchange or an over-the-counter market, including local and regional markets); or

   b. That files, or is in the process of filing, its financial statements with a securities commission or other regulatory organisation for the purpose of issuing any class of instruments in a public market; and

2. The consolidated financial statements of a group with a parent:

   a. Whose debt or equity instruments are traded in a public market (a domestic or foreign stock exchange or an over-the-counter market, including local and regional markets); or
   b. That files, or is in the process of filing, the consolidated financial statements with a securities commission or other regulatory organisation for the purpose of issuing any class of instruments in a public market.

Where an entity voluntarily applies this IFRS, the entity must comply with all the requirements in this IFRS. If the entity does not comply with all the requirements, such information cannot be disclosed as segment information.

If a financial report contains both the consolidated financial statements of a parent that is within the scope of this IFRS as well as the parent's separate financial statements, segment information is required only in the consolidated financial statements.

A regulatory requirement to file financial statements does not equate to financial statements linked to the process of issuing instruments to a public market. In such instances, the entity would not be subjected to the disclosure requirements of IFRS 8.

DEFINITIONS OF TERMS

Chief operating decision maker. The term "chief operating decision maker" identifies a function, not necessarily a manager with a specific title. That function is to allocate resources to and assess the performance of the operating segments of an entity. Often the chief operating decision maker of an entity is its chief executive officer or chief operating officer but, for example, it may be a group of executive directors or others. Deciding who the chief operating decision maker is can be difficult and judgement is needed to ensure that the right person or persons have been identified. Where the board of directors include non-executive directors, it may not be appropriate to classify the board as the chief operating decision maker. This is because the non-executive directors are not usually involved in the day-to-day activities of the entity (and therefore the resource allocation decisions); their role is a governance one and not a management one.

Common costs. Operating expenses incurred by the enterprise for the benefit of more than one business segment.

Corporate assets. Assets maintained for general corporate purposes and not used in the operations of any business segment.

General corporate expenses. Expenses incurred for the benefit of the corporation as a whole, which cannot be reasonably allocated to any segment.

Identifiable assets. Those tangible and intangible assets used by a business segment, including those the segment uses exclusively, and an allocated portion of assets used jointly by more than one segment.

Intersegment sales. Transfers of products or services, similar to those sold to unaffiliated customers, between business segments or geographic areas of the entity.

Intrasegment sales. Transfers within a business segment or geographic area.

Operating activities. The principal revenue producing activities of an entity and other activities that are not investing or financing activities.

Operating profit or loss. A business segment's revenue minus all operating expenses, including an allocated portion of common costs.

Operating segment. A component of an entity:

- That engages in business activities from which it may earn revenues and incur expenses (including revenues and expenses relating to transactions with other components of the same entity);
- Whose operating results are regularly reviewed by the entity's chief operating decision maker to make decisions about resources to be allocated to the segments and assess its performance; and
- For which discrete financial information is available.

Reportable segment. Operating segments that:

- Have been identified in accordance with the above definition or result from aggregating two or more of those segments in accordance with aggregation criteria; and
- Exceed the quantitative thresholds.

Segment accounting policies. The policies adopted for reporting the consolidated financial statements of the entity, as well as for segment reporting.

Segment assets. Operating assets employed by a segment in operating activities, whether directly attributable or reasonably allocable to the segment; these should exclude those generating revenues or expenses which are excluded from the definitions of segment revenue and segment expense.

Segment expense. Expense that is directly attributable to a segment, or the relevant portion of expense that can be allocated on a reasonable basis to a segment; it excludes interest expense, losses on sales of investments or extinguishment of debt, equity method losses of associates and joint ventures, income taxes and corporate expenses not identified with specific segments.

Segment revenue. Revenue that is directly attributable to a segment, or the relevant portion of revenue that can be allocated on a reasonable basis to a segment, and that is derived from transactions with parties outside the enterprise and from other segments of the same entity; it excludes interest and dividend income, and gains on sales of investments or extinguishment of debt.

Transfer pricing. The pricing of products or services between business segments or geographic areas.

IDENTIFICATION

Identification of operating segments within business organisations has grown in complexity over the years, and the conglomerate form of organisation (where unrelated or dissimilar operations are united within one reporting entity, sometimes to provide the overall entity with benefits of counter cyclicality among the constituent operations) has become normal practice, and it consequently has become necessary to concede that financial statements which present the full scope of an entity's operations on an aggregated basis declined markedly in usefulness without further relevant detail.

While it is certainly possible to assess the overall financial health of the reporting entity using such financial reports, it is much more difficult to evaluate management's operating and financial strategies, particularly with regard to its emphasis on specific lines of business or geographic spheres of operation. For example, the extent to which operating results for a given period are the consequence of the development of new products having greater potential for future growth, compared to more mature product lines which nonetheless still account for a majority of the entity's total sales, would tend to be masked in financial statements which did not present results by business segment.

IFRS 8 does not define but requires an explanation of how segment profit or loss, segment assets and segment liabilities are determined and measured for each reportable segment. This standard also requires general and entity-wide disclosures, including information about products and services, geographical areas, major customers and important factors used to identify an entity's reportable segments.

CONCEPTS AND REQUIREMENTS UNDER IFRS 8

IFRS 8 establishes how an entity is to report information about its operating segments in *annual* financial statements. Additionally, due to a consequential amendment made to IAS 34, entities are required to report selected information about their operating segments in *interim* financial reports, when interim reports are issued. IFRS 8 also sets out requirements for related disclosures about products and services, geographical areas and major customers.

IFRS 8 requires that an entity report financial and descriptive information about its *reportable segments*. Reportable segments are defined as *operating segments* or aggregations thereof that meet certain defined criteria. Operating segments are components of an entity about which separate financial information is available that is evaluated regularly by the chief operating decision maker in deciding how to allocate resources and in assessing performance. Generally, segment financial information is required to be reported on the same basis as is used internally for evaluating operating segment performance and deciding how to allocate resources to operating segments. This conforms to the objective of putting users in the "shoes of management" in their ability to evaluate management performance.

In the past, there had been debate over the value and validity of disclosing results of operations on a segmental basis. IFRS 8 requires an entity to report a measure of operating segment profit or loss and of segment assets. It also requires the reporting entity to report a measure of segment liabilities and income and expense items if such measures are regularly provided to the chief operating decision maker. It requires reconciliations of total reportable segment revenues, total profit or loss, total assets, liabilities and other amounts disclosed for reportable segments to corresponding amounts in the entity's financial statements.

IFRS 8 also generally requires certain informational disclosures apart from any correspondence to information used in making management operating decisions. This includes information about the revenues derived from its products or services (or groups of similar products and services), about the countries in which it earns revenues and holds assets and about major customers. However, information that is not prepared for internal use need not be reported if the necessary information is not available and the cost to develop it would be excessive.

Descriptive information about the way the operating segments were determined, the products and services provided by the segments, differences between the measurements used in reporting segment information and those used in the entity's financial statements, and changes in the measurement of segment amounts from period to period must also be provided in the notes to the financial statements. This information is necessary for users to meaningfully interpret the operating segment financial data, including making comparisons to prior periods.

Operating Segments and Reportable Segments

IFRS 8 defines reportable segments as being a subset of operating segments. In other words, there may be certain operating segments that fail to meet the threshold test for being reportable under this standard. Therefore, an entity must first determine its operating segments and then identify which of those operating segments are reportable segments. To do this one must have a clear understanding of the definitions of an operating segment as opposed to a reportable segment.

Operating segments

An operating segment is a component of an entity:

1. That engages in business activities from which it may earn revenues and incur expenses (including revenues and expenses relating to transactions with other components of the same entity);
2. Whose operating results are regularly reviewed by the entity's chief operating decision maker to make decisions about resources to be allocated to the segment and assess its performance; and
3. For which discrete financial information is available.

Revenue generation is not an absolute threshold test for an operating segment. An operating segment may engage in business activities for which it has yet to earn revenues; for example, start-up operations may be operating segments before earning revenues.

By the same token, not every part of an entity is necessarily an operating segment or part of an operating segment. Thus, a corporate headquarters, as well as certain functional departments, may earn no revenues, or may generate revenues that are merely incidental to the activities of the entity. These would not be deemed to be operating segments under the definitions set forth under IFRS 8. For the purposes of IFRS 8, an entity's post-employment benefit plans are not operating segments either.

Start-up operations may be operating segments, even where the entity is not yet earning any revenues from its operations. In situations where all of the segment's revenues and expenses are derived from intra-group transactions, these segments may still qualify as operating segments. Such a situation may occur in a vertically integrated operation. Vertically integrated operations are structures that combine many or all of the production and selling processes within one entity.

For many entities, the three characteristics of operating segments set forth above will serve to clearly identify its operating segments. In other situations, an entity may produce reports in which its business activities are presented in a variety of ways (particularly in so-called "matrix organisation" structures, where there are multiple and overlapping lines of reporting responsibilities). If the chief operating decision maker uses more than one set of segment information, other factors may be necessary to identify a single set of components as constituting an entity's operating segments, including the nature of the business activities of each component, the existence of managers responsible for them, and information presented to the board of directors. Of course, any such decision should be documented, and should be maintained over time, to the extent possible, to ensure comparability of disclosures. The chief operating decision maker should review segment definitions to ensure accuracy and consistency.

A discontinued operation can meet the definition of an operating segment, if it continues to engage in business activities, the operating results are regularly reviewed by the chief operating decision maker and there is discrete financial information available to facilitate the review.

A practical example is where the company has a research and development division as well as a head office. The head office carries out support functions, such as accounting, treasury, information technology, legal, human resource, environmental and internal audit. Generally, the head office would not be an operating segment as its functions are only incidental to the entity's business. However, the research and development division may meet the definition of an operating segment as its activities may serve as an integral component of the entity's business.

In some instances, it may be difficult to determine the operating segments. Factors to consider when identifying the operating segments include:

a. The entity has managers responsible for each product area;
b. The entity has just one sales manager;
c. The chief operating decision maker receives information regularly on development costs of new products and employee numbers in each product area;
d. Information on each product area is regularly supplied to the whole board; or
e. The board only receives information on total sales of the entity.

Chief operating decision maker

The standard notes that the term "chief operating decision maker" does not necessarily refer to a person but rather to a function; the function being the ability to allocate resources to operating segments and assessing their performance.

Care should be taken when determining who the CODM is; generally, a board of directors that consist of both executive and non-executive directors cannot be seen as the chief operating decision maker as the non-executive directors are not involved in the day-to-day operations, except at a very high level. Non-executive directors' role is generally that of a governance role rather than a management role.

Reportable segments

Only reportable segments give rise to the financial statement disclosures set forth by IFRS 8. Reportable segments are operating segments as defined above, or *aggregations* of two or more such operating segments, that exceed the quantitative thresholds described below.

Operating segments often exhibit similar long-term financial performance if they have similar economic characteristics. For example, similar long-term average gross margins for two operating segments would be expected if their economic characteristics were similar. Two or more operating segments may *optionally* be aggregated into a single operating segment if aggregation is consistent with the core principle of IFRS 8, the segments have similar economic characteristics and segments are similar in each of the following respects:

1. The nature of the products and services;
2. The nature of the production processes;
3. The type or class of customer for their products and services;
4. The methods used to distribute their products or provide their services; and
5. If applicable, the nature of the regulatory environment, for example banking, insurance or public utilities.

It should be noted that the aggregation criteria are tests and not indicators and that all criteria must be satisfied before operating segments may be aggregated.

The process for determining reportable segments is not straightforward; IFRS 8 has a useful flowchart that can assist in the determination of reportable segments. This flowchart is summarised below:

1. Identify operating segments;
2. Determine whether any operating segments meet all the aggregation criteria and, if so, aggregate them;
3. Review the identified operating segments and aggregated groups of operating segments to see if they individually meet the quantitative thresholds. Those that do are treated as reportable segments;
4. For the remainder, check whether any of the identified operating segments or aggregated groups of operating segments meet a majority of the aggregation criteria. If they do, aggregate them and treat as reportable segments if desired. Individual operating segments can also be treated as reportable segments even if they are not aggregated with another segment or do not meet the quantitative threshold;
5. Test whether the external revenues of reportable segments identified so far represent 75% or more of the entity's external revenue. If they do, then aggregate the remaining segments into a segment called "All other segments," which is not a reportable segment as defined by IFRS 8. If they do not, then additional reportable segments must be identified until the total of reportable segments reaches the 75% point.

Once it has been determined which operating segments may be aggregated, any one of the following quantitative thresholds must also be met when identifying reportable segments:

1. The segment's reported revenue, including both sales to external customers and intersegment sales or transfers, is 10% or more of the combined revenue, internal and external, of all operating segments;
2. The absolute amount of its reported profit or loss is 10% or more of the greater, in absolute amount, of (i) the combined reported profit of all operating segments that did not report a loss, and (ii) the combined reported loss of all operating segments that reported a loss;
3. Its assets are 10% or more of the combined assets of all operating segments.

Furthermore, if the total external revenue reported by operating segments constitutes less than 75% of the entity's revenue, additional operating segments must be identified as reportable segments, even if they do not meet the criteria established under IFRS 8, until at least 75% of the entity's revenue is included in reportable segments.

A reporting entity may combine information about more than one operating segment that does not meet the quantitative thresholds to produce a reportable segment only if the operating segments have similar economic characteristics and share a majority of the aggregation criteria set forth above. Thus, a catch-all ("all other segments") category should not be used, unless truly immaterial. The sources of the revenue included in the "all other segments" category must be described.

More segments may be optionally defined by management as being reportable, even if the foregoing criteria are not met. Operating segments that do not meet any of the quantitative thresholds may be considered reportable, and separately disclosed, if management believes that information about the segment would be useful to users of the financial statements.

This may be particularly relevant if, for various reasons, an operating segment traditionally meeting the test as a reportable segment falls below each threshold in the current year, but management expects the segment to regain its former prominence within a relatively brief time. To ensure interperiod comparability, it may be maintained as a reportable segment notwithstanding its current diminished significance. If management judges that an operating segment identified as a reportable segment in the immediately preceding periods is of continuing significance, information about that segment must, per IFRS 8, continue to be reported separately in the current period even if it no longer meets the criteria for reportability.

It is important to note that the above is different from the aggregation of segments that may be done prior to the initial determination of reportable segments, where all of the criteria must be satisfied. The distinction between the two stages of aggregation is due to the following:

a. In the first stage, the aggregation takes place before determining the reportable segments. Each of the aggregation criteria is considered to be significant; accordingly, all criteria must be satisfied;
b. In the second stage, the reportable segments have already been identified and the segments that are being aggregated are those that do not meet the thresholds for treatment as reportable segments. Accordingly, the aggregation criterion is less important.

If an operating segment is identified as a reportable segment in the current period in accordance with the above-stated quantitative thresholds, segment data for a prior period presented for comparative purposes is to be restated to reflect the newly reportable segment as a separate segment, even if that segment did not satisfy the criteria for reportability in the prior period, unless the necessary information is not available and the cost to develop it would be excessive.

The standard notes that there may be a practical limit to the number of reportable segments that an entity separately discloses beyond which segment information may become too detailed (the so-called information overload situation). Although no precise limit has been determined, as the number of segments that are reportable increases above 10, the entity should consider whether a practical limit has been reached. However, there is no absolute requirement to limit the number of segments.

Example of determining the reportable segments

Below are details of the operating segments of which information is provided to the chief operating decision maker.

Segment	Sales €	Profit €	Loss €	Assets €
Segment A	700,000	300,000		500,000
Segment B	500,000		250,000	1,000,000
Segment C	2,300,000		1,000,000	1,500,000
Segment D	900,000		450,000	600,000
Segment E	800,000	200,000		1,000,000
Segment F	4,000,000	2,700,000		1,000,000
	9,200,000	**3,200,000**	**1,700,000**	**5,600,000**

Individual reportable segments are identified if the contribution falls into the quantitative thresholds below:

1. Contribution of 10% or more to total sales, calculated as €920,000;
2. Contribution of 10% or more to total profit, calculated as €320,000:
   a. Only total profit is used as this is the greater of total profit and loss;
3. Contribution of 10% or more of total assets, calculated as €560,000.

   Accordingly:

Segment	Sales threshold met	Profit/(loss) threshold met	Assets threshold met	Reportable segment
Segment A	No	No	No	No
Segment B	No	No	Yes	Yes
Segment C	Yes	Yes	Yes	Yes
Segment D	No	Yes	Yes	Yes
Segment E	No	No	Yes	Yes
Segment F	Yes	Yes	Yes	Yes

DISCLOSURE REQUIREMENTS

A reporting entity is required to disclose information to enable users of its financial statements to evaluate the nature and financial effects of the business activities in which it engages and the economic environments in which it operates.

The reporting entity is required to disclose the following *for each period for which a statement of comprehensive income* is presented:

1. General information:
   a. The factors used to identify the entity's reportable segments, including the basis of organisation (for example, whether management has chosen to organise the entity around differences in products and services, geographical areas, regulatory environments, or a combination of factors, and whether operating segments have been aggregated);

b. The judgements made by management in applying the aggregation criteria in paragraph 12 of IFRS 8. This includes a brief description of the operating segments that have been aggregated in this way and the economic indicators that have been assessed in determining that the aggregated operating segments share similar economic characteristics; and
c. The types of products and services from which each reportable segment derives its revenues.

2. Information about reported segment profit or loss, including specified revenues and expenses included in reported segment profit or loss, segment assets, segment liabilities and the basis of measurement, as follows:

   a. A measure of profit or loss for each reportable segment;
   b. A measure of total assets and liabilities for each reportable segment if such amounts are regularly provided to the chief operating decision maker;
   c. The following information about each reportable segment if the specified amounts are included in the measure of segment profit or loss reviewed by the chief operating decision maker or are otherwise regularly provided to the chief operating decision maker even if not included in that measure of segment profit or loss:

      i. Revenues from contracts with customers;
      ii. Revenues from transactions with other operating segments of the same entity;
      iii. Interest revenue;
      iv. Interest expense;
      v. Depreciation and amortisation;
      vi. Material items of income and expense disclosed in accordance with IAS 1, *Presentation of Financial Statements*;
      vii. The entity's interest in the profit or loss of associates and joint ventures accounted for by the equity method;
      viii. Income tax expense or income; and
      ix. Material non-cash items other than depreciation and amortisation.

      An entity is to report interest revenue separately from interest expense for each reportable segment unless a majority of the segment's revenues are from interest and the chief operating decision maker relies primarily on net interest revenue to assess the performance of the segment and make decisions about resources to be allocated to the segment. In that situation, an entity may report that segment's interest revenue net of its interest expense and disclose that it has done so.
   d. The reporting entity is to disclose the following about each reportable segment if the specified amounts are included in the measure of segment assets reviewed by the chief operating decision maker or are otherwise regularly provided to the chief operating decision maker, even if not included in the measure of segment assets:

      i. The amount of investment in associates and joint ventures accounted for by the equity method; and

ii. The amounts of additions to non-current assets other than financial instruments, deferred tax assets, net defined benefit assets and rights arising under insurance contracts. If the entity does not present a classified statement of financial position, non-current assets are to be deemed those that include amounts expected to be recovered more than 12 months after the date of the statement of financial position.

e. An entity shall provide an explanation of the measurements of segment profit or loss, segment assets and segment liabilities for each reportable segment. At a minimum, an entity shall disclose the following:

   i. The basis of accounting for any transactions between reportable segments;
   ii. The nature of any differences between the measurements of the reportable segments' profits or losses and the entity's profit or loss before tax and discontinued operations (if not apparent from reconciliations as per Point 3 below);
   iii. The nature of any differences between the measurements of the reportable segments' assets and the entity's assets operations (if not apparent from reconciliations as per Point 3 below);
   iv. The nature of any differences between the measurements of the reportable segments' liabilities and the entity's liabilities operations (if not apparent from reconciliations as per Point 3 below);
   v. The nature of any changes from prior periods in the measurement methods used to determine reported segment profit or loss and the effect, if any, of those changes on the measurement of segment profit or loss; and
   vi. The nature and effect of any asymmetrical allocations to reportable segments.

3. Reconciliations of the totals of segment revenues, reported segment profit or loss, segment assets, segment liabilities and other material segment items to corresponding entity amounts as follows:

   a. The total of the reportable segments' revenues to the entity's revenue;
   b. The total of the reportable segments' measures of profit or loss to the entity's profit or loss before tax expense (tax income) and discontinued operations. However, if an entity allocates to reportable segments items such as tax expense (tax income), the entity may reconcile the total of the segments' measures of profit or loss to the entity's profit or loss after those items;
   c. The total of the reportable segments' assets to the entity's assets if the segment assets are reported in accordance with Point 2 above;
   d. The total of the reportable segments' liabilities to the entity's liabilities if segment liabilities are reported to the entity's chief operating decision maker;
   e. The total of the reportable segments' amounts for every other material item of information disclosed to the corresponding amount for the entity.

IFRS 8 dictates that all material reconciling items are to be separately identified and described. For example, the amount of each material adjustment needed to reconcile reportable segment profit or loss to the entity's profit or loss arising from different accounting policies is required to be separately identified and described.

IFRS 8 also mandates that reconciliations of statements of financial position amounts for reportable segments to the entity's statement of financial position amounts be presented for *each date* at which a *statement of financial position* is presented. If, as is typical, comparative statements of financial position are presented, information for prior periods is to be presented.

If the reporting entity changes the structure of its internal organisation in a manner that causes the composition of its reportable segments to change, the corresponding information for earlier periods, including interim periods, is to be restated, unless the information is not available and the cost to develop it would be excessive. The determination of whether the information is not available and the cost to develop it would be excessive must be made separately for each individual item of disclosure—thus, a blanket conclusion regarding impracticability would normally not be appropriate. Following a change in the composition of its reportable segments, the entity discloses whether it has restated the corresponding items of segment information for earlier periods.

Furthermore, if the reporting entity has changed the structure of its internal organisation in a manner that causes the composition of its reportable segments to change, and if segment information for earlier periods, including interim periods, is *not* restated to reflect the change, it must disclose in the year in which the change occurs segment information for the current period on both the old basis and the new basis of segmentation, unless the necessary information is not available and the cost to develop it would be excessive. This requirement is expected to discourage frequent changes in structure affecting segment reporting.

Entity-wide disclosure requirements

IFRS 8 also mandates disclosures of certain entity-wide data. These disclosures are required regardless of whether the entity has multiple reportable segment disclosures to be made under this standard. These disclosures need not be provided, if already part of the reportable segment disclosures.

1. *Information about products and services.* Revenues from external customers for each product and service, or each group of similar products and services, are to be identified, unless the necessary information is not available and the cost to develop it would be excessive, in which case that fact shall be disclosed. The amounts of revenues reported are to be based on the financial information used to produce the entity's financial statements.
2. *Information about geographical areas.* Unless the necessary information is not available and the cost to develop it would be excessive, the following information is required:

    a. Revenues from contracts with customers (1) attributed to the entity's country of domicile, and (2) attributed to all foreign countries in total from which the entity derives revenues. If revenues from an individual foreign country are material, those revenues are to be disclosed separately. An entity is required to disclose the basis for attributing revenues from external customers to individual countries.
    b. Non-current assets other than financial instruments, deferred tax assets, post-employment benefit assets and rights arising under insurance contracts (1) located in the entity's country of domicile, and (2) located in all foreign countries in

total in which the entity holds assets. If assets in an individual foreign country are material, those assets shall be disclosed separately. Non-current assets are to be defined as assets that include amounts expected to be recovered more than 12 months after the reporting date.

The amounts reported are to be based on the financial information that is used to produce the entity's financial statements. If the necessary information is not available and the cost to develop it would be excessive, that fact shall be disclosed. An entity may provide, in addition to the information required by this paragraph, subtotals of geographical information about groups of countries.

3. *Information about major customers*. Information about the extent of the reporting entity's reliance on its major customers must be provided. If revenues from transactions with a single external customer amount to 10% or more of the entity's revenues, it is required to disclose that fact, the total amount of revenues from each such customer and the identity of segment or segments reporting the revenues. The entity need not disclose the identity of a major customer or amount of revenues that each segment reports from that customer.

IFRS 8 requires the application of judgement to assess whether a government (including government agencies and similar bodies whether local, national or international) and entities known to the reporting entity to be under the control of that government are considered a single customer. In assessing this, the reporting entity should consider the extent of economic integration between those entities.

EXAMPLE OF FINANCIAL STATEMENT DISCLOSURES UNDER IFRS

Roche Group
Annual Report 201X

Notes to the Consolidated Financial Statements

1. Summary of significant accounting policies

6. Segment information

(a) Information on reportable segments

Management has determined the operating segments based on the reports regularly reviewed by the chief operating decision maker ("CODM") in making strategic decisions. Each operating segment is managed separately by a dedicated Chief Executive Officer and management team allowing management to maintain and develop the specific identity of each Maison. These operating segments have been aggregated into four reportable segments as follows:

- Jewelry Maisons—businesses whose heritage is in the design, manufacture and distribution of jewelry products; these comprise Cartier and Van Cleef & Arpels;
- Specialist Watchmakers—businesses whose primary activity includes the design, manufacture and distribution of precision timepieces. The Group's Specialist Watchmakers comprise Piaget, A. Lange & Sohne, Jaeger-LeCoultre, Vacheron Constantin, Officine Panerai, IWC, Baume & Mercier and Roger Dubuis;

- Montblanc Maison—a business whose primary activity includes the design, manufacture and distribution of writing instruments; and
- Other—other operations mainly comprise Alfred Dunhill, Lancel, Chloe, Net-a-Porter, Purdey, textile brands and other manufacturing entities.

The entire product range of a particular Maison, which may include jewelry, watches, writing instruments and leather goods, is reflected in the sales and operating result for that segment. The non-separable costs of operating multibrand regional platforms are allocated to individual operating segments using allocation keys most relevant to the nature of the expense being allocated. Unallocated corporate costs represent the costs of the Group's corporate operations which are not attributed to the segments. Performance measurement is based on segment contribution before corporate costs, interest and tax, as management believes that such information is most relevant in evaluating the results of segments relative to other entities that operate within similar markets. Intersegment transactions between different fiscal entities are transacted at prices that reflect the risk and rewards transferred and are entered into under normal commercial terms and conditions. Intersegment transactions within the same fiscal entity are transacted at cost. All such transactions are eliminated in the reports reviewed by the CODM.

The segment results for the years ended March 31 are as follows:

	201X	*201X-1*
	€m	*€m*
External sales		
Jewelry Maisons	4,590	3,479
Specialist Watchmakers	2,323	1,774
Montblanc Maison	723	672
Other	1,231	967
	8,867	**6,892**
Operating result		
Jewelry Maisons	1,510	1,062
Specialist Watchmakers	539	379
Montblanc Maison	119	109
Other	(35)	(34)
Operating profit from reportable segments	**2,133**	**1,516**
Unallocated corporate costs	(93)	(161)
Consolidated operating profit before finance and tax	**2,040**	**1,355**
Finance costs	(314)	(292)
Finance income	79	111
Share of post-tax results of associated undertakings	(1)	101
Profit before taxation	**1,804**	**1,275**
Taxation	(264)	(196)
Profit for the year	**1,540**	**1,079**

An impairment charge of €2 million is included within the Other reportable segment for 201X (201X-1: €1 million included within each of the Jewelry Maisons and the Other reportable segment). The segment assets which are reviewed by the CODM comprise inventories and trade debtors.

	201X	*201X-1*
	€m	*€m*
Segment assets		
Jewelry Maisons	2,149	1,590
Specialist Watchmakers	1,219	956
Montblanc Maison	357	307
Other	417	328
	4,142	**3,181**
Total assets for reportable segments	4,142	3,181
Property, plant and equipment	1,529	1,267
Goodwill	479	441
Other intangible assets	316	314
Investment property	64	–
Investments in associated undertakings	10	7
Deferred income tax assets	443	349
Financial assets at fair value through profit or loss	2,469	2,224
Other non-current assets	248	211
Other receivables	274	205
Derivative financial instruments	27	148
Prepayments	116	119
Cash at bank and on hand	1,636	1,227
Total assets	**11,753**	**9,693**

The CODM also reviews additions to property, plant and equipment and other intangible assets as follows:

	201X	*201X-1*
	€m	*€m*
Additions to non-current assets:		
Property, plant and equipment, and other intangible assets		
Jewelry Maisons	185	125
Specialist Watchmakers	119	65
Montblanc Maison	31	24
Other	101	60
Unallocated	81	34
	517	**308**

(b) Information about geographical areas

Each reporting segment operates on a worldwide basis. External sales presented in the three main geographical areas where the Group's reportable segments operate are as follows:

	201X	*201X-1*
	€m	*€m*
Europe	**3,097**	**2,588**
France	669	551
Switzerland	347	303
Germany, Italy and Spain	670	606
Other Europe	1,411	1,128

	201X	*201X-1*
Asia	**4,517**	**3,306**
China/Hong Kong	2,412	1,645
Japan	833	737
Other Asia	1,272	924
Americas	**1,253**	**998**
USA	973	758
Other Americas	280	240
	8,867	**6,892**

Sales are allocated based on the location of the wholesale customer, the boutique or the shipping address for online transactions. The total non-current assets other than financial instruments and deferred tax assets located in Switzerland, the Company's domicile, and the rest of the world are as follows:

	201X	*201X-1*
	€m	*€m*
Switzerland	1,217	1,056
Rest of the world	1,331	1,104
	2,548	**2,160**

Segment assets are allocated based on where the assets are located.

(c) Information about products

External sales by product are as follows:

	201X	*201X-1*
	€m	*€m*
Watches	4,404	3,320
Jewelry	2,248	1,685
Leather goods	721	602
Writing instruments	357	359
Clothing and other	1,137	926
	8,867	**6,892**

(d) Major customers

Sales to no single customer represented more than 10% of total revenue. Given the local nature of the luxury goods wholesale and retail businesses, there are no major customer relationships.

Hays plc
Financial Year 201X

1. Segmental Information

Adoption of IFRS 8, Operating Segments

The Group has adopted IFRS 8, *Operating Segments*, with effect from July 1, 2009. IFRS 8 requires operating segments to be identified on the basis of internal reports about components of the Group that are regularly reviewed by the chief operating decision maker to allocate resources to segments and to assess their performance.

As a result, the Group continues to segment the business into three regions, Asia Pacific, Continental Europe & Rest of World, and United Kingdom & Ireland.

The Group's continuing operations comprise one class of business, that of qualified, professional and skilled recruitment.

Net fees and operating profit from continuing operations

The Group's Management Board, which is regarded as the chief operating decision maker, uses net fees by segment as its measure of revenue in internal reports. This is because net fees exclude the remuneration of temporary workers, and payments to other recruitment agencies where the Group acts as principal, which are not considered relevant in allocating resources to segments. The Group's Management Board considers net fees for the purpose of making decisions about allocating resources. The reconciliation of turnover to net fees can be found in Note 6.

(In € million)	**201X**	201X-1
Net fees from continuing operations		
Asia Pacific	**242.2**	210.0
Continental Europe & Rest of World	**266.5**	220.4
United Kingdom & Ireland	**225.3**	241.7
	734.0	672.1

(In € million)	**201X**	201X-1 Before exceptional items	201X-1 Exceptional items	201X-1
Operating profit from continuing operations				
Asia Pacific	**90.9**	78.1	–	78.1
Continental Europe & Rest of World	**43.7**	32.4	–	32.4
United Kingdom & Ireland	**(6.5)**	3.6	4.1	7.7
	128.1	114.1	4.1	118.2

The Group does not report items below operating profit by segment in its internal management reporting. The full detail of these items can be seen in the Group Consolidated Income Statement.

There is no material difference between the segmentation of the Group's turnover by geographic origin and destination.

Net Trade Receivables

For the purpose of monitoring performance and allocating resources from a balance sheet perspective, the Group's Management Board monitors trade receivables net of provisions for impairments only on a segment by segment basis. These are monitored on a constant currency basis for comparability through the year. These are shown below and reconciled to the totals as shown in Note 18.

(In € million)	As reported internally	Foreign exchange	**201X**	As reported internally	Foreign exchange	201X-1
Net trade receivables						
Asia Pacific	76.1	(1.7)	**74.4**	59.9	9.9	69.8
Continental Europe & Rest of World	157.3	(17.4)	**139.9**	104.7	10.6	115.3
United Kingdom & Ireland	137.7	(0.6)	**137.1**	160.0	0.5	160.5
	371.1	(19.7)	**351.4**	324.6	21.0	345.6

Major Customers

Included in turnover is an amount of approximately €587 million (201X-1: €540 million) which arose from sales to the Group's largest customer, which were generated within the United Kingdom & Ireland. This is the only customer to exceed 10% of the Group's turnover; however, as it includes a significant element of remuneration of temporary workers and remuneration of other recruitment agencies, it represents less than 2% of the Group's net fees.

US GAAP COMPARISON

The IASB and FASB converged their segment reporting guidance in 2009. Consequently, the standards are nearly identical, with the following exceptions:

- Similar to IFRS, US GAAP requires an entity to provide a measure of assets that the chief operating decision maker uses in evaluating the performance of the segments. This includes expenditures on long-lived assets (some are excluded). US GAAP excludes goodwill. IFRS does not.
- US GAAP does not require disclosure of a measure of segment liabilities. IAS 8 requires disclosure of segment liabilities if such a measure is regularly provided to the chief operating decision maker.
- A matrix organisation employs multiple management reporting relationships for the functions of people. US GAAP requires that an entity, with a matrix form of organisation to determine operating segments, is based on products and services. IFRS requires such an entity to determine operating segments by reference to the core principle of the IFRS.
- US GAAP provides specific guidance for determining operating segments in certain circumstances (e.g., for equity method investees, certain corporate divisions and divisions that do not have assets allocated for internal reporting purposes).
- The revenue recognition standard that was jointly issued by IFRS and FASB ASU 2014-09 *Revenue Contracts with Customers (Topic 606)* have some minor definition changes though out Topic 280 *Segment Reporting*, that bring in to line the language to be consistent with the new revenue standard and are effective concurrent with the new revenue standard under which most companies are operating under using US GAAP.

In March 2017, the IASB proposed several changes to IFRS 8; the amendments clarify and emphasise the criteria that must be met before two operating segments may be aggregated and include the following disclosures not currently required under US GAAP:

- With respect to the person or group that performs the function of the chief operating decision maker, companies are to disclose the title and role of the person or group; and
- Requires disclosure when the the segments reported in the financial statements differ from the annual report segments.

For contracts that are permitted to be settled in either common stock or cash at the entity's option, the presumption that the contract will be settled in ordinary shares if the effect is dilutive can be overcome if the entity has an existing practice or stated policy that provides a reasonable basis to conclude that the contract will be settled partially or wholly in cash.

Instruments that contain embedded conversion features that are contingently convertible or exercisable on the basis of a market price trigger are included in diluted earnings per share (if dilutive) regardless of whether the market price trigger has been met. The presentation of cash flow per share, or similar information, in the financial statements is specifically prohibited.

29 RELATED PARTY DISCLOSURES

INTRODUCTION

Relationships, transactions and outstanding balances between entities that are considered *related parties*, as defined by IAS 24, *Related Party Disclosures*, must be adequately disclosed in financial statements of a reporting entity. Such disclosures have long been a common feature of financial reporting, and most national accounting standard-setting bodies have imposed similar mandates. The rationale for compelling such disclosures is the concern that entities which are related to each other, whether by virtue of an ability to control or to exercise significant influence or where a person is a member of key management of a reporting entity (all as defined under IFRS), usually have leverage in influencing transaction terms, including values.

If these events and transactions were simply mingled with transactions conducted with other unrelated parties on normal arm's-length terms or negotiated terms, the users of the financial statements would likely be impeded in their ability to project future earnings and cash flows for the reporting entity, given that related party transaction terms could arbitrarily be altered at any time. Thus, to ensure financial reporting transparency, reporting entities are required to disclose the nature, type and components of transactions with related parties. Reporting entities need also to disclose related party transactions to enable readers of financial statements to understand what part of commercial and other activity is undertaken by the entity and third parties and to what extent the reporting entity is reliant on its related parties.

Although IAS 24 states "related party relationships are a normal feature of commerce and business," it nevertheless recognises that a related party relationship could have a material effect on the financial position and operating results of a reporting entity, due to the possibility that transactions with related parties may not be effected at the same amounts or terms as are those between unrelated parties. For that reason, extensive disclosure of such transactions is deemed necessary to convey a full picture of a reporting entity's financial position and results of operations.

While IAS 24 has been operative for over two decades, it is commonly observed that related party transactions are not being properly disclosed in all instances. This is due in part, perhaps, to the perceived sensitive nature of such disclosures and fear of giving out too much information that may be detrimental to a reporting entity. As a consequence, even when a note to financial statements that is captioned "related party transactions" is disclosed, it is often fairly evident that the spectrum of disclosures required by IAS 24 has not been included. Historically, there seems to be particular resistance to reporting certain types of related party transactions, such as loans to directors, key management personnel or close members of the executives' families.

IAS 1 demands, as a prerequisite to asserting that financial statements have been prepared in conformity with IFRS, that there is *full compliance* with all IFRS. This requirement pertains to all recognition and measurement standards and extends to the disclosures to be made as well. As a practical matter, it becomes incumbent upon the management and directors as those responsible for preparation of financial statements to ascertain whether disclosures, including related party disclosures, comply with IFRS when the financial statements represent such to be the case.

Sources of IFRS

IAS 24, 28, *IFRS* 10, 11

DEFINITIONS OF TERMS

Close members of the family of an individual. For the purpose of IAS 24, close members of the family of an individual are defined as "those family members that may be expected to influence, or be influenced by, that person in their dealings with the entity." An individual's domestic partner, spouse and children, children of the individual's spouse or domestic partner, and dependants of the individual or the individual's spouse or domestic partner may be considered close members of the family.

Compensation. Compensation includes all employee benefits (as defined in IAS 19), including employee benefits in the form of share-based payment as envisaged in IFRS 2. Employee benefits include all forms of consideration paid, payable or provided by the entity, or on behalf of the entity, in exchange for services rendered to the entity. It also includes such consideration paid on behalf of a parent of the entity in respect of activities of the entity. Compensation thus includes short-term employee benefits (such as wages, salaries, paid annual and sick leave, profit-sharing and bonuses and non-monetary benefits); post-employment benefits (such as pensions); other long-term benefits (such as long-term disability benefits); termination benefits; and share-based payments.

Government. Refers to government, government agencies and similar bodies whether local, national or international.

Government-related entity. An entity that is controlled, jointly controlled or significantly influenced by a government.

Key management personnel. IAS 24 defines key management personnel as "those persons having authority and responsibility for planning, directing, and controlling the activities of the reporting entity, including directors (whether executive or otherwise) of the entity." Key management personnel would include the board and departmental heads.

Related party. For the purpose of IAS 24, a related party is a person or entity that is related to an entity that is preparing its financial statements (referred to as a "reporting entity"):

a. A person or a close member of that person's family is related to a reporting entity if that person:

    1. Has control or joint control over the reporting entity;
    2. Has significant influence over the reporting entity; or
    3. Is a member of the key management personnel of the reporting entity or of a parent of the reporting entity.

b. An entity is related to a reporting entity if any of the following conditions apply:

    1. The entity and the reporting entity are members of the same group (which means that each parent, subsidiary and fellow subsidiary is related to the others).
    2. One entity is an associate or joint venture of the other entity (or an associate or joint venture of a member of a group of which the other entity is a member).
    3. Both entities are joint ventures of the same third party.
    4. One entity is a joint venture of a third entity and the other entity is an associate of the third entity.
    5. The entity is a post-employment defined benefit plan for the benefit of employees of either the reporting entity or an entity related to the reporting entity. If the reporting entity is itself such a plan, the sponsoring employers are also related to the reporting entity.
    6. The entity is controlled or jointly controlled by a person identified in (a).
    7. A person identified in (a)(1) has significant influence over the entity or is a member of the key management personnel of the entity (or of a parent of the entity).
    8. The entity, or any member of a group of which it is a part, provides key management personnel services to the reporting entity or to the parent of the reporting entity.

Related party transaction. A related party transaction is a transfer of resources, services or obligations between a reporting entity and a related party, regardless of whether a price is charged.

The definition terms for "control," "investment entities" and "significant influence" are included in IFRS 10, 11 and IAS 28 (refer to Chapter 14).

IDENTIFICATION

The Need for Related Party Disclosures

For strategic or other reasons, entities will sometimes carry out certain aspects of their business activities through associates, joint ventures or subsidiaries. For example, to ensure that it has a guaranteed supply of raw materials, an entity may decide to purchase a portion of its requirements (of raw materials) through a subsidiary or, alternatively, will make a direct investment in its vendor to assure continuity of supply. In this way, the entity might be able to control or exercise significant influence over the financial and operating decisions of its major supplier (the investee), including ensuring a source of supply and, perhaps, affecting the prices charged. Such related party relationships and transactions are thus a normal feature of commerce and business and need not suggest any inappropriate behaviour.

A related party relationship could have an impact on the financial position and operating results of the reporting entity because:

1. Related parties may enter into certain transactions with each other which unrelated parties may not normally want to enter into (e.g., uneconomic transactions and transactions done at negotiated terms).
2. Amounts charged for transactions between related parties may not be comparable to amounts charged for similar transactions between unrelated parties (either higher or lower prices than arm's length).
3. The mere existence of the relationship may sometimes be sufficient to affect the dealings of the reporting entity with other (unrelated) parties. (For instance, an entity may cease purchasing from its former major supplier upon acquiring a subsidiary which is the other supplier's competitor.)
4. Transactions between entities would not have taken place if the related party relationship had not existed. For example, a company sells its entire output to an associate at cost. The producing entity might not have survived but for these related party sales to the associate, if it did not have enough business with arm's-length customers for the kind of goods it manufactures.
5. The existence of related party relationships may result in certain transactions *not* taking place, which otherwise would have occurred. Thus, even in the absence of actual transactions with related entities, the mere fact that these relationships exist could constitute material information from the viewpoints of various users of financial statements, including current and potential vendors, customers and employees. Related party information is thus unique, in that even an absence of transactions might be deemed a material disclosure matter.
6. Certain related party transactions may have tax implications, especially if transactions are carried out at negotiated terms across borders.

Because of issues such as those mentioned above, which often distinguish related party transactions from those with unrelated entities, accounting standards (including IFRS) have almost universally mandated financial statement disclosure of such transactions. Disclosures of related party transactions in financial statements is a means of conveying to users of financial statements the messages that certain related party relationships exist as of the date of the financial statements, and that certain transactions were consummated with related parties during the period which the financial statements cover, together with the financial impacts of these related party transactions in the financial statements. Since related party transactions could have an effect on the financial position and operating results of the reporting entity, disclosure of such transactions would be prudent based on the increasingly cited principle of transparency (in financial reporting). Only if such information is disclosed to the users of financial statements will they be able to make informed decisions.

Scope of the Standard

IAS 24 is to be applied in dealing with related parties and transactions between a reporting entity and its related parties. The requirements of this standard apply to the financial statements of each reporting entity. IAS 24 sets forth disclosure requirements only; it does not prescribe the accounting for related party transactions, nor does it address the measurements to be applied in the instance of such transactions. IAS 24 is to be employed in determining the existence of related party relationships and transactions; identifying the outstanding balances, including commitments, between related parties; concluding on whether disclosures are required under the circumstances; and determining the content of such disclosures.

Related party disclosures are required not only in the consolidated (group) financial statements, but also in the separate financial statements of the parent entity, venturer or investor. In separate statements, any intragroup transactions and balances must be disclosed in the related party note, although these will be eliminated in consolidated financial reports. When intragroup transactions and balances are eliminated on consolidation such transactions and balances are not required to be disclosed under IAS 24. However, transactions and balances between an investment entity and its subsidiaries that are accounted for at fair value through profit or loss (and therefore not consolidated) need to be disclosed.

Applicability

The requirements of the standard should be applied to related parties as identified in the definition of a related party.

Substance over Form

The standard clarifies that in applying the provisions of IAS 24 to each possible related party relationship, consideration should be given to the substance of the relationship and not merely to its legal form. Thus, certain relationships might not rise to the level of related parties for the purpose of necessitating disclosure under the provisions of IAS 24. Examples of such situations:

1. Two entities having only common director or other key management personnel, notwithstanding the specific requirements of IAS 24 above.
2. Agencies and entities such as:

    a. Providers of finance (e.g., banks and creditors);
    b. Trade unions;
    c. Public utilities;
    d. Government departments and agencies.

3. Entities upon which the reporting entity may be economically dependent, due to the volume of business the entity transacts with them. For example:

    a. A single customer;
    b. A major supplier;
    c. A franchisor;
    d. A distributor; or
    e. A general agent.

4. Two venturers, simply because they share joint control over a joint venture.

Example

The following scenarios apply in the business model of Entity A

Entity A is a manufacturer of electronic products. All of its supplies are sourced from one vendor for guaranteed supplies of the right quality and within time since the company operates a just-in-time (JIT) model. The finished products are sold to entities it (Entity A) can either control or exercise significant influence over. The entity also transacts with members of its top management and their relatives. The transactions are as follows:

a. Entity A purchases all its raw materials and parts from Entity B. Due to the high quality of the material that Entity B has provided over the last 15 years, Entity A has never purchased from any other supplier. Thus, it may be considered economically dependent on Entity B.
b. Entity A sells 65% of its output to a company owned by one of the directors (Entity C), 25% to a company that is its "associate" by virtue of owning 25% of the share capital (Entity D) and the balance through a company owned by Entity A's sole financiers (Entity E).
c. Entity A stores the raw material and the finished goods in a warehouse that is leased from another company (Entity F) where the managing director is a non-executive director.
d. Entity A has provided an interest-free loan to a company owned by its managing director (Entity G) for the purposes of financing the purchase of delivery vans which Entity G is using for transporting goods from the warehouse of the supplier to the warehouse used by Entity A for storing inventory.

Analysis of the transactions

Which of the transactions above warrant disclosure as related party transactions under IAS 24?

a. Notwithstanding the fact that Entity A purchases all its raw materials and parts from Entity B and is economically dependent on it, Entity B does not automatically become a related party. Thus, for the purpose of IAS 24, purchases made from Entity B are not considered related party transactions and hence would not need to be disclosed.
b. 65% of the sales are to an entity owned by a "director" of Entity C (i.e., an entity controlled by a member of key management), and 25% of the sales are made to an entity over which Entity A has "significant influence." Thus, both sales are to related parties as defined in IAS 24 and would need to be disclosed as such. The sales to Entity E do not qualify to be disclosed as related party transactions simply because the financier does not have any control or significant influence over Entity A.
c. Even though Entity A and Entity F share one director, the two companies are not related and thus the transaction need not be disclosed in Entity A's financial statements.
d. The interest-free loan to an entity owned by a director needs to be disclosed as a related party transaction. The fact that it is interest free may warrant disclosure because it may not be construed as an "arm's-length transaction" since Entity A would not normally provide unrelated parties with interest-free loans.

Significant Influence

The existence of the ability to exercise significant influence is an important concept in relation to this standard. It is one of the two criteria stipulated in the definition of a related party, which when present would, for the purposes of this standard, make one party related to another. In other words, for the purposes of this standard, if one party is considered to have the ability to exercise significant influence over another, then the two parties are considered to be related.

The existence of the ability to exercise significant influence may be evidenced in one or more of the following ways:

1. By representation on the board of directors of the other entity;
2. By one company having influence over a decision by virtue of a casting vote at a meeting of directors or shareholders;
3. By participation in the policy-making process of the other entity;
4. By having material intercompany transactions between two entities;
5. By interchange of managerial personnel between two entities; or
6. By dependence on another entity for technical information.

Significant influence may be gained through agreement, by statute or by means of share ownership. Under the provisions of IAS 24, similar to the presumption of significant influence under IAS 28, an entity is deemed to possess the ability to exercise significant influence if it directly or indirectly through subsidiaries holds 20% or more of the voting power of another entity (unless it can be clearly demonstrated that despite holding such voting power the investor does not have the ability to exercise significant influence over the investee).

Conversely, if an entity, directly or indirectly through subsidiaries, owns less than 20% of the voting power of another entity, it is presumed that the investor does not possess the ability to exercise significant influence (unless it can be clearly demonstrated that the investor does have such an ability despite holding less than 20% of the voting power). Further, while explaining the concept of significant influence, IAS 28 also clarifies that "a substantial or majority ownership by another investor does not *necessarily* preclude an investor from having significant influence" (emphasis added).

Example: Consideration of subsidiaries, associates and joint ventures

The following is a group structure of Entity A, "The Parent."

Entity A has a controlling interest in Entities B and C. Further the company has significant influence over an Associate (Entity D) whereas one of the Subsidiaries (Entity C) has significant influence over another Associate (Entity E).

Entity A controls a Joint Venture (JV) together with a company called Capital Investors Inc.

Analysis of the disclosures' considerations

In Entity A's separate financial statements, all the Subsidiaries, Associates and JVs are related parties. The joint venturer, Capital Investors Inc., does not qualify to be disclosed as a related party.

In Entity B's financial statements, The Parent, Entity C, the Associates and the JV are related parties.

In Entity C's separate financial statements, The Parent, Entity B, the Associates and the JV are related parties.

In the financial statements of Associates D and E, The Parent and Subsidiaries and the JV are related parties. Associates D and E are not related to each other though.

DISCLOSURES

Financial Statement Disclosures

IAS 24 does not address the issue of timing when two parties become or cease to become related and whether disclosures are required of transactions with a party that was related for only part of the reporting period. The recommended practice is that where a transaction took place while the party was related, it should be disclosed. In respect of balances with related parties, these should be disclosed either if the transaction took place when the parties were related, or if the parties were related at the reporting date. In respect of parent and ultimate parent disclosures, where there was a change during the reporting period, this change should be disclosed including details of the previous parent, new parent and ultimate controlling party

IAS 24 recognises that in many countries certain related party disclosures are prescribed by law. In particular, transactions with directors, because of the fiduciary nature of their relationship with the entity, are mandated financial statement disclosures in some jurisdictions. In fact, corporate legislation in some countries goes further and requires certain disclosures which are even more stringent than the disclosure requirements under IAS 24, or under most national GAAP.

For example, under one regulation, in addition to the usual disclosures pertaining to related party transactions, companies are required to disclose not just year-end balances that are due to or due from directors or certain other related parties but are also required to disclose the highest balances for the period (for which financial statements are presented) which were due to or due from them to the corporate entity. Such a requirement may exist since in the absence of this disclosure, balances at year-end can be "cleaned up" (e.g., via short-term bank borrowings) and the artificially low amounts reported can provide a misleading picture to financial statement users regarding the real magnitude of such transactions and balances.

There is nothing in IAS 24 that prohibits supplemental information from being provided over and above the requirements of the standard. Commitment to a "substance over form" approach, with the goal of maximising representational faithfulness and ensuring transparency of the financial reporting process, would, indeed, make expanded disclosures appear all but mandatory. While many do seek to satisfy the mere letter of the requirements under IFRS, the "principles-based" approach of these standards would, it could easily be argued, demand that preparers (and their auditors) undertake to comply with the spirit of the rules as well.

IAS 24 provides examples of situations where related party transactions may lead to disclosures by a reporting entity in the period that they affect:

- Purchases or sales of goods (finished or unfinished, meaning work in progress).
- Purchases or sales of property and other assets.
- Rendering or receiving of services.
- Agency arrangements.
- Leasing arrangement.
- Transfer of research and development.
- Licence agreements.
- Finance (including loans and equity participation in cash or in kind).
- Guarantees and collaterals.

- Commitments linked to the occurrence or non-occurrence of particular events, including executory contracts (recognised and unrecognised).
- Settlement of liabilities on behalf of the entity or by the entity on behalf of another party.

The foregoing should not be considered an exhaustive list of situations requiring disclosure. As very clearly stated in the standard, these are only "examples of situations which may lead to disclosures." In practice, many other situations are encountered which would warrant disclosure. For example, a contract for maintaining and servicing computers, entered into with a subsidiary company, would need to be disclosed by the reporting entity in parent company financial statements.

Disclosure of Parent-Subsidiary Relationships

IAS 24 requires disclosure of relationships between parent and subsidiaries irrespective of whether there have been transactions between the related parties. The name of the parent entity must be provided in the subsidiary's financial statement disclosures; if the ultimate controlling party is a different entity, its name must be disclosed. One reason for this requirement is to enable users of the reporting entity's financial statements to seek out the financial statements of the parent or ultimate controlling party for possible review. If neither of these produces consolidated financial statements available for public use, IAS 24 provides that the name of the "next most senior parent" that produces financial statements must be stated in addition. These requirements are in addition to those set forth by IFRS 10, IFRS 11, IFRS 12 and IAS 28.

To illustrate this point, consider the following example:

> Apex, who owns 25% of Bellweather, and by virtue of share ownership has more than 20% of the voting power, would be considered to possess the ability to exercise significant influence over Bellweather. During the year, Apex entered into an agency agreement with Bellweather; however, no transactions took place during the year between the two companies based on the agency contract. Since Apex is considered a related party to Bellweather by virtue of the ability to exercise significant influence, rather than control (i.e., there is not a parent-subsidiary relationship), no disclosure of this related party relationship would be needed under IAS 24. If, however, Apex owned 51% or more of the voting power of Bellweather it would thereby be considered related to Bellweather on the basis of control and disclosure of this relationship would be needed, irrespective of whether any transactions actually took place between them.

Disclosures to Be Provided

Per IAS 24, if there have been transactions between related parties, the reporting entity should disclose:

1. The nature of the related party transaction; and
2. Information about transactions and outstanding balances necessary to understand the potential effect of the relationship on the financial statements.

At a minimum, the following disclosure shall be made:

a. The amount of the transaction;
b. The amount of outstanding balances and their terms and conditions, including whether they are secured, and details of any guarantees given or received;

c. Provision for doubtful debts related to the amount of the outstanding balances;
d. Any expense recognised during the period in respect of bad or doubtful debts due from the related parties.

The disclosures required are to be made *separately* for each of the following categories:

1. The parent;
2. Entities with joint control or significant influence over the entity;
3. Subsidiaries;
4. Associates;
5. Joint venture in which the entity is a venturer;
6. Key management personnel of the entity or its parent; and
7. Other related parties.

Arm's-length transaction price assertions

The assertion that related party transactions were made at terms that are normal or that the related party transactions are at arm's length can be made only if it can be supported. It is presumed that it would rarely be prudent to make such an assertion. The default presumption is that related party transactions are not *necessarily* conducted on arm's-length terms, which is not taken to imply that transactions were conducted on other bases either.

For example, when an entity purchases raw materials amounting to €5 million from an associated company, these are at normal commercial terms (which can be supported, e.g., by competitive bids), and these purchases account for 75% of its total purchases for the year, the following disclosures would seem appropriate:

> During the year, purchases amounting to €5 million were made from an associated company. These purchases were made at normal commercial terms, at prices equivalent to those offered by competitive unrelated vendors. At December 31, 20XX, the balance remaining outstanding and owed to this associated company amount to €2.3 million.

Note that the obtaining of sufficient competent evidence to support an assertion that terms including prices for related party transactions were equivalent to those which would have prevailed for transactions with unrelated parties may be difficult. For example, if the reporting entity formerly purchased from multiple unrelated vendors but, after acquiring a captive source of supply, moves a large portion of its purchases to that vendor, even if prices are the same as had been formerly negotiated with the many unrelated suppliers, this might not warrant an assertion such as the above. The reason is that, with 75% of all purchases being made with this single, related party supplier, it might not be valid to compare those prices with the process previously negotiated with multiple vendors each providing only a smaller fraction of the reporting entity's needs. Had a large (almost single-source) supply arrangement been executed with any one of the previous suppliers, it might have been possible to negotiate a lower schedule of prices, making comparison of former prices paid for small purchases inapplicable to support this assertion.

Aggregation of disclosures

IAS 24 requires that items of a similar nature may be disclosed in the aggregate. However, when separate disclosure is necessary for an understanding of the effects of the related party transactions on the financial statements of the reporting entity, aggregation would not be appropriate.

A good example of the foregoing is an aggregated disclosure of total sales made during the year to a number of associated companies, instead of separately disclosing sales made to each associated company. On the other hand, an example of separate disclosure (as opposed to aggregated disclosure) is the disclosure of year-end balances due from various related parties disclosed by category (e.g., advances to directors, associated companies, etc.). In the latter case, it makes sense to disclose separately by categories of related parties, instead of aggregating all balances from various related parties together and disclosing, say, the total amount due from all related parties as one amount, since the character of the transactions could well be at variance, as might be the likelihood of timely collection. In fact, separate disclosure in this case seems necessary for an understanding of the effects of related party transactions on the financial statements of the reporting entity.

IAS 24 specifically cites other IFRS which also establish requirements for disclosures of related party transactions. These include:

- IFRS 10, which requires disclosure of a listing of significant subsidiaries;
- IAS 28, which requires disclosure of a listing of significant associates;
- IFRS 11, which requires disclosure of a listing of interests in significant joint arrangements;
- IFRS 12, which requires disclosure of interests in other entities.

Compensation

A controversial topic is the disclosure of details regarding key management compensation. In some jurisdictions, such disclosures (at least for the upper echelon of management) are required, but in other instances these are secrets closely kept by the reporting entities. The IASB considered deleting these disclosures, given privacy and other concerns, and the belief that other "approval processes" (i.e., internal controls) regulated these arrangements, which therefore would not be subject to frequent abuse. However, these disclosures were maintained in the standard because these are deemed relevant for decision making by financial statement users and are clearly within the definition of related party transactions.

The reporting entity is required to disclose key management personnel compensation in total and for each of the following categories:

- Short-term employee benefits;
- Post-employment benefits;
- Other long-term benefits;
- Terminal benefit; and
- Share-based payment.

Comparatives

IAS 24 does not address the basis on which comparative financial information should be presented. Often, challenges arise in respect of parties that are related in one period but not in the other. However, under the objectives of IAS 24 as set out above, it is recommended that disclosures be provided for transactions and balances with parties that were related during the respective years presented.

For example, A sold goods to B in 20XX and 20XX-1. In 20XX, A acquired a 25% interest in B. Related party transactions would only be disclosed for the 20XX financial statements because the transactions in 20XX-1 were not carried out and influenced by relationship as defined under IAS 24.

On the other hand, if A had a 25% interest in B in 20XX-1 which was disposed of at the end of 20XX-1, the transactions for 20XX-1 should be disclosed under IAS 24 but not the transactions for 20XX.

Government-Related Entities

The reporting entity is exempt from the disclosure requirements for related party transactions and outstanding balances, including commitments for the following entities:

1. A government that has control, joint control or significant influence over the reporting entity; and
2. Another entity that is a related party because the same government has control, joint control or significant influence over both the reporting entity and the other entity.

If the exemption is applicable, the reporting entity must disclose the following:

1. The name of the government and the nature of its relationship with the reporting entity (i.e., control, joint control or significant influence);
2. The following information in sufficient detail to enable users of the entity's financial statements to understand the effect of related party transactions on its financial statements:

    a. The nature and amount of each individually significant transaction; and
    b. For other transactions that are collectively, but not individually, significant, a qualitative or quantitative indication of their extent.

Judgement is used to determine the level of detail to be disclosed for significant transactions. The reporting entity should consider the closeness of the related party relationship and the following factors in establishing the level of significance of the transaction:

1. Significance in terms of size.
2. Whether or not the transaction was carried out on non-market-related terms.
3. Whether or not the transaction was outside the entity's normal day-to-day business operations, such as the purchase and sale of businesses.
4. Whether or not the transaction was disclosed to regulatory or supervisory authorities.
5. Whether or not the transaction was reported to senior management.
6. Whether or not the transaction was subject to shareholder approval.

EXAMPLE OF FINANCIAL STATEMENT DISCLOSURES

Exemplum Reporting PLC
Financial Statements
For the Year Ended December 31, 20XX

The group's investments in subsidiaries, associates and joint ventures have been disclosed in notes XX and XX. The group is controlled by XYZ plc. XYZ plc is also the group's ultimate controlling company

Transactions:

Relationship	**Sale of goods**		**Purchase of goods**	**Related party**	**Amounts owed to related party**		**Amounts owed by related party**	
	20XX	**20XX-1**	**20XX**	**20XX-1**	**20XX**	**20XX-1**	**20XX**	**20XX-1**
Parent	X	X	X	X	X	X	X	X
Associates	X	X	X	X	X	X	X	X
Joint venture	X	X	X	X	X	X	X	X
Key management personnel compensation	–	–	–	–	X	X	X	X

Amounts owed to and by related parties are unsecured, interest free, and have 110 fixed terms of repayment.

The balances will be settled in cash. There are no guarantees that have been given or received.

No provision for impairment has been recognised against amounts outstanding, and no expense has been recognised during the period in respect of bad or doubtful debts due from related parties.

	20XX	20XX-1
Key management personnel compensation:		
Short-term employee benefits	X	X
Post-employment benefits	X	X
Other long-term benefits	X	X
Termination benefits	X	X
Share-based payments	X	X
Dividends	X	X
	X	X

US GAAP COMPARISON

Similar to IFRS, US GAAP, mainly found at ASC 850, *Related Party Disclosures*, requires disclosure of related party transactions and relationships, so users can assess the impact of such arrangements on the financial statements. However, unlike IFRS, disclosures about relationships with government bodies are subject to the general disclosures of other topics.

Transactions between related parties, with some exceptions, whether reflected in the financial statements or not (e.g., exchange of the services between subsidiaries under common control of a parent that are not reflected in the books of record) are disclosed. Exceptions are compensation, expense allowances or similar items in the ordinary course of business. However, receivables from employees, officers and affiliated entities must be presented separately from others.

The disclosures for related party transactions are the nature of the relationships involved, description of the transactions, the values of such transactions, amounts due to or from related parties and transaction terms. The name of the related party should be included if necessary, to obtain an understanding of the relationship. Additionally, if an entity is a member of a group that is under common control and the existence of that control could result in operating results or a financial position substantially different from those that would have resulted without that relationship, the disclosures must include the nature of the relationship.

Amounts disclosed can be aggregated by type, provided that doing so does not obscure the nature or amount with a significant related party. General disclosures cannot imply that transactions with related parties are made on an arm's-length basis unless it can be substantiated.

30 ACCOUNTING AND REPORTING BY RETIREMENT BENEFIT PLANS

INTRODUCTION

IAS 26 sets out the form and content of the general-purpose financial reports of retirement benefit plans. The standard applies to:

- Defined contribution plans where benefits are determined by contributions to the plan together with investment earnings thereon; and
- Defined benefit plans where benefits are determined by a formula based on employees' earnings and/or years of service.

IAS 26 may be compared to IAS 19. The former addresses the financial reporting considerations for the benefit plan itself, as the reporting entity, while the latter deals with employers' accounting for the cost of such benefits as they are earned by the employees. While these standards are thus somewhat related, there will not be any direct interrelationship between amounts reported in benefit plan financial statements and amounts reported under IAS 19 by employers.

Source of IFRS
IAS 26

DEFINITIONS OF TERMS

Actuarial present value of promised retirement benefits. The present value of the expected payments by a retirement benefit plan to existing and past employees, attributable to the service already rendered.

Defined benefit plans. Retirement benefit plans under which amounts to be paid as retirement benefits are determined by reference to a formula usually based on employees' earnings and/or years of service.

Defined contribution plans. Retirement benefit plans under which amounts to be paid as retirement benefits are determined by contributions to a fund together with investment earnings thereon.

Funding. The transfer of assets to an entity (the fund) separate from the employer's entity to meet future obligations for the payment of retirement benefits.

Net assets available for benefits. The assets of a retirement benefit plan less its liabilities other than the actuarial present value of promised retirement benefits.

Participants. The members of a retirement benefit plan and others who are entitled to benefits under the plan.

Retirement benefit plans. Arrangements whereby an entity provides benefits for employees on or after termination of service (either in the form of an annual income or as a lump sum) when such benefits or the contributions towards them can be determined or estimated in advance of retirement from the provisions of a document (i.e., based on a formal arrangement) or from the entity's practices (which is referred to as an informal arrangement).

Vested benefits. Benefits, the rights to which, under the terms of a retirement benefit plan, are not conditional on continued employment.

SCOPE

IAS 26 should be applied in accounting and reporting by retirement benefit plans. IAS 26 does not establish a mandate for the publication of such reports by retirement plans. However, if such reports are prepared by a retirement plan, then the requirements of this standard should be applied to them.

IAS 26 regards a retirement benefit plan as a separate entity, distinct from the employer of the plan's participants. It is noteworthy that this standard also applies to retirement benefit plans that have sponsors other than the employer (e.g., trade associations or groups of employers). Furthermore, this standard deals with accounting and reporting by retirement benefit plans to all participants as a group and does not deal with reports to individual participants with respect to their retirement benefit entitlements.

The standard applies the same basis of accounting and reporting to both formal and informal retirement benefit plans. It is also worthy of mention that this standard applies whether or not a separate fund is created and regardless of whether there are trustees. The requirements of this standard also apply to retirement benefit plans with assets invested with an insurance company, unless the contract with the insurance company is in the name of a specified participant or a group of participants and the responsibility is solely of the insurance company.

This standard does not deal with other forms of employment benefits such as employment termination indemnities, deferred compensation arrangements, long-service leave benefits, special early retirement or redundancy plans, health and welfare plans or bonus plans.

Retirement benefit plans are usually described as being either defined contribution or defined benefit plans. When the quantum of the future benefits payable to the retirement benefit plan participants is determined by the contributions paid (by the participants' employer, the participants, or both) together with investment earnings thereon, such plans are defined contribution plans. Defined benefit plans, by contrast, promise certain benefits, often determined by formulae which involve factors such as years of service and salary level at the time of retirement, without regard to whether the plan has sufficient assets.

Under defined benefit plans the ultimate responsibility for payment (which may be guaranteed by an insurance company, the government or some other entity, depending on local law and custom) remains with the employer. In rare circumstances, a retirement benefit plan may contain characteristics of both defined contribution and defined benefit plans. Such a hybrid plan is deemed to be a defined benefit plan for the purposes of this standard.

DEFINED CONTRIBUTION PLANS

IAS 26 requires that the reporting of a defined contribution plan contains a statement of the net assets available for benefits and a description of the funding policy. In preparing the statement of the net assets available for benefits, the plan investments should be carried at fair value, which for marketable securities would be market value. In cases where an estimate of fair value is not possible, disclosure is required of the reason as to why fair value has not been used. As a practical matter, most plan assets will have determinable market values, since the plans' trustees' discharge of their fiduciary responsibilities will generally mandate that only marketable investments be held.

An example of a statement of net assets available for plan benefits, for a defined contribution plan, is set forth below.

XYZ Defined Contribution Plan
Statement of Net Assets Available for Benefits
December 31, 20XX
(€000)

Assets	
Investments at fair value	
Government securities	5,000
Municipal bonds	3,000
Local equity securities	3,000
Foreign equity securities	3,000
Local debt securities	2,000
Foreign corporate bonds	2,000
Other	1,000
Total investments	19,000
Receivables	
Amounts due from stockbrokers on sale of securities	15,000
Accrued interest	5,000
Dividends receivable	2,000
Total receivables	22,000
Cash	5,000
Total assets	**46,000**
Liabilities	
Accounts payable	
Amounts due to stockbrokers on purchase of securities	10,000
Benefits payable to participants—due and unpaid	11,000
Total accounts payable	21,000
Accrued expenses	11,000
Total liabilities	**32,000**
Net assets available for benefits	**14,000**

DEFINED BENEFIT PLANS

When amounts to be paid as retirement benefits are determined by reference to a formula, usually based on employees' earnings and/or years of service, such retirement benefit plans are defined benefit plans. The key factor is that the benefits are fixed or determinable, without regard to the adequacy of assets which may have been set aside for payment of the benefits.

The reporting objective for a defined benefit plan is periodically to provide information about the financial resources and activities of the plan that is useful in assessing the relationship between the accumulated resources and the plan benefits over time. To achieve the objective the financial statement usually includes the following:

1. A description of significant activities for the period and the effect of changes relating to the plan, its membership and terms and conditions.
2. A statement of performance for the period and the financial position at the end of the period.
3. Actual information either as part of the financial statements or separately.
4. A description of the investment policies.

The standard requires that the report of a defined benefit plan should contain *either*:

1. A statement that shows:
    a. The net assets available for benefits;
    b. The actuarial present value of promised retirement benefits, distinguishing between vested and non-vested benefits; and
    c. The resulting excess or deficit;

or

2. A statement of net assets available for benefits, including *either*:
    a. A note disclosing the actuarial present value of promised retirement benefits, distinguishing between vested and non-vested benefits; *or*
    b. A reference to this information in an accompanying actuarial report.

The standard does not make it incumbent upon the plan to obtain annual actuarial valuations. If an actuarial valuation has not been prepared on the date of the report, the most recent valuation should be used as the basis for preparing the financial statement. The date of the valuation used should be disclosed. Actuarial present values of promised benefits should be based either on current or projected salary levels. Whichever basis is used should be disclosed. The effect of any changes in actuarial assumptions that had a material impact on the actuarial present value of promised retirement benefits should also be disclosed. The report should explain the relationship between actuarial present values of promised benefits, the net assets available for benefits and the policy for funding the promised benefits.

As in the case of defined contribution plans, investments of a defined benefit plan should be carried at fair value, which for marketable securities would be market value.

The following are examples of the alternative types of reports prescribed for a defined benefit plan:

ABC Defined Benefit Plan
Statement of Net Assets Available for Benefits, Actuarial Present Value of Accumulated Retirement Benefits and Plan Excess or Deficit
December 31, 20XX
(€000)

1. Statement of net assets available for benefits	
Assets	
Investments at fair value	
Government securities	50,000
Municipal bonds	30,000
Local equity securities	30,000
Foreign equity securities	30,000
Local debt securities	20,000
Foreign corporate bonds	20,000
Other	10,000
Total investments	190,000
Receivables	
Amounts due from stockbrokers on sale of securities	150,000
Accrued interest	50,000
Dividends receivable	20,000
Total receivables	220,000
Cash	50,000
Total assets	460,000
Liabilities	
Accounts payable	
Amounts due to stockbrokers on purchase of securities	100,000
Benefits payable to participants—due and unpaid	110,000
Total accounts payable	210,000
Accrued expenses	110,000
Total liabilities	320,000
Net assets available for benefits	140,000
2. Actuarial present value of accumulated plan benefits	
Vested benefits	100,000
Non-vested benefits	20,000
Total	120,000
3. Excess of net assets available for benefits over actuarial present value of accumulated plan benefits	20,000

ABC Defined Benefit Plan
Statement of Changes in Net Assets Available for Benefits
December 31, 20XX
(€000)

Investment income	
Interest income	40,000
Dividend income	10,000
Net appreciation (unrealised gain) in fair value of investments	10,000
Total investment income	60,000
Plan contributions	
Employer contributions	50,000
Employee contributions	50,000
Total plan contributions	100,000

Total additions to net asset value	160,000
Plan benefit payments	
Pensions (annual)	30,000
Lump sum payments on retirement	30,000
Severance pay	10,000
Commutation of superannuation benefits	15,000
Total plan benefit payments	85,000
Total deductions from net asset value	85,000
Net increase in asset value	75,000
Net assets available for benefits	
Beginning of year	65,000
End of year	140,000

DISCLOSURES

IAS 26 requires that the reports of a retirement benefit plan, both defined benefit plans and defined contribution plans, should also contain the following information:

1. A statement of changes in net assets available for benefits;
2. A summary of significant accounting policies; and
3. A description of the plan and the effect of any changes in the plan during the period.

Reports provided by retirement benefits plans may include the following, if applicable:

1. A statement of net assets available for benefits disclosing:
   a. Assets at the end of the period suitably classified;
   b. The basis of valuation of assets;
   c. Details of any single investment exceeding either 5% of the net assets available for benefits or 5% of any class or type of security;
   d. Details of any investment in the employer; and
   e. Liabilities other than the actuarial present value of promised retirement benefits.
2. A statement of changes in net assets available for benefits showing the following:
   a. Employer contributions;
   b. Employee contributions;
   c. Investment income such as interest and dividends;
   d. Other income;
   e. Benefits paid or payable (analysed, for example, as retirement, death and disability benefits, and lump sum payments);
   f. Administrative expenses;
   g. Other expenses;
   h. Taxes on income;
   i. Profits and losses on disposal of investments and changes in value of investments; and
   j. Transfers from and to other plans.
3. A description of the funding policy;
4. For defined benefit plans, the actuarial present value of promised retirement benefits (which may distinguish between vested benefits and non-vested benefits) based

on the benefits promised under the terms of the plan, on service rendered to date and using either current salary levels or projected salary levels. This information may be included in an accompanying actuarial report to be read in conjunction with the related information; and

5. For defined benefit plans, a description of the significant actuarial assumptions made and the method used to calculate the actuarial present value of promised retirement benefits.

According to the standard, since the report of a retirement benefit plan contains a description of the plan, either as part of the financial information or in a separate report, it may contain the following:

1. The names of the employers and the employee groups covered;
2. The number of participants receiving benefits and the number of other participants, classified as appropriate;
3. The type of plan—defined contribution or defined benefit;
4. A note as to whether participants contribute to the plan;
5. A description of the retirement benefits promised to participants;
6. A description of any plan termination terms; and
7. Changes in items 1 through 6 during the period covered by the report.

Furthermore, it is not uncommon to refer to other documents that are readily available to users and in which the plan is described, and to include only information on subsequent changes in the report.

US GAAP COMPARISON

The US GAAP codification has separate sections for the reporting by defined benefit plans (ASC 960), defined contribution plans (ASC 962) and health and welfare plans (ASC 965). Like IFRS, actuarial measurement of the obligation is necessary and shall include estimates of participant vesting.

The obligations for these three types of plans must include future expected increases in salary rates (if applicable). There is no option as there is under IFRS to choose current salary levels. US GAAP, like IFRS, includes future increases in benefits costs. Plan assets are recorded at fair value with reductions for costs to sell. Benefit-responsive insurance contracts are reported both at fair value and contract value.

The accounting for benefit plans under US GAAP is heavily influenced by US regulations, primarily the Employment Retirement and Income Security Act of 1974 (ERISA). Certain disclosures are required only because ERISA mandates them, although the plan need not be under the jurisdiction of ERISA. Additionally, certain US government-defined plans are specifically presented in the financial statements of the plans.

Generally, all three types of plans require the following statements:

- A statement that includes information regarding the net assets available for benefits as of the end of the plan year;
- A statement that includes information regarding the changes during the year in the net assets available for benefits;
- Except for defined contribution plans, information regarding the actuarial present value of accumulated plan benefits as of either the beginning or end of the plan year.

31 AGRICULTURE

INTRODUCTION

Historically, agricultural activities received scant, if any, attention from the world's accounting standard setters. This may have been because the major national and international accounting standard setters have been those of the US and the UK, whose economies are far less dependent upon agriculture than those of many less-developed nations of the world. For developing nations, agriculture is indeed disproportionately significant, and given the IASC's role in establishing financial reporting standards for those nations, this focus on agriculture was perhaps to be expected. The culmination of this lengthy project, IAS 41, is by far the most comprehensive addressing of this financial reporting topic ever undertaken.

Prior to the development of IAS 41, assets related to agricultural activity and changes in those assets were excluded from the scope of International Accounting Standards. For instance, IAS 2, *Inventories*, excluded "producers" of livestock, agricultural and forest products "...to the extent that they are measured at net realisable value in accordance with well-established practices in certain industries." Additionally, national standard setters have produced guidelines that are relatively piecemeal and were aimed at resolving a specific issue. Also, the traditional accountancy models are based on a historic cost and realisation basis which conflicts with the rationale of change in altering biological assets. These factors led to a diversity in accounting treatments, which IAS 41 addresses.

The earlier exclusion of agriculture from most established accounting and financial reporting rules can best be understood in the context of certain unique features of the industry. These include biological transformations (growth, procreation, production, degeneration) which alter the very substance of the biological assets; the wide variety of characteristics of the living assets which challenge traditional classification schemes; the nature of management functions in the industry; and the predominance of small, closely held ownership. On the other hand, since in many nations agriculture is a major industry, in some cases accounting for over 50% of gross national product, logic would suggest that comprehensive systems of financial reporting for business entities cannot be deemed complete while excluding so large a segment of the economy.

A review of published financial statements for agriculture-related entities would have revealed the consequences of the lack of a single method of accounting. A wide range of methods and principles has been applied to such businesses as forest products, livestock and grain production.

For example, some forest products companies have accounted for timberlands at original cost, charging depreciation only to the extent of net harvesting, with reforestation costs charged to expense as incurred. Others in the same industry capitalised reforestation costs and even carrying costs and charged depletion on a units-of-production basis. Still others have been valuing forest lands at the net present value of expected future cash flows. This wide disparity obviously has impaired users' ability to gauge the relative performance of entities operating within a single industry group, hindering investment and other decision making by them.

Source of IFRS
IAS 41

SCOPE

IAS 41 applies to the following when they relate to agricultural activity:

- Biological assets, except for bearer plants;
- Agricultural produce at the point of harvest; or
- Unconditional government grants as much as it relates to a biological asset.

The accounting for assets such as inventories and plant and equipment will be guided by such existing standards as IAS 2 and IAS 16. In other words, once the biological transformation process is complete (e.g., when grain is harvested, fruit is picked, animals are slaughtered or trees are felled), the accounting principles imposed on agriculture in this chapter will cease to apply.

The following matters are excluded from the scope of this standard:

Matter	**Relevant standard**
Land related to agricultural activity	IAS 16, *Property, Plant and Equipment* IAS 40, *Investment Property*
Bearer plants related to agricultural activities (excluding produce of those bearer plants)	IAS 16, *Property, Plant and Equipment*
Government grants related to bearer plants	IAS 20, *Accounting for Government Grants and Disclosure of Government Assistance*
Intangible assets related to agricultural activity	IAS 38, *Intangible Assets*

In addition to the above, right-of-use assets arising from a lease of land related to agricultural activity will be excluded from the scope of IAS 41, *Agriculture*, once an entity adopts IFRS 16, *Leases*.

The table below provides examples of biological assets, agricultural produce and products that are the result of processing after harvest:

Biological assets	Agricultural produce	Products that are the result of processing after harvest
Sheep	Wool	Yarn, carpet
Trees in a timber plantation	Felled trees	Logs, lumber
Dairy cattle	Milk	Cheese
Pigs	Carcasses	Sausages, cured hams
Cotton plants	Harvested cotton	Thread, clothing
Sugarcane	Harvested cane	Sugar
Tobacco plants	Picked leaves	Cured tobacco
Tea bushes	Picked leaves	Tea
Grape vines	Picked grapes	Wine
Fruit trees	Picked fruit	Processed fruit
Oil palms	Picked fruit	Palm oil
Rubber trees	Harvested latex	Rubber products

All of the above categories fall into the scope of this standard, except for biological assets that may be classified as bearer plants and accordingly fall into the scope of IAS 16, *Property, Plant and Equipment*. Examples of these bearer plants included in the table above could be cotton plants, tea bushes, grape vines, fruit trees and oil palms. When determining whether a biological asset falls into the scope of this standard, judgement is required as to whether the asset meets the definition of a bearer plant; the definition of a bearer plant is discussed later on in this section.

DEFINITIONS OF TERMS

Active market. Market for which all these conditions exist: the items traded within the market are homogeneous; willing buyers and sellers can normally be found at any time; and prices are available to the public.

Agricultural activity. Management by an entity of the biological transformation and harvest of biological assets for sale or for conversion into agricultural produce or into additional biological assets.

Agricultural land. Land used directly to support and sustain biological assets in agricultural activity; however, the land itself is not a biological asset.

Agricultural produce. The harvested product of the entity's biological assets.

Bearer plants. A living plant that:

a. Is used in the production or supply of agricultural produce;
b. Is expected to bear produce for more than one period; and

c. Has a remote likelihood of being sold as agricultural produce, except for incidental scrap sales.

The following are not bearer plants:

a. Plants cultivated to be harvested as agricultural produce, such as trees grown for use as lumber;
b. Plants cultivated to produce agricultural produce where there is more than a remote likelihood that the entity will also harvest and sell the plants as agricultural produce, other than as incidental scrap sales, such as trees that are cultivated both for their fruit and lumber; and
c. Annual crops, such as maize and wheat.

Biological assets. Living plants and animals controlled by the entity as a result of past events. Control may be through ownership or through another type of legal arrangement.

Biological transformation. The processes of growth, degeneration, production and procreation, which cause qualitative and quantitative changes in a biological asset.

Carrying amount. Amount at which an asset is recognised in the statement of financial position after deducting any accumulated depreciation or amortisation and accumulated impairment losses thereon.

Costs to sell. Incremental costs directly attributable to the disposal of an asset, excluding finance costs and income taxes.

Fair value. The price that would be received to sell an asset or paid to transfer a liability in an orderly transaction between market participants at the measurement date.

Group of biological assets. An aggregation of similar living animals or plants. For instance, a herd, flock, etc., that is managed jointly to ensure that the group is sustainable on an ongoing basis.

Harvest. The detachment of agricultural produce from the biological asset or the cessation of a biological asset's life processes.

IDENTIFICATION

Agriculture is defined as the management of the biological transformation of plants and animals to yield produce for consumption or further processing. The term agriculture encompasses livestock, forestry, annual and perennial cropping, orchards, plantations and aquaculture. Agriculture is distinguished from "pure exploitation" where resources are simply removed from the environment (e.g., by fishing or deforestation) without management initiatives such as the operation of hatcheries, reforestation or other attempts to manage their regeneration. IAS 41 does not apply to pure exploitation activities, nor does it apply to agricultural produce, which is harvested and is thus a non-living product of the biological assets.

However, when bearer plants are no longer used and sold as scrap, such as cherry trees sold for firewood, these sales are seen as incidental sales and IAS 16 will still apply to the date that the bearer plant is scrapped. The standard furthermore does not govern accounting for agriculture produce which is incorporated in further processing, as occurs in integrated agribusiness entities that involve activities which are not unique to agriculture.

IAS 41 sets forth a three-part test or set of criteria for agricultural activities. First, the plants or animals which are the object of the activities must be alive and capable of transformation. Secondly, the change must be managed, which implies a range of activities (e.g., fertilising the soil and weeding in the case of crop growing; feeding and providing health care in the instance of animal husbandry; etc.). Thirdly, there must be a basis for the measurement of change, such as the ripeness of vegetables, the weight of animals, circumference of trees and so forth. If these three criteria are all satisfied, the activity will be impacted by the financial reporting requirements imposed by IAS 41.

A practical example would be where a zoo also has a breeding programme. Animals are held mainly for recreational purposes rather than agricultural activities; the animals in the zoo would therefore not fall into the scope of this standard due to the absence of management of biological transformation and IAS 16, *Property, Plant and Equipment*, would apply.

Biological assets are the principal assets of agricultural activities, and they are held for their transformative potential. This results in two major types of outcomes: the first may involve asset changes—as through growth or quality improvement, degeneration or procreation. The second involves the creation of separable products initially qualifying as agricultural produce. The management of the biological transformation process is the distinguishing characteristic of agricultural activities.

Biological assets often are managed in groups, as exemplified by herds of animals, groves of trees and fields of crops. To be considered a group, however, the components must be homogeneous in nature and there must further be homogeneity in the activity for which the group is deployed. For example, cherry trees maintained for their production of fruit are not in the same group as cherry trees grown for lumber.

IAS 41 applies to forests and similar regenerative resources excluded from IAS 16; producers' inventories of livestock, agriculture and forest products, including those excluded from IAS 2, to the extent they are to be measured at net realisable value; and natural increases in herds and agricultural and forest products excluded from IFRS 15. In other words, the produce grown on bearer plants are included in the scope of IAS 41, whereas the bearer plant itself is included in the scope of IAS 16 *Property, Plant and Equipment*.

Biological assets are categorised as either consumable or bearer and mature or immature. Consumable biological assets are those that are to be harvested as agricultural produce or sold as biological assets, such as beef cattle or crops for harvest such as wheat. Bearer biological assets are those from which other biological assets or agricultural produce are obtained, such as dairy cattle or fruit trees. Mature biological assets are those that have attained harvestable specifications or are able to sustain regular harvests whereas immature biological assets have not yet reached that stage.

RECOGNITION AND MEASUREMENT

Basic Principles of IAS 41

IAS 41 applies to all entities which undertake agricultural activities. Animals or plants are to be recognised as biological assets or agricultural produce only when all of the following requirements have been met:

a. The entity controls the asset as a result of past events. Control may be evidenced by legal ownership of cattle and the branding or otherwise marketing of the cattle on acquisition, birth or weaning;

b. It is probable that future economic benefits associated with the asset will flow to the entity. The future benefits are normally assessed by measuring the significant physical attributes; and
c. The fair value or cost of the asset can be measured reliably.

The standard also governs the initial measurement of agricultural produce, which is the end product of the biological transformation process; it furthermore guides the accounting for government grants pertaining to agricultural assets. This is in line with the *Framework* when determining whether an item classifies for recognition as an asset.

The most important feature of the standard is the requirement that biological assets are to be measured at their respective fair values less cost to sell as of each date of the statements of financial position, and agricultural produce harvested from an entity's biological assets is also measured at its fair value less costs to sell at the point of harvest, before it is transferred to inventories. The imperative to deploy fair value accounting springs from the fact that there are long production periods for many crops (an extreme being forests under management for as long as 30 years before being harvested) and, even more typically, for livestock. In the absence of fair value accounting with changes in value being reported in operating results, the entire earnings of a long-term production process might only be reported at lengthy intervals, which would not faithfully represent the underlying economic activities being carried out. This is entirely analogous to long-term construction projects, for which percentage-of-completion accounting is commonly prescribed for very similar reasons.

An example of determining whether to recognise a biological asset is a pregnant ewe that is a biological asset and its offspring will also be biological assets, but they will not be recognised as separate assets until all of the recognition criteria have been met. As control will generally not be an issue and the fair value of the new-born lambs should be readily ascertainable, it will normally only be necessary to determine when it is probable that future economic benefits associated with the lambs will flow to the owner. The lambs will therefore be recognised as separate biological assets when the lambing has proved successful and the offspring are healthy. Also bear in mind that the fair value of ewes after birth will decrease.

Determining Fair Values

The primary determinant of fair value is observable market prices, just as it is for financial instruments having active markets (as defined in IFRS 9, discussed at length in Chapter 24). Chapter 25 discusses fair value measurements under IFRS 13, *Fair Value Measurement*, in more depth. The required use of "farm gate" market prices will reflect both the "as is" and "where is" attributes of the biological assets. That is, the value is meant to pertain to the assets as they exist, where they are located, in the condition they are in as of the measurement (statement of financial position) date. They are not hypothetical values, as, for instance, are hogs when delivered to the slaughterhouse. Where these "farm gate" prices are not available, market values will have to be reduced by transaction costs, including transport, to arrive at net market values which would equate to fair values as intended by IAS 41.

The cost of a biological asset may, however, sometimes approximate the fair value, particularly when:

a. Little biological transformation has taken place since initial cost incurrence, such as for seedlings planted immediately prior to the end of a reporting period or newly acquired livestock; or
b. The impact of the biological transformation on price is not expected to be material, such as for the initial growth in a 30-year pine plantation production cycle.

In the case of products for which market values might not be readily available, other approaches to fair value determination will have to be employed. This is most likely to become an issue where market values exist but, due to market imperfections, are not deemed to be useful. For example, when access to markets is restricted or unduly influenced by temporary monopoly or monopsony conditions, or when no market exists as of the date of the statement of financial position, alternative measures will be called for. In such circumstances, it might be necessary to refer to such indicators as the most recent market prices for the class of asset at issue, market prices for similar assets (e.g., different varieties of the same crop), sector benchmarks (e.g., relating value of a dairy farm to the kilograms of milk solids or fat produced), net present value of expected future cash flows discounted at a risk-class rate or net realisable values for short-cycle products for which most growth has already occurred. Last and probably least useful would be historical costs, which might be particularly suited to biological assets that have thus far experienced little transformation.

When fair value is determined using a valuation technique due to quoted prices not being available or applicable, it is important to note than any cash flows relating to the financing of the assets, taxation or re-establishment of biological assets after harvest (such as the cost of replanting trees in a plantation forest after harvest) may not be included in the fair value determination.

One practical problem arises when an indirect method of valuation implicitly values both the crop and the land itself, taken together as a whole. IAS 41 indicates that such valuations must be allocated to the different assets to give a better indication of the future economic benefits each will confer. If a combined market price, for example, can be obtained for the land plus the immature growing crops situated thereon, and a quotation for the land alone can also be obtained, this will permit a fair value assessment of the immature growing crops (while the land itself will generally be presented on the statement of financial position at cost, not fair value, under IAS 16). Another technique would involve the subdivision of the assets into classes based on age, quality or other traits, and the valuation of each subgroup by reference to market prices. While these methods may involve added effort, IAS 41 concludes that the usefulness of the resulting financial statements will be materially enhanced if this is done.

Increases in fair value due to the growth of the biological asset is only one-half of the accounting equation, of course, since there will normally have been cost inputs incurred to foster the growth (e.g., applications of fertiliser to the fields, etc.). Under the provisions of IAS 41, costs of producing and harvesting biological assets are to be charged to expense as incurred. This is necessary, since if costs were added to the assets' carrying amount (analogous to interest on borrowings in connection with long-term construction projects) and the assets were then also adjusted to fair value, there would be risk of double-counting cost or value increases. As mandated, however, value increases due to either price changes or growth, or both, will be taken into current income, where costs of production will be appropriately matched against them, resulting in a meaningful measure of the net result of periodic operations.

However, in some instances the fair value for a biological asset may not be possible to determine. An entity is only allowed to rebut the presumption that fair value can be measured reliably on initial recognition if the following criteria are satisfied:

a. Quoted market prices are not available;
b. Alternative fair value measurements are determined to be clearly unreliable.

An entity must continuously assess whether fair value of these assets recognised at cost can now be determined; once it can be determined, the asset must be measured subsequently at fair value less cost to sell.

Where a biological asset was previously measured at fair value, an entity cannot apply this rebuttal to subsequent measurement. It should be noted that if an entity applies the above rebuttal, the judgements made by management of the entity must be detailed in the financial statements, if significant.

Recognition and Measurement

The recognition and measurement requirements of IAS 41 are as follows:

1. Biological assets are to be measured on initial recognition and at the end of each reporting period at their fair value, less estimated costs to sell, except where fair value cannot be measured reliably. In which case, it is valued at its historical cost less any accumulated depreciation and accumulated impairment losses.
2. Agricultural produce harvested from an entity's biological assets should be measured at fair value less estimated costs to sell at the point of harvest. That amount effectively becomes the cost basis, to which further processing costs may be added, as the conditions warrant, with accounting thereafter guided by IAS 2, *Inventories*, or another applicable standard.
3. If an active market exists for a biological asset or for agricultural produce, the quoted price in that market is the appropriate basis for determining the fair value of that asset. If an active market does not exist, however, the reporting entity should use market-determined prices or values, such as the most recent market transaction price, when available. It must be noted that existing contracts to sell biological assets or agricultural harvest at a future date are not necessarily relevant in measuring fair value, because fair value reflects the current market conditions in which market participant buyers and sellers would enter into a transaction. The mere existence of a contract should therefore not be considered when determining fair value at a date earlier than execution of the contract.
4. Under certain circumstances, market-determined prices or values may not be available for an asset, as it exists in its current condition. In these circumstances, the entity should use the present value of expected net cash flows from the asset discounted at a current market-determined pre-tax rate, in determining fair value.
5. The gain or loss which is reported upon initial recognition of biological assets, and those arising from changes in fair value less estimated point-of-sales costs, should be included in net profit or loss for the period in which the gain or loss arises. That is, these are reported in current period results of operations, and not taken directly into equity.
6. The gain or loss arising from the initial recognition of agricultural produce should be included in net profit or loss for the period in which it arises.
7. Land is to be accounted for under IAS 16, *Property, Plant, and Equipment*, or IAS 40, *Investment Property*, as is appropriate under the circumstances. Biological assets that are physically attached to land are recognised and measured at their fair value less estimated point-of-sales costs, separately from the land.
8. If the entity receives an unconditional government grant related to a biological asset measured at its fair value less estimated point-of-sales costs, the grant should be recognised as income when it first becomes receivable. If the grant related to a

biological asset measured at its fair value less estimated costs to sell is conditional, including grants which require an entity not to engage in specified agricultural activity, the grant should be recognised in income when the conditions attaching to it are first met.

9. For government grants pertaining to biological assets which are measured at cost less accumulated depreciation and any accumulated impairment losses, IAS 20, *Accounting for Government Grants and Disclosure of Government Assistance*, should be applied. (See Chapter 21.)
10. Some contracts for the sale of biological assets or agricultural produce are not within the scope of IFRS 9, *Financial Instruments*, because the reporting entity expects to deliver the commodity, rather than settle up in cash. Under IAS 41, such biological assets are to be measured at fair value until the biological assets are sold or the produce is harvested.

Example: Recognising gains and losses as a result of fair value measurement and sale of biological assets

Entity A purchased 100 lambs at an auction for €100,000 on December 31, 20XX. Transportation costs were €1,000. Entity A would have to incur the same transportation costs if it had sold its lambs in the auction. In addition, there would be a 2% auctioneer's fee on the market price of the lamb payable by the seller. Entity A also incurred €500 on veterinary expenses.

On June 30, 20X+1, the fair value of the cattle in the most relevant market increases to €110,000.

On September 1, 20X+1, Entity A sold 18 lambs at auction for €20,000 and incurred transportation charges of €150. In addition, there would be a 2% auctioneer's fee on the market price of the lamb payable by the seller.

On December 15, 20X+1, the fair value of the 82 remaining lambs was €82,820. Forty-two lambs were slaughtered on that day and the total cost was €4,200. The fair value of the carcasses on that day was €48,300 and the estimated transportation cost to sell the carcasses is €420. No other selling costs are expected.

On December 31, 20X+1, the fair value of the remaining 40 lambs was €44,800. The estimated transportation cost is €400. In addition, there would be a 2% auctioneer's fee on the market price of the lamb payable by the seller.

Initial recognition of lambs at December 31, 20XX:

Dr	Biological assets		€97,000*	
Dr	Loss on initial recognition		4,000	
	Cr	Bank		€101,000

**Calculation*:*	
Fair value in most relevant market	*100,000*
Less transport costs	*(1,000)*
Less auctioneer's fees	*(2,000)*

Dr	Veterinary expenses		€500	
	Cr	Bank		€500

Subsequent measurement of lambs at June 30, 20X+1:

Dr	Biological asset		€9,800*	
	Cr	Gain on changes in fair value less costs to sell		€9,800

**Calculation*:*	
Fair value in most relevant market	*110,000*
Less transportation costs	*(1,000)*
Less auctioneer's fee	*(2,200)*

Sale of lambs on September 1, 20X+1:

Dr	Bank		€19,450	
Dr	Selling expenses (150 + 400)		550	
	Cr	Revenue		€20,000

Transfer of biological assets to inventory on December 15, 20X+1:

Dr	Inventory		€47,880*	
Dr	Fair value loss on cattle		1,176	
	Cr	Biological asset (106,800 × 42/100)		€44,856
	Cr	Bank (slaughter cost)		4,200

**Calculation*:*	
Fair value of carcasses	*48,300*
Less transport costs	*(420)*

Subsequent Expenditure on Biological Assets

Where subsequent expenditure (biological transformation) are incurred of biological assets measured at fair value less costs to sell, an entity can either capitalize these subsequent costs or recognize it as an expense when incurred. This is accordingly an accounting policy choice.

Either method is acceptable in terms of IAS 41, however care should be taken when disclosing the subsequent costs either separately in the Statement of Comprehensive Income or as part of the analysis of expenses. In applying either method, entities will need to determine the needs of the users of the financial statements, in line with the requirements of IAS 1 *Presentation of Financial Statements.*

Agricultural Produce (Measurement)

Agricultural produce is distinguished from biological assets and is not to be measured at fair value other than at the point of harvest, which is the point where biological assets become agricultural produce. For example, when crops are harvested they become agricultural produce and are initially valued at the fair value as of the date of harvest, at the location of harvest (i.e., the value of harvested crops at a remote point of delivery would not be a pertinent measure). If there has been a time interval between the last valuation and the harvest, the value as of the harvest date should be determined or estimated; any increase or decrease since the last valuation would be taken into earnings.

PRESENTATION AND DISCLOSURES

Financial Statement Presentation

Statement of financial position

IAS 41 requires that the carrying amount of biological assets be presented separately on the face of the statement of financial position (i.e., not included with other, non-biological assets). Preparers are encouraged to describe the nature and stage of production of each group of biological assets in narrative format in the notes to the financial statements, optionally quantified. Consumable biological assets are to be differentiated from bearer assets, with further subdivisions into mature and immature subgroups for each of these broad categories. The purpose of these disclosures is to give the users of the financial statements some insight into the timing of future cash flows, since the mature subgroups will presumably be realised through market transactions soon, and the pattern of cash flows resulting from bearer assets differs from those deriving from consumables. In addition, the entity must disclose the nature of its activities involving each group of biological assets and non-financial measures or estimates of the physical quantities of each group of biological assets at the end of the period and output of agricultural produce during the period.

Statement of profit or loss and other comprehensive income

The changes in fair value should be presented on the face of the statement of profit or loss and other comprehensive income, ideally broken down between groups of biological assets. However, group level detail may be reserved to the notes to the financial statements.

IAS 1 permits the presentation of expenses in accordance with either a natural classification (e.g., materials purchases, depreciation, etc.) or a functional basis (cost of sales, administrative, selling, etc.). The draft standard on agriculture had urged that the natural classification of income and expenses be adopted for the statement of profit or loss and other comprehensive income. Sufficient detail is to be included in the face of the statement of profit or loss and other comprehensive income to support an analysis of operating performance. However, these are recommendations, not strict requirements.

Additional disclosures

1. An entity shall disclose:
   a. The existence and carrying amounts of biological assets whose title is restricted, and the carrying amounts of biological assets pledged as security for liabilities;
   b. The amount of commitments for the development or acquisition of biological assets; and
   c. Financial risk management strategies related to agricultural activity.
2. An entity shall present a reconciliation of changes in the carrying amount of biological assets between the beginning and the end of the current period. The reconciliation shall include:
   a. The gain or loss arising from changes in fair value less costs to sell;
   b. Increases due to purchases;

c. Decreases attributable to sales and biological assets classified as held for sale (or included in a disposal group that is classified as held for sale) in accordance with IFRS 5, *Non-current Assets Held for Sale and Discontinued Operations*;
d. Decreases due to harvest;
e. Increases resulting from business combinations;
f. Net exchange differences arising on the translation of financial statements into a different presentation currency, and on the translation of a foreign operation into the presentation currency of the reporting entity; and
g. Other changes.

3. Where fair value cannot be measured reliably, the following additional disclosure is required:

 a. A description of the biological assets;
 b. An explanation of why fair value cannot be measured reliably;
 c. If possible, the range of estimates within which fair value is highly likely to lie;
 d. The depreciation method used;
 e. The useful lives or the depreciation rates used;
 f. The gross carrying amount and the accumulated depreciation (aggregated with accumulated impairment losses) at the beginning and end of the period;
 g. Impairment losses;
 h. Reversals of impairment losses; and
 i. Depreciation.

4. Where fair value has become determinable, the following must be disclosed:

 a. A description of the biological assets;
 b. An explanation of why fair value has become reliably measurable; and
 c. The effect of the change.

EXAMPLES OF FINANCIAL STATEMENT DISCLOSURES

Sappi 201X Integrated Report
at September 201X

2.3 Critical accounting policies and estimates

2.3.5 Plantations

Plantations are stated at fair value less estimated cost to sell at the harvesting stage.

In arriving at plantation fair values, the key assumptions are estimated prices less cost of delivery, discount rates and volume and growth estimations. All changes in fair value are recognised in the period in which they arise.

The impact of changes in estimate prices, discount rates and volume and growth assumptions may have on the calculated fair value and other key financial information on plantations is disclosed in Note 10.

- **Estimated prices less cost of delivery**

The group uses a 12 quarter rolling historical average price to estimate the fair value of all immature timber and mature timber that is to be felled in more than 12 months from the reporting date. Twelve quarters is considered a reasonable period of time after taking the length of the growth cycle of the plantations into account. Expected future price trends and recent market transactions involving comparable plantations are also considered in estimating fair value.

Mature timber that is expected to be felled within 12 months from the end of the reporting period is valued using unadjusted current market prices. Such timber is expected to be used in the short term and consequently current market prices are considered an appropriate reflection of fair value.

The fair value is derived by using the prices as explained above reduced by the estimated cost of delivery. Cost of delivery includes all costs associated with getting the harvested agricultural produce to the market, including harvesting, loading, transport and allocated fixed overheads.

- **Discount rate**

The discount rate used is the applicable pre-tax weighted-average cost of capital of the business unit.

- **Volume and growth estimations and cost assumptions**

The group focuses on good husbandry techniques, which include ensuring that the rotation of plantations is met with adequate planting activities for future harvesting. The age threshold used for quantifying immature timber is dependent on the rotation period of the specific timber genus, which varies between 8 and 18 years. In the Southern African region, softwood less than eight years and hardwood less than five years are classified as immature timber.

Trees are generally felled at the optimum age when ready for intended use. At the time the tree is felled it is taken out of plantations and accounted for under inventory and reported as depletion cost (fellings).

Depletion costs include the fair value of timber felled, which is determined on the average method, plus amounts written off against standing timber to cover loss or damage caused by fire, disease and stunted growth. These costs are accounted for on a cost per metric ton allocation method multiplied by unadjusted current market prices. Tons are calculated using the projected growth to rotation age and are extrapolated to current age on a straight-line basis.

The group has projected growth estimation over a period of 8 to 18 years per rotation. In deriving this estimate, the group established a long-term sample plot network which is representative of the species and sites on which trees are grown and the measured data from these permanent sample plots were used as input into the group's growth estimation. Periodic adjustments are made to existing models for new genetic material.

The group directly manages plantations established on land that is either owned or leased from third parties. Indirectly managed plantations represent plantations established on land held by independent commercial farmers where Sappi provides technical advice on the growing and tendering of trees. The associated costs for managing the plantations are recognised as silviculture costs in cost of sales (see Note 4).

10. Plantations	**20X1**	**20X1-1**
€ million		
Plantations		
Fair value of plantations at beginning of year	**580**	**687**
Gains arising from growth	**83**	**81**
Fire, hazardous weather and other damages	**(4)**	–
(Loss) gain arising from fair value price changes	**(15)**	**(16)**
Harvesting—agriculture produce (fellings)	**(73)**	**(82)**
Disposals	**(1)**	
Translation difference	**(15)**	**(90)**
Fair value of plantations at end of year	**555**	**580**

Sappi manages the establishment, maintenance and harvesting of its plantations on a compartmentalised basis. These plantations are comprised of pulpwood and saw logs and are managed in such a way to ensure that the optimum fibre balance is supplied to its paper and pulping operations in Southern Africa.

As the group manages its plantations on a rotational basis, the respective increases by means of growth are negated by depletions over the rotation period for the group's own production or sales.

The group owns plantations on land that we own, as well as on land that we lease. The group discloses both as directly managed plantations. With regard to indirectly managed plantations, the group has several different types of agreements with many independent farmers. The terms of the agreements depend on the type and specific needs of the farmer and the areas planted ranging in duration from one to more than 20 years. In certain circumstances, we provide loans to farmers that are disclosed as accounts receivable on the group balance sheets (these loans are considered, individually and in aggregate, immaterial to the group). If the group provides seedlings, silviculture and/or technical assistance, the costs are expensed when incurred by the group.

The group is exposed to financial risks arising from climatic changes, disease and other natural risks such as fire, flooding and storms and human-induced losses arising from strikes, civil commotion and malicious damage. These risks are covered by an appropriate level of insurance as determined by management. The plantations have an integrated management system that complies with FSC standards.

Changes in estimate prices, the discount rate, costs to sell and volume and growth assumptions applied in the valuation of immature timber may impact the calculated fair value as tabled below:

€ million	**20X1**	**20X1-1**	**20X1-2**
Market price changes			
1% increase in market prices	4	4	2
1% decrease in market prices	(4)	(4)	(2)
Discount rate (for immature timber)			
1% increase in market rate	(4)	(4)	(5)
1% decrease in market rate	4	4	5
Volume assumption			
1% increase in estimate of volume	5	6	9
1% decrease in estimate of volume	(5)	(6)	(9)
Costs to sell			
1% increase in costs to sell	(3)	(3)	(1)
1% decrease in costs to sell	3	3	1
Growth assumption			
1% increase in rate of growth	2	1	2
1% decrease in rate of growth	(2)	(1)	(2)

OTHER ISSUES

Agricultural Land

Agricultural land is not deemed a biological asset; thus, the principles espoused in IAS 41 for biological and agricultural assets do not apply to land. The requirements of IAS 16, which are applicable to other categories of property, plant and equipment, apply equally to agricultural land. The use of the allowed alternative method (i.e., revaluation), particularly for land-based systems such as orchards, plantations and forests, where the fair value of the biological asset was determined from net realisable values which included the underlying land, would be logical and advisable, but is not actually a requirement. It would also enhance the usefulness of the financial statements if land held by entities engaged in agricultural activities is further classified in the statement of financial position according to specific uses. Alternatively, this information can be conveyed in the notes to the financial statements.

Intangible Assets Related to Agriculture

Under IAS 38, intangible assets may be carried at cost or at revalued amounts, but only to the extent that active markets exist for the intangibles. In general, it is not expected that such markets will exist for commonly encountered classes of intangible assets. On the other hand, agricultural activities are expected to frequently involve intangibles such as water rights, production quotas and pollution rights, and it is anticipated that for these intangibles active markets may exist.

To enhance the internal consistency of financial statements of entities engaged in biological and agriculture operations, if intangibles which pertain to the entity's agricultural activities have active markets, these should be presented in the statement of financial position at their fair values. This is not, however, an actual requirement.

US GAAP COMPARISON

US GAAP provides specific incremental guidance for the accounting, reporting and disclosure of agricultural activities. Agricultural products and activities include animals (livestock) and plants. However, ASC 905 does not apply to growers of timber, sugarcane and pineapple in tropical regions, breeding animals in competitive sports or merchants or non-co-operative processors of agricultural products that purchase commodities from growers, contract harvesters or others serving agricultural producers.

The carrying amount of agricultural products is historical cost. For assets deemed property, plant and equipment, depreciation is systematic and rational based on its utility. Permanent improvements to land, such as grading, are not depreciated because their utility does not diminish with time. Short-lived animals, such as chickens, are classified as inventory. The costs of reclaiming productive capacity from the land that relates specifically to the current year harvest are accrued as part of the costs, even though these costs will benefit subsequent years' harvest. In instances where additional costs are required after harvest of a particular crop to overcome a physical or noxious condition, those costs are estimated and accrued as costs of the harvested crop. Costs involved in raising progeny to a productive state (i.e., a calf to the point it produces milk) are accumulated as part of the costs and depreciated when the livestock reaches maturity.

Market prices for valuing crops or livestock are only used in valuing inventory or property, plant and equipment in exceptional circumstances when it is not practicable to determine an appropriate cost basis for products. Per ASC 905-330-30-1, a market basis is acceptable if the products meet all of the following criteria: (1) the products have immediate marketability at quoted market prices that cannot be influenced by the producer, (2) the products have characteristics of unit interchangeability, and (3) the products have relatively insignificant costs of disposal.

US GAAP also provides guidance for agricultural co-operatives. An agricultural co-operative is an organisation which performs any of following on behalf of its patrons: sale, processing, marketing and other activities. Co-operatives can provide services for non-patrons, but the results and financial positions must be separately presented. Co-operatives generally distribute all profits to patrons, except for retains, which are reserves to insulate the co-operative from financial shocks. Revenue is recorded by patrons whenever title passes to the co-operative. If title does not pass, the revenue is accounted for on a consignment basis, with revenue deferred until sale to the third-party buyer takes place. The equity section of an agricultural co-operative must separate earnings and balance between patrons and non-patrons. This is because the co-operative's mission is to perform service on behalf of the patrons, and each patron may have different rights and obligations, although bylaws or other agreements generally govern most of the activities. Frequently, co-operatives pool products from patrons and remit proceeds to each patron based on the volume sold.

Investments by patrons in co-operatives are accounted for under the cost method or the equity method if it has significant influence (per applicable US GAAP). The investment balance includes retains. The investment balance is reduced if co-operative losses will likely not be recovered by the patron.

32 EXTRACTIVE INDUSTRIES

INTRODUCTION

IFRS 6 deals with the accounting of exploration for, and the evaluation of, mineral resources. In April 2010, the IASB published the results of an international research project on a possible future IFRS for extractive activities in the form of a discussion paper—*Extractive Activities*. This chapter reports both on IFRS 6 and possible future developments. However, the IASB has paused the project and moved extractive activities to an inactive phase. At the time of writing, the project is not included on the IASB's work plan.

IFRS 6 does not address other aspects of accounting by entities engaged in the exploration for and evaluation of mineral resources. An entity shall not apply IFRS 6 to expenditures incurred:

a. Before the exploration for and evaluation of mineral resources, such as expenditures incurred before the entity has obtained the legal rights to explore a specific area;
b. After the technical feasibility and commercial viability of extracting a mineral resource are demonstrable.

Sources of IFRS	
IFRS 6	*IFRIC* 20

DEFINITIONS OF TERMS

Exploration and evaluation assets. Exploration and evaluation expenditures recognised as assets in accordance with the reporting entity's accounting policy.

Exploration and evaluation expenditures. Expenditures incurred by a reporting entity in connection with the exploration for and evaluation of mineral resources, before the technical feasibility and commercial viability of extracting a mineral resource have been demonstrated.

Exploration for and evaluation of mineral resources. The search for mineral resources, including minerals, oil, natural gas and similar non-regenerative resources after the entity has obtained legal rights to explore in a specific area, as well as the determination of the technical feasibility and commercial viability of extracting the mineral resources.

EXPLORATION AND EVALUATION OF MINERAL RESOURCES

Background

In December 2004, the IASB issued IFRS 6, *Exploration for and Evaluation of Mineral Resources*, which proposed an interim solution designed to facilitate compliance with IFRS by entities reporting exploration and evaluation assets, without making substantial changes to existing accounting practices. The reasons cited by the IASB for the development of an interim standard addressing exploration for and evaluation of mineral resources were as follows:

1. There were no extant IFRS that specifically addressed the exploration for and evaluation of mineral resources, which had been excluded from the scope of IAS 38. Furthermore, mineral rights and mineral resources such as oil, natural gas and similar non-regenerative resources were excluded from the scope of IAS 16. Accordingly, a reporting entity having such assets and activities is required to determine accounting policies for such expenditures in accordance with IAS 8.
2. There were alternative views on how the exploration for and evaluation of mineral resources and, particularly, the recognition of exploration and evaluation assets, were required to be accounted for under IFRS.
3. Accounting practices for exploration and evaluation expenditures under various national GAAP standards were quite diverse, and often differed from practices in other sectors for items that could have been considered similar (e.g., the accounting practices for research costs under IAS 38).
4. Exploration and evaluation expenditures represented a significant cost to entities engaged in extractive activities.

IFRS 6 in Greater Detail

IFRS 6 sets forth a set of generalised principles for reporting entities that have activities involving the exploration for and evaluation of mineral resources. These principles are as follows:

1. IFRS fully applies to these entities, except when they are specifically excluded from the scope of a given standard.
2. Reporting entities may continue employing their existing accounting policies to account for exploration and evaluation assets, but any change in accounting will have to qualify under the criteria set forth by IAS 8.

3. A reporting entity that recognises exploration and evaluation assets must assess those assets for impairment when the facts and circumstances surrounding the assets suggest that the carrying amount of the assets may exceed their recoverable amounts. However, the entity may conduct the assessment at the level of "a cash-generating unit for exploration and evaluation assets," rather than at the level otherwise required by IAS 36. As set out in IFRS 6, this is a higher level of aggregation than would have been the case under a strict application of the criteria in IAS 36. A cash-generating unit for exploration and evaluation assets can be no larger than an operating segment as determined by IFRS 8, *Operating Segments*.

Thus, according to IFRS 6, entities that have assets used for exploration and evaluation of mineral resources are to report under IFRS, but certain assets may be subject to alternative measurement requirements.

Cash-Generating Units for Exploration and Evaluation Assets

The most significant aspect of IFRS 6 concerns its establishment of a unique definition of *cash-generating units* for impairment testing. It created a different level of aggregation for mineral exploration and evaluation assets, when compared to all other assets subject to impairment considerations under IAS 36. The reason for this distinction is that the IASB was concerned that requiring entities to use the standard definition of a cash-generating unit, as set out in IAS 36, when assessing exploration and evaluation assets for impairment might have negated the effects of the other aspects of the proposal, thereby resulting in the inappropriate recognition of impairment losses under certain circumstances. Specifically, the IASB was of the opinion that the standard definition of a cash-generating unit could cause there to be uncertainty about whether the reporting entity's existing accounting policies were consistent with IFRS, because exploration and evaluation assets would often not be expected to:

1. Be the subject of future cash inflow and outflow projections relating to the development of the project, on a reasonable and consistent basis, without being heavily discounted because of uncertainty and lead times;
2. Have a determinable net selling price; or
3. Be readily identifiable with other assets that generate cash inflows as a specific cash-generating unit.

In the IASB's view, the implications were that an exploration and evaluation asset would often be deemed to be impaired, inappropriately, if the IAS 36 definition of a cash-generating unit was applied without at least the potential for modification.

IFRS 6 provides that the reporting entity is to determine an accounting policy for allocating exploration and evaluation assets to cash-generating units or groups of cash-generating units for the purpose of assessing those assets for impairment as that need arises. Accordingly, each cash-generating unit or group of units to which an exploration and evaluation asset is allocated is not to be larger than an operating segment, determined in accordance with IFRS 8 (See discussion in Chapter 28). The level identified by the entity for the purposes of testing exploration and evaluation assets for impairment can comprise one or more cash-generating units.

IFRS 6 provides that exploration and evaluation assets are to be assessed for impairment when facts and circumstances suggest that the carrying amount of an exploration and evaluation asset might exceed the recoverable amount, as with other impairment testing prescribed by IAS 36. When facts and circumstances indicate that the carrying amount might exceed the respective recoverable amount, the reporting entity is required to measure, present and disclose any resulting impairment loss in accordance with IAS 36, with the exception that the extent of aggregation may be greater than for other assets.

In addition to the criteria set out in IAS 36, IFRS 6 identifies certain indications that impairment may have occurred regarding the exploration and evaluation assets. It states that one or more of the following facts and circumstances indicate that the reporting entity should test exploration and evaluation assets for impairment:

1. The period for which the entity has the right to explore in the specific area has expired during the period or will expire in the near future and is not expected to be renewed.
2. Substantive expenditure by the entity on further exploration for and evaluation of mineral resources in the specific area is neither budgeted nor planned.
3. Exploration for and evaluation of mineral resources in the specific area have not resulted in the discovery of commercially viable quantities of mineral resources, and accordingly the reporting entity decided to discontinue such activities in the specific area.
4. Sufficient data exist to suggest that, although a development in the specific area is likely to proceed, the carrying amount from the exploration and evaluation asset is unlikely to be fully recovered.

If testing identifies impairment, the consequent adjustment of carrying amounts to the lower, impaired value results in a charge to current operating results, just as described by IAS 36 (discussed in Chapter 13).

ASSETS SUBJECT TO IFRS 6

Categorisation

IFRS 6 provides a listing of assets that would fall within the definition of exploration and evaluation expenditures. These assets are those that are related to the following activities:

1. Acquisition of rights to explore;
2. Topographical, geological, geochemical and geophysical studies;
3. Exploratory drilling;
4. Trenching;
5. Sampling; and
6. Activities in relation to evaluating technical feasibility and commercial viability of extracting a mineral resource.

The qualifying expenditures notably *exclude* those that are incurred in connection with the development of a mineral resource once technical feasibility and commercial viability of extracting a mineral resource have been established. Additionally, any administration and other general overhead costs are explicitly excluded from the definition of qualifying expenditures.

Availability of Cost or Revaluation Models

Consistent with IAS 16, IFRS 6 requires initial recognition of exploration and evaluation assets based on actual cost, but subsequent recognition can be done using either the historical cost model or the revaluation model. The standard does not offer guidance regarding these accounting treatments and the requirements of IAS 16 or IAS 38 should be applied. (See discussion in Chapters 9 and 11.)

Financial Statement Classification

IFRS 6 provides that the reporting entity is to classify exploration and evaluation assets as tangible or intangible according to the nature of the assets acquired and apply the classification consistently. It notes that certain exploration and evaluation assets, such as drilling rights, have traditionally been considered intangible assets, while other assets have historically been identified as tangible (such as vehicles and drilling rigs). The standard states that, to the extent that a tangible asset is consumed in developing an intangible asset, the amount reflecting that consumption (which would otherwise be reported as depreciation) becomes part of the cost of the intangible asset. Using a tangible asset to develop an intangible asset, however, does not warrant classifying the tangible asset as an intangible asset.

In the statement of financial position, exploration and evaluation assets are to be presented as a separate class of assets. Disclosures required by IAS 16 or IAS 38 must be made depending on how the exploration and evaluation assets are classified.

IFRS 6 only addresses exploration and evaluation. It holds that once the technical feasibility and commercial viability of extracting a mineral resource have been demonstrated, exploration and evaluation assets are no longer to be classified as such. At that point, the exploration and evaluation assets are to be assessed for impairment, and any impairment loss recognised, before reclassification.

Disclosure Requirements under IFRS 6

A reporting entity is required to disclose information that identifies and explains the amounts recognised in its financial statements that pertain to the exploration for and evaluation of mineral resources. This could be accomplished by disclosing:

1. Its accounting policies for exploration and evaluation expenditures, including the recognition of exploration and evaluation assets;
2. The amounts of assets, liabilities, income and expense and operating and investment cash flows arising from the exploration for and evaluation of mineral resources.

The Exposure Draft preceding IFRS 6 had proposed that the mandatory disclosures identify the level at which the entity assesses exploration and evaluation assets for impairment. While this is not set forth in IFRS 6, it is obviously good practice, and is therefore strongly recommended by the authors.

EXAMPLE OF FINANCIAL STATEMENT DISCLOSURES

Since IFRS 6 is only an interim standard that does not deal with all aspects of the recognition and measurement of mining assets and liabilities it is important to illustrate how the recognition and measurement of mining assets are applied through a practical example.

Anglo American
2017 Annual Report

Accounting policy: exploration and evaluation expenditure

Exploration and evaluation expenditure is expensed in the year in which it is incurred. Exploration expenditure is the cost of exploring for mineral resources other than that occurring at existing operations and projects and comprises geological and geophysical studies, exploratory drilling and sampling and mineral resource development. Evaluation expenditure includes the cost of conceptual and pre-feasibility studies and evaluation of mineral resources at existing operations. When a decision is taken that a mining project is technically feasible and commercially viable, usually after a pre-feasibility study has been completed, subsequent directly attributable expenditure, including feasibility study costs, are considered development expenditure and are capitalised within property, plant and equipment. Exploration properties acquired are recognised on the balance sheet when management considers that their value is recoverable. These properties are measured at cost less any accumulated impairment losses.

IFRIC 20, *STRIPPING COSTS IN THE PRODUCTION PHASE OF A SURFACE MINE*

In August 2011, the IASB published IFRIC 20, *Stripping Costs in the Production Phase of a Surface Mine*. This IFRIC addresses the following three questions:

1. How and what production stripping costs to recognise as an asset;
2. How to initially measure the stripping activity asset; and
3. How to subsequently measure the stripping activity asset.

In summary, the IFRIC concludes that:

- When benefits from the stripping activity are realised in the form of inventory produced, the principles of IAS 2, *Inventories*, shall be applied. However, to the extent that the benefit is the improved access to ore, the entity shall recognise these costs as a non-current asset. This non-current asset will be known as the "stripping activity asset."
- The stripping activity asset will be accounted for as part of an existing asset (an enhancement of an existing asset) and will be classified as either tangible or intangible according to the nature of the existing asset of which it forms a part.
- The stripping activity asset will be initially measured at cost.
- The stripping activity asset will be subsequently measured at cost or revalued amount less depreciation or amortisation and less impairment losses, in the same way as the existing asset of which it is a part.
- The stripping activity asset will be depreciated or amortised on a systematic basis, over the expected useful life of the identified component of the ore body that becomes more accessible as a result of the stripping activity.

This IFRIC becomes effective for annual periods beginning on or after January 1, 2013. Earlier application is permitted. The Interpretation applies to production stripping costs incurred on or after the beginning of the earliest period presented. Any "predecessor stripping asset" at that date is required to be reclassified as a part of the existing asset to which the stripping activity is related (to the extent there remains an identifiable component of the ore body to which it can be associated), or otherwise recognised in opening retained earnings at the beginning of the earliest period presented.

The following is a practical example of an accounting policy and illustrates how deferred stripping is applied in practice.

EXAMPLE OF FINANCIAL STATEMENT DISCLOSURES

Anglo American
2017 Annual Report

Accounting judgements: deferred stripping

In certain mining operations, rock or soil overlying a mineral deposit, known as overburden, and other waste materials must be removed to access the orebody. The process of removing overburden and other mine waste materials is referred to as stripping. The group defers stripping costs onto the balance sheet where they are considered to improve access to ore in future periods. Where the amount to be capitalised cannot be specifically identified it is determined based on the volume of waste extracted compared with expected volume for the identified component of the orebody. This determination is dependent on an individual mine's design and life of mine plan and therefore changes to the design or life of mine plan will result in changes to these estimates. Identification of the components of a mine's orebody is made by reference to the life of mine plan. The assessment depends on a range of factors, including each mine's specific operational features and materiality.

Accounting policy: deferred stripping

The removal of rock or soil overlying a mineral deposit, overburden and other waste minerals is often necessary during the initial development of an open pit mine site to access the orebody. The process of removing overburden and other mine waste materials is referred to as stripping. The directly attributable cost of this activity is capitalised in full within "Mining properties and leases," until the point at which the mine is considered to be capable of operating in the manner intended by management. This is classified as expansionary capital expenditure, within investing cash flows.

The removal of waste material after the point at which depreciation commences is referred to as production stripping. When the waste removal activity improves access to ore extracted in the current period, the costs of production stripping are charged to the income statement as operating costs in accordance with the principles of IAS 2, *Inventories*.

Where production stripping activity both produces inventory and improves access to ore in future periods the associated costs of waste removal are allocated between the two elements. The portion that benefits future ore extraction is capitalised within "Mining properties and leases." This is classified as stripping and development capital expenditure, within investing cash flows. If the amount to be capitalised cannot be specifically identified it is determined based on the volume of the waste extracted compared with expected volume for the identified component of the orebody. The determination is dependent on an individual mine's design and life of mine plan and therefore changes to the design or life of mine plan will result in changes to these estimates. Identification of the components of a mine's orebody is made by reference to the life of mine plan. The assessment depends on a range of factors, including each mine's specific operational features and materiality.

In certain instances, significant levels of waste removal may occur during the production phase with little or no associated production. This may occur at both open pit and underground mines, for example longwall development.

The cost of this waste removal is capitalised in full to "Mining properties and leases."

All amounts capitalised in respect of waste removal are depreciated using the unit of production method for the component of the orebody to which they relate, consistent with depreciation of property, plant and equipment.

The effects of changes to the life of mine plan on the expected cost of waste removal or remaining ore reserves for a component are accounted for prospectively as a change in estimate.

The IASB has decided to open a research project on extractive industries again to assess whether accounting requirements for exploration, evaluation, development and production of minerals, and oil and gas, should be introduced. No documents are published yet.

FUTURE DEVELOPMENTS

The IASB is in the process of gathering evidence to decide whether a project on extractive industries should be included in their work plan.

US GAAP COMPARISON

US GAAP separately addresses extractive industries (ASC 930), specifically for mining and oil- and gas-producing companies (ASC 932), accounting for the acquisition of property, exploration, development, production and support equipment and facilities. Specific guidance regarding the presentation of costs and revenues, capitalisation, depreciation, derecognition and disclosure of costs related to oil and gas extraction is also provided. However, extracted resources are valued at cost with very few exceptions.

Disclosures for oil and gas activities are substantial and require specialised engineering estimates. Some of these disclosures are:

- Proved oil and gas reserve quantities;
- Capitalised costs relating to oil- and gas-producing activities;
- Continued capitalisation of exploratory well costs;
- Costs incurred for property acquisition, exploration and development;
- Results of operations of oil- and gas-producing activities;
- A standardised measure of discounted future net cash flows related to proven oil and gas reserve quantities.

There are additional disclosures for public companies. Disclosures also include net quantities for equity-accounted entities. The unit of account for impairments is specifically at the field level. Additionally, if a field is proved non-productive after the balance sheet date, but before the financial statements are available for issue, it should be considered for an adjusting subsequent event, not merely a disclosure as is required for other impairments related to conditions occurring after the reporting date.

Under US GAAP all costs related to oil- and gas-producing activities are accounted for under either the successful efforts method or the full cost method, and the type of exploration and evaluation costs capitalised under each method differ. For other extractive industries, exploration and evaluation costs are generally expensed as they are incurred unless an identifiable asset is created by the activity.

Additionally, oil- and gas-producing entities do not segregate capitalised exploration and evaluation costs into tangible and intangible components; instead all capitalised costs are classified as tangible assets. Furthermore, the test for recoverability is usually conducted at the oil and gas field level under the successful efforts method, or by geographic region under the full cost method.

33 ACCOUNTING FOR INSURANCE CONTRACTS

INTRODUCTION

IFRS 4, *Insurance Contracts*, mainly addresses the identification of insurance contracts by an entity that issues these contracts—which is not limited to insurance companies—and limited other recognition and measurement issues. It applies to insurance contracts issued, reinsurance contracts held and financial instruments issued with a discretionary participation feature. The matter of the actual accounting for insurance contracts is not addressed in IFRS 4.

IFRS 17, *Insurance Contracts*, was issued in May 2017 to create a comprehensive standard to deal with the identification, recognition, measurement, presentation and disclosure of insurance contracts. IFRS 17 is effective for annual reporting periods beginning on or after January 1, 2022. Earlier adoption is permitted provided that the entity also applies IFRS 9, *Financial Instruments*, and IFRS 15, *Revenue from Contracts with Customers*, on or before the date of initial application of IFRS 17.

Source of IFRS
IFRS 4

DEFINITIONS OF TERMS

Cedant. The policyholder under a reinsurance contract.

Deposit component. A contractual component that is not accounted for as a derivative under IFRS 9 and would be within the scope of IFRS 9 if it were a separate instrument.

Direct insurance contract. An insurance contract that is not a reinsurance contract.

Discretionary participation feature. A contractual right to receive, as a supplement to guaranteed benefits, additional benefits:

1. That are likely to be a significant portion of the total contractual benefits;
2. Whose amount or timing is contractually at the discretion of the issuer; and
3. That are contractually based on:
    a. The performance of a specified pool of contracts or a specified type of contract;
    b. Realised and/or unrealised investment returns on a specific pool of assets held by the issuer; or
    c. The profit or loss of the company, fund or other entity that issues the contract.

Fair value. The amount for which an asset could be exchanged, or a liability settled, between knowledgeable, willing parties in an arm's-length transaction.

Financial guarantee contract. A contract that requires the issuer to make specified payments to reimburse the holder for a loss it incurs because a specified debtor fails to make payment when due in accordance with the original or modified terms of a debt instrument.

Financial risk. The risk of a possible future change in one or more of a specified interest rate, financial instrument price, commodity price, foreign exchange rate, index of prices or rates, credit rating or credit index or other variable, provided in the case of a non-financial variable that the variable is not specific to a party to the contract.

Guaranteed benefits. Payments or other benefits to which a particular policyholder or investor has an unconditional right that is not subject to the contractual discretion of the issuer.

Guaranteed element. An obligation to pay guaranteed benefits included in a contract that contains a discretionary participation feature.

Insurance asset. An insurer's net contractual rights under an insurance contract.

Insurance contract. A contract under which one party (the insurer) accepts significant insurance risk from another party (the policyholder) by agreeing to compensate the policyholder if a specified uncertain future event (the insured event) adversely affects the policyholder.

Insurance liability. An insurer's net contractual obligations under an insurance contract.

Insurance risk. Risk, other than financial risk, transferred from the holder of a contract to the issuer.

Insured event. An uncertain future event that is covered by an insurance contract and creates insurance risk.

Insurer. The party that has an obligation under an insurance contract to compensate a policyholder if an insured event occurs.

Liability adequacy test. An assessment of whether the carrying amount of an insurance liability needs to be increased (or the carrying amount of related deferred acquisition costs or related intangible assets decreased), based on a review of future cash flows.

Policyholder. A party that has a right to compensation under an insurance contract if an insured event occurs.

Reinsurance assets. A cedant's net contractual rights under a reinsurance contract.

Reinsurance contract. An insurance contract issued by one insurer (the reinsurer) to compensate another insurer (the cedant) for losses on one or more contracts issued by the cedant.

Reinsurer. The party that has an obligation under a reinsurance contract to compensate a cedant if an insured event occurs.

Unbundle. Account for the components of a contract as if they were separate contracts.

INSURANCE CONTRACTS

An insurance contract is defined in IFRS 4 as a contract under which one party (the insurer) accepts significant insurance risk from another party (the policyholder) by agreeing to compensate the policyholder if a specified uncertain future event (the insured event) adversely affects the policyholder.

A contract creates sufficient insurance risk to qualify as an insurance contract only if there is a reasonable possibility that an event affecting the policyholder or other beneficiary will cause a significant change in the present value of the insurer's net cash flows arising from that contract. In considering whether there is a reasonable possibility of such significant change, it is necessary to consider the probability of the event and the magnitude of its effect. Also, a contract that qualifies as an insurance contract at inception or later remains an insurance contract until all rights and obligations are extinguished or expire. If a contract did not qualify as an insurance contract at inception, it should be subsequently reclassified as an insurance contract if, and only if, a significant change in the present value of the insurer's net cash flows becomes a reasonable possibility.

A range of other arrangements, which share certain characteristics with insurance contracts, would be excluded from any imposed insurance contracts accounting standard, since they are dealt with under other standards. These include financial guarantees (including credit insurance) measured at fair value; product warranties issued directly by a manufacturer, dealer or retailer; employers' assets and liabilities under employee benefit plans (including equity compensation plans); retirement benefit obligations reported by defined benefit retirement plans; contingent consideration payable or receivable in a business combination; and contractual rights or contractual obligations that are contingent on the future use of, or right to use, a non-financial item (for example, certain licence fees, royalties, lease payments and similar items).

IFRS 4 applies to all insurance contracts, including reinsurance. Thus, the standard does not relate only to insurance companies, but all entities engaging in insurance contracts.

IFRS 4 does not apply to product warranties issued directly by a manufacturer, dealer or retailer; employers' assets and liabilities under employee benefit plans and retirement benefit obligations reported by defined benefit retirement plans; contractual rights or obligations that are contingent on the future use of or right to use a non-financial item, as well as lessee's residual value guarantees on finance leases; financial guarantees entered into or retained on transferring financial assets or financial liabilities within the scope of IFRS 9; contingent consideration payable or receivable in a business combination; or direct insurance contracts that an entity holds as a policyholder.

Insurance risk

IFRS 4 replaces what had been an indirect definition of an insurance contract under IAS 32 with a positive definition based on the transfer of significant insurance risk from the policyholder to the insurer. This definition covers most motor, travel, life, annuity, medical, property, reinsurance and professional indemnity contracts. Some catastrophe bonds and weather derivatives would also qualify, as long as payments are linked to a specific climatic or other insured future event that would adversely affect the policyholder. On the other hand, policies that transfer no significant insurance risk—such as some savings and pensions plans—will be deemed financial instruments, addressed by IFRS 9, regardless of their legal form. IFRS 9 also applies to contracts that principally transfer financial risk, such as credit derivatives and some forms of financial reinsurance.

There may be some difficulty in classifying the more complex products (including certain hybrids). To facilitate this process, the IASB has explained that insurance risk will be deemed *significant* only if an insured event could cause an insurer to pay significant additional benefits in *any* scenario, apart from a scenario that lacks commercial substance. As a practical matter, reporting entities should compare the cash flows from (1) the occurrence of the insured event against (2) all other events. If the cash flows under the former are significantly larger than under the latter, significant insurance risk is present.

For example, when the insurance benefits payable upon death are significantly larger than the benefits payable upon surrender or maturity, there is significant insurance risk. The significance of the additional benefits is to be measured irrespective of the probability of the insured event, if the scenario has commercial substance. Reporting entities have to develop internal quantitative guidance to ensure the definition is applied consistently throughout the entity. To qualify as significant, the insurance risk also needs to reflect a *pre-existing* risk for the policyholder, rather than having arisen from the terms of the contract.

This requirement would specifically exclude from the cash flow comparison features such as waivers of early redemption penalties within investment plans or mortgages in the event of death. Since it is the contract itself that brought the charges into place, the waiver does not represent an additional benefit received for the transfer of a pre-existing insurance risk.

The application of this IFRS 4 definition may result in the redesignation of a significant fraction of existing insurance contracts as investment contracts. In other situations, the impact could be the opposite. For example, a requirement to pay benefits earlier if an insured event occurs could make a contract insurance; this means that many pure endowment contracts are likely to meet the definition of insurance. All told, insuring entities will need to set clear, consistent and justifiable contract classification criteria and rigorously apply these.

RECOGNITION AND MEASUREMENT GUIDANCE

Adequacy of insurance liabilities

IFRS 4 imposes a *liability adequacy test*, which requires that at each reporting date the "insurer" must assess whether its recognised insurance liabilities are adequate, using then-current estimates of future cash flows under the outstanding insurance contracts. If as a result of that assessment it is determined that the carrying amount of insurance liabilities (less related deferred acquisition costs and related intangible assets, if appropriate—see discussion below) is insufficient given the estimated future cash flows, the full amount of such deficiency must be reported currently in earnings.

The standard defines minimum requirements for the adequacy test that is to be applied to the liability account. These minimum requirements are that:

1. The test considers the current estimates of all contractual cash flows, and of such related cash flows as claims handling costs, as well as cash flows that will result from embedded options and guarantees.

2. If the test shows that the liability is inadequate, the entire deficiency is recognised in profit or loss.

In situations where the insuring entity's accounting policies do not require a liability adequacy test, or provide for a test that does not meet the minimum requirements noted above, then the entity is required under IFRS 4 to:

1. Determine the carrying amount of the relevant insurance liabilities, less the carrying amount of:
    a. Any related deferred acquisition costs; and
    b. Any related intangible assets, such as those acquired in a business combination or portfolio transfer. However, related reinsurance assets are not considered because an insurer accounts for them separately.
2. Determine whether the carrying amount of the relevant net insurance liabilities is less than the carrying amount that would be required if the relevant insurance liabilities were within the scope of IAS 37. If it is less, the insurer shall recognise the entire difference in profit or loss and decrease the carrying amount of the related deferred acquisition costs or related intangible assets or increase the carrying amount of the relevant insurance liabilities.

The IAS 37-based amount is the required minimum liability to be presented. Therefore, if the current carrying amount is less, the insuring entity must recognise the entire shortfall in current period earnings. The corresponding credit to this loss recognition will either decrease the carrying amount of the related deferred acquisition costs or related intangible assets or increase the carrying amount of the relevant insurance liabilities, or both, dependent upon the facts and circumstances.

In applying the foregoing procedures, any related reinsurance assets are not considered, because an insuring entity accounts for these separately, as noted later in this discussion.

If an insuring entity's liability adequacy test meets the minimum requirements set forth above, this test is applied at the level of aggregation specified above. On the other hand, if the liability adequacy test does not meet the stipulated minimum requirements, the comparison must instead be made at the level of a portfolio of contracts that are subject to broadly similar risks and which are managed together as a single portfolio.

For purposes of comparing the recorded liability to the amount required under IAS 37, it is acceptable to reflect future investment margins only if the carrying amount of the liability also reflects those same margins. Future investment margins are defined under IFRS 4 as being employed if the discount rate used reflects the estimated return on the insuring entity's assets, or if the returns on those assets are projected at an estimated rate of return, and discounted at a different rate, with the result included in the measurement of the liability. There is a rebuttable presumption that future investment margins should not be used; however, exceptions (see below) can exist.

Impairment testing of reinsurance assets

When an insuring entity obtains reinsurance (making it the *cedant*), an asset is created in its financial statements. As with other assets, the reporting entity must consider whether an impairment has occurred as of the reporting date. Under IFRS 4, a reinsurance asset is impaired only when there is objective evidence that the cedant may not receive all amounts due to it under the terms of the contract, as a consequence of an event that occurred after initial recognition of the reinsurance asset, and furthermore the impact of that event is reliably measurable in terms of the amounts that the cedant will receive from the reinsurer.

When the reinsurance asset is found to be impaired, the carrying amount is adjusted downward and a loss is recognised in current period earnings for the full amount.

Selection of accounting principles

IFRS requires certain accounting practices to be adopted with regard to insurance contracts, but also allows other, existing procedures to remain in place under defined conditions. An insuring entity may, under the provisions of IFRS 4, change accounting policies for insurance contracts only if such change makes the financial statements more relevant to the economic decision-making needs of users and no less reliable or more reliable and no less relevant to those needs. Relevance and reliability are to be assessed by applying the criteria set forth in IAS 8.

To justify changing its accounting policies for insurance contracts, an insuring entity must demonstrate that the change brings its financial statements nearer to satisfying the criteria of IAS 8, but the change does not necessarily have to achieve full compliance with those criteria. The standard addresses changes in accounting policies in the context of current interest rates; continuation of existing reporting practices; prudence; future investment margins; and "shadow accounting." These are discussed in the following paragraphs.

Regarding interest rates, IFRS 4 provides that an insuring entity is permitted, although it is not required, to change its accounting policies such that it remeasures designated insurance liabilities to reflect current market interest rates, and recognises changes in those liabilities in current period earnings. It may also adopt accounting policies that require other current estimates and assumptions for the designated liabilities. IFRS 4 permits an insuring entity to change its accounting policies for designated liabilities, without consistently applying those policies to all similar liabilities, as the requirements under IAS 8 would suggest. If the insuring entity designates liabilities for this policy choice, it must continue to apply current market interest rates consistently in all periods to all these liabilities until they are later eliminated.

An unusual feature of IFRS 4 is that it offers affected reporting entities the option to continue with their existing accounting policies. Specifically, an insuring entity is allowed to continue the following practices if in place prior to the effective date of IFRS 4:

1. Measuring insurance liabilities on an *undiscounted* basis.
2. Measuring contractual rights to future investment management fees at an amount that exceeds their fair value as implied by a comparison with current fees charged by other market participants for similar services. It is likely that the fair value at inception of those contractual rights equals the origination costs paid, unless future investment management fees and related costs are out of line with market comparables.
3. Employing non-uniform accounting policies for the insurance contracts (and related deferred acquisition costs and intangible assets, if any) of subsidiaries, except as permitted by the above-noted interest provision. If those accounting policies are not uniform, the insuring entity may change them if the change does not make the accounting policies more diverse, and also satisfies the other requirements of the standard.

The concept of *prudence*, as set forth in IFRS 4, is meant to excuse an insuring entity from a need to change its accounting policies for insurance contracts to eliminate excessive prudence (i.e., conservatism). However, if the insuring entity already measures its insurance contracts with sufficient prudence, it is not permitted to introduce additional prudence following adoption of IFRS 4.

The matter of *future investment margins* requires some explanation. Under IFRS 4 it is clearly preferred that the measurement of insurance contracts should not reflect future investment margins, but the standard does not require reporting entities to change accounting policies for insurance contracts to eliminate future investment margins. On the other hand, adopting a policy that would reflect this is presumed to be improper (the standard states that there is a rebuttable presumption that the financial statements would become less relevant and reliable if an accounting policy that reflects future investment margins in the measurement of insurance contracts is adopted, unless those margins affect the contractual payments). The standard offers two examples of accounting policies that reflect those margins. The first is using a discount rate that reflects the estimated return on the insurer's assets, while the second is projecting the returns on those assets at an estimated rate of return, discounting those projected returns at a different rate and including the result in the measurement of the liability.

IFRS 4 states that the insuring entity could possibly overcome this rebuttable presumption if the other components of a change in accounting policies increase the relevance and reliability of its financial statements sufficiently to outweigh the decrease in relevance and reliability caused by the inclusion of future investment margins. As an example, it cites the situation where the existing accounting policies for insurance contracts involve excessively prudent (i.e., conservative) assumptions set at inception, and a statutory discount rate not directly referenced to market conditions and ignore some embedded options and guarantees. This entity might make its financial statements more relevant and no less reliable by switching to a comprehensive investor-oriented basis of accounting that is widely used and involves current estimates and assumptions; a reasonable (but not excessively prudent) adjustment to reflect risk and uncertainty; measurements that reflect both the intrinsic value and time value of embedded options and guarantees; and a current market discount rate, even if that discount rate reflects the estimated return on the insuring entity's assets.

The actual ability to overcome IFRS 4's rebuttable presumption is fact dependent. Thus, in some measurement approaches, the discount rate is used to determine the present value of a future profit margin, which is then attributed to different periods using a formula. In such approaches, the discount rate affects the measurement of the liability only indirectly, and the use of a less appropriate discount rate has limited or no effect on the measurement of the liability at inception. In yet other approaches, the discount rate determines the measurement of the liability directly, and because the introduction of an asset-based discount rate has a more significant effect, it is highly unlikely that an insurer could overcome the rebuttable presumption noted above.

Finally, there is the matter of *shadow accounting*. According to IFRS 4, an insurer is permitted, but not required, to change its accounting policies so that a recognised but unrealised gain or loss on an asset affects those measurements in the same way that a realised gain or loss does. This is because, under some accounting models, realised gains or losses on an insurer's assets have a direct effect on the measurement of some or all of (1) its insurance liabilities; (2) related deferred acquisition costs; and (3) related intangible assets. IFRS 4 provides that the related adjustment to the insurance liability (or deferred acquisition costs or intangible assets) may be recognised in equity if, and only if, the unrealised gains or losses are recognised directly in equity.

Unbundling

Specific requirements pertain to *unbundling* of elements of insurance contracts, and dealing with embedded derivatives, options and guarantees.

Unbundling refers to the accounting for components of a contract as if they were separate contracts. Some insurance contracts consist of an insurance component and a deposit component. IFRS 4 in some cases requires the reporting entity to unbundle those components, and in other fact situations provides the entity with the option of unbundled accounting. Specifically, unbundling is *required* if both the following conditions are met:

1. The insuring entity can measure the deposit component (inclusive of any embedded surrender options) separately (i.e., without considering the insurance component); *and*
2. The insuring entity's accounting policies do not otherwise require it to recognise all obligations and rights arising from the deposit component.

On the other hand, unbundling is permitted, but not required, if the insuring entity can measure the deposit component separately but its accounting policies require it to recognise all obligations and rights arising from the deposit component, regardless of the basis used to measure those rights and obligations.

Unbundling is actually prohibited if an insuring entity cannot measure the deposit component separately. If unbundling is applied to a contract, the insuring entity applies IFRS 4 to the insurance component of the contract, while using IFRS 9 to account for the deposit component of that contract.

Recognition

IFRS 4 prohibits the recognition of a liability for any provisions for possible future claims, if those claims arise under insurance contracts that are not in existence at the reporting date. Catastrophe and equalisation provisions are thus prohibited, because they do not reflect loss events that have already occurred and therefore recognition would be inconsistent with IAS 37. Loss recognition testing is required for losses already incurred at each date of the statement of financial position, as described above. An insurance liability (or a part of an insurance liability) is to be removed from the statement of financial position only when it is extinguished (i.e., when the obligation specified in the contract is discharged or cancelled or expires).

In terms of display, offsetting of reinsurance assets against the related insurance liabilities is prohibited, as is offsetting of income or expense from reinsurance contracts against the expense or income from the related insurance contracts.

Discretionary participation features in insurance contracts

Insurance contracts sometimes contain a discretionary participation feature, as well as a guaranteed element. (That is, some portion of the return to be accrued to policyholders is at the discretion of the insuring entity.) Under the provisions of IFRS 4, the issuer of such a contract may, but is not required to, recognise the guaranteed element separately from the discretionary participation feature. If the issuer does not recognise them separately, it must classify the entire contract as a liability. If, on the other hand, the issuer classifies them separately, it will classify the guaranteed element as a liability. If the entity recognises the discretionary participation feature separately from the guaranteed element, the discretionary participation feature can be classified either as a liability or as a separate component of equity; the standard does not specify how the decision should be reached. In fact, the issuer may even split that feature into liability and equity components, if a consistent accounting policy is used to determine that split.

When there is a discretionary participation feature which is reported in equity, the reporting entity is permitted to recognise all premiums received as revenue, without separating any portion that relates to the equity component. Changes in the guaranteed element and in the portion of the discretionary participation feature classified as a liability are to be reported in earnings, while changes in the part of the discretionary participation feature classified as equity are to be accounted for as an allocation of earnings, similar to how minority interest is reported.

Embedded derivatives

If the contract contains an embedded derivative within the scope of IFRS 9, that standard must be applied to that embedded derivative.

DISCLOSURE

Under the provisions of IFRS 4, insuring entities must disclose information that identifies and explains the amounts in its financial statements arising from insurance contracts. This is accomplished by disclosure of accounting policies for insurance contracts and related assets, liabilities, income and expense; of recognised assets, liabilities, income and expense (and, if it presents its statement of cash flows using the direct method, cash flows) arising from insurance contracts. Additionally, if the insuring entity is a cedant, it must also disclose gains and losses recognised in profit or loss on buying reinsurance; and, if the cedant defers and amortises gains and losses arising on buying reinsurance, the amortisation for the period and the amounts remaining unamortised at the beginning and end of the period.

Disclosure is also required of the process used to determine the assumptions that have the greatest effect on the measurement of the recognised amounts described above. When practicable, quantified disclosure of those assumptions is to be presented as well. The effect of changes in assumptions used to measure insurance assets and insurance liabilities is required, reporting separately the effect of each change that has a material effect on the financial statements.

Finally, reconciliation of changes in insurance liabilities, reinsurance assets and, if any, related deferred acquisition costs are mandated by IFRS 4.

Regarding the amount, timing and uncertainty of cash flows, the entity is required to disclose information that helps users to understand these matters as they result from insurance contracts. This is accomplished if the insuring entity discloses its objectives in managing risks arising from insurance contracts and its policies for mitigating those risks.

Applying IFRS 9 with IFRS 4

IFRS 4 was amended September 2016 to create a temporary exception for insurers to remain applying IAS 39 rather than IFRS 9 for annual periods beginning before January

1, 2021, if the insurer's activities are predominantly connected with insurance. If the entities activities are not predominantly connected with insurance, an overlay approach may be applied, under which the difference between the IFRS 9 and IAS 39 treatment is recognised in other comprehensive income.

The temporary exemptions from IFRS 9 and the overlay approach are also available to an issuer of a financial instrument that contains a discretionary participation feature.

Temporary exemption from IFRS 9

An insurer may apply the temporary exemption from IFRS 9 if it has not previously applied any version of IFRS 9 (except for applying the requirement in IFRS 9 that the effect of changes in credit risk of a liability are recognised in other comprehensive income for financial liability designated at fair value through profit or loss) and its activities are predominantly connected with insurance, at its annual reporting date that immediately precedes April 1, 2016, or at a subsequent annual reporting date specified.

After April 1, 2016 an entity applying the temporary exception should reassess whether its activities are predominantly connected with insurance at a subsequent annual reporting date if there was a change in the entity's activities. An entity that previously did not qualify for the temporary exemption from IFRS 9 is permitted to reassess whether its activities are predominantly connected with insurance at subsequent annual reporting dates before December 31, 2018 only if there was a change in the entity's activities during that annual period. The standard provides additional guidance on what constitutes a change in an entity's activities.

If an entity no longer qualifies for the temporary exemption from IFRS 9 as a result of a reassessment, then the entity is permitted to continue to apply the temporary exemption from IFRS 9 only until the end of the annual period that began immediately after that reassessment. An insurer that previously elected to apply the temporary exemption from IFRS 9 may at the beginning of any subsequent annual period irrevocably elect to apply IFRS 9.

An entity applying the temporary exception from IFRS 9 may apply the requirement in IFRS 9 that the effect of changes in credit risk of a liability are recognised in other comprehensive income for financial liability designated at fair value through profit or loss.

An insurer's activities are predominantly connected with insurance if:

1. The carrying amount of its liabilities arising from contracts within the scope of IFRS 4, which includes any deposit components or embedded derivatives unbundled from insurance contracts, is significant compared to the total carrying amount of all its liabilities; and
2. The percentage of the total carrying amount of its liabilities connected with insurance relative to the total carrying amount of all its liabilities is:

    a. Greater than 90%; or
    b. Less than or equal to 90% but greater than 80%, and the insurer does not engage in a significant activity unconnected with insurance. The standard provides further guidance on assessing whether an entity engages in significant unconnected activities.

Liabilities connected with insurance comprise:

1. Liabilities arising from contracts within the scope of IFRS 4;
2. Non-derivative investment contract liabilities measured at fair value through profit or loss applying IAS 39 (including those designated as at fair value through profit or

loss to which the insurer has applied the requirements in IFRS 9 for the presentation of gains and losses); and

3. Liabilities that arise because the insurer issues, or fulfils obligations arising from, the above contracts. Examples of such liabilities include derivatives used to mitigate risks arising from those contracts and from the assets backing those contracts, relevant tax liabilities such as the deferred tax liabilities for taxable temporary differences on liabilities arising from those contracts and debt instruments issued that are included in the insurer's regulatory capital.

A first-time adopter of IFRS may apply the temporary exemption from IFRS 9 if it meets the criteria for applying the temporary exemption as described above.

Situations may exist where an insurer applies the temporary exceptions from IFRS 9 but its associates or joint ventures do not, or vice versa. For annual periods beginning before January 1, 2021, the entity is permitted to retain the relevant accounting policies applied by the associate or joint venture as follows:

1. The entity applies IFRS 9 but the associate or joint venture applies the temporary exemption from IFRS 9; or
2. The entity applies the temporary exemption from IFRS 9 but the associate or joint venture applies IFRS 9.

An entity may apply the requirements separately for each associate or joint venture.

When an entity uses the equity method to account for its investment in an associate or joint venture:

1. IFRS 9 shall continue to be applied, if it was previously applied in the financial statements used to apply the equity method to that associate or joint venture (after reflecting any adjustments made by the entity).
2. IFRS 9 might be subsequently applied, if the temporary exemption from IFRS 9 was previously applied in the financial statements used to apply the equity method to that associate or joint venture (after reflecting any adjustments made by the entity).

An entity may apply the requirements above separately for each associate or joint venture.

Disclosures about the temporary exemption from IFRS 9

The disclosure objective for an insurer that elects to apply the temporary exemption from IFRS 9 is to disclose information to enable users of financial statements:

1. To understand how the insurer qualified for the temporary exemption; and
2. To compare insurers applying the temporary exemption with entities applying IFRS 9.

To achieve this disclosure objective, an insurer shall disclose:

1. The fact that it is applying the temporary exemption from IFRS 9 and how the insurer concluded that it qualified for the temporary exemption from IFRS 9, including:

    a. If the carrying amount of its liabilities arising from contracts within the scope of this IFRS was less than or equal to 90% of the total carrying amount of all its liabilities, the nature and carrying amounts of the liabilities connected with insurance that are not liabilities arising from contracts within the scope of this IFRS;

b. If the percentage of the total carrying amount of its liabilities connected with insurance relative to the total carrying amount of all its liabilities was less than or equal to 90% but greater than 80%, how the insurer determined that it did not engage in a significant activity unconnected with insurance, including what information it considered; and
c. If the insurer qualified for the temporary exemption from IFRS 9 on the basis of a reassessment:

    i. The reason for the reassessment;
    ii. The date on which the relevant change in its activities occurred; and
    iii. A detailed explanation of the change in its activities and a qualitative description of the effect of that change on the insurer's financial statements.

2. If an entity concludes that its activities are no longer predominantly connected with insurance, the following information in each reporting period before it begins to apply IFRS 9:

    a. The fact that it no longer qualifies for the temporary exemption from IFRS 9;
    b. The date on which the relevant change in its activities occurred and a detailed explanation of the change in its activities; and
    c. A qualitative description of the effect of that change on the entity's financial statements.

3. To comply, the fair value at the end of the reporting period and the amount of change in the fair value during that period for the following two groups of financial assets separately:

    a. Financial assets with contractual terms that give rise on specified dates to cash flows that are solely payments of principal and interest on the principal amount outstanding, excluding any financial asset that meets the definition of held for trading in IFRS 9, or that is managed and whose performance is evaluated on a fair value basis;
    b. All financial assets other than those specified in Paragraph 3.a. above; that is, any financial asset:

        i. With contractual terms that do not give rise on specified dates to cash flows that are solely payments of principal and interest on the principal amount outstanding;
        ii. That meets the definition of held for trading in IFRS 9; or
        iii. That is managed and whose performance is evaluated on a fair value basis.

4. When disclosing the information in Point 3., the insurer:

    a. May deem the carrying amount of the financial asset measured applying IAS 39 to be a reasonable approximation of its fair value if the insurer is not required to disclose its fair value applying IFRS 7 (e.g., short-term trade receivables); and
    b. Shall consider the level of detail necessary to enable users of financial statements to understand the characteristics of the financial assets.

5. Information about the credit risk exposure, including significant credit risk concentrations inherent in the financial assets. At a minimum, an insurer shall disclose the following information for those financial assets at the end of the reporting period:

   a. By credit risk rating grades as defined in IFRS 7, the carrying amounts applying IAS 39 (in the case of financial assets measured at amortised cost, before adjusting for any impairment allowances).
   b. For the financial assets that do not have low credit risk at the end of the reporting period, the fair value and the carrying amount applying IAS 39 (in the case of financial assets measured at amortised cost, before adjusting for any impairment allowances). IFRS 9 provides the relevant requirements for assessing whether the credit risk on a financial instrument is considered low.

6. Information about where a user of financial statements can obtain any publicly available IFRS 9 information that relates to an entity within the group that is not provided in the group's consolidated financial statements for the relevant reporting period. For example, such IFRS 9 information could be obtained from the publicly available individual or separate financial statements of an entity within the group that has applied IFRS 9.
7. The fact that an entity elected to apply the exemption from uniform accounting policy requirements in IAS 28 for associates and joint ventures.
8. If an entity applied the temporary exemption from IFRS 9 when accounting for its investment in an associate or joint venture using the equity method, the following, in addition to the information required by IFRS 12, *Disclosure of Interests in Other Entities*:

   a. The information described in the disclosure paragraphs above for each associate or joint venture that is material to the entity. The amounts disclosed shall be those included in the IFRS financial statements of the associate or joint venture after reflecting any adjustments made by the entity when using the equity method, rather than the entity's share of those amounts.
   b. The quantitative information described above in aggregate for all individually immaterial associates or joint ventures. The aggregate amounts:

      i. Disclosed shall be the entity's share of those amounts; and
      ii. For associates shall be disclosed separately from the aggregate amounts disclosed for joint ventures.

The overlay approach

An insurer is permitted to apply the overlay approach to designated financial assets. An insurer that applies the overlay approach shall:

1. Reclassify between profit or loss and other comprehensive income an amount that results in the profit or loss at the end of the reporting period for the designated financial assets being the same as if the insurer had applied IAS 39 to the designated financial assets. Accordingly, the amount reclassified is equal to the difference between:

   a. The amount reported in profit or loss for the designated financial assets applying IFRS 9; and
   b. The amount that would have been reported in profit or loss for the designated financial assets if the insurer had applied IAS 39.

2. Apply all other applicable IFRS to its financial instruments.

An insurer may elect to apply the overlay approach only when it first applies IFRS 9. An insurer may also apply the overlay approach if the temporary exception from IFRS 9 is no longer available because the insurers' activities are no longer predominantly connected with insurance.

An insurer shall present the amount reclassified between profit or loss and other comprehensive income applying the overlay approach:

1. In profit or loss as a separate line item; and
2. In other comprehensive income as a separate component of other comprehensive income.

A financial asset is eligible for designation for the overlay approach if the following criteria are met:

1. It is measured at fair value through profit or loss applying IFRS 9 but would not have been measured at fair value through profit or loss in its entirety applying IAS 39; and
2. It is not held in respect of an activity that is unconnected with contracts within the scope of IFRS 4. Examples of financial assets that would not be eligible for the overlay approach are those assets held in respect of banking activities or financial assets held in funds relating to investment contracts that are outside the scope of IFRS 4.

An insurer may designate an eligible financial asset for the overlay approach when it elects to apply the overlay approach. An insurer is permitted to designate eligible financial assets for the overlay approach on an instrument-by-instrument basis. Subsequently, it may designate an eligible financial asset for the overlay approach when:

1. That asset is initially recognised; or
2. That asset is held in respect of an activity that is connected with contracts within the scope of this IFRS 4 for the first time.

When relevant, for the purposes of applying the overlay approach to a newly designated financial asset in Point 2., above:

1. Its fair value at the date of designation shall be its new amortised cost carrying amount; and
2. The effective interest rate shall be determined based on its fair value at the date of designation.

An entity shall continue to apply the overlay approach to a designated financial asset until that financial asset is derecognised. However, an entity:

1. Shall de-designate a financial asset when the financial asset is no longer held in respect of an activity that is connected with contracts within the scope of IFRS 4. For example, a financial asset will no longer meet that criterion when an entity transfers that asset so that it is held in respect of its banking activities or when an entity ceases to be an insurer.
2. May, at the beginning of any annual period, stop applying the overlay approach to all designated financial assets. An entity that elects to stop applying the overlay approach shall apply IAS 8 to account for the change in accounting policy.

When an entity de-designates a financial asset, it shall reclassify from accumulated other comprehensive income to profit or loss as a reclassification adjustment any balance relating to that financial asset.

If an entity stops using the overlay approach applying by election or because it is no longer an insurer, it shall not subsequently apply the overlay approach. An insurer that has elected to apply the overlay approach but has no eligible financial assets may subsequently apply the overlay approach when it has eligible financial assets.

Disclosures about the overlay approach

The disclosure objective is that an insurer that applies the overlay approach shall disclose information to enable users of financial statements to understand:

1. How the total amount reclassified between profit or loss and other comprehensive income in the reporting period is calculated; and
2. The effect of that reclassification on the financial statements.

To achieve the disclosure objective, an insurer shall disclose:

1. The fact that it is applying the overlay approach.
2. The carrying amount at the end of the reporting period of financial assets to which the insurer applies the overlay approach by class of financial asset.
3. The basis for designating financial assets for the overlay approach, including an explanation of any designated financial assets that are held outside the legal entity that issues contracts within the scope of this IFRS.
4. An explanation of the total amount reclassified between profit or loss and other comprehensive income in the reporting period in a way that enables users of financial statements to understand how that amount is derived, including:

    a. The amount reported in profit or loss for the designated financial assets applying IFRS 9; and
    b. The amount that would have been reported in profit or loss for the designated financial assets if the insurer had applied IAS 39.

5. The effect of the reclassification between profit or loss and other comprehensive income on each affected line item in profit or loss.
6. If during the reporting period, the insurer has changed the designation of financial assets:

    a. The amount reclassified between profit or loss and other comprehensive income in the reporting period relating to newly designated financial assets applying the overlay approach;
    b. The amount that would have been reclassified between profit or loss and other comprehensive income in the reporting period if the financial assets had not been de-designated; and
    c. The amount reclassified in the reporting period to profit or loss from accumulated other comprehensive income for financial assets that have been de-designated.

If an entity applied the overlay approach when accounting for its investment in an associate or joint venture using the equity method, the entity shall disclose the following, in addition to the information required by IFRS 12:

1. The information described above for each associate or joint venture that is material to the entity. The amounts disclosed shall be those included in the IFRS financial statements of the associate or joint venture after reflecting any adjustments made by the entity when using the equity method, rather than the entity's share of those amounts.
2. The quantitative information described above, and the effect of the reclassification on profit or loss and other comprehensive income in aggregate for all individually immaterial associates or joint ventures. The aggregate amounts:

    a. Disclosed shall be the entity's share of those amounts; and
    b. For associates shall be disclosed separately from the aggregate amounts disclosed for joint ventures.

Interaction with other requirements

Reclassifying an amount between profit or loss and other comprehensive income applying the overlay approach may have consequential effects for including other amounts in other comprehensive income, such as income taxes. An insurer shall apply the relevant IFRS, such as IAS 12, *Income Taxes*, to determine any such consequential effects.

If a first-time adopter elects to apply the overlay approach, it shall restate comparative information to reflect the overlay approach if, and only if, it restates comparative information to comply with IFRS 9.

Transitional Provisions

Temporary exemption from IFRS 9

The temporary exemption from IFRS 9 is for annual periods beginning on or after January 1, 2018. An entity that discloses the information required for this temporary exemption from IFRS 9 shall use the transitional provisions in IFRS 9 that are relevant to making the assessments required for those disclosures. The date of initial application for this purpose shall be deemed to be the beginning of the first annual period beginning on or after January 1, 2018.

The overlay approach

An entity shall apply the amendments, which permit insurers to apply the overlay approach to designated financial assets, when it first applies IFRS 9. An entity that elects to apply the overlay approach shall:

1. Apply that approach retrospectively to designated financial assets on transition to IFRS 9. Accordingly, for example, the entity shall recognise as an adjustment to the opening balance of accumulated other comprehensive income an amount equal to the difference between the fair value of the designated financial assets determined applying IFRS 9 and their carrying amount determined applying IAS 39.

2. Restate comparative information to reflect the overlay approach if, and only if, the entity restates comparative information applying IFRS 9.

FUTURE DEVELOPMENTS

IFRS 17, Insurance Contracts

IFRS 17, *Insurance Contracts*, was issued in May 2017 to create a comprehensive standard to deal with the identification, recognition, measurement, presentation and disclosure of insurance contracts. IFRS 17 is effective for annual reporting periods beginning on or after January 1, 2021 (might be extended to January 1, 2022). IFRS 17 will replace IFRS 4. Earlier adoption is permitted provided that the entity also applies IFRS 9, *Financial Instruments*, and IFRS 15, *Revenue from Contracts with Customers*, on or before the date of initial application of IFRS 17.

IFRS 17 in principle transfers all the requirements to identify an insurance contract from IFRS 4. New rules are created for the unbundling of deposits and non-insurance revenue components. The following process is followed for unbundling:

1. Identify and account for embedded derivatives by applying IFRS 9.
2. Separate from a host insurance contract an investment component when that investment component is distinct and then apply IFRS 9 to the investment component.
3. Separate from the host insurance contract any promise to transfer distinct goods or non-insurance services to a policyholder by applying IFRS 15.

The benchmark approach in IFRS 17 is based on the principle that insurance contracts create a bundle of rights and obligations that work together to generate a package of cash inflows (premiums) and outflows (benefits and claims). An insurer would apply to that package of cash flows a measurement approach, called the *fulfilment value approach*, that uses the following building blocks:

1. A current estimate of the expected future net cash flows from premiums, claims, benefits and expenses.
2. An explicit risk adjustment for uncertainty about the amount of future cash flows.
3. A discount rate that adjusts those cash flows for the time value of money.
4. A contract service margin.

Components of the building block approach are defined in IFRS 17 as follows:

Component	**Definition**
Fulfilment cash flows	An explicit, unbiased and probability-weighted estimate (i.e., *expected value*) of the *present value* of the *future cash outflows* minus the present value of *future cash inflows* that arises as the entity *fulfils* insurance contracts, including a *risk adjustment* for non-financial risks.
Risk adjustment for non-financial risks	The *compensation* an entity requires for *bearing the uncertainty* about the *amount and timing* of the cash flows that arises from *non-financial risk* as the entity fulfils the insurance contracts.
Contract service margin	A component of the carrying amount of the asset or liability for a group of insurance contacts presenting the *unearned profits* the entity will recognise as it provides *services* under the insurance contract

The first three building blocks are regarded to be the fulfilment cash flows and the contract service margin reflects the entity's risk-adjusted expected profit from the contract. The contract services eliminate the recognition of any gain at inception of the contract. The contractual service margin is therefore the unearned profits on the contract and is reduced as the profits are earned over the duration of the contract. The contract service margin is updated for changes in future service-related estimations. The effect of the fulfilment value approach is that the profit from a group of insurance contracts is spread over the period the entity provides insurance coverage, and therefore is released from insurance risks. However, if a group of contracts is loss-making, the loss is recognised immediately.

A simplified *premium allocation approach* is also available for entities that:

- expect that the liability for future coverage would not sufficiently differ from the fulfilment value approach; and
- the coverage period for each contract in the group is one year or less.

The premium allocation approach allows an entity to measure the amount relating to remaining service by recognising the unearned premiums received as a liability. The coverage period of one year and less is, however, problematic since in unclear instances the assessment is based on when the boundary of insurance contracts ends. The boundary of insurance contracts ends when the substantive rights in the contracts end:

- For individual policyholders: when a practical ability to reassess risks of the contract and reset benefits (prices) exists;
- For portfolio of contracts: a practical ability exists to (1) reassess the risks of the contracts and reset benefits (prices) and (2) when pricing of the contracts is only determined to the next reset date.

Insurance contracts are classified in different portfolios to apply the applicable measurement basis based on three steps:

1. Whether the contracts have similar risks and are managed together.
2. Each portfolio of contracts must then be further divided at initial recognition into:
    - onerous contracts (loss-making contracts);
    - contracts that have no significant possibility of becoming onerous (profitable contracts);
    - remaining contracts in the portfolio (less profitable contracts).
3. Each portfolio of contracts is further limited to a yearly grouping (yearly cohort).

IFRS 17 determines that a group of insurance contracts is recognised at the earlier of:

- The beginning of the *coverage period*;
- The date when the first payment from a policyholder becomes due;
- When a group of contracts becomes onerous.

Under both the fulfilment value approach and the premium allocation approach a liability for remaining coverage and a liability for incurred claims must be recognised. These terms are defined as follows:

Liability for remaining coverage	An entity's obligation to investigate and pay valid claims under existing insurance contacts for insured events that have not yet occurred (i.e., the obligation that relates to the unexpired portion of the coverage period).
Liability for incurred claims	An entity's obligation to investigate and pay valid claims for insured events that have already occurred, including events that have occurred but for which claims have not been reported and other incurred insurance expenses.

Under the fulfilment value approach, the liability for remaining coverage is the fulfilment value determined for a group of contracts, while for the premium allocation approach it is the revenue received in advance (unearned premiums received) minus deferred acquisition cost (if not expensed). Under the fulfilment value approach acquisition cost is deducted from the contract service margin and spread as the net profit is recognised. The liability for incurred claims includes both claims reported but which are not paid or settled and claims incurred but not reported.

The presentation of an insurance entity's performance is divided into insurance service results and financial results to separate them. The financial results are further divided into finance (investment) results and finance expense. The presentation in the income statement will then be as follows:

Insurance revenue	X
Incurred claims and other expenses	(X)
Insurance service results	**X**
Investment income	X
Insurance finance expenses	(X)
Net financial results	**X**
Profit or loss	**X**

Insurance finance expenses resulting from changes in interest rates may be transferred to other comprehensive income. Income and expenses from reinsurance contracts should be presented separately. The new format of the income statement is applicable to both entities that previously were regarded as short-term or long-term insurers. The IASB wants to create comparability between insurance and other entities. Revenue is regarded as the amount charged for insurance coverage as it is earned. Revenue should therefore specially be calculated when the fulfilment value approach is followed. Under the premium allocation approach revenue represents the earned premiums.

Reinsurance contracts issued by the insurance entity are treated similarly to other direct insurance business and included in the liability for remaining coverage and the liability for incurred claims. Reinsurance contracts held by the insurance entity are treated similarly but oppositely. However, if the fulfilment value approach is followed, no contract service margin is created since the profit in the contract is regarded as part of the cost of reinsurance.

IFRS 17 also deals with contracts with participation features. For insurance contracts with direct participation features the entity's share of the changes in the fair value of the underlying items is included in the contract service margin. For investment contracts with discretionary participation features, the requirements for insurance contracts are modified as follows:

- The date of initial recognition is the date the entity becomes a party to the contract (similar to IFRS 9).

- Cash flows are regarded to be within the contract boundary when they result from a substantive obligation of the entity to deliver cash at a present or future date. No substantive obligation to deliver cash is regarded to exist when the entity has the practical ability to set a price for the promise to deliver the cash that fully reflects the amount of cash promised and related risks.
- The contractual service margin is recognised over the duration of the group of contracts in a systematic way that reflects the transfer of investment services under the contract.

IFRS 17 provides detailed disclosure requirements. IFRS 17 should be applied retrospectively on transition. However, if impracticable, a modified retrospective approach or a fair value approach may be applied.

Proposed Amendments in Exposure Draft

The IASB has issued an exposure draft to proposed amendments to IFRS 17. These proposed amendments are summarised below:

- A scope exclusion to exclude credit cards and loan contracts.
- A choice to apply IFRS 17 or IFRS 9 to contracts that meet the definition of an insurance contracts but limit the compensation for insurance events to the amount required to settle the policyholder's obligations created by the contract, such a loans contracts who would be regarded to be paid on death of the person responsible for paying the loan.
- Allocation of insurance acquisition cash flows on a systematic or rational basis that are directly attributable to a group of insurance contracts and recognising and asset for such acquisition cash flows paid before they are allocated as an expense. Such recognised asset is subjective to impairment provisions.
- An entity that identify coverage units for insurance contracts without direct participation features should consider the quantity of benefits and expected period of both insurance coverage and investment related services in establishing the contractual service margin and allocation the contractual service margin to investment-return service and investment-related services.
- An entity is required to identify coverage units for insurance contracts with direct participation features considering the quantity of benefits and expected period of both insurance coverage and investment-related services.
- Disclose quantitative information about when an entity expects to recognise in profit or loss the contractual service margin remaining at the end of the reporting period. The approached used to determine the relative weighting of the benefits provided by insurance coverage of insurance coverage and investment-return services or investment-related services should also be disclosed.
- The contractual service margin is adjusted for a group of reinsurance contracts held that provides proportionate coverage, and as a result recognise income, when the entity recognises a loss on initial recognition of an onerous group of underlying insurance contracts, or on addition of onerous contracts to that group. The amount of the adjustment and resulting income is determined by multiplying:
    - the loss recognised on the group of underlying insurance contracts; and
    - the fixed percentage of claims on the group of underlying contracts the entity has a right to recover from the group of reinsurance contracts held.

- To present separately in the statement of financial position the carrying amount of portfolios of insurance contracts issued that are assets and those that are liabilities. Applying the existing requirements, an entity would present the carrying amount of groups of insurance contracts issued that are assets and those that are liabilities. The amendment would also apply to portfolios of reinsurance contracts held that are assets and those that are liabilities.
- Extend the risk mitigation option available when an entity uses derivatives to mitigate financial risk arising from insurance contracts with direct participation features. That option would apply in circumstances when an entity uses reinsurance contracts held to mitigate financial risk arising from insurance contracts with direct participation features.
- Defer the effective date of IFRS 17 by one year to annual reporting periods beginning on or after 1 January 2022. The temporary exemption of applying IFRs 9 is also extended by one year.
- An additional modification in the modified retrospective approach that require an entity, to the extent permitted, to classify as a liability for incurred claims as a liability for settlement of claims incurred before an insurance contract was acquired. An entity applying the fair value approach could choose to classify such a liability as a liability for incurred claims.
- Permit an entity to apply the option to not recognise a change in the contract service margin in the effect of financial risk (paragraph B115) prospectively from the transition date, rather than the date of initial application. To apply the option prospectively on or after the transition date, an entity would be required to designate risk mitigation relationships at or before the date it applies the option.
- An entity that can apply IFRS 17 retrospectively to a group of insurance contracts be permitted to instead apply the fair value approach to that group if it meets specified criteria relating to risk mitigation.
- To add the definition "insurance contract services": The definition includes the following services that an entity provides to a policyholder of an insurance contract:
    - coverage for an **insured event** (insurance coverage);
    - for insurance contracts without direct participation features, the generation of an investment return for the policyholder, if applicable (investment-return service); and for insurance contracts with direct participation features, the management of underlying items on behalf of the policyholder (investment-related service).
    - for insurance contracts with direct participation features, the management of underlying items on behalf of the policyholder (investment-related service).

US GAAP COMPARISON

The US GAAP guidance at ASC 944, *Financial Services—Insurance*, covers insurance contracts issued by insurance-type companies, that is they have qualified as an insurance company through registration of their insurance domiciling state. If you are an insurance company then you would comply with ASC 944 with respect to insurance activities, acquisition costs, claim costs and liabilities for future policy benefits, policyholder dividends and separate accounts. If you do not fall under ASC 944 then your revenue and expense are accounted for under other US GAAP codification. Additionally, US GAAP does not consider an insurance contract to be a financial instrument whereas IFRS does.

ASC 944 lists four methods for recognition of premium revenue and contract liabilities: one method was developed for short-duration contract accounting and three methods for long-duration contract accounting (i.e., traditional life, universal life and participating contracts). Generally, the four methods reflect the nature of the insurance entity's obligations and policyholder rights under the provisions of the contract. Acquisition costs are amortised over the life of the policy and subject to impairment based on the adequacy of premiums for policies in light of circumstances at the balance sheet date.

Short-duration contracts, which are for a short period, usually one year, generally require revenue recognition on a straight-line basis. Long-duration contracts, in most cases, require offsetting of receivables or cash against unrecognised revenue. This revenue is recognised commensurate with the risk insured. Another feature of long-duration contract accounting is that for each reporting period, liabilities for coverage risk are assessed and increased if needed. The offset is recognised in the current period expense.

Current US GAAP has special disclosure requirements that are required supplementary information for short-term contracts. Long-term contracts requirements are covered by ASU 2018-12 Financial Services—Insurance (Topic 944): Targeted Improvements to the Accounting for Long-Duration Contracts.

US GAAP contains a provision to ensure there are adequate reserves to cover premiums under what is called a premium deficiency test, which is required. The premium deficiency test would be adequate if used for the IFRS's "liability adequacy test."

US GAAP also covers accounting for reinsurance contracts. These arrangements transfer some or all of the risk of insurance to a third party (not the insured). Generally, the accounting is similar to insurance contracts, although there are specific criteria for determining if the original insurer has transferred the risks to the reinsurer.

The concept of separate accounts specifies accounting when assets are specifically segregated for a particular policyholder, for example variable annuity contracts that guarantee some minimum level of benefits.

34 INTERIM FINANCIAL REPORTING

INTRODUCTION

Interim financial reports are financial statements covering periods of less than a full financial year. Most commonly such reports will be for a period of six months (which are referred to as semi-annual financial reports) or three months (which are referred to as quarterly financial reports), depending on relevant jurisdictions. The purpose of interim financial reports is to provide financial statement users with more timely information for making investment and credit decisions, based on the expectation that full-year results will be a reasonable extrapolation from interim performance. Additionally, interim reports can yield significant information concerning trends affecting the business and seasonality effects, both of which could be obscured in annual reports.

The basic objective of interim reporting is to provide frequent and timely assessments of an entity's performance. However, interim reporting has inherent limitations. As the reporting period is shortened, the effects of errors in estimation and allocation are magnified. The proper allocation of annual operating expenses to interim periods is also a significant concern. Because the progressive tax rates of most jurisdictions are applied to total annual income and various tax credits may arise, the accurate determination of interim period income tax expense is often difficult. Other annual operating expenses may be concentrated in one interim period yet benefit the entire year's operations. Examples include advertising expenses and major repairs or maintenance of equipment, which may be seasonal in nature. The effects of seasonal fluctuations and temporary market conditions further limit the reliability, comparability and predictive value of interim reports. Because of this reporting environment, the issue of independent auditor association with interim financial reports remains problematic.

Sources of IFRS	
IAS 1, 34	*IFRIC* 10
IASB's Framework for the Preparation and Presentation of Financial Statements	

SCOPE

IAS 34, *Interim Financial Reporting*, does not mandate which entities should be required to publish interim financial reports, how frequently, or how soon after the end of an interim period. Local governments, securities regulators, security exchanges or accounting bodies often govern the application of IAS 34 for entities whose debt or equity securities are publicly traded. IAS 34 applies if an entity elects or is required to apply IAS 34.

An entity's annual financial statements are evaluated independently, from its interim reports, for compliance with IFRS. If an entity's interim report is described as complying with IFRS, it must apply all the requirements of IAS 34.

DEFINITIONS OF TERMS

Interim financial report. An interim financial report means a financial report containing either a complete set of financial statements for an interim period (as described in IAS 1), or a set of condensed financial statements (as described in IAS 34) for an interim period.

Interim period. A financial reporting period shorter than a full financial year (e.g., a period of three or six months).

OBJECTIVES OF INTERIM FINANCIAL REPORTING

The purpose of interim financial reporting is to provide information that will be useful in making economic decisions (as, of course, is the purpose of annual financial information). Furthermore, interim financial reporting is expected to provide information specifically about the financial position, performance and change in financial position of an entity. The objective is general enough to embrace the preparation and presentation of either full financial statements or condensed information.

While accounting is often criticised for looking at an entity's performance through the rearview mirror, in fact it is well understood by standard setters that to be useful, such information must provide insights into future performance. As outlined in the objective of the IASB's standard on interim financial reporting, IAS 34, the primary, but not exclusive, purpose of timely interim period reporting is to provide interested parties (e.g., investors and creditors) with an understanding of the entity's earnings-generating capacity and its cash flow-generating capacity, which are clearly future oriented. Furthermore, the interim data are expected to give interested parties insights not only into such matters as seasonal volatility or irregularity, and provide timely notice about changes in patterns or trends, both to income or cash-generating behaviour, but also into balance sheet-based phenomena such as liquidity.

APPLICATION OF ACCOUNTING POLICIES

There is no requirement under IFRS that entities must prepare interim financial statements. Furthermore, even if annual financial statements are prepared in accordance with IFRS, the reporting entity is free to present interim financial statements on bases other than IFRS, as long as they are not misrepresented as being IFRS compliant.

If interim financial statements are IFRS based, IAS 34 states that interim financial data should be prepared in conformity with accounting policies used in its annual financial statements. The only exception noted is when a change in accounting policy has been adopted since the last year-end financial report was issued. However, IAS 34 specifically states that the frequency of an entity's reporting shall not effect the measurement of its annual results. To achieve this objective, certain measurements in the interim reporting purposes shall be made on a year-to-date basis. It is thus acknowledged that interim reports are part of the financial year. Recognition of assets, liabilities, expenses and income, however, is the same as for the annual financial statements.

Consistency

The standard logically states that interim period financial statements should be prepared using the same accounting principles that had been employed in the most recent annual financial statements, subject to any changes in accounting policies or adoption of new IFRS for the financial reporting period which the interim accounts are a component of. This is consistent with the idea that the latest annual report provides the frame of reference that will be employed by users of the interim information. The fact that interim data are expected to be useful in making projections of the forthcoming full-year's reported results of operations makes consistency of accounting principles between the interim period and prior year important, since the projected results for the current year will undoubtedly be evaluated in the context of year-earlier performance. Unless the accounting principles applied in both periods are consistent, any such comparison is likely to be impeded.

The decision to require consistent application of accounting policies across interim periods and in comparison with the earlier fiscal year is a logical implication of the view of interim reporting as being largely a means of predicting the next fiscal year's results. It is also driven by the conclusion that those interim reporting periods stand alone (rather than being merely an integral portion of the full year).

Consolidated Reporting Requirement

The standard also requires that, if the entity's most recent annual financial statements were presented on a consolidated basis, then the interim financial reports in the immediate succeeding year should also be presented similarly. This is entirely in keeping with the notion of consistency of application of accounting policies. The rule does not, however, either preclude or require publishing additional "parent company only" interim reports, even if the most recent annual financial statements did include such additional financial statements.

Restatement of Accounting Policies

A change in accounting policy other than one for which the transition is specified by a new standard should be reflected by restating the financial statements of prior interim periods of the current year and the comparable interim periods of the prior financial year. However, when it is impracticable to determine the cumulative effect at the beginning of the financial year of applying a new accounting policy to prior periods, the interim periods are only adjusted prospectively from the earliest date practicable.

One of the objectives of this requirement of IAS 34 is to ensure that a single accounting policy is applied to a particular class of transactions throughout the entire financial year. To allow differing accounting policies to be applied to the same class of transactions within a single financial year would be troublesome since it would result in "interim allocation difficulties, obscured operating results, and complicated analysis and understandability of interim period information."

Materiality as Applied to Interim Financial Statements

Materiality is one of the most fundamental concepts underlying financial reporting. At the same time, it has largely been resistant to attempts at precise definition. Some IFRS do require that items be disclosed if material or significant, or if of "such size" as would warrant separate disclosure. Guidelines for performing an arithmetical calculation of a threshold for materiality (to measure "such size") are not prescribed in IAS 1, or for that matter in any other IFRS. Rather, this determination is left to the devices of each individual charged with responsibility for financial reporting.

IAS 34 advanced the notion that materiality for interim reporting purposes may differ from that defined in the context of an annual period. This follows from the decision to endorse the discrete view of interim financial reporting generally. Thus, for example, discontinuing operations would have to be evaluated for disclosure purposes against whatever benchmark, such as gross revenue, is deemed appropriate as that item is being reported in the interim financial statements—not as it was shown in the prior year's financial statements or is projected to be shown in the current full year's results.

The effect of the foregoing would normally be to lower the threshold level for reporting such items. Thus, it is deemed likely that some items separately set forth in the interim financials may not be so presented in the subsequent full year's annual report that includes that same interim period.

Example of interim period materiality consideration

To illustrate, assume that Xanadu Corp. has gross revenues of €2.8 million in the first fiscal quarter and will, in fact, go on to generate revenues of €12 million for the full year. Traditionally, for this company's financial reporting, materiality is defined as 5% of revenues. If in the first quarter income from discontinued operations amounting to €200,000 is earned, this would be separately categorised in the quarterly financial statements since it exceeds the defined 5% threshold for materiality. If there are no other discontinued operations results for the balance of the year, Xanadu Corp might validly be concluded that disclosure in the year-end financials may be omitted, since the €200,000 income item is not material in the context of €12 million of full-year revenues. Thus, Xanadu's first quarter report would detail the discontinued operations, but that is later subsumed in continuing operations in the annual financial statements.

PRESENTATION

Content of an Interim Financial Report

Instead of repeating information previously presented in annual financial statements, interim financial reports should preferably focus on new activities, events and circumstances that have occurred since the date of publication of the latest complete set of financial statements. IAS 34 recognises the need to keep financial statement users informed about the latest financial condition of the reporting entity and has moderated the presentation and disclosure requirements of interim financial reports. In the interest of timeliness and with a sensitivity to cost considerations, and also to avoid repetition of information previously (and recently) reported, the standard allows an entity, at its option, to provide information relating to its financial position in a condensed format, in lieu of comprehensive information provided in a complete set of financial statements prepared in accordance with IAS 1.

IAS 34 sets forth the following important aspects of interim financial reporting:

- By permitting presentation of condensed financial information, the standard is not intended to either prohibit or discourage the reporting entity from presenting a complete set of interim financial statements, as defined by IAS 1;
- When the choice is made to present condensed interim financial statements, if an entity chooses to add line items or additional explanatory notes to the condensed financial statements, over and above the minimum prescribed by this standard, the standard does not, in any way, prohibit or discourage the addition of such extra information; and
- The recognition and measurement guidance in IAS 34 applies equally to a complete set of interim financial statements as to condensed interim financial statements. A complete set of interim financial statements would include not only the disclosures specifically prescribed by this standard, but also disclosures required by other IFRS standards. For example, disclosures required by IFRS 7, such as those pertaining to credit risk, would need to be incorporated in a complete set of interim financial statements, in addition to the selected note disclosures prescribed by IAS 34.

Minimum Components of an Interim Financial Report

IAS 34 sets forth minimum requirements in relation to condensed interim financial reports. The standard mandates that the following financial statements components be presented when an entity opts for the condensed format:

- A condensed statement of financial position;
- A condensed statement of profit or loss and other comprehensive income, either as:
  - A condensed single statement; or
  - A condensed separate statement of profit or loss and a condensed statement of comprehensive income;

- A condensed statement of changes in equity;
- A condensed statement of cash flows; and
- Selected explanatory notes.

Form and Content of Interim Financial Statements

1. IAS 34 mandates that if an entity chooses to present the "complete set of (interim) financial statements" instead of opting for the allowed method of presenting only "condensed" interim financial statements, then the form and content of those statements should conform to the requirements set by IAS 1 for a complete set of financial statements.
2. However, if an entity opts for the condensed format approach to interim financial reporting, then IAS 34 requires that, at a minimum, those condensed financial statements include each of the headings and the subtotals that were included in the entity's most recent annual financial statements, along with selected explanatory notes, as prescribed by the standard.

   It is interesting to note that IAS 34 mandates expansiveness in certain cases. The standard notes that extra line items or notes may need to be added to the minimum disclosures prescribed above, if their omission would make the condensed interim financial statements misleading. This concept can be best explained through the following illustration:

   > At December 20XX-1, an entity's comparative statement of financial position had trade receivables that were considered doubtful, and hence were fully provided for as of that date. On the face of the statement of financial position as of December 31, 20XX-1, the amount disclosed against trade receivables, net of provision, was a zero balance (and the comparative figure disclosed as of December 31, 20XX-2, under the prior year column was a positive amount, since at that earlier point of time, that is, at the end of the previous year, a small portion of the receivable was still considered collectible). At December 31, 20XX-1, the fact that the receivable (net of the provision) ended up being presented as a zero balance on the face of the statement of financial position was well explained in the notes to the annual financial statements (which clearly showed the provision being deducted from the gross amount of the receivable that caused the resulting figure to be a zero balance that was then carried forward to the statement of financial position). If at the end of the first quarter of the following year the trade receivables were still doubtful of collection, thereby necessitating creation of a 100% provision against the entire balance of trade receivables as of March 31, 20XX, and the entity opted to present a condensed statement of financial position as part of the interim financial report, it would be misleading in this case to disclose the trade receivables as of March 31, 20XX, as a zero balance, without adding a note to the condensed statement of financial position explaining this phenomenon.

3. IAS 34 requires disclosure of earnings per share (EPS) (both basic EPS and diluted EPS) on the face of the interim statement of comprehensive income. This disclosure is mandatory whether condensed or complete interim financial statements are presented. However, since EPS is only required (by IAS 33) for publicly held companies, it is likewise only mandated for interim financial statements of such reporting entities.
4. IAS 34 mandates that an entity should follow the same format in its interim statement showing changes in equity as it did in its most recent annual financial statements.
5. IAS 34 requires that an interim financial report be prepared on a consolidated basis if the entity's most recent annual financial statements were consolidated statements.

Regarding presentation of separate interim financial statements of the parent company in addition to consolidated interim financial statements, if they were included in the most recent annual financial statements, this standard neither requires nor prohibits such inclusion in the interim financial report of the entity.

Significant Events and Transactions

While a number of notes would potentially be required at an interim date, there could clearly be far less disclosure than is prescribed under other IFRS. IAS 34 reiterates that it is superfluous to provide the same notes in the interim financial report that appeared in the most recent annual financial statements, since financial statement users are presumed to have access to those statements. The interim financial report provides an explanation of events and transactions that are significant to an understanding of the changes in financial position and performance of the entity since the last annual reporting. This information updates the relevant information presented in the most recent annual financial report. In keeping with this line of thinking, the following is a non-exhaustive list of events and transactions that are disclosed, if they are significant:

1. The write-down of inventories to net realisable value (NRV) and any reversal.
2. Losses from the impairment of financial assets; property, plant and equipment; intangible or other assets and any reversal.
3. The reversal of any provision for restructuring cost.
4. Acquisitions and disposal of property, plant and equipment.
5. Commitments for the purchase of property, plant and equipment.
6. Litigation settlements.
7. Corrections of prior period errors.
8. Changes in the business or economic circumstances that effect the entity's financial assets and liabilities (recognised at fair value or amortised cost).
9. Any loan default or breach of a loan agreement that has not been remedied.
10. Related-party transactions.
11. Transfers between levels of the fair value hierarchy used for the measuring of financial instruments.
12. Changes in the classification of financial assets due to changes in purpose or use.
13. Changes in contingent liabilities and contingent assets.

Other Disclosures

The additional disclosure below must also be provided in the notes to the interim financial statements on a financial year-to-year basis. These disclosures could also be incorporated by cross-reference from the interim financial statements to some other statement (such as management commentary or risk report) that is available to users of the financial statements on the same terms as the interim financial statements and at the same time. If users of the financial statements do not have access to the information incorporated by cross-reference on the same terms and at the same time, the interim financial report is incomplete.

1. A statement that the same accounting policies and methods of computation are applied in the interim financial statements compared with the most recent annual financial statements, or if those policies or methods have changed, a description of the nature and effect of the change;

2. Explanatory comments about seasonality or cyclicality of interim operations;
3. The nature and amount of significant items affecting interim results that are unusual because of nature, size or incidence;
4. Dividends paid, either in the aggregate or on a per-share basis, presented separately for ordinary (common) shares and other classes of shares;
5. The following segment information (if the entity is required to report IFRS 8, *Operating Segments*, in its annual financial statements):
   - Revenues from external customers and intersegment revenue if reported to the chief operating decision maker.
   - A measure of profit or loss.
   - Total assets and total liabilities (if these amounts are provided to the chief operating decision maker on a regular basis and secondly, there has been a significant change from the amount disclosed in the last annual financial statements for that segment).
   - A description of any change in the basis of segmentation or in the basis of measuring segment profits.
   - A reconciliation of the total segments' profit or loss to the entity's profit or loss before tax and discontinued operations (or after tax if used).
6. Any events occurring subsequent to the end of the interim period that have not been reflected in the interim financial statements;
7. Issues, repurchases and repayments of debt and equity securities;
8. The nature and quantum of changes in estimates of amounts reported in prior interim periods of the current financial year, or changes in estimates of amounts reported in prior financial years, if those changes have a material effect in the current interim period;
9. The effect of changes in the composition of the entity during the interim period, like business combinations, acquisitions or disposal of subsidiaries, and long-term investments, restructuring and discontinuing operations;
10. Certain fair value disclosure regarding financial instruments in IFRS 7 and IFRS 13;
11. For entities becoming, or ceasing to be, investment entities, certain disclosures in IFRS 12; and
12. The disaggregation of revenue from contracts with customers required by IFRS 15.

Finally, in the case of a complete set of interim financial statements, the standard allows additional disclosures mandated by other IFRS. However, if the condensed format is used, then additional disclosures required by other IFRS are *not* required.

Comparative Interim Financial Statements

IAS 34 endorses the concept of comparative reporting, which is generally acknowledged to be more useful than is the presentation of information about only a single period. The other components of the interim financial statements should present the following data for the two periods:

- The statement of financial position as of the end of the current interim period and a comparative statement of financial position as of the end of the immediately preceding financial year (*not* as of the comparable year or earlier date);

- Statements of profit or loss and other comprehensive income for the current interim period and cumulatively for the current financial year to date, with comparative statements of profit or loss and other comprehensive income for the comparable interim periods (current and year to date) of the immediately preceding financial year. As permitted by IAS 1, an interim report may present for each period a statement or statements of profit or loss and other comprehensive income;
- The statement of cash flows cumulatively for the current financial year to date, with a comparative statement for the comparable year-to-date period of the immediately preceding financial year; and
- The statement of changes in equity cumulatively for the current financial year to date, with a comparative statement for the comparable year-to-date period of the immediately preceding financial year.

The following illustration should amply explain the above-noted requirements of IAS 34. XYZ Limited presents quarterly interim financial statements and its financial year ends on December 31 each year. For the second quarter of 20XX, XYZ Limited should present the following financial statements (condensed or complete) as of June 30, 20XX:

1. A statement of financial position with two columns, presenting information as of June 30, 20XX, and as of December 31, 20XX-1.
2. A statement of comprehensive income with four columns, presenting information for the three-month periods ended June 30, 20XX, and June 30, 20XX-1; and for the six-month periods (year to date) ended June 30, 20XX, and June 30, 20XX-1.
3. A statement of cash flows with two columns presenting information for the six-month periods (year to date) ended June 30, 20XX, and June 30, 20XX-1.
4. A statement of changes in equity with two columns presenting information for the six-month periods (year to date) ended June 30, 20XX, and June 30, 20XX-1.

IAS 34 recommends that, for highly seasonal businesses, the inclusion of additional financial information for the 12 months ending on the date of the interim report and comparative information for the prior 12-month period (also referred to as rolling 12-month statements) would be deemed very useful. The objective of recommending rolling 12-month statements is that seasonality concerns would be thereby eliminated, since by definition each rolling period contains all the seasons of the year. (Rolling statements, however, cannot correct cyclicality that encompasses more than one year, such as that of secular business expansions and recessions.) Accordingly, IAS 34 encourages companies affected by seasonality to consider including these additional statements, which could result in an interim statement of comprehensive income comprising six or more columns of data.

RECOGNITION AND MEASUREMENT ISSUES

General Concepts

The definitions of assets, liabilities, income and expense are the same for interim period reporting as for annual reporting. These items are defined in the IASB's *Conceptual Framework*. The effect of stipulating that the same definitions apply to interim reporting is to further underscore the concept of interim periods being discrete units of time upon which the statements report. For example, given the definition of assets as resources generating future economic benefits for the entity, expenditures that could not be capitalised at year-end because of a failure to meet this definition could similarly not be capitalised at interim dates. Applying the same definitions at interim dates, IAS 34 has mandated the same recognition rules as are applicable at the end of full annual reporting periods.

While the overall implication is that identical recognition rules are to be applied to interim financial statements, there is a requirement that measurements of the interim reporting purposes are made on a year-to-date basis. This means that specific measurements such as fair value, impairment and estimates would be applied at the interim period as if were applied by the annual year-end. Changes in the measurement amount in the next interim period would be a change of estimate in that period. However, expenses such as income tax that are payable on a yearly basis would be measured in the interim reports on the yearly weighted-average income tax rate expected for the full financial year. The recognition and measure at each interim report are based on the information when the interim report is prepared and only updated in the next interim report.

Application of the Recognition and Measurement Basis

Recognition is based on the general recognition guidance for assets, liabilities, income and expenses. The year-to-date measurement basis means that items are measured on a specific interim date if a measure is available on that date, but are measured on a yearly basis if the measurements are related to a year assessment of the total amount receivable or payable. The Illustrative Examples provide the following examples to explain the general recognition and measurement guidance:

- *Major planned periodical maintenance and overhaul, and other planned but irregular costs.* The cost of such maintenance and overhaul or other seasonal expenditure expected to be incurred late in the year is not anticipated for an interim period, unless an event occurred that creates a legal or constructive obligation at the interim ending date.
- *Provisions.* Provisions are only recognised when the entity has no realistic alternative but to make the transfer as a result of a past event that creates a legal or constructive obligation. Estimated changes in measurement of recognised provisions are updated in each interim report.
- *Year-end bonuses.* The nature of bonuses might differ significantly. A year-end bonus is only anticipated in an interim period if the bonus is (a) a legal or constructive obligation that the entity has no realistic alternative to avoid the payment and (b) a realistic estimate could be made. Specifically, the guidance in IAS 19 should be applied (see Chapter 19). The assessment will be based on the expectation whether a bonus will be paid at year-end based on the performance until the end of the interim period.
- *Contingent lease payments.* Contingent leases based on a required level of annual sales will be recognised pro rata in the interim report based on the expectation that the annual level will be achieved, based on the information available in the interim period. This is based on the fact that the entity has no realistic alternative to making the future lease payment.
- *Intangible assets.* All costs incurred in an interim period on an intangible asset are expensed if the criteria for capitalisation is not met at the end of the interim period.
- *Pensions cost.* Pension cost in an interim period is based on a year-to-date basis based on the actuarial determined pension rate anticipated at the end of the year, adjusted for significant market fluctuations and events, which might change that rate.

- *Short-term compensation absence*. In terms of the requirements of IAS 19 the amount outstanding at the end of the interim period will only be recognised if the short-term compensation is accumulating.

Revenues Received Seasonally, Cyclically or Occasionally

IAS 34 is clear in stipulating that revenues such as dividend income and interest earned cannot be anticipated or deferred at interim dates, unless such practice would be acceptable under IFRS at year-end. Interest income is typically accrued, since it is well established that this represents a contractual commitment. Dividend income, on the other hand, is not recognised until declared, even when highly predictable based on past experience; these are not obligations of the paying corporation until actually declared.

Furthermore, seasonality factors should not be smoothed out of the financial statements. For example, for many retail stores a high percentage of annual revenues occur during the holiday shopping period, and the quarterly or other interim financial statements should fully reflect such seasonality. That is, revenues should be recognised as they occur.

Recognition of Annual Costs Incurred Unevenly during the Year

IAS 34 clarifies that cost incurred unevenly during an entity's financial year shall not be anticipated or deferred for interim reporting purposes, unless anticipation or deferral would be appropriate at the end of the financial year. The Illustrated Examples provide the following examples to demonstrate this principle:

- *Employer payroll tax and insurance contributions*. If such contributions are assessed on an annual basis the expense recognised in the interim reports is estimated using an estimated annual effective payroll tax or contribution rate. If a progressive tax rate is applied for individuals, it means that the rate will be based on the total expected remuneration of the employee for the year.

Income Taxes

The fact that income taxes are assessed annually by the taxing authorities is the primary reason for reaching the conclusion that taxes are to be accrued based on the estimated average annual effective tax rate for the full fiscal year. Furthermore, if rate changes have been enacted to take effect later in the fiscal year (while some rate changes take effect in midyear, more likely this would be an issue if the entity reports on a fiscal year and the new tax rates become effective at the start of a calendar year), the expected effective rate should take into account the rate changes as well as the anticipated pattern of earnings to be experienced over the course of the year.

Thus, the rate to be applied to interim period earnings (or losses, as discussed further below) will take into account the expected level of earnings for the entire forthcoming year, as well as the effect of enacted (or substantially enacted) changes in the tax rates to become operative later in the fiscal year. In other words, and as the standard puts it, the estimated average annual rate would "reflect a blend of the progressive tax rate structure expected to be applicable to the full year's earnings including enacted or substantially enacted changes in the income tax rates scheduled to take effect later in the financial year."

IAS 34 addresses in detail the various computational aspects of an effective interim period tax rate, which are summarised in the following paragraphs.

Difference in Financial Reporting Year and Tax Year

When the financial reporting year and the income tax year differ, the tax expense is calculated at a different average estimated tax rate for each portion of a tax year falling in the interim period.

Multiplicity of Taxing Jurisdictions and Different Categories of Income

Many entities are subject to a multiplicity of taxing jurisdictions, and in some instances the amount of income subject to tax will vary from one to the next, since different laws will include and exclude disparate items of income or expense from the tax base. For example, interest earned on government-issued bonds may be exempted from tax by the jurisdiction that issued them but be defined as fully taxable by other tax jurisdictions the entity is subject to. To the extent feasible, the appropriate estimated average annual effective tax rate should be separately ascertained for each taxing jurisdiction and applied individually to the interim period pre-tax income of each jurisdiction, so that the most accurate estimate of income taxes can be developed at each interim reporting date. In general, an overall estimated effective tax rate will not be as satisfactory for this purpose as would a more carefully constructed set of estimated rates, since the pattern of taxable and deductible items will fluctuate from one period to the next.

Similarly, if the tax law prescribes different income tax rates for different categories of income (e.g., the tax rate on capital gains may differ from the tax rate applicable to business income in many countries), then to the extent practicable, a separate tax rate should be applied to each category of interim period pre-tax income. The standard, while mandating such detailed rules of computing and applying tax rates across jurisdictions or across categories of income, recognises that in practice such a degree of precision may not be achievable in all cases. Thus, in all such cases, IAS 34 softens its stand and allows usage of a "weighted-average of rates across jurisdictions or across categories of income" provided "it is a reasonable approximation of the effect of using more specific rates."

Tax Credits

In calculating an expected effective tax rate for a given tax jurisdiction, all relevant features of the tax regulations should be taken into account. Jurisdictions may provide for tax credits based on new investment in plant and machinery, relocation of facilities to backward or underdeveloped areas, research and development expenditures, levels of export sales, etc. and the expected credits against the tax for the full year should be given consideration in the determination of an expected effective tax rate. The tax effect of new investment in plant and machinery, when the local taxing body offers an investment credit for qualifying investment in tangible productive assets, will be reflected in those interim periods of the fiscal year in which the new investment occurs (assuming it can be forecast to occur later in a given fiscal year), and not merely in the period in which the new investment occurs. This is consistent with the underlying concept that taxes are strictly an annual phenomenon, but it is at variance with the purely discrete view of interim financial reporting.

IAS 34 notes that, although tax credits and similar modifying elements are to be taken into account in developing the expected effective tax rate to apply to interim earnings, tax benefits which will relate to onetime events are to be reflected in the interim period when those events take place. This is perhaps most likely to be encountered in the context of capital gains taxes incurred in connection with occasional disposal of investments and other capital assets; since it is not feasible to project the rate at which such transactions will occur over the course of a year, the tax effects should be recognised only as the underlying events transpire.

While in most cases tax credits are to be handled as suggested in the foregoing paragraphs, in some jurisdictions tax credits, particularly those that relate to export revenue or capital expenditures, are in effect government grants. The accounting for government grants is set forth in IAS 20; in brief, grants are recognised in income over the period necessary to properly match them to the costs which the grants are intended to offset or defray. To ensure compliance with both IAS 20 and IAS 34, tax credits will need to be carefully analysed to identify those which are, in substance, grants, and then accounting for the credit consistent with its true nature.

Tax Loss Tax Credit Carrybacks and Carryforwards

When an interim period loss gives rise to a tax loss carryback, it should be fully reflected in that interim period. Similarly, if a loss in an interim period produces a tax loss carryforward, it should be recognised immediately, but only if the criteria set forth in IAS 12 are met. It must be deemed probable that the benefits will be realisable before the loss benefits can be given formal recognition in the financial statements. In the case of interim period losses, it may be necessary to assess not only whether the entity will be profitable enough in future fiscal years to utilise the tax benefits associated with the loss, but, furthermore, whether interim periods later in the same year will provide earnings of sufficient magnitude to absorb the losses of the current period.

IAS 12 provides that changes in expectations regarding the realisability of benefits related to net operating loss carryforwards should be reflected currently in tax expense. Similarly, if a net operating loss carryforward benefit is not deemed probable of being realised until the interim (or annual) period when it in fact becomes realised, the tax effect will be included in tax expense of that period. Appropriate explanations must be included in the notes to the financial statements, even on an interim basis, to provide the user with an understanding of the unusual relationship between pre-tax accounting income and the provision for income taxes.

Volume Rebates or Other Anticipated Price Changes in Interim Reporting Periods

IAS 34 prescribes that where volume rebates or other contractual changes in the prices of goods and services are anticipated to occur over the annual reporting period, these should be anticipated in the interim financial statements for periods within that year. The logic is that the effective cost of materials, labour or other inputs will be altered later in the year as a consequence of the volume of activity during earlier interim periods, among others, and it would be a distortion of the reported results of those earlier periods if this were not taken into account. Clearly this must be based on estimates, since the volume of purchases, etc., in later portions of the year may not materialise as anticipated. As with other estimates, however, as more accurate information becomes available this will be adjusted on a prospective basis, meaning that the results of earlier periods should not be revised or corrected. This is consistent with the accounting prescribed for contingent rentals and is furthermore consistent with IAS 37's guidance on provisions.

The requirement to take volume rebates and similar adjustments into effect in interim period financial reporting applies equally to vendors or providers, as well as to customers or consumers of the goods and services. In both instances, however, it must be deemed probable that such adjustments have been earned or will occur before giving recognition to them in the financial statements. This high threshold has been set because the definitions of assets and liabilities in the IASB's *Conceptual Framework* require that they be recognised only when it is probable that the benefits will flow into or out from the entity. An accrual would only be appropriate for contractual price adjustments and related matters. Discretionary rebates and other price adjustments, even if typically experienced in earlier periods, would not be given formal recognition in the interim financial statements.

Depreciation and Amortisation in Interim Periods

The rule regarding depreciation and amortisation in interim periods is more consistent with the discrete view of interim reporting. Charges to be recognised in the interim periods are to be related only to those assets actually employed during the period; planned acquisitions for later periods of the fiscal year are not to be taken into account.

While this rule seems entirely logical, it can give rise to a problem that is not encountered in the context of most other types of revenue or expense items. This occurs when the tax laws or financial reporting conventions permit or require that special allocation formulas be used during the year of acquisition (and often disposition) of an asset. In such cases, depreciation or amortisation will be an amount other than the amount that would be computed based purely on the fraction of the year the asset was in service. For example, assume that the convention is that one half-year of depreciation is charged during the year the asset is acquired, irrespective of how many months it is in service. Further assume that a particular asset is acquired at the inception of the fourth quarter of the year. Under the requirements of IAS 34, the first three quarters would not be charged with any depreciation expense related to this asset (even if it was known in advance that the asset would be placed in service in the fourth quarter). However, this would then necessitate charging fourth quarter operations with one half-year's (i.e., two quarters') depreciation, which arguably would distort that final period's results of operations.

IAS 34 does address this problem area. It states that an adjustment should be made in the final interim period so that the sum of interim depreciation and amortisation equals an independently computed annual charge for these items. However, there is no requirement that financial statements be separately presented for a final interim period (and most entities, in fact, do not report for a final period); such an adjustment might be implicit in the annual financials, and presumably would be explained in the notes if material (the standard does not explicitly require this, however).

The alternative financial reporting strategy, that is, projecting annual depreciation, including the effect of asset dispositions and acquisitions planned for or reasonably anticipated to occur during the year, and then allocating this ratably to interim periods, has been rejected. Such an approach might have been rationalised in the same way that the use of the effective annual tax rate was in assigning tax expense or benefits to interim periods, but this has not been done.

Inventories

Inventories represent a major category for most manufacturing and merchandising entities, and some inventory costing methods pose unique problems for interim financial reporting. In general, however, the same inventory costing principles should be utilised for interim reporting as for annual reporting. The use of estimates in determining quantities, costs and NRVs at interim dates will be more pervasive.

Two particular difficulties are addressed in IAS 34. These are the matters of determining NRVs at interim dates and the allocation of manufacturing variances.

Regarding NRV determination, the standard expresses the belief that the determination of NRV at interim dates should be based on selling prices and costs to complete at those dates. Projections should therefore not be made regarding conditions which possibly might exist at the time of the fiscal year-end. Furthermore, write-downs to NRV taken at interim reporting dates should be reversed in a subsequent interim reporting period only if it would be appropriate to do so at the end of the financial year.

The last of the special issues related to inventories that are addressed by IAS 34 concerns allocation of variances at interim dates. When standard costing methods are employed, the resulting variances are typically allocated to cost of sales and inventories in proportion to the monetary magnitude of those two captions, or according to some other rational system. IAS 34 requires that the price, efficiency, spending and volume variances of a manufacturing entity are recognised in income at interim reporting dates to the extent those variances would be recognised at the end of the financial year. It should be noted that some national standards have prescribed deferral of such variances to year end based on the premise that some of the variances will tend to offset over the course of a full fiscal year, particularly if the result of volume fluctuations is due to seasonal factors.

When variance allocation is thus deferred, the full balances of the variances are placed onto the statement of financial position, typically as additions to or deductions from the inventory accounts. However, IAS 34 expresses a preference that these variances be disposed of at interim dates (instead of being deferred to year-end) since to not do so could result in reporting inventory at interim dates at more or less than actual cost.

Example of interim reporting of product costs

Dakar Corporation encounters the following product cost situations as part of its quarterly reporting:

- It only conducts inventory counts at the end of the second quarter and end of the fiscal year. Its typical gross profit is 30%. The actual gross profit at the end of the second quarter is determined to have been 32% for the first six months of the year. The actual gross profit at the end of the year is determined to have been 29% for the entire year.
- It determines that, at the end of the second quarter, due to peculiar market conditions, there is an NRV adjustment to certain inventory required in the amount of €90,000. Dakar expects that this market anomaly will be corrected by year-end, which indeed does occur in late December.
- It suffers a decline of €65,000 in the market value of its inventory during the third quarter. This inventory value increases by €75,000 in the fourth quarter.
- It suffers a clearly temporary decline of €10,000 in the market value of a specific part of its inventory in the first quarter, which it recovers in the second quarter.

Dakar uses the following calculations to record these situations and determine quarterly cost of goods sold:

	Quarter 1	*Quarter 2*	*Quarter 3*	*Quarter 4*	*Full Year*
Sales	€10,000,000	€8,500,000	€7,200,000	€11,800,000	€37,500,000
(1—Gross profit percentage)	70%		70%		
Cost of goods, gross profit method	7,000,000		5,040,000		
Cost of goods, based on actual physical count		5,580,000[1]		9,005,000[2]	26,625,000
Temporary NRV decline in specific inventory[3]		90,000		(90,000)	0
Decline in inventory value with subsequent increase[4]	65,000	(65,000)	0		
Temporary decline in inventory value[5]	10,000	(10,000)	0	0	0
Total cost of goods sold	**7,010,000**	**5,660,000**	**5,105,000**	**8,850,000**	**26,625,000**

[1]*Calculated as [€18,500,000 sales × (1 – 32% gross margin)] – €7,000,000 (quarter 1 cost of sales).*
[2]*Calculated as [€37,500,000 sales × (1 – 29% gross margin)] – €17,620,000 (quarters 1–3 cost of sales).*
[3]*Even though anticipated to recover, the NRV decline must be recognised.*
[4]*Full recognition of market value decline, followed by recognition of market value increase, but only in the amount needed to offset the amount of the initial decline.*
[5]*No deferred recognition to temporary decline in value.*

Example of interim reporting of other expenses

Dakar Corporation encounters the following expense situations as part of its quarterly reporting:

- Its largest customer, Festive Fabrics, has placed firm orders for the year that will result in sales of €1,500,000 in the first quarter, €2,000,000 in the second quarter, €750,000 in the third quarter and €1,650,000 in the fourth quarter. Dakar gives Festive Fabrics a 5% rebate if Festive Fabrics buys at least €5 million of goods each year. Festive Fabrics exceeded the €5 million goal in the preceding year and was expected to do so again in the current year.
- It incurs €24,000 of trade show fees in the first quarter for a trade show that will occur in the third quarter.
- It pays €64,000 *in advance* in the second quarter for a series of advertisements that will run through the third and fourth quarters.
- It receives a €32,000 property tax bill in the second quarter that applies to the *following* 12 months.
- It incurs annual factory air filter replacement costs of €6,000 in the first quarter.
- Its management team is entitled to a year-end bonus of €120,000 if it meets a sales target of €40 million, prior to any sales rebates, with the bonus dropping by €10,000 for every million dollars of sales not achieved.

Dakar uses the following calculations to record these situations:

	Quarter 1	Quarter 2	Quarter 3	Quarter 4	Full year
Sales	€10,000,000	€8,500,000	€7,200,000	€11,800,000	€37,500,000
Deduction from sales	(75,000)[1]	(100,000)	(37,500)	(82,500)	(295,000)
Marketing expense			24,000[2]		24,000
Advertising expense			32,000[3]	32,000	64,000
Property tax expense		8,000[4]	8,000	8,000	24,000
Maintenance expense	1,500[5]	1,500	1,500	1,500	6,000
Bonus expense	30,000[6]	25,500	21,600	17,900	95,000

[1]*The sales rebate is based on 5% of the actual sales to the customer in the quarter when the sale is incurred. The actual payment back to the customer does not occur until the end of the year, when the €5 million goal is definitively reached. Since the firm orders for the full year exceed the threshold for rebates, the obligation is deemed probable and must be recorded.*

[2]*The €24,000 trade show payment is initially recorded as a prepaid expense and then charged to marketing expense when the trade show occurs.*

[3]*The €64,000 advertising payment is initially recorded as a prepaid expense and then charged to advertising expense when the advertisements run.*

[4]*The €32,000 property tax payment is initially recorded as a prepaid expense and then charged to property tax expense on a straight-line basis over the next four quarters.*

[5]*The €6,000 air filter replacement payment is initially recorded as a prepaid expense and then charged to maintenance expense over the one-year life of the air filters.*

[6]*The management bonus is recognised in proportion to the amount of revenue recognised in each quarter. Once it becomes apparent that the full sales target will not be reached, the bonus accrual should be adjusted downward. In this case, the downward adjustment is assumed to be in the fourth quarter, since past history and seasonality factors made non-achievement of the full goal unlikely until fourth quarter results were known. (Note: with other fact patterns, quarterly accruals may have differed.)*

Foreign Currency Translation Adjustments at Interim Dates

IAS 21 prescribes rules for translating the financial statements for foreign operations into either the functional currency or the presentation currency and also includes guidelines for using historical, average or closing foreign exchange rates. It also lays down rules for including the resulting adjustments either in income or in equity. IAS 34 requires that, consistent with IAS 21, the actual average and closing rates for the interim period be used in translating financial statements of foreign operations at interim dates. In other words, the future changes to exchange rates (in the current financial year) are not allowed to be anticipated by IAS 34.

Where IAS 21 provides for translation adjustments to be recognised in the statement of profit or loss and other comprehensive income in the period it arises, IAS 34 stipulates that the same approach be applied during each interim period. If the adjustments are expected to reverse before the end of the financial year, IAS 34 requires that entities not defer some foreign currency translation adjustments at an interim date.

Use of Estimates in Interim Periods

IAS 34 recognises that preparation of interim financial statements will require a greater use of estimates than annual financial statements. Appendix C to the standard provides examples of use of estimates to illustrate the application of this standard in this regard. The appendix provides nine examples covering areas ranging from inventories to pensions.

Readers are advised to read the other illustrations contained in Appendix C of IAS 34 for further guidance on the subject.

Impairment of Assets in Interim Periods

IAS 34 stipulated that an entity was to apply the same impairment testing, recognition and reversal criteria at an interim period as it would at the end of its financial year. The frequency of interim financial reporting, however, was not to affect the annual financial statements. This prescription created unanticipated conflicts, since certain impairments were not, according to other standards, subject to later reversals.

One apparent conflict between IAS 34's directives and the IAS 36 requirement is that an impairment loss recognised on goodwill cannot be later reversed. If, for example, an impairment of goodwill was indicated in the first fiscal quarter, but at year end that impairment no longer existed, it would be impossible to comply with the proscription against having interim reporting affect annual results unless the impairment in the first quarter were reversed later in the year.

IFRIC Interpretation 10, *Interim Financial Reporting and Impairment*, directs that impairments of goodwill recognised in interim periods may not be later reversed, even if at year's end no impairment would otherwise have been reported. This interpretation therefore brings to an end the IAS 34-based mandate that the frequency of interim reporting cannot itself impact annual financial reporting.

IFRS 9, issued in October 2010, amended a number of paragraphs under IFRIC 10. The revision of IFRIC 10 states that entities may not reverse an impairment loss recognised in a previous interim period in respect of goodwill. However, this restriction will not extend to other areas of potential conflict between IAS 34 and other standards.

Interim Financial Reporting in Hyperinflationary Economies

IAS 34 requires that interim financial reports in hyperinflationary economies be prepared using the same principles as at the financial year end. Thus, the provisions of IAS 29 would need to be complied with in this regard. IAS 34 stipulates that in presenting interim data in the measuring unit, entities should report the resulting gain or loss on the net monetary position in the interim period's statement of comprehensive income. IAS 34 also requires that entities do not need to annualise the recognition of the gain or loss or use estimated annual inflation rates in preparing interim period financial statements in a hyperinflationary economy.

US GAAP COMPARISON

While both US GAAP and IFRS require interim reporting for public companies, there are significant differences with regard to how and when the elements of the financial statements are recognised and measured.

US GAAP, under ASC 270, *Interim Reporting*, requires that product-related or variable costs be recognised in full in the interim period as they are incurred, the same way that is required for annual financial statements. However, production cost allocation variances expected to be made up by the end of the period are deferred. Additionally, generally, practice and policies applied in annual periods shall be applied at interim periods. However, for other expenses, when the expenditure can be shown to clearly benefit a future period, the expense is allocated among those periods, resulting in deferral or accrual of certain costs. IFRS regards each interim period as a discrete period. In other words, under US GAAP, except for seasonal effects, each period should be predictive of the remaining periods of the fiscal year. Seasonal effects are disclosed. Entities are encouraged to present rolling full-year results for material seasonal effects if doing so would improve comparability. However, if an expense is unusual or cannot be reasonably attributed to future periods, it is not deferred. Allocations of these costs to current and future periods cannot be arbitrary. The effective income tax rate is based on full-year income estimates. Changes in income tax rates are recognised in the current interim period, unless attributed to an error.

US GAAP is more explicit about the types of transactions that require disclosures related to fourth-quarter activity. In particular, the following fourth-quarter activity must be disclosed:

- Activity related to a change in accounting principle;
- Disposals of components of an entity;
- Unusual or infrequently occurring items recognised in the fourth quarter; and
- The aggregate effect of year-end adjustments that are material to the results of the fourth quarter.

US GAAP, unlike IFRS, does not allow decreases in inventory value recorded in annual financial statements to be reversed. However, for interim reporting, if the price of inventory rises in a subsequent interim period within the same fiscal year, a reversal gain is recognised up to the amount of previous losses. The LIFO method of inventory cost flow is prohibited under IFRS, but not under US GAAP. When a LIFO-layer liquidation is expected to be restored by the end of the year, a debit to inventory is made with an offset to current liabilities in the interim period and replacement costs of the inventory are recognised in cost of goods sold.

Materiality of an adjustment is determined with regard to the expected results for the fiscal year. IFRS use the current interim period results. Similar to IFRS, costs that are accrued during the year because the amount is based on full-year activities (e.g., sales and purchase discounts, bonuses) are estimated and recognised at each interim period.

Under US GAAP, a statement of changes in equity is not required in interim financial statements.

35 HYPERINFLATION

INTRODUCTION

IAS 29 addresses financial reporting in *hyperinflationary* economies. While, in general, this applies the same principles as are employed when using general price level accounting, the objective is to convert the financial statements of entities operating under conditions that render unadjusted financial statements of little or no value into meaningful measures of financial position and performance.

	Sources of IFRS	
IAS 29	*IFRS* 1	*IFRIC* 7

FINANCIAL REPORTING IN HYPERINFLATIONARY ECONOMIES

Hyperinflation is a condition that is difficult to define precisely, as there is not a clear demarcation between merely rampant inflation and true hyperinflation. However, in any given economic system, when the general population has lost faith in the stability of the local economy, and business transactions are commonly either denominated in a stable reference currency of another country, or are structured to incorporate an indexing feature intended to compensate for the distortive effects of inflation, hyperinflation may be present. As a benchmark, when cumulative inflation over three years approaches or exceeds 100%, it must be conceded that the economy is suffering from hyperinflation.

Hyperinflation is obviously a major problem for any economy, as it creates severe distortions and, left unaddressed, results in uncontrolled acceleration of the rate of price changes, ending in inevitable collapse, as was witnessed in post-World War I Germany. From a financial reporting perspective, there are also major problems, since even over a brief interval such as a year or even a quarter, the statement of comprehensive income will contain transactions with such a variety of purchasing power units that aggregation becomes meaningless, as would adding dollars, sterling or euros.

In a truly hyperinflationary economy, users of financial statements are unable to make meaningful use of such statements unless they have been recast into currency units having purchasing power defined by prices at or near the date of the statements. Unless this common denominator is employed, the financial statements are too difficult to interpret for purposes of making management, investing and credit decisions. Although some sophisticated users, particularly in those countries where hyperinflation has been endemic, such as some of the South American nations, including Brazil and Argentina, and for certain periods nations such as Israel, are able to apply rules of thumb to cope with this problem, in general modifications must be made to general-purpose financial statements if they are to have any value.

Under international accounting standards, if hyperinflation is deemed to characterise the economy, a form of price level accounting must be applied to the financial statements to conform to generally accepted accounting principles. IAS 29 requires that all the financial statements be adjusted to reflect year-end general price levels, which entails applying a broad-based index to all non-monetary items on the statement of financial position and to all transactions reported in the statement of comprehensive income and the statement of cash flows.

Severe Hyperinflation According to IFRS 1

In 2010 the IASB was asked to clarify how an entity should resume presenting financial statements in accordance with IFRS after a period of severe hyperinflation, during which the entity had been unable to comply with IAS 29, *Financial Reporting in Hyperinflationary Economies*. It should be noted that an entity would be unable to comply with IAS 29 if a reliable general price index is not available to all entities with that same functional currency, and exchangeability between the currency and a relatively stable foreign currency does not exist. However, once the functional currency changes to a non-hyperinflationary currency, or the currency ceases to be severely hyperinflationary, an entity would be able to start applying IFRS to subsequent transactions.

IFRS 1 was amended to provide guidance on how an entity can present IFRS financial statements after its currency ceases to be severely hyperinflationary, by presenting an opening IFRS statement of financial position on or after the functional currency normalisation date.

It was believed that allowing an entity to apply the exemption when presenting an opening IFRS statement of financial position after, and not just on, the functional currency normalisation date would address practical concerns that may arise if the functional currency normalisation date and the entity's date of transition to IFRS are different. This amendment would also be available to entities that were emerging from a period of severe hyperinflation but had not applied IFRS in the past.

IFRS 1 permits an entity emerging from a period of severe hyperinflation to elect to measure its assets and liabilities at fair value. That fair value could then be used as the deemed cost in its opening IFRS statement of financial position. This approach expands the scope of the deemed cost exemptions in IFRS 1. However, because severe hyperinflation is a specific set of circumstances, the IASB wanted to ensure that the fair value measurement option was applied only to those assets and liabilities that were held before the functional currency normalisation date, and not to other assets and liabilities held by the entity at the time it made the transition to IFRS. Furthermore, where a parent entity's functional currency has been subject to severe hyperinflation, but its subsidiary company's functional currency has not been subject to severe hyperinflation, IFRS 1 does not require such a subsidiary company to apply this exemption.

Any adjustments arising on electing to measure assets and liabilities at fair value in the opening IFRS statement of financial position arise from events and transactions before the date of transition to IFRS. Thus, an entity should recognise those adjustments directly in retained earnings (or, if appropriate, in another category of equity) at the date of transition to IFRS.

Entities are required to prepare and present comparative information in accordance with IFRS. Furthermore, it should be noted that the preparation of information in accordance with IFRS for periods before the functional currency normalisation date may not be possible; hence, the exemption refers to a date of transition on or after the functional currency normalisation date. This may lead to a comparative period of less than 12 months. Entities should consider whether disclosure of non-IFRS comparative information and historical summaries would provide useful information to users of financial statements. In all such cases entities should explain the transition to IFRS.

Restating Historical Cost Financial Statements under Hyperinflation Conditions

The precise adjustments to be made depend on whether the financial reporting system is based on historical costs or on current costs. Although in both cases the goal is to restate the financial statements into the measuring unit that exists at the date of the statement of financial position, the mechanics will vary to some extent.

If the financial reporting system is based on historical costing, the process used to adjust the statement of financial position can be summarised as follows:

1. Monetary assets and liabilities are already presented in units of year-end purchasing power and receive no further adjustment. (See the appendix for a categorisation of different assets and liabilities as to their status as monetary or non-monetary.)
2. Monetary assets and liabilities that are linked to price changes, such as indexed debt securities, are adjusted according to the terms of the contractual arrangement. This does not change the characterisation of these items as monetary, but it does serve to reduce or even eliminate the purchasing power gain or loss that would have otherwise been experienced as a result of holding these items during periods of changing general prices.
3. Non-monetary items are adjusted by applying a ratio of indices, the numerator of which is the general price level index at the date of the statement of financial position and the denominator is of which is the index as of the acquisition or inception date of the item in question. For some items, such as plant assets, this is a straightforward process, while for others, such as work-in-process inventories, this can be more complex.
4. Certain assets cannot be adjusted as described above, because even in nominally historical cost financial statements these items have been revised to some other basis, such as fair value or net realisable amounts. For example, under the allowed alternative method of IAS 16, property, plant and equipment can be adjusted to fair value. In such a case, no further adjustment would be warranted, assuming that

the adjustment to fair value was made as of the latest date of the statement of financial position. If the latest revaluation was as of an earlier date, the carrying amounts should be further adjusted to compensate for changes in the general price level from that date to the date of the statement of financial position, using the indexing technique noted above.

5. Consistent with the established principles of historical cost accounting, if the restated amounts of non-monetary assets exceed the recoverable amounts, these must be reduced appropriately. This can easily occur, since specific prices of goods will vary by differing amounts, even in a hyperinflationary environment, and in fact some may decline in terms of current cost even in such cases, particularly when technological change occurs rapidly. Since the application of price level accounting, whether for ordinary inflation or for hyperinflation, does not imply an abandonment of historical costing, being a mere translation into more timely and relevant purchasing power units, the rules of that mode of financial reporting still apply. Generally accepted accounting principles require that assets not be stated at amounts in excess of realisable amounts, and this constraint applies even when price level adjustments are reflected.
6. Equity accounts must also be restated to compensate for changing prices. Paid-in capital accounts are indexed by reference to the dates when the capital was contributed, which are usually a discrete number of identifiable transactions over the life of the entity. Revaluation accounts, if any, are eliminated entirely, as these will be subsumed in restated retained earnings. The retained earnings account itself is the most complex to analyse and in practice is often treated as a balancing figure after all other statement of financial position accounts have been restated. However, it is possible to compute the adjustment to this account directly, and that is the recommended course of action, lest other errors go undetected. To adjust retained earnings, each year's earnings should be adjusted by a ratio of indices, the numerator being the general price level as of the date of the statement of financial position, and the denominator being the price level as of the end of the year for which the earnings were reported. Reductions of retained earnings for dividends paid should be adjusted similarly.
7. IAS 29 addresses a few other special problem areas. For example, the standard notes that borrowing costs typically already reflect the impact of inflation (more accurately, interest rates reflect inflationary expectations), and thus it would represent a form of double counting to fully index capital asset costs for price level changes when part of the cost of the asset was capitalised interest, as required by IAS 23, *Borrowing Costs*. As a practical matter, interest costs are often not a material component of recorded asset amounts, and the inflation-related component would only be a fraction of interest costs capitalised. However, the general rule is to delete that fraction of the capitalised borrowing costs which represents inflationary compensation, since the entire cost of the asset will be indexed to current purchasing units.

To restate the current period's statement of comprehensive income, a reasonably accurate result can be obtained if revenue and expense accounts are multiplied by the ratio of end-of-period prices to average prices for the period. Where price changes were not relatively constant throughout the period, or when transactions did not occur ratably, as when there was a distinct seasonal pattern to sales activity, a more precise measurement effort might be needed. This can be particularly important when a devaluation of the currency took place during the year.

While IAS 29 addresses the statement of cash flows only perfunctorily (its issuance was prior to the revision of IAS 7), this financial statement must also be modified to report all items in terms of year-end purchasing power units. For example, changes in working capital accounts, used to convert net income into cash flow from operating activities, will be altered to reflect the real (i.e., inflation-adjusted) changes.

To illustrate, if beginning accounts receivable were €500,000 and ending receivables were €650,000, but prices rose by 40% during the year, the apparent €150,000 increase in receivables (which would be a use of cash) is really a €50,000 decrease [(€500,000 × 1.4 = €700,000) – €650,000], which in cash flow terms is a source of cash. Other items must be handled similarly. Investing and financing activities should be adjusted on an item-by-item basis, since these are normally discrete events that do not occur ratably throughout the year.

Additionally, the adjusted statement of comprehensive income will report a gain or loss on net monetary items held. As an approximation, this will be computed by applying the change in general prices for the year to the average net monetary assets (or liabilities) outstanding during the year. If net monetary items changed materially at one or more times during the year, a more detailed computation would be warranted. In the statement of comprehensive income, the gain or loss on net monetary items should be associated with the adjustment relating to items that are linked to price level changes (indexed debt, etc.) as well as with interest income and expense and foreign exchange adjustments, since theoretically at least, all these items contain a component that reflects inflationary behaviour.

Restating Current Cost Financial Statements under Hyperinflation Conditions

If the financial reporting system is based on current costing (as described earlier in the chapter), the process used to adjust the statement of financial position can be summarised as follows:

1. Monetary assets and liabilities are already presented in units of year-end purchasing power and receive no further adjustment. (See the appendix for a categorisation of different assets and liabilities as to their status as monetary or non-monetary.)
2. Monetary assets and liabilities that are linked to price changes, such as indexed debt securities, are adjusted according to the terms of the contractual arrangement. This does not change the characterisation of these items as monetary, but it does serve to reduce or even eliminate the purchasing power gain or loss that would have otherwise been experienced as a result of holding these items during periods of changing general prices.
3. Non-monetary items are already stated at year-end current values or replacement costs and need no further adjustments. Issues related to recoverable amounts and other complications associated with price level adjusted historical costs should not normally arise.
4. Equity accounts must also be restated to compensate for changing prices. Paid-in capital accounts are indexed by reference to the dates when the capital was contributed, which are usually a discrete number of identifiable transactions over the life of the entity. Revaluation accounts are eliminated entirely, as these will be subsumed in restated retained earnings. The retained earnings account itself will typically be a "balancing account" under this scenario, since detailed analysis would be very difficult, although certainly not impossible, to accomplish.

The current cost statement of comprehensive income, excluding the price level component, will reflect transactions at current costs as of the transaction dates. For example, cost of sales will be comprised of the costs as of each transaction date (usually approximated on an average basis). To report these as of the date of the statement of financial position, these costs will have to be further inflated to year-end purchasing power units, by means of the ratio of general price level indices, as suggested above.

In addition, the adjusted statement of comprehensive income will report a gain or loss on net monetary items held. This will be similar to that discussed under the historical cost reporting above. However, current cost statements of comprehensive income, if prepared, already will include the net gain or loss on monetary items held, which need not be computed again.

To the extent that restated earnings differ from earnings on which income taxes are computed, there will be a need to provide more or less tax accrual, which will be a deferred tax obligation or asset, depending on the circumstances.

Comparative Financial Statements

Consistent with the underlying concept of reporting in hyperinflationary economies, all prior-year financial statement amounts must be updated to purchasing power units as of the most recent date of the statement of financial position. This will be a relatively simple process of applying a ratio of indices of the current year-end price level to the year earlier price level.

Consolidated Financial Statements

A parent reporting in the currency of a hyperinflationary economy may have subsidiaries that also report in the currencies of hyperinflationary economies. The financial statements of any such subsidiary need first to be restated before they are included in the consolidated financial statements by applying a general price index of the country in whose currency it reports. Where such a subsidiary is a foreign subsidiary, its restated financial statements are translated at closing rates. The financial statements of subsidiaries that do not report in the currencies of hyperinflationary economies are dealt with in accordance with the normal translation principles in IAS 21.

If financial statements with different reporting period ends are consolidated, all items, whether non-monetary or monetary, need to be restated into the measuring unit current at the date of the consolidated financial statements.

Other Disclosure Issues

IAS 29 requires that when the standard is applied, the fact that hyperinflation adjustments have been made must be noted. The underlying basis of accounting, historical cost or current cost should be stipulated, as should the price level index that was utilised in making the adjustments.

Economies which Cease Being Hyperinflationary

When application of IAS 29 is discontinued, the amounts reported in the last statement of financial position that had been adjusted become, effectively, the new cost basis. The previously applied adjustments are not reversed, since an end to a period of hyperinflation generally means only that prices have reached a plateau, not that they have deflated to earlier levels.

Guidance on Applying the Restatement Approach

IFRIC issued an Interpretation of IAS 29 (IFRIC 7, *Applying the Restatement Approach*) that addresses the matter of differentiating between monetary and non-monetary items. IAS 29 requires that when the reporting entity identifies the existence of hyperinflation in the economy of its functional currency, it must restate its financial statements for the effects of inflation. The restatement approach distinguishes between monetary and non-monetary items, but in practice it has been noted that there is uncertainty about how to restate the financial statements for the first time, particularly with regard to deferred tax balances, and concerning comparative information for prior periods. IFRIC 7 addresses these matters.

Under IFRIC 7, in the first year that an entity identifies the existence of hyperinflation, it would start applying IAS 29 as if it had always applied that standard—that is, as if the economy had always been hyperinflationary. It must recreate an opening statement of financial position at the beginning of the earliest annual accounting period presented in the restated financial statements for the first year it applies IAS 29.

The implication of this Interpretation is that restatements of non-monetary items that are carried at historical cost are effected as of the dates of first recognition (e.g., acquisition). The restatements cannot be effected merely from the opening date of the statement of financial position (which would commonly be at the beginning of the comparative financial statement year). For example, if the year-end 2013 statement of financial position is the first one under IAS 29, with two-year comparative reporting employed, but various plant assets acquired, say, in 2005, the application of IFRIC 7 would require restatements for price level changes from 2005 to year-end 2012.

Non-monetary assets that are not reported at historical costs (e.g., plant assets revalued for IFRS-basis financial reporting, per IAS 16) require a different mode of adjustment. In this situation, the restatements are applied only for the period of time elapsed since the latest revaluation dates (which should, per IAS 16, be recent dates in most instances). For example, if revaluation was performed at year-end 2010, then only the period from year-end 2010 to year-end 2012 would be subject to adjustment, as the year-end 2010 revaluation already served to address hyperinflation occurring to that date.

IFRIC 7 provides that if detailed records of the acquisition dates for items of property, plant and equipment are not available or are not capable of estimation, the reporting entity should use an independent professional assessment of the fair value of the items as the basis for restatement. Likewise, if a general price index is not available, it may be necessary to use an estimate based on the changes in the exchange rate between the functional currency and a relatively stable foreign currency, for example when the entity restates its financial statements.

IFRIC 7 also provides specific guidance on the difficult topic of deferred tax balances in the *opening* statement of financial position of the entity subject to IAS 29 restatement. A two-step computational procedure is required to effect the restatement of deferred tax assets and liabilities. First, deferred tax items are remeasured in accordance with IAS 12 *after* having restated the nominal carrying amounts of all other non-monetary items in the opening statement of financial position as of that date. Secondly, the remeasured deferred tax assets and/or liabilities are restated for hyperinflation's effects from the opening date of the statement of financial position to the reporting date (the most recent date of the statement of financial position).

US GAAP COMPARISON

US GAAP does not generally permit inflation-adjusted financial statements. However, under US GAAP, entities under hyperinflation conditions are deemed to use a functional currency of a highly inflationary economy if the cumulative inflation rate for three years exceeds 100%. No such bright-line exists under IFRS to identify hyperinflation. A 100% cumulative inflation rate over three years is only an indicator that must be considered.

Under US GAAP, subsidiaries (both consolidated or equity-method accounted) that use highly inflationary currencies must substitute the hyperinflation currency with a reporting currency. Accordingly, remeasurement effects from the transaction currency into the reporting currency are recognised in profit and loss. If the currency of a subsidiary ceases to be highly inflationary, the reporting currency at the date of change shall be translated into the local currency at current exchange rates.

APPENDIX: MONETARY VS. NON-MONETARY ITEMS

Item	*Monetary*	*Non-monetary*	*Requires analysis*
Cash on hand, demand deposits and time deposits	X		
Foreign currency and claims to foreign currency	X		
Securities			
Common stock (passive investment)		X	
Preferred stock (convertible or participating) and convertible bonds			X
Other preferred stock or bonds	X		
Accounts and notes receivable and allowance for doubtful accounts	X		
Mortgage loan receivables	X		
Inventories		X	
Loans made to employees	X		
Prepaid expenses			X
Long-term receivables	X		
Refundable deposits	X		
Advances to unconsolidated subsidiaries	X		
Equity in unconsolidated subsidiaries		X	
Pension and other funds			X
Property, plant and equipment and accumulated depreciation		X	
Cash surrender value of life insurance	X		
Purchase commitments (portion paid on fixed-price contracts)		X	
Advances to suppliers (not on fixed-price contracts)	X		
Deferred income tax charges	X		
Patents, trademarks, goodwill and other intangible assets		X	
Deferred life insurance policy acquisition costs	X		
Deferred property and casualty insurance policy acquisition costs		X	
Accounts payable and accrued expenses	X		
Accrued vacation pay			X

Cash dividends payable	X		
Obligations payable in foreign currency	X		
Sales commitments (portion collected on fixed-price contracts)		X	
Advances from customers (not on fixed-price contracts)	X		
Accrued losses on purchase commitments	X		
Deferred revenue			X
Refundable deposits	X		
Bonds payable, other long-term debt and related discount or premium	X		
Accrued pension obligations			X
Obligations under product warranties		X	
Deferred income tax obligations	X		
Deferred investment tax credits		X	
Life or property and casualty insurance policy reserves	X		
Unearned insurance premiums		X	
Deposit liabilities of financial institutions	X		

36 FIRST-TIME ADOPTION OF INTERNATIONAL FINANCIAL REPORTING STANDARDS

INTRODUCTION

When a reporting entity undertakes the preparation of its financial statements in accordance with IFRS for the first time, a number of implementation questions must be addressed and resolved. These questions relate to recognition, classification and measurement, as well as presentation and disclosure issues. Consequently, the IASB decided to promulgate a standard on this subject as its maiden pronouncement, notwithstanding the limited guidance issued by its predecessor, the IASC.

In principle, IFRS 1 requires companies implementing international standards to apply retrospectively all IFRS effective at the end of the company's first IFRS reporting period to all comparative periods presented, as if they had always been applied. However, the standard provides a number of mandatory exceptions and optional exemptions to the requirement for a full retrospective application of IFRS, which override the transitional provisions included in other IFRS. These exceptions and exemptions cover primarily two types of situations: (1) those requiring judgements by management about past conditions after the outcome of a particular situation is already known, and (2) those in which the cost of full retrospective application of IFRS would exceed the potential benefit to investors and other users of the financial statements. In addition, the standard specifies certain disclosure requirements.

IFRS 1 provides guidance that all companies must follow on initial adoption of IFRS. Although IFRS is considered a principles-based framework, the provisions of IFRS 1 are rules based and must be followed as written. The standard is quite complex and companies in transition to IFRS must carefully analyse it to determine the most appropriate accounting treatment and take advantage of an opportunity to reassess all financial reporting.

Source of IFRS
IFRS 1

DEFINITIONS OF TERMS

Date of transition to IFRS. This refers to the beginning of the earliest period for which an entity presents full comparative information under IFRS in its "first IFRS financial statements" (defined below).

Deemed cost. An amount substituted for "cost" or "depreciated cost" at a given date. In subsequent periods, this value is used as the basis for depreciation or amortisation.

Fair value. The amount for which an asset could be exchanged, or a liability settled, between knowledgeable, willing parties in an arm's-length transaction.

First IFRS financial statements. The first annual financial statements in which an entity adopts IFRS by making an explicit and unreserved statement of compliance with IFRS.

First IFRS reporting period. The latest reporting period covered by an entity's first IFRS financial statements that contains an explicit and unreserved statement of compliance with IFRS.

First-time adopter (of IFRS). An entity is referred to as a first-time adopter in the period in which it presents its first IFRS financial statements.

International Financial Reporting Standards (IFRS). The standards issued by the International Accounting Standards Board (IASB). More generally, the term connotes the currently outstanding standards (IFRS), the interpretations issued by the IFRS Interpretations Committee (IFRIC), as well as all still-effective previous standards (IAS) issued by the predecessor International Accounting Standards Committee (IASC), and the interpretations issued by the IASC's Standing Interpretations Committee (SIC).

Opening IFRS statement of financial position. The statement of financial position prepared in accordance with the requirements of IFRS 1 as of the "date of transition to IFRS." IFRS 1 requires that a first-time adopter *prepare* and *present* an opening statement of financial position. Thus, this statement is *published* along with the "first IFRS financial statements."

Previous GAAP. This refers to the basis of accounting (e.g., national standards) a first-time adopter used immediately prior to IFRS adoption.

Reporting date. The end of the latest period covered by financial statements or by an interim financial report.

FIRST-TIME ADOPTION GUIDANCE

Objective and Scope of IFRS 1

IFRS 1 applies to an entity that presents its *first IFRS financial statements.* It specifies the requirements that an entity must follow when it first adopts IFRS as the basis for preparing its general-purpose financial statements. IFRS 1 refers to these entities as *first-time adopters.*

The objective of this standard is to ensure that an entity's first IFRS financial statements, including interim financial reports, present high-quality information that:

1. Is transparent and comparable over all periods presented;
2. Provides a suitable starting point for accounting in accordance with IFRS; and
3. Can be prepared at a cost that does not exceed the benefits.

First-time IFRS adopters' financial statements should be comparable over time and between entities applying IFRS for the first time, as well as those already applying IFRS.

Per IFRS 1, an entity must apply the standard in its first IFRS financial statements and in *each interim financial report* it presents under IAS 34, *Interim Financial Reporting*, for a part of the period covered by its first IFRS financial statements. For example, if 20XX is the first annual period for which IFRS financial statements are being prepared, the quarterly or semiannual statements for 20XX, if presented, must also comply with IFRS.

According to the standard, an entity's first IFRS financial statements refer to the first annual financial statements in which the entity adopts IFRS by making an *explicit and unreserved statement* (in the financial statements) of compliance with IFRS (with *all* IFRS!).

IFRS 1 clarifies that an entity, which in a previous period fully complied with IFRS, but whose most recent previous annual financial statements did not contain an explicit and unreserved statement of compliance with IFRS, and in the current period makes an explicit and unreserved statement of compliance with IFRS, has the choice of either applying IFRS 1 (in full) or to retrospectively apply IFRS in accordance with the provision of IAS 8, *Accounting Policies, Changes in Estimates and Errors* (application of this is discussed in more detail in Chapter 7). Under both options an entity needs to disclose the reason it stops to apply IFRS and the reason it is resuming applying IFRS and when IAS 8 is applied, the reason for electing to apply IFRS as if it had never stopped applying IFRS.

An entity, in its first IFRS financial statements, has the choice between applying an existing and currently effective IFRS or applying early a new or revised IFRS that is not yet mandatorily effective, provided that the new or revised IFRS permits early application. An entity is required to apply the same version of the IFRS throughout the periods covered by those first IFRS financial statements. Early adoption is, however, possible and entities are permitted to early adopt any individual amendment within the cycle without early adopting all other amendments.

IFRS-compliant financial statements presented in the current year would qualify as first IFRS financial statements if the reporting entity presented its most recent previous financial statements:

- Under national GAAP or standards that were inconsistent with IFRS in all respects;
- In conformity with IFRS in all respects, but without an explicit and unreserved statement to that effect;

- With an explicit statement that the financial statements complied with certain IFRS, but not with all applicable standards;
- Under national GAAP or standards that differ from IFRS but using some individual IFRS to account for items which were not addressed by its national GAAP or other standards;
- Under national GAAP or standards, but with a reconciliation of selected items to amounts determined under IFRS.

Other examples of situations where an entity's current year's financial statements would qualify as its first IFRS financial statements are when:

- The entity prepared financial statements in the previous period under IFRS, but the financial statements had been identified as being "for internal use only" and had not been made available to the entity's owners or any other external users;
- The entity presented IFRS-compliant financial reporting in the previous period under IFRS for consolidation purposes without preparing a complete set of financial statements as mandated by IAS 1, *Presentation of Financial Statements*; and
- The entity did not present financial statements for the previous periods at all.

Example to illustrate the implications of the standard

Excellent Inc., incorporated in Mysteryland, is a progressive multinational corporation that has always presented its financial statements under the national GAAP of the country of incorporation, with additional disclosures made in its footnotes. The supplementary data included value-added statements and a reconciliation of major items on its statement of financial position to IFRS. Excellent Inc. has significant borrowings from international financial institutions, and these have certain restrictive financial covenants—such as a defined upper limit on the ratio of external debt to equity, and minimum annual return on investments. To monitor compliance with these covenants, Excellent Inc. also prepared a separate set of financial statements in accordance with IFRS, but these were never made available to the international financial institutions or to the shareholders of Excellent Inc.

In 20XX it was publicly announced that IFRS would be adopted as Mysteryland's national GAAP from 20XX.

Excellent Inc. had always presented its financial statements under its national GAAP but had also voluntarily provided a reconciliation of major items on its statement of financial position to IFRS in its footnotes, and "for internal purposes" had also prepared a separate set of financial statements under IFRS. Despite these previous overtures towards IFRS compliance, in the year 20XX—when Excellent Inc. moves to IFRS as its national GAAP and presents its financial statements to the outside world under IFRS, with an explicit and unreserved statement that these financial statements comply with IFRS—it will nonetheless be considered a first-time adopter and will have to comply with the requirements of IFRS 1.

In cases when the reporting entity's financial statements in the previous year contained an explicit and unreserved statement of compliance with IFRS, but in fact did not fully comply with all accounting policies under IFRS, such an entity would *not* be considered a first-time adopter for the purposes of IFRS 1. The disclosed or undisclosed departures from IFRS in previous years' financial statements of this entity would be treated as an "error" under IFRS 1, which warrants correction made in the manner prescribed by IAS 8, *Accounting Policies, Changes in Accounting Estimates and Errors*. In addition, an entity making changes in accounting policies as a result of specific transitional requirements in other IFRS is also not considered a first-time adopter.

IFRS 1 identifies three situations in which IFRS 1 would *not* apply. These exceptions include, for example, when an entity:

1. Stops presenting its financial statements under national requirements (i.e., its national GAAP) along with another set of financial statements that contained an explicit or unreserved statement of compliance with IFRS;
2. Presented its financial statements in the previous year under national requirements (its national GAAP) and those financial statements contained (improperly) an explicit and unreserved statement of IFRS compliance; or
3. Presented its financial statements in the previous year that contained an explicit and unreserved statement of compliance with IFRS, and its auditors qualified their report on those financial statements.

Key Dates

In transition to IFRS, two important dates that must be clearly determined are the first IFRS *reporting date* and *transition date*. "Reporting date" for an entity's first IFRS financial statements refers to the end of the latest period covered by the annual financial statements, or interim financial statements, if any, that the entity presents under IAS 34 for the period covered by its first IFRS financial statements. This is illustrated in the following examples.

Examples to illustrate the reporting date

Example 1: Xodus Inc. presents its first annual financial statements under IFRS for the calendar year 20XX, which include an explicit and unreserved statement of compliance with IFRS. It also presents full comparative financial information for the calendar year 20XX-1. In this case, the latest period covered by these annual financial statements would end on December 31, 20XX, and the *reporting date* for the purposes of IFRS 1 is December 31, 20XX (presuming the entity does not present financial statements under IAS 34 for interim periods within calendar year 20XX).

Example 2: Similarly, if Xodus Inc. decides to present its first IFRS interim financial statements in accordance with IAS 34 for the six months ended June 30, 20XX, in addition to the first IFRS annual financial statements for the year ended December 31, 20XX, the *reporting date* would be June 30, 20XX (and not December 31, 20XX).

"Transition date" refers to the beginning of the earliest period for which an entity presents full comparative information under IFRS as part of its first IFRS financial statements. Thus, the date of transition to IFRS depends on two factors: the date of adoption of IFRS and the number of years of comparative information that the entity decides to present along with the financial information of the year of adoption. In accordance with IFRS 1, at least one year of comparative information is required. The "first IFRS reporting period" is the latest reporting period covered by an entity's first IFRS financial statements.

The financial reporting requirements under IFRS 1 are presented below.

Example of IFRS 1 reporting requirements

Assume that Adaptability Inc. decides to implement IFRS in 20XX and to present comparative information for one year only. The end of Adaptability's first IFRS reporting period is December 31, 20XX. The last reporting period under previous GAAP is 20XX-2. The example below illustrates reporting requirements under IFRS 1 applicable to this entity.

Date of transition >Reporting date

I--------------------------------I---------------------------------------I--I

1/1/20XX-1 12/31/20XX-1 03/31/20XX 12/31/20XX

- Adaptability Inc. must prepare and present an opening IFRS statement of financial position at the date of transition to IFRS, that is the beginning of business on January 1, 20XX-1 (or, equivalently, close of business on December 31, 20XX-2). Its last reporting period under "previous GAAP" is 20XX-2 and end of comparative period is on December 31, 20XX-1.
- Adaptability Inc. will produce its first IFRS financial statements for the annual period ending December 31, 20XX. The first IFRS reporting period is 20XX.
- Adaptability Inc. will prepare and present its statement of financial position for December 31, 20XX (including comparative amounts for December 31, 20XX-1), statement of comprehensive income, statement of changes in equity and statement of cash flows for the year ending December 31, 20XX (including comparative amounts for 20XX-1) and disclosures (including comparative amounts for 20XX-1).

Adaptability Inc. has quarterly reporting requirements; the entity will comply with IAS 34 and present the first IFRS-compliant interim report—the March 31, 20XX quarterly report. Consequently, the first IFRS reporting date is March 31, 20XX.

If Adaptability Inc. would be required (or choose) to present two years of comparative information under IFRS, the transition date would be January 1, 20XX-2.

Steps in Transition to IFRS

Transition to IFRS involves the following steps:

- Selection of accounting policies that comply with IFRS standards effective at the reporting date.
- Preparation of an opening IFRS statement of financial position at the date of transition to IFRS as the starting point for subsequent accounting under IFRS. *Recognise* all assets and liabilities whose recognition is required under IFRS:
    - *Derecognise* items as assets or liabilities if IFRS does not permit such recognition;
    - *Reclassify* items in the financial statements in accordance with IFRS; and
    - *Measure* all recognised assets and liabilities according to principles set forth in IFRS.
- Presentation and disclosure in an entity's first IFRS financial statements and interim financial reports.

Selection of Accounting Policies

IFRS 1 stipulates that an entity should use the same accounting policies throughout all periods presented in its first IFRS financial statements, and also in its opening IFRS statement of financial position. Furthermore, the standard requires that those accounting policies must comply with each IFRS effective at the "reporting date" (as explained before) for its first IFRS financial statements, with certain exceptions. It requires full retrospective application of all IFRS effective at the reporting date for an entity's first IFRS financial statements, except under certain defined circumstances wherein the entity is prohibited by IFRS from applying IFRS retrospectively (mandatory exceptions) or it may elect to use one or more exemptions from some requirements of other IFRS (optional exemptions). Both concepts are discussed later in this chapter.

If a new IFRS has been issued on the reporting date, but application is not yet mandatory, although reporting entities have been encouraged to apply it before the effective date, the first-time adopter is permitted, but not required, to apply it as well. As stated before, an entity's first reporting date under IFRS refers to the end of the latest period covered by the first annual financial statements in accordance with IFRS, or interim financial statements, if any, that the entity presents under IAS 34. For example, if an entity's first IFRS reporting date is December 31, 20XX, consequently:

- First IFRS financial statements must comply with IFRS in effect at December 31, 20XX; and
- Opening statement of financial position at January 1, 20XX-1, and comparative information presented for 20XX-1, must comply with IFRS effective at December 31, 20XX (at the end of the first IFRS reporting period).

On first-time adoption of IFRS, the first most important step that an entity has to take is the selection of accounting policies that comply with IFRS. Management must select initial IFRS accounting policies based on relevance and reliability as these choices will affect the company's financial reporting for years to come. While many accounting policy choices will simply reflect relevant circumstances (e.g., method of depreciation, percentage of completion vs. completed contract accounting), other choices will result from IFRS flexibility.

The several areas where a choice of accounting policies under IFRS exists include:

- IFRS 1—Optional exemptions from the full retrospective application of IFRS for some types of transactions on first-time IFRS adoption (see optional exemptions from other IFRS);
- IFRS 3—In acquisitions of less than 100%, the option to measure non-controlling interest at fair value or proportionate share of the acquiree's identifiable net assets (this choice will result in recognising 100% of goodwill or only the parent's share of goodwill);
- IFRS 4—Remeasure insurance liabilities to fair value during each accounting period;
- IAS 1—
    a. Present one statement of comprehensive income or separate income statement and comprehensive income statement;
    b. Presentation of expenses in the income statement by nature or by function;
- IAS 2—
    a. Value inventories at FIFO or weighted-average;
    b. Measure certain inventories, for example agricultural produce, minerals and commodities, at net realisable value rather than cost;

- IAS 7—
    a. Direct or indirect method for presenting operating cash flows;
    b. Classify interest and dividends as operating, investing or financing;
- IAS 16—Measure property, plant and equipment using the cost-depreciation model or the revaluation through equity model;
- IAS 19—Many options available for recognising actuarial gains and losses (immediately in profit or loss, immediately in equity or different methods of spreading the cost);
- IAS 20—Various options of accounting for government grants;
- IAS 23—Borrowing costs;
- IAS 27, IAS 28, IAS 31—Cost or fair value model for investments in subsidiaries, associates and joint ventures in the *separate* financial statements;
- IAS 31—Equity method or proportionate consolidation for joint ventures;
- IAS 38—The cost-depreciation model or revaluation through equity model for intangible assets with quoted market prices;
- IFRS 9—
    a. Optional hedge accounting;
    b. Option to designate individual financial assets and financial liabilities to be measured at fair value through P&L;
    c. Option to designate non-trading instruments as fair value through other comprehensive income;
    d. Option to reclassify out of fair-value-through-profit or loss, and out of other comprehensive income categories;
    e. Option to adjust the carrying amount of a hedged item for gains and losses on the hedging instrument;
    f. Option of trade date or settlement date accounting; and
    g. Option to separate an embedded derivative or account for the entire contract at fair-value-through-profit or loss;
- IAS 40—
    a. The cost-depreciation model or fair value model for investment property; and
    b. Option to classify land use rights as investment property.

IFRS 1 requires a first-time adopter to use the current version of IFRS (or future standards, if early adoption permitted) without considering the superseded versions. This obviates the need to identify varying iterations of the standards that would have guided the preparation of the entity's financial statements at each prior reporting date, which would have been a very time-consuming and problematic task. This means that the comparative financial statements accompanying the first IFRS-compliant reporting may differ—perhaps materially—from what would have been presented in those earlier periods had the entity commenced reporting consistent with IFRS at an earlier point in time. Entities can early adopt new standards if early adoption is permitted by the standards but cannot apply standards that are not published at the first IFRS reporting period.

The IASB's original thinking was to grant the first-time adopter an option to elect application of IFRS *as if it had always applied IFRS* (i.e., from the entity's inception). However, to have actualised this, the first-time adopter would have had to consider the various iterations of IFRS that had historically existed over the period of time culminating with its actual adoption of IFRS. Upon reflection, this would have created not merely great practical difficulties for preparers but would have negatively impacted comparability among periods and across reporting entities. Thus, IFRS 1, as promulgated, offers no such option.

The amendment to IFRS 1 as part of the 2010 *Improvement to IFRS* clarified that, if a first-time adopter changes its accounting policies or its use of the exemptions in IFRS 1 after it has published an interim financial report in accordance with IAS 34, *Interim Financial Reporting*, but before its first IFRS financial statements are issued, it should explain those changes and update the reconciliations between previous GAAP and IFRS. The requirements in IAS 8 do not apply to such changes.

Opening IFRS Statement of Financial Position

A first-time adopter must prepare and present an opening IFRS statement of financial position at the date of transition to IFRS. This statement serves as the starting point for the entity's accounting under IFRS. Logically, preparation of an opening statement of financial position is a necessary step to accurately restate the first year's statements of comprehensive income, changes in equity and cash flows.

Example to illustrate the date of the opening statement of financial position

Adaptability Inc. decided to adopt IFRS in its annual financial statements for the fiscal year ending December 31, 20XX, and to present comparative information for the year 20XX-1. Thus, the beginning of the earliest period for which the entity should present full comparative information under IFRS would be January 1, 20XX-1. Accordingly, the opening IFRS statement of financial position for purposes of compliance with IFRS 1 would be that as of the beginning of business on January 1, 20XX-1 (equivalent to the closing of business on December 31, 20XX-2).

Alternatively, if Adaptability Inc. decided (or was required, e.g., by the stock listing authorities) to present two years of comparative information (i.e., for both 20XX-2 and 20XX-1), as well as for the current year 20XX, then the beginning of the earliest period for which the entity would present full comparative information would be January 1, 20XX-2 (equivalent to close of business on December 31, 20XX-3). Accordingly, the opening IFRS statement of financial position for purposes of compliance with IFRS 1 would be that as of January 1, 20XX-2, under these circumstances.

The opening statement of financial position, prepared at the transition date, must be based on standards applied at the end of the first reporting period. This implies that advance planning will be required for several items, including hedging, and that the opening statement of financial position cannot be finalised until the end of the first IFRS reporting period (reporting date).

Example to illustrate IFRS to be applied in the opening statement of financial position

ABC entity's first IFRS reporting period will end on December 31, 20XX, and its transition date is January 1, 20XX-1, since only one comparative period will be presented. In the first IFRS financial statements ABC will apply IFRS 7, as amended in 2010, in all periods presented in the first IFRS financial statements. The amendment in question clarifies the intended interaction between qualitative and quantitative disclosures of the nature and extent of risks arising from financial instruments and removed some disclosure items which were seen to be superfluous or misleading and was effective for all accounting periods beginning on or after January 1, 20XX-1.

In preparing the opening IFRS statement of financial position in transition from previous GAAP to IFRS, several adjustments to the financial statements are required. A first-time IFRS adopter should apply the following (except in cases where IFRS 1 prohibits retrospective application or grants certain exemptions):

1. *Recognise* all assets and liabilities whose recognition is required under IFRS. It is expected that many companies will recognise additional assets and liabilities under IFRS reporting, when compared with the national GAAP formerly employed. Areas which may result in this effect include:

   - Defined benefit pension plans (IAS 19);
   - Deferred taxation (IAS 12);
   - Assets and liabilities under certain finance leases (IAS 17);
   - Provisions where there is a legal or constructive obligation (IAS 37);
   - Derivative financial instruments (IFRS 9);
   - Internal development costs (IAS 38); and
   - Share-based payments (IFRS 2).

2. *Derecognise* items as assets or liabilities if IFRS does not permit such recognition. Some assets and liabilities recognised under an entity's previous (national) GAAP will have to be derecognised. For example:

   - Provisions where there is no legal or constructive obligation (e.g., general reserves, post-acquisition restructuring) (IAS 37);
   - Internally generated intangible assets (IAS 38); and
   - Deferred tax assets where recovery is not probable (IAS 12).

3. *Reclassify* items that are recognised under previous GAAP as one type of asset, liability or component of equity, but are a different type of asset, liability or component of equity under IFRS. Assets and liabilities that might be reclassified to conform to IFRS include:

   - Certain financial instruments previously classified as equity;
   - Any assets and liabilities that have been offset where the criteria for offsetting in IFRS are not met—for example, the offset of an insurance recovery against a provision;
   - Non-current assets held for sale (IFRS 5); and
   - Non-controlling interest (IFRS 10).

4. *Measure* all recognised assets and liabilities according to principles set forth in IFRS. This remeasurement may be required when the accounting basis is the same but measured differently (e.g., cost basis under IFRS may not be the same as under US GAAP), when the basis is changed (e.g., from cost to fair value) or there are differences in the applicability of discounting (e.g., provisions or impairments). Assets and liabilities that might have to be measured differently include:

   - Receivables (IAS 18);
   - Inventory (IAS 2);
   - Employee benefit obligations (IAS 19);

- Deferred taxation (IAS 12);
- Financial instruments (IFRS 9);
- Provisions (IAS 37);
- Impairments of property, plant and equipment, and intangible assets (IAS 36);
- Assets held for disposal (IFRS 5); and
- Share-based payments (IFRS 2).

Example to illustrate adjustments required to IFRS opening statement of financial position on transition

ABC Inc. presented its most recent financial statements under national GAAP through 20XX-1. It adopted IFRS from 20XX and is required to prepare an opening IFRS statement of financial position as at January 1, 20XX-1. In preparing the IFRS opening statement of financial position, ABC Inc. noted the following.

Under its previous GAAP, ABC Inc. sold certain financial receivables as well as trade receivables for the amount of €250,000 to special-purpose entities (SPEs) that are not consolidated although they conduct activities on behalf of the ABC Inc. Group (the Group). In addition, ABC Inc. was using the LIFO method to account for certain inventories, and, consequently, reported the carrying value of inventory reduced by €150,000, as compared to the value under the FIFO method. Furthermore, it had not discounted, to present value, long-term provisions for warranty of €100,000 although the effect of discounting would be material (€10,000). Finally, all research and development costs of €500,000 (of which total €300,000 relates to research costs) for the invention of new products were expensed when incurred.

To prepare the opening IFRS statement of financial position at January 1, 20XX-1, ABC Inc. would need to make the following adjustments to its statement of financial position at December 31, 20XX-2, presented under its previous GAAP:

1. IFRS 10 requires ABC Inc. to consolidate an SPE where it is deemed to control it. Indicators of control include the SPE conducting activities on behalf of the Group and/or the Group holding the majority of the risks and rewards of the SPE. Thus, SPEs should be consolidated and €250,000 of receivables is recognised under IFRS;
2. IAS 2 prohibits the use of LIFO. Consequently, the Group adopted the FIFO method and had to increase inventory by €150,000 under IFRS;
3. IAS 37 states that long-term provisions must be discounted to their present value if the effect from discounting is material. As a result, the Group adjusted the amount of provisions for warranty by €10,000, the effect from discounting;
4. IAS 38 allows that development costs are capitalised as intangible assets if the technical and economic feasibility of a project can be demonstrated. Thus, €200,000 incurred on development costs should be capitalised as an intangible asset under IFRS.

Mandatory Exceptions to the Retrospective Application of Other IFRS

IFRS 1 *prohibits* retrospective application of some aspects of other IFRS when a judgement would have been required about the past and the outcome is known on first-time adoption. For example, practical implementation difficulties could arise from the retrospective application of aspects of IFRS 9 or could lead to selective designation of some hedges to report a particular result. Mandatory exceptions relate to estimates, derecognition of non-derivative financial assets and non-derivative financial liabilities, hedge accounting and non-controlling interests.

Estimates

An entity's estimates under IFRS at the date of transition to IFRS should be consistent with estimates made for the same date under its previous GAAP (after adjustments to reflect any difference in accounting policies), unless there is objective evidence that those estimates were in error, as that term is defined under IFRS. In particular, such estimates as those of market prices, interest rates or foreign exchange rates should reflect market conditions at the date of transition to IFRS. Revisions based on information developed after the transition date should only be recognised as income or expense (reflected in results of operations) in the period when the entity made the revision and may not be "pushed back" to the opening IFRS statement of financial position prepared at the transition date at which, historically, the new information had not been known. Any information an entity receives after the date of transition to IFRS about estimates it made under previous GAAP should be treated as a *non-adjusting* event after the date of the statement of financial position, and accorded the treatment prescribed by IAS 10, *Events after the Reporting Period*.

Example to illustrate mandatory exception applicable to estimates

ABC Inc. recognised a provision for legal claims of €8,000,000 in accordance with previous GAAP at the date of transition to IFRS on January 1, 20XX-1. The settlement amount is €9,000,000, which is known on June 11, 20XX, and requires the revision of this estimate. The entity should not reflect that new information in its opening IFRS statement of financial position (unless the estimate needs adjustment for any differences in accounting policies or there is objective evidence that the estimate was in error, in accordance with IAS 8). Instead, ABC Inc. will reflect that new information as an expense of €1,000,000 in profit or loss for the year ended December 31, 20XX.

Derecognition of financial assets and financial liabilities (IFRS 9)

If a first-time adopter derecognised non-derivative financial assets or non-derivative financial liabilities under its previous GAAP, it should not recognise those assets and liabilities under IFRS, unless they qualify for recognition as a result of a later transaction or event. However, an entity may apply the derecognition requirements retrospectively, from a date of the entity's choice, if the information needed to apply IFRS 9 to derecognised items as a result of past transactions was obtained at the time of initially accounting for those transactions.

A first-time adopter should recognise all derivatives and other interests retained after derecognition and still existing and consolidate all SPEs that it controls at the date of transition to IFRS (even if the SPE existed before the date of transition to IFRS or holds financial assets or financial liabilities that were derecognised under previous GAAP).

Hedge accounting (IFRS 9)

A first-time adopter is required, at the date of transition to IFRS, to measure all derivatives at fair value and eliminate all deferred losses and gains on derivatives that were reported under its previous GAAP. However, a first-time adopter is not permitted to reflect a hedging relationship in its opening IFRS statement of financial position if it does not qualify for hedge accounting under IFRS 9. But if an entity designated a net position as a hedged item under its previous GAAP, it may designate an individual item within that net position as a hedged item under IFRS, provided it does so prior to the date of transition to IFRS. Transitional provisions of IFRS 9 apply to hedging relationships of a first-time adopter at the date of transition to IFRS.

Non-controlling interests (IFRS 10)

A first-time adopter should apply the following requirements prospectively from the date of transition to IFRS:

- Attribution of total comprehensive income to the owners of the parent and to the non-controlling interests even if this results in the non-controlling interests having a deficit balance;
- Accounting for changes in the parent's ownership interest in a subsidiary that do not result in a loss of control; and
- Accounting for a loss of control over a subsidiary, and the related requirements.

OPTIONAL EXEMPTIONS

IFRS 1 allows a first-time adopter to elect to use one or more optional (voluntary) exemptions from the retrospective application of other IFRS. Optional exemptions from the retrospective application of other IFRS are granted on first-time adoption in specific areas where the cost of complying with the requirements of IFRS 1 would be likely to exceed the benefits to users of financial statements or where the retrospective application is impractical. A parent company and all of its subsidiaries must analyse these exemptions to determine which exemptions to apply and how to apply them, but it should be emphasised that the exemptions do not impact future accounting policy choices and cannot be applied by analogy to other items.

The application of these optional exemptions is explained in detail below. A first-time adopter of IFRS may elect to use exemptions from the general measurement and restatement principles in one or more of the following instances.

Business Combinations

IFRS 1 exempts the first-time adopter from mandatory retrospective application in the case of business combinations that occurred before the date of transition to IFRS. That is, requirements under IFRS 3 can be applied in accounting for combinations that occurred before the transition date under IFRS, but this *need not be done*. Thus, under IFRS 1, an entity may elect to use previous national GAAP accounting relating to such business combinations. The IASB provided this exemption because, if retrospective application of IFRS 3 had been made obligatory, it could have forced entities to estimate (or make educated guesses) about conditions that presumably prevailed at the respective dates of past business combinations. This would have been particularly challenging where data from past business combinations had not been preserved. The use of such estimates could have adversely affected the relevance and reliability of the financial statements, and was thus seen as a situation to be avoided.

In evaluating responses to the draft of its standard on first-time adoption of IFRS, the IASB concluded that notwithstanding the fact that restatement of past business combinations to conform with IFRS was conceptually preferable, a pragmatic assessment of cost versus benefit weighed in favour of *permitting* but *not requiring* such restatement. However, the IASB did place an important limitation on this election: if a first-time adopter having multiple acquisition transactions restates *any* business combination, it must restate *all* business combinations that took place subsequent to the date of that restated combination transaction. First-time adopters thus cannot "cherry pick" among past business combinations to apply IFRS opportunistically to certain of them.

Example to illustrate business combination exemption

	Business combination 1 selected for IFRS conversion	Business combination 2	Transition date	
I	I	I	I	I
1/1/20XX-1	6/6/20XX-1	3/31/20XX	12/31/20XX	12/31/20XX

For instance, if ABC Inc., a first-time adopter, did not seek this exemption, and instead opted to apply IFRS 3 retrospectively, and restated a major business combination that took place on June 6, 20XX-1, then, under this requirement of IFRS 1, ABC Inc. is required to restate business combinations that took place subsequent to the date of that major business combination to which it applied IFRS 3 retrospectively. Earlier combinations would *not* have to be restated.

If the entity employs the exemption under IFRS 1 and does not apply IFRS 3 retrospectively to a past business combination, it must observe these rules:

1. The first-time adopter should preserve the same classification (an *acquisition* or a *uniting of interests*) as was applied in its previous GAAP financial statements.
2. The first-time adopter should recognise all assets and liabilities at the date of transition to IFRS that were acquired or assumed in a past business combination, except:
    a. Certain financial assets and financial liabilities that were derecognised under its previous GAAP; and
    b. Assets (including goodwill) and liabilities that were not recognised in the acquirer's consolidated statement of financial position under previous GAAP and also would not qualify for recognition under IFRS in the separate statement of financial position of the acquiree.

    Any resulting change should be recognised by the first-time adopter in retained earnings (or another component of equity, if appropriate) unless the change results from the recognition of an intangible asset that was previously incorporated within goodwill.
3. The first-time adopter should derecognise (i.e., exclude) from its opening IFRS statement of financial position any item recognised under previous GAAP that does not qualify for recognition, either as an asset or liability, under IFRS. The resulting change from this derecognition should be accounted by the first-time adopter as follows: first, if the first-time adopter had classified a past business combination as an acquisition and recognised as an intangible asset an item that does not qualify for recognition as an asset under IAS 38, it should reclassify that item (and any related deferred tax and non-controlling interests) as part of goodwill (unless it deducted goodwill from equity, instead of presenting it as an asset, under its previous GAAP); and secondly, the first-time adopter should recognise all other resulting changes in retained earnings.
4. In cases where IFRS require subsequent measurement of some assets and liabilities on a basis other than original cost, such as fair value, the first-time adopter should measure these

assets and liabilities on that basis in its opening IFRS statement of financial position, even if these assets and liabilities were acquired or assumed in a preceding business combination. Any resulting change in the carrying amount should be recognised by the first-time adopter in retained earnings (or another component of equity, if appropriate), instead of as an adjustment to goodwill.

5. Subsequent to the business combination, the carrying amount under previous GAAP of assets acquired and liabilities assumed in the business combination should be treated as their *deemed cost* under IFRS at that date. If IFRS require a cost-based measurement of those assets and liabilities at a later date, deemed cost should be used instead (e.g., as the basis for cost-based depreciation or amortisation from the date of the business combination).
6. If assets acquired or liabilities assumed were not recognised in a past business combination under the previous GAAP, the first-time adopter should recognise and measure them in its consolidated statement of financial position on the basis that IFRS would require in the separate statement of financial position of the acquiree.
7. The carrying amount of goodwill in the opening IFRS statement of financial position should be its carrying amount under previous GAAP at the date of transition to IFRS, after the following adjustments:

   a. The carrying amount of goodwill should be increased due to a reclassification that would be needed for an intangible asset recognised under previous GAAP but which does not qualify as an intangible asset under IAS 38. Similarly, the carrying amount of goodwill should be decreased due to inclusion of an intangible asset as part of goodwill under previous GAAP but which requires separate recognition under IFRS.
   b. If the purchase consideration of a past business combination was based on a contingency which was resolved prior to the date of transition to IFRS, and a reliable estimate of the adjustment relating to the contingency can be made and it is probable that a payment will be made, the first-time adopter should adjust the carrying amount of goodwill by that amount. Similarly, if a previously recognised contingency can no longer be measured reliably, or its payment is no longer probable, the first-time adopter should adjust the carrying amount of goodwill accordingly.
   c. Whether or not there is evidence of impairment of goodwill, the first-time adopter should apply IAS 36 in testing goodwill for impairment, if any, and should recognise the resulting impairment loss in retained earnings (or, if so, required by IAS 36, in revaluation surplus).

      The impairment test should be based on conditions at the date of transition to IFRS.

8. No other adjustments are permitted by IFRS 1 to the carrying amount of goodwill at the date of transition to IFRS. The following adjustments would be prohibited:

   a. Reducing goodwill to separately reflect in-process research and development acquired in that business combination;
   b. Adjusting previous amortisation of goodwill; or
   c. Reversing adjustments to goodwill that IFRS 3 would not permit but which were appropriately made under previous GAAP.

9. If under its previous GAAP a first-time adopter did not consolidate a subsidiary acquired in a business combination (i.e., because the parent did not treat it as a subsidiary under previous GAAP), the first-time adopter should adjust the carrying amounts of the subsidiary's assets and liabilities to the amounts that IFRS would require in the subsidiary's separate statement of financial position. The deemed cost of goodwill would be equal to the

difference at the date of transition to IFRS between the parent's interest in those adjusted carrying amounts and the cost in the parent's separate financial statements of its investment in the subsidiary.

10. The non-controlling interest should be adjusted to reflect its share of the adjustments to recognised assets and liabilities.

IFRS 1 states that these exemptions for past business combinations also apply to past acquisitions of investments in associates and in joint ventures. Furthermore, the date chosen for electing to apply IFRS 3 retrospectively to past business combinations applies equally to associates and joint ventures.

Example to illustrate the effects of first-time adoption of IFRS

ABC Inc., a first-time adopter, has a transition date of January 1, 20XX. ABC acquired entity DEF on June 1, 20XX-1. Under previous GAAP, in accounting for this acquisition, ABC (1) did not separately recognise development costs of €100 at 1/1/20XX; (2) recognised a general restructuring provision of €200, which was 75% outstanding at 1/1/20XX; (3) did not recognise a deferred tax asset of €50 resulting from temporary differences associated with assets acquired and liabilities assumed. In transition to IFRS, ABC elects not to restate previous business combinations.

At the date of transition, ABC has to make the following adjustments: (1) recognise development costs of €100, with the adjustment taken to goodwill; (2) derecognise the general restructuring provision of €200, with the adjustment recognised in retained earnings; (3) recognise a deferred tax asset of €50, with the adjustment recognised in retained earnings.

In addition, the concept of "push-down accounting," required under SEC guidance in special circumstances, does not exist in IFRS. It means that previous revaluations to fair value at acquisition made by subsidiaries to apply push-down accounting need to be reversed on transition to IFRS, but those revaluations can be used as deemed cost of property, plant and equipment, certain intangible assets and investment property.

Deemed Cost

An entity may elect to measure an item of property, plant and equipment at fair value at the date of its transition to IFRS and use the fair value as its deemed cost at that date. In accordance with IFRS 1, "deemed cost" is an amount substituted for "cost" or "depreciated cost" at a given date, and this value is subsequently used as the basis for depreciation or amortisation. A first-time adopter may elect to use a previous GAAP revaluation of an item of property, plant and equipment at, or before, the date of transition to IFRS as deemed costs at the date of revaluation if the revaluation amount, when determined, was broadly comparable to either fair value or cost (or depreciated cost under IFRS adjusted for changes in general or specific price index).

These elections are equally available for investment property measured under the cost model and intangible assets that meet the recognition criteria and the criteria for revaluation (including the existence of an active market).

Example to illustrate the effect of the deemed cost exemption

ABC Inc., a first-time adopter, has a transition date of January 1, 20XX. ABC revalued buildings under previous GAAP and on the last revaluation date at 12/31/11, the buildings were valued at €500. Depreciation of €60 has been charged since the revaluation and the expected remaining useful life is 20 years. At 1/1/20XX ABC had a cumulative balance in the revaluation reserve of €100. At the date of transition to IFRS, ABC elects the deemed cost exemption. ABC makes the following adjustments to its opening IFRS statement of financial position: (1) buildings are recognised at the deemed cost of €500; (2) the revaluation reserve of €100 is taken to retained earnings; (3) accumulated depreciation of €6 must be recognised for the period 12/31/11 to 1/1/20XX [(500 − 60)/20 = 22 annually; (22 × 3 = 66) − 60 = 6].

If a first-time adopter has established a deemed cost under previous GAAP for any of its assets or liabilities by measuring them at their fair values at a particular date because of the occurrence of an event such as privatisation or an initial public offering, it is allowed to use such an event-driven fair value as deemed cost for IFRS at the date of that measurement. The May 2010 *Improvements to IFRS* amended IFRS 1 to clarify that a first-time adopter is also permitted to use an event-driven fair value as "deemed cost" at the measurement date for measurement events that occurred after the date of transition to IFRS but during the period covered by the first IFRS financial statements. Any resulting adjustment is recognised directly in equity at the measurement date.

First-time adopters must assess and evaluate available accounting options under IAS 16 and determine which options would be more advantageous going forward, when adopting IFRS. For example, the first IFRS financial statements must present property, plant and equipment as if the requirements of IAS 16 had always been applied. While the "component approach" to depreciation is allowed but rarely used under US GAAP, this approach is required under IFRS and may result in significant adjustments in conversion for US adopters discussed in detail in Chapter 9, Property, Plant and Equipment.

It is common in some countries to account for exploration and development costs for properties in development or production in cost centres that include all properties in a large geographical area (often referred to as "full cost accounting"). Since this approach is not allowed under IFRS, the process of remeasuring the assets on the first-time adoption of IFRS would likely be tedious and expensive. The amendments to IFRS 1, in effect for annual periods beginning on or after January 1, 2011, would allow an entity that used full cost accounting under its previous GAAP to measure exploration and evaluation assets, as well as oil and gas assets in the development or production phases, at the date of transition to IFRS, at the amount determined under the entity's previous GAAP.

The amendments allow an entity that used such accounting under previous GAAP to elect to measure oil and gas assets at the date of transition on the following basis:

1. Exploration and evaluation assets at the amount determined under previous GAAP; and
2. Assets in the development or production phases at the amount determined for the cost centre under previous GAAP. This amount is allocated pro rata to the underlying assets, using reserve volumes or reserve values as of that date.

To avoid the use of deemed costs resulting in an oil and gas asset being measured at more than its recoverable amount, the first-time adopter should test exploration and evaluation assets and assets in the development and production phases for impairment at the date of transition to IFRS in accordance with IFRS 6, *Exploration for and Evaluation of Mineral Resources*, or IAS 36, *Impairments of Assets*, and, if necessary, reduce the amount determined in accordance with (1) and (2). This paragraph considers only those oil and gas assets that are used in the exploration, evaluation, development or production of oil and gas.

In addition, in the May 2010 *Improvements to IFRS*, the IASB amended IFRS 1 to allow entities with rate-regulated activities that hold, or previously held, items of property, plant and equipment or intangible assets for use in such operations (and recognised separately as regulatory assets) that may not be eligible for capitalisation under IFRS to recognise such items and to elect to use the previous GAAP carrying amount of such items as their deemed cost at the date of transition to IFRS. This exemption is available on an item-by-item basis, but entities are required to immediately (at the date of transition to IFRS) test for impairment in accordance with IAS 36 each item for which this exemption is used. (See discussion of rate-regulated activities in Chapter 32, Extractive Industries.)

Leases

In accordance with IFRIC 4, *Determining Whether an Arrangement Contains a Lease*, a first-time adopter may determine whether an arrangement existing at the date of transition to IFRS contains a lease on the basis of facts and circumstances existing at that date.

IFRS 1 exempts entities with existing leasing contracts that made, under previous GAAP, the same determination as that required by IFRIC 4, but that assessment was at a date other than that required by IFRIC 4, from reassessing the classification of those contracts when adopting IFRS.

Below Market Rate Government Loans

In the amendment to IFRS 1 issued in March 2012, it was clarified that first-time adopters will not be required to recognise the corresponding benefit of a government loan at a below-market rate of interest as a government grant. An entity may still elect to retrospectively apply the requirements in IAS 20 if the information needed to do so was obtained at the time of initially accounting for that loan. The amendment will give first-time adopters the same relief as existing preparers of IFRS financial statements.

Cumulative Translation Differences

A first-time IFRS adopter has the option to reset to zero all cumulative translation differences arising on monetary items that are part of a company's net investment in foreign operations existing at the transition date. IAS 21 requires an entity to classify certain translation differences as a separate component of equity, and upon disposal of the foreign operation, to transfer the cumulative translation difference relating to the foreign operation to the statement of comprehensive income as part of the gain or loss on disposal.

Under IFRS 1, a first-time adopter is exempted from recognising cumulative translation differences on foreign operations prior to the date of transition to IFRS. If it elects this exemption, the cumulative translation adjustment for all foreign operations would be deemed to be zero and the gain or loss on subsequent disposal of any foreign operation should exclude translation differences that arose before the date of transition to IFRS, but would include all subsequent translation adjustments recognised in accordance with IAS 21.

A company on transition to IFRS may also need to change the functional currency of one or more subsidiaries under IAS 21, due to differences in existing guidance in this respect. This could possibly create the need to revalue property, plant and equipment on first-time adoption rather than restating non-monetary assets measured at historical cost, which could be onerous.

Investments in Subsidiaries, Jointly Controlled Entities and Associates

In accordance with IAS 27 a company may value its investments in subsidiaries, jointly controlled entities and associates either at cost or in accordance with IFRS 9. Under IFRS 1, a first-time adopter electing deemed cost to account for these investments may choose either fair value, determined in accordance with IFRS 9, at the entity's date of transition to IFRS, or carrying amount under previous GAAP at that date.

Assets and Liabilities of Subsidiaries, Associates and Joint Ventures

IFRS 1 provides exemptions under two circumstances as follows:

1. If a subsidiary becomes a first-time adopter later than its parent, the subsidiary must, in its separate (stand-alone) financial statements, measure its assets and liabilities at either:
    a. The carrying amounts that would be included in its parent's consolidated financial statements, based on its parent's date of transition to IFRS (if no adjustments were made for consolidation procedures and for the effect of the business combination in which the parent acquired the subsidiary); or
    b. The carrying amounts required by the other provisions of IFRS 1, based on the subsidiary's date of transition to IFRS.

    A similar choice can be made by associates or joint ventures that adopt IFRS later than the entity.
2. If a reporting entity (parent) becomes a first-time adopter after its subsidiary (or associate or joint venture) the entity is required, in its consolidated financial statements, to measure the assets and liabilities of the subsidiary (or associate or joint venture) at the same carrying amounts as in the separate (stand-alone) financial statements of the subsidiary (or associate or joint venture), after adjusting for consolidation and equity accounting adjustments and for effects of the business combination in which an entity acquired the subsidiary. In a similar manner, if a parent becomes a first-time adopter for its separate financial statements earlier or later than for its consolidated financial statements, it shall measure its assets and liabilities at the same amounts in both financial statements, except for consolidation adjustments.

In cases where a subsidiary decided to elect different exemptions from those the parent selects for the preparation of consolidated financial statements, this may create permanent differences between the subsidiaries' and parents' books, requiring adjustments in consolidation. This exemption does not impact the requirement in IAS 1 that uniform accounting policies must be applied in the consolidated entities for all entities within a group.

Compound Financial Instruments

If an entity has issued a compound financial instrument, such as a convertible debenture, with characteristics of both debt and equity, IFRS requires that at inception, it should split and separate the liability component of the compound financial instrument from equity. If the liability portion is no longer outstanding at the date of adoption of IFRS, a retrospective and literal application of the standard would require separating two portions of equity. The first portion, which is in retained earnings, represents the cumulative interest accreted on the liability component. The other portion represents the original equity component of the instrument and would be in paid-in capital.

IFRS 1 exempts a first-time adopter from this split accounting if the former liability component is no longer outstanding at the date of transition to IFRS. This exemption can be significant to companies that routinely issue compound financial instruments.

Designation of Previously Recognised Financial Instruments

IFRS 1 permits a first-time adopter to designate a financial asset at fair value through other comprehensive income and a financial instrument (provided it meets certain criteria) as a financial asset or financial liability at fair value through profit or loss, at the *date of transition* to IFRS. IFRS 9 requires such designation to be made on *initial* recognition.

Fair Value Measurement of Financial Assets or Financial Liabilities at Initial Recognition

A first-time adopter may apply requirements of IFRS 9 regarding (1) the best evidence of the fair value of a financial instrument at initial recognition, and (2) the subsequent measurement of the financial asset or financial liability and the subsequent recognition of gains and losses, prospectively to transactions entered into on or after the date of transition to IFRS.

Decommissioning Liabilities included in the Cost of Property, Plant and Equipment

IFRS 1 provides that a first-time adopter need not comply with the requirements of IFRIC 1, *Changes in Existing Decommissioning, Restoration and Similar Liabilities*, for changes in such liabilities that occurred before the date of transition to IFRS. Adjustments to liabilities on first-time IFRS adoption arise from events and transactions before the date of transition to IFRS and are generally recognised in retained earnings. For entities using this exemption, certain measurements and disclosures are required. If a first-time adopter uses these exemptions, it should:

1. Measure the liability at the date of transition in accordance with IAS 37;
2. Estimate the amount of the liability (which is within the scope of IFRIC 1) that would have been included in the cost of the related asset when the liability was first incurred, by discounting the liability to that date using its best estimate of the historical risk-adjusted discount rate(s) that would have applied for that liability over the intervening period; and
3. Calculate the accumulated depreciation on that amount, as of the date of transition to IFRS, on the basis of the current estimate of the useful life of the asset, using the depreciation policy in accordance with IFRS.

In addition, an entity that uses the exemption in IFRS 1 to value at deemed cost determined under previous GAAP oil and gas assets in the development or production phases in cost centres that include all properties in a large geographical area should, instead of following the above rules (1.–3.) or IFRIC 1:

1. Measure decommissioning, restoration and similar liabilities as of the date of transition to IFRS under IAS 37; and
2. Recognise directly in retained earnings any difference between that amount and the carrying amount of those liabilities at the date of transition determined under previous GAAP.

Service Concession Arrangements

A first-time adopter may apply the transitional provisions of IFRIC 12.

Borrowing Costs

IFRS 1 permits a first-time adopter to apply the transitional provisions included in IAS 23 (as revised in 2007). The effective date in IAS 23 should be interpreted as the later of July 1, 2009, or the date of transition to IFRS. With the amendment to IFRS 1, per the Annual Improvements 2009–2011 Cycle published in May 2012, the first-time adopter may designate any date before the effective date and capitalise borrowing costs relating to all qualifying assets in accordance with IAS 23 for which the commencement date for capitalisation is on or after that date. Additionally, once the first-time adopter applies this provision, they may not restate any previously capitalised borrowing costs as capitalised under the previous GAAP. This amendment is effective for annual periods beginning on January 1, 2013, and early adoption is allowed.

Based on the experience of EU and Australian companies, exceptions most likely to be elected by first-time adopters pertain to the following: business combinations, deemed cost, employee benefits, share-based payment and cumulative translation differences.

These exemptions from the full retrospective application of IFRS should benefit first-time adopters, by reducing the cost of implementing IFRS. Entities should evaluate potential impacts of electing to use the proposed exemptions, including implications for information systems, taxes and reported results of operations.

Severe Hyperinflation

IFRS 1 permits a first-time adopter, if it has a functional currency that was, or is, the currency of a hyperinflationary economy, to determine whether it was subject to severe hyperinflation before the date of transition to IFRS.

The currency of a hyperinflationary economy is subject to severe hyperinflation if it has both of the following characteristics:

1. A reliable general price index is not available to all entities with transactions and balances in the currency;
2. Exchangeability between the currency and a relatively stable foreign currency does not exist.

The functional currency of an entity ceases to be subject to severe hyperinflation on the functional currency's normalisation date. That is the date when the functional currency no longer has either, or both, of the characteristics in the above paragraph, or when there is a change in the entity's functional currency to a currency that is not subject to severe hyperinflation. When an entity's date of transition to IFRS is on, or after, the functional currency normalisation date, the entity may elect to measure all assets and liabilities held before the functional currency normalisation date at fair value on the date of transition to IFRS. The entity may use that fair value as the deemed cost of those assets and liabilities in the opening IFRS statement of financial position.

When the functional currency normalisation date falls within a 12-month comparative period, the comparative period may be less than 12 months, provided that a complete set of financial statements as required by IAS 1 is provided for that shorter period.

PRESENTATION AND DISCLOSURE

IFRS 1 does not provide exemptions from the presentation and disclosure requirements in other IFRS.

Explanation of Transition to IFRS

A first-time adopter that applied IFRS in a previous period and whose most recent previous annual financial statements did not contain an explicit and unreserved statement of compliance with IFRS standards, and in the current period makes an *explicit and unreserved statement* of compliance with IFRS, has the choice of either (1) applying IFRS 1 (in full), or (2) retrospectively applying IFRS in accordance with the provision of IAS 8, *Accounting Policies, Changes in Estimates and Errors*. Should option 1 be applied, the first-time adopter must disclose its reason for not fully complying with IFRS in prior periods and the reason why it now does fully comply with IFRS. Should option 2 be applied, the first-time adopter must disclose its reasons for electing to apply IAS 8 full retrospective treatment to fully comply with IFRS (as if it had never stopped applying IFRS in the first place).

Comparative Information

A first-time adopter must prepare and present an opening statement of financial position as of its transition date, in accordance with IFRS in effect as of the company's first reporting date. At least one year of comparative financial statement information has to be presented. To comply with IAS 1, *Presentation of Financial Statements*, an entity's first IFRS financial statements should include at least three statements of financial position, two statements of comprehensive income, two separate income statements (if presented), two statements of cash flows and two statements of changes in equity and related notes, including comparative information.

If an entity also presents historical summaries of selected data for periods prior to the first period that it presents full comparative information under IFRS, and IFRS does not require the summary data to be in compliance with IFRS, such data should be labelled prominently as not being in compliance with IFRS and also disclose the nature of the adjustment that would make that data IFRS compliant.

Reconciliations

A first-time adopter must explain how the transition to IFRS affected its reported financial position, financial performance and cash flows. To comply with the above requirement, reconciliation of equity and profit and loss as reported under previous GAAP to IFRS should be included in the entity's first IFRS financial statements. Specifically, an entity should include a reconciliation of its equity reported under previous GAAP to its equity under IFRS, for both of the following dates: (1) the date of transition to IFRS, and (2) the end of the latest period presented in the entity's most recent annual financial statements under previous GAAP. Consequently, IFRS 1 requires the following reconciliations to be presented in first IFRS financial statements:

- Reconciliations of the entity's equity reported under previous GAAP to its equity restated under IFRS for both of the following dates:
    - The date of transition to IFRS; and

    - The end of the latest period presented in the entity's most recent annual financial statements under previous GAAP.
- A reconciliation of the entity's total comprehensive income reported in most recent financial statements under previous GAAP to its comprehensive income under IFRS for the same period. The starting point for that reconciliation should be the amount of comprehensive income reported under previous GAAP for the same period. If an entity did not report such a total, the reconciliation starts with profit or loss under previous GAAP.
- In addition to the reconciliations of its equity and comprehensive income, if the entity recognised or reversed any impairment losses for the first time in preparing its opening IFRS statement of financial position, the entity is required to make the disclosures that would have been required in accordance with IAS 36, if the entity had recognised or reversed those impairment losses in the period beginning with the date of transition to IFRS.

Consequently, for an entity adopting IFRS for the first time in its December 31, 20XX financial statements, the reconciliation of equity would be required as of January 1, 20XX-1, and December 31, 20XX-1; and the reconciliation of comprehensive income for the year 20XX-1. These reconciliations must provide sufficient detail enabling users to understand material adjustments to the statement of financial position and comprehensive income. Material adjustments to the statement of cash flows should also be disclosed. For all reconciliations, entities must distinguish the changes in accounting policies from corrections of errors.

Other Disclosures

IFRS 1 requires first-time adopters to present other disclosures, including:

- Entities that designated a previously recognised financial asset or financial liability as a financial asset or financial liability at fair value through profit or loss, or a financial asset at fair value through other comprehensive income should disclose the fair value designated into each category when this designation was made and the carrying amount in the previous financial statements.
- Entities that recognised or reversed any impairment losses for the first time in preparing their opening IFRS statement of financial position need to present the disclosures required by IAS 36 as if those impairment losses or reversals had been recognised in the first period beginning with the date of transition to IFRS.
- Entities that used fair values in their opening IFRS statement of financial position as deemed cost for an item of property, plant and equipment, an investment property or an intangible asset, should disclose for each line item in the opening IFRS statement of financial position the aggregate of those fair values and the aggregate adjustments made to the carrying amounts reported under previous GAAP.
- Also, entities that apply the exemption to measure oil and gas assets in the development or production phases at the amount determined for the cost centre under previous GAAP (and this amount is allocated pro rata to the underlying assets, using reserve volumes or reserve values as of that date) should disclose that fact and the basis on which carrying amounts determined under previous GAAP were allocated.

Interim Reporting

An entity adopting IFRS in an interim report (e.g., in quarterly or half-yearly financial statements) that is presented in accordance with IAS 34 is required to comply with IFRS 1, adopt IFRS effective at the end of the interim period and prepare comparative financial information for interim periods.

Example to illustrate the effect on interim reporting

Xodus Inc. decides to present its first IFRS interim financial statements for the three months ended March 31, 20XX, in accordance with IAS 34, within its first IFRS reporting period ending on December 31, 20XX. Consequently, the first reporting date is March 31, 20XX, and the company will be required to provide comparative IFRS financial information for the quarterly periods. If the company decided to present comparative information for one year only, then the March 31, 20XX-1, comparatives would have to be presented.

In accordance with IFRS 1, entities must be able to generate profit or loss statements also for interim periods and prepare certain reconciliations between amounts reported under previous GAAP and IFRS. In addition to satisfying the requirements of IAS 34, if an entity presented an interim financial report for the comparable interim period of the preceding financial year, the following reconciliations must be included:

- A reconciliation of the entity's equity reported under previous GAAP at the end of that comparable interim period, to its equity restated under IFRS at that date; and
- A reconciliation of the entity's comprehensive income reported under previous GAAP for that comparable interim period (if an entity did not report such a total, reconciliation of profit or loss under previous GAAP) to its restated comprehensive income under IFRS for the same period.

In addition to the reconciliations listed above, an entity's first interim financial report prepared under IAS 34 for part of the period covered by its first IFRS financial statements should also include reconciliations and other disclosures for the fiscal year. Also, IAS 34 requires an entity to disclose "any events or transactions that are material to an understanding of the current interim report."

It is anticipated, and recommended, that transition-period disclosures be presented as a complete package, covering:

- A full set of restated financial statements (statements of financial position, comprehensive income, cash flows and changes in equity);
- Notes explaining the restatement, including reconciliations from amounts reported under previous GAAP to restated amounts under IFRS; and
- Notes on the accounting policies to be applied under IFRS and exemptions applied at transition.

Additional footnote detail in the annual financial statements for the first year IFRS is applied may also be useful. At a minimum, however, to provide a thorough understanding of the transition, it will be advisable to identify all the relevant factors considered by the preparer (the reporting entity) in converting to IFRS in the transition disclosure package itself.

Options With and Within the Accounting Standards

An entity adopting IFRS for the first time may have a choice among accounting standards as well as accounting policies as a result of (1) options with accounting standards (newly issued IFRS), and (2) options within accounting standards.

In conformity with IFRS 1, an entity should adopt IFRS issued and effective at the reporting date of the entity's first IFRS financial statements. Some IFRS may not be issued as of the date of an entity's transition to IFRS but will be effective at the reporting date. It is also possible to adopt a standard whose application is not yet mandatory for the reporting period but whose early adoption is permitted. The IASB has a number of projects currently on its agenda where standards are expected to be finalised in the near future with application dates beyond that date, including those dealing with such matters as derecognition, liabilities, share-based payments and accounting for income taxes. An entity is required to apply the same version of the IFRS throughout the periods covered by those first IFRS financial statements.

On first-time adoption of IFRS, an entity must choose which accounting policies will be adopted. IFRS require an entity to measure some assets and liabilities at fair value, and some others (for example, pension liabilities) at net realisable value or other forms of current value that reflect explicit current projections of future cash flows. An entity will have a choice between different options of accounting policies within accounting standards that may be applied in preparing its first IFRS financial statements. Examples of areas where options within IFRS exist include: cost versus revaluation model of accounting for property, plant and equipment and intangible assets (IAS 16, IAS 38); cost versus fair value model of accounting for investment property (IAS 40); cost versus fair value of jointly controlled entities (IFRS 11, IAS 27); and fair value versus proportionate share of the acquiree's identifiable net assets to measure non-controlling interest in consolidated financial statements (IFRS 3). There are several other areas where there is a choice of accounting policies under IFRS which may have a significant impact on an entity's future results. Once an accounting policy is adopted, opportunities to change may be restricted to justified situations where the change would result in a more appropriate presentation.

In many respects, entities are given a "fresh start" and are required to redetermine their accounting policies under IFRS, fully restating past comparative information. The limited optional exceptions also present some opportunities for entities to determine optimal outcomes.

Transition from US GAAP to IFRS: The Case of DaimlerChrysler

DaimlerChrysler (former Daimler Benz, today Daimler AG) adopted US GAAP in 1998 for purposes of listing on the NYSE. Since it reported under US GAAP in 2005, DaimlerChrysler was exempted until 2007 from implementing the EU Regulation on adopting IFRS. In May 2007, DaimlerChrysler announced that it would sell 80.1% of its stake in the Chrysler Group. Although the company no longer operates the Chrysler Group, it continues to trade on the NYSE and to carry US-issued debt. In November 2007, the SEC eliminated the requirement for foreign registrants reporting under IFRS to reconcile their financial statements to US GAAP. In 2007, DaimlerChrysler had to implement IFRS and its 2007 financial statements were prepared in accordance with IFRS, as issued by the IASB and endorsed by the EU.

DaimlerChrysler followed the provisions of IFRS 1, *First-time Adoption of IFRS*, to prepare its opening IFRS statement of financial position at the transition date. In accordance with IFRS 1, DaimlerChrysler's *date of transition* to IFRS, on which the opening IFRS statement of financial position was prepared, was January 1, 2005, since the company presented two years of comparative financial statements (2005 and 2006). As required by

IFRS 1, each IFRS effective at the reporting date of DaimlerChrysler's first IFRS-compliant financial statements (December 31, 2007) was retrospectively applied.

Certain of DaimlerChrysler's IFRS accounting policies applied in the opening statement of financial position differed from its US GAAP policies applied on that date. The resulting adjustments which arose from events and transactions before the date of transition to IFRS were recognised directly in retained earnings (or another category of equity where appropriate, as of January 1, 2005). The impacts of IFRS adoption on the financial statements are presented in Examples 1 and 2 below along with the footnote, and Example 3, taken from the reissued 2006 report which provides explanation of the differences between IFRS and US GAAP that had major impacts on the financial reports.

Example 1: Statement of financial position impacts of DaimlerChrysler's transition to IFRS

Reconciliations of DaimlerChrysler's equity reported under US GAAP to its equity under IFRS at the transition date (January 1, 2005) and at the end of two comparative periods, 2005 and 2006, presented under US GAAP.

(In millions of €)	*At December 31, 2006*	*At December 31, 2005*	*At January 1, 2005*
Stockholders' equity under US GAAP (as reported)	34,155	36,449	33,522
Adjustments	154	131	169
Stockholders' equity under US GAAP (adjusted)	34,309	36,580	33,691
Minority interest (a)	663	653	909
Stockholders' equity under US GAAP (adjusted) and minority interest	34,972	37,233	34,600
Development costs (b)	5,066	5,142	4,710
Borrowing costs (c)	(843)	(977)	(910)
Investment in EADS (d)	810	1,142	972
Inventories (LIFO) (e)	477	495	349
Transfer of financial assets/ leveraged leases (f)	(517)	(556)	(552)
Pension and other post-employment benefits (g)	(752)	(7,670)	(7,728)
Provisions (h)	321	764	678
Other adjustments (i)	(677)	(872)	(740)
Income taxes (j)	(1,408)	1,359	1,392
Total reconciling items	2,477	(1,173)	(1,829)
Equity under IFRS	37,449	36,060	32,771

Example 2: Income statement impacts of DaimlerChrysler's transition to IFRS

Reconciliation of DaimlerChrysler's net income reported under US GAAP to its net profit under IFRS for two comparative periods, 2005 and 2006, presented under US GAAP.

(In millions of €)	*2006*	*2005*
Net income under US GAAP (as reported)	3,227	2,846
Adjustments	19	(43)
Net income under US GAAP (adjusted)	3,246	2,803
Minority interest (a)	56	74
Net income under US GAAP (adjusted) including minority interest	3,302	2,877
Development costs (b)	145	274
Borrowing costs	47	52
Investment in EADS (c)	(468)	165
Inventories (LIFO) (d)	12	55
Transfer of financial assets/leveraged leases (e)	(61)	(4)
Pension and other post-employment benefits	1,558	1,081
Provisions (f)	(374)	24
Other adjustments (g)	212	60
Income taxes (h)	(590)	(369)
Total reconciling items	481	1,338
Net profit under IFRS	3,783	4,215

Example 3: Required explanation

An explanation of how the transition from US GAAP to IFRS has affected DaimlerChrysler's earnings, financial position and cash flows is presented in the following tables and notes that accompany the tables.

a. *Minority interest*. Under IFRS, minority interests are included in equity, and net profit includes the portion allocated to the minority interest holders. Under US GAAP net income only includes the income attributable to the shareholders of DaimlerChrysler AG. The amounts of the reconciling items (b)–(j) presented in the tables above also include the amounts allocable to minority interest holders.
b. *Development costs*. Under US GAAP, with the exception of certain software development costs, all development costs are expensed as incurred in accordance with ASC 730, *Accounting for Research and Development Costs*. Under IFRS, development costs are capitalised as intangible assets if the technical and economic feasibility of a project can be demonstrated. These costs are subsequently amortised on a straight-line basis over the expected useful lives of the products for which they were incurred (i.e., they become a part of the production costs in which the component for which such costs were incurred is used). Once these vehicles are sold, the amortisation of development costs is included in cost of sales.
c. *Investment in EADS*. Differences between US GAAP and IFRS also affect the carrying amount and DaimlerChrysler's equity in the earnings of EADS, a significant equity investee. DaimlerChrysler accounts for its investment in EADS at a three-month time-lag. Under US GAAP, transactions and events that occur during the intervening period between September 30, 2006, and DaimlerChrysler's reporting date do not result in adjustments, but are disclosed if significant. Under IFRS, the financial information of EADS has to be adjusted for significant transactions and events that occurred after September 30, 2006, but before DaimlerChrysler's reporting date. EADS recorded significant charges in the fourth quarter of 2006, primarily in connection with problems with the A380 programme and resulting delivery delays and the decision to launch the industrial programme for the new A350XWB aircraft family.

In 2003, under US GAAP, DaimlerChrysler determined that the decline in fair value below the carrying value of its investment in EADS was other than temporary and reduced the carrying value by €1.96 billion to its market value. The fair value was determined using the quoted market price, which approximated €3.5 billion at that time. Under IFRS, the investment would not have been considered impaired because the fair value would have been determined using the higher of fair value or value in use, which at that time exceeded the carrying amount.

d. *Inventories (LIFO)*. Under US GAAP, the Group accounted for certain inventories of US subsidiaries using the LIFO principle. Under IFRS, the use of LIFO is prohibited, as set forth in IAS 2, *Inventories*.

e. *Transfer of financial assets/leveraged leases*. As part of its financing activities, the Group regularly sells certain financial receivables from its financial services business as well as trade receivables to SPEs and other third parties ("transfer of financial assets").

In the US GAAP financial statements, transferred receivables meeting the derecognition conditions are removed from the balance sheet, any consideration received, including retained interests, is recognised, and gains or losses from the sale of such receivables are recognised in income. In contrast, in the IFRS consolidated balance sheets as of December 31, 2006 and 2005, receivables of €21.7 billion and €21.3 billion, respectively (primarily receivables from financial services), and liabilities of €21.7 billion and €21.3 billion, respectively (primarily financing liabilities), were reported which are not recorded on the balance sheets in accordance with US GAAP.

Under US GAAP, investments in leveraged leases are recorded on a net basis (i.e., non-recourse financing has been offset against the rental receivable of the lessor). The investment in leveraged leases is included in the line item receivables from financial services in the consolidated balance sheets. Revenue from leveraged leases is recognised under the effective interest method using an after-tax rate of return on the net investment. Under IFRS, investments in leveraged leases are generally recorded on a gross basis on the consolidated balance sheet as receivables from financial services, including the unguaranteed residual value, while the related non-recourse debt is presented as a financial liability. Interest on the receivable is recognised as revenue based on a constant rate of return before taxes, at the rate implicit in the lease. As a result, in the IFRS consolidated balance sheets as of December 31, 2006 and 2005, the Group reported additional receivables from financial services of €1.5 billion and €2.0 billion and liabilities of €1.8 billion and €2.3 billion, respectively, compared to the US GAAP carrying amounts. In addition, certain investments in leveraged cross-border leases are not accounted for as leases at all under IFRS, but represent financial instruments for which revenue is recognised based on their rate of return before income taxes.

f. *Provisions*. In accordance with IFRS, long-term provisions must be discounted to their present value if the effect from discounting is material. Under US GAAP, discounting is only permissible for specific types of provisions if the amount and timing of the cash flows can be reasonably predicted.

This item also includes differences between US GAAP and IFRS relative to the accounting for early retirement agreements concluded in the framework of the German Altersteilzeit benefits. Under US GAAP, all payments during the inactive phase are accrued with a corresponding charge to earnings over the period from reaching an early retirement agreement to the end of the employment. Under IFRS, however, the incremental benefit payments are fully recognised as expenses at the time the early retirement agreement is signed. In 2006, DaimlerChrysler changed its estimates of the effects of employee bonuses and other benefits upon adoption of EITF 05-5, *Accounting for Early Retirement or Post-employment Programs with Specific Features (Such as Terms Specified in Altersteilzeit Early Retirement Arrangements)*, and recognised a gain of €166 million, or €102 million, net of taxes.

g. *Other adjustments*. Other adjustments consist of a number of individually small different recognition and measurement provisions, including the effects of the elections to adjust retained earnings at the transition date for accumulated foreign currency translation differences upon transition to IFRS on gains or losses from disposals of foreign operations, the recognition of gains from sales of real estate leased back under the terms of operating leases, puttable minority interest and other items.
h. *Income taxes*. The adjustments for income taxes are mainly due to the tax effects of differences between IFRS and US GAAP.

This reconciliation item also includes adjustments owing to the use of different tax rates in the elimination of intercompany profits, different valuation allowances on deferred taxes and differences in recognition of uncertain income tax benefits.

The differing valuation allowances, mainly for state and local taxes in the US, are a result of the varying temporary differences under US GAAP compared to IFRS.

Until December 31, 2006, DaimlerChrysler recognised in its US GAAP financial statements the benefit of an uncertain income tax position only when it was probable that the tax position would be sustained based solely on the technical merits of the position and the application of the law. Under IFRS, the potential tax exposure from an uncertain income tax position has to be determined by using the best estimate of the probable amount which results in the recognition of the benefit from a tax position when it is more likely than not that it will be realised.

Information on the statement of cash flows. The presentation of cash flows between IFRS and US GAAP differs primarily because of investments in development projects which are capitalised and reported as investing activities under IFRS, accounting for transfers of receivables which fail derecognition under IFRS and are presented as a secured borrowing under IFRS and inventory-related operating leases between DaimlerChrysler and a customer which are presented as operating activities under IFRS.

(In millions of €)	*2006*	*2005*
Cash provided by operating activities under US GAAP	14,016	12,353
Difference	321	(1,321)
Cash provided by operating activities under IFRS	14,337	11,032
Cash used for investing activities under US GAAP	(14,581)	(11,222)
Differences	(1,276)	985
Cash used for investing activities under IFRS	(15,857)	(10,237)
Cash provided by (used for) financing activities under US GAAP	496	(1,513)
Differences	1,900	229
Cash provided by (used for) financing activities under IFRS	2,396	(1,284)

Example 4: First-time adoption by Meikles Group

2. Basis of preparation

The Group's financial statements have been prepared in accordance with IFRS. The financial statements are prepared from statutory records that are maintained under the historical cost convention as modified by the revaluation of property, plant and equipment, biological assets and financial instruments which are measured at fair value in the opening statement of financial position.

2.1 Transition to IFRS

The Group is resuming presentation of IFRS financial statements after the Group issued financial statements in the prior reporting period ended December 31, 2009, which could not include an explicit and unreserved statement of compliance with IFRS due to the effects of severe hyperinflation. As discussed in note 2.5, the group has early adopted the amendments to IFRS 1 and is therefore applying that standard in returning to compliance with IFRS. The Group's functional currency for the period before January 1, 2009, the Zimbabwe dollar (ZW$), was subject to severe hyperinflation because it had both the following characteristics:

- A reliable general price index was not available to all entities with transactions and balances in ZW$ because the Zimbabwe Central Statistical Office did not release the consumer price indices from August 1, 2008, while the existence of market distortions made measurement of inflation by alternative means unreliable; and
- Exchangeability between the ZW$ and a relatively stable foreign currency did not exist.

The Group's functional currency ceased to be subject to severe hyperinflation from January 1, 2009, when the Group changed its functional currency from ZW$ to US$.

2.2 Exemption for fair value as deemed cost

The Group elected to measure certain items of property, plant and equipment, biological assets, bank balances and cash, inventories, other financial assets, other financial liabilities and trade and other payables at fair value and to use the fair values as the deemed cost of those assets and liabilities in the opening statement of financial position as of January 1, 2009.

2.3 Comparative financial information

The financial statements comprise three statements of financial position, and two statements of comprehensive income, two statements of changes in equity and two statements of cash flows, as a result of the retrospective application of the amendments to IFRS 1. The comparative statements of comprehensive income, changes in equity and cash flows are for 12 months.

2.4 Reconciliation to previous basis of preparation

The Group's financial statements for the prior period ended December 31, 2009, claimed compliance with IFRS, except certain of the requirements of IAS 1, *Presentation of Financial Statements*, IAS 21, *The Effects of Changes in Foreign Exchange Rates*, and IAS 29, *Financial Reporting in Hyperinflationary Economies*. Certain prior year errors were identified during the period and a reconciliation of the amounts previously stated in the December 31, 2009 financial statements and the comparative amounts as presented in this report is given in Note 32.

32. Prior year adjustments

32.1 Opening balances of property, plant and equipment

During the period errors were identified on the January 1, 2009 carrying amounts of certain property, plant and equipment for the stores and agricultural operations. The assets were omitted from the valuation exercise carried out at January 1, 2009, when the functional currency was changed from ZW$ to US$. This has been corrected by the restatement of the 2009 comparatives included in these financial statements.

32.2 Opening balances of biological assets, other receivables and nursery stocks

During the period, it was discovered that the carrying amounts of certain biological assets of the agricultural segment were understated while certain receivables and nursery stocks were incorrectly valued at January 1, 2009, resulting in a misstatement of the opening carrying amounts. The error has been corrected in the comparative statements of financial position.

Presented below are only those statements of comprehensive income and statements of financial position items which have been impacted by the prior year adjustments.

32.3 Prior year costs reclassification

Certain prior year costs have been reclassified to conform to current year presentation.
Statement of comprehensive income

	December 31, 2009 previously stated US$	*Adjustments of property, plant and equipment US$*	*Adjustments to biological assets US$*	*December 31, 2009 restated US$*
Other operating costs	(16,067,056)	(862,866)	–	(16,929,922)
Fair value adjustments	(35,712)	–	2,116,946	2,081,234
Income tax	5,449,453	384,330	(545,114)	5,288,669
Loss for the year from continuing operations	(3,747,889)	(478,536)	1,571,832	(2,654, 593)
Total comprehensive loss for the year	(3,824, 645)	(478,536)	1,571, 832	(2,731, 349)

Statements of financial position

January 1, 2009	*January 1, 2009 as previously stated US$*	*Adjustments of property, plant and equipment US$*	*Adjustments to inventories US$*	*Adjustments to trade and other receivables US$*	*January 1, 2009 restated US$*
Property, plant and equipment	89,650, 542	4,720, 754	–	–	94,371, 296
Inventories	5,565, 764	–	(502,194)	–	5,063, 570
Trade and other receivables	10,280, 439	–	–	(152,007)	10,128, 432
Total assets	200,489, 141	4,720, 754	(502,194)	(152,007)	204,555, 694
Non-distributable reserves	(148,118, 994)	(3,476, 943)	502,194	152,007	(150,941,736)
Deferred tax liability	(23,074, 660)	(1,243, 811)	–	–	(24,318, 471)
Total equity and liabilities	(200,489, 141)	(4,720, 754)	502,194	152,007	(204,555, 694)

December 31, 2009	*December 31, 2009 as previously stated US$*	*January 1, 2009 net adjustments as above US $*	*Adjustments of property, plant and equipment US$*	*Adjustments to biological assets US$*	*December 31, 2009 restated US$*
Property, plant and equipment	76,672, 807	4,720, 754	(862,866)	–	80,530, 695
Biological assets	4,193, 614	–	–	2,116, 946	6,310, 560
Inventory	17,617, 464	(502,194)	–	–	17,115, 270
Trade and other receivables	7,485, 896	(152,007)	–	–	7,333, 889
Total assets	271,429, 262	4,066, 553	(862,866)	2,116, 946	276,749, 895
Non-distributable reserves	(107,160, 978)	(2,822, 742)	–	–	(109,983, 720)
Accumulated loss	22,418, 679	–	478,536	(1,571, 832)	21,325, 383
Deferred tax	(13,941, 913)	(1,243, 811)	384,330	(545,114)	(15,346, 508)
Total equity and liabilities	(271,429, 262)	(4,066, 553)	862,866	(2,116, 946)	(276,749, 895)

INDEX